Format for Bank Reconciliation:

Cash balance according to bank statement		\$XXX
Add: Additions by company not on bank statement	\$XXX	
Bank errors	XXX	XXX
		\$XXX
Deduct: Deductions by company not on bank statement	\$XXX	
Bank errors	XXX	XXX
Adjusted balance		\$XXX

Cash balance according to company's records		\$XXX
Add: Additions by bank not recorded by company	\$XXX	
Company errors	XXX	XXX
		\$XXX
Deduct: Deductions by bank not recorded by company	\$XXX	
Company errors	XXX	XXX
Adjusted balance		\$XXX

Note: Additions and deductions to company records require journal entries by the company.

Inventory Costing Methods:

- First-in, First-out (FIFO)
- Last-in, First-out (LIFO)
- Weighted-Average

Interest Computations:

Interest = Face Amount (or Principal) × Rate × Time

Methods of Determining Annual Depreciation:

Straight-Line: $\frac{\text{Cost} - \text{Estimated Residual Value}}{\text{Estimated Life}}$

Double-Declining-Balance: Rate* × Book Value at Beginning of Period

*Rate is commonly twice the straight-line rate (1 ÷ Estimated Life).

Units-of-Activity: $\frac{\text{Cost} - \text{Residual Value}}{\text{Total Estimated Units of Activity}} \times$ Units of Activity for Period

Adjustments to Net Income (Loss) Using the Indirect Method:

	Increase (Decrease)
Net income (loss)	\$ XXX
Adjustments to reconcile net income to net cash flow from operating activities:	
Depreciation of fixed assets	XXX
Amortization of intangible assets	XXX
Losses on disposal of assets	XXX
Gains on disposal of assets	(XXX)
Changes in current operating assets and liabilities:	
Increases in noncash current operating assets	(XXX)
Decreases in noncash current operating assets	XXX
Increases in current operating liabilities	XXX
Decreases in current operating liabilities	(XXX)
Net cash flow from operating activities	\$ XXX or \$(XXX)

Contribution Margin Ratio = $\frac{\text{Sales} - \text{Variable Costs}}{\text{Sales}}$

Break-Even Sales (Units) = $\frac{\text{Fixed Costs}}{\text{Unit Contribution Margin}}$

Sales (Units) = $\frac{\text{Fixed Costs} + \text{Target Profit}}{\text{Unit Contribution Margin}}$

Margin of Safety = $\frac{\text{Sales} - \text{Sales at Break-Even Point}}{\text{Sales}}$

Operating Leverage = $\frac{\text{Contribution Margin}}{\text{Income from Operations}}$

Variances:

Direct Materials Price Variance = (Actual Price − Standard Price) × Actual Quantity

Direct Materials Quantity Variance = (Actual Quantity − Standard Quantity) × Standard Price

Direct Labor Rate Variance = (Actual Rate per Hour − Standard Rate per Hour) × Actual Hours

Direct Labor Time Variance = (Actual Direct Labor Hours − Standard Direct Labor Hours) × Standard Rate per Hour

Variable Factory Overhead Controllable Variance = Actual Variable Factory Overhead − Budgeted Variable Factory Overhead

Fixed Factory Overhead Volume Variance = (Standard Hours for 100% of Normal Capacity − Standard Hours for Actual Units Produced) × Fixed Factory Overhead Rate

Rate of Return on Investment (ROI) = $\frac{\text{Income from Operations}}{\text{Invested Assets}}$

Alternative ROI Computation:

$$\text{ROI} = \frac{\text{Income from Operations}}{\text{Sales}} \times \frac{\text{Sales}}{\text{Invested Assets}}$$

Capital Investment Analysis Methods:

Methods That Ignore Present Values:

- Average Rate of Return Method
- Cash Payback Method

Methods That Use Present Values:

- Net Present Value Method
- Internal Rate of Return Method

Average Rate of Return = $\frac{\text{Estimated Average Annual Income}}{\text{Average Investment}}$

Present Value Index = $\frac{\text{Total Present Value of Net Cash Flow}}{\text{Amount to Be Invested}}$

Present Value Factor for an Annuity of \$1 = $\frac{\text{Amount to Be Invested}}{\text{Equal Annual Net Cash Flows}}$

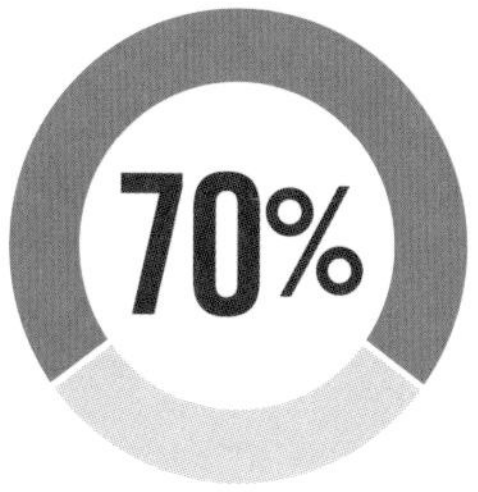

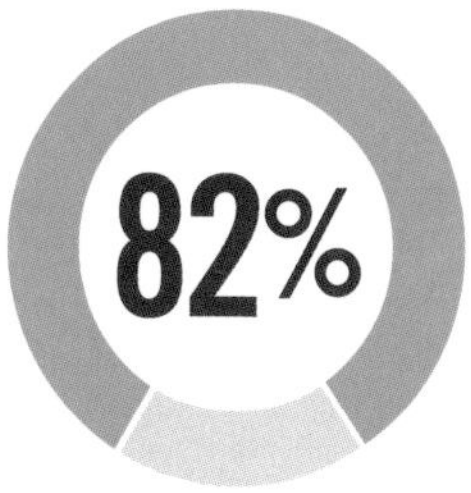

FINANCIAL ACCOUNTING

16e

Carl S. Warren
Professor Emeritus of Accounting
University of Georgia, Athens

Contributing Authors

Christine A. Jonick
Professor of Accounting
University of North Georgia, Gainesville

Jennifer S. Schneider
Assistant Professor of Accounting
University of North Georgia, Gainesville

Australia • Brazil • Mexico • Singapore • United Kingdom • United States

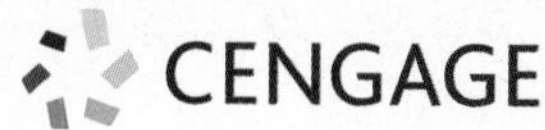

Financial Accounting, 16th edition
Carl S. Warren, Christine A. Jonick, and Jennifer S. Schneider

Senior Vice President, Higher Education & Skills Product: Erin Joyner

Product Director: Jason Fremder

Senior Product Manager: Matthew Filimonov

Product Assistant: Matt Schiesl

Senior Digital Delivery Lead: Jessica Robbe

Senior Content Manager: Diane Bowdler

Executive Marketing Manager: Nathan Anderson

Intellectual Property Analyst: Ashley Maynard

Intellectual Property Project Manager: Carly Belcher

Production Service: Lumina Datamatics, Inc.

Text and Cover Designer: Christopher Doughman

Cover Image: iStock.com/ExperienceInteriors

Throughout this text, real-world companies are used in the narrative, illustrations, and end-of-chapter assignments. These companies are identified in **boldface** type, and any data presented was adapted from or based upon annual reports, Securities and Exchange Commission filings, or other publicly available sources. Any other individuals or companies used in illustrations or homework are fictional, and any resemblance to actual persons, living or dead, businesses or companies is entirely coincidental.

Library of Congress Control Number: 2019954868
ISBN: 978-1-337-91310-2

Cengage
200 Pier 4 Boulevard
Boston, MA 02210

Printed in the United States of America
Print Number: 01 Print Year: 2019

Brief Contents

Preface

Roadmap for Success

Warren's *Financial Accounting 16e* makes it easy for you to give students a solid foundation in accounting without overwhelming students. Warren covers the fundamentals AND motivates students to learn by showing how accounting is important to a business.

The Warren presentation style provides content in a way that this generation reads and assimilates information.

- Short, concise paragraphs and bullets
- Stepwise progression
- Meaningful illustrations and graphs

Hallmarks

Schemas provide a roadmap of accounting that emphasizes the big picture. Each chapter begins with a graphic Schema, or Roadmap of Accounting, that shows readers how the chapter material fits within the larger context of the overall book. With this approach, students view chapter concepts as part of a larger whole rather than as mere independent pieces of knowledge, for a truly functional understanding of accounting.

A four-part schema (Chs. 1–4) demonstrates how chapter content integrates within the accounting cycle. The financial accounting chapters' schema (Chs. 5–17) highlights chapter content within a set of integrated financial statements.

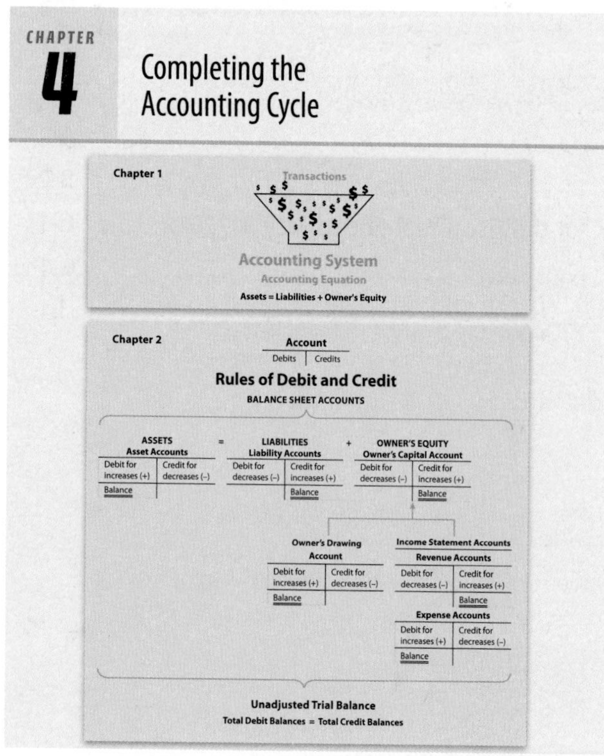

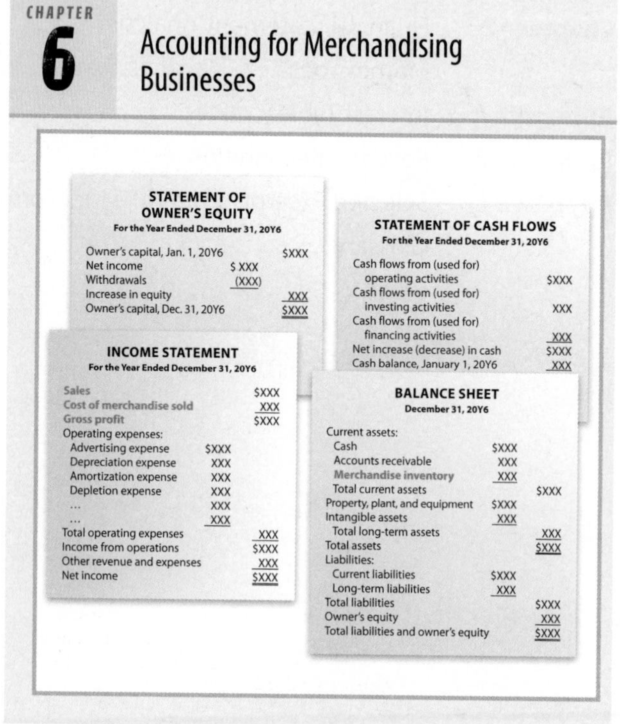

Revised and refreshed real company chapter openers engage readers from the start. Chapter openers introduce and briefly describe a real company and how its challenges relate to the chapter content. Links to this opening company appear throughout the chapter to reinforce the importance of what readers are learning.

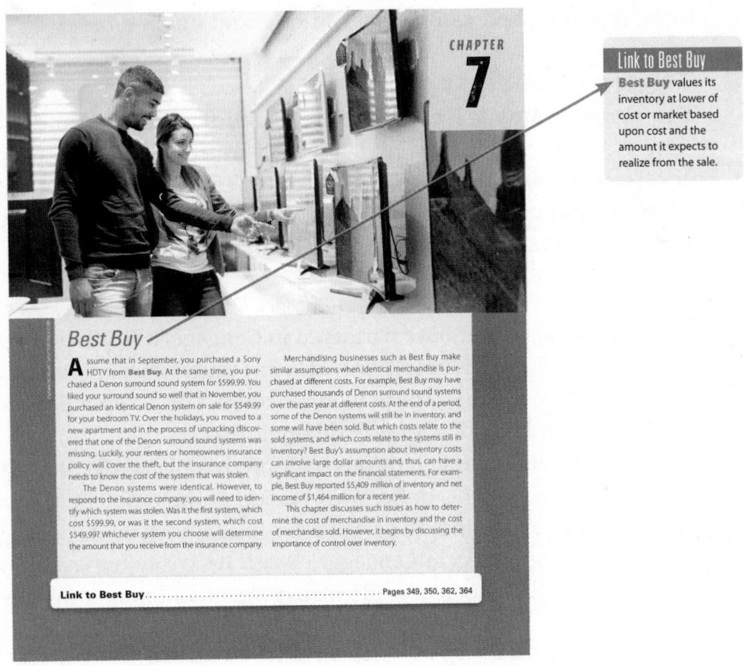

CHAPTER 7

Link to Best Buy

Best Buy values its inventory at lower of cost or market based upon cost and the amount it expects to realize from the sale.

Best Buy

Assume that in September, you purchased a Sony HDTV from **Best Buy**. At the same time, you purchased a Denon surround sound system for $599.99. You liked your surround sound so well that in November, you purchased an identical Denon system on sale for $549.99 for your bedroom TV. Over the holidays, you moved to a new apartment and in the process of unpacking discovered that one of the Denon surround sound systems was missing. Luckily, your renters or homeowners insurance policy will cover the theft, but the insurance company needs to know the cost of the system that was stolen.

The Denon systems were identical. However, to respond to the insurance company, you will need to identify which system was stolen. Was it the first system, which cost $599.99, or was it the second system, which cost $549.99? Whichever system you choose will determine the amount that you receive from the insurance company.

Merchandising businesses such as Best Buy make similar assumptions when identical merchandise is purchased at different costs. For example, Best Buy may have purchased thousands of Denon surround sound systems over the past year at different costs. At the end of a period, some of the Denon systems will still be in inventory, and some will have been sold. But which costs relate to the sold systems, and which costs relate to the systems still in inventory? Best Buy's assumption about inventory costs can involve large dollar amounts and, thus, can have a significant impact on the financial statements. For example, Best Buy reported $5,409 million of inventory and net income of $1,464 million for a recent year.

This chapter discusses such issues as how to determine the cost of merchandise in inventory and the cost of merchandise sold. However, it begins by discussing the importance of control over inventory.

Link to Best Buy .... Pages 349, 350, 362, 364

Revised end-of-chapter assignments (homework) provide important hands-on practice. Refined, meaningful review and applications at the end of each chapter include Discussion Questions, Practice Exercises (A and B versions), Exercises, Problems (Series A and B), and Cases & Projects that emphasize ethics, teamwork, and communication skills.

Cases & Projects

ETHICS

CP 5-1 Ethics in Action

Netbooks Inc. provides accounting applications for business customers on the Internet for a monthly subscription. Netbooks' customers run their accounting system on the Internet; thus, the business data and accounting software reside on the servers of Netbooks Inc. The senior management of Netbooks believes that once a customer begins to use Netbooks, it is very difficult to cancel the service. That is, customers are "locked in" because it is difficult to move the business data from Netbooks to another accounting application even though the customers own their own data. Therefore, Netbooks has decided to entice customers with an initial low monthly price that is half the normal monthly rate for the first year of services. After a year, the price will be increased to the regular monthly rate. Netbooks management believes that customers will have to accept the full price because customers will be locked in after one year of use.

a. Discuss whether the half-price offer is an ethical business practice.

b. Discuss whether customer "lock-in" is an ethical business practice.

TEAM ACTIVITY

REAL WORLD

CP 5-2 Team Activity

The two leading software application providers for supply chain management (SCM) and customer relationship management (CRM) software are **JDA** and **Salesforce.com**, respectively. In groups of two or three, go to the website of each company (www.jda.com and www.salesforce.com, respectively) and list the services provided by each company's software.

COMMUNICATION

REAL WORLD

CP 5-3 Communication

Internet-based accounting software is a recent trend in business computing. Major software firms such as **Oracle**, **SAP**, and **NetSuite** are running their core products on the Internet using cloud computing. NetSuite is one of the most popular small-business Internet-based accounting systems.

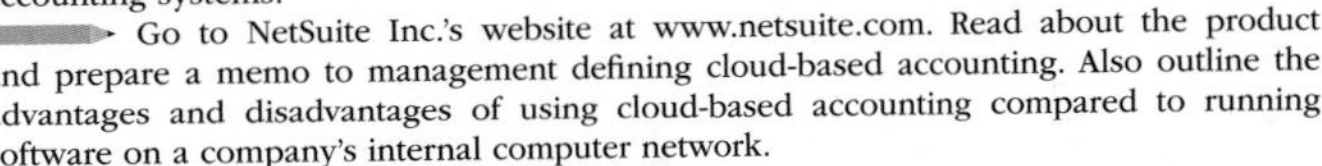

Go to NetSuite Inc.'s website at www.netsuite.com. Read about the product and prepare a memo to management defining cloud-based accounting. Also outline the advantages and disadvantages of using cloud-based accounting compared to running software on a company's internal computer network.

CengageNOWv2

CengageNOWv2 is a powerful course management and online homework resource that provides control and customization to optimize the student learning experience. Included are many proven resources, such as algorithmic activities, a test bank, course management tools, reporting and assessment options, and much more.

Cengage Mobile App

The *Cengage Mobile App* lets students study wherever and whenever the mood strikes. Now available with *CengageNOWv2,* it features a full interactive eBook—readable online or off—with 24/7 course access and study tools to power on-the-go learning. Plus, the app allows you to engage your students with instant in-class polling and take attendance with a tap. Find details at **www.cengage.com/mobile-app/**.

Excel Online

Cengage and Microsoft have partnered in CengageNOWv2 to provide students with a uniform, authentic Excel experience. It provides instant feedback, built-in video tips, and easily accessible spreadsheet work. These features allow you to spend more time teaching accounting applications and less time troubleshooting Excel.

These new algorithmic activities offer pre-populated data directly in Microsoft Excel Online. Each student receives his or her own version of the problem to perform the necessary data calculations in Excel Online. Their work is constantly saved in Cengage cloud storage as a part of homework assignments in CengageNOWv2. It's easily retrievable so students can review their answers without cumbersome file management and numerous downloads/uploads.

Motivation: Set Expectations and Prepare Students for the Course

CengageNOWv2 helps motivate students and get them ready to learn by reshaping their misconceptions about the introductory accounting course and providing a powerful tool to engage students.

CengageNOWv2 Start-Up Center

Students are often surprised by the amount of time they need to spend outside of class working through homework assignments in order to succeed. The CengageNOWv2 Start-Up Center will help students identify what they need to do and where they need to focus in order to be successful with a variety of new resources.

- What Is Accounting? Module ensures students understand course expectations and how to be successful in the introductory accounting course. This module consists of two assignable videos: Introduction to Accounting and Success Strategies. The Student Advice Videos offer advice from real students about what it takes to do well in the course.
- Math Review Module, designed to help students get up to speed with necessary math skills, includes math review assignments and Show Me How math review videos to ensure that students have an understanding of basic math skills.
- How to Use CengageNOWv2 Module focuses on learning accounting, not on a particular software system. Quickly familiarize your students with CengageNOWv2 and direct them to all of its built-in student resources.

Motivation: Prepare Them for Class

With all the outside obligations accounting students have, finding time to read the textbook before class can be a struggle. Point students to the key concepts they need to know before they attend class.

- **Video: Tell Me More.** Short Tell Me More lecture activities explain the core concepts of the chapter through an engaging auditory and visual presentation. Available either on a stand-alone basis or as an assignment, they are ideal for all class formats—flipped model, online, hybrid, or face-to-face.

Provide Help Right When Students Need It

The best way to learn accounting is through practice, but students often get stuck when attempting homework assignments on their own.

- **Video: Show Me How.** Created for the most frequently assigned end-of-chapter items, Show Me How problem demonstration videos provide a step-by-step model of a similar problem. Embedded tips help students avoid common mistakes and pitfalls.

MindTap eReader

The MindTap eReader for Warren's *Financial Accounting* is the most robust digital reading experience available. Hallmark features include:

- Fully optimized for the iPad.
- Note taking, highlighting, and more.
- The MindTap eReader also features ReadSpeaker®, an online text-to-speech application that vocalizes, or "speech-enables," online educational content. This feature is ideally suited for both instructors and learners who would like to listen to content instead of (or in addition to) reading it.

CENGAGE UNLIMITED

Cengage Unlimited

Cengage Unlimited is a first of-its-kind digital subscription designed specifically to lower costs. Students get total access to everything Cengage has to offer on demand—in one place. That's over 20,000 eBooks, 2,300 digital learning products, and dozens of study tools across 70 disciplines and over 675 courses. Currently available in select markets. Find details at **www.cengage.com/unlimited**.

New to This Edition

- Updated dates and real company information for currency.
- Refreshed end-of-chapter assignments with different numerical values and updated information.
- A new "Time Period Concept" discussion has been added to the "Generally Accepted Accounting Principles" section of Chapter 1. This discussion defines and illustrates the natural business year and fiscal year accounting periods.
- The fiscal year discussion was moved from the prior edition's Chapter 4. In addition, the notation of 20Y1, 20Y2, ... is introduced for indicating years throughout the text.
- In Chapter 2, the discussion on "Errors Not Affecting the Trial Balance" has been revised to better aid student understanding and to simplify the preparation of correcting journal entries.
- In Chapter 4, the Accounting Cycle illustration in Exhibit 8 has been revised to facilitate student review.
- In Chapter 4, the "Fiscal Year" discussion has been moved to Chapter 1.
- In Chapter 4, the "Reversing Entry" appendix has been moved to an online appendix.
- A new "Why Is the Accrual Basis of Accounting Required by GAAP?" discussion has been added as Appendix 2 to Chapter 4. The understanding of why accrual accounting is required by GAAP is important for students' ability to analyze and evaluate financial statements. Why accrual accounting is required is illustrated by comparing NetSolutions' financial statements under the accrual basis (Chapters 1–4) with related cash basis financial statements.
- To simplify and give the instructor more flexibility in Chapter 6, the discussion of the accounting for customer merchandise refunds, including the related adjusting entries, has been moved to Appendix 2 at the end of the chapter.
- For those instructors who prefer to cover sales discounts using the gross method, Appendix 1, "Gross Method of Recording Sales Discounts," has been added to the end of Chapter 6.

About the Authors

Carl S. Warren

Terry R. Spray/InHisImage Studios

Dr. Carl S. Warren is Professor Emeritus of Accounting at the University of Georgia, Athens. Dr. Warren has taught classes at the University of Georgia, University of Iowa, Michigan State University, and University of Chicago. He focused his teaching efforts on principles of accounting and auditing. Dr. Warren received his PhD from Michigan State University and his BBA and MA from the University of Iowa. During his career, Dr. Warren published numerous articles in professional journals, including *The Accounting Review*, *Journal of Accounting Research*, *Journal of Accountancy*, *The CPA Journal*, and *Auditing: A Journal of Practice & Theory*. Dr. Warren has served on numerous committees of the American Accounting Association, the American Institute of Certified Public Accountants, and the Institute of Internal Auditors. He also has consulted with numerous companies and public accounting firms. His outside interests include handball, golf, skiing, backpacking, and fly-fishing.

Christine A. Jonick

Courtesy of Christine Jonick

Dr. Christine A. Jonick is Professor of Accounting at University of North Georgia, Gainesville. She received her Ed.D from the University of Georgia, her MBA from Adelphi University, and her BA from State University of New York at Binghamton. Dr. Jonick has focused her teaching efforts on principles of accounting and intermediate financial accounting. She is the recipient of several teaching awards, including one for excellence in online instruction. She has published accounting-related articles in research journals and a case study in the *Institute of Management Accountants (IMA) Educational Case Journal*. Dr. Jonick serves on numerous professional committees, is an active board member for the American Accounting Association SE, and is a recent past president of the Georgia Association of Accounting Educators. Dr. Jonick has worked with accounting textbook publishers for over a decade as a technology consultant, subject matter expert, and content developer. Her outside interests include travel, biking, technology development, and family activities.

Jennifer S. Schneider

Courtesy of Jennifer Schneider

Jennifer S. Schneider is an Assistant Professor at the University of North Georgia, Gainesville. Professor Schneider has taught principles of accounting, survey of accounting, principles of finance, accounting information systems, and auditing. She is a Florida CPA and began her career at PwC. She has 15+ years' experience with Fortune 500 companies, primarily in audit and financial/SEC reporting. Prior to coming to the University of North Georgia, Professor Schneider taught at the University of Amsterdam. Her research interests are in the Scholarship of Teaching and Learning. Professor Schneider has published several articles including an article in the *Institute of Management Accountants (IMA) Educational Case Journal*. She has also served as faculty advisor for Beta Alpha Psi, which is an international honors organization for financial information students and professionals. She enjoys spending time with her two sons, Luke and Graeme, both students at the University of Georgia, Athens.

Contents

Chapter **16** Statement of Cash Flows 765

Chapter **17** Financial Statement Analysis 821

CHAPTER 1

Introduction to Accounting and Business

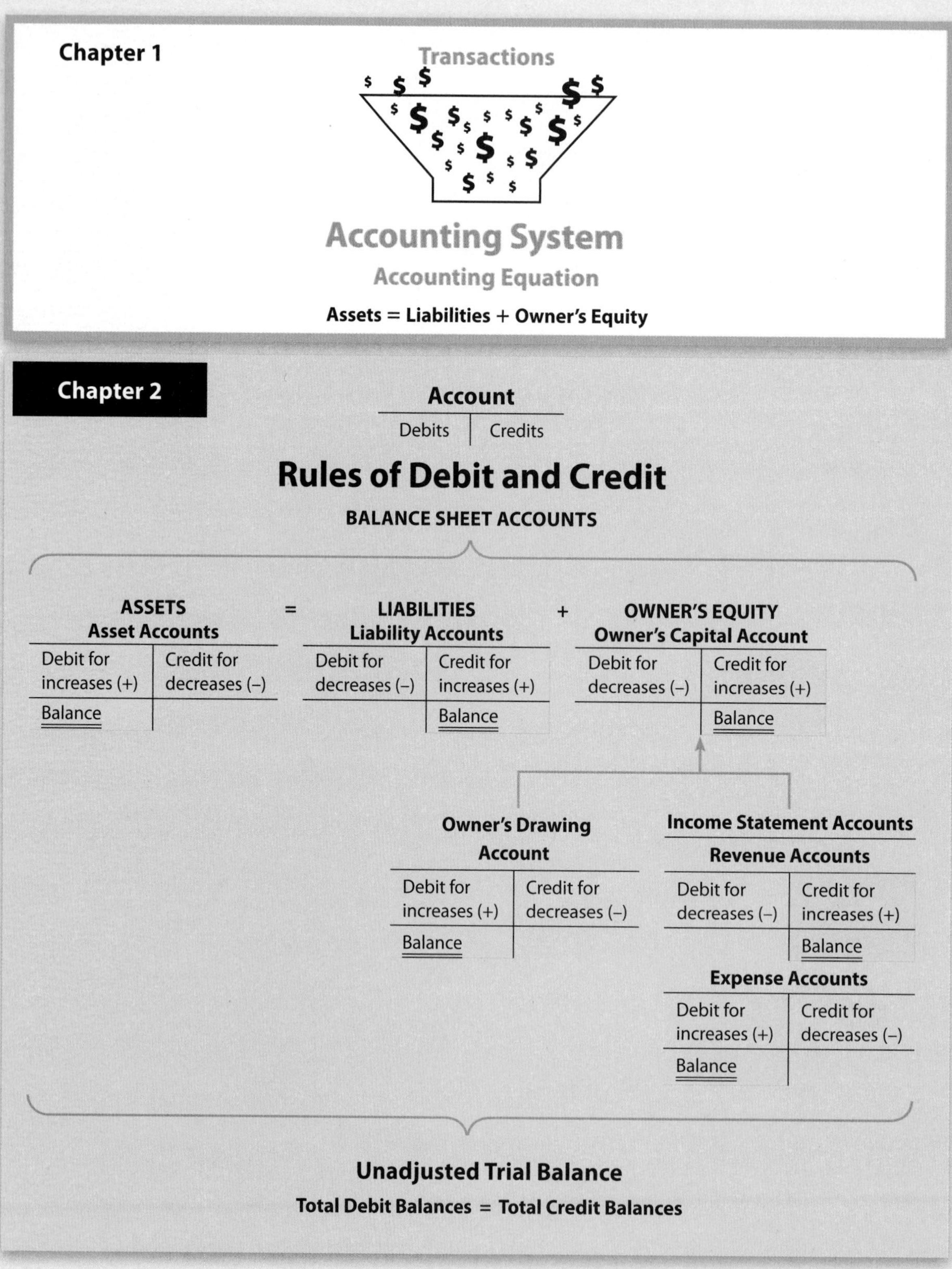

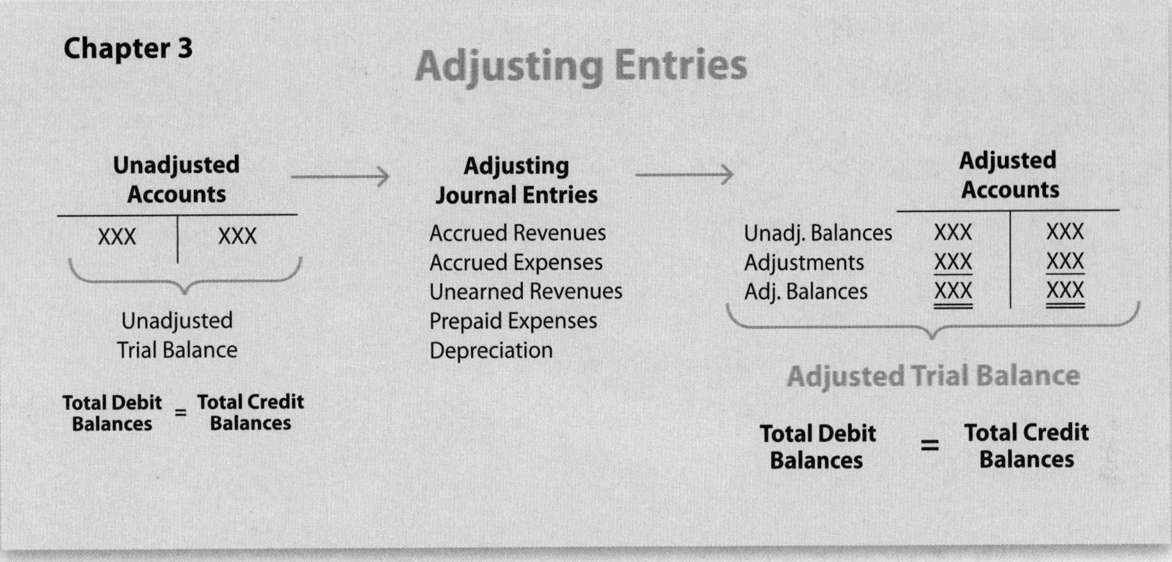
Chapter 3
Adjusting Entries
Unadjusted Accounts
XXX
XXX
Unadjusted Trial Balance
Total Debit Balances = Total Credit Balances
Adjusting Journal Entries
Accrued Revenues
Accrued Expenses
Unearned Revenues
Prepaid Expenses
Depreciation
Adjusted Accounts
Unadj. Balances XXX XXX
Adjustments XXX XXX
Adj. Balances XXX XXX
Adjusted Trial Balance
Total Debit Balances = Total Credit Balances

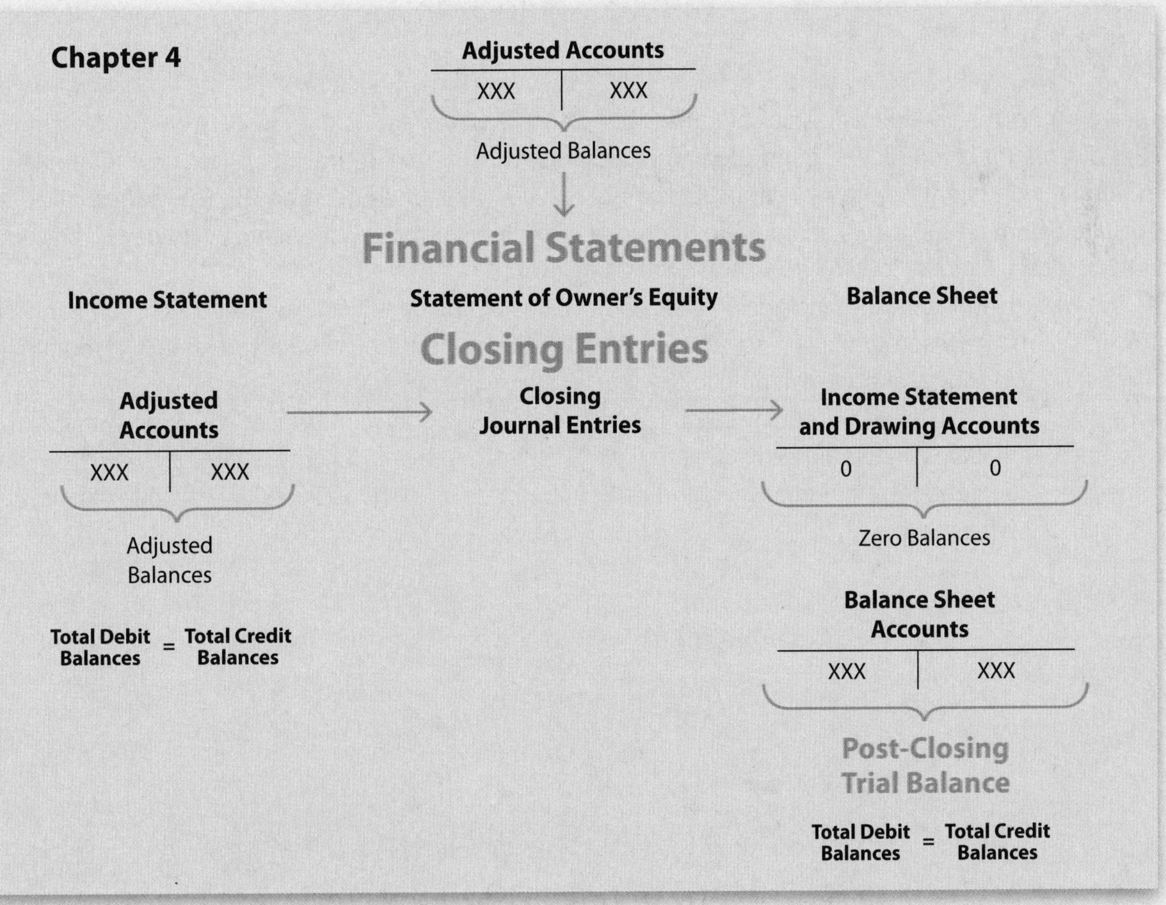
Chapter 4
Adjusted Accounts
XXX
XXX
Adjusted Balances
Financial Statements
Income Statement
Statement of Owner's Equity
Balance Sheet
Closing Entries
Adjusted Accounts
XXX
XXX
Adjusted Balances
Total Debit Balances = Total Credit Balances
Closing Journal Entries
Income Statement and Drawing Accounts
0
0
Zero Balances
Balance Sheet Accounts
XXX
XXX
Post-Closing Trial Balance
Total Debit Balances = Total Credit Balances

CHAPTER

1

PHOTOMIX-COMPANY/PIXABAY

Twitter

When two teams pair up for a game of football, there is often a lot of noise. The band plays, the fans cheer, and fireworks light up the scoreboard. Obviously, the fans are committed and care about the outcome of the game. Just like fans at a football game, the owners of a business want their business to "win" against their competitors in the marketplace. While having your football team win can be a source of pride, winning in the marketplace goes beyond pride and has many tangible benefits. Companies that are winners are better able to serve customers, provide good jobs for employees, and make money for their owners.

Twitter, Inc. is one of the most visible companies on the Internet. It provides a real-time information network where members can post messages, called *tweets*, for free. Millions post tweets every day throughout the world.

Do you think Twitter is a successful company? Does it make money? How would you know? Accounting helps to answer these questions.

This textbook introduces you to accounting, the language of business. Chapter 1 begins by discussing what a business is, how it operates, and the role that accounting plays.

Link to Twitter .... Pages 6, 12, 14, 20, 24

LEARNING OBJECTIVES

After studying this chapter, you should be able to:

Example Exercises (EE) are shown in **red.**

Nature of Business and Accounting

OBJ. 1 Describe the nature of business and the role of accounting and ethics in business.

A **business**[1] is an organization in which basic resources (inputs), such as materials and labor, are assembled and processed to provide goods or services (outputs) to customers. Businesses come in all sizes, from a local coffee house to **Starbucks**, which sells over $24 billion of coffee and related products each year.

The objective of most businesses is to earn a **profit**. Profit is the difference between the amounts received from customers for goods or services and the amounts paid for the inputs used to provide the goods or services. This text focuses on businesses operating to earn a profit. However, many of the same concepts and principles also apply to not-for-profit organizations such as hospitals, churches, and government agencies.

Types of Businesses

Three types of businesses operating for profit include service, merchandising, and manufacturing businesses. Some examples of each type of business follow:

- **Service businesses** provide services rather than products to customers.
  - **Delta Air Lines** (transportation services)
  - **The Walt Disney Company** (entertainment services)

1 A complete glossary of terms appears at the end of the text.

Link to Twitter

Twitter is a service company that provides a platform for individuals to send text messages called *tweets*.

- **Merchandising businesses** sell products they purchase from other businesses to customers.
  - **Wal-Mart Stores, Inc.** (general merchandise)
  - **Amazon.com** (general merchandise)
- **Manufacturing businesses** convert basic inputs into products that are sold to customers.
  - **Ford Motor Co.** (cars, trucks, vans)
  - **Dell Inc.** (personal computers)

Role of Accounting in Business

The role of accounting in business is to provide information for managers to use in operating the business. In addition, accounting provides information to other users in assessing the economic performance and condition of the business.

Note

Accounting is an information system that provides reports to users about the economic activities and condition of a business.

Thus, **accounting** can be defined as an information system that provides reports to users about the economic activities and condition of a business. You could think of accounting as the "language of business." This is because accounting is the means by which businesses' financial information is communicated to users.

The process by which accounting provides information to users is as follows:

1. Identify users.
2. Assess users' information needs.
3. Design the accounting information system to meet users' needs.
4. Record economic data about business activities and events.
5. Prepare accounting reports for users.

As illustrated in Exhibit 1, users of accounting information can be divided into two groups: internal users and external users.

Managerial Accounting Internal users of accounting information include managers and employees. These users are directly involved in managing and operating the business. The area of accounting that provides internal users with information is called **managerial accounting** or **management accounting**.

The objective of managerial accounting is to provide relevant and timely information for managers' and employees' decision-making needs. Oftentimes, such information is sensitive and is not distributed outside the business. Examples of sensitive information might include information about customers, prices, and plans to expand the business. Managerial accountants employed by a business are employed in **private accounting**.

Link to Twitter

One of the ways **Twitter** provides information to its investors is by publishing an annual report, which includes general-purpose financial statements.

Financial Accounting External users of accounting information include investors, creditors, customers, and the government. These users are not directly involved in managing and operating the business. The area of accounting that provides external users with information is called **financial accounting**.

The objective of financial accounting is to provide relevant and timely information for the decision-making needs of users outside the business. For example, financial reports on the operations and condition of the business are useful for banks and other creditors in deciding whether to lend money to the business. **General-purpose financial statements** are one type of financial accounting report that is distributed to external users. The term *general-purpose* refers to the wide range of decision-making needs that these reports are designed to serve. Later in this chapter, general-purpose financial statements are described and illustrated.

ETHICS

Role of Ethics in Accounting and Business

The objective of accounting is to provide relevant, timely information for user decision making. Accountants must behave in an ethical manner so that the information they provide users will be trustworthy and, thus, useful for decision making. Managers and employees must also behave in an ethical manner in managing and operating a business. Otherwise, no one will be willing to invest in or loan money to the business.

Accounting as an Information System **EXHIBIT 1**

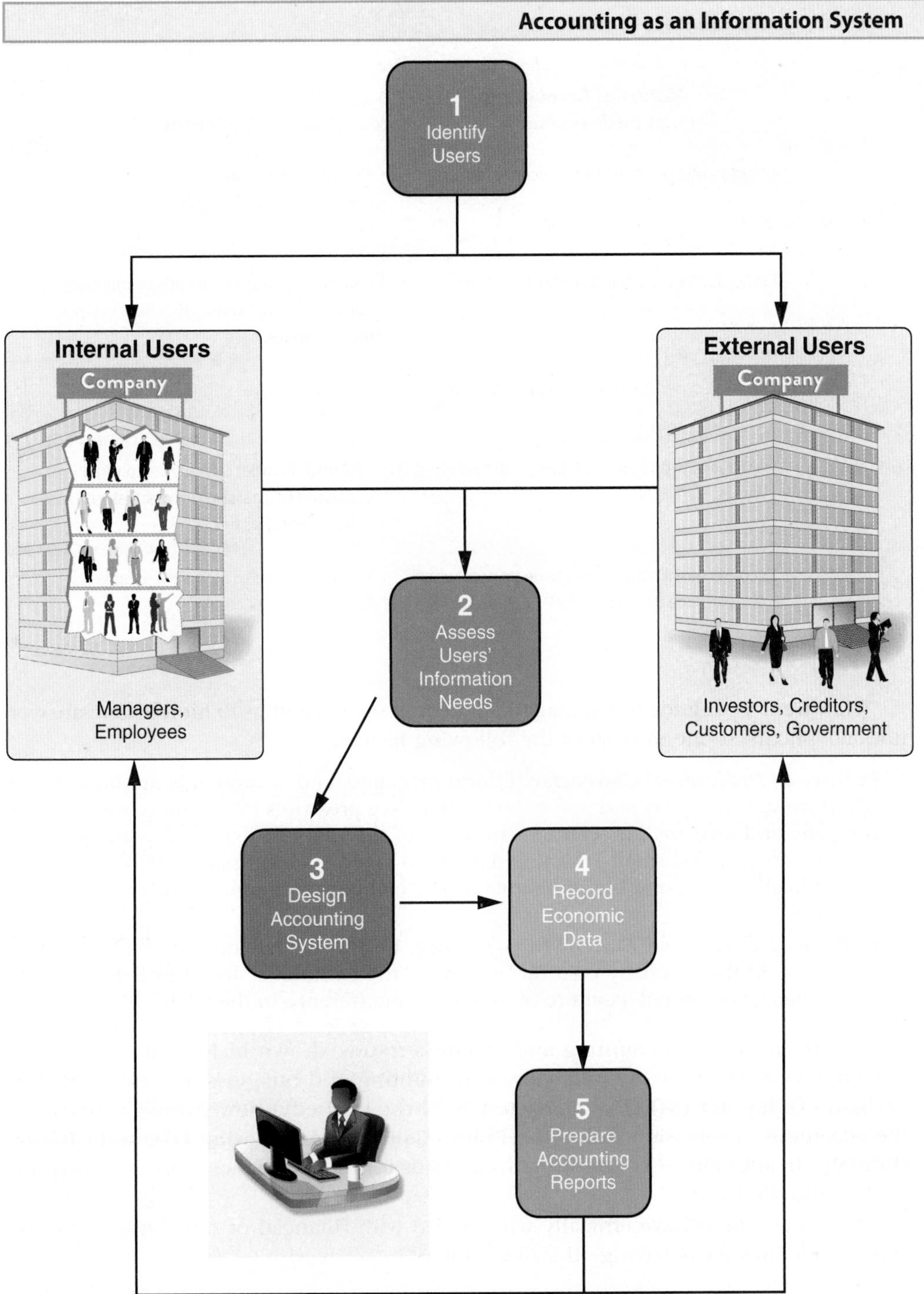

Ethics are moral principles that guide the conduct of individuals. Unfortunately, business managers and accountants sometimes behave in an unethical manner. Many of the managers of the companies listed in Exhibit 2 engaged in accounting or business fraud. These ethical violations led to fines, firings, and lawsuits. In some cases, managers were criminally prosecuted, convicted, and sent to prison.

EXHIBIT 2 **Accounting and Business Frauds**

Company	Nature of Accounting or Business Fraud	Result
Computer Associates International, Inc.	Fraudulently reported its financial results.	CEO and senior executives indicted. Five executives pled guilty. $225 million fine.
Enron	Fraudulently reported its financial results.	Bankrupcty. Senior executives criminally convicted. More than $60 billion in stock market losses.
HealthSouth	Overstated performance by $4 billion in false entries.	Senior executives criminally convicted.
Qwest Communications International, Inc.	Improperly reported $3 billion in false receipts.	CEO and six other executives criminally convicted of "massive financial fraud." $250 million SEC fine.
Xerox Corporation	Recognized $3 billion in revenue prior to when it should have been recorded.	$10 million fine to SEC. Six executives forced to pay $22 million.

What went wrong for the managers and companies listed in Exhibit 2? The answer normally involved one or both of the following factors:

- ***Failure of Individual Character.*** Ethical managers and accountants are honest and fair. However, managers and accountants often face pressures from supervisors to meet company and investor expectations. In many of the cases in Exhibit 2, managers and accountants justified small ethical violations to avoid such pressures. However, these small violations became big violations as the company's financial problems became worse.
- ***Culture of Greed and Ethical Indifference.*** By their behavior and attitude, senior managers set the company culture. In most of the companies listed in Exhibit 2, the senior managers created a culture of greed and indifference to the truth.

As a result of the accounting and business frauds shown in Exhibit 2, Congress passed laws to monitor the behavior of accounting and business. For example, the **Sarbanes-Oxley Act (SOX)** was enacted. SOX established a new oversight body for the accounting profession called the **Public Company Accounting Oversight Board (PCAOB)**. In addition, SOX established standards for independence, corporate responsibility, and disclosure.

How does one behave ethically when faced with financial or other types of pressure? Guidelines for behaving ethically follow:[2]

1. Identify an ethical decision by using your personal ethical standards of honesty and fairness.
2. Identify the consequences of the decision and its effect on others.
3. Consider your obligations and responsibilities to those who will be affected by your decision.
4. Make a decision that is ethical and fair to those affected by it.

2 Many companies have ethical standards of conduct for managers and employees. In addition, the Institute of Management Accountants and the American Institute of Certified Public Accountants have professional codes of conduct, which can be obtained from their websites at www.imanet.org and www.aicpa.org, respectively.

Integrity, Objectivity, and Ethics in Business

BERNIE MADOFF

In June 2009, Bernard L. "Bernie" Madoff was sentenced to 150 years in prison for defrauding thousands of investors in one of the biggest frauds in American history. Madoff's fraud started several decades earlier when he began a Ponzi scheme in his investment management firm, **Bernard L. Madoff Investment Securities LLC**.

In a Ponzi scheme, the investment manager uses funds received from new investors to pay a return to existing investors, rather than basing investment returns on the fund's actual performance. As long as the investment manager is able to attract new investors, he or she will have new funds to pay existing investors and continue the fraud. While most Ponzi schemes collapse quickly when the investment manager runs out of new investors, Madoff's reputation, popularity, and personal contacts provided a steady stream of investors, which allowed the fraud to survive for decades.

Opportunities for Accountants

Numerous career opportunities are available for students majoring in accounting. Currently, the demand for accountants exceeds the number of new graduates entering the job market. This is partly due to the increased regulation of business caused by the accounting and business frauds shown in Exhibit 2. Also, more and more businesses have come to recognize the importance and value of accounting information.

As indicated earlier, accountants who work for a business are employed in private accounting. Private accountants have a variety of possible career options within a company. Some of these career options are shown in Exhibit 3 along with their starting salaries. Accountants who provide audit services, called auditors, attest to the accuracy of financial records, accounts, and systems. As shown in Exhibit 3, several private accounting careers have certification options.

Accounting Career Paths and Salaries EXHIBIT 3

Accounting Career Track	Description	Career Options	Annual Starting Salaries*	Certification
Private Accounting	Accountants employed by companies, government, and not-for-profit entities.	Bookkeeper	$43,000	
		Payroll clerk	$39,000	Certified Payroll Professional (CPP)
		General accountant	$47,000	
		Budget analyst	$51,000	
		Cost accountant	$49,000	Certified Management Accountant (CMA)
		Internal auditor	$46,000	Certified Internal Auditor (CIA)
		Information technology auditor	$51,000	Certified Information Systems Auditor (CISA)
Public Accounting	Accountants employed individually or within a public accounting firm in audit, tax, or management advisory services.		$47,000	Certified Public Accountant (CPA)

*Average salaries rounded to the nearest thousand. Salaries may vary by size of company and region.
Source: Robert Half *2019 U.S. Salary Guide (Finance and Accounting)*, Robert Half International, Inc. (www.roberthalf.com/workplace-research/salary-guides).

Accountants who provide services on a fee basis are said to be employed in **public accounting**. In public accounting, an accountant may practice as an individual or as a member of a public accounting firm. Public accountants who have met a state's education, experience, and examination requirements may become **Certified Public Accountants (CPAs)**.

Because all functions within a business use accounting information, experience in private or public accounting provides a solid foundation for a career. Many high-level positions in industry and in government agencies are held by individuals with accounting backgrounds.

Business Connection

PATHWAYS COMMISSION

The Pathways Commission issued its study titled *Charting a National Strategy for the Next Generation of Accountants*. The Commission was made up of diverse members and was jointly sponsored by the American Institute of Certified Public Accountants (AICPA) and the American Accounting Association (AAA). The Commission emphasized the importance of accounting for a prosperous society and good decision making. The Commission also emphasized that accountants must be critical thinkers who are comfortable addressing the shades of gray required by accounting judgments.

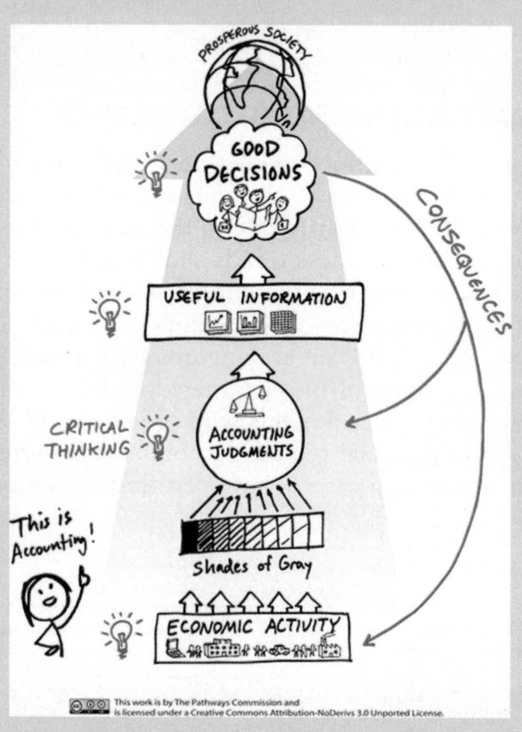

Source: *Charting a National Strategy for the Next Generation of Accountants*, The Pathways Commission, July 2012.

OBJ. 2 Summarize the development of accounting principles and relate them to practice.

Generally Accepted Accounting Principles

If companies did not follow the same rules when reporting financial information, comparisons among companies would be difficult, if not impossible. Thus, financial accountants follow **generally accepted accounting principles (GAAP)** in preparing reports. These reports allow investors and other users to compare one company to another.

Accounting principles and concepts develop from research, accepted accounting practices, and pronouncements of regulators. Within the United States, the

Financial Accounting Standards Board (FASB) has the primary responsibility for developing accounting principles. The FASB maintains an electronic database, called the **Accounting Standards Codification**, that contains all the accounting standards that make up GAAP. Changes in the FASB Codification are made using **Accounting Standards Updates**.

The **Securities and Exchange Commission (SEC),** an agency of the U.S. government, has authority over the accounting and financial disclosures for companies whose shares of ownership (stock) are traded and sold to the public. The SEC normally accepts the accounting principles set forth by the FASB. However, the SEC may issue *Staff Accounting Bulletins* on accounting matters that may not have been addressed by the FASB.

Many countries outside the United States use accounting principles adopted by the **International Accounting Standards Board (IASB)**. The IASB issues *International Financial Reporting Standards (IFRS)*. Differences currently exist between FASB and IASB accounting principles. Investors and other stakeholders should be aware of these differences in analyzing financial reports of international companies. Throughout this text, International Connection boxes, such as the one at the bottom of this page, highlight many of these differences. In addition, Appendix B at the end of this text summarizes differences between U.S. GAAP and IFRS.

In this chapter and text, accounting principles and concepts are emphasized. It is through this emphasis on the "why" as well as the "how" that you will gain an understanding of accounting.

Business Entity Concept

The **business entity concept** limits the economic data in an accounting system to data related directly to the activities of the business. In other words, the business is viewed as an entity separate from its owners, creditors, or other businesses. For example, the accountant for a business with one owner would record the activities of the business only and would not record the personal activities, property, or debts of the owner.

Note

Under the business entity concept, the activities of a business are recorded separately from the activities of its owners, creditors, or other businesses.

A business entity may take the form of a proprietorship, partnership, corporation, or **limited liability company (LLC)**. Each of these forms and their major characteristics are listed in Exhibit 4.

The three types of businesses discussed earlier—service, merchandising, and manufacturing—may be organized as proprietorships, partnerships, corporations, or limited liability companies. Because of the large amount of resources required to operate a manufacturing business, most manufacturers such as **Ford Motor Company** are corporations. Most large retailers such as **Wal-Mart** and **The Home Depot** are also corporations.

International Connection

INTERNATIONAL FINANCIAL REPORTING STANDARDS (IFRS)

IFRS are considered to be more "principles-based" than U.S. GAAP, which is considered to be more "rules-based." For example, U.S. GAAP consists of approximately 17,000 pages, which include numerous industry-specific accounting rules. In contrast, IFRS allow more judgment in deciding how business transactions are recorded. Many believe that the strong regulatory and litigation environment in the United States is the cause for the more rules-based GAAP approach. Regardless, IFRS and GAAP share many common principles.

EXHIBIT 4 Forms of Business Entities

Form of Business Entity	Characteristics	Examples
Proprietorship is owned by one individual.	• 70% of business entities in the United States. • Easy and inexpensive to organize. • Resources are limited to those of the owner. • Used by small businesses.	• A & B Painting
Partnership is owned by two or more individuals.	• 10% of business organizations in the United States (combined with limited liability companies). • Combines the skills and resources of more than one person.	• Jones & Smith, Architects
Corporation is organized under state or federal statutes as a separate legal taxable entity.	• Generates 90% of business revenues. • 20% of the business organizations in the United States. • Ownership is divided into shares called stock. • Can obtain large amounts of resources by issuing stock. • Used by large businesses.	• **Alphabet (Google)** • **Apple** • **Ford Motor Company** • **Twitter**
Limited liability company (LLC) combines the attributes of a partnership and a corporation.	• 10% of business organizations in the United States (combined with partnerships). • Often used as an alternative to a partnership. • Has tax and legal liability advantages for owners.	• Mosel & Farmer, CPAs, LLC

Time Period Concept

The **time period concept** requires a company to report its economic activities on a regular basis for a specific period. In doing so, financial condition and operating results of the company are reported periodically on a consistent basis. Financial accounting reports are often prepared monthly, quarterly, and yearly.

The annual accounting period adopted by a company is called its **fiscal year**. The fiscal year most commonly used is the calendar year beginning January 1 and ending December 31. However, other periods are not unusual, especially for companies organized as corporations.

> **Link to Twitter**
>
> **Twitter** uses an annual accounting period ending December 31.

Corporations often use a fiscal year that ends when business activities have reached the lowest point in their annual operating cycle, which allows more time to prepare financial reports. Such a fiscal year is called the **natural business year**. For example, the natural business year for most retail businesses is January 31, which is after the busy holiday season and end-of-year sales. To illustrate, **Wal-Mart Stores, Inc.** recently reported its annual financial results for the year ending January 31.

Throughout this text, we use the notation 20Y1, 20Y2, 20Y3, etc., to indicate years.[3] For example, a company's fiscal year could begin August 1, 20Y7, and end on July 31, 20Y8, as follows:

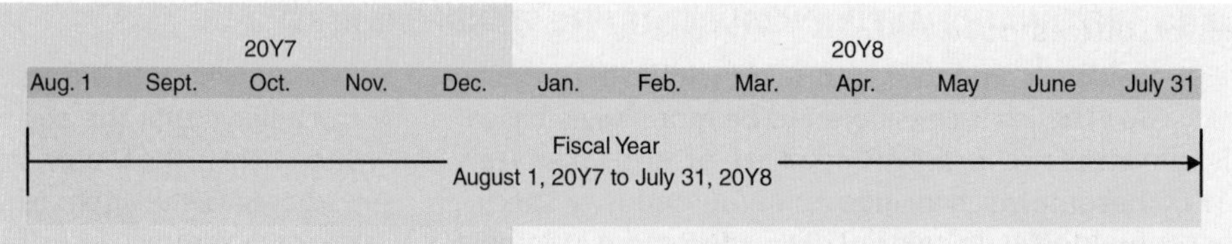

3 We use this notation to reduce the number of changes necessary when revising this and future editions of the text. This, in turn, reduces the cost of each revision, which helps reduce the need to increase the retail price of the text.

Cost Concept

Under the **cost concept**, amounts are initially recorded in the accounting records at their cost or purchase price. To illustrate, assume that Aaron Publishers purchased a building on February 20, 20Y2, for $150,000. The following additional information applies to the building:

Price listed by seller on January 1, 20Y2	$160,000
Aaron Publishers' initial offer to buy on January 31, 20Y2	140,000
Purchase price on February 20, 20Y2	150,000
Estimated selling price on December 31, 20Y7	220,000
Assessed value for property taxes, December 31, 20Y7	190,000

Under the cost concept, Aaron Publishers records the purchase of the building on February 20, 20Y2, at the purchase price of $150,000. The other amounts listed have no effect on the accounting records.

The fact that the building has an estimated selling price of $220,000 on December 31, 20Y7, indicates that the building has increased in value. However, to use the $220,000 in the accounting records would be to record a profit before selling the building. If Aaron Publishers sells the building on January 9, 20Y9, for $240,000, a profit of $90,000 ($240,000 – $150,000) is then realized and recorded. The new owner would record $240,000 as its cost of the building.

The cost concept also involves the objectivity and unit of measure concepts. The **objectivity concept** requires that the amounts recorded in the accounting records be based on unbiased evidence. In exchanges between a buyer and a seller, both try to get the best price. Only the final agreed-upon amount is objective enough to be recorded in the accounting records. If amounts in the accounting records were constantly being revised upward or downward based on offers, appraisals, and opinions, accounting reports could become unstable and unreliable.

The **unit of measure concept** requires that economic data be recorded in dollars. Money is a common unit of measurement for reporting financial data and reports.

EXAMPLE EXERCISE 1-1 Cost Concept **OBJ. 2**

On August 25, Gallatin Repair Service extended an offer of $400,000 for land that had been priced for sale at $500,000. On September 3, Gallatin Repair Service accepted the seller's counteroffer of $460,000. On October 20, the land was assessed at a value of $300,000 for property tax purposes. On December 4, a national retail chain offered Gallatin Repair Service $525,000 for the land. At what value should the land be recorded in Gallatin Repair Service's records?

Follow My Example 1-1

$460,000. Under the cost concept, the land should be recorded at the cost to Gallatin Repair Service.

Practice Exercises: PE 1-1A, PE 1-1B

The Accounting Equation

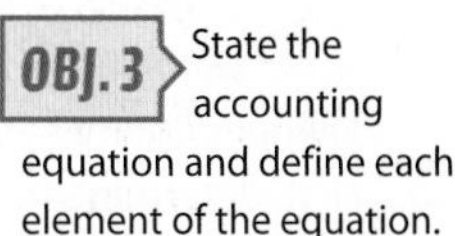

The resources owned by a business are its **assets**. Examples of assets include cash, land, buildings, and equipment. The rights or claims to the assets are divided into two types: (1) the rights of creditors and (2) the rights of owners. The rights of creditors are the debts of the business and are called **liabilities**. The rights of the owners of a proprietorship, partnership, or limited liability company are called **owner's equity**. Since stockholders own a corporation, the rights of owners of a corporation are called **stockholders' equity**.

Link to Twitter

Twitter's accounting equation for a recent year: Assets ($10,163 million) = Liabilities ($3,357 million) + Stockholders' Equity ($6,806 million)

The following equation shows the relationship among assets, liabilities, and owner's equity:

Assets = Liabilities + Owner's Equity

This equation is called the **accounting equation**. Liabilities usually are shown before owner's equity in the accounting equation because creditors have first rights to the assets.

Given any two amounts, the accounting equation may be solved for the third unknown amount. To illustrate, if the assets owned by a business amount to $100,000 and the liabilities amount to $30,000, the owner's equity is equal to $70,000, computed as follows:

Assets	−	**Liabilities**	=	**Owner's Equity**
$100,000	−	$30,000	=	$70,000

Business Connection

THE ACCOUNTING EQUATION

The accounting equation serves as the basic foundation for the accounting systems of all companies. From the smallest business, such as the local convenience store, to the largest business, such as **The Coca-Cola Company**, companies use the accounting equation. Some examples taken from recent financial reports of well-known corporations follow:

Company	Assets*	= Liabilities	+ Stockholders' Equity
Alphabet (Google)	$232,792 =	$55,164 +	$177,628
The Coca-Cola Company	$83,216 =	$66,235 +	$16,981
DowDuPont	$188,030 =	$93,459 +	$94,571
eBay	$22,819 =	$16,538 +	$6,281
Target	$37,431 =	$26,478 +	$10,953
Microsoft Corporation	$258,848 =	$176,130 +	$82,718
Southwest Airlines Co.	$26,243 =	$16,390 +	$9,853
Wal-Mart Stores, Inc.	$204,522 =	$123,700 +	$80,822

*Amounts are shown in millions of dollars.

EXAMPLE EXERCISE 1-2 Accounting Equation — OBJ. 3

John Joos is the owner and operator of You're A Star, a motivational consulting business. At the end of its accounting period, December 31, 20Y8, You're A Star has assets of $800,000 and liabilities of $350,000. Using the accounting equation, determine the following amounts:

a. Owner's equity as of December 31, 20Y8.
b. Owner's equity as of December 31, 20Y9, assuming that assets increased by $130,000 and liabilities decreased by $25,000 during 20Y9.

Follow My Example 1-2

a. Assets = Liabilities + Owner's Equity
$800,000 = $350,000 + Owner's Equity
Owner's Equity = $450,000

b. First, determine the change in owner's equity during 20Y9 as follows:
Assets = Liabilities + Owner's Equity
$130,000 = −$25,000 + Owner's Equity
Owner's Equity = $155,000

Next, add the change in owner's equity during 20Y9 to the owner's equity on December 31, 20Y8, to arrive at owner's equity on December 31, 20Y9, as follows:

Owner's Equity on December 31, 20Y9 = $450,000 (Owner's Equity on December 31, 20Y8) + $155,000 (change in Owner's Equity) = $605,000

Practice Exercises: PE 1-2A, PE 1-2B

Business Transactions and the Accounting Equation

OBJ. 4 Describe and illustrate how business transactions can be recorded in terms of the resulting change in the elements of the accounting equation.

Paying a monthly bill, such as a telephone bill of $168, affects a business's financial condition because it now has less cash on hand. Such an economic event or condition that directly changes an entity's financial condition or its results of operations is a **business transaction**. For example, purchasing land for $50,000 is a business transaction. In contrast, a change in a business's credit rating does not directly affect cash or any other asset, liability, or owner's equity amount.

All business transactions can be stated in terms of changes in the elements of the accounting equation. How business transactions affect the accounting equation can be illustrated by using some typical transactions. As a basis for illustration, a business organized by Chris Clark is used.

Note

All business transactions can be stated in terms of changes in the elements of the accounting equation.

Assume that on November 1, 20Y3, Chris Clark begins a business that will be known as **NetSolutions**. The first phase of Chris's business plan is to operate NetSolutions as a service business assisting individuals and small businesses in developing web pages and installing computer software. Chris expects this initial phase of the business to last one to two years. During this period, Chris plans on gathering information on the software and hardware needs of customers. During the second phase of the business plan, Chris plans to expand NetSolutions into a personalized retailer of software and hardware for individuals and small businesses.

Each transaction during NetSolutions' first month of operations is described in the following paragraphs. The effect of each transaction on the accounting equation is then shown.

Nov. 1, 20Y3 Chris Clark deposited $25,000 in a bank account in the name of NetSolutions.

Transaction A

This transaction increases the asset cash (on the left side of the equation) by $25,000. To balance the equation, the owner's equity (on the right side of the equation) increases by the same amount. The equity of the owner is identified using the owner's name and "Capital," such as "Chris Clark, Capital."

The effect of this transaction on NetSolutions' accounting equation is as follows:

Assets	=	Owner's Equity
Cash		Chris Clark, Capital
a. 25,000	=	25,000

Since Chris Clark is the sole owner, NetSolutions is a proprietorship. Also, the preceding accounting equation is only for the business, NetSolutions. Under the business entity assumption, Chris's personal assets, such as his home, personal bank account, and personal liabilities are excluded from the equation.

Nov. 5, 20Y3 NetSolutions paid $20,000 for the purchase of land as a future building site.

Transaction B

The land is located in a business park with access to transportation facilities. Chris Clark plans to rent office space and equipment during the first phase of the business plan. During the second phase, Chris plans to build an office and a warehouse on the land.

The purchase of the land changes the makeup of the assets, but it does not change the total assets. The items in the equation prior to this transaction and the effect of the transaction follow. The new amounts are called *balances*.

	Assets		=	Owner's Equity
	Cash	+ Land	=	Chris Clark, Capital
Bal.	25,000			25,000
b.	−20,000	+20,000		
Bal.	5,000	20,000		25,000
	25,000		=	25,000

Transaction C *Nov. 10, 20Y3 NetSolutions purchased supplies for $1,350 and agreed to pay the supplier in the near future.*

You have probably used a credit card to buy clothing or other merchandise. In this type of transaction, you received clothing for a promise to pay your credit card bill in the future. That is, you received an asset and incurred a liability to pay a future bill. NetSolutions entered into a similar transaction by purchasing supplies for $1,350 and agreeing to pay the supplier in the near future. This type of transaction is called a purchase *on account* and is often described as follows: *Purchased supplies on account, $1,350.*

The liability created by a purchase on account is called an **account payable**. Items such as supplies that will be used in the business in the future are called **prepaid expenses**, which are assets. Thus, the effect of this transaction is to increase assets (Supplies) and liabilities (Accounts Payable) by $1,350, as follows:

	Assets			=	Liabilities + Owner's Equity	
	Cash	+ Supplies +	Land	=	Accounts Payable +	Chris Clark, Capital
Bal.	5,000		20,000			25,000
c.		+1,350			+1,350	
Bal.	5,000	1,350	20,000		1,350	25,000
	26,350			=	26,350	

Transaction D *Nov. 18, 20Y3 NetSolutions received cash of $7,500 for providing services to customers.*

You may have earned money by painting houses or mowing lawns. If so, you received money for rendering services to a customer. Likewise, a business earns money by selling goods or services to its customers. This amount is called **revenue**.

During its first month of operations, NetSolutions received cash of $7,500 for providing services to customers. The receipt of cash increases NetSolutions' assets and also increases Chris Clark's equity in the business. The revenues of $7,500 are recorded in a Fees Earned column to the right of Chris Clark, Capital. The effect of this transaction is to increase Cash and Fees Earned by $7,500, as follows:

	Assets			=	Liabilities +	Owner's Equity	
	Cash	+ Supplies +	Land	=	Accounts Payable +	Chris Clark, Capital	+ Fees Earned
Bal.	5,000	1,350	20,000		1,350	25,000	
d.	+7,500						+7,500
Bal.	12,500	1,350	20,000		1,350	25,000	7,500
	33,850			=	33,850		

Different terms are used for the various types of revenues. As illustrated for NetSolutions, revenue from providing services is recorded as **fees earned**. Revenue from the sale of merchandise is recorded as **sales**. Other examples of revenue include rent, which is recorded as **rent revenue**, and interest, which is recorded as **interest revenue**.

Instead of receiving cash at the time services are provided or goods are sold, a business may accept payment at a later date. Such revenues are described as *fees earned on account* or *sales on account*. For example, if NetSolutions had provided services on account instead of for cash, transaction (d) would have been described as follows: *Fees earned on account, $7,500.*

In such cases, the firm has an asset, called an **account receivable**, which is a claim against the customer. Fees earned on account are recorded as increases in Accounts Receivable and Fees Earned. When customers pay their accounts, Cash increases, and Accounts Receivable decreases.

Nov. 30, 20Y3 NetSolutions paid the following expenses during the month: wages, $2,125; rent, $800; utilities, $450; and miscellaneous, $275. ***Transaction E***

During the month, NetSolutions spent cash or used up other assets in earning revenue. Assets used in this process of earning revenue are called **expenses**. Expenses include supplies used and payments for employee wages, utilities, and other services.

NetSolutions paid the following expenses during the month: wages, $2,125; rent, $800; utilities, $450; and miscellaneous, $275. Miscellaneous expenses include small amounts paid for such items as postage, coffee, and newspapers. The effect of expenses is the opposite of revenues in that expenses reduce assets and owner's equity. Like fees earned, the expenses are recorded in columns to the right of Chris Clark, Capital. However, since expenses reduce owner's equity, the expenses are entered as negative amounts. The effect of this transaction is as follows:

	Assets			=	**Liabilities +**	**Owner's Equity**					
	Cash +	Supplies +	Land	=	Accounts Payable +	Chris Clark, Capital +	Fees Earned −	Wages Exp. −	Rent Exp. −	Utilities Exp. −	Misc. Exp.
Bal.	12,500	1,350	20,000		1,350	25,000	7,500				
e.	−3,650							−2,125	−800	−450	−275
Bal.	8,850	1,350	20,000		1,350	25,000	7,500	−2,125	−800	−450	−275
		30,200		=			30,200				

Businesses usually record each revenue and expense transaction as it occurs. However, to simplify, NetSolutions' revenues and expenses are summarized for the month in transactions (d) and (e).

Nov. 30, 20Y3 NetSolutions paid creditors on account, $950. ***Transaction F***

When you pay your monthly credit card bill, you decrease the cash and decrease the amount you owe to the credit card company. Likewise, when NetSolutions pays $950 to creditors during the month, it reduces assets and liabilities, as follows:

	Assets			=	**Liabilities +**	**Owner's Equity**					
	Cash +	Supplies +	Land	=	Accounts Payable +	Chris Clark, Capital +	Fees Earned −	Wages Exp. −	Rent Exp. −	Utilities Exp. −	Misc. Exp.
Bal.	8,850	1,350	20,000		1,350	25,000	7,500	−2,125	−800	−450	−275
f.	−950				−950						
Bal.	7,900	1,350	20,000		400	25,000	7,500	−2,125	−800	−450	−275
		29,250		=			29,250				

Paying an amount on account is different from paying an expense. The paying of an expense reduces owner's equity, as illustrated in transaction (e). Paying an amount on account reduces the amount owed on a liability.

Nov. 30, 20Y3 Chris Clark determined that the cost of supplies on hand at the end of the month was $550. ***Transaction G***

The cost of the supplies on hand (not yet used) at the end of the month is $550. Thus, $800 ($1,350 − $550) of supplies must have been used during the month. This decrease in supplies is recorded as an expense, as follows:

	Assets			=	Liabilities +	Owner's Equity						
	Cash	+ Supplies +	Land	=	Accounts Payable +	Chris Clark, Capital	+ Fees Earned −	Wages Exp. −	Rent Exp. −	Supplies Exp. −	Utilities Exp. −	Misc. Exp.
Bal.	7,900	1,350	20,000		400	25,000	7,500	−2,125	−800		−450	−275
g.		−800								−800		
Bal.	7,900	550	20,000		400	25,000	7,500	−2,125	−800	−800	−450	−275
	28,450			=	28,450							

Transaction H *Nov. 30, 20Y3 Chris Clark withdrew $2,000 from NetSolutions for personal use.*

At the end of the month, Chris Clark withdrew $2,000 in cash from the business for personal use. This transaction is the opposite of an investment in the business by the owner. Withdrawals by the owner should not be confused with expenses. Withdrawals *do not* represent assets or services used in the process of earning revenues. Instead, withdrawals are a distribution of capital to the owner. Owner withdrawals are identified by the owner's name and *Drawing*. For example, Chris's withdrawal is identified as Chris Clark, Drawing. Like expenses, withdrawals are recorded in a column to the right of Chris Clark, Capital. The effect of the $2,000 withdrawal is as follows:

	Assets			=	Liabilities +	Owner's Equity							
	Cash	+ Supp. +	Land	=	Accounts Payable +	Chris Clark, Capital	− Chris Clark, Drawing	+ Fees Earned −	Wages Exp. −	Rent Exp. −	Supplies Exp. −	Utilities Exp. −	Misc. Exp.
Bal.	7,900	550	20,000		400	25,000		7,500	−2,125	−800	−800	−450	−275
h.	−2,000						−2,000						
Bal.	5,900	550	20,000		400	25,000	−2,000	7,500	−2,125	−800	−800	−450	−275
	26,450			=	26,450								

Summary

The transactions of **NetSolutions** are summarized in Exhibit 5. Each transaction is identified by letter, and the balance of each accounting equation element is shown after every transaction.

EXHIBIT 5 **Summary of Transactions for NetSolutions**

	Assets			=	Liabilities +	Owner's Equity							
	Cash	+ Supp. +	Land	=	Accounts Payable +	Chris Clark, Capital	− Chris Clark, Drawing	+ Fees Earned −	Wages Exp. −	Rent Exp. −	Supplies Exp. −	Utilities Exp. −	Misc. Exp.
a.	+25,000					+25,000							
b.	−20,000		+20,000										
Bal.	5,000		20,000			25,000							
c.		+1,350			+1,350								
Bal.	5,000	+1,350	20,000		+1,350	25,000							
d.	+7,500							+7,500					
Bal.	12,500	1,350	20,000		1,350	25,000		7,500					
e.	−3,650								−2,125	−800		−450	−275
Bal.	8,850	1,350	20,000		1,350	25,000		7,500	−2,125	−800		−450	−275
f.	−950				−950								
Bal.	7,900	1,350	20,000		400	25,000		7,500	−2,125	−800		−450	−275
g.		−800									−800		
Bal.	7,900	550	20,000		400	25,000		7,500	−2,125	−800	−800	−450	−275
h.	−2,000						−2,000						
Bal.	5,900	550	20,000		400	25,000	−2,000	7,500	−2,125	−800	−800	−450	−275
	26,450			=	26,450								

You should note the following:

- The effect of every transaction *is an increase or a decrease in one or more of the accounting equation elements.*
- The two sides of the accounting equation are *always equal.*
- The owner's equity is *increased by amounts invested by the owner* and is *decreased by withdrawals by the owner.* In addition, the owner's equity is *increased by revenues* and is *decreased by expenses.*

The four types of transactions affecting owner's equity are illustrated in Exhibit 6.

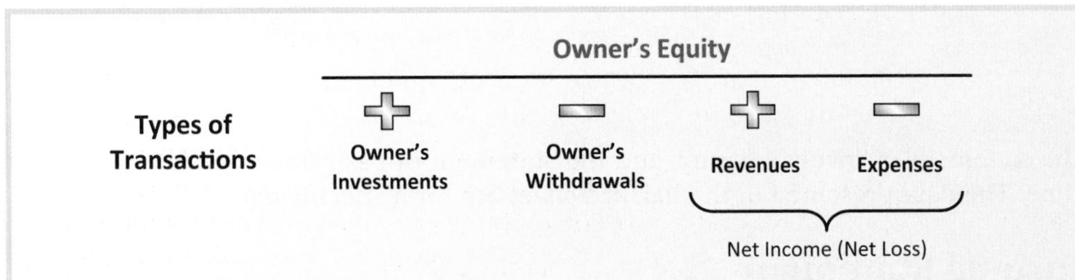

EXHIBIT 6
Types of Transactions Affecting Owner's Equity

EXAMPLE EXERCISE 1-3 Transactions **OBJ. 4**

Salvo Delivery Service is owned and operated by Joel Salvo. The following selected transactions were completed by Salvo Delivery Service during February:

1. Received cash from owner as additional investment, $35,000.
2. Paid creditors on account, $1,800.
3. Billed customers for delivery services on account, $11,250.
4. Received cash from customers on account, $6,740.
5. Paid cash to owner for personal use, $1,000.

Indicate the effect of each transaction on the accounting equation elements (Assets, Liabilities, Owner's Equity, Drawing, Revenue, and Expense). Also indicate the specific item within the accounting equation element that is affected. To illustrate, the answer to (1) follows:

(1) Asset (Cash) increases by $35,000; Owner's Equity (Joel Salvo, Capital) increases by $35,000.

Follow My Example 1-3

(2) Asset (Cash) decreases by $1,800; Liability (Accounts Payable) decreases by $1,800.

(3) Asset (Accounts Receivable) increases by $11,250; Revenue (Delivery Service Fees) increases by $11,250.

(4) Asset (Cash) increases by $6,740; Asset (Accounts Receivable) decreases by $6,740.

(5) Asset (Cash) decreases by $1,000; Drawing (Joel Salvo, Drawing) increases by $1,000.

Practice Exercises: PE 1-3A, PE 1-3B

Financial Statements

OBJ. 5 Describe the financial statements of a proprietorship and explain how they interrelate.

After transactions have been recorded and summarized, reports are prepared for users. The accounting reports providing this information are called **financial statements**. The primary financial statements of a proprietorship are the income statement, the statement of owner's equity, the balance sheet, and the statement of cash flows. The order in which the financial statements are prepared and the nature of each statement are described in Exhibit 7.

The four financial statements and their interrelationships are illustrated later in this chapter. The data for the statements are taken from the summary of **NetSolutions**' transactions in Exhibit 5.

All financial statements are identified by the name of the business, the title of the statement, and the *date* or *period of time*. The data presented in the income statement,

EXHIBIT 7
Financial Statements

Order Prepared	Financial Statement	Description of Statement
1.	**Income statement**	A summary of the revenue and expenses *for a specific period of time*, such as a month or a year.
2.	**Statement of owner's equity**	A summary of the changes in the owner's equity that have occurred *during a specific period of time*, such as a month or a year.
3.	**Balance sheet**	A list of the assets, liabilities, and owner's equity *as of a specific date*, usually at the close of the last day of a month or a year.
4.	**Statement of cash flows**	A summary of the cash receipts and cash payments for a *specific period of time*, such as a month or a year.

the statement of owner's equity, and the statement of cash flows are for a period of time. The data presented in the balance sheet are for a specific date.

Note

When revenues exceed expenses, it is referred to as *net income, net profit,* or *earnings*. When expenses exceed revenues, it is referred to as *net loss*.

Link to Twitter

For a recent year, **Twitter** reported net income of $1.2 billion.

Income Statement

The income statement reports the revenues and expenses for a *period of time*, based on the **matching concept**. This concept is applied by *matching* the expenses incurred during a period with the revenue that those expenses generated. The excess of the revenue over the expenses is called **net income**, **net profit**, or **earnings**. If the expenses exceed the revenue, the excess is a **net loss**.

The revenue and expenses for NetSolutions were shown in the accounting equation as separate increases and decreases. Net income for a period increases the owner's equity (capital) for the period. A net loss decreases the owner's equity (capital) for the period.

The revenue, the expenses, and the net income of $3,050 for NetSolutions are reported in the income statement in Exhibit 8. The order in which the expenses are listed in the income statement varies among businesses. Most businesses list expenses in order of size, beginning with the larger items. Miscellaneous expense is usually shown as the last item, regardless of the amount.

EXAMPLE EXERCISE 1-4 Income Statement **OBJ. 5**

The revenues and expenses of Chickadee Travel Service for the year ended December 31, 20Y9, follow:

Fees earned	$263,200
Miscellaneous expense	12,950
Office expense	63,000
Wages expense	131,700

Prepare an income statement for the year ended December 31, 20Y9.

Follow My Example 1-4

Chickadee Travel Service
Income Statement
For the Year Ended December 31, 20Y9

Fees earned		$263,200
Expenses:		
Wages expense	$131,700	
Office expense	63,000	
Miscellaneous expense	12,950	
Total expenses		207,650
Net income		$ 55,550

Practice Exercises: PE 1-4A, PE 1-4B

Statement of Owner's Equity

The statement of owner's equity reports the changes in the owner's equity for a period of time. It is prepared *after* the income statement because the net income or net loss for the period must be reported in this statement. Similarly, it is prepared *before* the balance sheet because the amount of owner's equity at the end of the period must be reported on the balance sheet. As a result, the statement of owner's equity is often viewed as the connecting link between the income statement and balance sheet.

Three types of transactions affected owner's equity of NetSolutions during November:

- the original investment of $25,000,
- the revenue of $7,500 and expenses of $4,450 that resulted in net income of $3,050 for the month, and
- a withdrawal of $2,000 by the owner.

The preceding information is summarized in the statement of owner's equity in Exhibit 8.

EXAMPLE EXERCISE 1-5 Statement of Owner's Equity **OBJ. 5**

Using the income statement for Chickadee Travel Service shown in Example Exercise 1-4, prepare a statement of owner's equity for the year ended December 31, 20Y9. Adam Cellini, the owner, invested an additional $50,000 in the business and withdrew cash of $30,000 for personal use during the year. The capital of Adam Cellini was $80,000 on January 1, 20Y9.

Follow My Example 1-5

Chickadee Travel Service
Statement of Owner's Equity
For the Year Ended December 31, 20Y9

Adam Cellini, capital, January 1, 20Y9		$ 80,000
Additional investment by owner during year	$ 50,000	
Net income for the year	55,550	
Withdrawals	(30,000)	
Increase in owner's equity		75,550
Adam Cellini, capital, December 31, 20Y9		$155,550

Practice Exercises: PE 1-5A, PE 1-5B

Balance Sheet

The balance sheet in Exhibit 8 reports the amounts of NetSolutions' assets, liabilities, and owner's equity as of November 30, 20Y3. The asset and liability amounts are taken from the last line of the summary of transactions in Exhibit 5. Chris Clark, Capital as of November 30, 20Y3, is taken from the statement of owner's equity. The form of balance sheet shown in Exhibit 8 is called the **account form**. This is because it resembles the basic format of the accounting equation, with assets on the left side and the liabilities and owner's equity sections on the right side.

The Assets section of the balance sheet presents assets in the order that they will be converted into cash or used in operations. Cash is presented first, followed by receivables, supplies, prepaid insurance, and other assets. The assets of a more permanent nature are shown next, such as land, buildings, and equipment.

In the Liabilities section of the balance sheet in Exhibit 8, accounts payable is the only liability. When there are two or more liabilities, each should be listed and the total amount of liabilities presented as follows:

Liabilities		
Accounts payable	$12,900	
Wages payable	2,570	
Total liabilities		$15,470

REAL WORLD

Bank loan officers use a business's financial statements in deciding whether to grant a loan to the business. Once the loan is granted, the borrower may be required to maintain a certain level of assets in excess of liabilities. The business's financial statements are used to monitor this level.

EXHIBIT 8

Financial Statements for NetSolutions

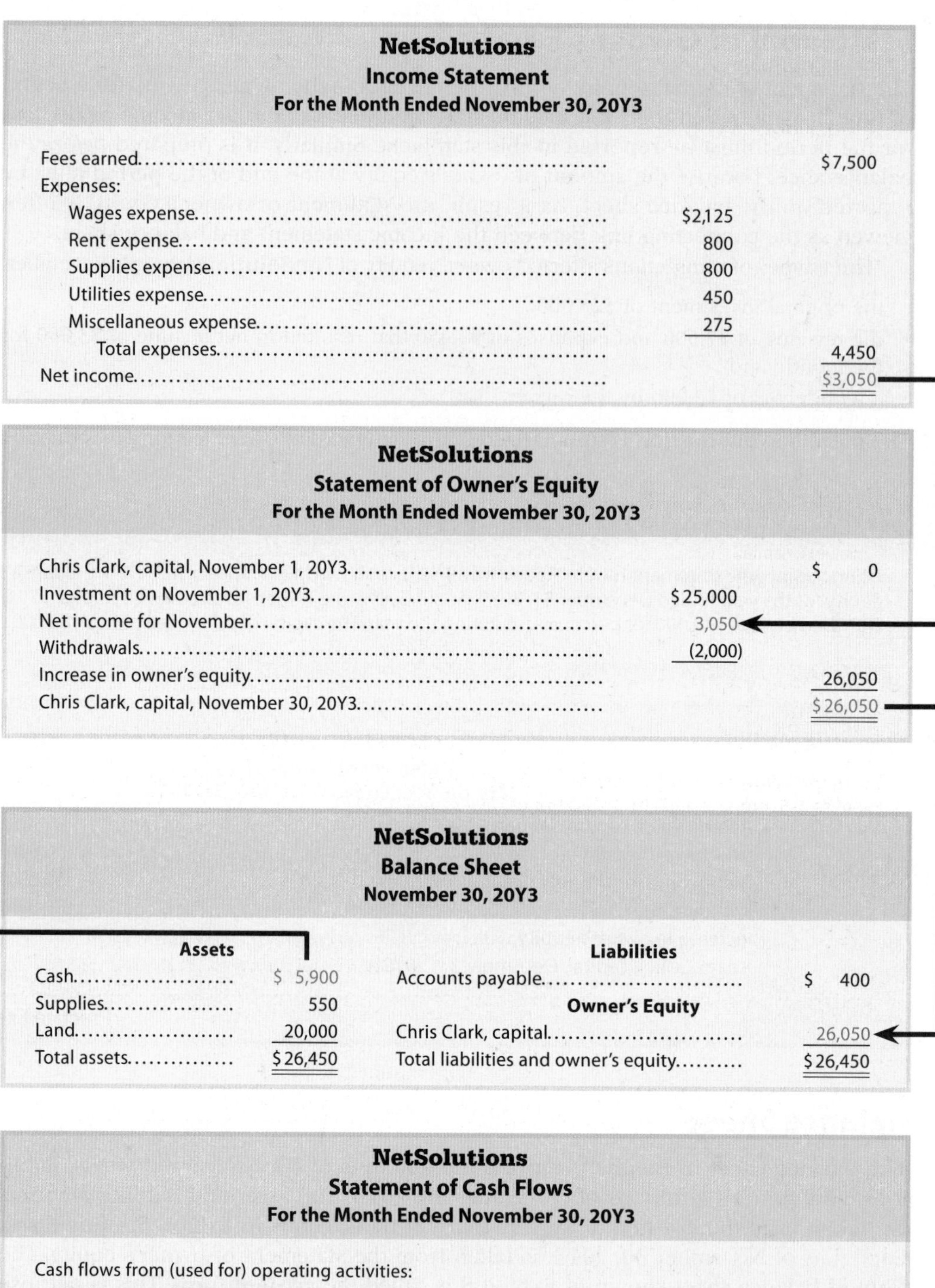

NetSolutions
Income Statement
For the Month Ended November 30, 20Y3

Fees earned		$7,500
Expenses:		
Wages expense	$2,125	
Rent expense	800	
Supplies expense	800	
Utilities expense	450	
Miscellaneous expense	275	
Total expenses		4,450
Net income		$3,050

NetSolutions
Statement of Owner's Equity
For the Month Ended November 30, 20Y3

Chris Clark, capital, November 1, 20Y3		$ 0
Investment on November 1, 20Y3	$25,000	
Net income for November	3,050	
Withdrawals	(2,000)	
Increase in owner's equity		26,050
Chris Clark, capital, November 30, 20Y3		$26,050

NetSolutions
Balance Sheet
November 30, 20Y3

Assets		Liabilities	
Cash	$ 5,900	Accounts payable	$ 400
Supplies	550	**Owner's Equity**	
Land	20,000	Chris Clark, capital	26,050
Total assets	$26,450	Total liabilities and owner's equity	$26,450

NetSolutions
Statement of Cash Flows
For the Month Ended November 30, 20Y3

Cash flows from (used for) operating activities:		
Cash received from customers	$ 7,500	
Cash paid for expenses and to creditors	(4,600)	
Net cash flows from operating activities		$ 2,900
Cash flows from (used for) for investing activities:		
Cash paid for acquisition of land		(20,000)
Cash flows from (used for) financing activities:		
Cash received from owner's investment	$ 25,000	
Cash withdrawal by owner	(2,000)	
Net cash flows from financing activities		23,000
Net increase in cash		$ 5,900
Cash balance, November 1, 20Y3		0
Cash balance, November 30, 20Y3		$ 5,900

The form of balance sheet shown in Exhibit 9 is called the **report form**. It lists the assets, liabilities, and owner's equity in a downward sequence. The report form is the most common form of reporting the balance sheet and for that reason is used in the remainder of this text.

EXHIBIT 9

Report Form of Balance Sheet

NetSolutions
Balance Sheet
November 30, 20Y3

Assets	
Cash	$ 5,900
Supplies	550
Land	20,000
Total assets	$26,450
Liabilities	
Accounts payable	$ 400
Owner's Equity	
Chris Clark, capital	26,050
Total liabilities and owner's equity	$26,450

EXAMPLE EXERCISE 1-6 Balance Sheet

OBJ. 5

Using the following data for Chickadee Travel Service as well as the statement of owner's equity shown in Example Exercise 1-5, prepare a balance sheet as of December 31, 20Y9.

Accounts payable	$12,200
Accounts receivable	31,350
Cash	53,050
Land	80,000
Supplies	3,350

Follow My Example 1-6

Chickadee Travel Service
Balance Sheet
December 31, 20Y9

Assets	
Cash	$ 53,050
Accounts receivable	31,350
Supplies	3,350
Land	80,000
Total assets	$167,750
Liabilities	
Accounts payable	$ 12,200
Owner's Equity	
Adam Cellini, capital	155,550
Total liabilities and owner's equity	$167,750

Practice Exercises: PE 1-6A, PE 1-6B

Statement of Cash Flows

The statement of cash flows consists of the following three sections, as shown in Exhibit 8:

1. operating activities
2. investing activities
3. financing activities

Each of these sections is briefly described in this section.

Cash Flows from (Used for) Operating Activities This section reports a summary of cash receipts and cash payments from operations. The net cash flows from operating activities normally differs from the amount of net income for the period. In Exhibit 8, **NetSolutions** reported net cash flows from operating activities of $2,900 and net income of $3,050. This difference occurs because revenues and expenses may not be recorded at the same time that cash is received from customers or paid to creditors.

Cash Flows from (Used for) Investing Activities This section reports the cash transactions for the acquisition and sale of relatively permanent assets such as land, buildings, and equipment. Exhibit 8 reports that **NetSolutions** paid $20,000 for the purchase of land during November.

Cash Flows from (Used for) Financing Activities This section reports the cash transactions related to cash investments by the owner, borrowings, and withdrawals by the owner. Exhibit 8 shows that Chris Clark invested $25,000 in **NetSolutions** and withdrew $2,000 during November.

Link to Twitter

For a recent year, **Twitter** reported $1,340 million of cash inflows from operating activities, $2,056 million of cash used for investing activities, $978 million of cash from financing activities, and net increase in cash of $262 million.

Preparing NetSolutions' Statement of Cash Flows Preparing the statement of cash flows requires that each of the November cash transactions for **NetSolutions** be classified as an operating, investing, or financing activity. Using the summary of transactions shown in Exhibit 5, the November cash transactions for NetSolutions are classified as follows:

Transaction	Amount	Cash Flow Activity
a.	$25,000	Financing (Investment by Chris Clark)
b.	−20,000	Investing (Purchase of land)
d.	7,500	Operating (Fees earned)
e.	−3,650	Operating (Payment of expenses)
f.	−950	Operating (Payment of account payable)
h.	−2,000	Financing (Withdrawal by Chris Clark)

Transactions (c) and (g) are not listed since they did not involve a cash receipt or payment. In addition, the payment of accounts payable in transaction (f) is classified as an operating activity because the account payable arose from the purchase of supplies, which are used in operations. Using the preceding classifications of November cash transactions, the statement of cash flows is prepared as shown in Exhibit 8.[4]

The ending cash balance shown on the statement of cash flows is also reported on the balance sheet as of the end of the period. To illustrate, the ending cash of $5,900 reported on the November statement of cash flows in Exhibit 8 is also reported as the amount of cash on hand in the November 30, 20Y3, balance sheet.

Since November is NetSolutions' first period of operations, the increase in cash for November and the November 30, 20Y3, cash balance are the same amount, $5,900, as shown in Exhibit 8. In later periods, NetSolutions will report in its statement of cash flows a beginning cash balance, an increase or a decrease in cash for the period, and an ending cash balance. For example, assume that for December NetSolutions has

4 This method of preparing the statement of cash flows is called the "direct method." This method and the indirect method are discussed further in Chapter 16.

a decrease in cash of $3,835. The last three lines of NetSolutions' statement of cash flows for December would be as follows:

Net decrease in cash	$(3,835)
Cash balance, December 1, 20Y3	5,900
Cash balance, December 31, 20Y3	$2,065

EXAMPLE EXERCISE 1-7 Statement of Cash Flows **OBJ. 5**

A summary of cash flows for Chickadee Travel Service for the year ended December 31, 20Y9, follows:

Cash receipts:	
Cash received from customers	$251,000
Cash received from additional investment of owner	50,000
Cash payments:	
Cash paid for expenses	210,000
Cash paid for land	80,000
Cash paid to owner for personal use	30,000

The cash balance as of January 1, 20Y9, was $72,050. Prepare a statement of cash flows for Chickadee Travel Service for the year ended December 31, 20Y9.

Follow My Example 1-7

Chickadee Travel Service
Statement of Cash Flows
For the Year Ended December 31, 20Y9

Cash flows from (used for) operating activities:		
Cash received from customers	$ 251,000	
Cash paid for expenses	(210,000)	
Net cash flows from operating activities		$ 41,000
Cash flows from (used for) investing activities:		
Cash payments for purchase of land		(80,000)
Cash flows from (used for) financing activities:		
Cash received from owner as investment	$ 50,000	
Cash withdrawals by owner	(30,000)	
Net cash flows from financing activities		20,000
Net decrease in cash		$(19,000)
Cash balance, January 1, 20Y9		72,050
Cash balance, December 31, 20Y9		$ 53,050

Practice Exercises: PE 1-7A, PE 1-7B

Interrelationships Among Financial Statements

Financial statements are prepared in the order of the income statement, statement of owner's equity, balance sheet, and statement of cash flows. This order is important because the financial statements are interrelated. These interrelationships for NetSolutions are shown in Exhibit 8 and are described in Exhibit 10.[5]

The preceding interrelationships are important in analyzing financial statements and the impact of transactions on a business. In addition, these interrelationships serve as a check on whether the financial statements are prepared correctly. For example, if the ending cash on the statement of cash flows does not agree with the balance sheet cash, then an error has occurred.

5 Depending on the method of preparing the Cash Flows from (Used for) Operating Activities section of the statement of cash flows, net income (or net loss) may also appear on the statement of cash flows. This interrelationship or method of preparing the statement of cash flows, called the "indirect method," is described and illustrated in Chapter 16.

EXHIBIT 10 **Financial Statement Interrelationships**

Financial Statements	Interrelationship	NetSolutions Example (Exhibit 8)
Income Statement *and* Statement of Owner's Equity	Net income or net loss reported on the income statement is also reported on the statement of owner's equity as either an addition (net income) to or deduction (net loss) from the beginning owner's equity and any additional investments by the owner during the period.	NetSolutions' net income of $3,050 for November is added to Chris Clark's investment of $25,000 on the statement of owner's equity.
Statement of Owner's Equity *and* Balance Sheet	Owner's capital at the end of the period reported on the statement of owner's equity is also reported on the balance sheet as owner's capital.	Chris Clark, Capital of $26,050 as of November 30, 20Y3, on the statement of owner's equity also appears on the November 30, 20Y3, balance sheet as Chris Clark, Capital.
Balance Sheet *and* Statement of Cash Flows	The cash reported on the balance sheet is also reported as the end-of-period cash on the statement of cash flows.	Cash of $5,900 reported on the balance sheet as of November 30, 20Y3, is also reported on the November statement of cash flows as the end-of-period cash.

Describe and illustrate the use of the ratio of liabilities to owner's equity in evaluating a company's financial condition.

FAI

Financial Analysis and Interpretation: Ratio of Liabilities to Owner's Equity

The basic financial statements illustrated in this chapter are useful to bankers, creditors, owners, and others in analyzing and interpreting the financial performance and condition of a company. Throughout this text, various tools and techniques that are often used to analyze and interpret a company's financial performance and condition are described and illustrated. The first such tool that is discussed is useful in analyzing the ability of a company to pay its creditors.

The relationship between liabilities and owner's equity, expressed as a **ratio of liabilities to owner's equity**, is computed as follows:

$$\text{Ratio of Liabilities to Owner's Equity} = \frac{\text{Total Liabilities}}{\text{Total Owner's Equity (or Total Stockholders' Equity)}}$$

NetSolutions' ratio of liabilities to owner's equity at the end of November is 0.015, computed as follows:

$$\text{Ratio of Liabilities to Owner's Equity} = \frac{\$400}{\$26{,}050} = 0.015 \text{ (Rounded)}$$

Corporations refer to total owner's equity as total stockholders' equity. Thus, total stockholders' equity is substituted for total owner's equity when computing this ratio.

To illustrate, recent balance sheet data (in millions) for **Alphabet (Google) Inc.** and **Amazon.com, Inc.** follow:

	Recent Year	Prior Year
Alphabet Inc.		
Total liabilities	$ 55,164	$ 44,793
Total stockholders' equity	177,628	152,502
Amazon.com, Inc.		
Total liabilities	$119,099	$103,601
Total stockholders' equity	43,549	27,709

The ratio of liabilities to stockholders' equity for Alphabet and Amazon.com for a recent year and the prior year is computed as follows:

	Recent Year*	Prior Year*
Alphabet Inc.		
Ratio of liabilities to stockholders' equity	0.31	0.29
	($55,164 ÷ $177,628)	($44,793 ÷ $152,502)
Amazon.com, Inc.		
Ratio of liabilities to stockholders' equity	2.73	3.74
	($119,099 ÷ $43,549)	($103,601 ÷ $27,709)

*Rounded to two decimal places.

The rights of creditors to a business's assets come before the rights of the owners or stockholders. Thus, the lower the ratio of liabilities to owner's equity, the better able the company is to withstand poor business conditions and to pay its obligations to creditors.

Alphabet is unusual in that it has a very low amount of liabilities. Its ratio of liabilities to stockholders' equity of 0.31 in the recent year and 0.29 in the prior year is low. In contrast, Amazon.com, Inc. has more liabilities; its ratio of liabilities to stockholders' equity is 2.73 in the recent year and 3.74 in the prior year. Because Amazon.com, Inc.'s ratio of liabilities to stockholders' equity decreased, its creditors are less at risk at the end of the recent year. However, Amazon.com, Inc.'s creditors are more at risk than are Alphabet's creditors.

EXAMPLE EXERCISE 1-8 Ratio of Liabilities to Owner's Equity

OBJ. 6

The following data were taken from Hawthorne Company's balance sheet:

	Dec. 31, 20Y5	Dec. 31, 20Y4
Total liabilities	$120,000	$105,000
Total owner's equity	80,000	75,000

a. Compute the ratio of liabilities to owner's equity.

b. Has the creditors' risk increased or decreased from December 31, 20Y4, to December 31, 20Y5?

Follow My Example 1-8

a.

	Dec. 31, 20Y5	Dec. 31, 20Y4
Total liabilities	$120,000	$105,000
Total owner's equity	80,000	75,000
Ratio of liabilities to owner's equity	1.50	1.40
	($120,000 ÷ $80,000)	($105,000 ÷ $75,000)

b. Increased

Practice Exercises: PE 1-8A, PE 1-8B

At a Glance 1

OBJ. 1 Describe the nature of business and the role of accounting and ethics in business.

Key Points A business provides goods or services (outputs) to customers with the objective of earning a profit. Three types of businesses include service, merchandising, and manufacturing businesses.

Accounting is an information system that provides reports to users about the economic activities and condition of a business.

Ethics are moral principles that guide the conduct of individuals. Good ethical conduct depends on individual character and firm culture.

Accountants are engaged in private accounting or public accounting.

Learning Outcomes	Example Exercises	Practice Exercises
• Distinguish among service, merchandising, and manufacturing businesses.		
• Describe the role of accounting in business and explain why accounting is called the "language of business."		
• Define ethics and list two factors affecting ethical conduct.		
• Differentiate between private and public accounting.		

OBJ. 2 Summarize the development of accounting principles and relate them to practice.

Key Points Generally accepted accounting principles (GAAP) are used in preparing financial statements. Accounting principles and assumptions develop from research, practice, and pronouncements of authoritative bodies.

The business entity assumption views the business as an entity separate from its owners, creditors, or other businesses. Businesses may be organized as proprietorships, partnerships, corporations, and limited liability companies. The time period concept requires businesses to report their financial condition and results on a regular basis for a specific period of time. The cost concept requires that purchases by a business be recorded in terms of actual cost. The objectivity concept requires that the accounting records and reports be based on unbiased evidence. The unit of measure concept requires that economic data be recorded in dollars.

Learning Outcomes	Example Exercises	Practice Exercises
• Explain what is meant by generally accepted accounting principles.		
• Describe how generally accepted accounting principles are developed.		
• Describe and give an example of what is meant by the business entity concept.		
• Describe the characteristics of a proprietorship, partnership, corporation, and limited liability company.		
• Describe and give an example of the time period concept.		
• Describe and give an example of what is meant by the cost concept.	EE1-1	PE1-1A, 1-1B
• Describe and give an example of what is meant by the objectivity concept.		
• Describe and give an example of what is meant by the unit of measure concept.		

OBJ. 3 State the accounting equation and define each element of the equation.

Key Points The resources owned by a business and the rights or claims to these resources may be stated in the form of an equation, as follows: Assets = Liabilities + Owner's Equity

Learning Outcomes	Example Exercises	Practice Exercises
• State the accounting equation.		
• Define assets, liabilities, and owner's equity.		
• Given two elements of the accounting equation, solve for the third element.	EE1-2	PE1-2A, 1-2B

OBJ. 4 Describe and illustrate how business transactions can be recorded in terms of the resulting change in the elements of the accounting equation.

Key Points All business transactions can be stated in terms of the change in one or more of the three elements of the accounting equation.

Learning Outcomes	Example Exercises	Practice Exercises
• Define a business transaction.		
• Using the accounting equation as a framework, record transactions.	EE1-3	PE1-3A, 1-3B

OBJ. 5 Describe the financial statements of a proprietorship and explain how they interrelate.

Key Points The primary financial statements of a proprietorship are the income statement, the statement of owner's equity, the balance sheet, and the statement of cash flows. The income statement reports a period's net income or net loss, which is also reported on the statement of owner's equity. The ending owner's capital reported on the statement of owner's equity is also reported on the balance sheet. The ending cash balance is reported on the balance sheet and the statement of cash flows.

Learning Outcomes	Example Exercises	Practice Exercises
• List and describe the financial statements of a proprietorship.		
• Prepare an income statement.	EE1-4	PE1-4A, 1-4B
• Prepare a statement of owner's equity.	EE1-5	PE1-5A, 1-5B
• Prepare a balance sheet.	EE1-6	PE1-6A, 1-6B
• Prepare a statement of cash flows.	EE1-7	PE1-7A, 1-7B
• Explain how the financial statements of a proprietorship are interrelated.		

OBJ. 6 Describe and illustrate the use of the ratio of liabilities to owner's equity in evaluating a company's financial condition.

Key Points A ratio useful in analyzing the ability of a business to pay its creditors is the ratio of liabilities to owner's (stockholders') equity. The lower the ratio of liabilities to owner's equity, the better able the company is to withstand poor business conditions and to pay its obligations to creditors.

Learning Outcomes	Example Exercises	Practice Exercises
• Describe the usefulness of the ratio of liabilities to owner's (stockholders') equity.		
• Compute the ratio of liabilities to owner's (stockholders') equity.	EE1-8	PE1-8A, 1-8B

Illustrative Problem

Cecil Jameson, Attorney-at-Law, is a proprietorship owned and operated by Cecil Jameson. On July 1, 20Y5, the company has the following assets and liabilities: cash, $1,000; accounts receivable, $3,200; supplies, $850; land, $10,000; accounts payable, $1,530. Office space and office equipment are currently being rented, pending the construction of an office complex on land purchased last year. Business transactions during July are summarized as follows:

a. Received cash from clients for services, $3,928.

b. Paid creditors on account, $1,055.

c. Received cash from Cecil Jameson as an additional investment, $3,700.

d. Paid office rent for the month, $1,200.

e. Charged clients for legal services on account, $2,025.

f. Purchased supplies on account, $245.

g. Received cash from clients on account, $3,000.

h. Received invoice for paralegal services from Legal Aid Inc. for July (to be paid on August 10), $1,635.

i. Paid the following: wages expense, $850; utilities expense, $325; answering service expense, $250; and miscellaneous expense, $75.

j. Determined that the cost of supplies on hand was $980; therefore, the cost of supplies used during the month was $115.

k. Jameson withdrew $1,000 in cash from the business for personal use.

Instructions

1. Determine the amount of owner's equity (Cecil Jameson's capital) as of July 1, 20Y5.
2. State the assets, liabilities, and owner's equity as of July 1 in equation form similar to that shown in this chapter. In tabular form below the equation, indicate the increases and decreases resulting from each transaction and the new balances after each transaction.
3. Prepare an income statement for July, a statement of owner's equity for July, and a balance sheet as of July 31, 20Y5.
4. (Optional) Prepare a statement of cash flows for July.

Solution

1.

Assets – Liabilities	=	Owner's Equity (Cecil Jameson, capital)
($1,000 + $3,200 + $850 + $10,000) – $1,530	=	Owner's Equity (Cecil Jameson, capital)
$15,050 – $1,530	=	Owner's Equity (Cecil Jameson, capital)
$13,520	=	Owner's Equity (Cecil Jameson, capital)

2.

	Assets				= Liabilities +	Owner's Equity									
	Cash +	Accts. Rec. +	Supp. +	Land =	Accts. Pay. +	Cecil Jameson, Capital −	Cecil Jameson, Drawing +	Fees Earned −	Paralegal Exp. −	Rent Exp. −	Wages Exp. −	Utilities Exp. −	Answering Service Exp. −	Supp. Exp. −	Misc. Exp.
Bal.	1,000	3,200	850	10,000	1,530	13,520									
a.	+3,928							3,928							
Bal.	4,928	3,200	850	10,000	1,530	13,520		3,928							
b.	−1,055				−1,055										
Bal.	3,873	3,200	850	10,000	475	13,520		3,928							
c.	+3,700					+3,700									
Bal.	7,573	3,200	850	10,000	475	17,220		3,928							
d.	−1,200									−1,200					
Bal.	6,373	3,200	850	10,000	475	17,220		3,928		−1,200					
e.		+ 2,025						+ 2,025							
Bal.	6,373	5,225	850	10,000	475	17,220		5,953		−1,200					
f.			+245		+245										
Bal.	6,373	5,225	1,095	10,000	720	17,220		5,953		−1,200					
g.	+3,000	−3,000													
Bal.	9,373	2,225	1,095	10,000	720	17,220		5,953		−1,200					
h.					+1,635				−1,635						
Bal.	9,373	2,225	1,095	10,000	2,355	17,220		5,953	−1,635	−1,200					
i.	−1,500										−850	−325	−250		−75
Bal.	7,873	2,225	1,095	10,000	2,355	17,220		5,953	−1,635	−1,200	−850	−325	−250		−75
j.			−115											−115	
Bal.	7,873	2,225	980	10,000	2,355	17,220		5,953	−1,635	−1,200	−850	−325	−250	−115	−75
k.	−1,000						−1,000								
Bal.	6,873	2,225	980	10,000	2,355	17,220	−1,000	5,953	−1,635	−1,200	−850	−325	−250	−115	−75

3.

Cecil Jameson, Attorney-at-Law
Income Statement
For the Month Ended July 31, 20Y5

Fees earned		$5,953
Expenses:		
Paralegal expense	$1,635	
Rent expense	1,200	
Wages expense	850	
Utilities expense	325	
Answering service expense	250	
Supplies expense	115	
Miscellaneous expense	75	
Total expenses		4,450
Net income		$1,503

Cecil Jameson, Attorney-at-Law
Statement of Owner's Equity
For the Month Ended July 31, 20Y5

Cecil Jameson, capital, July 1, 20Y5		$13,520
Additional investment by owner	$ 3,700	
Net income for the month	1,503	
Withdrawals	(1,000)	
Increase in owner's equity		4,203
Cecil Jameson, capital, July 31, 20Y5		$17,723

(Continued)

Cecil Jameson, Attorney-at-Law
Balance Sheet
July 31, 20Y5

Assets	
Cash	$ 6,873
Accounts receivable	2,225
Supplies	980
Land	10,000
Total assets	$20,078
Liabilities	
Accounts payable	$ 2,355
Owner's Equity	
Cecil Jameson, capital	17,723
Total liabilities and owner's equity	$20,078

4. (Optional)

Cecil Jameson, Attorney-at-Law
Statement of Cash Flows
For the Month Ended July 31, 20Y5

Cash flows from (used for) operating activities:		
Cash received from customers	$ 6,928*	
Cash paid for operating expenses	(3,755)**	
Net cash flows from operating activities		$ 3,173
Cash flows from (used for) investing activities		—
Cash flows from (used for) financing activities:		
Cash received from owner as investment	$ 3,700	
Cash withdrawal by owner	(1,000)	
Net cash flows from financing activities		2,700
Net increase in cash		$ 5,873
Cash balance, July 1, 20Y5		1,000
Cash balance, July 31, 20Y5		$ 6,873

*$6,928 = $3,928 + $3,000 (from Cash column in Part 2)

**$3,755 = $1,055 + $1,200 + $1,500 (from Cash column in Part 2)

Key Terms

account form (21)
account payable (16)
account receivable (17)
accounting (6)
accounting equation (14)
Accounting Standards Codification (11)
Accounting Standards Updates (11)
assets (13)
balance sheet (20)
business (5)
business entity concept (11)
business transaction (15)
Certified Public Accountant (CPA) (10)
corporation (12)
cost concept (13)
earnings (20)
ethics (7)
expenses (17)
fees earned (16)
financial accounting (6)
Financial Accounting Standards Board (FASB) (11)
financial statements (19)
fiscal year (12)
generally accepted accounting principles (GAAP) (10)
general-purpose financial statements (6)
income statement (20)
interest revenue (16)
International Accounting Standards Board (IASB) (11)
liabilities (13)
limited liability company (LLC) (11)

management (or managerial) accounting (6)
manufacturing business (6)
matching concept (20)
merchandising business (6)
natural business year (12)
net income (or net profit) (20)
net loss (20)
objectivity concept (13)
owner's equity (13)
partnership (12)
prepaid expenses (16)
private accounting (6)
profit (5)
proprietorship (12)
public accounting (10)
Public Company Accounting Oversight Board (PCAOB) (8)
ratio of liabilities to owner's (stockholders') equity (26)
rent revenue (16)
report form (23)
revenue (16)
sales (16)
Sarbanes-Oxley Act (SOX) (8)
Securities and Exchange Commission (SEC) (11)
service business (5)
statement of cash flows (20)
statement of owner's equity (20)
stockholders' equity (13)
time period concept (12)
unit of measure concept (13)

Discussion Questions

1. Name some users of accounting information.
2. What is the role of accounting in business?
3. REAL WORLD Why are most large companies like **Microsoft**, **PepsiCo**, **Caterpillar**, and **AutoZone** organized as corporations?
4. Josh Reilly is the owner of Dispatch Delivery Service. Recently, Josh paid interest of $4,500 on a personal loan of $75,000 that he used to begin the business. Should Dispatch Delivery Service record the interest payment? Explain.
5. On July 12, Reliable Repair Service extended an offer of $150,000 for land that had been priced for sale at $185,000. On September 3, Reliable Repair Service accepted the seller's counteroffer of $167,500. Describe how Reliable Repair Service should record the land.
6. a. Land with an assessed value of $750,000 for property tax purposes is acquired by a business for $900,000. Ten years later, the plot of land has an assessed value of $1,200,000 and the business receives an offer of $2,000,000 for it. Should the monetary amount assigned to the land in the business records now be increased?
   b. Assuming that the land acquired in (a) was sold for $2,125,000, how would the various elements of the accounting equation be affected?
7. Describe the difference between an account receivable and an account payable.
8. A business had revenues of $679,000 and operating expenses of $588,000. Did the business (a) incur a net loss or (b) realize net income?
9. A business had revenues of $640,000 and operating expenses of $715,000. Did the business (a) incur a net loss or (b) realize net income?
10. The financial statements are interrelated. (a) What item of financial or operating data appears on both the income statement and the statement of owner's equity? (b) What item appears on both the balance sheet and the statement of owner's equity? (c) What item appears on both the balance sheet and the statement of cash flows?

Practice Exercises

Example Exercises

SHOW ME HOW

EE 1-1 *p. 13*

PE 1-1A Cost concept **OBJ. 2**

On February 3, Boulder Repair Service extended an offer of $566,000 for land that had been priced for sale at $629,000. On February 28, Boulder Repair Service accepted the seller's counteroffer of $597,000. On October 23, the land was assessed at a value of $613,000 for property tax purposes. On January 15 of the next year, Boulder Repair Service was offered $708,000 for the land by a national retail chain. At what value should the land be recorded in Boulder Repair Service's records?

EE 1-1 *p. 13*

PE 1-1B Cost concept **OBJ. 2**

On March 31, Clementine Repair Service extended an offer of $350,500 for land that had been priced for sale at $388,500. On April 15, Clementine Repair Service accepted the seller's counteroffer of $369,500. On September 9, the land was assessed at a value

(Continued)

of $316,700 for property tax purposes. On December 8, Clementine Repair Service was offered $401,200 for the land by a national retail chain. At what value should the land be recorded in Clementine Repair Service's records?

SHOW ME HOW

EE 1-2 *p. 14*

PE 1-2A Accounting equation **OBJ. 3**

Patrick Miller is the owner and operator of Chicopee LLC, a motivational consulting business. At the end of its accounting period, December 31, 20Y8, Chicopee has assets of $518,000 and liabilities of $165,000. Using the accounting equation, determine the following amounts:

a. Owner's equity as of December 31, 20Y8.

b. Owner's equity as of December 31, 20Y9, assuming that assets increased by $86,200 and liabilities increased by $25,000 during 20Y9.

SHOW ME HOW

EE 1-2 *p. 14*

PE 1-2B Accounting equation **OBJ. 3**

Pauline Emm is the owner and operator of Power Thoughts, a motivational consulting business. At the end of its accounting period, December 31, 20Y8, Power Thoughts has assets of $382,000 and liabilities of $94,000. Using the accounting equation, determine the following amounts:

a. Owner's equity as of December 31, 20Y8.

b. Owner's equity as of December 31, 20Y9, assuming that assets decreased by $63,000 and liabilities increased by $35,000 during 20Y9.

SHOW ME HOW

EE 1-3 *p. 19*

PE 1-3A Transactions **OBJ. 4**

Peachtree Delivery Service is owned and operated by Terry Young. The following selected transactions were completed by Peachtree Delivery Service during February:

1. Received cash from owner as additional investment, $65,200.
2. Billed customers for delivery services on account, $22,400.
3. Paid creditors on account, $4,100.
4. Received cash from customers on account, $14,700.
5. Paid cash to owner for personal use, $1,600.

Indicate the effect of each transaction on the accounting equation elements (Assets, Liabilities, and Owner's Equity). Also indicate the specific item within the accounting equation element that is affected. To illustrate, the answer to (1) follows:

(1) Asset (Cash) increases by $65,200; Owner's Equity (Terry Young, Capital) increases by $65,200.

SHOW ME HOW

EE 1-3 *p. 19*

PE 1-3B Transactions **OBJ. 4**

Cross Country Delivery Service is owned and operated by Pedro Gonzalez. The following selected transactions were completed by Cross Country Delivery Service during May:

1. Received cash from owner as additional investment, $25,050.
2. Paid advertising expense, $6,750.
3. Purchased supplies on account, $2,920.
4. Billed customers for delivery services on account, $20,460.
5. Received cash from customers on account, $11,410.

Indicate the effect of each transaction on the accounting equation elements (Assets, Liabilities, and Owner's Equity). Also indicate the specific item within the accounting equation element that is affected. To illustrate, the answer to (1) follows:

(1) Asset (Cash) increases by $25,050; Owner's Equity (Pedro Gonzalez, Capital) increases by $25,050.

SHOW ME HOW

EE 1-4 *p. 20* **PE 1-4A Income statement** **OBJ. 5**

The revenues and expenses of Up-in-the-Air Travel Service for the year ended April 30, 20Y7, follow:

Fees earned	$1,870,000
Office expense	343,000
Miscellaneous expense	21,000
Wages expense	1,115,000

Prepare an income statement for the year ended April 30, 20Y7.

SHOW ME HOW

EE 1-4 *p. 20* **PE 1-4B Income statement** **OBJ. 5**

The revenues and expenses of Zenith Travel Service for the year ended August 31, 20Y4, follow:

Fees earned	$899,600
Office expense	353,800
Miscellaneous expense	14,400
Wages expense	539,800

Prepare an income statement for the year ended August 31, 20Y4.

SHOW ME HOW

EE 1-5 *p. 21* **PE 1-5A Statement of owner's equity** **OBJ. 5**

Using the income statement for Up-in-the-Air Travel Service shown in Practice Exercise 1-4A, prepare a statement of owner's equity for the year ended April 30, 20Y7. Jerome Foley, the owner, invested an additional $52,000 in the business during the year and withdrew cash of $34,000 for personal use. Jerome Foley, capital as of May 1, 20Y6, was $876,000.

SHOW ME HOW

EE 1-5 *p. 21* **PE 1-5B Statement of owner's equity** **OBJ. 5**

Using the income statement for Zenith Travel Service shown in Practice Exercise 1-4B, prepare a statement of owner's equity for the year ended August 31, 20Y4. Megan Cox, the owner, invested an additional $43,200 in the business during the year and withdrew cash of $21,600 for personal use. Megan Cox, capital as of September 1, 20Y3, was $456,000.

SHOW ME HOW

EE 1-6 *p. 23* **PE 1-6A Balance sheet** **OBJ. 5**

Using the following data for Up-in-the-Air Travel Service as well as the statement of owner's equity shown in Practice Exercise 1-5A, prepare a report form balance sheet as of April 30, 20Y7:

Accounts payable	$ 90,000
Accounts receivable	417,000
Cash	170,000
Land	772,000
Supplies	16,000

SHOW ME HOW

EE 1-6 *p. 23* **PE 1-6B Balance sheet** **OBJ. 5**

Using the following data for Zenith Travel Service as well as the statement of owner's equity shown in Practice Exercise 1-5B, prepare a report form balance sheet as of August 31, 20Y4:

Accounts payable	$ 53,500
Accounts receivable	90,600
Cash	54,500
Land	372,000
Supplies	5,600

EE 1-7 p. 25 **PE 1-7A Statement of cash flows** **OBJ. 5**

A summary of cash flows for Up-in-the-Air Travel Service for the year ended April 30, 20Y7, follows:

Cash receipts:	
Cash received from customers	$1,803,000
Cash received from additional investment of owner	52,000
Cash payments:	
Cash paid for operating expenses	1,479,000
Cash paid for land	347,000
Cash paid to owner for personal use	34,000

The cash balance as of May 1, 20Y6, was $175,000.

Prepare a statement of cash flows for Up-in-the-Air Travel Service for the year ended April 30, 20Y7.

EE 1-7 p. 25 **PE 1-7B Statement of cash flows** **OBJ. 5**

A summary of cash flows for Zenith Travel Service for the year ended August 31, 20Y4, follows:

Cash receipts:	
Cash received from customers	$881,000
Cash received from additional investment of owner	43,200
Cash payments:	
Cash paid for operating expenses	895,000
Cash paid for land	60,000
Cash paid to owner for personal use	21,600

The cash balance as of September 1, 20Y3, was $106,900.

Prepare a statement of cash flows for Zenith Travel Service for the year ended August 31, 20Y4.

EE 1-8 p. 27 **PE 1-8A Ratio of liabilities to owner's equity** **OBJ. 6**

The following data were taken from Nakajima Company's balance sheet:

	Dec. 31, 20Y6	Dec. 31, 20Y5
Total liabilities	$598,000	$569,900
Total owner's equity	460,000	410,000

a. Compute the ratio of liabilities to owner's equity.

b. Has the creditor's risk increased or decreased from December 31, 20Y5, to December 31, 20Y6?

EE 1-8 p. 27 **PE 1-8B Ratio of liabilities to owner's equity** **OBJ. 6**

The following data were taken from McClean Company's balance sheet:

	Dec. 31, 20Y6	Dec. 31, 20Y5
Total liabilities	$4,042,000	$3,096,000
Total owner's equity	4,300,000	3,600,000

a. Compute the ratio of liabilities to owner's equity.

b. Has the creditor's risk increased or decreased from December 31, 20Y5, to December 31, 20Y6?

Exercises

EX 1-1 Types of businesses **OBJ. 1**

The following is a list of well-known companies:

1. **Alcoa Inc.**
2. **Boeing**
3. **Caterpillar**
4. **Citigroup Inc.**
5. **CVS**
6. **Delta Air Lines**
7. **eBay Inc.**
8. **FedEx**
9. **Ford Motor Company**
10. **Gap Inc.**
11. **H&R Block**
12. **Hilton Hospitality, Inc.**
13. **Procter & Gamble**
14. **SunTrust**
15. **Wal-Mart Stores, Inc.**

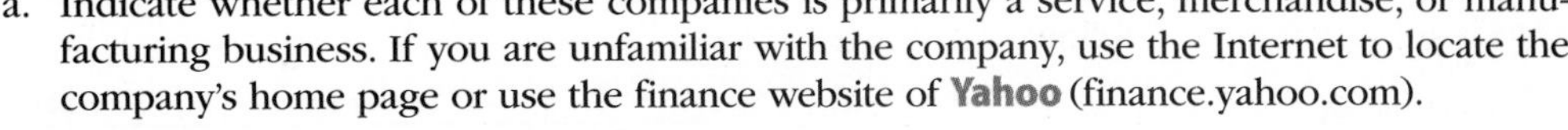

a. Indicate whether each of these companies is primarily a service, merchandise, or manufacturing business. If you are unfamiliar with the company, use the Internet to locate the company's home page or use the finance website of **Yahoo** (finance.yahoo.com).

b. For which of the preceding companies is the accounting equation relevant?

ETHICS

EX 1-2 Professional ethics **OBJ. 1**

A fertilizer manufacturing company wants to relocate to Lakeside County. A report from a fired researcher at the company indicates the company's product is releasing toxic by-products. The company suppressed that report. A later report commissioned by the company shows there is no problem with the fertilizer.

Should the company's chief executive officer reveal the content of the unfavorable report in discussions with Lakeside County representatives? Discuss.

EX 1-3 Business entity assumption **OBJ. 2**

Big Sky Sports sells hunting and fishing equipment and provides guided hunting and fishing trips. Big Sky Sports is owned and operated by Joe Flannery, a well-known sports enthusiast and hunter. Joe's wife, Pam, owns and operates Glacier Boutique, a women's clothing store. Joe and Pam have established a trust fund to finance their children's college education. The trust fund is maintained by Kalispell State Bank in the name of the children, Trey and Brooke.

a. For each of the following transactions, identify which of the entities listed should record the transaction in its records:

Entities	
G	Glacier Boutique
K	Kalispell State Bank
B	Big Sky Sports
X	None of the above

1. Pam deposited a $2,000 personal check in the trust fund at Kalispell State Bank.
2. Pam purchased two dozen spring dresses from a Spokane designer for a special spring sale.
3. Joe paid a breeder's fee for an English Springer Spaniel to be used as a hunting guide dog.
4. Pam authorized the trust fund to purchase mutual fund shares.
5. Joe paid a local doctor for his annual physical, which was required by the workmen's compensation insurance policy carried by Big Sky Sports.
6. Received a cash advance from customers for a guided hunting trip.
7. Pam paid her dues to the YWCA.
8. Pam donated several dresses from inventory for a local charity auction for the benefit of a women's abuse shelter.

(Continued)

9. Joe paid for dinner and a movie to celebrate their thirtieth wedding anniversary.
10. Joe paid for an advertisement in a hunters' magazine.

b. What is a business transaction?

✔ Starbucks, $1,175

SHOW ME HOW

REAL WORLD

EX 1-4 Accounting equation **OBJ. 3**

The total assets and total liabilities (in millions) of **Dunkin Brands Group** and **Starbucks Corporation** follow:

	Dunkin Brands Group	Starbucks
Assets	$3,457	$24,156
Liabilities	4,170	22,981

Determine the stockholders' equity of each company.

✔ Dollar Tree, $5,643

REAL WORLD

EX 1-5 Accounting equation **OBJ. 3**

The total assets and total liabilities (in millions) of **Dollar Tree Inc.** and **Target Corporation** follow:

	Dollar Tree	Target
Assets	$13,501	$41,290
Liabilities	7,858	29,993

Determine the stockholders' equity of each company.

✔ a. $4,474,000

SHOW ME HOW

EX 1-6 Accounting equation **OBJ. 3**

Determine the missing amount for each of the following:

	Assets	=	Liabilities	=	Owner's Equity
a.	X	=	$633,000	+	$3,841,000
b.	$6,124,500	=	X	+	$5,737,000
c.	$1,981,800	=	$748,900	+	X

✔ b. $555,000

SHOW ME HOW

EXCEL ONLINE

EX 1-7 Accounting equation **OBJ. 3, 4**

Penny Lyman is the owner and operator of Go109, a motivational consulting business. At the end of its accounting period, December 31, 20Y1, Go109 has assets of $659,000 and liabilities of $165,000. Using the accounting equation and considering each case independently, determine the following amounts:

a. Penny Lyman, capital, as of December 31, 20Y1.

b. Penny Lyman, capital, as of December 31, 20Y2, assuming that assets increased by $88,000 and liabilities increased by $27,000 during 20Y2.

c. Penny Lyman, capital, as of December 31, 20Y2, assuming that assets decreased by $151,000 and liabilities increased by $13,000 during 20Y2.

d. Penny Lyman, capital, as of December 31, 20Y2, assuming that assets increased by $152,000 and liabilities decreased by $16,000 during 20Y2.

e. Net income (or net loss) during 20Y2, assuming that as of December 31, 20Y2, assets were $782,000, liabilities were $196,000, and there were no additional investments or withdrawals.

EX 1-8 Asset, liability, and owner's equity items **OBJ. 3**

Indicate whether each of the following is identified with (1) an asset, (2) a liability, or (3) owner's equity:

a. accounts receivable
b. accounts payable
c. cash
d. fees earned
e. land
f. rent expense
g. supplies

EX 1-9 Effect of transactions on accounting equation **OBJ. 4**

Describe how the following business transactions affect the three elements of the accounting equation:

a. Invested cash in business.
b. Paid for utilities used in the business.
c. Purchased supplies for cash.
d. Purchased supplies on account.
e. Received cash for services performed.

EX 1-10 Effect of transactions on accounting equation **OBJ. 4**

✔ a. (1) increase $183,000

SHOW ME HOW

a. A vacant lot acquired for $115,000 is sold for $298,000 in cash. What is the effect of the sale on the total amount of the seller's (1) assets, (2) liabilities, and (3) owner's equity?
b. Assume that the seller owes $80,000 on a loan for the land. After receiving the $298,000 cash in (a), the seller pays the $80,000 owed. What is the effect of the payment on the total amount of the seller's (1) assets, (2) liabilities, and (3) owner's equity?
c. Is it true that a transaction always affects at least two elements (Assets, Liabilities, or Owner's Equity) of the accounting equation? Explain.

EX 1-11 Effect of transactions on owner's equity **OBJ. 4**

Indicate whether each of the following types of transactions will either (a) increase owner's equity or (b) decrease owner's equity:

1. expenses
2. owner's investments
3. owner's withdrawals
4. revenues

EX 1-12 Transactions **OBJ. 4**

The following selected transactions were completed by Silverado Delivery Service during February:

1. Received cash from owner as additional investment, $25,000.
2. Purchased supplies for cash, $750.
3. Paid rent for February, $3,000.
4. Paid advertising expense, $1,500.
5. Received cash for providing delivery services, $16,800.
6. Billed customers for delivery services on account, $32,500.
7. Paid creditors on account, $1,400.
8. Received cash from customers on account, $23,770.
9. Determined that the cost of supplies on hand was $275 and $475 of supplies had been used during the month.
10. Paid cash to owner for personal use, $5,000.

Indicate the effect of each transaction on the accounting equation by listing the numbers identifying the transactions, (1) through (10), in a column and inserting at the right of each number the appropriate letter from the following list:

a. Increase in an asset, decrease in another asset.
b. Increase in an asset, increase in a liability.
c. Increase in an asset, increase in owner's equity.
d. Decrease in an asset, decrease in a liability.
e. Decrease in an asset, decrease in owner's equity.

EX 1-13 Nature of transactions

OBJ. 4

✔ **d. $22,800**

SHOW ME HOW

Teri West operates her own catering service. Summary financial data for July are presented in equation form as follows. Each line designated by a number indicates the effect of a transaction on the equation. Each increase and decrease in owner's equity, except transaction (5), affects net income.

	Assets			= Liabilities +	Owner's Equity			
	Cash	+ Supplies +	Land	= Accounts Payable +	Teri West, Capital	– Teri West, Drawing	+ Fees Earned	– Expenses
Bal.	40,000	3,000	82,000	7,500	117,500			
1.	+71,800						+71,800	
2.	–15,000		+15,000					
3.	–47,500							–47,500
4.		+1,100		+1,100				
5.	–5,000					–5,000		
6.	–4,000			–4,000				
7.		–1,500						–1,500
Bal.	40,300	2,600	97,000	4,600	117,500	–5,000	71,800	–49,000

a. Describe each transaction.

b. What is the amount of the net increase in cash during the month?

c. What is the amount of the net increase in owner's equity during the month?

d. What is the amount of the net income for the month?

e. How much of the net income for the month was retained in the business?

EX 1-14 Net income and owner's withdrawals

OBJ. 5

The income statement of a proprietorship for the month of February indicates a net income of $17,500. During the same period, the owner withdrew $25,500 in cash from the business for personal use.

Would it be correct to say that the business had incurred a net loss of $8,000 during the month? Discuss.

EX 1-15 Net income and owner's equity for four businesses

OBJ. 5

✔ **Jersey: Net income, $248,000**

SHOW ME HOW

Four different proprietorships, Dakota, Jersey, Carolina, and Iowa, show the same balance sheet data at the beginning and end of a year. These data, exclusive of the amount of owner's equity, are summarized as follows:

	Total Assets	Total Liabilities
Beginning of the year	$605,000	$237,000
End of the year	928,000	352,000

On the basis of the preceding data and the following additional information for the year, determine the net income (or loss) of each company for the year. (*Hint:* First, determine the amount of increase or decrease in owner's equity during the year.)

Dakota: The owner had made no additional investments in the business and had made no withdrawals from the business.

Jersey: The owner had made no additional investments in the business but had withdrawn $40,000.

Carolina: The owner had made an additional investment of $66,000 but had made no withdrawals.

Iowa: The owner had made an additional investment of $66,000 and had withdrawn $40,000.

EX 1-16 Balance sheet items **OBJ. 5**

From the following list of selected items taken from the records of Rosewood Appliance Service as of a specific date, identify those that would appear on the balance sheet:

1. Accounts Payable
2. Accounts Receivable
3. Andrew King, Capital
4. Cash
5. Fees Earned
6. Land
7. Rent Expense
8. Supplies
9. Wages Expense
10. Wages Payable

EX 1-17 Income statement items **OBJ. 5**

Based on the data presented in Exercise 1-16, identify those items that would appear on the income statement.

EX 1-18 Statement of owner's equity **OBJ. 5**

✔ **Brian Walinsky, capital, April 30, 20Y7: $510,000**

SHOW ME HOW

Financial information related to Pegasus Products Company, a proprietorship, for the month ended April 30, 20Y7, is as follows:

Net income for April	$161,000
Brian Walinsky's withdrawals during April	24,000
Brian Walinsky's capital, April 1, 20Y7	373,000

a. Prepare a statement of owner's equity for the month ended April 30, 20Y7.

b. Why is the statement of owner's equity prepared before the April 30, 20Y7, balance sheet?

EX 1-19 Income statement **OBJ. 5**

✔ **Net income: $142,600**

SHOW ME HOW

Hermes Services was organized on August 1, 20Y2. A summary of the revenue and expense transactions for August follows:

Fees earned	$627,600
Wages expense	440,800
Rent expense	28,100
Supplies expense	6,800
Miscellaneous expense	9,300

Prepare an income statement for the month ended August 31.

EX 1-20 Missing amounts from balance sheet and income statement data **OBJ. 5**

✔ **(a) $135,000**

SHOW ME HOW

EXCEL ONLINE

One item is omitted in each of the following summaries of balance sheet and income statement data for the following four different proprietorships:

	Freeman	**Heyward**	**Jones**	**Ramirez**
Beginning of the year:				
Assets	$ 900,000	$490,000	$115,000	(d)
Liabilities	360,000	260,000	81,000	$120,000
End of the year:				
Assets	1,260,000	675,000	100,000	270,000
Liabilities	330,000	220,000	80,000	136,000
During the year:				
Additional investment in the business	(a)	150,000	10,000	55,000
Withdrawals from the business	75,000	32,000	(c)	39,000
Revenue	570,000	(b)	115,000	115,000
Expenses	240,000	128,000	122,500	128,000

Determine the missing amounts, identifying them by letter. (*Hint:* First, determine the amount of increase or decrease in owner's equity during the year.)

EX 1-21 Balance sheets, net income **OBJ. 5**

✔ b. $122,000

Financial information related to the proprietorship of Rockwell Interiors for February and March 20Y0 is as follows:

	February 29, 20Y0	March 31, 20Y0
Accounts payable	$280,000	$360,000
Accounts receivable	720,000	870,000
Cash	290,000	340,000
David Patel, capital	?	?
Supplies	30,000	32,000

a. Prepare balance sheets for Rockwell Interiors as of February 29 and March 31, 20Y0.

b. Determine the amount of net income for March, assuming that the owner made no additional investments or withdrawals during the month.

c. Determine the amount of net income for March, assuming that the owner made no additional investments but withdrew $50,000 during the month.

EX 1-22 Financial statements **OBJ. 5**

Each of the following items is shown in the financial statements of **Exxon Mobil Corporation**:

1. Accounts payable
2. Cash equivalents
3. Crude oil inventory
4. Equipment
5. Exploration expenses
6. Income taxes payable
7. Investments
8. Long-term debt
9. Materials inventory
10. Notes and loans payable
11. Notes receivable
12. Production expenses
13. Supplies
14. Sales
15. Selling expenses

a. Identify the financial statement (balance sheet or income statement) in which each item would appear.

b. Can an item appear on more than one financial statement?

c. Is the accounting equation relevant for Exxon Mobil Corporation?

EX 1-23 Statement of cash flows **OBJ. 5**

Indicate whether each of the following activities would be reported on the statement of cash flows as (a) an operating activity, (b) an investing activity, or (c) a financing activity:

1. Cash received from fees earned.
2. Cash paid for expenses.
3. Cash paid for land.
4. Cash paid to owner for personal use.

EX 1-24 Statement of cash flows **OBJ. 5**

✔ Net increase in cash, $117,500

A summary of cash flows for Ethos Consulting Group for the year ended May 31, 20Y6, follows:

Cash receipts:	
Cash received from customers	$637,500
Cash received from additional investment of owner	62,500
Cash payments:	
Cash paid for operating expenses	475,000
Cash paid for land	90,000
Cash paid to owner for personal use	17,500

The cash balance as of June 1, 20Y5, was $58,000.

Prepare a statement of cash flows for Ethos Consulting Group for the year ended May 31, 20Y6.

EX 1-25 Financial statements OBJ. 5

✔ Correct amount of total assets is $51,500.

We-Sell Realty, organized August 1, 20Y9, is owned and operated by Omar Farah. How many errors can you find in the following statements for We-Sell Realty, prepared after its first month of operations?

We-Sell Realty
Income Statement
August 31, 20Y9

Sales commissions		$140,000
Expenses:		
Office salaries expense	$87,000	
Rent expense	18,000	
Automobile expense	7,500	
Miscellaneous expense	2,200	
Supplies expense	1,150	
Total expenses		115,850
Net income		$ 25,000

Omar Farah
Statement of Owner's Equity
August 31, 20Y8

Omar Farah, capital, August 1, 20Y9	$ 0
Withdrawals during August	(10,000)
	$(10,000)
Investment on August 1, 20Y9	15,000
	$ 5,000
Net income for August	25,000
Omar Farah, capital, August 31, 20Y9	$ 30,000

Balance Sheet
For the Month Ended August 31, 20Y9

Assets	
Cash	$ 8,900
Accounts payable	22,350
Total assets	$31,250
Liabilities	
Accounts receivable	$38,600
Supplies	4,000
Owner's Equity	
Omar Farah, capital	30,000
Total liabilities and owner's equity	$72,600

EX 1-26 Ratio of liabilities to stockholders' equity OBJ. 6

✔ a. Year 2: $43,075

The Home Depot is the world's largest home improvement retailer and one of the largest retailers in the United States based on net sales volume. The Home Depot operates over 2,200 Home Depot® stores that sell a wide assortment of building materials and home improvement and lawn and garden products.

The Home Depot recently reported the following balance sheet data (in millions):

	Year 2	Year 1
Total assets	$44,529	$42,966
Total stockholders' equity	1,454	4,333

a. Determine the total liabilities at the end of Years 2 and 1.

b. Determine the ratio of liabilities to stockholders' equity for Year 2 and Year 1. Round to two decimal places.

c. What conclusions regarding the margin of protection to the creditors can you draw from (b)?

EX 1-27 Ratio of liabilities to stockholders' equity OBJ. 6

✔ b. Year 2: 5.01

Lowe's Companies Inc., a major competitor of **The Home Depot** in the home improvement business, operates over 1,800 stores. Lowe's recently reported the following balance sheet data (in millions):

	Year 2	Year 1
Total assets	$35,291	$34,408
Total liabilities	29,418	27,974

a. Determine the total stockholders' equity at the end of Years 2 and 1.

b. Determine the ratio of liabilities to stockholders' equity for Year 2 and Year 1. Round to two decimal places.

c. What conclusions regarding the risk to the creditors can you draw from (b)?

d. Using the balance sheet data for The Home Depot in Exercise 1-26, how does the ratio of liabilities to stockholders' equity of Lowe's compare to that of The Home Depot?

Problems: Series A

PR 1-1A Transactions OBJ. 4

✔ Cash bal. at end of June: $38,430

On June 1 of the current year, Pamela Schatz established a business to manage rental property. She completed the following transactions during June:

a. Opened a business bank account with a deposit of $55,000 from personal funds.

b. Purchased office supplies on account, $3,300.

c. Received cash from fees earned for managing rental property, $18,300.

d. Paid rent on office and equipment for the month, $8,300.

e. Paid creditors on account, $2,290.

f. Billed customers for fees earned for managing rental property, $30,800.

g. Paid automobile expenses (including rental charges) for the month, $1,380, and miscellaneous expenses, $1,800.

h. Paid office salaries, $7,300.

i. Determined that the cost of supplies on hand was $1,250; therefore, the cost of supplies used was $2,050.

j. Withdrew cash for personal use, $13,800.

Instructions

1. Indicate the effect of each transaction and the balances after each transaction, using the following tabular headings:

Assets			= Liabilities +	Owner's Equity							
Cash +	Accounts Receivable +	Supplies =	Accounts Payable +	Pamela Schatz, Capital −	Pamela Schatz, Drawing +	Fees Earned −	Rent Expense −	Salaries Expense −	Supplies Expense −	Auto Expense −	Misc. Expense

2. Briefly explain why the owner's investment and revenues increased owner's equity, while withdrawals and expenses decreased owner's equity.

3. Determine the net income for June.

4. How much did June's transactions increase or decrease Pamela Schatz's capital?

PR 1-2A Financial statements OBJ. 5

✔ 1. Net income: $347,200

The amounts of the assets and liabilities of Excalibur Travel Agency at December 31, 20Y5, the end of the year, and its revenue and expenses for the year follow. The capital of James Brewster, owner, was $710,000 on January 1, 20Y5, the beginning of the year. During the year, James withdrew $44,500.

Accounts payable	$ 73,500	Rent expense	$ 38,100
Accounts receivable	302,000	Supplies	5,800
Cash	201,900	Supplies expense	4,300
Fees earned	967,000	Utilities expense	30,200
Land	576,500	Wages expense	540,400
Miscellaneous expense	6,800		

Instructions

1. Prepare an income statement for the year ended December 31, 20Y5.
2. Prepare a statement of owner's equity for the year ended December 31, 20Y5.
3. Prepare a balance sheet as of December 31, 20Y5.
4. What item appears on both the statement of owner's equity and the balance sheet?

PR 1-3A Financial statements

OBJ. 5

✔ 1. Net income: $31,200

Seth Feye established Reliance Financial Services on July 1, 20Y2. Reliance Financial Services offers financial planning advice to its clients. The effect of each transaction and the balances after each transaction for July follow:

	Assets			= Liabilities +	Owner's Equity							
	Cash	+ Accounts Receivable	+ Supplies	= Accounts Payable	+ Seth Feye, Capital	− Seth Feye, Drawing	+ Fees Earned	− Salaries Expense	− Rent Expense	− Auto Expense	− Supplies Expense	− Misc. Expense
a.	+50,000				+50,000							
b.			+7,000	+7,000								
Bal.	50,000		7,000	7,000	50,000							
c.	−3,600			−3,600								
Bal.	46,400		7,000	3,400	50,000							
d.	+110,000						+110,000					
Bal.	156,400		7,000	3,400	50,000		110,000					
e.	−33,000								−33,000			
Bal.	123,400		7,000	3,400	50,000		110,000		−33,000			
f.	−20,800									−16,000		−4,800
Bal.	102,600		7,000	3,400	50,000		110,000		−33,000	−16,000		−4,800
g.	−55,000							−55,000				
Bal.	47,600		7,000	3,400	50,000		110,000	−55,000	−33,000	−16,000		−4,800
h.			−4,500								−4,500	
Bal.	47,600		2,500	3,400	50,000		110,000	−55,000	−33,000	−16,000	−4,500	−4,800
i.		+34,500					+ 34,500					
Bal.	47,600	34,500	2,500	3,400	50,000		144,500	−55,000	−33,000	−16,000	−4,500	−4,800
j.	−15,000					−15,000						
Bal.	32,600	34,500	2,500	3,400	50,000	−15,000	144,500	−55,000	−33,000	−16,000	−4,500	−4,800

Instructions

1. Prepare an income statement for the month ended July 31, 20Y2.
2. Prepare a statement of owner's equity for the month ended July 31, 20Y2.
3. Prepare a balance sheet as of July 31, 20Y2.
4. *(Optional)* Prepare a statement of cash flows for the month ending July 31, 20Y2.

PR 1-4A Transactions; financial statements

OBJ. 4, 5

✔ 2. Net income: $27,350

On July 1, 20Y7, Pat Glenn established Half Moon Realty. Pat completed the following transactions during the month of July:

a. Opened a business bank account with a deposit of $25,000 from personal funds.
b. Purchased office supplies on account, $1,850.

(Continued)

c. Paid creditor on account, $1,200.
d. Earned sales commissions, receiving cash, $41,500.
e. Paid rent on office and equipment for the month, $3,600.
f. Withdrew cash for personal use, $4,000.
g. Paid automobile expenses (including rental charge) for the month, $3,050, and miscellaneous expenses, $1,600.
h. Paid office salaries, $5,000.
i. Determined that the cost of supplies on hand was $950; therefore, the cost of supplies used was $900.

Instructions

1. Indicate the effect of each transaction and the balances after each transaction, using the following tabular headings:

Assets	= Liabilities +	Owner's Equity							
Cash + Supplies =	Accounts Payable +	Pat Glenn, Capital −	Pat Glenn, Drawing +	Sales Commissions −	Salaries Expense −	Rent Expense −	Auto Expense −	Supplies Expense −	Misc. Expense

2. Prepare an income statement for July, a statement of owner's equity for July, and a balance sheet as of July 31.

PR 1-5A Transactions; financial statements

OBJ. 4, 5

✔ **3. Net income: $63,775**

D'Lite Dry Cleaners is owned and operated by Joel Palk. A building and equipment are currently being rented, pending expansion to new facilities. The actual work of dry cleaning is done by another company for a fee. The assets and liabilities of the business on July 1, 20Y6, are as follows: Cash, $45,000; Accounts Receivable, $93,000; Supplies, $7,000; Land, $75,000; Accounts Payable, $40,000. Business transactions during July are summarized as follows:

a. Joel Palk invested additional cash in the business with a deposit of $35,000 in the business bank account.
b. Paid $50,000 for the purchase of land adjacent to land currently owned by D'Lite Dry Cleaners as a future building site.
c. Received cash from cash customers for dry cleaning revenue, $32,125.
d. Paid rent for the month, $6,000.
e. Purchased supplies on account, $2,500.
f. Paid creditors on account, $22,800.
g. Charged customers for dry cleaning revenue on account, $84,750.
h. Received monthly invoice for dry cleaning expense for July (to be paid on August 10), $29,500.
i. Paid the following: wages expense, $7,500; truck expense, $2,500; utilities expense, $1,300; miscellaneous expense, $2,700.
j. Received cash from customers on account, $88,000.
k. Determined that the cost of supplies on hand was $5,900; therefore, the cost of supplies used during the month was $3,600.
l. Withdrew $12,000 cash for personal use.

Instructions

1. Determine the amount of Joel Palk's capital as of July 1, 20Y6.
2. State the assets, liabilities, and owner's equity as of July 1 in equation form similar to that shown in Exhibit 5. In tabular form below the equation, indicate increases and decreases resulting from each transaction and the new balances after each transaction.
3. Prepare an income statement for July, a statement of owner's equity for July, and a balance sheet as of July 31.
4. *(Optional)* Prepare a statement of cash flows for July.

✔ k. $362,500

PR 1-6A Missing amounts from financial statements **OBJ. 5**

The financial statements at the end of Wolverine Realty's first month of operations are as follows:

Wolverine Realty
Income Statement
For the Month Ended April 30, 20Y3

Fees earned		$ (a)
Expenses:		
Wages expense	$300,000	
Rent expense	100,000	
Supplies expense	(b)	
Utilities expense	20,000	
Miscellaneous expense	25,000	
Total expenses		475,000
Net income		$275,000

Wolverine Realty
Statement of Owner's Equity
For the Month Ended April 30, 20Y3

Dakota Rowe, capital, April 1, 20Y3		$ (c)
Investment on April 1, 20Y3	$ 375,000	
Net income for April	(d)	
Withdrawals	(125,000)	
Increase in owner's equity		(e)
Dakota Rowe, capital, April 30, 20Y3		$ (f)

Wolverine Realty
Balance Sheet
April 30, 20Y3

Assets	
Cash	$462,500
Supplies	12,500
Land	150,000
Total assets	$ (g)
Liabilities	
Accounts payable	$ 100,000
Owner's Equity	
Dakota Rowe, capital	(h)
Total liabilities and owner's equity	$ (i)

Wolverine Realty
Statement of Cash Flows
For the Month Ended April 30, 20Y3

Cash flows from (used for) operating activities:		
Cash received from customers	$ (j)	
Cash paid for operating expenses and to creditors	(387,500)	
Net cash flows from operating activities		$ (k)
Cash flows from (used for) investing activities:		
Cash paid for acquisition of land		(l)
Cash flows from (used for) financing activities:		
Cash received from owner as investment	$ (m)	
Cash withdrawals by owner	(n)	
Net cash flows from financing activities		(o)
Net increase (decrease) in cash		$ (p)
Cash balance, April 1, 20Y3		0
Cash balance, April 30, 20Y3		$ (q)

Instructions

By analyzing the interrelationships among the four financial statements, determine the proper amounts for (a) through (q).

Problems: Series B

PR 1-1B Transactions

OBJ. 4

✔ Cash bal. at end of March: $48,650

SHOW ME HOW

Amy Austin established an insurance agency on March 1 of the current year and completed the following transactions during March:

a. Opened a business bank account with a deposit of $50,000 from personal funds.
b. Purchased supplies on account, $4,000.
c. Paid creditors on account, $2,300.
d. Received cash from fees earned on insurance commissions, $13,800.
e. Paid rent on office and equipment for the month, $5,000.
f. Paid automobile expenses for the month, $1,150, and miscellaneous expenses, $300.
g. Paid office salaries, $2,500.
h. Determined that the cost of supplies on hand was $2,700; therefore, the cost of supplies used was $1,300.
i. Billed insurance companies for sales commissions earned, $12,500.
j. Withdrew cash for personal use, $3,900.

Instructions

1. Indicate the effect of each transaction and the balances after each transaction, using the following tabular headings:

Assets			= Liabilities +	Owner's Equity							
Cash +	Accounts Receivable +	Supplies =	Accounts Payable +	Amy Austin, Capital –	Amy Austin, Drawing +	Fees Earned –	Rent Expense –	Salaries Expense –	Supplies Expense –	Auto Expense –	Misc. Expense

2. Briefly explain why the owner's investment and revenues increased owner's equity, while withdrawals and expenses decreased owner's equity.
3. Determine the net income for March.
4. How much did March's transactions increase or decrease Amy Austin's capital?

PR 1-2B Financial statements

OBJ. 5

✔ 1. Net income: $200,000

SHOW ME HOW

The amounts of the assets and liabilities of Wilderness Travel Service at April 30, 20Y5, the end of the year, and its revenue and expenses for the year follow. The capital of Harper Borg, owner, was $180,000 at May 1, 20Y4, the beginning of the year, and the owner withdrew $40,000 during the year.

Accounts payable	$ 25,000	Supplies	$ 9,000
Accounts receivable	210,000	Supplies expense	12,000
Cash	146,000	Taxes expense	10,000
Fees earned	875,000	Utilities expense	38,000
Miscellaneous expense	15,000	Wages expense	525,000
Rent expense	75,000		

Instructions

1. Prepare an income statement for the year ended April 30, 20Y5.
2. Prepare a statement of owner's equity for the year ended April 30, 20Y5.
3. Prepare a balance sheet as of April 30, 20Y5.
4. What item appears on both the income statement and statement of owner's equity?

✔ 1. Net income: $10,900

PR 1-3B Financial statements

OBJ. 5

Jose Loder established Bronco Consulting on August 1, 20Y2. The effect of each transaction and the balances after each transaction for August follow:

	Assets			=Liabilities+	Owner's Equity							
	Cash	+ Accounts Receivable	+ Supplies	= Accounts Payable	+ Jose Loder, Capital	− Jose Loder, Drawing	+ Fees Earned	− Salaries Expense	− Rent Expense	− Auto Expense	− Supplies Expense	− Misc. Expense
a.	+75,000				+75,000							
b.			+9,000	+9,000								
Bal.	75,000		9,000	9,000	75,000							
c.	+92,000						+92,000					
Bal.	167,000		9,000	9,000	75,000		92,000					
d.	−27,000								−27,000			
Bal.	140,000		9,000	9,000	75,000		92,000		−27,000			
e.	−6,000			−6,000								
Bal.	134,000		9,000	3,000	75,000		92,000		−27,000			
f.		+33,000					+33,000					
Bal.	134,000	33,000	9,000	3,000	75,000		125,000		−27,000			
g.	−23,000									−15,500		−7,500
Bal.	111,000	33,000	9,000	3,000	75,000		125,000		−27,000	−15,500		−7,500
h.	−58,000							−58,000				
Bal.	53,000	33,000	9,000	3,000	75,000		125,000	−58,000	−27,000	−15,500		−7,500
i.			−6,100								−6,100	
Bal.	53,000	33,000	2,900	3,000	75,000		125,000	−58,000	−27,000	−15,500	−6,100	−7,500
j.	−15,000					−15,000						
Bal.	38,000	33,000	2,900	3,000	75,000	−15,000	125,000	−58,000	−27,000	−15,500	−6,100	−7,500

Instructions

1. Prepare an income statement for the month ended August 31, 20Y2.
2. Prepare a statement of owner's equity for the month ended August 31, 20Y2.
3. Prepare a balance sheet as of August 31, 20Y2.
4. *(Optional)* Prepare a statement of cash flows for the month ending August 31, 20Y2.

✔ 2. Net income: $10,850

PR 1-4B Transactions; financial statements

OBJ. 4, 5

On April 1, 20Y7, Maria Adams established Custom Realty. Maria completed the following transactions during the month of April:

a. Opened a business bank account with a deposit of $24,000 from personal funds.
b. Paid rent on office and equipment for the month, $3,600.
c. Paid automobile expenses (including rental charge) for the month, $1,350, and miscellaneous expenses, $600.
d. Purchased office supplies on account, $1,200.
e. Earned sales commissions (revenue) from selling real estate, receiving cash, $19,800.
f. Paid creditor on account, $750.
g. Paid office salaries, $2,500.
h. Withdrew cash for personal use, $3,500.
i. Determined that the cost of supplies on hand was $300; therefore, the cost of supplies used was $900.

(Continued)

Instructions

1. Indicate the effect of each transaction and the balances after each transaction, using the following tabular headings:

Assets		= Liabilities +	Owner's Equity							
		Accounts	Maria Adams,	Maria Adams,	Sales	Rent	Salaries	Auto	Supplies	Misc.
Cash + Supplies	=	Payable +	Capital –	Drawing +	Commissions –	Expense –	Expense –	Expense –	Expense –	Expense

2. Prepare an income statement for April, a statement of owner's equity for April, and a balance sheet as of April 30.

PR 1-5B Transactions; financial statements

OBJ. 4, 5

✔ 3. Net income: $40,150

Bev's Dry Cleaners is owned and operated by Beverly Zahn. A building and equipment are currently being rented, pending expansion to new facilities. The actual work of dry cleaning is done by another company for a fee. The assets and the liabilities of the business on November 1, 20Y6, are as follows: Cash, $39,000; Accounts Receivable, $80,000; Supplies, $11,000; Land, $50,000; Accounts Payable, $31,500. Business transactions during November are summarized as follows:

a. Beverly Zahn invested additional cash in the business with a deposit of $21,000 in the business bank account.

b. Purchased land adjacent to land currently owned by Bev's Dry Cleaners to use in the future as a parking lot, paying cash of $35,000.

c. Paid rent for the month, $4,000.

d. Charged customers for dry cleaning revenue on account, $72,000.

e. Paid creditors on account, $20,000.

f. Purchased supplies on account, $8,000.

g. Received cash from cash customers for dry cleaning revenue, $38,000.

h. Received cash from customers on account, $77,000.

i. Received monthly invoice for dry cleaning expense for November (to be paid on December 10), $29,450.

j. Paid the following: wages expense, $24,000; truck expense, $2,100; utilities expense, $1,800; miscellaneous expense, $1,300.

k. Determined that the cost of supplies on hand was $11,800; therefore, the cost of supplies used during the month was $7,200.

l. Withdrew $5,000 for personal use.

Instructions

1. Determine the amount of Beverly Zahn's capital as of November 1.
2. State the assets, liabilities, and owner's equity as of November 1 in equation form similar to that shown in Exhibit 5. In tabular form below the equation, indicate increases and decreases resulting from each transaction and the new balances after each transaction.
3. Prepare an income statement for November, a statement of owner's equity for November, and a balance sheet as of November 30.
4. *(Optional)* Prepare a statement of cash flows for November.

✔ i. $120,000

PR 1-6B Missing amounts from financial statements

OBJ. 5

The financial statements at the end of Atlas Realty's first month of operations follow:

Atlas Realty
Income Statement
For the Month Ended May 31, 20Y3

Fees earned		$400,000
Expenses:		
Wages expense	$ (a)	
Rent expense	48,000	
Supplies expense	17,600	
Utilities expense	14,400	
Miscellaneous expense	4,800	
Total expenses		288,000
Net income		$ (b)

Atlas Realty
Statement of Owner's Equity
For the Month Ended May 31, 20Y3

LuAnn Martin, capital, May 1, 20Y3		$ (c)
Investment on May 1, 20Y3	$ (d)	
Net income for May	(e)	
Withdrawals	(f)	
Increase in owner's equity		(g)
LuAnn Martin, capital, May 31, 20Y3		$ (h)

Atlas Realty
Balance Sheet
May 31, 20Y3

Assets	
Cash	$ 123,200
Supplies	12,800
Land	(i)
Total assets	$ (j)
Liabilities	
Accounts payable	$ 48,000
Owner's Equity	
LuAnn Martin, capital	(k)
Total liabilities and owner's equity	$ (l)

Atlas Realty
Statement of Cash Flows
For the Month Ended May 31, 20Y3

Cash flows from (used for) operating activities:		
Cash received from customers	$ (m)	
Cash paid for operating expenses and to creditors	(252,800)	
Net cash flows from operating activities		$ (n)
Cash flows from (used for) investing activities:		
Cash paid for acquisition of land		(120,000)
Cash flows from (used for) financing activities:		
Cash received from owner as investment	$ 160,000	
Cash withdrawals by owner	(64,000)	
Net cash flows from financing activities		(o)
Net increase (decrease) in cash		$ (p)
Cash balance, May 1, 20Y3		0
Cash balance, May 31, 20Y3		$ (q)

Instructions

By analyzing the interrelationships among the four financial statements, determine the proper amounts for (a) through (q).

Continuing Problem

✔ **2. Net income: $1,340**

Peyton Smith enjoys listening to all types of music and owns countless CDs. Over the years, Peyton has gained a local reputation for knowledge of music from classical to rap and the ability to put together sets of recordings that appeal to all ages.

During the last several months, Peyton served as a guest disc jockey on a local radio station. In addition, Peyton has entertained at several friends' parties as the host deejay.

On June 1, 20Y9, Peyton established a proprietorship known as PS Music. Using an extensive collection of music MP3 files, Peyton will serve as a disc jockey on a fee basis for weddings, college parties, and other events. During June, Peyton entered into the following transactions:

June 1. Deposited $4,000 in a checking account in the name of PS Music.

2. Received $3,500 from a local radio station for serving as the guest disc jockey for June.

2. Agreed to share office space with a local real estate agency, Pinnacle Realty. PS Music will pay one-fourth of the rent. In addition, PS Music agreed to pay a portion of the wages of the receptionist and to pay one-fourth of the utilities. Paid $800 for the rent of the office.

4. Purchased supplies from City Office Supply Co. for $350. Agreed to pay $100 within 10 days and the remainder by July 5, 20Y9.

6. Paid $500 to a local radio station to advertise the services of PS Music twice daily for two weeks.

8. Paid $675 to a local electronics store for renting digital recording equipment.

12. Paid $350 (music expense) to Cool Music for the use of its current music demos to make various music sets.

13. Paid City Office Supply Co. $100 on account.

16. Received $300 from a dentist for providing two music sets for the dentist to play for her patients.

22. Served as disc jockey for a wedding party. The father of the bride agreed to pay $1,000 in July.

25. Received $500 for serving as the disc jockey for a cancer charity ball hosted by the local hospital.

29. Paid $240 (music expense) to Galaxy Music for the use of its library of music demos.

30. Received $900 for serving as PS disc jockey for a local club's monthly dance.

30. Paid Pinnacle Realty $400 for PS Music's share of the receptionist's wages for June.

30. Paid Pinnacle Realty $300 for PS Music's share of the utilities for June.

30. Determined that the cost of supplies on hand is $170. Therefore, the cost of supplies used during the month was $180.

30. Paid for miscellaneous expenses, $415.

30. Paid $1,000 royalties (music expense) to National Music Clearing for use of various artists' music during the month.

30. Withdrew $500 of cash from PS Music for personal use.

Instructions

1. Indicate the effect of each transaction and the balances after each transaction, using the following tabular headings:

Assets			= Liabilities +	Owner's Equity										
Cash +	Accts. Rec. +	Supplies =	Accounts Payable	+ Peyton Smith, Capital	− Peyton Smith, Drawing	+ Fees Earned	− Music Exp.	− Office Rent Exp.	− Equipment Rent Exp.	− Advertising Exp.	− Wages Exp.	− Utilities Exp.	− Supplies Exp.	− Misc. Exp.

2. Prepare an income statement for PS Music for the month ended June 30, 20Y9.
3. Prepare a statement of owner's equity for PS Music for the month ended June 30, 20Y9.
4. Prepare a balance sheet for PS Music as of June 30, 20Y9.

Cases & Projects

ETHICS

CP 1-1 Ethics in Action

Marco Brolo is one of three partners who own and operate Silkroad Partners, a global import–export business. Marco is the partner in charge of recording partnership transactions in the accounts. On his way to work one day, Marco's car broke down. At the repair shop, Marco learned that his car's engine had significant damage, and it will cost over $2,000 to repair the damage. He does not have enough money in his bank account to cover the cost of the repair, and his credit cards are at their limit. This car is the only form of transportation that Marco has to get to and from work every day. He does not use his car for any business travel.

After considering his options, Marco decides to take $2,000 from the partnership for the repair and record it as an expense of the partnership. He believes that this is appropriate since he needs his car to get to work every day.

1. Is Marco behaving ethically? Why or why not?
2. Who is affected by Marco's decision?
3. What other alternatives might Marco consider?

ETHICS

CP 1-2 Ethics in Action

Colleen Fernandez, president of Rhino Enterprises, applied for a $175,000 loan from First Federal Bank. The bank requested financial statements from Rhino Enterprises as a basis for granting the loan. Colleen has told her accountant to provide the bank with a balance sheet. Colleen has decided to omit the other financial statements because there was a net loss during the past year.

In groups of three or four, discuss the following questions:

1. Is Colleen behaving in a professional manner by omitting some of the financial statements?
2. a. What types of information about their businesses would owners be willing to provide bankers? What types of information would owners not be willing to provide?
   b. What types of information about a business would bankers want before extending a loan?
   c. What common interests are shared by bankers and business owners?

TEAM ACTIVITY

CP 1-3 Team Activity

In teams, select a public company that interests you. Obtain the company's most recent annual report on Form 10-K. The Form 10-K is a company's annually required filing with the Securities and Exchange Commission (SEC). It includes the company's financial statements and accompanying notes. The Form 10-K can be obtained either (a) by referring to the investor relations section of the company's website or (b) by using the company search feature of the SEC's EDGAR database service found at www.sec.gov/edgar/searchedgar/companysearch.html.

Based on the information in the company's most recent annual report, answer the following questions:

1. What is the official name of the company?
2. Where are the company's principal offices located?

(Continued)

3. Who is the company's chief executive officer?
4. Is the company primarily a service, merchandising, or manufacturing business?
5. How does the company describe its business?
6. Which financial statements are included in the annual report?

CP 1-4 Communication

COMMUNICATION

There are two common causes of business and accounting fraud:

- A failure of individual character
- A culture of greed or ethical indifference within an organization

Write a brief memo describing how these two factors could lead to accounting fraud.

CP 1-5 Net income

On January 1, 20Y8, Dr. Marcie Cousins established Health-Wise Medical, a medical practice organized as a proprietorship. The following conversation occurred the following August between Dr. Cousins and a former medical school classmate, Dr. Avi Abu, at an American Medical Association convention in Seattle:

Dr. Abu: Marcie, good to see you again. Why didn't you call when you were in Miami? We could have had dinner together.

Dr. Cousins: Actually, I never made it to Miami this year. My husband and kids went up to our Vail condo twice, but I got stuck in Jacksonville. I opened a new consulting practice this January and haven't had any time for myself since.

Dr. Abu: I heard about it . . . Health . . . something . . . right?

Dr. Cousins: Yes, Health-Wise Medical. My husband chose the name.

Dr. Abu: I've thought about doing something like that. Are you making any money? I mean, is it worth your time?

Dr. Cousins: You wouldn't believe it. I started by opening a bank account with $25,000, and my July bank statement has a balance of $80,000. Not bad for six months—all pure profit.

Dr. Abu: Maybe I'll try it in Miami! Let's have breakfast together tomorrow, and you can fill me in on the details.

Comment on Dr. Cousins' statement that the difference between the opening bank balance ($25,000) and the July statement balance ($80,000) is pure profit.

CP 1-6 Transactions and financial statements

Lisa Duncan, a junior in college, has been seeking ways to earn extra spending money. As an active sports enthusiast, Lisa plays tennis regularly at the Phoenix Tennis Club, where her family has a membership. The president of the club recently approached Lisa with the proposal that she manage the club's tennis courts. Lisa's primary duty would be to supervise the operation of the club's 4 indoor and 10 outdoor courts, including court reservations.

In return for her services, the club would pay Lisa $325 per week, plus Lisa could keep whatever she earned from lessons. The club and Lisa agreed to a one-month trial, after which both would consider an arrangement for the remaining two years of Lisa's college career. On this basis, Lisa organized Serve-N-Volley. During September 20Y7, Lisa managed the tennis courts and entered into the following transactions:

a. Opened a business account by depositing $950.
b. Paid $300 for tennis supplies (practice tennis balls, etc.).
c. Paid $275 for the rental of video equipment to be used in offering lessons during September.
d. Arranged for the rental of two ball machines during September for $250. Paid $100 in advance, with the remaining $150 due October 1.
e. Received $1,750 for lessons given during September.

f. Received $600 in fees from the use of the ball machines during September.

g. Paid $800 for salaries of part-time employees who answered the telephone and took reservations while Lisa was giving lessons.

h. Paid $290 for miscellaneous expenses.

i. Received $1,300 from the club for managing the tennis courts during September.

j. Determined that the cost of supplies on hand at the end of the month totaled $180; therefore, the cost of supplies used was $120.

k. Withdrew $400 for personal use on September 30.

As a friend and an accounting student, you have been asked by Lisa to aid her in assessing the venture.

1. Indicate the effect of each transaction and the balances after each transaction, using the following tabular headings:

Assets	= Liabilities +			Owner's Equity				
	Accounts	Lisa Duncan,	Lisa Duncan,	Fees	Salaries	Rent	Supplies	Misc.
Cash + Supplies =	Payable +	Capital −	Drawing +	Earned −	Expense −	Expense −	Expense −	Expense

2. Prepare an income statement for September.
3. Prepare a statement of owner's equity for September.
4. Prepare a balance sheet as of September 30.
5. a. Assume that Lisa Duncan could earn $10 per hour working 30 hours a week as a waitress. Evaluate which of the two alternatives, working as a waitress or operating Serve-N-Volley, would provide Lisa with the most income per month.

   b. Discuss any other factors that you believe Lisa should consider before discussing a long-term arrangement with the Phoenix Tennis Club.

CP 1-7 Certification requirements for accountants

By satisfying certain specific requirements, accountants may become certified as public accountants (CPAs), management accountants (CMAs), or internal auditors (CIAs). Find the certification requirements for one of these accounting groups by accessing one of the following websites:

Site	Description
www.ais-cpa.com	This site lists the address and/or Internet link for each state's board of accountancy. Find your state's requirements.
www.imanet.org	This site lists the requirements for becoming a CMA.
www.theiia.org	This site lists the requirements for becoming a CIA.

CP 1-8 Cash flows

Amazon.com, an Internet retailer, was incorporated and began operation in the mid-1990s. On the statement of cash flows, would you expect Amazon.com's net cash flows from operating, investing, and financing activities to be positive or negative for its first three years of operations? Use the following format for your answers and briefly explain your logic.

	First Year	Second Year	Third Year
Net cash flows from (used for) operating activities	negative		
Net cash flows from (used for) investing activities			
Net cash flows from (used for) financing activities			

CHAPTER

2

Analyzing Transactions

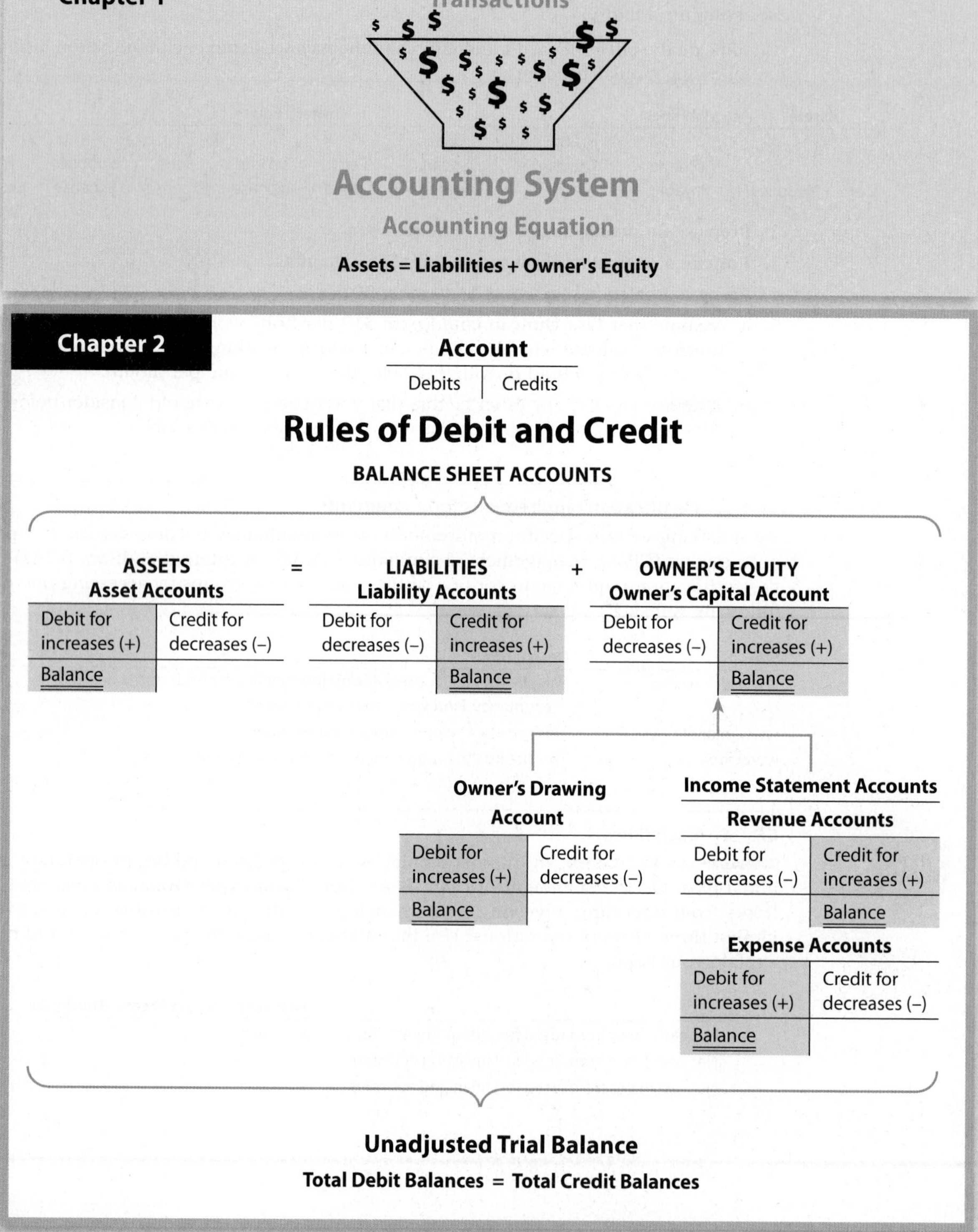

CHAPTER

2

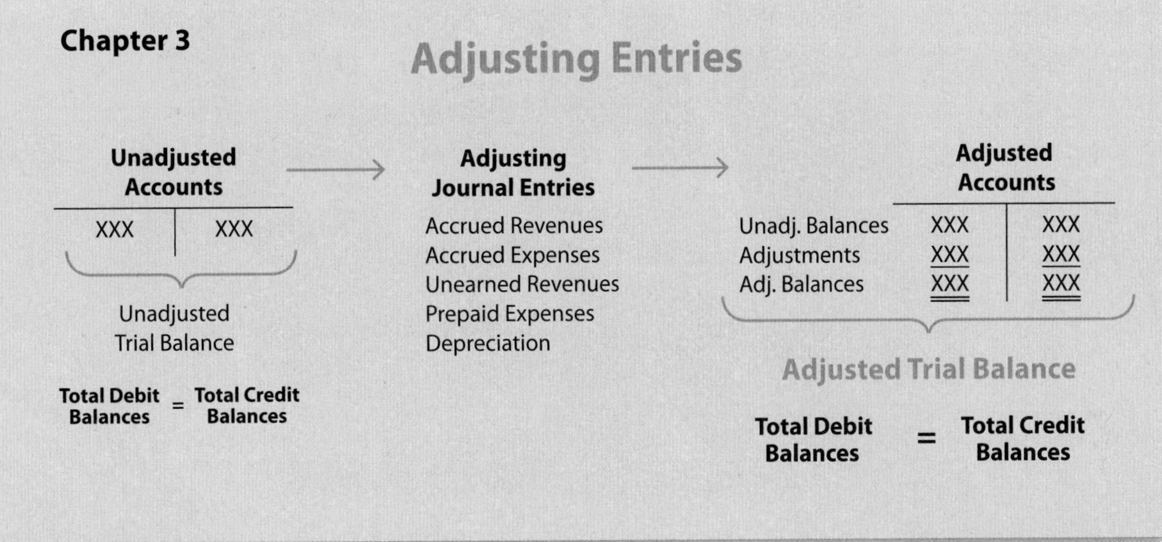

Chapter 3
Adjusting Entries
Unadjusted Accounts
XXX
XXX
Unadjusted Trial Balance
Total Debit Balances = Total Credit Balances
Adjusting Journal Entries
Accrued Revenues
Accrued Expenses
Unearned Revenues
Prepaid Expenses
Depreciation
Adjusted Accounts
Unadj. Balances XXX XXX
Adjustments XXX XXX
Adj. Balances XXX XXX
Adjusted Trial Balance
Total Debit Balances = Total Credit Balances

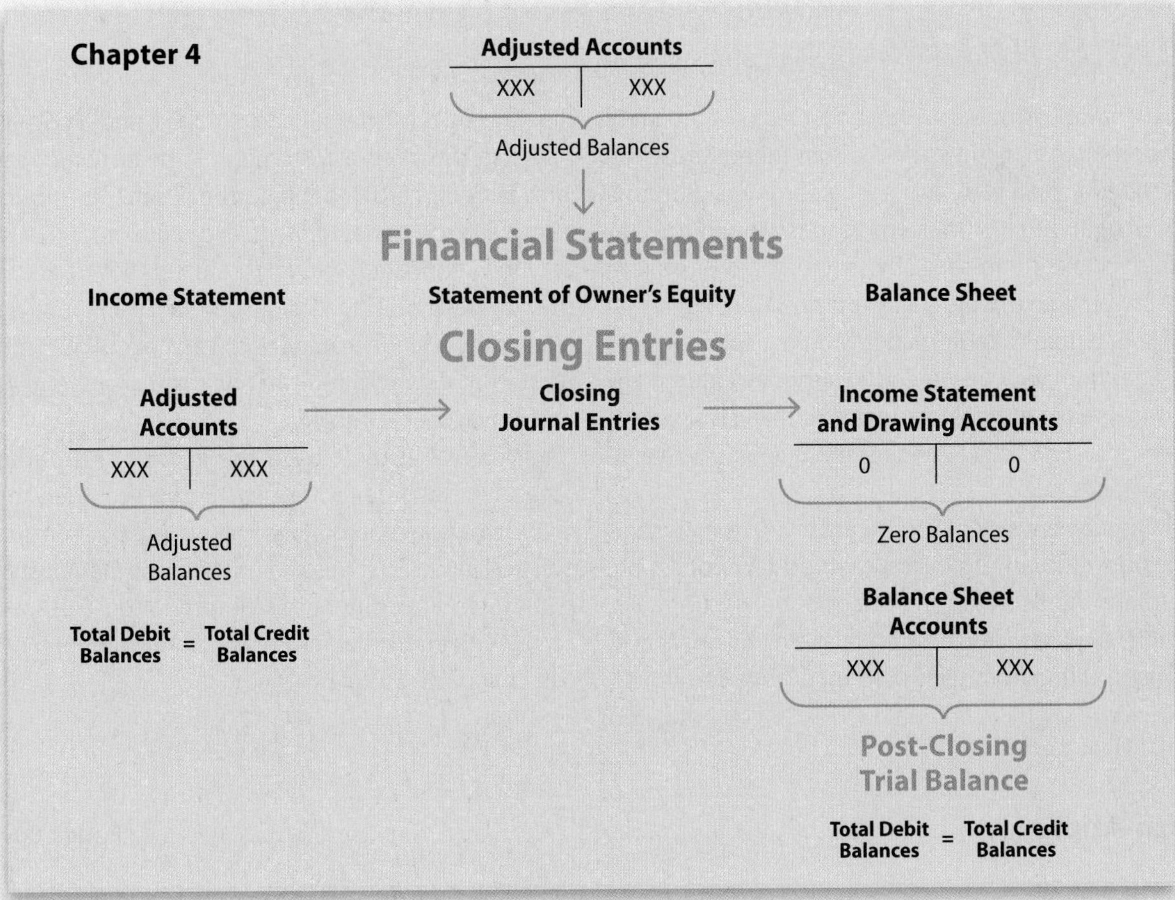

Chapter 4
Adjusted Accounts
XXX
XXX
Adjusted Balances
Financial Statements
Income Statement
Statement of Owner's Equity
Balance Sheet
Closing Entries
Adjusted Accounts
XXX
XXX
Adjusted Balances
Total Debit Balances = Total Credit Balances
Closing Journal Entries
Income Statement and Drawing Accounts
0
0
Zero Balances
Balance Sheet Accounts
XXX
XXX
Post-Closing Trial Balance
Total Debit Balances = Total Credit Balances

NOAH BERGER/BLOOMBERG/GETTY IMAGES

Apple Inc.™

Every day it seems like we get an incredible amount of incoming e-mail messages—from friends, relatives, subscribed e-mail lists, and even spammers! But how do you organize all of these messages? You might create folders to sort messages by sender, topic, or project. Perhaps you use keyword search utilities. You might even use filters or rules to automatically delete spam or send messages from your best friend to a special folder. In any case, you are organizing information so that it is simple to retrieve and allows you to understand, respond, or refer to the messages.

In the same way that you organize your e-mail, companies develop an organized method for processing, recording, and summarizing financial transactions. For example, **Apple Inc.** has a huge volume of financial transactions, resulting from sales of its innovative computers, digital media (iTunes), iPods, iPhones, and iPads. When Apple sells an iPad, a customer has the option of paying with a credit card, a debit or check card, an Apple gift card, a financing arrangement, or cash. In order to analyze only the information related to Apple's cash transactions, the company must record or summarize all these similar sales using a single category or "cash" account. Similarly, Apple will record sales from financing arrangements in different accounts (records).

While Chapter 1 used the accounting equation (Assets = Liabilities + Owner's Equity) to analyze and record financial transactions, this chapter presents more practical and efficient recording methods that most companies use. In addition, this chapter discusses possible accounting errors that may occur, along with methods to detect and correct them.

Link to Apple .... Pages 60, 62, 78

LEARNING OBJECTIVES

After studying this chapter, you should be able to:

Example Exercises (EE) are shown in **red.**

OBJ. 1 **Describe the characteristics of an account and a chart of accounts.**

Using Accounts to Record Transactions
Chart of Accounts

OBJ. 2 **Describe and illustrate journalizing transactions using the double-entry accounting system.**

Double-Entry Accounting System
Balance Sheet Accounts
Income Statement Accounts
Owner Withdrawals
Normal Balances — EE **2-1**
Journalizing: Asset Purchase — EE **2-2**

OBJ. 3 **Describe and illustrate the journalizing and posting of transactions to accounts.**

Journalizing and Posting to Accounts
Journalizing: Fees Earned — EE **2-3**
Journalizing: Withdrawals — EE **2-4**
Missing Amount from Account — EE **2-5**

OBJ. 4 **Prepare an unadjusted trial balance and explain how it can be used to discover errors.**

Trial Balance
Errors Affecting the Trial Balance — EE **2-6**
Correcting Entries — EE **2-7**

OBJ. 5 **Describe and illustrate the use of horizontal analysis in evaluating a company's performance and financial condition.**

Financial Analysis and Interpretation: Horizontal Analysis
Horizontal Analysis Report — EE **2-8**

At a Glance 2 Page 83

Using Accounts to Record Transactions

OBJ. 1 Describe the characteristics of an account and a chart of accounts.

In Chapter 1, the November transactions for **NetSolutions** were recorded using the accounting equation format shown in Exhibit 1. However, this format is not efficient or practical for companies that have to record thousands or millions of transactions daily. As a result, accounting systems are designed to show the increases and decreases in each accounting equation element as a separate record. This record is called an **account**.

To illustrate, the Cash column of NetSolutions' November transactions in Exhibit 1 records the increases and decreases in cash. Likewise, the other columns in Exhibit 1 record the increases and decreases in the other accounting equation elements. Each of these columns can be organized into a separate account.

An account, in its simplest form, has three parts.

- A title, which is the name of the accounting equation element recorded in the account
- A space for recording increases in the amount of the element
- A space for recording decreases in the amount of the element

The account form that follows is called a **T account** because it resembles the letter T. The left side of the account is called the *debit* side, and the right side is called the *credit* side:[1]

Title	
Left side *debit*	Right side *credit*

1 The terms *debit* and *credit* are derived from the Latin *debere* and *credere*, respectively.

EXHIBIT 1 **NetSolutions' November Transactions**

	Assets			= Liabilities +	Owner's Equity							
	Cash +	Supp. +	Land =	Accounts Payable +	Chris Clark, Capital −	Chris Clark, Drawing +	Fees Earned −	Wages Exp. −	Rent Exp. −	Supplies Exp. −	Utilities Exp. −	Misc. Exp.
a.	+25,000				+25,000							
b.	−20,000		+20,000									
Bal.	5,000		20,000		25,000							
c.		+1,350		+1,350								
Bal.	5,000	1,350	20,000	1,350	25,000							
d.	+7,500						+7,500					
Bal.	12,500	1,350	20,000	1,350	25,000		7,500					
e.	−3,650							−2,125	−800		−450	−275
Bal.	8,850	1,350	20,000	1,350	25,000		7,500	−2,125	−800		−450	−275
f.	−950			−950								
Bal.	7,900	1,350	20,000	400	25,000		7,500	−2,125	−800		−450	−275
g.		−800								−800		
Bal.	7,900	550	20,000	400	25,000		7,500	−2,125	−800	−800	−450	−275
h.	−2,000					−2,000						
Bal.	5,900	550	20,000	400	25,000	−2,000	7,500	−2,125	−800	−800	−450	−275

Note

Amounts entered on the left side of an account are debits, and amounts entered on the right side of an account are credits.

The amounts shown in the Cash column of Exhibit 1 would be recorded in a cash account as follows:

Cash

Debit Side of Account	(a)	25,000	(b)	20,000	Credit Side of Account
	(d)	7,500	(e)	3,650	
			(f)	950	
			(h)	2,000	
	Balance	5,900			

Balance of Account

Recording transactions in accounts must follow certain rules. For example, increases in assets are recorded on the **debit** (left) side of an account. Likewise, decreases in assets are recorded on the **credit** (right) side of an account. The excess of the debits of an asset account over its credits is the **balance of the account.**

To illustrate, the receipt (increase in Cash) of $25,000 in transaction (a) is entered on the debit (left) side of the cash account. The letter or date of the transaction is also entered into the account. That way, if any questions later arise related to the entry, the entry can be traced back to the underlying transaction data. In contrast, the payment (decrease in Cash) of $20,000 to purchase land in transaction (b) is entered on the credit (right) side of the account.

The balance of the cash account of $5,900 is the excess of the debits over the credits, computed as follows:

Debits ($25,000 + $7,500)	$32,500
Less credits ($20,000 + $3,650 + $950 + $2,000)	26,600
Balance of Cash as of November 30, 20Y3	$ 5,900

Link to Apple

In a recent balance sheet, **Apple Inc.** reported $25.9 billion of cash.

The balance of the cash account is inserted in the account in the Debit column. In this way, the balance is identified as a debit balance.[2] This balance represents NetSolutions' cash on hand as of November 30, 20Y3. This balance of $5,900 is reported on the November 30, 20Y3, balance sheet for NetSolutions as shown in Exhibit 8 of Chapter 1.

In an actual accounting system, more formal account forms replace the T account. Later in this chapter, a four-column account is illustrated. The T account, however, is

2 The totals of the Debit and Credit columns may be shown separately in an account. When this is done, these amounts should be identified in some way so that they are not mistaken for entries or the ending balance of the account.

a simple way to illustrate the effects of transactions on accounts and financial statements. For this reason, T accounts are often used in business to explain transactions.

Each of the columns in Exhibit 1 can be converted into an account form in a similar manner as was done for the Cash column of Exhibit 1. However, as mentioned earlier, recording increases and decreases in accounts must follow certain rules. These rules are discussed after the chart of accounts is described.

Chart of Accounts

A group of accounts for a business entity is called a **ledger**. A list of the accounts in the ledger is called a **chart of accounts**. The accounts are normally listed in the order in which they appear in the financial statements. The balance sheet accounts are listed first, in the order of assets, liabilities, and owner's equity. The income statement accounts are then listed in the order of revenues and expenses.

Assets **Assets** are resources owned by the business entity. These resources can be physical items, such as cash and supplies, or intangibles that have value. Examples of intangible assets include patent rights, copyrights, and trademarks. Assets also include accounts receivable, prepaid expenses (such as insurance), buildings, equipment, and land.

Liabilities **Liabilities** are debts owed to outsiders (creditors). Liabilities are often identified on the balance sheet by titles that include *payable*. Examples of liabilities include accounts payable, notes payable, and wages payable. Cash received before services are delivered creates a liability to perform the services. These future service commitments are called *unearned revenues*. Examples of unearned revenues include magazine subscriptions received by a publisher and tuition received at the beginning of a term by a college.

Owner's Equity **Owner's equity** is the owner's right to the assets of the business after all liabilities have been paid. For a proprietorship, the owner's equity is represented by the balance of the owner's **capital account**. A **drawing** account represents the amount of withdrawals made by the owner.

Revenues **Revenues** are increases in assets and owner's equity as a result of selling services or products to customers. Examples of revenues include fees earned, fares earned, commissions revenue, and rent revenue.

Business Connection

THE HIJACKING RECEIVABLE

A company's chart of accounts should reflect the basic nature of its operations. Occasionally, however, transactions take place that give rise to unusual accounts. The following is a story of one such account.

Before strict airport security was implemented across the United States, several airlines experienced hijacking incidents. One such incident occurred when a **Southern Airways** jet en route from Memphis to Miami was hijacked during a stopover in Birmingham, Alabama. The three hijackers boarded the plane in Birmingham armed with handguns and hand grenades. At gunpoint, the hijackers took the plane, the plane's crew, and the passengers to nine American cities, Toronto, and eventually Havana, Cuba.

During the long flight, the hijackers demanded a ransom of $10 million. Southern Airways, however, was only able to come up with $2 million. Eventually, the pilot talked the hijackers into settling for the $2 million when the plane landed in Chattanooga for refueling.

Upon landing in Havana, the Cuban authorities arrested the hijackers and, after a brief delay, sent the plane, passengers, and crew back to the United States. The hijackers and the $2 million stayed in Cuba.

How did Southern Airways account for and report the hijacking payment in its subsequent financial statements? As you might have analyzed, the initial entry credited Cash for $2 million. The debit was to an account entitled "Hijacking Payment." This account was reported as a type of receivable under "other assets" on Southern Airways' balance sheet. The company maintained that it would be able to collect the cash from the Cuban government and that, therefore, a receivable existed. In fact, Southern Airways was later repaid $2 million by the Cuban government, which was, at that time, attempting to improve relations with the United States.

Expenses **Expenses** result from using up assets or consuming services in the process of generating revenues. Examples of expenses include wages expense, rent expense, utilities expense, supplies expense, and miscellaneous expense.

Illustration of Chart of Accounts A chart of accounts should meet the needs of a company's managers and other users of its financial statements. The accounts within the chart of accounts are numbered for use as references. A numbering system is normally used so that new accounts can be added without affecting other account numbers.

Exhibit 2 is **NetSolutions**' chart of accounts that is used in this chapter. Additional accounts will be introduced in later chapters. In Exhibit 2, each account number has two digits. The first digit indicates the major account group of the ledger in which the account is located. Accounts beginning with 1 represent assets; 2, liabilities; 3, owner's equity; 4, revenue; and 5, expenses. The second digit indicates the location of the account within its group.

EXHIBIT 2

Chart of Accounts for NetSolutions

Balance Sheet Accounts	**Income Statement Accounts**
1. Assets	**4. Revenue**
11 Cash	41 Fees Earned
12 Accounts Receivable	**5. Expenses**
14 Supplies	51 Wages Expense
15 Prepaid Insurance	52 Supplies Expense
17 Land	53 Rent Expense
18 Office Equipment	54 Utilities Expense
2. Liabilities	59 Miscellaneous Expense
21 Accounts Payable	
23 Unearned Rent	
3. Owner's Equity	
31 Chris Clark, Capital	
32 Chris Clark, Drawing	

Each of the columns in Exhibit 1 has been assigned an account number in the chart of accounts shown in Exhibit 2. In addition, Accounts Receivable, Prepaid Insurance, Office Equipment, and Unearned Rent have been added. These accounts will be used in recording NetSolutions' December transactions.

OBJ. 2 Describe and illustrate journalizing transactions using the double-entry accounting system.

Double-Entry Accounting System

All businesses use what is called the **double-entry accounting system**. This system is based on the accounting equation and requires:

- Every business transaction to be recorded in at least two accounts.
- The total debits recorded for each transaction to be equal to the total credits recorded.

The double-entry accounting system also has specific **rules of debit and credit** for recording transactions in the accounts.

Link to Apple

Apple records transactions using double-entry accounting.

Balance Sheet Accounts

The debit and credit rules for balance sheet accounts are as follows:

Balance Sheet Accounts

ASSETS Asset Accounts		=	LIABILITIES Liability Accounts		+	OWNER'S EQUITY Owner's Equity Accounts	
Debit for increases (+)	Credit for decreases (–)		Debit for decreases (–)	Credit for increases (+)		Debit for decreases (–)	Credit for increases (+)

Income Statement Accounts

The debit and credit rules for income statement accounts are based on their relationship with owner's equity. As shown for balance sheet accounts, owner's equity accounts are increased by credits. Because revenues increase owner's equity, revenue accounts are increased by credits and decreased by debits. Because owner's equity accounts are decreased by debits, expense accounts are increased by debits and decreased by credits. Thus, the rules of debit and credit for revenue and expense accounts are as follows:

Income Statement Accounts			
Revenue Accounts		**Expense Accounts**	
Debit for decreases (–)	Credit for increases (+)	Debit for increases (+)	Credit for decreases (–)

Owner Withdrawals

The debit and credit rules for recording owner withdrawals are based on the effect of owner withdrawals on owner's equity. Because an owner's withdrawals decrease owner's equity, the owner's drawing account is increased by debits. Likewise, the owner's drawing account is decreased by credits. Thus, the rules of debit and credit for the owner's drawing account are as follows:

Drawing Account	
Debit for increases (+)	Credit for decreases (–)

Normal Balances

The sum of the increases in an account is usually equal to or greater than the sum of the decreases in the account. Thus, the **normal balance of an account** is either a debit or credit depending on whether increases in the account are recorded as debits or credits. For example, because asset accounts are increased with debits, asset accounts normally have debit balances. Likewise, liability accounts normally have credit balances.

The rules of debit and credit and the normal balances of the various types of accounts are summarized in Exhibit 3. Debits and credits are sometimes abbreviated as Dr. for debit and Cr. for credit.

Rules of Debit and Credit, Normal Balances of Accounts EXHIBIT 3

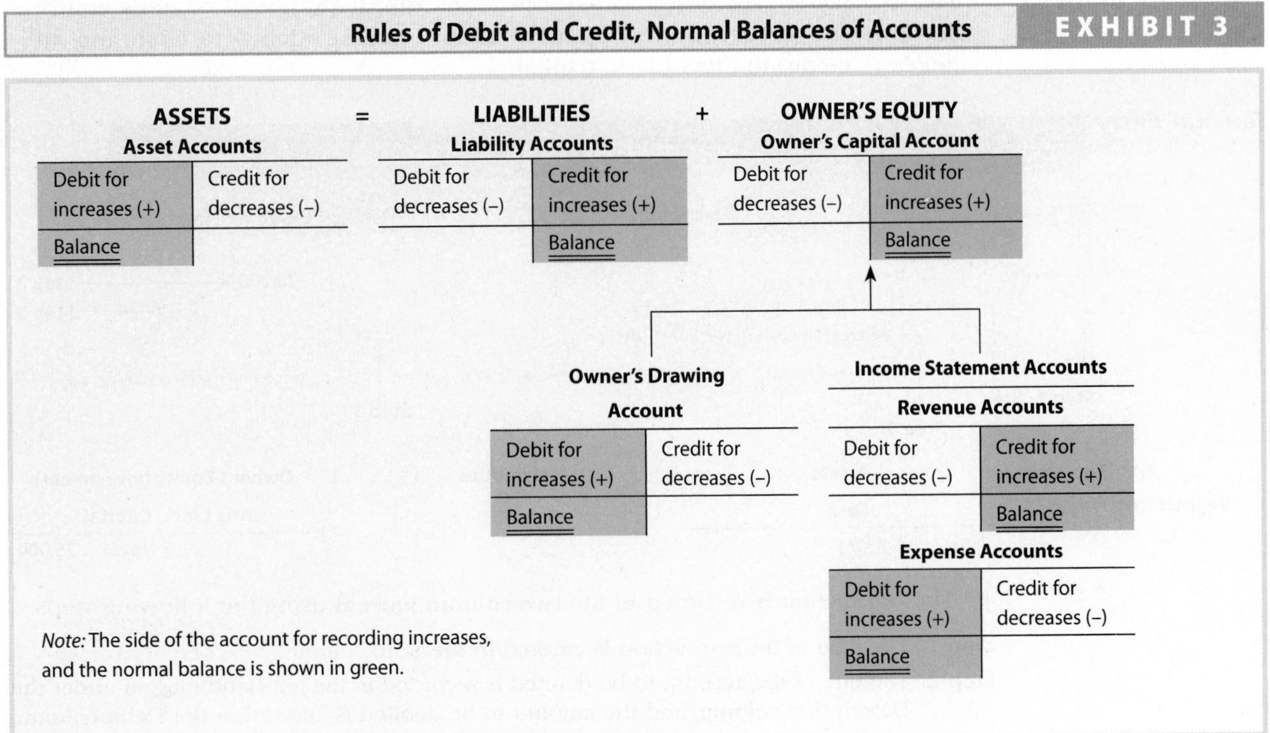

When an account with a normal debit balance has a credit balance, or vice versa, an error may have occurred or an unusual situation may exist. For example, a credit balance in the office equipment account could result only from an error. This is because a business cannot have more decreases than increases of office equipment. On the other hand, a debit balance in an accounts payable account could result from an overpayment.

EXAMPLE EXERCISE 2-1 Rules of Debit and Credit and Normal Balances **OBJ. 2**

State for each account whether it is likely to have (a) debit entries only, (b) credit entries only, or (c) both debit and credit entries. Also indicate its normal balance.

1. Amber Saunders, Drawing
2. Accounts Payable
3. Cash
4. Fees Earned
5. Supplies
6. Utilities Expense

Follow My Example 2-1

1. Debit entries only; normal debit balance
2. Debit and credit entries; normal credit balance
3. Debit and credit entries; normal debit balance
4. Credit entries only; normal credit balance
5. Debit and credit entries; normal debit balance
6. Debit entries only; normal debit balance

Practice Exercises: PE 2-1A, PE 2-1B

Journalizing

Using the rules of debit and credit, transactions are initially entered in a record called a **journal**. In this way, the journal serves as a record of when transactions occurred and were recorded. To illustrate, the November transactions of **Net Solutions** from Chapter 1 are used.

Transaction A *Nov. 1* *Chris Clark deposited $25,000 in a bank account in the name of NetSolutions.*

Analysis This transaction increases an asset account and increases an owner's equity account. It is recorded in the journal as an increase (debit) to Cash and an increase (credit) to Chris Clark, Capital.

Journal Entry

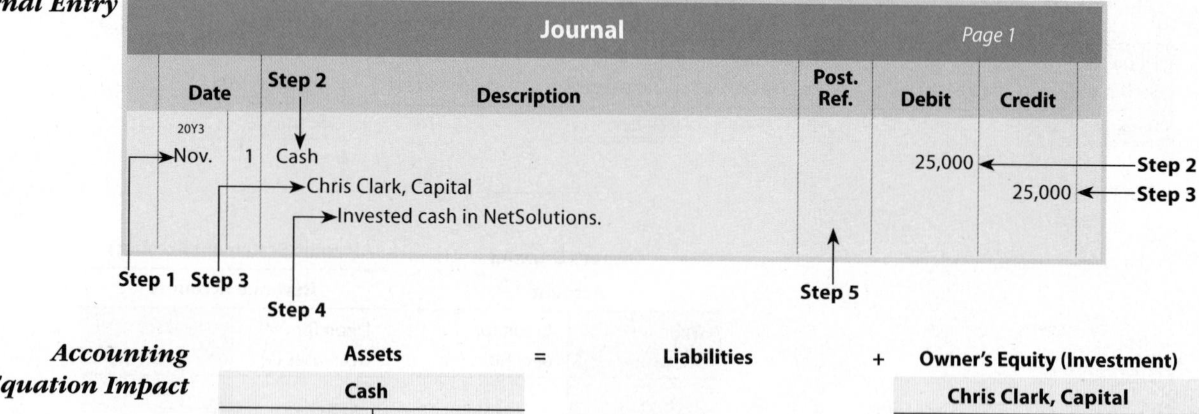

Accounting Equation Impact

Assets	=	Liabilities	+	Owner's Equity (Investment)
Cash				**Chris Clark, Capital**
Nov. 1 25,000				Nov. 1 25,000

The transaction is recorded in the **two-column journal** using the following steps:

Step 1. The date of the transaction is entered in the Date column.

Step 2. The title of the account to be debited is recorded in the left-hand margin under the Description column, and the amount to be debited is entered in the Debit column.

Step 3. The title of the account to be credited is listed below and to the right of the debited account title, and the amount to be credited is entered in the Credit column.

Step 4. A brief description may be entered below the credited account.

Step 5. The Post. Ref. (Posting Reference) column is left blank when the journal entry is initially recorded. This column is used later in this chapter when the journal entry amounts are transferred to the accounts in the ledger.

The process of recording a transaction in the journal is called **journalizing**. The entry in the journal is called a **journal entry**.

A useful method for analyzing and journalizing transactions is as follows:

Step 1. Carefully read the description of the transaction to determine whether an asset, a liability, an owner's equity, a revenue, an expense, or a drawing account is affected.

Step 2. For each account affected by the transaction, determine whether the account increases or decreases.

Step 3. Determine whether each increase or decrease should be recorded as a debit or a credit to the account, following the rules of debit and credit shown in Exhibit 3.

Step 4. Record the transaction using a journal entry.

Exhibit 4 summarizes terminology that is often used in describing a transaction along with the related accounts that would be debited and credited.

EXHIBIT 4

Transaction Terminology and Related Journal Entry Accounts

	Journal Entry Account	
Common Transaction Terminology	**Debit**	**Credit**
Received cash for services provided	Cash	Fees Earned
Services provided on account	Accounts Receivable	Fees Earned
Received cash on account	Cash	Accounts Receivable
Purchased on account	Asset account	Accounts Payable
Paid on account	Accounts Payable	Cash
Paid cash	Asset or expense account	Cash
Owner investments	Cash and/or other assets	(Owner's name), Capital
Owner withdrawals	(Owner's name), Drawing	Cash

The remaining transactions of **NetSolutions** for November are analyzed and journalized next.

Transaction B

Nov. 5 NetSolutions paid $20,000 for the purchase of land as a future building site.

Analysis

This transaction increases one asset account and decreases another. It is recorded in the journal as a $20,000 increase (debit) to Land and a $20,000 decrease (credit) to Cash.

Journal Entry

	Nov.	5	Land		20,000	
			Cash			20,000
			Purchased land for building site.			

Accounting Equation Impact

Assets = **Liabilities** + **Owner's Equity**

Land	
Nov. 5 20,000	

Cash	
	Nov. 5 20,000

Transaction C *Nov. 10 NetSolutions purchased supplies on account for $1,350.*

Analysis

This transaction increases an asset account and increases a liability account. It is recorded in the journal as a $1,350 increase (debit) to Supplies and a $1,350 increase (credit) to Accounts Payable.

Journal Entry

Nov.	10	Supplies		1,350	
		Accounts Payable			1,350
		Purchased supplies on account.			

Accounting Equation Impact

Assets = **Liabilities** + **Owner's Equity**

Supplies	
Nov. 10 1,350	

Accounts Payable	
	Nov. 10 1,350

Transaction D *Nov. 18 NetSolutions received cash of $7,500 from customers for services provided.*

Analysis

This transaction increases an asset account and increases a revenue account. It is recorded in the journal as a $7,500 increase (debit) to Cash and a $7,500 increase (credit) to Fees Earned.

Journal Entry

Nov.	18	Cash		7,500	
		Fees Earned			7,500
		Received fees from customers.			

Accounting Equation Impact

Assets = **Liabilities** + **Owner's Equity (Revenue)**

Cash	
Nov. 18 7,500	

Fees Earned	
	Nov. 18 7,500

Transaction E *Nov. 30 NetSolutions incurred the following expenses: wages, $2,125; rent, $800; utilities, $450; and miscellaneous, $275.*

Analysis

This transaction increases various expense accounts and decreases an asset (Cash) account. You should note that regardless of the number of accounts, *the sum of the debits is always equal to the sum of the credits in a journal entry.* It is recorded in the journal with increases (debits) to the expense accounts (Wages Expense, $2,125; Rent Expense, $800; Utilities Expense, $450; and Miscellaneous Expense, $275) and a decrease (credit) to Cash, $3,650.

Journal Entry

Nov.	30	Wages Expense		2,125	
		Rent Expense		800	
		Utilities Expense		450	
		Miscellaneous Expense		275	
		Cash			3,650
		Paid expenses.			

Accounting Equation Impact

Assets = **Liabilities** + **Owner's Equity (Expense)**

Cash	
	Nov. 30 3,650

Wages Expense	
Nov. 30 2,125	

Rent Expense	
Nov. 30 800	

Utilities Expense	
Nov. 30 450	

Miscellaneous Expense	
Nov. 30 275	

Nov. 30 NetSolutions paid creditors on account, $950.

Transaction F

Analysis

This transaction decreases a liability account and decreases an asset account. It is recorded in the journal as a $950 decrease (debit) to Accounts Payable and a $950 decrease (credit) to Cash.

Journal Entry

Nov.	30	Accounts Payable		950	
		Cash			950
		Paid creditors on account.			

Accounting Equation Impact

Assets = **Liabilities** + **Owner's Equity**

Cash			Accounts Payable	
	Nov. 30 950		Nov. 30 950	

Nov. 30 Chris Clark determined that the cost of supplies on hand at November 30 was $550.

Transaction G

Analysis

NetSolutions purchased $1,350 of supplies on November 10. Thus, $800 ($1,350 purchased – $550 on hand) of supplies have been used during November. This transaction is recorded in the journal as an $800 increase (debit) to Supplies Expense and an $800 decrease (credit) to Supplies.

Journal Entry

Nov.	30	Supplies Expense		800	
		Supplies			800
		Supplies used during November.			

Accounting Equation Impact

Assets = **Liabilities** + **Owner's Equity (Expense)**

Supplies			Supplies Expense	
	Nov. 30 800		Nov. 30 800	

Nov. 30 Chris Clark withdrew $2,000 from NetSolutions for personal use.

Transaction H

Analysis

This transaction decreases assets and owner's equity. It is recorded in the journal as a $2,000 increase (debit) to Chris Clark, Drawing and a $2,000 decrease (credit) to Cash.

Journal Entry

Journal *Page 2*

Date		Description	Post. Ref.	Debit	Credit
20Y3					
Nov.	30	Chris Clark, Drawing		2,000	
		Cash			2,000
		Chris Clark withdrew cash for personal use.			

Accounting Equation Impact

Assets = **Liabilities** + **Owner's Equity (Drawing)**

Cash			Chris Clark, Drawing	
	Nov. 30 2,000		Nov. 30 2,000	

Integrity, Objectivity, and Ethics in Business

WILL JOURNALIZING PREVENT FRAUD?

While journalizing transactions reduces the possibility of fraud, it by no means eliminates it. For example, embezzlement can be hidden within the double-entry bookkeeping system by creating fictitious suppliers to whom checks are issued.

EXAMPLE EXERCISE 2-2 Journal Entry for Asset Purchase **OBJ. 2**

Prepare a journal entry for the purchase of a truck on June 3 for $42,500, paying $8,500 cash and the remainder on account.

Follow My Example 2-2

June 3	Truck	42,500	
	Cash		8,500
	Accounts Payable		34,000

Practice Exercises: PE 2-2A, PE 2-2B

OBJ. 3 Describe and illustrate the journalizing and posting of transactions to accounts.

Journalizing and Posting to Accounts

As illustrated, a transaction is first recorded in a journal. Periodically, the journal entries are transferred to the accounts in the ledger. The process of transferring the debits and credits from the journal entries to the accounts is called **posting**.

The December transactions of **NetSolutions** are used to illustrate posting from the journal to the ledger. By using the December transactions, an additional review of analyzing and journalizing transactions is provided.

Transaction *Dec. 1* *NetSolutions paid a premium of $2,400 for an insurance policy for liability, theft, and fire. The policy covers a one-year period.*

Analysis

Prepayments of expenses, such as for insurance premiums, are called prepaid expenses. Prepaid expenses are assets. For NetSolutions, the asset purchased is insurance protection for 12 months. This transaction is recorded as a $2,400 increase (debit) to Prepaid Insurance and a $2,400 decrease (credit) to Cash.

Journal Entry

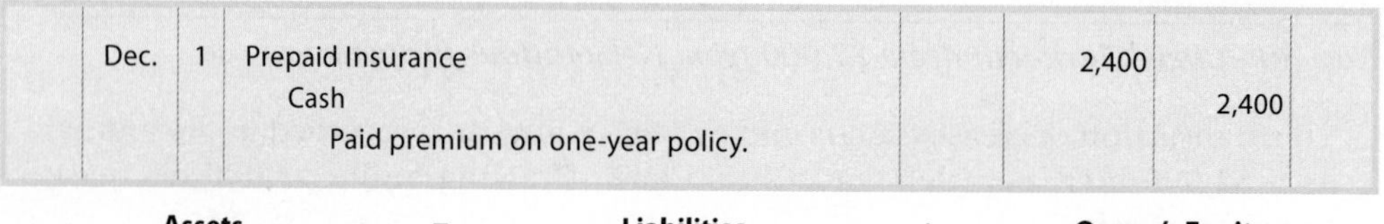

Dec.	1	Prepaid Insurance		2,400	
		Cash			2,400
		Paid premium on one-year policy.			

Accounting Equation Impact

Assets = **Liabilities** + **Owner's Equity**

Cash 11	
	Dec. 1 2,400

Prepaid Insurance 15	
Dec. 1 2,400	

Although T accounts are useful for illustrating the recording and posting of transactions, more formal, multi-column accounts are used in practice. For example, a **four-column account** has Date, Item, and Posting Reference (Post. Ref.) columns as well as Debit and Credit columns for posting transactions. In addition, the four-column account has Balance (Debit and Credit) columns for indicating the current balance of the account, sometimes called a running balance.[3] The posting of the preceding December 1 transaction to four-column accounts is shown in Exhibit 5.

The debits and credits for each journal entry are posted to the accounts in the order in which they occur in the journal. To illustrate, the debit portion of the December 1 journal entry is posted to the prepaid insurance account in Exhibit 5 using the following four steps:

Step 1. The date (Dec. 1) of the journal entry is entered in the Date column of Prepaid Insurance.

Step 2. The amount (2,400) is entered into the Debit column of Prepaid Insurance.

3 In a computerized, digital environment, accounts may take a variety of forms and include additional data useful for managing the company. However, as a minimum all accounts will include the columns of a four-column account.

Step 3. The journal page number (2) is entered in the Posting Reference (Post. Ref.) column of Prepaid Insurance.

Step 4. The account number (15) is entered in the Posting Reference (Post. Ref.) column in the journal.

As shown in Exhibit 5, the credit portion of the December 1 journal entry is posted to the cash account in a similar manner.

Diagram of the Recording and Posting of a Debit and a Credit Ledger, NetSolutions **EXHIBIT 5**

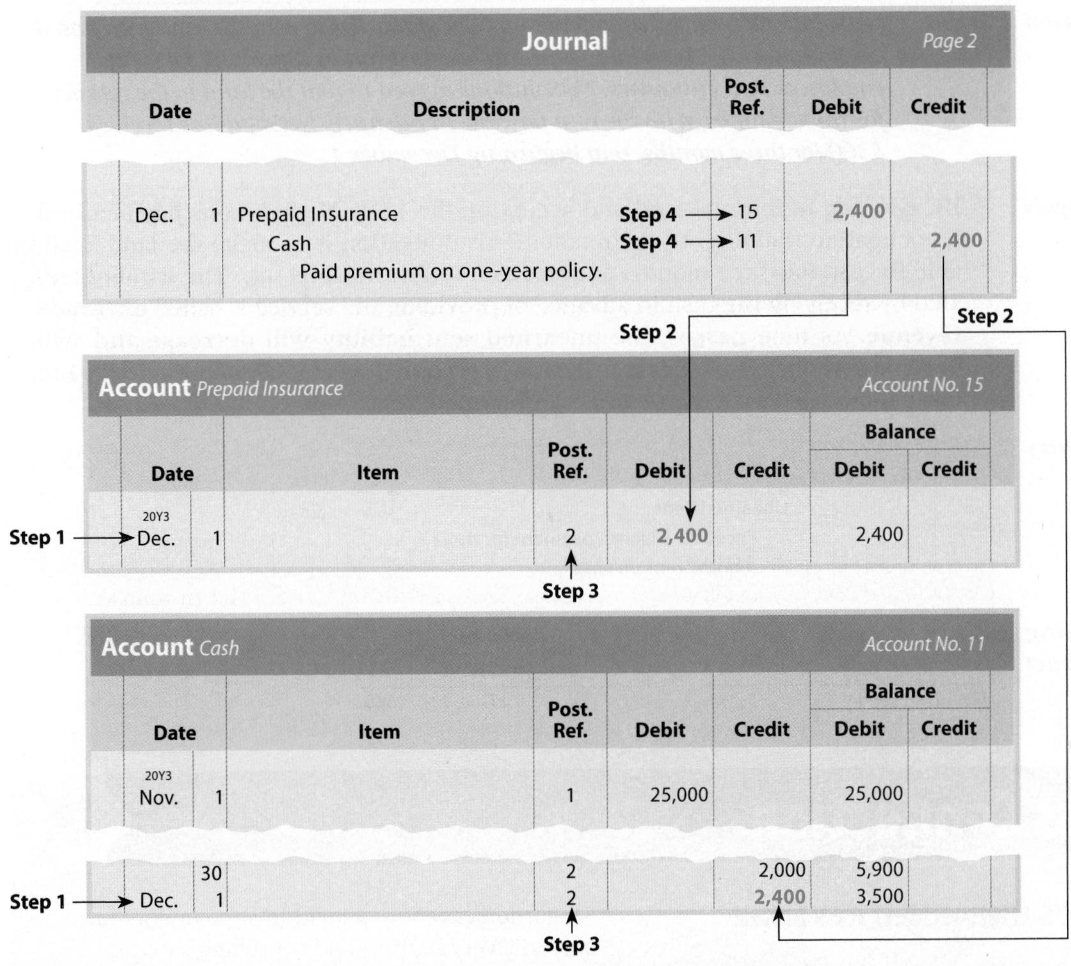

Journal *Page 2*

Date		Description	Post. Ref.	Debit	Credit
Dec.	1	Prepaid Insurance	15	2,400	
		Cash	11		2,400
		Paid premium on one-year policy.			

Account *Prepaid Insurance* *Account No. 15*

Date		Item	Post. Ref.	Debit	Credit	Balance Debit	Balance Credit
20Y3 Dec.	1		2	2,400		2,400	

Account *Cash* *Account No. 11*

Date		Item	Post. Ref.	Debit	Credit	Balance Debit	Balance Credit
20Y3 Nov.	1		1	25,000		25,000	
	30		2		2,000	5,900	
Dec.	1		2		2,400	3,500	

The remaining December transactions for **NetSolutions** are analyzed and journalized in the following paragraphs. These transactions are posted to the ledger later in this chapter (see Exhibit 6). To simplify, some of the December transactions are stated in summary form. For example, cash received for services is normally recorded on a daily basis. However, only summary totals are recorded at the middle and end of the month for NetSolutions.

Transaction

Dec. 1 NetSolutions paid rent for December, $800. The company from which NetSolutions is renting its office space now requires the payment of rent on the first of each month rather than at the end of the month.

Analysis

The prepayment of rent is an asset, much like the advance payment of the insurance premium in the preceding transaction. However, unlike the insurance premium, this prepaid rent will expire in one month. When an asset is purchased with the expectation that it will be used up in a short period of time, such as a month, it is normal to debit an expense account initially. This avoids having to transfer the balance from an asset account (Prepaid Rent) to an expense account (Rent Expense) at the end of the month. Thus, this transaction is recorded as an $800 increase (debit) to Rent Expense and an $800 decrease (credit) to Cash.

Journal Entry

Dec.	1	Rent Expense	53	800	
		Cash	11		800
		Paid rent for December.			

Accounting Equation Impact

Assets		=	Liabilities	+	Owner's Equity (Expense)	
Cash	11				**Rent Expense**	53
	Dec. 1 800				Dec. 1 800	

Transaction *Dec. 1* ***NetSolutions received an offer from a local retailer to rent the land purchased on November 5. The retailer plans to use the land as a parking lot for its employees and customers. NetSolutions agreed to rent the land to the retailer for three months, with the rent payable in advance. NetSolutions received $360 for three months' rent beginning December 1.***

Analysis

By agreeing to rent the land and accepting the $360, NetSolutions has incurred an obligation (liability) to the retailer. This obligation is to make the land available for use for three months and not to interfere with its use. The liability created by receiving the cash in advance of providing the service is called **unearned revenue**. As time passes, the unearned rent liability will decrease and will become revenue. Thus, this transaction is recorded as a $360 increase (debit) to Cash and a $360 increase (credit) to Unearned Rent.

Journal Entry

Dec.	1	Cash	11	360	
		Unearned Rent	23		360
		Received advance payment for three months' rent on land.			

Accounting Equation Impact

Assets		=	Liabilities		+	Owner's Equity
Cash	11		**Unearned Rent**	23		
Dec. 1 360				Dec. 1 360		

Business Connection

MICROSOFT'S UNEARNED REVENUE

Microsoft Corporation develops, manufactures, licenses, and supports a wide range of computer software products, including, Word®, Excel®, and the Xbox® gaming system. When Microsoft sells its products, it also provides technical support and periodic updates on those products for a period of time. Thus, at the time of sale, a portion of the proceeds is unearned (deferred) for these services. As time passes and services are provided to customers, Microsoft records a portion of its unearned (deferred) revenue as revenue.[4]

To illustrate, the following excerpt was taken from a recent financial statement of Microsoft:

Unearned revenue ... include(s) payments for: post-delivery support and consulting services to be performed in the future; Xbox Live subscriptions and prepaid points; Microsoft Dynamics business solutions products; Office 365 subscriptions; Skype prepaid credits and subscriptions; Bundled Offerings; and other offerings for which we have been paid in advance....

During a recent year, Microsoft recognized as revenue $55,078 million of unearned revenue, which is 50% of its total revenues. For a recent year ending June 30, Microsoft also reported on its balance sheet a liability for unearned revenue of $32,720 million. Thus, the recording of unearned revenue is a significant item for Microsoft.

Source: Microsoft Corporation, Form 10-K, For the Year Ended June 30, 2018.

4 Separating unearned revenue from the initial sale of a product or service is consistent with *Revenue from Contracts with Customers (Topic 606)*, FASB, 2014.

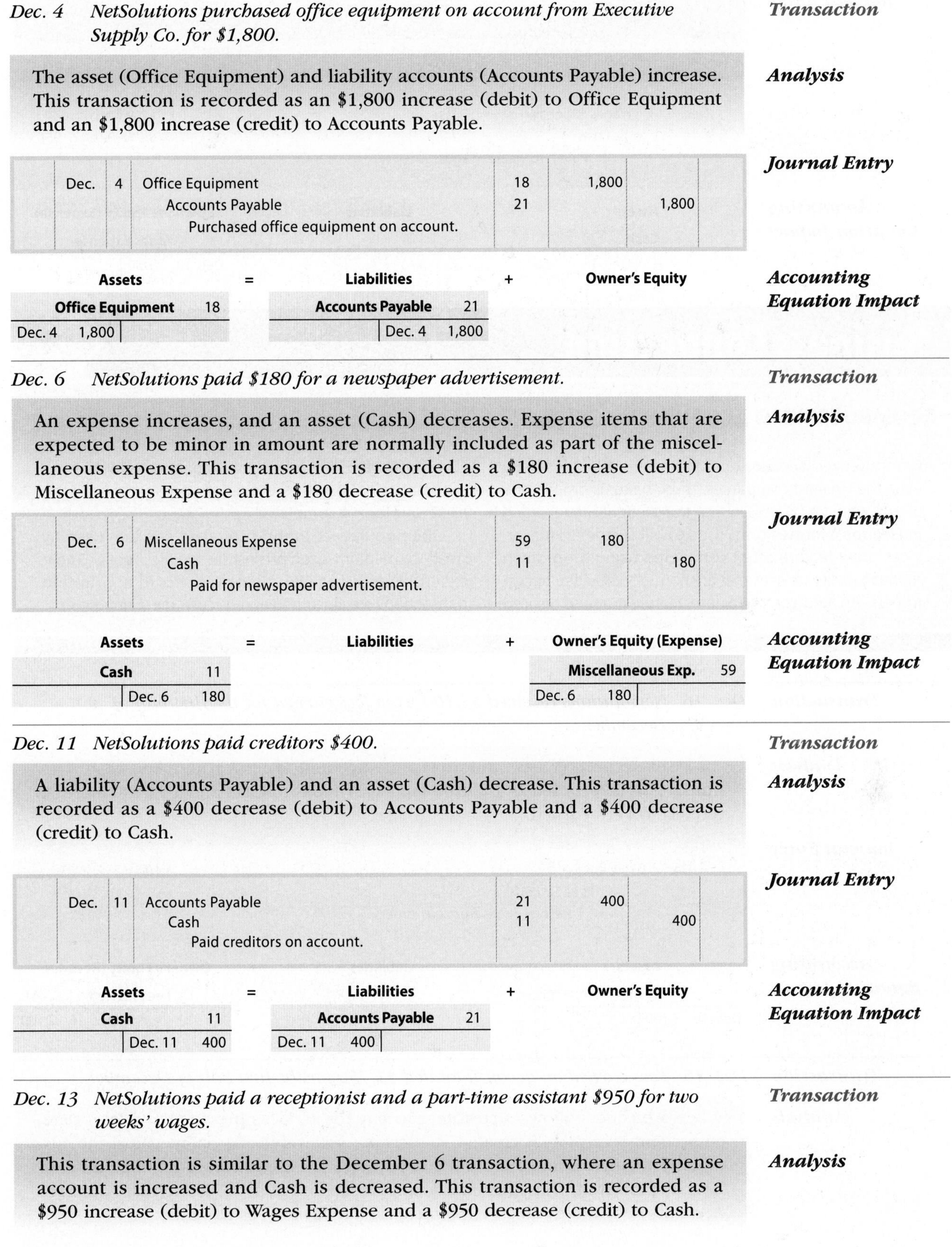

Dec. 4 NetSolutions purchased office equipment on account from Executive Supply Co. for $1,800. — ***Transaction***

Analysis

The asset (Office Equipment) and liability accounts (Accounts Payable) increase. This transaction is recorded as an $1,800 increase (debit) to Office Equipment and an $1,800 increase (credit) to Accounts Payable.

Journal Entry

Dec.	4	Office Equipment	18	1,800	
		Accounts Payable	21		1,800
		Purchased office equipment on account.			

Accounting Equation Impact

Assets	=	Liabilities	+	Owner's Equity
Office Equipment 18		**Accounts Payable** 21		
Dec. 4 1,800 |		| Dec. 4 1,800		

Dec. 6 NetSolutions paid $180 for a newspaper advertisement. — ***Transaction***

Analysis

An expense increases, and an asset (Cash) decreases. Expense items that are expected to be minor in amount are normally included as part of the miscellaneous expense. This transaction is recorded as a $180 increase (debit) to Miscellaneous Expense and a $180 decrease (credit) to Cash.

Journal Entry

Dec.	6	Miscellaneous Expense	59	180	
		Cash	11		180
		Paid for newspaper advertisement.			

Accounting Equation Impact

Assets	=	Liabilities	+	Owner's Equity (Expense)
Cash 11				**Miscellaneous Exp.** 59
| Dec. 6 180				Dec. 6 180 |

Dec. 11 NetSolutions paid creditors $400. — ***Transaction***

Analysis

A liability (Accounts Payable) and an asset (Cash) decrease. This transaction is recorded as a $400 decrease (debit) to Accounts Payable and a $400 decrease (credit) to Cash.

Journal Entry

Dec.	11	Accounts Payable	21	400	
		Cash	11		400
		Paid creditors on account.			

Accounting Equation Impact

Assets	=	Liabilities	+	Owner's Equity
Cash 11		**Accounts Payable** 21		
| Dec. 11 400		Dec. 11 400 |		

Dec. 13 NetSolutions paid a receptionist and a part-time assistant $950 for two weeks' wages. — ***Transaction***

Analysis

This transaction is similar to the December 6 transaction, where an expense account is increased and Cash is decreased. This transaction is recorded as a $950 increase (debit) to Wages Expense and a $950 decrease (credit) to Cash.

Journal Entry

Journal					Page 3
Date		Description	Post. Ref.	Debit	Credit
20Y3					
Dec.	13	Wages Expense	51	950	
		Cash	11		950
		Paid two weeks' wages.			

Accounting Equation Impact

Assets = Liabilities + Owner's Equity (Expense)

Cash	11
	Dec. 13 950

Wages Expense	51
Dec. 13 950	

Business Connection

COMPUTERIZED ACCOUNTING SYSTEMS

Computerized accounting systems are widely used by even the smallest companies. These systems simplify the record-keeping process in that transactions are recorded in electronic forms. Forms used to bill customers for services provided are often completed using drop-down menus that list services that are normally provided to customers. An auto-complete entry feature may also be used to fill in customer names. For example, type "ca" to display customers with names beginning with "Ca" (Caban, Cahill, Carey, and Caswell). And to simplify data entry, entries are automatically posted to the ledger accounts when the electronic form is completed.

One popular accounting software package used by small- to medium-sized businesses is QuickBooks®. Some examples of using QuickBooks to record accounting transactions are illustrated and discussed in Chapter 5.

Transaction *Dec. 16 NetSolutions received $3,100 from fees earned for the first half of December.*

Analysis

An asset account (Cash) and a revenue account (Fees Earned) increase. This transaction is recorded as a $3,100 increase (debit) to Cash and a $3,100 increase (credit) to Fees Earned.

Journal Entry

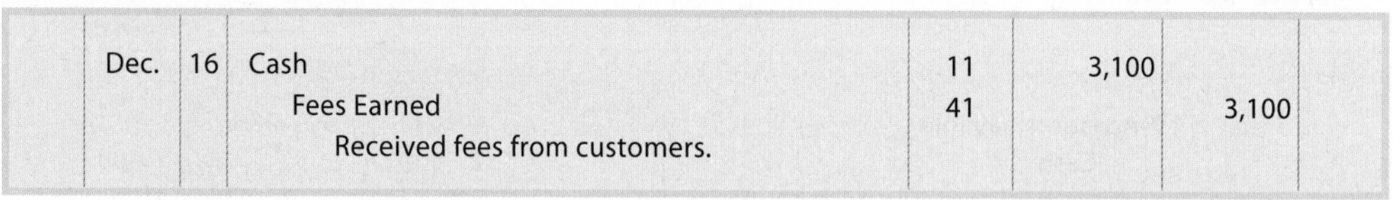

Dec.	16	Cash	11	3,100	
		Fees Earned	41		3,100
		Received fees from customers.			

Accounting Equation Impact

Assets = Liabilities + Owner's Equity (Revenue)

Cash	11
Dec. 16 3,100	

Fees Earned	41
	Dec. 16 3,100

Transaction *Dec. 16 Fees earned on account totaled $1,750 for the first half of December.*

Analysis

When a business allows a customer to pay for services provided at a later date, an **account receivable** is created. An account receivable is a claim against the customer, and, thus, is an asset for the seller. Revenue is earned even though no cash has been received. Thus, this transaction is recorded as a $1,750 increase (debit) to Accounts Receivable and a $1,750 increase (credit) to Fees Earned.

Journal Entry

Dec.	16	Accounts Receivable	12	1,750	
		Fees Earned	41		1,750
		Fees earned on account.			

Assets	=	Liabilities	+	Owner's Equity (Revenue)
Accounts Receivable 12				**Fees Earned** 41
Dec. 16 1,750 |				| Dec. 16 1,750

Accounting Equation Impact

EXAMPLE EXERCISE 2-3 Journal Entry for Fees Earned

OBJ. 3

Prepare a journal entry on August 7 for the fees earned on account, $115,000.

Follow My Example 2-3

Aug. 7	Accounts Receivable.	115,000	
	Fees Earned.		115,000

Practice Exercises: PE 2-3A, PE 2-3B

Dec. 20 NetSolutions paid $900 to Executive Supply Co. on the $1,800 debt owed from the December 4 transaction.

Transaction

This is similar to the transaction of December 11. This transaction is recorded as a $900 decrease (debit) to Accounts Payable and a $900 decrease (credit) to Cash.

Analysis

Dec.	20	Accounts Payable	21	900	
		Cash	11		900
		Paid creditors on account.			

Journal Entry

Assets	=	Liabilities	+	Owner's Equity
Cash 11		**Accounts Payable** 21		
| Dec. 20 900		Dec. 20 900 |		

Accounting Equation Impact

Dec. 21 NetSolutions received $650 from customers in payment of their accounts.

Transaction

When customers pay amounts owed for services they have previously received, one asset increases and another asset decreases. This transaction is recorded as a $650 increase (debit) to Cash and a $650 decrease (credit) to Accounts Receivable.

Analysis

Dec.	21	Cash	11	650	
		Accounts Receivable	12		650
		Received cash from customers on account.			

Journal Entry

Assets	=	Liabilities	+	Owner's Equity
Cash 11				
Dec. 21 650 |				
Accounts Receivable 12				
| Dec. 21 650				

Accounting Equation Impact

Dec. 23 NetSolutions paid $1,450 for supplies.

Transaction

One asset account (Supplies) increases, and another asset account (Cash) decreases. This transaction is recorded as a $1,450 increase (debit) to Supplies and a $1,450 decrease (credit) to Cash.

Analysis

Journal Entry

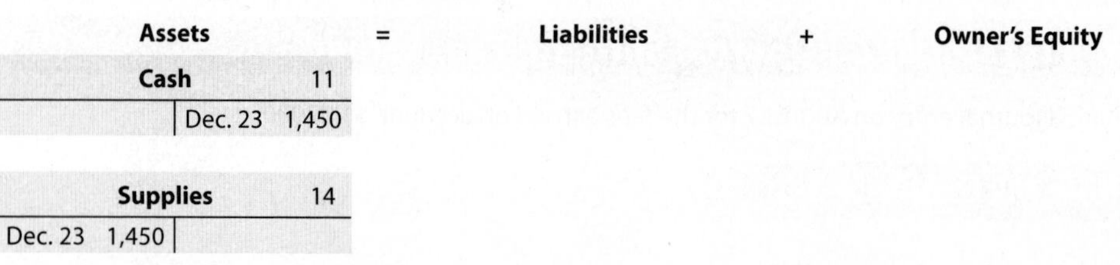

Dec.	23	Supplies	14	1,450	
		Cash	11		1,450
		Purchased supplies.			

Accounting Equation Impact

Assets = **Liabilities** + **Owner's Equity**

Cash	11
	Dec. 23 1,450

Supplies	14
Dec. 23 1,450	

Transaction *Dec. 27 NetSolutions paid the receptionist and the part-time assistant $1,200 for two weeks' wages.*

Analysis This transaction is similar to the transaction of December 13. This transaction is recorded as a $1,200 increase (debit) to Wages Expense and a $1,200 decrease (credit) to Cash.

Journal Entry

Dec.	27	Wages Expense	51	1,200	
		Cash	11		1,200
		Paid two weeks' wages.			

Accounting Equation Impact

Assets = **Liabilities** + **Owner's Equity (Expense)**

Cash	11
	Dec. 27 1,200

Wages Expense	51
Dec. 27 1,200	

Transaction *Dec. 31 NetSolutions paid its $310 telephone (utility) bill for the month.*

Analysis This is similar to the transaction of December 6. This transaction is recorded as a $310 increase (debit) to Utilities Expense and a $310 decrease (credit) to Cash.

Journal Entry

Dec.	31	Utilities Expense	54	310	
		Cash	11		310
		Paid telephone bill.			

Accounting Equation Impact

Assets = **Liabilities** + **Owner's Equity (Expense)**

Cash	11
	Dec. 31 310

Utilities Expense	54
Dec. 31 310	

Transaction *Dec. 31 NetSolutions paid its $225 electric (utility) bill for the month.*

Analysis This is similar to the preceding transaction. This transaction is recorded as a $225 increase (debit) to Utilities Expense and a $225 decrease (credit) to Cash.

Journal Entry

Journal *Page 4*

Date		Description	Post. Ref.	Debit	Credit
20Y3					
Dec.	31	Utilities Expense	54	225	
		Cash	11		225
		Paid electric bill.			

Assets	=	Liabilities	+	Owner's Equity (Expense)
Cash 11				**Utilities Expense** 54
| Dec. 31 225				Dec. 31 225 |

Accounting Equation Impact

Dec. 31 NetSolutions received $2,870 from fees earned for the second half of December. ***Transaction***

Analysis

This is similar to the transaction of December 16. This transaction is recorded as a $2,870 increase (debit) to Cash and a $2,870 increase (credit) to Fees Earned.

Journal Entry

Dec.	31	Cash	11	2,870	
		Fees Earned	41		2,870
		Received fees from customers.			

Assets	=	Liabilities	+	Owner's Equity (Revenue)
Cash 11				**Fees Earned** 41
Dec. 31 2,870 |				| Dec. 31 2,870

Accounting Equation Impact

Dec. 31 Fees earned on account totaled $1,120 for the second half of December. ***Transaction***

Analysis

This is similar to the transaction of December 16. This transaction is recorded as a $1,120 increase (debit) to Accounts Receivable and a $1,120 increase (credit) to Fees Earned.

Journal Entry

Dec.	31	Accounts Receivable	12	1,120	
		Fees Earned	41		1,120
		Fees earned on account.			

Assets	=	Liabilities	+	Owner's Equity (Revenue)
Accounts Receivable 12				**Fees Earned** 41
Dec. 31 1,120 |				| Dec. 31 1,120

Accounting Equation Impact

Dec. 31 Chris Clark withdrew $2,000 for personal use. ***Transaction***

Analysis

This transaction decreases owner's equity and assets. This transaction is recorded as a $2,000 increase (debit) to Chris Clark, Drawing and a $2,000 decrease (credit) to Cash.

Journal Entry

Dec.	31	Chris Clark, Drawing	32	2,000	
		Cash	11		2,000
		Chris Clark withdrew cash for personal use.			

Assets	=	Liabilities	+	Owner's Equity (Drawing)
Cash 11				**Chris Clark, Drawing** 32
| Dec. 31 2,000				Dec. 31 2,000 |

Accounting Equation Impact

EXAMPLE EXERCISE 2-4 Journal Entry for Owner's Withdrawal — OBJ. 3

Prepare a journal entry on December 29 for the payment of $12,000 to the owner of Smartstaff Consulting Services, Dominique Walsh, for personal use.

Follow My Example 2-4

Dec. 29	Dominique Walsh, Drawing	12,000	
	Cash		12,000

Practice Exercises: PE 2-4A, PE 2-4B

Exhibit 6 shows the December 31, 20Y3, ledger for NetSolutions after the transactions for both November and December have been posted.

EXHIBIT 6 **General Ledger for NetSolutions on December 31, 20Y3**

Ledger

Account Cash — *Account No. 11*

Date	Item	Post. Ref.	Debit	Credit	Balance Debit	Balance Credit
20Y3						
Nov. 1		1	25,000		25,000	
5		1		20,000	5,000	
18		1	7,500		12,500	
30		1		3,650	8,850	
30		1		950	7,900	
30		2		2,000	5,900	
Dec. 1		2		2,400	3,500	
1		2		800	2,700	
1		2	360		3,060	
6		2		180	2,880	
11		2		400	2,480	
13		3		950	1,530	
16		3	3,100		4,630	
20		3		900	3,730	
21		3	650		4,380	
23		3		1,450	2,930	
27		3		1,200	1,730	
31		3		310	1,420	
31		4		225	1,195	
31		4	2,870		4,065	
31		4		2,000	2,065	

Account Accounts Receivable — *Account No. 12*

Date	Item	Post. Ref.	Debit	Credit	Balance Debit	Balance Credit
20Y3						
Dec. 16		3	1,750		1,750	
21		3		650	1,100	
31		4	1,120		2,220	

Account Supplies — *Account No. 14*

Date	Item	Post. Ref.	Debit	Credit	Balance Debit	Balance Credit
20Y3						
Nov. 10		1	1,350		1,350	
30		1		800	550	
Dec. 23		3	1,450		2,000	

Account Prepaid Insurance — *Account No. 15*

Date	Item	Post. Ref.	Debit	Credit	Balance Debit	Balance Credit
20Y3						
Dec. 1		2	2,400		2,400	

Account Land — *Account No. 17*

Date	Item	Post. Ref.	Debit	Credit	Balance Debit	Balance Credit
20Y3						
Nov. 5		1	20,000		20,000	

Account Office Equipment — *Account No. 18*

Date	Item	Post. Ref.	Debit	Credit	Balance Debit	Balance Credit
20Y3						
Dec. 4		2	1,800		1,800	

Account Accounts Payable — *Account No. 21*

Date	Item	Post. Ref.	Debit	Credit	Balance Debit	Balance Credit
20Y3						
Nov. 10		1		1,350		1,350
30		1	950			400
Dec. 4		2		1,800		2,200
11		2	400			1,800
20		3	900			900

Account Unearned Rent — *Account No. 23*

Date	Item	Post. Ref.	Debit	Credit	Balance Debit	Balance Credit
20Y3						
Dec. 1		2		360		360

Account Chris Clark, Capital — *Account No. 31*

Date	Item	Post. Ref.	Debit	Credit	Balance Debit	Balance Credit
20Y3						
Nov. 1		1		25,000		25,000

Account Chris Clark, Drawing — *Account No. 32*

Date	Item	Post. Ref.	Debit	Credit	Balance Debit	Balance Credit
20Y3						
Nov. 30		2	2,000		2,000	
Dec. 31		4	2,000		4,000	

General Ledger for NetSolutions on December 31, 20Y3 (*Concluded*) EXHIBIT 6

Account *Fees Earned* *Account No. 41*

Date	Item	Post. Ref.	Debit	Credit	Balance Debit	Balance Credit
20Y3						
Nov. 18		1		7,500		7,500
Dec. 16		3		3,100		10,600
16		3		1,750		12,350
31		4		2,870		15,220
31		4		1,120		16,340

Account *Wages Expense* *Account No. 51*

Date	Item	Post. Ref.	Debit	Credit	Balance Debit	Balance Credit
20Y3						
Nov. 30		1	2,125		2,125	
Dec. 13		3	950		3,075	
27		3	1,200		4,275	

Account *Supplies Expense* *Account No. 52*

Date	Item	Post. Ref.	Debit	Credit	Balance Debit	Balance Credit
20Y3						
Nov. 30		1	800		800	

Account *Rent Expense* *Account No. 53*

Date	Item	Post. Ref.	Debit	Credit	Balance Debit	Balance Credit
20Y3						
Nov. 30		1	800		800	
Dec. 1		2	800		1,600	

Account *Utilities Expense* *Account No. 54*

Date	Item	Post. Ref.	Debit	Credit	Balance Debit	Balance Credit
20Y3						
Nov. 30		1	450		450	
Dec. 31		3	310		760	
31		4	225		985	

Account *Miscellaneous Expense* *Account No. 59*

Date	Item	Post. Ref.	Debit	Credit	Balance Debit	Balance Credit
20Y3						
Nov. 30		1	275		275	
Dec. 6		2	180		455	

EXAMPLE EXERCISE 2-5 Missing Amount from an Account

OBJ. 3

On March 1, the cash account balance was $22,350. During March, cash receipts totaled $241,880, and the March 31 balance was $19,125. Determine the cash payments made during March.

Follow My Example 2-5

Using the following T account, solve for the amount of cash payments (indicated by ?):

Cash

Mar. 1 Bal.	22,350	?	Cash payments
Cash receipts	241,880		
Mar. 31 Bal.	19,125		

$19,125 = $22,350 + $241,880 – Cash payments
Cash payments = $22,350 + $241,880 – $19,125
Cash payments = $245,105

Practice Exercises: PE 2-5A, PE 2-5B

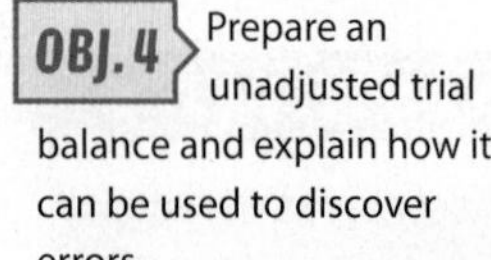

Prepare an unadjusted trial balance and explain how it can be used to discover errors.

Trial Balance

Errors may occur in posting debits and credits from the journal to the ledger. One way to detect such errors is by preparing a **trial balance**. Double-entry accounting requires that debits must always equal credits. The trial balance verifies this equality. The steps in preparing a trial balance are as follows:

Step 1. List the name of the company, the title of the trial balance, and the date the trial balance is prepared.

Step 2. List the accounts from the ledger, and enter their debit or credit balance in the Debit or Credit column of the trial balance.

Step 3. Total the Debit and Credit columns of the trial balance.

Step 4. Verify that the total of the Debit column equals the total of the Credit column.

The trial balance for **NetSolutions** as of December 31, 20Y3, is shown in Exhibit 7. The account balances in Exhibit 7 are taken from the ledger shown in Exhibit 6. Before a trial balance is prepared, each account balance in the ledger must be determined. When the standard account form is used as in Exhibit 6, the balance of each account appears in the balance column on the same line as the last posting to the account.

The trial balance shown in Exhibit 7 is titled an **unadjusted trial balance**. This is to distinguish it from other trial balances that will be prepared in later chapters. These other trial balances include an adjusted trial balance and a post-closing trial balance.[5]

EXHIBIT 7 Trial Balance

Link to Apple

Recently, **Apple** reported $23.2 billion in accounts receivable.

Step 1 — **NetSolutions**
Unadjusted Trial Balance
December 31, 20Y3

Step 2

	Account No.	Debit Balances	Credit Balances
Cash	11	2,065	
Accounts Receivable	12	2,220	
Supplies	14	2,000	
Prepaid Insurance	15	2,400	
Land	17	20,000	
Office Equipment	18	1,800	
Accounts Payable	21		900
Unearned Rent	23		360
Chris Clark, Capital	31		25,000
Chris Clark, Drawing	32	4,000	
Fees Earned	41		16,340
Wages Expense	51	4,275	
Supplies Expense	52	800	
Rent Expense	53	1,600	
Utilities Expense	54	985	
Miscellaneous Expense	59	455	
		42,600	42,600

Step 3
Step 4

5 The adjusted trial balance will be discussed in Chapter 3 and the post-closing trial balance in Chapter 4.

Errors Affecting the Trial Balance

If the trial balance totals are not equal, an error has occurred. In this case, the error must be found and corrected. A method useful in discovering errors is as follows:

1. If the difference between the Debit and Credit column totals is 10, 100, or 1,000, an error in addition may have occurred. In this case, re-add the trial balance column totals. If the error still exists, recompute the account balances.
2. If the difference between the Debit and Credit column totals can be evenly divisible by 2, the error may be due to the entering of a debit balance as a credit balance, or vice versa. In this case, review the trial balance for account balances of one-half the difference that may have been entered in the wrong column. For example, if the Debit column total is $20,640 and the Credit column total is $20,236, the difference of $404 ($20,640 − $20,236) may be due to a credit account balance of $202 that was entered as a debit account balance.
3. If the difference between the Debit and Credit column totals is evenly divisible by 9, trace the account balances back to the ledger to see if an account balance was incorrectly copied from the ledger. Two common types of copying errors are transpositions and slides. A **transposition** occurs when the order of the digits is copied incorrectly, such as writing $542 as $452 or $524. In a **slide**, the entire number is copied incorrectly one or more spaces to the right or the left, such as writing $542.00 as $54.20 or $5,420.00. In both cases, the resulting error will be evenly divisible by 9.
4. If the difference between the Debit and Credit column totals is not evenly divisible by 2 or 9, review the ledger to see if an account balance in the amount of the error has been omitted from the trial balance. If the error is not discovered, review the journal postings to see if a posting of a debit or credit may have been omitted.
5. If an error is not discovered by the preceding steps, the accounting process must be retraced, beginning with the last journal entry.

The trial balance does not provide complete proof of the accuracy of the ledger. It indicates only that the debits and the credits are equal. This proof is of value, however, because errors often affect the equality of debits and credits.

EXAMPLE EXERCISE 2-6 Errors Affecting the Trial Balance — OBJ. 4

For each of the following errors, considered individually, indicate whether the error would cause the trial balance totals to be unequal. If the error would cause the trial balance totals to be unequal, indicate whether the debit or credit total is higher and by how much.

a. Payment of a cash withdrawal of $5,600 was journalized and posted as a debit of $6,500 to Salary Expense and a credit of $6,500 to Cash.

b. A fee of $2,850 earned from a client was debited to Accounts Receivable for $2,580 and credited to Fees Earned for $2,850.

c. A payment of $3,500 to a creditor was posted as a debit of $3,500 to Accounts Payable and a debit of $3,500 to Cash.

Follow My Example 2-6

a. The trial balance totals are equal since both the debit and credit entries were journalized and posted for $6,500.

b. The trial balance totals are unequal. The credit total is higher by $270 ($2,850 – $2,580).

c. The trial balance totals are unequal. The debit total is higher by $7,000 ($3,500 + $3,500).

Practice Exercises: PE 2-6A, PE 2-6B

Errors Not Affecting the Trial Balance

An error may occur that does not cause the trial balance totals to be unequal. Such an error may be discovered when preparing the trial balance or may be indicated by an unusual account balance. For example, a credit balance in the supplies account indicates an error has occurred. This is because a business cannot have "negative" supplies. When such errors are discovered, they should be corrected. If the error has already been journalized and posted to the ledger, a **correcting journal entry** is normally prepared.

To illustrate, assume that on May 5 a $12,500 purchase of office equipment for cash was incorrectly journalized and posted as a debit to Supplies and a credit to Cash for $12,500, as follows:

May	5	Supplies	14	12,500	
		Cash	11		12,500

The error was discovered on May 31. Before making a correcting journal entry, the journal entry that was made in error is compared to the entry that should have been made. By comparing these two journal entries, the correcting journal entry can be determined, as shown in Exhibit 8.

EXHIBIT 8 **Correcting Journal Entry**

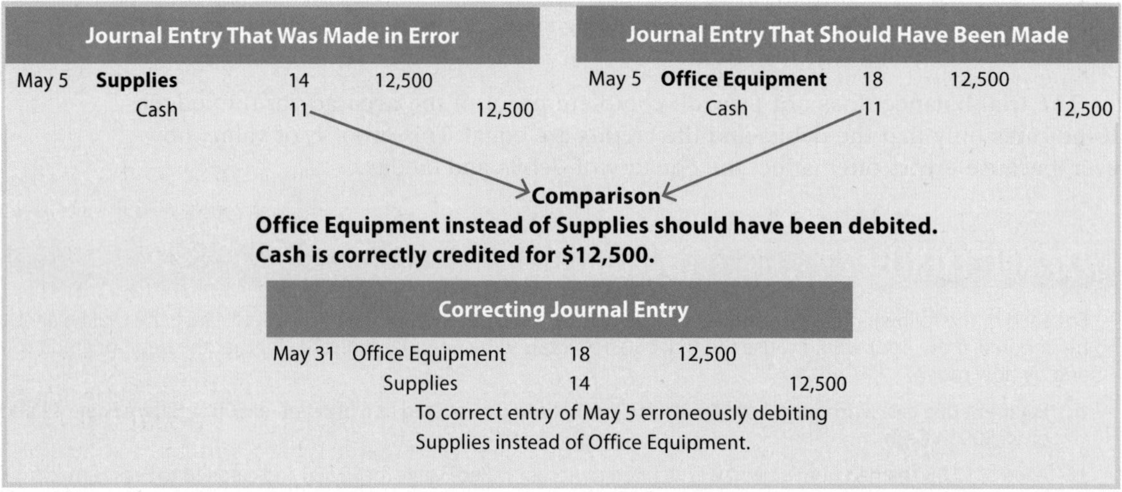

Journal Entry That Was Made in Error

May 5	**Supplies**	14	12,500	
	Cash	11		12,500

Journal Entry That Should Have Been Made

May 5	**Office Equipment**	18	12,500	
	Cash	11		12,500

Comparison
Office Equipment instead of Supplies should have been debited.
Cash is correctly credited for $12,500.

Correcting Journal Entry

May 31	Office Equipment	18	12,500	
	Supplies	14		12,500
	To correct entry of May 5 erroneously debiting Supplies instead of Office Equipment.			

Exhibit 8 indicates that the correcting journal entry debits Office Equipment and credits Supplies for $12,500. Because correcting journal entries are unusual, an explanation is often inserted below the correcting journal entry. After the correcting journal entry is posted, the office equipment and supplies accounts will have correct balances.

EXAMPLE EXERCISE 2-7 Correcting Entries **OBJ. 4**

The following errors took place in journalizing and posting transactions:

a. A withdrawal of $6,000 by Cheri Ramey, owner of the business, was recorded as a debit to Office Salaries Expense and a credit to Cash.

b. Utilities Expense of $4,500 paid for the current month was recorded as a debit to Miscellaneous Expense and a credit to Accounts Payable.

Journalize the entries to correct the errors. Omit explanations.

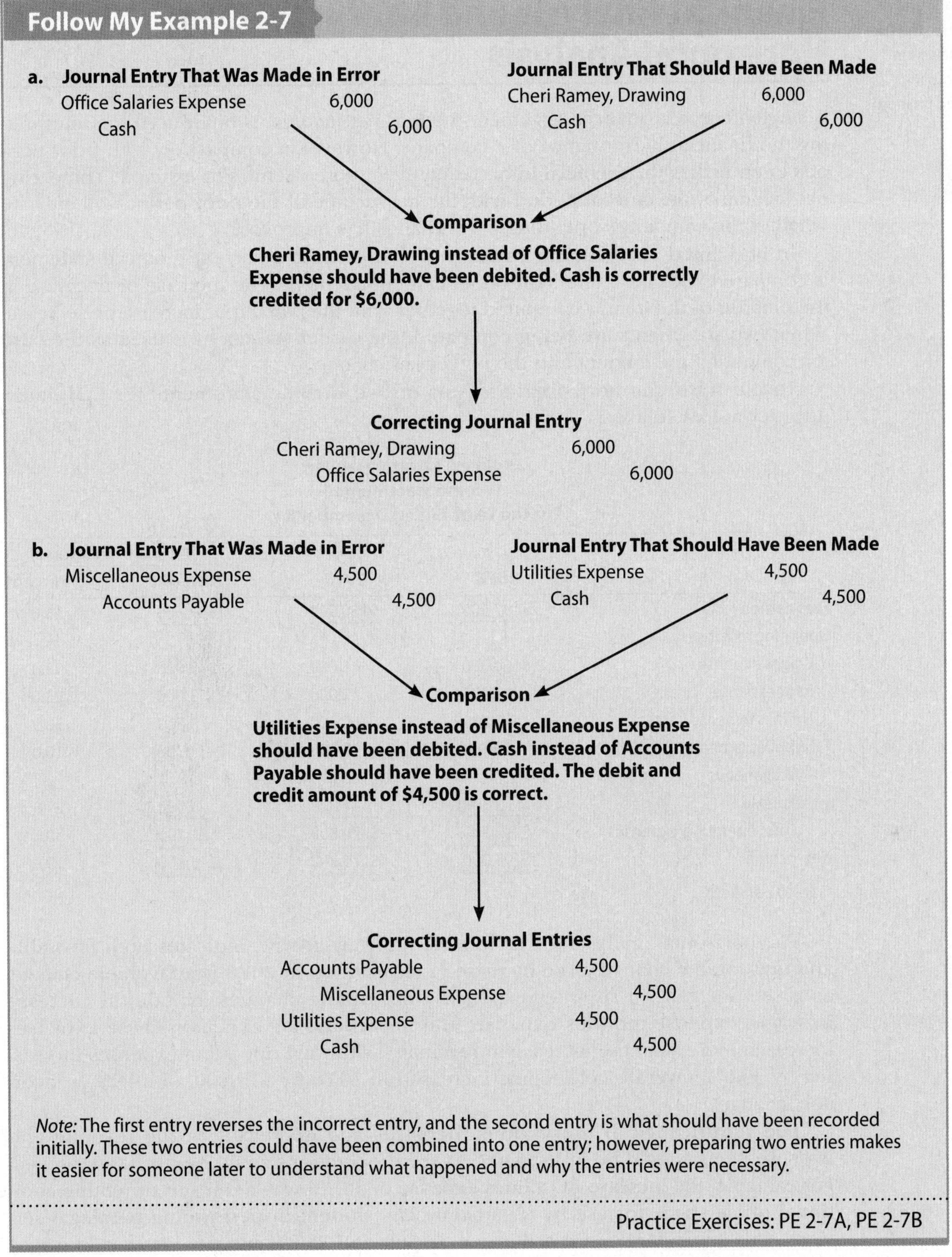

Follow My Example 2-7

a.

Journal Entry That Was Made in Error

Office Salaries Expense	6,000	
Cash		6,000

Journal Entry That Should Have Been Made

Cheri Ramey, Drawing	6,000	
Cash		6,000

Comparison

Cheri Ramey, Drawing instead of Office Salaries Expense should have been debited. Cash is correctly credited for $6,000.

Correcting Journal Entry

Cheri Ramey, Drawing	6,000	
Office Salaries Expense		6,000

b.

Journal Entry That Was Made in Error

Miscellaneous Expense	4,500	
Accounts Payable		4,500

Journal Entry That Should Have Been Made

Utilities Expense	4,500	
Cash		4,500

Comparison

Utilities Expense instead of Miscellaneous Expense should have been debited. Cash instead of Accounts Payable should have been credited. The debit and credit amount of $4,500 is correct.

Correcting Journal Entries

Accounts Payable	4,500	
Miscellaneous Expense		4,500
Utilities Expense	4,500	
Cash		4,500

Note: The first entry reverses the incorrect entry, and the second entry is what should have been recorded initially. These two entries could have been combined into one entry; however, preparing two entries makes it easier for someone later to understand what happened and why the entries were necessary.

Practice Exercises: PE 2-7A, PE 2-7B

Describe and illustrate the use of horizontal analysis in evaluating a company's performance and financial condition.

FAI

Financial Analysis and Interpretation: Horizontal Analysis

A single item in a financial statement, such as net income, is often useful in interpreting the financial performance of a company. However, a comparison with prior periods often makes the financial information even more useful. For example, comparing net income of the current period with the net income of the prior period will indicate whether the company's operating performance has improved.

In **horizontal analysis**, the amount of each item on a current financial statement is compared with the same item on an earlier statement. The increase or decrease in the *amount* of the item is computed together with the *percent* of increase or decrease. When two statements are being compared, the earlier statement is used as the base for computing the amount and the percent of change.

To illustrate, the horizontal analysis of two income statements for J. Holmes, Attorney-at-Law follows:

J. Holmes, Attorney-at-Law
Income Statements
For the Years Ended December 31

			Increase (Decrease)	
	20Y8	**20Y7**	**Amount**	**Percent**
Fees earned	$187,500	$150,000	$37,500	25.0%*
Operating expenses:				
Wages expense	$ 60,000	$ 45,000	$15,000	33.3
Rent expense	15,000	12,000	3,000	25.0
Utilities expense	12,500	9,000	3,500	38.9
Supplies expense	2,700	3,000	(300)	(10.0)
Miscellaneous expense	2,300	1,800	500	27.8
Total operating expenses	$ 92,500	$ 70,800	$21,700	30.6
Net income	$ 95,000	$ 79,200	$15,800	19.9

*$37,500 ÷ $150,000

The horizontal analysis for J. Holmes, Attorney-at-Law, indicates both favorable and unfavorable changes. The increase in fees earned in 20Y8 is a favorable change, as is the decrease in supplies expense. Unfavorable changes include the increase in wages expense, utilities expense, and miscellaneous expense. These expenses increased more than the increase in revenues, with total operating expenses increasing by 30.6%. Overall, net income increased in 20Y8 by $15,800, or 19.9%, a favorable change.

The significance of the various increases and decreases in the revenue and expense items should be investigated to see if operations could be further improved. For example, the increase in utilities expense of 38.9% was the result of renting additional office space for use by a part-time law student in performing paralegal services. This explains the increase in rent expense of 25.0% and the increase in wages expense of 33.3%. The increase in revenues of 25.0% reflects the fees generated by the new paralegal.

The preceding example illustrates how horizontal analysis can be useful in interpreting and analyzing the income statement. Horizontal analyses can also be performed for the balance sheet, the statement of owner's equity, and the statement of cash flows.

EXAMPLE EXERCISE 2-8 Horizontal Analysis

OBJ. 5

Two income statements for McCorkle Company follow:

McCorkle Company
Income Statements
For the Years Ended December 31

	20Y7	20Y6
Fees earned	$210,000	$175,000
Operating expenses	172,500	150,000
Net income	$ 37,500	$ 25,000

Prepare a horizontal analysis of McCorkle Company's income statements.

Follow My Example 2-8

McCorkle Company
Income Statements
For the Years Ended December 31

			Increase (Decrease)	
	20Y7	**20Y6**	**Amount**	**Percent**
Fees earned	$210,000	$175,000	$35,000	20%
Operating expenses	172,500	150,000	22,500	15
Net income	$ 37,500	$ 25,000	$12,500	50

Practice Exercises: PE 2-8A, PE 2-8B

At a Glance 2

OBJ. 1 Describe the characteristics of an account and a chart of accounts.

Key Points The simplest form of an account, a T account, has three parts: (1) a title, which is the name of the item recorded in the account; (2) a left side, called the debit side; and (3) a right side, called the credit side. Periodically, the debits in an account are added, the credits in the account are added, and the balance of the account is determined.

The system of accounts that make up a ledger is called a chart of accounts.

Learning Outcomes	Example Exercises	Practice Exercises
• Record transactions in T accounts.		
• Determine the balance of a T account.		
• Prepare a chart of accounts for a proprietorship.		

OBJ. 2 Describe and illustrate journalizing transactions using the double-entry accounting system.

Key Points Transactions are initially entered in a record called a journal. The rules of debit and credit for recording increases or decreases in accounts are shown in Exhibit 3. Each transaction is recorded so that the sum of the debits is always equal to the sum of the credits. The normal balance of an account is indicated by the side of the account (debit or credit) that receives the increases.

Learning Outcomes	*Example Exercises*	*Practice Exercises*
• Indicate the normal balance of an account.	**EE2-1**	**PE2-1A, 2-1B**
• Journalize transactions using the rules of debit and credit.	**EE2-2**	**PE2-2A, 2-2B**

OBJ. 3 Describe and illustrate the journalizing and posting of transactions to accounts.

Key Points Transactions are journalized and posted to the ledger using the rules of debit and credit. The debits and credits for each journal entry are posted to the accounts in the order in which they occur in the journal.

Learning Outcomes	*Example Exercises*	*Practice Exercises*
• Journalize transactions using the rules of debit and credit.	**EE2-3**	**PE2-3A, 2-3B**
• Given other account data, determine the missing amount of an account entry.	**EE2-4**	**PE2-4A, 2-4B**
• Post journal entries to a standard account.	**EE2-5**	**PE2-5A, 2-5B**
• Post journal entries to a T account.		

OBJ. 4 Prepare an unadjusted trial balance and explain how it can be used to discover errors.

Key Points A trial balance is prepared by listing the accounts from the ledger and their balances. The totals of the Debit column and Credit column of the trial balance must be equal. If the two totals are not equal, an error has occurred. Errors may occur even though the trial balance totals are equal. Such errors may require a correcting journal entry.

Learning Outcomes	*Example Exercises*	*Practice Exercises*
• Prepare an unadjusted trial balance.	**EE2-6**	**PE2-6A, 2-6B**
• Discover errors that cause unequal totals in the trial balance.		
• Prepare correcting journal entries for various errors.	**EE2-7**	**PE2-7A, 2-7B**

OBJ. 5 Describe and illustrate the use of horizontal analysis in evaluating a company's performance and financial condition.

Key Points In horizontal analysis, the amount of each item on a current financial statement is compared with the same item on an earlier statement. The increase or decrease in the *amount* of the item is computed, together with the *percent* of increase or decrease. When two statements are being compared, the earlier statement is used as the base for computing the amount and the percent of change.

Learning Outcomes	*Example Exercises*	*Practice Exercises*
• Describe horizontal analysis.		
• Prepare a horizontal analysis report of a financial statement.	**EE2-8**	**PE2-8A, 2-8B**

Illustrative Problem

J. F. Outz, M.D., has been practicing as a cardiologist for three years. During April 20Y6, Outz completed the following transactions in her practice of cardiology:

Apr. 1. Paid office rent for April, $800.

3. Purchased equipment on account, $2,100.

5. Received cash on account from patients, $3,150.

8. Purchased X-ray film and other supplies on account, $245.

9. One of the items of equipment purchased on April 3 was defective. It was returned with the permission of the supplier, who agreed to reduce the account for the amount charged for the item, $325.

12. Paid cash to creditors on account, $1,250.

17. Paid cash for renewal of a six-month property insurance policy, $370.

20. Discovered that the balances of the cash account and the accounts payable account as of April 1 were overstated by $200. A payment of that amount to a creditor in March had not been recorded. Journalize the $200 payment as of April 20.

24. Paid cash for laboratory analysis, $545.

27. Dr. Outz withdrew $1,250 for personal use.

30. Recorded the cash received in payment of services to patients during April, $1,720.

30. Paid salaries of receptionist and nurses, $1,725.

30. Paid various utility expenses, $360.

30. Recorded fees charged to patients on account for services performed in April, $5,145.

30. Paid miscellaneous expenses, $132.

Outz's account titles, numbers, and balances as of April 1 (all normal balances) are listed as follows: Cash, 11, $4,123; Accounts Receivable, 12, $6,725; Supplies, 13, $290; Prepaid Insurance, 14, $465; Equipment, 18, $19,745; Accounts Payable, 22, $765; J. F. Outz, Capital, 31, $30,583; J. F. Outz, Drawing, 32, $0; Professional Fees, 41, $0; Salary Expense, 51, $0; Rent Expense, 53, $0; Laboratory Expense, 55, $0; Utilities Expense, 56, $0; Miscellaneous Expense, 59, $0.

Instructions

1. Open a ledger of standard four-column accounts for Dr. Outz as of April 1. Enter the balances in the appropriate balance columns and place a check mark (✓) in the Posting Reference column. (*Hint:* Verify the equality of the debit and credit balances in the ledger before proceeding with the next instruction.)
2. Journalize each transaction in a two-column journal.
3. Post the journal to the ledger, extending the balances to the appropriate balance columns after each posting.
4. Prepare an unadjusted trial balance as of April 30.

Solution 1., 2., and 3.

Journal *Page 27*

Date	Description	Post. Ref.	Debit	Credit
20Y6				
Apr. 1	Rent Expense	53	800	
	Cash	11		800
	Paid office rent for April.			
3	Equipment	18	2,100	
	Accounts Payable	22		2,100
	Purchased equipment on account.			
5	Cash	11	3,150	
	Accounts Receivable	12		3,150
	Received cash on account.			
8	Supplies	13	245	
	Accounts Payable	22		245
	Purchased supplies.			
9	Accounts Payable	22	325	
	Equipment	18		325
	Returned defective equipment.			
12	Accounts Payable	22	1,250	
	Cash	11		1,250
	Paid creditors on account.			
17	Prepaid Insurance	14	370	
	Cash	11		370
	Renewed six-month property policy.			
20	Accounts Payable	22	200	
	Cash	11		200
	Recorded March payment to creditor.			

Account *Cash* *Account No. 11*

Date	Item	Post. Ref.	Debit	Credit	Balance Debit	Balance Credit
20Y6						
Apr. 1	Balance	✓			4,123	
1		27		800	3,323	
5		27	3,150		6,473	
12		27		1,250	5,223	
17		27		370	4,853	
20		27		200	4,653	
24		28		545	4,108	
27		28		1,250	2,858	
30		28	1,720		4,578	
30		28		1,725	2,853	
30		28		360	2,493	
30		28		132	2,361	

Journal *Page 28*

Date	Description	Post. Ref.	Debit	Credit
20Y6				
Apr. 24	Laboratory Expense	55	545	
	Cash	11		545
	Paid for laboratory analysis.			
27	J. F. Outz, Drawing	32	1,250	
	Cash	11		1,250
	J. F. Outz withdrew cash for personal use.			
30	Cash	11	1,720	
	Professional Fees	41		1,720
	Received fees from patients.			
30	Salary Expense	51	1,725	
	Cash	11		1,725
	Paid salaries.			
30	Utilities Expense	56	360	
	Cash	11		360
	Paid utilities.			
30	Accounts Receivable	12	5,145	
	Professional Fees	41		5,145
	Recorded fees earned on account.			
30	Miscellaneous Expense	59	132	
	Cash	11		132
	Paid expenses.			

Account *Accounts Receivable* *Account No. 12*

Date	Item	Post. Ref.	Debit	Credit	Balance Debit	Balance Credit
20Y6						
Apr. 1	Balance	✓			6,725	
5		27		3,150	3,575	
30		28	5,145		8,720	

Account *Supplies* *Account No. 13*

Date	Item	Post. Ref.	Debit	Credit	Balance Debit	Balance Credit
20Y6						
Apr. 1	Balance	✓			290	
8		27	245		535	

Account *Prepaid Insurance* — *Account No. 14*

Date	Item	Post. Ref.	Debit	Credit	Balance Debit	Balance Credit
20Y6						
Apr. 1	Balance	✓			465	
17		27	370		835	

Account *Equipment* — *Account No. 18*

Date	Item	Post. Ref.	Debit	Credit	Balance Debit	Balance Credit
20Y6						
Apr. 1	Balance	✓			19,745	
3		27	2,100		21,845	
9		27		325	21,520	

Account *Accounts Payable* — *Account No. 22*

Date	Item	Post. Ref.	Debit	Credit	Balance Debit	Balance Credit
20Y6						
Apr. 1	Balance	✓				765
3		27		2,100		2,865
8		27		245		3,110
9		27	325			2,785
12		27	1,250			1,535
20		27	200			1,335

Account *J. F. Outz, Capital* — *Account No. 31*

Date	Item	Post. Ref.	Debit	Credit	Balance Debit	Balance Credit
20Y6						
Apr. 1	Balance	✓				30,583

Account *J. F. Qutz, Drawing* — *Account No. 32*

Date	Item	Post. Ref.	Debit	Credit	Balance Debit	Balance Credit
20Y6						
Apr. 27		28	1,250		1,250	

Account *Professional Fees* — *Account No. 41*

Date	Item	Post. Ref.	Debit	Credit	Balance Debit	Balance Credit
20Y6						
Apr. 30		28		1,720		1,720
30		28		5,145		6,865

Account *Salary Expense* — *Account No. 51*

Date	Item	Post. Ref.	Debit	Credit	Balance Debit	Balance Credit
20Y6						
Apr. 30		28	1,725		1,725	

Account *Rent Expense* — *Account No. 53*

Date	Item	Post. Ref.	Debit	Credit	Balance Debit	Balance Credit
20Y6						
Apr. 1		27	800		800	

Account *Laboratory Expense* — *Account No. 55*

Date	Item	Post. Ref.	Debit	Credit	Balance Debit	Balance Credit
20Y6						
Apr. 24		28	545		545	

Account *Utilities Expense* — *Account No. 56*

Date	Item	Post. Ref.	Debit	Credit	Balance Debit	Balance Credit
20Y6						
Apr. 30		28	360		360	

Account *Miscellaneous Expense* — *Account No. 59*

Date	Item	Post. Ref.	Debit	Credit	Balance Debit	Balance Credit
20Y6						
Apr. 30		28	132		132	

4.

J. F. Outz, M.D.
Unadjusted Trial Balance
April 30, 20Y6

	Account No.	Debit Balances	Credit Balances
Cash	11	2,361	
Accounts Receivable	12	8,720	
Supplies	13	535	
Prepaid Insurance	14	835	
Equipment	18	21,520	
Accounts Payable	22		1,335
J. F. Outz, Capital	31		30,583
J. F. Outz, Drawing	32	1,250	
Professional Fees	41		6,865
Salary Expense	51	1,725	
Rent Expense	53	800	
Laboratory Expense	55	545	
Utilities Expense	56	360	
Miscellaneous Expense	59	132	
		38,783	38,783

Key Terms

account (59)
account receivable (72)
assets (61)
balance of the account (60)
capital account (61)
chart of accounts (61)
correcting journal entry (80)
credit (60)
debit (60)
double-entry accounting system (62)
drawing (61)
expenses (62)
four-column account (68)
horizontal analysis (82)
journal (64)
journal entry (65)
journalizing (65)
ledger (61)
liabilities (61)
normal balance of an account (63)
owner's equity (61)
posting (68)
revenues (61)
rules of debit and credit (62)
slide (79)
T account (59)
transposition (79)
trial balance (78)
two-column journal (64)
unadjusted trial balance (78)
unearned revenue (70)

Discussion Questions

1. What is the difference between an account and a ledger?
2. Do the terms *debit* and *credit* signify increase or decrease, or can they signify either? Explain.
3. McIntyre Company adheres to a policy of depositing all cash receipts in a bank account and making all payments by check. The cash account as of December 31 has a credit balance of $1,850, and there is no undeposited cash on hand. (a) Assuming that no errors occurred during journalizing or posting, what caused this unusual balance? (b) Is the $1,850 credit balance in the cash account an asset, a liability, owner's equity, a revenue, or an expense?
4. eCatalog Services Company performed services in October for a specific customer for a fee of $7,890. Payment was received the following November.

(a) Was the revenue earned in October or November? (b) What accounts should be debited and credited in (1) October and (2) November?

5. If the two totals of a trial balance are equal, does it mean that there are no errors in the accounting records? Explain.
6. Assume that a trial balance is prepared with an account balance of $8,900 listed as $9,800 and an account balance of $1,000 listed as $100. Identify the transposition and the slide.
7. Assume that when a purchase of supplies of $2,650 for cash was recorded, both the debit and the credit were journalized and posted as $2,560. (a) Would this error cause the trial balance to be out of balance? (b) Would the trial balance be out of balance if the $2,650 entry had been journalized correctly but the credit to Cash had been posted as $2,560?
8. Assume that Muscular Consulting erroneously recorded the payment of $7,500 of owner withdrawals as a debit to Salary Expense. (a) How would this error affect the equality of the trial balance? (b) How would this error affect the income statement, statement of owner's equity, and balance sheet?
9. Assume that Sunshine Realty Co. borrowed $300,000 from Columbia First Bank and Trust. In recording the transaction, Sunshine erroneously recorded the receipt as a debit to Cash, $300,000, and a credit to Fees Earned, $300,000. (a) How would this error affect the equality of the trial balance? (b) How would this error affect the income statement, statement of owner's equity, and balance sheet?
10. Checking accounts are a common form of deposits for banks. Assume that Surety Storage has a checking account at Ada Savings Bank. What type of account (asset, liability, owner's equity, revenue, expense, drawing) does the account balance of $11,375 represent from the viewpoint of (a) Surety Storage and (b) Ada Savings Bank?

Practice Exercises

Example Exercises

SHOW ME HOW

EE 2-1 p. 64

PE 2-1A Rules of debit and credit and normal balances

OBJ. 2

State for each account whether it is likely to have (a) debit entries only, (b) credit entries only, or (c) both debit and credit entries. Also indicate its normal balance.

1. Accounts Receivable
2. Commissions Earned
3. Heidi Schmidt, Capital
4. Rent Expense
5. Rent Revenue
6. Wages Payable

SHOW ME HOW

EE 2-1 p. 64

PE 2-1B Rules of debit and credit and normal balances

OBJ. 2

State for each account whether it is likely to have (a) debit entries only, (b) credit entries only, or (c) both debit and credit entries. Also indicate its normal balance.

1. Accounts Payable
2. Cash
3. Del Robinson, Drawing
4. Miscellaneous Expense
5. Insurance Expense
6. Fees Earned

SHOW ME HOW

EE 2-2 p. 68

PE 2-2A Journal entry for asset purchase

OBJ. 2

Prepare a journal entry for the purchase of office equipment on February 19 for $14,800 paying $3,600 cash and the remainder on account.

SHOW ME HOW

EE 2-2 p. 68

PE 2-2B Journal entry for asset purchase

OBJ. 2

Prepare a journal entry for the purchase of office supplies on September 30 for $1,900, paying $600 cash and the remainder on account.

SHOW ME HOW

EE 2-3 p. 73

PE 2-3A Journal entry for fees earned **OBJ. 3**

Prepare a journal entry on April 30 for fees earned on account, $12,980.

SHOW ME HOW

EE 2-3 p. 73

PE 2-3B Journal entry for fees earned **OBJ. 3**

Prepare a journal entry on August 13 for cash received for services rendered, $7,480.

SHOW ME HOW

EE 2-4 p. 75

PE 2-4A Journal entry for owner's withdrawal **OBJ. 3**

Prepare a journal entry on December 23 for the withdrawal of $27,000 by Graeme Schneider for personal use.

SHOW ME HOW

EE 2-4 p. 75

PE 2-4B Journal entry for owner's withdrawal **OBJ. 3**

Prepare a journal entry on June 30 for the withdrawal of $9,500 by Claire Hope for personal use.

SHOW ME HOW

EE 2-5 p. 77

PE 2-5A Missing amount from an account **OBJ. 3**

On July 1, the cash account balance was $42,830. During July, cash payments totaled $132,500 and the July 31 balance was $33,850. Determine the cash receipts during July.

SHOW ME HOW

EE 2-5 p. 77

PE 2-5B Missing amount from an account **OBJ. 3**

On August 1, the supplies account balance was $1,240. During August, supplies of $3,760 were purchased, and $1,600 of supplies were on hand as of August 31. Determine supplies expense for August.

SHOW ME HOW

EE 2-6 p. 79

PE 2-6A Errors affecting the trial balance **OBJ. 4**

For each of the following errors, considered individually, indicate whether the error would cause the trial balance totals to be unequal. If the error would cause the trial balance totals to be unequal, indicate whether the debit or credit total is higher and by how much.

a. The payment of an insurance premium of $9,800 for a three-year policy was debited to Prepaid Insurance for $9,800 and credited to Cash for $8,900.

b. A payment of $350 on account was debited to Accounts Payable for $530 and credited to Cash for $530.

c. A purchase of supplies on account for $2,900 was debited to Supplies for $2,900 and debited to Accounts Payable for $2,900.

SHOW ME HOW

EE 2-6 p. 79

PE 2-6B Errors affecting the trial balance **OBJ. 4**

For each of the following errors, considered individually, indicate whether the error would cause the trial balance totals to be unequal. If the error would cause the trial balance totals to be unequal, indicate whether the debit or credit total is higher and by how much.

a. The payment of cash for the purchase of office equipment of $14,200 was debited to Land for $14,200 and credited to Cash for $14,200.

b. The payment of $1,730 on account was debited to Accounts Payable for $1,370 and credited to Cash for $1,730.

c. The receipt of cash on account of $2,750 was recorded as a debit to Cash for $7,250 and a credit to Accounts Receivable for $2,750.

EE 2-7 *p. 80*

PE 2-7A Correcting entries **OBJ. 4**

The following errors took place in journalizing and posting transactions:

a. Rent expense of $3,220 paid for the current month was recorded as a debit to Miscellaneous Expense and a credit to Rent Expense.

b. The payment of $5,080 from a customer on account was recorded as a debit to Cash and a credit to Accounts Payable.

Journalize the entries to correct the errors. Omit explanations.

EE 2-7 *p. 80*

PE 2-7B Correcting entries **OBJ. 4**

The following errors took place in journalizing and posting transactions:

a. The receipt of $10,700 for services rendered was recorded as a debit to Accounts Receivable and a credit to Fees Earned.

b. The purchase of supplies of $4,300 on account was recorded as a debit to Office Equipment and a credit to Supplies.

Journalize the entries to correct the errors. Omit explanations.

FAI

EE 2-8 *p. 83*

PE 2-8A Horizontal analysis **OBJ. 5**

Two income statements for Vaughn Company follow:

Vaughn Company
Income Statements
For the Years Ended December 31

	20Y1	20Y0
Fees earned	$716,800	$896,000
Operating expenses	557,760	672,000
Net income	$159,040	$224,000

Prepare a horizontal analysis of Vaughn Company's income statements.

EE 2-8 *p. 83*

PE 2-8B Horizontal analysis **OBJ. 5**

Two income statements for Satterfield Company follow:

Satterfield Company
Income Statements
For the Years Ended December 31

	20Y1	20Y0
Fees earned	$3,068,200	$2,645,000
Operating expenses	2,281,600	1,984,000
Net income	$ 786,600	$ 661,000

Prepare a horizontal analysis of Satterfield Company's income statements.

Exercises

EX 2-1 Chart of accounts **OBJ. 1**

The following accounts appeared in recent financial statements of **Delta Air Lines**:

Accounts Payable	Fuel Inventory
Accounts Receivable	Landing Fees (Expense)
Accrued Salaries (Obligations)	Loyalty Program (Obligations)
Aircraft Fuel (Expense)	Parts and Supplies
Aircraft Maintenance (Expense)	Passenger Commissions (Expense)
Aircraft Rent (Expense)	Passenger Revenue
Air Traffic Liability	Prepaid Expenses
Cargo Revenue	Property and Equipment
Cash	Regional Carriers Expense

(Continued)

Identify each account as either a balance sheet account or an income statement account. For each balance sheet account, identify it as an asset, a liability, or owner's equity. For each income statement account, identify it as a revenue or an expense.

EX 2-2 Chart of accounts

OBJ. 1

Oak Interiors is owned and operated by Fred Biggs, an interior decorator. In the ledger of Oak Interiors, the first digit of the account number indicates its major account classification (1—assets, 2—liabilities, 3—owner's equity, 4—revenues, 5—expenses). The second digit of the account number indicates the specific account within each of the preceding major account classifications.

Match each account number with its most likely account in the list that follows. The account numbers are 11, 12, 13, 21, 31, 32, 41, 51, 52, and 53.

Accounts Payable	Fred Biggs, Drawing
Accounts Receivable	Land
Cash	Miscellaneous Expense
Fees Earned	Supplies Expense
Fred Biggs, Capital	Wages Expense

EX 2-3 Chart of accounts

OBJ. 1

Outdoor Leadership School is a newly organized business that teaches people how to inspire and influence others. The list of accounts to be opened in the general ledger is as follows:

Accounts Payable	Miscellaneous Expense
Accounts Receivable	Prepaid Insurance
Cash	Rent Expense
Equipment	Supplies
Fees Earned	Supplies Expense
Lorri Ross, Capital	Unearned Rent
Lorri Ross, Drawing	Wages Expense

List the accounts in the order in which they should appear in the ledger of Outdoor Leadership School and assign account numbers. Each account number is to have two digits: the first digit is to indicate the major classification (1 for assets, for example), and the second digit is to identify the specific account within each major classification (11 for Cash, for example).

EX 2-4 Rules of debit and credit

OBJ. 1, 2

The following table summarizes the rules of debit and credit. For each of the items (a) through (l), indicate whether the proper answer is a debit or a credit.

	Increase	Decrease	Normal Balance
Balance sheet accounts:			
Asset	(a)	(b)	(c)
Liability	(d)	Debit	(e)
Owner's equity:			
Capital	Credit	(f)	Credit
Drawing	(g)	(h)	(i)
Income statement accounts:			
Revenue	(j)	(k)	Credit
Expense	(l)	Credit	Debit

EX 2-5 Normal entries for accounts

OBJ. 2

During the month, Midwest Labs Co. has a substantial number of transactions affecting each of the following accounts. State for each account whether it is likely to have (a) debit entries only, (b) credit entries only, or (c) both debit and credit entries.

1. Accounts Payable
2. Accounts Receivable
3. Cash
4. Fees Earned
5. Insurance Expense
6. Jerri Holt, Drawing
7. Utilities Expense

EX 2-6 Normal balances of accounts OBJ. 1, 2

Identify each of the following accounts of Dispatch Services Co. as asset, liability, owner's equity, revenue, or expense and state in each case whether the normal balance is a debit or a credit:

a. Accounts Payable
b. Accounts Receivable
c. Ashley Griffin, Capital
d. Ashley Griffin, Drawing
e. Cash
f. Fees Earned
g. Office Equipment
h. Rent Expense
i. Supplies
j. Wages Expense

EX 2-7 Transactions OBJ. 2

Simmons Consulting Co. has the following accounts in its ledger: Cash; Accounts Receivable; Supplies; Office Equipment; Accounts Payable; Michael Short, Capital; Michael Short, Drawing; Fees Earned; Rent Expense; Advertising Expense; Utilities Expense; Miscellaneous Expense.

Journalize the following selected transactions for October 20Y3 in a two-column journal. Journal entry explanations may be omitted.

Oct. 1. Paid rent for the month, $4,800.
3. Paid advertising expense, $2,500.
5. Paid cash for supplies, $1,390.
6. Purchased office equipment on account, $10,670.
10. Received cash from customers on account, $19,730.
15. Paid creditors on account, $9,480.
27. Paid cash for miscellaneous expenses, $530.
30. Paid telephone bill (utility expense) for the month, $220.
31. Fees earned and billed to customers for the month, $38,620.
31. Paid electricity bill (utility expense) for the month, $1,540.
31. Withdrew cash for personal use, $6,700.

EX 2-8 Journalizing and posting OBJ. 2, 3

On September 18, 20Y4, Carbon Company purchased $8,710 of supplies on account. In Carbon Company's chart of accounts, the supplies account is No. 15, and the accounts payable account is No. 21.

a. Journalize the September 18, 20Y4, transaction on Page 87 of Carbon Company's two-column journal. Include an explanation of the entry.
b. Prepare a four-column account for Supplies. Enter a debit balance of $2,960 as of September 1, 20Y4. Place a check mark (✓) in the Posting Reference column.
c. Prepare a four-column account for Accounts Payable. Enter a credit balance of $38,400 as of September 1, 20Y4. Place a check mark (✓) in the Posting Reference column.
d. Post the September 18, 20Y4, transaction to the accounts.
e. Do the rules of debit and credit apply to all companies?

EX 2-9 Transactions and T accounts OBJ. 2, 3

The following selected transactions were completed during August of the current year:

1. Billed customers for fees earned, $73,900.
2. Purchased supplies on account, $1,960.
3. Received cash from customers on account, $62,770.
4. Paid creditors on account, $820.

a. Journalize these transactions in a two-column journal, using the appropriate number to identify the transactions. Journal entry explanations may be omitted.

(Continued)

b. Post the entries prepared in (a) to the following T accounts: Cash, Supplies, Accounts Receivable, Accounts Payable, Fees Earned. To the left of each amount posted in the accounts, place the appropriate number to identify the transactions.

c. Assume that the unadjusted trial balance on August 31 shows a credit balance for Accounts Receivable. Does this credit balance mean that an error has occurred?

EX 2-10 Cash account balance **OBJ. 1, 2, 3**

During the month, Warwick Co. received $515,000 in cash and paid out $375,000 in cash.

a. Do the data indicate that Warwick Co. had net income of $140,000 during the month? Explain.

b. If the balance of the cash account is $200,000 at the end of the month, what was the cash balance at the beginning of the month?

EX 2-11 Account balances **OBJ. 1, 2, 3**

✔ c. $249,020

SHOW ME HOW

EXCEL ONLINE

a. During February, $194,500 was paid to creditors on account, and purchases on account were $210,400. Assuming that the February 28 balance of Accounts Payable was $62,500, determine the account balance on February 1.

b. On October 1, the accounts receivable account balance was $121,100. During October, $470,500 was collected from customers on account. Assuming that the October 31 balance was $136,800, determine the fees billed to customers on account during October.

c. On April 1, the cash account balance was $48,350. During April, cash receipts totaled $260,060 and the April 30 balance was $59,390. Determine the cash payments made during April.

EX 2-12 Capital account balance **OBJ. 1, 2**

SHOW ME HOW

As of January 1, Terrace Waters, Capital had a credit balance of $500,000. During the year, withdrawals totaled $10,000, and the business incurred a net loss of $320,000.

a. Compute the balance of Terrace Waters, Capital as of the end of the year.

b. Assuming that there have been no recording errors, will the balance sheet prepared at December 31 balance? Explain.

EX 2-13 Identifying transactions **OBJ. 1, 2**

Emerald Tours Co. is a travel agency. The nine transactions recorded by Emerald Tours during May 20Y5, its first month of operations, are indicated in the following T accounts:

Cash

	Debit		Credit
(1)	97,000	(2)	1,160
(7)	10,540	(3)	2,070
		(4)	8,120
		(6)	3,490
		(9)	3,200

Equipment

	Debit		Credit
(3)	10,350		

Mary Silva, Drawing

	Debit		Credit
(9)	3,200		

Accounts Receivable

	Debit		Credit
(5)	15,910	(7)	10,540

Accounts Payable

	Debit		Credit
(6)	3,490	(3)	8,280

Fees Earned

	Debit		Credit
		(5)	15,910

Supplies

	Debit		Credit
(2)	1,160	(8)	850

Mary Silva, Capital

	Debit		Credit
		(1)	97,000

Operating Expenses

	Debit		Credit
(4)	8,120		
(8)	850		

Indicate for each debit and each credit (a) whether an asset, liability, owner's equity, drawing, revenue, or expense account was affected and (b) whether the account was increased (+) or decreased (–). Present your answers in the following form, with transaction (1) given as an example:

	Account Debited		Account Credited	
Transaction	Type	Effect	Type	Effect
(1)	asset	+	owner's equity	+

SHOW ME HOW

EX 2-14 Journal entries **OBJ. 1, 2**

Based upon the T accounts in Exercise 2-13, prepare the nine journal entries from which the postings were made. Journal entry explanations may be omitted.

✔ (a) Total of Debit column: $117,700

SHOW ME HOW

EX 2-15 Trial balance **OBJ. 4**

Based upon the data presented in Exercise 2-13, (a) prepare an unadjusted trial balance, listing the accounts in their proper order. (b) Based upon the unadjusted trial balance, determine the net income or net loss.

✔ Total of Credit column: $925,000

SHOW ME HOW

EX 2-16 Trial balance **OBJ. 4**

The accounts in the ledger of Hickory Furniture Company as of December 31, 20Y6, are listed in alphabetical order below. All accounts have normal balances. The balance of the cash account has been intentionally omitted.

Accounts Payable	$ 42,770	Notes Payable	$ 50,000
Accounts Receivable	116,900	Prepaid Insurance	21,600
Cash	?	Rent Expense	48,000
Elaine Wells, Capital	75,000	Supplies	4,275
Elaine Wells, Drawing	24,000	Supplies Expense	6,255
Fees Earned	745,230	Unearned Rent	12,000
Insurance Expense	3,600	Utilities Expense	26,850
Land	50,000	Wages Expense	580,700
Miscellaneous Expense	9,500		

Prepare an unadjusted trial balance, listing the accounts in their normal order and inserting the missing figure for cash.

EX 2-17 Effect of errors on trial balance **OBJ. 4**

Indicate which of the following errors, each considered individually, would cause the trial balance totals to be unequal:

a. A fee of $21,000 earned and due from a client was not debited to Accounts Receivable or credited to a revenue account, because the cash had not been received.

b. A receipt of $11,300 from an account receivable was journalized and posted as a debit of $11,300 to Cash and a credit of $11,300 to Fees Earned.

c. A payment of $4,950 to a creditor was posted as a debit of $4,950 to Accounts Payable and a debit of $4,950 to Cash.

d. A payment of $5,000 for equipment purchased was posted as a debit of $500 to Equipment and a credit of $500 to Cash.

e. Payment of a cash withdrawal of $19,000 was journalized and posted as a debit of $1,900 to Salary Expense and a credit of $19,000 to Cash.

Indicate which of the preceding errors would require a correcting entry.

EX 2-18 Errors in trial balance

OBJ. 4

✔ Total of Credit column: $525,000

The following preliminary unadjusted trial balance of Ranger Co., a sports ticket agency, does not balance:

Ranger Co.
Unadjusted Trial Balance
August 31, 20Y7

	Debit Balances	Credit Balances
Cash	77,600	
Accounts Receivable	37,750	
Prepaid Insurance		12,000
Equipment	19,000	
Accounts Payable		29,100
Unearned Rent		10,800
Carmen Meeks, Capital	110,000	
Carmen Meeks, Drawing	13,000	
Fees Earned		385,000
Wages Expense		213,000
Advertising Expense	16,350	
Miscellaneous Expense		18,400
	273,700	668,300

When the ledger and other records are reviewed, you discover the following: (1) the debits and credits in the cash account total $77,600 and $62,100, respectively; (2) a billing of $9,000 to a customer on account was not posted to the accounts receivable account; (3) a payment of $4,500 made to a creditor on account was not posted to the accounts payable account; (4) the balance of the unearned rent account is $5,400; (5) the correct balance of the equipment account is $190,000; and (6) each account has a normal balance.

Prepare a corrected unadjusted trial balance.

EX 2-19 Effect of errors on trial balance

OBJ. 4

The following errors occurred in posting from a two-column journal:

1. A credit of $6,000 to Accounts Payable was not posted.
2. An entry debiting Accounts Receivable and crediting Fees Earned for $5,300 was not posted.
3. A debit of $2,700 to Accounts Payable was posted as a credit.
4. A debit of $480 to Supplies was posted twice.
5. A debit of $3,600 to Cash was posted to Miscellaneous Expense.
6. A credit of $780 to Cash was posted as $870.
7. A debit of $12,620 to Wages Expense was posted as $12,260.

Considering each case individually (i.e., assuming that no other errors had occurred), indicate (a) by "yes" or "no" whether the trial balance would be out of balance; (b) if answer to (a) is "yes," the amount by which the trial balance totals would differ; and (c) whether the Debit or Credit column of the trial balance would have the larger total. Answers should be presented in the following form, with error (1) given as an example:

	(a)	(b)	(c)
Error	Out of Balance	Difference	Larger Total
1.	yes	$6,000	debit

EX 2-20 Errors in trial balance OBJ. 4

✔ Total of Credit column: $1,040,000

Identify the errors in the following trial balance. All accounts have normal balances.

Mascot Co.
Unadjusted Trial Balance
For the Month Ending July 31, 20Y3

	Account No.	Debit Balances	Credit Balances
Cash	11	36,000	
Accounts Receivable	12		112,600
Prepaid Insurance	13	18,000	
Equipment	14	375,000	
Accounts Payable	21	53,300	
Salaries Payable	22		7,500
Samuel Parson, Capital	31		297,200
Samuel Parson, Drawing	32		17,000
Fees Earned	41		682,000
Salary Expense	51	396,800	
Advertising Expense	52		73,000
Miscellaneous Expense	59	11,600	
		1,189,300	1,189,300

EX 2-21 Entries to correct errors OBJ. 4

The following errors took place in journalizing and posting transactions:

a. Insurance of $18,000 paid for the current year was recorded as a debit to Insurance Expense and a credit to Prepaid Insurance.

b. A withdrawal of $10,000 by Brian Phillips, owner of the business, was recorded as a debit to Wages Expense and a credit to Cash.

Journalize the entries to correct the errors. Omit explanations.

EX 2-22 Entries to correct errors OBJ. 4

SHOW ME HOW

The following errors took place in journalizing and posting transactions:

a. Cash of $8,800 received on account was recorded as a debit to Fees Earned and a credit to Cash.

b. A $1,760 purchase of supplies for cash was recorded as a debit to Supplies Expense and a credit to Accounts Payable.

Journalize the entries to correct the errors. Omit explanations.

EX 2-23 Horizontal analysis of income statement OBJ. 5

✔ a. 1. 3.6% decrease

SHOW ME HOW

The following data (in millions) were taken from the financial statements of **Target Corporation**:

	Recent Year	Prior Year
Revenue	$75,356	$72,714
Operating expenses	71,246	68,490
Operating income	$ 4,110	$ 4,224

a. For Target Corporation, determine the amount of change in millions and the percent of change (round to one decimal place) from the prior year to the recent year for:

1. Revenue
2. Operating expenses
3. Operating income

b. What conclusions can you draw from your analysis of the revenue and the total operating expenses?

EX 2-24 Horizontal analysis of income statement **OBJ. 5**

✔ a. 2. 9.8% increase

The following data (in millions) were taken from the financial statements of **Costco Wholesale Corporation**:

	Recent Year	Prior Year
Revenue	$141,576	$129,025
Operating expenses	137,096	124,914
Operating income	$ 4,480	$ 4,111

a. For Costco, determine the amount of change in millions and the percent of change (round to one decimal place) from the prior year to the recent year for:

1. Revenue
2. Operating expenses
3. Operating income

b. Comment on the results of your horizontal analysis in part (a).

c. Based upon Exercise 2-23, compare and comment on the operating results of Target and Costco for the recent year.

Problems: Series A

PR 2-1A Entries into T accounts and trial balance **OBJ. 1, 2, 3, 4**

✔ 3. Total of Debit column: $93,890

Connie Young, an architect, opened an office on October 1, 20Y4. During the month, she completed the following transactions connected with her professional practice:

a. Transferred cash from a personal bank account to an account to be used for the business, $36,000.

b. Paid October rent for office and workroom, $2,400.

c. Purchased used automobile for $32,800, paying $7,800 cash and giving a note payable for the remainder.

d. Purchased office and computer equipment on account, $9,000.

e. Paid cash for supplies, $2,150.

f. Paid cash for annual insurance policies, $4,000.

g. Received cash from client for plans delivered, $12,200.

h. Paid cash for miscellaneous expenses, $815.

i. Paid cash to creditors on account, $4,500.

j. Paid $5,000 on note payable.

k. Received invoice for blueprint service, due in November, $2,890.

l. Recorded fees earned on plans delivered, payment to be received in November, $18,300.

m. Paid salary of assistants, $6,450.

n. Paid gas, oil, and repairs on automobile for October, $1,020.

Instructions

1. Record these transactions directly in the following T accounts, without journalizing: Cash; Accounts Receivable; Supplies; Prepaid Insurance; Automobiles; Equipment; Accounts Payable; Notes Payable; Connie Young, Capital; Professional Fees; Salary Expense; Blueprint Expense; Rent Expense; Automobile Expense; Miscellaneous Expense. To the left of the amount entered in the accounts, place the appropriate letter to identify the transaction.
2. Determine account balances of the T accounts. Accounts containing a single entry only (such as Prepaid Insurance) do not need a balance.
3. Prepare an unadjusted trial balance for Connie Young, Architect, as of October 31, 20Y4.
4. Determine the net income or net loss for October.

PR 2-2A Journal entries and trial balance

OBJ. 1, 2, 3, 4

✔ 4. c. $4,690

SHOW ME HOW

On January 1, 20Y5, Fahad Ali established Mountain Top Realty, which completed the following transactions during the month:

a. Fahad Ali transferred cash from a personal bank account to an account to be used for the business, $53,000.
b. Paid rent on office and equipment for the month, $7,950.
c. Purchased supplies on account, $4,240.
d. Paid creditor on account, $2,320.
e. Earned fees, receiving cash, $24,180.
f. Paid automobile expenses (including rental charge) for month, $2,490, and miscellaneous expenses, $560.
g. Paid office salaries, $6,630.
h. Determined that the cost of supplies used was $1,860.
i. Withdrew cash for personal use, $2,600.

Instructions

1. Journalize entries for transactions (a) through (i), using the following account titles: Cash; Supplies; Accounts Payable; Fahad Ali, Capital; Fahad Ali, Drawing; Fees Earned; Rent Expense; Office Salaries Expense; Automobile Expense; Supplies Expense; Miscellaneous Expense. Explanations may be omitted.
2. Prepare T accounts, using the account titles in (1). Post the journal entries to these accounts, placing the appropriate letter to the left of each amount to identify the transactions. Determine the account balances after all posting is complete. Accounts containing only a single entry do not need a balance.
3. Prepare an unadjusted trial balance as of January 31, 20Y5.
4. Determine the following:
   a. Amount of total revenue recorded in the ledger.
   b. Amount of total expenses recorded in the ledger.
   c. Amount of net income for January.
5. Determine the increase or decrease in owner's equity for January.

PR 2-3A Journal entries and trial balance

OBJ. 1, 2, 3, 4

✔ 3. Total of Credit column: $125,990

SHOW ME HOW

On June 1, 20Y6, Hannah Ellis established an interior decorating business, Whitworth Designs. During the month, Hannah completed the following transactions related to the business:

June 1. Hannah transferred cash from a personal bank account to an account to be used for the business, $48,000.
1. Paid rent for period of June 1 to end of month, $6,510.
6. Purchased office equipment on account, $19,340.
8. Purchased a van for $39,100 paying $6,200 cash and giving a note payable for the remainder.
10. Purchased supplies for cash, $3,260.
12. Received cash for job completed, $16,730.
15. Paid annual premiums on property and casualty insurance, $4,940.
23. Recorded jobs completed on account and sent invoices to customers, $16,320.
24. Received an invoice for van expenses, to be paid in July, $2,060.

(Continued)

Enter the following transactions on Page 2 of the two-column journal:

June 29. Paid utilities expense, $4,250.
29. Paid miscellaneous expenses, $1,300.
30. Received cash from customers on account, $10,050.
30. Paid wages of employees, $6,950.
30. Paid creditor a portion of the amount owed for equipment purchased on June 6, $9,360.
30. Withdrew cash for personal use, $2,200.

Instructions

1. Journalize each transaction in a two-column journal beginning on Page 1, referring to the following chart of accounts in selecting the accounts to be debited and credited. (Do not insert the account numbers in the journal at this time.) Explanations may be omitted.

11 Cash	31 Hannah Ellis, Capital
12 Accounts Receivable	32 Hannah Ellis, Drawing
13 Supplies	41 Fees Earned
14 Prepaid Insurance	51 Wages Expense
16 Equipment	53 Rent Expense
18 Van	54 Utilities Expense
21 Notes Payable	55 Van Expense
22 Accounts Payable	59 Miscellaneous Expense

2. Post the journal to a ledger of four-column accounts, inserting appropriate posting references as each item is posted. Extend the balances to the appropriate balance columns after each transaction is posted.
3. Prepare an unadjusted trial balance for Whitworth Designs as of June 30, 20Y6.
4. Determine the excess of revenues over expenses for June.
5. Can you think of any reason why the amount determined in (4) might not be the net income for June?

PR 2-4A Journal entries and trial balance **OBJ. 1, 2, 3, 4**

✔ 4. Total of Debit column: $532,525

Elite Realty acts as an agent in buying, selling, renting, and managing real estate. The unadjusted trial balance on March 31, 20Y7, follows:

Elite Realty
Unadjusted Trial Balance
March 31, 20Y7

	Account No.	Debit Balances	Credit Balances
Cash	11	26,300	
Accounts Receivable	12	61,500	
Prepaid Insurance	13	3,000	
Office Supplies	14	1,800	
Land	16	—	
Accounts Payable	21		14,000
Unearned Rent	22		—
Notes Payable	23		—
Lester Wagner, Capital	31		46,000
Lester Wagner, Drawing	32	2,000	
Fees Earned	41		240,000
Salary and Commission Expense	51	148,200	
Rent Expense	52	30,000	
Advertising Expense	53	17,800	
Automobile Expense	54	5,500	
Miscellaneous Expense	59	3,900	
		300,000	300,000

The following business transactions were completed by Elite Realty during April 20Y7:

Apr. 1. Paid rent on office for month, $6,500.
2. Purchased office supplies on account, $2,300.
5. Paid insurance premiums, $6,000.
10. Received cash from clients on account, $52,300.
15. Purchased land for a future building site for $200,000, paying $30,000 in cash and giving a note payable for the remainder.
17. Paid creditors on account, $6,450.
20. Returned a portion of the office supplies purchased on April 2, receiving full credit for their cost, $325.
23. Paid advertising expense, $4,300.

Enter the following transactions on Page 19 of the two-column journal:

27. Discovered an error in computing a commission; received cash from the salesperson for the overpayment, $2,500.
28. Paid automobile expense (including rental charges for an automobile), $1,500.
29. Paid miscellaneous expenses, $1,400.
30. Recorded revenue earned and billed to clients during the month, $57,000.
30. Paid salaries and commissions for the month, $11,900.
30. Withdrew cash for personal use, $4,000.
30. Rented land purchased on April 15 to local merchants association for use as a parking lot in May and June, during a street rebuilding program; received advance payment of $10,000.

Instructions

1. Record the April 1, 20Y7, balance of each account in the appropriate balance column of a four-column account, write *Balance* in the item column, and place a check mark (✓) in the Posting Reference column.
2. Journalize the transactions for April in a two-column journal beginning on Page 18. Journal entry explanations may be omitted.
3. Post to the ledger, extending the account balance to the appropriate balance column after each posting.
4. Prepare an unadjusted trial balance of the ledger as of April 30, 20Y7.
5. Assume that the April 30 transaction for salaries and commissions should have been $19,100. (a) Why did the unadjusted trial balance in (4) balance? (b) Journalize the correcting entry. (c) Is this error a transposition or slide?

PR 2-5A Corrected trial balance

OBJ. 4

✓ **1. Total of Debit column: $725,000**

The Colby Group has the following unadjusted trial balance as of August 31, 20Y8:

The Colby Group
Unadjusted Trial Balance
August 31, 20Y8

	Debit Balances	Credit Balances
Cash	17,300	
Accounts Receivable	37,000	
Supplies	7,400	
Prepaid Insurance	1,900	
Equipment	196,000	
Notes Payable		97,600
Accounts Payable		26,000
Terry Colby, Capital		129,150
Terry Colby, Drawing	56,000	
Fees Earned		454,450
Wages Expense	270,000	
Rent Expense	51,800	
Advertising Expense	25,200	
Miscellaneous Expense	5,100	
	667,700	707,200

(Continued)

The debit and credit totals are not equal as a result of the following errors:

a. The cash entered on the trial balance was understated by $6,000.
b. A cash receipt of $5,600 was posted as a debit to Cash of $6,500.
c. A debit of $11,000 to Accounts Receivable was not posted.
d. A return of $150 of defective supplies was erroneously posted as a $1,500 credit to Supplies.
e. An insurance policy acquired at a cost of $1,200 was posted as a credit to Prepaid Insurance.
f. The balance of Notes Payable was understated by $20,000.
g. A credit of $4,800 in Accounts Payable was overlooked when determining the balance of the account.
h. A debit of $7,000 for a withdrawal by the owner was posted as a credit to Terry Colby, Capital.
i. The balance of $58,100 in Rent Expense was entered as $51,800 in the trial balance.
j. Gas, Electricity, and Water Expense, with a balance of $24,150, was omitted from the trial balance.

Instructions

1. Prepare a corrected unadjusted trial balance as of August 31, 20Y8.
2. Does the fact that the unadjusted trial balance in (1) is balanced mean that there are no errors in the accounts? Explain.

Problems: Series B

PR 2-1B Entries into T accounts and trial balance

OBJ. 1, 2, 3, 4

✔ 3. Total of Debit column: $69,550

Ken Jones, an architect, opened an office on April 1, 20Y4. During the month, he completed the following transactions connected with his professional practice:

a. Transferred cash from a personal bank account to an account to be used for the business, $18,000.
b. Purchased used automobile for $19,500, paying $2,500 cash and giving a note payable for the remainder.
c. Paid April rent for office and workroom, $3,150.
d. Paid cash for supplies, $1,450.
e. Purchased office and computer equipment on account, $6,500.
f. Paid cash for annual insurance policies on automobile and equipment, $2,400.
g. Received cash from a client for plans delivered, $12,000.
h. Paid cash to creditors on account, $1,800.
i. Paid cash for miscellaneous expenses, $375.
j. Received invoice for blueprint service, due in May, $2,500.
k. Recorded fees earned on plans delivered, payment to be received in May, $15,650.
l. Paid salary of assistant, $2,800.
m. Paid cash for miscellaneous expenses, $200.
n. Paid $300 on note payable.
o. Paid gas, oil, and repairs on automobile for April, $550.

Instructions

1. Record these transactions directly in the following T accounts without journalizing: Cash; Accounts Receivable; Supplies; Prepaid Insurance; Automobiles; Equipment; Accounts Payable; Notes Payable; Ken Jones, Capital; Professional Fees; Rent Expense; Salary Expense; Blueprint Expense; Automobile Expense; Miscellaneous Expense. To the left of each amount entered in the accounts, place the appropriate letter to identify the transaction.
2. Determine account balances of the T accounts. Accounts containing a single entry only (such as Prepaid Insurance) do not need a balance.

3. Prepare an unadjusted trial balance for Ken Jones, Architect, as of April 30, 20Y4.
4. Determine the net income or net loss for April.

PR 2-2B Journal entries and trial balance OBJ. 1, 2, 3, 4

✔ 4. c. $4,550

On August 1, 20Y5, Rafael Masey established Planet Realty, which completed the following transactions during the month:

a. Rafael Masey transferred cash from a personal bank account to an account to be used for the business, $17,500.
b. Purchased supplies on account, $2,300.
c. Earned fees, receiving cash, $13,300.
d. Paid rent on office and equipment for the month, $3,000.
e. Paid creditor on account, $1,150.
f. Withdrew cash for personal use, $1,800.
g. Paid automobile expenses (including rental charge) for month, $1,500, and miscellaneous expenses, $400.
h. Paid office salaries, $2,800.
i. Determined that the cost of supplies used was $1,050.

Instructions

1. Journalize entries for transactions (a) through (i), using the following account titles: Cash; Supplies; Accounts Payable; Rafael Masey, Capital; Rafael Masey, Drawing; Fees Earned; Rent Expense; Office Salaries Expense; Automobile Expense; Supplies Expense; Miscellaneous Expense. Journal entry explanations may be omitted.
2. Prepare T accounts, using the account titles in (1). Post the journal entries to these accounts, placing the appropriate letter to the left of each amount to identify the transactions. Determine the account balances after all posting is complete. Accounts containing only a single entry do not need a balance.
3. Prepare an unadjusted trial balance as of August 31, 20Y5.
4. Determine the following:
   a. Amount of total revenue recorded in the ledger.
   b. Amount of total expenses recorded in the ledger.
   c. Amount of net income for August.
5. Determine the increase or decrease in owner's equity for August.

PR 2-3B Journal entries and trial balance OBJ. 1, 2, 3, 4

✔ 3. Total of Credit column: $70,300

On October 1, 20Y6, Jay Pryor established an interior decorating business, Pioneer Designs. During the month, Jay completed the following transactions related to the business:

Oct. 1. Jay transferred cash from a personal bank account to an account to be used for the business, $18,000.
4. Paid rent for period of October 4 to end of month, $3,000.
10. Purchased a used truck for $23,750, paying $3,750 cash and giving a note payable for the remainder.
13. Purchased equipment on account, $10,500.
14. Purchased supplies for cash, $2,100.
15. Paid annual premiums on property and casualty insurance, $3,600.
15. Received cash for job completed, $8,950.

Enter the following transactions on Page 2 of the two-column journal:

21. Paid creditor a portion of the amount owed for equipment purchased on October 13, $2,000.
24. Recorded jobs completed on account and sent invoices to customers, $14,150.
26. Received an invoice for truck expenses, to be paid in November, $700.
27. Paid utilities expense, $2,240.
27. Paid miscellaneous expenses, $1,100.

(Continued)

Oct. 29. Received cash from customers on account, $7,600.

30. Paid wages of employees, $4,800.

31. Withdrew cash for personal use, $3,500.

Instructions

1. Journalize each transaction in a two-column journal beginning on Page 1, referring to the following chart of accounts in selecting the accounts to be debited and credited. (Do not insert the account numbers in the journal at this time.) Journal entry explanations may be omitted.

11 Cash	31 Jay Pryor, Capital
12 Accounts Receivable	32 Jay Pryor, Drawing
13 Supplies	41 Fees Earned
14 Prepaid Insurance	51 Wages Expense
16 Equipment	53 Rent Expense
18 Truck	54 Utilities Expense
21 Notes Payable	55 Truck Expense
22 Accounts Payable	59 Miscellaneous Expense

2. Post the journal to a ledger of four-column accounts, inserting appropriate posting references as each item is posted. Extend the balances to the appropriate balance columns after each transaction is posted.
3. Prepare an unadjusted trial balance for Pioneer Designs as of October 31, 20Y6.
4. Determine the excess of revenues over expenses for October.
5. Can you think of any reason why the amount determined in (4) might not be the net income for October?

PR 2-4B Journal entries and trial balance **OBJ. 1, 2, 3, 4**

✔ 4. Total of Debit column: $945,000

Valley Realty acts as an agent in buying, selling, renting, and managing real estate. The unadjusted trial balance on July 31, 20Y7, follows:

Valley Realty
Unadjusted Trial Balance
July 31, 20Y7

	Account No.	Debit Balances	Credit Balances
Cash	11	52,500	
Accounts Receivable	12	100,100	
Prepaid Insurance	13	12,600	
Office Supplies	14	2,800	
Land	16	—	
Accounts Payable	21		21,000
Unearned Rent	22		—
Notes Payable	23		—
Cindy Getman, Capital	31		87,500
Cindy Getman, Drawing	32	44,800	
Fees Earned	41		591,500
Salary and Commission Expense	51	385,000	
Rent Expense	52	49,000	
Advertising Expense	53	32,200	
Automobile Expense	54	15,750	
Miscellaneous Expense	59	5,250	
		700,000	700,000

The following business transactions were completed by Valley Realty during August 20Y7:

Aug. 1. Purchased office supplies on account, $3,150.

2. Paid rent on office for month, $7,200.

3. Received cash from clients on account, $83,900.

5. Paid insurance premiums, $12,000.

9. Returned a portion of the office supplies purchased on August 1, receiving full credit for their cost, $400.

Aug. 17. Paid advertising expense, $8,000.

23. Paid creditors on account, $13,750.

Enter the following transactions on Page 19 of the two-column journal:

29. Paid miscellaneous expenses, $1,700.

30. Paid automobile expense (including rental charges for an automobile), $2,500.

31. Discovered an error in computing a commission during July; received cash from the salesperson for the overpayment, $2,000.

31. Paid salaries and commissions for the month, $53,000.

31. Recorded revenue earned and billed to clients during the month, $183,500.

31. Purchased land for a future building site for $75,000, paying $7,500 in cash and giving a note payable for the remainder.

31. Withdrew cash for personal use, $1,000.

31. Rented land purchased on August 31 to a local university for use as a parking lot during football season (September, October, and November); received advance payment of $5,000.

Instructions

1. Record the August 1 balance of each account in the appropriate balance column of a four-column account, write *Balance* in the item column, and place a check mark (✓) in the Posting Reference column.
2. Journalize the transactions for August in a two-column journal beginning on Page 18. Journal entry explanations may be omitted.
3. Post to the ledger, extending the account balance to the appropriate balance column after each posting.
4. Prepare an unadjusted trial balance of the ledger as of August 31, 20Y7.
5. Assume that the August 31 transaction for Cindy Getman's cash withdrawal should have been $10,000. (a) Why did the unadjusted trial balance in (4) balance? (b) Journalize the correcting entry. (c) Is this error a transposition or slide?

PR 2-5B Corrected trial balance **OBJ. 4**

✓ **1. Total of Debit column: $712,500**

Tech Support Services has the following unadjusted trial balance as of January 31, 20Y8:

Tech Support Services
Unadjusted Trial Balance
January 31, 20Y8

	Debit Balances	Credit Balances
Cash	25,550	
Accounts Receivable	44,050	
Supplies	6,660	
Prepaid Insurance	3,600	
Equipment	162,000	
Notes Payable		75,000
Accounts Payable		13,200
Thad Engelberg, Capital		101,850
Thad Engelberg, Drawing	33,000	
Fees Earned		534,000
Wages Expense	306,000	
Rent Expense	62,550	
Advertising Expense	23,850	
Gas, Electricity, and Water Expense	17,000	
	684,260	724,050

The debit and credit totals are not equal as a result of the following errors:

a. The cash entered on the trial balance was overstated by $8,000.

b. A cash receipt of $4,100 was posted as a debit to Cash of $1,400.

(Continued)

c. A debit of $12,350 to Accounts Receivable was not posted.

d. A return of $235 of defective supplies was erroneously posted as a $325 credit to Supplies.

e. An insurance policy acquired at a cost of $3,000 was posted as a credit to Prepaid Insurance.

f. The balance of Notes Payable was overstated by $21,000.

g. A credit of $3,450 in Accounts Payable was overlooked when the balance of the account was determined.

h. A debit of $6,000 for a withdrawal by the owner was posted as a debit to Thad Engelberg, Capital.

i. The balance of $28,350 in Advertising Expense was entered as $23,850 in the trial balance.

j. Miscellaneous Expense, with a balance of $4,600, was omitted from the trial balance.

Instructions

1. Prepare a corrected unadjusted trial balance as of January 31, 20Y8.
2. Does the fact that the unadjusted trial balance in (1) is balanced mean that there are no errors in the accounts? Explain.

Continuing Problem

✔ **4. Total of Debit column: $40,750**

The transactions completed by PS Music during June 20Y9 were described at the end of Chapter 1. The following transactions were completed during July, the second month of the business's operations:

July 1. Peyton Smith made an additional investment in PS Music by depositing $5,000 in PS Music's checking account.

1. Instead of continuing to share office space with a local real estate agency, Peyton decided to rent office space near a local music store. Paid rent for July, $1,750.

1. Paid a premium of $2,700 for a comprehensive insurance policy covering liability, theft, and fire. The policy covers a one-year period.

2. Received $1,000 cash from customers on account.

3. On behalf of PS Music, Peyton signed a contract with a local radio station, KXMD, to provide guest spots for the next three months. The contract requires PS Music to provide a guest disc jockey for 80 hours per month for a monthly fee of $3,600. Any additional hours beyond 80 will be billed to KXMD at $40 per hour. In accordance with the contract, Peyton received $7,200 from KXMD as an advance payment for the first two months.

3. Paid $250 to creditors on account.

4. Paid an attorney $900 for reviewing the July 3 contract with KXMD. (Record as Miscellaneous Expense.)

5. Purchased office equipment on account from Office Mart, $7,500.

8. Paid for a newspaper advertisement, $200.

11. Received $1,000 for serving as a disc jockey for a party.

13. Paid $700 to a local audio electronics store for rental of digital recording equipment.

14. Paid wages of $1,200 to receptionist and part-time assistant.

Enter the following transactions on Page 2 of the two-column journal:

16. Received $2,000 for serving as a disc jockey for a wedding reception.

18. Purchased supplies on account, $850.

July 21. Paid $620 to Upload Music for use of its current music demos in making various music sets.

22. Paid $800 to a local radio station to advertise the services of PS Music twice daily for the remainder of July.

23. Served as disc jockey for a party for $2,500. Received $750, with the remainder due August 4, 20Y9.

27. Paid electric bill, $915.

28. Paid wages of $1,200 to receptionist and part-time assistant.

29. Paid miscellaneous expenses, $540.

30. Served as a disc jockey for a charity ball for $1,500. Received $500, with the remainder due on August 9, 20Y9.

31. Received $3,000 for serving as a disc jockey for a party.

31. Paid $1,400 royalties (music expense) to National Music Clearing for use of various artists' music during July.

31. Withdrew $1,250 cash from PS Music for personal use.

PS Music's chart of accounts and the balance of accounts as of July 1, 20Y9 (all normal balances), are as follows:

Account	Balance	Account	Balance
11 Cash	$3,920	41 Fees Earned	$6,200
12 Accounts Receivable	1,000	50 Wages Expense	400
14 Supplies	170	51 Office Rent Expense	800
15 Prepaid Insurance	—	52 Equipment Rent Expense	675
17 Office Equipment	—	53 Utilities Expense	300
21 Accounts Payable	250	54 Music Expense	1,590
23 Unearned Revenue	—	55 Advertising Expense	500
31 Peyton Smith, Capital	4,000	56 Supplies Expense	180
32 Peyton Smith, Drawing	500	59 Miscellaneous Expense	415

Instructions

1. Enter the July 1, 20Y9, account balances in the appropriate balance column of a four-column account. Write *Balance* in the Item column and place a check mark (✓) in the Posting Reference column. (*Hint:* Verify the equality of the debit and credit balances in the ledger before proceeding with the next instruction.)
2. Analyze and journalize each transaction in a two-column journal beginning on Page 1, omitting journal entry explanations.
3. Post the journal to the ledger, extending the account balance to the appropriate balance column after each posting.
4. Prepare an unadjusted trial balance as of July 31, 20Y9.

Cases & Projects

CP 2-1 Ethics in Action

ETHICS

Buddy Dupree is the accounting manager for On-Time Geeks, a tech support company for individuals and small businesses. As part of his job, Buddy is responsible for preparing the company's trial balance. His supervisor placed a "hard deadline" of Friday at 5 PM for the completion of the trial balance. Unfortunately, Buddy was unable to get the trial balance to balance by the due date. The credit side of the trial balance exceeded the debit side by $3,000. To make the deadline, Buddy decided to add a $3,000 debit to the vehicles account balance. He selected the vehicles account because it will not be significantly affected by the additional $3,000.

1. Is Buddy behaving ethically? Why or why not?
2. Who is affected by Buddy's decision?
3. How should Buddy have handled this situation?

CP 2-2 Team Activity

In teams, select a public company that interests you. Obtain the company's most recent annual report on Form 10-K. The Form 10-K is a company's annually required filing with the Securities and Exchange Commission (SEC). It includes the company's financial statements and accompanying notes. The Form 10-K can be obtained either (a) by referring to the investor relations section of the company's website or (b) by using the company search feature of the SEC's EDGAR database service found at www.sec.gov/edgar/searchedgar/companysearch.html.

Based on the information in the company's most recent annual report, answer the following questions:

1. What amount of total assets does the company report on its balance sheet?
2. What amount of total liabilities does the company report on its balance sheet?
3. Using the accounting equation, determine the company's stockholders' equity. Compare this amount to the amount of stockholders' equity reported on the company's balance sheet.
4. How many years of information are reported on the company's income statement?
5. How many years of information are reported on the company's balance sheet?
6. What is the difference between the information reported on the income statement and the information reported on the balance sheet?

CP 2-3 Team Activity

The following excerpt is from a conversation between Kate Purvis, the president and chief operating officer of Light House Company, and her neighbor, Dot Evers:

Dot: Kate, I'm taking a course in night school, "Intro to Accounting." I was wondering—could you answer a couple of questions for me?

Kate: Well, I will if I can.

Dot: Okay, our instructor says that it's critical we understand the basic concepts of accounting, or we'll never get beyond the first test. My problem is with those rules of debit and credit . . . you know, assets increase with debits, decrease with credits, etc.

Kate: Yes, pretty basic stuff. You just have to memorize the rules. It shouldn't be too difficult.

Dot: Sure, I can memorize the rules, but my problem is I want to be sure I understand the basic concepts behind the rules. For example, why can't assets be increased with credits and decreased with debits like revenue? As long as everyone did it that way, why not? It would seem easier if we had the same rules for all increases and decreases in accounts. Also, why is the left side of an account called the debit side? Why couldn't it be called something simple . . . like the "LE" for Left Entry? The right side could be called just "RE" for Right Entry. Finally, why are there just two sides to an entry? Why can't there be three or four sides to an entry?

In a group of four or five, select one person to play the role of Kate and one person to play the role of Dot.

1. After listening to the conversation between Kate and Dot, help Kate answer Dot's questions.
2. What information (other than just debit and credit journal entries) could the accounting system gather that might be useful to Kate in managing Light House Company?

CP 2-4 Communication

The complexity of the current business and regulatory environment has increased the demand for individuals in all fields of business who have the ability to analyze business transactions and interpret their effects on the financial statements. Search the Internet or your local newspaper for job opportunities in business. One possible website is www.careerbuilder.com.

Select a job opportunity to explore further. Write a brief memo to your instructor describing how the ability to analyze business transactions and interpret their effects on the financial statements would be needed for the job opportunity you have selected.

CP 2-5 Account for revenue

Bozeman College requires students to pay tuition each term before classes begin. Students who have not paid their tuition are not allowed to enroll or to attend classes.

What journal entry do you think Bozeman College would use to record the receipt of the students' tuition payments? Describe the nature of each account in the entry.

CP 2-6 Record transactions

The following discussion took place between Tony Cork, the office manager of Hallmark Data Company, and a new accountant, Cassie Miles:

Cassie: I've been thinking about our method of recording entries. It seems inefficient.

Tony: In what way?

Cassie: Well—correct me if I'm wrong—it seems like we have unnecessary steps in the process. We could easily develop a trial balance by posting our transactions directly into the ledger and bypassing the journal altogether. In this way, we could combine the recording and posting process into one step and save ourselves a lot of time. What do you think?

Tony: We need to have a talk.

What should Tony say to Cassie?

CP 2-7 Transactions and income statement

Cory Neece is planning to manage and operate Eagle Caddy Service at Canyon Lake Golf and Country Club during June through August 20Y9. Cory will rent a small maintenance building from the country club for $500 per month and will offer caddy services, including cart rentals, to golfers. Cory has had no formal training in record keeping.

Cory keeps notes of all receipts and expenses in a shoe box. An examination of Cory's shoe box records for June revealed the following:

June 1. Transferred $2,000 from personal bank account to be used to operate the caddy service.
1. Paid rent expense to Canyon Lake Golf and Country Club, $500.
2. Paid for golf supplies (practice balls, for example), $750.
3. Arranged for the rental of 40 regular (pulling) golf carts and 20 gasoline-driven carts for $3,000 per month. Paid $600 in advance, with the remaining $2,400 due June 20.
7. Purchased supplies, including gasoline, for the golf carts on account, $1,000. Canyon Lake Golf and Country Club has agreed to allow Cory to store the gasoline in one of its fuel tanks at no cost.
15. Received cash for services from June 1–15, $5,400.
17. Paid cash to creditors on account, $1,000.
20. Paid remaining rental on golf carts, $2,400.
22. Purchased supplies, including gasoline, on account, $850.
25. Earned fees from customers on account, $1,800.
28. Paid miscellaneous expenses, $395.
30. Received cash for services from June 16–30, $4,200.
30. Paid telephone and electricity (utilities) expenses, $340.
30. Paid wages of part-time employees, $850.
30. Received cash on account, $1,500.
30. Determined the amount of supplies on hand at the end of June, $675.

Cory has asked you several questions concerning his financial affairs to date, and he has asked you to assist with his record keeping and reporting of financial data.

a. To assist Cory with his record keeping, prepare a chart of accounts that would be appropriate for Eagle Caddy Service.

b. Prepare an income statement for June in order to help Cory assess the profitability of Eagle Caddy Service. For this purpose, the use of T accounts may be helpful in analyzing the effects of each June transaction.

c. Based on Cory's records of receipts and payments, compute the amount of cash on hand on June 30. For this purpose, a T account for cash may be useful.

d. A count of the cash on hand on June 30 totaled $6,175. Briefly discuss the possible causes of the difference between the amount of cash computed in (c) and the actual amount of cash on hand.

CHAPTER 3

The Adjusting Process

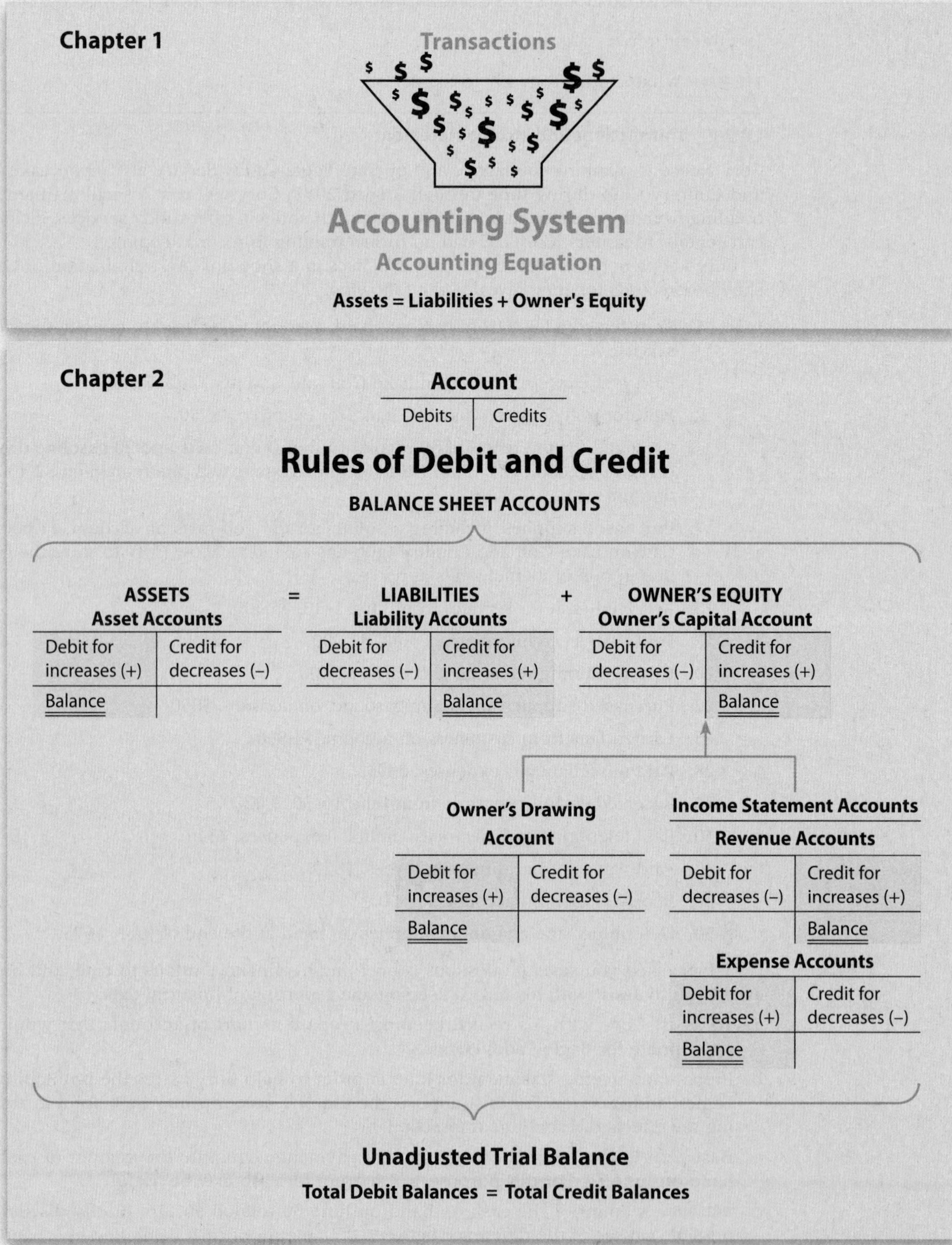

CHAPTER

3

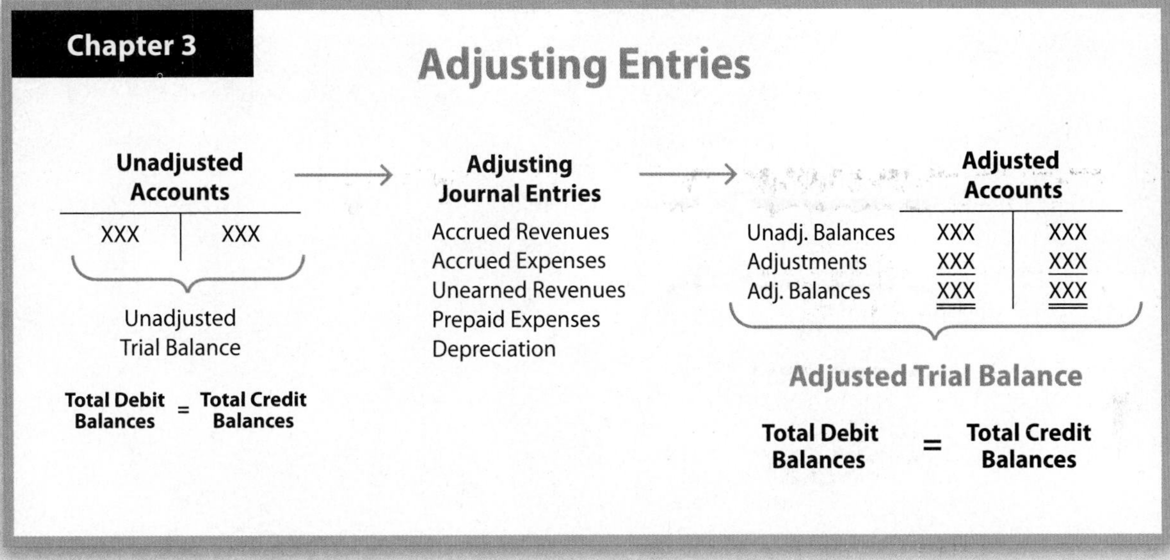

Chapter 3
Adjusting Entries
Unadjusted Accounts
XXX
XXX
Unadjusted Trial Balance
Total Debit Balances = Total Credit Balances
Adjusting Journal Entries
Accrued Revenues
Accrued Expenses
Unearned Revenues
Prepaid Expenses
Depreciation
Adjusted Accounts
Unadj. Balances XXX XXX
Adjustments XXX XXX
Adj. Balances XXX XXX
Adjusted Trial Balance
Total Debit Balances = Total Credit Balances

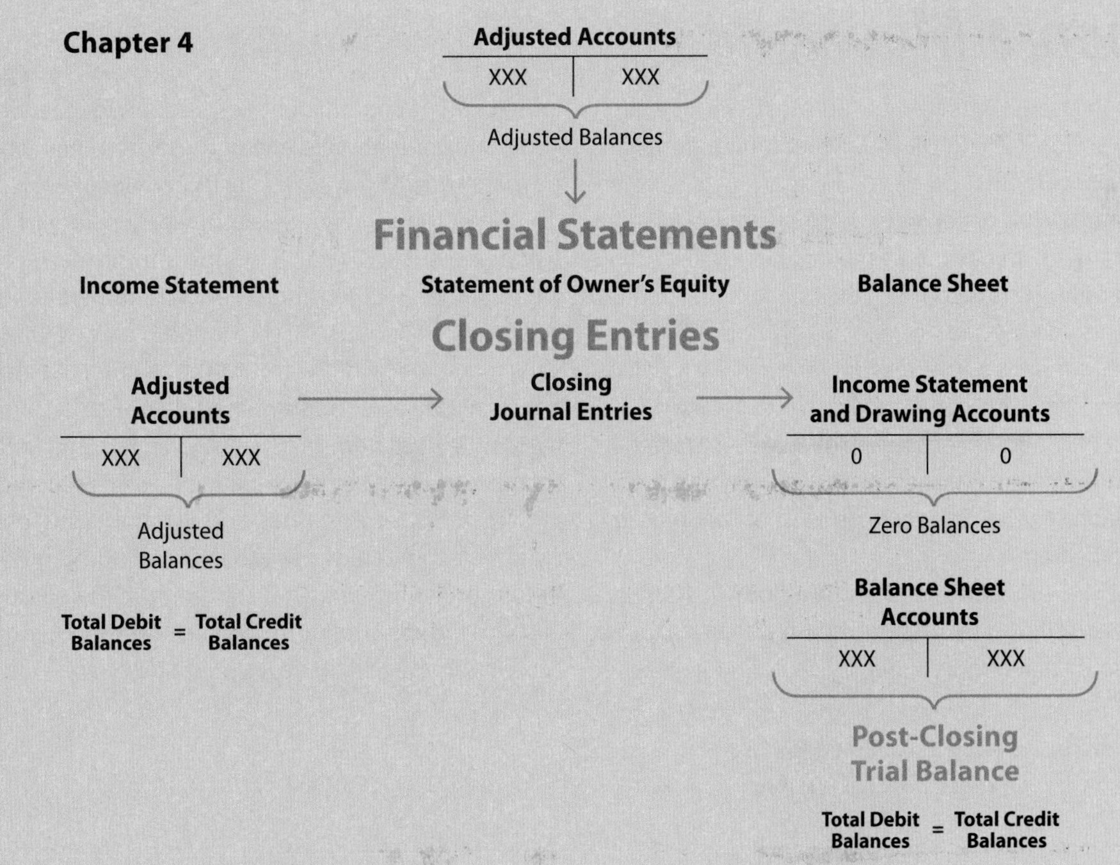

Chapter 4
Adjusted Accounts
XXX
XXX
Adjusted Balances
Financial Statements
Income Statement
Statement of Owner's Equity
Balance Sheet
Closing Entries
Adjusted Accounts
XXX
XXX
Adjusted Balances
Total Debit Balances = Total Credit Balances
Closing Journal Entries
Income Statement and Drawing Accounts
0
0
Zero Balances
Balance Sheet Accounts
XXX
XXX
Post-Closing Trial Balance
Total Debit Balances = Total Credit Balances

CHAPTER 3

WESTEND61/GETTY IMAGES

Pandora Media, Inc.[1]

Do you use an Internet-based music service such as Pandora? Using playlist-generating algorithms, **Pandora Media, Inc.** predicts a listener's music preferences based on his or her initial music selections. Pandora selects music it thinks the listener will enjoy, including music of new artists that match the listener's preferences. Pandora also developed similar comedy-generating algorithms that match a listener's preferences for comedy with more than 3,000 comedians.

Most of Pandora's services are offered free to listeners with approximately 20% of its revenues generated from subscription services. So, where do most of Pandora's revenues come from?

Pandora generates more than 70% of its revenues from selling advertising banners that surround the video displays on its tuner. By analyzing its listener interactions, Pandora identifies listener age, gender, zip code, and content preferences. These attributes can then be matched with advertiser needs and desires.

When should Pandora record revenue from its advertisers and subscribers? Revenue should be recorded when earned. Advertising revenue is earned as ads are displayed, while subscriber revenue is earned when the service has been delivered to the listener. As a result, companies like Pandora must update their accounting records for such items as unearned advertising and subscription revenue before preparing financial statements.

This chapter describes and illustrates the process by which companies update their accounting records before preparing financial statements. This discussion includes the adjustments to update revenue and expense accounts at the end of the accounting period.

1 Sirius XM Holdings Inc. acquired Pandora Media, Inc. on February 1, 2019.

Link to Pandora . . . . Pages 113, 114, 118, 120, 121, 123, 125

LEARNING OBJECTIVES

After studying this chapter, you should be able to:

Example Exercises (EE) are shown in **red**.

OBJ. 1 **Describe the nature of the adjusting process.**

OBJ. 2 **Prepare adjusting entries for accruals.**

OBJ. 3 **Prepare adjusting entries for deferrals.**

OBJ. 4 **Prepare adjusting entries for depreciation.**

OBJ. 5 **Summarize the adjusting process.**

OBJ. 6 **Prepare an adjusted trial balance.**

OBJ. 7 **Describe and illustrate the use of vertical analysis in evaluating a company's performance and financial condition.**

At a Glance 3 Page 134

Nature of the Adjusting Process

OBJ. 1 Describe the nature of the adjusting process.

In Chapter 2, the November and December transactions for **NetSolutions** were recorded using the double-entry accounting system. After the transactions were recorded, an unadjusted trial balance was prepared on December 31 verifying that the total debit balances equal the total credit balances. Before financial statements can be prepared, however, some accounts on the unadjusted trial balance must be adjusted. These adjustments are necessary because the transactions for NetSolutions were recorded using the accrual basis of accounting.

Accrual and Cash Basis of Accounting

Under the **accrual basis of accounting**, revenues and their related expenses are reported on the income statement in the period in which a service has been performed or a product has been delivered. Cash may or may not be received from customers during this period. For example, a cleaning company will record revenue after it cleans an office building, even if it is not paid for several weeks. The accrual basis of accounting also requires expenses to be recorded when they are incurred, not necessarily when cash is paid.

Although generally accepted accounting principles (GAAP) require the accrual basis of accounting, most individuals and some businesses use the cash basis of accounting. Under the **cash basis of accounting**, revenues and expenses are reported on the income statement in the period in which cash is received or paid. For example, fees are recorded when cash is received from clients; likewise, wages are recorded when cash is paid to employees. The net income (or net loss) is the difference between the cash receipts (revenues) and the cash payments (expenses).

Link to Pandora

Pandora uses the accrual basis of accounting in preparing its financial statements.

Small service businesses may use the cash basis because they have few receivables and payables. For example, attorneys, physicians, and real estate agents may use the cash basis. For them, the cash basis provides financial statements similar to those of the accrual basis. For most large businesses, however, the cash basis will not provide accurate financial statements for user needs. For this reason, the accrual basis is required by GAAP and is used in this text.[2]

Revenue and Expense Recognition

Link to Pandora

Subscription revenues from **Pandora**'s customers are recorded equally over the subscription periods. For example, a yearly subscription would be recorded equally over 12 months.

To be useful for decision making, financial statements must be provided on a periodic basis. As a result, the economic life of a business is divided into time periods such as a month, quarter of a year, or full year. Under accrual accounting, the net income of a period is reported using revenue and expense recognition principles.

Under the **revenue recognition principle**, revenues are recorded when they are earned, which is when services have been performed or products have been delivered to customers. Revenue is measured as the value of the assets received, such as cash or accounts receivable.[3] The process of recognizing revenues is called **revenue recognition**.[4]

Under the **expense recognition principle**, the expenses incurred in generating revenue must be reported in the same period as the related revenue. This is also called the **matching principle**. By matching revenues and expenses, net income or loss for the period is properly reported on the income statement. Adjusting entries are required to properly match revenues and expenses.

The Adjusting Process

At the end of an accounting period, an unadjusted trial balance is prepared to verify that the total debit balances equal the total credit balances. Many of these account balances are reported on the financial statements without change. For example, the balances of the cash and land accounts are normally the amounts reported on the balance sheet.

Some accounts on the unadjusted trial balance, however, require adjustments for the following reasons:

Link to Pandora

Pandora computes royalty expense paid to an artist for a song that is streamed to listeners based upon the number of times it is played/streamed.

- Some revenues and expenses may be unrecorded at the end of the accounting period. For example, a company may have provided services to customers that it has not billed or recorded at the end of the accounting period. Likewise, a company may not pay its employees until the next accounting period even though the employees have earned their wages in the current period.
- Some expenses are not recorded daily. For example, the daily use of supplies would require many entries with small amounts. Also, information about the amount of supplies on hand on a day-to-day basis is normally not needed.
- Some revenues and expenses are incurred as time passes rather than as separate transactions. For example, rent received in advance (unearned rent) expires and becomes revenue with the passage of time. Likewise, prepaid insurance expires and becomes an expense with the passage of time.

The analysis and updating of accounts at the end of the period before the financial statements are prepared is called the **adjusting process**. The journal entries that bring the accounts up to date at the end of the accounting period are called **adjusting entries**. All adjusting entries affect at least one income statement account and one balance sheet account. Thus, an adjusting entry will always involve a revenue or an expense account *and* an asset or a liability account.

2 The accrual and cash bases of accounting are further described and illustrated in Appendix 2 to Chapter 4, "Why Is the Accrual Basis of Accounting Required by GAAP?"

3 As will be illustrated later in this chapter, revenues may also be measured as a decrease in a liability such as unearned revenue.

4 FASB Accounting Standards Update, Revenue from Contracts with Customers (Topic 606), Financial Accounting Standards Board, May 2014, Norwalk, CT.

EXAMPLE EXERCISE 3-1 Accounts Requiring Adjustment **OBJ. 1**

Indicate with a Yes or No whether or not each of the following accounts normally requires an adjusting entry:

a. Cash
b. Supplies Expense
c. Wages Expense
d. Land
e. Accounts Receivable
f. Unearned Rent

Follow My Example 3-1

a. No
b. Yes
c. Yes
d. No
e. Yes
f. Yes

Practice Exercises: PE 3-1A, PE 3-1B

Types of Accounts Requiring Adjustment

The two general classifications of accounts requiring adjustment are as follows:

- Accruals
- Deferrals

Accruals An **accrual** occurs when revenue has been earned or an expense has been incurred but has not been recorded. If the accrual is for revenue, the adjusting entry debits an asset such as Accounts Receivable and credits a revenue account. If the accrual is for an expense, the adjusting entry debits an expense account and credits a related liability account such as Accounts Payable or Wages Payable. Exhibit 1 summarizes the accounting for accruals.

EXHIBIT 1
Accruals

ACCRUED REVENUE			
Initial Recording		**End-of-Period**	
Transaction Revenue has been earned.	**Journal Entry** No journal entry has been made.	**Adjustment Data** Revenue earned.	**Adjusting Entry** Accounts Receivable XXX Revenue XXX
ACCRUED EXPENSE			
Initial Recording		**End-of-Period**	
Transaction Expense has been incurred.	**Journal Entry** No journal entry has been made.	**Adjustment Data** Expense incurred.	**Adjusting Entry** Expense XXX Liability XXX

Deferrals A **deferral** occurs when cash related to a future revenue or expense has been initially recorded as a liability or an asset. If the cash received is related to future revenue, it is initially recorded as a liability called **unearned revenue**. The adjusting entry in the period when the revenue is earned debits an unearned revenue account and credits a revenue account. If the cash paid is related to a future expense, it is initially recorded as an asset called **prepaid expense**. The adjusting entry in the period when the expense is incurred debits an expense account and credits a prepaid expense (asset) account. Exhibit 2 summarizes the accounting for deferrals.

EXHIBIT 2 **Deferrals**

UNEARNED REVENUE

Initial Recording		End-of-Period	
Transaction	**Journal Entry**	**Adjustment Data**	**Adjusting Entry**
Cash has been received for revenue that will be earned in a future period.	Cash XXX Unearned Revenue XXX	Revenue has been earned.	**Unearned Revenue XXX** **Revenue XXX**

PREPAID EXPENSE

Initial Recording		End-of-Period	
Transaction	**Journal Entry**	**Adjustment Data**	**Adjusting Entry**
Cash has been paid for a future expense.	Prepaid Expense XXX Cash XXX	Prepaid expense has been used to generate revenue.	**Expense XXX** **Prepaid Expense XXX**

EXAMPLE EXERCISE 3-2 Type of Adjustment **OBJ. 1**

Classify the following items as (1) prepaid expense, (2) unearned revenue, (3) accrued expense, or (4) accrued revenue:

a. Wages owed but not yet paid.
b. Supplies on hand.
c. Fees received but not yet earned.
d. Fees earned but not yet received.

Follow My Example 3-2

a. Accrued expense
b. Prepaid expense
c. Unearned revenue
d. Accrued revenue

Practice Exercises: PE 3-2A, PE 3-2B

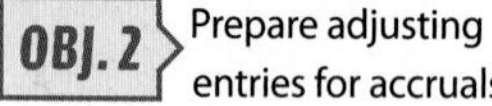
Prepare adjusting entries for accruals.

Adjusting Entries for Accruals

To illustrate adjusting entries, the December 31, 20Y3, unadjusted trial balance of NetSolutions, shown in Exhibit 3, is used. An expanded chart of accounts for NetSolutions is shown in Exhibit 4. The additional accounts used in this chapter are highlighted. The rules of debit and credit shown in Exhibit 3 of Chapter 2 are used to record the adjusting entries.

EXHIBIT 3

Unadjusted Trial Balance for NetSolutions

NetSolutions
Unadjusted Trial Balance
December 31, 20Y3

	Account No.	Debit Balances	Credit Balances
Cash	11	2,065	
Accounts Receivable	12	2,220	
Supplies	14	2,000	
Prepaid Insurance	15	2,400	
Land	17	20,000	
Office Equipment	18	1,800	
Accounts Payable	21		900
Unearned Rent	23		360
Chris Clark, Capital	31		25,000
Chris Clark, Drawing	32	4,000	
Fees Earned	41		16,340
Wages Expense	51	4,275	
Supplies Expense	52	800	
Rent Expense	53	1,600	
Utilities Expense	54	985	
Miscellaneous Expense	59	455	
		42,600	42,600

EXHIBIT 4

Expanded Chart of Accounts for NetSolutions

Balance Sheet Accounts	Income Statement Accounts
1. Assets	**4. Revenue**
11 Cash	41 Fees Earned
12 Accounts Receivable	42 Rent Revenue
14 Supplies	**5. Expenses**
15 Prepaid Insurance	51 Wages Expense
17 Land	52 Supplies Expense
18 Office Equipment	53 Rent Expense
19 Accumulated Depreciation—Office Equipment	54 Utilities Expense
2. Liabilities	55 Insurance Expense
21 Accounts Payable	56 Depreciation Expense
22 Wages Payable	59 Miscellaneous Expense
23 Unearned Rent	
3. Owner's Equity	
31 Chris Clark, Capital	
32 Chris Clark, Drawing	

Accrued Revenues

During an accounting period, some revenues are recorded only when cash is received. Thus, at the end of an accounting period, there may be revenue that has been earned *but has not been recorded.* In such cases, the revenue is recorded by increasing (debiting) an asset account (Accounts Receivable) and increasing (crediting) a revenue account (Fees Earned).

To illustrate, assume that **NetSolutions** signed an agreement with Dankner Co. on December 15. The agreement provides that NetSolutions will answer computer questions and render assistance to Dankner Co.'s employees. The services will be billed to Dankner Co. on the fifteenth of each month at a rate of $20 per hour. As of December 31, NetSolutions had provided 25 hours of assistance to Dankner Co. The revenue of $500 (25 hours × $20) will be billed on January 15. However, NetSolutions earned the revenue in December.

The claim against the customer for payment of the $500 is an account receivable (*an asset*). Thus, the accounts receivable account is increased (debited) by $500, and the fees earned account is increased (credited) by $500. The adjusting journal entry and T accounts are as follows:

Adjusting Journal Entry

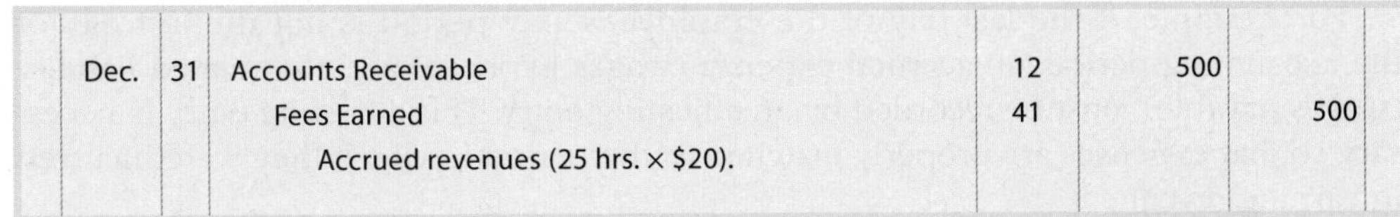

Dec.	31	Accounts Receivable	12	500	
		Fees Earned	41		500
		Accrued revenues (25 hrs. × $20).			

Accounting Equation Impact

Assets = **Liabilities** + **Owner's Equity (Revenue)**

Accounts Receivable	12	
Bal.	2,220	
Dec. 31	500	
Adj. Bal.	2,720	

Fees Earned		41
	Bal.	16,340
	Dec. 31	500
	Adj. Bal.	16,840

If the adjustment for the accrued revenue ($500) is not recorded, Fees Earned and the net income will be understated by $500 on the income statement. On the balance sheet, assets (Accounts Receivable) and owner's equity (Chris Clark, Capital) will be understated by $500. The effects of omitting this adjusting entry are as follows:

Link to Pandora

Pandora's accrued revenues from advertising are recorded in its accounts receivable at the end of the year.

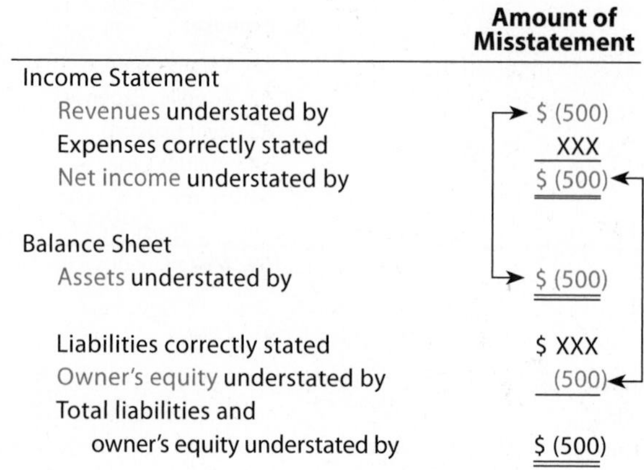

	Amount of Misstatement
Income Statement	
Revenues understated by	$ (500)
Expenses correctly stated	XXX
Net income understated by	$ (500)
Balance Sheet	
Assets understated by	$ (500)
Liabilities correctly stated	$ XXX
Owner's equity understated by	(500)
Total liabilities and owner's equity understated by	$ (500)

EXAMPLE EXERCISE 3-3 Adjustment for Accrued Revenues **OBJ. 2**

At the end of the current year, $13,680 of fees have been earned but have not been billed to clients. Journalize the adjusting entry to record the accrued fees.

Follow My Example 3-3

Accounts Receivable	13,680	
Fees Earned		13,680
Accrued fees.		

Practice Exercises: PE 3-3A, PE 3-3B

Accrued Expenses

Some types of services used in earning revenues are paid for *after* the service has been performed. For example, wages expense is incurred hour by hour but is paid only daily, weekly, biweekly, or monthly. At the end of the accounting period, the amount of such *accrued* but unpaid items is an expense and a liability.

For example, if the last day of the employees' pay period is not the last day of the accounting period, an accrued expense (wages expense) and the related liability (wages payable) must be recorded by an adjusting entry. This adjusting entry is necessary so that expenses are properly matched to the period in which they were incurred in earning revenue.

To illustrate, **NetSolutions** pays its employees biweekly. During December, NetSolutions paid wages of $950 on December 13 and $1,200 on December 27. These payments covered pay periods ending on those days as shown in Exhibit 5.

As of December 31, NetSolutions owes $250 of wages to employees for Monday and Tuesday, December 30 and 31. Thus, the wages expense account is increased

EXHIBIT 5
Accrued Wages

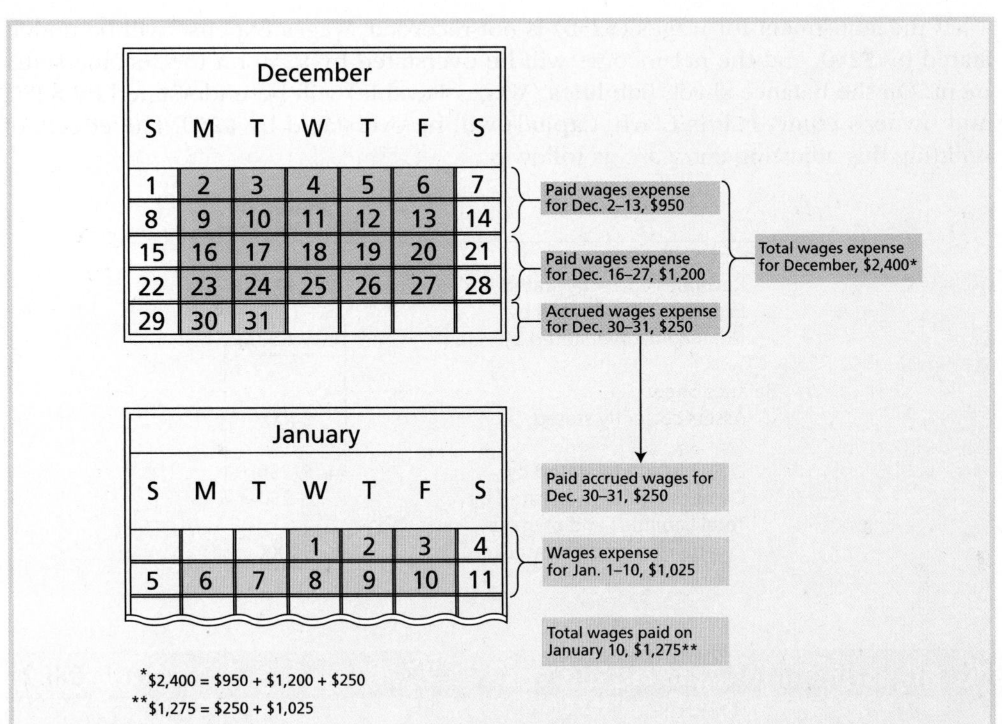

(debited) by $250, and the wages payable account is increased (credited) by $250. The adjusting journal entry and T accounts are as follows:

Adjusting Journal Entry

Dec.	31	Wages Expense	51	250	
		Wages Payable	22		250
		Accrued wages.			

Accounting Equation Impact

Assets = **Liabilities** + **Owner's Equity (Expense)**

Wages Payable			**22**
		Dec. 31	250

Wages Expense		**51**
Bal.	4,275	
Dec. 31	250	
Adj. Bal.	4,525	

After the adjusting entry is recorded and posted, the debit balance of the wages expense account is $4,525. This balance of $4,525 is the wages expense for two months, November and December. The credit balance of $250 in Wages Payable is the liability for wages owed on December 31.

As shown in Exhibit 5, NetSolutions paid wages of $1,275 on January 10. This payment includes the $250 of accrued wages recorded on December 31. Thus, on January 10, the wages payable account is decreased (debited) by $250. Also, the wages expense account is increased (debited) by $1,025 ($1,275 – $250), which is the wages expense for January 1–10. Finally, the cash account is decreased (credited) by $1,275. The journal entry for the payment of wages on January 10 follows:[5]

Jan.	10	Wages Expense	51	1,025	
		Wages Payable	22	250	
		Cash	11		1,275

5 To simplify the subsequent recording of the following period's transactions, some accountants use what is known as reversing entries for certain types of adjustments. Reversing entries are discussed and illustrated in an online appendix at Cengage.com.

If the adjustment for wages ($250) is not recorded, Wages Expense will be understated by $250, and the net income will be overstated by $250 on the income statement. On the balance sheet, liabilities (Wages Payable) will be understated by $250, and owner's equity (Chris Clark, Capital) will be overstated by $250. The effects of omitting this adjusting entry are as follows:

Link to Pandora

On a recent balance sheet, **Pandora** reported accrued content acquisition costs (a payable) of $97.8 million, which it pays to owners of the music it plays.

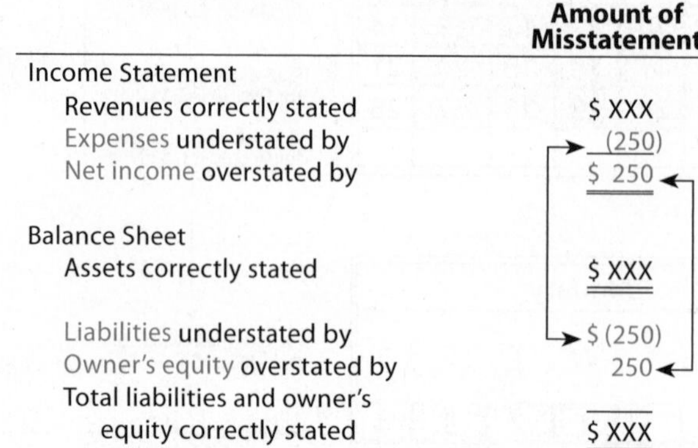

	Amount of Misstatement
Income Statement	
Revenues correctly stated	$ XXX
Expenses understated by	(250)
Net income overstated by	$ 250
Balance Sheet	
Assets correctly stated	$ XXX
Liabilities understated by	$ (250)
Owner's equity overstated by	250
Total liabilities and owner's equity correctly stated	$ XXX

EXAMPLE EXERCISE 3-4 Adjustment for Accrued Expense **OBJ. 2**

Sanregret Realty Co. pays weekly salaries of $12,500 on Friday for a five-day week ending on that day. Journalize the necessary adjusting entry at the end of the accounting period, assuming that the period ends on Thursday.

Follow My Example 3-4

Salaries Expense	10,000	
Salaries Payable		10,000
Accrued salaries [($12,500 ÷ 5 days) × 4 days].		

Practice Exercises: PE 3-4A, PE 3-4B

Business Connection

EARNING REVENUES FROM SEASON TICKETS

Madison Square Garden Company owns the New York Knicks basketball team and the New York Rangers hockey team. The company sells season tickets prior to the season. The amounts received for season tickets are recognized as unearned revenue, a current liability. Madison Square Garden recognizes revenue and reduces unearned revenue as the games are played through the season.

OBJ. 3 Prepare adjusting entries for deferrals.

Adjusting Entries for Deferrals

The unadjusted trial balance for **NetSolutions** in Exhibit 3 indicates Unearned Rent of $360. In addition, Exhibit 3 indicates that NetSolutions has prepaid assets consisting of Supplies of $2,000 and Prepaid Insurance of $2,400. Each of these deferrals requires an adjusting entry.

Unearned Revenues

The December 31 unadjusted trial balance of **NetSolutions** indicates a balance in the unearned rent account of $360. This balance represents the receipt of three months' rent on December 1 for December, January, and February. At the end of December, one month's rent has been earned. Thus, the unearned rent account is decreased (debited) by $120, and the rent revenue account is increased (credited) by $120. The $120 represents the rental revenue for one month ($360 ÷ 3). The adjusting journal entry and T accounts are as follows:

Adjusting Journal Entry

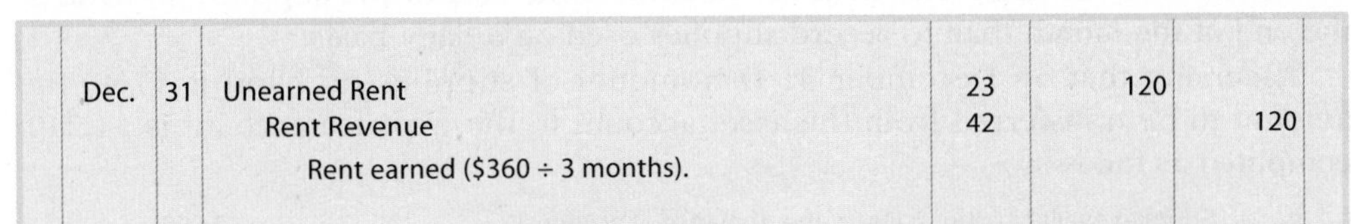

Dec.	31	Unearned Rent	23	120	
		Rent Revenue	42		120
		Rent earned ($360 ÷ 3 months).			

Accounting Equation Impact

Assets = Liabilities + Owner's Equity (Revenue)

Unearned Rent			23
Dec. 31	120	Bal.	360
		Adj. Bal.	240

Rent Revenue			42
		Dec. 31	120

After the adjusting entry is recorded and posted, the unearned rent account has a credit balance of $240. This balance is a liability that will become revenue in a future period. Rent Revenue has a balance of $120, which is revenue earned during the current period.

If the preceding adjustment of unearned rent and rent revenue is not recorded, the financial statements prepared on December 31 will be misstated. On the income statement, Rent Revenue and the net income will be understated by $120. On the balance sheet, liabilities (Unearned Rent) will be overstated by $120, and owner's equity (Chris Clark, Capital) will be understated by $120. The effects of omitting this adjusting entry are as follows:

> **Link to Pandora**
>
> On a recent balance sheet, **Pandora** reported unearned (deferred) revenue of $31.5 million.

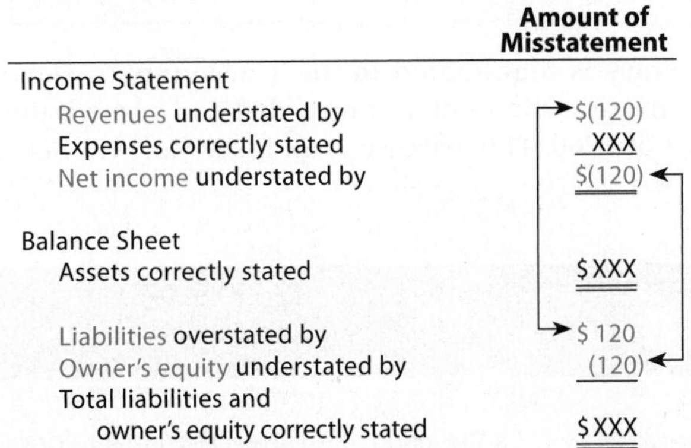

	Amount of Misstatement
Income Statement	
Revenues understated by	$(120)
Expenses correctly stated	XXX
Net income understated by	$(120)
Balance Sheet	
Assets correctly stated	$ XXX
Liabilities overstated by	$ 120
Owner's equity understated by	(120)
Total liabilities and owner's equity correctly stated	$ XXX

EXAMPLE EXERCISE 3-5 Adjustment for Unearned Revenue — OBJ. 3

The balance in the unearned fees account, before adjustment at the end of the year, is $44,900. Journalize the adjusting entry required if the amount of unearned fees at the end of the year is $12,300.

Follow My Example 3-5

Unearned Fees	32,600	
Fees Earned		32,600
Fees earned ($44,900 – $12,300).		

Practice Exercises: PE 3-5A, PE 3-5B

Prepaid Expenses

The December 31, 20Y3, unadjusted trial balance of **NetSolutions** indicates a balance in the supplies account of $2,000. In addition, the prepaid insurance account has a balance of $2,400. Each of these accounts requires an adjusting entry.

Supplies The balance in NetSolutions' supplies account on December 31 is $2,000. Some of these supplies (paper and envelopes, for example) were used during December, and some are still on hand (not used). If either amount is known, the other can be determined. It is normally easier to determine the cost of the supplies on hand at the end of the month than to record supplies used on a daily basis.

Assuming that on December 31 the amount of supplies on hand is $760, the amount to be transferred from the asset account to the expense account is $1,240, computed as follows:

Supplies available during December (balance of account)	$2,000
Supplies on hand, December 31	760
Supplies used (amount of adjustment)	$1,240

At the end of December, the supplies expense account is increased (debited) for $1,240, and the supplies account is decreased (credited) for $1,240 to record the supplies used during December. The adjusting journal entry and T accounts for Supplies and Supplies Expense are as follows:

Adjusting Journal Entry

Dec.	31	Supplies Expense	52	1,240	
		Supplies	14		1,240
		Supplies used ($2,000 – $760).			

Accounting Equation Impact

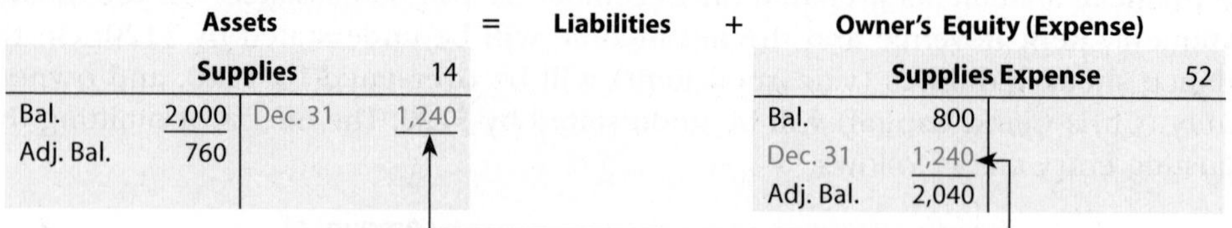

Assets = Liabilities + Owner's Equity (Expense)

Supplies			14
Bal.	2,000	Dec. 31	1,240
Adj. Bal.	760		

Supplies Expense		52
Bal.	800	
Dec. 31	1,240	
Adj. Bal.	2,040	

The adjusting entry is highlighted in the T accounts to separate it from other transactions. After the adjusting entry is recorded and posted, the supplies account has a debit balance of $760. This balance is an asset that will become an expense in a future period.

Business Connection

SPORTS SIGNING BONUS

The **National Football League** (NFL), **National Basketball Association** (NBA), and **National Hockey League** (NHL) all have team salary caps that are used to create parity in the sport league. The salary cap limits the total salaries that a team can pay each year. Teams use signing bonuses as a way to reduce the impact of salaries on the salary cap. Under cap rules, the bonus is spread over the length of the player's contract. For example, if a player receives a $6 million bonus for a six-year contract, the player will receive the complete $6 million upon signing the contract, but only $1 million will be applied to the salary cap for each year of the contract. This is similar to how GAAP accounts for the bonus. The bonus is treated as a prepaid salary expense that is amortized over the life of the contract. If a player is released prior to the end of the contract, any remaining unamortized balance is expensed immediately.

Prepaid Insurance The debit balance of $2,400 in **NetSolutions**' prepaid insurance account represents a December 1 prepayment of insurance for 12 months. At the end of December, the insurance expense account is increased (debited) and the prepaid insurance account is decreased (credited) by $200, the insurance for one month. The adjusting journal entry and T accounts for Prepaid Insurance and Insurance Expense are as follows:

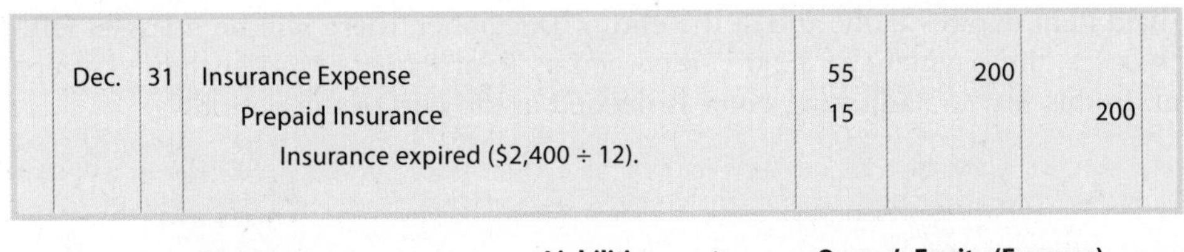

Dec.	31	Insurance Expense	55	200	
		Prepaid Insurance	15		200
		Insurance expired ($2,400 ÷ 12).			

Adjusting Journal Entry

Assets = **Liabilities** + **Owner's Equity (Expense)**

Prepaid Insurance		15	
Bal.	2,400	Dec. 31	200
Adj. Bal.	2,200		

Insurance Expense		55
Dec. 31	200	

Accounting Equation Impact

After the adjusting entry is recorded and posted, the prepaid insurance account has a debit balance of $2,200. This balance is an asset that will become an expense in future periods. The insurance expense account has a debit balance of $200, which is an expense of the current period.

If the preceding adjustments for supplies ($1,240) and insurance ($200) are not recorded, the financial statements prepared as of December 31 will be misstated. On the income statement, Supplies Expense and Insurance Expense will be understated by a total of $1,440 ($1,240 + $200), and net income will be overstated by $1,440. On the balance sheet, Supplies and Prepaid Insurance will be overstated by a total of $1,440. Because net income increases owner's equity, Chris Clark, Capital will also be overstated by $1,440 on the balance sheet. The effects of omitting these adjusting entries on the income statement and balance sheet are as follows:

Link to Pandora

On a recent balance sheet, **Pandora** reported prepaid expenses and other current assets of $19 million.

	Amount of Misstatement
Income Statement	
Revenues correctly stated	$ XXX
Expenses understated by	(1,440)
Net income overstated by	$1,440
Balance Sheet	
Assets overstated by	$1,440
Liabilities correctly stated	$ XXX
Owner's equity overstated by	1,440
Total liabilities and owner's equity overstated by	$1,440

Integrity, Objectivity, and Ethics in Business

FREE ISSUE

Office supplies are often available to employees on a "free issue" basis. This means that employees do not have to "sign" for the release of office supplies but merely obtain the necessary supplies from a local storage area as needed. Just because supplies are easily available, however, doesn't mean they can be taken for personal use. There are many instances where employees have been terminated for taking supplies home for personal use.

Payments for prepaid expenses are sometimes made at the beginning of the period in which they will be *entirely used or consumed*. To illustrate, the following December 1 transaction of NetSolutions is used:

Dec. 1 NetSolutions paid rent of $800 for the month.

On December 1, the rent payment of $800 represents Prepaid Rent. However, the Prepaid Rent expires daily, and at the end of December, there will be no asset left. In such cases, the payment of $800 is recorded as Rent Expense rather than as Prepaid Rent. In this way, no adjusting entry is needed at the end of the period.

EXAMPLE EXERCISE 3-6 Adjustment for Prepaid Expense OBJ. 3

The prepaid insurance account had a beginning balance of $2,400 and was debited for $3,600 of additional premiums paid during the year. Journalize the adjusting entry required at the end of the year, assuming the amount of unexpired insurance related to future periods is $3,250.

Follow My Example 3-6

Insurance Expense	2,750	
Prepaid Insurance		2,750
Insurance expired ($2,400 + $3,600 – $3,250).		

Practice Exercises: PE 3-6A, PE 3-6B

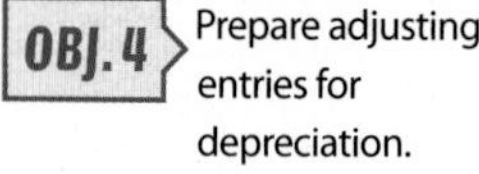

Prepare adjusting entries for depreciation.

Adjusting Entries for Depreciation

Fixed assets, or **plant assets**, are physical resources that are owned and used by a business and are permanent or have a long life. Examples of fixed assets include land, buildings, and equipment. In a sense, fixed assets are a type of *long-term* prepaid expense. However, because of their normally high dollar amount and long life, they are discussed separately from other prepaid expenses.

Fixed assets, such as office equipment, are used to generate revenue much like supplies are used to generate revenue. Unlike supplies, however, there is no visible reduction in the quantity of the equipment. Instead, as time passes, the equipment loses its ability to provide useful services. This decrease in usefulness is called **depreciation**.

All fixed assets, except land, lose their usefulness and, thus, are said to **depreciate**. As a fixed asset depreciates, a portion of its cost should be recorded as an expense. This periodic expense is called **depreciation expense**.

The adjusting entry to record depreciation expense is similar to the adjusting entry for supplies used. The depreciation expense account is increased (debited) for the amount of depreciation. However, the fixed asset account is not decreased (credited). This is because both the original cost of a fixed asset and the depreciation recorded since its purchase are reported on the balance sheet. Instead, an account entitled **Accumulated Depreciation** is increased (credited).

Accumulated depreciation accounts are called **contra accounts**, or **contra asset accounts**. This is because accumulated depreciation accounts are deducted from their related fixed asset accounts on the balance sheet. The normal balance of a contra account is opposite the account from which it is deducted. Because the normal balance of a fixed asset account is a debit, the normal balance of an accumulated depreciation account is a credit.

The normal titles for fixed asset accounts and their related contra asset accounts are as follows:

Fixed Asset Account	Contra Asset Account
Land	None—Land is not depreciated.
Buildings	Accumulated Depreciation—Buildings
Store Equipment	Accumulated Depreciation—Store Equipment
Office Equipment	Accumulated Depreciation—Office Equipment

The December 31, 20Y3, unadjusted trial balance of **NetSolutions** (Exhibit 3) indicates that NetSolutions owns two fixed assets: land and office equipment. Land does not depreciate and therefore does not have a contra account or an adjusting entry. Office equipment, however, does depreciate and requires an adjusting entry. Assume that the office equipment depreciates $50 during December. The depreciation expense account is increased (debited) by $50, and the contra account Accumulated Depreciation—Office Equipment is increased (credited) by $50.[6] The adjusting journal entry and T accounts are as follows:

Adjusting Journal Entry

Dec.	31	Depreciation Expense	56	50	
		Accumulated Depreciation—Office Equip.	19		50
		Depreciation on office equipment.			

Accounting Equation Impact

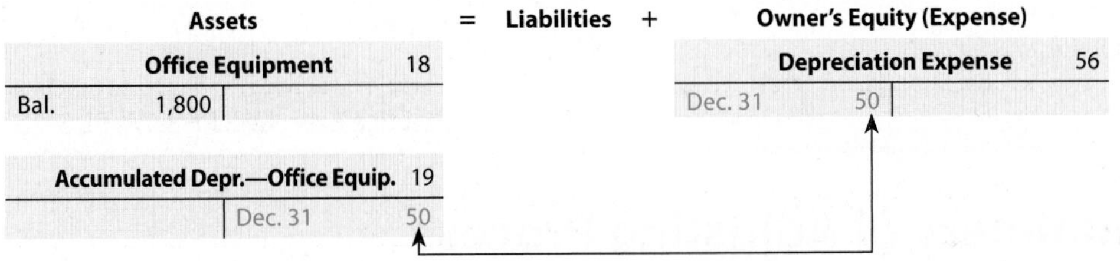

After the adjusting journal entry is recorded and posted, the office equipment account still has a debit balance of $1,800. This is the original cost of the office equipment that was purchased on December 4. The accumulated depreciation—office equipment account has a credit balance of $50. The difference between these two balances is the cost of the office equipment that has not yet been depreciated. This amount, called the **book value of the asset** (or **net book value**), is computed as follows:

Book Value of Asset = Cost of Asset – Accumulated Depreciation of Asset

Thus, the book value of NetSolutions' office equipment at the end of December is $1,750 ($1,800 – $50). The office equipment and its related accumulated depreciation are reported on the December 31, 20Y3, balance sheet as follows:

Office equipment	$1,800	
Less accumulated depreciation	50	$1,750

The market value of a fixed asset usually differs from its book value. This is because depreciation is an *allocation* method, not a *valuation* method. That is, depreciation allocates the cost of a fixed asset to expense over its estimated life. Depreciation does not measure changes in market values, which vary from year to year. Thus, on December 31, 20Y3, the market value of NetSolutions' office equipment could be more or less than $1,750.

If the adjustment for depreciation ($50) is not recorded, Depreciation Expense on the income statement will be understated by $50, and the net income will be overstated by $50. On the balance sheet, assets (the book value of Office Equipment) and

Link to Pandora

On a recent balance sheet, **Pandora** reported property, plant, and equipment of $248 million, accumulated depreciation of $131 million, and a net book value of $117 million.

6 Methods of computing depreciation expense are described and illustrated in Chapter 10.

owner's equity (Chris Clark, Capital) will be overstated by $50. The effects of omitting the adjustment for depreciation are as follows:

	Amount of Misstatement
Income Statement	
Revenues correctly stated	$ XX
Expenses understated by	(50)
Net income overstated by	$ 50
Balance Sheet	
Assets overstated by	$ 50
Liabilities correctly stated	$ XX
Owner's equity overstated by	50
Total liabilities and owner's equity overstated by	$ 50

EXAMPLE EXERCISE 3-7 Adjustment for Depreciation

OBJ. 4

The estimated amount of depreciation on equipment for the current year is $4,250. Journalize the adjusting entry to record the depreciation.

Follow My Example 3-7

Depreciation Expense	4,250	
Accumulated Depreciation—Equipment		4,250
Depreciation on equipment.		

Practice Exercises: PE 3-7A, PE 3-7B

OBJ. 5 Summarize the adjusting process.

Summary of Adjusting Process

A summary of the basic types of adjusting entries is shown in Exhibit 6. The adjusting entries for **NetSolutions** are shown in Exhibit 7. The adjusting entries are dated as of the last day of the period. However, because collecting the adjustment data requires time, the entries are usually recorded at a later date. An explanation is normally included with each adjusting entry.

NetSolutions' adjusting entries are posted to the ledger shown in Exhibit 8. The adjustments are highlighted in Exhibit 8 to distinguish them from other transactions.

Business Connection

MICROSOFT'S DEFERRED REVENUES

Microsoft Corporation develops, manufactures, licenses, and supports a wide range of computer software products, including Windows® operating systems, Word®, Excel®, and the Xbox® gaming system. When Microsoft sells its products, it incurs an obligation to support its software with technical support and periodic updates. As a result, not all the revenue is earned on the date of sale; some of the revenue on the date of sale is unearned. The portion of revenue related to support services, such as updates and technical support, is earned as time passes and support is provided to customers. Thus, each year Microsoft makes adjusting entries transferring some of its unearned revenue to revenue. The following were taken from recent financial statements of Microsoft:

	Year 2	Year 1
Unearned revenue (in millions)	$32,720	$26,656

During Year 3, Microsoft expects to recognize $28,905 of revenue from the $32,720 of unearned revenue, which will have a significant impact on its operating results. At the same time, Microsoft will record additional unearned revenue from Year 3 sales.

Summary of Adjustments — EXHIBIT 6

Examples	Reason for Adjustment	Adjusting Entry			Examples from NetSolutions			Financial Statement Impact if Adjusting Entry Is Omitted	
ACCRUED REVENUES									
Services performed but not billed, interest to be received	Services have been provided to the customer but have not been billed or recorded. Interest has been earned but has not been received or recorded.	Asset Revenue	Dr.	 Cr.	Accounts Receivable Fees Earned	500	 500	Income Statement: Revenues Expenses Net income Balance Sheet: Assets Liabilities Owner's equity (Owner's Capital)	 Understated No effect Understated Understated No effect Understated
ACCRUED EXPENSES									
Wages or salaries incurred but not paid, interest incurred but not paid	Expenses have been incurred, but have not been paid or recorded.	Expense Liability	Dr.	 Cr.	Wages Expense Wages Payable	250	 250	Income Statement: Revenues Expenses Net income Balance Sheet: Assets Liabilities Owner's equity (Owner's Capital)	 No effect Understated Overstated No effect Understated Overstated
UNEARNED REVENUES									
Unearned rent, magazine subscriptions received in advance, fees received in advance of services	Cash received before the services have been provided is recorded as a liability. Some services have been provided to the customer before the end of the accounting period.	Liability Revenue	Dr.	 Cr.	Unearned Rent Rent Revenue	120	 120	Income Statement: Revenues Expenses Net income Balance Sheet: Assets Liabilities Owner's equity (Owner's Capital)	 Understated No effect Understated No effect Overstated Understated
PREPAID EXPENSES									
Supplies, prepaid insurance	Prepaid expenses (assets) have been used or consumed in the business operations.	Expense Asset	Dr.	 Cr.	Supplies Expense Supplies Insurance Expense Prepaid Insurance	1,240 200	 1,240 200	Income Statement: Revenues Expenses Net income Balance Sheet: Assets Liabilities Owner's equity (Owner's Capital)	 No effect Understated Overstated Overstated No effect Overstated
DEPRECIATION									
Depreciation of equipment and buildings	Fixed assets depreciate as they are used or consumed in the business operations.	Expense Contra Asset	Dr.	 Cr.	Depreciation Expense Accum. Depr.—Office Equipment	50	 50	Income Statement: Revenues Expenses Net income Balance Sheet: Assets Liabilities Owner's equity (Owner's Capital)	 No effect Understated Overstated Overstated No effect Overstated

EXHIBIT 7

Adjusting Entries—NetSolutions

Journal *Page 5*

Date		Description	Post. Ref.	Debit	Credit
20Y3		Adjusting Entries			
Dec.	31	Accounts Receivable	12	500	
		Fees Earned	41		500
		Accrued fees (25 hrs. × $20).			
	31	Wages Expense	51	250	
		Wages Payable	22		250
		Accrued wages.			
	31	Unearned Rent	23	120	
		Rent Revenue	42		120
		Rent earned ($360 ÷ 3 months).			
	31	Supplies Expense	52	1,240	
		Supplies	14		1,240
		Supplies used ($2,000 – $760).			
	31	Insurance Expense	55	200	
		Prepaid Insurance	15		200
		Insurance expired ($2,400 ÷ 12 months).			
	31	Depreciation Expense	56	50	
		Accum. Depreciation—Office Equipment	19		50
		Depreciation on office equipment.			

EXHIBIT 8 **Ledger with Adjusting Entries—NetSolutions**

Account *Cash* *Account No. 11*

Date	Item	Post. Ref.	Debit	Credit	Balance Debit	Balance Credit
20Y3						
Nov. 1		1	25,000		25,000	
5		1		20,000	5,000	
18		1	7,500		12,500	
30		1		3,650	8,850	
30		1		950	7,900	
30		2		2,000	5,900	
Dec. 1		2		2,400	3,500	
1		2		800	2,700	
1		2	360		3,060	
6		2		180	2,880	
11		2		400	2,480	
13		3		950	1,530	
16		3	3,100		4,630	
20		3		900	3,730	
21		3	650		4,380	
23		3		1,450	2,930	
27		3		1,200	1,730	
31		3		310	1,420	
31		4		225	1,195	
31		4	2,870		4,065	
31		4		2,000	2,065	

Account *Accounts Receivable* *Account No. 12*

Date	Item	Post. Ref.	Debit	Credit	Balance Debit	Balance Credit
20Y3						
Dec. 16		3	1,750		1,750	
21		3		650	1,100	
31		4	1,120		2,220	
31	Adjusting	5	500		2,720	

Account *Supplies* Account No. 14

Date	Item	Post. Ref.	Debit	Credit	Balance Debit	Balance Credit
20Y3						
Nov. 10		1	1,350		1,350	
30		1		800	550	
Dec. 23		3	1,450		2,000	
31	Adjusting	5		1,240	760	

Ledger with Adjusting Entries—NetSolutions *(Continued)* EXHIBIT 8

Account *Prepaid Insurance* — Account No. 15

Date	Item	Post. Ref.	Debit	Credit	Balance Debit	Balance Credit
20Y3						
Dec. 1		2	2,400		2,400	
31	Adjusting	5		200	2,200	

Account *Land* — Account No. 17

Date	Item	Post. Ref.	Debit	Credit	Balance Debit	Balance Credit
20Y3						
Nov. 5		1	20,000		20,000	

Account *Office Equipment* — Account No. 18

Date	Item	Post. Ref.	Debit	Credit	Balance Debit	Balance Credit
20Y3						
Dec. 4		2	1,800		1,800	

Account *Accum. Depr.—Office Equip.* — Account No. 19

Date	Item	Post. Ref.	Debit	Credit	Balance Debit	Balance Credit
20Y3						
Dec. 31	Adjusting	5		50		50

Account *Accounts Payable* — Account No. 21

Date	Item	Post. Ref.	Debit	Credit	Balance Debit	Balance Credit
20Y3						
Nov. 10		1		1,350		1,350
30		1	950			400
Dec. 4		2		1,800		2,200
11		2	400			1,800
20		3	900			900

Account *Wages Payable* — Account No. 22

Date	Item	Post. Ref.	Debit	Credit	Balance Debit	Balance Credit
20Y3						
Dec. 31	Adjusting	5		250		250

Account *Unearned Rent* — Account No. 23

Date	Item	Post. Ref.	Debit	Credit	Balance Debit	Balance Credit
20Y3						
Dec. 1		2		360		360
31	Adjusting	5	120			240

Account *Chris Clark, Capital* — Account No. 31

Date	Item	Post. Ref.	Debit	Credit	Balance Debit	Balance Credit
20Y3						
Nov. 1		1		25,000		25,000

Account *Chris Clark, Drawing* — Account No. 32

Date	Item	Post. Ref.	Debit	Credit	Balance Debit	Balance Credit
20Y3						
Nov. 30		2	2,000		2,000	
Dec. 31		4	2,000		4,000	

Account *Fees Earned* — Account No. 41

Date	Item	Post. Ref.	Debit	Credit	Balance Debit	Balance Credit
20Y3						
Nov. 18		1		7,500		7,500
Dec. 16		3		3,100		10,600
16		3		1,750		12,350
31		4		2,870		15,220
31		4		1,120		16,340
31	Adjusting	5		500		16,840

Account *Rent Revenue* — Account No. 42

Date	Item	Post. Ref.	Debit	Credit	Balance Debit	Balance Credit
20Y3						
Dec. 31	Adjusting	5		120		120

Account *Wages Expense* — Account No. 51

Date	Item	Post. Ref.	Debit	Credit	Balance Debit	Balance Credit
20Y3						
Nov. 30		1	2,125		2,125	
Dec. 13		3	950		3,075	
27		3	1,200		4,275	
31	Adjusting	5	250		4,525	

(Continued)

EXHIBIT 8 **Ledger with Adjusting Entries—NetSolutions (*Concluded*)**

Account *Supplies Expense* — Account No. *52*

Date	Item	Post. Ref.	Debit	Credit	Balance Debit	Balance Credit
20Y3						
Nov. 30		1	800		800	
Dec. 31	Adjusting	5	1,240		2,040	

Account *Rent Expense* — Account No. *53*

Date	Item	Post. Ref.	Debit	Credit	Balance Debit	Balance Credit
20Y3						
Nov. 30		1	800		800	
Dec. 1		2	800		1,600	

Account *Utilities Expense* — Account No. *54*

Date	Item	Post. Ref.	Debit	Credit	Balance Debit	Balance Credit
20Y3						
Nov. 30		1	450		450	
Dec. 31		3	310		760	
31		4	225		985	

Account *Insurance Expense* — Account No. *55*

Date	Item	Post. Ref.	Debit	Credit	Balance Debit	Balance Credit
20Y3						
Dec. 31	Adjusting	5	200		200	

Account *Depreciation Expense* — Account No. *56*

Date	Item	Post. Ref.	Debit	Credit	Balance Debit	Balance Credit
20Y3						
Dec. 31	Adjusting	5	50		50	

Account *Miscellaneous Expense* — Account No. *59*

Date	Item	Post. Ref.	Debit	Credit	Balance Debit	Balance Credit
20Y3						
Nov. 30		1	275		275	
Dec. 6		2	180		455	

EXAMPLE EXERCISE 3-8 Effects of Omitting Adjustments **OBJ. 5**

For the year ending December 31, 20Y5, Mann Medical Co. mistakenly omitted adjusting entries for (1) $8,600 of unearned revenue that was earned, (2) earned revenue of $12,500 that was not billed, and (3) accrued wages of $2,900. Indicate the combined effect of the errors on (a) revenues, (b) expenses, and (c) net income for the year ended December 31, 20Y5.

Follow My Example 3-8

a. Revenues were understated by $21,100 ($8,600 + $12,500).
b. Expenses were understated by $2,900.
b. Net income was understated by $18,200 ($8,600 + $12,500 – $2,900).

Practice Exercises: PE 3-8A, PE 3-8B

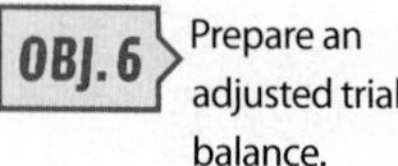
Prepare an adjusted trial balance.

Adjusted Trial Balance

After the adjusting entries are posted, an **adjusted trial balance** is prepared. The adjusted trial balance verifies the equality of the total debit and credit balances before the financial statements are prepared. If the adjusted trial balance does not balance, an error has occurred. However, as discussed in Chapter 2, errors may occur even though the adjusted trial balance totals agree. For example, if an adjusting entry were omitted, the adjusted trial balance totals would still agree.

Exhibit 9 shows the adjusted trial balance for **NetSolutions** as of December 31, 20Y3. Chapter 4 discusses how financial statements, including a classified balance sheet, are prepared from an adjusted trial balance.

EXHIBIT 9

Adjusted Trial Balance

NetSolutions
Adjusted Trial Balance
December 31, 20Y3

	Account No.	Debit Balances	Credit Balances
Cash	11	2,065	
Accounts Receivable	12	2,720	
Supplies	14	760	
Prepaid Insurance	15	2,200	
Land	17	20,000	
Office Equipment	18	1,800	
Accumulated Depreciation—Office Equipment	19		50
Accounts Payable	21		900
Wages Payable	22		250
Unearned Rent	23		240
Chris Clark, Capital	31		25,000
Chris Clark, Drawing	32	4,000	
Fees Earned	41		16,840
Rent Revenue	42		120
Wages Expense	51	4,525	
Supplies Expense	52	2,040	
Rent Expense	53	1,600	
Utilities Expense	54	985	
Insurance Expense	55	200	
Depreciation Expense	56	50	
Miscellaneous Expense	59	455	
		43,400	43,400

EXAMPLE EXERCISE 3-9 Effect of Errors on Adjusted Trial Balance **OBJ. 6**

For each of the following errors, considered individually, indicate whether the error would cause the adjusted trial balance totals to be unequal. If the error would cause the adjusted trial balance totals to be unequal, indicate whether the debit or credit total is higher and by how much.

a. The adjustment for accrued fees of $5,340 was journalized as a debit to Accounts Payable for $5,340 and a credit to Fees Earned of $5,340.

b. The adjustment for depreciation of $3,260 was journalized as a debit to Depreciation Expense for $3,620 and a credit to Accumulated Depreciation for $3,260.

Follow My Example 3-9

a. The totals are equal even though the debit should have been to Accounts Receivable instead of Accounts Payable.

b. The totals are unequal. The debit total is higher by $360 ($3,620 – $3,260).

Practice Exercises: PE 3-9A, PE 3-9B

Financial Analysis and Interpretation: Vertical Analysis

OBJ. 7 Describe and illustrate the use of vertical analysis in evaluating a company's performance and financial condition.

Comparing each item on a financial statement with a total amount from the same statement is useful in analyzing relationships within the financial statement. **Vertical analysis** is the term used to describe such comparisons.

In vertical analysis of a balance sheet, each asset item is stated as a percent of the total assets. Each liability and owner's equity item is stated as a percent of total liabilities and owner's equity. In vertical analysis of an income statement, each item is stated as a percent of revenues or fees earned.

Vertical analysis is also useful for analyzing changes in financial statements over time. To illustrate, a vertical analysis of two years of income statements for J. Holmes, Attorney-at-Law, follows:

J. Holmes, Attorney-at-Law
Income Statements
For the Years Ended December 31

	20Y8		20Y7	
	Amount	**Percent***	**Amount**	**Percent***
Fees earned	$187,500	100.0%	$150,000	100.0%
Operating expenses:				
Wages expense	$ 60,000	32.0%	$ 45,000	30.0%
Rent expense	15,000	8.0%	12,000	8.0%
Utilities expense	12,500	6.7%	9,000	6.0%
Supplies expense	2,700	1.4%	3,000	2.0%
Miscellaneous expense	2,300	1.2%	1,800	1.2%
Total operating expenses	$ 92,500	49.3%	$ 70,800	47.2%
Net income	$ 95,000	50.7%	$ 79,200	52.8%

*Rounded to one decimal place

The preceding vertical analysis indicates both favorable and unfavorable trends affecting the income statement of J. Holmes, Attorney-at-Law. The increase in 20Y8 in wages expense of 2.0% (32.0% − 30.0%) is an unfavorable trend, as is the increase in utilities expense of 0.7% (6.7% − 6.0%). A favorable trend is the decrease in supplies expense of 0.6% (2.0% − 1.4%). Rent expense and miscellaneous expense as a percent of fees earned were constant. The net result of these trends is that net income decreased as a percent of fees earned from 52.8% in 20Y7 to 50.7% in 20Y8.

The analysis of the various percentages shown for J. Holmes, Attorney-at-Law, can be enhanced by comparisons with industry averages. Such averages are published by trade associations and financial information services. Any major differences between industry averages should be investigated.

A vertical analysis of operating income taken from two recent years of income statements for **Pandora Media, Inc.** follows:

Pandora Media, Inc.
Operating Income Statements
For the Years Ended December 31
(in thousands)

	Year 2		Year 1	
	Amount	**Percent***	**Amount**	**Percent***
Revenues:				
Advertising	$1,074,927	73.3%	$1,072,490	77.4%
Subscription	315,853	21.5%	225,786	16.3%
Ticketing service	76,032	5.2%	86,550	6.3%
Total revenues	$1,466,812	100.0%	$1,384,826	100.0%
Expenses:				
Cost of revenues	$ 967,067	65.9%	$ 896,350	64.7%
Sales and marketing	492,542	33.6%	490,364	35.4%
General and administrative	190,711	13.0%	176,164	12.7%
Product development	154,325	10.5%	140,707	10.2%
Other	155,041	10.6%	—	—
Total expenses	$1,959,686	133.6%	$ 1,703,585	123.0%
Income (loss) from operations	$ (492,874)	(33.6)%	$ (318,759)	(23.0)%

*Rounded to one decimal place

The preceding illustration shows the usefulness of vertical analysis. Since Year 2 revenues are significantly larger than those of Year 1, it is difficult to compare operating results using only dollar amounts. Vertical analysis, however, provides a relative comparison. The analysis reveals that the operating loss increased from 23.0% to 33.6% as a percent of total revenues. This significant decline was the result of the net change in expenses as a percent of revenue. The cost of revenues increased from 64.7% to 65.9% of revenues. General and administrative and product development expenses also increased as a percent of sales. The percentage increase in these expenses was less than the percentage decrease in sales and marketing expenses. Thus, total expenses increased from 123.0% to 133.6% as a percent of revenues.

EXAMPLE EXERCISE 3-10 Vertical Analysis

OBJ. 7

Two income statements for Fortson Company follow:

Fortson Company
Income Statements
For the Years Ended December 31

	20Y2	20Y1
Fees earned	$425,000	$375,000
Operating expenses	263,500	210,000
Income from operations	$161,500	$165,000

a. Prepare a vertical analysis of Fortson Company's income statements.

b. Does the vertical analysis indicate a favorable or an unfavorable change?

Follow My Example 3-10

a.

Fortson Company
Income Statements
For the Years Ended December 31

	20Y2		20Y1	
	Amount	**Percent**	**Amount**	**Percent**
Fees earned	$425,000	100%	$375,000	100%
Operating expenses	263,500	62	210,000	56
Income from operations	$161,500	38%	$165,000	44%

b. An unfavorable change of increasing operating expenses and decreasing income from operations is indicated.

Practice Exercises: PE 3-10A, PE 3-10B

At a Glance 3

OBJ. 1 Describe the nature of the adjusting process.

Key Points The accrual basis of accounting requires that revenues be reported in the period in which they are earned and expenses be matched with the revenues they generate. The updating of accounts at the end of the accounting period is called the adjusting process. Each adjusting entry affects an income statement and balance sheet account. The two general classifications for accounts requiring adjustment are accruals and deferrals. Accruals include accrued revenues and accrued expenses. Deferrals include unearned revenues and prepaid expenses.

Learning Outcomes	*Example Exercises*	*Practice Exercises*
• Explain why accrual accounting requires adjusting entries.		
• Describe the revenue and expense recognition principles.		
• List accounts that do and do *not* require adjusting entries at the end of the accounting period.	**EE3-1**	**PE3-1A, 3-1B**
• Give an example of accrued revenue, accrued expense, deferrred (unearned) revenue, and deferred (prepaid) expense.	**EE3-2**	**PE3-2A, 3-2B**

OBJ. 2 Prepare adjusting entries for accruals.

Key Points Adjusting entries for accruals include accrued revenues and expenses. The adjusting entry for an accrued revenue debits an asset such as Accounts Receivable and credits a revenue account such as Fees Earned. The adjusting entry for an accrued expense debits an expense account such as Wages Expense and credits a liability account such as Wages Payable.

Learning Outcomes	*Example Exercises*	*Practice Exercises*
• Prepare an adjusting entry for an accrued revenue.	**EE3-3**	**PE3-3A, 3-3B**
• Prepare an adjusting entry for an accrued expense.	**EE3-4**	**PE3-4A, 3-4B**

OBJ. 3 Prepare adjusting entries for deferrals.

Key Points Adjusting entries for deferrals include unearned revenues and prepaid expenses. The adjusting entry for an unearned revenue debits an unearned revenue account such as Unearned Rent and credits a revenue account such as Rent Revenue. The adjusting entry for a prepaid expense debits an expense account such as Insurance Expense and credits an asset account such as Prepaid Insurance.

Learning Outcomes	*Example Exercises*	*Practice Exercises*
• Prepare an adjusting entry for an unearned revenue.	**EE3-5**	**PE3-5A, 3-5B**
• Prepare an adjusting entry for a prepaid expense.	**EE3-6**	**PE3-6A, 3-6B**

OBJ. 4 Prepare adjusting entries for depreciation.

Key Points The adjusting entry for depreciation of a fixed asset debits Depreciation Expense and credits a contra asset account, Accumulated Depreciation. The book value of a fixed asset equals its cost less its accumulated depreciation. Land is a fixed asset that does not depreciate.

Learning Outcomes	Example Exercises	Practice Exercises
• Describe assets that require the recording of an adjusting entry for depreciation.		
• Prepare an adjusting entry for depreciation expense.	EE3-7	PE3-7A, 3-7B

OBJ. 5 Summarize the adjusting process.

Key Points A summary of adjustments, including the type of adjustment, reason for the adjustment, the adjusting entry, and the effect of omitting an adjustment on the financial statements, is shown in Exhibit 6.

Learning Outcomes	Example Exercises	Practice Exercises
• Determine the effect on the income statement and balance sheet of omitting an adjusting entry for a prepaid expense, an unearned revenue, an accrued revenue, an accrued expense, and depreciation.	EE3-8	PE3-8A, 3-8B

OBJ. 6 Prepare an adjusted trial balance.

Key Points After all of the adjusting entries have been posted, the equality of the total debit balances and the total credit balances is verified using an adjusted trial balance.

Learning Outcomes	Example Exercises	Practice Exercises
• Prepare an adjusted trial balance.		
• Determine the effect of errors on the equality of the adjusted trial balance.	EE3-9	PE3-9A, 3-9B

OBJ. 7 Describe and illustrate the use of vertical analysis in evaluating a company's performance and financial condition.

Key Points Comparing each item on a financial statement with a total amount from the same statement is called vertical analysis. On the balance sheet, each asset is expressed as a percent of total assets, and each liability and owner's equity is expressed as a percent of total liabilities and owner's equity. On the income statement, each revenue and expense is expressed as a percent of total revenues or fees earned.

Learning Outcomes	Example Exercises	Practice Exercises
• Describe vertical analysis.		
• Prepare a vertical analysis report of a financial statement.	EE3-10	PE3-10A, 3-10B

Illustrative Problem

Three years ago, T. Roderick organized Harbor Realty. At July 31, 20Y8, the end of the current year, the unadjusted trial balance of Harbor Realty was as follows:

Harbor Realty
Unadjusted Trial Balance
July 31, 20Y8

	Debit Balances	Credit Balances
Cash	3,425	
Accounts Receivable	7,000	
Supplies	1,270	
Prepaid Insurance	620	
Office Equipment	51,650	
Accumulated Depreciation—Office Equipment		9,700
Accounts Payable		925
Wages Payable		0
Unearned Fees		1,250
T. Roderick, Capital		29,000
T. Roderick, Drawing	5,200	
Fees Earned		59,125
Wages Expense	22,415	
Depreciation Expense	0	
Rent Expense	4,200	
Utilities Expense	2,715	
Supplies Expense	0	
Insurance Expense	0	
Miscellaneous Expense	1,505	
	100,000	100,000

The data needed to determine year-end adjustments follow:

- Supplies on hand at July 31, 20Y8, $380.
- Insurance premiums expired during the year, $315.
- Depreciation of equipment during the year, $4,950.
- Wages accrued but not paid at July 31, 20Y8, $440.
- Accrued fees earned but not recorded at July 31, 20Y8, $1,000.
- Unearned fees on July 31, 20Y8, $750.

Instructions

1. Prepare the necessary adjusting journal entries on July 31, 20Y8. Include journal entry explanations.
2. Determine the balance of the accounts affected by the adjusting entries and prepare an adjusted trial balance.

Solution

1.

Journal

Date		Description	Post. Ref.	Debit	Credit
20Y8 July	31	Supplies Expense		890	
		Supplies			890
		Supplies used ($1,270 – $380).			
	31	Insurance Expense		315	
		Prepaid Insurance			315
		Insurance expired.			
	31	Depreciation Expense		4,950	
		Accumulated Depreciation—Office Equipment			4,950
		Depreciation expense.			
	31	Wages Expense		440	
		Wages Payable			440
		Accrued wages.			
	31	Accounts Receivable		1,000	
		Fees Earned			1,000
		Accrued fees.			
	31	Unearned Fees		500	
		Fees Earned			500
		Fees earned ($1,250 – $750).			

2.

Harbor Realty
Adjusted Trial Balance
July 31, 20Y8

	Debit Balances	Credit Balances
Cash	3,425	
Accounts Receivable	8,000	
Supplies	380	
Prepaid Insurance	305	
Office Equipment	51,650	
Accumulated Depreciation—Office Equipment		14,650
Accounts Payable		925
Wages Payable		440
Unearned Fees		750
T. Roderick, Capital		29,000
T. Roderick, Drawing	5,200	
Fees Earned		60,625
Wages Expense	22,855	
Depreciation Expense	4,950	
Rent Expense	4,200	
Utilities Expense	2,715	
Supplies Expense	890	
Insurance Expense	315	
Miscellaneous Expense	1,505	
	106,390	106,390

Key Terms

accrual (115)
accrual basis of accounting (113)
Accumulated Depreciation (124)
adjusted trial balance (130)
adjusting entries (114)
adjusting process (114)
book value of the asset (or net book value) (125)
cash basis of accounting (113)
contra accounts (or contra asset accounts) (124)
deferral (115)
depreciate (124)
depreciation (124)
depreciation expense (124)
expense recognition principle (114)
fixed assets (or plant assets) (124)
matching principle (114)
prepaid expense (115)
revenue recognition (114)
revenue recognition principle (114)
unearned revenue (115)
vertical analysis (131)

Discussion Questions

1. How are revenues and expenses reported on the income statement under (a) the cash basis of accounting and (b) the accrual basis of accounting?
2. Is the matching concept related to (a) the cash basis of accounting or (b) the accrual basis of accounting?
3. Why are adjusting entries needed at the end of an accounting period?
4. What is the difference between adjusting entries and correcting entries?
5. Identify the four different categories of adjusting entries frequently required at the end of an accounting period.
6. If the effect of the debit portion of an adjusting entry is to increase the balance of an asset account, which of the following statements describes the effect of the credit portion of the entry?
   a. Increases the balance of a revenue account.
   b. Increases the balance of an expense account.
   c. Increases the balance of a liability account.
7. If the effect of the credit portion of an adjusting entry is to increase the balance of a liability account, which of the following statements describes the effect of the debit portion of the entry?
   a. Increases the balance of a revenue account.
   b. Increases the balance of an expense account.
   c. Increases the balance of an asset account.
8. Does every adjusting entry affect net income for a period? Explain.
9. On November 1 of the current year, a business paid the November rent on the building that it occupies. (a) Do the rights acquired at November 1 represent an asset or an expense? (b) What is the justification for debiting Rent Expense at the time of payment?
10. (a) Explain the purpose of the two accounts: Depreciation Expense and Accumulated Depreciation. (b) What is the normal balance of each account? (c) Is it customary for the balances of the two accounts to be equal in amount? (d) In what financial statements, if any, will each account appear?

Practice Exercises

Example Exercises

SHOW ME HOW

EE 3-1 *p. 115*

PE 3-1A Accounts requiring adjustment **OBJ. 1**

Indicate with a Yes or No whether or not each of the following accounts normally requires an adjusting entry:

a. Building
b. Cash
c. Wages Expense
d. Miscellaneous Expense
e. Nancy Palmer, Capital
f. Prepaid Insurance

EE 3-1 *p. 115*

PE 3-1B Accounts requiring adjustment **OBJ. 1**

Indicate with a Yes or No whether or not each of the following accounts normally requires an adjusting entry:

a. Accumulated Depreciation
b. Frank Kent, Drawing
c. Land
d. Salaries Payable
e. Supplies
f. Unearned Rent

EE 3-2 *p. 116*

PE 3-2A Type of adjustment **OBJ. 1, 2, 3**

Classify the following items as (1) prepaid expense, (2) unearned revenue, (3) accrued revenue, or (4) accrued expense:

a. Cash received for use of land next month.
b. Fees earned but not received.
c. Wages owed but not yet paid.
d. Supplies on hand.

EE 3-2 *p. 116*

PE 3-2B Type of adjustment **OBJ. 1, 2, 3**

Classify the following items as (1) prepaid expense, (2) unearned revenue, (3) accrued revenue, or (4) accrued expense:

a. Cash received for services not yet rendered.
b. Insurance paid for the next year.
c. Interest revenue earned but not received.
d. Salaries owed but not yet paid.

EE 3-3 *p. 118*

PE 3-3A Adjustment for accrued revenues **OBJ. 2**

At the end of the current year, $18,540 of fees have been earned but have not been billed to clients. Journalize the adjusting entry (include an explanation) to record the accrued fees.

EE 3-3 *p. 118*

PE 3-3B Adjustment for accrued revenues **OBJ. 2**

At the end of the current year, $27,480 of fees have been earned but have not been billed to clients. Journalize the adjusting entry (include an explanation) to record the accrued fees.

EE 3-4 *p. 120*

PE 3-4A Adjustment for accrued expense **OBJ. 2**

Blue Ocean Realty Co. pays weekly salaries of $33,300 for a six-day workweek (Monday through Saturday). Journalize the necessary adjusting entry (include an explanation) assuming that the accounting period ends on Thursday.

EE 3-4 *p. 120*

PE 3-4B Adjustment for accrued expense **OBJ. 2**

Silver Star Realty Co. pays weekly salaries of $16,200 on Friday for a five-day workweek ending on that day. Journalize the necessary adjusting entry (include an explanation) assuming that the accounting period ends on Tuesday.

EE 3-5 *p. 121*

PE 3-5A Adjustment for unearned revenue **OBJ. 3**

On August 1, 20Y1, Newhouse Co. received $13,200 for the rent of land for 12 months. Journalize the adjusting entry (include an explanation) required for unearned rent on December 31, 20Y1.

EE 3-5 *p. 121*

PE 3-5B Adjustment for unearned revenue **OBJ. 3**

The balance in the unearned fees account, before adjustment at the end of the year, is $316,290. Journalize the adjusting entry (include an explanation) required if the amount of unearned fees at the end of the year is $220,240.

SHOW ME HOW

EE 3-6 p. 124

PE 3-6A Adjustment for prepaid expense OBJ. 3

The prepaid insurance account had a beginning balance of $6,800 and was debited for $25,100 of premiums paid during the year. Journalize the adjusting entry (include an explanation) required at the end of the year, assuming the amount of unexpired insurance related to future periods is $8,500.

SHOW ME HOW

EE 3-6 p. 124

PE 3-6B Adjustment for prepaid expense OBJ. 3

The supplies account had a beginning balance of $4,085 and was debited for $7,810 for supplies purchased during the year. Journalize the adjusting entry (include an explanation) required at the end of the year, assuming the amount of supplies on hand is $3,610.

SHOW ME HOW

EE 3-7 p. 126

PE 3-7A Adjustment for depreciation OBJ. 4

The estimated amount of depreciation on equipment for the current year is $14,400. Journalize the adjusting entry (include an explanation) to record the depreciation.

SHOW ME HOW

EE 3-7 p. 126

PE 3-7B Adjustment for depreciation OBJ. 4

The estimated amount of depreciation on a building for the current year is $8,120. Journalize the adjusting entry (include an explanation) to record the depreciation.

SHOW ME HOW

EE 3-8 p. 130

PE 3-8A Effects of omitting adjustments OBJ. 5

For the year ending April 30, Safeguard Medical Services Co. mistakenly omitted adjusting entries for (1) $1,700 of supplies that were used, (2) unearned revenue of $8,000 that was earned, and (3) insurance of $10,900 that expired. Indicate the effect of the errors on (a) revenues, (b) expenses, and (c) net income for the year ended April 30.

SHOW ME HOW

EE 3-8 p. 130

PE 3-8B Effects of omitting adjustments OBJ. 5

For the year ending August 31, Solstice Medical Co. mistakenly omitted adjusting entries for (1) depreciation of $8,400, (2) fees earned that were not billed of $64,400, and (3) accrued wages of $10,600. Indicate the effect of the errors on (a) revenues, (b) expenses, and (c) net income for the year ended August 31.

SHOW ME HOW

EE 3-9 p. 131

PE 3-9A Effects of errors on adjusted trial balance OBJ. 6

For each of the following errors, considered individually, indicate whether the error would cause the adjusted trial balance totals to be unequal. If the error would cause the adjusted trial balance totals to be unequal, indicate whether the debit or credit total is higher and by how much.

a. The adjustment for accrued wages of $6,900 was journalized as a debit to Wages Expense for $6,900 and a credit to Accounts Payable for $6,900.

b. The entry for $1,519 of supplies used during the period was journalized as a debit to Supplies Expense of $1,519 and a credit to Supplies of $1,591.

SHOW ME HOW

EE 3-9 p. 131

PE 3-9B Effect of errors on adjusted trial balance OBJ. 6

For each of the following errors, considered individually, indicate whether the error would cause the adjusted trial balance totals to be unequal. If the error would cause the adjusted trial balance totals to be unequal, indicate whether the debit or credit total is higher and by how much.

a. The adjustment of $9,700 for accrued fees earned was journalized as a debit to Accounts Receivable for $9,700 and a credit to Fees Earned for $7,900.

b. The adjustment of depreciation of $18,700 was omitted from the end-of-period adjusting entries.

EE 3-10 *p. 133*

PE 3-10A Vertical analysis

OBJ. 7

Two income statements for Upward Company follow:

Upward Company
Income Statements
For the Years Ended December 31

	20Y5	20Y4
Fees earned	$924,000	$784,000
Operating expenses	545,160	478,240
Income from operations	$378,840	$305,760

a. Prepare a vertical analysis of Upward Company's income statements.

b. Does the vertical analysis indicate a favorable or an unfavorable change?

FAI

EE 3-10 *p. 133*

PE 3-10B Vertical analysis

OBJ. 7

Two income statements for Versatile Company follow:

Versatile Company
Income Statements
For the Years Ended December 31

	20Y5	20Y4
Fees earned	$1,468,000	$1,164,000
Operating expenses	822,080	628,560
Income from operations	$ 645,920	$ 535,440

a. Prepare a vertical analysis of Versatile Company's income statements.

b. Does the vertical analysis indicate a favorable or an unfavorable change?

Exercises

EX 3-1 Classifying types of adjustments

OBJ. 1, 2, 3

Classify the following items as (a) accrued revenue, (b) accrued expense, (c) unearned revenue, or (d) prepaid expense:

1. Bill for ads that appeared in prior month's local newspaper.
2. Fees received but not yet earned.
3. Fees earned but not yet received.
4. Premium paid on a one-year insurance policy.
5. Rent received in advance for rental of office space.
6. Supplies on hand.
7. Rent paid in advance.
8. Wages owed but payable in the following period.

EX 3-2 Classifying adjusting entries

OBJ. 1, 2, 3

The following accounts were taken from the unadjusted trial balance of Legislative Results Inc., a congressional lobbying firm. Indicate whether or not each account would normally require an adjusting entry. If the account normally requires an adjusting entry, use the following notation to indicate the type of adjustment:

AR—Accrued Revenue
AE—Accrued Expense
UR—Unearned Revenue
PE—Prepaid Expense

(Continued)

To illustrate, the answer for the first account follows:

Account	Answer
Accounts Receivable	Normally requires adjustment (AR).
Cash	
Harriet Kasun, Capital	
Interest Expense	
Interest Receivable	
Land	
Office Equipment	
Prepaid Rent	
Supplies	
Unearned Fees	
Wages Expense	

EX 3-3 Adjusting entry for accrued fees **OBJ. 2**

At the end of the current year, $59,500 of fees have been earned but have not been billed to clients.

a. Journalize the adjusting entry to record the accrued fees.

b. If the cash basis rather than the accrual basis had been used, would an adjusting entry have been necessary? Explain.

EX 3-4 Effect of omitting adjusting entry **OBJ. 2, 5**

The adjusting entry for accrued fees was omitted at the end of the current year. Indicate which items will be in error, because of the omission, on (a) the income statement for the current year and (b) the balance sheet at the end of the year. Also indicate whether the items in error will be overstated or understated.

✔ a. Amount of entry: $8,880

EX 3-5 Adjusting entries for accrued salaries **OBJ. 2**

Perimeter Realty Co. pays weekly salaries of $14,800 on Friday for a five-day workweek ending on that day. Journalize the necessary adjusting entry at the end of the accounting period, assuming that the period ends (a) on Wednesday and (b) on Thursday.

EX 3-6 Determining wages paid **OBJ. 2**

The wages payable and wages expense accounts at May 31, after adjusting entries have been posted at the end of the first month of operations, are shown in the following T accounts:

Wages Payable			Wages Expense	
	Bal. 7,175		Bal. 73,250	

Determine the amount of wages paid during the month.

EX 3-7 Effect of omitting adjusting entry **OBJ. 2, 5**

Accrued salaries owed to employees for October 30 and 31 are not considered in preparing the financial statements for the year ended October 31. Indicate which items will be erroneously stated, because of the error, on (a) the income statement for the year and (b) the balance sheet as of October 31. Also indicate whether the items in error will be overstated or understated.

EX 3-8 Effect of omitting adjusting entry **OBJ. 2, 5**

When preparing the financial statements for the year ended October 31, accrued salaries owed to employees for October 30 and 31 were omitted. The accrued salaries were included in the first salary payment in November. Indicate which items will be erroneously stated, because of failure to correct the initial error, on (a) the income statement for the month of November and (b) the balance sheet as of November 30.

SHOW ME HOW

EX 3-9 Adjusting entries for unearned fees **OBJ. 3**

The balance in the unearned fees account, before adjustment at the end of the year, is $23,100. Journalize the adjusting entry required if the amount of unearned fees at the end of the year is $4,620.

EX 3-10 Effect of omitting adjusting entry **OBJ. 3, 5**

At the end of January, the first month of the business year, the usual adjusting entry transferring rent earned from the unearned rent account to a revenue account was omitted. Indicate which items will be incorrectly stated, because of the error, on (a) the income statement for January and (b) the balance sheet as of January 31. Also indicate whether the items in error will be overstated or understated.

SHOW ME HOW

EX 3-11 Adjusting entry for supplies **OBJ. 3**

The balance in the supplies account, before adjustment at the end of the year, is $10,680. Journalize the adjusting entry required if the amount of supplies on hand at the end of the year is $1,940.

SHOW ME HOW

EX 3-12 Determining supplies purchased **OBJ. 3**

The supplies and supplies expense accounts at February 28, after adjusting entries have been posted at the end of the first year of operations, are shown in the following T accounts:

Supplies			Supplies Expense		
Bal.	1,310		Bal.	7,800	

Determine the amount of supplies purchased during the year.

EX 3-13 Effect of omitting adjusting entry **OBJ. 3, 5**

At August 31, the end of the first month of operations, the usual adjusting entry transferring prepaid insurance expired to an expense account is omitted. Which items will be incorrectly stated, because of the error, on (a) the income statement for August and (b) the balance sheet as of August 31? Also indicate whether the items in error will be overstated or understated.

SHOW ME HOW

EX 3-14 Adjusting entries for prepaid insurance **OBJ. 3**

The balance in the prepaid insurance account, before adjustment at the end of the year, is $27,000. Journalize the adjusting entry required under each of the following alternatives for determining the amount of the adjustment: (a) the amount of insurance expired during the year is $20,250; (b) the amount of unexpired insurance applicable to future periods is $6,750.

SHOW ME HOW

EX 3-15 Adjusting entries for prepaid insurance **OBJ. 3**

The prepaid insurance account had a balance of $3,000 at the beginning of the year. The account was debited for $32,500 for premiums on policies purchased during the year. Journalize the adjusting entry required under each of the following alternatives for determining the amount of the adjustment: (a) the amount of unexpired insurance applicable to future periods is $4,800; (b) the amount of insurance expired during the year is $30,700.

SHOW ME HOW

EX 3-16 Adjusting entries for unearned and accrued fees **OBJ. 2, 3**

The balance in the unearned fees account, before adjustment at the end of the year, is $97,770. Of these fees, $39,750 have been earned. In addition, $24,650 of fees have been earned but have not been billed. Journalize the adjusting entries (a) to adjust the unearned fees account and (b) to record the accrued fees.

EX 3-17 Adjusting entries for prepaid and accrued taxes **OBJ. 2, 3**

✔ b. $57,320

SHOW ME HOW

A-Z Construction Company was organized on May 1 of the current year. On May 2, A-Z Construction prepaid $18,480 to the city for taxes (license fees) for the *next* 12 months and debited the prepaid taxes account. A-Z Construction is also required to pay in January an annual tax (on property) for the current calendar year of $45,000.

a. Journalize the two adjusting entries required to bring the accounts affected by the two taxes up to date as of December 31, the end of the current year.

b. What is the amount of tax expense for the current year?

SHOW ME HOW

EX 3-18 Adjustment for depreciation **OBJ. 4**

The estimated amount of depreciation on equipment for the current year is $8,200. Journalize the adjusting entry to record the depreciation.

SHOW ME HOW

EXCEL ONLINE

EX 3-19 Determining fixed asset's book value **OBJ. 4**

The balance in the equipment account is $3,240,000, and the balance in the accumulated depreciation—equipment account is $2,134,000.

a. What is the book value of the equipment?

b. Does the balance in the accumulated depreciation account mean that the equipment's loss of value is $2,134,000? Explain.

EX 3-20 Book value of fixed assets **OBJ. 4**

In a recent balance sheet, **Microsoft Corporation** reported property, plant, and equipment of $58,683 million and accumulated depreciation of $29,223 million.

a. What was the book value of the fixed assets?

b. Would the book value of Microsoft's fixed assets normally approximate their market values?

EX 3-21 Effects of errors on financial statements **OBJ. 2, 5**

For a recent period, the balance sheet for **Costco Wholesale Corporation** reported accrued expenses of $5,675 million. For the same period, Costco reported income before income taxes of $4,442 million. Assume that the adjusting entry for $5,675 million of accrued expenses was not recorded at the end of the current period. What would have been the income (loss) before income taxes?

EX 3-22 Effects of errors on financial statements **OBJ. 2, 5**

For a recent year, the balance sheet for **The Campbell Soup Company** includes accrued expenses of $676 million. The income before taxes for Campbell for the year was $272 million.

a. Assume the adjusting entry for $676 million of accrued expenses was not recorded at the end of the year. By how much would income before taxes have been misstated?

b. What is the percentage of the misstatement in (a) to the reported income of $272 million? Round to one decimal place.

EX 3-23 Effects of errors on financial statements **OBJ. 2, 3, 5**

✔ 1. a. Revenue understated, $34,900

The accountant for Healthy Life Company, a medical services consulting firm, mistakenly omitted adjusting entries for (a) unearned revenue earned during the year ($34,900) and (b) accrued wages ($12,770). Indicate the effect of each error, considered individually, on the income statement for the current year ended July 31. Also indicate the effect of each error on the July 31 balance sheet. Set up a table similar to the following, and record your answers by inserting the dollar amount in the appropriate spaces. Insert a zero if the error does not affect the item.

	Error (a)		Error (b)	
	Over-stated	Under-stated	Over-stated	Under-stated
1. Revenue for the year would be	$____	$____	$____	$____
2. Expenses for the year would be	$____	$____	$____	$____
3. Net income for the year would be	$____	$____	$____	$____
4. Assets at July 31 would be	$____	$____	$____	$____
5. Liabilities at July 31 would be	$____	$____	$____	$____
6. Owner's equity at July 31 would be	$____	$____	$____	$____

EX 3-24 Effects of errors on financial statements **OBJ. 2, 3, 5**

If the net income for the current year had been $196,400 in Exercise 3-23, what would have been the correct net income if the proper adjusting entries had been made?

SHOW ME HOW

EX 3-25 Adjusting entries for depreciation; effect of error **OBJ. 4, 5**

On December 31, a business estimates depreciation on equipment used during the first year of operations to be $13,900.

a. Journalize the adjusting entry required as of December 31.

b. If the adjusting entry in (a) were omitted, which items would be erroneously stated on (1) the income statement for the year and (2) the balance sheet as of December 31?

SHOW ME HOW

EX 3-26 Adjusting entries from trial balances **OBJ. 6**

The unadjusted and adjusted trial balances for American Leaf Company on October 31, 20Y2, follow:

(*Continued*)

American Leaf Company
Trial Balances
October 31, 20Y2

	Unadjusted		Adjusted	
	Debit Balances	Credit Balances	Debit Balances	Credit Balances
Cash	16		16	
Accounts Receivable	38		44	
Supplies	12		10	
Prepaid Insurance	20		8	
Land	26		26	
Equipment	40		40	
Accumulated Depreciation—Equipment		8		12
Accounts Payable		26		26
Wages Payable		0		2
Les Huff, Capital		92		92
Les Huff, Drawing	8		8	
Fees Earned		74		80
Wages Expense	24		26	
Rent Expense	8		8	
Insurance Expense	0		12	
Utilities Expense	4		4	
Depreciation Expense	0		4	
Supplies Expense	0		2	
Miscellaneous Expense	4		4	
	200	200	212	212

Journalize the five entries that adjusted the accounts at October 31, 20Y2. None of the accounts were affected by more than one adjusting entry.

EX 3-27 Adjusting entries from trial balances **OBJ. 6**

✔ **Corrected trial balance totals, $369,000**

The accountant for Eva's Laundry prepared the following unadjusted and adjusted trial balances. Assume that all balances in the unadjusted trial balance and the amounts of the adjustments are correct. Identify the errors in the accountant's adjusting entries, assuming that none of the accounts were affected by more than one adjusting entry.

Eva's Laundry
Trial Balances
May 31, 20Y3

	Unadjusted		Adjusted	
	Debit Balances	Credit Balances	Debit Balances	Credit Balances
Cash	7,500		7,500	
Accounts Receivable	18,250		23,250	
Laundry Supplies	3,750		6,750	
Prepaid Insurance*	5,200		1,600	
Laundry Equipment	190,000		177,000	
Accumulated Depreciation—Laundry Equipment		48,000		48,000
Accounts Payable		9,600		9,600
Wages Payable				1,000
Eva Baldwin, Capital		110,300		110,300
Eva Baldwin, Drawing	28,775		28,775	
Laundry Revenue		182,100		182,100
Wages Expense	49,200		49,200	
Rent Expense	25,575		25,575	
Utilities Expense	18,500		18,500	
Depreciation Expense			13,000	
Laundry Supplies Expense			3,000	
Insurance Expense			600	
Miscellaneous Expense	3,250		3,250	
	350,000	350,000	358,000	351,000

*$3,600 of insurance expired during the year.

EX 3-28 Vertical analysis **OBJ. 7**

Amazon.com, Inc. is the largest Internet retailer in the United States. Amazon's income statements through operating income for two recent years are as follows (in millions):

Amazon.com, Inc.
Operating Income Statements
For the Years Ended December 31
(in millions)

	Year 2	Year 1
Product sales	$141,915	$118,573
Service sales	90,972	59,293
Total sales	$232,887	$177,866
Cost of sales	$139,156	$111,934
Fulfillment	34,027	25,249
Marketing	13,814	10,069
Technology and content	28,837	22,620
General and administrative	4,336	3,674
Other operating expense, net	296	214
Total operating expenses	$220,466	$173,760
Operating income	$ 12,421	$ 4,106

a. Prepare a vertical analysis of the two operating income statements. Round percentages to one decimal place.

b. Use the vertical analysis to explain the decrease in operating income.

EX 3-29 Vertical analysis **OBJ. 7**

The following data are taken from recent financial statements of **Nike, Inc.** (in millions):

	Year 2	Year 1
Sales (revenues)	$36,397	$34,350
Net income	1,933	4,240

a. Determine the amount of change (in millions) and percent of change in net income from Year 1 to Year 2. Round to one decimal place.

b. Determine the percentage relationship between net income and sales for Year 2 and Year 1. Round to one decimal place.

c. What conclusions can you draw from your analyses?

EX 3-30 Vertical analysis **OBJ. 7**

The following income statement data for **AT&T Inc.** and **Verizon Communications Inc.** were taken from their recent annual reports (in millions):

	AT&T	Verizon
Revenues	$170,756	$130,863
Cost of services (expense)	79,419	55,508
Selling and marketing expense	36,765	31,083
Depreciation and other expenses	28,476	21,994
Operating income	$ 26,096	$ 22,278

a. Prepare a vertical analysis of the income statement for AT&T. Round to one decimal place.

b. Prepare a vertical analysis of the income statement for Verizon. Round to one decimal place.

c. Based on parts (a) and (b), how does AT&T compare to Verizon?

Problems: Series A

SHOW ME HOW

PR 3-1A Adjusting entries

OBJ. 2, 3, 4

On December 31, the following data were accumulated for preparing the adjusting entries for Flagship Realty:

- The supplies account balance on December 31 is $1,585. The supplies on hand on December 31 are $320.
- The unearned rent account balance on December 31 is $10,350 representing the receipt of an advance payment on December 1 of five months' rent from tenants.
- Wages accrued but not paid at December 31 are $3,710.
- Fees earned but unbilled at December 31 are $21,610.
- Depreciation of office equipment is $3,340.

Instructions

1. Journalize the adjusting entries required at December 31.
2. Briefly explain the difference between adjusting entries and entries that would be made to correct errors.

SHOW ME HOW

PR 3-2A Adjusting entries

OBJ. 2, 3, 4, 5

Selected account balances before adjustment for Atlantic Coast Realty at July 31, the end of the current year, are as follows:

	Debits	Credits
Accounts Receivable	$ 75,000	
Equipment	345,700	
Accumulated Depreciation—Equipment		$112,500
Prepaid Rent	9,000	
Supplies	3,350	
Wages Payable		—
Unearned Fees		12,000
Fees Earned		660,000
Wages Expense	325,000	
Rent Expense	—	
Depreciation Expense	—	
Supplies Expense	—	

Data needed for year-end adjustments are as follows:

- Unbilled fees at July 31, $11,150.
- Supplies on hand at July 31, $900.
- Rent expired, $6,000.
- Depreciation of equipment during year, $8,950.
- Unearned fees at July 31, $2,000.
- Wages accrued but not paid at July 31, $4,840.

Instructions

1. Journalize the six adjusting entries required at July 31, based on the data presented.
2. What would be the effect on the income statement if the adjustments for unbilled fees and accrued wages were omitted at the end of the year?
3. What would be the effect on the balance sheet if the adjustments for unbilled fees and accrued wages were omitted at the end of the year?
4. What would be the effect on "Net increase or decrease in cash" on the statement of cash flows if the adjustments for unbilled fees and accrued wages were omitted at the end of the year?

PR 3-3A Adjusting entries

OBJ. 2, 3, 4, 5

Milbank Repairs & Service, an electronics repair store, prepared the following unadjusted trial balance at the end of its first year of operations:

Milbank Repairs & Service
Unadjusted Trial Balance
June 30, 20Y4

	Debit Balances	Credit Balances
Cash	10,350	
Accounts Receivable	67,500	
Supplies	16,200	
Equipment	166,100	
Accounts Payable		15,750
Unearned Fees		18,000
Nancy Townes, Capital		171,500
Nancy Townes, Drawing	13,500	
Fees Earned		294,750
Wages Expense	94,500	
Rent Expense	72,000	
Utilities Expense	51,750	
Miscellaneous Expense	8,100	
	500,000	500,000

For preparing the adjusting entries, the following data were assembled:

- Fees earned but unbilled on June 30 were $7,380.
- Supplies on hand on June 30 were $2,775.
- Depreciation of equipment was estimated to be $11,000 for the year.
- The balance in unearned fees represented the June 1 receipt in advance for services to be provided. During June, $16,500 of the services were provided.
- Unpaid wages accrued on June 30 were $3,880.

Instructions

1. Journalize the adjusting entries necessary on June 30, 20Y4.
2. Determine the revenues, expenses, and net income of Milbank Repairs & Service before the adjusting entries.
3. Determine the revenues, expenses, and net income of Milbank Repairs & Service after the adjusting entries.
4. Determine the effect of the adjusting entries on Nancy Townes, Capital.

PR 3-4A Adjusting entries

OBJ. 2, 3, 4, 5, 6

Good Note Company specializes in the repair of music equipment and is owned and operated by Robin Stahl. On November 30, 20Y5, the end of the current year, the accountant for Good Note prepared the following trial balances:

Good Note Company
Trial Balances
November 30, 20Y5

	Unadjusted		Adjusted	
	Debit Balances	Credit Balances	Debit Balances	Credit Balances
Cash	38,250		38,250	
Accounts Receivable	89,500		89,500	
Supplies	11,250		2,400	
Prepaid Insurance	14,250		3,850	
Equipment	290,450		290,450	
Accumulated Depreciation—Equipment		94,500		106,100
Automobiles	129,500		129,500	
Accumulated Depreciation—Automobiles		54,750		62,050
Accounts Payable		24,930		26,130
Salaries Payable		—		8,100
Unearned Service Fees		18,000		9,000
Robin Stahl, Capital		324,020		324,020
Robin Stahl, Drawing	75,000		75,000	
Service Fees Earned		733,800		742,800
Salary Expense	516,900		525,000	
Rent Expense	54,000		54,000	
Supplies Expense	—		8,850	
Depreciation Expense—Equipment	—		11,600	
Depreciation Expense—Automobiles	—		7,300	
Utilities Expense	12,900		14,100	
Taxes Expense	8,175		8,175	
Insurance Expense	—		10,400	
Miscellaneous Expense	9,825		9,825	
	1,250,000	1,250,000	1,278,200	1,278,200

Instructions

Journalize the seven entries that adjusted the accounts at November 30. None of the accounts were affected by more than one adjusting entry.

PR 3-5A Adjusting entries and adjusted trial balances

OBJ. 2, 3, 4, 5, 6

✔ 2. Total of Debited Balances column on adjusted trial balance: $849,750

Emerson Company is a small editorial services company owned and operated by Suzanne Emerson. On October 31, 20Y6, Emerson Company's accounting clerk prepared the unadjusted trial balance shown on the next page.

The data needed to determine year-end adjustments are as follows:

- Unexpired insurance at October 31, $550.
- Supplies on hand at October 31, $610.
- Depreciation of building for the year, $10,920.
- Depreciation of equipment for the year, $7,830.
- Unearned rent at October 31, $2,050.
- Accrued salaries and wages at October 31, $2,550.
- Fees earned but unbilled on October 31, $9,140.

Emerson Company
Unadjusted Trial Balance
October 31, 20Y6

	Debit Balances	Credit Balances
Cash	6,820	
Accounts Receivable	34,940	
Prepaid Insurance	6,550	
Supplies	1,800	
Land	102,400	
Building	273,200	
Accumulated Depreciation—Building		79,660
Equipment	123,110	
Accumulated Depreciation—Equipment		89,130
Accounts Payable		11,060
Unearned Rent		6,140
Suzanne Emerson, Capital		338,000
Suzanne Emerson, Drawing	14,000	
Fees Earned		295,320
Salaries and Wages Expense	175,950	
Utilities Expense	38,560	
Advertising Expense	20,750	
Repairs Expense	15,700	
Miscellaneous Expense	5,530	
	819,310	819,310

Instructions

1. Journalize the adjusting entries using the following additional accounts: Salaries and Wages Payable, Rent Revenue, Insurance Expense, Depreciation Expense—Building, Depreciation Expense—Equipment, and Supplies Expense.
2. Determine the balances of the accounts affected by the adjusting entries and prepare an adjusted trial balance.

PR 3-6A Adjusting entries and errors

OBJ. 2, 3, 4, 5

✔ **2. Corrected net income: $137,750**

At the end of April, the first month of operations, the following selected data were taken from the financial statements of Shelby Crawford, an attorney:

Net income for April	$120,000
Total assets at April 30	750,000
Total liabilities at April 30	300,000
Total owner's equity at April 30	450,000

In preparing the financial statements, adjustments for the following data were overlooked:

- Supplies used during April, $2,750.
- Unbilled fees earned at April 30, $23,700.
- Depreciation of equipment for April, $1,800.
- Accrued wages at April 30, $1,400.

Instructions

1. Journalize the entries to record the omitted adjustments.
2. Determine the correct amount of net income for April and the total assets, liabilities, and owner's equity at April 30. In addition to indicating the corrected amounts, indicate the effect of each omitted adjustment by setting up and completing a columnar table similar to the following. The adjustment for supplies used is presented as an example.

(Continued)

	Net Income	Total Assets	=	Total Liabilities	+	Total Owner's Equity
Reported amounts	$120,000	$750,000		$300,000		$450,000
Corrections:						
Supplies used	−2,750	−2,750		0		−2,750
Unbilled fees earned						
Equipment depreciation						
Accrued wages						
Corrected amounts						

Problems: Series B

SHOW ME HOW

PR 3-1B Adjusting entries

OBJ. 2, 3, 4

On May 31, the following data were accumulated to assist the accountant in preparing the adjusting entries for Oceanside Realty:

- Fees accrued but unbilled at May 31 are $19,750.
- The supplies account balance on May 31 is $12,300. The supplies on hand at May 31 are $4,150.
- Wages accrued but not paid at May 31 are $2,700.
- The unearned rent account balance at May 31 is $9,000, representing the receipt of an advance payment on May 1 of three months' rent from tenants.
- Depreciation of office equipment is $3,200.

Instructions

1. Journalize the adjusting entries required at May 31.
2. Briefly explain the difference between adjusting entries and entries that would be made to correct errors.

SHOW ME HOW

PR 3-2B Adjusting entries

OBJ. 2, 3, 4, 5

Selected account balances before adjustment for Intuit Realty at November 30, the end of the current year, follow:

	Debits	Credits
Accounts Receivable	$ 75,000	
Equipment	250,000	
Accumulated Depreciation—Equipment		$ 12,000
Prepaid Rent	12,000	
Supplies	3,170	
Wages Payable		—
Unearned Fees		10,000
Fees Earned		400,000
Wages Expense	140,000	
Rent Expense	—	
Depreciation Expense	—	
Supplies Expense	—	

Data needed for year-end adjustments are as follows:

- Supplies on hand at November 30, $550.
- Depreciation of equipment during year, $1,675.
- Rent expired during year, $8,500.
- Wages accrued but not paid at November 30, $2,000.
- Unearned fees at November 30, $4,000.
- Unbilled fees at November 30, $5,380.

Instructions

1. Journalize the six adjusting entries required at November 30, based on the data presented.
2. What would be the effect on the income statement if the adjustments for equipment depreciation and unearned fees were omitted at the end of the year?
3. What would be the effect on the balance sheet if the adjustments for equipment depreciation and unearned fees were omitted at the end of the year?
4. What would be the effect on "Net increase or decrease in cash" on the statement of cash flows if the adjustments for equipment depreciation and unearned fees were omitted at the end of the year?

PR 3-3B Adjusting entries

OBJ. 2, 3, 4, 5

Crazy Mountain Outfitters Co., an outfitter store for fishing treks, prepared the following unadjusted trial balance at the end of its first year of operations:

Crazy Mountain Outfitters Co.
Unadjusted Trial Balance
April 30, 20Y4

	Debit Balances	Credit Balances
Cash	11,400	
Accounts Receivable	72,600	
Supplies	7,200	
Equipment	112,000	
Accounts Payable		12,200
Unearned Fees		19,200
John Bridger, Capital		137,800
John Bridger, Drawing	10,000	
Fees Earned		305,800
Wages Expense	157,800	
Rent Expense	55,000	
Utilities Expense	42,000	
Miscellaneous Expense	7,000	
	475,000	475,000

For preparing the adjusting entries, the following data were assembled:

- Supplies on hand on April 30 were $1,380.
- Fees earned but unbilled on April 30 were $3,900.
- Depreciation of equipment was estimated to be $3,000 for the year.
- Unpaid wages accrued on April 30 were $2,475.
- The balance in unearned fees represented the April 1 receipt in advance for services to be provided. Only $14,140 of the services was provided between April 1 and April 30.

Instructions

1. Journalize the adjusting entries necessary on April 30, 20Y4.
2. Determine the revenues, expenses, and net income of Crazy Mountain Outfitters Co. before the adjusting entries.
3. Determine the revenues, expenses, and net income of Crazy Mountain Outfitters Co. after the adjusting entries.
4. Determine the effect of the adjusting entries on John Bridger, Capital.

PR 3-4B Adjusting entries

OBJ. 2, 3, 4, 5, 6

The Signage Company specializes in the maintenance and repair of signs, such as billboards. On March 31, 20Y5, the accountant for The Signage Company prepared the trial balances shown at the top of the following page.

(Continued)

The Signage Company
Trial Balances
March 31, 20Y5

	Unadjusted		Adjusted	
	Debit Balances	Credit Balances	Debit Balances	Credit Balances
Cash	4,750		4,750	
Accounts Receivable	17,400		17,400	
Supplies	6,200		2,175	
Prepaid Insurance	9,000		1,150	
Land	100,000		100,000	
Buildings	170,000		170,000	
Accumulated Depreciation—Buildings		51,500		61,000
Trucks	75,000		75,000	
Accumulated Depreciation—Trucks		12,000		17,000
Accounts Payable		6,920		8,750
Salaries Payable		—		1,400
Unearned Service Fees		10,500		3,850
Mary Bakken, Capital		256,400		256,400
Mary Bakken, Drawing	7,500		7,500	
Service Fees Earned		162,680		169,330
Salary Expense	80,000		81,400	
Depreciation Expense—Trucks	—		5,000	
Rent Expense	11,900		11,900	
Supplies Expense	—		4,025	
Utilities Expense	6,200		8,030	
Depreciation Expense—Buildings	—		9,500	
Taxes Expense	2,900		2,900	
Insurance Expense	—		7,850	
Miscellaneous Expense	9,150		9,150	
	500,000	500,000	517,730	517,730

Instructions

Journalize the seven entries that adjusted the accounts at March 31. None of the accounts were affected by more than one adjusting entry.

PR 3-5B Adjusting entries and adjusted trial balances

OBJ. 2, 3, 4, 5, 6

✔ **2. Total of Debit Balances column on adjusted trial balance: $420,300**

Reece Financial Services Co., which specializes in appliance repair services, is owned and operated by Joni Reece. Reece Financial Services' accounting clerk prepared the following unadjusted trial balance at July 31, 20Y6:

Reece Financial Services Co.
Unadjusted Trial Balance
July 31, 20Y6

	Debit Balances	Credit Balances
Cash	10,200	
Accounts Receivable	34,750	
Prepaid Insurance	6,000	
Supplies	1,725	
Land	50,000	
Building	155,750	
Accumulated Depreciation—Building		62,850
Equipment	45,000	
Accumulated Depreciation—Equipment		17,650
Accounts Payable		3,750
Unearned Rent		3,600
Joni Reece, Capital		153,550
Joni Reece, Drawing	8,000	
Fees Earned		158,600
Salaries and Wages Expense	56,850	
Utilities Expense	14,100	
Advertising Expense	7,500	
Repairs Expense	6,100	
Miscellaneous Expense	4,025	
	400,000	400,000

The data needed to determine year-end adjustments are as follows:

- Depreciation of building for the year, $6,400.
- Depreciation of equipment for the year, $2,800.
- Accrued salaries and wages at July 31, $900.
- Unexpired insurance at July 31, $1,500.
- Fees earned but unbilled on July 31, $10,200.
- Supplies on hand at July 31, $615.
- Rent unearned at July 31, $300.

Instructions

1. Journalize the adjusting entries using the following additional accounts: Salaries and Wages Payable, Rent Revenue, Insurance Expense, Depreciation Expense—Building, Depreciation Expense—Equipment, and Supplies Expense.
2. Determine the balances of the accounts affected by the adjusting entries and prepare an adjusted trial balance.

PR 3-6B Adjusting entries and errors

OBJ. 2, 3, 4, 5

✔ **2. Corrected net income: $128,700**

At the end of August, the first month of operations, the following selected data were taken from the financial statements of Tucker Jacobs, an attorney:

Net income for August	$112,500
Total assets at August 31	650,000
Total liabilities at August 31	225,000
Total owner's equity at August 31	425,000

In preparing the financial statements, adjustments for the following data were overlooked:

- Unbilled fees earned at August 31, $31,900.
- Depreciation of equipment for August, $7,500.
- Accrued wages at August 31, $5,200.
- Supplies used during August, $3,000.

Instructions

1. Journalize the entries to record the omitted adjustments.
2. Determine the correct amount of net income for August and the total assets, liabilities, and owner's equity at August 31. In addition to indicating the corrected amounts, indicate the effect of each omitted adjustment by setting up and completing a columnar table similar to the following. The first adjustment is presented as an example.

	Net Income	Total Assets	=	Total Liabilities	+	Total Owner's Equity
Reported amounts	$112,500	$650,000		$225,000		$425,000
Corrections:						
Unbilled fees earned	+31,900	+31,900		0		+31,900
Equipment depreciation						
Accrued wages						
Supplies used						
Corrected amounts						

Continuing Problem

✔ 3. Total of Debit column: $42,340

The unadjusted trial balance that you prepared for PS Music at the end of Chapter 2 should appear as follows:

PS Music
Unadjusted Trial Balance
July 31, 20Y9

	Account No.	Debit Balances	Credit Balances
Cash	11	9,945	
Accounts Receivable	12	2,750	
Supplies	14	1,020	
Prepaid Insurance	15	2,700	
Office Equipment	17	7,500	
Accounts Payable	21		8,350
Unearned Revenue	23		7,200
Peyton Smith, Capital	31		9,000
Peyton Smith, Drawing	32	1,750	
Fees Earned	41		16,200
Wages Expense	50	2,800	
Office Rent Expense	51	2,550	
Equipment Rent Expense	52	1,375	
Utilities Expense	53	1,215	
Music Expense	54	3,610	
Advertising Expense	55	1,500	
Supplies Expense	56	180	
Miscellaneous Expense	59	1,855	
		40,750	40,750

The data needed to determine adjustments are as follows:

- During July, PS Music provided guest disc jockeys for KXMD for a total of 115 hours. For information on the amount of the accrued revenue to be billed to KXMD, see the contract described in the July 3 transaction at the end of Chapter 2.
- Supplies on hand at July 31, $275.
- The balance of the prepaid insurance account relates to the July 1 transaction in Chapter 2.
- Depreciation of the office equipment is $50.
- The balance of the unearned revenue account relates to the contract between PS Music and KXMD, described in the July 3 transaction in Chapter 2.
- Accrued wages as of July 31 were $140.

Instructions

1. Prepare adjusting journal entries. You will need the following additional accounts:
   18 Accumulated Depreciation—Office Equipment
   22 Wages Payable
   57 Insurance Expense
   58 Depreciation Expense
2. Post the adjusting entries, inserting balances in the accounts affected.
3. Prepare an adjusted trial balance.

Cases & Projects

CP 3-1 Ethics in Action

Chris P. Bacon is the chief accountant for CV Industries, a large manufacturing company. In addition to its normal business activities, the company has excess warehouse space that it rents out to local businesses. Because the typical renter is a small business, CV Industries requires renters to make lease payments for the entire rental period on the day the lease is signed. As a result, CV Industries typically reports a large unearned rent balance on its balance sheet.

After making adjusting entries for the current year, Chris prepares the adjusted trial balance and notices that the company's earnings will decline significantly. He presents the adjusted trial balance to the company's CFO, Antonio Beldin, who is concerned about the earnings decline. Mr. Beldin notices the large unearned rent balance and proposes making an additional end-of-period adjusting entry to recognize the entire unearned rent balance as revenue in the current period. Chris protests, reminding Mr. Beldin that the adjusting entry for unearned rent has already been made. Mr. Beldin assures Chris that his proposal is acceptable, reminding Chris that "because we have already received the cash, we have the right to recognize the revenue in the current period." He instructs Chris to make the additional adjusting journal entry. Chris is hesitant to follow these instructions, but he is sensitive to the company's emphasis on earnings growth and makes the adjusting entry as instructed.

1. Is Chris behaving ethically? Why or why not?
2. Who is affected by Chris's decision?

CP 3-2 Ethics in Action

Daryl Kirby opened Squid Realty Co. on January 1, 20Y7. At the end of the first year, the business needed additional capital. On behalf of Squid Realty Co., Daryl applied to Ocean National Bank for a loan of $375,000. Based on Squid Realty Co.'s financial statements, which had been prepared on a cash basis, the Ocean National Bank loan officer rejected the loan as too risky.

After receiving the rejection notice, Daryl instructed his accountant to prepare the financial statements on an accrual basis. These statements included $65,000 in accounts receivable and $25,000 in accounts payable. Daryl then instructed his accountant to record an additional $30,000 of accounts receivable for commissions on property for which a contract had been signed on December 28, 20Y7. The title to the property is to transfer on January 5, 20Y8, when an attorney formally records the transfer of the property to the buyer.

Daryl then applied for a $375,000 loan from Free Spirit Bank, using the revised financial statements. On this application, Daryl indicated that he had not previously been rejected for credit.

Discuss the ethical and professional conduct of Daryl Kirby in applying for the loan from Free Spirit Bank.

CP 3-3 Team Activity

In teams, select a public company that interests you. Obtain the company's most recent annual report on Form 10-K. The Form 10-K is a company's annually required filing with the Securities and Exchange Commission (SEC). It includes the company's financial statements and accompanying notes. The Form 10-K can be obtained either (a) by referring to the investor relations section of the company's website or (b) by using the company search feature of the SEC's EDGAR database service found at www.sec.gov/edgar/searchedgar/companysearch.html.

(Continued)

Based on the information in the company's most recent annual report, answer the following questions:

1. In what industry does the company operate?
2. How many years of information are reported on the company's income statement?
3. How much net income does the company report on its income statement for each year presented?
4. How much revenue does the company report on its income statement for each year presented?
5. Within the notes to the financial statements, find the note on significant accounting policies. Based on the information in this note, when does the company recognize revenue?
6. Based solely on the company's net income, has the company's performance improved, remained constant, or deteriorated over the periods presented? Briefly explain your answer.

CP 3-4 Communication

COMMUNICATION

REAL WORLD

Delta Air Lines is a major passenger airline headquartered in the United States. Most Delta passengers purchase their tickets several weeks prior to taking their trip and use a credit card such as VISA or American Express to pay for their tickets. The credit card company pays the airline at the time the flight is booked, several weeks prior to the flight.

Write a brief memo to your instructor explaining when Delta should recognize revenue from ticket sales.

CP 3-5 Adjustments and financial statements

Several years ago, your brother opened Magna Appliance Repairs. He made a small initial investment and added money from his personal bank account as needed. He withdrew money for living expenses at irregular intervals. As the business grew, he hired an assistant. He is now considering adding more employees, purchasing additional service trucks, and purchasing the building he now rents. To secure funds for the expansion, your brother submitted a loan application to the bank and included the most recent financial statements (which follow) prepared from accounts maintained by a part-time bookkeeper.

Magna Appliance Repairs
Income Statement
For the Year Ended October 31, 20Y8

Service revenue		$675,000
Less: Rent paid	$187,200	
Wages paid	148,500	
Supplies paid	42,000	
Utilities paid	39,000	
Insurance paid	21,600	
Miscellaneous payments	54,600	492,900
Net income		$ 182,100

Magna Appliance Repairs
Balance Sheet
October 31, 20Y8

Assets	
Cash	$ 95,400
Amounts due from customers	112,500
Truck	332,100
Total assets	$540,000
Equities	
Owner's capital	$540,000

After reviewing the financial statements, the loan officer at the bank asked your brother if he used the accrual basis of accounting for revenues and expenses. Your brother responded that he did and that is why he included an account for "Amounts Due from Customers." The loan officer then asked whether or not the accounts were adjusted prior to the preparation of the statements. Your brother answered that they had not been adjusted.

a. Why do you think the loan officer suspected that the accounts had not been adjusted prior to the preparation of the statements?

b. Indicate possible accounts that might need to be adjusted before an accurate set of financial statements could be prepared.

CHAPTER

4 Completing the Accounting Cycle

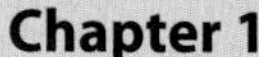

Chapter 1

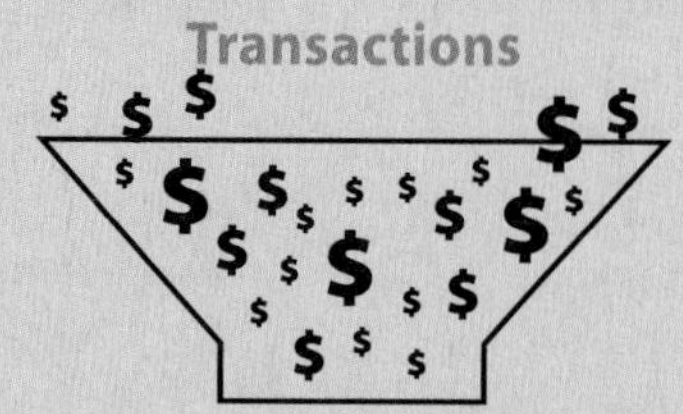

Accounting System

Accounting Equation

Assets = Liabilities + Owner's Equity

Chapter 2

Account

Debits	Credits

Rules of Debit and Credit

BALANCE SHEET ACCOUNTS

ASSETS = **LIABILITIES** + **OWNER'S EQUITY**

Asset Accounts

Debit for increases (+)	Credit for decreases (–)
Balance	

Liability Accounts

Debit for decreases (–)	Credit for increases (+)
	Balance

Owner's Capital Account

Debit for decreases (–)	Credit for increases (+)
	Balance

Owner's Drawing Account

Debit for increases (+)	Credit for decreases (–)
Balance	

Income Statement Accounts

Revenue Accounts

Debit for decreases (–)	Credit for increases (+)
	Balance

Expense Accounts

Debit for increases (+)	Credit for decreases (–)
Balance	

Unadjusted Trial Balance

Total Debit Balances = Total Credit Balances

CHAPTER 4

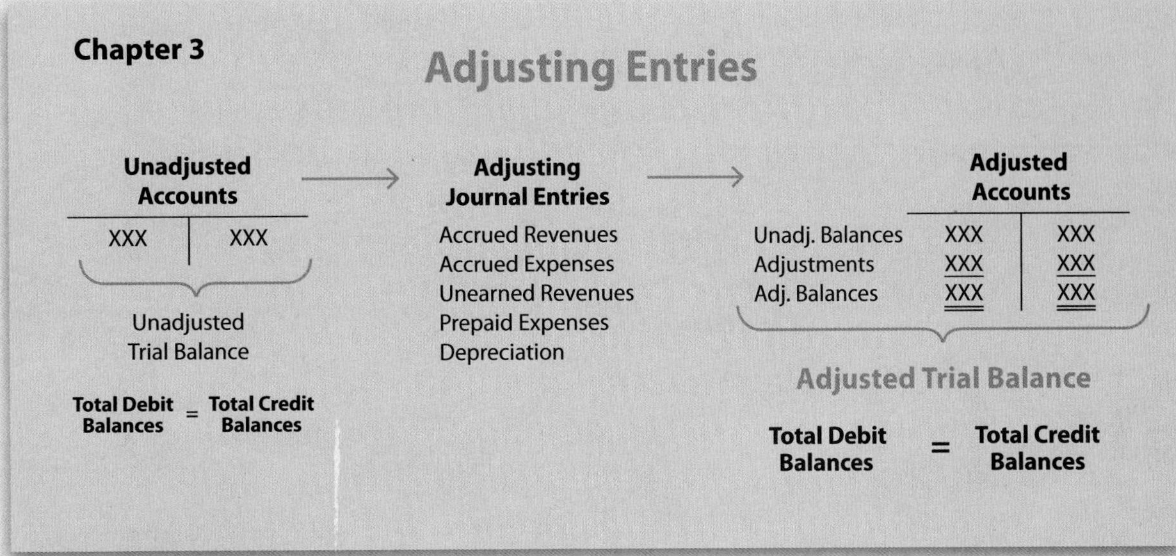

Chapter 3
Adjusting Entries
Unadjusted Accounts
XXX
XXX
Unadjusted Trial Balance
Total Debit Balances = Total Credit Balances
Adjusting Journal Entries
Accrued Revenues
Accrued Expenses
Unearned Revenues
Prepaid Expenses
Depreciation
Adjusted Accounts
Unadj. Balances XXX XXX
Adjustments XXX XXX
Adj. Balances XXX XXX
Adjusted Trial Balance
Total Debit Balances = Total Credit Balances

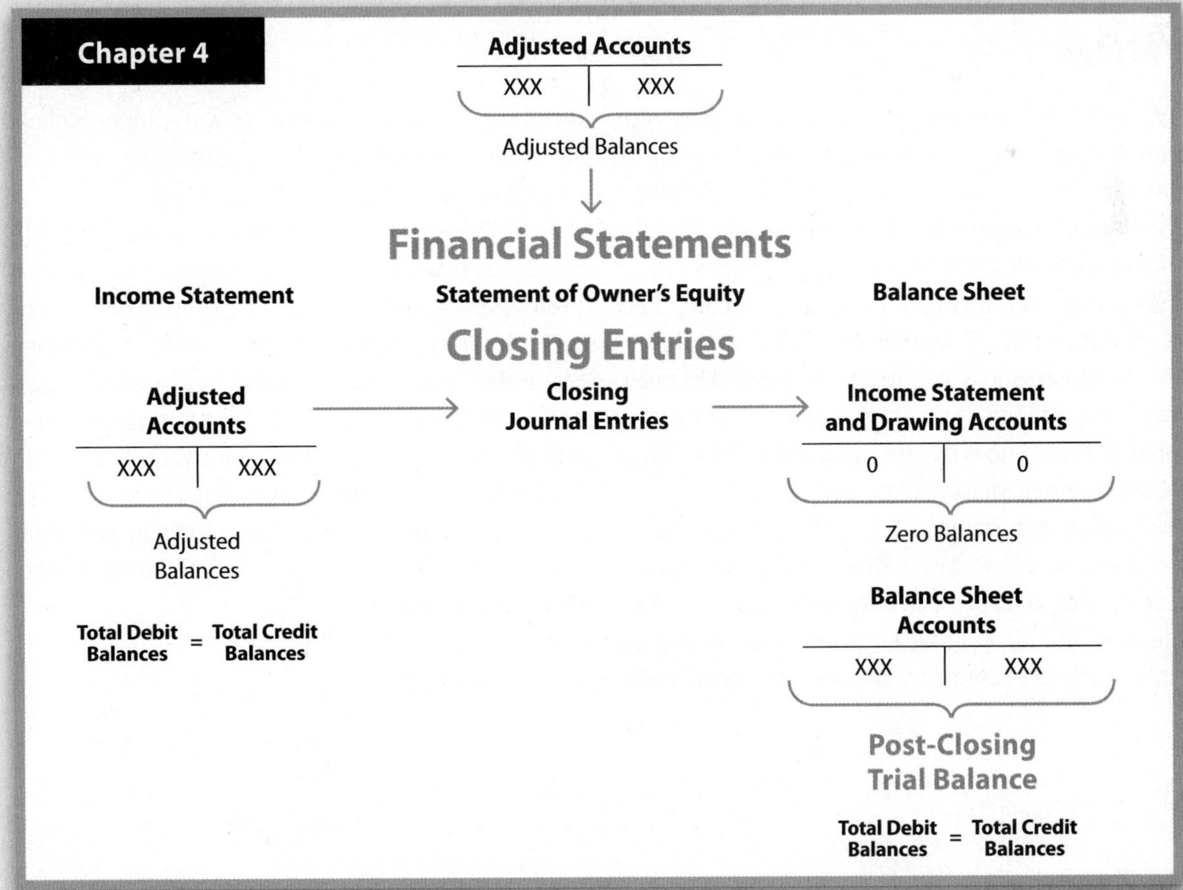

Chapter 4
Adjusted Accounts
XXX
XXX
Adjusted Balances
Financial Statements
Income Statement
Statement of Owner's Equity
Balance Sheet
Closing Entries
Adjusted Accounts
XXX
XXX
Adjusted Balances
Total Debit Balances = Total Credit Balances
Closing Journal Entries
Income Statement and Drawing Accounts
0
0
Zero Balances
Balance Sheet Accounts
XXX
XXX
Post-Closing Trial Balance
Total Debit Balances = Total Credit Balances

CHAPTER

4

JAKE CHARLES/ALAMY STOCK PHOTO

Zynga

Zynga is a leading provider of social games with more than 85 million active players per month. Zynga's games, such as CityVille, FarmVille, CastleVille, and Café World, can be played on a variety of platforms including **Facebook**, **Google** Android, and **Apple** iOS.

Zynga was founded in 2007 and is named after CEO (chief executive officer) Mark Pincus's dog. Zinga is an American Bulldog who is known for her human-like qualities, which include sitting on chairs and eating at the dinner table. Because she is playful, loyal, and lovable, Zinga is considered the guiding spirit of the company.

In developing its games, Zynga goes through a game development cycle that starts with the initial gaming concept, continues with program development, and ends with testing and debugging errors. Businesses also go through a cycle of accounting activities that begins with recording transactions and ends with preparing financial statements and getting the accounting records ready for recording the next period's transactions.

In Chapter 1, the initial accounting cycle for **NetSolutions** began with Chris Clark's investment in the business on November 1, 20Y3. The cycle continued with recording NetSolutions' transactions for November and December, as we discussed and illustrated in Chapters 1 and 2. In Chapter 3, the cycle continued when the adjusting entries for the two months ending December 31, 20Y3, were recorded. In this chapter, the cycle is completed for NetSolutions by preparing financial statements and getting the accounts ready for recording transactions of the next period.

Source: Zynga.com

Link to Zynga..Pages 165, 168

LEARNING OBJECTIVES

After studying this chapter, you should be able to:

Example Exercises (EE) are shown in **red.**

OBJ. 1 **Describe the flow of accounting information from the unadjusted trial balance into the adjusted trial balance and financial statements.**

Flow of Accounting Information
Flow of Accounts into Financial Statements — EE **4-1**

OBJ. 2 **Prepare financial statements from adjusted account balances.**

Financial Statements
Income Statement
Statement of Owner's Equity — EE **4-2**
Balance Sheet — EE **4-3**

OBJ. 3 **Prepare closing entries.**

Closing Entries
Journalizing and Posting Closing Entries — EE **4-4**
Post-Closing Trial Balance

OBJ. 4 **Describe the accounting cycle.**

Accounting Cycle
Steps of the Accounting Cycle — EE **4-5**

OBJ. 5 **Illustrate the accounting cycle for one period.**

Illustration of the Accounting Cycle

OBJ. 6 **Describe and illustrate the use of working capital and the current ratio in evaluating a company's financial condition.**

Financial Analysis and Interpretation: Working Capital and Current Ratio
Computing Working Capital and Current Ratio — EE **4-6**

APP. 1 OBJ. **Describe and illustrate the use of an end-of-period spreadsheet for preparing financial statements.**

APP. 2 OBJ. **Describe and explain why generally accepted accounting principles (GAAP) require the accrual basis of accounting.**

At a Glance 4 Page 198

Flow of Accounting Information

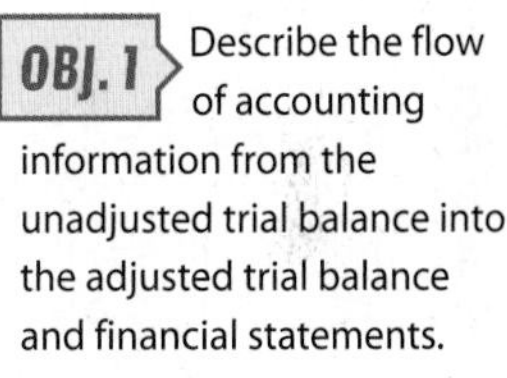
OBJ. 1 Describe the flow of accounting information from the unadjusted trial balance into the adjusted trial balance and financial statements.

The process of adjusting the accounts and preparing financial statements is one of the most important in accounting. Using the **NetSolutions** illustration from Chapters 1–3 and an end-of-period spreadsheet, the flow of accounting data in adjusting accounts and the preparation of financial statements are summarized in Exhibit 1.

The end-of-period spreadsheet in Exhibit 1 begins with the unadjusted trial balance. The unadjusted trial balance verifies that the total of the debit balances equals the total of the credit balances. If the trial balance totals are unequal, an error has occurred. Any errors must be found and corrected before the end-of-period process can continue.

Many companies use **Microsoft**'s Excel® software to prepare end-of-period spreadsheets.

The adjustments for NetSolutions from Chapter 3 are shown in the Adjustments columns of the spreadsheet. Cross-referencing (by letters) the debit and credit of each adjustment is useful in reviewing the effect of the adjustments on the unadjusted account balances. The adjustments are normally entered in the order in which the data are assembled. If the titles of the accounts to be adjusted do not appear in the unadjusted trial balance, the accounts are inserted in their proper order in the Account Title column. The total of the Adjustments columns verifies that the total debits equal the total credits for the adjusting entries. The total of the Debit column must equal the total of the Credit column.

The adjustments in the spreadsheet are added to or subtracted from the amounts in the Unadjusted Trial Balance columns to arrive at the amounts inserted in the Adjusted Trial Balance columns. In this way, the Adjusted Trial Balance columns of the spreadsheet illustrate the effect of the adjusting entries on the unadjusted accounts. The totals of the Adjusted Trial Balance columns verify that the totals of the debit and credit balances are equal after adjustment.

EXHIBIT 1 End-of-Period Spreadsheet and Flow of Accounting Data—NetSolutions

	A	B	C	D	E	F	G
1		NetSolutions					
2		End-of-Period Spreadsheet					
3		For the Two Months Ended December 31, 20Y3					
4		Unadjusted				Adjusted	
5		Trial Balance		Adjustments		Trial Balance	
6	Account Title	Dr.	Cr.	Dr.	Cr.	Dr.	Cr.
7							
8	Cash	2,065				2,065	
9	Accounts Receivable	2,220		(a) 500		2,720	
10	Supplies	2,000			(d) 1,240	760	
11	Prepaid Insurance	2,400			(e) 200	2,200	
12	Land	20,000				20,000	
13	Office Equipment	1,800				1,800	
14	Accumulated Depreciation				(f) 50		50
15	Accounts Payable		900				900
16	Wages Payable				(b) 250		250
17	Unearned Rent		360	(c) 120			240
18	Chris Clark, Capital		25,000				25,000
19	Chris Clark, Drawing	4,000				4,000	
20	Fees Earned		16,340		(a) 500		16,840
21	Rent Revenue				(c) 120		120
22	Wages Expense	4,275		(b) 250		4,525	
23	Supplies Expense	800		(d) 1,240		2,040	
24	Rent Expense	1,600				1,600	
25	Utilities Expense	985				985	
26	Insurance Expense			(e) 200		200	
27	Depreciation Expense			(f) 50		50	
28	Miscellaneous Expense	455				455	
29		42,600	42,600	2,360	2,360	43,400	43,400
30							

NetSolutions
Income Statement
For the Two Months Ended December 31, 20Y3

Revenues:		
Fees earned	$16,840	
Rent revenue	120	
Total revenues		$16,960
Expenses:		
Wages expense	$ 4,525	
Supplies expense	2,040	
Rent expense	1,600	
Utilities expense	985	
Insurance expense	200	
Depreciation expense	50	
Miscellaneous expense	455	
Total expenses		9,855
Net income		$ 7,105

NetSolutions
Balance Sheet
December 31, 20Y3

Assets

Current assets:			
Cash		$ 2,065	
Accounts receivable		2,720	
Supplies		760	
Prepaid insurance		2,200	
Total current assets			$ 7,745
Property, plant, and equipment:			
Land		$20,000	
Office equipment	$1,800		
Less accum. depreciation	50	1,750	
Total property, plant, and equipment			21,750
Total assets			$29,495

Liabilities

Current liabilities:		
Accounts payable	$ 900	
Wages payable	250	
Unearned rent	240	
Total liabilities		$ 1,390

Owner's Equity

Chris Clark, capital	28,105
Total liabilities and owner's equity	$29,495

NetSolutions
Statement of Owner's Equity
For the Two Months Ended December 31, 20Y3

Chris Clark, capital, November 1, 20Y3		$ 0
Investment on November 1, 20Y3	$25,000	
Net income for November and December	7,105	
Withdrawals for November and December	(4,000)	
Increase in owner's equity		28,105
Chris Clark, capital, December 31, 20Y3		$28,105

Exhibit 1 illustrates the flow of accounts from the adjusted trial balance into the financial statements as follows:

1. The revenue and expense accounts (spreadsheet lines 20–28) flow into the income statement.
2. The owner's capital account, Chris Clark, Capital (spreadsheet line 18), and owner's drawing account, Chris Clark, Drawing (spreadsheet line 19), flow into the statement of owner's equity. The net income of $7,105 also flows into the statement of owner's equity from the income statement.
3. The asset and liability accounts (spreadsheet lines 8–17) flow into the balance sheet. The end-of-period owner's equity (Chris Clark, Capital of $28,105) also flows into the balance sheet from the statement of owner's equity.

To summarize, Exhibit 1 illustrates the process by which accounts are adjusted. In addition, Exhibit 1 illustrates how the adjusted accounts flow into the financial statements. The financial statements for NetSolutions can be prepared directly from Exhibit 1.

The spreadsheet in Exhibit 1 is not required. However, many accountants prepare such a spreadsheet, sometimes called a *work sheet*, as part of the normal end-of-period process. The primary advantage in doing so is that it allows managers and accountants to see the effect of adjustments on the financial statements. This is especially useful for adjustments that depend upon estimates. Such estimates and their effect on the financial statements are discussed in later chapters.[1]

EXAMPLE EXERCISE 4-1 Flow of Accounts into Financial Statements — OBJ. 1

The balances for the accounts that follow appear in the Adjusted Trial Balance columns of the end-of-period spreadsheet. Indicate whether each account would flow into the income statement, statement of owner's equity, or balance sheet.

1. Office Equipment
2. Utilities Expense
3. Accumulated Depreciation
4. Unearned Rent
5. Fees Earned
6. Doug Johnson, Drawing
7. Rent Revenue
8. Supplies

Follow My Example 4-1

1. Balance sheet
2. Income statement
3. Balance sheet
4. Balance sheet
5. Income statement
6. Statement of owner's equity
7. Income statement
8. Balance sheet

Practice Exercises: PE 4-1A, PE 4-1B

Financial Statements

OBJ. 2 Prepare financial statements from adjusted account balances.

Using the adjusted trial balance shown in Exhibit 1, the financial statements for NetSolutions can be prepared. The income statement, the statement of owner's equity, and the balance sheet are shown in Exhibit 2.[2]

Income Statement

The income statement is prepared directly from the Adjusted Trial Balance columns of the Exhibit 1 spreadsheet, beginning with fees earned of $16,840. The expenses in the income statement in Exhibit 2 are listed in order of size, beginning with the larger items. Miscellaneous expense is the last item, regardless of its amount.

Link to Zynga

In a recent income statement, **Zynga** reported a net income from operations of $15.4 million.

1 Appendix 1 to this chapter describes and illustrates how to prepare an end-of-period spreadsheet that includes financial statement columns.

2 The financial statements in Exhibit 2 are based upon the accrual basis of accounting. Appendix 2 illustrates and explains why generally accepted accounting principles (GAAP) require the accrual basis of accounting.

EXHIBIT 2

Financial Statements, NetSolutions

NetSolutions
Income Statement
For the Two Months Ended December 31, 20Y3

Revenues:		
Fees earned	$16,840	
Rent revenue	120	
Total revenues		$16,960
Expenses:		
Wages expense	$ 4,525	
Supplies expense	2,040	
Rent expense	1,600	
Utilities expense	985	
Insurance expense	200	
Depreciation expense	50	
Miscellaneous expense	455	
Total expenses		9,855
Net income		$ 7,105

NetSolutions
Statement of Owner's Equity
For the Two Months Ended December 31, 20Y3

Chris Clark, capital, November 1, 20Y3		$ 0
Investment on November 1, 20Y3	$25,000	
Net income for November and December	7,105	
Withdrawals during November and December	(4,000)	
Increase in owner's equity		28,105
Chris Clark, capital, December 31, 20Y3		$28,105

NetSolutions
Balance Sheet
December 31, 20Y3

Assets			
Current assets:			
Cash		$ 2,065	
Accounts receivable		2,720	
Supplies		760	
Prepaid insurance		2,200	
Total current assets			$ 7,745
Property, plant, and equipment:			
Land		$20,000	
Office equipment	$1,800		
Less accumulated depreciation	50	1,750	
Total property, plant, and equipment			21,750
Total assets			$29,495
Liabilities			
Current liabilities:			
Accounts payable		$ 900	
Wages payable		250	
Unearned rent		240	
Total liabilities			$ 1,390
Owner's Equity			
Chris Clark, capital			28,105
Total liabilities and owner's equity			$29,495

Integrity, Objectivity, and Ethics in Business

CEO'S HEALTH?

How much and what information to disclose in financial statements and to investors presents a common ethical dilemma for managers and accountants. For example, Steve Jobs, co-founder and CEO of **Apple Inc.**, had been diagnosed and treated for pancreatic cancer. Apple Inc. had insisted that the status of Steve Jobs's health was a "private" matter and did not have to be disclosed to investors. Apple maintained this position even though Jobs was a driving force behind Apple's innovation and financial success.

Steve Jobs's health deteriorated significantly, however, and that disclosure was eventually provided. On October 5, 2011, Steve Jobs died at the age of 56.

Statement of Owner's Equity

The first item presented on the statement of owner's equity is the balance of the owner's capital account at the beginning of the period. The amount listed as owner's capital in the spreadsheet, however, is not always the account balance at the beginning of the period. The owner may have invested additional assets in the business during the period. For the beginning balance and any additional investments, it is necessary to refer to the owner's capital account in the ledger. These amounts, along with the net income (or net loss) and the drawing account balance, are used to determine the ending owner's capital account balance.

The basic form of the statement of owner's equity is shown in Exhibit 2. For NetSolutions, the amount of drawings by the owner was less than the net income. If the owner's withdrawals had exceeded the net income, the difference between the two items would then be deducted from the beginning capital account balance. Other factors, such as additional investments or a net loss, also require some change in the form, as follows:

Allan Johnson, capital, January 1, 20Y3		$39,000
Investment during year	$ 6,000	
Net loss for year	(5,600)	
Withdrawals	(9,500)	
Decrease in owner's equity		(9,100)
Allan Johnson, capital, December 31, 20Y3		$29,900

EXAMPLE EXERCISE 4-2 Statement of Owner's Equity **OBJ. 2**

Zack Gaddis owns and operates Gaddis Employment Services. On January 1, 20Y9, Zack Gaddis, Capital had a balance of $186,000. During the year, Zack invested an additional $40,000 and withdrew $25,000. For the year ended December 31, 20Y9, Gaddis Employment Services reported a net income of $18,750. Prepare a statement of owner's equity for the year ended December 31, 20Y9.

Follow My Example 4-2

Gaddis Employment Services
Statement of Owner's Equity
For the Year Ended December 31, 20Y9

Zack Gaddis, capital, January 1, 20Y9		$186,000
Investment during 20Y9	$ 40,000	
Net income	18,750	
Withdrawals	(25,000)	
Increase in owner's equity		33,750
Zack Gaddis, capital, December 31, 20Y9		$219,750

Practice Exercises: PE 4-2A, PE 4-2B

Balance Sheet

The balance sheet is prepared directly from the Adjusted Trial Balance columns of the Exhibit 1 spreadsheet, beginning with Cash of $2,065. The asset and liability amounts are taken from the spreadsheet. The owner's equity amount, however, is taken from the statement of owner's equity, as illustrated in Exhibit 2.

The balance sheet in Exhibit 2 shows subsections for assets and liabilities. Such a balance sheet is a *classified balance sheet*. These subsections are described next.

Note

Two common classes of assets are current assets and property, plant, and equipment.

Link to Zynga

In a recent balance sheet, **Zynga** reported current assets of $747 million; property, plant, and equipment and other assets of $1.4 billion; and total assets of $2.1 billion.

Assets

Assets are commonly divided into two sections on the balance sheet: (1) current assets and (2) property, plant, and equipment.

Current Assets Cash and other assets that are expected to be converted to cash or sold or used up usually within one year or less, through the normal operations of the business, are called **current assets**. In addition to cash, the current assets may include notes receivable, accounts receivable, supplies, and other prepaid expenses.

Notes receivable are amounts that customers owe. They are written promises to pay the amount of the note and interest. Accounts receivable are also amounts customers owe, but they are less formal than notes. Accounts receivable normally result from providing services or selling merchandise on account. Notes receivable and accounts receivable are current assets because they are usually converted to cash within one year or less.

Property, Plant, and Equipment The Property, Plant, and Equipment section may also be described as **fixed assets** or **plant assets**. These assets include equipment, machinery, buildings, and land. With the exception of land, as discussed in Chapter 3, fixed assets depreciate over a period of time. The original cost, accumulated depreciation, and book value of each major type of fixed asset are normally reported on the balance sheet or in the notes to the financial statements.

Note

Two common classes of liabilities are current liabilities and long-term liabilities.

Link to Zynga

In a recent balance sheet, **Zynga** reported current liabilities of $480 million, long-term and other liabilities of $70 million, and total liabilities of $550 million.

Liabilities

Liabilities are the amounts the business owes to creditors. Liabilities are commonly divided into two sections on the balance sheet: (1) current liabilities and (2) long-term liabilities.

Current Liabilities Liabilities that will be due within a short time (usually one year or less) and that are to be paid out of current assets are called **current liabilities**. The most common liabilities in this group are notes payable and accounts payable. Other current liability accounts may include Wages Payable, Interest Payable, Taxes Payable, and Unearned Fees.

Long-Term Liabilities Liabilities that will not be due for a long time (usually more than one year) are called **long-term liabilities**. If NetSolutions had long-term liabilities, they would be reported below the current liabilities. As long-term liabilities come due and are to be paid within one year, they are reported as current liabilities. If they are to be renewed rather than paid, they would continue to be reported as long term. When a long-term asset, such as a building, is pledged as security for a liability, the obligation may be called a *mortgage note payable* or a *mortgage payable*.

Owner's Equity

The owner's right to the assets of the business is presented on the balance sheet below the liabilities section. The owner's equity is added to the total liabilities, and this total must be equal to the total assets.

EXAMPLE EXERCISE 4-3 Classified Balance Sheet — OBJ. 2

The following accounts appear in an adjusted trial balance of Hindsight Consulting. Indicate whether each account would be reported as (a) a current asset; (b) property, plant, and equipment; (c) a current liability; (d) a long-term liability; or (e) owner's equity on the December 31, 20Y1, balance sheet of Hindsight Consulting.

1. Jason Corbin, Capital
2. Notes Receivable (due in six months)
3. Note Payable (due in 10 years)
4. Land
5. Cash
6. Unearned Rent (three months)
7. Accumulated Depreciation—Equipment
8. Accounts Payable

Follow My Example 4-3

1. Owner's equity
2. Current asset
3. Long-term liability
4. Property, plant, and equipment
5. Current asset
6. Current liability
7. Property, plant, and equipment
8. Current liability

Practice Exercises: PE 4-3A, PE 4-3B

International Connection

IFRS INTERNATIONAL DIFFERENCES

Financial statements prepared under accounting practices in other countries often differ from those prepared under generally accepted accounting principles in the United States. This is to be expected because cultures and market structures differ from country to country.

To illustrate, **BMW Group** prepares its financial statements under International Financial Reporting Standards as adopted by the European Union. In doing so, BMW's balance sheet reports fixed assets first, followed by current assets. It also reports owner's equity before the liabilities. In contrast, balance sheets prepared under U.S. accounting principles report current assets followed by fixed assets and current liabilities followed by long-term liabilities and owner's equity. The U.S. form of balance sheet is organized to emphasize creditor interpretation and analysis. For example, current assets and current liabilities are presented first to facilitate their interpretation and analysis by creditors. Likewise, to emphasize their importance, liabilities are reported before owner's equity.*

Regardless of these differences, the basic principles underlying the accounting equation and the double-entry accounting system are the same in Germany and the United States. Even though differences in recording and reporting exist, the accounting equation holds true: The total assets still equal the total liabilities and owner's equity.

*Examples of U.S. and IFRS financial statement reporting differences are further discussed and illustrated in Appendix B.

Closing Entries

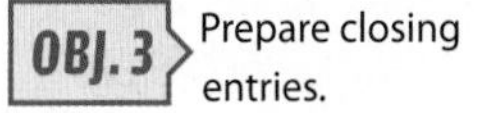

Prepare closing entries.

As discussed in Chapter 3, the adjusting entries are recorded in the journal at the end of the accounting period. For **NetSolutions**, the adjusting entries are shown in Exhibit 7 of Chapter 3. After the adjusting entries are posted to NetSolutions' ledger, shown in Exhibit 6 of this chapter, the ledger agrees with the data reported on the financial statements.

The balances of the accounts reported on the balance sheet are carried forward from period to period. Because these accounts are carried forward from period to period, they are called **permanent accounts** or **real accounts**. For example, Cash, Accounts Receivable, Equipment, Accumulated Depreciation, Accounts Payable, and Owner's Capital are permanent accounts.

The balances of the accounts reported on the income statement are not carried forward from year to year. Also, the balance of the owner's drawing account, which is reported on the statement of owner's equity, is not carried forward. Because these accounts report amounts for only one period, they are called **temporary accounts** or **nominal accounts**. Temporary accounts are not carried forward because they relate only to one period. For example, the Fees Earned of $16,840 and Wages Expense of $4,525 for NetSolutions shown in Exhibit 2 are for the two months ending December 31, 20Y3, and should not be carried forward to 20Y4.

Closing entries transfer the balances of temporary accounts to the owner's capital account.

At the beginning of the next period, temporary accounts should have zero balances. To achieve this, temporary account balances are transferred to permanent accounts at the end of the accounting period. The entries that transfer these balances are called **closing entries**. The transfer process is called the **closing process** and is sometimes referred to as **closing the books**.

The closing process involves the following two closing journal entries.

First Closing Entry:
Revenue and expense account balances are transferred to the owner's capital account.

Second Closing Entry:
The balance of the owner's drawing account is transferred to the owner's capital account.

Exhibit 3 diagrams the closing process.

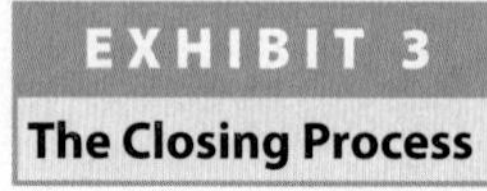

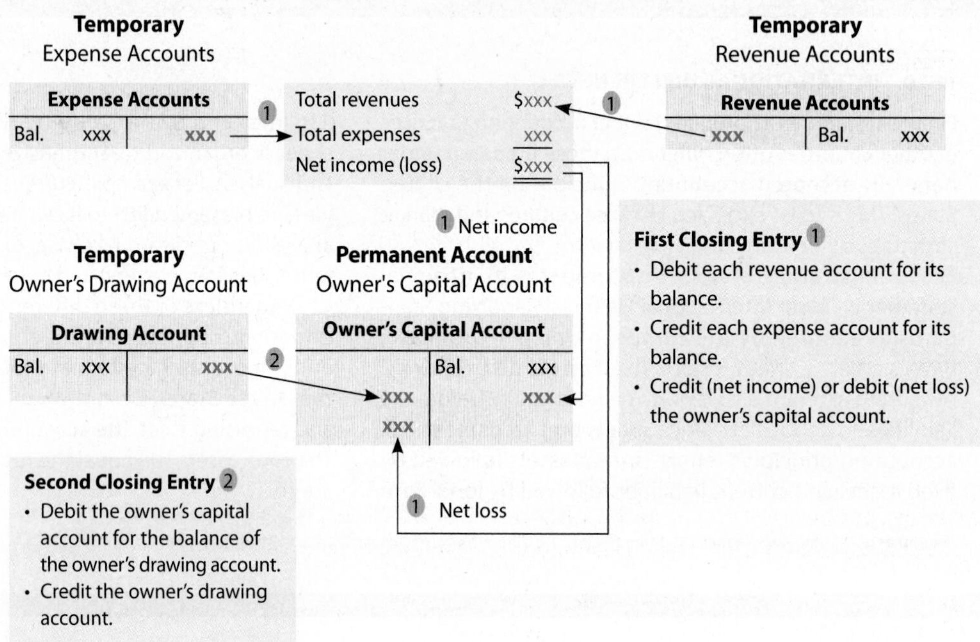

The two closing entries required in the closing process are as follows:[3]

1. Debit each revenue account for its balance, credit each expense account for its balance, and credit (net income) or debit (net loss) the owner's capital account.
2. Debit the owner's capital account for the balance of the drawing account and credit the drawing account.

Closing entries are recorded in the journal and are dated as of the last day of the accounting period. In the journal, closing entries are recorded immediately following the adjusting entries. The caption, *Closing Entries*, may be inserted above the closing entries to separate them from the adjusting entries.

Journalizing and Posting Closing Entries

A flowchart of the two closing entries for **NetSolutions** is shown in Exhibit 4. The balances in the accounts are those shown in the Adjusted Trial Balance columns of the end-of-period spreadsheet shown in Exhibit 1.

3 It is possible to close the temporary revenue and expense accounts using a clearing account such as Income Summary, Revenue and Expense Summary, or Profit and Loss Summary. In this case, four closing entries are made. The first entry closes the revenue accounts to Income Summary. The second entry closes the expense accounts to Income Summary. The third entry closes the income summary account to owner's equity. The fourth entry closes the owner's drawing account to owner's equity.

Flowchart of Closing Entries for NetSolutions EXHIBIT 4

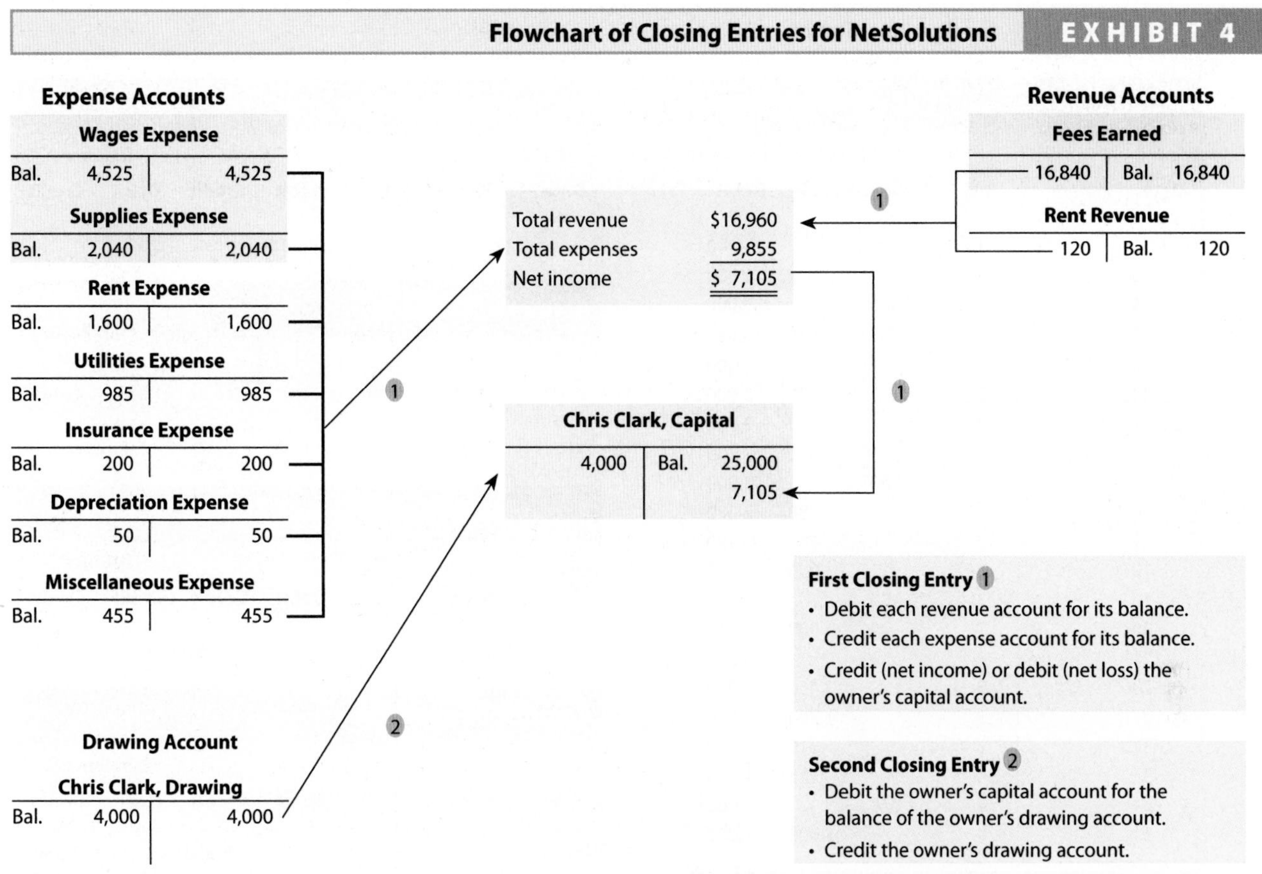

The closing entries for NetSolutions are shown in Exhibit 5. The account titles and balances for these entries may be obtained from the end-of-period spreadsheet, the adjusted trial balance, the income statement, the statement of owner's equity, or the ledger.

EXHIBIT 5
Closing Entries, NetSolutions

Journal *Page 6*

Date		Description	Post. Ref.	Debit	Credit
		Closing Entries			
20Y3 Dec.	31	Fees Earned	41	16,840	
		Rent Revenue	42	120	
		Wages Expense	51		4,525
		Supplies Expense	52		2,040
		Rent Expense	53		1,600
		Utilities Expense	54		985
		Insurance Expense	55		200
		Depreciation Expense	56		50
		Miscellaneous Expense	59		455
		Chris Clark, Capital	31		7,105
	31	Chris Clark, Capital	31	4,000	
		Chris Clark, Drawing	32		4,000

The closing entries are posted to NetSolutions' ledger as shown in Exhibit 6. After the closing entries are posted, NetSolutions' ledger has the following characteristics:

- The balance of Chris Clark, Capital of $28,105 agrees with the amount reported on the statement of owner's equity and the balance sheet.
- The revenue, expense, and drawing accounts will have zero balances.

EXHIBIT 6 **Ledger, NetSolutions**

Account *Cash* *Account No. 11*

Date	Item	Post. Ref.	Debit	Credit	Balance Debit	Balance Credit
20Y3						
Nov. 1		1	25,000		25,000	
5		1		20,000	5,000	
18		1	7,500		12,500	
30		1		3,650	8,850	
30		1		950	7,900	
30		2		2,000	5,900	
Dec. 1		2		2,400	3,500	
1		2		800	2,700	
1		2	360		3,060	
6		2		180	2,880	
11		2		400	2,480	
13		3		950	1,530	
16		3	3,100		4,630	
20		3		900	3,730	
21		3	650		4,380	
23		3		1,450	2,930	
27		3		1,200	1,730	
31		3		310	1,420	
31		4		225	1,195	
31		4	2,870		4,065	
31		4		2,000	2,065	

Account *Accounts Receivable* *Account No. 12*

Date	Item	Post. Ref.	Debit	Credit	Balance Debit	Balance Credit
20Y3						
Dec. 16		3	1,750		1,750	
21		3		650	1,100	
31		4	1,120		2,220	
31	Adjusting	5	500		2,720	

Account *Supplies* *Account No. 14*

Date	Item	Post. Ref.	Debit	Credit	Balance Debit	Balance Credit
20Y3						
Nov. 10		1	1,350		1,350	
30		1		800	550	
Dec. 23		3	1,450		2,000	
31	Adjusting	5		1,240	760	

Account *Prepaid Insurance* *Account No. 15*

Date	Item	Post. Ref.	Debit	Credit	Balance Debit	Balance Credit
20Y3						
Dec. 1		2	2,400		2,400	
31	Adjusting	5		200	2,200	

Account *Land* *Account No. 17*

Date	Item	Post. Ref.	Debit	Credit	Balance Debit	Balance Credit
20Y3						
Nov. 5		1	20,000		20,000	

Account *Office Equipment* *Account No. 18*

Date	Item	Post. Ref.	Debit	Credit	Balance Debit	Balance Credit
20Y3						
Dec. 4		2	1,800		1,800	

Account *Accumulated Depreciation* *Account No. 19*

Date	Item	Post. Ref.	Debit	Credit	Balance Debit	Balance Credit
20Y3						
Dec. 31	Adjusting	5		50		50

Account *Accounts Payable* *Account No. 21*

Date	Item	Post. Ref.	Debit	Credit	Balance Debit	Balance Credit
20Y3						
Nov. 10		1		1,350		1,350
30		1	950			400
Dec. 4		2		1,800		2,200
11		2	400			1,800
20		3	900			900

Account *Wages Payable* *Account No. 22*

Date	Item	Post. Ref.	Debit	Credit	Balance Debit	Balance Credit
20Y3						
Dec. 31	Adjusting	5		250		250

Account *Unearned Rent* *Account No. 23*

Date	Item	Post. Ref.	Debit	Credit	Balance Debit	Balance Credit
20Y3						
Dec. 1		2		360		360
31	Adjusting	5	120			240

Account *Chris Clark, Capital* *Account No. 31*

Date	Item	Post. Ref.	Debit	Credit	Balance Debit	Balance Credit
20Y3						
Nov. 1		1		25,000		25,000
Dec. 31	Closing	6		7,105		32,105
31	Closing	6	4,000			28,105

Ledger, NetSolutions (*Concluded*) **EXHIBIT 6**

Account *Chris Clark, Drawing* *Account No. 32*

Date	Item	Post. Ref.	Debit	Credit	Balance Debit	Balance Credit
20Y3						
Nov. 30		2	2,000		2,000	
Dec. 31		4	2,000		4,000	
31	Closing	6		4,000	—	—

Account *Fees Earned* *Account No. 41*

Date	Item	Post. Ref.	Debit	Credit	Balance Debit	Balance Credit
20Y3						
Nov. 18		1		7,500		7,500
Dec. 16		3		3,100		10,600
16		3		1,750		12,350
31		4		2,870		15,220
31		4		1,120		16,340
31	Adjusting	5		500		16,840
31	Closing	6	16,840		—	—

Account *Rent Revenue* *Account No. 42*

Date	Item	Post. Ref.	Debit	Credit	Balance Debit	Balance Credit
20Y3						
Dec. 31	Adjusting	5		120		120
31	Closing	6	120		—	—

Account *Wages Expense* *Account No. 51*

Date	Item	Post. Ref.	Debit	Credit	Balance Debit	Balance Credit
20Y3						
Nov. 30		1	2,125		2,125	
Dec. 13		3	950		3,075	
27		3	1,200		4,275	
31	Adjusting	5	250		4,525	
31	Closing	6		4,525	—	—

Account *Supplies Expense* *Account No. 52*

Date	Item	Post. Ref.	Debit	Credit	Balance Debit	Balance Credit
20Y3						
Nov. 30		1	800		800	
Dec. 31	Adjusting	5	1,240		2,040	
31	Closing	6		2,040	—	—

Account *Rent Expense* *Account No. 53*

Date	Item	Post. Ref.	Debit	Credit	Balance Debit	Balance Credit
20Y3						
Nov. 30		1	800		800	
Dec. 1		2	800		1,600	
31	Closing	6		1,600	—	—

Account *Utilities Expense* *Account No. 54*

Date	Item	Post. Ref.	Debit	Credit	Balance Debit	Balance Credit
20Y3						
Nov. 30		1	450		450	
Dec. 31		3	310		760	
31		4	225		985	
31	Closing	6		985	—	—

Account *Insurance Expense* *Account No. 55*

Date	Item	Post. Ref.	Debit	Credit	Balance Debit	Balance Credit
20Y3						
Dec. 31	Adjusting	5	200		200	
31	Closing	6		200	—	—

Account *Depreciation Expense* *Account No. 56*

Date	Item	Post. Ref.	Debit	Credit	Balance Debit	Balance Credit
20Y3						
Dec. 31	Adjusting	5	50		50	
31	Closing	6		50	—	—

Account *Miscellaneous Expense* *Account No. 59*

Date	Item	Post. Ref.	Debit	Credit	Balance Debit	Balance Credit
20Y3						
Nov. 30		1	275		275	
Dec. 6		2	180		455	
31	Closing	6		455	—	—

As shown in Exhibit 6, the closing entries are normally identified in the ledger as "Closing." In addition, a line is often inserted in both balance columns after a closing entry is posted. This separates next period's revenue, expense, and withdrawal transactions from those of the current period. Next period's transactions will be posted directly below the closing entry.

EXAMPLE EXERCISE 4-4 Closing Entries **OBJ. 3**

After the accounts have been adjusted at July 31, the end of the year, the following balances are taken from the ledger of Cabriolet Services Co.:

Terry Lambert, Capital	$615,850
Terry Lambert, Drawing	25,000
Fees Earned	380,450
Wages Expense	250,000
Rent Expense	65,000
Supplies Expense	18,250
Miscellaneous Expense	6,200

Journalize the two entries required to close the accounts.

Follow My Example 4-4

July	31	Fees Earned	380,450	
		Wages Expense		250,000
		Rent Expense		65,000
		Supplies Expense		18,250
		Miscellaneous Expense		6,200
		Terry Lambert, Capital		41,000
	31	Terry Lambert, Capital	25,000	
		Terry Lambert, Drawing		25,000

Practice Exercises: PE 4-4A, PE 4-4B

Post-Closing Trial Balance

A post-closing trial balance is prepared after the closing entries have been posted. The purpose of the post-closing (after closing) trial balance is to verify that the ledger is in balance at the beginning of the next period. The accounts and amounts should agree exactly with the accounts and amounts listed on the balance sheet at the end of the period. The post-closing trial balance for **NetSolutions** is shown in Exhibit 7.

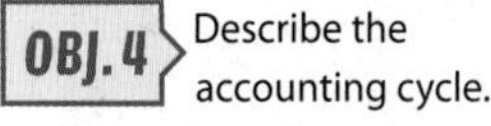

Accounting Cycle

The accounting process that begins with analyzing and journalizing transactions and ends with the post-closing trial balance is called the **accounting cycle**. The steps in the accounting cycle are as follows:

Step 1. Transactions are analyzed and recorded in the journal.
Step 2. Transactions are posted to the ledger.
Step 3. An unadjusted trial balance is prepared.
Step 4. Adjustment data are assembled and analyzed.
Step 5. (Optional) An optional end-of-period spreadsheet is prepared.

Step 6. Adjusting entries are journalized and posted to the ledger.
Step 7. An adjusted trial balance is prepared.
Step 8. Financial statements are prepared.
Step 9. Closing entries are journalized and posted to the ledger.
Step 10. A post-closing trial balance is prepared.[4]

EXHIBIT 7

Post-Closing Trial Balance, NetSolutions

NetSolutions
Post-Closing Trial Balance
December 31, 20Y3

	Account No.	Debit Balances	Credit Balances
Cash	11	2,065	
Accounts Receivable	12	2,720	
Supplies	14	760	
Prepaid Insurance	15	2,200	
Land	17	20,000	
Office Equipment	18	1,800	
Accumulated Depreciation	19		50
Accounts Payable	21		900
Wages Payable	22		250
Unearned Rent	23		240
Chris Clark, Capital	31		28,105
		29,545	29,545

Exhibit 8 illustrates the accounting cycle in graphic form. It also illustrates how the accounting cycle begins with the source documents for a transaction and flows through the accounting system and into the financial statements.

EXAMPLE EXERCISE 4-5 Accounting Cycle

OBJ. 4

From the following list of steps in the accounting cycle, identify what two steps are missing:

a. Transactions are analyzed and recorded in the journal.
b. Transactions are posted to the ledger.
c. Adjustment data are assembled and analyzed.
d. An optional end-of-period spreadsheet is prepared.
e. Adjusting entries are journalized and posted to the ledger.
f. Financial statements are prepared.
g. Closing entries are journalized and posted to the ledger.
h. A post-closing trial balance is prepared.

Follow My Example 4-5

The following two steps are missing: (1) the preparation of an unadjusted trial balance and (2) the preparation of the adjusted trial balance. The unadjusted trial balance should be prepared after step (b). The adjusted trial balance should be prepared after step (e).

Practice Exercises: PE 4-5A, PE 4-5B

4 Some accountants include the journalizing and posting of "reversing entries" as the last step in the accounting cycle. Because reversing entries are not required, they are described and illustrated in an online appendix at Cengage.com.

EXHIBIT 8

Accounting Cycle

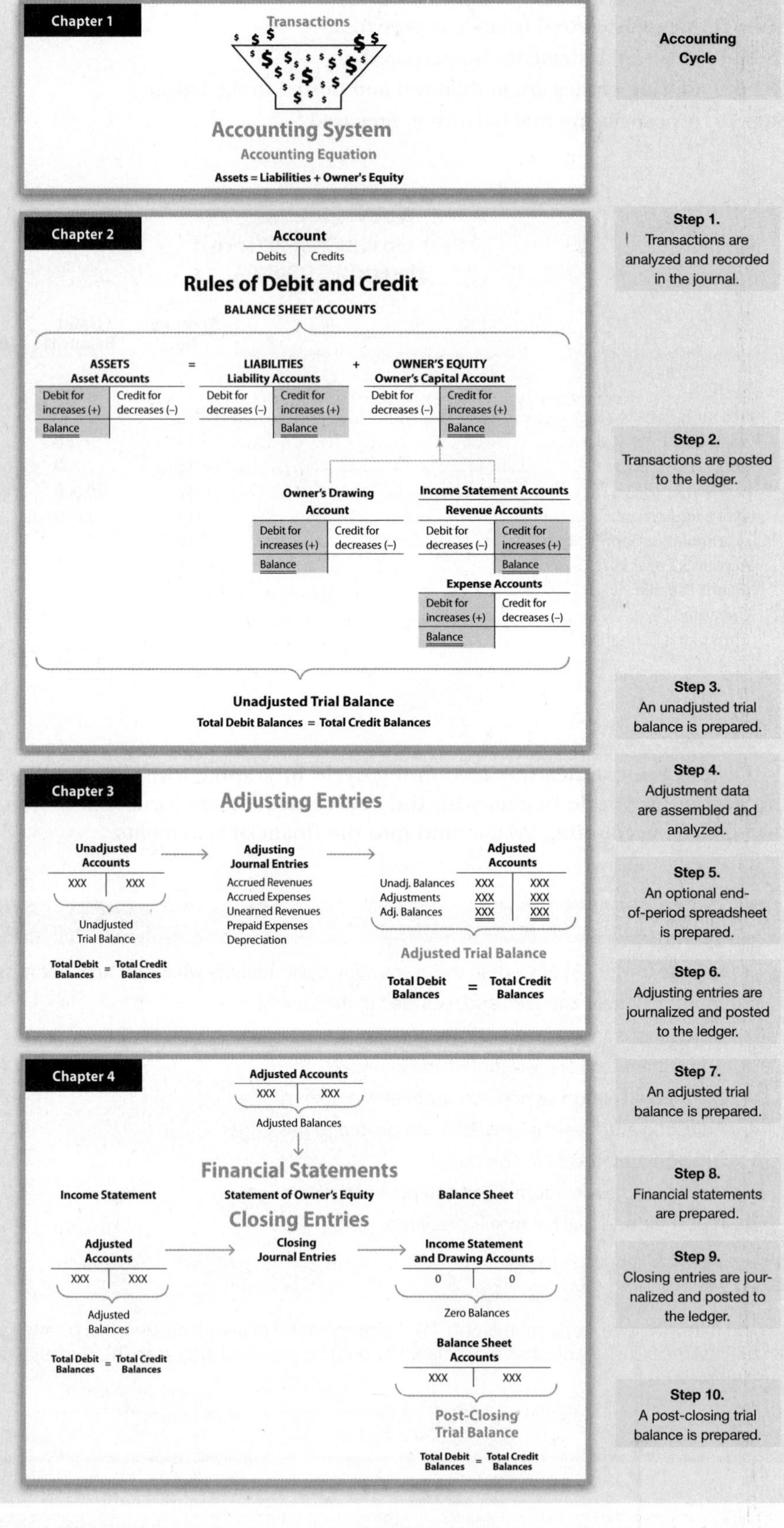

Illustration of the Accounting Cycle

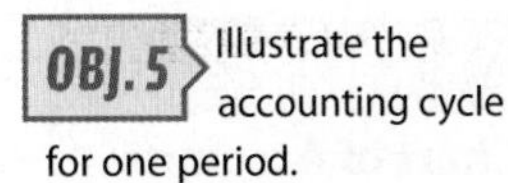

Illustrate the accounting cycle for one period.

In this section, the complete accounting cycle for one period is illustrated. Assume that for several years Kelly Pitney has operated a part-time consulting business from her home. As of April 1, 20Y5, Kelly decided to move to rented quarters and to operate the business on a full-time basis. The business will be known as Kelly Consulting. During April, Kelly Consulting entered into the following transactions:

Apr. 1. The following assets were received from Kelly Pitney: cash, $13,100; accounts receivable, $3,000; supplies, $1,400; and office equipment, $12,500. There were no liabilities received.

1. Paid three months' rent on a lease rental contract, $4,800.
2. Paid the premiums on property and casualty insurance policies, $1,800.
4. Received cash from clients as an advance payment for services to be provided and recorded it as unearned fees, $5,000.
5. Purchased additional office equipment on account from Office Station Co., $2,000.
6. Received cash from clients on account, $1,800.
10. Paid cash for a newspaper advertisement, $120.
12. Paid Office Station Co. for part of the debt incurred on April 5, $1,200.
12. Provided services on account for the period April 1–12, $4,200.
14. Paid part-time receptionist for two weeks' salary, $750.
17. Received cash from cash clients for fees earned during the period April 1–16, $6,250.
18. Paid cash for supplies, $800.
20. Provided services on account for the period April 13–20, $2,100.
24. Recorded cash from cash clients for fees earned for the period April 17–24, $3,850.
26. Received cash from clients on account, $5,600.
27. Paid part-time receptionist for two weeks' salary, $750.
29. Paid telephone bill for April, $130.
30. Paid electricity bill for April, $200.
30. Received cash from cash clients for fees earned for the period April 25–30, $3,050.
30. Provided services on account for the remainder of April, $1,500.
30. Kelly withdrew $6,000 for personal use.

Step 1. Analyzing and Recording Transactions in the Journal

The first step in the accounting cycle is to analyze and record transactions in the journal using the double-entry accounting system. As illustrated in Chapter 2, transactions are analyzed and journalized using the following steps:

Step 1. Carefully read the description of the transaction to determine whether an asset, liability, owner's equity, revenue, expense, or drawing account is affected.

Step 2. For each account affected by the transaction, determine whether the account increases or decreases.

Step 3. Determine whether each increase or decrease should be recorded as a debit or a credit, following the rules of debit and credit shown in Exhibit 3 of Chapter 2.

Step 4. Record the transaction using a journal entry.

The company's chart of accounts is useful in determining which accounts are affected by the transaction. The chart of accounts for Kelly Consulting is shown in Exhibit 9.

EXHIBIT 9

Chart of Accounts for Kelly Consulting

11 Cash	31 Kelly Pitney, Capital
12 Accounts Receivable	32 Kelly Pitney, Drawing
14 Supplies	41 Fees Earned
15 Prepaid Rent	51 Salary Expense
16 Prepaid Insurance	52 Rent Expense
18 Office Equipment	53 Supplies Expense
19 Accumulated Depreciation	54 Depreciation Expense
21 Accounts Payable	55 Insurance Expense
22 Salaries Payable	59 Miscellaneous Expense
23 Unearned Fees	

After analyzing each of Kelly Consulting's transactions for April, the journal entries are recorded as shown in Exhibit 10.

EXHIBIT 10

Journal Entries for April, Kelly Consulting

Journal *Page 1*

Date		Description	Post. Ref.	Debit	Credit
20Y5					
Apr.	1	Cash	11	13,100	
		Accounts Receivable	12	3,000	
		Supplies	14	1,400	
		Office Equipment	18	12,500	
		Kelly Pitney, Capital	31		30,000
	1	Prepaid Rent	15	4,800	
		Cash	11		4,800
	2	Prepaid Insurance	16	1,800	
		Cash	11		1,800
	4	Cash	11	5,000	
		Unearned Fees	23		5,000
	5	Office Equipment	18	2,000	
		Accounts Payable	21		2,000
	6	Cash	11	1,800	
		Accounts Receivable	12		1,800
	10	Miscellaneous Expense	59	120	
		Cash	11		120
	12	Accounts Payable	21	1,200	
		Cash	11		1,200
	12	Accounts Receivable	12	4,200	
		Fees Earned	41		4,200
	14	Salary Expense	51	750	
		Cash	11		750

Journal *Page 2*

Date		Description	Post. Ref.	Debit	Credit
20Y5					
Apr.	17	Cash	11	6,250	
		Fees Earned	41		6,250
	18	Supplies	14	800	
		Cash	11		800

EXHIBIT 10

Journal Entries for April, Kelly Consulting (*Concluded*)

Journal				Page 2
Date	**Description**	**Post. Ref.**	**Debit**	**Credit**
20	Accounts Receivable	12	2,100	
	Fees Earned	41		2,100
24	Cash	11	3,850	
	Fees Earned	41		3,850
26	Cash	11	5,600	
	Accounts Receivable	12		5,600
27	Salary Expense	51	750	
	Cash	11		750
29	Miscellaneous Expense	59	130	
	Cash	11		130
30	Miscellaneous Expense	59	200	
	Cash	11		200
30	Cash	11	3,050	
	Fees Earned	41		3,050
30	Accounts Receivable	12	1,500	
	Fees Earned	41		1,500
30	Kelly Pitney, Drawing	32	6,000	
	Cash	11		6,000

Step 2. Posting Transactions to the Ledger

Periodically, the transactions recorded in the journal are posted to the accounts in the ledger. The debits and credits for each journal entry are posted to the accounts in the order in which they occur in the journal. As illustrated in Chapters 2 and 3, journal entries are posted to the accounts using the following four steps:

Step 1. The date is entered in the Date column of the account.

Step 2. The amount is entered in the Debit or Credit column of the account.

Step 3. The journal page number is entered in the Posting Reference column.

Step 4. The account number is entered in the Posting Reference (Post. Ref.) column in the journal.

The journal entries for Kelly Consulting have been posted to the ledger shown in Exhibit 18.

Step 3. Preparing an Unadjusted Trial Balance

An unadjusted trial balance is prepared to determine whether any errors have been made in posting the debits and credits to the ledger. The unadjusted trial balance shown in Exhibit 11 does not provide complete proof of the accuracy of the ledger. It indicates only that the debits and the credits are equal. This proof is of value, however, because errors often affect the equality of debits and credits. If the two totals of a trial balance are not equal, an error has occurred that must be discovered and corrected.

The unadjusted account balances shown in Exhibit 11 were taken from Kelly Consulting's ledger shown in Exhibit 18, before any adjusting entries were recorded.

EXHIBIT 11

Unadjusted Trial Balance, Kelly Consulting

Kelly Consulting
Unadjusted Trial Balance
April 30, 20Y5

	Account No.	Debit Balances	Credit Balances
Cash	11	22,100	
Accounts Receivable	12	3,400	
Supplies	14	2,200	
Prepaid Rent	15	4,800	
Prepaid Insurance	16	1,800	
Office Equipment	18	14,500	
Accumulated Depreciation	19		0
Accounts Payable	21		800
Salaries Payable	22		0
Unearned Fees	23		5,000
Kelly Pitney, Capital	31		30,000
Kelly Pitney, Drawing	32	6,000	
Fees Earned	41		20,950
Salary Expense	51	1,500	
Rent Expense	52	0	
Supplies Expense	53	0	
Depreciation Expense	54	0	
Insurance Expense	55	0	
Miscellaneous Expense	59	450	
		56,750	56,750

Step 4. Assembling and Analyzing Adjustment Data

Before the financial statements can be prepared, the accounts must be updated. The four types of accounts that normally require adjustment (updating) include prepaid expenses, unearned revenue, accrued revenue, and accrued expenses. In addition, depreciation expense must be recorded for fixed assets other than land. The following data have been assembled on April 30, 20Y5, for analysis of possible adjustments for Kelly Consulting:

a. Insurance expired during April is $300.
b. Supplies on hand on April 30 are $1,350.
c. Depreciation of office equipment for April is $330.
d. Accrued receptionist salary on April 30 is $120.
e. Rent expired during April is $1,600.
f. Unearned fees on April 30 are $2,500.

Step 5. Preparing an Optional End-of-Period Spreadsheet

Although an end-of-period spreadsheet is not required, it is useful in showing the flow of accounting information from the unadjusted trial balance to the adjusted trial balance. In addition, an end-of-period spreadsheet is useful in analyzing the impact of proposed adjustments on the financial statements. The end-of-period spreadsheet for Kelly Consulting is shown in Exhibit 12. The use of an end-of-period spreadsheet is further discussed in Appendix 1 to this chapter.

Step 6. Journalizing and Posting Adjusting Entries

Based on the adjustment data shown in Step 4, adjusting entries for Kelly Consulting are prepared as shown in Exhibit 13. Each adjusting entry affects at least one income statement account and one balance sheet account. Explanations for each adjustment including any computations are normally included with each adjusting entry.

EXHIBIT 12

End-of-Period Spreadsheet, Kelly Consulting

	A	B	C	D	E	F	G
1		**Kelly Consulting**					
2		**End-of-Period Spreadsheet**					
3		**For the Month Ended April 30, 20Y5**					
4		**Unadjusted**				**Adjusted**	
5		**Trial Balance**		**Adjustments**		**Trial Balance**	
6	**Account Title**	**Dr.**	**Cr.**	**Dr.**	**Cr.**	**Dr.**	**Cr.**
7							
8	Cash	22,100				22,100	
9	Accounts Receivable	3,400				3,400	
10	Supplies	2,200			(b) 850	1,350	
11	Prepaid Rent	4,800			(e) 1,600	3,200	
12	Prepaid Insurance	1,800			(a) 300	1,500	
13	Office Equipment	14,500				14,500	
14	Accum. Depreciation				(c) 330		330
15	Accounts Payable		800				800
16	Salaries Payable				(d) 120		120
17	Unearned Fees		5,000	(f) 2,500			2,500
18	Kelly Pitney, Capital		30,000				30,000
19	Kelly Pitney, Drawing	6,000				6,000	
20	Fees Earned		20,950		(f) 2,500		23,450
21	Salary Expense	1,500		(d) 120		1,620	
22	Rent Expense			(e) 1,600		1,600	
23	Supplies Expense			(b) 850		850	
24	Depreciation Expense			(c) 330		330	
25	Insurance Expense			(a) 300		300	
26	Miscellaneous Expense	450				450	
27		56,750	56,750	5,700	5,700	57,200	57,200
28							

EXHIBIT 13

Adjusting Entries, Kelly Consulting

Journal *Page 3*

Date		Description	Post. Ref.	Debit	Credit
		Adjusting Entries			
20Y5 Apr.	30	Insurance Expense	55	300	
		Prepaid Insurance	16		300
		Expired insurance.			
	30	Supplies Expense	53	850	
		Supplies	14		850
		Supplies used ($2,200 – $1,350).			
	30	Depreciation Expense	54	330	
		Accumulated Depreciation	19		330
		Depreciation of office equipment.			
	30	Salary Expense	51	120	
		Salaries Payable	22		120
		Accrued salary.			
	30	Rent Expense	52	1,600	
		Prepaid Rent	15		1,600
		Rent expired during April.			
	30	Unearned Fees	23	2,500	
		Fees Earned	41		2,500
		Fees earned ($5,000 – $2,500).			

Each of the adjusting entries shown in Exhibit 13 is posted to Kelly Consulting's ledger shown in Exhibit 18. The adjusting entries are identified in the ledger as "Adjusting."

Step 7. Preparing an Adjusted Trial Balance

After the adjustments have been journalized and posted, an adjusted trial balance is prepared to verify the equality of the total of the debit and credit balances. This is the last step before preparing the financial statements. If the adjusted trial balance does not balance, an error has occurred and must be found and corrected. The adjusted trial balance for Kelly Consulting as of April 30, 20Y5, is shown in Exhibit 14.

EXHIBIT 14

Adjusted Trial Balance, Kelly Consulting

Kelly Consulting
Adjusted Trial Balance
April 30, 20Y5

	Account No.	Debit Balances	Credit Balances
Cash	11	22,100	
Accounts Receivable	12	3,400	
Supplies	14	1,350	
Prepaid Rent	15	3,200	
Prepaid Insurance	16	1,500	
Office Equipment	18	14,500	
Accumulated Depreciation	19		330
Accounts Payable	21		800
Salaries Payable	22		120
Unearned Fees	23		2,500
Kelly Pitney, Capital	31		30,000
Kelly Pitney, Drawing	32	6,000	
Fees Earned	41		23,450
Salary Expense	51	1,620	
Rent Expense	52	1,600	
Supplies Expense	53	850	
Depreciation Expense	54	330	
Insurance Expense	55	300	
Miscellaneous Expense	59	450	
		57,200	57,200

Step 8. Preparing the Financial Statements

The most important outcome of the accounting cycle is the financial statements. The income statement is prepared first, followed by the statement of owner's equity and then the balance sheet. The statements can be prepared directly from the adjusted trial balance, the end-of-period spreadsheet, or the ledger. The net income or net loss shown on the income statement is reported on the statement of owner's equity along with any additional investments by the owner and any withdrawals. The ending owner's capital is reported on the balance sheet and is added with total liabilities to equal total assets.

The financial statements for Kelly Consulting are shown in Exhibit 15. Kelly Consulting earned net income of $18,300 for April. As of April 30, 20Y5, Kelly Consulting has total assets of $45,720, total liabilities of $3,420, and total owner's equity of $42,300.

EXHIBIT 15

Financial Statements, Kelly Consulting

Kelly Consulting
Income Statement
For the Month Ended April 30, 20Y5

Fees earned		$23,450
Expenses:		
Salary expense	$1,620	
Rent expense	1,600	
Supplies expense	850	
Depreciation expense	330	
Insurance expense	300	
Miscellaneous expense	450	
Total expenses		5,150
Net income		$18,300

Kelly Consulting
Statement of Owner's Equity
For the Month Ended April 30, 20Y5

Kelly Pitney, capital, April 1, 20Y5		$ 0
Investment during the month	$30,000	
Net income for the month	18,300	
Withdrawals	(6,000)	
Increase in owner's equity		42,300
Kelly Pitney, capital, April 30, 20Y5		$42,300

Kelly Consulting
Balance Sheet
April 30, 20Y5

Assets		
Current assets:		
Cash	$22,100	
Accounts receivable	3,400	
Supplies	1,350	
Prepaid rent	3,200	
Prepaid insurance	1,500	
Total current assets		$31,550
Property, plant, and equipment:		
Office equipment	$14,500	
Less accumulated depreciation	330	
Total property, plant, and equipment		14,170
Total assets		$45,720
Liabilities		
Current liabilities:		
Accounts payable	$ 800	
Salaries payable	120	
Unearned fees	2,500	
Total liabilities		$ 3,420
Owner's Equity		
Kelly Pitney, capital		42,300
Total liabilities and owner's equity		$45,720

Step 9. Journalizing and Posting Closing Entries

As described earlier in this chapter, two closing entries are required at the end of an accounting period. These two closing entries are as follows:

First Closing Entry:
Debit each revenue account for its balance, credit each expense account for its balance, and credit (net income) or debit (net loss) the owner's capital account.

Second Closing Entry:
Debit the owner's capital account for the balance of the drawing account and credit the drawing account.

The two closing entries for Kelly Consulting are shown in Exhibit 16. The closing entries are posted to Kelly Consulting's ledger as shown in Exhibit 18. After the closing entries are posted, Kelly Consulting's ledger has the following characteristics:

- The balance of Kelly Pitney, Capital of $42,300 agrees with the amount reported on the statement of owner's equity and the balance sheet.
- The revenue, expense, and drawing accounts will have zero balances.

EXHIBIT 16

Closing Entries, Kelly Consulting

Journal — Page 4

Date		Description	Post. Ref.	Debit	Credit
20Y5		Closing Entries			
Apr.	30	Fees Earned	41	23,450	
		Salary Expense	51		1,620
		Rent Expense	52		1,600
		Supplies Expense	53		850
		Depreciation Expense	54		330
		Insurance Expense	55		300
		Miscellaneous Expense	59		450
		Kelly Pitney, Capital	31		18,300
	30	Kelly Pitney, Capital	31	6,000	
		Kelly Pitney, Drawing	32		6,000

The closing entries are normally identified in the ledger as "Closing." In addition, a line is often inserted in both balance columns after a closing entry is posted. This separates next period's revenue, expense, and withdrawal transactions from those of the current period.

Step 10. Preparing a Post-Closing Trial Balance

A post-closing trial balance is prepared after the closing entries have been posted. The purpose of the post-closing trial balance is to verify that the ledger is in balance at the beginning of the next period. The accounts and amounts in the post-closing trial balance should agree exactly with the accounts and amounts listed on the balance sheet at the end of the period.

The post-closing trial balance for Kelly Consulting is shown in Exhibit 17. The balances shown in the post-closing trial balance are taken from the ending balances in the ledger shown in Exhibit 18. These balances agree with the amounts shown on Kelly Consulting's balance sheet in Exhibit 15.

EXHIBIT 17

Post-Closing Trial Balance, Kelly Consulting

Kelly Consulting
Post-Closing Trial Balance
April 30, 20Y5

	Account No.	Debit Balances	Credit Balances
Cash	11	22,100	
Accounts Receivable	12	3,400	
Supplies	14	1,350	
Prepaid Rent	15	3,200	
Prepaid Insurance	16	1,500	
Office Equipment	18	14,500	
Accumulated Depreciation	19		330
Accounts Payable	21		800
Salaries Payable	22		120
Unearned Fees	23		2,500
Kelly Pitney, Capital	31		42,300
		46,050	46,050

Ledger, Kelly Consulting **EXHIBIT 18**

Ledger

Account *Cash* — *Account No. 11*

Date	Item	Post. Ref.	Debit	Credit	Balance Debit	Balance Credit
20Y5 Apr. 1		1	13,100		13,100	
1		1		4,800	8,300	
2		1		1,800	6,500	
4		1	5,000		11,500	
6		1	1,800		13,300	
10		1		120	13,180	
12		1		1,200	11,980	
14		1		750	11,230	
17		2	6,250		17,480	
18		2		800	16,680	
24		2	3,850		20,530	
26		2	5,600		26,130	
27		2		750	25,380	
29		2		130	25,250	
30		2		200	25,050	
30		2	3,050		28,100	
30		2		6,000	22,100	

Account *Accounts Receivable* — *Account No. 12*

Date	Item	Post. Ref.	Debit	Credit	Balance Debit	Balance Credit
20Y5 Apr. 1		1	3,000		3,000	
6		1		1,800	1,200	
12		1	4,200		5,400	
20		2	2,100		7,500	
26		2		5,600	1,900	
30		2	1,500		3,400	

Account *Supplies* — *Account No. 14*

Date	Item	Post. Ref.	Debit	Credit	Balance Debit	Balance Credit
20Y5 Apr. 1		1	1,400		1,400	
18		2	800		2,200	
30	Adjusting	3		850	1,350	

Account *Prepaid Rent* — *Account No. 15*

Date	Item	Post. Ref.	Debit	Credit	Balance Debit	Balance Credit
20Y5 Apr. 1		1	4,800		4,800	
30	Adjusting	3		1,600	3,200	

Account *Prepaid Insurance* — *Account No. 16*

Date	Item	Post. Ref.	Debit	Credit	Balance Debit	Balance Credit
20Y5 Apr. 2		1	1,800		1,800	
30	Adjusting	3		300	1,500	

Account *Office Equipment* — *Account No. 18*

Date	Item	Post. Ref.	Debit	Credit	Balance Debit	Balance Credit
20Y5 Apr. 1		1	12,500		12,500	
5		1	2,000		14,500	

(Continued)

EXHIBIT 18 **Ledger, Kelly Consulting (*Continued*)**

Account *Accumulated Depreciation* — *Account No. 19*

Date	Item	Post. Ref.	Debit	Credit	Balance Debit	Balance Credit
20Y5						
Apr. 30	Adjusting	3		330		330

Account *Accounts Payable* — *Account No. 21*

Date	Item	Post. Ref.	Debit	Credit	Balance Debit	Balance Credit
20Y5						
Apr. 5		1		2,000		2,000
12		1	1,200			800

Account *Salaries Payable* — *Account No. 22*

Date	Item	Post. Ref.	Debit	Credit	Balance Debit	Balance Credit
20Y5						
Apr. 30	Adjusting	3		120		120

Account *Unearned Fees* — *Account No. 23*

Date	Item	Post. Ref.	Debit	Credit	Balance Debit	Balance Credit
20Y5						
Apr. 4		1		5,000		5,000
30	Adjusting	3	2,500			2,500

Account *Kelly Pitney, Capital* — *Account No. 31*

Date	Item	Post. Ref.	Debit	Credit	Balance Debit	Balance Credit
20Y5						
Apr. 1		1		30,000		30,000
30	Closing	4		18,300		48,300
30	Closing	4	6,000			42,300

Account *Kelly Pitney, Drawing* — *Account No. 32*

Date	Item	Post. Ref.	Debit	Credit	Balance Debit	Balance Credit
20Y5						
Apr. 30		2	6,000		6,000	
30	Closing	4		6,000	—	—

Account *Fees Earned* — *Account No. 41*

Date	Item	Post. Ref.	Debit	Credit	Balance Debit	Balance Credit
20Y5						
Apr. 12		1		4,200		4,200
17		2		6,250		10,450
20		2		2,100		12,550
24		2		3,850		16,400
30		2		3,050		19,450
30		2		1,500		20,950
30	Adjusting	3		2,500		23,450
30	Closing	4	23,450		—	—

Account *Salary Expense* — *Account No. 51*

Date	Item	Post. Ref.	Debit	Credit	Balance Debit	Balance Credit
20Y5						
Apr. 14		1	750		750	
27		2	750		1,500	
30	Adjusting	3	120		1,620	
30	Closing	4		1,620	—	—

Account *Rent Expense* — *Account No. 52*

Date	Item	Post. Ref.	Debit	Credit	Balance Debit	Balance Credit
20Y5						
Apr. 30	Adjusting	3	1,600		1,600	
30	Closing	4		1,600	—	—

Account *Supplies Expense* — *Account No. 53*

Date	Item	Post. Ref.	Debit	Credit	Balance Debit	Balance Credit
20Y5						
Apr. 30	Adjusting	3	850		850	
30	Closing	4		850	—	—

Account *Depreciation Expense* — *Account No. 54*

Date	Item	Post. Ref.	Debit	Credit	Balance Debit	Balance Credit
20Y5						
Apr. 30	Adjusting	3	330		330	
30	Closing	4		330	—	—

Ledger, Kelly Consulting (*Concluded*) EXHIBIT 18

Account *Insurance Expense* — *Account No. 55*

Date	Item	Post. Ref.	Debit	Credit	Balance Debit	Balance Credit
20Y5						
Apr. 30	Adjusting	3	300		300	
30	Closing	4		300	—	—

Account *Miscellaneous Expense* — *Account No. 59*

Date	Item	Post. Ref.	Debit	Credit	Balance Debit	Balance Credit
20Y5						
Apr. 10		1	120		120	
29		2	130		250	
30		2	200		450	
30	Closing	4		450	—	—

Financial Analysis and Interpretation: Working Capital and Current Ratio

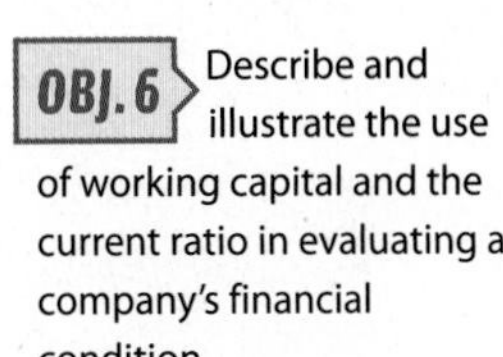

Describe and illustrate the use of working capital and the current ratio in evaluating a company's financial condition.

The ability to convert assets into cash is called **liquidity**, while the ability of a business to pay its debts is called **solvency**. Two financial measures for evaluating a business's liquidity and solvency are working capital and the current ratio.

Working capital is the excess of the current assets of a business over its current liabilities, computed as follows:

$$\text{Working Capital} = \text{Current Assets} - \text{Current Liabilities}$$

Current assets are more liquid than long-term assets. Thus, an increase in a company's current assets increases or improves its liquidity. An increase in working capital increases or improves liquidity in the sense that current assets are available for uses other than paying current liabilities.

A positive working capital implies that the business is able to pay its current liabilities and is solvent. Thus, an increase in working capital increases or improves a company's short-term solvency.

To illustrate, NetSolutions' working capital at the end of 20Y3 is \$6,355, computed as follows:

$$\begin{aligned}\text{Working Capital} &= \text{Current Assets} - \text{Current Liabilities}\\ &= \$7{,}745 - \$1{,}390\\ &= \$6{,}355\end{aligned}$$

This amount of working capital implies that NetSolutions is able to pay its current liabilities.

The **current ratio** is another means of expressing the relationship between current assets and current liabilities. The current ratio is computed by dividing current assets by current liabilities, as follows:

$$\text{Current Ratio} = \frac{\text{Current Assets}}{\text{Current Liabilities}}$$

To illustrate, the current ratio for NetSolutions at the end of 20Y3 is 5.6, computed as follows:

$$\begin{aligned}\text{Current Ratio} &= \frac{\text{Current Assets}}{\text{Current Liabilities}}\\ &= \frac{\$7{,}745}{\$1{,}390}\\ &= 5.6 \text{ (Rounded)}\end{aligned}$$

The current ratio is more useful than working capital in making comparisons across companies or with industry averages. To illustrate, the following data (in millions) were taken from recent financial statements of **Electronic Arts Inc.**, **Take-Two Interactive Software, Inc.**, and **Zynga, Inc.**:

	Electronic Arts		Take-Two		Zynga	
	Year 2	Year 1	Year 2	Year 1	Year 2	Year 1
Current assets	$6,004	$5,199	$2,409	$2,195	$747	$831
Current liabilities	2,491	2,415	1,727	1,686	480	283
Working capital	$3,513	$2,784	$ 682	$ 509	$267	$548
Current ratio*	2.41	2.15	1.39	1.30	1.56	2.94

*Rounded to two decimal places.

Comparing current ratios in Year 2, Electronic Arts has the strongest liquidity position with a current ratio of 2.41. This compares to Zynga's current ratio of 1.56 and Take-Two's current ratio of 1.39. Zynga's current ratio has decreased from 2.94 in Year 1 to 1.56 in Year 2. Electronic Arts' current ratio increased from 2.15 in Year 1 to 2.41 in Year 2, and Take-Two's current ratio increased slightly from 1.30 in Year 1 to 1.39 in Year 2. Overall, all three companies have current ratios exceeding 1; thus, there is little risk to short-term creditors that the companies will not meet their current liabilities. However, Zynga's significant decrease in working capital and current ratio in Year 2 raises some concern and should be investigated.

EXAMPLE EXERCISE 4-6 Working Capital and Current Ratio

OBJ. 6

Current assets and current liabilities for Fortson Company follow:

	20Y7	20Y6
Current assets	$310,500	$262,500
Current liabilities	172,500	150,000

a. Determine the working capital and current ratio for 20Y7 and 20Y6.

b. Is the change in the current ratio from 20Y6 to 20Y7 favorable or unfavorable?

Follow My Example 4-6

a.

	20Y7	20Y6
Current assets	$310,500	$262,500
Current liabilities	172,500	150,000
Working capital	$138,000	$112,500
Current ratio	1.80	1.75
	($310,500 ÷ $172,500)	($262,500 ÷ $150,000)

b. The change from 1.75 to 1.80 is favorable.

Practice Exercises: PE 4-6A, PE 4-6B

APPENDIX 1

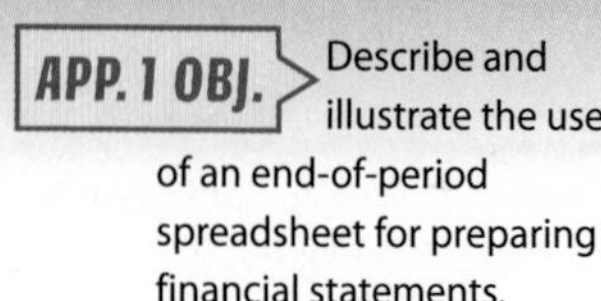

Describe and illustrate the use of an end-of-period spreadsheet for preparing financial statements.

End-of-Period Spreadsheet

Accountants often use spreadsheets for analyzing and summarizing data. Such spreadsheets are not a formal part of the accounting records. This is in contrast to the chart of accounts, the journal, and the ledger, which are essential parts of an accounting system. Spreadsheets are usually prepared by using a computer program such as Microsoft's Excel.®

Exhibit 1 is an end-of-period spreadsheet used to summarize adjusting entries and their effects on the accounts. As illustrated in the chapter, the financial statements for NetSolutions can be prepared directly from the spreadsheet's Adjusted Trial Balance columns.

Some accountants prefer to expand the end-of-period spreadsheet shown in Exhibit 1 to include financial statement columns. Exhibits 19 through 23 illustrate the step-by-step process of how to prepare this expanded spreadsheet. As a basis for illustration, NetSolutions is used.

Step 1. Enter the Title

The spreadsheet is started by entering the following data:

1. Name of the business: *NetSolutions*
2. Type of spreadsheet: *End-of-Period Spreadsheet*
3. The period of time: *For the Two Months Ended December 31, 20Y3*

Exhibit 19 shows the preceding data entered for NetSolutions.

Spreadsheet with Unadjusted Trial Balance Entered EXHIBIT 19

	A	B	C	D	E	F	G	H	I	J	K
1			NetSolutions								
2			End-of-Period Spreadsheet								
3			For the Two Months Ended December 31, 20Y3								
4		Unadjusted				Adjusted					
5		Trial Balance		Adjustments		Trial Balance		Income Statement		Balance Sheet	
6	Account Title	Dr.	Cr.	Dr.	Cr.	Dr.	Cr.	Dr.	Cr.	Dr.	Cr.
7											
8	Cash	2,065									
9	Accounts Receivable	2,220									
10	Supplies	2,000									
11	Prepaid Insurance	2,400									
12	Land	20,000									
13	Office Equipment	1,800									
14	Accumulated Depreciation										
15	Accounts Payable		900								
16	Wages Payable										
17	Unearned Rent		360								
18	Chris Clark, Capital		25,000								
19	Chris Clark, Drawing	4,000									
20	Fees Earned		16,340								
21	Rent Revenue										
22	Wages Expense	4,275									
23	Supplies Expense	800									
24	Rent Expense	1,600									
25	Utilities Expense	985									
26	Insurance Expense										
27	Depreciation Expense										
28	Miscellaneous Expense	455									
29		42,600	42,600								
30											

The spreadsheet is used for summarizing the effects of adjusting entries. It also aids in preparing financial statements.

Step 2. Enter the Unadjusted Trial Balance

Enter the unadjusted trial balance on the spreadsheet. The spreadsheet in Exhibit 19 shows the unadjusted trial balance for NetSolutions at December 31, 20Y3.

Step 3. Enter the Adjustments

The adjustments for NetSolutions from Chapter 3 are entered in the Adjustments columns, as shown in Exhibit 20. Cross-referencing (by letters) the debit and credit of each adjustment is useful in reviewing the spreadsheet. It is also helpful for identifying the adjusting entries that need to be recorded in the journal. This cross-referencing process is sometimes referred to as *keying* the adjustments.

EXHIBIT 20 **Spreadsheet with Unadjusted Trial Balance and Adjustments**

	A	B	C	D	E	F	G	H	I	J	K
1				NetSolutions							
2				End-of-Period Spreadsheet							
3				For the Two Months Ended December 31, 20Y3							
4		Unadjusted				Adjusted					
5		Trial Balance		Adjustments		Trial Balance		Income Statement		Balance Sheet	
6	Account Title	Dr.	Cr.	Dr.	Cr.	Dr.	Cr.	Dr.	Cr.	Dr.	Cr.
7											
8	Cash	2,065									
9	Accounts Receivable	2,220		(a) 500							
10	Supplies	2,000			(d) 1,240						
11	Prepaid Insurance	2,400			(e) 200						
12	Land	20,000									
13	Office Equipment	1,800									
14	Accumulated Depreciation				(f) 50						
15	Accounts Payable		900								
16	Wages Payable				(b) 250						
17	Unearned Rent		360	(c) 120							
18	Chris Clark, Capital		25,000								
19	Chris Clark, Drawing	4,000									
20	Fees Earned		16,340		(a) 500						
21	Rent Revenue				(c) 120						
22	Wages Expense	4,275		(b) 250							
23	Supplies Expense	800		(d) 1,240							
24	Rent Expense	1,600									
25	Utilities Expense	985									
26	Insurance Expense			(e) 200							
27	Depreciation Expense			(f) 50							
28	Miscellaneous Expense	455									
29		42,600	42,600	2,360	2,360						
30											

The adjustments on the spreadsheet are used in preparing the adjusting journal entries.

The adjustments are normally entered in the order in which the data are assembled. If the titles of the accounts to be adjusted do not appear in the unadjusted trial balance, the accounts are inserted in their proper order in the Account Title column.

The adjusting entries for NetSolutions that are entered in the Adjustments columns are as follows:

(a) **Accrued Fees.** Fees accrued at the end of December but not recorded total $500. This amount is an increase in an asset and an increase in revenue. The adjustment is entered as (1) $500 in the Adjustments Debit column on the same line as Accounts Receivable and (2) $500 in the Adjustments Credit column on the same line as Fees Earned.

(b) **Wages.** Wages accrued but not paid at the end of December total $250. This amount is an increase in expenses and an increase in liabilities. The adjustment is entered as (1) $250 in the Adjustments Debit column on the same line as Wages Expense and (2) $250 in the Adjustments Credit column on the same line as Wages Payable.

(c) **Unearned Rent.** The unearned rent account has a credit balance of $360. This balance represents the receipt of three months' rent, beginning with December. Thus, the rent revenue for December is $120 ($360 ÷ 3). The adjustment is entered as (1) $120 in the Adjustments Debit column on the same line as Unearned Rent and (2) $120 in the Adjustments Credit column on the same line as Rent Revenue.

(d) **Supplies.** The supplies account has a debit balance of $2,000. The cost of the supplies on hand at the end of the period is $760. The supplies expense for December is the difference between the two amounts, or $1,240 ($2,000 – $760). The adjustment is entered as (1) $1,240 in the Adjustments Debit column on the same line as Supplies Expense and (2) $1,240 in the Adjustments Credit column on the same line as Supplies.

(e) **Prepaid Insurance.** The prepaid insurance account has a debit balance of $2,400. This balance represents the prepayment of insurance for 12 months beginning December 1. Thus, the insurance expense for December is $200 ($2,400 ÷ 12). The adjustment is entered as (1) $200 in the Adjustments Debit column on the same line as Insurance Expense and (2) $200 in the Adjustments Credit column on the same line as Prepaid Insurance.

(f) **Depreciation.** Depreciation of the office equipment is $50 for December. The adjustment is entered as (1) $50 in the Adjustments Debit column on the same line as Depreciation Expense and (2) $50 in the Adjustments Credit column on the same line as Accumulated Depreciation.

After the adjustments have been entered, the Adjustments columns are totaled to verify the equality of the debits and credits. The total of the Debit column must equal the total of the Credit column.

Step 4. Enter the Adjusted Trial Balance

The adjusted trial balance is entered by combining the adjustments with the unadjusted balances for each account. The adjusted amounts are then extended to the Adjusted Trial Balance columns, as shown in Exhibit 21.

Spreadsheet with Unadjusted Trial Balance, Adjustments, and Adjusted Trial Balance Entered EXHIBIT 21

	A	B	C	D	E	F	G	H	I	J	K
1				NetSolutions							
2				End-of-Period Spreadsheet							
3				For the Two Months Ended December 31, 20Y3							
4		Unadjusted				Adjusted					
5		Trial Balance		Adjustments		Trial Balance		Income Statement		Balance Sheet	
6	Account Title	Dr.	Cr.	Dr.	Cr.	Dr.	Cr.	Dr.	Cr.	Dr.	Cr.
7											
8	Cash	2,065				2,065					
9	Accounts Receivable	2,220		(a) 500		2,720					
10	Supplies	2,000			(d) 1,240	760					
11	Prepaid Insurance	2,400			(e) 200	2,200					
12	Land	20,000				20,000					
13	Office Equipment	1,800				1,800					
14	Accumulated Depreciation				(f) 50		50				
15	Accounts Payable		900				900				
16	Wages Payable				(b) 250		250				
17	Unearned Rent		360	(c) 120			240				
18	Chris Clark, Capital		25,000				25,000				
19	Chris Clark, Drawing	4,000				4,000					
20	Fees Earned		16,340		(a) 500		16,840				
21	Rent Revenue				(c) 120		120				
22	Wages Expense	4,275		(b) 250		4,525					
23	Supplies Expense	800		(d) 1,240		2,040					
24	Rent Expense	1,600				1,600					
25	Utilities Expense	985				985					
26	Insurance Expense			(e) 200		200					
27	Depreciation Expense			(f) 50		50					
28	Miscellaneous Expense	455				455					
29		42,600	42,600	2,360	2,360	43,400	43,400				
30											

The adjusted trial balance amounts are determined by adding the adjustments to or subtracting the adjustments from the trial balance amounts. For example, the Wages Expense debit of $4,525 is the trial balance amount of $4,275 plus the $250 adjustment debit.

To illustrate, the cash amount of $2,065 is extended to the Adjusted Trial Balance Debit column since no adjustments affected Cash. Accounts Receivable has an initial balance of $2,220 and a debit adjustment of $500. Thus, $2,720 ($2,220 + $500) is entered in the Adjusted Trial Balance Debit column for Accounts Receivable. The same process continues until all account balances are extended to the Adjusted Trial Balance columns.

After the accounts and adjustments have been extended, the Adjusted Trial Balance columns are totaled to verify the equality of debits and credits. The total of the Debit column must equal the total of the Credit column.

Step 5. Extend the Accounts to the Income Statement and Balance Sheet Columns

The adjusted trial balance amounts are extended to the Income Statement and Balance Sheet columns. The amounts for revenues and expenses are extended to the Income Statement columns. The amounts for assets, liabilities, owner's capital, and drawing are extended to the Balance Sheet columns.[5]

The first account listed in the Adjusted Trial Balance columns is Cash with a debit balance of $2,065. Cash, an asset, is listed on the balance sheet and has a debit balance. Therefore, $2,065 is extended to the Balance Sheet Debit column. The Fees Earned balance of $16,840 is extended to the Income Statement Credit column. The same process continues until all account balances have been extended to the proper columns, as shown in Exhibit 22.

Step 6. Total the Income Statement and Balance Sheet Columns, Compute the Net Income or Net Loss, and Complete the Spreadsheet

After the account balances are extended to the Income Statement and Balance Sheet columns, each of the columns is totaled. The difference between the two Income Statement column totals is the amount of the net income or the net loss for the period. This difference (net income or net loss) will also be the difference between the two Balance Sheet column totals.

If the Income Statement Credit column total (total revenue) is greater than the Income Statement Debit column total (total expenses), the difference is the net income. If the Income Statement Debit column total is greater than the Income Statement Credit column total, the difference is a net loss.

As shown in Exhibit 23, the total of the Income Statement Credit column is $16,960, and the total of the Income Statement Debit column is $9,855. Thus, the net income for NetSolutions is $7,105, computed as follows:

Total of Income Statement Credit column (revenues)	$16,960
Total of Income Statement Debit column (expenses)	9,855
Net income (excess of revenues over expenses)	$ 7,105

The amount of the net income, $7,105, is entered in the Income Statement Debit column and the Balance Sheet Credit column. *Net income* is also entered in the Account Title column. Entering the net income of $7,105 in the Balance Sheet Credit column has the effect of transferring the net balance of the revenue and expense accounts to the owner's capital account.

If there was a net loss instead of net income, the amount of the net loss would be entered in the Income Statement Credit column and the Balance Sheet Debit column. *Net loss* would also be entered in the Account Title column.

After the net income or net loss is entered on the spreadsheet, the Income Statement and Balance Sheet columns are totaled. The totals of the two Income Statement columns must now be equal. The totals of the two Balance Sheet columns must also be equal.

5 The balance of the drawing account is extended to the Balance Sheet columns because the spreadsheet does not have separate Statement of Owner's Equity columns.

Spreadsheet with Amounts Extended to Income Statement and Balance Sheet Columns **EXHIBIT 22**

	A	B	C	D	E	F	G	H	I	J	K
1				NetSolutions							
2				End-of-Period Spreadsheet							
3				For the Two Months Ended December 31, 20Y3							
4		Unadjusted				Adjusted					
5		Trial Balance		Adjustments		Trial Balance		Income Statement		Balance Sheet	
6	Account Title	Dr.	Cr.	Dr.	Cr.	Dr.	Cr.	Dr.	Cr.	Dr.	Cr.
7											
8	Cash	2,065				2,065				2,065	
9	Accounts Receivable	2,220		(a) 500		2,720				2,720	
10	Supplies	2,000			(d) 1,240	760				760	
11	Prepaid Insurance	2,400			(e) 200	2,200				2,200	
12	Land	20,000				20,000				20,000	
13	Office Equipment	1,800				1,800				1,800	
14	Accumulated Depreciation				(f) 50		50				50
15	Accounts Payable		900				900				900
16	Wages Payable				(b) 250		250				250
17	Unearned Rent		360	(c) 120			240				240
18	Chris Clark, Capital		25,000				25,000				25,000
19	Chris Clark, Drawing	4,000				4,000				4,000	
20	Fees Earned		16,340		(a) 500		16,840		16,840		
21	Rent Revenue				(c) 120		120		120		
22	Wages Expense	4,275		(b) 250		4,525		4,525			
23	Supplies Expense	800		(d) 1,240		2,040		2,040			
24	Rent Expense	1,600				1,600		1,600			
25	Utilities Expense	985				985		985			
26	Insurance Expense			(e) 200		200		200			
27	Depreciation Expense			(f) 50		50		50			
28	Miscellaneous Expense	455				455		455			
29		42,600	42,600	2,360	2,360	43,400	43,400				
30											

The revenue and expense amounts are extended to (entered in) the Income Statement columns.

The asset, liability, owner's capital, and drawing amounts are extended to (entered in) the Balance Sheet columns.

Preparing the Financial Statements from the Spreadsheet

The spreadsheet can be used to prepare the income statement, the statement of owner's equity, and the balance sheet shown in Exhibit 2. The income statement is normally prepared directly from the spreadsheet. The expenses are listed in the income statement in Exhibit 2 in order of size, beginning with the larger items. Miscellaneous expense is the last item, regardless of its amount.

The first item normally presented on the statement of owner's equity is the balance of the owner's capital account at the beginning of the period. The amount listed as owner's capital in the spreadsheet, however, is not always the account balance at the beginning of the period. The owner may have invested additional assets in the business during the period. Thus, for the beginning balance and any additional investments, it is necessary to refer to the capital account in the ledger. These amounts, along with the net income (or net loss) and the drawing amount shown in the spreadsheet, are used to determine the ending capital account balance.

EXHIBIT 23 **Completed Spreadsheet with Net Income Shown**

	A	B	C	D	E	F	G	H	I	J	K
1				NetSolutions							
2				End-of-Period Spreadsheet							
3				For the Two Months Ended December 31, 20Y3							
4		Unadjusted				Adjusted					
5		Trial Balance		Adjustments		Trial Balance		Income Statement		Balance Sheet	
6	Account Title	Dr.	Cr.	Dr.	Cr.	Dr.	Cr.	Dr.	Cr.	Dr.	Cr.
7											
8	Cash	2,065				2,065				2,065	
9	Accounts Receivable	2,220		(a) 500		2,720				2,720	
10	Supplies	2,000			(d) 1,240	760				760	
11	Prepaid Insurance	2,400			(e) 200	2,200				2,200	
12	Land	20,000				20,000				20,000	
13	Office Equipment	1,800				1,800				1,800	
14	Accumulated Depreciation				(f) 50		50				50
15	Accounts Payable		900				900				900
16	Wages Payable				(b) 250		250				250
17	Unearned Rent		360	(c) 120			240				240
18	Chris Clark, Capital		25,000				25,000				25,000
19	Chris Clark, Drawing	4,000				4,000				4,000	
20	Fees Earned		16,340		(a) 500		16,840		16,840		
21	Rent Revenue				(c) 120		120		120		
22	Wages Expense	4,275		(b) 250		4,525		4,525			
23	Supplies Expense	800		(d) 1,240		2,040		2,040			
24	Rent Expense	1,600				1,600		1,600			
25	Utilities Expense	985				985		985			
26	Insurance Expense			(e) 200		200		200			
27	Depreciation Expense			(f) 50		50		50			
28	Miscellaneous Expense	455				455		455			
29		42,600	42,600	2,360	2,360	43,400	43,400	9,855	16,960	33,545	26,440
30	Net income							7,105			7,105
31								16,960	16,960	33,545	33,545
32											

The difference between the Income Statement column totals of $7,105 is the net income for the period. The difference between the Balance Sheet column totals is also $7,105, the net income for the period.

The balance sheet can be prepared directly from the spreadsheet columns except for the ending balance of owner's capital. The ending balance of owner's capital is taken from the statement of owner's equity.

When a spreadsheet is used, the adjusting and closing entries are normally not journalized or posted until after the spreadsheet and financial statements have been prepared. The data for the adjusting entries are taken from the Adjustments columns of the spreadsheet. The data for the first two closing entries are taken from the Income Statement columns of the spreadsheet. The amount for the third closing entry is the net income or net loss appearing at the bottom of the spreadsheet. The amount for the fourth closing entry is the drawing account balance that appears in the Balance Sheet Debit column of the spreadsheet.

APPENDIX 2

Why Is the Accrual Basis of Accounting Required by GAAP?

APP. 2 OBJ. Describe and explain why generally accepted accounting principles (GAAP) require the accrual basis of accounting.

The accrual basis of accounting was used in this chapter as well as in Chapters 1–3 to illustrate the transactions and financial statements for NetSolutions. Why the accrual basis of accounting is required by generally accepted accounting principles (GAAP) is described and illustrated in this appendix. This understanding is important for your ability to analyze and evaluate financial statements.

Cash Basis of Accounting

To understand why the accrual basis of accounting is required, it is first necessary to consider alternative bases of accounting. The primary alternative basis of accounting is the cash basis, which is simple and is often used by small companies and individuals operating a part-time business.[6]

Under the cash basis of accounting, revenues and expenses are recorded (recognized) when *cash is received or paid.* For example, revenue is recorded when cash is received from a customer regardless of when the services or goods have been provided or delivered. Likewise, expenses are recorded when the cash is paid regardless of when the related revenues are recorded. In other words, revenues and expenses are reported on the income statement in the period in which cash is received or paid.

Under the cash basis, accrual transactions such as purchasing on credit (accounts payable) or selling on credit (accounts receivable) are not recorded until the cash is paid or received. In addition, deferrals are not recorded under the cash basis until the cash is paid or received. As a result, adjusting entries, which originate from accruals and deferrals, are not recorded under the cash basis.

Companies that have few receivables or payables, such as attorneys, physicians, and real estate agents, may use the cash basis. For these types of companies, the cash basis provides financial statements similar to those under the accrual basis. For most large businesses, however, the cash basis will not provide adequate financial statements for user needs. As a result, almost all large companies use the accrual basis.

Accrual Basis of Accounting

As illustrated in this and preceding chapters, the accrual basis reports net income using revenue and expense recognition principles. Under the *revenue recognition principle*, revenues are recorded when earned, which is when the services have been performed or products have been delivered to customers. Revenue is recorded at the amount expected to be received.[7]

Under the *expense recognition principle*, the expenses incurred in generating revenue are recorded in the same period as the related revenue. This is also called the *matching principle.* To ensure revenues and expenses are properly matched, adjusting entries are required at the end of an accounting period, as illustrated in Chapter 3.

6 Some companies use a *modified cash basis of accounting*, which includes "some" accrual accounting. Modified cash bases of accounting are discussed in advanced accounting courses.

7 *Revenue from Contracts with Customers, Topic 606, FASB Accounting Standards Update,* Financial Accounting Standards Board, Norwalk, CT., May 2014.

Illustration of Cash and Accrual Accounting

NetSolutions is used to illustrate how the accrual basis better reports the operating performance (net income or net loss) of a company. The November and December income statements for NetSolutions using the accrual basis and the cash basis are shown in Exhibit 24.[8]

EXHIBIT 24 Accrual- and Cash-Basis Income Statements for NetSolutions

Accrual Basis

NetSolutions
Income Statement
For the Month Ended November 30, 20Y3

Fees earned		$7,500
Expenses:		
Wages expense	$2,125	
Rent expense	800	
Supplies expense	800	
Utilities expense	450	
Miscellaneous expense	275	
Total expenses		4,450
Net income		$3,050

NetSolutions
Income Statement
For the Two Months Ended December 31, 20Y3

Fees earned	$9,340	
Rent revenue	120	
Total revenues		$9,460
Expenses:		
Wages expense	$2,400	
Supplies expense	1,240	
Rent expense	800	
Utilities expense	535	
Insurance expense	200	
Depreciation expense	50	
Miscellaneous expense	180	
Total expenses		5,405
Net income		$4,055

Cash Basis

NetSolutions
Income Statement
For the Month Ended November 30, 20Y3

Fees earned		$7,500
Expenses:		
Wages expense	$2,125	
Supplies expense	950	
Rent expense	800	
Utilities expense	450	
Miscellaneous expense	275	
Total expenses		4,600
Net income		$2,900

NetSolutions
Income Statement
For the Two Months Ended December 31, 20Y3

Fees earned	$6,620	
Rent revenue	360	
Total revenues		$ 6,980
Expenses:		
Insurance expense	$2,400	
Wages expense	2,150	
Supplies expense	1,850	
Rent expense	800	
Utilities expense	535	
Miscellaneous expense	180	
Total expenses		7,915
Net loss		$ (935)

The November income statements in Exhibit 24 for the cash and accrual bases are similar. Specifically, the November accrual net income is $3,050 compared to a cash net income of $2,900. This similarity exists because NetSolutions entered into only one accrual accounting transaction in November. In this transaction on November 10, supplies of $1,350 were purchased on account. At the end of November, $800 of these supplies had been used and were recorded as Supplies Expense. The amount of $800 is used for supplies expense on the accrual-basis income statement. Cash of $950 was paid on account toward the supplies purchase in November, so $950 is used for supplies expense on the cash-basis statement.

8 The cash-basis income statements for November and December are prepared by analyzing the transactions posted to the cash account in Exhibit 6. The accrual-basis income statement for November is shown in Chapter 1. The December income statement is prepared from the Exhibit 6 ledger using only the December postings, including December 31 adjusting entries.

In December, NetSolutions entered into a variety of accrual accounting transactions. As a result, the net income under the accrual and cash bases differs significantly. For example, the December accrual-basis net income of $4,055 is in stark contrast to the cash-basis net loss of $(935). Which of the two December net income statements better reflects the operating performance of NetSolutions? The answer can be determined by analyzing NetSolutions' operating results for November and December.

NetSolutions' operating results for November and December are summarized in Exhibit 25. Under the accrual basis of accounting, revenues increased by 26.1% in December while expenses increased by only 21.5%. As a result, net income increased by 33.0%. These results suggest that NetSolutions is a profitable, rapidly expanding company.

In contrast, Exhibit 25 indicates that under the cash basis of accounting, revenues decreased by 6.9% while expenses increased by 72.1%. As a result, NetSolutions reported a net loss of $935 or a decrease of 132.2% from November's net income of $2,900. These results suggest that NetSolutions is in trouble and may not be able to continue as a viable company.

Exhibit 25 illustrates why generally accepted accounting principles (GAAP) require the accrual basis of accounting. Specifically, accrual accounting better reflects the underlying operating performance of a company. Accrual accounting does this by better recording and matching revenues and expenses. As a result, accrual accounting is a better indicator of a company's current and future operating performance.

Accrual versus Cash Basis of Accounting, NetSolutions EXHIBIT 25

Accrual Basis of Accounting

			Increase (Decrease)		Interpretation
	December	**November**	**Amount**	**Percent**	
Revenues	$9,460	$7,500	$1,960	26.1%	NetSolutions is profitable and rapidly expanding.
Expenses	5,405	4,450	955	21.5%	
Net income (loss)	$4,055	$3,050	1,005	33.0%	

Cash Basis of Accounting

			Increase (Decrease)		Interpretation
	December	**November**	**Amount**	**Percent**	
Revenues	$6,980	$7,500	$ (520)	(6.9)%	NetSolutions is in trouble with declining revenues and increasing expenses, which generated a net loss. This suggests that NetSolutions may not be able to continue as a viable company without significant operational changes.
Expenses	7,915	4,600	3,315	(72.1)%	
Net income (loss)	$ (935)	$2,900	(3,835)	(132.2)%	

The significant differences in the accrual- and cash-basis income statements for December shown in Exhibits 24 and 25 are caused by the various accrual and deferral transactions that NetSolutions entered into in December. For example, NetSolutions earned $3,370 ($1,750 + $1,120 + $500) of fees from customers by providing services on account. However, only $650 of these fees were collected in December and, as a result, only $650 was included with the revenues reported under the cash basis. Likewise, NetSolutions paid a premium of $2,400 for a one-year (12-month) insurance policy. Under the cash basis, the entire payment of $2,400 was recorded as insurance expense for December. Under the accrual basis, only $200 (one month's premium) was recorded as a December expense.

At a Glance 4

OBJ. 1 Describe the flow of accounting information from the unadjusted trial balance into the adjusted trial balance and financial statements.

Key Points Exhibit 1 illustrates the end-of-period process by which accounts are adjusted and how the adjusted accounts flow into the financial statements.

Learning Outcomes	Example Exercises	Practice Exercises
• Using an end-of-period spreadsheet, describe how the unadjusted trial balance accounts are affected by adjustments and how the adjusted trial balance accounts flow into the income statement and balance sheet.	**EE4-1**	**PE4-1A, 4-1B**

OBJ. 2 Prepare financial statements from adjusted account balances.

Key Points Using the end-of-period spreadsheet shown in Exhibit 1, the income statement and balance sheet for NetSolutions can be prepared. The statement of owner's equity is prepared by referring to transactions that have been posted to owner's capital accounts in the ledger. A classified balance sheet has sections for current assets; property, plant, and equipment; current liabilities; long-term liabilities; and owner's equity.

Learning Outcomes	Example Exercises	Practice Exercises
• Describe how the net income or net loss from the period can be determined from an end-of-period spreadsheet.		
• Prepare an income statement, a statement of owner's equity, and a balance sheet.	**EE4-2**	**PE4-2A, 4-2B**
• Indicate how accounts would be reported on a classified balance sheet.	**EE4-3**	**PE4-3A, 4-3B**

OBJ. 3 Prepare closing entries.

Key Points Two entries are required in closing the temporary accounts. The first entry debits each revenue account for its balance, credits each expense account for its balance, and credits (net income) or debits (net loss) the owner's capital account. The second entry closes the drawing account to the owner's capital account.

After the closing entries have been posted to the ledger, the balance in the capital account agrees with the amount reported on the statement of owner's equity and balance sheet. In addition, the revenue, expense, and drawing accounts will have zero balances.

Learning Outcomes	Example Exercises	Practice Exercises
• Prepare the closing entry for revenues and expenses.	**EE4-4**	**PE4-4A, 4-4B**
• Prepare the closing entry for the owner's drawing account.	**EE4-4**	**PE4-4A, 4-4B**

OBJ. 4 Describe the accounting cycle.

Key Points The ten basic steps of the accounting cycle are as follows:

1. Transactions are analyzed and recorded in the journal.
2. Transactions are posted to the ledger.
3. An unadjusted trial balance is prepared.
4. Adjustment data are assembled and analyzed.
5. An optional end-of-period spreadsheet is prepared.
6. Adjusting entries are journalized and posted to the ledger.
7. An adjusted trial balance is prepared.
8. Financial statements are prepared.
9. Closing entries are journalized and posted to the ledger.
10. A post-closing trial balance is prepared.

Learning Outcomes	Example Exercises	Practice Exercises
• List the ten steps of the accounting cycle.		
• Determine whether any steps are out of order in a listing of accounting cycle steps.		
• Determine whether there are any missing steps in a listing of accounting cycle steps.	**EE4-5**	**PE4-5A, 4-5B**

OBJ. 5 Illustrate the accounting cycle for one period.

Key Points The complete accounting cycle for Kelly Consulting for the month of April is described and illustrated in this chapter.

Learning Outcomes	Example Exercises	Practice Exercises
• Complete the accounting cycle for a period from beginning to end.		

OBJ. 6 Describe and illustrate the use of working capital and the current ratio in evaluating a company's financial condition.

Key Points The ability to convert assets into cash is called liquidity, while the ability of a business to pay its debts is called solvency. Two financial measures for evaluating a business's liquidity and solvency are working capital and the current ratio. Working capital is computed by subtracting current liabilities from current assets. An excess of current assets over current liabilities implies that the business is able to pay its current liabilities. The current ratio is computed by dividing current assets by current liabilities. The current ratio is more useful than working capital in making comparisons across companies or with industry averages.

Learning Outcomes	Example Exercises	Practice Exercises
• Define liquidity and solvency.		
• Compute working capital.	**EE4-6**	**PE4-6A, 4-6B**
• Compute the current ratio.	**EE4-6**	**PE4-6A, 4-6B**

Illustrative Problem

Three years ago, T. Roderick organized Harbor Realty. At July 31, 20Y8, the end of the fiscal year, the following end-of-period spreadsheet was prepared:

	A	B	C	D	E	F	G
1		Harbor Realty					
2		End-of-Period Spreadsheet					
3		For the Year Ended July 31, 20Y8					
4		Unadjusted				Adjusted	
5		Trial Balance		Adjustments		Trial Balance	
6	**Account Title**	**Dr.**	**Cr.**	**Dr.**	**Cr.**	**Dr.**	**Cr.**
7							
8	Cash	3,425				3,425	
9	Accounts Receivable	7,000		(e) 1,000		8,000	
10	Supplies	1,270			(a) 890	380	
11	Prepaid Insurance	620			(b) 315	305	
12	Office Equipment	51,650				51,650	
13	Accum. Depreciation		9,700		(c) 4,950		14,650
14	Accounts Payable		925				925
15	Unearned Fees		1,250	(f) 500			750
16	Wages Payable				(d) 440		440
17	T. Roderick, Capital		29,000				29,000
18	T. Roderick, Drawing	5,200				5,200	
19	Fees Earned		59,125		(e) 1,000		60,625
20					(f) 500		
21	Wages Expense	22,415		(d) 440		22,855	
22	Depreciation Expense			(c) 4,950		4,950	
23	Rent Expense	4,200				4,200	
24	Utilities Expense	2,715				2,715	
25	Supplies Expense			(a) 890		890	
26	Insurance Expense			(b) 315		315	
27	Miscellaneous Expense	1,505				1,505	
28		100,000	100,000	8,095	8,095	106,390	106,390
29							

Instructions

1. Prepare an income statement, a statement of owner's equity (no additional investments were made during the year), and a balance sheet.
2. On the basis of the data in the end-of-period spreadsheet, journalize the closing entries.

Solution

1.

Harbor Realty
Income Statement
For the Year Ended July 31, 20Y8

Fees earned		$60,625
Expenses:		
Wages expense	$22,855	
Depreciation expense	4,950	
Rent expense	4,200	
Utilities expense	2,715	
Supplies expense	890	
Insurance expense	315	
Miscellaneous expense	1,505	
Total expenses		37,430
Net income		$23,195

Harbor Realty
Statement of Owner's Equity
For the Year Ended July 31, 20Y8

T. Roderick, capital, August 1, 20Y7		$29,000
Net income for the year	$23,195	
Withdrawals	(5,200)	
Increase in owner's equity		17,995
T. Roderick, capital, July 31, 20Y8		$46,995

Harbor Realty
Balance Sheet
July 31, 20Y8

Assets		
Current assets:		
Cash	$ 3,425	
Accounts receivable	8,000	
Supplies	380	
Prepaid insurance	305	
Total current assets		$12,110
Property, plant, and equipment:		
Office equipment	$51,650	
Less accumulated depreciation	14,650	
Total property, plant, and equipment		37,000
Total assets		$49,110
Liabilities		
Current liabilities:		
Accounts payable	$ 925	
Unearned fees	750	
Wages payable	440	
Total liabilities		$ 2,115
Owner's Equity		
T. Roderick, capital		46,995
Total liabilities and owner's equity		$49,110

2.

Journal					Page
Date		**Description**	**Post. Ref.**	**Debit**	**Credit**
		Closing Entries			
20Y8 July	31	Fees Earned		60,625	
		Wages Expense			22,855
		Depreciation Expense			4,950
		Rent Expense			4,200
		Utilities Expense			2,715
		Supplies Expense			890
		Insurance Expense			315
		Miscellaneous Expense			1,505
		T. Roderick, Capital			23,195
	31	T. Roderick, Capital		5,200	
		T. Roderick, Drawing			5,200

Key Terms

accounting cycle (174)
closing entries (170)
closing process (170)
closing the books (170)
current assets (168)
current liabilities (168)
current ratio (187)
first closing entry (170)
fixed (plant) assets (168)
liquidity (187)
long-term liabilities (168)
notes receivable (168)
real (permanent) accounts (169)
second closing entry (170)
solvency (187)
temporary (nominal) accounts (169)
working capital (187)

Discussion Questions

1. Why do some accountants prepare an end-of-period spreadsheet?
2. Describe the nature of the assets that compose the following sections of a balance sheet: (a) Current Assets and (b) Property, Plant, and Equipment.
3. What is the difference between a current liability and a long-term liability?
4. What types of accounts are referred to as temporary accounts?
5. Identify the permanent accounts from the following accounts: Cash; Chris Hawkins, Drawing; Fees Earned; Office Equipment; Wages Expense.
6. Why are closing entries required at the end of an accounting period?
7. What is the difference between adjusting entries and closing entries?
8. Are closing entries recorded before or after preparing the (a) adjusted trial balance, (b) financial statements, (c) post-closing trial balance?
9. What is the purpose of the post-closing trial balance?
10. (a) What is the most important output of the accounting cycle? (b) Do all companies have an accounting cycle? Explain.

Practice Exercises

Example Exercises

SHOW ME HOW

EE 4-1 *p. 165*

PE 4-1A Flow of accounts into financial statements **OBJ. 1**

The balances for the accounts that follow appear in the Adjusted Trial Balance columns of the end-of-period spreadsheet. Indicate whether each account would flow into the income statement, statement of owner's equity, or balance sheet.

1. Accounts Payable
2. Depreciation Expense
3. Nat Hager, Capital (beginning of period)
4. Office Equipment
5. Rent Revenue
6. Supplies Expense
7. Unearned Rent
8. Wages Payable

SHOW ME HOW

EE 4-1 *p. 165*

PE 4-1B Flow of accounts into financial statements **OBJ. 1**

The balances for the accounts that follow appear in the Adjusted Trial Balance columns of the end-of-period spreadsheet. Indicate whether each account would flow into the income statement, statement of owner's equity, or balance sheet.

1. Accumulated Depreciation
2. Cash
3. Fees Earned
4. Insurance Expense
5. Prepaid Rent
6. Supplies
7. Tina Greer, Drawing
8. Wages Expense

SHOW ME HOW

EE 4-2 *p. 167*

PE 4-2A Statement of owner's equity **OBJ. 2**

Cyrus Bautista owns and operates Aquarius Advertising Services. On January 1, 20Y3, Cyrus Bautista, Capital had a balance of $471,900. During the year, Cyrus invested an additional $72,000 and withdrew $17,000. For the year ended December 31, 20Y3, Aquarius Advertising Services reported a net income of $103,000. Prepare a statement of owner's equity for the year ended December 31, 20Y3.

SHOW ME HOW

EE 4-2 *p. 167*

PE 4-2B Statement of owner's equity **OBJ. 2**

Ava Marie Rowland owns and operates Road Runner Delivery Services. On January 1, 20Y3, Ava Marie Rowland, Capital had a balance of $781,000. During the year, Ava Marie made no additional investments and withdrew $19,000. For the year ended December 31, 20Y3, Road Runner Delivery Services reported a net loss of $34,500. Prepare a statement of owner's equity for the year ended December 31, 20Y3.

SHOW ME HOW

EE 4-3 *p. 168*

PE 4-3A Classified balance sheet **OBJ. 2**

The following accounts appear in an adjusted trial balance of Carbinaro Consulting. Indicate whether each account would be reported as (a) a current asset; (b) property, plant, and equipment; (c) a current liability; (d) a long-term liability; or (e) owner's equity on the December 31, 20Y4, balance sheet of Carbinaro Consulting.

1. Building
2. Cindy Sue Delaney, Capital
3. Note Payable (due in five years)
4. Prepaid Rent
5. Salaries Payable
6. Supplies
7. Taxes Payable
8. Unearned Service Fees

EE 4-3 p. 168

PE 4-3B Classified balance sheet

OBJ. 2

The following accounts appear in an adjusted trial balance of Kangaroo Consulting. Indicate whether each account would be reported as (a) a current asset; (b) property, plant, and equipment; (c) a current liability; (d) a long-term liability; or (e) owner's equity on the December 31, 20Y4, balance sheet of Kangaroo Consulting.

1. Accounts Payable
2. Accounts Receivable
3. Accumulated Depreciation—Building
4. Cash
5. Lea Gabel, Capital
6. Note Payable (due in 10 years)
7. Supplies
8. Wages Payable

EE 4-4 p. 174

PE 4-4A Closing entries

OBJ. 3

After the accounts have been adjusted at December 31, the end of the fiscal year, the following balances were taken from the ledger of Magenta Delivery Services Co.:

Ellie Liu, Capital	$8,366,300
Ellie Liu, Drawing	70,000
Fees Earned	1,644,500
Wages Expense	1,239,200
Rent Expense	109,400
Supplies Expense	26,800
Miscellaneous Expense	19,300

Journalize the two entries required to close the accounts.

EE 4-4 p. 174

PE 4-4B Closing entries

OBJ. 3

After the accounts have been adjusted at April 30, the end of the fiscal year, the following balances were taken from the ledger of Twin Trees Landscaping Co.:

Oscar Killingsworth, Capital	$503,900
Oscar Killingsworth, Drawing	8,200
Fees Earned	279,100
Wages Expense	221,600
Rent Expense	43,800
Supplies Expense	9,000
Miscellaneous Expense	10,200

Journalize the two entries required to close the accounts.

EE 4-5 p. 175

PE 4-5A Accounting cycle

OBJ. 4

From the following list of steps in the accounting cycle, identify what two steps are missing:

a. Transactions are analyzed and recorded in the journal.
b. An unadjusted trial balance is prepared.
c. Adjustment data are assembled and analyzed.
d. An optional end-of-period spreadsheet is prepared.
e. Adjusting entries are journalized and posted to the ledger.
f. An adjusted trial balance is prepared.
g. Closing entries are journalized and posted to the ledger.
h. A post-closing trial balance is prepared.

EE 4-5 p. 175

PE 4-5B Accounting cycle

OBJ. 4

From the following list of steps in the accounting cycle, identify what two steps are missing:

a. Transactions are analyzed and recorded in the journal.
b. Transactions are posted to the ledger.

c. An unadjusted trial balance is prepared.
d. An optional end-of-period spreadsheet is prepared.
e. Adjusting entries are journalized and posted to the ledger.
f. An adjusted trial balance is prepared.
g. Financial statements are prepared.
h. A post-closing trial balance is prepared.

EE 4-6 p. 188

FAI

PE 4-6A Working capital and current ratio **OBJ. 6**

Current assets and current liabilities for Konex Properties Company follow:

	20Y9	20Y8
Current assets	$2,042,400	$1,759,500
Current liabilities	1,380,000	1,150,000

a. Determine the working capital and current ratio for 20Y9 and 20Y8.
b. Is the change in the current ratio from 20Y8 to 20Y9 favorable or unfavorable?

EE 4-6 p. 188

FAI

EXCEL ONLINE

PE 4-6B Working capital and current ratio **OBJ. 6**

Current assets and current liabilities for Sandstone Company follow:

	20Y9	20Y8
Current assets	$2,133,800	$1,613,300
Current liabilities	940,000	730,000

a. Determine the working capital and current ratio for 20Y9 and 20Y8.
b. Is the change in the current ratio from 20Y8 to 20Y9 favorable or unfavorable?

Exercises

EX 4-1 Flow of accounts into financial statements **OBJ. 1, 2**

The balances for the accounts that follow appear in the Adjusted Trial Balance columns of the end-of-period spreadsheet. Indicate whether each account would flow into the income statement, statement of owner's equity, or balance sheet.

1. Accounts Payable
2. Accounts Receivable
3. Cash
4. Eddy Rosewood, Drawing
5. Fees Earned
6. Supplies
7. Unearned Rent
8. Utilities Expense
9. Wages Expense
10. Wages Payable

EX 4-2 Classifying accounts **OBJ. 1, 2**

Balances for each of the following accounts appear in an adjusted trial balance. Identify each as (a) asset, (b) liability, (c) revenue, or (d) expense.

1. Accounts Receivable
2. Equipment
3. Fees Earned
4. Insurance Expense
5. Land
6. Prepaid Rent
7. Rent Revenue
8. Salary Expense
9. Salary Payable
10. Supplies
11. Unearned Rent
12. Wages Payable

SHOW ME HOW

EX 4-3 Financial statements from the end-of-period spreadsheet **OBJ. 1, 2**

Bamboo Consulting is a consulting firm owned and operated by Lisa Gooch. The following end-of-period spreadsheet was prepared for the year ended July 31, 20Y5:

	A	B	C	D	E	F	G
1		Bamboo Consulting					
2		End-of-Period Spreadsheet					
3		For the Year Ended July 31, 20Y5					
4		Unadjusted				Adjusted	
5		Trial Balance		Adjustments		Trial Balance	
6	Account Title	Dr.	Cr.	Dr.	Cr.	Dr.	Cr.
7							
8	Cash	58,000				58,000	
9	Accounts Receivable	106,200				106,200	
10	Supplies	11,900			(a) 7,500	4,400	
11	Office Equipment	515,000				515,000	
12	Accumulated Depreciation		28,000		(b) 5,600		33,600
13	Accounts Payable		20,500				20,500
14	Salaries Payable				(c) 2,500		2,500
15	Lisa Gooch, Capital		516,700				516,700
16	Lisa Gooch, Drawing	25,000				25,000	
17	Fees Earned		348,500				348,500
18	Salary Expense	186,500		(c) 2,500		189,000	
19	Supplies Expense			(a) 7,500		7,500	
20	Depreciation Expense			(b) 5,600		5,600	
21	Miscellaneous Expense	11,100				11,100	
22		913,700	913,700	15,600	15,600	921,800	921,800
23							

Based on the preceding spreadsheet, prepare an income statement, statement of owner's equity, and balance sheet for Bamboo Consulting.

SHOW ME HOW

EX 4-4 Financial statements from the end-of-period spreadsheet **OBJ. 1, 2**

Elliptical Consulting is a consulting firm owned and operated by Jayson Neese. The following end-of-period spreadsheet was prepared for the year ended June 30, 20Y6:

	A	B	C	D	E	F	G
1		Elliptical Consulting					
2		End-of-Period Spreadsheet					
3		For the Year Ended June 30, 20Y6					
4		Unadjusted				Adjusted	
5		Trial Balance		Adjustments		Trial Balance	
6	Account Title	Dr.	Cr.	Dr.	Cr.	Dr.	Cr.
7							
8	Cash	27,000				27,000	
9	Accounts Receivable	53,500				53,500	
10	Supplies	3,000			(a) 2,100	900	
11	Office Equipment	30,500				30,500	
12	Accumulated Depreciation		4,500		(b) 1,500		6,000
13	Accounts Payable		3,300				3,300
14	Salaries Payable				(c) 375		375
15	Jayson Neese, Capital		82,200				82,200
16	Jayson Neese, Drawing	2,000				2,000	
17	Fees Earned		60,000				60,000
18	Salary Expense	32,000		(c) 375		32,375	
19	Supplies Expense			(a) 2,100		2,100	
20	Depreciation Expense			(b) 1,500		1,500	
21	Miscellaneous Expense	2,000				2,000	
22		150,000	150,000	3,975	3,975	151,875	151,875
23							

Based on the preceding spreadsheet, prepare an income statement, statement of owner's equity, and balance sheet for Elliptical Consulting.

✔ Net income, $168,800

EX 4-5 Income statement OBJ. 2

The following account balances were taken from the adjusted trial balance for Capstone Messenger Service, a delivery service firm, for the fiscal year ended April 30, 20Y7:

Depreciation Expense	$ 6,700	Rent Expense	$ 46,500
Fees Earned	522,000	Salaries Expense	260,900
Insurance Expense	1,200	Supplies Expense	3,200
Miscellaneous Expense	2,800	Utilities Expense	31,900

Prepare an income statement.

✔ Net loss, $(18,900)

EX 4-6 Income statement; net loss OBJ. 2

The following revenue and expense account balances were taken from the ledger of Guardian Health Services Co. after the accounts had been adjusted on February 28, 20Y0, the end of the fiscal year:

Depreciation Expense	$ 6,800	Service Revenue	$407,900
Insurance Expense	2,700	Supplies Expense	2,500
Miscellaneous Expense	7,400	Utilities Expense	30,800
Rent Expense	49,100	Wages Expense	327,500

Prepare an income statement.

✔ Net income, $4,572

EX 4-7 Income statement OBJ. 2

FedEx Corporation had the following revenue and expense account balances (in millions) for a recent year ending May 31:

Depreciation Expense	$ 3,095	Purchased Transportation	$15,101
Fuel Expense	3,374	Rentals and Landing Fees	3,361
Maintenance and Repairs Expense	2,622	Revenues	65,450
Other Expense	10,337	Salaries and Employee Benefits	23,207
Provision for Income Taxes (Benefit)	(219)		

Prepare an income statement.

✔ Farhan Wasti, capital, Dec. 31, 20Y1: $1,789,000

EX 4-8 Statement of owner's equity OBJ. 2

Serenity Systems Co. offers its services to residents in the Minneapolis area. Selected accounts from the ledger of Serenity Systems Co. for the fiscal year ended December 31, 20Y1, are as follows:

Farhan Wasti, Capital

Dec. 31	98,000	Jan. 1 (20Y1)	1,502,000
		Dec. 31	385,000

Farhan Wasti, Drawing

Mar. 31	24,500	Dec. 31	98,000
June 30	24,500		
Sept. 30	24,500		
Dec. 31	24,500		

Prepare a statement of owner's equity for the year.

✔ Angelo Phelps, capital, April 30, 20Y2: $492,700

EX 4-9 Statement of owner's equity; net loss OBJ. 2

Selected accounts from the ledger of Masterpiece Arts for the fiscal year ended April 30, 20Y2, are as follows:

Angelo Phelps, Capital

Apr. 30	35,200	May 1 (20Y1)	537,100
30	9,200		

Angelo Phelps, Drawing

July 31	2,300	Apr. 30	9,200
Oct. 31	2,300		
Jan. 31	2,300		
Apr. 30	2,300		

Prepare a statement of owner's equity for the year.

EX 4-10 Classifying assets OBJ. 2

Identify each of the following as (a) a current asset or (b) property, plant, and equipment:

1. Accounts Receivable
2. Building
3. Cash
4. Land
5. Prepaid Insurance
6. Supplies

EX 4-11 Balance sheet classification **OBJ. 2**

At the balance sheet date, a business owes a mortgage note payable of $375,000, the terms of which provide for monthly payments of $1,250.

Explain how the liability should be classified on the balance sheet.

EX 4-12 Balance sheet **OBJ. 2**

✔ **Total assets: $920,300**

SHOW ME HOW

MaxFit Weight Loss Co. offers personal weight reduction consulting services to individuals. After all the accounts have been closed on November 30, 20Y4, the end of the fiscal year, the balances of selected accounts from the ledger of MaxFit Weight Loss Co. are as follows:

Accounts Payable	$ 44,800	Prepaid Insurance	$ 8,500
Accounts Receivable	138,600	Prepaid Rent	24,900
Accumulated Depreciation	221,300	Salaries Payable	10,700
Cash	?	Supplies	5,700
Equipment	563,000	Unearned Fees	21,400
Land	356,200	Vanessa Freeman, Capital	843,400

Prepare a classified balance sheet that includes the correct balance for Cash.

EX 4-13 Balance sheet **OBJ. 2**

✔ **Corrected balance sheet, total assets: $625,000**

List the errors you find in the following balance sheet. Prepare a corrected balance sheet.

Labyrinth Services Co.
Balance Sheet
For the Year Ended August 31, 20Y3

Assets		
Current assets:		
Cash	$ 18,500	
Accounts payable	31,300	
Supplies	6,500	
Prepaid insurance	16,600	
Land	225,000	
Total current assets		$297,900
Property, plant, and equipment:		
Building	$400,000	
Equipment	97,000	
Total property, plant, and equipment		635,400
Total assets		$933,300
Liabilities		
Current liabilities:		
Accounts receivable	$ 41,400	
Accumulated depreciation—building	155,000	
Accumulated depreciation—equipment	25,000	
Net income	118,200	
Total liabilities		$339,600
Owner's Equity		
Wages payable	$ 6,500	
Ruben Daniel, capital	587,200	
Total owner's equity		593,700
Total liabilities and owner's equity		$933,300

EX 4-14 Identifying accounts to be closed **OBJ. 3**

From the list that follows, identify the accounts that should be closed to the owner's capital account at the end of the fiscal year:

a. Accounts Receivable
b. Accumulated Depreciation
c. Building
d. Depreciation Expense
e. Fees Earned
f. Jackie Lindsay, Capital
g. Jackie Lindsay, Drawing
h. Land
i. Supplies
j. Supplies Expense
k. Unearned Rent
l. Wages Expense

EX 4-15 Closing entries **OBJ. 3**

Prior to closing, total revenues were $8,315,000 and total expenses were $6,460,000. During the year, the owner made no additional investments and withdrew $408,000. After the closing entries, how much did the owner's capital account change?

EX 4-16 Closing entries with net income **OBJ. 3**

Assume that the entry closing total revenues of $3,190,000 and total expenses of $2,350,000 has been made for the year. At the end of the fiscal year, Teresa Schafer, Capital has a credit balance of $1,885,000 and Teresa Schafer, Drawing has a balance of $770,000. (a) Journalize the entry required to close the Teresa Schafer, drawing account. (b) Determine the amount of Teresa Schafer, Capital at the end of the period.

EX 4-17 Closing entries with net loss **OBJ. 3**

Creative Images Co. offers its services to individuals desiring to improve their personal images. After the accounts have been adjusted at July 31, the end of the fiscal year, the following balances were taken from the ledger of Creative Images Co.:

Violet Lozano, Capital	$934,500	Rent Expense	$52,900
Violet Lozano, Drawing	66,000	Supplies Expense	17,200
Fees Earned	545,000	Miscellaneous Expense	5,400
Wages Expense	342,400		

Journalize the two entries required to close the accounts.

EX 4-18 Identifying permanent accounts **OBJ. 3**

Which of the following accounts will usually appear in the post-closing trial balance?

a. Accounts Receivable
b. Cash
c. Depreciation Expense
d. Fees Earned
e. Doug Woods, Capital
f. Doug Woods, Drawing
g. Equipment
h. Land
i. Salaries Payable
j. Unearned Rent
k. Wages Expense

EX 4-19 Post-closing trial balance

OBJ. 3

✔ Correct column totals, $300,000

SHOW ME HOW

An accountant prepared the following post-closing trial balance:

La Casa Services Co.
Post-Closing Trial Balance
March 31, 20Y6

	Debit Balances	Credit Balances
Cash	46,540	
Accounts Receivable	122,260	
Supplies		4,000
Equipment		127,200
Accumulated Depreciation	33,600	
Accounts Payable	52,100	
Salaries Payable		6,400
Unearned Rent	9,000	
Sonya Flynn, Capital	198,900	
	462,400	137,600

Prepare a corrected post-closing trial balance. Assume that all accounts have normal balances and that the amounts shown are correct.

EX 4-20 Steps in the accounting cycle

OBJ. 4

Rearrange the following steps in the accounting cycle in proper sequence:

a. Transactions are analyzed and recorded in the journal.
b. An unadjusted trial balance is prepared.
c. Transactions are posted to the ledger.
d. Adjustment data are assembled and analyzed.
e. An adjusted trial balance is prepared.
f. Adjusting entries are journalized and posted to the ledger.
g. An optional end-of-period spreadsheet is prepared.
h. A post-closing trial balance is prepared.
i. Financial statements are prepared.
j. Closing entries are journalized and posted to the ledger.

EX 4-21 Working capital and current ratio

OBJ. 6

SHOW ME HOW

The following data (in thousands) were taken from recent financial statements of **Under Armour, Inc.**:

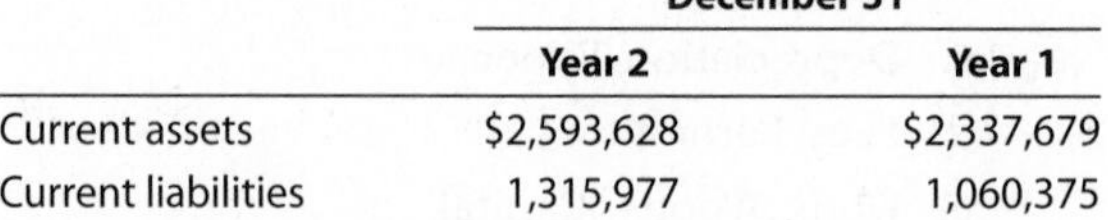

	December 31	
	Year 2	Year 1
Current assets	$2,593,628	$2,337,679
Current liabilities	1,315,977	1,060,375

a. Compute the working capital and the current ratio as of December 31, Year 2 and Year 1. Round to two decimal places.

b. What conclusions concerning the company's ability to meet its financial obligations can you draw from part (a)?

EX 4-22 Working capital and current ratio

OBJ. 6

The following data (in thousands) were taken from recent financial statements of **Starbucks Corporation**:

	Year 2	Year 1
Current assets	$12,494,200	$5,283,400
Current liabilities	5,684,200	4,220,700

a. Compute the working capital and the current ratio for Year 2 and Year 1. Round to two decimal places.

b. What conclusions concerning the company's ability to meet its financial obligations can you draw from part (a)?

Appendix 1

EX 4-23 Completing an end-of-period spreadsheet

List (a) through (j) in the order they would be performed in preparing and completing an end-of-period spreadsheet.

a. Add the Debit and Credit columns of the Unadjusted Trial Balance columns of the spreadsheet to verify that the totals are equal.

b. Add the Debit and Credit columns of the Balance Sheet and Income Statement columns of the spreadsheet to verify that the totals are equal.

c. Add or deduct adjusting entry data to trial balance amounts, and extend amounts to the Adjusted Trial Balance columns.

d. Add the Debit and Credit columns of the Adjustments columns of the spreadsheet to verify that the totals are equal.

e. Add the Debit and Credit columns of the Balance Sheet and Income Statement columns of the spreadsheet to determine the amount of net income or net loss for the period.

f. Add the Debit and Credit columns of the Adjusted Trial Balance columns of the spreadsheet to verify that the totals are equal.

g. Enter the adjusting entries into the spreadsheet, based on the adjustment data.

h. Enter the amount of net income or net loss for the period in the proper Income Statement column and Balance Sheet column.

i. Enter the unadjusted account balances from the general ledger into the Unadjusted Trial Balance columns of the spreadsheet.

j. Extend the adjusted trial balance amounts to the Income Statement columns and the Balance Sheet columns.

Appendix 1

EX 4-24 Adjustment data on an end-of-period spreadsheet

✔ **Total debits of Adjustments column: $31**

Alert Security Services Co. offers security services to business clients. The trial balance for Alert Security Services Co. has been prepared on the following end-of-period spreadsheet for the year ended October 31, 20Y5:

Alert Security Services Co.
End-of-Period Spreadsheet
For the Year Ended October 31, 20Y5

	Unadjusted Trial Balance		Adjustments		Adjusted Trial Balance	
Account Title	**Dr.**	**Cr.**	**Dr.**	**Cr.**	**Dr.**	**Cr.**
Cash	12					
Accounts Receivable	90					
Supplies	8					
Prepaid Insurance	12					
Land	190					
Equipment	50					

(Continued)

Accumulated Depreciation		4
Accounts Payable		36
Wages Payable		0
Brenda Schultz, Capital		260
Brenda Schultz, Drawing	8	
Fees Earned		200
Wages Expense	110	
Rent Expense	12	
Insurance Expense	0	
Utilities Expense	6	
Supplies Expense	0	
Depreciation Expense	0	
Miscellaneous Expense	2	
	500	500

The data for year-end adjustments are as follows:

a. Fees earned but not yet billed, $13.
b. Supplies on hand, $4.
c. Insurance premiums expired, $10.
d. Depreciation expense, $3.
e. Wages accrued but not paid, $1.

Enter the adjustment data and place the balances in the Adjusted Trial Balance columns.

Appendix 1

EX 4-25 Completing an end-of-period spreadsheet

✔ Net income: $65

Alert Security Services Co. offers security services to business clients. Complete the following end-of-period spreadsheet for Alert Security Services Co.:

Alert Security Services Co.
End-of-Period Spreadsheet
For the Year Ended October 31, 20Y7

	Adjusted Trial Balance		Income Statement		Balance Sheet	
Account Title	**Dr.**	**Cr.**	**Dr.**	**Cr.**	**Dr.**	**Cr.**
Cash	12					
Accounts Receivable	103					
Supplies	4					
Prepaid Insurance	2					
Land	190					
Equipment	50					
Accumulated Depreciation		7				
Accounts Payable		36				
Wages Payable		1				
Brenda Schultz, Capital		260				
Brenda Schultz, Drawing	8					
Fees Earned		213				
Wages Expense	111					
Rent Expense	12					
Insurance Expense	10					
Utilities Expense	6					
Supplies Expense	4					
Depreciation Expense	3					
Miscellaneous Expense	2					
	517	517				

Appendix 1

EX 4-26 Financial statements from an end-of-period spreadsheet

✔ Brenda Schultz, capital, October 31, 20Y7: $317

Based on the data in Exercise 4-25, prepare an income statement, statement of owner's equity, and balance sheet for Alert Security Services Co.

Appendix 1

EX 4-27 Adjusting entries from an end-of-period spreadsheet

Based on the data in Exercise 4-24, prepare the adjusting entries for Alert Security Services Co.

Appendix 1

EX 4-28 Closing entries from an end-of-period spreadsheet

Based on the data in Exercise 4-25, prepare the two closing entries for Alert Security Services Co.

Problems: Series A

PR 4-1A Financial statements and closing entries **OBJ. 1, 2, 3**

✔ 3. Total assets: $659,460

SHOW ME HOW

Outreach Signals Company maintains and repairs warning lights, such as those found on radio towers and lighthouses. Outreach Signals Company prepared the following end-of-period spreadsheet at December 31, 20Y1, the end of the fiscal year:

	A	B	C	D	E	F	G
1		Outreach Signals Company					
2		End-of-Period Spreadsheet					
3		For the Year Ended December 31, 20Y1					
4		Unadjusted				Adjusted	
5		Trial Balance		Adjustments		Trial Balance	
6	Account Title	Dr.	Cr.	Dr.	Cr.	Dr.	Cr.
7							
8	Cash	20,500				20,500	
9	Accounts Receivable	63,800		(a) 19,700		83,500	
10	Prepaid Insurance	6,600			(b) 4,700	1,900	
11	Supplies	4,700			(c) 3,540	1,160	
12	Land	154,300				154,300	
13	Building	787,000				787,000	
14	Accum. Depr.—Building		402,000		(d) 14,200		416,200
15	Equipment	192,000				192,000	
16	Accum. Depr.—Equipment		157,600		(e) 7,100		164,700
17	Accounts Payable		24,700				24,700
18	Salaries and Wages Payable				(f) 7,700		7,700
19	Unearned Rent		3,300	(g) 2,000			1,300
20	Inez Villanueva, Capital		375,000				375,000
21	Inez Villanueva, Drawing	16,000				16,000	
22	Fees Earned		612,000		(a) 19,700		631,700
23	Rent Revenue				(g) 2,000		2,000
24	Salaries and Wages Expense	256,820		(f) 7,700		264,520	
25	Advertising Expense	34,200				34,200	
26	Utilities Expense	17,900				17,900	
27	Depr. Exp.—Building			(d) 14,200		14,200	
28	Repairs Expense	13,930				13,930	
29	Depr. Exp.—Equipment			(e) 7,100		7,100	
30	Insurance Expense			(b) 4,700		4,700	
31	Supplies Expense			(c) 3,540		3,540	
32	Misc. Expense	6,850				6,850	
33		1,574,600	1,574,600	58,940	58,940	1,623,300	1,623,300
34							

(Continued)

Instructions

1. Prepare an income statement for the year ended December 31.
2. Prepare a statement of owner's equity for the year ended December 31. No additional investments were made during the year.
3. Prepare a balance sheet as of December 31.
4. Based upon the end-of-period spreadsheet, journalize the closing entries.
5. Prepare a post-closing trial balance.

PR 4-2A Financial statements and closing entries **OBJ. 2, 3**

✔ 1. Stacy Tanner, capital, June 30: $483,300

Finders Investigative Services is an investigative services firm that is owned and operated by Stacy Tanner. On June 30, 20Y3, the end of the fiscal year, the accountant for Finders Investigative Services prepared an end-of-period spreadsheet, a part of which follows:

	A	F	G
1	**Finders Investigative Services**		
2	**End-of-Period Spreadsheet**		
3	**For the Year Ended June 30, 20Y3**		
4		**Adjusted**	
5		**Trial Balance**	
6	**Account Title**	**Dr.**	**Cr.**
7			
8	Cash	28,000	
9	Accounts Receivable	69,600	
10	Supplies	4,600	
11	Prepaid Insurance	2,500	
12	Building	439,500	
13	Accumulated Depreciation—Building		44,200
14	Accounts Payable		11,700
15	Salaries Payable		3,000
16	Unearned Rent		2,000
17	Stacy Tanner, Capital		373,800
18	Stacy Tanner, Drawing	12,000	
19	Service Fees		718,000
20	Rent Revenue		12,000
21	Salaries Expense	522,100	
22	Rent Expense	48,000	
23	Supplies Expense	10,800	
24	Depreciation Expense—Building	8,750	
25	Utilities Expense	7,150	
26	Repairs Expense	3,000	
27	Insurance Expense	2,500	
28	Miscellaneous Expense	6,200	
29		1,164,700	1,164,700

Instructions

1. Prepare an income statement, a statement of owner's equity (no additional investments were made during the year), and a balance sheet.
2. Journalize the entries that were required to close the accounts at June 30.
3. If Stacy Tanner, Capital has instead decreased $30,000 after the closing entries were posted, and the withdrawals remained the same, what would have been the amount of net income or net loss?

PR 4-3A T accounts, adjusting entries, financial statements, and closing entries; optional end-of-period spreadsheet

OBJ. 2, 3

✔ 5. Net income: $10,700

The unadjusted trial balance of Epicenter Laundry at June 30, 20Y3, the end of the fiscal year, follows:

Epicenter Laundry
Unadjusted Trial Balance
June 30, 20Y3

	Debit Balances	Credit Balances
Cash	11,000	
Laundry Supplies	21,500	
Prepaid Insurance	9,600	
Laundry Equipment	232,600	
Accumulated Depreciation		125,400
Accounts Payable		11,800
Sophie Perez, Capital		105,600
Sophie Perez, Drawing	10,000	
Laundry Revenue		232,200
Wages Expense	125,200	
Rent Expense	40,000	
Utilities Expense	19,700	
Miscellaneous Expense	5,400	
	475,000	475,000

The data needed to determine year-end adjustments are as follows:

a. Laundry supplies on hand at June 30 are $3,600.
b. Insurance premiums expired during the year are $5,700.
c. Depreciation of laundry equipment during the year is $6,500.
d. Wages accrued but not paid at June 30 are $1,100.

Instructions

1. For each account listed in the unadjusted trial balance, enter the balance in a T account. Identify the balance as "June 30 Bal." In addition, add T accounts for Wages Payable, Depreciation Expense, Laundry Supplies Expense, and Insurance Expense.
2. *(Optional)* Enter the unadjusted trial balance on an end-of-period spreadsheet and complete the spreadsheet. Add the accounts listed in part (1) as needed.
3. Journalize and post the adjusting entries. Identify the adjustments as "Adj." and the new balances as "Adj. Bal."
4. Prepare an adjusted trial balance.
5. Prepare an income statement, a statement of owner's equity (no additional investments were made during the year), and a balance sheet.
6. Journalize and post the closing entries. Identify the closing entries as "Clos."
7. Prepare a post-closing trial balance.

PR 4-4A Ledger accounts, adjusting entries, financial statements, and closing entries; optional spreadsheet

OBJ. 2, 3

✔ 5. Net income: $51,150

The unadjusted trial balance of Lakota Freight Co. at March 31, 20Y7, the end of the year, follows:

Lakota Freight Co.
Unadjusted Trial Balance
March 31, 20Y7

	Account No.	Debit Balances	Credit Balances
Cash	11	12,000	
Supplies	13	30,000	
Prepaid Insurance	14	3,600	
Equipment	16	110,000	
Accumulated Depreciation—Equipment	17		25,000
Trucks	18	60,000	
Accumulated Depreciation—Trucks	19		15,000
Accounts Payable	21		4,000
Kaya Tarango, Capital	31		96,000
Kaya Tarango, Drawing	32	15,000	
Service Revenue	41		160,000
Wages Expense	51	45,000	
Rent Expense	53	10,600	
Truck Expense	54	9,000	
Miscellaneous Expense	59	4,800	
		300,000	300,000

The data needed to determine year-end adjustments are as follows:

a. Supplies on hand at March 31 are $7,500.

b. Insurance premiums expired during the year are $1,800.

c. Depreciation of equipment during the year is $8,350.

d. Depreciation of trucks during the year is $6,200.

e. Wages accrued but not paid at March 31 are $600.

Instructions

1. For each account listed in the trial balance, enter the balance in the appropriate Balance column of a four-column account and place a check mark (✓) in the Posting Reference column.
2. *(Optional)* Enter the unadjusted trial balance on an end-of-period spreadsheet and complete the spreadsheet. Add the accounts listed in part (3) as needed.
3. Journalize and post the adjusting entries, inserting balances in the accounts affected. Record the adjusting entries on Page 26 of the journal. The following additional accounts from Lakota Freight Co.'s chart of accounts should be used: Wages Payable, 22; Supplies Expense, 52; Depreciation Expense—Equipment, 55; Depreciation Expense—Trucks, 56; Insurance Expense, 57.
4. Prepare an adjusted trial balance.
5. Prepare an income statement, a statement of owner's equity (no additional investments were made during the year), and a balance sheet.
6. Journalize and post the closing entries. Record the closing entries on Page 27 of the journal. Indicate closed accounts by inserting a line in both Balance columns opposite the closing entry.
7. Prepare a post-closing trial balance.

✔ 8. Net income: $68,130

PR 4-5A Complete accounting cycle **OBJ. 4, 5**

For the past several years, Samantha Hogan has operated a part-time consulting business from her home. As of July 1, 20Y9, Samantha decided to move to rented quarters and to operate the business, which was to be known as Arborvite Consulting, on a full-time basis. Arborvite Consulting entered into the following transactions during July:

July 1. The following assets were received from Samantha Hogan: cash, $25,700; accounts receivable, $30,200; supplies, $5,100; and office equipment, $12,100. There were no liabilities received.

1. Paid three months' rent on a lease rental contract, $8,100.

2. Paid the premiums on property and casualty insurance policies, $6,100.

3. Received cash from clients as an advance payment for services to be provided and recorded it as unearned fees, $10,800.

5. Purchased additional office equipment on account from Office Necessities Co., $6,900.

6. Received cash from clients on account, $17,300.

10. Paid cash for a newspaper advertisement, $680.

12. Paid Office Necessities Co. for part of the debt incurred on July 5, $4,100.

12. Provided services on account for the period July 1–12, $19,200.

14. Paid receptionist for two weeks' salary, $2,000.

Record the following transactions on Page 2 of the journal:

17. Received cash from cash clients for fees earned during the period July 1–17, $14,100.

18. Paid cash for supplies, $1,400.

20. Provided services on account for the period July 13–20, $12,200.

24. Received cash from cash clients for fees earned for the period July 17–24, $11,500.

26. Received cash from clients on account, $16,300.

27. Paid receptionist for two weeks' salary, $2,000.

29. Paid telephone bill for July, $440.

31. Paid electricity bill for July, $910.

31. Received cash from cash clients for fees earned for the period July 25–31, $9,600.

31. Provided services on account for the remainder of July, $7,400.

31. Samantha withdrew $27,100 for personal use.

Instructions

1. Journalize each transaction in a two-column journal starting on Page 1, referring to the following chart of accounts in selecting the accounts to be debited and credited. (Do not insert the account numbers in the journal at this time.)

11	Cash	31	Samantha Hogan, Capital
12	Accounts Receivable	32	Samantha Hogan, Drawing
14	Supplies	41	Fees Earned
15	Prepaid Rent	51	Salary Expense
16	Prepaid Insurance	52	Rent Expense
18	Office Equipment	53	Supplies Expense
19	Accumulated Depreciation	54	Depreciation Expense
21	Accounts Payable	55	Insurance Expense
22	Salaries Payable	59	Miscellaneous Expense
23	Unearned Fees		

(Continued)

2. Post the journal to a ledger of four-column accounts.
3. Prepare an unadjusted trial balance.
4. At the end of July, the following adjustment data were assembled. Analyze and use these data to complete parts (5) and (6).
   a. Insurance expired during July is $510.
   b. Supplies on hand on July 31 are $3,900.
   c. Depreciation of office equipment for July is $540.
   d. Accrued receptionist salary on July 31 is $190.
   e. Rent expired during July is $2,700.
   f. Unearned fees on July 31 are $4,100.
5. *(Optional)* Enter the unadjusted trial balance on an end-of-period spreadsheet and complete the spreadsheet.
6. Journalize and post the adjusting entries. Record the adjusting entries on Page 3 of the journal.
7. Prepare an adjusted trial balance.
8. Prepare an income statement, a statement of owner's equity, and a balance sheet.
9. Prepare and post the closing entries. Record the closing entries on Page 4 of the journal. Indicate closed accounts by inserting a line in both Balance columns opposite the closing entry.
10. Prepare a post-closing trial balance.

Problems: Series B

PR 4-1B Financial statements and closing entries

OBJ. 1, 2, 3

✔ 3. Total assets: $342,425

SHOW ME HOW

Last Chance Company offers legal consulting advice to prison inmates. Last Chance Company prepared the end-of-period spreadsheet shown at the top of the following page at June 30, 20Y1, the end of the fiscal year.

Instructions

1. Prepare an income statement for the year ended June 30.
2. Prepare a statement of owner's equity for the year ended June 30. No additional investments were made during the year.
3. Prepare a balance sheet as of June 30.
4. On the basis of the end-of-period spreadsheet, journalize the closing entries.
5. Prepare a post-closing trial balance.

	A	B	C	D	E	F	G
1		**Last Chance Company**					
2		**End-of-Period Spreadsheet**					
3		**For the Year Ended June 30, 20Y1**					
4		**Unadjusted**				**Adjusted**	
5		**Trial Balance**		**Adjustments**		**Trial Balance**	
6	**Account Title**	**Dr.**	**Cr.**	**Dr.**	**Cr.**	**Dr.**	**Cr.**
7							
8	Cash	5,100				5,100	
9	Accounts Receivable	22,750		(a) 3,750		26,500	
10	Prepaid Insurance	3,600			(b) 1,300	2,300	
11	Supplies	2,025			(c) 1,500	525	
12	Land	80,000				80,000	
13	Building	340,000				340,000	
14	Accum. Depr.—Building		190,000		(d) 3,000		193,000
15	Equipment	140,000				140,000	
16	Accum. Depr.—Equipment		54,450		(e) 4,550		59,000
17	Accounts Payable		9,750				9,750
18	Salaries and Wages Payable				(f) 1,900		1,900
19	Unearned Rent		4,500	(g) 3,000			1,500
20	Tami Garrigan, Capital		361,300				361,300
21	Tami Garrigan, Drawing	20,000				20,000	
22	Fees Earned		280,000		(a) 3,750		283,750
23	Rent Revenue				(g) 3,000		3,000
24	Salaries and Wages Expense	145,100		(f) 1,900		147,000	
25	Advertising Expense	86,800				86,800	
26	Utilities Expense	30,000				30,000	
27	Travel Expense	18,750				18,750	
28	Depr. Exp.—Equipment			(e) 4,550		4,550	
29	Depr. Exp.—Building			(d) 3,000		3,000	
30	Supplies Expense			(c) 1,500		1,500	
31	Insurance Expense			(b) 1,300		1,300	
32	Misc. Expense	5,875				5,875	
33		900,000	900,000	19,000	19,000	913,200	913,200
34							

PR 4-2B Financial statements and closing entries

OBJ. 2, 3

✔ 1. Nicole Gorman, capital, October 31: $313,000

The Gorman Group is a financial planning services firm owned and operated by Nicole Gorman. As of October 31, 20Y3, the end of the fiscal year, the accountant for The Gorman Group prepared an end-of-period spreadsheet, part of which follows:

	A	F	G
1	**The Gorman Group**		
2	**End-of-Period Spreadsheet**		
3	**For the Year Ended October 31, 20Y3**		
4		**Adjusted**	
5		**Trial Balance**	
6	**Account Title**	**Dr.**	**Cr.**
7			
8	Cash	11,000	
9	Accounts Receivable	28,150	
10	Supplies	6,350	
11	Prepaid Insurance	9,500	
12	Land	75,000	
13	Buildings	250,000	
14	Accumulated Depreciation—Buildings		117,200
15	Equipment	240,000	
16	Accumulated Depreciation—Equipment		151,700
17	Accounts Payable		33,300
18	Salaries Payable		3,300
19	Unearned Rent		1,500
20	Nicole Gorman, Capital		220,000
21	Nicole Gorman, Drawing	20,000	
22	Service Fees		468,000
23	Rent Revenue		5,000
24	Salaries Expense	291,000	
25	Depreciation Expense—Equipment	17,500	
26	Rent Expense	15,500	
27	Supplies Expense	9,000	
28	Utilities Expense	8,500	
29	Depreciation Expense—Buildings	6,600	
30	Repairs Expense	3,450	
31	Insurance Expense	3,000	
32	Miscellaneous Expense	5,450	
33		1,000,000	1,000,000

(Continued)

Instructions

1. Prepare an income statement, a statement of owner's equity (no additional investments were made during the year), and a balance sheet.
2. Journalize the entries that were required to close the accounts at October 31.
3. If the balance of Nicole Gorman, Capital had instead increased $115,000 after the closing entries were posted and the withdrawals remained the same, what would have been the amount of net income or net loss?

✔ 5. Net income: $27,350

PR 4-3B T accounts, adjusting entries, financial statements, and closing entries; optional end-of-period spreadsheet

OBJ. 2, 3

The unadjusted trial balance of La Mesa Laundry at August 31, 20Y5, the end of the fiscal year, follows:

La Mesa Laundry
Unadjusted Trial Balance
August 31, 20Y5

	Debit Balances	Credit Balances
Cash	3,800	
Laundry Supplies	9,000	
Prepaid Insurance	6,000	
Laundry Equipment	180,800	
Accumulated Depreciation		49,200
Accounts Payable		7,800
Bobbi Downey, Capital		95,000
Bobbi Downey, Drawing	2,400	
Laundry Revenue		248,000
Wages Expense	135,800	
Rent Expense	43,200	
Utilities Expense	16,000	
Miscellaneous Expense	3,000	
	400,000	400,000

The data needed to determine year-end adjustments are as follows:

a. Wages accrued but not paid at August 31 are $2,200.
b. Depreciation of equipment during the year is $8,150.
c. Laundry supplies on hand at August 31 are $2,000.
d. Insurance premiums expired during the year are $5,300.

Instructions

1. For each account listed in the unadjusted trial balance, enter the balance in a T account. Identify the balance as "Aug. 31 Bal." In addition, add T accounts for Wages Payable, Depreciation Expense, Laundry Supplies Expense, and Insurance Expense.
2. *(Optional)* Enter the unadjusted trial balance on an end-of-period spreadsheet and complete the spreadsheet. Add the accounts listed in part (1) as needed.
3. Journalize and post the adjusting entries. Identify the adjustments as "Adj." and the new balances as "Adj. Bal."
4. Prepare an adjusted trial balance.
5. Prepare an income statement, a statement of owner's equity (no additional investments were made during the year), and a balance sheet.
6. Journalize and post the closing entries. Identify the closing entries as "Clos."
7. Prepare a post-closing trial balance.

✔ 5. Net income: $46,150

PR 4-4B Ledger accounts, adjusting entries, financial statements, and closing entries; optional end-of-period spreadsheet

OBJ. 2, 3

The unadjusted trial balance of Recessive Interiors at January 31, 20Y7, the end of the year, follows:

Recessive Interiors
Unadjusted Trial Balance
January 31, 20Y7

	Account No.	Debit Balances	Credit Balances
Cash	11	13,100	
Supplies	13	8,000	
Prepaid Insurance	14	7,500	
Equipment	16	113,000	
Accumulated Depreciation—Equipment	17		12,000
Trucks	18	90,000	
Accumulated Depreciation—Trucks	19		27,100
Accounts Payable	21		4,500
Jeanne McQuay, Capital	31		126,400
Jeanne McQuay, Drawing	32	3,000	
Service Revenue	41		155,000
Wages Expense	51	72,000	
Rent Expense	52	7,600	
Truck Expense	53	5,350	
Miscellaneous Expense	59	5,450	
		325,000	325,000

The data needed to determine year-end adjustments are as follows:

a. Supplies on hand at January 31 are $2,850.
b. Insurance premiums expired during the year are $3,150.
c. Depreciation of equipment during the year is $5,250.
d. Depreciation of trucks during the year is $4,000.
e. Wages accrued but not paid at January 31 are $900.

Instructions

1. For each account listed in the unadjusted trial balance, enter the balance in the appropriate Balance column of a four-column account and place a check mark (✓) in the Posting Reference column.
2. *(Optional)* Enter the unadjusted trial balance on an end-of-period spreadsheet and complete the spreadsheet. Add the accounts listed in part (3) as needed.
3. Journalize and post the adjusting entries, inserting balances in the accounts affected. Record the adjusting entries on Page 26 of the journal. The following additional accounts from Recessive Interiors' chart of accounts should be used: Wages Payable, 22; Depreciation Expense—Equipment, 54; Supplies Expense, 55; Depreciation Expense—Trucks, 56; Insurance Expense, 57.
4. Prepare an adjusted trial balance.
5. Prepare an income statement, a statement of owner's equity (no additional investments were made during the year), and a balance sheet.
6. Journalize and post the closing entries. Record the closing entries on Page 27 of the journal. Indicate closed accounts by inserting a line in both Balance columns opposite the closing entry.
7. Prepare a post-closing trial balance.

✔ 8. Net income: $53,775

PR 4-5B Complete accounting cycle

OBJ. 4, 5

For the past several years, Jeff Horton has operated a part-time consulting business from his home. As of April 1, 20Y9, Jeff decided to move to rented quarters and to operate the business, which was to be known as Rosebud Consulting, on a full-time basis. Rosebud Consulting entered into the following transactions during April:

Apr. 1. The following assets were received from Jeff Horton: cash, $20,000; accounts receivable, $14,700; supplies, $3,300; and office equipment, $12,000. There were no liabilities received.

1. Paid three months' rent on a lease rental contract, $6,000.

2. Paid the premiums on property and casualty insurance policies, $4,200.

4. Received cash from clients as an advance payment for services to be provided and recorded it as unearned fees, $9,400.

5. Purchased additional office equipment on account from Smith Office Supply Co., $8,000.

6. Received cash from clients on account, $11,700.

10. Paid cash for a newspaper advertisement, $350.

12. Paid Smith Office Supply Co. for part of the debt incurred on April 5, $6,400.

12. Provided services on account for the period April 1–12, $21,900.

14. Paid receptionist for two weeks' salary, $1,650.

Record the following transactions on Page 2 of the journal:

17. Received cash from cash clients for fees earned during the period April 1–16, $6,600.

18. Paid cash for supplies, $725.

20. Provided services on account for the period April 13–20, $16,800.

24. Received cash from cash clients for fees earned for the period April 17–24, $4,450.

26. Received cash from clients on account, $26,500.

27. Paid receptionist for two weeks' salary, $1,650.

29. Paid telephone bill for April, $540.

30. Paid electricity bill for April, $760.

30. Received cash from cash clients for fees earned for the period April 25–30, $5,160.

30. Provided services on account for the remainder of April, $2,590.

30. Jeff withdrew $18,000 for personal use.

Instructions

1. Journalize each transaction in a two-column journal starting on Page 1, referring to the following chart of accounts in selecting the accounts to be debited and credited. (Do not insert the account numbers in the journal at this time.)

11	Cash	31	Jeff Horton, Capital
12	Accounts Receivable	32	Jeff Horton, Drawing
14	Supplies	41	Fees Earned
15	Prepaid Rent	51	Salary Expense
16	Prepaid Insurance	52	Supplies Expense
18	Office Equipment	53	Rent Expense
19	Accumulated Depreciation	54	Depreciation Expense
21	Accounts Payable	55	Insurance Expense
22	Salaries Payable	59	Miscellaneous Expense
23	Unearned Fees		

2. Post the journal to a ledger of four-column accounts.
3. Prepare an unadjusted trial balance.

4. At the end of April, the following adjustment data were assembled. Analyze and use these data to complete parts (5) and (6).
   a. Insurance expired during April is $350.
   b. Supplies on hand on April 30 are $1,225.
   c. Depreciation of office equipment for April is $400.
   d. Accrued receptionist salary on April 30 is $275.
   e. Rent expired during April is $2,000.
   f. Unearned fees on April 30 are $2,350.
5. *(Optional)* Enter the unadjusted trial balance on an end-of-period spreadsheet and complete the spreadsheet.
6. Journalize and post the adjusting entries. Record the adjusting entries on Page 3 of the journal.
7. Prepare an adjusted trial balance.
8. Prepare an income statement, a statement of owner's equity, and a balance sheet.
9. Prepare and post the closing entries. Record the closing entries on Page 4 of the journal. Indicate closed accounts by inserting a line in both Balance columns opposite the closing entry.
10. Prepare a post-closing trial balance.

Continuing Problem

✔ **2. Net income: $4,955**

The unadjusted trial balance of PS Music as of July 31, 20Y9, along with the adjustment data for the two months ended July 31, 20Y9, are shown in Chapter 3. Based upon the adjustment data, the following adjusted trial balance was prepared:

PS Music
Adjusted Trial Balance
July 31, 20Y9

	Debit Balances	Credit Balances
Cash	9,945	
Accounts Receivable	4,150	
Supplies	275	
Prepaid Insurance	2,475	
Office Equipment	7,500	
Accumulated Depreciation		50
Accounts Payable		8,350
Wages Payable		140
Unearned Revenue		3,600
Peyton Smith, Capital		9,000
Peyton Smith, Drawing	1,750	
Fees Earned		21,200
Music Expense	3,610	
Wages Expense	2,940	
Office Rent Expense	2,550	
Advertising Expense	1,500	
Equipment Rent Expense	1,375	
Utilities Expense	1,215	
Supplies Expense	925	
Insurance Expense	225	
Depreciation Expense	50	
Miscellaneous Expense	1,855	
	42,340	42,340

(Continued)

Instructions

1. *(Optional)* Using the data from Chapter 3, prepare an end-of-period spreadsheet.
2. Prepare an income statement, a statement of owner's equity, and a balance sheet. (*Note:* Peyton Smith made investments in PS Music on June 1 and July 1, 20Y9.)
3. Journalize and post the closing entries. Indicate closed accounts by inserting a line in both Balance columns opposite the closing entry.
4. Prepare a post-closing trial balance.

Comprehensive Problem 1

✔ 8. Net income, $33,425

Kelly Pitney began her consulting business, Kelly Consulting, on April 1, 20Y5. The accounting cycle for Kelly Consulting for April, including financial statements, was illustrated in this chapter. During May, Kelly Consulting entered into the following transactions:

May 3. Received cash from clients as an advance payment for services to be provided and recorded it as unearned fees, $4,500.
5. Received cash from clients on account, $2,450.
9. Paid cash for a newspaper advertisement, $225.
13. Paid Office Station Co. for part of the debt incurred on April 5, $640.
15. Provided services on account for the period May 1–15, $9,180.
16. Paid part-time receptionist for two weeks' salary including the amount owed on April 30, $750.
17. Received cash from cash clients for fees earned during the period May 1–16, $8,360.

Record the following transactions on Page 6 of the journal:

20. Purchased supplies on account, $735.
21. Provided services on account for the period May 16–20, $4,820.
25. Received cash from cash clients for fees earned for the period May 17–23, $7,900.
27. Received cash from clients on account, $9,520.
28. Paid part-time receptionist for two weeks' salary, $750.
30. Paid telephone bill for May, $260.
31. Paid electricity bill for May, $810.
31. Received cash from cash clients for fees earned for the period May 26–31, $3,300.
31. Provided services on account for the remainder of May, $2,650.
31. Kelly withdrew $10,500 for personal use.

Instructions

1. The chart of accounts for Kelly Consulting is shown in Exhibit 9, and the post-closing trial balance as of April 30, 20Y5, is shown in Exhibit 17. For each account in the post-closing trial balance, enter the balance in the appropriate Balance column of a four-column account. Date the balances May 1, 20Y5, and place a check mark (✓) in the Posting Reference column. Journalize each of the May transactions in a two-column journal starting on Page 5 of the journal and using Kelly Consulting's chart of accounts. (Do not insert the account numbers in the journal at this time.)
2. Post the journal to a ledger of four-column accounts.
3. Prepare an unadjusted trial balance.
4. At the end of May, the following adjustment data were assembled. Analyze and use these data to complete parts (5) and (6).
   a. Insurance expired during May is $275.
   b. Supplies on hand on May 31 are $715.

c. Depreciation of office equipment for May is $330.
d. Accrued receptionist salary on May 31 is $325.
e. Rent expired during May is $1,600.
f. Unearned fees on May 31 are $3,210.

5. *(Optional)* Enter the unadjusted trial balance on an end-of-period spreadsheet and complete the spreadsheet.
6. Journalize and post the adjusting entries. Record the adjusting entries on Page 7 of the journal.
7. Prepare an adjusted trial balance.
8. Prepare an income statement, a statement of owner's equity, and a balance sheet.
9. Prepare and post the closing entries. Record the closing entries on Page 8 of the journal. Indicate closed accounts by inserting a line in both Balance columns opposite the closing entry.
10. Prepare a post-closing trial balance.

Cases & Projects

ETHICS

CP 4-1 Ethics in Action

New Wave Images is a graphics design firm that prepares its financial statements using a calendar year. Manny Kinn, the company treasurer and vice president of finance, has prepared a classified balance sheet as of December 31. In January, this balance sheet will be submitted along with an application for a loan from First Peoples Community Bank. An excerpt from the balance sheet follows:

Cash	$ 25,000
Accounts receivable	85,000
......	
Total assets	$250,000

The accounts receivable balance includes a $56,000 loan to Tom Morrow, the company president. Tom borrowed the money from New Wave 18 months earlier for a down payment on a new home. Tom has orally assured Manny that he will pay off the loan within the next year. Because Tom is the company president, Manny treats the amount due as part of its normal accounts receivable. In addition, Manny knows that the bank will consider a large balance in accounts receivable more favorably than a large personal loan to a single individual. Manny reported the $56,000 in the same manner on the preceding year's balance sheet.

1. Is Manny behaving ethically by reporting the loan to Tom as a trade account receivable? Why or why not?
2. Who will be affected by Manny's decision?

TEAM ACTIVITY

REAL WORLD

CP 4-2 Team Activity

In teams, select two public companies of different industries that interest you. Obtain each company's most recent annual report on Form 10-K. The Form 10-K is a company's annually required filing with the Securities and Exchange Commission (SEC). It includes the company's financial statements and accompanying notes. The Form 10-K can be obtained either (a) by referring to the investor relations section of the company's website or (b) by using the company search feature of the SEC's EDGAR database service found at www.sec.gov/edgar/searchedgar/companysearch.html.

Find the balance sheet for each of the two companies you have selected. Compare the balance sheets of the two companies as follows:

(Continued)

1. Which balance sheet accounts do the two companies have in common?
2. Which balance sheet accounts stand out as different between the two companies? Why do these differences exist?

CP 4-3 Communication

COMMUNICATION

Your friend, Daniel Nat, recently began work as the lead accountant for Asheville Company. Daniel prepared the following balance sheet for December 31, 20Y4:

Asheville Company **Balance Sheet** **For the Year Ended December 31, 20Y4**	
Assets	
Land	$100,000
Accounts payable	10,000
Accounts receivable	12,500
Cash	10,000
Daniel Nat, capital	235,000
Total assets	$367,500
Liabilities	
Equipment	$125,000
Wages payable	2,500
Total liabilities	$127,500

Write a brief memo to Daniel explaining the errors in the Asheville Company balance sheet and the correct presentation for the balance sheet.

CP 4-4 Financial statements

The following is an excerpt from a telephone conversation between Ben Simpson, president of Main Street Co., and Tami Lundgren, owner of Reliable Employment Co.:

Ben: Tami, you're going to have to do a better job of finding me a new computer programmer. That last guy was great at programming, but he didn't have any common sense.

Tami: What do you mean? The guy had a master's degree with straight A's.

Ben: Yes, well, last month he developed a new financial reporting system. He said we could do away with manually preparing an end-of-period spreadsheet and financial statements. The computer would automatically generate our financial statements with "a push of a button."

Tami: So what's the big deal? Sounds to me like it would save you time and effort.

Ben: Right! The balance sheet showed a minus for supplies!

Tami: Minus supplies? How can that be?

Ben: That's what I asked.

Tami: So, what did he say?

Ben: Well, after he checked the program, he said that it must be right. The minuses were greater than the pluses. . . .

Tami: Didn't he know that Supplies can't have a credit balance—it must have a debit balance?

Ben: He asked me what a debit and credit were.

Tami: I see your point.

1. Comment on (a) the desirability of computerizing Main Street Co.'s financial reporting system, (b) the elimination of the end-of-period spreadsheet in a computerized accounting system, and (c) the computer programmer's lack of accounting knowledge.
2. Explain to the programmer why Supplies could not have a credit balance.

CP 4-5 Financial statements

Assume that you recently accepted a position with Five Star National Bank & Trust as an assistant loan officer. As one of your first duties, you have been assigned the responsibility of evaluating a loan request for $300,000 from West Gate Auto Co., a small proprietorship. In support of the loan application, Joan Whalen, owner, submitted a "Statement of Accounts" (trial balance) for the first year of operations ended October 31, 20Y6.

West Gate Auto Co.
Statement of Accounts
October 31, 20Y6

Cash	5,000	
Billings Due from Others	40,000	
Supplies (chemicals, etc.)	7,500	
Building	222,300	
Equipment	50,000	
Amounts Owed to Others		31,000
Investment in Business		179,000
Service Revenue		215,000
Wages Expense	75,000	
Utilities Expense	10,000	
Rent Expense	8,000	
Insurance Expense	6,000	
Other Expenses	1,200	
	425,000	425,000

1. Explain to Joan Whalen why a set of financial statements (income statement, statement of owner's equity, and balance sheet) would be useful to you in evaluating the loan request.
2. In discussing the "Statement of Accounts" with Joan Whalen, you discovered that the accounts had not been adjusted at October 31. Analyze the "Statement of Accounts" and indicate possible adjusting entries that might be necessary before an accurate set of financial statements could be prepared.
3. Assuming that an accurate set of financial statements will be submitted by Joan Whalen in a few days, what other considerations or information would you require before making a decision on the loan request?

CHAPTER

5

Accounting Systems

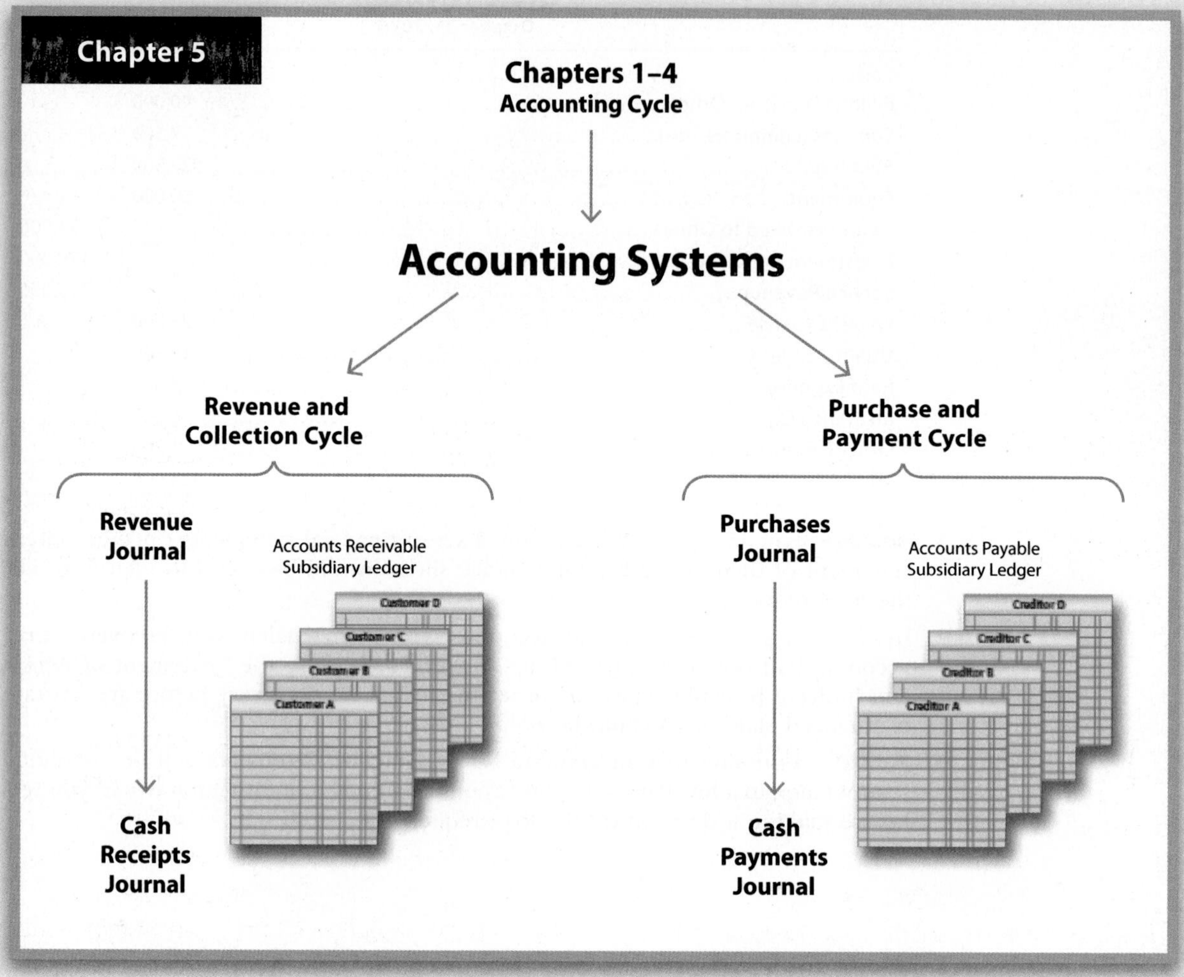

NAN728/SHUTTERSTOCK.COM

CHAPTER 5

Intuit Inc.

You likely interact with accounting systems as part of your everyday life. For example, your bank statement is a type of accounting system. When you make a deposit, the bank records an addition to your cash; when you withdraw cash, the bank records a reduction in your cash. Such a simple accounting system works well for a person with just a few transactions per month. However, over time, you may find that your financial affairs will become more complex and involve many different types of transactions, including investments and loan payments. At this point, relying on your bank statement may not be sufficient for managing your financial affairs. Personal financial planning software, such as **Intuit**'s Quicken®, can be useful when your financial affairs become more complex.

What happens if you decide to begin a small business? Transactions expand to include customers, vendors, and employees. As a result, the accounting system will need to adjust to this complexity. Thus, many small businesses use small-business accounting software, such as Intuit's QuickBooks®, as their first accounting system. As a business grows, more sophisticated accounting systems will be needed. Companies, such as **SAP**, **Oracle**, **Microsoft**, and **Sage Software, Inc.**, offer accounting system solutions for businesses that become larger with more complex accounting needs.

Accounting systems used by large and small businesses employ the basic principles of the accounting cycle discussed in the previous chapters. However, these accounting systems include features that simplify the recording and summary process. In this chapter, we will discuss these simplifying procedures as they apply to both manual and computerized systems.

Link to Intuit.......... Pages 231, 238, 244, 246

LEARNING OBJECTIVES

After studying this chapter, you should be able to:

Example Exercises (EE) are shown in **red.**

OBJ. 1 **Define and describe an accounting system.**

Basic Accounting Systems

OBJ. 2 **Journalize and post transactions in a manual accounting system that uses subsidiary ledgers and special journals.**

Manual Accounting Systems

Subsidiary Ledgers	
Special Journals	
Revenue Journal	EE **5-1**
Cash Receipts Journal	
Accounts Receivable Control Account and Subsidiary Ledger	EE **5-2**
Purchases Journal	EE **5-3**
Cash Payments Journal	
Accounts Payable Control Account and Subsidiary Ledger	EE **5-4**

OBJ. 3 **Describe and illustrate the use of a computerized accounting system.**

Computerized Accounting Systems

OBJ. 4 **Describe the basic features of e-commerce.**

E-Commerce

OBJ. 5 **Use segment analysis in evaluating the operating performance of a company.**

Financial Analysis and Interpretation: Segment Analysis

Evaluate Segment Operating Performance EE **5-5**

At a Glance 5 Page 250

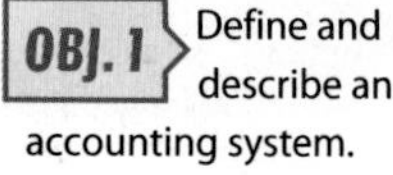

Define and describe an accounting system.

Basic Accounting Systems

In Chapters 1–4, an accounting system for **NetSolutions** was described and illustrated. An **accounting system** is the methods and procedures for collecting, classifying, summarizing, and reporting a business's financial and operating information. Most accounting systems, however, are more complex than NetSolutions'. For example, **Southwest Airlines**' accounting system not only records basic transaction data but also records data on such items as ticket reservations, credit card collections, frequent-flier mileage, and aircraft maintenance.

As a business grows and changes, its accounting system also changes in a three-step process. This three-step process is as follows:

Step 1. *Analyze* user information needs.
Step 2. *Design* the system to meet the user needs.
Step 3. *Implement* the system.

For NetSolutions, our analysis determined that Chris Clark needed financial statements for the new business (Step 1). In Chapters 1–4, we designed the system that included a chart of accounts, a two-column journal, and a general ledger (Step 2). Finally, we implemented the system to record transactions and prepare financial statements (Step 3).

Once a system has been implemented, input from users is used to analyze and improve the system. For example, in later chapters, NetSolutions expands its chart of accounts to record more complex transactions.

The accounting system design consists of:

- internal controls and
- information processing methods.

Internal controls are the policies and procedures that protect assets from misuse, ensure that business information is accurate, and ensure that laws and regulations are being followed. Internal controls are discussed in Chapter 8.

Processing methods are the means by which the accounting system collects, summarizes, and reports accounting information. These methods may be either *manual* or *computerized.* We begin by describing and illustrating a simple manual accounting system that uses special journals and subsidiary ledgers. This is followed by a discussion of more complex computerized accounting systems.

Manual Accounting Systems

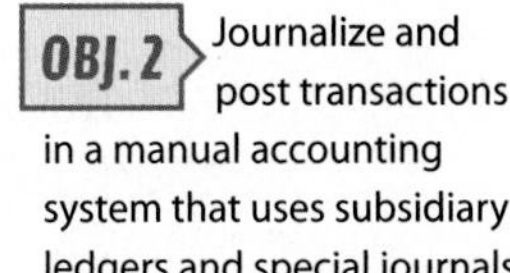

Journalize and post transactions in a manual accounting system that uses subsidiary ledgers and special journals.

Accounting systems are manual or computerized. Understanding a manual accounting system is useful in identifying relationships between accounting data and reports. Also, most computerized systems use principles from manual systems.

In Chapters 1–4, the transactions for **NetSolutions** were manually recorded in an all-purpose (two-column) journal. The journal entries were then posted individually to the accounts in the ledger. Such a system is simple to use and easy to understand when there are a small number of transactions. However, when a business has a large number of *similar* transactions, using an all-purpose journal is inefficient and impractical. In such cases, subsidiary ledgers and special journals are useful.

Subsidiary Ledgers

A large number of individual accounts with a common characteristic can be grouped together in a separate ledger called a **subsidiary ledger**. The primary ledger, which contains all of the balance sheet and income statement accounts, is then called the **general ledger**. Each subsidiary ledger is represented in the general ledger by a summarizing account, called a **controlling account**. The sum of the balances of the accounts in a subsidiary ledger must equal the balance of the related controlling account. Thus, a subsidiary ledger is a secondary ledger that supports a controlling account in the general ledger.

Two of the most common subsidiary ledgers are as follows:

- Accounts receivable subsidiary ledger
- Accounts payable subsidiary ledger

Note

Subsidiary ledgers provide detail of individual accounts that are summarized in a controlling account in the general ledger.

The **accounts receivable subsidiary ledger**, or *customers ledger*, lists the individual customer accounts in alphabetical order. The controlling account in the general ledger that summarizes the debits and credits to the individual customer accounts is Accounts Receivable.

The **accounts payable subsidiary ledger**, *or creditors ledger*, lists individual creditor accounts in alphabetical order. The related controlling account in the general ledger is Accounts Payable.

The relationship between the general ledger and the accounts receivable and accounts payable subsidiary ledgers is illustrated in Exhibit 1.

Many businesses use subsidiary ledgers for other accounts in addition to Accounts Receivable and Accounts Payable. For example, businesses often use an equipment subsidiary ledger to keep track of each item of equipment purchased, its cost, location, and other data. Moreover, merchandising and manufacturing businesses use additional types of subsidiary ledgers that are unique to them. We simplify by illustrating accounting systems for a service business.

Special Journals

One method of processing transactions more efficiently in a manual system is to use special journals. **Special journals** are designed to record a single kind of transaction that occurs frequently. For example, since most businesses have many transactions in which cash is paid out, they will likely use a special journal for recording cash payments. Likewise, they will use another special journal for recording cash receipts.

Link to Intuit

Intuit has subsidiary ledgers for property and equipment, inventory, and investments.

EXHIBIT 1

General Ledger and Subsidiary Ledgers

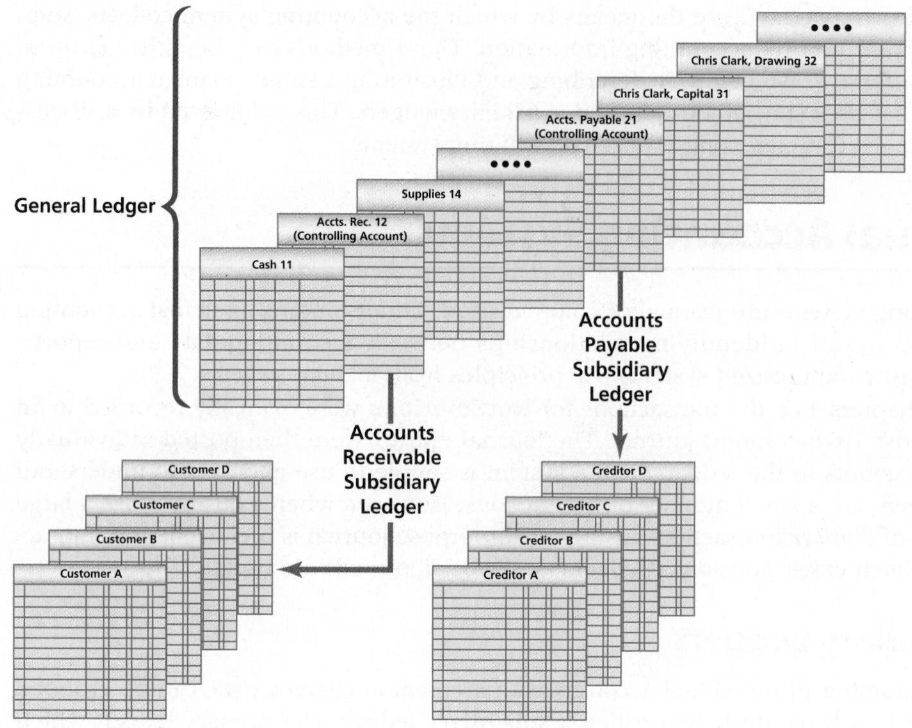

Note

Special journals summarize common transactions that are used frequently.

The format and number of special journals that a business uses depends on the nature of the business. The common transactions and their related special journals used by small service businesses are as follows:

Transaction		Special Journal
Providing services *on account*	**recorded in** →	**Revenue journal**
Receipt of cash from *any* source	**recorded in** →	**Cash receipts journal**
Purchase of items *on account*	**recorded in** →	**Purchases journal**
Payment of cash for *any* purpose	**recorded in** →	**Cash payments journal**

The all-purpose two-column journal, called the **general journal** or simply the *journal*, can be used for entries that do not fit into any of the special journals. For example, adjusting and closing entries are recorded in the general journal.

The following types of transactions, special journals, and subsidiary ledgers are described and illustrated for **NetSolutions**:

Transaction	**Special Journal**	**Subsidiary Ledger**
Fees earned on account	Revenue journal	Accounts receivable subsidiary ledger
Cash receipts	Cash receipts journal	Accounts receivable subsidiary ledger
Purchases on account	Purchases journal	Accounts payable subsidiary ledger
Cash payments	Cash payments journal	Accounts payable subsidiary ledger

As shown, transactions that are recorded in the revenue and cash receipts journals will affect the accounts receivable subsidiary ledger as part of the *revenue and collection cycle*. Likewise, transactions that are recorded in the purchases and cash payments journals will affect the accounts payable subsidiary ledger as part of the *purchases and payments cycle*.

To illustrate, we will assume that NetSolutions had the following selected general ledger balances on March 1, 20Y5:

Account Number	Account	Balance
11	Cash	$6,200
12	Accounts Receivable	3,400
14	Supplies	2,500
18	Office Equipment	2,500
21	Accounts Payable	1,230

Revenue Journal

Fees earned on account would be recorded in the **revenue journal**. *Cash fees earned* would be recorded in the cash receipts journal.

To illustrate the efficiency of using a revenue journal, an example for **NetSolutions** is used. Specifically, assume that NetSolutions recorded the following four revenue transactions for March in its general journal:

Date		Description	Post. Ref.	Debit	Credit
20Y5					
Mar.	2	Accounts Receivable—Accessories By Claire	12/✓	2,200	
		Fees Earned	41		2,200
	6	Accounts Receivable—RapZone	12/✓	1,750	
		Fees Earned	41		1,750
	18	Accounts Receivable—Web Cantina	12/✓	2,650	
		Fees Earned	41		2,650
	27	Accounts Receivable—Accessories By Claire	12/✓	3,000	
		Fees Earned	41		3,000

For the preceding entries, NetSolutions recorded eight accounts and eight amounts. In addition, NetSolutions made 12 postings to the ledgers—four to Accounts Receivable in the general ledger, four to the accounts receivable subsidiary ledger (indicated by each check mark), and four to Fees Earned in the general ledger.

The preceding revenue transactions could be recorded more efficiently in a revenue journal, as shown in Exhibit 2. In each revenue transaction, the amount of the debit to Accounts Receivable is the same as the amount of the credit to Fees Earned. Thus, only a single amount column is necessary. The date, invoice number, customer name, and amount are entered separately for each transaction.

Revenues are normally recorded in the revenue journal when the company sends an invoice to the customer. An **invoice** is the bill that is sent to the customer by the company. Each invoice is normally numbered in sequence for future reference.

To illustrate, assume that on March 2, NetSolutions issued Invoice No. 615 to Accessories By Claire for fees earned of $2,200. This transaction is entered in the revenue journal, shown in Exhibit 2, by entering the following items:

1. Date column: *Mar. 2*
2. Invoice No. column: *615*
3. Account Debited column: *Accessories By Claire*
4. Accts. Rec. Dr./Fees Earned Cr. column: *2,200*

EXHIBIT 2
Revenue Journal

Revenue Journal					Page 35
Date		**Invoice No.**	**Account Debited**	**Post. Ref.**	**Accts. Rec. Dr. Fees Earned Cr.**
20Y5					
Mar.	2	615	Accessories By Claire		2,200
	6	616	RapZone		1,750
	18	617	Web Cantina		2,650
	27	618	Accessories By Claire		3,000
	31				9,600

The process of posting from a revenue journal, shown in Exhibit 3, is as follows:

Step 1. Each transaction is posted individually to a customer account in the accounts receivable subsidiary ledger. Postings to customer accounts should be made on a regular basis. In this way, the customer's account will show a current balance.

To illustrate, Exhibit 3 shows the posting of the $2,200 debit to Accessories By Claire in the accounts receivable subsidiary ledger. After the posting, Accessories By Claire has a debit balance of $2,200.

Step 2. To provide a trail of the entries posted to the general and subsidiary ledgers, the source of these entries is indicated in the Posting Reference column of each account by inserting the letter R (for revenue journal) and the page number of the revenue journal.

To illustrate, Exhibit 3 shows that after $2,200 is posted to Accessories By Claire's account, R35 is inserted in the Post. Ref. column of the account.

Step 3. To indicate that the transaction has been posted to the accounts receivable subsidiary ledger, a check mark (✓) is inserted in the Post. Ref. column of the revenue journal, as shown in Exhibit 3.

To illustrate, Exhibit 3 shows that a check mark (✓) has been inserted in the Post. Ref. column next to Accessories By Claire in the revenue journal to indicate that the $2,200 has been posted.

Step 4. A single monthly total is posted to Accounts Receivable and Fees Earned in the general ledger. This total is equal to the sum of the month's debits to the individual accounts in the subsidiary ledger. It is posted in the general ledger as a debit to Accounts Receivable and a credit to Fees Earned, as shown in Exhibit 3. The accounts receivable account number (12) and the fees earned account number (41) are then inserted below the total in the revenue journal to indicate that the posting is completed.

To illustrate, Exhibit 3 shows that the monthly total of $9,600 was posted as a debit to Accounts Receivable (12) and as a credit to Fees Earned (41).

Exhibit 3 illustrates the efficiency gained by using the revenue journal rather than the general journal. Specifically, all of the transactions for fees earned during the month are posted to the general ledger only once—at the end of the month.

Revenue Journal and Postings **EXHIBIT 3**

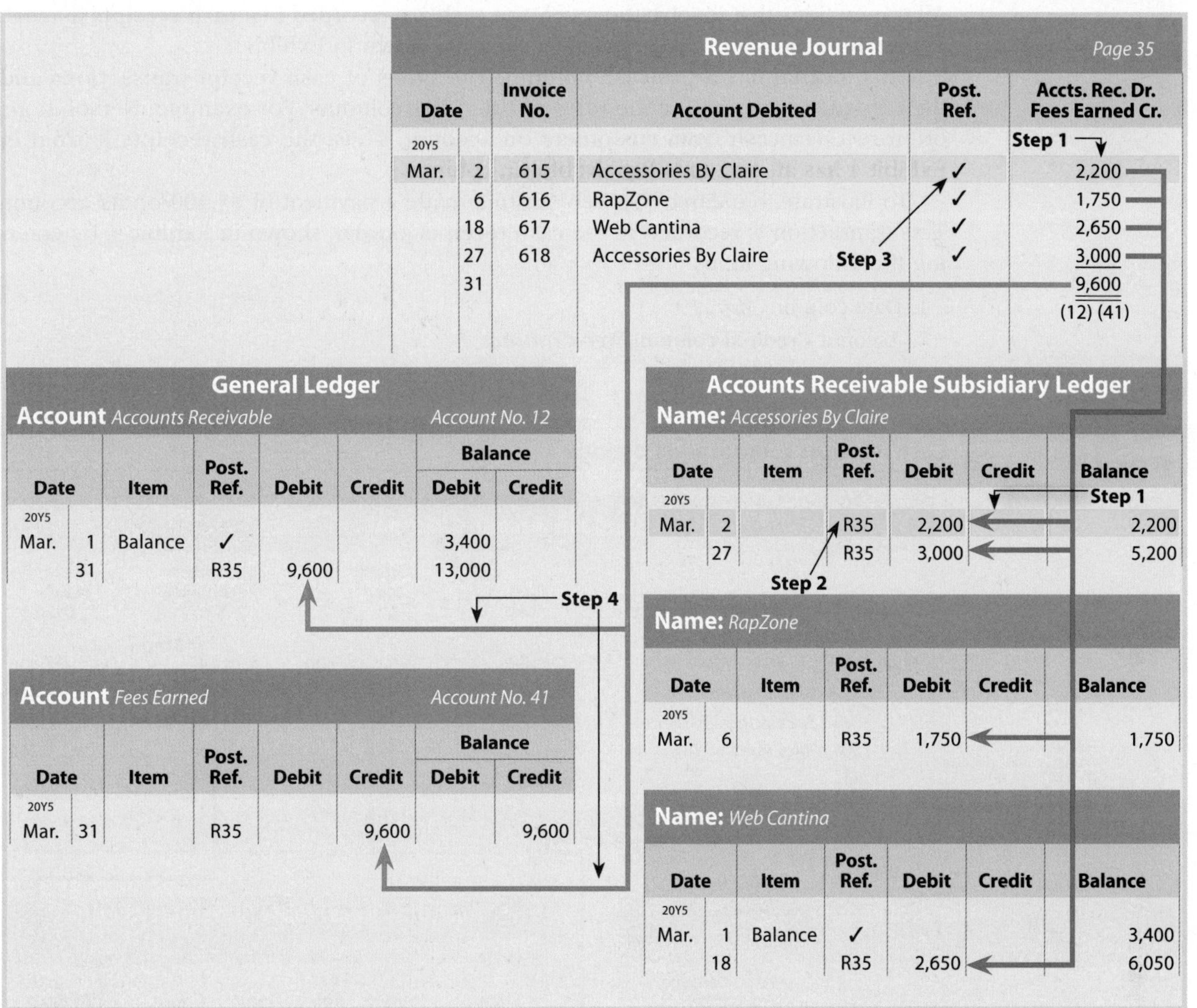

EXAMPLE EXERCISE 5-1 Revenue Journal

OBJ. 2

The following revenue transactions occurred during December:

Dec. 5. Issued Invoice No. 302 to Butler Company for services provided on account, $5,000.
9. Issued Invoice No. 303 to JoJo Enterprises for services provided on account, $2,100.
15. Issued Invoice No. 304 to Salinas Inc. for services provided on account, $3,250.

Record these transactions in a revenue journal as illustrated in Exhibit 2.

Follow My Example 5-1

REVENUE JOURNAL

Date	Invoice No.	Account Debited	Post. Ref.	Accts. Rec. Dr. Fees Earned Cr.
Dec. 5	302	Butler Company		5,000
9	303	JoJo Enterprises		2,100
15	304	Salinas Inc.		3,250

Practice Exercises: PE 5-1A, PE 5-1B

Cash Receipts Journal

All transactions that involve the receipt of cash are recorded in a **cash receipts journal**. The cash receipts journal for **NetSolutions** is shown in Exhibit 4.

This journal has a Cash Dr. column. The types of cash receipt transactions and their frequency determine the titles of the other columns. For example, NetSolutions often receives cash from customers on account. Thus, the cash receipts journal in Exhibit 4 has an Accounts Receivable Cr. column.

To illustrate, on March 19, Web Cantina made a payment of $3,400 on its account. This transaction is recorded in the cash receipts journal, shown in Exhibit 4, by entering the following items:

1. Date column: *Mar. 19*
2. Account Credited column: *Web Cantina*

EXHIBIT 4 **Cash Receipts Journal and Postings**

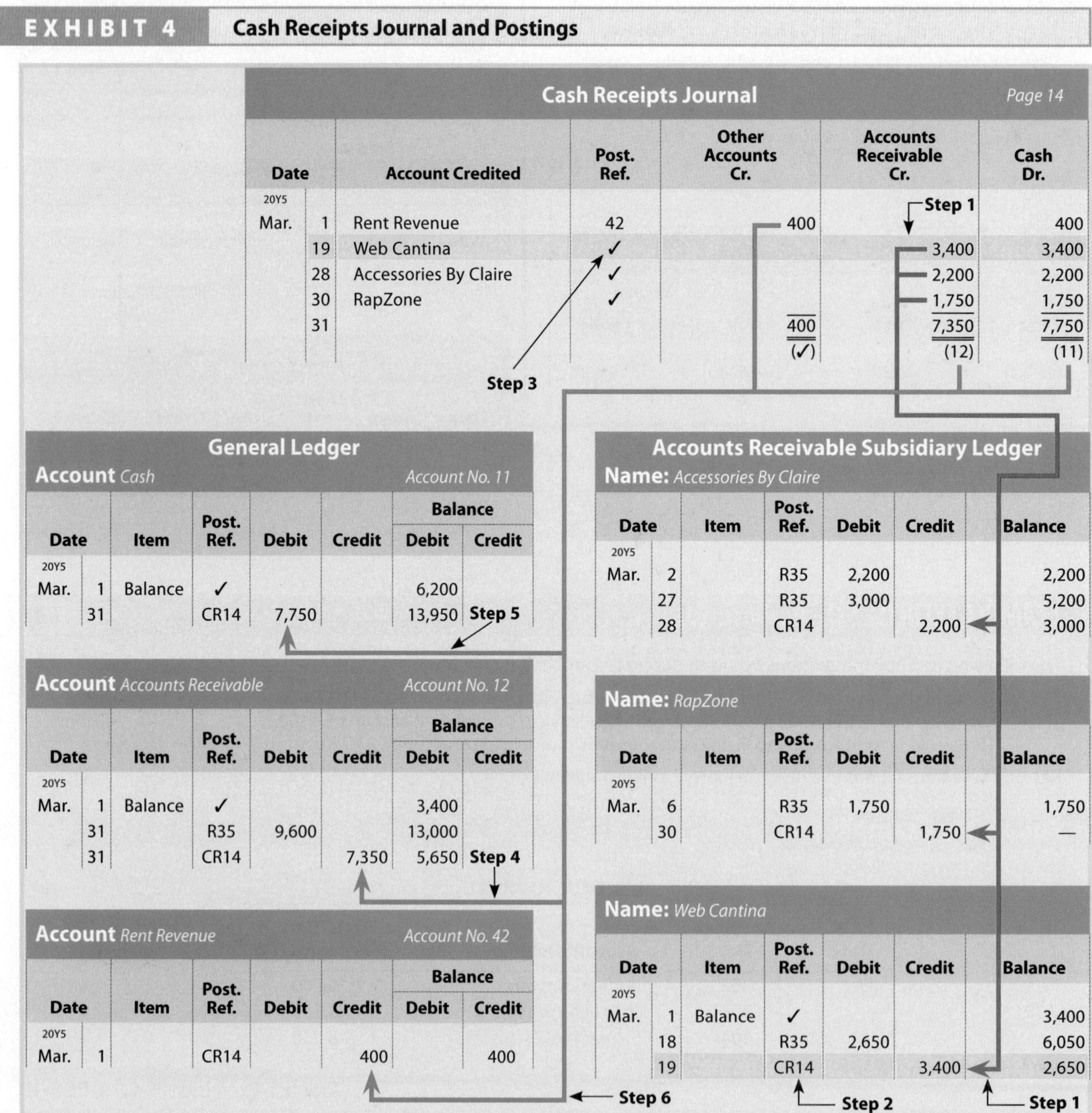

Cash Receipts Journal *Page 14*

Date		Account Credited	Post. Ref.	Other Accounts Cr.	Accounts Receivable Cr.	Cash Dr.
20Y5						
Mar.	1	Rent Revenue	42	400		400
	19	Web Cantina	✓		3,400	3,400
	28	Accessories By Claire	✓		2,200	2,200
	30	RapZone	✓		1,750	1,750
	31			400	7,350	7,750
				(✓)	(12)	(11)

General Ledger

Account *Cash* — *Account No. 11*

Date		Item	Post. Ref.	Debit	Credit	Balance Debit	Balance Credit
20Y5							
Mar.	1	Balance	✓			6,200	
	31		CR14	7,750		13,950	

Account *Accounts Receivable* — *Account No. 12*

Date		Item	Post. Ref.	Debit	Credit	Balance Debit	Balance Credit
20Y5							
Mar.	1	Balance	✓			3,400	
	31		R35	9,600		13,000	
	31		CR14		7,350	5,650	

Account *Rent Revenue* — *Account No. 42*

Date		Item	Post. Ref.	Debit	Credit	Balance Debit	Balance Credit
20Y5							
Mar.	1		CR14		400		400

Accounts Receivable Subsidiary Ledger

Name: *Accessories By Claire*

Date		Item	Post. Ref.	Debit	Credit	Balance
20Y5						
Mar.	2		R35	2,200		2,200
	27		R35	3,000		5,200
	28		CR14		2,200	3,000

Name: *RapZone*

Date		Item	Post. Ref.	Debit	Credit	Balance
20Y5						
Mar.	6		R35	1,750		1,750
	30		CR14		1,750	—

Name: *Web Cantina*

Date		Item	Post. Ref.	Debit	Credit	Balance
20Y5						
Mar.	1	Balance	✓			3,400
	18		R35	2,650		6,050
	19		CR14		3,400	2,650

3. Accounts Receivable Cr. column: *3,400*
4. Cash Dr. column: *3,400*

The Other Accounts Cr. column in Exhibit 4 is used for recording credits to any account for which there is no special credit column. For example, NetSolutions received cash on March 1 for rent. Since no special column exists for Rent Revenue, Rent Revenue is entered in the Account Credited column. Thus, this transaction is recorded in the cash receipts journal, shown in Exhibit 4, by entering the following items:

1. Date column: *Mar. 1*
2. Account Credited column: *Rent Revenue*
3. Other Accounts Cr. column: *400*
4. Cash Dr. column: *400*

The process of posting from the cash receipts journal, shown in Exhibit 4, is as follows:

Step 1. Each transaction involving the receipt of cash on account is posted individually to a customer account in the accounts receivable subsidiary ledger. Postings to customer accounts should be made on a regular basis. In this way, the customer's account will show a current balance.

To illustrate, Exhibit 4 shows on March 19 the receipt of $3,400 on account from Web Cantina. The posting of the $3,400 credit to Web Cantina in the accounts receivable subsidiary ledger is also shown in Exhibit 4. After the posting, Web Cantina has a debit balance of $2,650.

Step 2. To provide a trail of the entries posted to the subsidiary ledger, the source of these entries is indicated in the Posting Reference column of each account by inserting the letters CR (for cash receipts journal) and the page number of the cash receipts journal.

To illustrate, Exhibit 4 shows that after $3,400 is posted to Web Cantina's account in the accounts receivable subsidiary ledger, CR14 is inserted in the Post. Ref. column of the account.

Step 3. To indicate that the transaction has been posted to the accounts receivable subsidiary ledger, a check mark (✓) is inserted in the Posting Reference column of the cash receipts journal.

To illustrate, Exhibit 4 shows that a check mark (✓) has been inserted in the Post. Ref. column next to Web Cantina to indicate that the $3,400 has been posted.

Step 4. A single monthly total of the Accounts Receivable Cr. column is posted to the accounts receivable general ledger account. This is the total cash received on account and is posted as a credit to Accounts Receivable. The accounts receivable account number (12) is then inserted below the Accounts Receivable Cr. column to indicate that the posting is complete.

To illustrate, Exhibit 4 shows that the monthly total of $7,350 was posted as a credit to Accounts Receivable (12).

Step 5. A single monthly total of the Cash Dr. column is posted to the cash general ledger account. This is the total cash received during the month and is posted as a debit to Cash. The cash account number (11) is then inserted below the Cash Dr. column to indicate that the posting is complete.

To illustrate, Exhibit 4 shows that the monthly total of $7,750 was posted as a debit to Cash (11).

Step 6. The accounts listed in the Other Accounts Cr. column are posted on a regular basis as a separate credit to each account. The account number is then inserted in the Post. Ref. column to indicate that the posting is complete. Because accounts in the

Other Accounts Cr. column are posted individually, a check mark is placed below the column total at the end of the month to show that no further action is needed.

To illustrate, Exhibit 4 shows that $400 was posted as a credit to Rent Revenue in the general ledger and the rent revenue account number (42) was entered in the Post. Ref. column of the cash receipts journal. Also, at the end of the month, a check mark (✓) is entered below the Other Accounts Cr. column to indicate that no further action is needed.

Accounts Receivable Control Account and Subsidiary Ledger

Note

The balance of the accounts receivable controlling account equals the sum of the customer account balances.

After all posting has been completed for the month, the balances in the accounts receivable subsidiary ledger should be totaled. This total can be summarized in a separate schedule of customer balances. The total should then be compared with the balance of the accounts receivable controlling account in the general ledger. If the controlling account and the subsidiary ledger do not agree, an error has occurred and must be located and corrected.

The total of **NetSolutions**' accounts receivable customer balances is $5,650. This total agrees with the balance of its accounts receivable controlling account on March 31, 20Y5, as follows:

Link to Intuit

Helm Inc., an **Intuit** customer, will be represented by a subsidiary customer ledger in Intuit's accounting system.

Accounts Receivable (Controlling)

Balance, March 1, 20Y5	$ 3,400
Total debits (from revenue journal)	9,600
Total credits (from cash receipts journal)	(7,350)
Balance, March 31, 20Y5	$ 5,650

NetSolutions
Accounts Receivable Customer Balances
March 31, 20Y5

Accessories By Claire	$3,000
RapZone	0
Web Cantina	2,650
Total accounts receivable	$5,650

Equal debit balances

EXAMPLE EXERCISE 5-2 Accounts Receivable Subsidiary Ledger — OBJ. 2

The debits and credits from two transactions are presented in the following customer account:

NAME *Sweet Tooth Confections*
ADDRESS *1212 Lombard St.*

Date	Item	Post. Ref.	Debit	Credit	Balance
July 1	Balance	✓			625
7	Invoice 35	R12	86		711
31	Invoice 31	CR4		122	589

Describe each transaction and the source of each posting.

Follow My Example 5-2

July 7. Provided $86 of services on account to Sweet Tooth Confections, itemized on Invoice No. 35. Amount posted from Page 12 of the revenue journal.

31. Collected cash of $122 from Sweet Tooth Confections (Invoice No. 31). Amount posted from Page 4 of the cash receipts journal.

Practice Exercises: PE 5-2A, PE 5-2B

Purchases Journal

All *purchases on account* are recorded in the **purchases journal**. *Cash purchases would be recorded in the cash payments journal.* The purchases journal for **NetSolutions** is shown in Exhibit 5.

Purchases Journal and Postings EXHIBIT 5

Purchases Journal

Page 11

Date		Account Credited	Post. Ref.	Accounts Payable Cr.	Supplies Dr.	Other Accounts Dr.	Post. Ref.	Amount
20Y5					Step 1			
Mar.	3	Howard Supplies	✓	600	600			
	7	Donnelly Supplies	✓	420	420			
	12	Jewett Business Systems	✓	2,800		Office Equipment	18	2,800
	19	Donnelly Supplies	✓	1,450	1,450			
	27	Howard Supplies	✓	960	960			
	31			6,230	3,430			2,800
				(21)	(14)			(✓)

Step 3

General Ledger

Account *Supplies* — *Account No. 14*

Date		Item	Post. Ref.	Debit	Credit	Balance Debit	Balance Credit
20Y5							
Mar.	1	Balance	✓			2,500	
	31		P11	3,430		5,930	

Step 5

Account *Office Equipment* — *Account No. 18*

Date		Item	Post. Ref.	Debit	Credit	Balance Debit	Balance Credit
20Y5							
Mar.	1	Balance	✓			2,500	
	12		P11	2,800		5,300	

Step 6

Account *Accounts Payable* — *Account No. 21*

Date		Item	Post. Ref.	Debit	Credit	Balance Debit	Balance Credit
20Y5							
Mar.	1	Balance	✓				1,230
	31		P11		6,230		7,460

Step 4

Accounts Payable Subsidiary Ledger

Name: *Donnelly Supplies*

Date		Item	Post. Ref.	Debit	Credit	Balance
20Y5						
Mar.	7		P11		420	420
	19		P11		1,450	1,870

Name: *Grayco Supplies*

Date		Item	Post. Ref.	Debit	Credit	Balance
20Y5						
Mar.	1	Balance	✓			1,230

Step 1

Name: *Howard Supplies*

Date		Item	Post. Ref.	Debit	Credit	Balance
20Y5						
Mar.	3		P11		600	600
	27		P11		960	1,560

Step 2

Name: *Jewett Business Systems*

Date		Item	Post. Ref.	Debit	Credit	Balance
20Y5						
Mar.	12		P11		2,800	2,800

The amounts purchased on account are recorded in the purchases journal in an Accounts Payable Cr. column. The items most often purchased on account determine the titles of the other columns. For example, NetSolutions often purchases supplies on account. Thus, the purchases journal in Exhibit 5 has a Supplies Dr. column.

To illustrate, on March 3, NetSolutions purchased $600 of supplies on account from Howard Supplies. This transaction is recorded in the purchases journal, shown in Exhibit 5, by entering the following items:

1. Date column: *Mar. 3*
2. Account Credited column: *Howard Supplies*
3. Accounts Payable Cr. column: *600*
4. Supplies Dr. column: *600*

The Other Accounts Dr. column in Exhibit 5 is used to record purchases on account of any item for which there is no special debit column. The title of the account to be debited is entered in the Other Accounts Dr. column, and the amount is entered in the Amount column.

At the end of the month, all of the amount columns are totaled. The debits must equal the credits. If the debits do not equal the credits, an error has occurred. Before proceeding further, the error must be found and corrected.

The process of posting from the purchases journal shown in Exhibit 5 is as follows:

Step 1. Each transaction involving a purchase on account is posted individually to a creditor's account in the accounts payable subsidiary ledger. Postings to creditor accounts should be made on a regular basis. In this way, the creditor's account will show a current balance.

To illustrate, Exhibit 5 shows on March 3 the purchase of supplies of $600 on account from Howard Supplies. The posting of the $600 credit to Howard Supplies accounts payable subsidiary ledger is also shown in Exhibit 5. After the posting, Howard Supplies has a credit balance of $600.

Step 2. To provide a trail of the entries posted to the subsidiary and general ledgers, the source of these entries is indicated in the Posting Reference column of each account by inserting the letter P (for purchases journal) and the page number of the purchases journal.

To illustrate, Exhibit 5 shows that after $600 is posted to Howard Supplies account, P11 is inserted in the Post. Ref. column of the account.

Step 3. To indicate that the transaction has been posted to the accounts payable subsidiary ledger, a check mark (✓) is inserted in the Posting Reference column of the purchases journal, as shown in Exhibit 5.

To illustrate, Exhibit 5 shows that a check mark (✓) has been inserted in the Post. Ref. column next to Howard Supplies to indicate that the $600 has been posted.

Step 4. A single monthly total of the Accounts Payable Cr. column is posted to the accounts payable general ledger account. This is the total amount purchased on account and is posted as a credit to Accounts Payable. The accounts payable account number (21) is then inserted below the Accounts Payable Cr. column to indicate that the posting is complete.

To illustrate, Exhibit 5 shows that the monthly total of $6,230 was posted as a credit to Accounts Payable (21).

Step 5. A single monthly total of the Supplies Dr. column is posted to the supplies general ledger account. This is the total supplies purchased on account during the month and is posted as a debit to Supplies. The supplies account number (14) is then inserted below the Supplies Dr. column to indicate that the posting is complete.

To illustrate, Exhibit 5 shows that the monthly total of $3,430 was posted as a debit to Supplies (14).

Step 6. The accounts listed in the Other Accounts Dr. column are posted on a regular basis as a separate debit to each account. The account number is then inserted in the Post. Ref. column to indicate that the posting is complete. Because accounts in the Other Accounts Dr. column are posted individually, a check mark is placed below the column total at the end of the month to show that no further action is needed.

To illustrate, Exhibit 5 shows that $2,800 was posted as a debit to Office Equipment in the general ledger and the office equipment account number (18) was entered in the Post. Ref. column of the purchases journal. Also, at the end of the month, a check mark (✓) is entered below the Amount column to indicate that no further action is needed.

EXAMPLE EXERCISE 5-3 Purchases Journal OBJ. 2

The following purchase transactions occurred during October for Helping Hand Cleaners:

Oct. 11. Purchased cleaning supplies for $235, on account, from General Supplies.
19. Purchased cleaning supplies for $110, on account, from Hubble Supplies.
24. Purchased office equipment for $850, on account, from Office Warehouse.

Record these transactions in a purchases journal as illustrated at the top of Exhibit 5.

Follow My Example 5-3

PURCHASES JOURNAL

Date	Account Credited	Post. Ref.	Accounts Payable Cr.	Cleaning Supplies Dr.	Other Accounts Dr.	Post. Ref.	Amount
Oct. 11	General Supplies		235	235			
19	Hubble Supplies		110	110			
24	Office Warehouse		850		Office Equipment		850

Practice Exercises: PE 5-3A, PE 5-3B

Cash Payments Journal

All transactions that involve the payment of cash are recorded in a **cash payments journal**. The cash payments journal for NetSolutions is shown in Exhibit 6.

The cash payments journal shown in Exhibit 6 has a Cash Cr. column. The kinds of transactions in which cash is paid and how often they occur determine the titles of the other columns. For example, NetSolutions often pays cash to creditors on account. Thus, the cash payments journal in Exhibit 6 has an Accounts Payable Dr. column. In addition, NetSolutions makes all payments by check. Thus, a check number is entered for each payment in the Ck. No. (Check Number) column to the right of the Date column. The check numbers are helpful in controlling cash payments and provide a useful cross-reference.

To illustrate, on March 15, NetSolutions issued Check No. 151 for $1,230 to Grayco Supplies for payment on its account. This transaction is recorded in the cash payments journal shown in Exhibit 6 by entering the following items:

1. Date column: *Mar. 15*
2. Ck. No. column: *151*
3. Account Debited column: *Grayco Supplies*
4. Accounts Payable Dr. column: *1,230*
5. Cash Cr. column: *1,230*

The Other Accounts Dr. column in Exhibit 6 is used for recording debits to any account for which there is no special debit column. For example, NetSolutions issued Check No. 150 on March 2 for $1,600 in payment of March rent. This transaction is recorded in the cash payments journal, shown in Exhibit 6, by entering these items:

1. Date column: *Mar. 2*
2. Ck. No. column: *150*
3. Account Debited column: *Rent Expense*
4. Other Accounts Dr. column: *1,600*
5. Cash Cr. column: *1,600*

EXHIBIT 6 Cash Payments Journal and Postings

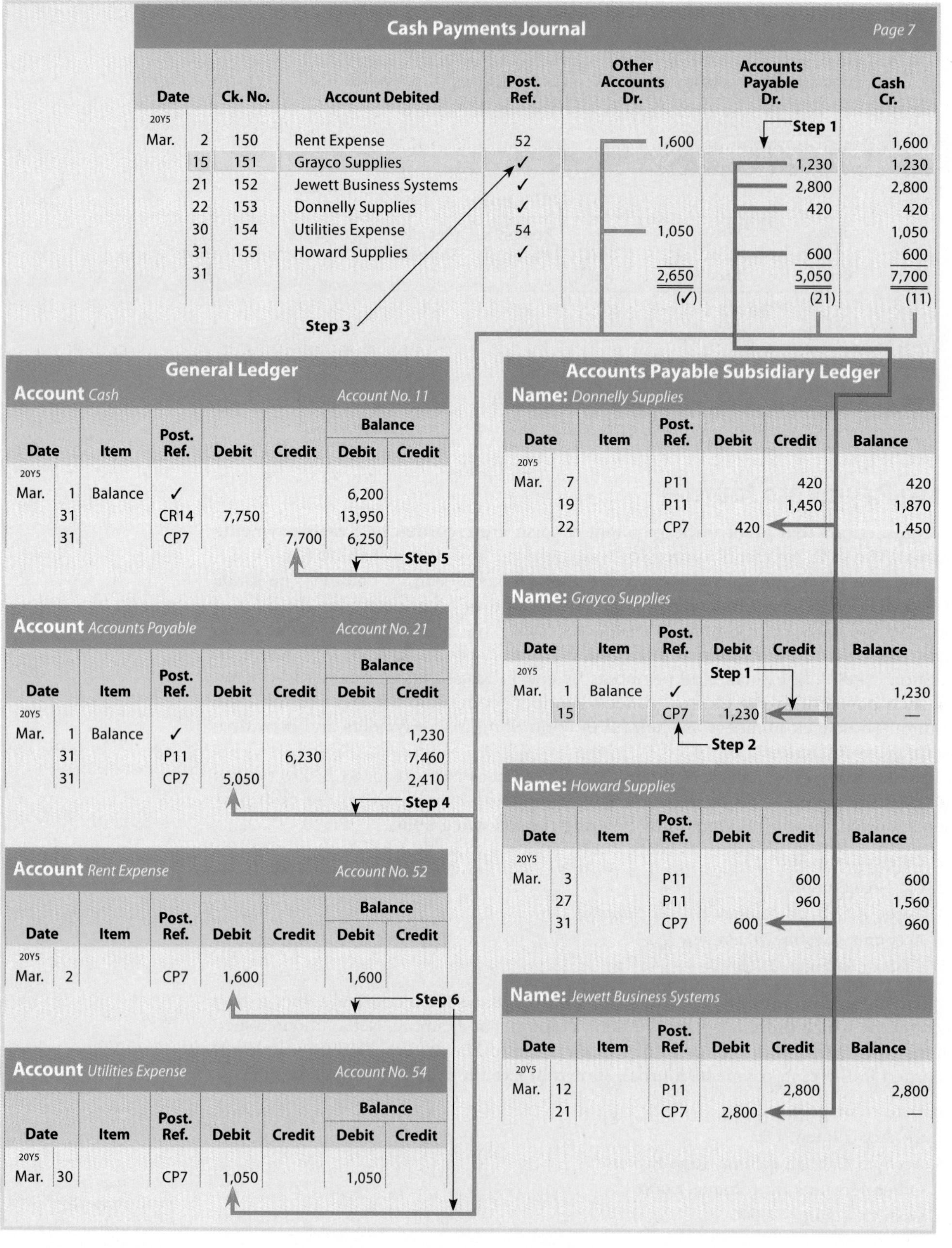

Cash Payments Journal — Page 7

Date		Ck. No.	Account Debited	Post. Ref.	Other Accounts Dr.	Accounts Payable Dr.	Cash Cr.
20Y5							
Mar.	2	150	Rent Expense	52	1,600		1,600
	15	151	Grayco Supplies	✓		1,230	1,230
	21	152	Jewett Business Systems	✓		2,800	2,800
	22	153	Donnelly Supplies	✓		420	420
	30	154	Utilities Expense	54	1,050		1,050
	31	155	Howard Supplies	✓		600	600
	31				2,650	5,050	7,700
					(✓)	(21)	(11)

General Ledger

Account Cash — Account No. 11

Date		Item	Post. Ref.	Debit	Credit	Balance Debit	Balance Credit
20Y5							
Mar.	1	Balance	✓			6,200	
	31		CR14	7,750		13,950	
	31		CP7		7,700	6,250	

Account Accounts Payable — Account No. 21

Date		Item	Post. Ref.	Debit	Credit	Balance Debit	Balance Credit
20Y5							
Mar.	1	Balance	✓				1,230
	31		P11		6,230		7,460
	31		CP7	5,050			2,410

Account Rent Expense — Account No. 52

Date		Item	Post. Ref.	Debit	Credit	Balance Debit	Balance Credit
20Y5							
Mar.	2		CP7	1,600		1,600	

Account Utilities Expense — Account No. 54

Date		Item	Post. Ref.	Debit	Credit	Balance Debit	Balance Credit
20Y5							
Mar.	30		CP7	1,050		1,050	

Accounts Payable Subsidiary Ledger

Name: Donnelly Supplies

Date		Item	Post. Ref.	Debit	Credit	Balance
20Y5						
Mar.	7		P11		420	420
	19		P11		1,450	1,870
	22		CP7	420		1,450

Name: Grayco Supplies

Date		Item	Post. Ref.	Debit	Credit	Balance
20Y5						
Mar.	1	Balance	✓			1,230
	15		CP7	1,230		—

Name: Howard Supplies

Date		Item	Post. Ref.	Debit	Credit	Balance
20Y5						
Mar.	3		P11		600	600
	27		P11		960	1,560
	31		CP7	600		960

Name: Jewett Business Systems

Date		Item	Post. Ref.	Debit	Credit	Balance
20Y5						
Mar.	12		P11		2,800	2,800
	21		CP7	2,800		—

The process of posting from the cash payments journal, Exhibit 6, is as follows:

Step 1. Each transaction involving the payment of cash on account is posted individually to a creditor account in the accounts payable subsidiary ledger. Postings to creditor accounts should be made on a regular basis. In this way, the creditor's account will show a current balance.

To illustrate, Exhibit 6 shows on March 15 the payment of $1,230 on account to Grayco Supplies. The posting of the $1,230 debit to Grayco Supplies in the accounts payable subsidiary ledger is also shown in Exhibit 6. After the posting, Grayco Supplies has a zero balance.

Step 2. To provide a trail of the entries posted to the subsidiary and general ledgers, the source of these entries is indicated in the Posting Reference column of each account by inserting the letters CP (for cash payments journal) and the page number of the cash payments journal.

To illustrate, Exhibit 6 shows that after $1,230 is posted to Grayco Supplies account, CP7 is inserted in the Post. Ref. column of the account.

Step 3. To indicate that the transaction has been posted to the accounts payable subsidiary ledger, a check mark (✓) is inserted in the Posting Reference column of the cash payments journal.

To illustrate, Exhibit 6 shows that a check mark (✓) has been inserted in the Post. Ref. column next to Grayco Supplies to indicate that the $1,230 has been posted.

Step 4. A single monthly total of the Accounts Payable Dr. column is posted to the accounts payable general ledger account. This is the total cash paid on account and is posted as a debit to Accounts Payable. The accounts payable account number (21) is then inserted below the Accounts Payable Dr. column to indicate that the posting is complete.

To illustrate, Exhibit 6 shows that the monthly total of $5,050 was posted as a debit to Accounts Payable (21).

Step 5. A single monthly total of the Cash Cr. column is posted to the cash general ledger account. This is the total cash payments during the month and is posted as a credit to Cash. The cash account number (11) is then inserted below the Cash Cr. column to indicate that the posting is complete.

To illustrate, Exhibit 6 shows that the monthly total of $7,700 was posted as a credit to Cash (11).

Step 6. The accounts listed in the Other Accounts Dr. column are posted on a regular basis as a separate debit to each account. The account number is then inserted in the Post. Ref. column to indicate that the posting is complete. Because accounts in the Other Accounts Dr. column are posted individually, a check mark is placed below the column total at the end of the month to show that no further action is needed.

To illustrate, Exhibit 6 shows that $1,600 was posted as a debit to Rent Expense (52) and $1,050 was posted as a debit to Utilities Expense (54) in the general ledger. The account numbers (52 and 54, respectively) were entered in the Post. Ref. column of the cash payments journal. Also, at the end of the month, a check mark (✓) is entered below the Other Accounts Dr. column to indicate that no further action is needed.

Accounts Payable Control Account and Subsidiary Ledger

After all posting has been completed for the month, the balances in the accounts payable subsidiary ledger should be totaled. This total can be summarized in a separate schedule of creditor balances. The total should then be compared with the balance of the accounts payable controlling account in the general ledger. If the controlling account and the subsidiary ledger do not agree, an error has occurred and must be located and corrected.

Note

The balance of the accounts payable controlling account equals the sum of the creditor account balances.

> **Link to Intuit**
>
> **Ernst and Young, LLP,** is **Intuit's** financial statement auditor and, as such, will be represented by an accounts payable subsidiary ledger account in Intuit's accounting system.

The total of **NetSolutions'** accounts payable creditor balances is $2,410. This total agrees with the balance of its accounts payable controlling account on March 31, 20Y5, as follows:

Accounts Payable (Controlling)	
Balance, March 1, 20Y5	$ 1,230
Total credits (from purchases journal)	6,230
Total debits	
(from cash payments journal)	(5,050)
Balance, March 31, 20Y5	$ 2,410

NetSolutions Accounts Payable Creditor Balances March 31, 20Y5	
Donnelly Supplies	$1,450
Grayco Supplies	0
Howard Supplies	960
Jewett Business Systems	0
Total accounts payable	$2,410

Equal credit balances

EXAMPLE EXERCISE 5-4 Accounts Payable Subsidiary Ledger — OBJ. 2

The debits and credits from two transactions are presented in the following creditor's (supplier's) account:

NAME *Lassiter Services Inc.*
ADDRESS *301 St. Bonaventure Ave.*

Date	Item	Post. Ref.	Debit	Credit	Balance
Aug. 1	Balance	✓			320
12	Invoice No. 101	CP36	200		120
22	Invoice No. 106	P16		140	260

Describe each transaction and the source of each posting.

Follow My Example 5-4

Aug. 12. Paid $200 to Lassiter Services Inc. on account (Invoice No. 101). Amount posted from Page 36 of the cash payments journal.

22. Purchased $140 of services on account from Lassiter Services Inc. itemized on Invoice No. 106. Amount posted from Page 16 of the purchases journal.

Practice Exercises: PE 5-4A, PE 5-4B

Business Connection

ACCOUNTING SYSTEMS AND PROFIT MEASUREMENT

A Greek restaurant owner in Canada had his own system of accounting. He kept his accounts payable in a cigar box on the left-hand side of his cash register, his daily cash returns in the cash register, and his receipts for paid bills in another cigar box on the right. A truly "manual" system.

When his youngest son graduated as an accountant, he was appalled by his father's primitive methods. "I don't know how you can run a business that way," he said. "How do you know what your profits are?"

"Well, son," the father replied, "when I got off the boat from Greece, I had nothing but the pants I was wearing. Today, your brother is a doctor. You are an accountant. Your sister is a speech therapist. Your mother and I have a nice car, a city house, and a country home. We have a good business, and everything is paid for. . . ."

"So, you add all that together, subtract the pants, and there's your profit!"

Computerized Accounting Systems

OBJ. 3 Describe and illustrate the use of a computerized accounting system.

Computerized accounting systems are widely used by even the smallest of companies. Computerized accounting systems have the following three main advantages over manual systems:

- Computerized systems simplify the record-keeping process by recording transactions in electronic journals or forms and, at the same time, posting them electronically to general and subsidiary ledger accounts.
- Computerized systems are generally more accurate than manual systems.
- Computerized systems provide management with current account balance information to support decision making, since account balances are posted as the transactions occur.

The popular QuickBooks accounting software for small- to medium-sized businesses is used to illustrate a computerized accounting system for **NetSolutions**. To simplify, the illustration is limited to transactions involving revenue earned on account and the subsequent recording of cash collections. Exhibit 7 illustrates the use of QuickBooks for NetSolutions to record transactions as follows:

Large companies have their accounting systems integrated within the company's automated business systems. Such integrated software is termed ERP, or enterprise resource planning.

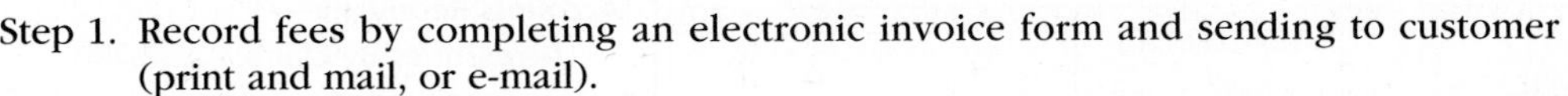

Step 1. Record fees by completing an electronic invoice form and sending to customer (print and mail, or e-mail).

Sales transactions are entered using an electronic invoice form. The electronic form appears like a paper form with fields to input transaction data. The fields may have drop-down lists to ease data entry. After the form is completed, it is printed out and mailed, or e-mailed, to the customer.

To illustrate, on March 2, NetSolutions earned $2,200 on account from Accessories By Claire. As shown in Exhibit 7, Invoice No. 615 was created using an electronic form. Upon submitting the invoice form, QuickBooks automatically posts a $2,200 debit to the Accessories By Claire customer account and a credit to Fees Earned. An invoice is either e-mailed or printed for mailing to Accessories By Claire.

Step 2. Record collection of payment by completing a "receive payment" form.

Upon collection from the customer, a "receive payment" electronic form is opened and completed. As with the "invoice form," data are input into the various fields directly or by using drop-down lists.

To illustrate, a $2,200 payment was collected from Accessories By Claire on March 28. The $2,200 was applied to Invoice No. 615, as shown by the check mark (✓) next to the March 2 date at the bottom of the form in Exhibit 7. As shown at the bottom of the form, the March 27 invoice of $3,000 remains uncollected. When the screen is completed and submitted, a debit of $2,200 is automatically posted to the cash account and a credit for $2,200 is posted to the Accessories By Claire account. This causes the balance of the Accessories By Claire account to be reduced from $5,200 to $3,000.

Step 3. Prepare reports.

At any time, managers may request reports from the software. Three such reports include the following:

- "Accounts Receivable Customer Balances" lists as of a specific date the accounts receivable balances by customer.

  To illustrate, the Accounts Receivable Customer Balances report shown in Exhibit 7 for NetSolutions was generated as of March 31, 20Y5. The total of the balances of the Accounts Receivable Customer Balances report of $5,650 agrees with the accounts receivable subsidiary ledger balance total we illustrated using a manual system for NetSolutions in Exhibit 4.

- "Fees Earned by Customer" lists revenue by customer for the month. It is created from the electronic invoice form used in Step 1.

  To illustrate, the Fees Earned by Customer report shown in Exhibit 7 for NetSolutions is for the month of March 20Y5. The $9,600 of total consulting fees earned agrees with the total of the revenue journal we illustrated using a manual system for NetSolutions in Exhibits 2 and 3.

- "Cash Receipts" lists the cash receipts during the month.

  To illustrate, the Cash Receipts report shown in Exhibit 7 for NetSolutions is for the month of March 20Y5. The total cash receipts of $7,750 agree with the total of the Cash Dr. column of the cash receipts journal we illustrated using a manual system for NetSolutions in Exhibit 4.

> **Link to Intuit**
>
> **Intuit** derives 50% of its revenues from small business accounting software.

Quickbooks and other computerized accounting systems use electronic forms. Alternatively, some computerized systems use electronic special journals. Such journals are designed similar to those illustrated in the text. Additionally, electronic general journals are found in all computerized systems.

EXHIBIT 7 **Revenue and Cash Receipts in QuickBooks**

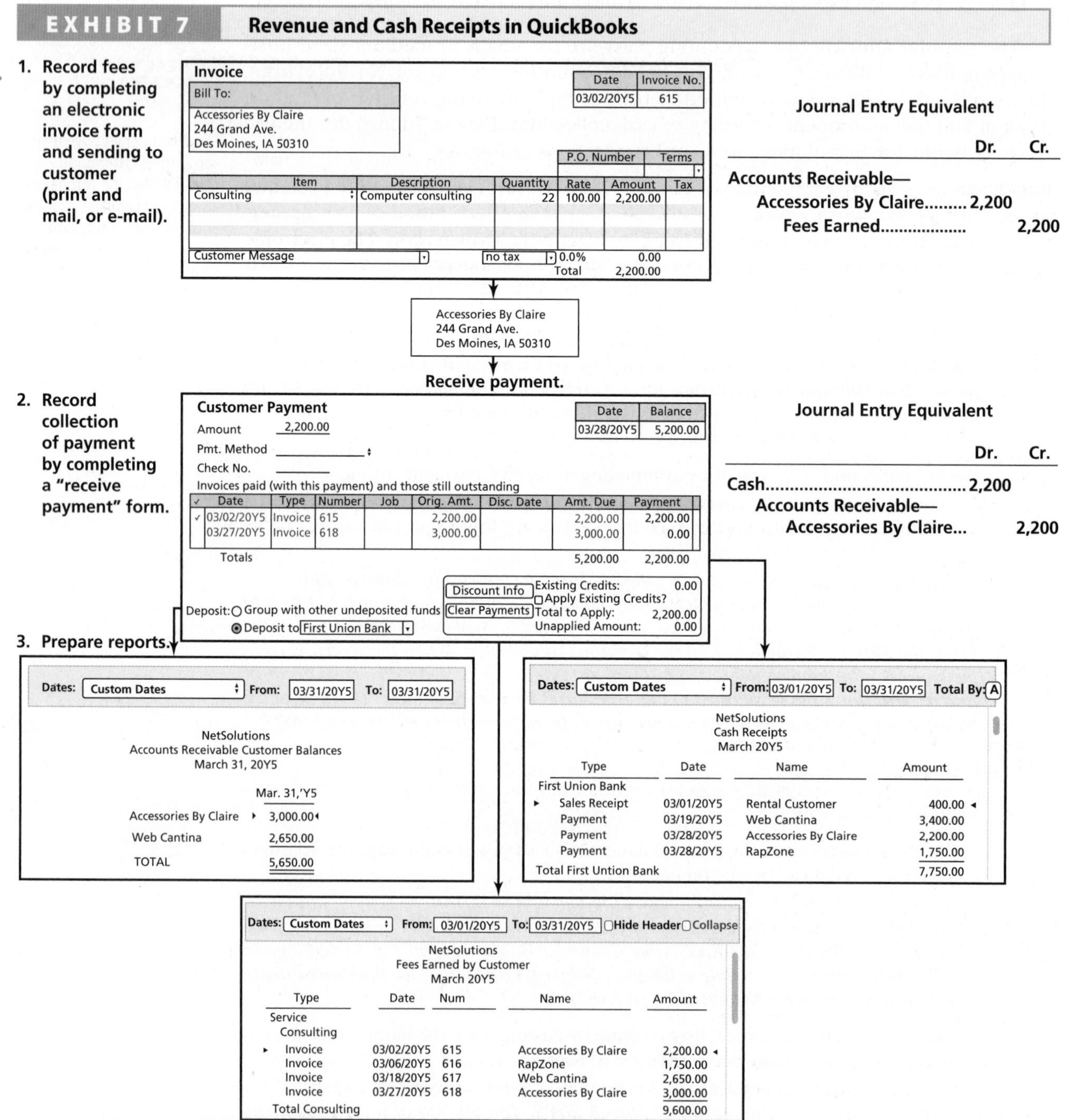

1. Record fees by completing an electronic invoice form and sending to customer (print and mail, or e-mail).

Invoice

Bill To:
Accessories By Claire
244 Grand Ave.
Des Moines, IA 50310

Date	Invoice No.
03/02/20Y5	615

P.O. Number	Terms

Item	Description	Quantity	Rate	Amount	Tax
Consulting	Computer consulting	22	100.00	2,200.00	

Customer Message — no tax — 0.0% — 0.00
Total 2,200.00

Journal Entry Equivalent

	Dr.	Cr.
Accounts Receivable— Accessories By Claire.........	2,200	
Fees Earned..................		2,200

Accessories By Claire
244 Grand Ave.
Des Moines, IA 50310

Receive payment.

2. Record collection of payment by completing a "receive payment" form.

Customer Payment

Amount 2,200.00
Pmt. Method
Check No.

Date	Balance
03/28/20Y5	5,200.00

Invoices paid (with this payment) and those still outstanding

✓	Date	Type	Number	Job	Orig. Amt.	Disc. Date	Amt. Due	Payment
✓	03/02/20Y5	Invoice	615		2,200.00		2,200.00	2,200.00
	03/27/20Y5	Invoice	618		3,000.00		3,000.00	0.00
	Totals						5,200.00	2,200.00

Discount Info — Existing Credits: 0.00
Apply Existing Credits?
Clear Payments — Total to Apply: 2,200.00
Unapplied Amount: 0.00

Deposit: ○ Group with other undeposited funds
◉ Deposit to First Union Bank

Journal Entry Equivalent

	Dr.	Cr.
Cash..	2,200	
Accounts Receivable— Accessories By Claire...		2,200

3. Prepare reports.

Dates: Custom Dates From: 03/31/20Y5 To: 03/31/20Y5

NetSolutions
Accounts Receivable Customer Balances
March 31, 20Y5

	Mar. 31,'Y5
Accessories By Claire	3,000.00
Web Cantina	2,650.00
TOTAL	5,650.00

Dates: Custom Dates From: 03/01/20Y5 To: 03/31/20Y5 Total By: A

NetSolutions
Cash Receipts
March 20Y5

Type	Date	Name	Amount
First Union Bank			
Sales Receipt	03/01/20Y5	Rental Customer	400.00
Payment	03/19/20Y5	Web Cantina	3,400.00
Payment	03/28/20Y5	Accessories By Claire	2,200.00
Payment	03/28/20Y5	RapZone	1,750.00
Total First Untion Bank			7,750.00

Dates: Custom Dates From: 03/01/20Y5 To: 03/31/20Y5 Hide Header Collapse

NetSolutions
Fees Earned by Customer
March 20Y5

Type	Date	Num	Name	Amount
Service				
Consulting				
Invoice	03/02/20Y5	615	Accessories By Claire	2,200.00
Invoice	03/06/20Y5	616	RapZone	1,750.00
Invoice	03/18/20Y5	617	Web Cantina	2,650.00
Invoice	03/27/20Y5	618	Accessories By Claire	3,000.00
Total Consulting				9,600.00

Business Connection

TURBOTAX

Intuit sells TurboTax®, one of the most popular tax preparation software products for individuals. With this roduct, the tax return is prepared using electronic tax forms. Thus, the familiar Form 1040 is presented as an electronic form with data-entry fields provided for the various line items. The advantage of this approach is that all the arithmetic and linking between forms is done automatically. A change in one field automatically updates all other linked fields.

In using these tools, the computer program prevents transactions in which the total debits do not equal the total credits. In such cases, an error screen will notify the user to correct data inputs. Likewise, the software will not make posting or mathematical errors.

In this section, revenue and cash receipt transactions are illustrated for NetSolutions using QuickBooks accounting software. Similar illustrations could be provided for purchases and cash payment transactions. A complete illustration of a computerized accounting system is beyond the scope of this text. However, this chapter provides a solid foundation for applying accounting system concepts in either a manual or a computerized system.

E-Commerce

OBJ. 4 Describe the basic features of e-commerce.

Using the Internet to perform business transactions is termed **e-commerce**. The U.S. Census Bureau indicates that e-commerce represents more than $513 billion in retail sales, or more than 9% of all retail sales.[1] When transactions are between a company and a consumer, it is termed *B2C (business-to-consumer) e-commerce*. Examples of companies engaged in B2C e-commerce include **Amazon.com**, **priceline.com Incorporated**, and **Apple Inc.** The B2C business allows consumers to shop and receive goods at home, rather than going to the store. For example, Apple Inc. allows consumers to use its website to select and purchase Apple products for direct shipment to the home.

When transactions are conducted between two companies, it is termed *B2B (business-to-business) e-commerce*. Examples of companies engaged in B2B e-commerce include **Cisco Systems, Inc.**, an Internet equipment manufacturer, and **Union Pacific Corporation**, a railroad. Union Pacific, for example, allows its business customers to order freight transportation services from its website.

The Internet creates opportunities for improving the speed and efficiency of transactions. As discussed, many companies are realizing these benefits of using e-commerce. Three additional areas where the Internet is being used for business purposes are as follows:

- **Supply chain management (SCM):** Internet applications to plan supply needs and coordinate them with suppliers.
- **Customer relationship management (CRM):** Internet applications to plan and coordinate marketing and sales efforts.
- **Product life-cycle management (PLM):** Internet applications to plan and coordinate the product development and design processes.

Many web applications generate accounting transactions as they occur. For example, shopping cart transactions on e-commerce sites generate the accounting revenue transactions for the seller.

1 Quarterly Retail E-commerce Sales, *U.S. Census Bureau News*, U.S. Department of Commerce, March 13, 2019, p. 1.

Integrity, Objectivity, and Ethics in Business

ONLINE FRAUD

Online fraud accounted for losses equal to approximately 0.9% of all online revenue. As a result, online retailers are using address verification and credit card security codes as additional security measures. Address verification matches the customer's address to the address on file with the credit card company, while the security code is the additional three- or four-digit code designed to reduce fictitious credit card transactions. In addition, merchants are using Google Maps lookups to verify that order addresses match real locations. Online fraud has been decreasing the last several years as a result of these and other measures.

Source: 15th Annual CyberSource Online Fraud Benchmark Survey, *CyberSource*, January 2015.

As the Internet continues to become the preferred method of conducting business, new applications will be developed. Many of these applications will be linked to the accounting system as transactions flow inside and outside the organization.

OBJ. 5 Use segment analysis in evaluating the operating performance of a company.

Financial Analysis and Interpretation: Segment Analysis

Accounting systems often use computers to collect, classify, summarize, and report financial and operating information in a variety of ways. One way is to report revenue earned by different segments of business. Businesses may be segmented by region, by product or service, or by type of customer. Segment revenues are determined from the invoice data that are entered into the accounting system.

For example, **Intuit Inc.** uses invoice data from the accounting system to determine the amount of revenue earned by different products and services. Segment analysis uses horizontal and vertical comparisons to analyze the contributions of various segments to the total operating performance of a company. To illustrate, selected product and service segment revenue information from the notes to Intuit's financial statements for two recent fiscal years follows:

Segment	Recent Year (in millions)	Prior Year (in millions)
Small Business	$2,994	$2,539
Consumer	2,517	2,201
Strategic Partner	453	437
Total revenues	$5,964	$5,177

This segment information can be used to perform horizontal analysis using the prior year as the base year as follows:

Segment	Recent Year (in millions)	Prior Year (in millions)	Increase (Decrease)	
			Amount	Percent
Small Business	$2,994	$2,539	$455	17.9%
Consumer	2,517	2,201	316	14.4
Strategic Partner	453	437	16	3.7
Total revenues	$5,964	$5,177	$787	15.2

Intuit's total revenues increased by more than 15%. This increase is primarily due to growth in the Small Business and Consumer segments.

In addition, vertical analysis could be performed on the segment disclosures as follows:

	Recent Year		Prior Year	
Segment	**Amount (in millions)**	**Percent**	**Amount (in millions)**	**Percent**
Small Business	$2,994	50.2%	$2,539	49.0%
Consumer	2,517	42.2	2,201	42.5
Strategic Partner	453	7.6	437	8.4
Total revenues	$5,964	100.0%	$5,177	100.0%*

*Difference due to rounding.

The preceding analysis shows that revenue in the Small Business segment increased as a percent of total revenues between the two years. The Consumer and Strategic Partner segments decreased slightly as a percent of total revenues between the two years.

Both analyses together show that Intuit has increasing revenue between the two years, caused mostly by an increase in Small Business, its largest segment. The Consumer and Strategic Partner segments exhibited revenue growth between the two years although their share of the total revenue has declined slightly between the two years.

EXAMPLE EXERCISE 5-5 Segment Analysis

OBJ. 5

Morse Company does business in two regional segments: East and West. The following annual revenue information was determined from the accounting system's invoice information:

Segment	20Y9	20Y8
East	$25,000	$20,000
West	50,000	60,000
Total revenues	$75,000	$80,000

Prepare horizontal and vertical analyses of the segments. Round to one decimal place.

Follow My Example 5-5

Horizontal analysis:

			Increase (Decrease)	
Segment	**20Y9**	**20Y8**	**Amount**	**Percent**
East	$25,000	$20,000	$ 5,000	25.0%
West	50,000	60,000	(10,000)	(16.7)
Total revenues	$75,000	$80,000	$ (5,000)	(6.3)

Vertical analysis:

	20Y9		20Y8	
Segment	**Amount**	**Percent**	**Amount**	**Percent**
East	$25,000	33.3%	$20,000	25.0%
West	50,000	66.7	60,000	75.0
Total revenues	$75,000	100.0%	$80,000	100.0%

Practice Exercises: PE 5-5A, PE 5-5B

At a Glance 5

OBJ. 1 Define and describe an accounting system.

Key Points An accounting system is the methods and procedures for collecting, classifying, summarizing, and reporting a business's financial information. The three steps through which an accounting system evolves are (1) analysis of information needs, (2) design of the system, and (3) implementation of the system design.

Learning Outcomes	Example Exercises	Practice Exercises
• Define an accounting system.		
• Describe the three steps for designing an accounting system: (1) analysis, (2) design, and (3) implementation.		

OBJ. 2 Journalize and post transactions in a manual accounting system that uses subsidiary ledgers and special journals.

Key Points Subsidiary ledgers may be used to maintain separate records for customers and creditors (vendors). A controlling account in the general ledger summarizes the subsidiary ledger accounts. The sum of the subsidiary ledger account balances must agree with the balance in the related controlling account.

Learning Outcomes	Example Exercises	Practice Exercises
• Prepare a revenue journal and post services provided on account to individual customer accounts and the column total to the corresponding general ledger accounts.	**EE5-1**	**PE5-1A, 5-1B**
• Prepare a cash receipts journal and post collections on account to individual customer accounts. Post Other Accounts column entries individually and special column totals to the corresponding general ledger accounts.	**EE5-2**	**PE5-2A, 5-2B**
• Prepare a purchases journal and post amounts owed to individual creditor accounts. Post Other Accounts column entries individually and special column totals to the corresponding general ledger accounts.	**EE5-3**	**PE5-3A, 5-3B**
• Prepare a cash payments journal and post the amounts paid to individual creditor accounts. Post Other Accounts column entries individually and special column totals to the corresponding general ledger accounts.	**EE5-4**	**PE5-4A, 5-4B**

OBJ. 3 Describe and illustrate the use of a computerized accounting system.

Key Points Computerized accounting systems are similar to manual systems. The main advantages of a computerized accounting system are the simultaneous recording and posting of transactions, high degree of accuracy, and timeliness of reporting.

Learning Outcomes	Example Exercises	Practice Exercises
• Differentiate between a manual and a computerized accounting system.		
• Illustrate revenue and cash receipts transactions using QuickBooks.		

OBJ. 4 Describe the basic features of e-commerce.

Key Points Using the Internet to perform business transactions is termed e-commerce. B2C e-commerce involves Internet transactions between a business and consumer, while B2B e-commerce involves Internet transactions between businesses. More elaborate e-commerce involves planning and coordinating suppliers, customers, and product design.

Learning Outcomes	Example Exercises	Practice Exercises
• Define e-commerce and describe the major trends in e-commerce.		

OBJ. 5 Use segment analysis in evaluating the operating performance of a company.

Key Points Businesses may be segmented by region, by product or service, or by type of customer. Segment revenues can be analyzed using horizontal and vertical analyses. Such analyses are useful to management for evaluating the causes of business performance.

Learning Outcomes	Example Exercises	Practice Exercises
• Prepare horizontal and vertical analyses for business segments.	EE5-5	PE5-5A, 5-5B

Illustrative Problem

Selected transactions of O'Malley Co. for the month of May are as follows:

a. May 1. Issued Check No. 1001 in payment of rent for May, $1,200.
b. 2. Purchased office supplies on account from McMillan Co., $3,600.
c. 4. Issued Check No. 1003 in payment of freight charges on the supplies purchased on May 2, $320.
d. 8. Provided services on account to Waller Co., Invoice No. 51, $4,500.
e. 9. Issued Check No. 1005 for office supplies purchased, $450.
f. 10. Received cash for monthly rental of unused storage space, $120.
g. 11. Purchased office equipment on account from Fender Office Products, $15,000.
h. 12. Issued Check No. 1010 in payment of the supplies purchased from McMillan Co. on May 2, $3,600.
i. 16. Provided services on account to Riese Co., Invoice No. 58, $8,000.
j. 18. Received $4,500 from Waller Co. in payment of May 8 invoice.
k. 20. Invested additional cash in the business, $10,000.
l. 25. Provided services for cash, $15,900.
m. 30. Issued Check No. 1040 for withdrawal of cash for personal use, $1,000.
n. 30. Issued Check No. 1041 in payment of electricity and water invoices, $690.
o. 30. Issued Check No. 1042 in payment of office and sales salaries for May, $15,800.
p. 31. Journalized adjusting entries from the work sheet prepared for the fiscal year ended May 31.

(Continued)

O'Malley Co. maintains journals and subsidiary ledgers as follows:

Journals	Subsidiary Ledgers
Revenue	Accounts receivable
Purchases	Accounts payable
Cash receipts	
Cash payments	
General	

Instructions

1. Indicate the journal in which each of the preceding transactions, (a) through (p), would be recorded.
2. Indicate whether an account in the accounts receivable or accounts payable subsidiary ledgers would be affected for each of the preceding transactions.
3. Journalize transactions (b), (c), (d), (h), and (j) in the appropriate journals.

Solution

1. Journal	2. Subsidiary Ledger
a. Cash payments journal	None
b. Purchases journal	Accounts payable ledger
c. Cash payments journal	None
d. Revenue journal	Accounts receivable ledger
e. Cash payments journal	None
f. Cash receipts journal	None
g. Purchases journal	Accounts payable ledger
h. Cash payments journal	Accounts payable ledger
i. Revenue journal	Accounts receivable ledger
j. Cash receipts journal	Accounts receivable ledger
k. Cash receipts journal	None
l. Cash receipts journal	None
m. Cash payments journal	None
n. Cash payments journal	None
o. Cash payments journal	None
p. General journal	None

3.

Transaction (b):

Purchases Journal

Date		Account Credited	Post. Ref.	Accounts Payable Cr.	Office Supplies Dr.	Other Accounts Dr.	Post. Ref.	Amount
May	2	McMillan Co.		3,600	3,600			

Transactions (c) and (h):

Cash Payments Journal

Date		Ck. No.	Account Debited	Post. Ref.	Other Accounts Dr.	Accounts Payable Dr.	Cash Cr.
May	4	1003	Freight Expense		320		320
	12	1010	McMillan Co.			3,600	3,600

Transaction (d):

Revenue Journal					
Date		Invoice No.	Account Debited	Post. Ref.	Accts. Rec. Dr. Fees Earned Cr.
May	8	51	Waller Co.		4,500

Transaction (j):

Cash Receipts Journal						
Date		Account Credited	Post. Ref.	Other Accounts Cr.	Accounts Receivable Cr.	Cash Dr.
May	18	Waller Co.			4,500	4,500

Key Terms

accounting system (230)
accounts payable subsidiary ledger (231)
accounts receivable subsidiary ledger (231)
cash payments journal (241)
cash receipts journal (236)
controlling account (231)
e-commerce (247)
general journal (232)
general ledger (231)
internal controls (230)
invoice (233)
purchases journal (238)
revenue journal (233)
special journals (231)
subsidiary ledger (231)

Discussion Questions

1. Why would a company maintain separate accounts receivable ledgers for each customer, as opposed to maintaining a single accounts receivable ledger for all customers?
2. What are the major advantages of the use of special journals?
3. In recording 400 fees earned on account during a single month, how many times will it be necessary to write Fees Earned (a) if each transaction, including fees earned, is recorded individually in a two-column general journal; (b) if each transaction for fees earned is recorded in a revenue journal?
4. How many postings to Fees Earned for the month would be needed in Discussion Question 3 if the procedure described in (a) had been used; if the procedure described in (b) had been used?
5. During the current month, the following errors occurred in recording transactions in the purchases journal or in posting from it:
   a. An invoice for $1,875 of supplies from Kelly Co. was recorded as having been received from Kelley Co., another supplier.
   b. A credit of $420 to Blackstone Company was posted as $240 in the subsidiary ledger.
   c. An invoice for equipment of $4,800 was recorded as $4,000.
   d. The Accounts Payable column of the purchases journal was overstated by $3,600.

   How will each error come to the bookkeeper's attention, other than by chance discovery?
6. Assuming the use of a two-column general journal, a purchases journal, and a cash payments journal as illustrated in this chapter, indicate the journal in which each of the following transactions should be recorded:
   a. Purchase of office supplies on account.
   b. Purchase of supplies for cash.
   c. Purchase of store equipment on account.

(Continued)

d. Payment of cash on account to creditor.
e. Payment of cash for office supplies.

7. What is an electronic form, and how is it used in a computerized accounting system?
8. When are transactions posted in a computerized accounting system?
9. What happens to the special journal in a computerized accounting system that uses electronic forms?
10. How would e-commerce improve the revenue/collection cycle?

Practice Exercises

Example Exercises

SHOW ME HOW

EE 5-1 *p. 235* **PE 5-1A Revenue journal** **OBJ. 2**

The following revenue transactions occurred during August:

Aug. 4. Issued Invoice No. 162 to Oasis Enterprises Co. for services provided on account, $320.
15. Issued Invoice No. 163 to City Electric Inc. for services provided on account, $535.
25. Issued Invoice No. 164 to Juniper Co. for services provided on account, $170.

Record these three transactions in the following revenue journal format:

REVENUE JOURNAL

Date	Invoice No.	Account Debited	Post. Ref.	Accts. Rec. Dr. Fees Earned Cr.

SHOW ME HOW

EE 5-1 *p. 235* **PE 5-1B Revenue journal** **OBJ. 2**

The following revenue transactions occurred during April:

Apr. 6. Issued Invoice No. 78 to BlueBird Co. for services provided on account, $1,710.
11. Issued Invoice No. 79 to Hitchcock Inc. for services provided on account, $3,320.
19. Issued Invoice No. 80 to Fletcher Inc. for services provided on account, $550.

Record these three transactions in the following revenue journal format:

REVENUE JOURNAL

Date	Invoice No.	Account Debited	Post. Ref.	Accts. Rec. Dr. Fees Earned Cr.

SHOW ME HOW

EE 5-2 *p. 238* **PE 5-2A Accounts receivable subsidiary ledger** **OBJ. 2**

The debits and credits from two transactions are presented in the following customer account:

NAME *Central Entertainment*
ADDRESS *125 Wycoff Ave.*

Date	Item	Post. Ref.	Debit	Credit	Balance
Feb. 1	Balance	✓			460
22	Invoice No. 422	CR106		200	260
27	Invoice No. 445	R92	280		540

Describe each transaction and the source of each posting.

SHOW ME HOW

EE 5-2 p. 238

PE 5-2B Accounts receivable subsidiary ledger

OBJ. 2

The debits and credits from two transactions are presented in the following customer account:

NAME *Eclypse Products Inc.*
ADDRESS *46 W. Main St.*

Date	Item	Post. Ref.	Debit	Credit	Balance
Aug. 1	Balance	✓			1,420
10	Invoice No. 119	R24	890		2,310
17	Invoice No. 106	CR46		720	1,590

Describe each transaction and the source of each posting.

SHOW ME HOW

EE 5-3 p. 241

PE 5-3A Purchases journal

OBJ. 2

The following purchase transactions occurred during October for NonStop Inc.:

Oct. 6. Purchased office supplies for $310, on account from U-Save Supply Inc.
14. Purchased office equipment for $3,430, on account from Zell Computer Inc.
26. Purchased office supplies for $485, on account from U-Save Supply Inc.

Record these transactions in the following purchases journal format:

PURCHASES JOURNAL

Date	Account Credited	Post. Ref.	Accounts Payable Cr.	Office Supplies Dr.	Other Accounts Dr.	Post. Ref.	Amount

SHOW ME HOW

EE 5-3 p. 241

PE 5-3B Purchases journal

OBJ. 2

The following purchase transactions occurred during March for Celebration Catering Service:

Mar. 11. Purchased party supplies for $820, on account from Gift Pack Supplies Inc.
14. Purchased party supplies for $425, on account from Fun 4 All Supplies Inc.
27. Purchased office furniture for $3,330, on account from Office Space Inc.

Record these transactions in the following purchases journal format:

PURCHASES JOURNAL

Date	Account Credited	Post. Ref.	Accounts Payable Cr.	Party Supplies Dr.	Other Accounts Dr.	Post. Ref.	Amount

SHOW ME HOW

EE 5-4 p. 244

PE 5-4A Accounts payable subsidiary ledger

OBJ. 2

The debits and credits from two transactions are presented in the following creditor's (supplier's) account:

NAME *Sunstar Technology*
ADDRESS *2199 Commerce Place*

Date	Item	Post. Ref.	Debit	Credit	Balance
Nov. 1	Balance	✓			8,560
11	Invoice No. 85	P8		1,680	10,240
22	Invoice No. 43	CP46	2,980		7,260

Describe each transaction and the source of each posting.

SHOW ME HOW

EE 5-4 *p. 244* **PE 5-4B Accounts payable subsidiary ledger** **OBJ. 2**

The debits and credits from two transactions are presented in the following creditor's (supplier's) account:

NAME *Quinlan Inc.*
ADDRESS *5000 Grand Ave.*

Date	Item	Post. Ref.	Debit	Credit	Balance
Jan. 1	Balance	✓			163
11	Invoice No. 122	CP71	113		50
26	Invoice No. 139	P55		128	178

Describe each transaction and the source of each posting.

SHOW ME HOW

FAI

EE 5-5 *p. 249* **PE 5-5A Segment analysis** **OBJ. 5**

Verity Company does business in two customer segments: Retail and Wholesale. The following annual revenue information was determined from the accounting system's invoice information:

Segment	20Y5	20Y4
Retail	$145,400	$138,500
Wholesale	173,100	189,300
Total revenues	$318,500	$327,800

Prepare horizontal and vertical analyses of the segments. Round to one decimal place.

SHOW ME HOW

FAI

EE 5-5 *p. 249* **PE 5-5B Segment analysis** **OBJ. 5**

Navigator Life, Inc., does business in two product segments: Camping and Fishing. The following annual revenue information was determined from the accounting system's invoice information:

Segment	20Y3	20Y2
Camping	$336,900	$288,800
Fishing	168,500	192,500
Total revenues	$505,400	$481,300

Prepare horizontal and vertical analyses of the segments. Round to one decimal place.

Exercises

EX 5-1 Identify postings from revenue journal **OBJ. 2**

Using the following revenue journal for Westside Cleaners Inc., identify each of the posting references, indicated by a letter, as representing (1) posting to general ledger accounts or (2) posting to subsidiary ledger accounts:

REVENUE JOURNAL

Date	Invoice No.	Account Debited	Post. Ref.	Accounts Rec. Dr. Fees Earned Cr.
20Y3				
May 1	112	Hazmat Safety Co.	(a)	$ 3,740
10	113	Masco Co.	(b)	1,790
20	114	Alpha GenCorp	(c)	5,110
27	115	Jordan Inc.	(d)	2,260
31				$12,900
				(e)

EX 5-2 Accounts receivable ledger **OBJ. 2**

✔ **d. Total accounts receivable, $13,980**

Based on the data presented in Exercise 5-1, assume that the beginning balances for the customer accounts were zero, except for Jordan Inc., which had a $1,080 beginning balance. In addition, there were no collections during the period.

a. Set up a T account for Accounts Receivable and T accounts for the four accounts needed in the customer ledger.

b. Post to the T accounts.

c. Determine the balance in the accounts.

d. Prepare a listing of the accounts receivable customer balances as of May 31, 20Y3.

EX 5-3 Identify journals **OBJ. 2**

Assuming the use of a two-column (all-purpose) general journal, a revenue journal, and a cash receipts journal as illustrated in this chapter, indicate the journal in which each of the following transactions should be recorded:

a. Receipt of cash refund from overpayment of taxes.

b. Adjustment to record accrued salaries at the end of the year.

c. Providing services on account.

d. Investment of additional cash in the business by the owner.

e. Receipt of cash on account from a customer.

f. Receipt of cash for rent.

g. Receipt of cash from sale of office equipment.

h. Sale of used office equipment on account, at cost, to a neighboring business.

i. Closing of drawing account at the end of the year.

j. Providing services for cash.

EX 5-4 Identify journals **OBJ. 2**

Assuming the use of a two-column (all-purpose) general journal, a purchases journal, and a cash payments journal as illustrated in this chapter, indicate the journal in which each of the following transactions should be recorded:

a. Payment of six months' rent in advance.

b. Purchase of an office computer on account.

c. Purchase of office supplies on account.

d. Adjustment to record depreciation at the end of the month.

e. Adjustment to record accrued salaries at the end of the period.

f. Purchase of services on account.

g. Adjustment to prepaid rent at the end of the month.

h. Purchase of office equipment for cash.

i. Adjustment to prepaid insurance at the end of the month.

j. Purchase of office supplies for cash.

k. Advance payment of a one-year fire insurance policy on the office.

EX 5-5 Identify transactions in accounts receivable subsidiary ledger — OBJ. 2

The debits and credits from three related transactions are presented in the following customer's account taken from the accounts receivable subsidiary ledger:

NAME *Mission Design*
ADDRESS *1319 Elm Street*

Date	Item	Post. Ref.	Debit	Credit	Balance
20Y7					
Apr. 3		R44	740		740
6		J11		60	680
24		CR81		680	—

Describe each transaction and identify the source of each posting.

EX 5-6 Prepare journal entries in a revenue journal — OBJ. 2

Shannon Consulting Company had the following transactions during the month of October:

Oct. 2. Issued Invoice No. 321 to Pryor Corp. for services rendered on account, $1,625.
3. Issued Invoice No. 322 to Armor Inc. for services rendered on account, $850.
14. Issued Invoice No. 323 to Pryor Corp. for services rendered on account, $565.
24. Issued Invoice No. 324 to Rose Co. for services rendered on account, $2,320.
29. Collected Invoice No. 321 from Pryor Corp.

a. Record the October revenue transactions for Shannon Consulting Company in the following revenue journal format:

REVENUE JOURNAL

Date	Invoice No.	Account Debited	Post. Ref.	Accts. Rec. Dr. Fees Earned Cr.

b. What is the total amount posted to the accounts receivable and fees earned accounts from the revenue journal for October?

c. What is the October 31 balance of the Pryor Corp. customer account assuming a zero balance on October 1?

EX 5-7 Posting a revenue journal — OBJ. 2, 3

The revenue journal for Sapling Consulting Inc. follows. The accounts receivable controlling account has a July 1, 20Y2, balance of $625 consisting of an amount due from Aladdin Co. There were no collections during July.

REVENUE JOURNAL — **Page** *12*

Date	Invoice No.	Account Debited	Post. Ref.	Accts. Rec. Dr. Fees Earned Cr.
20Y2				
July 4	355	Clearmark Co.		1,890
9	356	Life Star Inc.		3,410
18	357	Aladdin Co.		950
22	359	Clearmark Co.		3,660
31				9,910

a. Prepare a T account for the accounts receivable customer accounts.

b. Post the transactions from the revenue journal to the customer accounts and determine their ending balances.

c. Prepare T accounts for the accounts receivable and fees earned accounts. Post control totals to the two accounts and determine the ending balances.

d. Prepare a schedule of the customer account balances to verify the equality of the sum of the customer account balances and the accounts receivable controlling account balance.

e. How might a computerized system differ from a revenue journal in recording revenue transactions?

EX 5-8 Accounts receivable subsidiary ledger

OBJ. 2

✔ Accounts Receivable balance, January 31, $10,310

The revenue and cash receipts journals for Birmingham Productions Inc. follow. The accounts receivable control account has a January 1, 20Y4, balance of $4,720 consisting of an amount due from Clear Pointe Studios Inc.

REVENUE JOURNAL — **Page 16**

Date	Invoice No.	Account Debited	Post. Ref.	Accts. Rec. Dr. Fees Earned Cr.
20Y4				
Jan. 6	1	Echo Broadcasting Co.	✓	2,860
14	2	Gold Coast Media Inc.	✓	6,350
22	3	Echo Broadcasting Co.	✓	3,710
25	4	Clear Pointe Studios Inc.	✓	2,050
29	5	Amber Communications Inc.	✓	4,550
31				19,520
				(12) (41)

CASH RECEIPTS JOURNAL — **Page 36**

Date	Account Credited	Post. Ref.	Fees Earned Cr.	Accts. Rec. Cr.	Cash Dr.
20Y4					
Jan. 6	Clear Pointe Studios Inc.	✓	—	4,720	4,720
11	Fees Earned		3,990		3,990
18	Echo Broadcasting Co.	✓	—	2,860	2,860
28	Gold Coast Media Inc.	✓	—	6,350	6,350
31			3,990	13,930	17,920
			(41)	(12)	(11)

Prepare a listing of the accounts receivable customer balances and verify that the total agrees with the ending balance of the accounts receivable controlling account.

EX 5-9 Revenue and cash receipts journals

OBJ. 2

Transactions related to revenue and cash receipts completed by Augusta Inc. during the month of March 20Y8 are as follows:

Mar. 2. Issued Invoice No. 512 to Santorini Co., $2,135.
4. Received cash from CMI Inc., on account, for $475.
8. Issued Invoice No. 513 to Gabriel Co., $520.
12. Issued Invoice No. 514 to Yarnell Inc., $1,985.
19. Received cash from Yarnell Inc., on account, $1,305.
20. Issued Invoice No. 515 to Electronic Central Inc., $455.
28. Received cash from Marshall Inc. for services provided, $380.
29. Received cash from Santorini Co. for Invoice No. 512 of March 2.
31. Received cash from McCleary Co. for services provided, $195.

Prepare a single-column revenue journal and a cash receipts journal to record these transactions. Use the following column headings for the cash receipts journal: Fees Earned Cr., Accounts Receivable Cr., and Cash Dr. Place a check mark (✓) in the Post. Ref. column to indicate when the accounts receivable subsidiary ledger should be posted.

✔ a. Revenue journal total, $8,700

EX 5-10 Revenue and cash receipts journals **OBJ. 2**

Lasting Summer Inc. has $2,510 in the October 1 balance of the accounts receivable account consisting of $1,060 from Champion Co. and $1,450 from Wayfarer Co. Transactions related to revenue and cash receipts completed by Lasting Summer Inc. during the month of October 20Y5 are as follows:

Oct. 3. Issued Invoice No. 622 for services provided to Palace Corp., $2,890.
5. Received cash from Champion Co., on account, for $1,060.
8. Issued Invoice No. 623 for services provided to Sunny Style Inc., $1,940.
12. Received cash from Wayfarer Co., on account, for $1,450.
18. Issued Invoice No. 624 for services provided to Amex Services Inc., $2,970.
23. Received cash from Palace Corp. for Invoice No. 622 of October 3.
28. Issued Invoice No. 625 to Wayfarer Co., on account, for $900.
30. Received cash from Rogers Co. for services provided, $120.

a. Prepare a single-column revenue journal and a cash receipts journal to record these transactions. Use the following column headings for the cash receipts journal: Fees Earned Cr., Accounts Receivable Cr., and Cash Dr. Place a check mark (✓) in the Post. Ref. column to indicate when the accounts receivable subsidiary ledger should be posted.

b. Prepare a listing of the accounts receivable customer balances and verify that the total of the accounts receivable customer balances equals the balance of the accounts receivable controlling account on October 31, 20Y5.

c. Why does Lasting Summer Inc. use a subsidiary ledger for accounts receivable?

EX 5-11 Identify postings from purchases journal **OBJ. 2**

Using the following purchases journal, identify each of the posting references, indicated by a letter, as representing (1) a posting to a general ledger account, (2) a posting to a subsidiary ledger account, or (3) that no posting is required:

PURCHASES JOURNAL **Page 49**

Date	Account Credited	Post. Ref.	Accounts Payable Cr.	Store Supplies Dr.	Office Supplies Dr.	Other Accounts Dr.	Post. Ref.	Amount
20Y9								
Jan. 4	Coastal Equipment Co.	(a)	5,325			Warehouse Equipment	(g)	5,325
6	Arrow Supply Co.	(b)	4,000		4,000			
9	Valley Products	(c)	1,875	1,600	275			
14	Office Warehouse	(d)	2,200			Office Equipment	(h)	2,200
20	Office Warehouse	(e)	6,000			Store Equipment	(i)	6,000
25	Metro Supply Co.	(f)	2,740	2,740				
31			22,140	4,340	4,275			13,525
			(j)	(k)	(l)			(m)

EX 5-12 Identify postings from cash payments journal **OBJ. 2**

Using the following cash payments journal, identify each of the posting references, indicated by a letter, as representing (1) a posting to a general ledger account, (2) a posting to a subsidiary ledger account, or (3) that no posting is required.

CASH PAYMENTS JOURNAL **Page 46**

Date	Ck. No.	Account Debited	Post. Ref.	Other Accounts Dr.	Accounts Payable Dr.	Cash Cr.
20Y1						
July 3	611	Energy Systems Co.	(a)		4,000	4,000
5	612	Utilities Expense	(b)	310		310
10	613	Prepaid Rent	(c)	3,200		3,200
16	614	Flowers to Go, Inc.	(d)		1,250	1,250
19	615	Advertising Expense	(e)	640		640
22	616	Office Equipment	(f)	3,600		3,600
25	617	Echo Co.	(g)		5,500	5,500
26	618	Office Supplies	(h)	250		250
31	619	Salaries Expense	(i)	1,750		1,750
31				9,750	10,750	20,500
				(j)	(k)	(l)

EX 5-13 Identify transactions in accounts payable subsidiary ledger **OBJ. 2**

The debits and credits from three related transactions are presented in the following creditor's account taken from the accounts payable ledger:

NAME *Apex Performance Co.*
ADDRESS *101 W. Stratford Ave.*

Date	Item	Post. Ref.	Debit	Credit	Balance
20Y7					
June 6		P49		12,000	12,000
14		J12	150		11,850
16		CP23	11,850		—

Describe each transaction and identify the source of each posting.

SHOW ME HOW

EX 5-14 Prepare journal entries in a purchases journal **OBJ. 2**

Fernandez Services Inc. had the following transactions during the month of April:

Apr. 4. Purchased office supplies from Officemate Inc. on account, $825.
9. Purchased office equipment on account from Tek Village Inc., $4,890.
16. Purchased office supplies from Officemate Inc. on account, $365.
19. Purchased office supplies from Paper-to-Go Inc. on account, $385.
27. Paid invoice on April 4 purchase from Officemate Inc.

a. Record the April purchase transactions for Fernandez Services Inc. in the following purchases journal format:

PURCHASES JOURNAL

Date	Account Credited	Post. Ref.	Accts. Payable Cr.	Office Supplies Dr.	Other Accounts Dr.	Post. Ref.	Amount

b. What is the total amount posted to the accounts payable and office supplies accounts from the purchases journal for April?

c. What is the April 30 balance of the Officemate Inc. creditor account assuming a zero balance on April 1?

EX 5-15 Posting a purchases journal

OBJ. 2, 3

✔ d. Total accounts payable, $5,840

The purchases journal for Newmark Exterior Cleaners Inc. follows. The accounts payable account has a March 1, 20Y2, balance of $580 for an amount owed to Nicely Co. No payments were made on creditor invoices during March.

PURCHASES JOURNAL **Page 16**

Date		Account Credited	Post. Ref.	Accts. Payable Cr.	Cleaning Supplies Dr.	Other Accounts Dr.	Post. Ref.	Amount
20Y2								
Mar.	4	Enviro-Wash Supplies Inc.		690	690			
	15	Nicely Co.		325	325			
	20	Office Mate Inc.		3,860		Office Equipment		3,860
	26	Enviro-Wash Supplies Inc.		385	385			
	31			5,260	1,400			3,860

a. Prepare a T account for the accounts payable creditor accounts.

b. Post the transactions from the purchases journal to the creditor accounts and determine their ending balances.

c. Prepare T accounts for the accounts payable control and cleaning supplies accounts. Post control totals to the two accounts, and determine their ending balances. Cleaning Supplies had a zero balance at the beginning of the month.

d. Prepare a schedule of the creditor account balances to verify the equality of the sum of the accounts payable creditor balances and the accounts payable controlling account balance.

e. How might a computerized accounting system differ from the use of a purchases journal in recording purchase transactions?

EX 5-16 Accounts payable subsidiary ledger

OBJ. 2

✔ Accts. Pay., June 30, $34,740

SHOW ME HOW

The cash payments and purchases journals for Magnolia Landscaping follow. The accounts payable control account has a June 1, 20Y1, balance of $3,590, consisting of an amount owed to Augusta Sod Co.

CASH PAYMENTS JOURNAL **Page 31**

Date		Ck. No.	Account Debited	Post. Ref.	Other Accounts Dr.	Accounts Payable Dr.	Cash Cr.
20Y1							
June	4	203	Augusta Sod Co.	✓		3,590	3,590
	5	204	Utilities Expense	54	710		710
	15	205	Home Centers Lumber Co.	✓		8,390	8,390
	24	206	Nu Lawn Fertilizer	✓		1,460	1,460
	30				710	13,440	14,150
					(✓)	(21)	(11)

PURCHASES JOURNAL **Page 22**

Date		Account Credited	Post. Ref.	Accounts Payable Cr.	Landscaping Supplies Dr.	Other Accounts Dr.	Post. Ref.	Amount
20Y1								
June	3	Home Centers Lumber Co.	✓	8,390	8,390			
	7	Concrete Equipment Co.	✓	10,790		Equipment	18	10,790
	14	Nu Lawn Fertilizer	✓	1,460	1,460			
	24	Augusta Sod Co.	✓	10,380	10,380			
	29	Home Centers Lumber Co.	✓	13,570	13,570			
	30			44,590	33,800			10,790
				(21)	(14)			(✓)

Prepare a schedule of the accounts payable creditor balances and determine that the total agrees with the ending balance of the accounts payable controlling account.

✔ Purchases journal, Accts. Pay., Total, $910

SHOW ME HOW

EX 5-17 Purchases and cash payments journals **OBJ. 2**

Transactions related to purchases and cash payments completed by Wisk Away Cleaning Services Inc. during the month of May 20Y5 are as follows:

May 1. Issued Check No. 57 to Bio Safe Supplies Inc. in payment of account, $345.
3. Purchased cleaning supplies on account from Brite N' Shine Products Inc., $200.
8. Issued Check No. 58 to purchase equipment from Carson Equipment Sales, $2,860.
12. Purchased cleaning supplies on account from Porter Products Inc., $360.
15. Issued Check No. 59 to Bowman Electrical Service in payment of account, $145.
18. Purchased supplies on account from Bio Safe Supplies Inc., $240.
20. Purchased electrical repair services from Bowman Electrical Service on account, $110.
26. Issued Check No. 60 to Brite N' Shine Products Inc. in payment of May 3 invoice.
31. Issued Check No. 61 in payment of salaries, $5,600.

Prepare a purchases journal and a cash payments journal to record these transactions. The forms of the journals are similar to those illustrated in the text. Place a check mark (✓) in the Post. Ref. column to indicate when the accounts payable subsidiary ledger should be posted. Wisk Away Cleaning Services Inc. uses the following accounts:

Cash	11
Cleaning Supplies	14
Equipment	18
Accounts Payable	21
Salary Expense	51
Electrical Service Expense	53

EX 5-18 Purchases and cash payments journals **OBJ. 2**

Happy Tails Inc. has a September 1, 20Y4, accounts payable balance of $620, which consists of $320 due Labradore Inc. and $300 due Meow Mart Inc. Transactions related to purchases and cash payments completed by Happy Tails Inc. during the month of September 20Y4 are as follows:

Sept. 4. Purchased pet supplies from Best Friend Supplies Inc. on account, $295.
6. Issued Check No. 345 to Labradore Inc. in payment of account, $320.
13. Purchased pet supplies from Poodle Pals Inc. on account, $790.
18. Issued Check No. 346 to Meow Mart Inc. in payment of account, $300.
19. Purchased office equipment from Office Helper Inc. on account, $2,510.
23. Issued Check No. 347 to Best Friend Supplies Inc. in payment of account from purchase made on September 4.
27. Purchased pet supplies from Meow Mart Inc. on account, $450.
30. Issued Check No. 348 to Jennings Inc. for cleaning expenses, $80.

a. Prepare a purchases journal and a cash payments journal to record these transactions. The forms of the journals are similar to those used in the text. Place a check mark (✓) in the Post. Ref. column to indicate when the accounts payable subsidiary ledger should be posted. Happy Tails Inc. uses the following accounts:

Cash	11
Pet Supplies	14
Office Equipment	18
Accounts Payable	21
Cleaning Expense	54

b. Prepare a listing of accounts payable creditor balances on September 30, 20Y4. Verify that the total of the accounts payable creditor balances equals the balance of the accounts payable controlling account on September 30, 20Y4.

c. Why does Happy Tails Inc. use a subsidiary ledger for accounts payable?

EX 5-19 Error in accounts payable subsidiary ledger **OBJ. 2**

After Bunker Hill Assay Services Inc. had completed all postings for March in the current year (20Y4), the sum of the balances in the following accounts payable ledger did not agree with the $36,600 balance of the controlling account in the general ledger:

NAME *C. D. Greer and Son*
ADDRESS *972 S. Tenth Street*

Date	Item	Post. Ref.	Debit	Credit	Balance
20Y4					
Mar. 17		P30		3,750	3,750
27		P31		12,000	15,750

NAME *Carbon Supplies Inc.*
ADDRESS *1170 Mattis Avenue*

Date	Item	Post. Ref.	Debit	Credit	Balance
20Y4					
Mar. 1	Balance	✓			8,300
9		P30		7,000	14,000
12		J7	300		13,700
20		CP23	5,800		7,900

NAME *Cutler and Powell*
ADDRESS *717 Elm Street*

Date	Item	Post. Ref.	Debit	Credit	Balance
20Y4					
Mar. 1	Balance	✓			6,100
18		CP23	6,100		—
29		P31		7,800	7,800

NAME *Hudson Bay Minerals Co.*
ADDRESS *1240 W. Main Street*

Date	Item	Post. Ref.	Debit	Credit	Balance
20Y4					
Mar. 1	Balance	✓			4,750
10		CP22	4,750		—
17		P30		3,700	3,700
25		J7	3,000		1,700

NAME *Valley Power*
ADDRESS *915 E. Walnut Street*

Date	Item	Post. Ref.	Debit	Credit	Balance
20Y4					
Mar. 5		P30		3,150	3,150

Assuming that the controlling account balance of $36,600 has been verified as correct, (a) determine the error(s) in the preceding accounts and (b) prepare a listing of accounts payable creditor balances (from the corrected accounts payable subsidiary ledger).

EX 5-20 Identify postings from special journals **OBJ. 2**

Pinnacle Consulting Company makes most of its sales and purchases on credit. It uses the five journals described in this chapter (revenue, cash receipts, purchases, cash payments, and general). Identify the journal most likely used in recording the postings for selected transactions indicated by letter in the T accounts, as follows:

	Cash		
a.	10,940	b.	6,500

	Prepaid Rent		
		e.	1,200

	Accounts Receivable		
c.	11,790	a.	10,940

	Accounts Payable		
b.	6,500	d.	7,400

	Office Supplies		
d.	7,400		

	Fees Earned		
		c.	11,790

	Rent Expense		
e.	1,200		

EX 5-21 Cash receipts journal

OBJ. 2

The following cash receipts journal headings have been suggested for a small service firm. List the errors you find in the headings.

CASH RECEIPTS JOURNAL **Page *12***

Date	Account Credited	Post. Ref.	Fees Earned Cr.	Accts. Rec. Cr.	Cash Cr.	Other Accounts Dr.

EX 5-22 Computerized accounting systems

OBJ. 3

Most computerized accounting systems use electronic forms to record transaction information, such as the invoice form illustrated at the top of Exhibit 7 in this chapter.

a. Identify the key input fields (spaces) in an electronic invoice form.

b. What accounts are posted from an electronic invoice form?

c. Why aren't special journal totals posted to control accounts at the end of the month in an electronic accounting system?

EX 5-23 Computerized accounting systems and e-commerce

OBJ. 3, 4

Apple Inc.'s iTunes® provides digital products, such as music, video, and software. Purchases from iTunes are made with credit cards that are on file with the credit card processing company. Such transactions are considered cash transactions. Once the purchases are made, consumers can access the requested digital products for their enjoyment and the charges will show up on their credit card bills.

a. What kind of e-commerce application is described by Apple iTunes?

b. Assume you purchased 12 songs for $1.25 each on iTunes. Provide the journal entry generated by Apple's e-commerce application.

c. If a special journal were used, what type of special journal would be used to record this sales transaction?

d. If an electronic form were used, what type of electronic form would be used to record this sales transaction?

e. Would it be appropriate for Apple to use either special journals or electronic forms for sales transactions from iTunes? Explain.

EX 5-24 E-commerce

OBJ. 4

For each of the following companies, determine what they primarily sell and whether their e-commerce strategy is primarily business-to-consumer (B2C), business-to-business (B2B), or both. Use the Internet to investigate each company's site in conducting your research.

a. **Amazon.com**

b. **Dell Inc.**

c. **DowDuPont Inc.**

d. **Intuit Inc.**

e. **L.L. Bean, Inc.**

f. **W.W. Grainger, Inc.**

EX 5-25 Segment revenue horizontal analysis **OBJ. 5**

Starbucks Corporation reported the following geographical segment revenues for a recent and a prior fiscal year:

	Recent Year (in millions, rounded)	Prior Year (in millions, rounded)
Americas	$16,732	$15,620
China/Asia Pacific	4,474	3,240
Channel Development*	2,297	2,257
EMEA**	1,048	959
Other	168	311
Total	$24,719	$22,387

*Sells packaged coffee and teas globally
**Europe, Middle East, and Africa

a. Prepare a horizontal analysis of the segment data using the prior year as the base year. Round whole percents to one decimal place.

b. Prepare a vertical analysis of the segment data. Round whole percents to one decimal place.

c. What conclusions can be drawn from your analyses?

EX 5-26 Segment revenue vertical analysis **OBJ. 5**

Twenty-First Century Fox, Inc. is one of the world's largest entertainment companies that includes Twentieth Century Fox films, Fox Broadcasting, Fox News, the FX, and various satellite properties. The company provided revenue disclosures by its major product segments in the notes to its financial statements as follows:

Major Product Segments	For a Recent Year (in millions)
Cable Network Programming	$17,946
Television	5,162
Filmed Entertainment	8,747
Total revenues of major segments	$31,855

a. Provide a vertical analysis of the product segment revenue. Round whole percents to one decimal place.

b. Are the revenues of Twenty-First Century Fox, Inc. diversified or concentrated within a product segment? Explain.

EX 5-27 Segment revenue horizontal and vertical analyses **OBJ. 5**

The comparative segment revenues for **Yum! Brands**, a global quick-serve restaurant company, are as follows:

	Recent Year (in millions)	Prior Year (in millions)
KFC	$2,644	$3,105
Taco Bell	2,056	1,880
Pizza Hut	988	893
Total	$5,688	$5,878

a. Provide a horizontal analysis of the segment revenues using the prior year as the base year. Round whole percents to one decimal place.

b. Provide a vertical analysis of the segment revenues for both years. Round whole percents to one decimal place.

c. What conclusions can be drawn from your analyses?

Problems: Series A

PR 5-1A Revenue journal; accounts receivable subsidiary and general ledgers **OBJ. 2, 3**

✔ **1. Revenue journal, total fees earned, $1,170**

Sage Learning Centers was established on July 20 to provide educational services. The services provided during the remainder of the month are as follows:

July 21. Issued Invoice No. 1 to J. Dunlop for $115 on account.
22. Issued Invoice No. 2 to K. Tisdale for $350 on account.
24. Issued Invoice No. 3 to T. Quinn for $85 on account.
25. Provided educational services, $300, to K. Tisdale in exchange for educational supplies.
27. Issued Invoice No. 4 to F. Mintz for $225 on account.
30. Issued Invoice No. 5 to D. Chase for $170 on account.
30. Issued Invoice No. 6 to K. Tisdale for $120 on account.
31. Issued Invoice No. 7 to T. Quinn for $105 on account.

Instructions

1. Journalize the transactions for July, using a single-column revenue journal and a two-column general journal. Post to the following customer accounts in the accounts receivable ledger and insert the balance immediately after recording each entry: D. Chase; J. Dunlop; F. Mintz; T. Quinn; K. Tisdale.
2. Post the revenue journal and the general journal to the following accounts in the general ledger, inserting the account balances only after the last postings:

   12 Accounts Receivable
   13 Supplies
   41 Fees Earned

3. a. What is the sum of the balances of the customer accounts in the subsidiary ledger at July 31?
   b. What is the balance of the accounts receivable controlling account at July 31?
4. Assume Sage Learning Centers began using a computerized accounting system to record the sales transactions on August 1. What are some of the benefits of the computerized system over the manual system?

PR 5-2A Revenue and cash receipts journals; accounts receivable subsidiary and general ledgers **OBJ. 2, 3**

✔ **3. Total cash receipts, $34,390**

SHOW ME HOW

Transactions related to revenue and cash receipts completed by Crowne Business Services Co. during the period April 2–30 are as follows:

Apr. 2. Issued Invoice No. 793 to Ohr Co., $4,680.
5. Received cash from Mendez Co. for the balance owed on its account.
6. Issued Invoice No. 794 to Pinecrest Co., $1,990.
13. Issued Invoice No. 795 to Shilo Co., $3,450.
Post revenue and collections to the accounts receivable subsidiary ledger.
15. Received cash from Pinecrest Co. for the balance owed on April 1.
16. Issued Invoice No. 796 to Pinecrest Co., $5,500.
Post revenue and collections to the accounts receivable subsidiary ledger.
19. Received cash from Ohr Co. for the balance due on invoice of April 2.
20. Received cash from Pinecrest Co. for balance due on invoice of April 6.
22. Issued Invoice No. 797 to Mendez Co., $7,470.
25. Received $3,200 note receivable in partial settlement of the balance due on the Shilo Co. account.

(Continued)

Apr. 30. Received cash from fees earned, $12,890.

Post revenue and collections to the accounts receivable subsidiary ledger.

Instructions

1. Insert the following balances in the general ledger as of April 1:

11	Cash	$11,350
12	Accounts Receivable	14,830
14	Notes Receivable	6,000
41	Fees Earned	—

2. Insert the following balances in the accounts receivable subsidiary ledger as of April 1:

Mendez Co.	$8,710
Ohr Co.	—
Pinecrest Co.	6,120
Shilo Co.	—

3. Prepare a single-column revenue journal (p. 40) and a cash receipts journal (p. 36). Use the following column headings for the cash receipts journal: Fees Earned Cr., Accounts Receivable Cr., and Cash Dr. The Fees Earned column is used to record cash fees. Insert a check mark (✓) in the Post. Ref. column when recording cash fees.
4. Using the two special journals and the two-column general journal (p. 1), journalize the transactions for April. Post to the accounts receivable subsidiary ledger, and insert the balances at the points indicated in the narrative of transactions. Determine the balance in the customer's account before recording a cash receipt.
5. Total each of the columns of the special journals and post the individual entries and totals to the general ledger. Insert account balances after the last posting.
6. Determine that the sum of the customer balances agrees with the accounts receivable controlling account in the general ledger.
7. Why would an automated system omit postings to a controlling account as performed in Step 5 for Accounts Receivable?

PR 5-3A Purchases, accounts payable subsidiary account, and accounts payable ledger **OBJ. 2, 4**

✓ 5b. $18,110

Sterling Forest Landscaping designs and installs landscaping. The landscape designers and office staff use office supplies, while field supplies (rock, bark, etc.) are used in the actual landscaping. Purchases on account completed by Sterling Forest Landscaping during October are as follows:

Oct. 2. Purchased office supplies on account from Meade Co., $400.
5. Purchased office equipment on account from Peach Computers Co., $3,980.
9. Purchased office supplies on account from Executive Office Supply Co., $320.
13. Purchased field supplies on account from Yamura Co., $1,420.
14. Purchased field supplies on account from Omni Co., $2,940.
17. Purchased field supplies on account from Yamura Co., $1,890.
24. Purchased field supplies on account from Omni Co., $3,880.
29. Purchased office supplies on account from Executive Office Supply Co., $310.
31. Purchased field supplies on account from Omni Co., $1,800.

Instructions

1. Insert the following balances in the general ledger as of October 1:

14	Field Supplies	$ 5,920
15	Office Supplies	750
18	Office Equipment	12,300
21	Accounts Payable	1,170

2. Insert the following balances in the accounts payable subsidiary ledger as of October 1:

Executive Office Supply Co.	$390
Meade Co.	780
Omni Co.	—
Peach Computers Co.	—
Yamura Co.	—

3. Journalize the transactions for October, using a purchases journal (p. 30) similar to the one illustrated in this chapter. Prepare the purchases journal with columns for Accounts Payable, Field Supplies, Office Supplies, and Other Accounts. Post to the creditor accounts in the accounts payable subsidiary ledger immediately after each entry.
4. Post the purchases journal to the accounts in the general ledger.
5. a. What is the sum of the creditor balances in the subsidiary ledger at October 31?
   b. What is the balance of the accounts payable controlling account at October 31?
6. What type of e-commerce application would be used to plan and coordinate transactions with suppliers?

PR 5-4A Purchases and cash payments journals; accounts payable subsidiary and general ledgers OBJ. 2

✔ 1. Total cash payments, $203,940

AquaFresh Water Testing Service was established on April 16. AquaFresh uses field equipment and field supplies (chemicals and other supplies) to analyze water for unsafe contaminants in streams, lakes, and ponds. Transactions related to purchases and cash payments during the remainder of April are as follows:

Apr. 16. Issued Check No. 1 in payment of rent for the remainder of April, $3,500.
16. Purchased field supplies on account from Hydro Supply Co., $5,340.
16. Purchased field equipment on account from Pure Equipment Co., $21,450.
17. Purchased office supplies on account from Best Office Supply Co., $510.
19. Issued Check No. 2 in payment of field supplies, $3,340, and office supplies, $400.
Post the journals to the accounts payable subsidiary ledger.
23. Purchased office supplies on account from Best Office Supply Co., $660.
23. Issued Check No. 3 to purchase land, $140,000.
24. Issued Check No. 4 to Hydro Supply Co. in payment of April 16 invoice, $5,340.
26. Issued Check No. 5 to Pure Equipment Co. in payment of April 16 invoice, $21,450.
Post the journals to the accounts payable subsidiary ledger.
30. Acquired land in exchange for field equipment having a cost of $12,000.
30. Purchased field supplies on account from Hydro Supply Co., $7,650.
30. Issued Check No. 6 to Best Office Supply Co. in payment of April 17 invoice, $510.
30. Purchased the following from Pure Equipment Co. on account: field supplies, $1,340, and field equipment, $4,700.
30. Issued Check No. 7 in payment of salaries, $29,400.
Post the journals to the accounts payable subsidiary ledger.

Instructions

1. Journalize the transactions for April. Use a purchases journal and a cash payments journal, similar to those illustrated in this chapter, and a two-column general journal. Use debit columns for Field Supplies, Office Supplies, and Other Accounts in the purchases journal. Refer to the following partial chart of accounts:

11	Cash	19	Land
14	Field Supplies	21	Accounts Payable
15	Office Supplies	61	Salary Expense
17	Field Equipment	71	Rent Expense

(Continued)

At the points indicated in the narrative of transactions, post to the following accounts in the accounts payable subsidiary ledger:

Best Office Supply Co.
Hydro Supply Co.
Pure Equipment Co.

2. Post the individual entries (Other Accounts columns of the purchases journal and the cash payments journal and both columns of the general journal) to the appropriate general ledger accounts.
3. Total each of the columns of the purchases journal and the cash payments journal and post the appropriate totals to the general ledger. (Because the problem does not include transactions related to cash receipts, the cash account in the ledger will have a credit balance.)
4. Prepare a schedule of the accounts payable creditor balances.
5. Why might AquaFresh consider using a subsidiary ledger for the field equipment?

PR 5-5A All journals and general ledger; trial balance — OBJ. 2

✔ 2. Total cash receipts, $67,460

The transactions completed by Fleetfoot Courier Company during December, the first month of the fiscal year, were as follows:

Dec. 1. Issued Check No. 610 for December rent, $5,260.
2. Issued Invoice No. 940 to Clifford Co., $2,180.
3. Received check for $6,010 from Ryan Co. in payment of account.
5. Purchased a vehicle on account from Platinum Motors, $46,700.
6. Purchased office equipment on account from Austin Computer Co., $5,630.
6. Issued Invoice No. 941 to Ernesto Co., $4,850.
9. Issued Check No. 611 for fuel expense, $750.
10. Received check from Sing Co. in payment of $5,060 invoice.
10. Issued Check No. 612 for $410 to Office To Go Inc. in payment of invoice.
10. Issued Invoice No. 942 to Joy Co., $2,470.
11. Issued Check No. 613 for $3,870 to Essential Supply Co. in payment of account.
11. Issued Check No. 614 for $630 to Porter Co. in payment of account.
12. Received check from Clifford Co. in payment of $2,180 invoice of December 2.
13. Issued Check No. 615 to Platinum Motors in payment of $46,700 balance of December 5.
16. Issued Check No. 616 for $49,830 for cash purchase of a vehicle.
16. Cash fees earned for December 1–16, $25,420.
17. Issued Check No. 617 for miscellaneous administrative expense, $630.
18. Purchased maintenance supplies on account from Essential Supply Co., $2,190.
19. Purchased the following on account from McClain Co.: maintenance supplies, $1,880; office supplies, $470.
20. Issued Check No. 618 in payment of advertising expense, $2,230.
20. Used $4,010 maintenance supplies to repair delivery vehicles.
23. Purchased office supplies on account from Office To Go Inc., $500.
24. Issued Invoice No. 943 to Sing Co., $7,640.
24. Issued Check No. 619 to S. Holmes as a personal withdrawal, $3,760.
25. Issued Invoice No. 944 to Ernesto Co., $6,920.
25. Received check for $5,130 from Ryan Co. in payment of balance.
26. Issued Check No. 620 to Austin Computer Co. in payment of $5,630 invoice of December 6.
30. Issued Check No. 621 for monthly salaries as follows: driver salaries, $21,160; office salaries, $8,890.

Dec. 31. Cash fees earned for December 17–31, $23,660.

31. Issued Check No. 622 in payment for office supplies, $430.

Instructions

1. Enter the following account balances in the general ledger as of December 1:

11	Cash	$202,430	32	S. Holmes, Drawing	—
12	Accounts Receivable	16,200	41	Fees Earned	—
14	Maintenance Supplies	13,580	51	Driver Salaries Expense	—
15	Office Supplies	6,130	52	Maintenance Supplies Exp.	—
16	Office Equipment	35,680	53	Fuel Expense	—
17	Accum. Depr.—Office Equip.	8,640	61	Office Salaries Expense	—
18	Vehicles	120,070	62	Rent Expense	—
19	Accum. Depr.—Vehicles	18,400	63	Advertising Expense	—
21	Accounts Payable	4,910	64	Miscellaneous Administrative Expense	—
31	S. Holmes, Capital	362,140			

2. Journalize the transactions for December, using the following journals similar to those illustrated in this chapter: cash receipts journal (p. 31), purchases journal (p. 37, with columns for Accounts Payable, Maintenance Supplies, Office Supplies, and Other Accounts), single-column revenue journal (p. 35), cash payments journal (p. 34), and two-column general journal (p. 1). Assume that the daily postings to the individual accounts in the accounts payable subsidiary ledger and the accounts receivable subsidiary ledger have been made.
3. Post the appropriate individual entries to the general ledger.
4. Total each of the columns of the special journals and post the appropriate totals to the general ledger; insert the account balances.
5. Prepare a trial balance.

Problems: Series B

PR 5-1B Revenue journal; accounts receivable subsidiary and general ledgers OBJ. 2, 3

✔ **1. Revenue journal, total fees earned, $2,875**

Guardian Security Services was established on January 15 to provide security services. The services provided during the remainder of the month are as follows:

Jan. 18. Issued Invoice No. 1 to Murphy Co. for $490 on account.

20. Issued Invoice No. 2 to Qwik-Mart Co. for $340 on account.

24. Issued Invoice No. 3 to Hopkins Co. for $750 on account.

27. Issued Invoice No. 4 to Carson Co. for $680 on account.

28. Issued Invoice No. 5 to Amber Waves Co. for $120 on account.

28. Provided security services, $100, to Qwik-Mart Co. in exchange for supplies.

30. Issued Invoice No. 6 to Qwik-Mart Co. for $200 on account.

31. Issued Invoice No. 7 to Hopkins Co. for $295 on account.

Instructions

1. Journalize the transactions for January, using a single-column revenue journal and a two-column general journal. Post to the following customer accounts in the accounts receivable ledger and insert the balance immediately after recording each entry: Amber Waves Co.; Carson Co.; Hopkins Co.; Murphy Co.; Qwik-Mart Co.
2. Post the revenue journal to the following accounts in the general ledger, inserting the account balances only after the last postings:

12 Accounts Receivable
14 Supplies
41 Fees Earned

(Continued)

3. a. What is the sum of the balances of the customer accounts in the subsidiary ledger at January 31?

   b. What is the balance of the accounts receivable controlling account at January 31?

4. Assume Guardian Security Services began using a computerized accounting system to record the sales transactions on February 1. What are some of the benefits of the computerized system over the manual system?

PR 5-2B Revenue and cash receipts journals; accounts receivable subsidiary and general ledgers **OBJ. 2, 3**

✔ 3. Total cash receipts, $14,320

SHOW ME HOW

Transactions related to revenue and cash receipts completed by Affiliate Engineering Services during the period June 2–30 are as follows:

June 2. Issued Invoice No. 717 to Yee Co., $2,210.

3. Received cash from Auto-Flex Co. for the balance owed on its account.

7. Issued Invoice No. 718 to Cooper Development Co., $1,040.

10. Issued Invoice No. 719 to Ridge Communities, $4,390.

Post revenue and collections to the accounts receivable subsidiary ledger.

14. Received cash from Cooper Development Co. for the balance owed on June 1.

16. Issued Invoice No. 720 to Cooper Development Co., $620.

Post revenue and collections to the accounts receivable subsidiary ledger.

18. Received cash from Yee Co. for the balance due on invoice of June 2.

20. Received cash from Cooper Development Co. for invoice of June 7.

23. Issued Invoice No. 721 to Auto-Flex Co., $1,330.

30. Received cash from fees earned, $6,980.

30. Received office equipment of $2,780 in partial settlement of balance due on the Ridge Communities account.

Post revenue and collections to the accounts receivable subsidiary ledger.

Instructions

1. Insert the following balances in the general ledger as of June 1:

11	Cash	$28,340
12	Accounts Receivable	4,090
18	Office Equipment	53,620
41	Fees Earned	—

2. Insert the following balances in the accounts receivable subsidiary ledger as of June 1:

Auto-Flex Co.	$2,580
Cooper Development Co.	1,510
Ridge Communities	—
Yee Co.	—

3. Prepare a single-column revenue journal (p. 40) and a cash receipts journal (p. 36). Use the following column headings for the cash receipts journal: Fees Earned Cr., Accounts Receivable Cr., and Cash Dr. The Fees Earned column is used to record cash fees. Insert a check mark (✓) in the Post. Ref. column when recording cash fees.
4. Using the two special journals and the two-column general journal (p. 1), journalize the transactions for June. Post to the accounts receivable subsidiary ledger and insert the balances at the points indicated in the narrative of transactions. Determine the balance in the customer's account before recording a cash receipt.
5. Total each of the columns of the special journals and post the individual entries and totals to the general ledger. Insert account balances after the last posting.

6. Determine that the sum of the customer accounts agrees with the accounts receivable controlling account in the general ledger.
7. Why would an automated system omit postings to a control account as performed in Step 5 for Accounts Receivable?

PR 5-3B Purchases, accounts payable account, and accounts payable subsidiary ledger

OBJ. 2, 4

✔ 5a. $31,300

SHOW ME HOW

Plumb Line Surveyors provides survey work for construction projects. The office staff use office supplies, while surveying crews use field supplies. Purchases on account completed by Plumb Line Surveyors during May are as follows:

May 1. Purchased field supplies on account from Wendell Co., $3,240.
3. Purchased office supplies on account from Lassiter Co., $340.
8. Purchased field supplies on account from Tri Cities Supplies, $4,500.
12. Purchased field supplies on account from Wendell Co., $3,670.
15. Purchased office supplies on account from J-Mart Co., $500.
19. Purchased office equipment on account from Accu-Vision Supply Co., $8,150.
23. Purchased field supplies on account from Tri Cities Supplies, $2,450.
26. Purchased office supplies on account from J-Mart Co., $265.
30. Purchased field supplies on account from Tri Cities Supplies, $3,040.

Instructions

1. Insert the following balances in the general ledger as of May 1:

14	Field Supplies	$ 6,200
15	Office Supplies	1,490
18	Office Equipment	19,400
21	Accounts Payable	5,145

2. Insert the following balances in the accounts payable subsidiary ledger as of May 1:

Accu-Vision Supply Co.	$3,900
J-Mart Co.	730
Lassiter Co.	515
Tri Cities Supplies	—
Wendell Co.	—

3. Journalize the transactions for May, using a purchases journal (p. 30) similar to the one illustrated in this chapter. Prepare the purchases journal with columns for Accounts Payable, Field Supplies, Office Supplies, and Other Accounts. Post to the creditor accounts in the accounts payable subsidiary ledger immediately after each entry.
4. Post the purchases journal to the accounts in the general ledger.
5. a. What is the sum of the creditor balances in the subsidiary ledger at May 31?
   b. What is the balance of the accounts payable controlling account at May 31?
6. What type of e-commerce application would be used to plan and coordinate transactions with suppliers?

PR 5-4B Purchases and cash payments journals; accounts payable subsidiary and general ledgers

OBJ. 2

✔ 1. Total cash payments, $327,920

West Texas Exploration Co. was established on October 15 to provide oil-drilling services. West Texas uses field equipment (rigs and pipe) and field supplies (drill bits and lubricants) in its operations. Transactions related to purchases and cash payments during the remainder of October are as follows:

Oct. 16. Issued Check No. 1 in payment of rent for the remainder of October, $7,000.
16. Purchased field equipment on account from Petro Services Inc., $32,600.

(Continued)

Oct. 17. Purchased field supplies on account from Midland Supply Co., $9,780.

18. Issued Check No. 2 in payment of field supplies, $4,570, and office supplies, $650.

20. Purchased office supplies on account from A-One Office Supply Co., $1,320.

Post the journals to the accounts payable subsidiary ledger.

24. Issued Check No. 3 to Petro Services Inc., in payment of October 16 invoice.

26. Issued Check No. 4 to Midland Supply Co. in payment of October 17 invoice.

28. Issued Check No. 5 to purchase land, $240,000.

28. Purchased office supplies on account from A-One Office Supply Co., $3,670.

Post the journals to the accounts payable subsidiary ledger.

30. Purchased the following from Petro Services Inc. on account: field supplies, $25,300 and office equipment, $5,500.

30. Issued Check No. 6 to A-One Office Supply Co. in payment of October 20 invoice.

30. Purchased field supplies on account from Midland Supply Co., $12,450.

31. Issued Check No. 7 in payment of salaries, $32,000.

31. Rented building for one year in exchange for field equipment having a cost of $15,000.

Post the journals to the accounts payable subsidiary ledger.

Instructions

1. Journalize the transactions for October. Use a purchases journal and a cash payments journal similar to those illustrated in this chapter and a two-column general journal. Set debit columns for Field Supplies, Office Supplies, and Other Accounts in the purchases journal. Refer to the following partial chart of accounts:

11	Cash	18	Office Equipment
14	Field Supplies	19	Land
15	Office Supplies	21	Accounts Payable
16	Prepaid Rent	61	Salary Expense
17	Field Equipment	71	Rent Expense

At the points indicated in the narrative of transactions, post to the following subsidiary accounts in the accounts payable ledger:

A-One Office Supply Co.
Midland Supply Co.
Petro Services Inc.

2. Post the individual entries (Other Accounts columns of the purchases journal and the cash payments journal; both columns of the general journal) to the appropriate general ledger accounts.
3. Total each of the columns of the purchases journal and the cash payments journal, and post the appropriate totals to the general ledger. (Because the problem does not include transactions related to cash receipts, the cash account in the ledger will have a credit balance.)
4. Sum the balances of the accounts payable creditor balances.
5. Why might West Texas consider using a subsidiary ledger for the field equipment?

PR 5-5B All journals and general ledger; trial balance — OBJ. 2

✔ 2. Total cash receipts, $96,050

The transactions completed by AM Express Company during March, the first month of the fiscal year, were as follows:

Mar. 1. Issued Check No. 205 for March rent, $2,450.

2. Purchased a vehicle on account from McIntyre Sales Co., $26,900.

3. Purchased office equipment on account from Office Mate Inc., $1,570.

5. Issued Invoice No. 91 to Ellis Co., $7,000.

6. Received check for $7,950 from Chavez Co. in payment of invoice.

Mar. 7. Issued Invoice No. 92 to Trent Co., $9,840.
9. Issued Check No. 206 for fuel expense, $820.
10. Received check for $10,000 from Sajeev Co. in payment of invoice.
10. Issued Check No. 207 to Office City in payment of $450 invoice.
10. Issued Check No. 208 to Bastille Co. in payment of $1,890 invoice.
11. Issued Invoice No. 93 to Jarvis Co., $7,200.
11. Issued Check No. 209 to Porter Co. in payment of $415 invoice.
12. Received check for $7,000 from Ellis Co. in payment of March 5 invoice.
13. Issued Check No. 210 to McIntyre Sales Co. in payment of $26,900 invoice of March 2.
16. Cash fees earned for March 1–16, $26,800.
16. Issued Check No. 211 for purchase of a vehicle, $28,500.
17. Issued Check No. 212 for miscellaneous administrative expense, $4,680.
18. Purchased maintenance supplies on account from Bastille Co., $2,430.
18. Received check for rent revenue on office space, $900.
19. Purchased the following on account from Master Supply Co.: maintenance supplies, $2,640, and office supplies, $1,500.
20. Issued Check No. 213 in payment of advertising expense, $8,590.
20. Used maintenance supplies with a cost of $4,400 to repair vehicles.
21. Purchased office supplies on account from Office City, $990.
24. Issued Invoice No. 94 to Sajeev Co., $9,200.
25. Received check for $14,000 from Chavez Co. in payment of invoice.
25. Issued Invoice No. 95 to Trent Co., $6,300.
26. Issued Check No. 214 to Office Mate Inc. in payment of $1,570 invoice of March 3.
27. Issued Check No. 215 to J. Wu as a personal withdrawal, $4,000.
30. Issued Check No. 216 in payment of driver salaries, $33,300.
31. Issued Check No. 217 in payment of office salaries, $21,200.
31. Issued Check No. 218 for office supplies, $600.
31. Cash fees earned for March 17–31, $29,400.

Instructions

1. Enter the following account balances in the general ledger as of March 1:

11	Cash	$ 65,200	32	J. Wu, Drawing	—
12	Accounts Receivable	31,950	41	Fees Earned	—
14	Maintenance Supplies	7,240	42	Rent Revenue	—
15	Office Supplies	3,690	51	Driver Salaries Expense	—
16	Office Equipment	17,300	52	Maintenance Supplies Expense	—
17	Accum. Depr.—Office Equip.	4,250	53	Fuel Expense	—
18	Vehicles	62,400	61	Office Salaries Expense	—
19	Accum. Depr.—Vehicles	17,800	62	Rent Expense	—
21	Accounts Payable	2,755	63	Advertising Expense	—
31	J. Wu, Capital	162,975	64	Miscellaneous Administrative Exp.	—

2. Journalize the transactions for March, using the following journals similar to those illustrated in this chapter: single-column revenue journal (p. 35), cash receipts journal (p. 31), purchases journal (p. 37, with columns for Accounts Payable, Maintenance Supplies, Office Supplies, and Other Accounts), cash payments journal (p. 34), and two-column general journal (p. 1). Assume that the daily postings to the individual accounts in the accounts payable subsidiary ledger and the accounts receivable subsidiary ledger have been made.

(Continued)

3. Post the appropriate individual entries to the general ledger.
4. Total each of the columns of the special journals and post the appropriate totals to the general ledger; insert the account balances.
5. Prepare a trial balance.

Cases & Projects

ETHICS

CP 5-1 Ethics in Action

Netbooks Inc. provides accounting applications for business customers on the Internet for a monthly subscription. Netbooks' customers run their accounting system on the Internet; thus, the business data and accounting software reside on the servers of Netbooks Inc. The senior management of Netbooks believes that once a customer begins to use Netbooks, it is very difficult to cancel the service. That is, customers are "locked in" because it is difficult to move the business data from Netbooks to another accounting application even though the customers own their own data. Therefore, Netbooks has decided to entice customers with an initial low monthly price that is half the normal monthly rate for the first year of services. After a year, the price will be increased to the regular monthly rate. Netbooks management believes that customers will have to accept the full price because customers will be locked in after one year of use.

a. Discuss whether the half-price offer is an ethical business practice.
b. Discuss whether customer "lock-in" is an ethical business practice.

TEAM ACTIVITY

REAL WORLD

CP 5-2 Team Activity

The two leading software application providers for supply chain management (SCM) and customer relationship management (CRM) software are **JDA** and **Salesforce.com**, respectively. In groups of two or three, go to the website of each company (www.jda.com and www.salesforce.com, respectively) and list the services provided by each company's software.

COMMUNICATION

REAL WORLD

CP 5-3 Communication

Internet-based accounting software is a recent trend in business computing. Major software firms such as **Oracle**, **SAP**, and **NetSuite** are running their core products on the Internet using cloud computing. NetSuite is one of the most popular small-business Internet-based accounting systems.

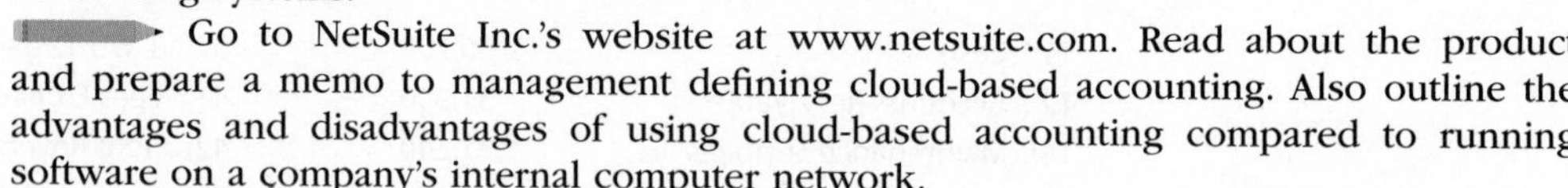

Go to NetSuite Inc.'s website at www.netsuite.com. Read about the product and prepare a memo to management defining cloud-based accounting. Also outline the advantages and disadvantages of using cloud-based accounting compared to running software on a company's internal computer network.

CP 5-4 Manual vs. computerized accounting systems

The following conversation took place between Durable Construction Co.'s bookkeeper, Kyle Byers, and the accounting supervisor, Sarah Nelson:

Sarah: Kyle, I'm thinking about bringing in a new computerized accounting system to replace our manual system. I guess this means that you will need to learn how to do computerized accounting.

Kyle: What does computerized accounting mean?

Sarah: I'm not sure, but you'll need to prepare for this new way of doing business.

Kyle: I'm not so sure we need a computerized system. I've been looking at some of the sample reports from the software vendor. It looks to me as if the computer will not add much to what we are already doing.

Sarah: What do you mean?

Kyle: Well, look at these reports. This Sales by Customer Report looks like our revenue journal, and the Deposit Detail Report looks like our cash receipts journal. Granted, the computer types them, so they look much neater than my special journals, but I don't see that we're gaining much from this change.

Sarah: Well, surely there's more to it than nice-looking reports. I've got to believe that a computerized system will save us time and effort someplace.

Kyle: I don't see how. We still need to key transactions into the computer. If anything, there may be more work when it's all said and done.

Do you agree with Kyle? Why might a computerized environment be preferred over the manual system?

CP 5-5 Accounts receivable and accounts payable

A subsidiary ledger is used for accounts receivable and accounts payable. Thus, transactions that are made "on account" are posted to the individual customer or creditor accounts.

a. Why do companies use subsidiary ledgers for accounts payable and accounts receivable?

b. Identify another account that could benefit from using a subsidiary ledger.

CP 5-6 Design of accounting systems

For the past few years, your client, Omni Care, has operated a small medical practice. Omni Care's current annual revenues are $945,000. Because the accountant has been spending more time each month recording all transactions in a two-column journal and preparing the financial statements, Omni Care is considering improving the accounting system by adding special journals and subsidiary ledgers. Omni Care has asked you to help with this project and has compiled the following information:

Type of Transaction	Estimated Frequency per Month
Fees earned on account	240
Purchase of medical supplies on account	190
Cash receipts from patients on account	175
Cash payments on account	160
Cash receipts from patients at time services are provided	120
Purchase of office supplies on account	35
Purchase of magazine subscriptions on account	5
Purchase of medical equipment on account	4
Cash payments for office salaries	3
Cash payments for utilities expense	3

1. Briefly discuss the circumstances under which special journals would be used in place of a two-column (all-purpose) journal. Include in your answer your recommendations for Omni Care's medical practice.
2. Assume that Omni Care has decided to use a revenue journal and a purchases journal. Design the format for each journal, giving special consideration to the needs of the medical practice.
3. Which subsidiary ledgers would you recommend for the medical practice?

CHAPTER

6 Accounting for Merchandising Businesses

STATEMENT OF OWNER'S EQUITY
For the Year Ended December 31, 20Y6

Owner's capital, Jan. 1, 20Y6		$XXX
Net income	$ XXX	
Withdrawals	(XXX)	
Increase in equity		XXX
Owner's capital, Dec. 31, 20Y6		$XXX

STATEMENT OF CASH FLOWS
For the Year Ended December 31, 20Y6

Cash flows from (used for) operating activities	$XXX
Cash flows from (used for) investing activities	XXX
Cash flows from (used for) financing activities	XXX
Net increase (decrease) in cash	$XXX
Cash balance, January 1, 20Y6	XXX

INCOME STATEMENT
For the Year Ended December 31, 20Y6

Sales		$XXX
Cost of merchandise sold		XXX
Gross profit		$XXX
Operating expenses:		
Advertising expense	$XXX	
Depreciation expense	XXX	
Amortization expense	XXX	
Depletion expense	XXX	
…	XXX	
…	XXX	
Total operating expenses		XXX
Income from operations		$XXX
Other revenue and expenses		XXX
Net income		$XXX

BALANCE SHEET
December 31, 20Y6

Current assets:		
Cash	$XXX	
Accounts receivable	XXX	
Merchandise inventory	XXX	
Total current assets		$XXX
Property, plant, and equipment	$XXX	
Intangible assets	XXX	
Total long-term assets		XXX
Total assets		$XXX
Liabilities:		
Current liabilities	$XXX	
Long-term liabilities	XXX	
Total liabilities		$XXX
Owner's equity		XXX
Total liabilities and owner's equity		$XXX

CHAPTER

6

RICHARD LEVINE/ALAMY STOCK PHOTO

Dollar Tree, Inc.

When you are low on cash but need to pick up party supplies, housewares, or other consumer items, where do you go? Many shoppers are turning to **Dollar Tree, Inc.**, the nation's largest single price point dollar retailer with more than 7,000 stores in 48 states and five Canadian provinces. For the fixed price of $1 on merchandise in its stores, Dollar Tree provides "new treasures" every week for the entire family.

Despite the fact that items cost only $1, the accounting for a merchandiser, like Dollar Tree, is more complex than for a service company. This is because a service company sells only services and has no inventory. Because of Dollar Tree's many locations and wide variety of merchandise, the company must design its accounting system to record the receipt of goods for sale and keep track of where the merchandise is located. The company must also record the sales and cost of merchandise sold for each of its stores. Finally, Dollar Tree must record such data as delivery costs, merchandise discounts, and merchandise returns.

This chapter focuses on the accounting principles and concepts for a merchandising business. In doing so, the basic differences between merchandiser and service company activities are highlighted. The financial statements of a merchandising business and accounting for merchandise transactions are also described and illustrated.

Link to Dollar Tree .... Pages 281, 283, 289, 290, 299

LEARNING OBJECTIVES

After studying this chapter, you should be able to:

Example Exercises (EE) are shown in **red.**

OBJ. 1 **Distinguish between the activities and financial statements of service and merchandising businesses.**

Nature of Merchandising Businesses
Operating Cycle
Gross Profit — EE **6-1**

OBJ. 2 **Describe and illustrate the accounting for merchandise transactions.**

Merchandising Transactions
Chart of Accounts for a Merchandising Business
Purchases Transactions — EE **6-2**
Sales Transactions — EE **6-3**
Freight — EE **6-4**
Summary: Recording Merchandise Inventory Transactions
Dual Nature of Merchandise Transactions — EE **6-5**
Sales Taxes and Trade Discounts

OBJ. 3 **Describe and illustrate the adjusting process for a merchandising business.**

The Adjusting Process
Adjusting Entry for Inventory Shrinkage — EE **6-6**
Adjusting Entries for Customer Refunds and Allowances — EE **6-7**

OBJ. 4 **Describe and illustrate the financial statements of a merchandising business.**

Financial Statements for a Merchandising Business
Multiple-Step Income Statement
Single-Step Income Statement
Statement of Owner's Equity
Balance Sheet
The Closing Process

OBJ. 5 **Describe and illustrate the use of asset turnover in evaluating a company's operating performance.**

Financial Analysis and Interpretation: Asset Turnover
Compute Asset Turnover — EE **6-8**

APP. 1 OBJ. **Describe and illustrate the gross method of accounting for sales discounts.**

APP. 2 OBJ. **Describe and illustrate the accounting for merchandise returns.**

APP. 3 OBJ. **Describe and illustrate the periodic method of accounting for merchandise transactions.**

At a Glance 6 Page 315

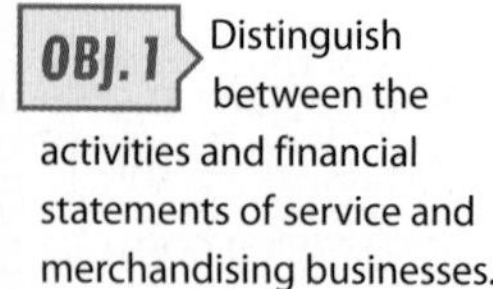

OBJ. 1 Distinguish between the activities and financial statements of service and merchandising businesses.

Nature of Merchandising Businesses

The activities of a service business differ from those of a merchandising business. These differences are reflected in the operating cycles of a service and merchandising business as well as in their financial statements.

Operating Cycle

The **operating cycle** is the process by which a company spends cash, generates revenues, and receives cash either at the time the revenues are generated or later by collecting an account receivable. The operating cycle of a service and merchandising business differs in that a merchandising business must purchase merchandise for sale to customers. The operating cycle for a merchandise business is shown in Exhibit 1.

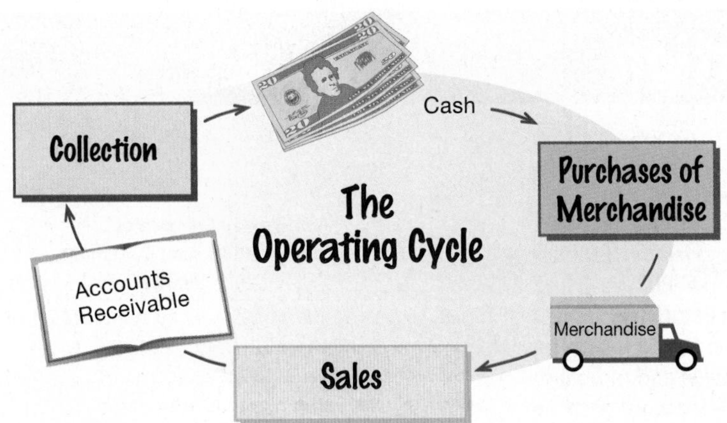

EXHIBIT 1

The Operating Cycle for a Merchandising Business

The time in days to complete an operating cycle differs significantly among merchandising businesses. Grocery stores normally have short operating cycles because of the nature of their merchandise. For example, many grocery items, such as milk, must be sold within their expiration dates of a week or two. In contrast, jewelry stores often carry expensive items that are displayed months before being sold to customers.

Financial Statements

The differences between service and merchandising businesses are also reflected in their financial statements. For example, these differences are illustrated in the following condensed income statements:

Service Business		Merchandising Business	
Fees earned	$XXX	Sales	$XXX
Operating expenses	XXX	Cost of merchandise sold	XXX
Operating income	$XXX	Gross profit	$XXX
		Operating expenses	XXX
		Operating income	$XXX

The revenue activities of a service business involve providing services to customers. On the income statement for a service business, the revenues from services are reported as *fees earned*. The operating expenses incurred in providing the services are subtracted from the fees earned to arrive at *operating income.*

In contrast, the revenue activities of a merchandising business involve the buying and selling of merchandise. A merchandising business first purchases merchandise to sell to its customers. When this merchandise is sold, the revenue is reported as **sales**, and its cost is recognized as an expense. This expense is called the **cost of merchandise sold**. The cost of merchandise sold is subtracted from sales to arrive at gross profit. This amount is called **gross profit** because it is the profit *before* deducting operating expenses.

Merchandise on hand (not sold) at the end of an accounting period is called **merchandise inventory**. Merchandise inventory is reported as a current asset on the balance sheet.

Link to Dollar Tree

In a recent income statement, **Dollar Tree** reported the following (in billions):

Sales............	$11.7
Cost of merch. sold.............	7.6
Gross profit.....	$ 4.1
Operating expenses........	2.6
Operating income..........	$ 1.5

Business Connection

COMCAST VERSUS LOWE'S

Comcast Corporation is a service business that offers cable communications, broadcast television (NBC television), filmed entertainment (Universal Pictures), and theme parks (Universal Parks) to its customers. **Lowe's Companies** is a large home improvement retailer. The differences in the operations of a service and merchandising business are illustrated in their recent income statements, as follows:

Comcast Corporation
Condensed Income Statement
(in millions)

Revenue	$94,507
Programming and production expenses	29,692
Selling and administrative expenses	34,789
Depreciation and amortization expenses	11,017
Operating income	$19,009

Lowe's Companies
Condensed Income Statement
(in millions)

Sales	$68,619
Cost of merchandise sold	45,210
Gross profit	$23,409
Selling, general, and administrative expenses	15,376
Depreciation expense	1,447
Operating income	$ 6,586

As a merchandising company, Lowe's subtracts cost of merchandise sold from sales to disclose gross profit. As a service company, Comcast shows neither cost of merchandise sold nor a gross profit line. Rather, service expenses are subtracted from revenue straight to operating income.

EXAMPLE EXERCISE 6-1 Gross Profit

OBJ. 1

During the current year, merchandise is sold for $250,000 cash and for $975,000 on account. The cost of the merchandise sold is $735,000. What is the amount of the gross profit?

Follow My Example 6-1

The gross profit is $490,000 ($250,000 + $975,000 – $735,000).

Practice Exercises: PE 6-1A, PE 6-1B

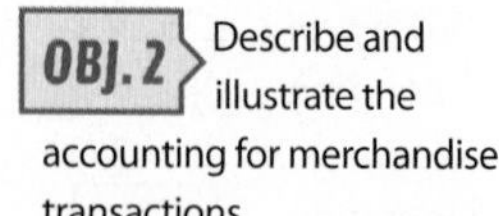

OBJ. 2 Describe and illustrate the accounting for merchandise transactions.

Merchandising Transactions

This section illustrates merchandise transactions for **NetSolutions** after it becomes a retailer of computer hardware and software. During 20Y6, Chris Clark implemented the second phase of NetSolutions' business plan. In doing so, Chris notified clients that beginning July 1, 20Y7, NetSolutions would no longer offer consulting services. Instead, it would become a merchandising business.

NetSolutions' business strategy is to offer personalized service to individuals and small businesses that are upgrading or purchasing new computer systems. NetSolutions' personal service includes a no-obligation, on-site assessment of the customer's computer needs. By providing personalized service and follow-up, Chris believes that NetSolutions can compete effectively against such retailers as **Best Buy**, **Office Depot**, and **Dell**.

Chart of Accounts for a Merchandising Business

NetSolutions' merchandise transactions are recorded in the accounts, using the rules of debit and credit that are described and illustrated in Chapter 2. However, since merchandising transactions differ from those of a service business, NetSolutions adopted the new chart of accounts shown in Exhibit 2.

EXHIBIT 2
Chart of Accounts for NetSolutions as a Merchandising Business

Balance Sheet Accounts	Income Statement Accounts
100 Assets	400 Revenues
110 Cash	410 Sales
112 Accounts Receivable	500 Costs and Expenses
115 Merchandise Inventory	510 Cost of Merchandise Sold
117 Office Supplies	520 Sales Salaries Expense
118 Prepaid Insurance	521 Advertising Expense
120 Land	522 Depreciation Expense—Store Equipment
123 Store Equipment	523 Delivery Expense
124 Accumulated Depreciation—Store Equipment	529 Miscellaneous Selling Expense
125 Office Equipment	530 Office Salaries Expense
126 Accumulated Depreciation—Office Equipment	531 Rent Expense
200 Liabilities	532 Depreciation Expense—Office Equipment
210 Accounts Payable	533 Insurance Expense
211 Salaries Payable	534 Office Supplies Expense
212 Unearned Rent	539 Misc. Administrative Expense
213 Customer Refunds Payable	600 Other Revenue
215 Notes Payable	610 Rent Revenue
300 Owner's Equity	700 Other Expense
310 Chris Clark, Capital	710 Interest Expense
311 Chris Clark, Drawing	

The accounts related to merchandising transactions are highlighted in Exhibit 2. The nature of these accounts will be described and illustrated as the related merchandising transactions are discussed.

As shown in Exhibit 2, NetSolutions' chart of accounts now consists of three-digit account numbers. The first digit indicates the major financial statement classification (1 for assets, 2 for liabilities, etc.). The second digit indicates the subclassification (e.g., 11 for current assets and 12 for noncurrent assets). The third digit identifies the specific account (e.g., 110 for Cash and 123 for Store Equipment).

Most merchandising companies use accounting systems with computerized reports that are similar to special journals and subsidiary ledgers illustrated in Chapter 5. For example, a merchandise accounting system typically produces sales and inventory reports. However, for the sake of simplicity, the transactions in this chapter will be illustrated using a two-column general journal.

Purchases Transactions

There are two systems for accounting for merchandise transactions: perpetual and periodic. In a **perpetual inventory system**, each purchase and sale of merchandise is recorded in the inventory account and related subsidiary ledger. In this way, the amount of merchandise available for sale and the amount sold are continuously (perpetually) updated in the inventory records. In a **periodic inventory system**, the inventory does not show the amount of merchandise available for sale and the amount sold. Instead, a listing of inventory on hand, called a **physical inventory**, is prepared at the end of the accounting period. This physical inventory is used to determine the cost of merchandise on hand at the end of the period and the cost of merchandise sold during the period.

Link to Dollar Tree

Dollar Tree uses point-of-sale computerized software to plan purchases and track inventory. This system automatically reorders key items based on sales and inventory levels.

Most merchandise companies use computerized perpetual inventory systems. Such systems use bar codes or radio frequency identification codes embedded in a product. An optical scanner or radio frequency identification device is then used to read the product codes and track inventory on hand and sold.

Because computerized perpetual inventory systems are widely used, this chapter illustrates merchandise transactions using a perpetual inventory system. The periodic system is described and illustrated in Appendix 3 at the end of this chapter.

Under the perpetual inventory system, cash purchases of $2,510 of merchandise are recorded as follows:

Journal — *Page 24*

Date		Description	Post. Ref.	Debit	Credit
20Y8					
Jan.	3	Merchandise Inventory		2,510	
		Cash			2,510
		Purchased inventory from Bowen Co.			

Purchases of $9,250 of merchandise on account are recorded as follows:

Date		Description	Post. Ref.	Debit	Credit
Jan.	4	Merchandise Inventory		9,250	
		Accounts Payable—Thomas Corporation			9,250
		Purchased inventory on account.			

The terms of purchases on account are normally indicated on the **invoice** or bill that the seller sends the buyer. An example of an invoice sent to NetSolutions by Alpha Technologies is shown in Exhibit 3.

EXHIBIT 3

Invoice

Alpha Technologies
1000 Matrix Blvd.
San Jose, CA 95116-1000

Made in U.S.A.

INVOICE 106-8

SOLD TO	CUSTOMER ORDER NO.	ORDER DATE
NetSolutions 5101 Washington Ave. Cincinnati, OH 45227-5101	412	Jan. 3, 20Y8

DATE SHIPPED	HOW SHIPPED AND ROUTE	TERMS	INVOICE DATE
Jan. 5, 20Y8	US Express Trucking Co.	2/10, n/30	Jan. 5, 20Y8

FROM	F.O.B.
San Jose	Cincinnati

QUANTITY	DESCRIPTION	UNIT PRICE	AMOUNT
20	HC9 Printer/Fax/Copier	150.00	3,000.00

The terms for when payments for merchandise are to be made are called the **credit terms**. If payment is required on delivery, the terms are cash or net cash. Otherwise, the buyer is allowed an amount of time, known as the **credit period**, in which to pay. The credit period usually begins with the date of the sale as shown on the invoice.

If payment is due within a stated number of days after the invoice date, such as 30 days, the terms are net 30 days. These terms may be written as *n/30*.[1] If payment is due by the end of the month in which the sale was made, the terms are written as *n/eom*.

Purchases Discounts To encourage the buyer to pay before the end of the credit period, the seller may offer a discount. For example, a seller may offer a 2% discount if the buyer pays within 10 days of the invoice date. If the buyer does not take the discount, the total invoice amount is due within 30 days. These terms are expressed as 2/10, n/30 and are read as "2% discount if paid within 10 days, net amount due within 30 days." The credit terms of 2/10, n/30 are summarized in Exhibit 4, using the invoice in Exhibit 3.

Credit Terms **EXHIBIT 4**

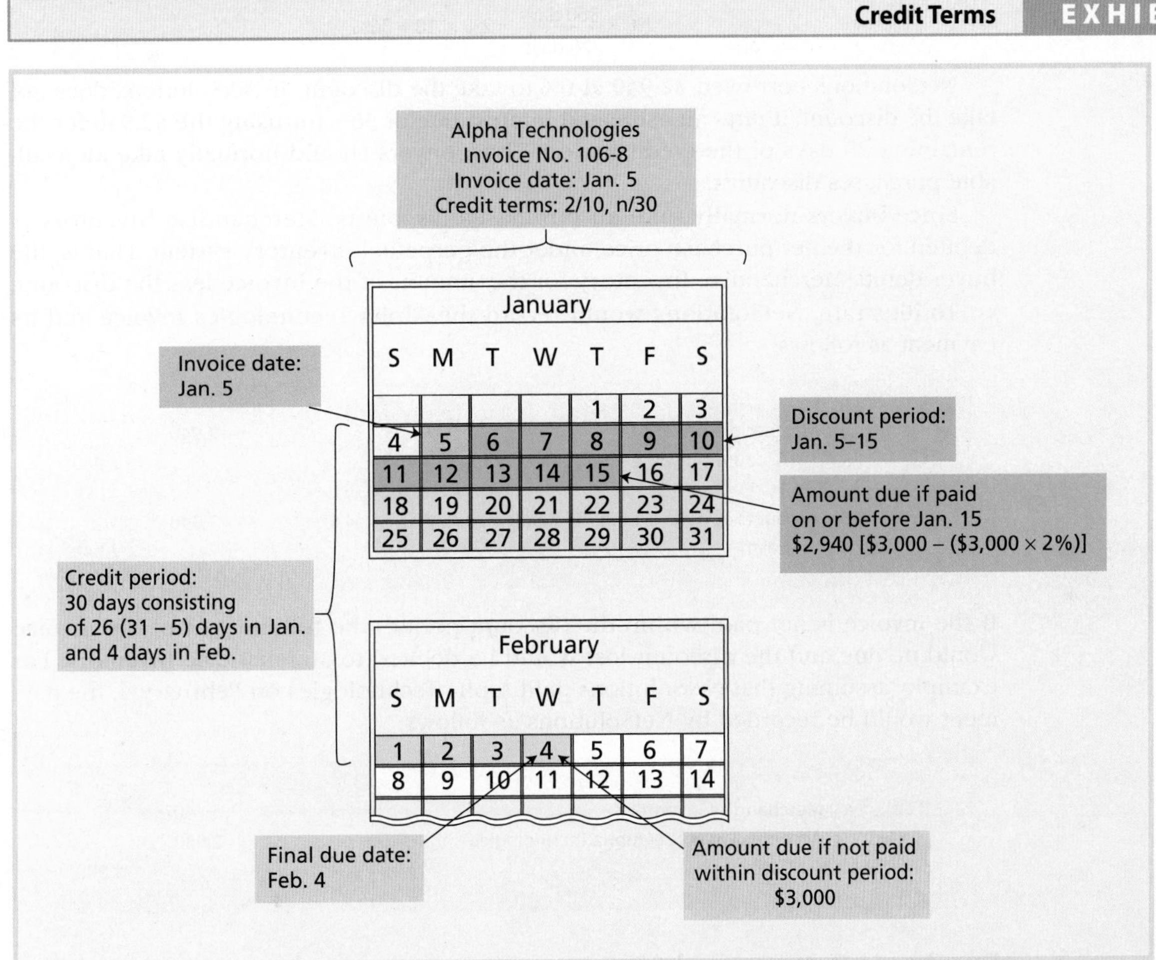

Discounts taken by the buyer for early payment of an invoice are called **purchases discounts**. Purchases discounts taken by a buyer reduce the cost of the merchandise purchased. Even if the buyer has to borrow to pay within a discount period, it is normally to the buyer's advantage to do so. For this reason, accounting systems are normally designed so that all available discounts are taken.

To illustrate, the invoice shown in Exhibit 3 is used. The last day of the discount period is January 15 (invoice date of January 5 plus 10 days). Assume that in order to pay the invoice on January 15, **NetSolutions** borrows $2,940, which is $3,000 less

1 The word *net* as used here does not have the usual meaning of a number after deductions have been subtracted, as in *net income*.

the discount of $60 ($3,000 × 2%). If an annual interest rate of 6% and a 360-day year is also assumed, the interest on the loan of $2,940 for the remaining 20 days of the credit period is $9.80 ($2,940 × 6% × 20 ÷ 360).[2]

The net savings to NetSolutions of taking the discount is $50.20, computed as follows:

Discount of 2% on $3,000	$60.00
Interest for 20 days at a rate of 6% on $2,940	9.80
Savings from taking the discount	$50.20

The savings can also be seen by comparing the interest rate on the money *saved* by taking the discount and the interest rate on the money *borrowed* to take the discount. The interest rate on the money saved in the prior example is estimated by converting 2% for 20 days to a yearly rate, as follows:

$$2\% \times \frac{360 \text{ days}}{20 \text{ days}} = 2\% \times 18 = 36\%$$

NetSolutions borrowed $2,940 at 6% to take the discount. If NetSolutions does not take the discount, it *pays* an estimated interest rate of 36% for using the $2,940 for the remaining 20 days of the credit period. Thus, buyers should normally take all available purchases discounts.

Since buyers normally take all purchases discounts, Merchandise Inventory is debited for the net purchase price under the perpetual inventory system. That is, the buyer debits Merchandise Inventory for the amount of the invoice less the discount.

To illustrate, NetSolutions would record the Alpha Technologies invoice and its payment as follows:

Jan.	5	Merchandise Inventory		2,940	
		Accounts Payable—Alpha Technologies			2,940
	15	Accounts Payable—Alpha Technologies		2,940	
		Cash			2,940

If the invoice is not paid within the discount period, the full amount of the invoice would be due and the discount lost would be debited to Merchandise Inventory. For example, assuming that NetSolutions paid Alpha Technologies on February 4, the payment would be recorded by NetSolutions as follows:

Feb.	4	Merchandise Inventory		60	
		Accounts Payable—Alpha Technologies		2,940	
		Cash			3,000

Purchases Returns and Allowances A buyer may request an allowance for merchandise that is returned (purchases return) or a price allowance (purchases allowance) for damaged or defective merchandise. From a buyer's perspective, such returns and allowances are called **purchases returns and allowances**. In both cases, the buyer normally sends the seller a debit memorandum to notify the seller of reasons for the return (purchase return) or to request a price reduction (purchase allowance).

A **debit memorandum**, often called a **debit memo**, is shown in Exhibit 5. A debit memo informs the seller of the amount the buyer proposes to *debit* to the account payable due the seller. It also states the reasons for the return or the request for the price allowance.

2 To simplify computations and rounding, we use a 360-day year rather than a 365-day year.

EXHIBIT 5
Debit Memo

NetSolutions **No. 18**
5101 Washington Ave.
Cincinnati, OH 45227-5101

DEBIT MEMO

TO	**DATE**
Maxim Systems 7519 East Wilson Ave. Seattle, WA 98101-7519	March 7, 20Y8

WE DEBITED YOUR ACCOUNT AS FOLLOWS

10	Server Network Interface Cards, your invoice No. 7291, are being returned via parcel post. Our order specified No. 825X, but we received No. 835c.	@ 90.00	900.00

The buyer may use the debit memo as the basis for recording the return or allowance or wait for approval from the seller (creditor). In either case, the buyer debits Accounts Payable and credits Merchandise Inventory.

To illustrate, **NetSolutions** records the return of the merchandise indicated in the debit memo in Exhibit 5 as follows:

Mar.	7	Accounts Payable—Maxim Systems		900	
		Merchandise Inventory			900
		Debit Memo No. 18.			

Before paying an invoice, a buyer may return merchandise or be granted a price allowance for an invoice with a purchase discount. In this case, the amount of the return is recorded at its invoice amount less the discount.

To illustrate, assume the following data concerning a purchase of merchandise by NetSolutions on May 2:

May 2. Purchased $5,000 of merchandise on account from Delta Data Link, terms 2/10, n/30.
4. Returned $1,000 of the merchandise purchased on May 2.
12. Paid for the purchase of May 2 less the return and discount.

NetSolutions would record these transactions as follows:

May	2	Merchandise Inventory		4,900	
		Accounts Payable—Delta Data Link			4,900
		Purchased merchandise [$5,000 – ($5,000 × 2%)].			
	4	Accounts Payable—Delta Data Link		980	
		Merchandise Inventory			980
		Returned portion of merch. purchased [$1,000 – ($1,000 × 2%)].			
	12	Accounts Payable—Delta Data Link		3,920	
		Cash			3,920
		($4,900 – $980)			

EXAMPLE EXERCISE 6-2 Purchases Transactions **OBJ. 2**

Rofles Company purchased merchandise on account from a supplier for $11,500, terms 2/10, n/30. Rofles Company returned $2,500 of the merchandise and received full credit.

a. If Rofles Company pays the invoice within the discount period, what is the amount of cash required for the payment?

b. Under a perpetual inventory system, what account is credited by Rofles Company to record the return?

Follow My Example 6-2

a. $8,820. Purchase of $11,270 [$11,500 – ($11,500 × 2%)] less the return of $2,450 [$2,500 – ($2,500 × 2%)].

b. Merchandise Inventory

Practice Exercises: PE 6-2A, PE 6-2B

Sales Transactions

Revenue from merchandise sales is usually recorded as *Sales*. Sometimes a business may use the title *Sales of Merchandise*.

Cash Sales A business may sell merchandise for cash. Cash sales are normally entered on a cash register and recorded in the accounts. To illustrate, assume that on March 3, **NetSolutions** sells merchandise for $1,800. These cash sales are recorded as follows:

Journal *Page 25*

Date		Description	Post. Ref.	Debit	Credit
20Y8					
Mar.	3	Cash		1,800	
		Sales			1,800
		To record cash sales.			

Using the perpetual inventory system, the cost of merchandise sold and the decrease in merchandise inventory are also recorded. In this way, the merchandise inventory account indicates the amount of merchandise on hand (not sold).

To illustrate, assume that the cost of merchandise sold on March 3 is $1,200. The entry to record the cost of merchandise sold and the decrease in the merchandise inventory is as follows:

Mar.	3	Cost of Merchandise Sold		1,200	
		Merchandise Inventory			1,200
		To record the cost of merchandise sold.			

Sales may be made to customers using credit cards such as **MasterCard** or **VISA**. Such sales are recorded as cash sales. This is because these sales are normally processed by a clearinghouse that contacts the bank that issued the card. The issuing bank then electronically transfers cash directly to the retailer's bank account.[3] Thus, the retailer normally receives cash within a few days of making the credit card sale.

3 CyberSource is one of the major credit card clearinghouses. For a more detailed description of how credit card sales are processed, see the following CyberSource Web page: www.cybersource.com. Click Products and under Payment Processing, click Payment Cards and then How it Works.

If customers use MasterCards to pay for their purchases, the sales would be recorded exactly as shown in the first March 3 entry illustrated in this section. Any processing fees charged by the clearinghouse or issuing bank are periodically recorded as an expense. This expense is normally reported on the income statement as an administrative expense. To illustrate, assume that NetSolutions paid credit card processing fees of $4,150 on March 31. These fees would be recorded as follows:

Mar.	31	Credit Card Expense		4,150	
		Cash			4,150
		To record service charges on credit card sales for the month.			

Link to Dollar Tree

Dollar Tree normally receives cash from credit card sales within three business days and thus records credit card sales as cash sales.

Sales on Account A business may sell merchandise on account. The seller records such sales as a debit to Accounts Receivable and a credit to Sales. An example of an entry for a **NetSolutions** sale on account of $6,000 to Jones Consulting follows. The cost of merchandise sold was $3,500.

Mar.	10	Accounts Receivable—Jones Consulting		6,000	
		Sales			6,000
		Invoice No. 7172.			
	10	Cost of Merchandise Sold		3,500	
		Merchandise Inventory			3,500
		Cost of merch. sold on Invoice No. 7172.			

Link to Dollar Tree

Dollar Tree only accepts cash, checks, credit cards, and debit cards from its customers.

Customer Discounts A seller may grant customers a variety of discounts, called **customer discounts**, as incentives to encourage customers to act in a way benefiting the seller. For example, a seller may offer customer discounts to encourage customers to purchase in volume or order early.

A common discount, called a **sales discount**, encourages customers to pay their invoice early. For example, a seller may offer credit terms of 2/10, n/30, which provides a 2% sales discount if the invoice is paid within 10 days. If not paid within 10 days, the total invoice amount is due within 30 days.[4]

To illustrate the accounting for sales discounts, assume that **NetSolutions** sold $18,000 of merchandise to Digital Technologies on March 10 with credit terms 2/10, n/30. The cost of merchandise sold was $10,800. The March 10 sale would be recorded as follows:[5]

Mar.	10	Accounts Receivable—Digital Technologies		17,640	
		Sales [$18,000 – ($18,000 × 2%)]			17,640
	10	Cost of Merchandise Sold		10,800	
		Merchandise Inventory			10,800

Link to Dollar Tree

Because **Dollar Tree** does not sell merchandise to customers on account, but only accepts cash, checks, credit cards, and debit cards, it did not report any accounts receivable on a recent balance sheet.

The sale to Digital Technologies is recorded by **NetSolutions** as $17,640, which is the invoice amount of $18,000 less the sales discount of $360 ($18,000 × 2%).[6]

4 From the buyer's perspective, a sales discount is referred to as a purchases discount, which was discussed earlier in this chapter.
5 The accounting for customer discounts other than sales discounts is discussed in advanced accounting courses.
6 This is consistent with *Revenue from Contracts with Customers, Topic 606, FASB Accounting Standards Update,* Financial Accounting Standards Board, Norwalk, CT, May 2014.

The payment by Digital Technologies on March 19 is recorded as follows:

Mar.	19	Cash	17,640	
		Accounts Receivable—Digital Technologies		17,640

If Digital Technologies did not pay within the discount period, NetSolutions would receive $18,000 and Sales would be credited for the amount of the discount. For example, assuming that Digital Technologies paid NetSolutions on April 9, the payment would be recorded by NetSolutions as follows:

Apr.	9	Cash	18,000	
		Accounts Receivable—Digital Technologies		17,640
		Sales		360

Cash Refunds and Allowances A buyer may receive merchandise that is defective, has been damaged during shipment, or does not meet the buyer's expectations. In these cases, the seller may pay the buyer a **cash refund** or grant a **customer allowance** that reduces the account receivable owed on the original selling price.

A seller estimates customer refunds and allowances for each year's sales. This estimate is used to record an adjusting entry that reduces current period sales and creates a liability for future refunds and allowances. The adjusting entry to record this liability, called **customer refunds payable**, is as follows.[7]

		Sales	XXX	
		Customer Refunds Payable		XXX

If the buyer is paid a refund, the seller debits Customer Refunds Payable and credits Cash. For example, assume that on March 4, **NetSolutions** pays Jones & Hunt a refund of $400 for merchandise that was damaged in shipment. Jones & Hunt has agreed to keep the merchandise and make any necessary repairs. Netsolutions would record the payment of the refund as follows:[8]

Mar.	4	Customer Refunds Payable	400	
		Cash		400

In some cases, a customer who is due a refund has an outstanding account receivable balance. Instead of paying a cash refund, the seller may grant the customer an allowance against the customer's account receivable. When this is done, the seller sends the buyer a **credit memorandum**, or **credit memo**, indicating its intent to credit the customer's account receivable.

To illustrate, assume that NetSolutions granted Blake & Sons a customer allowance of $900 against its outstanding accounts receivable. NetSolutions notifies Blake & Sons of the allowance by issuing the credit memo shown in Exhibit 6.

The credit memo indicates that NetSolutions intends to reduce Blake & Sons' accounts receivable for $900 due to merchandise damaged in shipment. NetSolutions would record the granting of the customer allowance as follows:

Link to Dollar Tree

Dollar Tree does not offer refunds, and all sales are final.

Mar.	4	Customer Refunds Payable	900	
		Accounts Receivable—Blake & Sons		900

7 The adjusting process for merchandise businesses is illustrated later in this chapter.

8 The accounting illustrated is based upon *Revenue from Contracts with Customers, Topic 606, FASB Accounting Standards Update*, Financial Accounting Standards Board, Norwalk, CT, May 2014.

NetSolutions
5101 Washington Ave.
Cincinnati, OH 45227-5101

CREDIT MEMO

TO	DATE
Blake & Sons 7608 Melton Avenue Los Angeles, CA 90025-3942	March 4, 20Y8

WE CREDITED YOUR ACCOUNT AS FOLLOWS

Allowance for merchandise damaged in shipment	900

EXHIBIT 6
Credit Memo

The journal entries for recording customer refunds and allowances are summarized in Exhibit 7. The journal entries in Exhibit 7 assume that the customer did not return merchandise. The accounting for merchandise returns is described and illustrated at the end of this chapter in Appendix 2.

Journal Entries to Record Customer Refunds and Allowances **EXHIBIT 7**

Cash Refund Paid			Credit Memorandum Issued		
Customer Refunds Payable	XXX		Customer Refunds Payable	XXX	
Cash		XXX	Accounts Receivable		XXX

EXAMPLE EXERCISE 6-3 Sales Transactions

OBJ. 2

Journalize the following merchandise transactions:

a. Sold merchandise on account to Smith Inc., $7,500, with terms 2/10, n/30. The cost of the merchandise sold was $5,625.
b. Received payment for the sale in (a) less the discount.
c. Issued a credit memo to Wilson Company for damaged merchandise of $800. Wilson Company agreed to keep the merchandise.

Follow My Example 6-3

a.	Accounts Receivable—Smith Inc. [$7,500 – ($7,500 × 2%)]	7,350	
	Sales		7,350
	Cost of Merchandise Sold	5,625	
	Merchandise Inventory		5,625
b.	Cash	7,350	
	Accounts Receivable—Smith Inc.		7,350
c.	Customer Refunds Payable	800	
	Accounts Receivable—Wilson Company		800

Practice Exercises: PE 6-3A, PE 6-3B

Integrity, Objectivity, and Ethics in Business

THE CASE OF THE FRAUDULENT PRICE TAGS

One of the challenges for a retailer is policing its sales return policy. There are many ways in which customers can unethically or illegally abuse such policies. In one case, a couple was accused of attaching **Marshalls'** store price tags to cheaper merchandise bought or obtained elsewhere. The couple then returned the cheaper goods and received the substantially higher refund amount. Company security officials discovered the fraud and had the couple arrested after they had allegedly bilked the company for more than $1 million.

Freight

Purchases and sales of merchandise often involve freight. The terms of a sale indicate when ownership (title and control) of the merchandise passes from the seller to the buyer. This point determines whether the buyer or the seller pays the freight costs.[9]

Note

The buyer bears the freight costs if the shipping terms are FOB shipping point.

The ownership of the merchandise may pass to the buyer when the seller delivers the merchandise to the freight carrier. In this case, the terms are said to be **FOB (free on board) shipping point**. This term means that the buyer pays the freight costs from the shipping point to the final destination. Such costs are part of the buyer's total cost of purchasing inventory and are added to the cost of the inventory by debiting Merchandise Inventory.

To illustrate, assume that on June 10, NetSolutions purchased merchandise as follows:

June 10. Purchased merchandise from Magna Data, $900, terms FOB shipping point.
10. Paid freight of $50 on June 10 purchase from Magna Data.

NetSolutions would record these two transactions as follows:

June	10	Merchandise Inventory		900	
		Accounts Payable—Magna Data			900
		Purchased merchandise, terms FOB shipping point.			
	10	Merchandise Inventory		50	
		Cash			50
		Paid shipping cost on merchandise purchased.			

Note

The seller bears the freight costs if the shipping terms are FOB destination.

The ownership of the merchandise may pass to the buyer when the buyer receives the merchandise. In this case, the terms are said to be **FOB (free on board) destination**. This term means that the seller pays the freight costs from the shipping point to the buyer's final destination. When the seller pays the delivery charges, the seller debits Delivery Expense or Freight Out. Delivery Expense is reported on the seller's income statement as a selling expense.

To illustrate, assume that NetSolutions sells merchandise as follows:

June 15. Sold merchandise to Kranz Company on account, $700, terms FOB destination. The cost of the merchandise sold is $480.
15. NetSolutions pays freight of $40 on the sale of June 15.

NetSolutions records the sale, the cost of the sale, and the freight cost as follows:

June	15	Accounts Receivable—Kranz Company		700	
		Sales			700
		Sold merchandise, terms FOB destination.			
	15	Cost of Merchandise Sold		480	
		Merchandise Inventory			480
		Recorded cost of merchandise sold to Kranz Company.			
	15	Delivery Expense		40	
		Cash			40
		Paid shipping cost on merchandise sold.			

9 The passage of title also determines whether the buyer or seller must pay other costs, such as the cost of insurance, while the merchandise is in transit.

The seller may prepay the freight even though the terms are FOB shipping point. The seller will then add the freight to the invoice. The buyer debits Merchandise Inventory for the total amount of the invoice, including the freight. Any discount terms would not apply to the prepaid freight.

To illustrate, assume that **NetSolutions** sells merchandise as follows:

June 20. Sold merchandise to Planter Company on account, $800, terms FOB shipping point. NetSolutions paid freight of $45, which was added to the invoice. The cost of the merchandise sold is $360.

NetSolutions records the sale, the cost of the sale, and the freight as follows:

June	20	Accounts Receivable—Planter Company		800	
		Sales			800
		Sold merchandise, terms FOB shipping point.			
	20	Cost of Merchandise Sold		360	
		Merchandise Inventory			360
		Recorded cost of merchandise sold to Planter Company.			
	20	Accounts Receivable—Planter Company		45	
		Cash			45
		Prepaid shipping cost on merchandise sold.			

Shipping terms, the passage of title (control), and whether the buyer or seller is to pay the freight costs are summarized in Exhibit 8.

Freight Terms **EXHIBIT 8**

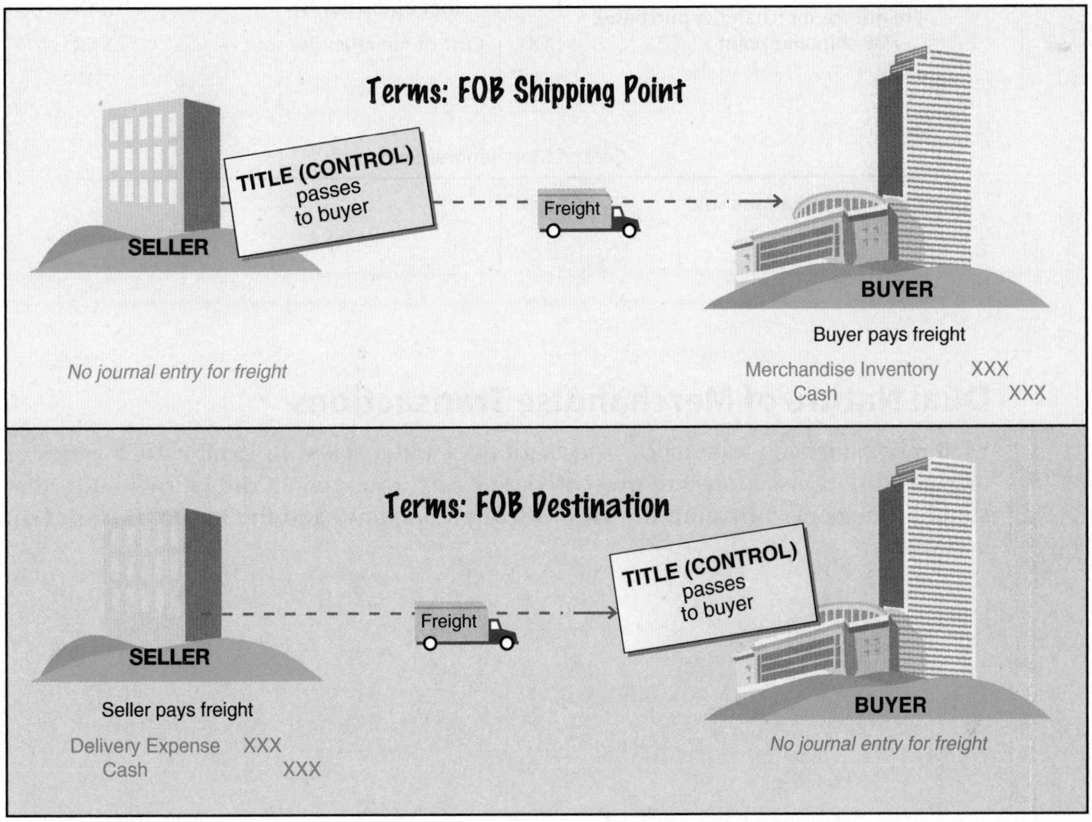

EXAMPLE EXERCISE 6-4 Freight Terms — OBJ. 2

Determine the amount to be paid in full settlement of each of the two invoices, (a) and (b), assuming that credit for refunds and allowances was received prior to payment and that all invoices were paid within the discount period.

	Merchandise	Freight Paid by Seller	Freight Terms	Credit for Refunds and Allowances
a.	$4,500	$200	FOB shipping point, 1/10, n/30	$ 800
b.	5,000	60	FOB destination, 2/10, n/30	2,500

Follow My Example 6-4

a. $3,863. Purchase of $4,455 [$4,500 – ($4,500 × 1%)] less credit of $792 [$800 – ($800 × 1%)] plus $200 of shipping.

b. $2,450. Purchase of $4,900 [$5,000 – ($5,000 × 2%)] less credit of $2,450 [$2,500 – ($2,500 × 2%)].

Practice Exercises: PE 6-4A, PE 6-4B

Summary: Recording Merchandise Inventory Transactions

Recording merchandise inventory transactions under the perpetual inventory system has been described and illustrated in the preceding sections. These transactions involved purchases, purchases returns and allowances, freight, and cost of merchandise sold (from sales). Exhibit 9 summarizes how these transactions are recorded in T account form.

EXHIBIT 9

Recording Merchandise Inventory Transactions

Merchandise Inventory

Debit		Credit	
Purchases (net of discounts)	XXX	Purchases returns and allowances (net of discounts)	XXX
Freight for merchandise purchased FOB shipping point	XXX	Cost of merchandise sold	XXX

Cost of Merchandise Sold

Debit		Credit
Cost of merchandise sold	XXX	

Dual Nature of Merchandise Transactions

Each merchandising transaction affects a buyer and a seller. In Exhibit 10, a series of merchandise transactions are presented. For each transaction, the journal entry that should be recorded by both the seller (Scully Company) and the buyer (Burton Co.) is shown.

Illustration of Merchandise Inventory Transactions for Seller and Buyer EXHIBIT 10

Transaction	Scully Company (Seller)			Burton Co. (Buyer)		
July 1. Scully Company sold merchandise on account to Burton Co., $7,500, terms FOB shipping point, n/45. The cost of the goods sold was $4,500.	Accounts Receivable—Burton Co.	7,500		Merchandise Inventory	7,500	
	Sales		7,500	Accounts Payable—Scully Co.		7,500
	Cost of Merchandise Sold	4,500				
	Merchandise Inventory		4,500			
July 2. Burton Co. paid freight of $150 on July 1 purchase from Scully Company.	No journal entry.			Merchandise Inventory	150	
				Cash		150
July 5. Scully Company sold merchandise on account to Burton Co., $5,000, terms FOB destination, n/15. The cost of the goods sold was $3,500.	Accounts Receivable—Burton Co.	5,000		Merchandise Inventory	5,000	
	Sales		5,000	Accounts Payable—Scully Co.		5,000
	Cost of Merchandise Sold	3,500				
	Merchandise Inventory		3,500			
July 7. Scully Company paid freight of $250 for delivery of merchandise sold to Burton Co. on July 5.	Delivery Expense	250		No journal entry.		
	Cash		250			
July 15. Scully Company received payment from Burton Co. for purchase of July 5.	Cash	5,000		Accounts Payable—Scully Co.	5,000	
	Accounts Receivable—Burton Co.		5,000	Cash		5,000
July 18. Scully Company sold merchandise on account to Burton Co., $12,000, terms FOB shipping point, 2/10, n/eom. Scully Company prepaid freight of $500, which was added to the invoice. The cost of the goods sold was $7,200.	Accounts Receivable—Burton Co.	11,760		Merchandise Inventory	12,260	
	Sales		11,760	Accounts Payable—Scully Co.		12,260
	Accounts Receivable—Burton Co.	500				
	Cash		500			
	Cost of Merchandise Sold	7,200				
	Merchandise Inventory		7,200			
July 22. Scully Company paid Burton Co. a refund of $750 for merchandise damaged in the July 5 purchase. Burton kept the merchandise.	Customer Refunds Payable	750		Cash	750	
	Cash		750	Merchandise Inventory		750
July 28. Scully Company received payment from Burton Co. for purchase of July 18.	Cash	12,260		Accounts Payable—Scully Co.	12,260	
	Accounts Receivable—Burton Co.		12,260	Cash		12,260

EXAMPLE EXERCISE 6-5 Transactions for Buyer and Seller **OBJ. 2**

Sievert Co. sold merchandise to Bray Co. on account, $11,500, terms 2/15, n/30. The cost of the merchandise sold is $6,900. Journalize the entries for Sievert Co. and Bray Co. for the sale, purchase, and payment of amount due. Assume that all discounts are taken.

Follow My Example 6-5

Sievert Co. journal entries:

Account	Debit	Credit
Accounts Receivable [$11,500 – ($11,500 × 2%)]	11,270	
Sales		11,270
Cost of Merchandise Sold	6,900	
Merchandise Inventory		6,900
Cash	11,270	
Accounts Receivable—Bray Co.		11,270

Bray Co. journal entries:

Account	Debit	Credit
Merchandise Inventory [$11,500 – ($11,500 × 2%)]	11,270	
Accounts Payable		11,270
Accounts Payable—Sievert Co.	11,270	
Cash		11,270

Practice Exercises: PE 6-5A, PE 6-5B

Sales Taxes and Trade Discounts

Sales of merchandise often involve sales taxes. Also, the seller may offer buyers trade discounts.

Sales Taxes Almost all states levy a tax on sales of merchandise.[10] The liability for the sales tax is incurred when the sale is made.

At the time of a cash sale, the seller collects the sales tax. When a sale is made on account, the seller charges the tax to the buyer by debiting Accounts Receivable. The seller credits the sales account for the amount of the sale and credits the tax to Sales Tax Payable. For example, the seller would record a sale of $100 on account to Lemon Co., subject to a tax of 6%, as follows:

				Debit	Credit
Aug.	12	Accounts Receivable—Lemon Co.		106	
		Sales			100
		Sales Tax Payable			6
		Invoice No. 339.			

On a regular basis, the seller pays to the taxing authority (state) the amount of the sales tax collected. The seller records such a payment of $2,900 as follows:

				Debit	Credit
Sept.	15	Sales Tax Payable		2,900	
		Cash			2,900
		Payment for sales taxes collected during August.			

10 Businesses that purchase merchandise for resale to others are normally exempt from paying sales taxes on their purchases. Only final buyers of merchandise normally pay sales taxes.

Business Connection

SALES TAXES

While there is no federal sales tax, most states have enacted statewide sales taxes. In addition, many states allow counties and cities to collect a "local option" sales tax. Delaware, Montana, New Hampshire, and Oregon have no state or local sales taxes. Tennessee (9.75%), California (10.25%), Washington (10.3%), and Louisiana (9.95%) have the highest average combined rates (including state and local option taxes). Several towns in Tuscaloosa County, Alabama, have the highest combined rates in the United States of 11%, while Chicago, Illinois, has the highest combined city rate of 10.25%.

What about companies that sell merchandise over the Internet? The general rule is that if the company ships merchandise to a customer in a state where the company does not have a physical location, no sales tax is due. For example, a customer in Montana who purchases merchandise online from a New York retailer (which has no physical location in Montana) does not have to pay sales tax to either Montana or New York.

Source: The Sales Tax Clearinghouse at www.thestc.com/FAQ.stm.

Trade Discounts **Wholesalers** are companies that sell merchandise to other businesses rather than to the public. Many wholesalers publish or upload sales catalogs online. However, wholesalers often offer special discounts to government agencies or businesses that order large quantities. Such discounts are called **trade discounts**.

Sellers and buyers do not normally record the list prices of merchandise and trade discounts in their accounts. For example, assume that an item has a list price of $1,000 and a 40% trade discount. The seller records the sale of the item at $600 [$1,000 less the trade discount of $400 ($1,000 × 40%)]. Likewise, the buyer records the purchase at $600.

The Adjusting Process

OBJ. 3 Describe and illustrate the adjusting process for a merchandising business.

Thus far, the chart of accounts and the recording of transactions for a merchandising business (NetSolutions) have been described and illustrated. Next, the adjusting process for a merchandising business is described and illustrated. This discussion focuses on the following adjusting entries that differ from those of a service business:[11]

- Inventory Shrinkage
- Customer Refunds and Allowances

Adjusting Entry for Inventory Shrinkage

Under the perpetual inventory system, the merchandise inventory account is continually updated for purchase and sales transactions. As a result, the balance of the inventory account is the amount of merchandise available for sale at that point in time. However, retailers normally experience some loss of inventory due to shoplifting, employee theft, or errors. Thus, the physical inventory on hand at the end of the accounting period is usually less than the balance of Merchandise Inventory. This difference is called **inventory shrinkage** or **inventory shortage**.

To illustrate, NetSolutions' inventory is as follows on December 31, 20Y8:

Account balance of Merchandise Inventory	$69,250
Physical inventory on hand	67,450
Inventory shrinkage	$ 1,800

11 The accounting for customer returns, including the related adjusting entry, is described and illustrated in Appendix 2 of this chapter.

At the end of the accounting period, inventory shrinkage is recorded by the following adjusting entry:

20Y8		Adjusting Entry			
Dec.	31	Cost of Merchandise Sold		1,800	
		Merchandise Inventory			1,800
		Inventory shrinkage ($63,950 – $62,150).			

After the preceding entry is recorded, the balance of Merchandise Inventory agrees with the physical inventory on hand at the end of the period. Since inventory shrinkage cannot be totally eliminated, it is considered a normal cost of operations. If, however, the amount of the shrinkage is unusually large, it may be disclosed separately on the income statement. In such cases, the shrinkage may be recorded in a separate account, such as Loss from Inventory Shrinkage.

EXAMPLE EXERCISE 6-6 Inventory Shrinkage **OBJ. 3**

Pulmonary Company's perpetual inventory records indicate that $382,800 of merchandise should be on hand on March 31, 20Y3. The physical inventory indicates that $371,250 of merchandise is actually on hand. Journalize the adjusting entry for the inventory shrinkage for Pulmonary Company for the year ended March 31, 20Y3. Assume that the inventory shrinkage is a normal amount.

Follow My Example 6-6

Mar. 31	Cost of Merchandise Sold	11,550	
	Merchandise Inventory		11,550
	Inventory shrinkage ($382,800 – $371,250).		

Practice Exercises: PE 6-6A, PE 6-6B

Integrity, Objectivity, and Ethics in Business

THE COST OF EMPLOYEE THEFT

One survey reported that the 21 largest U.S. retail store chains have lost between $13–18 billion to shoplifting and employee theft. The stores apprehended over 432,000 shoplifters and dishonest employees and recovered more than $188 million from these thieves. Approximately 1 out of every 35 employees was apprehended for theft from his or her employer. Each dishonest employee stole approximately 2.5 times the amount stolen by shoplifters ($966.61 versus $381.25).

Source: Jack L. Hayes International, *30th Annual Retail Theft Survey*, 2018.

Adjusting Entries for Customer Refunds and Allowances

Sellers are required to estimate refunds and allowances at the end of an accounting period and prepare an adjusting entry. The adjusting entry reduces the sales account and creates a customer refund liability account for the estimated refunds and allowances that will be granted to customers in the future.

To illustrate, assume the following for NetSolutions on December 31, 20Y8, before any adjustments:

Sales for the year ended December 31, 20Y8	$715,409
Estimated percent of refunds for 20Y8 sales	1%
Balance of Customer Refunds Payable	$800 (credit)

Based upon the preceding data, NetSolutions would make the following adjusting entry on December 31, 20Y8:[12]

Dec.	31	Sales (1% × $715,409)		7,154	
		Customer Refunds Payable			7,154

The adjusting entry reduces 20Y8 sales by the amount of estimated refunds that may occur in the next year. Since 1% of sales are expected to be refunded, Sales is debited for $7,154 (1% × $715,409). In addition, a liability is recorded for $7,154 by crediting Customer Refunds Payable for the estimated customer refunds that will be made in the next year.

EXAMPLE EXERCISE 6-7 Customer Refunds and Allowances **OBJ. 3**

Assume the following data for Bighorn Inc. before its year-end adjustments:

Sales for the year ended December 31, 20Y9	$18,440,000
Estimated percent of refunds for 20Y9 sales	1.5%

Journalize the adjusting entry for estimated customer refunds and allowances.

Follow My Example 6-7

Sales ($18,440,000 × 1.5%)	276,600	
Customer Refunds Payable		276,600

Practice Exercises: PE 6-7A, PE 6-7B

After the adjusting entry is posted to the ledger, Customer Refunds Payable will have a credit balance of $7,954 ($800 + $7,154). Customer refunds payable of $7,954 is reported as a current liability following Accounts Payable, as shown later in the chapter.

Financial Statements for a Merchandising Business

OBJ. 4 Describe and illustrate the financial statements of a merchandising business.

Although merchandising transactions affect the balance sheet in reporting inventory, they primarily affect the income statement. An income statement for a merchandising business is normally prepared using either a multiple-step or single-step format.

Multiple-Step Income Statement

The 20Y8 income statement for NetSolutions is shown in Exhibit 11. This form of income statement, called a **multiple-step income statement**, contains several sections, subsections, and subtotals.

Sales The total amount of sales to customers for cash and on account is reported in this section. NetSolutions reported sales of $708,255 for the year ended December 31, 20Y8.

Cost of Merchandise Sold As shown in Exhibit 11, NetSolutions reported cost of merchandise sold of $520,305 during 20Y8. This amount is the cost of merchandise sold to customers. Cost of merchandise sold may also be reported as Cost of Goods Sold or Cost of Sales.

Gross Profit The excess of sales over cost of merchandise sold is gross profit. As shown in Exhibit 11, NetSolutions reported gross profit of $187,950 in 20Y8.

Link to Dollar Tree

Dollar Tree reports its income using the multiple-step income statement format.

12 The accounting illustrated is based upon *Revenue from Contracts with Customers, Topic 606, FASB Accounting Standards Update*, Financial Accounting Standards Board, Norwalk, CT, May 2014.

Income from Operations **Income from operations**, sometimes called **operating income**, is determined by subtracting operating expenses from gross profit. Operating expenses are normally classified as either selling expenses or administrative expenses.

Selling expenses are incurred directly in the selling of merchandise. Examples of selling expenses include sales salaries, store supplies used, depreciation of store equipment, delivery expense, and advertising.

Administrative expenses, sometimes called **general expenses**, are incurred in the administration or general operations of the business. Examples of administrative expenses include office salaries, depreciation of office equipment, and office supplies used.

EXHIBIT 11

Multiple-Step Income Statement

NetSolutions Income Statement For the Year Ended December 31, 20Y8			
Sales			$708,255
Cost of merchandise sold			520,305
Gross profit			$187,950
Operating expenses:			
Selling expenses:			
Sales salaries expense	$53,430		
Advertising expense	10,860		
Depreciation expense—store equipment	3,100		
Delivery expense	2,800		
Miscellaneous selling expense	630		
Total selling expenses		$70,820	
Administrative expenses:			
Office salaries expense	$21,020		
Rent expense	8,100		
Depreciation expense—office equipment	2,490		
Insurance expense	1,910		
Office supplies expense	610		
Miscellaneous administrative expense	760		
Total administrative expenses		34,890	
Total operating expenses			105,710
Income from operations			$ 82,240
Other revenue and expense:			
Rent revenue		$ 600	
Interest expense		(2,440)	(1,840)
Net income			$ 80,400

Each selling and administrative expense may be reported separately as shown in Exhibit 11. However, many companies report selling, administrative, and operating expenses as single line items, as follows for NetSolutions:

IFRS

See Appendix B for more information.

Gross profit		$187,950
Operating expenses:		
Selling expenses	$70,820	
Administrative expenses	34,890	
Total operating expenses		105,710
Income from operations		$ 82,240

Other Revenue and Expense Other revenue and expense items are not related to the primary operations of the business. **Other revenue** is revenue from sources other than the primary operating activity of a business. Examples of other revenue include revenue from interest, rent, and gains resulting from the sale of fixed assets. **Other expense** is an expense that cannot be traced directly to the normal operations of the business. Examples of other expenses include interest expense and losses from disposing of fixed assets.

Other revenue and other expense are offset against each other on the income statement. If the total of other revenue exceeds the total of other expense, the difference is added to income from operations to determine net income. If the reverse is true, the difference is subtracted from income from operations. The other revenue and expense items of NetSolutions are reported as follows and in Exhibit 11:

Income from operations		$82,240
Other revenue and expense:		
Rent revenue	$ 600	
Interest expense	(2,440)	(1,840)
Net income		$80,400

Single-Step Income Statement

An alternate form of income statement is the **single-step income statement.** As shown in Exhibit 12, the income statement for NetSolutions deducts the total of all expenses *in one step* from the total of all revenues.

The single-step form emphasizes total revenues and total expenses in determining net income. A criticism of the single-step form is that gross profit and income from operations are not reported.

EXHIBIT 12

Single-Step Income Statement

NetSolutions
Income Statement
For the Year Ended December 31, 20Y8

Revenues:		
Sales		$708,255
Rent revenue		600
Total revenues		$708,855
Expenses:		
Cost of merchandise sold	$520,305	
Selling expenses	70,820	
Administrative expenses	34,890	
Interest expense	2,440	
Total expenses		628,455
Net income		$ 80,400

Statement of Owner's Equity

The statement of owner's equity for NetSolutions is shown in Exhibit 13. This statement is prepared in the same manner as for a service business.

EXHIBIT 13

Statement of Owner's Equity for Merchandising Business

NetSolutions
Statement of Owner's Equity
For the Year Ended December 31, 20Y8

Chris Clark, capital, January 1, 20Y8		$153,800
Net income for the year	$ 80,400	
Withdrawals	(18,000)	
Increase in owner's equity		62,400
Chris Clark, capital, December 31, 20Y8		$216,200

Balance Sheet

The balance sheet for NetSolutions is shown in Exhibit 14. In Exhibit 14, merchandise inventory of $67,450 is reported as a current asset, and the current portion of the note payable of $5,000 is reported as a current liability.

EXHIBIT 14

Balance Sheet for Merchandising Business

NetSolutions
Balance Sheet
December 31, 20Y8

Assets			
Current assets:			
Cash		$52,650	
Accounts receivable		91,080	
Merchandise inventory		67,450	
Office supplies		480	
Prepaid insurance		2,650	
Total current assets			$214,310
Property, plant, and equipment:			
Land		$20,000	
Store equipment	$27,100		
Less accumulated depreciation	5,700	21,400	
Office equipment	$15,570		
Less accumulated depreciation	4,720	10,850	
Total property, plant, and equipment			52,250
Total assets			$266,560
Liabilities			
Current liabilities:			
Accounts payable		$14,466	
Customer refunds payable		7,954	
Note payable (current portion)		5,000	
Salaries payable		1,140	
Unearned rent		1,800	
Total current liabilities			$ 30,360
Long-term liabilities:			
Note payable (final payment due in 10 years)			20,000
Total liabilities			$ 50,360
Owner's Equity			
Chris Clark, capital			216,200
Total liabilities and owner's equity			$266,560

The Closing Process

The closing entries for a merchandising business are similar to those for a service business. The two closing entries for a merchandising business are as follows:

1. Debit each revenue account for its balance, credit each expense account for its balance, and credit owner's capital account for net income. Debit the owner's capital account for a net loss. Cost of merchandise sold is a temporary account and is closed like an expense account.
2. Debit the owner's capital account for the balance of the drawing account and credit the drawing account.

The two closing entries for **NetSolutions** are as follows:

Journal					Page 29
Date		**Item**	**Post. Ref.**	**Debit**	**Credit**
20Y8		Closing Entries			
Dec.	31	Sales	410	708,255	
		Rent Revenue	610	600	
		Cost of Merchandise Sold	510		520,305
		Sales Salaries Expense	520		53,430
		Advertising Expense	521		10,860
		Depr. Expense—Store Equipment	522		3,100
		Delivery Expense	523		2,800
		Miscellaneous Selling Expense	529		630
		Office Salaries Expense	530		21,020
		Rent Expense	531		8,100
		Depr. Expense—Office Equipment	532		2,490
		Insurance Expense	533		1,910
		Office Supplies Expense	534		610
		Misc. Administrative Expense	539		760
		Interest Expense	710		2,440
		Chris Clark, Capital	310		80,400
	31	Chris Clark, Capital	310	18,000	
		Chris Clark, Drawing	311		18,000

After the closing entries are posted to the accounts, a post-closing trial balance is prepared. The only accounts that should appear on the post-closing trial balance are the asset, contra asset, liability, and owner's capital accounts with balances. These are the same accounts that appear on the end-of-period balance sheet. If the two totals of the trial balance columns are not equal, an error has occurred that must be found and corrected.

Financial Analysis and Interpretation: Asset Turnover

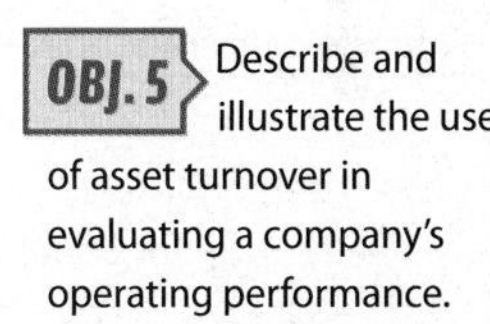

Asset turnover, sometimes called the ratio of sales to assets, measures how effectively a business is using its assets to generate sales. A high ratio indicates an effective use of assets.

The asset turnover is computed as follows:

$$\text{Asset Turnover} = \frac{\text{Sales}}{\text{Average Total Assets}}$$

To illustrate, the following data (in millions) were taken from recent annual reports of **Dollar Tree, Inc.**:

	Year 2	**Year 1**
Total revenues (sales)	$22,823	$22,246
Total assets:		
Beginning of year	16,333	15,702
End of year	13,501	16,333

The asset turnover for each year is as follows:

	Year 2	Year 1
Asset turnover*	1.53	1.39
	$22,823 ÷ [($16,333 + $13,501) ÷ 2]	$22,246 ÷ [($15,702 + $16,333) ÷ 2]

*Rounded to two decimal places.

Dollar Tree's asset turnover increased from 1.39 in Year 1 to 1.53 in Year 2. Thus, Dollar Tree's utilization of its assets to generate sales increased slightly in Year 2.

Using the asset turnover for comparisons to competitors and with industry averages could also be beneficial in interpreting Dollar Tree's use of its assets. For example, the following data (in millions) were taken from recent annual reports of **Dollar General Corporation**:

	Year 2
Total revenues (sales)	$25,625
Total assets:	
Beginning of year	12,517
End of year	13,204

Dollar General's asset turnover for Year 2 is as follows:

	Year 2
Asset turnover*	1.99
	$25,625 ÷ [($12,517 + $13,204) ÷ 2]

*Rounded to two decimal places.

Comparing Dollar General's Year 2 asset turnover of 1.99 to Dollar Tree's Year 2 ratio of 1.53 implies that Dollar General is using its assets more efficiently than is Dollar Tree.

EXAMPLE EXERCISE 6-8 Asset Turnover

OBJ. 5

Financial statement data for the years ending December 31, 20Y2 and 20Y1, for Gilbert Company follow:

	20Y2	20Y1
Sales	$1,305,000	$962,500
Total assets:		
Beginning of year	840,000	700,000
End of year	900,000	840,000

a. Determine the asset turnover for 20Y2 and 20Y1.

b. Is the change in the asset turnover from 20Y1 to 20Y2 favorable or unfavorable?

Follow My Example 6-8

a.

	20Y2	20Y1
Asset turnover	1.50	1.25
	$1,305,000 ÷ [($840,000 + $900,000) ÷ 2]	$962,500 ÷ [($700,000 + $840,000) ÷ 2]

b. The change from 1.25 to 1.50 is favorable, showing an improved use of assets to generate sales.

Practice Exercises: PE 6-8A, PE 6-8B

APPENDIX 1

Gross Method of Recording Sales Discounts

APP. 1 OBJ. Describe and illustrate the gross method of accounting for sales discounts.

In this chapter, sales discounts for early payment of an invoice were recorded using the net method. Under the *net method*, an invoice is recorded net of any discounts for early payment. This appendix illustrates the gross method of recording sales discounts.

Transactions

Under the **gross method**, a sales invoice with credit terms granting a discount for early payment is recorded at the gross amount of the invoice. If the customer pays within the discount period, Cash is debited for the amount received, the discount is recorded as a debit to Sales, and Accounts Receivable is credited for the invoice amount.

To illustrate, assume that NetSolutions uses the perpetual inventory system and sold $18,000 of merchandise to Digital Technologies on March 10, 20Y8, with credit terms of 2/10, n/30. The cost of the merchandise sold was $10,800. The sale would be recorded under the gross method as follows:

20Y8					
Mar.	10	Accounts Receivable—Digital Technologies		18,000	
		Sales			18,000
	10	Cost of Merchandise Sold		10,800	
		Merchandise Inventory			10,800

Assuming that Digital Technologies pays within the discount period on March 19, the payment would be recorded as follows:

Mar.	19	Cash		17,640	
		Sales		360	
		Accounts Receivable—Digital Technologies			18,000

Cash is debited for the amount received of $17,640, which is the invoice amount of $18,000 less the sales discount of $360 ($18,000 × 2%). Generally accepted accounting principles (GAAP) require that revenue (sales) be recognized in the amount of consideration received for the sale.[13] Since cash of $17,640 was received, Sales must be decreased (debited) for the sales discount of $360. The customer's account receivable is credited for its balance of $18,000.

Instead of paying within the discount period, assume the Digital Technologies pays the gross amount of $18,000 on April 9. The payments would be recorded as follows:

Apr.	9	Cash		18,000	
		Accounts Receivable—Digital Technologies			18,000

Since $18,000 was received, the revenue (sales) is $18,000; the amount recorded on March 10.

13 *Revenue from Contracts with Customers, Topic 606, FASB Accounting Standards Update,* Financial Accounting Standards Board, Norwalk, CT, May 2014.

Adjusting Entry

Since GAAP requires revenue (sales) to be recorded in the amount most likely to be received, the gross method requires an adjusting entry at the end of the accounting period. The adjusting entry reduces Sales for the estimated sales discounts related to the current period's sales that are expected to be taken in the next period.

To illustrate, assume the following data for NetSolutions on December 31, 20Y8:

	December 31, 20Y8 Balances	
	Debit	**Credit**
Sales		$709,955
Accounts Receivable	$92,880	
Allowance for Sales Discounts		100
Estimated sales discounts that will be taken in 20Y9	$ 1,700	

NetSolutions should record the following adjusting entry on December 31, 20Y8:

20Y8						
Dec.	31	Sales			1,700	
		Allowance for Sales Discounts				1,700

The preceding adjusting entry debits Sales for $1,700 and credits Allowance for Sales Discounts.

Allowance for Sales Discounts is a contra asset account similar to the contra asset account Accumulated Depreciation. Just as Accumulated Depreciation is a contra account to a fixed asset account, Allowance for Sales Discounts is a contra account to Accounts Receivable.

After the adjusting entry is posted, Allowance for Sales Discounts will have a credit balance of $1,800 ($100 + $1,700) and would be reported on the balance sheet as follows:

Accounts receivable	$92,880	
Less allowance for sales discounts	1,800	
Net accounts receivable		$91,080

NetSolutions would report sales of $708,255 ($709,955 – $1,700) on its income statement for the year ending December 31, 20Y8.

Subsequent Period

Customers with outstanding accounts receivable balances on December 31, 20Y8, will pay their balances in 20Y9. If a customer pays within the discount period, Allowance for Sales Discounts is debited instead of Sales. To illustrate, assume that Jay Smith pays his December 31, 20Y8, account receivable of $2,000 on January 4, 20Y9, and takes a 2/10 sales discount. The payment would be recorded as follows:

20Y9						
Jan.	4	Cash			1,960	
		Allowance for Sales Discounts			40	
		Accounts Receivable				2,000

Assume that Jay Smith paid on January 20 and did not take the sales discount. The payment would be recorded as follows:

20Y9				
Jan.	20	Cash	2,000	
		Accounts Receivable		2,000

At the end of 20Y9, Allowance for Sales Discounts will be adjusted for expected sales discounts related to 20Y9 sales that will be taken in the next year.

Comparison with the Net Method

Both the gross method and the net method are acceptable under GAAP. However, the gross method is more complex in that it requires an adjusting entry and a contra asset account. Exhibit 15 shows a comparison of the gross and net methods using the NetSolutions sale of $18,000 illustrated earlier.

EXHIBIT 15

Gross Method versus Net Method

			Gross Method		Net Method	
Sale:						
20Y8						
Mar. 10		Accounts Receivable—Digital Technologies	18,000		17,640	
		Sales		18,000		17,640
	10	Cost of Merchandise Sold	10,800		10,800	
		Merchandise Inventory		10,800		10,800
Discount Taken:						
Mar. 19		Cash	17,640		17,640	
		Sales	360			
		Accounts Receivable—Digital Technologies		18,000		17,640
Discount Not Taken:						
Apr. 9		Cash	18,000		18,000	
		Sales				360
		Accounts Receivable—Digital Technologies		18,000		17,640
Adjusting Entry:						
Dec. 31		Sales	1,700		No entry[14]	
		Allowance for Sales Discounts		1,700		

14 Customers with accounts receivable balances at the end of the period may have credit terms such as 2/10, n/30. We assume that the amount of consideration expected to be received from these receivables is the "most likely amount," which is net of the discount. However, the discount period for a customer's account receivable may have expired by the end of the period, and thus, a customer may pay more than the net amount. Any such missed discounts are likely to be insignificant (immaterial). Therefore, we assume no adjusting entry is required under the net method.

APPENDIX 2

Describe and illustrate the accounting for merchandise returns.

Returns of Merchandise

In the chapter examples, customers received refunds or allowances for damaged or defective goods but were not required to return the merchandise. In some situations, customers may return merchandise for a cash refund or allowance. When this happens, two journal entries are required. The first entry records the cash refund or allowance as was illustrated in the chapter. The second entry records the receipt of the returned inventory.

To illustrate, assume that on July 15 Bormann Enterprises returned merchandise that was purchased from Schultz Company for $3,000. The merchandise originally cost Schultz Company $2,100. Schultz Company would record the cash refund and the return with the following two entries:

July	15	Customer Refunds Payable	3,000	
		Cash		3,000
	15	Merchandise Inventory	2,100	
		Esimated Returns Inventory		2,100

The first entry records the cash refund payment of $3,000, as illustrated in the chapter. If Bormann Enterprises had an outstanding accounts receivable balance on July 15, Schultz Company could have issued a $3,000 credit memo to Bormann Enterprises. In this case, the seller would have credited Accounts Receivable—Bormann Enterprises instead of Cash.

The second entry uses an estimated returns of merchandise account that is created by the following adjusting entry:

		Estimated Returns Inventory	XXX	
		Cost of Merchandise Sold		XXX

The preceding adjusting entry estimates the amount of merchandise that will be returned by customers. The **estimated returns inventory** account is debited and is reported as a current asset account after Merchandise Inventory on the balance sheet. Since merchandise returns decrease Sales, the related estimated cost of merchandise sold is decreased (credited) in the adjusting entry.

When Bormann Enterprises returns the merchandise on July 15, the Merchandise Inventory account is debited for the merchandise's original cost to Schultz Company of $2,100.[15]

The Estimated Returns Inventory is then credited for $2,100.

15 Because of wear, tear, and damage, companies may segregate returned items from normal inventory and debit an inventory account other than Merchandise Inventory. For example, Returned Inventory might be debited rather than Merchandise Inventory.

As indicated in the preceding paragraphs, sellers are required to estimate returns at the end of the accounting period. To illustrate, assume the following data for **NetSolutions** before any adjustments on December 31, 20Y9:

	Unadjusted Balances December 31, 20Y9	
	Debit	**Credit**
Sales		$715,409
Cost of Merchandise Sold	$523,505	
Estimated Returns Inventory	300	
Customer Refunds Payable		800
Estimates:		
Cost of merchandise returned in next year	$ 5,000	
Percent of sales refunds and allowances	1%	

Based upon the preceding data, NetSolutions would make the following two adjusting entries on December 31, 20Y9:

20Y9					
Dec.	31	Sales (1% × $715,409)		7,154	
		Customer Refunds Payable			7,154
	31	Estimated Returns Inventory		5,000	
		Cost of Merchandise Sold			5,000

As illustrated in the chapter, the first adjusting entry reduces 20Y9 sales by the amount of estimated refunds that may occur in 20Y0. Since 1% of sales are expected to be refunded, Sales is debited for $7,154 (1% × $715,409). In addition, a liability is recorded for $7,154 by crediting Customer Refunds Payable for the estimated customer refunds in 20Y0.

The second adjusting entry debits the asset Estimated Returns Inventory and reduces Cost of Merchandise Sold for the cost of merchandise that is expected to be returned in 20Y0 of $5,000. Estimated Returns Inventory is debited rather than Merchandise Inventory because the type of merchandise returned will not be known until the returns actually occur.

After the adjusting entries are posted to the ledger, Estimated Returns Inventory will have an adjusted balance of $5,300 ($300 + $5,000), and Customer Refunds Payable will have a balance of $7,954 ($800 + $7,154). Estimated returns inventory of $5,300 is reported on the balance sheet as a current asset following Merchandise Inventory. Customer refunds payable of $7,954 is reported as a current liability following Accounts Payable. The adjusting entries ensure that the current period sales are matched with the related cost of merchandise sold on the income statement.

APPENDIX 3

APP. 3 OBJ. Describe and illustrate the periodic method of accounting for merchandise transactions.

The Periodic Inventory System

Throughout this chapter, the perpetual inventory system was used to record purchases and sales of merchandise. Not all merchandise businesses, however, use the perpetual inventory system. For example, small merchandise businesses, such as a local hardware store, may use a manual accounting system. A manual perpetual inventory system is time-consuming and costly to maintain. For these reasons, a business may elect to use the periodic inventory system.

Under the periodic inventory system, purchases are normally recorded at their invoice amount. If the invoice is paid within the discount period, the discount is recorded in a separate account called Purchases Discounts. Likewise, purchases returns are recorded in a separate account called Purchases Returns and Allowances.

Chart of Accounts Under the Periodic Inventory System

The chart of accounts for **NetSolutions** under a periodic inventory system is shown in Exhibit 16. The accounts used to record transactions under the periodic inventory system are highlighted.

EXHIBIT 16
Chart of Accounts Under the Periodic Inventory System

Balance Sheet Accounts	Income Statement Accounts
100 Assets	400 Revenues
110 Cash	410 Sales
112 Accounts Receivable	500 Costs and Expenses
115 Merchandise Inventory	510 Purchases
117 Office Supplies	511 Purchases Returns and Allowances
118 Prepaid Insurance	512 Purchases Discounts
120 Land	513 Freight In
123 Store Equipment	520 Sales Salaries Expense
124 Accumulated Depreciation—Store Equipment	521 Advertising Expense
125 Office Equipment	522 Depreciation Expense—Store Equipment
126 Accumulated Depreciation—Office Equipment	523 Delivery Expense
200 Liabilities	529 Miscellaneous Selling Expense
210 Accounts Payable	530 Office Salaries Expense
211 Salaries Payable	531 Rent Expense
212 Unearned Rent	532 Depreciation Expense—Office Equipment
213 Customer Refunds Payable	533 Insurance Expense
215 Notes Payable	534 Office Supplies Expense
300 Owner's Equity	539 Misc. Administrative Expense
310 Chris Clark, Capital	600 Other Revenue
311 Chris Clark, Drawing	610 Rent Revenue
	700 Other Expense
	710 Interest Expense

Recording Merchandise Transactions Under the Periodic Inventory System

Using the periodic inventory system, purchases of inventory are not recorded in the merchandise inventory account. Instead, purchases, purchases discounts, and purchases returns and allowances accounts are used. In addition, the sales of merchandise are not recorded in the merchandise inventory account. Thus, there is no detailed record of the amount of inventory on hand at any given time. At the end of the period, a physical count of merchandise inventory on hand is taken. This physical count is used to determine the cost of merchandise sold, as will be illustrated later.

The use of purchases, purchases discounts, purchases returns and allowances, and freight in accounts are described in this section.

Purchases Purchases of inventory are recorded in a purchases account rather than in the merchandise inventory account. Purchases is debited for the invoice amount of a purchase.

Purchases Discounts Purchases discounts are normally recorded in a separate purchases discounts account. The balance of the purchases discounts account is reported as a deduction from Purchases for the period. Thus, Purchases Discounts is a contra (or offsetting) account to Purchases.

Purchases Returns and Allowances Purchases returns and allowances are recorded in a similar manner as purchases discounts. A separate purchases returns and allowances account is used to record returns and allowances. Purchases returns and allowances are reported as a deduction from Purchases for the period. Thus, Purchases Returns and Allowances is a contra (or offsetting) account to Purchases.

Freight In When merchandise is purchased FOB shipping point, the buyer pays for the freight. Under the periodic inventory system, freight paid when purchasing merchandise FOB shipping point is debited to Freight In, Transportation In, or a similar account.

The preceding periodic inventory accounts and their effect on the cost of merchandise purchased are summarized as follows:

Account	Entry to Increase	Normal Balance	Effect on Cost of Merchandise Purchased
Purchases	Debit	Debit	Increases
Purchases Discounts	Credit	Credit	Decreases
Purchases Returns and Allowances	Credit	Credit	Decreases
Freight In	Debit	Debit	Increases

Exhibit 17 illustrates the recording of merchandise transactions using the periodic system.

Adjusting Process Under the Periodic Inventory System

The adjusting process is the same under the periodic and perpetual inventory systems except for the inventory shrinkage adjustment and customer refunds and allowances. The ending inventory is determined by a physical count under both systems.

Under the perpetual inventory system, the ending inventory physical count is compared to the balance of Merchandise Inventory. The difference is the amount of inventory shrinkage. The inventory shrinkage is then recorded as a debit to Cost of Merchandise Sold and a credit to Merchandise Inventory.

EXHIBIT 17

Transactions Using the Periodic Inventory System

Transaction	Periodic Inventory System		
June 5. Purchased $30,000 of merchandise on account, terms 2/10, n/30.	Purchases	30,000	
	Accounts Payable		30,000
June 8. Returned merchandise purchased on account on June 5, $500.	Accounts Payable	500	
	Purchases Returns and Allowances		500
June 15. Paid for purchase of June 5, less return of $500 and discount of $590 [($30,000 – $500) × 2%].	Accounts Payable	29,500	
	Cash		28,910
	Purchases Discounts		590
June 18. Sold merchandise on account, $12,500, 1/10, n/30. The cost of the merchandise sold was $9,000.	Accounts Receivable [$12,500 – ($12,500 × 1%)]	12,375	
	Sales		12,375
June 22. Purchased merchandise, $15,000, terms FOB shipping point, 2/15, n/30, with prepaid freight of $750 added to the invoice.	Purchases	15,000	
	Freight In	750	
	Accounts Payable		15,750
June 28. Received payment on account from June 18 sale.	Cash	12,375	
	Accounts Receivable		12,375
June 29. Received $19,600 from cash sales. The cost of the merchandise sold was $13,800.	Cash	19,600	
	Sales		19,600

Under the periodic inventory system, the merchandise inventory account is not kept up to date for purchases and sales. As a result, the inventory shrinkage cannot be directly determined. Instead, any inventory shrinkage is included indirectly in the computation of the cost of merchandise sold as shown in Exhibit 18. This is a major disadvantage of the periodic inventory system. That is, inventory shrinkage is not separately determined.

Like the perpetual inventory system, the periodic system records the same adjusting entry debiting Sales and crediting Customer Refunds Payable for estimated customer refunds and allowances of $7,154.

Financial Statements Under the Periodic Inventory System

The financial statements are similar under the perpetual and periodic inventory systems. When the multiple-step format of income statement is used, the cost of merchandise sold may be reported as shown in Exhibit 18.

EXHIBIT 18

Determining Cost of Merchandise Sold Using Periodic Inventory

Merchandise inventory, January 1, 20Y8		$ 59,700
Cost of merchandise purchased:		
Purchases	$521,980	
Purchases returns and allowances	(9,100)	
Purchases discounts	(2,525)	
Net purchases	$510,355	
Freight in	17,700	
Total cost of merchandise purchased		528,055
Merchandise available for sale		$587,755
Merchandise inventory, December 31, 20Y8		(67,450)
Cost of merchandise sold		$520,305

Closing Entries Under the Periodic Inventory System

In the periodic inventory system, the purchases, purchases discounts, purchases returns and allowances, and freight in accounts are closed to Chris Clark, Capital. In addition, the merchandise inventory account is adjusted to the end-of-period physical inventory count during the closing process.

The two closing entries under the periodic inventory system are as follows:

1. a. Debit Merchandise Inventory for its end-of-period balance based on the physical inventory.
   b. Debit each revenue account and the following temporary periodic inventory accounts for their balances.
      - Purchases Discounts
      - Purchases Returns and Allowances
   c. Credit Merchandise Inventory for its balance as of the beginning of the period.
   d. Credit each expense account and the following temporary periodic inventory accounts for their balances.
      - Purchases
      - Freight In
   e. Credit the owner's capital account (Chris Clark, Capital) for the net income. Debit the owner's capital account for a net loss.
2. Debit the owner's capital account (Chris Clark, Capital) and credit the owner's drawing account (Chris Clark, Drawing) for its balance.

The two closing entries for NetSolutions under the periodic inventory system are shown in Exhibit 19.

In the first closing entry, Merchandise Inventory is debited for $67,450. This is the ending physical inventory count on December 31, 20Y8. Merchandise Inventory is credited for its January 1, 20Y8, balance of $59,700. In this way, the closing entries reflect the effects of the beginning and ending inventory in determining the cost of merchandise sold, as shown in Exhibit 18. After the closing entries are posted, Merchandise Inventory will have a balance of $67,450, which is the amount reported on the December 31, 20Y8, balance sheet.

EXHIBIT 19

Closing Entries: Periodic Method

Journal

Date		Item	Post. Ref.	Debit	Credit
20Y8		Closing Entries			
Dec.	31	Merchandise Inventory (December 31, 20Y8)	115	67,450	
		Sales	410	708,255	
		Purchases Returns and Allowances	511	9,100	
		Purchases Discounts	512	2,525	
		Rent Revenue	610	600	
		Merchandise Inventory (January 1, 20Y8)	115		59,700
		Purchases	510		521,980
		Freight In	513		17,700
		Sales Salaries Expense	520		53,430
		Advertising Expense	521		10,860
		Depreciation Expense—Store Equipment	522		3,100
		Delivery Expense	523		2,800
		Miscellaneous Selling Expense	529		630
		Office Salaries Expense	530		21,020
		Rent Expense	531		8,100
		Depreciation Expense—Office Equipment	532		2,490
		Insurance Expense	533		1,910
		Office Supplies Expense	534		610
		Miscellaneous Administrative Expense	539		760
		Interest Expense	710		2,440
		Chris Clark, Capital	310		80,400
	31	Chris Clark, Capital	310	18,000	
		Chris Clark, Drawing	311		18,000

In Exhibit 19, the periodic inventory accounts are highlighted. Under the perpetual inventory system, the highlighted periodic inventory accounts are replaced with the cost of merchandise sold account.

At a Glance 6

OBJ. 1 Distinguish between the activities and financial statements of service and merchandising businesses.

Key Points Merchandising businesses purchase merchandise for selling to customers. On a merchandising business's income statement, revenue from selling merchandise is reported as sales. The cost of the merchandise sold is subtracted from sales to arrive at gross profit. The operating expenses are subtracted from gross profit to arrive at net income. Merchandise inventory, which is merchandise not sold at the end of the accounting period, is reported as a current asset on the balance sheet.

Learning Outcomes	Example Exercises	Practice Exercises
• Describe how the activities of a service and a merchandising business differ.		
• Describe the differences between the income statements of a service and a merchandising business.		
• Compute gross profit.	EE6-1	PE6-1A, 6-1B
• Describe how merchandise inventory is reported on the balance sheet.		

OBJ. 2 Describe and illustrate the accounting for merchandise transactions.

Key Points A chart of accounts for a merchandising business differs from that of a service business. The chart of accounts for NetSolutions as a merchandising business is shown in Exhibit 2. Under the perpetual inventory system, purchases of merchandise for cash or on account are recorded as Merchandise Inventory. Discounts for early payment of purchases on account are purchases discounts. Purchases of merchandise inventory subject to purchase discounts are recorded net of the discount. Price adjustments for returned merchandise are purchases returns and allowances. Price adjustments for returned merchandise are recorded net of any purchase discount.

Sales of merchandise for cash or on account are recorded as sales. The cost of merchandise sold and the reduction in merchandise inventory are also recorded at the time of sale.

A seller may grant customers a variety of discounts, called customer discounts. A sales discount encourages customers to pay their invoice early. Sales subject to a sales discount are recorded net of the discount.

A seller may pay a customer a refund or grant a price allowance for damaged merchandise, called customer refunds and allowances. When a customer is granted a refund, Customer Refunds Payable is debited and Cash is credited for the amount of the refund. When a customer with an outstanding accounts receivable is granted an allowance, Customer Refunds Payable is debited and Accounts Receivable is credited.

When merchandise is shipped FOB shipping point, the buyer pays the freight and debits Merchandise Inventory. When merchandise is shipped FOB destination, the seller pays the freight and debits Delivery Expense or Freight Out. Merchandise transactions can be summarized in T account form as shown in Exhibit 9. Each merchandising transaction affects a buyer and a seller. The liability for sales tax is incurred when the sale is made and is recorded by the seller as a credit to the sales tax payable account. Trade discounts are discounts off the list price of merchandise.

Learning Outcomes	Example Exercises	Practice Exercises
• Prepare a chart of accounts for a merchandising business.		
• Prepare journal entries to record the purchases of merchandise for cash.		
• Prepare journal entries to record the purchases of merchandise on account.	EE6-2	PE6-2A, 6-2B
• Prepare journal entries to record purchases discounts and purchases returns and allowances.	EE6-2	PE6-2A, 6-2B
• Prepare journal entries to record sales of merchandise for cash or using a credit card.		
• Prepare journal entries to record sales of merchandise on account.	EE6-3	PE6-3A, 6-3B
• Prepare journal entries to record sales discounts and customer refunds and allowances.	EE6-3	PE6-3A, 6-3B
• Prepare journal entries for freight from the point of view of the buyer and seller.		
• Determine the total cost of the purchase of merchandise under differing freight terms.	EE6-4	PE6-4A, 6-4B
• Record the same merchandise transactions for the buyer and seller.	EE6-5	PE6-5A, 6-5B
• Determine the cost of merchandise purchased when a trade discount is offered by the seller.		
• Record sales transactions involving sales taxes and trade discounts.		

OBJ. 3 Describe and illustrate the adjusting process for a merchandising business.

Key Points The normal adjusting entry for inventory shrinkage is to debit Cost of Merchandise Sold and credit Merchandise Inventory. The adjusting entry for customer refunds and allowances debits Sales and credits Customer Refunds Payable.

Learning Outcomes	Example Exercises	Practice Exercises
• Prepare the adjusting journal entry for inventory shrinkage.	EE6-6	PE6-6A, 6-6B
• Prepare the adjusting journal entry for customer refunds and allowances.	EE6-7	PE6-7A, 6-7B

OBJ. 4 **Describe and illustrate the financial statements of a merchandising business.**

Key Points The multiple-step income statement of a merchandiser reports sales. The cost of the merchandise sold is subtracted from sales to determine the gross profit. Operating income is determined by subtracting selling and administrative expenses from gross profit. Net income is determined by adding or subtracting the net of other revenue and expense. The income statement may also be reported in a single-step form.

The statement of owner's equity is similar to that for a service business.

The balance sheet reports merchandise inventory at the end of the period as a current asset. Also, customer refunds payable is reported as a current liability.

The closing entries for a merchandising business are similar to those for a service business except that the cost of merchandise sold is also closed.

Learning Outcomes	Example Exercises	Practice Exercises
• Prepare a multiple-step income statement for a merchandising business.		
• Prepare a single-step income statement.		
• Prepare a statement of owner's equity for a merchandising business.		
• Prepare a balance sheet for a merchandising business.		
• Prepare the closing entries for a merchandising business.		

OBJ. 5 **Describe and illustrate the use of asset turnover in evaluating a company's operating performance.**

Key Points Asset turnover measures how effectively a business is using its assets to generate sales. A high ratio indicates an effective use of assets. Asset turnover is computed as follows:

$$\text{Asset Turnover} = \frac{\text{Sales}}{\text{Average Total Assets}}$$

Learning Outcomes	Example Exercises	Practice Exercises
• Interpret a high asset turnover.		
• Compute the asset turnover.	**EE6-8**	**PE6-8A, 6-8B**

Illustrative Problem

The following transactions were completed by Montrose Company during May of the current year. Montrose Company uses a perpetual inventory system.

May 3. Purchased merchandise on account from Floyd Co., $4,000, terms FOB shipping point, 2/10, n/30, with prepaid freight of $120 added to the invoice.

5. Purchased merchandise on account from Kramer Co., $8,500, terms FOB destination, 1/10, n/30.

6. Sold merchandise on account to C. F. Howell Co., list price $4,000, trade discount 30%, terms 2/10, n/30. The cost of the merchandise sold was $1,125.

(Continued)

May 8. Purchased office supplies for cash, $150.

10. Returned merchandise purchased on May 5 from Kramer Co., $1,300.

13. Paid Floyd Co. on account for purchase of May 3.

14. Purchased merchandise for cash, $10,500.

15. Paid Kramer Co. on account for purchase of May 5, less return of May 10.

16. Received cash on account from sale of May 6 to C. F. Howell Co.

19. Sold merchandise on MasterCard credit cards, $2,450. The cost of the merchandise sold was $980.

22. Sold merchandise for cash to Comer Co., $3,480. The cost of the merchandise sold was $1,400.

24. Sold merchandise on account to Smith Co., $4,350, terms n/30. The cost of the merchandise sold was $1,750.

25. Refunded Comer Co. $600 for damaged merchandise from sale on May 22. Comer Co. agreed to keep the merchandise.

31. Paid a service processing fee of $140 for MasterCard sales.

Instructions

1. Journalize the preceding transactions.
2. Journalize the adjusting entry for merchandise inventory shrinkage, $3,750.
3. Journalize the adjusting entries for estimated customer refunds and allowances. Assume that sales of $3,000 are estimated to be refunded.

Solution

1.	May	3	Merchandise Inventory [$4,000 – ($4,000 × 2%)] + $120	4,040	
			Accounts Payable—Floyd Co.		4,040
		5	Merchandise Inventory [$8,500 – ($8,500 × 1%)]	8,415	
			Accounts Payable—Kramer Co.		8,415
		6	Accounts Receivable—C. F. Howell Co.	2,744	
			Sales		2,744
			[$4,000 – (30% × $4,000)] = $2,800		
			[$2,800 – ($2,800 × 2%)] = $2,744		
		6	Cost of Merchandise Sold	1,125	
			Merchandise Inventory		1,125
		8	Office Supplies	150	
			Cash		150
		10	Accounts Payable—Kramer Co. [$1,300 – ($1,300 × 1%)]	1,287	
			Merchandise Inventory		1,287
		13	Accounts Payable—Floyd Co.	4,040	
			Cash		4,040
		14	Merchandise Inventory	10,500	
			Cash		10,500
		15	Accounts Payable—Kramer Co. ($8,415 – $1,287)	7,128	
			Cash		7,128
		16	Cash	2,744	
			Accounts Receivable—C. F. Howell Co.		2,744
		19	Cash	2,450	
			Sales		2,450
		19	Cost of Merchandise Sold	980	
			Merchandise Inventory		980
		22	Cash	3,480	
			Sales		3,480

	May 22	Cost of Merchandise Sold	1,400	
		Merchandise Inventory		1,400
	24	Accounts Receivable—Smith Co.	4,350	
		Sales		4,350
	24	Cost of Merchandise Sold	1,750	
		Merchandise Inventory		1,750
	25	Customer Refunds Payable	600	
		Cash		600
	31	Credit Card Expense	140	
		Cash		140
2.	May 31	Cost of Merchandise Sold	3,750	
		Merchandise Inventory		3,750
3.	May 31	Sales	3,000	
		Customer Refunds Payable		3,000

Key Terms

administrative expenses (general expenses) (300)
asset turnover (303)
cash refund (290)
cost of merchandise sold (281)
credit memorandum (credit memo) (290)
credit period (284)
credit terms (284)
customer allowance (290)
customer discounts (289)
customer refunds payable (290)
debit memorandum (debit memo) (286)
estimated returns inventory (308)
FOB (free on board) destination (292)
FOB (free on board) shipping point (292)
gross method (of recording sales discounts) (305)
gross profit (281)
income from operations (operating income) (300)
inventory shrinkage (inventory shortage) (297)
invoice (284)
merchandise inventory (281)
multiple-step income statement (299)
operating cycle (280)
other expense (300)
other revenue (300)
periodic inventory system (283)
perpetual inventory system (283)
physical inventory (283)
purchases discounts (285)
purchases returns and allowances (286)
sales (281)
sales discount (289)
selling expenses (300)
single-step income statement (301)
trade discounts (297)
wholesalers (297)

Discussion Questions

1. What distinguishes a merchandising business from a service business?
2. Can a business earn a gross profit but incur a net loss? Explain.
3. The credit period during which the buyer of merchandise is allowed to pay usually begins with what date?
4. What is the meaning of (a) 1/15, n/60; (b) n/30; (c) n/eom?
5. How are sales to customers using MasterCard and VISA recorded?
6. What is the nature of (a) a credit memo issued by the seller of merchandise, (b) a debit memo issued by the buyer of merchandise?

7. Who bears the freight when the terms of sale are (a) FOB shipping point, (b) FOB destination?

8. Name three accounts that would normally appear in the chart of accounts of a merchandising business but would not appear in the chart of accounts of a service business.

9. Audio Outfitter Inc., which uses a perpetual inventory system, experienced a normal inventory shrinkage of $13,675. What accounts would be debited and credited to record the adjustment for the inventory shrinkage at the end of the accounting period?

10. Assume that Audio Outfitter Inc. in Discussion Question 9 experienced an abnormal inventory shrinkage of $98,600. Audio Outfitter Inc. has decided to record the abnormal inventory shrinkage so that it would be disclosed separately on the income statement. What account would be debited for the abnormal inventory shrinkage?

Practice Exercises

Example Exercises

EE 6-1 *p. 282*

PE 6-1A Gross profit

OBJ. 1

During the current year, merchandise is sold for $366,100 cash and $1,420,000 on account. The cost of the merchandise sold is $1,014,300. What is the amount of the gross profit?

EE 6-1 *p. 282*

PE 6-1B Gross profit

OBJ. 1

During the current year, merchandise is sold for $21,100 cash and $341,700 on account. The cost of the merchandise sold is $217,200. What is the amount of the gross profit?

EE 6-2 *p. 288*

PE 6-2A Purchases transactions

OBJ. 2

Flounder Company purchased merchandise on account from a supplier for $32,100, terms 2/10, n/30. Flounder Company returned $8,600 of the merchandise and received full credit.

a. If Flounder Company pays the invoice within the discount period, what is the amount of cash required for the payment?

b. What account is credited by Flounder Company to record the return?

EE 6-2 *p. 288*

PE 6-2B Purchases transactions

OBJ. 2

Wiseman Company purchased merchandise on account from a supplier for $85,000, terms 1/10, n/30. Wiseman Company returned $9,800 of the merchandise and received full credit.

a. If Wiseman Company pays the invoice within the discount period, what is the amount of cash required for the payment?

b. What account is debited by Wiseman Company to record the return?

EE 6-3 *p. 291*

PE 6-3A Sales transactions

OBJ. 2

Journalize the following merchandise transactions:

a. Sold merchandise on account, $94,800 with terms 2/10, n/30. The cost of the merchandise sold was $56,900.

b. Received payment less the discount.

c. Issued a $500 credit memo for damaged merchandise. The customer agreed to keep the merchandise.

SHOW ME HOW

EE 6-3 *p. 291*

PE 6-3B Sales transactions **OBJ. 2**

Journalize the following merchandise transactions:

a. Sold merchandise on account, $78,600 with terms 1/10, n/30. The cost of the merchandise sold was $47,200.

b. Received payment less the discount.

c. Issued a $900 credit memo for damaged merchandise. The customer agreed to keep the merchandise.

SHOW ME HOW

EE 6-4 *p. 294*

PE 6-4A Freight terms **OBJ. 2**

Determine the amount to be paid in full settlement of each of two invoices, (a) and (b), assuming that credit for returns and allowances was received prior to payment and that all invoices were paid within the discount period.

	Merchandise	Freight Paid by Seller	Freight Terms	Credit for Refunds and Allowances
a.	$120,800	$1,300	FOB shipping point, 1/10, n/30	$20,100
b.	147,700	2,100	FOB destination, 2/10, n/30	11,400

SHOW ME HOW

EE 6-4 *p. 294*

PE 6-4B Freight terms **OBJ. 2**

Determine the amount to be paid in full settlement of each of two invoices, (a) and (b), assuming that credit for returns and allowances was received prior to payment and that all invoices were paid within the discount period.

	Merchandise	Freight Paid by Seller	Freight Terms	Credit for Refunds and Allowances
a.	$58,600	$1,300	FOB destination, 1/10, n/30	$6,500
b.	73,100	600	FOB shipping point, 2/10, n/30	3,900

SHOW ME HOW

EE 6-5 *p. 296*

PE 6-5A Transactions for buyer and seller **OBJ. 2**

Sally Co. sold merchandise to Buck Co. on account, $58,900, terms 2/15, n/30. The cost of the merchandise sold is $35,200. Journalize the entries for Sally Co. and Buck Co. for the sale, purchase, and payment of amount due. Assume that all discounts are taken.

SHOW ME HOW

EE 6-5 *p. 296*

PE 6-5B Transactions for buyer and seller **OBJ. 2**

Statham Co. sold merchandise to Bloomingdale Co. on account, $147,600, terms FOB shipping point, 2/10, n/30. The cost of the merchandise sold is $88,600. Statham Co. paid freight of $2,400. Journalize the entries for Statham Co. and Bloomingdale Co. for the sale, purchase, and payment of amount due. Assume that all discounts are taken.

SHOW ME HOW

EE 6-6 *p. 298*

PE 6-6A Inventory shrinkage **OBJ. 3**

Novelty Furnishings Company's perpetual inventory records indicate that $755,000 of merchandise should be on hand on November 30, 20Y1. The physical inventory indicates that $742,000 of merchandise is actually on hand. Journalize the adjusting entry for the inventory shrinkage for Novelty Furnishings Company for the year ended November 30, 20Y1. Assume that the inventory shrinkage is a normal amount.

SHOW ME HOW

EE 6-6 *p. 298*

PE 6-6B Inventory shrinkage **OBJ. 3**

Stanley Flooring Company's perpetual inventory records indicate that $1,129,000 of merchandise should be on hand on December 31, 20Y1. The physical inventory indicates that $1,109,300 of merchandise is actually on hand. Journalize the adjusting entry for the inventory shrinkage for Stanley Flooring Company for the year ended December 31, 20Y1. Assume that the inventory shrinkage is a normal amount.

SHOW ME HOW

EE 6-7 *p. 299*

PE 6-7A Customer refunds and allowances

OBJ. 3

Assume the following data for Lusk Inc. before its year-end adjustments:

Sales for the year	$3,600,000
Estimated percent of refunds for the year	0.8%

Journalize the adjusting entry for customer refunds and allowances.

SHOW ME HOW

EE 6-7 *p. 299*

PE 6-7B Customer refunds and allowances

OBJ. 3

Assume the following data for Casper Company before its year-end adjustments:

Sales for the year	$1,750,000
Estimated percent of refunds for the year	0.6%

Journalize the adjusting entry for customer refunds and allowances.

SHOW ME HOW

EE 6-8 *p. 304*

PE 6-8A Asset turnover

OBJ. 5

FAI

Financial statement data for the years ending December 31, 20Y3 and 20Y2, for Linstrum Company follow:

	20Y3	20Y2
Sales	$2,310,000	$2,278,000
Total assets:		
Beginning of year	680,000	660,000
End of year	720,000	680,000

a. Determine the asset turnover for 20Y3 and 20Y2.

b. Is the change in the asset turnover from 20Y2 to 20Y3 favorable or unfavorable?

SHOW ME HOW

EE 6-8 *p. 304*

PE 6-8B Asset turnover

OBJ. 5

FAI

EXCEL ONLINE

Financial statement data for the years ending December 31, 20Y3 and 20Y2, for Lawson Company follow:

	20Y3	20Y2
Sales	$663,000	$516,000
Total assets:		
Beginning of year	240,000	190,000
End of year	270,000	240,000

a. Determine the asset turnover for 20Y3 and 20Y2.

b. Is the change in the asset turnover from 20Y2 to 20Y3 favorable or unfavorable?

Exercises

SHOW ME HOW

EXCEL ONLINE

EX 6-1 Determining gross profit

OBJ. 1

During the current year, merchandise is sold for $45,870,000. The cost of the merchandise sold is $33,026,400.

a. What is the amount of the gross profit?

b. Compute the gross profit percentage (gross profit divided by sales).

c. Will the income statement necessarily report a net income? Explain.

EX 6-2 Determining cost of merchandise sold OBJ. 1

For a recent year, **Best Buy** reported sales of $42,879 million. Its gross profit was $9,961 million. What was the amount of Best Buy's cost of merchandise sold?

EX 6-3 Chart of accounts OBJ. 2

Monet Paints Co. is a newly organized business with a list of accounts arranged in alphabetical order, as follows:

Accounts Payable	Merchandise Inventory
Accounts Receivable	Miscellaneous Administrative Expense
Accumulated Depreciation—Office Equipment	Miscellaneous Selling Expense
Accumulated Depreciation—Store Equipment	Notes Payable
Advertising Expense	Office Equipment
Cash	Office Salaries Expense
Cost of Merchandise Sold	Office Supplies
Customer Refunds Payable	Office Supplies Expense
Delivery Expense	Prepaid Insurance
Depreciation Expense—Office Equipment	Rent Expense
Depreciation Expense—Store Equipment	Salaries Payable
Insurance Expense	Sales
Interest Expense	Sales Salaries Expense
Kailey Garner, Capital	Store Equipment
Kailey Garner, Drawing	Store Supplies
Land	Store Supplies Expense

Construct a chart of accounts, assigning account numbers and arranging the accounts in balance sheet and income statement order, as illustrated in Exhibit 2. Each account number is three digits: the first digit is to indicate the major classification (1 for assets, for example); the second digit is to indicate the subclassification (11 for current assets, for example); and the third digit is to identify the specific account (110 for Cash, 112 for Accounts Receivable, 114 for Merchandise Inventory, etc.).

EX 6-4 Purchase-related transactions OBJ. 2

Oppenheimer Company purchased merchandise on account from a supplier for $84,000, terms 1/10, n/30. Oppenheimer Company returned $16,000 of the merchandise and received full credit.

a. What is the amount of cash required for the payment within the discount period?

b. Under a perpetual inventory system, what account is credited by Oppenheimer Company to record the return?

EX 6-5 Purchase-related transactions OBJ. 2

A retailer is considering the purchase of 500 units of a specific item from either of two suppliers. Their offers are as follows:

Supplier One: $40 a unit, total of $20,000, 1/10, n/30, no charge for freight.

Supplier Two: $39 a unit, total of $19,500, 2/10, n/30, plus freight of $500.

Which of the two offers, Supplier One or Supplier Two, yields the lower price?

EX 6-6 Purchase-related transactions **OBJ. 2**

The debits and credits for four related entries for a purchase of $40,000, terms 2/10, n/30, are presented in the following T accounts. Describe each transaction.

Cash

		(2)	450
		(4)	34,300

Accounts Payable

(3)	4,900	(1)	39,200
(4)	34,300		

Merchandise Inventory

(1)	39,200	(3)	4,900
(2)	450		

EX 6-7 Purchase-related transactions **OBJ. 2**

✔ c. Cash, cr. $45,080

SHOW ME HOW

Poff's Co., a women's clothing store, purchased $53,000 of merchandise from a supplier on account, terms FOB destination, 2/10, n/30. Poff's returned $7,000 of the merchandise, receiving a credit memo, and then paid the amount due within the discount period. Journalize Poff's entries to record (a) the purchase, (b) the merchandise return, and (c) the payment.

EX 6-8 Purchase-related transactions **OBJ. 2**

✔ e. Cash, dr. $4,480

SHOW ME HOW

Journalize entries for the following related transactions of Greenville Heating & Air Company:

a. Purchased $57,000 of merchandise from Foster Co. on account, terms 2/10, n/30.

b. Paid the amount owed on the invoice within the discount period.

c. Discovered that $11,000 of the merchandise purchased in (a) was defective and returned items, receiving credit for $10,780 [$11,000 − ($11,000 × 2%)].

d. Purchased $6,300 of merchandise from Foster Co. on account, terms n/30.

e. Received a refund from Foster Co. for return in (c) less the purchase in (d).

EX 6-9 Sales-related transactions, including the use of credit cards **OBJ. 2**

SHOW ME HOW

Journalize the entries for the following transactions:

a. Sold merchandise for cash, $116,300. The cost of the merchandise sold was $72,000.

b. Sold merchandise on account, $755,000. The cost of the merchandise sold was $400,000.

c. Sold merchandise to customers who used MasterCard and VISA, $1,950,000. The cost of the merchandise sold was $1,250,000.

d. Sold merchandise to customers who used American Express, $330,000. The cost of the merchandise sold was $230,000.

e. Paid $81,500 to National Clearing House Credit Co. for service fees for processing MasterCard, VISA, and American Express sales.

EX 6-10 Sales-related transactions **OBJ. 2**

SHOW ME HOW

After the amount due on a sale of $28,000, terms 2/10, n/eom, is received from a customer within the discount period, the seller consents to a $3,000 cash refund for defective merchandise. Journalize the entry to record the cash refund.

EX 6-11 Sales-related transactions **OBJ. 2**

The debits and credits for four related entries for a sale of $15,000, terms 1/10, n/30, are presented in the following T accounts. Describe each transaction.

Cash

	Debit		Credit
(4)	14,400		

Accounts Receivable

	Debit		Credit
(1)	14,850	(3)	450
		(4)	14,400

Merchandise Inventory

	Debit		Credit
		(2)	8,800

Customer Refunds Payable

	Debit		Credit
(3)	450		

Sales

	Debit		Credit
		(1)	14,850

Cost of Merchandise Sold

	Debit		Credit
(2)	8,800		

EX 6-12 Sales-related transactions **OBJ. 2**

✔ c. $57,470

SHOW ME HOW

Merchandise is sold on account to a customer for $56,500, terms FOB shipping point, 2/10, n/30. The seller paid the freight of $2,100. Determine the following: (a) amount of the sale, (b) amount debited to Accounts Receivable, and (c) amount received within the discount period.

EX 6-13 Determining amounts to be paid on invoices **OBJ. 2**

✔ a. $15,700

SHOW ME HOW

EXCEL ONLINE

Determine the amount to be paid in full settlement of each of the following invoices, assuming that credit for returns and allowances was received prior to payment and that all invoices were paid within the discount period:

	Merchandise	Freight Paid by Seller		Customer Refunds and Allowances
a.	$20,500	—	FOB destination, n/30	$4,800
b.	31,100	$560	FOB shipping point, 2/10, n/30	5,900
c.	24,000	—	FOB shipping point, 1/10, n/30	1,300
d.	11,000	370	FOB shipping point, 2/10, n/30	1,800
e.	42,200	—	FOB destination, 1/10, n/30	—

EX 6-14 Sales-related transactions **OBJ. 2**

SHOW ME HOW

Showcase Co., a furniture wholesaler, sells merchandise to Balboa Co. on account, $254,500, terms n/30. The cost of the merchandise sold is $152,700. Showcase Co. issues a credit memo for $30,000 as a price adjustment prior to Balboa Co. paying the original invoice. Journalize Showcase Co.'s entries for (a) the sale, including the cost of the merchandise sold; (b) the credit memo; and (c) the receipt of the check for the amount due from Balboa Co.

EX 6-15 Purchase-related transactions **OBJ. 2**

SHOW ME HOW

Based on the data presented in Exercise 6-14, journalize Balboa Co.'s entries for (a) the purchase, (b) the credit memo, and (c) the payment of the invoice.

EX 6-16 Sales tax **OBJ. 2**

✔ c. $38,880

SHOW ME HOW

A sale of merchandise on account for $36,000 is subject to an 8% sales tax. (a) Should the sales tax be recorded at the time of sale or when payment is received? (b) What is the amount recorded as sales? (c) What is the amount debited to Accounts Receivable? (d) What is the title of the account to which the $2,880 ($36,000 × 8%) is credited?

EX 6-17 Sales tax transactions **OBJ. 2**

Journalize the entries to record the following selected transactions:

a. Sold $62,800 of merchandise on account, subject to a sales tax of 5%. The cost of the merchandise sold was $37,500.

b. Paid $39,650 to the state sales tax department for taxes collected.

EX 6-18 Normal balances of merchandise accounts **OBJ. 2**

What is the normal balance of the following accounts: (a) Cost of Merchandise Sold, (b) Customer Refunds Payable, (c) Delivery Expense, (d) Merchandise Inventory, (e) Sales, (f) Sales Tax Payable.

EX 6-19 Adjusting entry for merchandise inventory shrinkage **OBJ. 3**

Paragon Tire Co.'s perpetual inventory records indicate that $2,780,000 of merchandise should be on hand on March 31, 20Y9. The physical inventory indicates that $2,734,800 of merchandise is actually on hand. Journalize the adjusting entry for the inventory shrinkage for Paragon Tire Co. for the year ended March 31, 20Y9.

EX 6-20 Adjusting entries for customer refunds and allowances **OBJ. 3**

Assume the following data for Oshkosh Company before its year-end adjustments:

Sales	$51,600,000
Estimated percent of refunds and allowances for current year sales	1.2%

Journalize the adjusting entry for customer refunds and allowances.

EX 6-21 Customer refunds and allowances **OBJ. 2, 3**

Zell Company had sales of $1,800,000 and related cost of merchandise sold of $1,150,000 for its first year of operations ending December 31, 20Y3. Zell Company provides customers refunds and allowances for any damaged merchandise. At the end of the year, Zell Company estimates that customers will request refunds and allowances for 1.5% of sales. Assume that on February 3, 20Y4, Zell Company paid a customer a $5,000 cash refund for damaged merchandise. (a) Journalize the adjusting entry on December 31, 20Y3, to record the expected customer refunds and allowances. (b) Journalize the entry to record the cash refund.

EX 6-22 Income statement and accounts for merchandiser **OBJ. 4**

For the fiscal year, sales were $191,350,000 and the cost of merchandise sold was $114,800,000.

a. What was the amount of gross profit?

b. If total operating expenses were $18,250,000, could you determine net income?

c. Is Customer Refunds Payable an asset, liability, or owner's equity account, and what is its normal balance?

EX 6-23 Income statement for merchandiser **OBJ. 4**

The following expenses were incurred by a merchandising business during the year. In which expense section of the income statement should each be reported: (a) selling, (b) administrative, or (c) other?

1. Advertising expense
2. Depreciation expense on store equipment

3. Insurance expense on office equipment
4. Interest expense on notes payable
5. Rent expense on office building
6. Salaries of office personnel
7. Salary of sales manager
8. Sales supplies used

SHOW ME HOW

EXCEL ONLINE

EX 6-24 Determining amounts for items omitted from income statement **OBJ. 4**

One item is omitted in each of the following four lists of income statement data. Determine the amounts of the missing items, identifying them by letter.

Sales	$463,400	(b)	$1,295,000	(d)
Cost of merchandise sold	(a)	$410,000	(c)	$900,000
Gross profit	83,500	277,500	275,000	600,000

✔ a. Net income: $751,000

SHOW ME HOW

EX 6-25 Multiple-step income statement **OBJ. 4**

On March 31, 20Y4, the balances of the accounts appearing in the ledger of Danns Furnishings Company, a furniture wholesaler, are as follows:

Accumulated Depreciation—Building	$ 419,000	Merchandise Inventory	$ 547,000
Administrative Expenses	302,000	Notes Payable	140,000
Building	1,397,000	Office Supplies	11,000
Cash	98,000	Salaries Payable	4,000
Cost of Merchandise Sold	2,123,000	Sales	3,582,000
Interest Expense	6,000	Selling Expenses	400,000
Kathy Melman, Capital	887,000	Store Supplies	50,000
Kathy Melman, Drawing	98,000		

a. Prepare a multiple-step income statement for the year ended March 31, 20Y4.

b. Compare the major advantages and disadvantages of the multiple-step and single-step forms of income statements.

EX 6-26 Multiple-step income statement **OBJ. 4**

Identify the errors in the following income statement:

Curbstone Company
Income Statement
For the Year Ended August 31, 20Y5

Sales		$8,595,000
Cost of merchandise sold		6,110,000
Income from operations		$2,485,000
Expenses:		
Selling expenses	$800,000	
Administrative expenses	575,000	
Delivery expense	425,000	
Total expenses		1,800,000
		$ 685,000
Other expense:		
Interest revenue		45,000
Gross profit		$ 640,000

EX 6-27 Single-step income statement OBJ. 4

✔ Net income: $1,277,500

Summary operating data for Custom Wire & Tubing Company during the year ended April 30, 20Y6, are as follows: cost of merchandise sold, $6,100,000; administrative expenses, $740,000; interest expense, $25,000; rent revenue, $60,000; sales, $9,332,500; and selling expenses, $1,250,000. Prepare a single-step income statement.

EX 6-28 Closing the accounts of a merchandiser OBJ. 4

From the following list, identify the accounts that should be closed to Tim Button, Capital at the end of the fiscal year under a perpetual inventory system: (a) Accounts Receivable, (b) Cost of Merchandise Sold, (c) Customer Refunds Payable, (d) Delivery Expense, (e) Merchandise Inventory, (f) Sales, (g) Supplies, (h) Supplies Expense, (i) Tim Button, Drawing, (j) Wages Expense.

EX 6-29 Closing entries; net income OBJ. 4

Based on the data presented in Exercise 6-25, journalize the closing entries.

EX 6-30 Closing entries OBJ. 4

On July 31, 20Y7, the balances of the accounts appearing in the ledger of Yang Interiors Company, a furniture wholesaler, are as follows:

Accumulated Depr.—Building	$443,000	Peter Bronsky, Capital	$ 644,000
Administrative Expenses	534,000	Peter Bronsky, Drawing	18,000
Building	984,000	Sales	1,745,000
Cash	95,000	Sales Tax Payable	4,500
Cost of Merchandise Sold	941,000	Selling Expenses	194,000
Interest Expense	7,000	Store Supplies	19,000
Merchandise Inventory	140,000	Store Supplies Expense	25,500
Notes Payable	121,000		

Prepare the July 31, 20Y7, closing entries for Yang Interiors Company.

EX 6-31 Asset turnover OBJ. 5

The Home Depot reported the following data (in millions) in its recent financial statements:

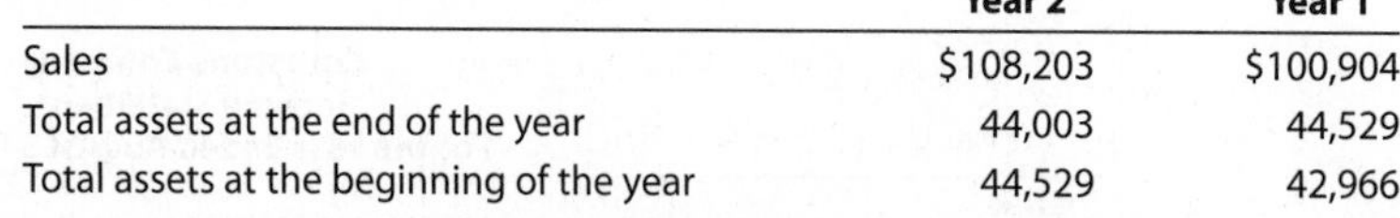

	Year 2	Year 1
Sales	$108,203	$100,904
Total assets at the end of the year	44,003	44,529
Total assets at the beginning of the year	44,529	42,966

a. Determine the asset turnover for The Home Depot for Year 2 and Year 1. Round to two decimal places.

b. What conclusions can be drawn concerning the trend in the ability of The Home Depot to effectively use its assets to generate sales?

EX 6-32 Asset turnover OBJ. 5

Kroger Co., a national supermarket chain, reported the following data (in millions) in its financial statements for a recent year:

Total revenue	$121,162
Total assets at end of year	38,118
Total assets at beginning of year	37,197

a. Compute the asset turnover. Round to two decimal places.

b. **Tiffany & Co.** is a large North American retailer of jewelry with an asset turnover of 0.82. Why would Tiffany's asset turnover be lower than that of Kroger?

Appendix 1
EX 6-33 Gross method for sales discounts

Schofield Co. sold merchandise on account to Bernard Retail Inc. for $15,000, terms 2/10, n/30. The cost of the merchandise sold was $8,000. Assuming Schofield Co. uses the gross method of recording sales discounts, journalize the entries to record (a) the sale, (b) the receipt of payment assuming it is made within the discount period, and (c) the receipt of payment assuming it is made beyond the discount period.

Appendix 1
EX 6-34 Gross method for sales discounts

The following were selected from among the transactions completed by Essex Company during March of the current year:

Mar. 2. Sold merchandise on account to Parsley Co., $32,000, terms 1/10, n/30. The cost of the merchandise sold was $18,500.

8. Sold merchandise on account to Tabor Co., $24,000, terms 2/10, n/30. The cost of the merchandise sold was $14,400.

11. Received payment on account for the sale of March 2 less the discount.

20. Received payment on account for the sale of March 8.

Journalize the March transactions using the gross method of recording sales discounts.

Appendix 1
EX 6-35 Adjusting entry for gross method

The following data were extracted from the accounting records of Sacajawea Mercantile Co. for the year ended June 30, 20Y4:

	June 30, 20Y4 Balances	
	Debit	**Credit**
Sales		$10,000,000
Accounts Receivable	$850,000	
Allowance for Sales Discounts		400
Estimated sales discounts that will be taken in fiscal year ending June 30, 20Y5	$ 7,000	

a. Journalize the June 30, 20Y4, adjusting entry for estimated sales discounts.
b. How would sales and accounts receivable be reported on the financial statements for the year ending June 30, 20Y4?

Appendix 1
EX 6-36 Discount taken in next fiscal year

Using the data for Sacajawea Mercantile Co. in Exercise 6-35, assume that Mark Bishop pays his June 30, 20Y4, account receivable of $1,500 on July 6, 20Y4, and takes a 2% sales discount. Journalize the entry to record the payment on account from Mark Bishop.

Appendix 1
EX 6-37 Gross and net methods for sales discounts

The following were selected from among the transactions completed by Strong Retail Group during August of the current year:

Aug. 5. Sold merchandise on account to M. Quinn, $7,500, terms 2/10, n/30. The cost of the merchandise sold was $4,200.

9. Sold merchandise on account to R. Busch., $4,000, terms 1/10, n/30. The cost of the merchandise sold was $2,100.

(Continued)

Aug. 15. Received payment on account for the sale of August 5 less the discount.

20. Sold merchandise on account to S. Mooney, $6,000, terms n/eom. The cost of the merchandise sold was $3,300.

25. Received payment on account for the sale of August 9.

31. Received payment on account for the sale of August 20.

a. Journalize the August transactions using the gross method of recording sales discounts.

b. Journalize the August transactions using the net method of recording sales discounts.

c. What is the total sales for August under each method?

d. Which method of recording sales discounts requires an end-of-period adjusting entry?

Appendix 2
EX 6-38 Customer refunds, allowances, and returns

On February 18, Silverman Enterprises sold $24,000 of merchandise to Brewster Co. with terms 2/10, n/30. The cost of the merchandise sold was $12,200. On February 23, Silverman Enterprises issued Brewster Co. a credit memo for returned merchandise. The invoice amount of the returned merchandise was $3,000, and the merchandise originally cost Silverman Enterprises $1,800.

a. Journalize the entries by Silverman Enterprises to record the February 18 sale.

b. Journalize the entries by Silverman Enterprises to record the merchandise returned by Brewster Co. on February 23.

c. Journalize the entry by Silverman Enterprises to record the payment of the amount due by Brewster on February 28.

Appendix 2
EX 6-39 Customer refunds, allowances, and returns

On April 23, Stilwell Inc. sold $15,000 of merchandise to Bosch Inc. with terms 2/10, n/30. The cost of the merchandise sold was $9,000. On May 2, Bosch Inc. paid Stilwell for the April 23 purchase less the discount. On May 11, Bosch Inc. returned merchandise to Stilwell Inc. and received a cash refund. The invoice amount of the returned merchandise was $2,500, and the merchandise originally cost Stilwell Inc. $1,300.

a. Journalize the entries by Stilwell Inc. to record the April 23 sale.

b. Journalize the entry by Stilwell Inc. to record the payment by Bosch Inc. on May 2.

c. Journalize the entries by Stilwell Inc. on May 11 to record the cash refund to Bosch Inc. and the returned merchandise.

d. How are Estimated Returns Inventory and Customer Refunds Payable reported on the financial statements of Stilwell Inc.?

Appendix 2
EX 6-40 Adjusting entries for customer refunds, allowances, and returns

Simons Company had sales of $24,000,000 and related cost of goods sold of $13,300,000 for its first year of operations ending December 31, 20Y6. Simons Company provides customers a refund for any returned or damaged merchandise. At the end of 20Y6, Simons Company estimates that customers will request refunds for 1.1% of sales and that merchandise costing $150,000 will be returned. Journalize the adjusting entries on December 31, 20Y6, to record the expected customer returns.

Appendix 2
EX 6-41 Adjusting entries for customer refunds, allowances, and returns

Swartz Company had sales of $7,800,000 and related cost of goods sold of $4,500,000 for its first year of operations ending December 31, 20Y3. Swartz Company provides customers a refund for any returned or damaged merchandise. At the end of 20Y3, Swartz Company estimates that customers will request refunds for 1.8% of sales and that merchandise costing $90,000 will be returned. Journalize the adjusting entries on December 31, 20Y3, to record the expected customer returns.

Appendix 2
EX 6-42 Adjusting entry for customer refunds, allowances, and returns; customer refund

Sinclair Company had sales of $12,000,000 and related cost of merchandise sold of $7,200,000 for its first year of operations ending December 31, 20Y1. Sinclair Company provides customers a refund for any returned or damaged merchandise. At the end of 20Y1, Sinclair Company estimates that customers will request refunds for 1.5% of sales and that merchandise costing $120,000 will be returned. Assume that on February 15, 20Y2, Brown Co. returned merchandise with an invoice amount of $8,000 for a cash refund. The returned merchandise originally cost Sinclair Company $5,500. (a) Journalize the adjusting entries on December 31, 20Y1, to record the expected customer returns. (b) Journalize the entries to record the returned merchandise and cash refund to Brown Co. on February 15, 20Y2.

Appendix 3
EX 6-43 Rules of debit and credit for periodic inventory accounts

Complete the following table by indicating for (a) through (g) whether the proper answer is debit or credit:

Account	Increase	Decrease	Normal Balance
Purchases	debit	(a)	(b)
Purchases Discounts	credit	(c)	credit
Purchases Returns and Allowances	(d)	(e)	(f)
Freight In	debit	(g)	debit

Appendix 3
EX 6-44 Journal entries using the periodic inventory system

The following selected transactions were completed by Air Systems Company during January of the current year. Air Systems Company uses the periodic inventory system.

Jan. 2. Purchased $18,200 of merchandise on account, FOB shipping point, terms 2/15, n/30.
5. Paid freight of $190 on the January 2 purchase.
6. Returned $2,750 of the merchandise purchased on January 2.
13. Sold merchandise on account, $37,300, FOB destination, 1/10, n/30. The cost of merchandise sold was $22,400.
15. Paid freight of $215 for the merchandise sold on January 13.
17. Paid for the purchase of January 2 less the return and discount.
23. Received payment on account for the sale of January 13 less the discount.

Journalize the entries to record the transactions of Air Systems Company.

Appendix 3
EX 6-45 Identify items missing in determining cost of merchandise sold

For (a) through (d), identify the items designated by X and Y.

a. Purchases − (X + Y) = Net purchases.
b. Net purchases + X = Cost of merchandise purchased.
c. Merchandise inventory (beginning) + Cost of merchandise purchased = X.
d. Merchandise available for sale − X = Cost of merchandise sold.

Appendix 3
EX 6-46 Cost of merchandise sold and related items

✔ a. Cost of merchandise sold, $3,540,000

The following data were extracted from the accounting records of Harkins Company for the year ended April 30, 20Y7:

Merchandise inventory, May 1, 20Y6	$ 380,000
Merchandise inventory, April 30, 20Y7	426,600
Purchases	3,800,000
Purchases returns and allowances	150,000
Purchases discounts	80,000
Sales	5,850,000
Freight in	16,600

a. Prepare the cost of merchandise sold section of the income statement for the year ended April 30, 20Y7, using the periodic inventory system.

b. Determine the gross profit to be reported on the income statement for the year ended April 30, 20Y7.

c. Would gross profit be different if the perpetual inventory system was used instead of the periodic inventory system?

Appendix 3
EX 6-47 Cost of merchandise sold

Based on the following data, determine the cost of merchandise sold for November:

Merchandise inventory, November 1	$ 28,000
Merchandise inventory, November 30	46,000
Purchases	475,000
Purchases returns and allowances	15,000
Purchases discounts	9,000
Freight in	7,000

Appendix 3
EX 6-48 Cost of merchandise sold

Based on the following data, determine the cost of merchandise sold for July:

Merchandise inventory, July 1	$ 190,850
Merchandise inventory, July 31	195,350
Purchases	1,126,000
Purchases returns and allowances	46,000
Purchases discounts	23,000
Freight in	17,500

Appendix 3
EX 6-49 Cost of merchandise sold

✔ Correct cost of merchandise sold, $990,000

Identify the errors in the following schedule of the cost of merchandise sold for the year ended May 31, 20Y4:

Cost of merchandise sold:		
Merchandise inventory, May 31, 20Y4		$ 148,300
Cost of merchandise purchased:		
Purchases	$1,110,000	
Purchases returns and allowances	55,000	
Purchases discounts	30,000	
Freight in	(22,000)	
Total cost of merchandise purchased		1,173,000
Merchandise available for sale		$1,321,300
Merchandise inventory, June 1, 20Y3		91,300
Cost of merchandise sold		$1,230,000

Appendix 3

Ex 6-50 Closing entries using periodic inventory system

United Rug Company is a small rug retailer owned and operated by Pat Kirwan. After the accounts have been adjusted on December 31, the following selected account balances were taken from the ledger:

Advertising Expense	$ 36,000
Depreciation Expense	13,000
Freight In	17,000
Merchandise Inventory, January 1	375,000
Merchandise Inventory, December 31	480,000
Miscellaneous Expense	9,000
Purchases	1,760,000
Purchases Discounts	35,000
Purchases Returns and Allowances	45,000
Pat Kirwan, Drawing	65,000
Salaries Expense	375,000
Sales	2,220,000

Journalize the closing entries on December 31.

Problems: Series A

PR 6-1A Purchase-related transactions using perpetual inventory system

OBJ. 2

The following selected transactions were completed by Capers Company during October of the current year:

Oct. 1. Purchased merchandise from UK Imports Co., $14,448, terms FOB destination, n/30.

3. Purchased merchandise from Hoagie Co., $9,950, terms FOB shipping point, 2/10, n/eom. Prepaid freight of $220 was added to the invoice.

4. Purchased merchandise from Taco Co., $13,650, terms FOB destination, 2/10, n/30.

6. Issued debit memo to Taco Co. for $4,550 of merchandise returned from purchase on October 4.

13. Paid Hoagie Co. for invoice of October 3.

14. Paid Taco Co. for invoice of October 4 less debit memo of October 6.

19. Purchased merchandise from Veggie Co., $27,300, terms FOB shipping point, n/eom.

19. Paid freight of $400 on October 19 purchase from Veggie Co.

20. Purchased merchandise from Caesar Salad Co., $22,000, terms FOB destination, 1/10, n/30.

30. Paid Caesar Salad Co. for invoice of October 20.

31. Paid UK Imports Co. for invoice of October 1.

31. Paid Veggie Co. for invoice of October 19.

Instructions

Journalize the entries to record the transactions of Capers Company for October.

PR 6-2A Sales-related transactions using perpetual inventory system OBJ. 2

The following selected transactions were completed by Amsterdam Supply Co., which sells office supplies primarily to wholesalers and occasionally to retail customers:

Mar. 2. Sold merchandise on account to Equinox Co., $18,900, terms FOB destination, 1/10, n/30. The cost of the merchandise sold was $13,300.

3. Sold merchandise for $11,350 plus 6% sales tax to retail cash customers. The cost of merchandise sold was $7,000.

4. Sold merchandise on account to Empire Co., $55,400, terms FOB shipping point, n/eom. The cost of merchandise sold was $33,200.

5. Sold merchandise for $30,000 plus 6% sales tax to retail customers who used MasterCard. The cost of merchandise sold was $19,400.

12. Received check for amount due from Equinox Co. for sale on March 2.

14. Sold merchandise to customers who used American Express cards, $13,700. The cost of merchandise sold was $8,350.

16. Sold merchandise on account to Targhee Co., $27,500, terms FOB shipping point, 1/10, n/30. The cost of merchandise sold was $16,000.

18. Issued credit memo for $1,000 to Targhee Co. for damaged merchandise from sale on March 16.

19. Sold merchandise on account to Vista Co., $8,250, terms FOB shipping point, 2/10, n/30. Added $75 to the invoice for prepaid freight. The cost of merchandise sold was $5,000.

26. Received check for amount due from Targhee Co. for sale on March 16 less credit memo of March 18.

28. Received check for amount due from Vista Co. for sale of March 19.

31. Received check for amount due from Empire Co. for sale of March 4.

31. Paid Fleetwood Delivery Service $5,600 for delivery of merchandise in March to customers under shipping terms of FOB destination.

Apr. 3. Paid City Bank $940 for service fees for handling MasterCard and American Express sales during March.

15. Paid $6,544 to state sales tax division for taxes owed on sales.

Instructions

Journalize the entries to record the transactions of Amsterdam Supply Co.

PR 6-3A Sales-related and purchase-related transactions using perpetual inventory system OBJ. 2

The following were selected from among the transactions completed by Harrison Company during November of the current year:

Nov. 3. Purchased merchandise on account from Moonlight Co., list price $120,000, trade discount 25%, terms FOB destination, 2/10, n/30.

4. Sold merchandise for cash, $53,500. The cost of the merchandise sold was $32,100.

5. Purchased merchandise on account from Papoose Creek Co., $67,400, terms FOB shipping point, 2/10, n/30, with prepaid freight of $1,150 added to the invoice.

6. Returned $19,200 ($25,600 list price less trade discount of 25%) of merchandise purchased on November 3 from Moonlight Co.

8. Sold merchandise on account to Quinn Co., $22,100 with terms n/15. The cost of the merchandise sold was $13,000.

13. Paid Moonlight Co. on account for purchase of November 3, less return of November 6.

14. Sold merchandise on VISA, $335,000. The cost of the merchandise sold was $198,700.

Nov. 15. Paid Papoose Creek Co. on account for purchase of November 5.

23. Received cash on account from sale of November 8 to Quinn Co.

24. Sold merchandise on account to Rabel Co., $80,800, terms 1/10, n/30. The cost of the merchandise sold was $48,300.

28. Paid VISA service fee of $5,030.

30. Paid Quinn Co. a cash refund of $1,770 for damaged merchandise from sale of November 8. Quinn Co. kept the merchandise.

Instructions

Journalize the transactions.

PR 6-4A Sales-related and purchase-related transactions for seller and buyer using perpetual inventory system **OBJ. 2**

The following selected transactions were completed during August between Summit Company and Beartooth Co.:

Aug. 1. Summit Company sold merchandise on account to Beartooth Co., $48,000, terms FOB destination, 2/15, n/eom. The cost of the merchandise sold was $28,800.

2. Summit Company paid freight of $1,150 for delivery of merchandise sold to Beartooth Co. on August 1.

5. Summit Company sold merchandise on account to Beartooth Co., $66,000, terms FOB shipping point, n/45. The cost of the merchandise sold was $40,000.

9. Beartooth Co. paid freight of $2,300 on August 5 purchase from Summit Company.

15. Summit Company sold merchandise on account to Beartooth Co., $58,700, terms FOB shipping point, 1/10, n/30. Summit Company paid freight of $1,675, which was added to the invoice. The cost of the merchandise sold was $35,000.

16. Beartooth Co. paid Summit Company for purchase of August 1.

20. Summit Company paid Beartooth Co. a refund of $1,800 for defective merchandise in the August 1 purchase. Beartooth Co. agreed to keep the merchandise.

25. Beartooth Co. paid Summit Company on account for purchase of August 15.

Instructions

Journalize the August transactions for (1) Summit Company and (2) Beartooth Co.

PR 6-5A Multiple-step income statement and balance sheet **OBJ. 3**

✔ 1. Net income $1,143,100

The following selected accounts and their current balances appear in the ledger of Druid Hills Co. for the fiscal year ended May 31, 20Y8:

Cash	$ 290,800	Kristina Marble, Drawing	$ 121,200
Accounts Receivable	1,170,600	Sales	13,746,000
Merchandise Inventory	2,075,300	Cost of Merchandise Sold	9,513,000
Office Supplies	16,400	Sales Salaries Expense	1,110,100
Prepaid Insurance	9,700	Advertising Expense	666,500
Office Equipment	1,005,800	Depreciation Expense—	
Accumulated Depreciation—		Store Equipment	169,700
Office Equipment	666,500	Miscellaneous Selling Expense	46,100
Store Equipment	4,362,700	Office Salaries Expense	787,700
Accumulated Depreciation—		Rent Expense	113,900
Store Equipment	2,205,600	Depreciation Expense—	
Accounts Payable	395,100	Office Equipment	60,600
Customer Refunds Payable	48,500	Insurance Expense	58,200
Salaries Payable	50,300	Office Supplies Expense	34,100
Note Payable		Miscellaneous Administrative Exp.	17,600
(final payment due in 10 years)	363,600	Interest Expense	25,400
Kristina Marble, Capital	4,179,800		

(Continued)

Instructions

1. Prepare a multiple-step income statement.
2. Prepare a statement of owner's equity.
3. Prepare a balance sheet, assuming that the current portion of the note payable is $60,600.
4. Briefly explain how multiple-step and single-step income statements differ.

PR 6-6A Single-step income statement **OBJ. 3**

Selected accounts and related amounts for Druid Hills Co. for the fiscal year ended May 31, 20Y8, are presented in Problem 6-5A.

Instructions

1. Prepare a single-step income statement in the format shown in Exhibit 12.
2. Prepare closing entries as of May 31, 20Y8.

Appendix 3
PR 6-7A Purchase-related transactions using periodic inventory system

Selected transactions for Capers Company during October of the current year are listed in Problem 6-1A.

Instructions

Journalize the entries to record the transactions of Capers Company for October using the periodic inventory system.

Appendix 3
PR 6-8A Sales-related and purchase-related transactions using periodic inventory system

Selected transactions for Harrison Company during November of the current year are listed in Problem 6-3A.

Instructions

Journalize the entries to record the transactions of Harrison Company for November using the periodic inventory system.

Appendix 3
PR 6-9A Periodic inventory accounts, multiple-step income statement, closing entries

✔ 2. Net income, $210,000

On December 31, 20Y6, the balances of the accounts appearing in the ledger of Wyman Company are as follows:

Cash	$ 13,500	Purchases	$2,650,000
Accounts Receivable	72,000	Purchases Returns and Allowances	93,000
Merchandise Inventory, January 1, 20Y6	257,000	Purchases Discounts	37,000
Office Supplies	3,000	Freight In	48,000
Prepaid Insurance	4,500	Sales Salaries Expense	300,000
Land	150,000	Advertising Expense	45,000
Store Equipment	270,000	Delivery Expense	9,000
Accumulated Depreciation—Store Equipment	55,900	Depreciation Expense—Store Equipment	6,000
Office Equipment	78,500	Miscellaneous Selling Expense	12,000
Accumulated Depreciation—Office Equipment	16,000	Office Salaries Expense	175,000
Accounts Payable	27,800	Rent Expense	28,000
Customer Refunds Payable	50,000	Insurance Expense	3,000
Salaries Payable	3,000	Office Supplies Expense	2,000
Unearned Rent	8,300	Depreciation Expense—Office Equipment	1,500
Notes Payable	50,000	Miscellaneous Administrative Expense	3,500
Shirley Wyman, Capital	530,500	Rent Revenue	7,000
Shirley Wyman, Drawing	25,000	Interest Expense	2,000
Sales	3,280,000		

Instructions

1. Does Wyman Company use a periodic or perpetual inventory system? Explain.
2. Prepare a multiple-step income statement for Wyman Company for the year ended December 31, 20Y6. The merchandise inventory as of December 31, 20Y6, was $335,000.
3. Prepare the closing entries for Wyman Company as of December 31, 20Y6.
4. What would the net income have been if the perpetual inventory system had been used?

Problems: Series B

PR 6-1B Purchase-related transactions using perpetual inventory system

OBJ. 2

The following selected transactions were completed by Niles Co. during March of the current year:

Mar. 1. Purchased merchandise from Haas Co., $43,250, terms FOB shipping point, 2/10, n/eom. Prepaid freight of $650 was added to the invoice.

5. Purchased merchandise from Whitman Co., $19,175, terms FOB destination, n/30.

10. Paid Haas Co. for invoice of March 1.

13. Purchased merchandise from Jost Co., $15,550, terms FOB destination, 2/10, n/30.

14. Issued debit memo to Jost Co. for $3,750 of merchandise returned from purchase on March 13.

18. Purchased merchandise from Fairhurst Company, $13,560, terms FOB shipping point, n/eom.

18. Paid freight of $140 on March 18 purchase from Fairhurst Company.

19. Purchased merchandise from Bickle Co., $6,500, terms FOB destination, 2/10, n/30.

23. Paid Jost Co. for invoice of March 13 less debit memo of March 14.

29. Paid Bickle Co. for invoice of March 19.

31. Paid Fairhurst Company for invoice of March 18.

31. Paid Whitman Co. for invoice of March 5.

Instructions

Journalize the entries to record the transactions of Niles Co. for March.

PR 6-2B Sales-related transactions using perpetual inventory system

OBJ. 2

The following selected transactions were completed by Green Lawn Supplies Co., which sells irrigation supplies primarily to wholesalers and occasionally to retail customers:

July 1. Sold merchandise on account to Landscapes Co., $33,450, terms FOB shipping point, n/eom. The cost of merchandise sold was $20,000.

2. Sold merchandise for $86,000 plus 8% sales tax to retail cash customers. The cost of merchandise sold was $51,600.

5. Sold merchandise on account to Peacock Company, $17,500, terms FOB destination, 1/10, n/30. The cost of merchandise sold was $10,000.

8. Sold merchandise for $112,000 plus 8% sales tax to retail customers who used VISA cards. The cost of merchandise sold was $67,200.

13. Sold merchandise to customers who used MasterCard cards, $96,000. The cost of merchandise sold was $57,600.

(Continued)

July 14. Sold merchandise on account to Loeb Co., $16,000, terms FOB shipping point, 1/10, n/30. The cost of merchandise sold was $9,000.
15. Received check for amount due from Peacock Company for sale on July 5.
16. Issued credit memo for $3,000 to Loeb Co. for damaged merchandise from sale on July 14. Loeb Co. kept the merchandise.
18. Sold merchandise on account to Jennings Company, $11,350, terms FOB shipping point, 2/10, n/30. Paid $475 for freight and added it to the invoice. The cost of merchandise sold was $6,800.
24. Received check for amount due from Loeb Co. for sale on July 14 less credit memo of July 16.
28. Received check for amount due from Jennings Company for sale of July 18.
31. Paid Black Lab Delivery Service $8,550 for delivery of merchandise in July to customers under shipping terms of FOB destination.
31. Received check for amount due from Landscapes Co. for sale of July 1.

Aug. 3. Paid Hays Federal Bank $3,770 for service fees for handling MasterCard and VISA sales during July.
10. Paid $41,260 to state sales tax division for taxes owed on sales.

Instructions

Journalize the entries to record the transactions of Green Lawn Supplies Co.

PR 6-3B Sales-related and purchase-related transactions using perpetual inventory system

OBJ. 2

The following were selected from among the transactions completed by Essex Company during July of the current year:

July 3. Purchased merchandise on account from Hamling Co., list price $72,000, trade discount 15%, terms FOB shipping point, 2/10, n/30, with prepaid freight of $1,450 added to the invoice.
5. Purchased merchandise on account from Kester Co., $33,450, terms FOB destination, 2/10, n/30.
6. Sold merchandise on account to Parsley Co., $36,000, terms n/15. The cost of the merchandise sold was $25,000.
7. Returned $6,850 of merchandise purchased on July 5 from Kester Co.
13. Paid Hamling Co. on account for purchase of July 3.
15. Paid Kester Co. on account for purchase of July 5, less return of July 7.
21. Received cash on account from sale of July 6 to Parsley Co.
21. Sold merchandise on MasterCard, $108,000. The cost of the merchandise sold was $64,800.
22. Sold merchandise on account to Tabor Co., $16,650, terms 2/10, n/30. The cost of the merchandise sold was $10,000.
23. Sold merchandise for cash, $91,200. The cost of the merchandise sold was $55,000.
28. Paid Parsley Co. a cash refund of $2,500 for damaged merchandise from sale of July 6. Parsley Co. kept the merchandise.
31. Paid MasterCard service fee of $1,650.

Instructions

Journalize the transactions.

PR 6-4B Sales-related and purchase-related transactions for seller and buyer using perpetual inventory system **OBJ. 2**

The following selected transactions were completed during April between Swan Company and Bird Company:

Apr. 2. Swan Company sold merchandise on account to Bird Company, $32,000, terms FOB shipping point, 2/10, n/30. Swan Company paid freight of $330, which was added to the invoice. The cost of the merchandise sold was $19,200.

8. Swan Company sold merchandise on account to Bird Company, $49,500, terms FOB destination, 1/15, n/30. The cost of the merchandise sold was $29,700.

8. Swan Company paid freight of $710 for delivery of merchandise sold to Bird Company on April 8.

12. Bird Company paid Swan Company for purchase of April 2.

18. Swan Company paid Bird Company a refund of $2,000 for defective merchandise in the April 2 purchase. Bird Company agreed to keep the merchandise.

23. Bird Company paid Swan Company for purchase of April 8.

24. Swan Company sold merchandise on account to Bird Company, $67,350, terms FOB shipping point, n/45. The cost of the merchandise sold was $40,400.

26. Bird Company paid freight of $875 on April 24 purchase from Swan Company.

Instructions

Journalize the April transactions for (1) Swan Company and (2) Bird Company.

PR 6-5B Multiple-step income statement and balance sheet **OBJ. 3**

✔ 1. Net income: $1,340,000

The following selected accounts and their current balances appear in the ledger of Kanpur Co. for the fiscal year ended June 30, 20Y5:

Account	Balance	Account	Balance
Cash	$ 92,000	Gerri Faber, Drawing	$ 300,000
Accounts Receivable	450,000	Sales	8,925,000
Merchandise Inventory	375,000	Cost of Merchandise Sold	5,620,000
Office Supplies	10,000	Sales Salaries Expense	850,000
Prepaid Insurance	12,000	Advertising Expense	420,000
Office Equipment	220,000	Depreciation Expense—	
Accumulated Depreciation—		Store Equipment	33,000
Office Equipment	58,000	Miscellaneous Selling Expense	18,000
Store Equipment	650,000	Office Salaries Expense	540,000
Accumulated Depreciation—		Rent Expense	48,000
Store Equipment	87,500	Insurance Expense	24,000
Accounts Payable	38,500	Depreciation Expense—	
Customer Refunds Payable	10,000	Office Equipment	10,000
Salaries Payable	4,000	Office Supplies Expense	4,000
Note Payable		Miscellaneous Administrative Exp.	6,000
(final payment due in eight years)	140,000	Interest Expense	12,000
Gerri Faber, Capital	431,000		

Instructions

1. Prepare a multiple-step income statement.
2. Prepare a statement of owner's equity.
3. Prepare a balance sheet, assuming that the current portion of the note payable is $7,000.
4. Briefly explain how multiple-step and single-step income statements differ.

PR 6-6B Single-step income statement

OBJ. 3

Selected accounts and related amounts for Kanpur Co. for the fiscal year ended June 30, 20Y5, are presented in Problem 6-5B.

Instructions

1. Prepare a single-step income statement in the format shown in Exhibit 12.
2. Prepare closing entries as of June 30, 20Y5.

Appendix 3

PR 6-7B Purchase-related transactions using periodic inventory system

Selected transactions for Niles Co. during March of the current year are listed in Problem 6-1B.

Instructions

Journalize the entries to record the transactions of Niles Co. for March using the periodic inventory system.

Appendix 3

PR 6-8B Sales-related and purchase-related transactions using periodic inventory system

Selected transactions for Essex Company during July of the current year are listed in Problem 6-3B.

Instructions

Journalize the entries to record the transactions of Essex Company for July using the periodic inventory system.

Appendix 3

PR 6-9B Periodic inventory accounts, multiple-step income statement, closing entries

✔ 2. Net income, $1,233,000

On June 30, 20Y9, the balances of the accounts appearing in the ledger of Simkins Company are as follows:

Cash	$ 125,000	Purchases	$4,100,000
Accounts Receivable	340,000	Purchases Returns and Allowances	32,000
Merchandise Inventory, July 1, 20Y8	415,000	Purchases Discounts	13,000
Office Supplies	9,000	Freight In	45,000
Prepaid Insurance	18,000	Sales Salaries Expense	580,000
Land	300,000	Advertising Expense	315,000
Store Equipment	550,000	Delivery Expense	18,000
Accumulated Depreciation—Store Equipment	190,000	Depreciation Expense—Store Equipment	12,000
Office Equipment	250,000	Miscellaneous Selling Expense	28,000
Accumulated Depreciation—Office Equipment	110,000	Office Salaries Expense	375,000
Accounts Payable	85,000	Rent Expense	43,000
Customer Refunds Payable	20,000	Insurance Expense	17,000
Salaries Payable	9,000	Office Supplies Expense	5,000
Unearned Rent	6,000	Depreciation Expense—Office Equipment	4,000
Notes Payable	50,000	Miscellaneous Administrative Expense	16,000
Amy Gant, Capital	705,000	Rent Revenue	32,500
Amy Gant, Drawing	275,000	Interest Expense	2,500
Sales	6,590,000		

Instructions

1. Does Simkins Company use a periodic or perpetual inventory system? Explain.
2. Prepare a multiple-step income statement for Simkins Company for the year ended June 30, 20Y9. The merchandise inventory as of June 30, 20Y9, was $541,000.

3. Prepare the closing entries for Simkins Company as of June 30, 20Y9.
4. What would the net income have been if the perpetual inventory system had been used?

Comprehensive Problem 2

✔ 8. Net income: $706,855

Palisade Creek Co. is a merchandising business that uses the perpetual inventory system. The account balances for Palisade Creek Co. as of May 1, 20Y7 (unless otherwise indicated), are as follows:

110	Cash	$ 83,600
112	Accounts Receivable	233,900
115	Merchandise Inventory	652,400
117	Prepaid Insurance	16,800
118	Store Supplies	11,400
123	Store Equipment	569,500
124	Accumulated Depreciation—Store Equipment	56,700
210	Accounts Payable	96,600
211	Customer Refunds Payable	50,000
212	Salaries Payable	—
310	Lynn Tolley, Capital, June 1, 20Y6	685,300
311	Lynn Tolley, Drawing	135,000
410	Sales	5,069,000
510	Cost of Merchandise Sold	2,823,000
520	Sales Salaries Expense	664,800
521	Advertising Expense	281,000
522	Depreciation Expense	—
523	Store Supplies Expense	—
529	Miscellaneous Selling Expense	12,600
530	Office Salaries Expense	382,100
531	Rent Expense	83,700
532	Insurance Expense	—
539	Miscellaneous Administrative Expense	7,800

During May, the last month of the fiscal year, the following transactions were completed:

May 1. Paid rent for May, $5,000.

3. Purchased merchandise on account from Martin Co., terms 2/10, n/30, FOB shipping point, $36,000.
4. Paid freight on purchase of May 3, $600.
6. Sold merchandise on account to Korman Co., terms 2/10, n/30, FOB shipping point, $68,500. The cost of the merchandise sold was $41,000.
7. Received $22,300 cash from Halstad Co. on account.
10. Sold merchandise for cash, $54,000. The cost of the merchandise sold was $32,000.
13. Paid for merchandise purchased on May 3.
15. Paid advertising expense for last half of May, $11,000.
16. Received cash from sale of May 6.
19. Purchased merchandise for cash, $18,700.
19. Paid $33,450 to Buttons Co. on account.
20. Paid Korman Co. a cash refund of $5,000 for damaged merchandise from sale of May 6. Korman Co. kept the merchandise.

(Continued)

Record the following transactions on Page 21 of the journal:

May 20. Sold merchandise on account to Crescent Co., terms 1/10, n/30, FOB shipping point, $110,000. The cost of the merchandise sold was $70,000.

21. For the convenience of Crescent Co., paid freight on sale of May 20, $2,300.

21. Received $42,900 cash from Gee Co. on account.

21. Purchased merchandise on account from Osterman Co., terms 1/10, n/30, FOB destination, $88,000.

24. Returned damaged merchandise purchased on May 21, receiving a credit memo from the seller for $5,000.

26. Refunded cash on sales made for cash, $800. The defective merchandise was not returned by the customer.

28. Paid sales salaries of $56,000 and office salaries of $29,000.

29. Purchased store supplies for cash, $2,400.

30. Sold merchandise on account to Turner Co., terms 2/10, n/30, FOB shipping point, $78,750. The cost of the merchandise sold was $47,000.

30. Received cash from sale of May 20 plus freight paid on May 21.

31. Paid for purchase of May 21, less return of May 24.

Instructions

1. Enter the balances of each of the accounts in the appropriate balance column of a four-column account. Write *Balance* in the Item column and place a check mark (✓) in the Posting Reference column. Journalize the transactions for May, starting on Page 20 of the journal.
2. Post the journal to the general ledger, extending the month-end balances to the appropriate balance columns after all posting is completed. In this problem, you are not required to update or post to the accounts receivable and accounts payable subsidiary ledgers.
3. Prepare an unadjusted trial balance.
4. At the end of May, the following adjustment data were assembled. Analyze and use these data to complete (5) and (6).

a.	Merchandise inventory on May 31		$585,200
b.	Insurance expired during the year		12,000
c.	Store supplies on hand on May 31		4,000
d.	Depreciation for the current year		14,000
e.	Accrued salaries on May 31:		
	Sales salaries	$7,000	
	Office salaries	6,600	13,600
f.	The adjustment for customer refunds and allowances is $60,000.		

5. *(Optional)* Enter the unadjusted trial balance on a 10-column end-of-period spreadsheet (work sheet), and complete the spreadsheet.
6. Journalize and post the adjusting entries. Record the adjusting entries on Page 22 of the journal.
7. Prepare an adjusted trial balance.
8. Prepare an income statement, a statement of owner's equity, and a balance sheet.
9. Prepare and post the closing entries. Record the closing entries on Page 23 of the journal. Indicate closed accounts by inserting a line in both Balance columns opposite the closing entry. Insert the new balance in the owner's capital account.
10. Prepare a post-closing trial balance.

Cases & Projects

ETHICS

CP 6-1 Ethics in Action

Margie Johnson is a staff accountant at ToolEx Company, a manufacturer of tools and equipment. The company is under pressure from investors to increase earnings, and the president of the company expects the accounting department to "make this happen." Margie's boss, who has been a mentor to her, is concerned that if earnings do not increase, he will be terminated.

Shortly after the end of the fiscal year, the company performs a physical count of the inventory. When Margie compares the physical count to the balance in the inventory account, she finds a significant amount of inventory shrinkage. The amount is so large that it will result in a significant drop in earnings this period. Margie's boss asks her not to make the adjusting entry for shrinkage this period. He assures her that they will get "caught up" on shrinkage in the next period, after the pressure is off to reach this period's earnings goal. Margie's boss asks her to do this as a personal favor to him.

What should Margie do in this situation? Why?

ETHICS

CP 6-2 Ethics in Action

On April 18, 20Y1, Bontanica Company, a garden retailer, purchased $9,800 of seed, terms 2/10, n/30, from Whitetail Seed Co. Even though the discount period had expired, Shelby Davey subtracted the discount of $196 when he processed the documents for payment on May 1, 20Y1.

Discuss whether Shelby Davey behaved in a professional manner by subtracting the discount even though the discount period had expired.

TEAM ACTIVITY

REAL WORLD

CP 6-3 Team Activity

In teams, select a public company that interests you. Obtain the company's most recent annual report on Form 10-K. The Form 10-K is a company's annually required filing with the Securities and Exchange Commission (SEC). It includes the company's financial statements and accompanying notes. The Form 10-K can be obtained either (a) by referring to the investor relations section of the company's website or (b) by using the company search feature of the SEC's EDGAR database service found at www.sec.gov/edgar/searchedgar/companysearch.html.

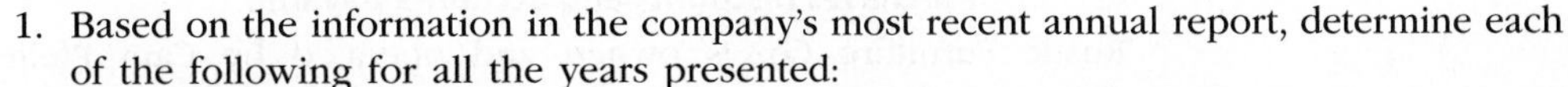

1. Based on the information in the company's most recent annual report, determine each of the following for all the years presented:
   a. Gross profit
   b. Gross profit rate (Gross profit ÷ Sales) (Round to one decimal place.)
   c. Income from operations
   d. Percentage change in income from operations (Round to one decimal place.)
   e. Net income
   f. Percentage change in net income (Round to one decimal place.)
2. Based solely on your responses to item 1, has the company's performance improved, remained constant, or deteriorated over the periods presented? Briefly explain your answer.

COMMUNICATION

CP 6-4 Communication

Suzi Nomro operates Watercraft Supply Company, an online boat parts distributorship that is in its third year of operation. The following income statement was prepared for the year ended October 31, 20Y2.

(Continued)

Watercraft Supply Company **Income Statement** **For the Year Ended October 31, 20Y2**		
Revenues:		
Sales		$1,350,000
Interest		15,000
Total revenues		$1,365,000
Expenses:		
Cost of merchandise sold	$810,000	
Selling expenses	140,000	
Administrative expenses	90,000	
Interest expense	4,000	
Total expenses		1,044,000
Net income		$ 321,000

Suzi is considering a proposal to increase net income by offering sales discounts of 2/15, n/30 and by shipping all merchandise FOB shipping point. Currently, no sales discounts are allowed and merchandise is shipped FOB destination. It is estimated that the new terms will increase sales by 10%. The ratio of the cost of merchandise sold to sales is expected to be 60%. All selling and administrative expenses are expected to remain unchanged, except for store supplies and miscellaneous selling expenses, which are expected to increase proportionately with increased sales. The amounts of these items for the year ended October 31, 20Y2, were as follows:

Store supplies expense	$12,000
Miscellaneous selling expenses	6,000

The interest revenue and expense items will remain unchanged. The shipment of all merchandise FOB shipping point will eliminate all delivery expenses, which for the year ended October 31, 20Y2, were $12,000.

Write a brief memo to Suzi discussing the potential benefits and limitations of this proposal. Include a determination of the net income that Watercraft Supply could generate for the year ending October 31, 20Y3, under the new proposal, assuming that all sales are collected within the discount period.

CP 6-5 Purchases discounts and accounts payable

Rustic Furniture Co. is owned and operated by Cam Pfeifer. The following is an excerpt from a conversation between Cam Pfeifer and Mitzi Wheeler, the chief accountant for Rustic Furniture Co.:

Cam: Mitzi, I've got a question about this recent balance sheet.

Mitzi: Sure, what's your question?

Cam: Well, as you know, I'm applying for a bank loan to finance our new store in Garden Grove, and I noticed that the accounts payable are listed as $320,000.

Mitzi: That's right. Approximately $275,000 of that represents amounts due our suppliers, and the remainder is miscellaneous payables to creditors for utilities, office equipment, supplies, etc.

Cam: That's what I thought. But as you know, we normally receive a 2% discount from our suppliers for earlier payment, and we always try to take the discount.

Mitzi: That's right. I can't remember the last time we missed a discount.

Cam: Well, in that case, it seems to me the accounts payable should be listed minus the 2% discount. Let's list the accounts payable due suppliers as $314,500 rather than $320,000. Every little bit helps. You never know. It might make the difference between getting and not getting the loan.

How would you respond to Cam Pfeifer's request?

CP 6-6 Determining cost of purchase

The following is an excerpt from a conversation between Mark Loomis and Krista Huff. Mark is debating whether to buy a stereo system from Tru-Sound Systems, a locally owned electronics store, or Wholesale Stereo, an online electronics company.

Mark: Krista, I don't know what to do about buying my new stereo.

Krista: What's the problem?

Mark: Well, I can buy it locally at Tru-Sound Systems for $1,175.00. However, Wholesale Stereo has the same system listed for $1,200.00.

Krista: What's the big deal? Buy it from Tru-Sound Systems.

Mark: It's not quite that simple. Wholesale Stereo charges $49.99 for shipping and handling. If I have Wholesale Stereo send it next-day air, it'll cost $89.99 for shipping and handling.

Krista: So?

Mark: But, that's not all. Tru-Sound Systems will give an additional 2% discount if I pay cash. Otherwise, they will let me use my VISA, or I can pay it off in three monthly installments. In addition, if I buy it from Tru-Sound Systems, I have to pay 9% sales tax. I won't have to pay sales tax if I buy it from Wholesale Stereo, since they are out of state.

Krista: Anything else???

Mark: Well . . . Wholesale Stereo says I have to charge it on my VISA. They don't accept checks.

Krista: I am not surprised. Many online stores don't accept checks.

Mark: I give up. What would you do?

1. Assuming that Wholesale Stereo doesn't charge sales tax on the sale to Mark, which company is offering the best buy?
2. What might be some considerations other than price that influence Mark's decision on where to buy the stereo system?

CHAPTER

7 Inventories

STATEMENT OF OWNER'S EQUITY
For the Year Ended December 31, 20Y6

Owner's capital, Jan. 1, 20Y6		$XXX
Net income	$ XXX	
Withdrawals	(XXX)	
Increase in equity		XXX
Owner's capital, Dec. 31, 20Y6		$XXX

STATEMENT OF CASH FLOWS
For the Year Ended December 31, 20Y6

Cash flows from (used for) operating activities	$XXX
Cash flows from (used for) investing activities	XXX
Cash flows from (used for) financing activities	XXX
Net increase (decrease) in cash	$XXX
Cash balance, January 1, 20Y6	XXX

INCOME STATEMENT
For the Year Ended December 31, 20Y6

Sales		$XXX
Cost of merchandise sold		XXX
Gross profit		$XXX
Operating expenses:		
Advertising expense	$XXX	
Depreciation expense	XXX	
Amortization expense	XXX	
Depletion expense	XXX	
...	XXX	
...	XXX	
Total operating expenses		XXX
Income from operations		$XXX
Other revenue and expenses		XXX
Net income		$XXX

BALANCE SHEET
December 31, 20Y6

Current assets:		
Cash	$XXX	
Accounts receivable	XXX	
Merchandise inventory	XXX	
Total current assets		$XXX
Property, plant, and equipment	$XXX	
Intangible assets	XXX	
Total long-term assets		XXX
Total assets		$XXX
Liabilities:		
Current liabilities	$XXX	
Long-term liabilities	XXX	
Total liabilities		$XXX
Owner's equity		XXX
Total liabilities and owner's equity		$XXX

CHAPTER 7

DUSAN PETKOVIC/SHUTTERSTOCK.COM

Best Buy

Assume that in September, you purchased a Sony HDTV from **Best Buy**. At the same time, you purchased a Denon surround sound system for $599.99. You liked your surround sound so well that in November, you purchased an identical Denon system on sale for $549.99 for your bedroom TV. Over the holidays, you moved to a new apartment and in the process of unpacking discovered that one of the Denon surround sound systems was missing. Luckily, your renters or homeowners insurance policy will cover the theft, but the insurance company needs to know the cost of the system that was stolen.

The Denon systems were identical. However, to respond to the insurance company, you will need to identify which system was stolen. Was it the first system, which cost $599.99, or was it the second system, which cost $549.99? Whichever system you choose will determine the amount that you receive from the insurance company.

Merchandising businesses such as Best Buy make similar assumptions when identical merchandise is purchased at different costs. For example, Best Buy may have purchased thousands of Denon surround sound systems over the past year at different costs. At the end of a period, some of the Denon systems will still be in inventory, and some will have been sold. But which costs relate to the sold systems, and which costs relate to the systems still in inventory? Best Buy's assumption about inventory costs can involve large dollar amounts and, thus, can have a significant impact on the financial statements. For example, Best Buy reported $5,409 million of inventory and net income of $1,464 million for a recent year.

This chapter discusses such issues as how to determine the cost of merchandise in inventory and the cost of merchandise sold. However, it begins by discussing the importance of control over inventory.

Link to Best Buy . . . . Pages 349, 350, 362, 364

LEARNING OBJECTIVES

After studying this chapter, you should be able to:

Example Exercises (EE) are shown in **red.**

OBJ. 1 **Describe the importance of control over inventory.**

Control of Inventory
Safeguarding Inventory
Reporting Inventory

OBJ. 2 **Describe three inventory cost flow assumptions and explain how they impact the income statement and balance sheet.**

Inventory Cost Flow Assumptions

Cost Flow Methods	EE **7-1**

OBJ. 3 **Determine the cost of inventory under the perpetual inventory system, using the FIFO, LIFO, and weighted average cost methods.**

Inventory Costing Methods Under a Perpetual Inventory System

First-In, First-Out Method	EE **7-2**
Last-In, First-Out Method	EE **7-3**
Weighted Average Cost Method	EE **7-4**

OBJ. 4 **Determine the cost of inventory under the periodic inventory system, using the FIFO, LIFO, and weighted average cost methods.**

Inventory Costing Methods Under a Periodic Inventory System

First-In, First-Out Method	EE **7-5**
Last-In, First-Out Method	EE **7-5**
Weighted Average Cost Method	EE **7-5**

OBJ. 5 **Compare and contrast the use of the three inventory costing methods.**

Comparing Inventory Costing Methods

OBJ. 6 **Describe and illustrate the reporting of merchandise inventory in the financial statements.**

Reporting Merchandise Inventory in the Financial Statements

Valuation at Lower of Cost or Market	EE **7-6**
Merchandise Inventory on the Balance Sheet	
Effect of Inventory Errors on the Financial Statements	EE **7-7**

OBJ. 7 **Describe and illustrate the inventory turnover and the days' sales in inventory in analyzing the efficiency and effectiveness of inventory management.**

Financial Analysis and Interpretation: Inventory Turnover and Days' Sales in Inventory

Compute Inventory Turnover and Day's Sales in Inventory	EE **7-8**

APP. OBJ. **Describe and illustrate the retail method and the gross profit method of estimating inventory.**

At a Glance 7 Page 372

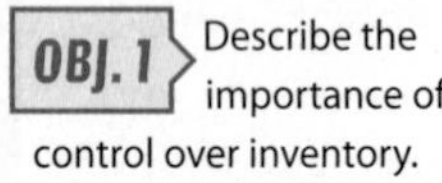
Describe the importance of control over inventory.

Control of Inventory

Two primary objectives of control over inventory are as follows:[1]

- Safeguarding the inventory from damage or theft.
- Reporting inventory in the financial statements.

Safeguarding Inventory

Controls for safeguarding inventory begin as soon as the inventory is ordered. The following documents are often used for inventory control:

- Purchase order
- Receiving report
- Vendor's invoice

The **purchase order** authorizes the purchase of the inventory from an approved vendor. As soon as the inventory is received, a receiving report is completed. The **receiving report** establishes an initial record of the receipt of the inventory. To make

1 Additional controls used by businesses are described and illustrated in Chapter 8, "Internal Control and Cash."

sure the inventory received is what was ordered, the receiving report is compared with the purchase order. The price, quantity, and description of the item on the purchase order and receiving report are then compared to the vendor's invoice. If the receiving report, purchase order, and vendor's invoice agree, the inventory is recorded in the accounting records. If any differences exist, they should be investigated and reconciled.

Recording inventory using a perpetual inventory system is also an effective means of control. The amount of inventory is always available in the **subsidiary inventory ledger**. This helps keep inventory quantities at proper levels. For example, comparing inventory quantities with maximum and minimum levels allows for the timely reordering of inventory and prevents ordering excess inventory.

Finally, controls for safeguarding inventory should include security measures to prevent damage and customer or employee theft. Some examples of security measures include the following:

- Storing inventory in areas that are restricted to only authorized employees
- Locking high-priced inventory in cabinets
- Using two-way mirrors, cameras, security tags, and guards

Link to Best Buy

Best Buy uses scanners to screen customers as they leave the store for merchandise that has not been purchased. In addition, Best Buy stations greeters at the store's entrance to keep customers from bringing in bags that can be used to shoplift merchandise.

Reporting Inventory

A **physical inventory** or *count of inventory* should be taken near year-end to make sure that the quantity of inventory reported in the financial statements is accurate. After the quantity of inventory on hand is determined, the cost of the inventory is assigned for reporting in the financial statements. Most companies assign costs to inventory using one of three inventory cost flow assumptions. If a physical count is not possible or inventory records are not available, the inventory cost may be estimated as described in the appendix at the end of this chapter.

Link to Best Buy

Best Buy conducts ongoing physical counts of inventory throughout the year as a basis for monitoring and predicting loss adjustments for theft.

Inventory Cost Flow Assumptions

OBJ. 2 Describe three inventory cost flow assumptions and explain how they impact the income statement and balance sheet.

An accounting issue arises when identical units of merchandise are acquired at different unit costs during a period. In such cases, when an item is sold, it is necessary to determine its cost using a cost flow assumption and related inventory costing method.

To illustrate, assume that three identical units of merchandise are purchased during May, as follows:

			Units	Cost
May	10	Purchase	1	$ 9
	18	Purchase	1	13
	24	Purchase	1	14
Total			3	$36

Average cost per unit: $12 ($36 ÷ 3 units)

Assume that one unit is sold on May 30 for $20. Depending upon which unit was sold, the gross profit varies from $11 to $6, computed as follows:

	May 10 Unit Sold	May 18 Unit Sold	May 24 Unit Sold
Sales	$20	$20	$20
Cost of merchandise sold	9	13	14
Gross profit	$11	$ 7	$ 6
Ending inventory	$27	$23	$22
	($13 + $14)	($9 + $14)	($9 + $13)

Under the **specific identification inventory cost flow method**, the unit sold is identified with a specific purchase. The ending inventory is made up of the remaining units on hand. Thus, the gross profit, cost of merchandise sold, and ending inventory can vary as illustrated. For example, if the May 18 unit was sold, the cost of merchandise sold is $13, the gross profit is $7, and the ending inventory is $23.

The specific identification method is not practical unless each inventory unit can be identified separately. For example, an automobile dealer may use the specific identification method because each automobile has a unique serial number. However, most businesses cannot identify each inventory unit separately. In such cases, one of the following three inventory cost flow methods is used.

Three common cost flow assumptions and related inventory costing methods are shown in Exhibit 1.

EXHIBIT 1 **Cost Flow Assumptions**

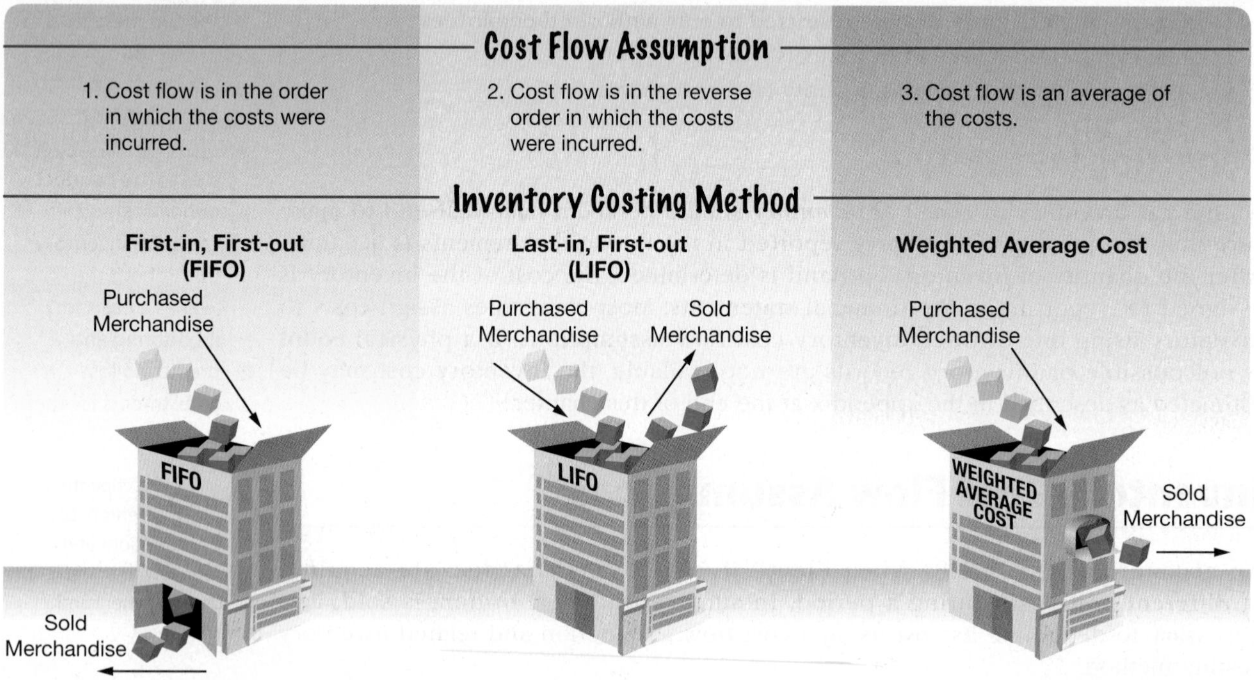

> **Link to Best Buy**
> **Best Buy** uses the first-in, first-out method for some of its inventory.

Under the **first-in, first-out (FIFO) inventory cost flow method**, the first units purchased are assumed to be sold and the ending inventory is made up of the most recent purchases. In the preceding example, the May 10 unit would be assumed to have been sold. Thus, the gross profit would be $11 ($20 – $9), and the ending inventory would be $27 ($13 + $14).

Under the **last-in, first-out (LIFO) inventory cost flow method**, the last units purchased are assumed to be sold and the ending inventory is made up of the first purchases. In the preceding example, the May 24 unit would be assumed to have been sold. Thus, the gross profit would be $6 ($20 – $14), and the ending inventory would be $22 ($9 + $13).

> **Link to Best Buy**
> **Best Buy** also uses the weighted average cost method for some of its inventory.

Under the **weighted average inventory cost flow method**, sometimes called the *average cost flow method*, the cost of the units sold and in ending inventory is a weighted average of the purchase costs. The purchase costs are weighted by the quantities purchased at each cost, thus the term *weighted average*. In the preceding example, the cost of the unit sold would be $12 ($36 ÷ 3 units), the gross profit would be $8 ($20 – $12), and the ending inventory would be $24 ($12 × 2 units). In this example, the purchase costs are weighted equally, since the same quantity (one) was purchased at each cost.

The three inventory cost flow methods, FIFO, LIFO, and weighted average, are shown in Exhibit 2. The FIFO method is used most frequently, followed by LIFO and weighted average methods.

EXHIBIT 2

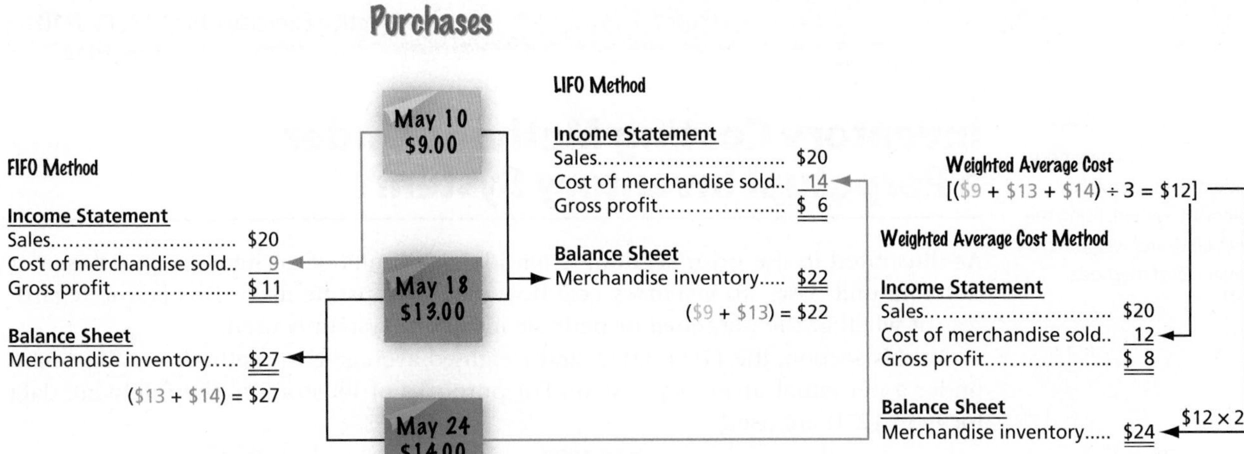

Business Connection

PAWN STARS AND SPECIFIC IDENTIFICATION

Pawn Stars is the History Channel's TV series featuring Rick Harrison's **Gold & Silver Pawn Shop** of Las Vegas, Nevada. As Rick says in the opening of every show, "you never know what is gonna come through that door." The show features the purchase of everything from antique pistols, original movie props, vintage cars and motorcycles, famous autographed memorabilia, and many other types of unusual collectibles. Each item needs to be appraised and a price negotiated with the seller. Once purchased, the pawn shop has an inventory to be presented to the public for sale. Gold & Silver Pawn uses the specific identification method for valuing inventory.

EXAMPLE EXERCISE 7-1 Cost Flow Methods

OBJ. 2

The following three identical units of Item QBM are purchased during February:

		Item QBM	Units	Cost
Feb.	8	Purchase	1	$ 45
	15	Purchase	1	48
	26	Purchase	1	51
		Total	3	$144
		Average cost per unit		$ 48 ($144 ÷ 3 units)

Assume that one unit is sold on February 27 for $70.

Determine the gross profit for February and ending inventory on February 28 using the (a) first-in, first-out (FIFO); (b) last-in, first-out (LIFO); and (c) weighted average cost methods.

(Continued)

Follow My Example 7-1

	Gross Profit	Ending Inventory
a. First-in, first-out (FIFO)...............	$25 ($70 − $45)	$99 ($48 + $51)
b. Last-in, first-out (LIFO)...............	$19 ($70 − $51)	$93 ($45 + $48)
c. Weighted average cost..............	$22 ($70 − $48)	$96 ($48 × 2)

Practice Exercises: PE 7-1A, PE 7-1B

OBJ. 3 Determine the cost of inventory under the perpetual inventory system, using the FIFO, LIFO, and weighted average cost methods.

Inventory Costing Methods Under a Perpetual Inventory System

As illustrated in the prior section, when identical units of an item are purchased at different unit costs, an inventory cost flow method must be used. This is true regardless of whether the perpetual or periodic inventory system is used.

In this section, the FIFO, LIFO, and weighted average cost methods are illustrated under a perpetual inventory system. For purposes of illustration, the following data for Item 127B are used:

	Item 127B	Units	Cost
Jan. 1	Inventory	1,000	$20.00
4	Sale at $30 per unit	700	
10	Purchase	500	22.40
22	Sale at $30 per unit	360	
28	Sale at $30 per unit	240	
30	Purchase	600	23.30

First-In, First-Out Method

When the FIFO method is used, costs are included in the cost of merchandise sold in the order in which they were purchased. This is often the same as the physical flow of the merchandise. Thus, the FIFO method often provides results that are about the same as those that would have been obtained using the specific identification method. For example, grocery stores shelve milk and other perishable products by expiration dates. Products with early expiration dates are stocked in front. In this way, the oldest products (earliest purchases) are sold first.

To illustrate, Exhibit 3 shows the use of FIFO under a perpetual inventory system for Item 127B. The journal entries and the subsidiary inventory ledger for Item 127B are shown in Exhibit 3 as follows:

1. The beginning balance on January 1 is $20,000 (1,000 units at a unit cost of $20).
2. On January 4, 700 units were sold at a price of $30 each for sales of $21,000 (700 units at a selling price of $30 per unit). The cost of merchandise sold is $14,000 (700 units at a unit cost of $20). After the sale, there remains $6,000 of inventory (300 units at a unit cost of $20).
3. On January 10, $11,200 is purchased (500 units at a unit cost of $22.40). After the purchase, the inventory is reported on two lines, $6,000 (300 units at a unit cost of $20.00) from the beginning inventory and $11,200 (500 units at a unit cost of $22.40) from the January 10 purchase.
4. On January 22, 360 units are sold at a price of $30 each for sales of $10,800 (360 units at a selling price of $30 per unit). Using FIFO, the cost of merchandise sold of $7,344 consists of $6,000 (300 units at a unit cost of $20.00) from the beginning inventory plus $1,344 (60 units at a unit cost of $22.40) from the January 10 purchase. After the sale, there remains $9,856 of inventory (440 units at a unit cost of $22.40) from the January 10 purchase.
5. The January 28 sale and January 30 purchase are recorded in a similar manner.

Entries and Perpetual Inventory Account (FIFO) EXHIBIT 3

		Debit	Credit
Jan. 4	Accounts Receivable	21,000	
	Sales		21,000
4	Cost of Merchandise Sold	14,000	
	Merchandise Inventory		14,000
10	Merchandise Inventory	11,200	
	Accounts Payable		11,200
22	Accounts Receivable	10,800	
	Sales		10,800
22	Cost of Merchandise Sold	7,344	
	Merchandise Inventory		7,344
28	Accounts Receivable	7,200	
	Sales		7,200
28	Cost of Merchandise Sold	5,376	
	Merchandise Inventory		5,376
30	Merchandise Inventory	13,980	
	Accounts Payable		13,980

Item 127B

	Purchases			Cost of Merchandise Sold			Inventory		
Date	Quantity	Unit Cost	Total Cost	Quantity	Unit Cost	Total Cost	Quantity	Unit Cost	Total Cost
Jan. 1							1,000	20.00	20,000
4				700	20.00	14,000	300	20.00	6,000
10	500	22.40	11,200				300	20.00	6,000
							500	22.40	11,200
22				300	20.00	6,000			
				60	22.40	1,344	440	22.40	9,856
28				240	22.40	5,376	200	22.40	4,480
30	600	23.30	13,980				200	22.40	4,480
							600	23.30	13,980
31	Balances					26,720			18,460

Cost of merchandise sold

January 31 inventory

6. The ending balance on January 31 is $18,460. This balance is made up of two layers of inventory as follows:

	Date of Purchase	Quantity	Unit Cost	Total Cost
Layer 1	Jan. 10	200	$22.40	$ 4,480
Layer 2	Jan. 30	600	23.30	13,980
Total		800		$18,460

EXAMPLE EXERCISE 7-2 Perpetual Inventory Using FIFO OBJ. 3

Beginning inventory, purchases, and sales for Item ER27 are as follows:

Nov. 1	Inventory	40 units at $5
5	Sale	30 units
11	Purchase	70 units at $7
21	Sale	36 units

Assuming a perpetual inventory system and using the first-in, first-out (FIFO) method, determine (a) the cost of merchandise sold on November 21 and (b) the inventory on November 30.

Follow My Example 7-2

a. Cost of merchandise sold (November 21):

10 units at $5	$ 50
26 units at $7	182
36 units	$232

b. Inventory, November 30:
$308 (44 units × $7)

Practice Exercises: PE 7-2A, PE 7-2B

Last-In, First-Out Method

When the LIFO method is used, the cost of the units sold is the cost of the most recent purchases. The LIFO method was originally used in those rare cases where the units sold were taken from the most recently purchased units. However, for tax purposes, LIFO is now widely used even when it does not represent the physical flow of units. The tax impact of LIFO is discussed later in this chapter.

To illustrate, Exhibit 4 shows the use of LIFO under a perpetual inventory system for Item 127B. The journal entries and the subsidiary inventory ledger for Item 127B are shown in Exhibit 4 as follows:

1. The beginning balance on January 1 is $20,000 (1,000 units at a unit of cost of $20.00).
2. On January 4, 700 units were sold at a price of $30 each for sales of $21,000 (700 units at a selling price of $30 per unit). The cost of merchandise sold is $14,000 (700 units at a unit cost of $20). After the sale, there remains $6,000 of inventory (300 units at a unit cost of $20).
3. On January 10, $11,200 is purchased (500 units at a unit cost of $22.40). After the purchase, the inventory is reported on two lines, $6,000 (300 units at a unit cost of $20.00) from the beginning inventory and $11,200 (500 units at $22.40 per unit) from the January 10 purchase.
4. On January 22, 360 units are sold at a price of $30 each for sales of $10,800 (360 units at a selling price of $30 per unit). Using LIFO, the cost of merchandise sold is $8,064 (360 units at unit cost of $22.40) from the January 10 purchase. After the sale, there remains $9,136 of inventory consisting of $6,000 (300 units at a unit cost of $20.00) from the beginning inventory and $3,136 (140 units at a unit cost of $22.40) from the January 10 purchase.
5. The January 28 sale and January 30 purchase are recorded in a similar manner.
6. The ending balance on January 31 is $17,980. This balance is made up of two layers of inventory as follows:

	Date of Purchase	Quantity	Unit Cost	Total Cost
Layer 1	Beg. inv. (Jan. 1)	200	$20.00	$ 4,000
Layer 2	Jan. 30	600	23.30	13,980
Total		800		$17,980

When the LIFO method is used, the subsidiary inventory ledger is sometimes maintained in units only. The units are converted to dollars when the financial statements are prepared at the end of the period.

EXHIBIT 4 **Entries and Perpetual Inventory Account (LIFO)**

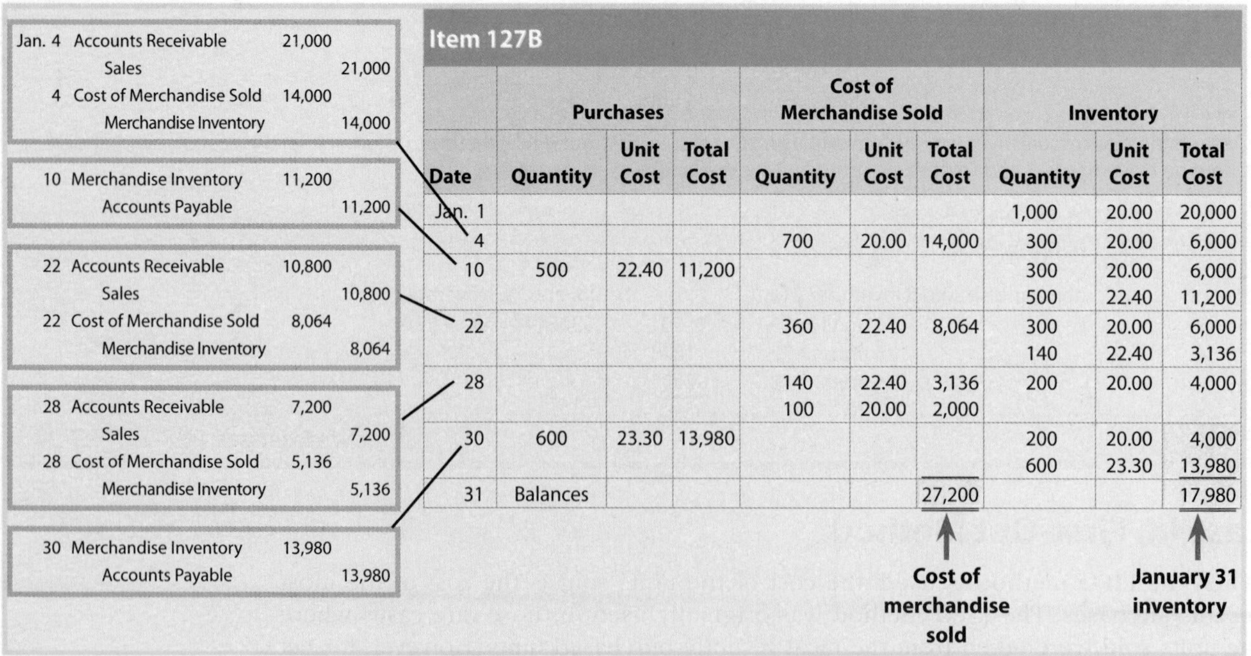

Date	Account	Debit	Credit
Jan. 4	Accounts Receivable	21,000	
	Sales		21,000
4	Cost of Merchandise Sold	14,000	
	Merchandise Inventory		14,000
10	Merchandise Inventory	11,200	
	Accounts Payable		11,200
22	Accounts Receivable	10,800	
	Sales		10,800
22	Cost of Merchandise Sold	8,064	
	Merchandise Inventory		8,064
28	Accounts Receivable	7,200	
	Sales		7,200
28	Cost of Merchandise Sold	5,136	
	Merchandise Inventory		5,136
30	Merchandise Inventory	13,980	
	Accounts Payable		13,980

Item 127B

	Purchases			Cost of Merchandise Sold			Inventory		
Date	Quantity	Unit Cost	Total Cost	Quantity	Unit Cost	Total Cost	Quantity	Unit Cost	Total Cost
Jan. 1							1,000	20.00	20,000
4				700	20.00	14,000	300	20.00	6,000
10	500	22.40	11,200				300	20.00	6,000
							500	22.40	11,200
22				360	22.40	8,064	300	20.00	6,000
							140	22.40	3,136
28				140	22.40	3,136	200	20.00	4,000
				100	20.00	2,000			
30	600	23.30	13,980				200	20.00	4,000
							600	23.30	13,980
31	Balances					27,200			17,980

EXAMPLE EXERCISE 7-3 Perpetual Inventory Using LIFO **OBJ. 3**

Beginning inventory, purchases, and sales for Item ER27 are as follows:

Nov. 1	Inventory	40 units at $5
5	Sale	30 units
11	Purchase	70 units at $7
21	Sale	36 units

Assuming a perpetual inventory system and using the last-in, first-out (LIFO) method, determine (a) the cost of the merchandise sold on November 21 and (b) the inventory on November 30.

Follow My Example 7-3

a. Cost of merchandise sold (November 21):
$252 (36 units × $7)

b. Inventory, November 30:

10 units at $5	$ 50
34 units at $7	238
44 units	$288

Practice Exercises: PE 7-3A, PE 7-3B

International Connection

IFRS INTERNATIONAL FINANCIAL REPORTING STANDARDS (IFRS)

IFRS permit the first-in, first-out (FIFO) and weighted average cost methods but prohibit the last-in, first-out (LIFO) method for determining inventory costs. Since LIFO is used in the United States, adoption of IFRS could have a significant impact on many U.S. companies. For example, **Caterpillar Inc.** uses LIFO. For a recent year, Caterpillar reported that its inventories would have been $2,009 million higher if FIFO had been used. Since Caterpillar reported profits of $6,147 million for the year, the adoption of IFRS would have significantly affected net income if IFRS and FIFO had been used.

Weighted Average Cost Method

When the weighted average cost method is used in a perpetual inventory system, a weighted average unit cost for each item is computed each time a purchase is made. This unit cost is used to determine the cost of each sale until another purchase is made and a new average is computed. This technique is called a *moving average.*

To illustrate, Exhibit 5 shows the use of weighted average under a perpetual inventory system for Item 127B.

The journal entries and the subsidiary inventory ledger for Item 127B are shown in Exhibit 5 as follows:

1. The beginning balance on January 1 is $20,000 (1,000 units at a unit cost of $20).
2. On January 4, 700 units were sold at a price of $30 each for sales of $21,000 (700 units at a selling price of $30 per unit). The cost of merchandise sold is $14,000 (700 units at a unit cost of $20.00). After the sale, there remains $6,000 of inventory (300 units at a unit cost of $20.00).
3. On January 10, $11,200 is purchased (500 units at a unit cost of $22.40). After the purchase, the weighted average unit cost of $21.50 is determined by dividing the total cost of the inventory on hand of $17,200 ($6,000 + $11,200) by the total quantity of inventory on hand of 800 (300 + 500) units. Thus, after the purchase, the inventory consists of 800 units at $21.50 per unit for a total cost of $17,200.

EXHIBIT 5 **Entries and Perpetual Inventory Account (Weighted Average)**

Jan. 4 Accounts Receivable	21,000	
Sales		21,000
4 Cost of Merchandise Sold	14,000	
Merchandise Inventory		14,000

10 Merchandise Inventory	11,200	
Accounts Payable		11,200

22 Accounts Receivable	10,800	
Sales		10,800
22 Cost of Merchandise Sold	7,740	
Merchandise Inventory		7,740

28 Accounts Receivable	7,200	
Sales		7,200
28 Cost of Merchandise Sold	5,160	
Merchandise Inventory		5,160

30 Merchandise Inventory	13,980	
Accounts Payable		13,980

Item 127B

	Purchases			Cost of Merchandise Sold			Inventory		
Date	Quantity	Unit Cost	Total Cost	Quantity	Unit Cost	Total Cost	Quantity	Unit Cost	Total Cost
Jan. 1							1,000	20.00	20,000
4				700	20.00	14,000	300	20.00	6,000
10	500	22.40	11,200				800	21.50	17,200
22				360	21.50	7,740	440	21.50	9,460
28				240	21.50	5,160	200	21.50	4,300
30	600	23.30	13,980				800	22.85	18,280
31	Balances					26,900	800	22.85	18,280

Cost of merchandise sold

January 31 inventory

4. On January 22, 360 units are sold at a price of $30 each for sales of $10,800 (360 units at a selling price of $30 per unit). Using weighted average, the cost of merchandise sold is $7,740 (360 units × $21.50 per unit). After the sale, there remains $9,460 of inventory (440 units × $21.50 per unit).
5. The January 28 sale and January 30 purchase are recorded in a similar manner.
6. The ending balance on January 31 is $18,280 (800 units × $22.85 per unit).

EXAMPLE EXERCISE 7-4 Perpetual Inventory Using Weighted Average — OBJ. 3

Beginning inventory, purchases, and sales for ER27 are as follows:

Nov. 1	Inventory	40 units at $5
5	Sale	30 units
11	Purchase	70 units at $7
21	Sale	36 units

Assuming a perpetual inventory system using the weighted average method, determine (a) the weighted average unit cost after the November 11 purchase, (b) the cost of the merchandise sold on November 21, and (c) the inventory on November 30.

Follow My Example 7-4

a. Weighted average unit cost: $6.75
Inventory total cost after purchase on November 21:

	Cost
10 units at $5	$ 50
70 units at $7	490
80 units	$540

Weighted average unit cost = $6.75 ($540 ÷ 80 units)

b. Cost of merchandise sold (November 21):
$243 (36 units × $6.75)

c. Inventory, November 30:
$297 (44 units at $6.75)

Practice Exercises: PE 7-4A, PE 7-4B

Business Connection

COMPUTERIZED PERPETUAL INVENTORY SYSTEMS

Your purchases are scanned when you go through the checkout line at **Best Buy**. The scanned data are used to identify the price and adjust the inventory levels. Computerized perpetual inventory systems are used like this when there are many inventory transactions and a manual system is simply not feasible.

Computerized perpetual inventory systems are useful to managers in controlling and managing inventory. For example, if Best Buy has fast-selling items, they can be reordered before the stock runs out. Sales patterns can also be analyzed to determine when to mark down merchandise or when to restock seasonal merchandise. Finally, computerized inventory data can be used to evaluate the effectiveness of advertising campaigns and promotions.

Inventory Costing Methods Under a Periodic Inventory System

OBJ. 4 Determine the cost of inventory under the periodic inventory system, using the FIFO, LIFO, and weighted average cost methods.

When the periodic inventory system is used, only revenue is recorded each time a sale is made. No entry is made at the time of the sale to record the cost of the merchandise sold. At the end of the accounting period, a physical inventory is taken to determine the cost of the inventory and the cost of the merchandise sold.[2]

Like the perpetual inventory system, a cost flow assumption must be made when identical units are acquired at different unit costs during a period. In such cases, the FIFO, LIFO, or weighted average cost method is used.

First-In, First-Out Method

To illustrate the use of the FIFO method in a periodic inventory system, we use the same data for Item 127B as in the perpetual inventory example. The beginning inventory and purchases of Item 127B in January are as follows:

Jan. 1	Inventory	1,000 units at	$20.00	$20,000
10	Purchase	500 units at	22.40	11,200
30	Purchase	600 units at	23.30	13,980
Available for sale during month		2,100		$45,180

The physical count on January 31 shows that 800 units are on hand. Using the FIFO method, the cost of the merchandise on hand at the end of the period is made up of the most recent costs. The cost of the 800 units in the ending inventory on January 31 is determined as follows:

Most recent costs, January 30 purchase	600 units at	$23.30	$13,980
Next most recent costs, January 10 purchase	200 units at	$22.40	4,480
Inventory, January 31	800 units		$18,460

Deducting the cost of the January 31 inventory of $18,460 from the cost of merchandise available for sale of $45,180 yields the cost of merchandise sold of $26,720, computed as follows:

Beginning inventory, January 1	$20,000
Purchases ($11,200 + $13,980)	25,180
Cost of merchandise available for sale in January	$45,180
Less ending inventory, January 31	18,460
Cost of merchandise sold	$26,720

2 Determining the cost of merchandise sold using the periodic system was illustrated in Appendix 3 in Chapter 6.

The $18,460 cost of the ending merchandise inventory on January 31 is made up of the most recent costs. The $26,720 cost of merchandise sold is made up of the beginning inventory and the earliest costs. Exhibit 6 shows the relationship of the cost of merchandise sold for January and the ending inventory on January 31.

EXHIBIT 6 First-In, First-Out Flow of Costs

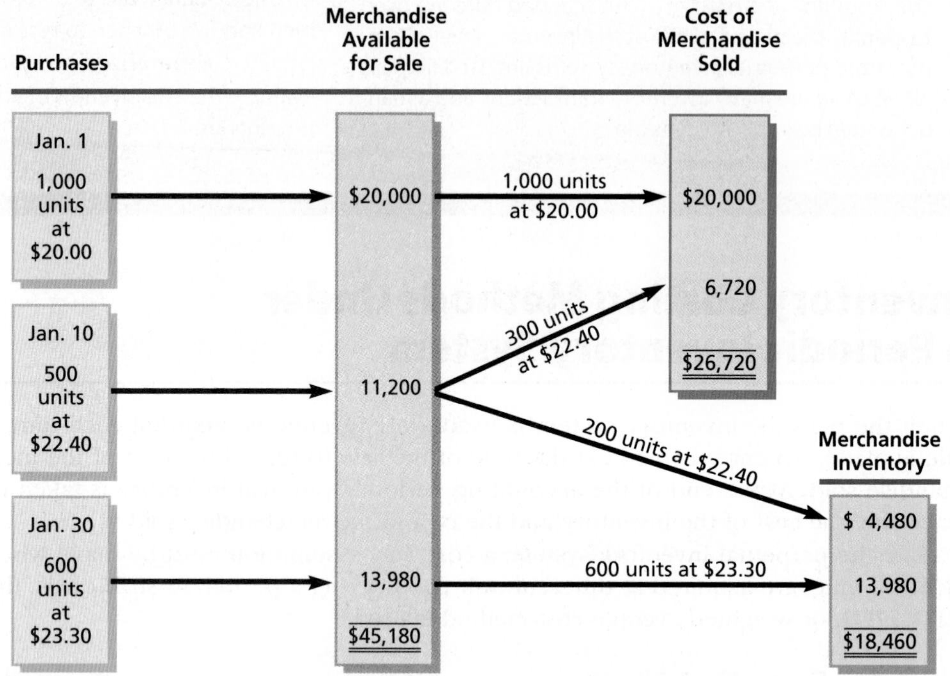

Last-In, First-Out Method

When the LIFO method is used, the cost of merchandise on hand at the end of the period is made up of the earliest costs. Based on the same data as in the FIFO example, the cost of the 800 units in ending inventory on January 31 is $16,000, which consists of 800 units from the beginning inventory at a cost of $20.00 per unit.

Deducting the cost of the January 31 inventory of $16,000 from the cost of merchandise available for sale of $45,180 yields the cost of merchandise sold of $29,180, computed as follows:

Beginning inventory, January 1	$20,000
Purchases ($11,200 + $13,980)	25,180
Cost of merchandise available for sale in January	$45,180
Less ending inventory, January 31	16,000
Cost of merchandise sold	$29,180

The $16,000 cost of the ending merchandise inventory on January 31 is made up of the earliest costs. The $29,180 cost of merchandise sold is made up of the most recent costs. Exhibit 7 shows the relationship of the cost of merchandise sold for January and the ending inventory on January 31.

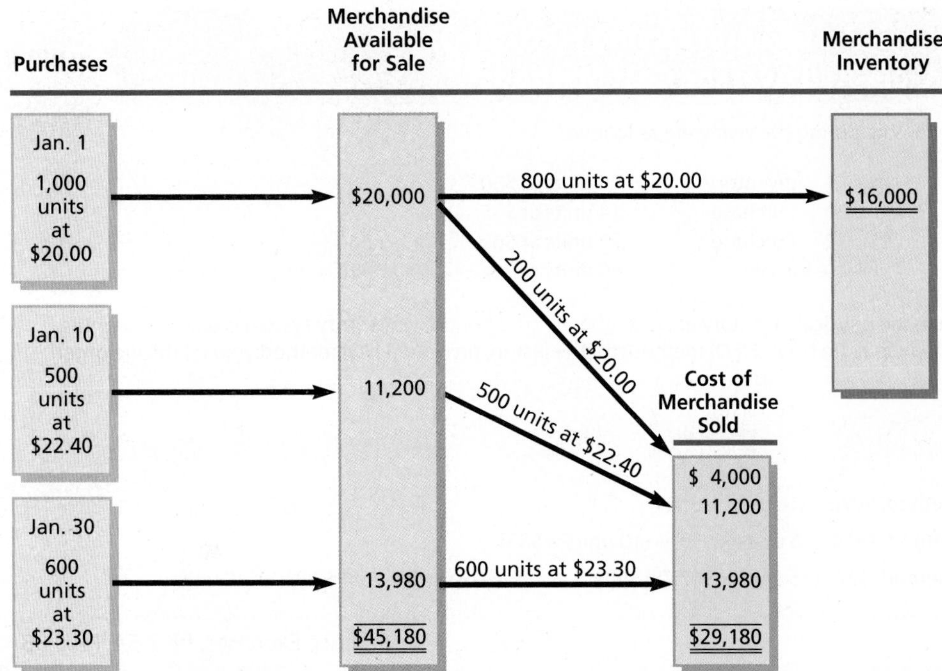

EXHIBIT 7

Last-In, First-Out Flow of Costs

Weighted Average Cost Method

The weighted average cost method uses the weighted average unit cost for determining the cost of merchandise sold and the ending merchandise inventory. If purchases are relatively uniform during a period, the weighted average cost method provides results that are similar to the physical flow of goods.

The weighted average unit cost is determined as follows:

$$\text{Weighted Average Unit Cost} = \frac{\text{Total Cost of Units Available for Sale}}{\text{Units Available for Sale}}$$

To illustrate, the data for Item 127B are used as follows:

$$\text{Weighted Average Unit Cost} = \frac{\text{Total Cost of Units Available for Sale}}{\text{Units Available for Sale}} = \frac{\$45{,}180}{2{,}100 \text{ units}}$$

$$= \$21.51 \text{ per unit (Rounded)}$$

The cost of the January 31 ending inventory is as follows:

Inventory, January 31: $17,208 (800 units × $21.51)

Deducting the cost of the January 31 inventory of $17,208 from the cost of merchandise available for sale of $45,180 yields the cost of merchandise sold of $27,972, computed as follows:

Beginning inventory, January 1	$20,000
Purchases ($11,200 + $13,980)	25,180
Cost of merchandise available for sale in January	$45,180
Less ending inventory, January 31	17,208
Cost of merchandise sold	$27,972

EXAMPLE EXERCISE 7-5 Periodic Inventory Using FIFO, LIFO, and Weighted Average Cost Methods **OBJ. 4**

The units of an item available for sale during the year were as follows:

Jan. 1	Inventory	6 units at $50	$ 300
Mar. 20	Purchase	14 units at $55	770
Oct. 30	Purchase	20 units at $62	1,240
Available for sale		40 units	$2,310

There are 16 units of the item in the physical inventory at December 31. The periodic inventory system is used. Determine the inventory cost using (a) the first-in, first-out (FIFO) method; (b) the last-in, first-out (LIFO) method; and (c) the weighted average cost method.

Follow My Example 7-5

a. First-in, first-out (FIFO) method: $992 = (16 units × $62)

b. Last-in, first-out (LIFO) method: $850 = (6 units × $50) + (10 units × $55)

c. Weighted average cost method: $924 (16 units × $57.75), where average cost = $57.75 = $2,310 ÷ 40 units

Practice Exercises: PE 7-5A, PE 7-5B

OBJ. 5 Compare and contrast the use of the three inventory costing methods.

Comparing Inventory Costing Methods

A different cost flow is assumed for the FIFO, LIFO, and weighted average inventory cost flow methods. As a result, the three methods normally yield different amounts for the following:

- Cost of merchandise sold
- Gross profit
- Net income
- Ending merchandise inventory

Using the perpetual inventory system illustration with sales of $39,000 (1,300 units × $30), the following differences are apparent:[3]

Partial Income Statements

	First-In, First-Out	Weighted Average Cost	Last-In, First-Out
Sales	$39,000	$39,000	$39,000
Cost of merchandise sold	26,720	26,900	27,200
Gross profit	$12,280	$12,100	$11,800
Merchandise Inventory, Jan. 31	$18,460	$18,280	$17,980

The preceding differences show the effect of increasing costs (prices). If costs (prices) remain the same, all three methods would yield the same results. However, costs (prices) normally do change. The effects of changing costs (prices) on the FIFO and LIFO methods are summarized in Exhibit 8. The weighted average cost method will always yield results between those of FIFO and LIFO.

FIFO reports higher gross profit and net income than the LIFO method when costs (prices) are increasing, as shown in Exhibit 8. However, in periods of rapidly rising costs, the inventory that is sold must be replaced at increasingly higher costs. In such cases, the larger FIFO gross profit and net income are sometimes called *inventory profits* or *illusory profits*.

3 Similar results would also occur when comparing inventory costing methods under a periodic inventory system.

	Increasing Costs (Prices)		Decreasing Costs (Prices)	
	Highest Amount	**Lowest Amount**	**Highest Amount**	**Lowest Amount**
Cost of merchandise sold	LIFO	FIFO	FIFO	LIFO
Gross profit	FIFO	LIFO	LIFO	FIFO
Net income	FIFO	LIFO	LIFO	FIFO
Ending merchandise inventory	FIFO	LIFO	LIFO	FIFO

EXHIBIT 8

Effects of Changing Costs (Prices): FIFO and LIFO Cost Methods

During a period of increasing costs, LIFO matches more recent costs against sales on the income statement. Thus, it can be argued that the LIFO method more nearly matches current costs with current revenues. LIFO also offers an income tax savings during periods of increasing costs. This is because LIFO reports the lowest amount of gross profit and, thus, taxable net income. However, under LIFO, the ending inventory on the balance sheet may be quite different from its current replacement cost. In such cases, the financial statements normally include a note that estimates what the inventory would have been if FIFO had been used.

The weighted average cost method is, in a sense, a compromise between FIFO and LIFO. The effect of cost (price) trends is averaged in determining the cost of merchandise sold and the ending inventory.

Integrity, Objectivity, and Ethics in Business

WHERE'S THE BONUS?

Managers are often given bonuses based on reported earnings numbers. This can create a conflict. LIFO can improve the value of the company through lower taxes. However, in periods of rising costs (prices), LIFO also produces a lower earnings number and, therefore, lower management bonuses. Ethically, managers should select accounting procedures that will maximize the value of the firm rather than their own compensation. Compensation specialists can help avoid this ethical dilemma by adjusting the bonus plan for the accounting procedure differences.

Reporting Merchandise Inventory in the Financial Statements

OBJ. 6 Describe and illustrate the reporting of merchandise inventory in the financial statements.

Cost is the primary basis for valuing and reporting inventories in the financial statements. However, inventory may be valued at other than cost in the following cases:

1. The cost of replacing items in inventory is below the recorded cost.
2. The inventory cannot be sold at normal prices due to imperfections, style changes, spoilage, damage, obsolescence, or other causes.

Valuation at Lower of Cost or Market

If the market is lower than the purchase cost, the **lower-of-cost-or-market (LCM) method** is used to value the inventory. *Market*, as used in *lower of cost or market*, is the **net realizable value** of the merchandise.[4] Net realizable value is determined as follows:

Net Realizable Value = Estimated Selling Price – Direct Costs of Disposal

Direct costs of disposal include selling expenses such as special advertising or sales commissions.

To illustrate, assume the following data about an item of damaged merchandise:

Original cost	$1,000
Estimated selling price	800
Estimated selling expenses	150

In applying LCM, the market value of the merchandise is $650, computed as follows:

Market Value (Net Realizable Value) = $800 – $150 = $650

Link to Best Buy

Best Buy values its inventory at lower of cost or market based upon cost and the amount it expects to realize from the sale.

Thus, the merchandise would be valued at $650, which is the lower of its cost of $1,000 and its market value of $650.

The amount of any price decline is included in the cost of merchandise sold. This, in turn, reduces gross profit and net income in the period in which the price declines occur. This matching of price declines to the period in which they occur is the primary advantage of using the lower-of-cost-or-market method.

To illustrate, assume the following data for 400 identical units of Item Echo in inventory on December 31:

Cost per unit	$10.25
Market value (net realizable value) per unit	9.50

Since the market value of Item Echo is $9.50 per unit, $9.50 is used under the lower-of-cost-or-market method.

Link to Best Buy

The excess of cost over the amount **Best Buy** expects to receive from the sale of an item is called a *markdown*.

Exhibit 9 illustrates applying the lower-of-cost-or-market method to each inventory item (Echo, Foxtrot, Sierra, Tango). As applied on an item-by-item basis, the total lower-of-cost-or-market is $15,070, which is a market decline of $450 ($15,520 – $15,070). This market decline of $450 is included in the cost of merchandise sold.

Rather than applying the LCM method to each item of inventory, LCM can be applied to the total inventory.[5] For example, assume that items Echo, Foxtrot, Sierra, and Tango make up the total inventory in Exhibit 9. In this case, the LCM as applied to the total inventory is determined by comparing the total cost of $15,520 to the total market value of $15,472. Thus, the LCM is $15,472 if applied to the total inventory.

EXHIBIT 9

Determining Inventory at Lower of Cost or Market (LCM)

	A	B	C	D	E	F	G
1				Market Value			
2		Inventory	Cost per	per Unit		Total	
3	Item	Quantity	Unit	(Net Realizable Value)	Cost	Market	LCM
4	Echo	400	$10.25	$ 9.50	$ 4,100	$ 3,800	$ 3,800
5	Foxtrot	120	22.50	24.10	2,700	2,892	2,700
6	Sierra	600	8.00	7.75	4,800	4,650	4,650
7	Tango	280	14.00	14.75	3,920	4,130	3,920
8	Total				$15,520	$15,472	$15,070
9							

4 Accounting Standards Update, *Inventory* (Topic 330): *Simplifying the Measurement of Inventory*, No. 2015-11, July 2015, FASB (Norwalk, CT).

5 The LCM can also be applied to different classes of inventory.

EXAMPLE EXERCISE 7-6 Lower-of-Cost-or-Market Method **OBJ. 6**

On the basis of the following data, determine the value of the inventory at the lower of cost or market. Apply lower of cost or market to each inventory item as shown in Exhibit 9.

Item	Inventory Quantity	Cost per Unit	Market Value per Unit (Net Realizable Value)
C17Y	10	$ 39	$40
B563	7	110	98

Follow My Example 7-6

	A	B	C	D	E	F	G
1				Market Value			
2		Inventory	Cost per	per Unit		Total	
3	Item	Quantity	Unit	(Net Realizable Value)	Cost	Market	LCM
4	C17Y	10	$ 39	$40	$ 390	$ 400	$ 390
5	B563	7	110	98	770	686	686
6	Total				$1,160	$1,086	$1,076
7							

Practice Exercises: PE 7-6A, PE 7-6B

Business Connection

GOOD SAMARITAN

A corporation may decide that the best way to dispose of unwanted inventory is to give it to charity. Under the Internal Revenue Code, a corporation may take an "enhanced" deduction for charitable contributions of select inventory, such as food, clothing, and medical supplies, used for the ill, the needy, or infants. Thus, for example, disaster relief contributions would be subject to the enhanced deduction. The enhanced deduction is for amounts up to half the planned profit on the item but not greater than twice what the company paid for it. Websites such as www.wastetocharity.org can help corporations donate unwanted items to recyclers and organizations.

Merchandise Inventory on the Balance Sheet

Merchandise inventory is usually reported in the Current Assets section of the balance sheet. In addition to this amount, the following are reported:

- The method of determining the cost of the inventory (FIFO, LIFO, or weighted average)
- The method of valuing the inventory (cost or the lower of cost or market)

The financial statement reporting for the topics covered in Chapters 7–15 is illustrated using excerpts from the financial statements of **Mornin' Joe**. Mornin' Joe is a fictitious company that offers drip and espresso coffee in a coffeehouse setting. The complete financial statements of Mornin' Joe are illustrated at the end of the last chapter.

The balance sheet presentation for merchandise inventory for Mornin' Joe is as follows:

Link to Best Buy

Best Buy uses the weighted average cost and first-in, first-out methods for recording inventory.

Mornin' Joe Balance Sheet December 31, 20Y6	
Current assets:	
Cash and cash equivalents	$235,000
Merchandise inventory—at lower of cost (first-in, first-out method) or market	120,000

It is not unusual for a large business to use different costing methods for segments of its inventories. Also, a business may change its inventory costing method. In such cases, the effect of the change and the reason for the change are disclosed in the financial statements.

Effect of Inventory Errors on the Financial Statements

Any errors in merchandise inventory will affect the balance sheet and income statement. Some reasons that inventory errors may occur include the following:

- Physical inventory on hand was miscounted.
- Costs were incorrectly assigned to inventory. For example, the FIFO, LIFO, or weighted average cost method was incorrectly applied.
- Inventory in transit was incorrectly included or excluded from inventory.
- Consigned inventory was incorrectly included or excluded from inventory.

Inventory errors often arise from merchandise that is in transit at year-end. As discussed in Chapter 6, shipping terms determine when the title to merchandise passes. When goods are purchased or sold *FOB shipping point*, title passes to the buyer when the goods are shipped. When the terms are *FOB destination*, title passes to the buyer when the goods are received.

To illustrate, assume that SysExpress ordered the following merchandise from American Products:

Date ordered:	December 27, 20Y1
Amount:	$10,000
Terms:	FOB shipping point, 2/10, n/30
Date shipped by seller:	December 30
Date delivered:	January 3, 20Y2

When SysExpress counts its physical inventory on December 31, 20Y1, the merchandise is still in transit. In such cases, it would be easy for SysExpress not to include the $10,000 of merchandise in its December 31 physical inventory. However, since the merchandise was purchased *FOB shipping point*, SysExpress owns the merchandise although it was not delivered until January 3. Thus, it should be included in the December 31 inventory even though it was not delivered until January 3. Likewise, any merchandise *sold* by SysExpress *FOB destination* is still SysExpress's inventory even if it is in transit to the buyer on December 31.

Inventory errors often arise from **consigned inventory**. Manufacturers sometimes ship merchandise to retailers who act as the manufacturer's selling agent. The manufacturer, called the **consignor**, retains title until the goods are sold. Such merchandise is said to be shipped *on consignment* to the retailer, called the **consignee**.

Any unsold merchandise at year-end is a part of the manufacturer's (consignor's) inventory even though the merchandise is at the retailer (consignee). At year-end, it would be easy for the retailer (consignee) to incorrectly include the consigned merchandise in its physical inventory. Likewise, the manufacturer (consignor) should include consigned inventory in its physical inventory even though the inventory is not on hand.

Income Statement Effects Inventory errors will misstate the income statement amounts for cost of merchandise sold, gross profit, and net income. The effects of inventory errors on the current period's income statement are summarized in Exhibit 10.

EXHIBIT 10

Effect of Inventory Errors on Current Period's Income Statement

Inventory Error	Income Statement Effect: Cost of Merchandise Sold	Gross Profit	Net Income
Beginning inventory is:			
Understated ↓	Understated ↓	↑ Overstated	↑ Overstated
↑ Overstated	↑ Overstated	Understated ↓	Understated ↓
Ending inventory is:			
Understated ↓	↑ Overstated	Understated ↓	Understated ↓
↑ Overstated	Understated ↓	↑ Overstated	↑ Overstated

To illustrate, the effects of inventory errors are shown on the income statements of SysExpress in Exhibit 11.[6] On December 31, 20Y1, assume that SysExpress incorrectly records its physical inventory as $50,000 instead of the correct amount of $60,000.

Effects of Inventory Errors on Two Years' Income Statements **EXHIBIT 11**

SysExpress
Income Statement
For the Years Ended December 31, 20Y1 and 20Y2

	20Y1 Correct		20Y1 Incorrect		20Y2 Incorrect		20Y2 Correct	
Sales		$980,000		$ 980,000		$1,100,000		$1,100,000
Merchandise inventory, January 1	$ 55,000		$ 55,000		$ 50,000		$ 60,000	
Purchases	650,000		650,000		700,000		700,000	
Merchandise available for sale	$705,000		$705,000		$750,000		$760,000	
Less merchandise inventory, December 31	60,000		50,000		70,000		70,000	
Cost of merchandise sold		645,000		655,000		680,000		690,000
Gross profit		$335,000		$325,000		$ 420,000		$ 410,000
Operating expenses		100,000		100,000		120,000		120,000
Net income		$235,000		$225,000		$ 300,000		$ 290,000

$10,000 Understatement of Net Income

$10,000 Overstatement of Net Income

Net Effect Is Zero for Two Years
The inventory errors reverse (or cancel) so that the combined net income for the two years of $525,000 ($225,000 + $300,000) is correct.

6 The effects of inventory errors will be illustrated using the periodic system. This is because it is easier to see the impacts of inventory errors on the income statement using the periodic system. The effects of inventory errors would be the same under the perpetual inventory system.

Thus, the December 31, 20Y1, inventory is understated by $10,000 ($60,000 – $50,000). As a result, the cost of merchandise sold is overstated by $10,000. The gross profit and the net income for the year will also be understated by $10,000.

The December 31, 20Y1, merchandise inventory becomes the January 1, 20Y2, inventory. Thus, the beginning inventory for 20Y2 is understated by $10,000. As a result, the cost of merchandise sold is understated by $10,000 for 20Y2. The gross profit and net income for 20Y2 will be overstated by $10,000.

As shown in Exhibit 11, because the ending inventory of one period is the beginning inventory of the next period, the effects of inventory errors carry forward to the next period. Specifically, if uncorrected, the effects of inventory errors reverse themselves in the next period. In Exhibit 11, the combined net income for the two years of $525,000 is correct even though the 20Y1 and 20Y2 income statements were incorrect.

Balance Sheet Effects Inventory errors misstate the merchandise inventory, current assets, total assets, and owner's equity on the balance sheet. The effects of inventory errors on the current period's balance sheet are summarized in Exhibit 12.

EXHIBIT 12

Effect of Inventory Errors on Current Period's Balance Sheet

	Balance Sheet Effect			
Ending Inventory Error	**Merchandise Inventory**	**Current Assets**	**Total Assets**	**Owner's Equity (Capital)**
Understated ↓	Understated ↓	Understated ↓	Understated ↓	Understated ↓
↑ Overstated	↑ Overstated	↑ Overstated	↑ Overstated	↑ Overstated

For the SysExpress illustration shown in Exhibit 11, the December 31, 20Y1, ending inventory was understated by $10,000. As a result, the merchandise inventory, current assets, and total assets would be understated by $10,000 on the December 31, 20Y1, balance sheet. Because the ending physical inventory is understated, the cost of merchandise sold for 20Y1 will be overstated by $10,000. Thus, the gross profit and the net income for 20Y1 are understated by $10,000. Because the net income is closed to owner's equity (capital) at the end of the period, the owner's equity on the December 31, 20Y1, balance sheet is also understated by $10,000.

Inventory errors reverse themselves within two years. As a result, the balance sheet will be correct as of December 31, 20Y2. Using the SysExpress illustration from Exhibit 11, these effects are summarized as follows:

	Amount of Misstatement	
Balance Sheet:	December 31, 20Y1	December 31, 20Y2
Merchandise inventory overstated (understated)	$(10,000)	Correct
Current assets overstated (understated)	(10,000)	Correct
Total assets overstated (understated)	(10,000)	Correct
Owner's equity overstated (understated)	(10,000)	Correct
Income Statement:	20Y1	20Y2
Cost of merchandise sold overstated (understated)	$ 10,000	$(10,000)
Gross profit overstated (understated)	(10,000)	10,000
Net income overstated (understated)	(10,000)	10,000

EXAMPLE EXERCISE 7-7 Effect of Inventory Errors OBJ. 6

Zula Repair Shop incorrectly counted its December 31, 20Y8, inventory as $250,000 instead of the correct amount of $220,000. Indicate the effect of the misstatement on Zula's December 31, 20Y8, balance sheet and income statement for the year ended December 31, 20Y8.

Follow My Example 7-7

	Amount of Misstatement Overstatement (Understatement)
Balance Sheet:	
Merchandise inventory overstated	$ 30,000
Current assets overstated	30,000
Total assets overstated	30,000
Owner's equity overstated	30,000
Income Statement:	
Cost of merchandise sold understated	$(30,000)
Gross profit overstated	30,000
Net income overstated	30,000

Practice Exercises: PE 7-7A, PE 7-7B

Financial Analysis and Interpretation: Inventory Turnover and Days' Sales in Inventory

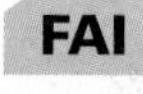

OBJ. 7 Describe and illustrate the inventory turnover and the days' sales in inventory in analyzing the efficiency and effectiveness of inventory management.

FAI

A merchandising business should keep enough inventory on hand to meet its customers' needs. A failure to do so may result in lost sales. However, too much inventory ties up funds that could be used to improve operations. Also, excess inventory increases expenses such as storage and property taxes. Finally, excess inventory increases the risk of losses due to price declines, damage, or changes in customer tastes.

Two measures to analyze the efficiency and effectiveness of inventory management are:

- inventory turnover and
- days' sales in inventory.

Inventory turnover measures the relationship between the cost of merchandise sold and the amount of inventory carried during the period. It is computed as follows:

$$\text{Inventory Turnover} = \frac{\text{Cost of Merchandise Sold}}{\text{Average Inventory}}$$

Business Connection

RAPID INVENTORY AT COSTCO

Costco Wholesale Corporation operates more than 650 membership warehouses that offer members low prices on a limited selection of nationally branded and selected private-label products. Costco emphasizes high sales volumes and rapid inventory turnover. This enables Costco to operate profitably at lower gross margins than traditional wholesalers, discount retailers, and supermarkets. In addition, Costco's rapid inventory turnover allows it to conserve its working capital, described as follows:

We operate membership warehouses ... [that] ... will produce high sales volumes and rapid inventory turnover.... We generally sell inventory before we are required to pay for it, even while taking advantage of early payment discounts when available.

Source: Costco Wholesale Corporation, *Form 10-K for the Fiscal Year Ended September 2, 2018.*

To illustrate, inventory turnover for **Best Buy** is computed from the following data (in millions) taken from two recent annual reports:

	For the Year Ended	
	Year 2	**Year 1**
Cost of merchandise sold	$32,918	$32,275
Inventories:		
Beginning of year	5,209	4,864
End of year	5,409	5,209
Average inventory:*		
($5,209 + $5,409) ÷ 2	5,309.0	
($4,864 + $5,209) ÷ 2		5,036.5
Inventory turnover:*		
$32,918 ÷ $5,309.0	6.20	
$32,275 ÷ $5,036.5		6.41

*Rounded to two decimal places.

Generally, the larger the inventory turnover is, the more efficient and effective the company is in managing inventory. In the preceding example, inventory turnover decreased slightly from 6.41 to 6.20 during Year 2, and thus Best Buy's inventory efficiency decreased during Year 2.

The **days' sales in inventory** measures the length of time it takes to acquire, sell, and replace the inventory. It is computed as follows:[7]

$$\text{Days' Sales in Inventory} = \frac{\text{Average Inventory}}{\text{Average Daily Cost of Merchandise Sold}}$$

The average daily cost of merchandise sold is determined by dividing the cost of merchandise sold by 365.[8] Based upon the preceding data, the days' sales in inventory for **Best Buy** is computed as follows:

	For the Year Ended	
	Year 2	**Year 1**
Cost of merchandise sold	$32,918	$32,275
Average daily cost of merchandise sold:*		
$32,918 ÷ 365 days	90.2	
$32,275 ÷ 365 days		88.4
Average inventory:*		
($5,209 + $5,409) ÷ 2	5,309.0	
($4,864 + $5,209) ÷ 2		5,036.5
Days' sales in inventory:*		
$5,309.0 ÷ $90.2	58.9 days	
$5,036.5 ÷ $88.4		57.0 days

*Rounded to one decimal place.

Generally, the lower the days' sales in inventory, the more efficient and effective the company is in managing inventory. As shown previously, the days' sales in inventory increased slightly from 57.0 to 58.9 during Year 2; thus, Best Buy's inventory management declined. This is consistent with the decrease in inventory turnover during the year.

7 Days' sales in inventory may also be computed as 365 days divided by the inventory turnover.
8 We use 365 days for all computations involving real-world companies and data. We do this to highlight differences among companies and because computations using real-world data normally require rounding.

As with most financial ratios, differences exist among industries. To illustrate, **Tiffany & Co.** is a large retailer of fine jewelry. Because jewelry doesn't sell as rapidly as Best Buy's consumer electronics, Tiffany's inventory turnover and days' sales in inventory should be significantly different from Best Buy's. For a recent year, this is confirmed as follows:

	Best Buy	Tiffany
Inventory turnover	6.20	0.70
Days' sales in inventory	58.9 days	520.2 days

EXAMPLE EXERCISE 7-8 Inventory Turnover and Days' Sales in Inventory — OBJ. 7

Financial statement data for years ending December 31 for Beadle Company follow:

	20Y4	20Y3
Cost of merchandise sold	$877,500	$615,000
Inventories:		
Beginning of year	225,000	185,000
End of year	315,000	225,000

a. Determine the inventory turnover for 20Y4 and 20Y3.

b. Determine the days' sales in inventory for 20Y4 and 20Y3, using 365 days.

c. Does the change in the inventory turnover and the days' sales in inventory from 20Y3 to 20Y4 indicate a favorable or an unfavorable trend?

Follow My Example 7-8

a. Inventory turnover:

	20Y4	20Y3
Average inventory:		
($225,000 + $315,000) ÷ 2	$270,000	
($185,000 + $225,000) ÷ 2		$205,000
Inventory turnover:		
$877,500 ÷ $270,000	3.25	
$615,000 ÷ $205,000		3.00

b. Days' sales in inventory:

Average daily cost of merchandise sold:		
$877,500 ÷ 365 days	$2,404	
$615,000 ÷ 365 days		$1,685
Average inventory:		
($225,000 + $315,000) ÷ 2	$270,000	
($185,000 + $225,000) ÷ 2		$205,000
Days' sales in inventory:		
$270,000 ÷ $2,404	112.3 days	
$205,000 ÷ $1,685		121.7 days

c. The increase in the inventory turnover from 3.00 to 3.25 and the decrease in the days' sales in inventory from 121.7 days to 112.3 days indicate favorable trends in managing inventory.

Practice Exercises: PE 7-8A, PE 7-8B

APPENDIX

APP. OBJ. Describe and illustrate the retail method and the gross profit method of estimating inventory.

Estimating Inventory Cost

A business may need to estimate the amount of inventory for the following reasons:

- Perpetual inventory records are not maintained.
- A fire or flood has destroyed inventory.
- A computer security breach has destroyed inventory records.
- Monthly or quarterly financial statements are needed, but a physical inventory is taken only once a year.

This appendix describes and illustrates two widely used methods of estimating inventory cost.

Retail Method of Inventory Costing

The **retail inventory method** of estimating inventory cost requires costs and retail prices to be maintained for the merchandise available for sale. A ratio of cost to retail price is then used to convert ending inventory at retail to estimate the ending inventory cost.

The retail inventory method is applied as follows:

Step 1. Determine the total merchandise available for sale at cost and retail.

Step 2. Determine the ratio of the cost to retail of the merchandise available for sale.

Step 3. Determine the ending inventory at retail by deducting the sales from the merchandise available for sale at retail.

Step 4. Estimate the ending inventory cost by multiplying the ending inventory at retail by the cost to retail ratio.

Exhibit 13 illustrates the retail inventory method.

EXHIBIT 13
Determining Inventory by the Retail Method

		A	B	C
	1		Cost	Retail
	2	Merchandise inventory, January 1	$19,400	$ 36,000
	3	Purchases in January (net)	42,600	64,000
Step 1 →	4	Merchandise available for sale	$62,000	$100,000
Step 2 →	5	Ratio of cost to retail price: $\frac{\$62,000}{\$100,000} = 62\%$		
	6	Sales for January		70,000
Step 3 →	7	Merchandise inventory, January 31, at retail		$ 30,000
Step 4 →	8	Merchandise inventory, January 31, at estimated cost		
	9	($30,000 × 62%)		$ 18,600
	10			

When estimating the cost to retail ratio, the mix of items in the ending inventory is assumed to be the same as the merchandise available for sale. If the ending inventory is made up of different classes of merchandise, cost to retail ratios may be developed for each class of inventory.

An advantage of the retail method is that it provides inventory figures for preparing monthly statements. Department stores and similar retailers often determine gross profit and operating income each month but may take a physical inventory only once or twice a year. Thus, the retail method allows management to monitor operations more closely.

The retail method may also be used as an aid in taking a physical inventory. In this case, the items are counted and recorded at their retail (selling) prices instead of their costs. The physical inventory at retail is then converted to cost by using the cost to retail ratio.

Gross Profit Method of Inventory Costing

The **gross profit method** uses the estimated gross profit for the period to estimate the inventory at the end of the period. The gross profit is estimated from the preceding year, adjusted for any current period changes in the cost and sales prices.

The gross profit method is applied as follows:

Step 1. Determine the merchandise available for sale at cost.

Step 2. Determine the estimated gross profit by multiplying the sales by the gross profit percentage.

Step 3. Determine the estimated cost of merchandise sold by deducting the estimated gross profit from the sales.

Step 4. Estimate the ending inventory cost by deducting the estimated cost of merchandise sold from the merchandise available for sale.

Exhibit 14 illustrates the gross profit method.

EXHIBIT 14

Estimating Inventory by Gross Profit Method

		A	B	C
	1			**Cost**
	2	Merchandise inventory, January 1		$ 57,000
	3	Purchases in January (net)		180,000
Step 1 →	4	Merchandise available for sale		$237,000
	5	Sales for January	$250,000	
Step 2 →	6	Less estimated gross profit ($250,000 × 30%)	75,000	
Step 3 →	7	Estimated cost of merchandise sold		175,000
Step 4 →	8	Estimated merchandise inventory, January 31		$ 62,000
	9			

The gross profit method is useful for estimating inventories for monthly or quarterly financial statements. It is also useful in estimating the cost of merchandise destroyed by fire or other disasters.

At a Glance 7

OBJ. 1 Describe the importance of control over inventory.

Key Points Two objectives of inventory control are safeguarding the inventory and properly reporting it in the financial statements. The perpetual inventory system and physical count enhance control over inventory.

Learning Outcomes	Example Exercises	Practice Exercises
• Describe controls for safeguarding inventory.		
• Describe how a perpetual inventory system enhances control over inventory.		
• Describe why taking a physical inventory enhances control over inventory.		

OBJ. 2 Describe three inventory cost flow assumptions and explain how they impact the income statement and balance sheet.

Key Points The three common inventory cost flow assumptions used in business are the (1) first-in, first-out method (FIFO); (2) last-in, first-out method (LIFO); and (3) weighted average cost method. The cost flow assumption affects the income statement and balance sheet.

Learning Outcomes	Example Exercises	Practice Exercises
• Describe the FIFO, LIFO, and weighted average cost flow methods.		
• Describe how the choice of a cost flow method affects the income statement and balance sheet.	**EE7-1**	**PE7-1A, 7-1B**

OBJ. 3 Determine the cost of inventory under the perpetual inventory system, using the FIFO, LIFO, and weighted average cost methods.

Key Points In a perpetual inventory system, the number of units and the cost of each type of merchandise are recorded in a subsidiary inventory ledger, with a separate account for each type of merchandise.

Learning Outcomes	Example Exercises	Practice Exercises
• Determine the cost of inventory and the cost of merchandise sold, using a perpetual inventory system under the FIFO method.	**EE7-2**	**PE7-2A, 7-2B**
• Determine the cost of inventory and the cost of merchandise sold, using a perpetual inventory system under the LIFO method.	**EE7-3**	**PE7-3A, 7-3B**
• Determine the cost of inventory and the cost of merchandise sold, using a perpetual inventory system under the weighted average cost method.	**EE7-4**	**PE7-4A, 7-4B**

OBJ. 4 Determine the cost of inventory under the periodic inventory system, using the FIFO, LIFO, and weighted average cost methods.

Key Points In a periodic inventory system, a physical inventory is taken to determine the cost of the inventory and the cost of merchandise sold.

Learning Outcomes	*Example Exercises*	*Practice Exercises*
• Determine the cost of inventory and the cost of merchandise sold, using a periodic inventory system under the FIFO method.	**EE7-5**	**PE7-5A, 7-5B**
• Determine the cost of inventory and the cost of merchandise sold, using a periodic inventory system under the LIFO method.	**EE7-5**	**PE7-5A, 7-5B**
• Determine the cost of inventory and the cost of merchandise sold, using a periodic inventory system under the weighted average cost method.	**EE7-5**	**PE7-5A, 7-5B**

OBJ. 5 Compare and contrast the use of the three inventory costing methods.

Key Points The three inventory costing methods will normally yield different amounts for (1) the ending inventory, (2) the cost of merchandise sold for the period, and (3) the gross profit (and net income) for the period.

Learning Outcomes	*Example Exercises*	*Practice Exercises*
• Indicate which inventory cost flow method will yield the highest and lowest ending inventory and net income during periods of increasing prices.		
• Indicate which inventory cost flow method will yield the highest and lowest ending inventory and net income during periods of decreasing prices.		

OBJ. 6 Describe and illustrate the reporting of merchandise inventory in the financial statements.

Key Points The lower of cost or market is used to value inventory. The market value is the net realizable value of the merchandise.

Merchandise inventory is usually presented in the Current Assets section of the balance sheet, following receivables. The method of determining the cost and valuing the inventory is reported.

Errors in reporting inventory based on the physical inventory will affect the balance sheet and income statement.

Learning Outcomes	*Example Exercises*	*Practice Exercises*
• Determine inventory using lower of cost or market.	**EE7-6**	**PE7-6A, 7-6B**
• Prepare the Current Assets section of the balance sheet that includes inventory.		
• Determine the effect of inventory errors on the balance sheet and income statement.	**EE7-7**	**PE7-7A, 7-7B**

OBJ. 7 **Describe and illustrate the inventory turnover and the days' sales in inventory in analyzing the efficiency and effectiveness of inventory management.**

Key Points Two measures to analyze the efficiency and effectiveness of inventory management are (1) inventory turnover and (2) days' sales in inventory.

Learning Outcomes	*Example Exercises*	*Practice Exercises*
• Describe the use of inventory turnover and days' sales in inventory in analyzing how well a company manages inventory.		
• Compute the inventory turnover.	EE7-8	PE7-8A, 7-8B
• Compute the days' sales in inventory.	EE7-8	PE7-8A, 7-8B

Illustrative Problem

Stewart Co.'s beginning inventory and purchases during the year ended December 31, 20Y2, were as follows:

		Unit	Unit Cost	Total Cost
January 1	Inventory	1,000	$50.00	$ 50,000
March 10	Purchase	3,000	52.00	156,000
June 25	Sold 1,600 units			
August 30	Purchase	2,600	55.00	143,000
October 5	Sold 4,000 units			
November 26	Purchase	1,000	57.68	57,680
December 31	Sold 800 units			
Total		7,600		$406,680

Instructions

1. Determine the cost of inventory on December 31, 20Y2, using the perpetual inventory system and each of the following inventory costing methods:
   a. first-in, first-out
   b. last-in, first-out
   c. weighted average
2. Determine the cost of inventory on December 31, 20Y2, using the periodic inventory system and each of the following inventory costing methods:
   a. first-in, first-out
   b. last-in, first-out
   c. weighted average cost
3. (Appendix) Assume that during the fiscal year ended December 31, 20Y2, sales were $530,000 and the estimated gross profit rate was 36%. Estimate the ending inventory at December 31, 20Y2, using the gross profit method.

Solution

1. The perpetual inventory ledgers follow:
   a. First-in, first-out method: $68,680 ($11,000 + $57,680)
   b. Last-in, first-out method: $61,536 ($50,000 + $11,536)
   c. Weighted average cost method: $66,600 (1,200 units × $55.50)

2. a. First-in, first-out method:

1,000 units at $57.68	$57,680
200 units at $55.00	11,000
1,200 units	$68,680

b. Last-in, first-out method:

1,000 units at $50.00	$50,000
200 units at $52.00	10,400
1,200 units	$60,400

c. Weighted average cost method:

Weighted average cost per unit: ($406,680 ÷ 7,600 units = $53.51 (Rounded)

Inventory, December 31, 20Y2: 1,200 units at $53.51 = $64,212

1. a. First-in, first-out method: $68,680 ($11,000 + $57,680)

	Purchases			Cost of Merchandise Sold			Inventory		
Date	**Quantity**	**Unit Cost**	**Total Cost**	**Quantity**	**Unit Cost**	**Total Cost**	**Quantity**	**Unit Cost**	**Total Cost**
20Y2									
Jan. 1							1,000	50.00	50,000
Mar. 10	3,000	52.00	156,000				1,000	50.00	50,000
							3,000	52.00	156,000
June 25				1,000	50.00	50,000	2,400	52.00	124,800
				600	52.00	31,200			
Aug. 30	2,600	55.00	143,000				2,400	52.00	124,800
							2,600	55.00	143,000
Oct. 5				2,400	52.00	124,800	1,000	55.00	55,000
				1,600	55.00	88,000			
Nov. 26	1,000	57.68	57,680				1,000	55.00	55,000
							1,000	57.68	57,680
Dec. 31				800	55.00	44,000	200	55.00	11,000
							1,000	57.68	57,680
31	Balances					338,000			68,680

b. Last-in, first-out method: $61,536 ($50,000 + $11,536)

	Purchases			Cost of Merchandise Sold			Inventory		
Date	**Quantity**	**Unit Cost**	**Total Cost**	**Quantity**	**Unit Cost**	**Total Cost**	**Quantity**	**Unit Cost**	**Total Cost**
20Y2									
Jan. 1							1,000	50.00	50,000
Mar. 10	3,000	52.00	156,000				1,000	50.00	50,000
							3,000	52.00	156,000
June 25				1,600	52.00	83,200	1,000	50.00	50,000
							1,400	52.00	72,800
Aug. 30	2,600	55.00	143,000				1,000	50.00	50,000
							1,400	52.00	72,800
							2,600	55.00	143,000
Oct. 5				2,600	55.00	143,000	1,000	50.00	50,000
				1,400	52.00	72,800			
Nov. 26	1,000	57.68	57,680				1,000	50.00	50,000
							1,000	57.68	57,680
Dec. 31				800	57.68	46,144	1,000	50.00	50,000
							200	57.68	11,536
31	Balances					345,144			61,536

(Continued)

c. Weighted average cost method: $66,600 (1,200 units × $55.50)

	Purchases			Cost of Merchandise Sold			Inventory		
Date	Quantity	Unit Cost	Total Cost	Quantity	Unit Cost	Total Cost	Quantity	Unit Cost	Total Cost
Jan. 1							1,000	50.00	50,000
Mar. 10	3,000	52.00	156,000				4,000	51.50	206,000
June 25				1,600	51.50	82,400	2,400	51.50	123,600
Aug. 30	2,600	55.00	143,000				5,000	53.32	266,600
Oct. 5				4,000	53.32	213,280	1,000	53.32	53,320
Nov. 26	1,000	57.68	57,680				2,000	55.50	111,000
Dec. 31				800	55.50	44,400	1,200	55.50	66,600
31	Balances					340,080	1,200	55.50	66,600

3. (Appendix)

Merchandise inventory, January 1, 20Y2		$ 50,000
Purchases (net)		356,680
Merchandise available for sale		$406,680
Sales	$530,000	
Less estimated gross profit ($530,000 × 36%)	190,800	
Estimated cost of merchandise sold		339,200
Estimated merchandise inventory, December 31, 20Y2		$ 67,480

Key Terms

consigned inventory (364)
consignee (364)
consignor (364)
days' sales in inventory (368)
first-in, first-out (FIFO) inventory cost flow method (350)
gross profit method (371)
inventory turnover (367)
last-in, first-out (LIFO) inventory cost flow method (350)
lower-of-cost-or-market (LCM) method (361)
net realizable value (362)
physical inventory (349)
purchase order (348)
receiving report (348)
retail inventory method (370)
specific identification inventory cost flow method (349)
subsidiary inventory ledger (349)
weighted average inventory cost flow method (350)

Discussion Questions

1. Before inventory purchases are recorded, the receiving report should be reconciled to what documents?
2. Why is it important to take a physical inventory periodically when using a perpetual inventory system?
3. Do the terms *FIFO, LIFO,* and *weighted average* refer to techniques used in determining quantities of the various classes of merchandise on hand? Explain.
4. If merchandise inventory is being valued at cost and the price level is decreasing, which of the three methods of costing—FIFO, LIFO, or weighted average cost—will yield (a) the highest inventory cost, (b) the lowest inventory cost, (c) the highest gross profit, and (d) the lowest gross profit?
5. Which of the three methods of inventory costing—FIFO, LIFO, or weighted average cost—will in general yield an inventory cost most nearly approximating current replacement cost?
6. If inventory is being valued at cost and the price level is steadily rising, which of the three methods of costing—FIFO, LIFO, or weighted average cost—will yield the lowest annual income tax expense? Explain.

7. Using the following data, how should the merchandise be valued under lower of cost or market?

Original cost	$1,350
Estimated selling price	1,475
Selling expenses	180

8. The inventory at the end of the year was understated by $14,750. (a) Did the error cause an overstatement or an understatement of the gross profit for the year? (b) Which items on the balance sheet at the end of the year were overstated or understated as a result of the error?

9. Hutch Co. sold merchandise to Bibbins Company on May 31, FOB shipping point. If the merchandise is in transit on May 31, the end of the fiscal year, which company would report it in its financial statements? Explain.

10. A manufacturer shipped merchandise to a retailer on a consignment basis. If the merchandise is unsold at the end of the period, in whose inventory should the merchandise be included?

Practice Exercises

Example Exercises

SHOW ME HOW

EE 7-1 *p. 351*

PE 7-1A Cost flow methods

OBJ. 2

The following three identical units of Item Alpha are purchased during April:

		Item Alpha	Units	Cost	
Apr.	2	Purchase	1	$ 76	
	14	Purchase	1	81	
	28	Purchase	1	83	
	Total		3	$240	
	Average cost per unit			$ 80	($240 ÷ 3 units)

Assume that one unit is sold on April 30 for $132.

Determine the gross profit for April and ending inventory on April 30 using the (a) first-in, first-out (FIFO); (b) last-in, first-out (LIFO); and (c) weighted average cost methods.

SHOW ME HOW

EE 7-1 *p. 351*

PE 7-1B Cost flow methods

OBJ. 2

The following three identical units of Item B are purchased during June:

		Item B	Units	Cost	
June	2	Purchase	1	$140	
	12	Purchase	1	152	
	23	Purchase	1	158	
	Total		3	$450	
	Average cost per unit			$150	($450 ÷ 3 units)

Assume that one unit is sold on June 27 for $270.

Determine the gross profit for June and ending inventory on June 30 using the (a) first-in, first-out (FIFO); (b) last-in, first-out (LIFO); and (c) weighted average cost methods.

SHOW ME HOW

EE 7-2 *p. 353*

PE 7-2A Perpetual inventory using FIFO

OBJ. 3

Beginning inventory, purchases, and sales for Item Copper are as follows:

Mar.	1	Inventory	450 units at $7
	9	Sale	390 units
	13	Purchase	410 units at $8
	25	Sale	340 units

Assuming a perpetual inventory system and using the first-in, first-out (FIFO) method, determine (a) the cost of merchandise sold on March 25 and (b) the inventory on March 31.

SHOW ME HOW

EE 7-2 *p. 353*

PE 7-2B Perpetual inventory using FIFO
OBJ. 3

Beginning inventory, purchases, and sales for Item Doodad are as follows:

July 1	Inventory	90 units at $21
7	Sale	79 units
15	Purchase	160 units at $24
24	Sale	70 units

Assuming a perpetual inventory system and using the first-in, first-out (FIFO) method, determine (a) the cost of merchandise sold on July 24 and (b) the inventory on July 31.

SHOW ME HOW

EE 7-3 *p. 355*

PE 7-3A Perpetual inventory using LIFO
OBJ. 3

Beginning inventory, purchases, and sales for Item FK7 are as follows:

Sept. 1	Inventory	115 units at $255
10	Sale	100 units
18	Purchase	110 units at $260
27	Sale	105 units

Assuming a perpetual inventory system and using the last-in, first-out (LIFO) method, determine (a) the cost of merchandise sold on September 27 and (b) the inventory on September 30.

SHOW ME HOW

EE 7-3 *p. 355*

PE 7-3B Perpetual inventory using LIFO
OBJ. 3

Beginning inventory, purchases, and sales for Item GY9 are as follows:

Mar. 1	Inventory	365 units at $24
8	Sale	305 units
15	Purchase	510 units at $26
27	Sale	325 units

Assuming a perpetual inventory system and using the last-in, first-out (LIFO) method, determine (a) the cost of merchandise sold on March 27 and (b) the inventory on March 31.

SHOW ME HOW

EE 7-4 *p. 356*

PE 7-4A Perpetual inventory using weighted average
OBJ. 3

Beginning inventory, purchases, and sales for H76 are as follows:

July 1	Inventory	300 units at $120
12	Sale	210 units
23	Purchase	360 units at $135
26	Sale	330 units

Assuming a perpetual inventory system and using the weighted average method, determine (a) the weighted average unit cost after the July 23 purchase, (b) the cost of the merchandise sold on July 26, and (c) the inventory on July 31.

SHOW ME HOW

EE 7-4 *p. 356*

PE 7-4B Perpetual inventory using weighted average
OBJ. 3

Beginning inventory, purchases, and sales for J101 are as follows:

Oct. 1	Inventory	480 units at $14
13	Sale	280 units
22	Purchase	600 units at $16
29	Sale	450 units

Assuming a perpetual inventory system and using the weighted average method, determine (a) the weighted average unit cost after the October 22 purchase, (b) the cost of the merchandise sold on October 29, and (c) the inventory on October 31.

SHOW ME HOW

EE 7-5 p. 360

PE 7-5A Periodic inventory using FIFO, LIFO, and weighted average cost methods OBJ. 4

The units of an item available for sale during the year were as follows:

Jan. 1	Inventory	15 units at $4,000	$ 60,000
Aug. 7	Purchase	21 units at $4,600	96,600
Dec. 11	Purchase	18 units at $5,100	91,800
Available for sale		54 units	$248,400

There are 17 units of the item in the physical inventory at December 31. The periodic inventory system is used. Determine the inventory cost using (a) the first-in, first-out (FIFO) method; (b) the last-in, first-out (LIFO) method; and (c) the weighted average cost method.

SHOW ME HOW

EE 7-5 p. 360

PE 7-5B Periodic inventory using FIFO, LIFO, and weighted average cost methods OBJ. 4

The units of an item available for sale during the year were as follows:

Jan. 1	Inventory	30 units at $460	$ 13,800
Aug. 13	Purchase	330 units at $437	144,210
Nov. 30	Purchase	50 units at $456	22,800
Available for sale		410 units	$180,810

There are 73 units of the item in the physical inventory at December 31. The periodic inventory system is used. Determine the inventory cost using (a) the first-in, first-out (FIFO) method; (b) the last-in, first-out (LIFO) method; and (c) the weighted average cost method.

SHOW ME HOW

EE 7-6 p. 363

PE 7-6A Lower-of-cost-or-market method OBJ. 6

On the basis of the following data, determine the value of the inventory at the lower of cost or market. Apply lower of cost or market to each inventory item, as shown in Exhibit 9.

Item	Inventory Quantity	Cost per Unit	Market Value per Unit (Net Realizable Value)
Raven 10	1,700	$163	$159
Dove 23	9,200	24	30

SHOW ME HOW

EE 7-6 p. 363

PE 7-6B Lower-of-cost-or-market method OBJ. 6

On the basis of the following data, determine the value of the inventory at the lower of cost or market. Apply lower of cost or market to each inventory item, as shown in Exhibit 9.

Item	Inventory Quantity	Cost per Unit	Market Value per Unit (Net Realizable Value)
JFW1	5,750	$ 9	$10
SAW9	1,040	27	24

SHOW ME HOW

EE 7-7 p. 367

PE 7-7A Effect of inventory errors OBJ. 6

During the taking of its physical inventory on August 31, 20Y7, Robin Interiors Company incorrectly counted its inventory as $543,500 instead of the correct amount of $560,700. Indicate the effect of the misstatement on Robin Interiors' August 31, 20Y7, balance sheet and income statement for the year ended August 31, 20Y7.

SHOW ME HOW

EE 7-7 p. 367

PE 7-7B Effect of inventory errors OBJ. 6

During the taking of its physical inventory on December 31, 20Y7, Combine Engine Company incorrectly counted its inventory as $274,100 instead of the correct amount of $270,700. Indicate the effect of the misstatement on Combine Engine's December 31, 20Y7, balance sheet and income statement for the year ended December 31, 20Y7.

SHOW ME HOW

EE 7-8 p. 369

PE 7-8A Inventory turnover and days' sales in inventory **OBJ. 7**

Financial statement data for years ending December 31 for Amsterdam Company follow:

	20Y4	20Y3
Cost of merchandise sold	$3,598,900	$3,015,630
Inventories:		
Beginning of year	593,000	589,600
End of year	648,000	593,000

a. Determine the inventory turnover for 20Y4 and 20Y3. Round to one decimal place.

b. Determine the days' sales in inventory for 20Y4 and 20Y3. Use 365 days and round to one decimal place.

c. Does the change in the inventory turnover and the days' sales in inventory from 20Y3 to 20Y4 indicate a favorable or an unfavorable trend?

SHOW ME HOW

EE 7-8 p. 369

PE 7-8B Inventory turnover and days' sales in inventory **OBJ. 7**

Financial statement data for years ending December 31 for Salsa Company follow:

	20Y7	20Y6
Cost of merchandise sold	$2,912,700	$3,009,790
Inventories:		
Beginning of year	489,000	481,900
End of year	533,000	489,000

a. Determine the inventory turnover for 20Y7 and 20Y6. Round to one decimal place.

b. Determine the days' sales in inventory for 20Y7 and 20Y6. Use 365 days and round to one decimal place.

c. Does the change in the inventory turnover and the days' sales in inventory from 20Y6 to 20Y7 indicate a favorable or an unfavorable trend?

Exercises

EX 7-1 Control of inventories **OBJ. 1**

Triple Creek Hardware Store currently uses a periodic inventory system. Kevin Carlton, the owner, is considering the purchase of a computer system that would make it feasible to switch to a perpetual inventory system.

Kevin is unhappy with the periodic inventory system because it does not provide timely information on inventory levels. Kevin has noticed on several occasions that the store runs out of good-selling items, while too many poor-selling items are on hand.

Kevin is also concerned about lost sales while a physical inventory is being taken. Triple Creek Hardware currently takes a physical inventory twice a year. To minimize distractions, the store is closed on the day inventory is taken. Kevin believes that closing the store is the only way to get an accurate inventory count.

Will switching to a perpetual inventory system strengthen Triple Creek Hardware's control over inventory items? Will switching to a perpetual inventory system eliminate the need for a physical inventory count? Explain.

EX 7-2 Control of inventories **OBJ. 1**

Hardcase Luggage Shop is a small retail establishment located in a large shopping mall. This shop has implemented the following procedures regarding inventory items:

a. Because the shop carries mostly high-quality, designer luggage, all inventory items are tagged with a control device that activates an alarm if a tagged item is removed from the store.

b. Because the display area of the store is limited, only a sample of each piece of luggage is kept on the selling floor. Whenever a customer selects a piece of luggage, the salesclerk gets the appropriate piece from the store's stockroom. Because all salesclerks need access to the stockroom, it is not locked. The stockroom is adjacent to the break room used by all mall employees.

c. Whenever Hardcase Luggage Shop receives a shipment of new inventory, the items are taken directly to the stockroom. Hardcase's accountant uses the vendor's invoice to record the amount of inventory received.

State whether each of these procedures is appropriate or inappropriate. If it is inappropriate, explain why.

✔ a. Inventory balance, April 30, $11,880

SHOW ME HOW

EX 7-3 Perpetual inventory using FIFO OBJ. 2, 3

Beginning inventory, purchases, and sales data for portable game players are as follows:

Apr.	1	Inventory	180 units at $40
	10	Sale	140 units
	15	Purchase	210 units at $42
	20	Sale	170 units
	24	Sale	60 units
	30	Purchase	240 units at $46

The business maintains a perpetual inventory system, costing by the first-in, first-out method.

a. Determine the cost of the merchandise sold for each sale and the inventory balance after each sale, presenting the data in the form illustrated in Exhibit 3.

b. Based upon the preceding data, would you expect the ending inventory to be higher or lower using the last-in, first-out method?

✔ Inventory balance, April 30, $11,840

SHOW ME HOW

EX 7-4 Perpetual inventory using LIFO OBJ. 2, 3

Assume that the business in Exercise 7-3 maintains a perpetual inventory system, costing by the last-in, first-out method. Determine the cost of merchandise sold for each sale and the inventory balance after each sale, presenting the data in the form illustrated in Exhibit 4.

✔ a. Inventory balance, May 31, $20,160

SHOW ME HOW

EX 7-5 Perpetual inventory using LIFO OBJ. 2, 3

Beginning inventory, purchases, and sales data for prepaid cell phones for May are as follows:

Inventory		Purchases		Sales	
May 1	1,550 units at $44	May 10	720 units at $45	May 12	1,200 units
		20	1,200 units at $48	14	830 units
				31	1,000 units

a. Assuming that the perpetual inventory system is used, costing by the LIFO method, determine the cost of merchandise sold for each sale and the inventory balance after each sale, presenting the data in the form illustrated in Exhibit 4.

b. Based upon the preceding data, would you expect the inventory to be higher or lower using the first-in, first-out method?

✔ Inventory balance, May 31, $21,120

SHOW ME HOW

EX 7-6 Perpetual inventory using FIFO OBJ. 2, 3

Assume that the business in Exercise 7-5 maintains a perpetual inventory system, costing by the first-in, first-out method. Determine the cost of merchandise sold for each sale and the inventory balance after each sale, presenting the data in the form illustrated in Exhibit 3.

EX 7-7 FIFO and LIFO costs under perpetual inventory system

OBJ. 2, 3

✔ b. $763,200

SHOW ME HOW

EXCEL ONLINE

The following units of an item were available for sale during the year:

Beginning inventory	21,600 units at $20.00
Sale	14,400 units at $40.00
First purchase	48,000 units at $25.20
Sale	36,000 units at $40.00
Second purchase	45,000 units at $26.40
Sale	33,000 units at $40.00

The firm uses the perpetual inventory system, and there are 31,200 units of the item on hand at the end of the year. What is the total cost of the ending inventory according to (a) FIFO, (b) LIFO?

EX 7-8 Weighted average cost flow method under perpetual inventory system

OBJ. 3

✔ Total Cost of Merchandise Sold, $2,110,500

SHOW ME HOW

The following units of a particular item were available for sale during the calendar year:

Jan. 1	Inventory	15,000 units at $60.00
Mar. 18	Sale	12,000 units
May 2	Purchase	27,000 units at $62.00
Aug. 9	Sale	22,500 units
Oct. 20	Purchase	10,500 units at $64.20

The firm uses the weighted average cost method with a perpetual inventory system. Determine the cost of merchandise sold for each sale and the inventory balance after each sale. Present the data in the form illustrated in Exhibit 5.

EX 7-9 Weighted average cost flow method under perpetual inventory system

OBJ. 3

✔ Total Cost of Merchandise Sold, $154,400

The following units of a particular item were available for sale during the calendar year:

Jan. 1	Inventory	4,000 units at $20
Apr. 19	Sale	2,500 units
June 30	Purchase	6,000 units at $24
Sept. 2	Sale	4,500 units
Nov. 15	Purchase	1,000 units at $25

The firm uses the weighted average cost method with a perpetual inventory system. Determine the cost of merchandise sold for each sale and the inventory balance after each sale. Present the data in the form illustrated in Exhibit 5.

EX 7-10 Perpetual inventory using FIFO

OBJ. 3

✔ Total Cost of Merchandise Sold, $152,000

EXCEL ONLINE

Assume that the business in Exercise 7-9 maintains a perpetual inventory system. Determine the cost of merchandise sold for each sale and the inventory balance after each sale, assuming the first-in, first-out method. Present the data in the form illustrated in Exhibit 3.

EX 7-11 Perpetual inventory using LIFO

OBJ. 3

✔ Total Cost of Merchandise Sold, $158,000

EXCEL ONLINE

Assume that the business in Exercise 7-9 maintains a perpetual inventory system. Determine the cost of merchandise sold for each sale and the inventory balance after each sale, assuming the last-in, first-out method. Present the data in the form illustrated in Exhibit 4.

EX 7-12 Periodic inventory by three methods

OBJ. 2, 4

✔ a. $167,700

The units of an item available for sale during the year were as follows:

Jan.	1	Inventory	1,000 units at $120
Feb.	17	Purchase	1,375 units at $128
July	21	Purchase	1,500 units at $136
Nov.	23	Purchase	1,125 units at $140

There are 1,200 units of the item in the physical inventory at December 31. The periodic inventory system is used. Determine the inventory cost by (a) the first-in, first-out method; (b) the last-in, first-out method; and (c) the weighted average cost method.

EX 7-13 Periodic inventory by three methods; cost of merchandise sold

OBJ. 2, 4

✔ a. Merchandise Inventory, $59,960

The units of an item available for sale during the year were as follows:

Jan.	1	Inventory	900 units at $54
Mar.	10	Purchase	1,120 units at $55
Aug.	30	Purchase	1,000 units at $58
Dec.	12	Purchase	980 units at $60

There are 1,000 units of the item in the physical inventory at December 31. The periodic inventory system is used. Determine the inventory cost and the cost of merchandise sold by three methods, presenting your answers in the following form:

	Cost	
Inventory Method	**Merchandise Inventory**	**Merchandise Sold**
a. First-in, first-out	$	$
b. Last-in, first-out		
c. Weighted average cost		

EX 7-14 Comparing inventory methods

OBJ. 5

Assume that a firm separately determined inventory under FIFO and LIFO and then compared the results.

a. In each space that follows, place the correct sign [less than (<), greater than (>), or equal (=)] for each comparison, assuming periods of rising prices.

1. FIFO inventory	________	LIFO inventory
2. FIFO cost of merchandise sold	________	LIFO cost of merchandise sold
3. FIFO net income	________	LIFO net income
4. FIFO income taxes	________	LIFO income taxes

b. Why would management prefer to use LIFO over FIFO in periods of rising prices?

EX 7-15 Lower-of-cost-or-market inventory

OBJ. 6

✔ LCM: $70,400

On the basis of the following data, determine the value of the inventory at the lower of cost or market. Assemble the data in the form illustrated in Exhibit 9.

Inventory Item	Inventory Quantity	Cost per Unit	Market Value per Unit (Net Realizable Value)
Birch	120	$150	$140
Cypress	90	120	130
Mountain Ash	200	110	100
Spruce	160	90	100
Willow	70	130	120

EX 7-16 Merchandise inventory on the balance sheet **OBJ. 6**

Based on the data in Exercise 7-15 and assuming that cost was determined by the FIFO method and lower of cost or market was determined on an individual item-by-item basis, show how the merchandise inventory would appear on the balance sheet.

EX 7-17 Effect of errors in physical inventory **OBJ. 6**

Missouri River Supply Co. sells canoes, kayaks, whitewater rafts, and other boating supplies. During the taking of its physical inventory on December 31, 20Y2, Missouri River Supply incorrectly counted its inventory as $233,400 instead of the correct amount of $238,600.

a. State the effect of the error on the December 31, 20Y2, balance sheet of Missouri River Supply.

b. State the effect of the error on the income statement of Missouri River Supply for the year ended December 31, 20Y2.

c. If uncorrected, what would be the effect of the error on the 20Y3 income statement?

d. If uncorrected, what would be the effect of the error on the December 31, 20Y3, balance sheet?

EX 7-18 Effect of errors in physical inventory **OBJ. 6**

Fonda Motorcycle Shop sells motorcycles, ATVs, and other related supplies and accessories. During the taking of its physical inventory on December 31, 20Y8, Fonda Motorcycle Shop incorrectly counted its inventory as $337,500 instead of the correct amount of $328,850.

a. State the effect of the error on the December 31, 20Y8, balance sheet of Fonda Motorcycle Shop.

b. State the effect of the error on the income statement of Fonda Motorcycle Shop for the year ended December 31, 20Y8.

c. If uncorrected, what would be the effect of the error on the 20Y9 income statement?

d. If uncorrected, what would be the effect of the error on the December 31, 20Y9, balance sheet?

EX 7-19 Error in inventory **OBJ. 6**

During 20Y5, the accountant discovered that the physical inventory at the end of 20Y4 had been understated by $42,750. Instead of correcting the error, however, the accountant assumed that the error would balance out (correct itself) in 20Y5.

Are there any flaws in the accountant's assumption? Explain.

EX 7-20 Inventory turnover **OBJ. 7**

SHOW ME HOW

FAI

The following data (in millions) were taken from recent annual reports of **Apple Inc.**, a manufacturer of personal computers and related products, and **Mattel Inc.**, a manufacturer of toys, including Barbie®, Hot Wheels®, and Disney Classics:

	Apple	Mattel
Cost of merchandise sold	$163,756	$2,716
Inventory, end of year	3,956	543
Inventory, beginning of the year	4,855	601

a. Determine the inventory turnover for Apple and Mattel. Round to one decimal place.

b. Would you expect Mattel's inventory turnover to be higher or lower than Apple's? Why?

EX 7-21 Inventory turnover and days' sales in inventory **OBJ. 7**

✔ a. Kroger, inventory turnover, 11.93

Kroger, **Sprouts Farmers Market, Inc.**, and **Ingles** are three grocery chains in the United States. Inventory management is an important aspect of the grocery retail business.

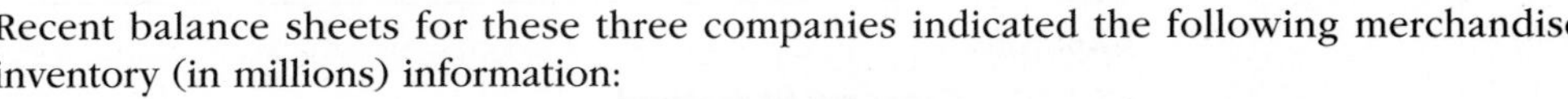

Recent balance sheets for these three companies indicated the following merchandise inventory (in millions) information:

	Kroger	Sprouts	Ingles
Cost of merchandise sold	$94,894	$3,460	$3,113
Inventory, end of year	8,123	264	372
Inventory, beginning of year	7,781	230	349

a. Determine the inventory turnover. Round to two decimal places.

b. Determine the days' sales in inventory. Round to one decimal place.

c. Interpret your results in parts (a) and (b).

d. If Ingles had Kroger's days' sales in inventory, how much additional cash flow (rounded to nearest million) would have been generated from the smaller inventory relative to its actual average inventory position?

Appendix

EX 7-22 Retail method

A business using the retail method of inventory costing determines that merchandise inventory at retail is $1,235,000. If the ratio of cost to retail price is 54%, what is the amount of inventory to be reported on the financial statements?

Appendix

EX 7-23 Retail method

A business using the retail method of inventory costing determines that merchandise inventory at retail is $396,400. If the ratio of cost to retail price is 61%, what is the amount of inventory to be reported on the financial statements?

Appendix

EX 7-24 Retail method

A business using the retail method of inventory costing determines that merchandise inventory at retail is $775,000. If the ratio of cost to retail price is 66%, what is the amount of inventory to be reported on the financial statements?

Appendix

EX 7-25 Retail method

On the basis of the following data, estimate the cost of the merchandise inventory at June 30 by the retail method:

		Cost	Retail
June 1	Merchandise inventory	$ 165,000	$ 275,000
June 1–30	Purchases (net)	2,361,500	3,800,000
June 1–30	Sales		3,550,000

Appendix

EX 7-26 Gross profit method

✔ **a. Merchandise destroyed: $414,000**

The merchandise inventory was destroyed by fire on December 13. The following data were obtained from the accounting records:

Jan. 1	Merchandise inventory	$ 350,000
Jan. 1–Dec. 31	Purchases (net)	2,950,000
	Sales	4,440,000
	Estimated gross profit rate	35%

a. Estimate the cost of the merchandise destroyed.

b. Briefly describe the situations in which the gross profit method is useful.

Appendix

EX 7-27 Gross profit method

Based on the following data, estimate the cost of the ending merchandise inventory:

Sales	$9,250,000
Estimated gross profit rate	36%
Beginning merchandise inventory	$ 180,000
Purchases (net)	5,945,000
Merchandise available for sale	$6,125,000

Appendix

EX 7-28 Gross profit method

Based on the following data, estimate the cost of the ending merchandise inventory:

Sales	$1,450,000
Estimated gross profit rate	42%
Beginning merchandise inventory	$ 100,000
Purchases (net)	860,000
Merchandise available for sale	$ 960,000

Problems: Series A

PR 7-1A FIFO perpetual inventory **OBJ. 2, 3**

✔ 3. $8,983,125

SHOW ME HOW

The beginning inventory at Midnight Supplies and data on purchases and sales for a three-month period ending March 31, are as follows:

Date		Transaction	Number of Units	Per Unit	Total
Jan.	1	Inventory	7,500	$ 75.00	$ 562,500
	10	Purchase	22,500	85.00	1,912,500
	28	Sale	11,250	150.00	1,687,500
	30	Sale	3,750	150.00	562,500
Feb.	5	Sale	1,500	150.00	225,000
	10	Purchase	54,000	87.50	4,725,000
	16	Sale	27,000	160.00	4,320,000
	28	Sale	25,500	160.00	4,080,000
Mar.	5	Purchase	45,000	89.50	4,027,500
	14	Sale	30,000	160.00	4,800,000
	25	Purchase	7,500	90.00	675,000
	30	Sale	26,250	160.00	4,200,000

Instructions

1. Record the inventory, purchases, and cost of merchandise sold data in a perpetual inventory record similar to the one illustrated in Exhibit 3, using the first-in, first-out method.
2. Determine the total sales and the total cost of merchandise sold for the period. Journalize the entries in the sales and cost of merchandise sold accounts. Assume that all sales were on account.
3. Determine the gross profit from sales for the period.

4. Determine the ending inventory cost as of March 31.
5. Based upon the preceding data, would you expect the inventory using the last-in, first-out method to be higher or lower?

PR 7-2A LIFO perpetual inventory **OBJ. 2, 3**

✔ 2. Gross profit, $8,853,750

SHOW ME HOW

The beginning inventory at Midnight Supplies and data on purchases and sales for a three-month period are shown in Problem 7-1A.

Instructions

1. Record the inventory, purchases, and cost of merchandise sold data in a perpetual inventory record similar to the one illustrated in Exhibit 4, using the last-in, first-out method.
2. Determine the total sales, the total cost of merchandise sold, and the gross profit from sales for the period.
3. Determine the ending inventory cost as of March 31.

PR 7-3A Weighted average cost method with perpetual inventory **OBJ. 2, 3**

✔ 2. Gross profit, $8,973,750

The beginning inventory for Midnight Supplies and data on purchases and sales for a three-month period are shown in Problem 7-1A.

Instructions

1. Record the inventory, purchases, and cost of merchandise sold data in a perpetual inventory record similar to the one illustrated in Exhibit 5, using the weighted average cost method.
2. Determine the total sales, the total cost of merchandise sold, and the gross profit from sales for the period.
3. Determine the ending inventory cost as of March 31.

PR 7-4A Periodic inventory by three methods **OBJ. 2, 4**

✔ 2. Inventory, $881,250

The beginning inventory for Midnight Supplies and data on purchases and sales for a three-month period are shown in Problem 7-1A.

Instructions

1. Determine the inventory on March 31 and the cost of merchandise sold for the three-month period, using the first-in, first-out method and the periodic inventory system.
2. Determine the inventory on March 31 and the cost of merchandise sold for the three-month period, using the last-in, first-out method and the periodic inventory system.
3. Determine the inventory on March 31 and the cost of merchandise sold for the three-month period, using the weighted average cost method and the periodic inventory system. Round the weighted average unit cost to the nearest cent.
4. Compare the gross profit and the March 31 inventories, using the following column headings:

	FIFO	LIFO	Weighted Average
Sales			
Cost of merchandise sold			
Gross profit			
Inventory, March 31			

PR 7-5A Periodic inventory by three methods

OBJ. 2, 4

✔ 1. $10,700

Dymac Appliances uses the periodic inventory system. Details regarding the inventory of appliances at January 1, purchases invoices during the next 12 months, and the inventory count at December 31 are summarized as follows:

Model	Inventory, January 1	Purchases Invoices 1st	2nd	3rd	Inventory Count, December 31
A10	—	4 at $ 64	4 at $ 70	4 at $ 76	6
B15	8 at $176	4 at 158	3 at 170	6 at 184	8
E60	3 at 75	3 at 65	15 at 68	9 at 70	5
G83	7 at 242	6 at 250	5 at 260	10 at 259	9
J34	12 at 240	10 at 246	16 at 267	16 at 270	15
M90	2 at 108	2 at 110	3 at 128	3 at 130	5
Q70	5 at 160	4 at 170	4 at 175	7 at 180	8

Instructions

1. Determine the cost of the inventory on December 31 by the first-in, first-out method. Present data in columnar form, using the following headings:

Model	Quantity	Unit Cost	Total Cost

   If the inventory of a particular model comprises one entire purchase plus a portion of another purchase acquired at a different unit cost, use a separate line for each purchase.
2. Determine the cost of the inventory on December 31 by the last-in, first-out method, following the procedures indicated in (1).
3. Determine the cost of the inventory on December 31 by the weighted average cost method, using the columnar headings indicated in (1).
4. Discuss which method (FIFO or LIFO) would be preferred for income tax purposes in periods of (a) rising prices and (b) declining prices.

PR 7-6A Lower-of-cost-or-market inventory

OBJ. 6

✔ Total LCM, $39,873

Data on the physical inventory of Ashwood Products Company as of December 31 follow:

Inventory Item	Inventory Quantity	Market Value per Unit (Net Realizable Value)
B12	38	$ 57
E41	18	180
G19	33	126
L88	18	550
N94	400	7
P24	90	18
R66	8	250
T33	140	20
Z16	15	752

Quantity and cost data from the last purchases invoice of the year and the next-to-the-last purchases invoice are summarized as follows:

	Last Purchases Invoice		Next-to-the-Last Purchases Invoice	
Inventory Item	Quantity Purchased	Unit Cost	Quantity Purchased	Unit Cost
B12	30	$ 60	30	$ 59
E41	35	178	20	180
G19	20	128	25	129
L88	10	563	10	560
N94	500	8	500	7
P24	80	22	50	21
R66	5	248	4	260
T33	100	21	100	19
Z16	10	750	9	745

Instructions

Determine the inventory at cost as well as at the lower of cost or market, using the first-in, first-out method. Record the appropriate unit costs on the inventory sheet and complete the pricing of the inventory. When there are two different unit costs applicable to an item, proceed as follows:

1. Draw a line through the quantity and insert the quantity and unit cost of the last purchase.
2. On the following line, insert the quantity and unit cost of the next-to-the-last purchase.
3. Total the cost and market columns and insert the lower of the two totals in the Lower of C or M column. The first item on the inventory sheet has been completed as an example.

Inventory Sheet
December 31

Inventory Item	Inventory Quantity	Cost per Unit	Market Value per Unit (Net Realizable Value)	Total Cost	Total Market	Total Lower of C or M
B12	~~38~~ 30	$60	$57	$1,800	$1,710	
	8	59	57	472	456	
				$2,272	$2,166	$2,166

Appendix

PR 7-7A Retail method; gross profit method

✔ 1. $483,600

Selected data on merchandise inventory, purchases, and sales for Celebrity Tan Co. and Ranchworks Co. are as follows:

	Cost	Retail
Celebrity Tan Co.		
Merchandise inventory, August 1	$ 300,000	$ 575,000
Transactions during August:		
Purchases (net)	2,149,000	3,375,000
Sales		3,170,000
Ranchworks Co.		
Merchandise inventory, March 1	$ 880,000	
Transactions during March through November:		
Purchases (net)	9,500,000	
Sales	15,800,000	
Estimated gross profit rate	38%	

Instructions

1. Determine the estimated cost of the merchandise inventory of Celebrity Tan Co. on August 31 by the retail method, presenting details of the computations.
2. a. Estimate the cost of the merchandise inventory of Ranchworks Co. on November 30 by the gross profit method, presenting details of the computations.

   b. Assume that Ranchworks Co. took a physical inventory on November 30 and discovered that $369,750 of merchandise was on hand. What was the estimated loss of inventory due to theft or damage during March through November?

Problems: Series B

PR 7-1B FIFO perpetual inventory

OBJ. 2, 3

✔ 3. $254,800

SHOW ME HOW

The beginning inventory of merchandise at Rhodes Co. and data on purchases and sales for a three-month period ending June 30 are as follows:

Date	Transaction	Number of Units	Per Unit	Total
Apr. 3	Inventory	40	$ 670	$ 26,800
8	Purchase	120	690	82,800
11	Sale	60	1,120	67,200
30	Sale	50	1,120	56,000
May 8	Purchase	100	700	70,000
10	Sale	80	1,120	89,600
19	Sale	30	1,120	33,600
28	Purchase	120	707	84,840
June 5	Sale	60	1,260	75,600
16	Sale	40	1,260	50,400
21	Purchase	180	712	128,160
28	Sale	190	1,260	239,400

Instructions

1. Record the inventory, purchases, and cost of merchandise sold data in a perpetual inventory record similar to the one illustrated in Exhibit 3, using the first-in, first-out method.
2. Determine the total sales and the total cost of merchandise sold for the period. Journalize the entries in the sales and cost of merchandise sold accounts. Assume that all sales were on account.
3. Determine the gross profit from sales for the period.
4. Determine the ending inventory cost on June 30.
5. Based upon the preceding data, would you expect the inventory using the last-in, first-out method to be higher or lower?

PR 7-2B LIFO perpetual inventory

OBJ. 2, 3

✔ 2. Gross profit, $253,070

The beginning inventory for Rhodes Co. and data on purchases and sales for a three-month period are shown in Problem 7-1B.

SHOW ME HOW

Instructions

1. Record the inventory, purchases, and cost of merchandise sold data in a perpetual inventory record similar to the one illustrated in Exhibit 4, using the last-in, first-out method.
2. Determine the total sales, the total cost of merchandise sold, and the gross profit from sales for the period.
3. Determine the ending inventory cost on June 30.

PR 7-3B Weighted average cost method with perpetual inventory

OBJ. 2, 3

✔ 2. Gross profit, $254,700

The beginning inventory for Rhodes Co. and data on purchases and sales for a three-month period are shown in Problem 7-1B.

Instructions

1. Record the inventory, purchases, and cost of merchandise sold data in a perpetual inventory record similar to the one illustrated in Exhibit 5, using the weighted average cost method.

2. Determine the total sales, the total cost of merchandise sold, and the gross profit from sales for the period.
3. Determine the ending inventory cost on June 30.

PR 7-4B Periodic inventory by three methods

OBJ. 2, 4

✔ 2. Inventory, June 30, $33,700

The beginning inventory for Rhodes Co. and data on purchases and sales for a three-month period are shown in Problem 7-1B.

Instructions

1. Determine the inventory on June 30 and the cost of merchandise sold for the three-month period, using the first-in, first-out method and the periodic inventory system.
2. Determine the inventory on June 30 and the cost of merchandise sold for the three-month period, using the last-in, first-out method and the periodic inventory system.
3. Determine the inventory on June 30 and the cost of merchandise sold for the three-month period, using the weighted average cost method and the periodic inventory system. Round the weighted average unit cost to the dollar.
4. Compare the gross profit and June 30 inventories using the following column headings:

	FIFO	LIFO	Weighted Average
Sales			
Cost of merchandise sold			
Gross profit			
Inventory, June 30			

PR 7-5B Periodic inventory by three methods

OBJ. 2, 4

✔ 1. $18,545

Pappa's Appliances uses the periodic inventory system. Details regarding the inventory of appliances at January 1, purchases invoices during the year, and the inventory count at December 31 are summarized as follows:

		Purchases Invoices			
Model	**Inventory, January 1**	**1st**	**2nd**	**3rd**	**Inventory Count, December 31**
C55	3 at $1,040	3 at $1,054	3 at $1,060	3 at $1,070	4
D11	9 at 639	7 at 645	6 at 666	6 at 675	11
F32	5 at 240	3 at 260	1 at 260	1 at 280	2
H29	6 at 305	3 at 310	3 at 316	4 at 317	4
K47	6 at 520	8 at 531	4 at 549	6 at 542	8
S33	—	4 at 222	4 at 232	—	2
X74	4 at 35	6 at 36	8 at 37	7 at 39	7

Instructions

1. Determine the cost of the inventory on December 31 by the first-in, first-out method. Present data in columnar form, using the following headings:

Model	Quantity	Unit Cost	Total Cost

   If the inventory of a particular model comprises one entire purchase plus a portion of another purchase acquired at a different unit cost, use a separate line for each purchase.
2. Determine the cost of the inventory on December 31 by the last-in, first-out method, following the procedures indicated in (1).
3. Determine the cost of the inventory on December 31 by the weighted average cost method, using the columnar headings indicated in (1).
4. Discuss which method (FIFO or LIFO) would be preferred for income tax purposes in periods of (a) rising prices and (b) declining prices.

PR 7-6B Lower-of-cost-or-market inventory

OBJ. 6

✔ Total LCM, $41,873

Data on the physical inventory of Katus Products Co. as of December 31 follow:

Inventory Item	Inventory Quantity	Market Value per Unit (Net Realizable Value)
A54	37	$ 56
C77	24	178
F66	30	132
H83	21	545
K12	375	5
Q58	90	18
S36	8	235
V97	140	20
Y88	17	744

Quantity and cost data from the last purchases invoice of the year and the next-to-the-last purchases invoice are summarized as follows:

	Last Purchases Invoice		Next-to-the-Last Purchases Invoice	
Inventory Item	Quantity Purchased	Unit Cost	Quantity Purchased	Unit Cost
A54	30	$ 60	40	$ 58
C77	25	174	15	180
F66	20	130	15	128
H83	6	547	15	540
K12	500	6	500	7
Q58	75	25	80	26
S36	5	256	4	260
V97	100	17	115	16
Y88	10	750	8	740

Instructions

Determine the inventory at cost as well as at the lower of cost or market, using the first-in, first-out method. Record the appropriate unit costs on the inventory sheet and complete the pricing of the inventory. When there are two different unit costs applicable to an item:

1. Draw a line through the quantity and insert the quantity and unit cost of the last purchase.
2. On the following line, insert the quantity and unit cost of the next-to-the-last purchase.
3. Total the cost and market columns and insert the lower of the two totals in the LCM column. The first item on the inventory sheet has been completed as an example.

Inventory Sheet
December 31

Inventory Item	Inventory Quantity	Cost per Unit	Market Value per Unit (Net Realizable Value)	Total Cost	Total Market	LCM
A54	~~37~~ 30	60	$56	$1,800	$1,680	
	7	58	56	406	392	
				$2,206	$2,072	$2,072

Appendix

PR 7-7B Retail method; gross profit method

✔ 1. $630,000

Selected data on merchandise inventory, purchases, and sales for Jaffe Co. and Coronado Co. are as follows:

	Cost	Retail
Jaffe Co.		
Merchandise inventory, February 1	$ 400,000	$ 615,000
Transactions during February:		
Purchases (net)	4,055,000	5,325,000
Sales		5,100,000

Coronado Co.	
Merchandise inventory, May 1	$ 400,000
Transactions during May through October:	
Purchases (net)	3,150,000
Sales	4,750,000
Estimated gross profit rate	35%

Instructions

1. Determine the estimated cost of the merchandise inventory of Jaffe Co. on February 28 by the retail method, presenting details of the computations.
2. a. Estimate the cost of the merchandise inventory of Coronado Co. on October 31 by the gross profit method, presenting details of the computations.
   b. Assume that Coronado Co. took a physical inventory on October 31 and discovered that $366,500 of merchandise was on hand. What was the estimated loss of inventory due to theft or damage during May through October?

Cases & Projects

ETHICS

CP 7-1 Ethics in Action

Sizemo Elektroniks sells semiconductors that are used in games and small toys. The company has been extremely successful in recent years, recording an increase in earnings each of the past six quarters. At the end of the current quarter, Jay Shulz, the company's staff accountant, calculated the ending inventory for the semiconductors and was surprised to find that the quantity of the Hayden 537X model had not changed during the quarter. Jay confirmed his calculation with the inventory control manager, who indicated that sales of the Hayden 537X had stopped when the Hayden 637X semiconductor was released early in the quarter. Jay researched the issue further and found that the Hayden 637X semiconductor has the same applications as the Hayden 537X, but has more computing power and a lower cost than the 537X. Jay e-mailed this information to Tina Vereen, the chief financial officer, and recommended that the company apply the lower-of-cost-or-market method to the Hayden 537X semiconductors in inventory. Later that day, Tina e-mailed Jay back, instructing him not to apply the lower-of-cost-or-market method to the 537X inventory because "the company is under considerable pressure to maintain its track record of earnings growth, and a lower-of-cost-or-market adjustment would result in a significant decline in earnings this quarter." Reluctantly, Jay followed Tina's instructions.

Evaluate the decision not to apply the lower-of-cost-or-market method in the current quarter.

1. Who benefits from this decision?
2. Who is harmed by this decision?
3. Are Jay and Tina acting in an ethical manner? Explain.

ETHICS

CP 7-2 Ethics in Action

Anstead Co. is experiencing a decrease in sales and operating income for the fiscal year ending October 31. Ryan Frazier, controller of Anstead Co., has suggested that all orders received before the end of the fiscal year be shipped by midnight, October 31, even if the shipping department must work overtime. Because Anstead Co. ships all merchandise FOB shipping point, it would record all such shipments as sales for the year ending October 31, thereby offsetting some of the decreases in sales and operating income.

Discuss whether Ryan Frazier is behaving in a professional manner.

TEAM ACTIVITY

CP 7-3 Team Activity

In teams, select a public company in the merchandising industry that interests you. Obtain the company's most recent annual report on Form 10-K. The Form 10-K is a company's annually required filing with the Securities and Exchange Commission (SEC). It includes the company's financial statements and accompanying notes. The Form 10-K can be obtained either (a) by referring to the investor relations section of the company's website or (b) by using the company search feature of the SEC's EDGAR database service found at www.sec.gov/edgar/searchedgar/companysearch.html.

(Continued)

1. Based on the information in the company's most recent annual report, answer the following questions:
   a. What types of items are included in the company's inventory?
   b. What inventory costing method or methods does the company use to determine the inventory amount reported on its balance sheet?
   c. How much inventory does the company have at the end of the most recent year?
   d. What percentage of total current assets is inventory during the two years presented? Has this percentage increased, decreased, or remained the same during this period?
   e. How much cost of merchandise sold does the company report for the most recent year?
2. Using the information presented in the company's annual report, determine the company's inventory turnover for the current and previous years. Based on this information, has the company's performance improved? Briefly explain your answer.

CP 7-4 Communication

COMMUNICATION

Golden Eagle Company began operations on April 1 by selling a single product. Data on purchases and sales for the year are as follows:

Purchases:

Date	Units Purchased	Unit Cost	Total Cost
April 6	31,000	$36.60	$1,134,600
May 18	33,000	39.00	1,287,000
June 6	40,000	39.60	1,584,000
July 10	40,000	42.00	1,680,000
August 10	27,200	42.75	1,162,800
October 25	12,800	43.50	556,800
November 4	8,000	44.85	358,800
December 10	8,000	48.00	384,000
	200,000		$8,148,000

Sales:

April	16,000 units
May	16,000
June	20,000
July	24,000
August	28,000
September	28,000
October	18,000
November	10,000
December	8,000
Total units	168,000
Total sales	$10,000,000

The president of the company, Connie Kilmer, has asked for your advice on which inventory cost flow method should be used for the 32,000-unit physical inventory that was taken on December 31. The company plans to expand its product line in the future and uses the periodic inventory system.

Write a brief memo to Ms. Kilmer comparing and contrasting the LIFO and FIFO inventory cost flow methods and their potential impacts on the company's financial statements.

CP 7-5 LIFO and inventory flow

The following is an excerpt from a conversation between Paula Marlo, the warehouse manager for Musick Foods Wholesale Co., and its accountant, Mike Hayes. Musick Foods operates a large regional warehouse that supplies produce and other grocery products to grocery stores in smaller communities.

Paula: Mike, can you explain what's going on here with these monthly statements?

Mike: Sure, Paula. How can I help you?

Paula: I don't understand this last-in, first-out inventory procedure. It just doesn't make sense.

Mike: Well, what it means is that we assume that the last goods we receive are the first ones sold. So the inventory consists of the items we purchased first.

Paula: Yes, but that's my problem. It doesn't work that way! We always distribute the oldest produce first. Some of that produce is perishable! We can't keep any of it very long or it'll spoil.

Mike: Paula, you don't understand. We only *assume* that the products we distribute are the last ones received. We don't actually have to distribute the goods in this way.

Paula: I always thought that accounting was supposed to show what really happened. It all sounds like "make believe" to me! Why not report what really happens?

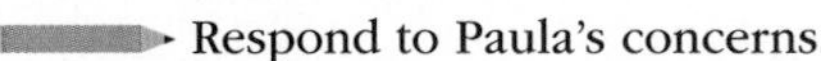 Respond to Paula's concerns.

CP 7-6 Comparing inventory ratios for two companies

Target Corp. sells merchandise primarily through its retail stores. On the other hand, **Amazon.com** uses its e-commerce services, features, and technologies to sell its products through the Internet. Recent balance sheet inventory disclosures for Target and Amazon.com (in millons) are as follows:

	Target	Amazon.com
Cost of merchandise sold	$53,299	$139,156
Inventory, end of year	9,497	17,174
Inventory, beginning of year	8,597	16,047

a. Determine the inventory turnover for Target and Amazon.com. Round to two decimal places.

b. Determine the days' sales in inventory for Target and Amazon.com. Use 365 days and round to one decimal place.

c. Interpret your results.

CP 7-7 Comparing inventory ratios for three companies

The general merchandise retail industry has a number of segments represented by the following companies:

Company Name	Merchandise Concept
Costco Wholesale Corporation	Membership warehouse
Wal-Mart	Discount general merchandise
JCPenney Company	Department store

For a recent year, the following cost of merchandise sold and beginning and ending inventories have been provided from corporate annual reports (in millions) for these three companies:

	Costco	Wal-Mart	JCPenney
Cost of merchandise sold	$123,152	$385,301	$7,870
Merchandise inventory, beginning	9,834	43,783	2,803
Merchandise inventory, ending	11,040	44,269	2,437

a. Determine the inventory turnover ratio for all three companies. Round to two decimal places.

b. Determine the days' sales in inventory for all three companies. Use 365 days and round to one decimal place.

c. Interpret these results based on each company's merchandise concept.

CHAPTER 8 Internal Control and Cash

STATEMENT OF OWNER'S EQUITY
For the Year Ended December 31, 20Y6

Owner's capital, Jan. 1, 20Y6		$XXX
Net income	$ XXX	
Withdrawals	(XXX)	
Increase in equity		XXX
Owner's capital, Dec. 31, 20Y6		$XXX

STATEMENT OF CASH FLOWS
For the Year Ended December 31, 20Y6

Cash flows from (used for) operating activities	$XXX
Cash flows from (used for) investing activities	XXX
Cash flows from (used for) financing activities	XXX
Net increase (decrease) in cash	$XXX
Cash balance, January 1, 20Y6	XXX

INCOME STATEMENT
For the Year Ended December 31, 20Y6

Sales		$XXX
Cost of merchandise sold		XXX
Gross profit		$XXX
Operating expenses:		
Advertising expense	$XXX	
Depreciation expense	XXX	
Amortization expense	XXX	
Depletion expense	XXX	
...	XXX	
...	XXX	
Total operating expenses		XXX
Income from operations		$XXX
Other revenue and expenses		XXX
Net income		$XXX

BALANCE SHEET
December 31, 20Y6

Current assets:		
Cash	$XXX	
Accounts receivable	XXX	
Merchandise inventory	XXX	
Total current assets		$XXX
Property, plant, and equipment	$XXX	
Intangible assets	XXX	
Total long-term assets		XXX
Total assets		$XXX
Liabilities:		
Current liabilities	$XXX	
Long-term liabilities	XXX	
Total liabilities		$XXX
Owner's equity		XXX
Total liabilities and owner's equity		$XXX

CHAPTER

8

eBay Inc.

Controls are a part of your everyday life. At one extreme, laws are used to limit your behavior. For example, speed limits are designed to control your driving for traffic safety. In addition, you may use many nonlegal controls. For example, you can keep credit card receipts in order to compare your transactions to the monthly credit card statement. Comparing receipts to the monthly statement is a control designed to catch mistakes made by the credit card company. In addition, banks give you a personal identification number (PIN) as a control against unauthorized access to your cash if you lose your automated teller machine (ATM) card. Dairies (milk producers) use freshness dating on their milk containers as a control to prevent the purchase or sale of soured milk. As you can see, you use and encounter controls every day.

Just as there are many examples of controls throughout society, businesses must also implement controls to help guide the behavior of their managers, employees, and customers. For example, **eBay Inc.** maintains an Internet-based marketplace for the sale of goods and services. Using eBay's online platform, buyers and sellers can browse, buy, and sell a wide variety of items including antiques and used cars. However, in order to maintain the integrity and trust of its buyers and sellers, eBay must have controls to ensure that buyers pay for their items and sellers don't misrepresent their items or fail to deliver sales. One such control eBay uses is a feedback forum that establishes buyers' and sellers' reputations. A prospective buyer or seller can view the member's reputation and feedback comments before completing a transaction. Dishonest or unfair trading can lead to a negative reputation and even suspension or cancellation of the member's ability to trade on eBay.

This chapter discusses controls that can be included in accounting systems to provide reasonable assurance that the financial statements are reliable. Controls to discover and prevent errors to a bank account are also discussed. This chapter begins by discussing the Sarbanes-Oxley Act and its impact on controls and financial reporting.

Link to eBay .... Pages 399, 401, 404, 405, 409, 418

LEARNING OBJECTIVES

After studying this chapter, you should be able to:

Example Exercises (EE) are shown in **red.**

OBJ. 1 **Describe the Sarbanes-Oxley Act and its impact on internal controls and financial reporting.**

Sarbanes-Oxley Act

OBJ. 2 **Describe and illustrate the objectives and elements of internal control.**

Internal Control

Objectives of Internal Control	
Elements of Internal Control	
Control Environment	EE **8-1**
Risk Assessment	EE **8-1**
Control Procedures	EE **8-1**
Monitoring	EE **8-1**
Information and Communication	EE **8-1**
Limitations of Internal Control	

OBJ. 3 **Describe and illustrate the application of internal controls to cash.**

Cash Controls over Receipts and Payments

Control of Cash Receipts
Control of Cash Payments

OBJ. 4 **Describe the nature of a bank account and its use in controlling cash.**

Bank Accounts

Bank Statement	EE **8-2**
Using the Bank Statement as a Control over Cash	

OBJ. 5 **Describe and illustrate the use of a bank reconciliation in controlling cash.**

Bank Reconciliation

Adjusted Balance and Entries	EE **8-3**

OBJ. 6 **Describe the accounting for special-purpose cash funds.**

Special-Purpose Cash Funds

Petty Cash Fund	EE **8-4**

OBJ. 7 **Describe and illustrate the reporting of cash and cash equivalents in the financial statements.**

Financial Statement Reporting of Cash

OBJ. 8 **Describe and illustrate the use of the ratio of cash to monthly cash expenses to assess the ability of a company to continue in business.**

Financial Analysis and Interpretation: Ratio of Cash to Monthly Cash Expenses

Compute Ratio of Cash to Monthly Cash Expenses	EE **8-5**

At a Glance 8 Page 421

OBJ. 1 Describe the Sarbanes-Oxley Act and its impact on internal controls and financial reporting.

Sarbanes-Oxley Act

The **Sarbanes-Oxley Act** is one of the most important laws affecting U.S. companies in recent history. The purpose of Sarbanes-Oxley is to foster public confidence and trust in the financial reporting of companies. In addition, Sarbanes-Oxley is designed to prevent fraud, theft, and financial scandals.

Sarbanes-Oxley applies only to companies whose stock is traded on public exchanges, referred to as *publicly held companies*. However, Sarbanes-Oxley highlighted the importance of assessing the financial controls and reporting of all companies. As a result, companies of all sizes have been influenced by Sarbanes-Oxley.

Sarbanes-Oxley emphasizes the importance of effective internal control.[1] **Internal control** is defined as the procedures and processes used by a company to:

- Safeguard its assets.
- Process information accurately.
- Ensure compliance with laws and regulations.

Sarbanes-Oxley requires companies to maintain effective internal controls over the recording of transactions and the preparing of financial statements. Such controls

1 Sarbanes-Oxley also has important implications for corporate governance and the regulation of the public accounting profession. This chapter, however, focuses on the internal control implications of Sarbanes-Oxley.

are important because they deter fraud and prevent misleading financial statements as shown in Exhibit 1.

EXHIBIT 1
Effect of Sarbanes-Oxley

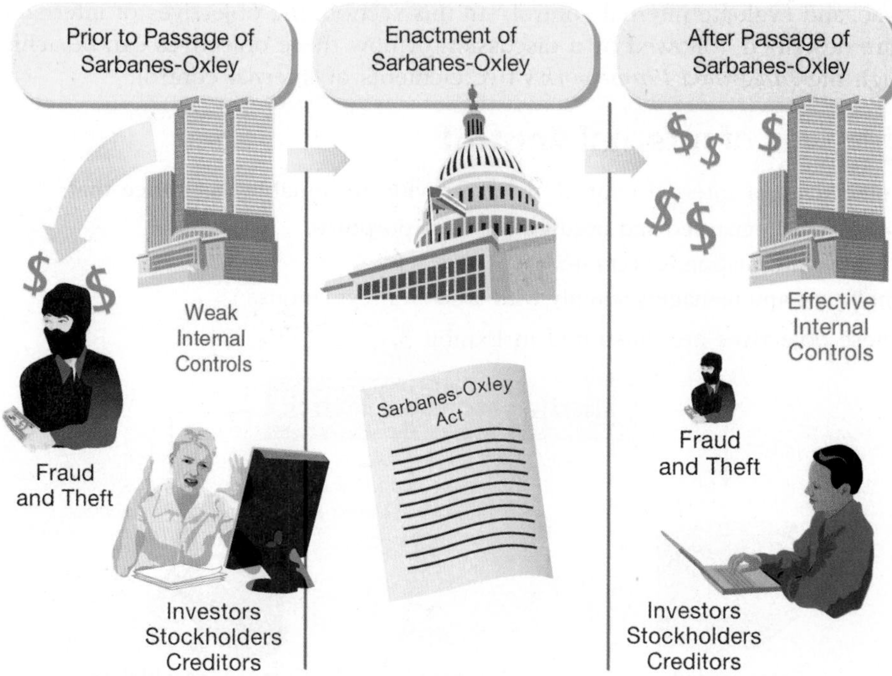

Sarbanes-Oxley also requires companies and their independent accountants to report on the effectiveness of the company's internal controls.[2] These reports are required to be filed with the company's annual 10-K report with the Securities and Exchange Commission. Companies are also encouraged to include these reports in their annual reports to stockholders. An example of such a report by the management of **eBay** is shown in Exhibit 2.

Link to eBay
Exhibit 2 is taken from the annual (10-K) report of **eBay**.

EXHIBIT 2
eBay's Report of Compliance with Sarbanes-Oxley

Management's Annual Report on Internal Control Over Financial Reporting

Our management is responsible for establishing and maintaining adequate internal control over financial reporting. Our management, including our principal executive officer and principal financial officer, conducted an evaluation of the effectiveness of our internal control over financial reporting based on the framework in *Internal Control—Integrated Framework (2013)* issued by the Committee of Sponsoring Organizations of the Treadway Commission. Based on its evaluation under the framework in *Internal Control—Integrated Framework*, our management concluded that our internal control over financial reporting was effective as of December 31, . . .

Source: eBay Inc., *Form 10-K for the Fiscal Year Ended December 31, 2018.*

Exhibit 2 indicates that the evaluation of internal controls is based on *Internal Control—Integrated Framework*, which was issued by the Committee of Sponsoring Organizations (COSO) of the Treadway Commission. This framework is the standard by which companies design, analyze, and evaluate internal controls. For this reason, this framework is used as the basis for discussing internal controls.[3]

2 These reporting requirements are required under Section 404 of the act. As a result, these requirements and reports are often referred to as 404 requirements and 404 reports.

3 Information on *Internal Control—Integrated Framework* can be found on COSO's website at www.coso.org/.

Describe and illustrate the objectives and elements of internal control.

Internal Control

Internal Control—Integrated Framework is the standard by which companies design, analyze, and evaluate internal control.[4] In this section, the objectives of internal control are described, followed by a discussion of how these objectives can be achieved through the *Integrated Framework's* five elements of internal control.

Objectives of Internal Control

The objectives of internal control are to provide reasonable assurance that:

- Assets are safeguarded and used for business purposes.
- Business information is accurate.
- Employees and managers comply with laws and regulations.

These objectives are illustrated in Exhibit 3.

EXHIBIT 3

Objectives of Internal Control

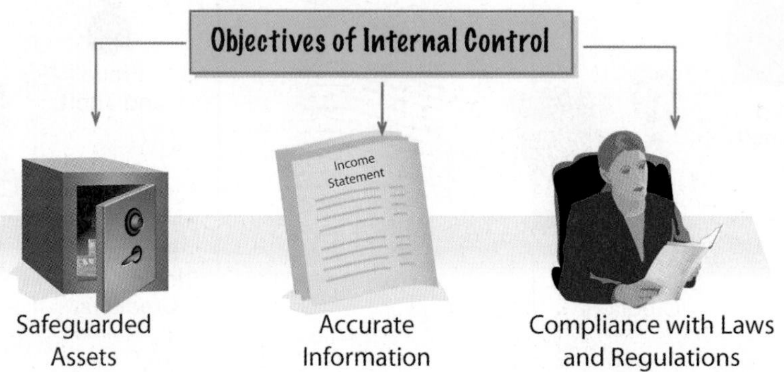

Internal control can safeguard assets by preventing theft, fraud, misuse, or misplacement. A serious concern of internal control is preventing employee fraud. **Employee fraud** is the intentional act of deceiving an employer for personal gain. Such fraud may range from minor overstating of a travel expense report to stealing millions of dollars. Employees stealing from a business often adjust the accounting records in order to hide their fraud. Thus, employee fraud usually affects the accuracy of business information.

Accurate information is necessary to operate a business successfully. Businesses must also comply with laws, regulations, and financial reporting standards. Examples of such standards include environmental regulations, safety regulations, and generally accepted accounting principles (GAAP).

Business Connection

EMPLOYEE FRAUD

The Association of Fraud Examiners estimates that 5% of annual revenues worldwide, or close to $4 trillion, is lost to employee fraud. A common cash receipts employee fraud can occur when employees accept cash payments from customers, do not record the sale, and then pocket the cash. A common cash payments employee fraud can occur when employees bill their employer for false services or personal items.

Source: *2018 Report to the Nation on Occupational Fraud and Abuse,* Association of Fraud Examiners.

Elements of Internal Control

The three internal control objectives can be achieved by applying the five **elements of internal control** set forth by the *Integrated Framework*.[5] These elements are as follows:

4 *Internal Control—Integrated Framework* by the Committee of Sponsoring Organizations of the Treadway Commission, 2013.
5 Ibid., pp. 12–14.

- Control environment
- Risk assessment
- Control procedures
- Monitoring
- Information and communication

The elements of internal control are illustrated in Exhibit 4.

EXHIBIT 4
Elements of Internal Control

Link to eBay

As technology changes, **eBay** must continually monitor and strengthen its controls over e-commerce transactions.

In Exhibit 4, the elements of internal control form an umbrella over the business to protect it from control threats. The control environment is the size of the umbrella. Risk assessment, control procedures, and monitoring are the fabric of the umbrella, which keep it from leaking. Information and communication connect the umbrella to management.

Control Environment

The **control environment** is the overall attitude of management and employees about the importance of controls. Three factors influencing a company's control environment include the following, as shown in Exhibit 5:

- Management's philosophy and operating style
- The company's organizational structure
- The company's personnel policies

EXHIBIT 5
Control Environment

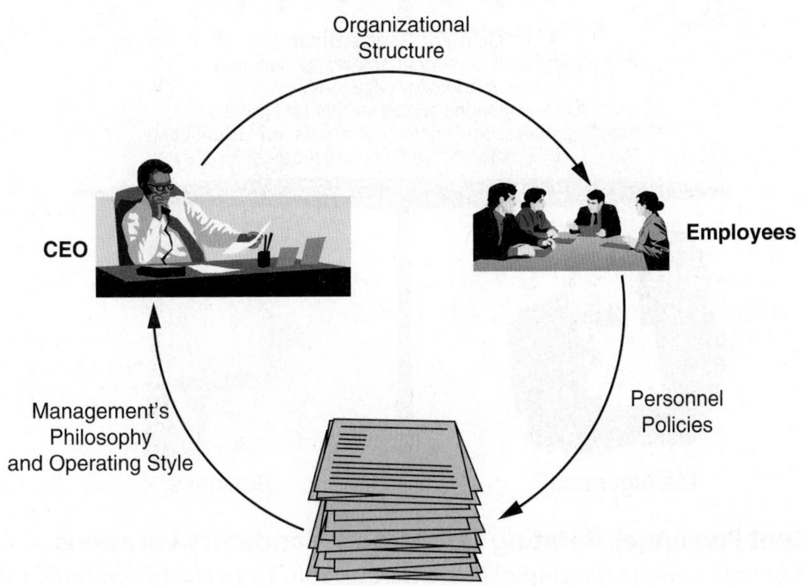

Management's philosophy and operating style relate to whether management emphasizes the importance of internal controls. An emphasis on controls and adherence to control policies creates an effective control environment. In contrast, overemphasizing operating goals and tolerating deviations from control policies creates an ineffective control environment.

The business's organizational structure is the framework for planning and controlling operations. For example, a retail store chain might organize each of its stores as separate business units. Each store manager has full authority over pricing and other operating activities. In such a structure, each store manager has the responsibility for establishing an effective control environment.

The business's personnel policies involve the hiring, training, evaluation, compensation, and promotion of employees. In addition, job descriptions, employee codes of ethics, and conflict-of-interest policies are part of the personnel policies. Such policies can enhance the internal control environment if they provide reasonable assurance that only competent, honest employees are hired and retained.

Risk Assessment

All businesses face risks such as changes in customer requirements, competitive threats, regulatory changes, and changes in economic factors. Management should identify such risks, analyze their significance, assess their likelihood of occurring, and take any necessary actions to minimize them.

Control Procedures

Control procedures provide reasonable assurance that business goals will be achieved, including the prevention of fraud. Control procedures, which constitute one of the most important elements of internal control, include the following as shown in Exhibit 6:

- Competent personnel, rotating duties, and mandatory vacations
- Separating responsibilities for related operations
- Separating operations, custody of assets, and accounting
- Proofs and security measures

EXHIBIT 6
Internal Control Procedures

Competent Personnel, Rotating Duties, and Mandatory Vacations A successful company needs competent employees who are able to perform the duties that they are assigned. Procedures should be established for properly training and supervising employees. It is also advisable to rotate duties of accounting personnel and mandate vacations for all employees. In this way, employees are encouraged to adhere to procedures. Cases of employee fraud are often discovered when a long-term employee, who never took vacations, missed work because of an illness or another unavoidable reason.

Separating Responsibilities for Related Operations The responsibility for related operations should be divided among two or more people. This decreases the possibility of errors and fraud. For example, if the same person orders supplies, verifies the receipt of the supplies, and pays the supplier, the following abuses may occur:

- Orders may be placed on the basis of friendship with a supplier rather than on price, quality, and other objective factors.
- The quantity and quality of supplies received may not be verified; thus, the company may pay for supplies that are not received or that are of poor quality.
- Supplies may be stolen by the employee.
- The validity and accuracy of invoices may not be verified; hence, the company may pay false or inaccurate invoices.

For the preceding reasons, the responsibilities for purchasing, receiving, and paying for supplies should be divided among three persons or departments.

Separating Operations, Custody of Assets, and Accounting The responsibilities for operations, custody of assets, and accounting should be separated. In this way, the accounting records serve as an independent check on the operating managers and the employees who have custody of assets.

To illustrate, employees who handle cash receipts should not record cash receipts in the accounting records. To do so would allow employees to borrow or steal cash and hide the theft in the accounting records. Likewise, operating managers should not record the results of operations. To do so would allow the managers to distort the accounting reports to show favorable results, which might allow them to receive larger bonuses.

Proofs and Security Measures Proofs and security measures are used to safeguard assets and ensure reliable accounting data. Proofs involve procedures such as authorization, approval, and reconciliation. For example, an employee planning to travel on company business may be required to complete a "travel request" form for a manager's authorization and approval.

Integrity, Objectivity, and Ethics in Business

TIPS ON PREVENTING EMPLOYEE FRAUD IN SMALL COMPANIES

- Do not have the same employee write company checks and keep the books. Look for payments to vendors you don't know or payments to vendors whose names appear to be misspelled.
- If your business has a computer system, restrict access to accounting files as much as possible. Also, keep a backup copy of your accounting files and store it at an off-site location.
- Be wary of anybody working in finance who declines to take vacations. They may be afraid that a replacement will uncover fraud.
- Require and monitor supporting documentation (such as vendor invoices) before signing checks.
- Track the number of credit card bills you sign monthly.
- Limit and monitor access to important documents and supplies, such as blank checks and signature stamps.
- Check W-2 forms against your payroll annually to make sure you're not carrying any fictitious employees.
- Rely on yourself, not on your accountant, to spot fraud.

Source: Steve Kaufman, "Embezzlement Common at Small Companies," Knight-Ridder Newspapers, reported in *Athens Daily News/Athens Banner-Herald,* March 10, 1996, p. 4D.

Documents used for authorization and approval should be prenumbered, accounted for, and safeguarded. Prenumbering of documents helps prevent transactions from being recorded more than once or not at all. In addition, accounting for and safeguarding prenumbered documents helps prevent fraudulent transactions from being recorded. For example, blank checks are prenumbered and safeguarded. Once a payment has been properly authorized and approved, the checks are filled out and issued.

Reconciliations are also an important control. Later in this chapter, the use of bank reconciliations as an aid in controlling cash is described and illustrated.

Security measures involve measures to safeguard assets. For example, cash on hand should be kept in a cash register or safe. Inventory not on display should be stored in a locked storeroom or warehouse. Accounting records such as the accounts receivable subsidiary ledger should also be safeguarded to prevent their loss. For example, electronically maintained accounting records should be safeguarded with access codes and backed up so that any lost or damaged files could be recovered if necessary.

Monitoring

Monitoring the internal control system is used to locate weaknesses and improve controls. Monitoring often includes observing employee behavior and the accounting system for indicators of control problems. Some such indicators are shown in Exhibit 7.[6]

EXHIBIT 7

Warning Signs of Internal Control Problems

Warning signs with regard to people

- Abrupt change in lifestyle (without winning the lottery).
- Close social relationships with suppliers.
- Refusing to take a vacation.
- Frequent borrowing from other employees.
- Excessive use of alcohol or drugs.

Warning signs from the accounting system

- Missing documents or gaps in transaction numbers (could mean documents are being used for fraudulent transactions).
- An unusual increase in customer refunds (refunds may be phony).
- Differences between daily cash receipts and bank deposits (could mean receipts are being pocketed before being deposited).
- Sudden increase in slow payments (employee may be pocketing the payments).
- Backlog in recording transactions (possibly an attempt to delay detection of fraud).

Evaluations of controls are often performed when there are major changes in strategy, senior management, business structure, or operations. Internal auditors, who are independent of operations, usually perform such evaluations. Internal auditors are also responsible for day-to-day monitoring of controls. External auditors also evaluate and report on internal control as part of their annual financial statement audit.

Link to eBay

eBay reduces fraudulent activities by restricting or suspending buyers and sellers with questionable transaction histories.

Information and Communication

Information and communication is an essential element of internal control. Information about the control environment, risk assessment, control procedures, and monitoring is used by management for guiding operations and ensuring compliance with reporting, legal, and regulatory requirements. Management also uses external information to assess events and conditions that impact decision making and external reporting. For example, management uses pronouncements of the Financial Accounting Standards Board (FASB) to assess the impact of changes in reporting standards on the financial statements.

6 Edwin C. Bliss, "Employee Theft," *Boardroom Reports*, July 15, 1994, pp. 5–6.

EXAMPLE EXERCISE 8-1 Internal Control Elements OBJ. 2

Identify each of the following as relating to (a) the control environment, (b) risk assessment, or (c) control procedures:

1. Mandatory vacations
2. Personnel policies
3. Report of outside consultants on future market changes

Follow My Example 8-1

1. (c) control procedures
2. (a) the control environment
3. (b) risk assessment

Practice Exercises: PE 8-1A, PE 8-1B

Limitations of Internal Control

Internal control systems can provide only reasonable assurance for safeguarding assets, processing accurate information, and complying with laws and regulations. In other words, internal controls are not a guarantee. This is due to the following factors:

- The human element of controls
- Cost-benefit considerations

The *human element* recognizes that controls are applied and used by humans. As a result, human errors can occur because of fatigue, carelessness, confusion, or misjudgment. For example, an employee may unintentionally shortchange a customer or miscount the amount of inventory received from a supplier. In addition, two or more employees may collude to defeat or circumvent internal controls. This latter case often involves fraud and the theft of assets. For example, the cashier and the accounts receivable clerk might collude to steal customer payments on account.

Cost-benefit considerations recognize that the cost of internal controls should not exceed their benefits. For example, retail stores could eliminate shoplifting by searching all customers before they leave the store. However, such a control procedure would upset customers and result in lost sales. Instead, retailers use cameras or signs saying, "*We prosecute all shoplifters.*"

Link to eBay

The auditor's report for **eBay** includes this statement: ". . . internal control over financial reporting is a process designed to provide reasonable assurance regarding the reliability of financial reporting . . ."

Cash Controls over Receipts and Payments

OBJ. 3 Describe and illustrate the application of internal controls to cash.

Cash includes coins, currency (paper money), checks, and money orders. Money on deposit with a bank or another financial institution that is available for withdrawal is also considered cash. Normally, you can think of cash as anything that a bank would accept for deposit in your account. For example, a check made payable to you could normally be deposited in a bank and, thus, is considered cash.

Businesses usually have several bank accounts. For example, a business might have one bank account for general cash payments and another for payroll. A separate ledger account is normally used for each bank account. For example, a bank account at City Bank could be identified in the ledger as *Cash in Bank—City Bank*. To simplify, this chapter assumes that a company has only *one* bank account, which is identified in the ledger as *Cash*.

Cash is the asset most likely to be stolen or used improperly in a business. For this reason, businesses must carefully control cash and cash transactions.

Business Connection

WHAT IS CRYPTOCURRENCY?

Cryptocurrency is a digital form of payment that is used as an alternative to the more common payment methods of cash, credit cards, and checks. The technology behind cryptocurrency allows you to send and receive payments directly online without going through a third party, such as a bank. When paying with a cryptocurrency, such as Bitcoin, you do not have to reveal personal information; your social security number, your credit score, and even your real name remain private. When receiving payments, you do not have to worry about payment fraud or invalid checks, because with cryptocurrency, people can only spend what they have.

Cryptocurrency relies on encryption, where text is converted into code that becomes unintelligible. Encryption makes transactions secure in terms of *confidentiality* (information transferred cannot be understood or decoded), *integrity* (information cannot be altered), and *authentication* (sender and receiver can confirm each other).

Cryptocurrencies are like virtual accounting systems in that they keep a record of all transactions. In the future, as cryptocurrencies become more prevalent, they may impact companies' internal control procedures.

> "Virtual currencies, perhaps most notably Bitcoin, have captured the imagination of some, struck fear among others, and confused the heck out of the rest of us."
>
> —Thomas Carper, U.S. Senator, Delaware

Control of Cash Receipts

To protect cash from theft and misuse, a business must control cash from the time it is received until it is deposited in a bank. Businesses normally receive cash from two main sources.

- Customers purchasing products or services
- Customers making payments on account

Cash Received from Cash Sales An important control used to protect cash received in over-the-counter sales is a cash register. The use of a cash register to control cash is shown in Exhibit 8.

EXHIBIT 8

Cash Register as a Control

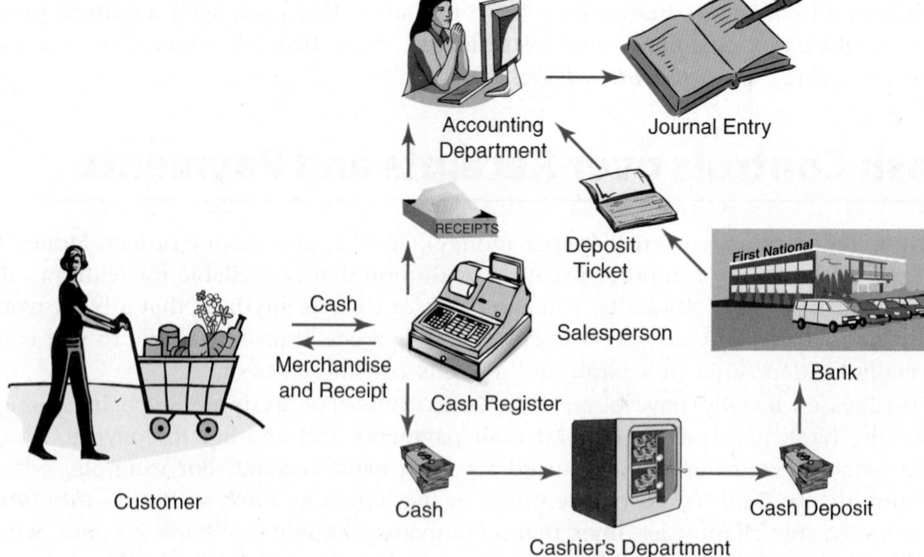

A cash register controls cash as follows:

1. At the beginning of every work shift, each cash register clerk is given a cash drawer containing a predetermined amount of cash. This amount is used for making change for customers and is sometimes called a *change fund*.
2. When a salesperson enters the amount of a sale, the cash register displays the amount to the customer. This allows the customer to verify that the clerk has charged the correct amount. The customer also receives a cash receipt.
3. At the end of the shift, the clerk and the supervisor count the cash in the clerk's cash drawer. The amount of cash in each drawer should equal the beginning amount of cash plus the cash sales for the day.
4. The supervisor takes the cash to the Cashier's Department where it is placed in a safe.
5. The supervisor forwards the clerk's cash register receipts to the Accounting Department.
6. The cashier prepares a bank deposit ticket.
7. The cashier deposits the cash in the bank, or the cash is picked up by an armored car service, such as **Wells Fargo**.
8. The Accounting Department summarizes the cash receipts and records the day's cash sales.
9. When cash is deposited in the bank, the bank normally stamps a duplicate copy of the deposit ticket with the amount received. This bank receipt is returned to the Accounting Department, where it is compared to the total amount that should have been deposited. This control helps ensure that all the cash is deposited and that no cash is lost or stolen on the way to the bank. Any shortages are thus promptly detected.

Salespersons may make errors in making change for customers or in ringing up cash sales. As a result, the amount of cash on hand may differ from the amount of cash sales. Such differences are recorded in a **cash short and over account**.

To illustrate, assume the following cash register data for May 3:

Cash register total for cash sales	$35,690
Cash receipts from cash sales	35,668

The cash sales, receipts, and shortage of $22 ($35,690 – $35,668) would be recorded as follows:

May	3	Cash		35,668	
		Cash Short and Over		22	
		Sales			35,690

If there had been cash over, Cash Short and Over would have been credited for the overage. At the end of the accounting period, a debit balance in Cash Short and Over is included in miscellaneous expense on the income statement. A credit balance is included in the Other Revenue section. If a salesperson consistently has large cash short and over amounts, the supervisor may require the clerk to take additional training.

Cash Received in the Mail Cash is received in the mail when customers pay their bills. This cash is usually in the form of checks and money orders. Most companies design their invoices so that customers return a portion of the invoice, called a *remittance advice*, with their payment. Remittance advices may be used to control cash received in the mail as follows:

1. An employee opens the incoming mail and compares the amount of cash received with the amount shown on the remittance advice. If a customer does not return a remittance advice, the employee prepares one. The remittance advice serves as a record of the cash initially received. It also helps ensure that the posting to the customer's account is for the amount of cash received.

2. The employee opening the mail stamps checks and money orders "For Deposit Only" in the bank account of the business.
3. The remittance advices and their summary totals are delivered to the Accounting Department.
4. All cash and money orders are delivered to the Cashier's Department.
5. The cashier prepares a bank deposit ticket.
6. The cashier deposits the cash in the bank, or the cash is picked up by an armored car service, such as **Wells Fargo**.
7. An accounting clerk records the cash received and posts the amounts to the customer accounts.
8. When cash is deposited in the bank, the bank normally stamps a duplicate copy of the deposit ticket with the amount received. This bank receipt is returned to the Accounting Department, where it is compared to the total amount that should have been deposited. This control helps ensure that all cash is deposited and that no cash is lost or stolen on the way to the bank. Any shortages are thus promptly detected.

Separating the duties of the Cashier's Department, which handles cash, and the Accounting Department, which records cash, is a control. If Accounting Department employees both handle and record cash, an employee could steal cash and change the accounting records to hide the theft.

Cash Received by EFT Cash may also be received from customers through **electronic funds transfer (EFT)**. For example, customers may authorize automatic electronic transfers from their checking accounts to pay monthly bills for such items as cell phone, Internet, and electric services. In such cases, the company sends the customer's bank a signed form from the customer authorizing the monthly electronic transfers. Each month, the company notifies the customer's bank of the amount of the transfer and the date the transfer should take place. On the due date, the company records the electronic transfer as a receipt of cash to its bank account and posts the amount paid to the customer's account.

Companies encourage customers to use EFT for the following reasons:

- EFTs cost less than receiving cash payments through the mail.
- EFTs enhance internal controls over cash, since the cash is received directly by the bank without any employees handling cash.
- EFTs reduce late payments from customers and speed up the processing of cash receipts.

Control of Cash Payments

Howard Schultz & Associates (HS&A) specializes in reviewing cash payments for its clients. HS&A searches for errors such as duplicate payments, failure to take discounts, and inaccurate computations. Amounts recovered for clients range from thousands to millions of dollars.

The control of cash payments should provide reasonable assurance that:

- Payments are made only for authorized transactions.
- Cash is used effectively and efficiently. For example, controls should ensure that all available purchase discounts are taken.

In a small business, an owner/manager may authorize payments based on personal knowledge. In a large business, however, purchasing goods, inspecting the goods received, and verifying the invoices are usually performed by different employees. These duties must be coordinated to ensure that proper payments are made to creditors. One system used for this purpose is the voucher system.

Voucher System A **voucher system** is a set of procedures for authorizing and recording liabilities and cash payments. A **voucher** is any document that serves as proof of authority to pay cash or issue an electronic funds transfer. An invoice that has been approved for payment could be considered a voucher. In many businesses, however, a voucher is a special form used to record data about a liability and the details of its payment.

In a manual system, a voucher is normally prepared after all necessary supporting documents have been received. For the purchase of goods, a voucher is supported by the supplier's invoice, a purchase order, and a receiving report. After a voucher is prepared, it is submitted for approval. Once approved, the voucher is recorded in the accounts and filed by due date. Upon payment, the voucher is recorded in the same manner as the payment of an account payable.

In a computerized system, data from the supporting documents (such as purchase orders, receiving reports, and suppliers' invoices) are entered directly into computer files. At the due date, the checks are automatically generated and mailed to creditors. At that time, the voucher is electronically transferred to a paid voucher file.

Cash Paid by EFT Cash can also be paid by electronic funds transfer (EFT) systems. For example, you can withdraw cash from your bank account using an ATM machine. Your withdrawal is a type of EFT transfer.

Companies also use EFT transfers. For example, many companies pay their employees via EFT. Under such a system, employees authorize the deposit of their payroll checks directly into their checking accounts. Each pay period, the company transfers the employees' net pay to their checking accounts through the use of EFT. Many companies also use EFT systems to pay their suppliers and other vendors.

Link to eBay

eBay purchased **PayPal**, which was developed to enable individuals and businesses to send and receive payments safely online. Because of new online payment systems such as Apple Pay™, eBay discontinued its PayPal operations in 2015 and established PayPal as a separate, publicly held company.

Business Connection

MOBILE PAYMENTS

A rapidly emerging method of payments using EFT is mobile payments, such as those made with Apple Pay™. With mobile payments, our phones become our wallets and our cash is transferred digitally from our bank accounts or credit cards.

Security is enhanced with fingerprint log-in to the smartphone. In this way, only the phone's owner can open the "wallet." Many of the internal control features required for managing cash payments are eliminated by this technology, much like EFT transactions. Moreover, even credit card slips are replaced by electronic authorizations and transactions. Internal controls are still required to verify that prices are accurate and goods are properly delivered for authenticated purchases.

Bank Accounts

OBJ. 4 Describe the nature of a bank account and its use in controlling cash.

A major reason that companies use bank accounts is for internal control. Some of the control advantages of using bank accounts are as follows:

- Bank accounts reduce the amount of cash on hand.
- Bank accounts provide an independent recording of cash transactions. Reconciling the balance of the cash account in the company's records with the cash balance according to the bank is an important control.
- Use of bank accounts facilitates the transfer of funds using EFT systems.

Bank Statement

Banks usually maintain a record of all checking account transactions. A summary of all transactions, called a **bank statement**, is mailed, usually each month, to the company (depositor) or made available online. The bank statement shows the beginning balance, additions, deductions, and the ending balance. A typical bank statement is shown in Exhibit 9.

EXHIBIT 9

Bank Statement

MEMBER FDIC — PAGE 1

VALLEY NATIONAL BANK
OF LOS ANGELES
LOS ANGELES, CA 90020-4253 (310)555-5151

POWER NETWORKING
1000 Belkin Street
Los Angeles, CA 90014 -1000

	ACCOUNT NUMBER	1627042
	FROM 6/30/20Y5 TO 7/31/20Y5	
	BALANCE	4,218.60
22	DEPOSITS	13,749.75
52	WITHDRAWALS	14,698.57
3	OTHER DEBITS AND CREDITS	90.00CR
	NEW BALANCE	3,359.78

CHECKS AND OTHER DEBITS				DEPOSITS	DATE	BALANCE
No. 850	819.40	No. 852	122.54	585.75	07/01	3,862.41
No. 854	369.50	No. 853	20.15	421.53	07/02	3,894.29
No. 851	600.00	No. 856	190.70	781.30	07/03	3,884.89
No. 855	25.93	No. 857	52.50		07/04	3,806.46
No. 860	921.20	No. 858	160.00	662.50	07/05	3,387.76
No. 862	91.07	NSF	300.00	503.18	07/07	3,499.87
No. 880	32.26	No. 877	535.09	ACH 932.00	07/29	4,136.66
No. 881	21.10	No. 879	732.26	705.21	07/30	4,088.51
No. 882	126.20	SC	18.00	MS 408.00	07/30	4,352.31
No. 874	26.12	ACH	1,615.13	648.72	07/31	3,359.78

EC — ERROR CORRECTION
ACH — AUTOMATED CLEARING HOUSE
MS — MISCELLANEOUS
NSF — NOT SUFFICIENT FUNDS
SC — SERVICE CHARGE

*** *** ***

THE RECONCILEMENT OF THIS STATEMENT WITH YOUR RECORDS IS ESSENTIAL.
ANY ERROR OR EXCEPTION SHOULD BE REPORTED IMMEDIATELY.

Checks or copies of the checks listed in the order they were paid by the bank may accompany the bank statement. If paid checks are returned, they are stamped "Paid," along with the date of payment. Many banks no longer return checks or check copies. Instead, the check payment information is available online.

The company's checking account balance *in the bank records* is a liability. Thus, in the bank's records, the company's account has a credit balance. Because the bank statement is prepared from the bank's point of view, a credit memo entry on the bank statement indicates an increase (a credit) to the company's account. Likewise, a debit memo entry on the bank statement indicates a decrease (a debit) in the company's account. This relationship is shown in Exhibit 10.

EXHIBIT 10

Checking Account: Company and Bank Perspectives

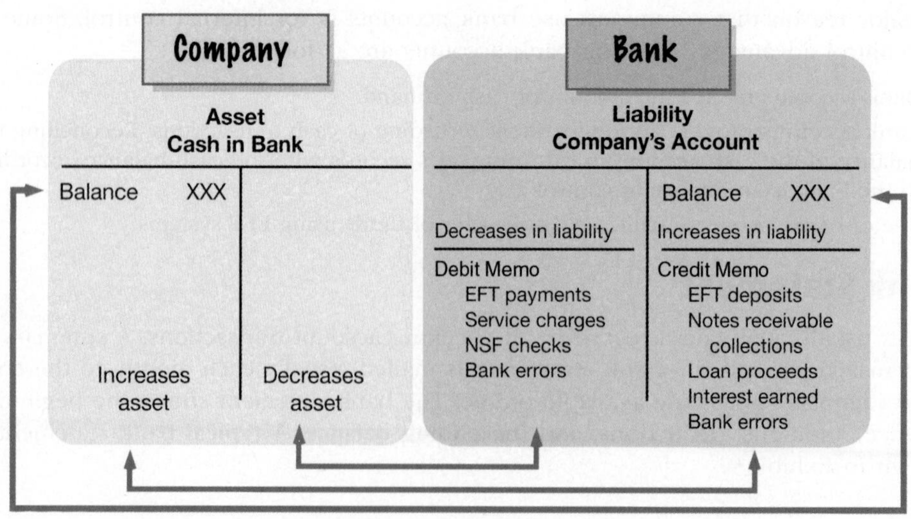

A bank makes credit entries (issues credit memos) for the following:

- Deposits made by electronic funds transfer (EFT)
- Collections of notes receivable for the company
- Proceeds for a loan made to the company by the bank
- Interest earned on the company's account
- Correction (if any) of bank errors

A bank makes debit entries (issues debit memos) for the following:

- Payments made by electronic funds transfer (EFT)
- Service charges
- Customer checks returned for not sufficient funds
- Correction (if any) of bank errors

Customers' checks returned for not sufficient funds, called *NSF checks*, are customer checks that were initially deposited but were not paid by the customer's bank. Because the company's bank credited the customer's check to the company's account when it was deposited, the bank debits the company's account (issues a debit memo) when the check is returned without payment.

The reason for a credit or debit memo entry is indicated on the bank statement. Exhibit 9 identifies the following types of credit and debit memo entries:

- EC: Error correction to correct bank error
- NSF: Not sufficient funds check
- SC: Service charge
- ACH: Automated clearing house entry for electronic funds transfer
- MS: Miscellaneous item such as collection of a note receivable on behalf of the company or receipt of a loan by the company from the bank

The preceding list includes the notation "ACH" for electronic funds transfers. ACH is a network for clearing electronic funds transfers among individuals, companies, and banks.[7] Because electronic funds transfers may be either deposits or payments, ACH entries may indicate either a debit or credit entry to the company's account. Likewise, entries to correct bank errors and miscellaneous items may indicate a debit or credit entry to the company's account.

EXAMPLE EXERCISE 8-2 Items on Company's Bank Statement

OBJ. 4

The following items may appear on a bank statement:

1. NSF check
2. EFT deposit
3. Service charge
4. Bank correction of an error from recording a $400 check issued by the company as $40

Using the following format, indicate whether the item would appear as a debit or credit memo on the bank statement and whether the item would increase or decrease the balance of the company's account:

Item No.	Appears on the Bank Statement as a Debit or Credit Memo	Increases or Decreases the Balance of the Company's Bank Account

Follow My Example 8-2

Item No.	Appears on the Bank Statement as a Debit or Credit Memo	Increases or Decreases the Balance of the Company's Bank Account
1	debit memo	decreases
2	credit memo	increases
3	debit memo	decreases
4	debit memo	decreases

Practice Exercises: PE 8-2A, PE 8-2B

7 For further information on ACH, go to www.nacha.org/. Click on "ACH."

Using the Bank Statement as a Control over Cash

The bank statement is a primary control that a company uses over cash. A company uses the bank's statement by comparing the company's recording of cash transactions to those recorded by the bank.

The cash balance shown by a bank statement is usually different from the company's cash balance, as shown in Exhibit 11 for Power Networking.

EXHIBIT 11

Power Networking's Records and Bank Statement

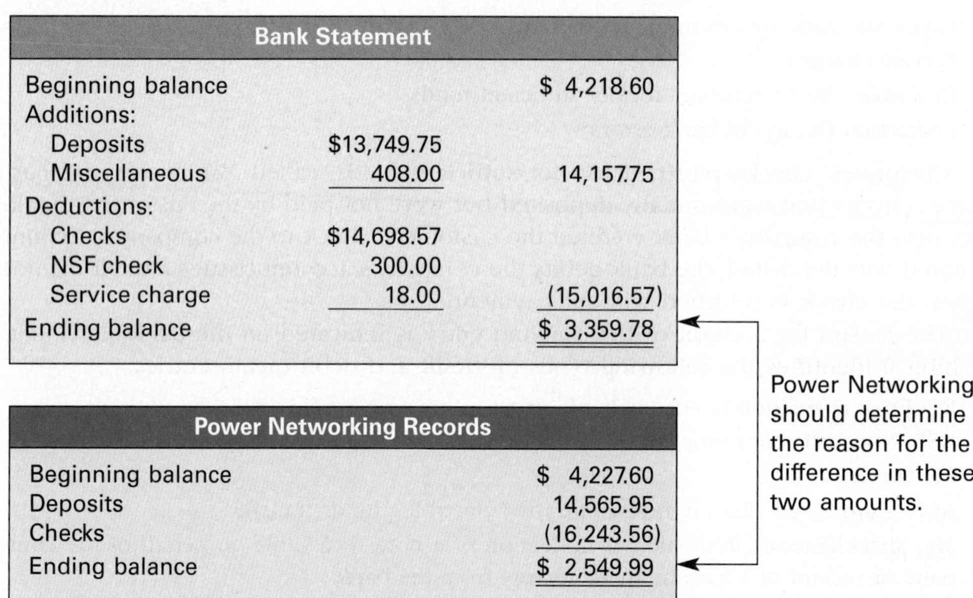

Bank Statement		
Beginning balance		$ 4,218.60
Additions:		
Deposits	$13,749.75	
Miscellaneous	408.00	14,157.75
Deductions:		
Checks	$14,698.57	
NSF check	300.00	
Service charge	18.00	(15,016.57)
Ending balance		$ 3,359.78

Power Networking Records	
Beginning balance	$ 4,227.60
Deposits	14,565.95
Checks	(16,243.56)
Ending balance	$ 2,549.99

Differences between the company and bank balance may arise because of a delay by either the company or bank in recording transactions. For example, there is normally a time lag of one or more days between the date a check is written and the date it is paid by the bank. Likewise, there is normally a time lag between when the company mails a deposit to the bank (or uses the night depository) and when the bank receives and records the deposit.

Differences may also arise because the bank has debited or credited the company's account for transactions that the company will not know about until the bank statement is received. Finally, differences may arise from errors made by either the company or the bank. For example, the company may incorrectly post to Cash a check written for $4,500 as $450. Likewise, a bank may incorrectly record the amount of a check.

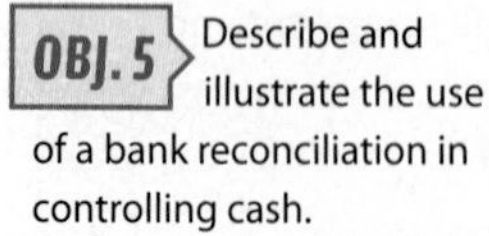

OBJ. 5 Describe and illustrate the use of a bank reconciliation in controlling cash.

Bank Reconciliation

A **bank reconciliation** is an analysis of the items and amounts that cause the cash balance reported in the bank statement to differ from the balance of the cash account in the ledger. The adjusted cash balance determined in the bank reconciliation is reported on the balance sheet.

A bank reconciliation is usually divided into two sections as follows:

- The *bank section* begins with the cash balance according to the bank statement and ends with the *adjusted balance.*
- The *company section* begins with the cash balance according to the company's records and ends with the *adjusted balance.*

The *adjusted balance* from bank and company sections must be equal. The format of the bank reconciliation is shown in Exhibit 12.

EXHIBIT 12
Bank Reconciliation Format

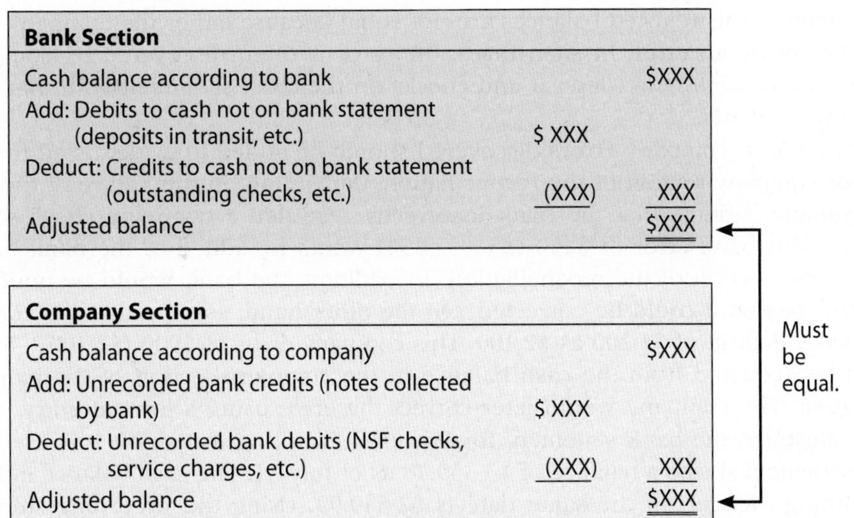

Bank Section		
Cash balance according to bank		$XXX
Add: Debits to cash not on bank statement (deposits in transit, etc.)	$ XXX	
Deduct: Credits to cash not on bank statement (outstanding checks, etc.)	(XXX)	XXX
Adjusted balance		$XXX

Company Section		
Cash balance according to company		$XXX
Add: Unrecorded bank credits (notes collected by bank)	$ XXX	
Deduct: Unrecorded bank debits (NSF checks, service charges, etc.)	(XXX)	XXX
Adjusted balance		$XXX

A bank reconciliation is prepared using the steps illustrated in Exhibit 13. The adjusted balances in the bank and company sections of the reconciliation must be equal. If the balances are not equal, an item has been overlooked and must be found.

EXHIBIT 13
How to Prepare a Bank Reconciliation

Bank Section

Step 1. Enter the *Cash balance according to bank* from the ending cash balance according to the bank statement.

Step 2. *Add deposits not recorded by the bank.*

Identify deposits not recorded by the bank by comparing each deposit listed on the bank statement with unrecorded deposits appearing in the preceding period's reconciliation and with the current period's deposits.

Examples: Deposits in transit at the end of the period

Step 3. *Deduct outstanding checks that have not been paid by the bank.*

Identify outstanding checks by comparing paid checks with outstanding checks appearing on the preceding period's reconciliation and with recorded checks.

Examples: Outstanding checks at the end of the period

Step 4. Determine the *Adjusted balance* by adding Step 2 and deducting Step 3.

Company Section

Step 5. Enter the *Cash balance according to company* from the ending cash balance in the ledger.

Step 6. *Add credit memos that have not been recorded.*

Identify the bank credit memos that have not been recorded by comparing the bank statement credit memos to entries in the journal.

Examples: A note receivable and interest that the bank has collected for the company

Step 7. *Deduct debit memos that have not been recorded.*

Identify the bank debit memos that have not been recorded by comparing the bank statement debit memos to entries in the journal.

Examples: Customers' not sufficient funds (NSF) checks; bank service charges

Step 8. Determine the *Adjusted balance* by adding Step 6 and deducting Step 7.

Verify That Adjusted Balances Are Equal

Step 9. Verify that the adjusted balances determined in Steps 4 and 8 are equal. If the adjusted balances in Steps 4 and 8 are unequal, search for any bank or company errors. Add or deduct the effects of any errors and verify that the adjusted balances are equal.

Sometimes the adjusted balances are not equal because either the company or the bank has made an error. In such cases, the error is often discovered by comparing the amount of each item (deposit and check) on the bank statement with that in the company's records.

Any bank or company errors discovered should be added to or deducted from the bank or company section of the reconciliation, depending on the nature of the error. For example, assume that the bank incorrectly recorded a company check for $50 as $500. This bank error of $450 ($500 – $50) would be added to the bank balance in the bank section of the reconciliation. In addition, the bank would be notified of the error so that it could be corrected. On the other hand, assume that the company recorded a deposit of $1,200 as $2,100. This company error of $900 ($2,100 – $1,200) would be deducted from the cash balance in the company section of the bank reconciliation. The company would later correct the error using a journal entry.

To illustrate, the bank statement for Power Networking in Exhibit 9 is used. This bank statement shows a balance of $3,359.78 as of July 31. The cash balance in Power Networking's ledger on the same date is $2,549.99. Using the preceding steps, the following reconciling items were identified:

Step 2. Deposit of July 31, not recorded on bank statement: $816.20

Step 3. Outstanding checks:

Check No. 812	$1,061.00
Check No. 878	435.39
Check No. 883	48.60
Total	$1,544.99

Step 6. Note receivable of $400 plus interest of $8 collected by bank not recorded in the journal as indicated by a credit memo of $408.00.

Step 7. Check from customer (Thomas Ivey) for $300 returned by bank because of insufficient funds (NSF) as indicated by a debit memo of $300.00.

Bank service charges of $18, not recorded in the journal as indicated by a debit memo of $18.00.

Step 9. An error of $9 was discovered. This error occurred when Check No. 879 for $732.26 to Taylor Co., on account, was recorded in the company's journal as $723.26.

The bank reconciliation, based on the Exhibit 9 bank statement and the preceding reconciling items, is shown in Exhibit 14. The company's records do not need to be

EXHIBIT 14 Bank Reconciliation for Power Networking

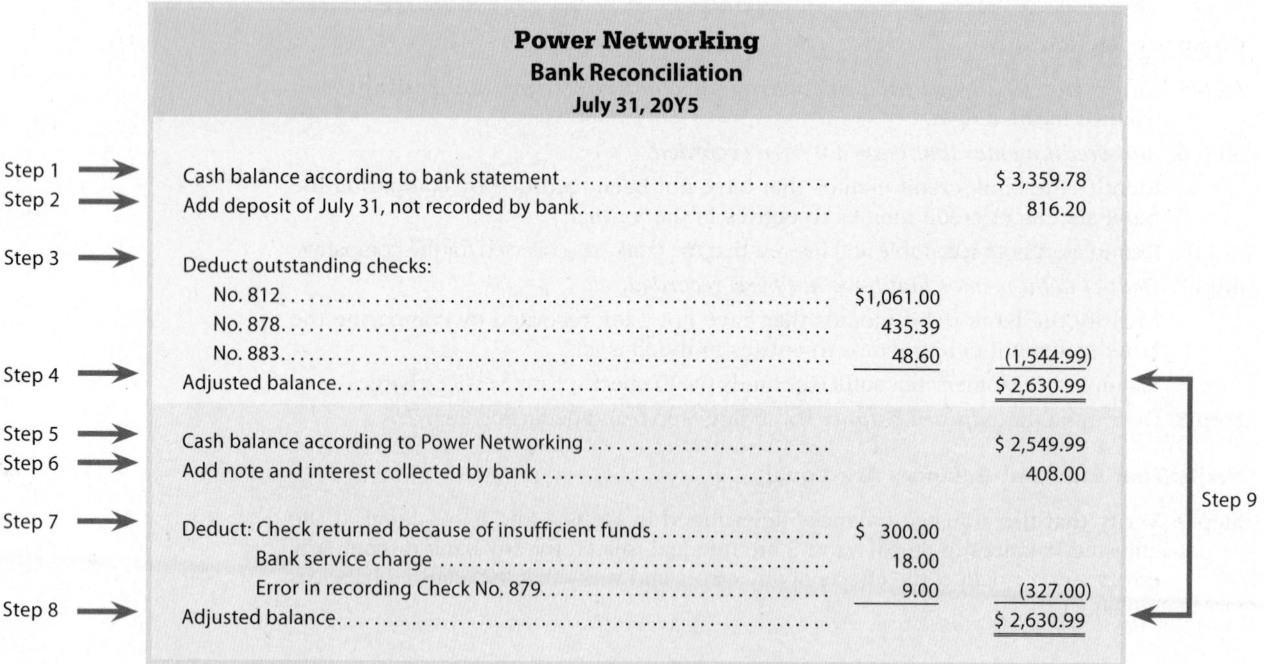

Power Networking
Bank Reconciliation
July 31, 20Y5

Step				
Step 1 →	Cash balance according to bank statement		$ 3,359.78	
Step 2 →	Add deposit of July 31, not recorded by bank		816.20	
Step 3 →	Deduct outstanding checks:			
	No. 812	$1,061.00		
	No. 878	435.39		
	No. 883	48.60	(1,544.99)	
Step 4 →	Adjusted balance		$ 2,630.99	← Step 9
Step 5 →	Cash balance according to Power Networking		$ 2,549.99	
Step 6 →	Add note and interest collected by bank		408.00	
Step 7 →	Deduct: Check returned because of insufficient funds	$ 300.00		
	Bank service charge	18.00		
	Error in recording Check No. 879	9.00	(327.00)	
Step 8 →	Adjusted balance		$ 2,630.99	← Step 9

updated for any items in the *bank section* of the reconciliation. This section begins with the cash balance according to the bank statement. However, the bank should be notified of any errors that need to be corrected.

The company's records do need to be updated for any items in the *company section* of the bank reconciliation. The company's records are updated using journal entries. For example, journal entries should be made for any unrecorded bank memos and any company errors.

The journal entries for Power Networking, based on the bank reconciliation shown in Exhibit 14, are as follows:

20Y5					
July	31	Cash		408	
		Notes Receivable			400
		Interest Revenue			8
	31	Accounts Receivable—Thomas Ivey		300	
		Miscellaneous Expense		18	
		Accounts Payable—Taylor Co.		9	
		Cash			327

After the preceding journal entries are recorded and posted, the cash account will have a debit balance of $2,630.99. This cash balance agrees with the adjusted balance shown on the bank reconciliation. This is the amount of cash on July 31 and is the amount that is reported on Power Networking's July 31 balance sheet.

Businesses may reconcile their bank accounts in a slightly different format from that shown in Exhibit 12. Regardless, the objective is to control cash by reconciling the company's records with the bank statement. In doing so, any errors or misuse of cash may be detected.

To enhance internal control, the bank reconciliation should be prepared by an employee who does not take part in or record cash transactions. Otherwise, mistakes may occur, and it is more likely that cash will be stolen or misapplied. For example, an employee who handles cash and also reconciles the bank statement could steal a cash deposit, omit the deposit from the accounts, and omit it from the reconciliation.

EXAMPLE EXERCISE 8-3 Bank Reconciliation

OBJ. 5

The following data were gathered to use in reconciling the bank account of Photo Op:

Balance per bank	$14,500
Balance per company records	13,875
Bank service charges	75
Deposit in transit	3,750
NSF check	800
Outstanding checks	5,250

a. What is the adjusted balance on the bank reconciliation?

b. Journalize any necessary entries for Photo Op based on the bank reconciliation.

Follow My Example 8-3

a. $13,000, computed as follows:

Bank section of reconciliation: $14,500 + $3,750 – $5,250 = $13,000
Company section of reconciliation: $13,875 – $75 – $800 = $13,000

b.

Accounts Receivable	800	
Miscellaneous Expense	75	
Cash		875

Practice Exercises: PE 8-3A, PE 8-3B

Bank reconciliations are also an important part of computerized systems where deposits and checks are stored in electronic files and records. Some systems use computer software to determine the difference between the bank statement and company cash balances. The software then adjusts for deposits in transit and outstanding checks. Any remaining differences are reported for further analysis.

Integrity, Objectivity, and Ethics in Business

BANK ERROR IN YOUR FAVOR (OR MAYBE NOT)

A New Zealand couple expected a $100,000 deposit into their checking account but discovered the bank accidentally deposited $10,000,000. The couple immediately transferred the $10,000,000 to another account and left the country, hoping to cash in on this supposed windfall. Not surprisingly, they were found, arrested, and prosecuted for fraud. So, if you find a bank error in your favor, it really isn't like getting a Monopoly card. You cannot keep the cash, but must return it to the bank. Banks typically have a long time to correct such errors, and if it can be reasonably determined that you knew of the error but failed to report it, you could be prosecuted for bank fraud.

Source: Nickel, "Bank Error in Your Favor?" *Forbes.com*, May 2012 (www.forbes.com/sites/moneybuilder/2012/05/24/bank-error-in-your-favor/).

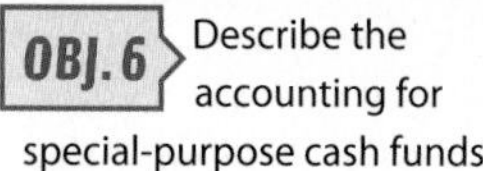

Describe the accounting for special-purpose cash funds.

Special-Purpose Cash Funds

A company often has to pay small amounts for such items as postage, office supplies, and minor repairs. Although small, such payments may occur often enough to total a significant amount. Thus, it is desirable to control such payments. However, writing a check for each small payment is not practical. Instead, a special cash fund, called a **petty cash fund**, is used.

A petty cash fund is established by estimating the amount of payments needed from the fund during a period, such as a week or a month. A check is then written and cashed for this amount. The money obtained from cashing the check is then given to an employee, called the *petty cash custodian*. The petty cash custodian disburses monies from the fund as needed. For control purposes, the company may place restrictions on the maximum amount and the types of payments that can be made from the fund. Each time money is paid from petty cash, the custodian records the details on a petty cash receipts form.

The petty cash fund is normally replenished at periodic intervals, when it is depleted, or when it reaches a minimum amount. When a petty cash fund is replenished, the accounts debited are determined by summarizing the petty cash receipts. A check is then written for this amount, payable to Petty Cash.

To illustrate, assume that a petty cash fund of $500 is established on August 1. The entry to record this transaction is as follows:

Aug.	1	Petty Cash		500	
		Cash			500

The only time Petty Cash is debited is when the fund is initially established, as shown in the preceding entry, or when the fund is being increased. The only time Petty Cash is credited is when the fund is being decreased or eliminated.

At the end of August, there is $30 of petty cash on hand and petty cash receipts indicate expenditures for the following items:

Office supplies	$380
Postage (debit Office Supplies)	22
Store supplies	35
Miscellaneous administrative expense	30
Total	$467

If the amount to replenish the petty cash fund does not equal the total of the petty cash receipts, the difference is recorded as "cash short and over." In this example, $470 ($500 less cash on hand of $30) is needed to replenish the petty cash fund. Since the total of the petty cash receipts is $467, Cash Short and Over is debited for $3, as shown in the following entry to replenish the petty cash fund.

Aug.	31	Office Supplies		402	
		Store Supplies		35	
		Miscellaneous Administrative Expense		30	
		Cash Short and Over		3	
		Cash			470

Petty Cash is not debited when the fund is replenished. Instead, only the accounts affected by the petty cash receipts and any cash short and over are recorded, as shown in the preceding entry. Replenishing the petty cash fund restores the fund to its original amount of $500.

Companies often use other cash funds for special needs, such as payroll or travel expenses. Such funds are called **special-purpose funds**. For example, each salesperson might be given $1,000 for travel-related expenses. Periodically, each salesperson submits an expense report, and the fund is replenished. Special-purpose funds are established and controlled in a manner similar to that of the petty cash fund.

EXAMPLE EXERCISE 8-4 Petty Cash Fund **OBJ. 6**

Journalize the necessary entries for each of the following:

a. Issued a check to establish a petty cash fund of $500.

b. The amount of cash in the petty cash fund is $120. Issued a check to replenish the fund, based on the following summary of petty cash receipts: office supplies, $300, and miscellaneous administrative expense, $75. Record any missing funds in the cash short and over account.

Follow My Example 8-4

a.	Petty Cash	500	
	Cash		500
b.	Office Supplies	300	
	Miscellaneous Administrative Expense	75	
	Cash Short and Over	5	
	Cash		380

Practice Exercises: PE 8-4A, PE 8-4B

Financial Statement Reporting of Cash

OBJ. 7 Describe and illustrate the reporting of cash and cash equivalents in the financial statements.

Cash is normally listed as the first asset in the Current Assets section of the balance sheet. Most companies present only a single cash amount on the balance sheet by combining all their bank and cash fund accounts.

A company may temporarily have excess cash. In such cases, the company usually invests in highly liquid investments in order to earn interest. These investments are called **cash equivalents**.[8] Examples of cash equivalents include U.S. Treasury bills,

8 To be classified as a cash equivalent, according to FASB *Accounting Standards Codification*, Section 305.10, the investment is expected to be converted to cash within three months.

notes issued by major corporations (referred to as *commercial paper*), and money market funds. In such cases, companies usually report *Cash and cash equivalents* as one amount on the balance sheet.

Link to eBay

On a recent balance sheet, **eBay** reported over $2 billion in cash and cash equivalents.

The balance sheet presentation for cash for **Mornin' Joe** follows:

Mornin' Joe
Balance Sheet
December 31, 20Y6

Assets	
Current assets:	
Cash and cash equivalents	$235,000

Banks may require that companies maintain minimum cash balances in their bank accounts. Such a balance is called a **compensating balance**. This is often required by the bank as part of a loan agreement or line of credit. A *line of credit* is a preapproved amount the bank is willing to lend to a customer upon request. Compensating balance requirements are normally disclosed in notes to the financial statements.

Business Connection

MANAGING APPLE'S CASH

Apple Inc. has investments and cash that total over $237 billion. This represents over 64% of Apple's total assets and thus requires significant management attention. How does Apple manage these assets? Apple owns **Braeburn Capital**, a Nevada-based asset management company. Braeburn was established for one purpose: to manage Apple's cash and investments. Braeburn operates under a veil of secrecy, and little is known about the firm. It is simply described as follows: "Braeburn Capital Inc. is the asset management arm of Apple Inc. The firm invests in the public equity markets." Apple's financial statement footnotes provide some detail describing its holdings. More than $25 billion is included as cash or cash equivalents, such as money market funds. The remainder is divided between short- and long-term investments.

Source: Apple Inc., *Form 10-K for the Year Ended September 29, 2018.*

OBJ. 8 Describe and illustrate the use of the ratio of cash to monthly cash expenses to assess the ability of a company to continue in business.

FAI

Financial Analysis and Interpretation: Ratio of Cash to Monthly Cash Expenses

For startup companies or companies in financial distress, cash is critical for survival. In their first few years, startup companies often report losses and negative net cash flows from operations. Moreover, companies in financial distress can also report losses and negative cash flows from operations. In such cases, the

ratio of cash to monthly cash expenses is useful for assessing how long a company can continue to operate without:

- Additional financing, or
- Positive cash flows generated from operations

The ratio of cash to monthly cash expenses is computed as follows:

$$\text{Ratio of Cash to Monthly Cash Expenses} = \frac{\text{Cash as of Year-End}}{\text{Monthly Cash Expenses}}$$

The cash, including any cash equivalents, is taken from the balance sheet as of year-end. The monthly cash expenses, sometimes called *cash burn*, are estimated from the Operating Activities section of the statement of cash flows as follows:

$$\text{Monthly Cash Expenses} = \frac{\text{Negative Cash Flow from Operations}}{12}$$

To illustrate, **Ocean Power Technologies, Inc.**, develops and markets systems that generate electricity from the rising and falling of ocean waves. The following data (in thousands) were taken from financial statements of Ocean Power Technologies:

	For Years Ended April 29			
	Year 4	**Year 3**	**Year 2**	**Year 1**
Cash and cash equivalents at year-end	$ 11,499	$ 8,421	$ 6,730	$ 17,336
Cash flow from operations	(10,696)	(10,038)	(10,930)	(17,174)

Based on the preceding data, the monthly cash expenses and ratio of cash to monthly cash expenses are computed as follows:

	For Years Ended April 29			
	Year 4	**Year 3**	**Year 2**	**Year 1**
Monthly cash expenses:*				
$10,696 ÷ 12	$891			
$10,038 ÷ 12		$837		
$10,930 ÷ 12			$911	
$17,174 ÷ 12				$1,431
Ratio of cash to monthly cash expenses:**				
$11,499 ÷ $891	12.9 months			
$8,421 ÷ $837		10.1 months		
$6,730 ÷ $911			7.4 months	
$17,336 ÷ $1,431				12.1 months

*Rounded to nearest dollar.

**Rounded to one decimal place.

The preceding computations indicate that Ocean Power had 12.1 months of cash available at the end of Year 1 to continue its operations. At the end of Year 2, Ocean Power had 7.4 months of cash available to continue its operations. During Year 2, Ocean Power reduced its monthly cash expenses from $1,431 in Year 1 to $911. At the end of Year 3, Ocean Power had 10.1 months of cash available to continue its operations. During Year 4, Ocean Power issued common stock of $14,654, which increased its ratio of cash to monthly cash expenses from 10.1 months at the end of Year 3 to 12.9 months at the end of Year 4.

The preceding analysis indicates that Ocean Power has generated negative cash flows from operations in each of the last four years. Ocean Power was able to fund its operations by issuing common stock. However, in the long term, Ocean Power must generate positive cash flows from its operations to survive and continue operating.

EXAMPLE EXERCISE 8-5 Ratio of Cash to Monthly Cash Expenses

OBJ. 8

Financial data for Chapman Company follow:

	For Year Ended December 31
Cash on December 31	$ 102,000
Cash flow from operations	(144,000)

a. Compute the ratio of cash to monthly cash expenses.

b. Interpret the results computed in (a).

Follow My Example 8-5

a. $$\text{Monthly Cash Expenses} = \frac{\text{Negative Cash Flow from Operations}}{12} = \frac{\$144{,}000}{12} = \$12{,}000 \text{ per month}$$

$$\text{Ratio of Cash to Monthly Cash Expenses} = \frac{\text{Cash as of Year-End}}{\text{Monthly Cash Expenses}} = \frac{\$102{,}000}{\$12{,}000 \text{ per month}} = 8.5 \text{ months}$$

b. The preceding computations indicate that Chapman Company has 8.5 months of cash remaining as of December 31. To continue operations beyond 8.5 months, Chapman Company will need to generate positive cash flows from operations or raise additional financing from its owners or by issuing debt.

Practice Exercises: PE 8-5A, PE 8-5B

Business Connection

MICROSOFT CORPORATION

Microsoft Corporation develops, manufactures, licenses, and supports software products for computing devices. Microsoft software products include computer operating systems, such as Windows®, and application software, such as Microsoft Word® and Excel®. Microsoft is actively involved in the video game market through its Xbox® and is also involved in online products and services.

Microsoft is known for its strong cash position. The following recent balance sheet of Microsoft reported more than $133 billion of cash and short-term investments:

Balance Sheet
(In millions)

Assets	
Current assets:	
Cash and equivalents	$ 11,946
Short-term investments	121,822
Total cash and short-term investments	$133,768

The cash and cash equivalents of $11,946 million are further described in the notes to the financial statements, as follows:

Cash and equivalents:	
Cash	$ 3,942
Mutual funds	246
Commercial paper	2,215
U.S. government and agency securities	3,678
Certificates of deposit	1,865
Total cash and equivalents	$11,946

Source: Microsoft Corporation, *Form 10-K for the Fiscal Year Ended June 30, 2018.*

At a Glance 8

OBJ. 1 Describe the Sarbanes-Oxley Act and its impact on internal controls and financial reporting.

Key Points Sarbanes-Oxley requires companies to maintain strong and effective internal controls and to report on the effectiveness of the internal controls.

Learning Outcomes	Example Exercises	Practice Exercises
• Describe why Congress passed Sarbanes-Oxley.		
• Describe the purpose of Sarbanes-Oxley.		
• Define internal control.		

OBJ. 2 Describe and illustrate the objectives and elements of internal control.

Key Points The objectives of internal control are to provide reasonable assurance that (1) assets are safeguarded and used for business purposes, (2) business information is accurate, and (3) the company is complying with laws and regulations. The elements of internal control are the control environment, risk assessment, control procedures, monitoring, and information and communication.

Learning Outcomes	Example Exercises	Practice Exercises
• List the objectives of internal control.		
• List the elements of internal control.		
• Describe each element of internal control and factors influencing each element.	EE8-1	PE8-1A, 8-1B

OBJ. 3 Describe and illustrate the application of internal controls to cash.

Key Points A cash register is a control for protecting cash received in over-the-counter sales. A remittance advice is a control for cash received through the mail. Separating the duties of handling cash and recording cash is also a control. A voucher system is a control system for cash payments. Many companies use electronic funds transfers for cash receipts and cash payments.

Learning Outcomes	Example Exercises	Practice Exercises
• Describe and give examples of controls for cash received from cash sales, cash received in the mail, and cash received by EFT.		
• Describe and give examples of controls for cash payments made using a voucher system and cash payments made by EFT.		

OBJ. 4 Describe the nature of a bank account and its use in controlling cash.

Key Points Bank accounts control cash by reducing the amount of cash on hand and facilitating the transfer of cash between businesses and locations. In addition, the bank statement allows a business to reconcile the cash transactions recorded in the accounting records to those recorded by the bank.

Learning Outcomes	Example Exercises	Practice Exercises
• Describe how the use of bank accounts helps control cash.	EE8-2	PE8-2A, 8-2B
• Describe a bank statement and provide examples of items that appear on a bank statement as debit and credit memos.		

OBJ. 5 Describe and illustrate the use of a bank reconciliation in controlling cash.

Key Points A bank reconciliation is prepared using the nine steps summarized in Exhibit 13. The items in the company section of a bank reconciliation must be journalized on the company's records.

Learning Outcomes	Example Exercises	Practice Exercises
• Describe a bank reconciliation.		
• Prepare a bank reconciliation.	EE8-3	PE8-3A, 8-3B
• Journalize any necessary entries on the company's records, based on the bank reconciliation.	EE8-3	PE8-3A, 8-3B

OBJ. 6 Describe the accounting for special-purpose cash funds.

Key Points Special-purpose cash funds, such as a petty cash fund or travel funds, are used by businesses to meet specific needs. Each fund is established by cashing a check for the amount of cash needed. At periodic intervals, the fund is replenished and the disbursements recorded.

Learning Outcomes	Example Exercises	Practice Exercises
• Describe the use of special-purpose cash funds.		
• Journalize the entry to establish a petty cash fund.	EE8-4	PE8-4A, 8-4B
• Journalize the entry to replenish a petty cash fund.	EE8-4	PE8-4A, 8-4B

OBJ. 7 Describe and illustrate the reporting of cash and cash equivalents in the financial statements.

Key Points Cash is listed as the first asset in the Current Assets section of the balance sheet. Companies that have invested excess cash in highly liquid investments usually report *Cash and cash equivalents* on the balance sheet.

Learning Outcomes	Example Exercises	Practice Exercises
• Describe the reporting of cash and cash equivalents in the financial statements.		
• Illustrate the reporting of cash and cash equivalents in the financial statements.		

OBJ. 8 **Describe and illustrate the use of the ratio of cash to monthly cash expenses to assess the ability of a company to continue in business.**

Key Points The ratio of cash to monthly cash expenses is useful for assessing how long a company can continue to operate without (1) additional financing or (2) generating positive cash flows from operations.

Learning Outcomes	Example Exercises	Practice Exercises
• Describe the use of the ratio of cash to monthly cash expenses.		
• Compute the ratio of cash to monthly cash expenses.	EE8-5	PE8-5A, 8-5B

Illustrative Problem

The bank statement for Urethane Company for June 30 indicates a balance of $9,293.11. All cash receipts are deposited in a night depository each evening after banking hours. The accounting records indicate the following summary data for cash receipts and payments for June:

Cash balance as of June 1	$ 3,943.50
Total cash receipts for June	28,971.60
Total amount of checks issued in June	28,388.85

Comparing the bank statement and the accompanying canceled checks and memos with the records reveals the following reconciling items:

a. The bank had collected for Urethane Company $1,030 on a note left for collection. The face amount of the note was $1,000.

b. A deposit of $1,852.21, representing receipts of June 30, had been made too late to appear on the bank statement.

c. Checks outstanding totaled $5,265.27.

d. A check drawn for $139 had been incorrectly charged by the bank as $157.

e. A check for $370 returned with the statement had been recorded in the company's records as $730. The check was for the payment of an obligation to Avery Equipment Company for the purchase of office supplies on account.

f. Bank service charges for June amounted to $18.20.

Instructions

1. Prepare a bank reconciliation for June.
2. Journalize the entries that should be made by Urethane Company.

Solution

1.

Urethane Company
Bank Reconciliation
June 30

Cash balance according to bank statement		$ 9,293.11
Add: Deposit of June 30, not recorded by bank	$1,852.21	
Bank error in charging check as $157 instead of $139	18.00	1,870.21
Deduct outstanding checks		(5,265.27)
Adjusted balance		$ 5,898.05
Cash balance according to company's records		$ 4,526.25*
Add: Note and interest collected by bank	$1,030.00	
Error in recording check	360.00**	1,390.00
Deduct bank service charges		(18.20)
Adjusted balance		$ 5,898.05

*$3,943.50 + $28,971.60 – $28,388.85

**$730 – $370 = $360

2.

June	30	Cash		1,390.00	
		Notes Receivable			1,000.00
		Interest Revenue			30.00
		Accounts Payable—Avery Equipment Company			360.00
	30	Miscellaneous Administrative Expense		18.20	
		Cash			18.20

Key Terms

bank reconciliation (412)
bank statement (409)
cash (405)
cash equivalents (417)
cash short and over account (407)
compensating balance (418)
control environment (401)
electronic funds transfer (EFT) (408)
elements of internal control (400)
employee fraud (400)
internal control (398)
petty cash fund (416)
ratio of cash to monthly cash expenses (419)
Sarbanes-Oxley Act (398)
special-purpose funds (417)
voucher (408)
voucher system (408)

Discussion Questions

1. (a) Name and describe the five elements of internal control. (b) Is any one element of internal control more important than another?
2. Why should the employee who handles cash receipts not have the responsibility for maintaining the accounts receivable records? Explain.
3. The ticket seller at a movie theater doubles as a ticket taker for a few minutes each day while the ticket taker is on a break. Which control procedure of a business's system of internal control is violated in this situation?

4. Why should the responsibility for maintaining the accounting records be separated from the responsibility for operations? Explain.

5. Assume that Brooke Miles, accounts payable clerk for West Coast Design Inc., stole $48,350 by paying fictitious invoices for goods that were never received. The clerk set up accounts in the names of the fictitious companies and cashed the checks at a local bank. Describe a control procedure that would have prevented or detected the fraud.

6. Before a voucher for the purchase of merchandise is approved for payment, supporting documents should be compared to verify the accuracy of the liability. Give an example of supporting documents for the purchase of merchandise.

7. The balance of Cash is likely to differ from the bank statement balance. What two factors are likely to be responsible for the difference?

8. What is the purpose of preparing a bank reconciliation?

9. Knott Inc. has a petty cash fund of $750. (a) Since the petty cash fund is only $750, should Knott Inc. implement controls over petty cash? (b) What controls, if any, could be used for the petty cash fund?

10. (a) How are cash equivalents reported in the financial statements? (b) What are some examples of cash equivalents?

Practice Exercises

Example Exercises

EE 8-1 *p. 405*

PE 8-1A Internal control elements **OBJ. 2**

Identify each of the following as relating to (a) the control environment, (b) control procedures, or (c) monitoring:

1. Hiring of external auditors to review the adequacy of controls
2. Personnel policies
3. Safeguarding inventory in a locked warehouse

EE 8-1 *p. 405*

PE 8-1B Internal control elements **OBJ. 2**

Identify each of the following as relating to (a) the control environment, (b) control procedures, or (c) information and communication:

1. Organizational structure
2. Report of company's conformity with environmental laws and regulations
3. Proofs and security measures

EE 8-2 *p. 411*

PE 8-2A Items on company's bank statement **OBJ. 4**

The following items may appear on a bank statement:

1. Bank correction of an error from posting another customer's check (disbursement) to the company's account
2. EFT deposit
3. Loan proceeds
4. NSF check

Using the following format, indicate whether each item would appear as a debit or credit memo on the bank statement and whether the item would increase or decrease the balance of the company's account:

Item No.	Appears on the Bank Statement as a Debit or Credit Memo	Increases or Decreases the Balance of the Company's Bank Account

EE 8-2 p. 411

PE 8-2B Items on company's bank statement OBJ. 4

The following items may appear on a bank statement:

1. Bank correction of an error from recording a $7,400 deposit as $4,700
2. EFT payment
3. Note collected for company
4. Service charge

Using the following format, indicate whether each item would appear as a debit or credit memo on the bank statement and whether the item would increase or decrease the balance of the company's account:

Item No.	Appears on the Bank Statement as a Debit or Credit Memo	Increases or Decreases the Balance of the Company's Bank Account

EE 8-3 p. 415

PE 8-3A Bank reconciliation OBJ. 5

The following data were gathered to use in reconciling the bank account of Donovan Company:

Balance per bank	$14,385
Balance per company records	11,200
Bank service charges	60
Deposit in transit	2,125
NSF check	1,480
Outstanding checks	6,850

a. What is the adjusted balance on the bank reconciliation?

b. Journalize any necessary entries for Donovan Company based on the bank reconciliation.

EE 8-3 p. 415

PE 8-3B Bank reconciliation OBJ. 5

The following data were gathered to use in reconciling the bank account of Crystal Company:

Balance per bank	$28,240
Balance per company records	10,280
Bank service charges	60
Deposit in transit	6,500
Note collected by bank with $530 interest	11,170
Outstanding checks	13,350

a. What is the adjusted balance on the bank reconciliation?

b. Journalize any necessary entries for Crystal Company based on the bank reconciliation.

EE 8-4 p. 417

PE 8-4A Petty cash fund OBJ. 6

Journalize the necessary entries for each of the following:

a. Issued a check to establish a petty cash fund of $1,410.

b. The amount of cash in the petty cash fund is $440. Issued a check to replenish the fund, based on the following summary of petty cash receipts: repair expense, $850, and miscellaneous selling expense, $80. Record any missing funds in the cash short and over account.

EE 8-4 p. 417

PE 8-4B Petty cash fund OBJ. 6

Journalize the necessary entries for each of the following:

a. Issued a check to establish a petty cash fund of $1,270.

b. The amount of cash in the petty cash fund is $160. Issued a check to replenish the fund, based on the following summary of petty cash receipts: store supplies, $780, and miscellaneous selling expense, $280. Record any missing funds in the cash short and over account.

SHOW ME HOW

FAI

EE 8-5 *p. 420*

PE 8-5A Ratio of cash to monthly cash expenses

OBJ. 8

Financial data for Abrams Company follow:

	For Year Ended December 31
Cash on December 31	$ 54,270
Cash flow from operations	(97,200)

a. Compute the ratio of cash to monthly cash expenses.

b. Interpret the results computed in (a).

SHOW ME HOW

FAI

EE 8-5 *p. 420*

PE 8-5B Ratio of cash to monthly cash expenses

OBJ. 8

Financial data for McMasters Company follow:

	For Year Ended December 31
Cash on December 31	$ 138,780
Cash flow from operations	(308,400)

a. Compute the ratio of cash to monthly cash expenses.

b. Interpret the results computed in (a).

Exercises

EX 8-1 Sarbanes-Oxley internal control report

OBJ. 1

Using Wikipedia (www.wikipedia.com), look up the entry for Sarbanes-Oxley Act. Look over the table of contents and find the section that describes Section 404.

What does Section 404 require of management's internal control report?

EX 8-2 Internal controls

OBJ. 2, 3

Jimmy Pace has recently been hired as the manager of Jittery Jon's Coffee Shop. Jittery Jon's Coffee Shop is a national chain of franchised coffee shops. During his first month as store manager, Jimmy encountered the following internal control situations:

a. Jittery Jon's Coffee Shop has one cash register. Prior to Jimmy's joining the coffee shop, each employee working on a shift would take a customer order, accept payment, and then prepare the order. Jimmy made one employee on each shift responsible for taking orders and accepting the customer's payment. Other employees prepare the orders.

b. Because only one employee uses the cash register, that employee is responsible for counting the cash at the end of the shift and verifying that the cash in the drawer matches the amount of cash sales recorded by the cash register. Jimmy expects each cashier to balance the drawer to the penny *every* time—no exceptions.

c. Jimmy caught an employee putting a case of 1,000 single-serving tea bags in her car. Not wanting to create a scene, Jimmy smiled and said, "I don't think you're putting those tea bags on the right shelf. Don't they belong inside the coffee shop?" The employee returned the tea bags to the stockroom.

State whether you agree or disagree with Jimmy's method of handling each situation and explain your answer.

EX 8-3 Internal controls

OBJ. 2, 3

Ramona's Clothing is a retail store specializing in women's clothing. The store has established a liberal return policy for the holiday season in order to encourage gift purchases. Any item purchased during November and December may be returned through January 31, with a receipt, for cash or exchange. If the customer does not have a receipt, cash will still be refunded for any item under $75. If the item is more than $75, a check is mailed to the customer.

Whenever an item is returned, a store clerk completes a return slip, which the customer signs. The return slip is placed in a special box. The store manager visits the return counter

(*Continued*)

approximately once every two hours to authorize the return slips. Clerks are instructed to place the returned merchandise on the proper rack on the selling floor as soon as possible.

This year, returns at Ramona's Clothing have reached an all-time high. There are a large number of returns under $75 without receipts.

a. How can salesclerks employed at Ramona's Clothing use the store's return policy to steal money from the cash register?

b. What internal control weaknesses do you see in the return policy that make cash thefts easier?

c. Would issuing a store credit in place of a cash refund for all merchandise returned without a receipt reduce the possibility of theft? List some advantages and disadvantages of issuing a store credit in place of a cash refund.

d. Assume that Ramona's Clothing is committed to the current policy of issuing cash refunds without a receipt. What changes could be made in the store's procedures regarding customer refunds to improve internal control?

EX 8-4 Internal controls for bank lending **OBJ. 2, 3**

Pacific Bank provides loans to businesses in the community through its Commercial Lending Department. Small loans (less than $100,000) may be approved by an individual loan officer, while larger loans (greater than $100,000) must be approved by a board of loan officers. Once a loan is approved, the funds are made available to the loan applicant under agreed-upon terms. Pacific Bank has instituted a policy whereby its president has the individual authority to approve loans up to $5,000,000. The president believes that this policy will allow flexibility to approve loans to valued clients much quicker than under the previous policy.

As an internal auditor of Pacific Bank, how would you respond to this change in policy?

EX 8-5 Internal controls **OBJ. 2, 3**

One of the largest losses in history from unauthorized securities trading involved a securities trader for the French bank **Societe Generale**. The trader was able to circumvent internal controls and create more than $7 billion in trading losses in six months. The trader apparently escaped detection by using knowledge of the bank's internal control systems learned from a previous back-office monitoring job. Much of this monitoring involved the use of software to monitor trades. In addition, traders were usually kept to tight trading limits. Apparently, these controls failed in this case.

What general weaknesses in Societe Generale's internal controls contributed to the occurrence and size of the losses?

EX 8-6 Internal controls **OBJ. 2, 3**

An employee of **JHT Holdings, Inc.**, a trucking company, was responsible for resolving roadway accident claims under $25,000. The employee created fake accident claims and wrote settlement checks of between $5,000 and $25,000 to friends or acquaintances acting as phony "victims." One friend recruited subordinates at his place of work to cash some of the checks. Beyond this, the JHT employee also recruited lawyers, whom he paid to represent both the trucking company and the fake victims in the bogus accident settlements. When the lawyers cashed the checks, they allegedly split the money with the corrupt JHT employee. This fraud went undetected for two years.

Why would it take so long to discover such a fraud?

EX 8-7 Internal controls **OBJ. 2, 3**

All-Around Sound Co. discovered a fraud whereby one of its front office administrative employees used company funds to purchase goods such as computers, digital cameras, and other electronic items for her own use. The fraud was discovered when employees noticed an increase in the frequency of deliveries from vendors and the use of unusual vendors. After some investigation, it was discovered that the employee would alter the description or change the quantity on an invoice in order to explain the cost on the bill.

What general internal control weaknesses contributed to this fraud?

EX 8-8 Financial statement fraud OBJ. 2, 3

A former chairman, CFO, and controller of **Donnkenny, Inc.**, an apparel company that makes sportswear for Pierre Cardin and Victoria Jones, pleaded guilty to financial statement fraud. These managers used false journal entries to record fictitious sales, hid inventory in public warehouses so that it could be recorded as "sold," and required sales orders to be backdated so that the sale could be moved to an earlier period. The combined effect of these actions caused $25 million out of $40 million in quarterly sales to be phony.

a. Why might control procedures listed in this chapter be insufficient in stopping this type of fraud?

b. How could this type of fraud be stopped?

EX 8-9 Internal control of cash receipts OBJ. 2, 3

The procedures used for over-the-counter receipts are as follows: At the close of each day's business, the salesclerks count the cash in their respective cash drawers, after which they determine the amount recorded by the cash register and prepare the memo cash form, noting any discrepancies. An employee from the cashier's office counts the cash, compares the total with the memo, and takes the cash to the cashier's office.

a. Indicate the weak link in internal control.

b. How can the weakness be corrected?

EX 8-10 Internal control of cash receipts OBJ. 2, 3

Sergio Flores works at the drive-through window of Big & Bad Burgers. Occasionally, when a drive-through customer orders, Sergio fills the order and pockets the customer's money. He does not ring up the order on the cash register.

Identify the internal control weaknesses that exist at Big & Bad Burgers and discuss what can be done to prevent this theft.

EX 8-11 Internal control of cash receipts OBJ. 2, 3

The mailroom employees send all remittances and remittance advices to the cashier. The cashier deposits the cash in the bank and forwards the remittance advices and duplicate deposit slips to the Accounting Department.

a. Indicate the weak link in internal control in the handling of cash receipts.

b. How can the weakness be corrected?

EX 8-12 Entry for cash sales; cash short OBJ. 2, 3

The actual cash received from cash sales was $25,538, and the amount indicated by the cash register total was $25,670. Journalize the entry to record the cash receipts and cash sales.

EX 8-13 Entry for cash sales; cash over OBJ. 2, 3

The actual cash received from cash sales was $66,670, and the amount indicated by the cash register total was $66,341. Journalize the entry to record the cash receipts and cash sales.

EX 8-14 Internal control of cash payments OBJ. 2, 3

Abbe Co. is a small merchandising company with a manual accounting system. An investigation revealed that in spite of a sufficient bank balance, a significant amount of available cash discounts had been lost because of failure to make timely payments. In addition, it was discovered that the invoices for several purchases had been paid twice.

Outline procedures for the payment of vendors' invoices so that the possibilities of losing available cash discounts and of paying an invoice a second time will be minimized.

EX 8-15 Internal control of cash payments **OBJ. 2, 3**

Paragon Tech Company, a communications equipment manufacturer, recently fell victim to a fraud scheme developed by one of its employees. To understand the scheme, it is necessary to review Paragon Tech's procedures for the purchase of services.

The purchasing agent is responsible for ordering services (such as repairs to a photocopy machine or office cleaning) after receiving a service requisition from an authorized manager. However, because no tangible goods are delivered, a receiving report is not prepared. When the Accounting Department receives an invoice billing Paragon Tech for a service call, the accounts payable clerk calls the manager who requested the service in order to verify that it was performed.

The fraud scheme involves Mae Jansma, the manager of plant and facilities. Mae arranged for her uncle's company, Radiate Systems, to be placed on Paragon Tech's approved vendor list. Mae did not disclose the family relationship.

On several occasions, Mae would submit a requisition for services to be provided by Radiate Systems. However, the service requested was really not needed, and it was never performed. Radiate Systems would bill Paragon Tech for the service and then split the cash payment with Mae.

Explain what changes should be made to Paragon Tech's procedures for ordering and paying for services in order to prevent such occurrences in the future.

EX 8-16 Bank reconciliation **OBJ. 5**

Identify each of the following reconciling items as: (a) an addition to the cash balance according to the bank statement, (b) a deduction from the cash balance according to the bank statement, (c) an addition to the cash balance according to the company's records, or (d) a deduction from the cash balance according to the company's records. (None of the transactions reported by bank debit and credit memos have been recorded by the company.)

1. Bank service charges, $90.
2. Check of a customer returned by bank to company because of insufficient funds, $520.
3. Check for $420 incorrectly recorded by the company as $240.
4. Check for $1,440 incorrectly charged by bank as $140.
5. Deposit in transit, $5,310.
6. Outstanding checks, $10,370.
7. Note collected by bank, $12,600.

EX 8-17 Entries based on bank reconciliation **OBJ. 5**

Which of the reconciling items listed in Exercise 8-16 require an entry in the company's accounts?

EX 8-18 Bank reconciliation **OBJ. 5**

The following data were accumulated for use in reconciling the bank account of Nakajima Co. for July:

1. Cash balance according to the company's records at July 31, $49,910.
2. Cash balance according to the bank statement at July 31, $48,250.
3. Checks outstanding, $4,460.
4. Deposit in transit, not recorded by bank, $6,450.
5. A check for $590 issued in payment of an account was erroneously recorded in the check register as $950.
6. Bank debit memo for service charges, $30.

a. Prepare a bank reconciliation, using the format shown in Exhibit 12.
b. If the balance sheet is prepared for Nakajima Co. on July 31, what amount should be reported for cash?
c. Must a bank reconciliation always balance (reconcile)?

SHOW ME HOW

EX 8-19 Entries for bank reconciliation **OBJ. 5**

Using the data presented in Exercise 8-18, journalize the entry or entries that should be made by the company.

SHOW ME HOW

EX 8-20 Entries for note collected by bank **OBJ. 5**

Accompanying a bank statement for Santee Company is a credit memo for $15,120 representing the principal ($14,000) and interest ($1,120) on a note that had been collected by the bank. The company had been notified by the bank at the time of the collection but had made no entries. Journalize the entry that should be made by the company to bring the accounting records up to date.

SHOW ME HOW

EX 8-21 Bank reconciliation **OBJ. 5**

An accounting clerk for Chesner Co. prepared the following bank reconciliation:

Chesner Co.
Bank Reconciliation
August 31

Cash balance according to company's records		$11,100
Add: Outstanding checks	$ 3,585	
Error by Chesner Co. in recording Check No. 1056 as $950 instead of $590	360	
Note for $12,000 collected by bank, including interest	12,480	16,425
		$27,525
Deduct: Deposit in transit on August 31	$ 7,200	
Bank service charges	25	7,225
Cash balance according to bank statement		$20,300

a. From the data in this bank reconciliation, prepare a new bank reconciliation for Chesner Co., using the format shown in Exhibit 12.

b. If a balance sheet is prepared for Chesner Co. on August 31, what amount should be reported for cash?

✔ Corrected adjusted balance: $19,780

EX 8-22 Bank reconciliation **OBJ. 5**

The following June 30 bank reconciliation was prepared for Poway Co.

Poway Co.
Bank Reconciliation
For the Month Ended June 30

Cash balance according to bank statement			$16,185
Add outstanding checks:			
No. 1067		$ 575	
1106		470	
1110		1,050	
1113		910	3,005
			$19,190
Deduct deposit of June 30, not recorded by bank			6,600
Adjusted balance			$12,590
Cash balance according to company's records			$ 8,985
Add: Proceeds of note collected by bank:			
Principal	$6,000		
Interest	300	$6,300	
Service charges		15	6,315
			$15,300
Deduct: Check returned because of insufficient funds		$ 890	
Error in recording June 17 deposit of $7,150 as $1,750		5,400	6,290
Adjusted balance			$ 9,010

a. Identify the errors in the bank reconciliation.

b. Prepare a new bank reconciliation for Poway Co., using the format shown in the illustrative problem.

EX 8-23 Using bank reconciliation to determine cash receipts stolen — OBJ. 2, 3, 5

Alaska Impressions Co. records all cash receipts on the basis of its cash register tapes. Alaska Impressions Co. discovered during October that one of its salesclerks had stolen an undetermined amount of cash receipts while taking the daily deposits to the bank. The following data have been gathered for October:

Cash in bank according to the general ledger	$11,680
Cash according to the October 31 bank statement	13,275
Outstanding checks as of October 31	3,670
Bank service charge for October	40
Note receivable, including interest collected by bank in October	2,100

No deposits were in transit on October 31.

a. Determine the amount of cash receipts stolen by the salesclerk.

b. What accounting controls would have prevented or detected this theft?

EX 8-24 Petty cash fund entries — OBJ. 6

Journalize the entries to record the following:

a. Check is issued to establish a petty cash fund of $1,290.

b. The amount of cash in the petty cash fund is now $303. Check is issued to replenish the fund, based on the following summary of petty cash receipts: office supplies, $427; miscellaneous selling expense, $365; miscellaneous administrative expense, $165. If the amount of the check to replenish the fund plus the balance in the fund do not equal $1,290, record the discrepancy in the cash short and over account.

EX 8-25 Variation in cash flows — OBJ. 7

Hasbro, Inc., designs, manufactures, and markets toy products worldwide. Hasbro's toys include Monopoly®, My Little Pony®, and Nerf brands. For a recent year, Hasbro reported the following net cash flows from operating activities (in thousands):

First quarter ending April 1	$317,789
Second quarter ending July 1	(76,938)
Third quarter ending September 30	(66,055)
Fourth quarter ending December 30	471,251

Explain why Hasbro reported negative net cash flows from operating activities during the second and third quarters and a large positive cash flow for the fourth quarter, with overall net positive cash flow for the year.

EX 8-26 Cash to monthly cash expenses ratio — OBJ. 8

El Dorado Inc. has monthly cash expenses of $168,500. On December 31, the cash balance is $1,415,400.

a. Compute the ratio of cash to monthly cash expenses.

b. Based on (a), what are the implications for El Dorado Inc.?

EX 8-27 Cash to monthly cash expenses ratio — OBJ. 8

Capstone Turbine Corporation produces and sells turbine generators for such applications as charging electric, hybrid vehicles. Capstone Turbine reported the following financial data for a recent year (in thousands):

Net cash flows from operating activities	$(8,641)
Cash and cash equivalents	14,408

a. Determine the monthly cash expenses. Round to one decimal place.

b. Determine the ratio of cash to monthly cash expenses. Round to one decimal place.

c. Based on your analysis, do you believe that Capstone Turbine will remain in business?

EX 8-28 Cash to monthly cash expenses ratio **OBJ. 8**

Amicus Therapeutics, Inc., is a biopharmaceutical company that develops drugs for the treatment of various diseases, including Parkinson's disease. Amicus Therapeutics reported the following financial data (in thousands) for three recent years:

	For Years Ended December 31		
	Year 3	Year 2	Year 1
Cash and cash equivalents	$ 79,749	$ 49,060	$ 187,026
Net cash flows from operations	(299,955)	(213,695)	(150,147)

a. Determine the monthly cash expenses for Year 3, Year 2, and Year 1. Round to one decimal place.

b. Determine the ratio of cash to monthly cash expenses for Year 3, Year 2, and Year 1 as of December 31. Round to one decimal place.

c. Based on (a) and (b), comment on Amicus Therapeutics' ratio of cash to monthly operating expenses for Years 1, 2, and 3.

Problems: Series A

PR 8-1A Evaluating internal control of cash **OBJ. 2, 3**

The following procedures were recently installed by Raspberry Creek Company:

a. After necessary approvals have been obtained for the payment of a voucher, the treasurer signs and mails the check. The treasurer then stamps the voucher and supporting documentation as paid and returns the voucher and supporting documentation to the accounts payable clerk for filing.

b. The accounts payable clerk prepares a voucher for each disbursement. The voucher along with the supporting documentation is forwarded to the treasurer's office for approval.

c. Along with petty cash expense receipts for postage, office supplies, etc., several postdated employee checks are in the petty cash fund.

d. At the end of the day, cash register clerks are required to use their own funds to make up any cash shortages in their registers.

e. At the end of each day, all cash receipts are placed in the bank's night depository.

f. At the end of each day, an accounting clerk compares the duplicate copy of the daily cash deposit slip with the deposit receipt obtained from the bank.

g. All mail is opened by the mail clerk, who forwards all cash remittances to the cashier. The cashier prepares a listing of the cash receipts and forwards a copy of the list to the accounts receivable clerk for recording in the accounts.

h. The bank reconciliation is prepared by the cashier, who works under the supervision of the treasurer.

Instructions

Indicate whether each of the procedures of internal control over cash represents (1) a strength or (2) a weakness. For each weakness, indicate why it exists.

PR 8-2A Transactions for petty cash, cash short and over **OBJ. 3, 6**

Jeremiah Restoration Company completed the following selected transactions during January:

Jan. 1. Established a petty cash fund of $900.

12. The cash sales for the day, according to the cash register records, totaled $6,148. The actual cash received from cash sales was $6,180.

31. Petty cash on hand was $75. Replenished the petty cash fund for the following disbursements, each evidenced by a petty cash receipt:

(Continued)

Jan. 3. Store supplies, $470.
7. Express charges on merchandise sold, $55 (Delivery Expense).
9. Office supplies, $30.
13. Office supplies, $11.
19. Postage stamps, $55 (Office Supplies).
21. Repair to office file cabinet lock, $60 (Miscellaneous Administrative Expense).
22. Postage due on special delivery letter, $30 (Miscellaneous Administrative Expense).
24. Express charges on merchandise sold, $85 (Delivery Expense).
30. Office supplies, $14.

Jan. 31. The cash sales for the day, according to the cash register records, totaled $4,550. The actual cash received from cash sales was $4,536.
31. Decreased the petty cash fund by $200.

Instructions

Journalize the transactions.

PR 8-3A Bank reconciliation and entries **OBJ. 5**

✔ 1. Adjusted balance: $446,000

SHOW ME HOW

The cash account for Norwegian Medical Co. at April 30 indicated a balance of $403,784. The bank statement indicated a balance of $468,460 on April 30. Comparing the bank statement and the accompanying canceled checks and memos with the records revealed the following reconciling items:

a. Checks outstanding totaled $73,870.
b. A deposit of $51,230, representing receipts of April 30, had been made too late to appear on the bank statement.
c. The bank collected $50,630 on a $48,220 note, including interest of $2,410.
d. A check for $9,160 returned with the statement had been incorrectly recorded by Norwegian Medical Co. as $916. The check was for the payment of an obligation to Universal Supply Co. for a purchase on account.
e. A check drawn for $680 had been erroneously charged by the bank as $860.
f. Bank service charges for April amounted to $170.

Instructions

1. Prepare a bank reconciliation.
2. Journalize the necessary entries. The accounts have not been closed.
3. If a balance sheet is prepared for Norwegian Medical Co. on April 30, what amount should be reported as cash?

PR 8-4A Bank reconciliation and entries **OBJ. 5**

✔ 1. Adjusted balance: $39,475

SHOW ME HOW

The cash account for Brentwood Bike Co. at May 1 indicated a balance of $34,250. During May, the total cash deposited was $140,300, and checks written totaled $138,880. The bank statement indicated a balance of $43,525 on May 31. Comparing the bank statement, the canceled checks, and the accompanying memos with the records revealed the following reconciling items:

a. Checks outstanding totaled $6,440.
b. A deposit of $1,850 representing receipts of May 31 had been made too late to appear on the bank statement.
c. The bank had collected for Brentwood Bike Co. $5,250 on a note left for collection. The face of the note was $5,000.
d. A check for $390 returned with the statement had been incorrectly charged by the bank as $930.
e. A check for $210 returned with the statement had been recorded by Brentwood Bike Co. as $120. The check was for the payment of an obligation to Adkins Co. on account.

f. Bank service charges for May amounted to $30.

g. A check for $1,325 from Jennings Co. was returned by the bank due to insufficient funds.

Instructions

1. Prepare a bank reconciliation as of May 31.
2. Journalize the necessary entries. The accounts have not been closed.
3. If a balance sheet is prepared for Brentwood Bike Co. on May 31, what amount should be reported as cash?

PR 8-5A Bank reconciliation and entries **OBJ. 5**

✔ 1. Adjusted balance: $13,216

Beeler Furniture Company deposits all cash receipts each Wednesday and Friday in a night depository after banking hours. The data required to reconcile the bank statement as of June 30 have been taken from various documents and records and are reproduced as follows. The sources of the data are printed in capital letters. All checks were written for payments on account.

CASH ACCOUNT:

Balance as of June 1	$9,317.40
CASH RECEIPTS FOR MONTH OF JUNE	$9,223.76

DUPLICATE DEPOSIT TICKETS:

Date and amount of each deposit in June:

Date	Amount	Date	Amount	Date	Amount
June 1	$1,080.50	June 10	$ 996.61	June 22	$ 897.34
3	854.17	15	882.95	24	947.21
8	840.50	17	1,606.74	30	1,117.74

CHECKS WRITTEN:

Number and amount of each check issued in June:

Check No.	Amount	Check No.	Amount	Check No.	Amount
740	$237.50	747	Void	754	$ 449.75
741	495.15	748	$450.90	755	272.75
742	501.90	749	640.13	756	113.95
743	761.30	750	276.77	757	407.95
744	506.88	751	299.37	758	259.60
745	117.25	752	537.01	759	901.50
746	298.66	753	380.95	760	486.39
Total amount of checks issued in June					$8,395.66

BANK RECONCILIATION FOR PRECEDING MONTH:

Beeler Furniture Company
Bank Reconciliation
May 31, 20Y2

Cash balance according to bank statement		$9,447.20
Add deposit for May 31, not recorded by bank		690.25
Deduct outstanding checks:		
No. 731	$162.15	
736	345.95	
738	251.40	
739	60.55	(820.05)
Adjusted balance		$9,317.40
Cash balance according to company's records		$9,352.50
Deduct bank service charges		(35.10)
Adjusted balance		$9,317.40

Instructions

1. Prepare a bank reconciliation as of June 30, 20Y2. If errors in recording deposits or checks are discovered, assume that the errors were made by the company. Assume that all deposits are from cash sales. All checks are written to satisfy accounts payable.

(Continued)

2. Journalize the necessary entries. The accounts have not been closed.
3. What is the amount of Cash that should appear on the balance sheet as of June 30?
4. Assume that a canceled check for $390 has been incorrectly recorded by the bank as $930. Briefly explain how the error would be included in a bank reconciliation and how it should be corrected.

JUNE BANK STATEMENT:

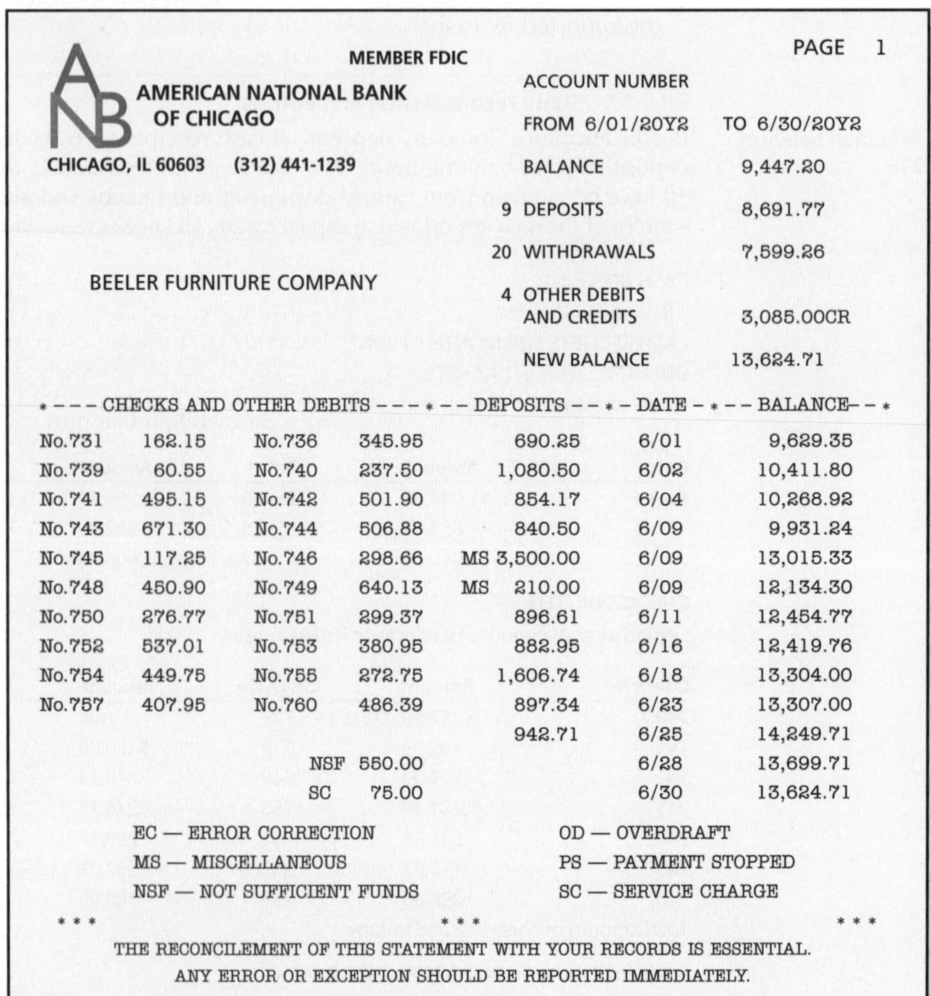

MEMBER FDIC

AMERICAN NATIONAL BANK
OF CHICAGO

CHICAGO, IL 60603 (312) 441-1239

BEELER FURNITURE COMPANY

PAGE 1

ACCOUNT NUMBER		
FROM 6/01/20Y2	TO 6/30/20Y2	
BALANCE		9,447.20
9	DEPOSITS	8,691.77
20	WITHDRAWALS	7,599.26
4	OTHER DEBITS AND CREDITS	3,085.00CR
NEW BALANCE		13,624.71

CHECKS AND OTHER DEBITS				DEPOSITS	DATE	BALANCE
No.731	162.15	No.736	345.95	690.25	6/01	9,629.35
No.739	60.55	No.740	237.50	1,080.50	6/02	10,411.80
No.741	495.15	No.742	501.90	854.17	6/04	10,268.92
No.743	671.30	No.744	506.88	840.50	6/09	9,931.24
No.745	117.25	No.746	298.66	MS 3,500.00	6/09	13,015.33
No.748	450.90	No.749	640.13	MS 210.00	6/09	12,134.30
No.750	276.77	No.751	299.37	896.61	6/11	12,454.77
No.752	537.01	No.753	380.95	882.95	6/16	12,419.76
No.754	449.75	No.755	272.75	1,606.74	6/18	13,304.00
No.757	407.95	No.760	486.39	897.34	6/23	13,307.00
				942.71	6/25	14,249.71
		NSF	550.00		6/28	13,699.71
		SC	75.00		6/30	13,624.71

EC — ERROR CORRECTION
MS — MISCELLANEOUS
NSF — NOT SUFFICIENT FUNDS
OD — OVERDRAFT
PS — PAYMENT STOPPED
SC — SERVICE CHARGE

THE RECONCILEMENT OF THIS STATEMENT WITH YOUR RECORDS IS ESSENTIAL.
ANY ERROR OR EXCEPTION SHOULD BE REPORTED IMMEDIATELY.

Problems: Series B

PR 8-1B Evaluating internal control of cash

OBJ. 2, 3

The following procedures were recently installed by The China Shop:

a. All sales are rung up on the cash register, and a receipt is given to the customer. All sales are recorded on a record locked inside the cash register.

b. Each cashier is assigned a separate cash register drawer to which no other cashier has access.

c. At the end of a shift, each cashier counts the cash in his or her cash register, unlocks the cash register record, and compares the amount of cash with the amount on the record to determine cash shortages and overages.

d. Checks received through the mail are given daily to the accounts receivable clerk for recording collections on account and for depositing in the bank.

e. Vouchers and all supporting documents are perforated with a PAID designation after being paid by the treasurer.

f. Disbursements are made from the petty cash fund only after a petty cash receipt has been completed and signed by the payee.

g. The bank reconciliation is prepared by the cashier.

Instructions

Indicate whether each of the procedures of internal control over cash represents (1) a strength or (2) a weakness. For each weakness, indicate why it exists.

SHOW ME HOW

PR 8-2B Transactions for petty cash, cash short and over **OBJ. 3, 6**

Cedar Springs Company completed the following selected transactions during June:

June 1. Established a petty cash fund of $1,000.

12. The cash sales for the day, according to the cash register records, totaled $9,440. The actual cash received from cash sales was $9,506.

30. Petty cash on hand was $46. Replenished the petty cash fund for the following disbursements, each evidenced by a petty cash receipt:

    June 2. Store supplies, $375.

    10. Express charges on merchandise purchased, $105 (Merchandise Inventory).

    14. Office supplies, $85.

    15. Office supplies, $90.

    18. Postage stamps, $33 (Office Supplies).

    20. Repair to fax, $100 (Miscellaneous Administrative Expense).

    21. Repair to office door lock, $25 (Miscellaneous Administrative Expense).

    22. Postage due on special delivery letter, $9 (Miscellaneous Administrative Expense).

    28. Express charges on merchandise purchased, $110 (Merchandise Inventory).

30. The cash sales for the day, according to the cash register records, totaled $13,390. The actual cash received from cash sales was $13,350.

30. Increased the petty cash fund by $200.

Instructions

Journalize the transactions.

✔ 1. Adjusted balance: $24,305

SHOW ME HOW

PR 8-3B Bank reconciliation and entries **OBJ. 5**

The cash account for Stone Systems at July 31 indicated a balance of $17,750. The bank statement indicated a balance of $33,650 on July 31. Comparing the bank statement and the accompanying canceled checks and memos with the records reveals the following reconciling items:

a. Checks outstanding totaled $17,865.

b. A deposit of $9,150, representing receipts of July 31, had been made too late to appear on the bank statement.

c. The bank had collected $6,095 on a note left for collection. The face of the note was $5,750.

d. A check for $390 returned with the statement had been incorrectly recorded by Stone Systems as $930. The check was for the payment of an obligation to Holland Co. for the purchase of office supplies on account.

e. A check drawn for $1,810 had been incorrectly charged by the bank as $1,180.

f. Bank service charges for July amounted to $80.

Instructions

1. Prepare a bank reconciliation.
2. Journalize the necessary entries. The accounts have not been closed.
3. If a balance sheet is prepared for Stone Systems on July 31, what amount should be reported as cash?

PR 8-4B Bank reconciliation and entries

OBJ. 5

✔ 1. Adjusted balance: $78,535

SHOW ME HOW

The cash account for Collegiate Sports Co. on November 1 indicated a balance of $81,145. During November, the total cash deposited was $293,150, and checks written totaled $307,360. The bank statement indicated a balance of $112,675 on November 30. Comparing the bank statement, the canceled checks, and the accompanying memos with the records revealed the following reconciling items:

a. Checks outstanding totaled $41,840.

b. A deposit of $12,200, representing receipts of November 30, had been made too late to appear on the bank statement.

c. A check for $7,250 had been incorrectly charged by the bank as $2,750.

d. A check for $760 returned with the statement had been recorded by Collegiate Sports Co. as $7,600. The check was for the payment of an obligation to Ramirez Co. on account.

e. The bank had collected for Collegiate Sports Co. $7,385 on a note left for collection. The face of the note was $7,000.

f. Bank service charges for November amounted to $125.

g. A check for $2,500 from Hallen Academy was returned by the bank because of insufficient funds.

Instructions

1. Prepare a bank reconciliation as of November 30.
2. Journalize the necessary entries. The accounts have not been closed.
3. If a balance sheet is prepared for Collegiate Sports Co. on November 30, what amount should be reported as cash?

PR 8-5B Bank reconciliation and entries

OBJ. 5

✔ 1. Adjusted balance: $11,494

Sunshine Interiors deposits all cash receipts each Wednesday and Friday in a night depository after banking hours. The data required to reconcile the bank statement as of July 31 have been taken from various documents and records and are reproduced as follows. The sources of the data are printed in capital letters. All checks were written for payments on account.

BANK RECONCILIATION FOR PRECEDING MONTH (DATED JUNE 30):		
Cash balance according to bank statement		$9,422.80
Add deposit of June 30, not recorded by bank		780.80
Deduct outstanding checks:		
No. 580	$310.10	
No. 602	85.50	
No. 612	92.50	
No. 613	137.50	(625.60)
Adjusted balance		$9,578.00
Cash balance according to company's records		$9,605.70
Deduct bank service charges		(27.70)
Adjusted balance		$9,578.00
CASH ACCOUNT:		
Balance as of July 1		$9,578.00
CASH RECEIPTS FOR MONTH OF JULY		6,465.42

DUPLICATE DEPOSIT TICKETS:

Date and amount of each deposit in July:

Date	Amount	Date	Amount	Date	Amount
July 2	$569.50	July 12	$580.70	July 23	$ 713.45
5	701.80	16	600.10	26	601.50
9	819.24	19	701.26	31	1,177.87

CHECKS WRITTEN:

Number and amount of each check issued in July:

Check No.	Amount	Check No.	Amount	Check No.	Amount
614	$243.50	621	$309.50	628	$ 837.70
615	350.10	622	Void	629	329.90
616	279.90	623	Void	630	882.80
617	395.50	624	707.01	631	1,081.56
618	435.40	625	158.63	632	325.40
619	320.10	626	550.03	633	310.08
620	238.87	627	381.73	634	241.71
Total amount of checks issued in July					$8,379.42

JULY BANK STATEMENT:

PAGE 1

MEMBER FDIC

AMERICAN NATIONAL BANK OF DETROIT

DETROIT, MI 48201-2500 (313) 933-8547

SUNSHINE INTERIORS

ACCOUNT NUMBER		
FROM 7/01/20Y5 TO 7/31/20Y5		
BALANCE		9,422.80
9	DEPOSITS	6,086.35
20	WITHDRAWALS	7,656.74
4	OTHER DEBITS AND CREDITS	3,749.00CR
NEW BALANCE		11,601.41

CHECKS AND OTHER DEBITS					DEPOSITS	DATE	BALANCE
No.580	310.10	No.612	92.50		780.80	07/01	9,801.00
No.602	85.50	No.614	243.50		569.50	07/03	10,041.50
No.615	350.10	No.616	279.90		701.80	07/06	10,113.30
No.617	395.50	No.618	435.40		819.24	07/11	10,101.64
No.619	320.10	No.620	238.87		580.70	07/13	10,123.37
No.621	309.50	No.624	707.01		MS 4,000.00	07/14	13,106.86
No.625	158.63	No.626	550.03		MS 160.00	07/14	12,558.20
No.627	318.73	No.629	329.90		600.10	07/17	12,509.67
No.630	882.80	No.631	1,081.56	NSF 375.00		07/20	10,170.31
No.632	325.40	No.634	241.71		701.26	07/21	10,304.46
					731.45	07/24	11,035.91
					601.50	07/28	11,637.41
		SC	36.00			07/31	11,601.41

EC — ERROR CORRECTION	OD — OVERDRAFT
MS — MISCELLANEOUS	PS — PAYMENT STOPPED
NSF — NOT SUFFICIENT FUNDS	SC — SERVICE CHARGE

* * * * * * * * *

THE RECONCILEMENT OF THIS STATEMENT WITH YOUR RECORDS IS ESSENTIAL.
ANY ERROR OR EXCEPTION SHOULD BE REPORTED IMMEDIATELY.

Instructions

1. Prepare a bank reconciliation as of July 31. If errors in recording deposits or checks are discovered, assume that the errors were made by the company. Assume that all deposits are from cash sales. All checks are written to satisfy accounts payable.
2. Journalize the necessary entries. The accounts have not been closed.
3. What is the amount of Cash that should appear on the balance sheet as of July 31?
4. Assume that a canceled check for $180 has been incorrectly recorded by the bank as $1,800. Briefly explain how the error would be included in a bank reconciliation and how it should be corrected.

Cases & Projects

CP 8-1 Ethics in Action

Tehra Dactyl is an accountant for Skeds, Inc., a footwear and apparel company. The company's revenue and net income have increased by more than 100% over the past three years. During the same period, Tehra and her colleagues in the Accounting Department have not received a raise or salary increase. Frustrated by not receiving a raise while the company has thrived, Tehra has begun submitting expense reimbursements for personal purchases. Tehra has a good relationship with her supervisor, and he simply "signs off" on Tehra's expense reimbursements. Tehra suspects that he knows she is submitting personal expenses for reimbursement and is "looking the other way" because Tehra has not received a raise in the past three years.

Are Tehra and her supervisor acting in an ethical manner? Why or why not?

CP 8-2 Ethics in Action

During the preparation of the bank reconciliation for Building Concepts Co., Joel Knolls, the assistant controller, discovered that Lone Peak National Bank incorrectly recorded a $3,290 check written by Building Concepts Co. as $329. Joel has decided not to notify the bank but wait for the bank to detect the error. Joel plans to record the $2,961 error as Other Income if the bank fails to detect the error within the next three months.

Discuss whether Joel is behaving in a professional manner.

CP 8-3 Team Activity

In teams, select a public company that interests you and is a business that requires inventory. Obtain the company's most recent annual report on Form 10-K. The Form 10-K is a company's annually required filing with the Securities and Exchange Commission (SEC). It includes the company's financial statements and accompanying notes. The Form 10-K can be obtained either (a) by referring to the investor relations section of the company's website or (b) by using the company search feature of the SEC's EDGAR database service found at www.sec.gov/edgar/searchedgar/companysearch.html.

1. Based on the information in the company's most recent annual report, answer the following questions:
   a. How much cash does the company have at the end of the most recent year?
   b. What percentage of total current assets is cash during the most recent two years presented? Has this percentage increased, decreased, or remained the same during this period?
2. Review Management's Annual Report on Internal Control Over Financial Reporting. Based on this information, answer the following questions:
   a. Who has responsibility for establishing and maintaining adequate internal controls over a company's financial reporting?
   b. How is "internal control over financial reporting" defined in this report?
   c. What level of assurance is provided that fraud will be detected?

CP 8-4 Team Activity

Select a business in your community and observe its internal controls over cash receipts and cash payments. The business could be a bank or a bookstore, a restaurant, a department store, or another retailer. In groups of three or four, identify and discuss the similarities and differences in each business's cash internal controls.

CP 8-5 Communication

Wholesome and Happy Foods is a farm-to-family grocery store located in the Pacific Northwest. The company recently installed four self-checkout lanes that allow customers to scan their own groceries and pay for their purchases using an automated checkout kiosk. The kiosks are monitored by a single attendant. In recent weeks, management has become concerned that some customers are not scanning all of the items when using the self-checkout lanes.

Write a brief memo to your instructor suggesting features and capabilities for the kiosks that would serve as control procedures, ensuring that all items brought through the self-checkout lanes are properly scanned and purchased.

CP 8-6 Internal controls

The following is an excerpt from a conversation between two salesclerks, Jean Moen and Sara Cheney. Jean and Sara are employed by Turpin Meadows Electronics, a locally owned and operated electronics retail store.

Jean: Did you hear the news?

Sara: What news?

Jean: Neal and Linda were both arrested this morning.

Sara: What? Arrested? You're putting me on!

Jean: No, really! The police arrested them first thing this morning. Put them in handcuffs, read them their rights—the whole works. It was unreal!

Sara: What did they do?

Jean: Well, apparently they were filling out merchandise refund forms for fictitious customers and then taking the cash.

Sara: I guess I never thought of that. How did they catch them?

Jean: The store manager noticed that returns were twice that of last year and seemed to be increasing. When he confronted Neal, he became flustered and admitted to taking the cash, apparently more than $9,000 in just three months. They're going over the transactions of the last six months to try to determine how much Linda stole. She apparently started stealing first.

Suggest appropriate control procedures that would have prevented or detected the theft of cash.

CP 8-7 Internal controls

The following is an excerpt from a conversation between the store manager of Wholesome Grocery Stores, Kara Dahl, and Lynn Shutes, president of Wholesome Grocery Stores:

Lynn: Kara, I'm concerned about this new scanning system.

Kara: What's the problem?

Lynn: Well, how do we know the clerks are ringing up all the merchandise?

Kara: That's one of the strong points about the system. The scanner automatically rings up each item based on its bar code. We update the prices daily, so we're sure the sale is rung up for the right price.

Lynn: That's not my concern. What keeps a clerk from pretending to scan items and then simply not charging his friends? If his friends were buying 10–15 items, it would be easy for the clerk to pass several items through putting his finger over the bar code or just pass the merchandise through the scanner with the wrong side showing. It would look normal for anyone observing. In the old days, we at least could hear the cash register ringing up each sale.

Kara: I see your point.

Suggest ways that Wholesome Grocery Stores could prevent or detect the theft of merchandise as described.

CP 8-8 Bank reconciliation and internal control

The records of Parker Company indicate a July 31 cash balance of $10,400, which includes undeposited receipts for July 30 and 31. The cash balance on the bank statement as of July 31 is $10,575. This balance includes a note of $2,250 plus $150 interest collected by the bank but not recorded in the journal. Checks outstanding on July 31 were as follows: No. 2670, $1,050; No. 3679, $675; No. 3690, $1,650; No. 5148, $225; No. 5149, $750; and No. 5151, $800.

(Continued)

On July 25, the cashier resigned, effective at the end of the month. Before leaving on July 31, the cashier prepared the following bank reconciliation:

Cash balance per books, July 31		$10,400
Add outstanding checks:		
No. 5148	$225	
5149	750	
5151	800	1,675
		$12,075
Less undeposited receipts		1,500
Cash balance per bank, July 31		$10,575
Deduct unrecorded note with interest		2,400
True cash, July 31		$ 8,175

Calculator Tape of Outstanding Checks:
0*
225+
750+
800+
1,675*

Subsequently, the owner of Parker Company discovered that the cashier had stolen an unknown amount of undeposited receipts, leaving only $1,500 to be deposited on July 31. The owner, a close family friend, has asked for your help in determining the amount that the former cashier stole.

1. Determine the amount the cashier stole from Parker Company. Show your computations in good form.
2. How did the cashier attempt to conceal the theft?
3. a. Identify two major weaknesses in internal controls that allowed the cashier to steal the undeposited cash receipts.
   b. Recommend improvements in internal controls so that similar types of thefts of undeposited cash receipts can be prevented.

CP 8-9 Cash to monthly cash expenses ratio

TearLab Corp. is a health care company that specializes in developing diagnostic devices for eye disease. TearLab reported the following data (in thousands) for three recent years:

	For Years Ended December 31		
	Year 3	**Year 2**	**Year 1**
Cash and cash equivalents	$ 7,272	$ 15,471	$ 13,838
Net cash flows from operations	(9,656)	(12,516)	(23,703)

1. Determine the monthly cash expenses for Year 3, Year 2, and Year 1. Round to one decimal place.
2. Determine the ratio of cash to monthly cash expenses as of December 31 for Year 3, Year 2, and Year 1. Round to one decimal place.
3. Based on (1) and (2), comment on TearLab's ratio of cash to monthly operating expenses for Years 1, 2, and 3.

CHAPTER 9 Receivables

STATEMENT OF OWNER'S EQUITY
For the Year Ended December 31, 20Y6

Owner's capital, Jan. 1, 20Y6		$XXX
Net income	$ XXX	
Withdrawals	(XXX)	
Increase in equity		XXX
Owner's capital, Dec. 31, 20Y6		$XXX

INCOME STATEMENT
For the Year Ended December 31, 20Y6

Sales		$XXX
Cost of merchandise sold		XXX
Gross profit		$XXX
Operating expenses:		
Advertising expense	$XXX	
Depreciation expense	XXX	
Amortization expense	XXX	
Depletion expense	XXX	
Bad debt expense	XXX	
…	XXX	
…	XXX	
Total operating expenses		XXX
Income from operations		$XXX
Other revenue and expenses		XXX
Interest revenue		XXX
Net income		$XXX

STATEMENT OF CASH FLOWS
For the Year Ended December 31, 20Y6

Cash flows from (used for) operating activities	$XXX
Cash flows from (used for) investing activities	XXX
Cash flows from (used for) financing activities	XXX
Net increase (decrease) in cash	$XXX
Cash balance, January 1, 20Y6	XXX

BALANCE SHEET
December 31, 20Y6

Current assets:		
Cash	$XXX	
Accounts receivable	XXX	
Allowance for doubtful accounts	XXX	
…	XXX	
Notes receivable	XXX	
Merchandise inventory	XXX	
Total current assets		$XXX
Property, plant, and equipment:	$XXX	
Intangible assets	XXX	
Total long-term assets		XXX
Total assets		$XXX
Liabilities:		
Current liabilities	$XXX	
Long-term liabilities	XXX	
Total liabilities		$XXX
Owner's equity		XXX
Total liabilities and owner's equity		$XXX

CHAPTER

9

Post Holdings, Inc.

A company generates revenues by providing goods or services to customers. For example, **Post Consumer Brands** sells breakfast cereals to supermarkets, convenience stores, club stores, restaurants, and hotels. Post also sells directly to consumers through its website at www.postconsumerbrands.com.

If you were to buy a case of cereal from Post online, you would use a credit card to complete the purchase. In this case, Post would record the transaction as a cash sale. However, Post allows its business customers to purchase its products "on account." Sales on account create accounts receivable with credit terms requiring payment within the credit period.

Unlike cash sales, not all credit sales will generate cash. That is, some customers will not pay their account receivable and the company will have to record a bad debt expense. Companies like Post try to reduce uncollectible accounts by reviewing a customer's credit rating and payment history prior to a sale. Even with such procedures, however, companies will experience bad debts.

This chapter describes common classifications of receivables, including notes receivable. In addition, methods of accounting for and estimating uncollectible accounts are described and illustrated. Finally, the reporting of receivables, the allowance for uncollectible accounts, and bad debt expense in the financial statements is described and illustrated.

Link to Post Holdings . . . . Pages 446, 447, 455, 462

LEARNING OBJECTIVES

After studying this chapter, you should be able to:

Example Exercises (EE) are shown in **red.**

OBJ. 1 Describe the common classes of receivables.

Classification of Receivables
Accounts Receivable
Notes Receivable
Other Receivables

OBJ. 2 Describe the accounting for uncollectible receivables.

Uncollectible Receivables

OBJ. 3 Describe the direct write-off method of accounting for uncollectible receivables.

Direct Write-Off Method for Uncollectible Accounts
Write-Offs to Bad Debt Expense — EE **9-1**

OBJ. 4 Describe the allowance method of accounting for uncollectible receivables.

Allowance Method for Uncollectible Accounts
Write-Offs to the Allowance Account — EE **9-2**
Percent of Sales Method — EE **9-3**
Analysis of Receivables Method — EE **9-4**

OBJ. 5 Compare the direct write-off and allowance methods of accounting for uncollectible accounts.

Comparing Direct Write-Off and Allowance Methods

OBJ. 6 Describe the accounting for notes receivable.

Notes Receivable
Characteristics of Notes Receivable
Accounting for Notes Receivable — EE **9-5**

OBJ. 7 Describe the reporting of receivables on the balance sheet.

Reporting Receivables on the Balance Sheet

OBJ. 8 Describe and illustrate the use of accounts receivable turnover and days' sales in receivables to evaluate a company's efficiency in collecting its receivables.

Financial Analysis and Interpretation: Accounts Receivable Turnover and Days' Sales in Receivables
Compute Accounts Receivable Turnover and Days' Sales in Receivables — EE **9-6**

At a Glance 9 Page 465

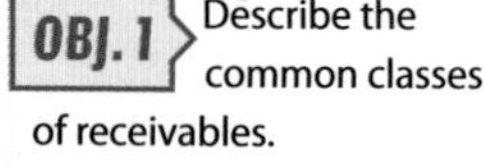

Describe the common classes of receivables.

Classification of Receivables

The receivables that result from sales on account are normally accounts receivable or notes receivable. The term **receivables** includes all money claims against other entities, including people, companies, and other organizations. Receivables are usually a significant portion of the total current assets.

Link to Post

In a recent annual report, **Post** reported that **Wal-Mart** is its largest customer, accounting for approximately 13% of sales.

Accounts Receivable

The most common transaction creating a receivable is selling merchandise or services on account (on credit). The receivable is recorded as a debit to Accounts Receivable. Such **accounts receivable** are normally collected within a short period, such as 30 or 60 days. They are classified on the balance sheet as a current asset.

Notes Receivable

Notes receivable are amounts that customers owe for which a formal, written instrument of credit has been issued. If notes receivable are expected to be collected within a year, they are classified on the balance sheet as a current asset.

Notes are often used for credit periods of more than 60 days. For example, a seller may require a down payment at the time of sale and accept a note or a series of notes for the remainder. Such notes usually provide for monthly payments.

Notes may also be used to settle a customer's account receivable. Notes and accounts receivable that result from sales transactions are sometimes called *trade receivables*. In this chapter, all notes and accounts receivable are from sales transactions.

Other Receivables

Other receivables include interest receivable, taxes receivable, and receivables from officers or employees. Other receivables are normally reported separately on the balance sheet. If they are expected to be collected within one year, they are classified as current assets. If collection is expected beyond one year, they are classified as noncurrent assets and reported under the caption *Investments*.

Uncollectible Receivables

OBJ. 2 Describe the accounting for uncollectible receivables.

In prior chapters, the accounting for sales of merchandise or services on account (on credit) was described and illustrated. A major issue that has not yet been discussed is that some customers will not pay their accounts. That is, some accounts receivable will be uncollectible.

Companies may shift the risk of uncollectible receivables to other companies. For example, some retailers do not accept sales on account but will only accept cash or credit cards. Such policies shift the risk to the credit card companies.

Companies may also sell their receivables. This is often the case when a company issues its own credit card. For example, **Macy's** and **JCPenney** issue their own credit cards. An advantage of a company selling its receivables is that it immediately receives cash for operating and other needs. Also, depending on the sales agreement, some of the risk of uncollectible accounts is shifted to the buyer.

Regardless of how careful a company is in granting credit, some credit sales will be uncollectible. The operating expense recorded from uncollectible receivables is called **bad debt expense**, *uncollectible accounts expense*, or *doubtful accounts expense*.

There is no general rule for when an account becomes uncollectible. Some indications that an account may be uncollectible include the following:

- The receivable is past due.
- The customer does not respond to the company's attempts to collect.
- The customer files for bankruptcy.
- The customer closes its business.
- The company cannot locate the customer.

If a customer doesn't pay, a company may turn the account over to a collection agency. After the collection agency attempts to collect payment, any remaining balance in the account is considered worthless.

The two methods of accounting for uncollectible receivables are as follows:

- The **direct write-off method** records bad debt expense only when an account is determined to be worthless.
- The **allowance method** records bad debt expense by estimating uncollectible accounts at the end of the accounting period.

The direct write-off method is often used by small companies and companies with few receivables.[1] Generally accepted accounting principles (GAAP), however, require companies with a large amount of receivables to use the allowance method. As a result, most well-known companies such as **General Electric**, **Pepsi**, **Intel**, and **FedEx** use the allowance method.

Link to Post

Post uses the allowance method and estimates uncollectible accounts based upon historical losses as well as the economic status of and its relationships with its customers, especially those identified as "at risk."

1 The direct write-off method is also required for federal income tax purposes.

Business Connection

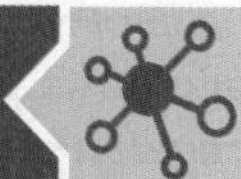

WARNING SIGNS

A business must manage the risk of extending credit. The following early warning signs can be used to signal the need to moderate future sales and accelerate collection efforts:

- You're only receiving partial payments.
- The customer's ordering pattern has declined dramatically, or the customer has stopped buying from you.
- The customer requests frequent changes in the payment schedule.
- You are repeatedly told that late payments are in process.
- The customer refuses to make payment, claiming dissatisfaction with the product.
- You can't reach your customer, or the customer refuses to acknowledge you.

Source: BMO Harris Bank website, Small Business Learning Center, Managing Your Trade Credit, 2015, www.bmoharris.com/us/small-business/learning-center/101/trade-credit.

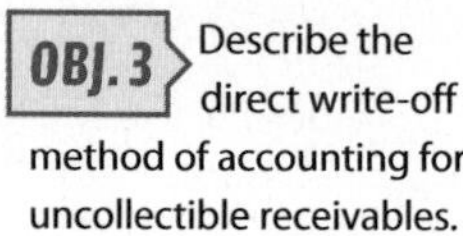

Describe the direct write-off method of accounting for uncollectible receivables.

Direct Write-Off Method for Uncollectible Accounts

Under the direct write-off method, Bad Debt Expense is not recorded until the customer's account is determined to be worthless. At that time, the customer's account receivable is written off.

To illustrate, assume that on May 10, a $4,200 account receivable from D. L. Ross has been determined to be uncollectible. The entry to write off the account is as follows:

May	10	Bad Debt Expense		4,200	
		Accounts Receivable—D. L. Ross			4,200

An account receivable that has been written off may be collected later. In such cases, the account is reinstated by an entry that reverses the write-off entry. The cash received in payment is then recorded as a receipt on account.

To illustrate, assume that the D. L. Ross account of $4,200 written off on May 10 is later collected on November 21. The reinstatement and receipt of cash is recorded as follows:

Nov.	21	Accounts Receivable—D. L. Ross		4,200	
		Bad Debt Expense			4,200
	21	Cash		4,200	
		Accounts Receivable—D. L. Ross			4,200

The direct write-off method is used by businesses that sell most of their goods or services for cash or through the acceptance of **MasterCard** or **VISA**, which are recorded as cash sales. In such cases, receivables are a small part of the current assets and any bad debt expense is small. Examples of such businesses are a restaurant, a convenience store, and a small retail store.

EXAMPLE EXERCISE 9-1 Direct Write-Off Method **OBJ. 3**

Journalize the following transactions, using the direct write-off method of accounting for uncollectible receivables:

July 9. Received $1,200 from Jay Burke and wrote off the remainder owed of $3,900 as uncollectible.

Oct. 11. Reinstated the account of Jay Burke and received $3,900 cash in full payment.

Follow My Example 9-1

July 9	Cash	1,200	
	Bad Debt Expense	3,900	
	Accounts Receivable—Jay Burke		5,100
Oct. 11	Accounts Receivable—Jay Burke	3,900	
	Bad Debt Expense		3,900
11	Cash	3,900	
	Accounts Receivable—Jay Burke		3,900

Practice Exercises: PE 9-1A, PE 9-1B

Allowance Method for Uncollectible Accounts

OBJ. 4 Describe the allowance method of accounting for uncollectible receivables.

The allowance method estimates the uncollectible accounts receivable at the end of the accounting period. Based on this estimate, Bad Debt Expense is recorded by an adjusting entry.

To illustrate, assume that ExTone Company began operations on August 1. As of the end of its accounting period on December 31, 20Y7, ExTone has outstanding accounts receivable of $200,000. This balance includes some past due accounts. Based on industry averages, ExTone estimates that $30,000 of the December 31 accounts receivable will be uncollectible. However, on December 31, ExTone doesn't know which customer accounts will be uncollectible. Thus, specific customer accounts cannot be decreased or credited. Instead, a contra asset account, **Allowance for Doubtful Accounts**, is credited for the estimated bad debts.

Using the $30,000 estimate, the following adjusting entry is made on December 31:

20Y7					
Dec.	31	Bad Debt Expense		30,000	
		Allowance for Doubtful Accounts			30,000
		Uncollectible accounts estimate.			

The preceding adjusting entry affects the income statement and balance sheet. On the income statement, the $30,000 of Bad Debt Expense will be matched against the related revenues of the period. On the balance sheet, the value of the receivables is reduced to the amount that is expected to be collected or realized. This amount, $170,000 ($200,000 – $30,000), is called the **net realizable value** of the receivables.

Note

The adjusting entry reduces receivables to their net realizable value and matches the uncollectible expense with revenues.

After the preceding adjusting entry is recorded, Accounts Receivable still has a debit balance of $200,000. This balance is the total amount owed by customers on account on December 31 as supported by the accounts receivable subsidiary ledger. The accounts receivable contra account, Allowance for Doubtful Accounts, has a credit balance of $30,000.

Integrity, Objectivity, and Ethics in Business

COLLECTING PAST DUE ACCOUNTS

Companies should make reasonable attempts (steps) to collect past due accounts. Many companies send a collection reminder as a first step. As a second step, a company may send a collection letter that offers options such as a willingness to negotiate a schedule for future payments. The next step is normally to turn the past due amount over to a collection agency or to file action in court. However, in no case should a company employee harass or misrepresent himself or herself to the customer as an attorney, a collection agent, or an agent of the court.

Write-Offs to the Allowance Account

When a customer's account is identified as uncollectible, it is written off against the allowance account. This requires the company to remove the specific accounts receivable and an equal amount from the allowance account.

To illustrate, on January 21, 20Y8, John Parker's account of $6,000 with ExTone Company is written off as follows:

20Y8					
Jan.	21	Allowance for Doubtful Accounts		6,000	
		Accounts Receivable—John Parker			6,000

At the end of a period, Allowance for Doubtful Accounts will normally have a balance. This is because Allowance for Doubtful Accounts is based on an estimate. As a result, the total write-offs to the allowance account during the period will rarely equal the balance of the account at the beginning of the period. The allowance account will have a credit balance at the end of the period if the write-offs during the period are less than the beginning balance. It will have a debit balance if the write-offs exceed the beginning balance.

Exhibit 1 illustrates the allowance method where the adjusting entry increases the Allowance for Doubtful Accounts (fills the bucket) while writing off accounts decreases the Allowance for Doubtful Accounts (empties the bucket).

EXHIBIT 1

The Allowance Method

To illustrate, assume that during 20Y8 ExTone Company writes off $26,750 of uncollectible accounts, including the $6,000 account of John Parker recorded on

January 21. Allowance for Doubtful Accounts will have a credit balance of $3,250 ($30,000 – $26,750), computed as follows:

ALLOWANCE FOR DOUBTFUL ACCOUNTS

				20Y8		
				Jan. 1	Balance	30,000
Total accounts written off $26,750	Jan. 21	6,000				
	Feb. 2	3,900				
	⋮	⋮				
				Dec. 31	Unadjusted balance	3,250

If ExTone had written off $32,100 in accounts receivable during 20Y8, Allowance for Doubtful Accounts would have had a debit balance of $2,100, computed as follows:

ALLOWANCE FOR DOUBTFUL ACCOUNTS

				20Y8		
				Jan. 1	Balance	30,000
Total accounts written off $32,100	Jan. 21	6,000				
	Feb. 2	3,900				
	⋮	⋮				
Dec. 31	Unadjusted balance	2,100				

The allowance account balances (credit balance of $3,250 and debit balance of $2,100) in the preceding illustrations are *before* the end-of-period adjusting entry. After the end-of-period adjusting entry is recorded, Allowance for Doubtful Accounts should always have a credit balance.

An account receivable that has been written off against the allowance account may be collected later. Like the direct write-off method, the account is reinstated by an entry that reverses the write-off entry. The cash received in payment is then recorded as a receipt on account.

To illustrate, assume that Nancy Smith's account of $5,000, which was written off on April 2, is collected later on June 10. ExTone Company records the reinstatement and the collection as follows:

				Debit	Credit
June	10	Accounts Receivable—Nancy Smith		5,000	
		Allowance for Doubtful Accounts			5,000
	10	Cash		5,000	
		Accounts Receivable—Nancy Smith			5,000

EXAMPLE EXERCISE 9-2 Allowance Method

OBJ. 4

Journalize the following transactions, using the allowance method of accounting for uncollectible receivables:

July 9. Received $1,200 from Jay Burke and wrote off the remainder owed of $3,900 as uncollectible.

Oct. 11. Reinstated the account of Jay Burke and received $3,900 cash in full payment.

Follow My Example 9-2

July 9	Cash	1,200	
	Allowance for Doubtful Accounts	3,900	
	Accounts Receivable—Jay Burke		5,100
Oct. 11	Accounts Receivable—Jay Burke	3,900	
	Allowance for Doubtful Accounts		3,900
11	Cash	3,900	
	Accounts Receivable—Jay Burke		3,900

Practice Exercises: PE 9-2A, PE 9-2B

Business Connection

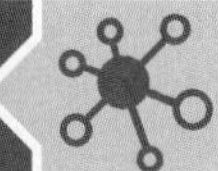

FAILURE TO COLLECT

When customers fail to pay their accounts, a business has the option of seeking payment through various means. The easiest recourse is simply to inquire about the cause of nonpayment and adjust terms to maximize the potential for collection. For large amounts, the cost and time of legal remedies can be appropriate. However, for smaller amounts, most businesses want to minimize the time, effort, and cost of collecting amounts that are past due. Thus, after exhausting their internal efforts to collect, businesses typically use the services of a collection agency to collect overdue accounts. Such services must abide by a number of consumer protection laws in collecting overdue accounts. The final amount collected will often be less than the full amount due, of which the collection agency will often keep 25–45% as a fee. Thus, the collection agency is often the last resort before a final write-off.

Estimating Uncollectibles

The allowance method requires an estimate of uncollectible accounts at the end of the period. This estimate is normally based on past experience, industry averages, and forecasts of the future.

The two methods used to estimate uncollectible accounts are as follows:

- Percent of sales method
- Analysis of receivables method

Percent of Sales Method Since accounts receivable are created by credit sales, uncollectible accounts can be estimated as a percent of credit sales. If the portion of credit sales to sales is relatively constant, the percent may be applied to total sales.

To illustrate, assume the following data for ExTone Company on December 31, 20Y8, before any adjustments:

Balance of Accounts Receivable	$ 240,000
Balance of Allowance for Doubtful Accounts	3,250 (Cr.)
Total credit sales	3,000,000
Bad debt as a percent of credit sales	¾%

Bad Debt Expense of $22,500 is estimated as follows:

Bad Debt Expense = Credit Sales × Bad Debt as a Percent of Credit Sales
Bad Debt Expense = $3,000,000 × ¾% = $22,500

The adjusting entry for uncollectible accounts on December 31, 20Y8, is as follows:

20Y8					
Dec.	31	Bad Debt Expense		22,500	
		Allowance for Doubtful Accounts			22,500
		Uncollectible accounts estimate			
		($3,000,000 × ¾% = $22,500).			

After the adjusting entry is posted to the ledger, Bad Debt Expense will have an adjusted balance of $22,500. Allowance for Doubtful Accounts will have an adjusted balance of $25,750 ($3,250 + $22,500). Both T accounts follow:

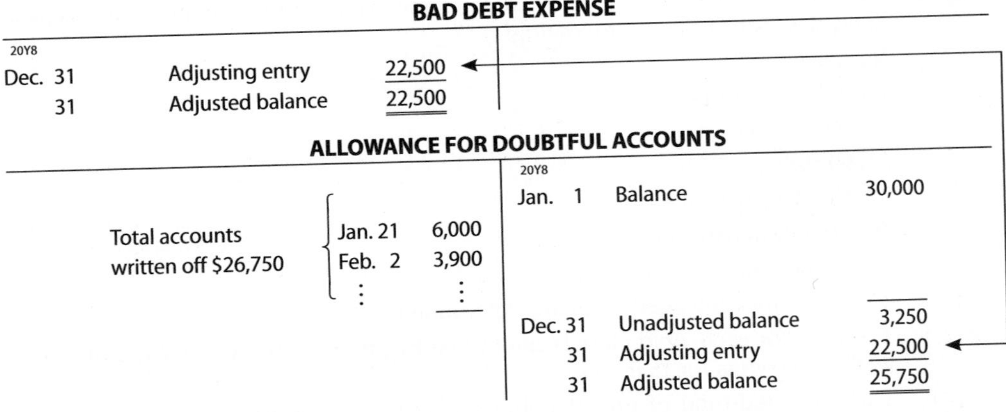

Under the percent of sales method, the amount of the adjusting entry is the amount estimated for Bad Debt Expense. This estimate is credited to whatever the unadjusted balance is for Allowance for Doubtful Accounts. For example, in the preceding illustration, the Allowance for Doubtful Accounts had a beginning credit balance of $3,250. After the adjusting entry, the balance of Allowance for Doubtful Accounts is an adjusted balance of $25,750 ($3,250 + $22,500), and the net realizable value of the receivables is $214,250 ($240,000 – $25,750).

Assume that in the preceding example, Allowance for Doubtful Accounts had a beginning debit balance of $2,100. After the adjusting entry, the balance of Allowance for Doubtful Accounts will have an adjusted balance of $20,400 ($22,500 – $2,100), and the net realizable value of the receivables is $219,600 ($240,000 – $20,400).

Note

The estimate based on sales is added to any balance in Allowance for Doubtful Accounts.

EXAMPLE EXERCISE 9-3 Percent of Sales Method

OBJ. 4

At the end of the current year, Accounts Receivable has a balance of $800,000; Allowance for Doubtful Accounts has a credit balance of $7,500; and sales for the year total $3,500,000. Bad debt expense is estimated at ½% of sales.

Determine (a) the amount of the adjusting entry for uncollectible accounts; (b) the adjusted balances of Accounts Receivable, Allowance for Doubtful Accounts, and Bad Debt Expense; and (c) the net realizable value of accounts receivable.

Follow My Example 9-3

a. $17,500 ($3,500,000 × ½%)

b.	Adjusted Balance Debt (Credit)
Accounts Receivable	$800,000
Allowance for Doubtful Accounts ($7,500 + $17,500)	(25,000)
Bad Debt Expense	17,500

c. $775,000 ($800,000 – $25,000)

Practice Exercises: PE 9-3A, PE 9-3B

Analysis of Receivables Method The analysis of receivables method is based on the assumption that the longer an account receivable is outstanding, the less likely it will be collected. The analysis of receivables method is applied as follows:

Step 1. The due date of each account receivable is determined.

Step 2. The number of days each account is past due is determined. This is the number of days between the due date of the account and the date of the analysis.

Step 3. Each account is placed in an aged class according to its days past due. Typical aged classes include the following:

Not past due
1–30 days past due
31–60 days past due
61–90 days past due
91–180 days past due
181–365 days past due
Over 365 days past due

Step 4. The totals for each aged class are determined.

Step 5. The total for each aged class is multiplied by an estimated percentage of uncollectible accounts for that class.

Step 6. The estimated total of uncollectible accounts is determined as the sum of the estimated uncollectible accounts for each aged class.

The preceding steps are summarized in an aging schedule, and this overall process is called **aging the receivables.**

To illustrate, assume that **ExTone Company** uses the analysis of receivables method instead of the percent of sales method. ExTone prepared an aging schedule for its accounts receivable of $240,000 as of December 31, 20Y8, as shown in Exhibit 2.

EXHIBIT 2 **Aging of Receivables Schedule, December 31, 20Y8**

		A	B	C	D	E	F	G	H	I
	1			Not			Days Past Due			
	2			Past						
Steps 1–3	3	Customer	Balance	Due	1–30	31–60	61–90	91–180	181–365	Over 365
	4	Ashby & Co.	1,500			1,500				
	5	B. T. Barr	6,100					3,500	2,600	
	6	Brock Co.	4,700	4,700						
	21									
	22	Saxon Woods Co.	600					600		
Step 4 →	23	Total	240,000	125,000	64,000	13,100	8,900	5,000	10,000	14,000
Step 5 →	24	Percent uncollectible		2%	5%	10%	20%	30%	50%	80%
Step 6 →	25	Estimate of uncollectible accounts	26,490	2,500	3,200	1,310	1,780	1,500	5,000	11,200
	26									

Assume that ExTone sold merchandise to Saxon Woods Co. on August 29 with terms 2/10, n/30. Thus, the due date (Step 1) of Saxon Woods' account is September 28, computed as follows:

Credit terms, net	30 days
Less: Aug. 29 to Aug. 31	2 days
Days in September	28 days

As of December 31, Saxon Woods' account is 94 days past due (Step 2), computed as follows:

Number of days past due in September	2 days (30 – 28)
Number of days past due in October	31 days
Number of days past due in November	30 days
Number of days past due in December	31 days
Total number of days past due	94 days

Exhibit 2 shows that the $600 account receivable for Saxon Woods Co. was placed in the 91–180 days past due class (Step 3).

The total for each of the aged classes is determined (Step 4). Exhibit 2 shows that $125,000 of the accounts receivable are not past due, while $64,000 are 1–30 days past due. ExTone applies a different estimated percentage of uncollectible accounts to the totals of each of the aged classes (Step 5). As shown in Exhibit 2, the percent is 2% for accounts not past due, while the percent is 80% for accounts over 365 days past due.

The sum of the estimated uncollectible accounts for each aged class (Step 6) is the estimated uncollectible accounts on December 31, 20Y8. This is the desired adjusted balance for Allowance for Doubtful Accounts. For ExTone, this amount is $26,490, as shown in Exhibit 2.

Comparing the estimate of $26,490 with the unadjusted balance of the allowance account determines the amount of the adjustment for Bad Debt Expense. For ExTone, the unadjusted balance of the allowance account is a credit balance of $3,250. The amount to be added to this balance is therefore $23,240 ($26,490 – $3,250). The adjusting entry is as follows:

Note

The estimate based on receivables is compared to the balance in the allowance account to determine the amount of the adjusting entry.

20Y8					
Dec.	31	Bad Debt Expense		23,240	
		Allowance for Doubtful Accounts			23,240
		Uncollectible accounts estimate ($26,490 – $3,250).			

After the preceding adjusting entry is posted to the ledger, Bad Debt Expense will have an adjusted balance of $23,240. Allowance for Doubtful Accounts will have an adjusted balance of $26,490, and the net realizable value of the receivables is $213,510 ($240,000 – $26,490). Both T accounts follow:

BAD DEBT EXPENSE

20Y8					
Dec. 31	Adjusting entry	23,240			
31	Adjusted balance	23,240			

ALLOWANCE FOR DOUBTFUL ACCOUNTS

			20Y8		
			Dec. 31	Unadjusted balance	3,250
			31	Adjusting entry	23,240
			31	Adjusted balance	26,490

Link to Post

In a recent balance sheet, **Post** reported an allowance for uncollectible accounts of $2,300,000 and a net realizable value of receivables of $462,300,000.

Under the analysis of receivables method, the amount of the adjusting entry is the amount that will yield an adjusted balance for Allowance for Doubtful Accounts equal to that estimated by the aging schedule. For example, assume that the unadjusted balance of the allowance account had been a debit of $2,100. The amount of the adjustment is $28,590 ($26,490 + $2,100). The Allowance for Doubtful Accounts will have an adjusted balance of $26,490 ($28,590 – $2,100), and the net realizable value of the receivables is $213,510 ($240,000 – $26,490). Bad Debt Expense will have an adjusted balance of $28,590. The T accounts appear as follows:

BAD DEBT EXPENSE

20Y8					
Dec. 31	Adjusting entry	28,590			
31	Adjusted balance	28,590			

ALLOWANCE FOR DOUBTFUL ACCOUNTS

20Y8			20Y8		
Dec. 31	Unadjusted balance	2,100	Dec. 31	Adjusting entry	28,590
			31	Adjusted balance	26,490

EXAMPLE EXERCISE 9-4 Analysis of Receivables Method — OBJ. 4

At the end of the current year, Accounts Receivable has a balance of $800,000, Allowance for Doubtful Accounts has a credit balance of $7,500, and sales for the year total $3,500,000. Using the aging method, the balance of Allowance for Doubtful Accounts is estimated as $30,000.

Determine (a) the amount of the adjusting entry for uncollectible accounts; (b) the adjusted balances of Accounts Receivable, Allowance for Doubtful Accounts, and Bad Debt Expense; and (c) the net realizable value of accounts receivable.

Follow My Example 9-4

a. $22,500 ($30,000 – $7,500)

	Adjusted Balance Debit (Credit)
b. Accounts Receivable	$800,000
Allowance for Doubtful Accounts	(30,000)
Bad Debt Expense	22,500

c. $770,000 ($800,000 – $30,000)

Practice Exercises: PE 9-4A, PE 9-4B

Comparing Estimation Methods Both the percent of sales and analysis of receivables methods estimate uncollectible accounts. However, each method has a slightly different focus and financial statement emphasis.

Under the percent of sales method, Bad Debt Expense is the focus of the estimation process. The percent of sales method places more emphasis on matching revenues and expenses and, thus, emphasizes the income statement. That is, the amount of the adjusting entry is based on the estimate of Bad Debt Expense for the period. Allowance for Doubtful Accounts is then credited for this amount.

Under the analysis of receivables method, Allowance for Doubtful Accounts is the focus of the estimation process. The analysis of receivables method places more emphasis on the net realizable value of the receivables and, thus, emphasizes the balance sheet. That is, the amount of the adjusting entry is the amount that will yield an adjusted balance for Allowance for Doubtful Accounts equal to that estimated by the aging schedule. Bad Debt Expense is then debited for this amount.

Exhibit 3 summarizes these differences between the percent of sales and the analysis of receivables methods. Exhibit 3 also shows the results of the ExTone Company

EXHIBIT 3

Difference Between Estimation Methods

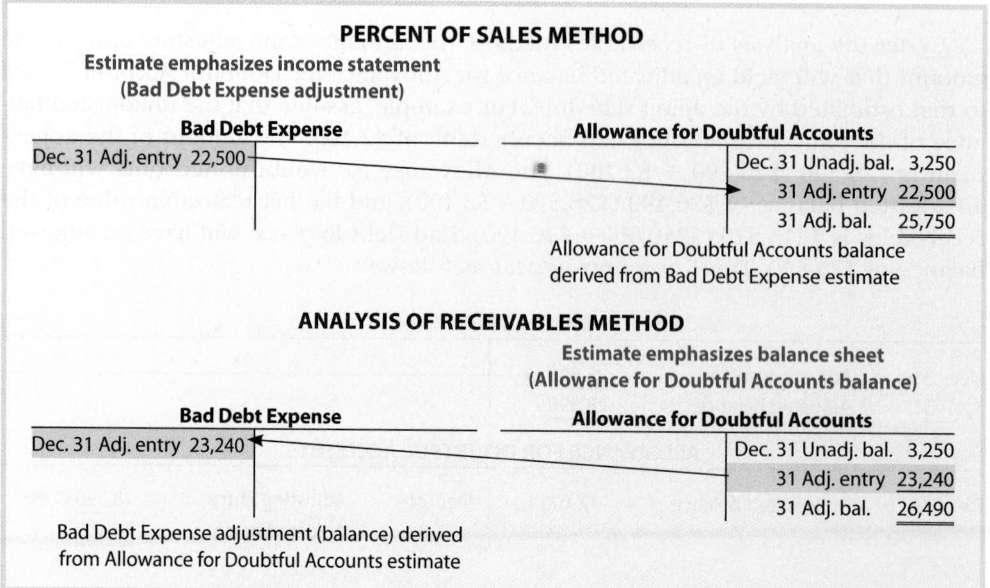

illustration for the percent of sales and analysis of receivables methods for 20Y8. The amounts shown in Exhibit 3 assume an unadjusted credit balance of $3,250 for Allowance for Doubtful Accounts. While the methods normally yield different amounts for any one period, over several periods, the amounts should be similar.

Business Connection

ALLOWANCE PERCENTAGES ACROSS COMPANIES

The percent of the allowance for doubtful accounts to total accounts receivable varies across companies and industries. For example, the following percentages were computed from recent annual reports:

Company	Industry	Percent of Allowance for Doubtful Accounts to Total Accounts Receivable
Coca-Cola	Beverages	11.5%
DuPont	Chemicals	2.1%
HCA	Health services	48.1%
Nike	Apparel	0.9%
Union Pacific	Transportation services	0.2%
Wynn Resorts	Casino gaming	10.6%

HCA's higher percentage is due in part to providing health care to patients without the means to pay. Wynn Resorts' high percentage is typical for casinos, representing the challenges in collecting gambling debts.

Comparing Direct Write-Off and Allowance Methods

OBJ. 5 Compare the direct write-off and allowance methods of accounting for uncollectible accounts.

Journal entries for the direct write-off and allowance methods are illustrated and compared in this section. As a basis for illustration, the following transactions, taken from the records of Hobbs Company for the year ending December 31, 20Y5, are used:

Mar. 1. Wrote off account of C. York, $3,650.

Apr. 12. Received $2,250 as partial payment on the $5,500 account of Cary Bradshaw. Wrote off the remaining balance as uncollectible.

June 22. Received the $3,650 from C. York, which had been written off on March 1. Reinstated the account and recorded the cash receipt.

Sept. 7. Wrote off the following accounts as uncollectible (record as one journal entry):

Jason Bigg	$1,100	Stanford Noonan	$1,360
Steve Bradey	2,220	Aiden Wyman	990
Samantha Neeley	775		

Dec. 31. Hobbs Company uses the percent of credit sales method of estimating uncollectible expenses. Based on past history and industry averages, 1.25% of credit sales are expected to be uncollectible. Hobbs recorded $3,400,000 of credit sales during the year.

Exhibit 4 illustrates the journal entries for Hobbs using the direct write-off and allowance methods. Using the direct write-off method, there is no adjusting entry on December 31 for uncollectible accounts. In contrast, the allowance method records an adjusting entry for estimated uncollectible accounts of $42,500.

EXHIBIT 4 **Comparing Direct Write-Off and Allowance Methods**

20Y5		Direct Write-Off Method			Allowance Method		
Mar.	1	Bad Debt Expense	3,650		Allowance for Doubtful Accounts	3,650	
		Accounts Receivable—C. York		3,650	Accounts Receivable—C. York		3,650
Apr.	12	Cash	2,250		Cash	2,250	
		Bad Debt Expense	3,250		Allowance for Doubtful Accounts	3,250	
		Accounts Receivable—Cary Bradshaw		5,500	Accounts Receivable—Cary Bradshaw		5,500
June	22	Accounts Receivable—C. York	3,650		Accounts Receivable—C. York	3,650	
		Bad Debt Expense		3,650	Allowance for Doubtful Accounts		3,650
	22	Cash	3,650		Cash	3,650	
		Accounts Receivable—C. York		3,650	Accounts Receivable—C. York		3,650
Sept.	7	Bad Debt Expense	6,445		Allowance for Doubtful Accounts	6,445	
		Accounts Receivable—Jason Bigg		1,100	Accounts Receivable—Jason Bigg		1,100
		Accounts Receivable—Steve Bradey		2,220	Accounts Receivable—Steve Bradey		2,220
		Accounts Receivable—Samantha Neeley		775	Accounts Receivable—Samantha Neeley		775
		Accounts Receivable—Stanford Noonan		1,360	Accounts Receivable—Stanford Noonan		1,360
		Accounts Receivable—Aiden Wyman		990	Accounts Receivable—Aiden Wyman		990
Dec.	31	No Entry			Bad Debt Expense	42,500	
					Allowance for Doubtful Accounts		42,500
					Uncollectible accounts estimate ($3,400,000 × 1.25% = $42,500).		

The primary differences between the direct write-off and allowance methods are summarized in Exhibit 5.

EXHIBIT 5 **Direct Write-Off and Allowance Methods**

	Direct Write-Off Method	Allowance Method
Bad debt expense is recorded	When a specific customer account is determined to be uncollectible.	Using an estimate based on (1) a percent of sales or (2) an analysis of receivables.
Allowance account	No allowance account is used.	The allowance account is used.
Primary users	Small companies and companies with few receivables.	Large companies and those with a large amount of receivables.

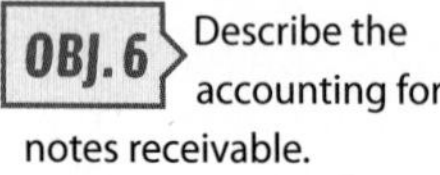
Describe the accounting for notes receivable.

Notes Receivable

A note has some advantages over an account receivable. By signing a note, the debtor recognizes the debt and agrees to pay it according to its terms. Thus, a note is a stronger legal claim.

Characteristics of Notes Receivable

A promissory note is a written promise to pay the face amount, usually with interest, on demand or at a date in the future.[2] Characteristics of a promissory note are as follows:

1. The *maker* is the party making the promise to pay.
2. The *payee* is the party to whom the note is payable.

2 You may see references to non-interest-bearing notes. Such notes are not widely used and carry an assumed or implicit interest rate.

3. The *face amount* is the amount for which the note is written on its face.
4. The *issuance date* is the date a note is issued.
5. The *due date* or *maturity date* is the date the note is to be paid.
6. The *term* of a note is the amount of time between the issuance and due dates.
7. The *interest rate* is that rate of interest that must be paid on the face amount for the term of the note.

Exhibit 6 illustrates a promissory note.

Promissory Note EXHIBIT 6

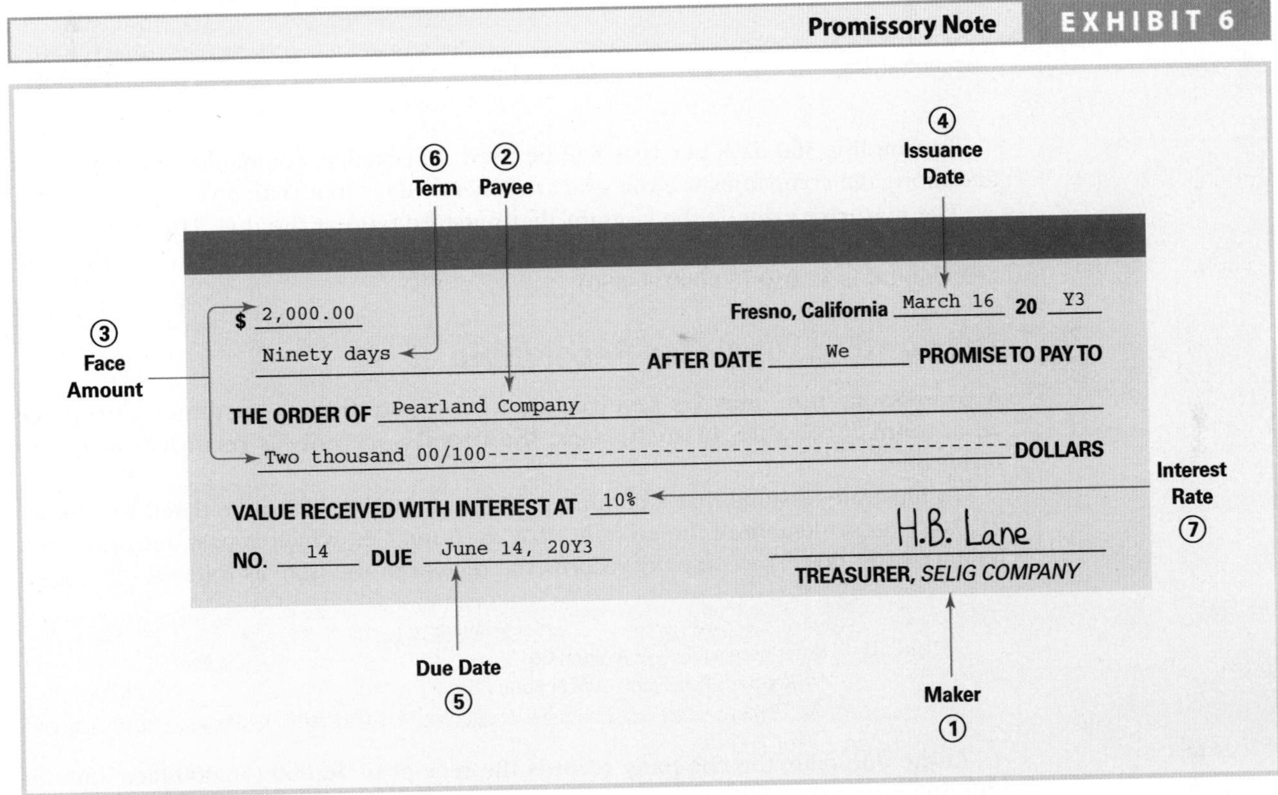

The maker of the note is Selig Company, and the payee is Pearland Company. The face value of the note is $2,000, the interest rate is 10%, and the issuance date is March 16, 20Y3. The term of the note is 90 days, which results in a due date of June 14, 20Y3, computed as follows and shown in Exhibit 7:

Days in March	31 days
Minus issuance date of note	16
Days remaining in March	15 days
Add days in April	30
Add days in May	31
Add days in June (due date of June 14)	14
Term of note	90 days

The interest on a note is computed as follows:

Interest = Face Amount × Interest Rate × (Term ÷ 360 days)

The interest rate is stated on an annual (yearly) basis, while the term is expressed as days. Thus, the interest on the note in Exhibit 6 is computed as follows:

Interest = $2,000 × 10% × (90 ÷ 360) = $50

EXHIBIT 7

Determining Due Date of Promissory Note

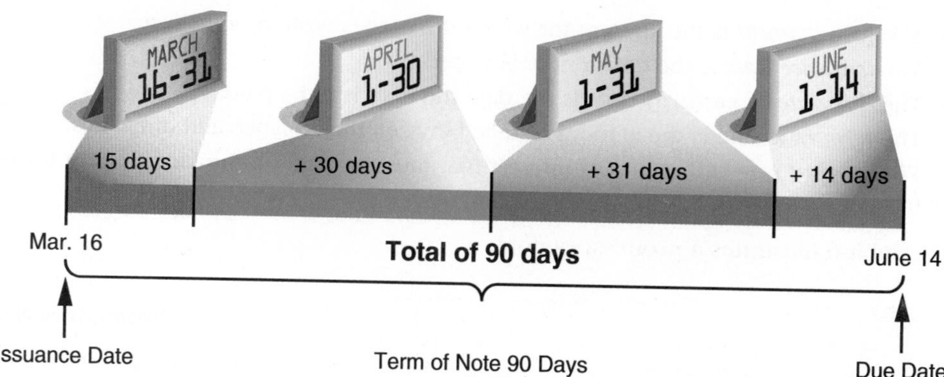

To simplify, 360 days per year will be used. In practice, companies such as banks and mortgage companies use the exact number of days in a year, 365.

The **maturity value** is the amount that must be paid at the due date of the note, which is the sum of the face amount and the interest. The maturity value of the note in Exhibit 6 is $2,050 ($2,000 + $50).

Accounting for Notes Receivable

A promissory note may be received by a company from a customer to replace an account receivable. In such cases, the promissory note is recorded as a note receivable.[3]

To illustrate, assume that a company accepts a 30-day, 12% note dated November 21, 20Y1, in settlement of the account of W. A. Bunn Co., which is past due and has a balance of $6,000. The company records the receipt of the note as follows:

20Y1					
Nov.	21	Notes Receivable—W. A. Bunn Co.		6,000	
		Accounts Receivable—W. A. Bunn Co.			6,000

At the due date, the company records the receipt of $6,060 ($6,000 face amount plus $60 interest) as follows:

20Y1					
Dec.	21	Cash		6,060	
		Notes Receivable—W. A. Bunn Co.			6,000
		Interest Revenue			60
		[$6,060 = $6,000 + ($6,000 × 12% × 30 ÷ 360)].			

If the maker of a note fails to pay the note on the due date, the note is a **dishonored note receivable**. A company that holds a dishonored note transfers the face amount of the note plus any interest due back to an accounts receivable account. For example, assume that the $6,000, 30-day, 12% note received from W. A. Bunn Co. and recorded on November 21 is dishonored. The company holding the note transfers the note and interest back to the customer's account as follows:

20Y1					
Dec.	21	Accounts Receivable—W. A. Bunn Co.		6,060	
		Notes Receivable—W. A. Bunn Co.			6,000
		Interest Revenue			60

3 The accounting for notes payable is described and illustrated in Chapter 14.

The company has earned the interest of $60, even though the note is dishonored. If the account receivable is uncollectible, the company will write off $6,060 against Allowance for Doubtful Accounts.

A company receiving a note should record an adjusting entry for any accrued interest at the end of the period. For example, assume that Crawford Company issues a $4,000, 90-day, 12% note dated December 1, 20Y4, to settle its account receivable. If the accounting period ends on December 31, the company receiving the note would record the following entries:

20Y4				
Dec.	1	Notes Receivable—Crawford Company	4,000	
		Accounts Receivable—Crawford Company		4,000
	31	Interest Receivable	40	
		Interest Revenue		40
		Accrued interest ($4,000 × 12% × 30 ÷ 360).		
20Y5				
Mar.	1	Cash	4,120	
		Notes Receivable—Crawford Company		4,000
		Interest Receivable		40
		Interest Revenue		80
		Total interest of $120 ($4,000 × 12% × 90 ÷ 360).		

The interest revenue account is closed at the end of each accounting period. The amount of interest revenue is normally reported in the Other Revenue section of the income statement.

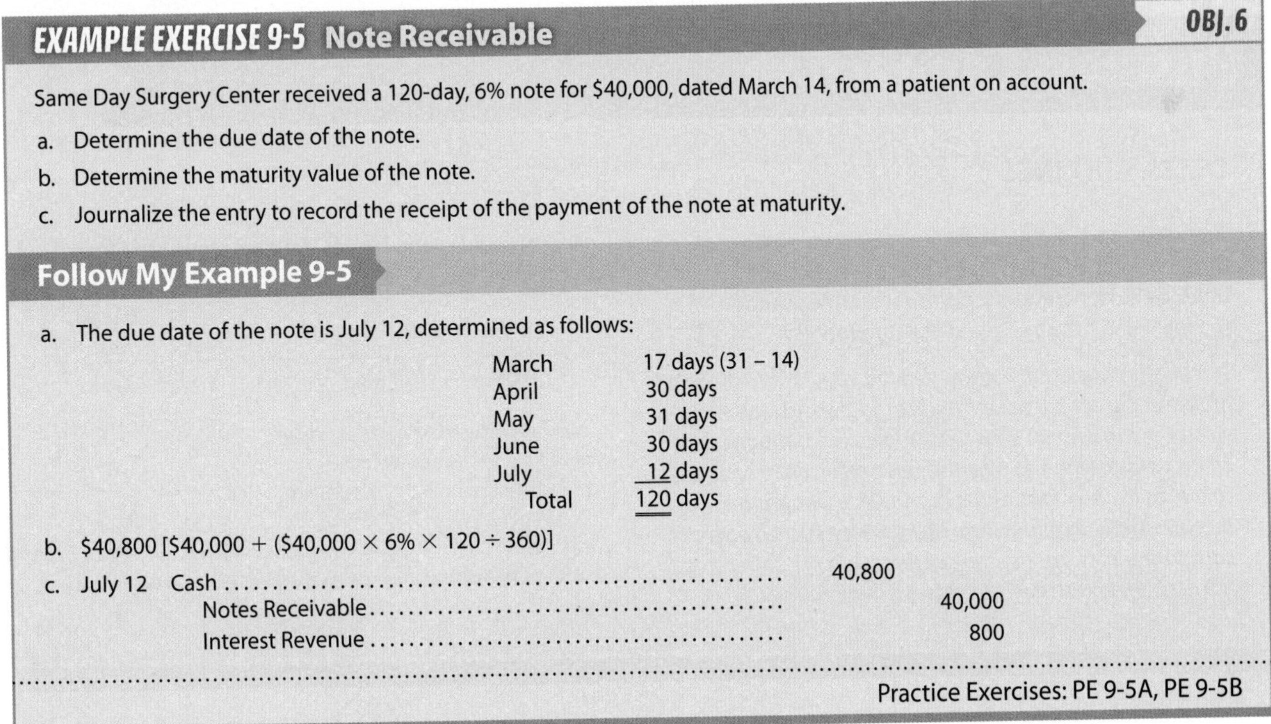

EXAMPLE EXERCISE 9-5 Note Receivable

OBJ. 6

Same Day Surgery Center received a 120-day, 6% note for $40,000, dated March 14, from a patient on account.

a. Determine the due date of the note.

b. Determine the maturity value of the note.

c. Journalize the entry to record the receipt of the payment of the note at maturity.

Follow My Example 9-5

a. The due date of the note is July 12, determined as follows:

March	17 days (31 – 14)
April	30 days
May	31 days
June	30 days
July	12 days
Total	120 days

b. $40,800 [$40,000 + ($40,000 × 6% × 120 ÷ 360)]

c. July 12	Cash	40,800	
	Notes Receivable		40,000
	Interest Revenue		800

Practice Exercises: PE 9-5A, PE 9-5B

OBJ. 7 Describe the reporting of receivables on the balance sheet.

Reporting Receivables on the Balance Sheet

All receivables that are expected to be realized in cash within a year are reported in the Current Assets section of the balance sheet. Current assets are normally reported in the order of their liquidity, beginning with cash and cash equivalents.

The balance sheet presentation for receivables for **Mornin' Joe** follows:

Mornin' Joe
Balance Sheet
December 31, 20Y6

Assets

Current assets:		
Cash and cash equivalents		$235,000
Accounts receivable	$305,000	
Less allowance for doubtful accounts	12,300	292,700

Link to Post

Post writes off a receivable against the allowance account when a customer files bankruptcy or is deemed to be uncollectible based upon the company's evaluation of the customer's solvency.

In Mornin' Joe's financial statements, the allowance for doubtful accounts is subtracted from accounts receivable. Some companies report receivables at their net realizable value with a note showing the amount of the allowance.

Other disclosures related to receivables are reported either on the face of the financial statements or in the financial statement notes. Such disclosures include the market (fair) value of the receivables. In addition, if unusual credit risks exist within the receivables, the nature of the risks are disclosed. For example, if the majority of the receivables are due from one customer or are due from customers located in one area of the country or one industry, these facts are disclosed.[4]

Business Connection

DELTA AIR LINES

Delta Air Lines is a major air carrier that services cities throughout the United States and the world. In its operations, Delta generates accounts receivable as reported in the following note to its financial statements:

Our accounts receivable are generated largely from the sale of passenger airline tickets and cargo transportation services, the majority of which are processed through major credit card companies. We also have receivables from the sale of mileage credits under our SkyMiles Program to participating airlines and non-airline businesses such as credit card companies, hotels, and car rental agencies. The credit risk associated with our receivables is minimal.

In a recent balance sheet, Delta reported the following accounts receivable (in millions):

	Dec. 31, Year 2	Dec. 31, Year 1
Current Assets:		
⋮		
Accounts receivable, net of an allowance for uncollectible accounts of $12 at December 31 (Year 2) and December 31 (Year 1)	$2,314	$2,377

Source: Delta Air Lines, Inc., *Form 10-K for the Fiscal Year Ended December 31, 2018.*

4 *FASB Accounting Standards Codification*, Section 210-10-50.

Financial Analysis and Interpretation: Accounts Receivable Turnover and Days' Sales in Receivables

OBJ. 8 Describe and illustrate the use of accounts receivable turnover and days' sales in receivables to evaluate a company's efficiency in collecting its receivables.

FAI

Two financial measures that are especially useful in evaluating efficiency in collecting receivables are the following:

- the accounts receivable turnover
- the days' sales in receivables

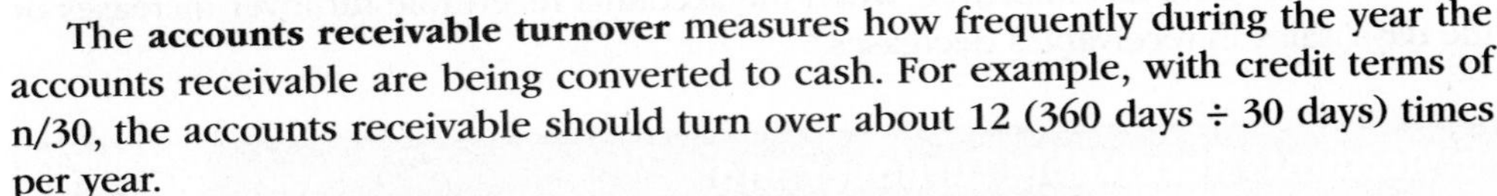

The **accounts receivable turnover** measures how frequently during the year the accounts receivable are being converted to cash. For example, with credit terms of n/30, the accounts receivable should turn over about 12 (360 days ÷ 30 days) times per year.

The accounts receivable turnover is computed as follows:[5]

$$\text{Accounts Receivable Turnover} = \frac{\text{Sales}}{\text{Average Accounts Receivable}}$$

The average accounts receivable can be determined by using monthly data or by simply adding the beginning and ending accounts receivable balances and dividing by two. For example, using the following financial data (in millions) for **Post**, the Year 2 and Year 1 accounts receivable turnover is 13.21 and 12.03, computed as follows:

	Year 2	Year 1
Sales	$6,257	$5,226
Accounts receivable:		
Beginning of year	482	387
End of year	465	482
Average accounts receivable:		
($482 + $465) ÷ 2	473.5	
($387 + $482) ÷ 2		434.5
Accounts receivable turnover:*		
$6,257 ÷ $473.5	13.21	
$5,226 ÷ $434.5		12.03

* Rounded to two decimal places.

The accounts receivable turnover has increased in Year 2. This suggests that Post was more efficient in collecting customer accounts in Year 2.

The **days' sales in receivables** is an estimate of the length of time the accounts receivable have been outstanding. With credit terms of n/30, the days' sales in receivables should be about 30 days. It is computed as follows:[6]

$$\text{Days' Sales in Receivables} = \frac{\text{Average Accounts Receivable}}{\text{Average Daily Sales}}$$

Average daily sales are determined by dividing sales by 365 days.[7] For example, using the preceding data for Post, the days' sales in receivables of 27.7 for Year 2 and 30.4 for Year 1 are computed as follows:

5 If known, credit sales can be used in the numerator. However, because credit sales are not normally disclosed to external users, most analysts use sales in the numerator.

6 Days' sales in receivables may also be computed as 365 days divided by the accounts receivable turnover.

7 We use 365 days for all computations involving real-world companies and data. We do this because it highlights differences among companies and because computations using real-world data normally require rounding.

	Year 2	Year 1
Average daily sales:*		
$6,257 ÷ 365	17.1	
$5,226 ÷ 365		14.3
Days' sales in receivables:*		
$473.5 ÷ 17.1	27.7	
$434.5 ÷ 14.3		30.4

*Rounded to one decimal place.

The days' sales in receivables confirms that Post's efficiency in collecting accounts receivable increased from Year 1 to Year 2. Generally, the efficiency in collecting accounts receivable has improved when the accounts receivable turnover increases or the days' sales in receivables decreases.[8]

EXAMPLE EXERCISE 9-6 Accounts Receivable Turnover and Days' Sales in Receivables

OBJ. 8

Financial statement data for years ending December 31 for Osterman Company follow:

	20Y9	20Y8
Sales	$4,284,000	$3,040,000
Accounts receivable:		
Beginning of year	550,000	400,000
End of year	640,000	550,000

Follow My Example 9-6

a. Determine the accounts receivable turnover for 20Y9 and 20Y8.

b. Determine the days' sales in receivables for 20Y9 and 20Y8. Use 365 days and round to one decimal place.

c. Does the change in accounts receivable turnover and the days' sales in receivables from 20Y8 to 20Y9 indicate a favorable or unfavorable change?

a. Accounts receivable turnover:

	20Y9	20Y8
Average accounts receivable:		
($550,000 + $640,000) ÷ 2	$595,000	
($400,000 + $550,000) ÷ 2		$475,000
Accounts receivable turnover:		
$4,284,000 ÷ $595,000	7.2	
$3,040,000 ÷ $475,000		6.4

b. Days' sales in receivables:

	20Y9	20Y8
Average daily sales:		
$4,284,000 ÷ 365 days	$11,737.0	
$3,040,000 ÷ 365 days		$8,328.8
Days' sales in receivables:		
$595,000 ÷ $11,737.0	50.7 days	
$475,000 ÷ $8,328.8		57.0 days

c. The increase in the accounts receivable turnover from 6.4 to 7.2 and the decrease in the days' sales in receivables from 57.0 days to 50.7 days indicate favorable changes in the efficiency of collecting accounts receivable.

Practice Exercises: PE 9-6A, PE 9-6B

8 Post's days in receivables could be computed by dividing 365 days by the accounts receivable turnover ratio. For example, Year 2 days' sales in receivables could be computed as 27.6 = 365 days ÷ 13.21 (difference from 27.7 due to rounding).

At a Glance 9

OBJ. 1 Describe the common classes of receivables.

Key Points *Receivables* includes all money claims against other entities. Receivables are normally classified as accounts receivable, notes receivable, or other receivables.

Learning Outcomes	Example Exercises	Practice Exercises
• Define the term *receivables*.		
• List some common classifications of receivables.		

OBJ. 2 Describe the accounting for uncollectible receivables.

Key Points The operating expense recorded from uncollectible receivables is called *bad debt expense*. The two methods of accounting for uncollectible receivables are the direct write-off method and the allowance method.

Learning Outcomes	Example Exercises	Practice Exercises
• Describe how a company may shift the risk of uncollectible receivables to other companies.		
• List factors that indicate an account receivable is uncollectible.		
• Describe two methods of accounting for uncollectible accounts receivable.		

OBJ. 3 Describe the direct write-off method of accounting for uncollectible receivables.

Key Points Under the direct write-off method, the entry to write off an account debits Bad Debt Expense and credits Accounts Receivable. Neither an allowance account nor an adjusting entry is needed at the end of the period.

Learning Outcomes	Example Exercises	Practice Exercises
• Prepare journal entries to write off an account, using the direct write-off method.	**EE9-1**	**PE9-1A, 9-1B**
• Prepare journal entries for the reinstatement and collection of an account previously written off.	**EE9-1**	**PE9-1A, 9-1B**

OBJ. 4 Describe the allowance method of accounting for uncollectible receivables.

Key Points Under the allowance method, an adjusting entry is made for uncollectible accounts. When an account is determined to be uncollectible, it is written off against the allowance account. The allowance account is a contra asset account that normally has a credit balance after the adjusting entry has been posted.

The estimate of uncollectibles may be based on a percent of sales or an analysis of receivables. Exhibit 3 compares and contrasts these two methods.

(*Continued*)

Learning Outcomes	Example Exercises	Practice Exercises
• Prepare journal entries to write off an account, using the allowance method.	EE9-2	PE9-2A, 9-2B
• Prepare journal entries for the reinstatement and collection of an account previously written off.	EE9-2	PE9-2A, 9-2B
• Determine the adjustment for uncollectible accounts, bad debt expense, and net realizable value of accounts receivable, using the percent of sales method.	EE9-3	PE9-3A, 9-3B
• Determine the adjustment for uncollectible accounts, bad debt expense, and net realizable value of accounts receivable, using the analysis of receivables method.	EE9-4	PE9-4A, 9-4B

OBJ. 5 Compare the direct write-off and allowance methods of accounting for uncollectible accounts.

Key Points Exhibit 4 illustrates the differences between the direct write-off and allowance methods of accounting for uncollectible accounts.

Learning Outcomes	Example Exercises	Practice Exercises
• Describe the differences in accounting for uncollectible accounts under the direct write-off and allowance methods.		
• Record journal entries, using the direct write-off and allowance methods.		

OBJ. 6 Describe the accounting for notes receivable.

Key Points A note received to settle an account receivable is recorded as a debit to Notes Receivable and a credit to Accounts Receivable. When a note is paid at maturity, Cash is debited, Notes Receivable is credited, and Interest Revenue is credited. If the maker of a note fails to pay, the dishonored note is recorded by debiting an account receivable for the amount due from the maker of the note.

Learning Outcomes	Example Exercises	Practice Exercises
• Describe the characteristics of a note receivable.		
• Determine the due date and maturity value of a note receivable.	EE9-5	PE9-5A, 9-5B
• Prepare journal entries for the receipt of the payment of a note receivable.	EE9-5	PE9-5A, 9-5B
• Prepare a journal entry for the dishonored note receivable.		

OBJ. 7 Describe the reporting of receivables on the balance sheet.

Key Points All receivables that are expected to be realized in cash within a year are reported in the Current Assets section of the balance sheet. In addition to the allowance for doubtful accounts, additional receivable disclosures include the market (fair) value and unusual credit risks.

Learning Outcomes	*Example Exercises*	*Practice Exercises*
• Describe how receivables are reported in the Current Assets section of the balance sheet.		
• Describe the disclosures related to receivables that should be reported in the financial statements.		

OBJ. 8 Describe and illustrate the use of accounts receivable turnover and days' sales in receivables to evaluate a company's efficiency in collecting its receivables.

Key Points Two financial measures that are especially useful in evaluating efficiency in collecting receivables are (1) the accounts receivable turnover and (2) the days' sales in receivables. Generally, the efficiency in collecting accounts receivable has improved when the accounts receivable turnover increases or there is a decrease in the days' sales in receivables.

Learning Outcomes	*Example Exercises*	*Practice Exercises*
• Describe two measures of the efficiency of managing receivables.		
• Compute and interpret the accounts receivable turnover and the days' sales in receivables.	**EE9-6**	**PE9-6A, 9-6B**

Illustrative Problem

Ditzler Company, a construction supply company, uses the allowance method of accounting for uncollectible accounts receivable. Selected transactions completed by Ditzler Company for the year ending December 31, 20Y2, are as follows:

Feb. 1. Sold merchandise on account to Ames Co., $8,000. The cost of the merchandise sold was $4,500.

Mar. 15. Accepted a 60-day, 12% note for $8,000 from Ames Co. on account.

Apr. 9. Wrote off a $2,500 account from Dorset Co. as uncollectible.

21. Loaned $7,500 cash to Jill Klein, receiving a 90-day, 14% note.

May 14. Received the interest due from Ames Co. and a new 90-day, 14% note as a renewal of the loan. (Record both the debit and the credit to the notes receivable account.)

June 13. Reinstated the account of Dorset Co., written off on April 9, and received $2,500 in full payment.

July 20. Jill Klein dishonored her note.

Aug. 12. Received from Ames Co. the amount due on its note of May 14.

19. Received from Jill Klein the amount owed on the dishonored note, plus interest for 30 days at 15%, computed on the maturity value of the note.

(Continued)

Dec. 16. Accepted a 60-day, 12% note for $12,000 from Global Company on account.
31. It is estimated that 3% of the credit sales of $1,375,000 for the year ended December 31 will be uncollectible.

Instructions

1. Journalize the transactions.
2. Journalize the adjusting entry to record the accrued interest on December 31, 20Y2, on the Global Company note.

Solution

1.

20Y2					
Feb.	1	Accounts Receivable—Ames Co.		8,000.00	
		Sales			8,000.00
	1	Cost of Merchandise Sold		4,500.00	
		Merchandise Inventory			4,500.00
Mar.	15	Notes Receivable—Ames Co.		8,000.00	
		Accounts Receivable—Ames Co.			8,000.00
Apr.	9	Allowance for Doubtful Accounts		2,500.00	
		Accounts Receivable—Dorset Co.			2,500.00
	21	Notes Receivable—Jill Klein		7,500.00	
		Cash			7,500.00
May	14	Notes Receivable—Ames Co.		8,000.00	
		Cash		160.00	
		Notes Receivable—Ames Co.			8,000.00
		Interest Revenue			160.00
		($8,000 × 12% × 60 ÷ 360).			
June	13	Accounts Receivable—Dorset Co.		2,500.00	
		Allowance for Doubtful Accounts			2,500.00
	13	Cash		2,500.00	
		Accounts Receivable—Dorset Co.			2,500.00
July	20	Accounts Receivable—Jill Klein		7,762.50	
		Notes Receivable—Jill Klein			7,500.00
		Interest Revenue			262.50
		($7,500 × 14% × 90 ÷ 360).			
Aug.	12	Cash		8,280.00	
		Notes Receivable—Ames Co.			8,000.00
		Interest Revenue			280.00
		($8,000 × 14% × 90 ÷ 360).			
	19	Cash		7,859.53	
		Accounts Receivable—Jill Klein			7,762.50
		Interest Revenue			97.03
		($7,762.50 × 15% × 30 ÷ 360).			
Dec.	16	Notes Receivable—Global Company		12,000.00	
		Accounts Receivable—Global Company			12,000.00
	31	Bad Debt Expense		41,250.00	
		Allowance for Doubtful Accounts			41,250.00
		Uncollectible accounts estimate			
		($1,375,000 × 3%).			

2.

20Y2					
Dec.	31	Interest Receivable		60.00	
		Interest Revenue			60.00
		Accrued interest			
		($12,000 × 12% × 15 ÷ 360).			

Key Terms

accounts receivable (446)
accounts receivable turnover (463)
aging the receivables (454)
Allowance for Doubtful Accounts (449)
allowance method (447)
bad debt expense (447)
days' sales in receivables (463)
direct write-off method (447)
dishonored note receivable (460)
maturity value (460)
net realizable value (449)
notes receivable (446)
receivables (446)

Discussion Questions

1. What are the three classifications of receivables?
2. Dan's Hardware is a small hardware store in the rural township of Twin Bridges. It rarely extends credit to its customers in the form of an account receivable. The few customers who are allowed to carry accounts receivable are long-time residents of Twin Bridges with a history of doing business at Dan's Hardware. What method of accounting for uncollectible receivables should Dan's Hardware use? Why?
3. What kind of an account (asset, liability, etc.) is Allowance for Doubtful Accounts, and is its normal balance a debit or a credit?
4. After the accounts are adjusted and closed at the end of the fiscal year, Accounts Receivable has a balance of $673,400 and Allowance for Doubtful Accounts has a balance of $11,900. Describe how the accounts receivable and the allowance for doubtful accounts are reported on the balance sheet.
5. A firm has consistently adjusted its allowance account at the end of the fiscal year by adding a fixed percent of the period's sales on account. After seven years, the balance in Allowance for Doubtful Accounts has become very large in relation to the balance in Accounts Receivable. Give two possible explanations.
6. Which of the two methods of estimating uncollectibles provides for the most accurate estimate of the current net realizable value of the receivables?
7. Neptune Company issued a note receivable to Sailfish Company. (a) Who is the payee? (b) What is the title of the account used by Sailfish Company in recording the note?
8. If a note provides for payment of principal of $85,000 and interest at the rate of 6%, will the interest amount to $5,100? Explain.
9. The maker of a $240,000, 6%, 90-day note receivable failed to pay the note on the due date of November 30. What accounts should be debited and credited by the payee to record the dishonored note receivable?
10. The note receivable dishonored in Discussion Question 9 is paid on December 30 by the maker, plus interest for 30 days at 9%. What entry should be made to record the receipt of the payment?

Practice Exercises

Example Exercises

SHOW ME HOW

EE 9-1 *p. 449*

PE 9-1A Direct write-off method **OBJ. 3**

Journalize the following transactions, using the direct write-off method of accounting for uncollectible receivables:

Apr. 15. Received $1,800 from Joe Brown and wrote off the remainder owed of $2,700 as uncollectible.

Aug. 7. Reinstated the account of Joe Brown and received $2,700 cash in full payment.

SHOW ME HOW

EE 9-1 *p. 449*

PE 9-1B Direct write-off method **OBJ. 3**

Journalize the following transactions, using the direct write-off method of accounting for uncollectible receivables:

Oct. 2. Received $1,140 from Elita Ramirez and wrote off the remainder owed of $2,570 as uncollectible.

Dec. 20. Reinstated the account of Elita Ramirez and received $2,570 cash in full payment.

SHOW ME HOW

EE 9-2 *p. 451*

PE 9-2A Allowance method **OBJ. 4**

Journalize the following transactions, using the allowance method of accounting for uncollectible receivables:

Apr. 15. Received $1,800 from Joe Brown and wrote off the remainder owed of $2,700 as uncollectible.

Aug. 7. Reinstated the account of Joe Brown and received $2,700 cash in full payment.

SHOW ME HOW

EE 9-2 *p. 451*

PE 9-2B Allowance method **OBJ. 4**

Journalize the following transactions, using the allowance method of accounting for uncollectible receivables:

Oct. 2. Received $1,140 from Elita Ramirez and wrote off the remainder owed of $2,570 as uncollectible.

Dec. 20. Reinstated the account of Elita Ramirez and received $2,570 cash in full payment.

SHOW ME HOW

EE 9-3 *p. 453*

PE 9-3A Percent of sales method **OBJ. 4**

At the end of the current year, Accounts Receivable has a balance of $2,450,000, Allowance for Doubtful Accounts has a credit balance of $14,860, and sales for the year total $31,600,000. Bad debt expense is estimated at ½ of 1% of sales.

Determine (a) the amount of the adjusting entry for uncollectible accounts; (b) the adjusted balances of Accounts Receivable, Allowance for Doubtful Accounts, and Bad Debt Expense; and (c) the net realizable value of accounts receivable.

SHOW ME HOW

EE 9-3 *p. 453*

PE 9-3B Percent of sales method **OBJ. 4**

At the end of the current year, Accounts Receivable has a balance of $4,770,000, Allowance for Doubtful Accounts has a debit balance of $17,230, and sales for the year total $63,800,000. Bad debt expense is estimated at ¾ of 1% of sales.

Determine (a) the amount of the adjusting entry for uncollectible accounts; (b) the adjusted balances of Accounts Receivable, Allowance for Doubtful Accounts, and Bad Debt Expense; and (c) the net realizable value of accounts receivable.

EE 9-4 *p. 456*

PE 9-4A Analysis of receivables method **OBJ. 4**

At the end of the current year, Accounts Receivable has a balance of $2,450,000, Allowance for Doubtful Accounts has a credit balance of $14,860, and sales for the year total $31,600,000. Using the aging method, the balance of Allowance for Doubtful Accounts is estimated as $250,000.

Determine (a) the amount of the adjusting entry for uncollectible accounts; (b) the adjusted balances of Accounts Receivable, Allowance for Doubtful Accounts, and Bad Debt Expense; and (c) the net realizable value of accounts receivable.

EE 9-4 *p. 456*

PE 9-4B Analysis of receivables method **OBJ. 4**

At the end of the current year, Accounts Receivable has a balance of $4,770,000, Allowance for Doubtful Accounts has a debit balance of $17,230, and sales for the year total $63,800,000. Using the aging method, the balance of Allowance for Doubtful Accounts is estimated as $380,000.

Determine (a) the amount of the adjusting entry for uncollectible accounts; (b) the adjusted balances of Accounts Receivable, Allowance for Doubtful Accounts, and Bad Debt Expense; and (c) the net realizable value of accounts receivable.

EE 9-5 *p. 461*

PE 9-5A Note receivable **OBJ. 6**

Linstrum Company received a 60-day, 9% note for $56,000, dated July 23, from a customer on account.

a. Determine the due date of the note.

b. Determine the maturity value of the note.

c. Journalize the entry to record the receipt of the payment of the note at maturity.

EE 9-5 *p. 461*

PE 9-5B Note receivable **OBJ. 6**

Maggiano Supply Company received a 120-day, 6% note for $420,000, dated June 12, from a customer on account.

a. Determine the due date of the note.

b. Determine the maturity value of the note.

c. Journalize the entry to record the receipt of the payment of the note at maturity.

EE 9-6 *p. 464*

PE 9-6A Accounts receivable turnover and days' sales in receivables **OBJ. 8**

Financial statement data for years ending December 31 for Schultze-Solutions Company follow:

	20Y2	20Y1
Sales	$1,848,000	$1,881,000
Accounts receivable:		
Beginning of year	195,300	184,700
End of year	224,700	195,300

a. Determine the accounts receivable turnover for 20Y2 and 20Y1. Round accounts receivable turnover to one decimal place.

b. Determine the days' sales in receivables for 20Y2 and 20Y1. Use 365 days and round to one decimal place.

c. Does the change in accounts receivable turnover and the days' sales in receivables from 20Y1 to 20Y2 indicate a favorable or unfavorable change?

EE 9-6 *p. 464*

PE 9-6B Accounts receivable turnover and days' sales in receivables **OBJ. 8**

Financial statement data for years ending December 31 for Cinderella Company follow:

	20Y9	20Y8
Sales	$9,525,000	$7,616,000
Accounts receivable:		
Beginning of year	715,000	645,000
End of year	785,000	715,000

(Continued)

a. Determine the accounts receivable turnover for 20Y9 and 20Y8. Round accounts receivable turnover to one decimal place.

b. Determine the days' sales in receivables for 20Y9 and 20Y8. Use 365 days and round to one decimal place.

c. Does the change in accounts receivable turnover and the days' sales in receivables from 20Y8 to 20Y9 indicate a favorable or unfavorable change?

Exercises

EX 9-1 Classifications of receivables **OBJ. 1**

Boeing is one of the world's major aerospace firms with operations involving commercial aircraft, military aircraft, missiles, satellite systems, and information and battle management systems. As of a recent year, Boeing had $1,877 million of receivables involving U.S. government contracts and $2,059 million of receivables involving commercial aircraft customers such as **Delta Air Lines** and **United Airlines**.

Should Boeing report these receivables separately in the financial statements or combine them into one overall accounts receivable amount? Explain.

EX 9-2 Nature of uncollectible accounts **OBJ. 2**

✔ a. 12.1%

MGM Resorts International owns and operates hotels and casinos including the MGM Grand and the Bellagio in Las Vegas, Nevada. As of a recent year, MGM reported accounts receivable of $747,981,000 and allowance for doubtful accounts of $90,775,000. **Johnson & Johnson** manufactures and sells a wide range of health care products including Band-Aid® bandages and Tylenol®. As of a recent year, Johnson & Johnson reported accounts receivable of $14,346,000,000 and allowance for doubtful accounts of $248,000,000.

a. Compute the percentage of the allowance for doubtful accounts to the accounts receivable for MGM Resorts International. Round to one decimal place.

b. Compute the percentage of the allowance for doubtful accounts to the accounts receivable for Johnson & Johnson. Round to one decimal place.

c. Discuss possible reasons for the difference in the two ratios computed in (a) and (b).

SHOW ME HOW

EX 9-3 Entries for uncollectible accounts, using direct write-off method **OBJ. 3**

Journalize the following transactions in the accounts of Arrow Medical Co., a medical equipment company that uses the direct write-off method of accounting for uncollectible receivables:

Jan. 19. Sold merchandise on account to Dr. Sinclair Welby, $77,000. The cost of the merchandise sold was $52,600.

July 7. Received $30,800 from Dr. Sinclair Welby and wrote off the remainder owed on the sale of January 19 as uncollectible.

Nov. 2. Reinstated the account of Dr. Sinclair Welby that had been written off on July 7 and received $46,200 cash in full payment.

EX 9-4 Entries for uncollectible receivables, using allowance method **OBJ. 4**

Journalize the following transactions in the accounts of Arizona Interiors Company, a restaurant supply company that uses the allowance method of accounting for uncollectible receivables:

May 1. Sold merchandise on account to Taiwan Palace Co., $25,800. The cost of the merchandise sold was $15,300.

Aug. 30. Received $10,900 from Taiwan Palace Co. and wrote off the remainder owed on the sale of May 1 as uncollectible.

Dec. 8. Reinstated the account of Taiwan Palace Co. that had been written off on August 30 and received $14,900 cash in full payment.

EX 9-5 Entries to write off accounts receivable

OBJ. 3, 4

Capstone Solutions Company, a computer consulting firm, has decided to write off the $45,800 balance of an account owed by a customer, Philadelphia Inc. Journalize the entry to record the write-off, assuming that (a) the direct write-off method is used and (b) the allowance method is used.

EX 9-6 Providing for doubtful accounts

OBJ. 4

✔ a. $162,000

✔ b. $155,100

SHOW ME HOW

EXCEL ONLINE

At the end of the current year, the accounts receivable account has a debit balance of $2,700,000 and sales for the year total $32,400,000. Determine the amount of the adjusting entry to provide for doubtful accounts under each of the following assumptions:

a. The allowance account before adjustment has a debit balance of $27,100. Bad debt expense is estimated at ½ of 1% of sales.

b. The allowance account before adjustment has a debit balance of $27,100. An aging of the accounts in the customer ledger indicates estimated doubtful accounts of $128,000.

c. The allowance account before adjustment has a credit balance of $17,900. Bad debt expense is estimated at ¾ of 1% of sales.

d. The allowance account before adjustment has a credit balance of $17,900. An aging of the accounts in the customer ledger indicates estimated doubtful accounts of $279,000.

EX 9-7 Number of days past due

OBJ. 4

✔ Avalanche Auto, 84 days

EXCEL ONLINE

Toot Auto Supply distributes new and used automobile parts to local dealers throughout the Midwest. Toot's credit terms are n/30. As of the end of business on October 31, the following accounts receivable were past due:

Account	Due Date	Amount
Avalanche Auto	August 8	$12,000
Bales Auto	October 11	2,400
Derby Auto Repair	June 23	3,900
Lucky's Auto Repair	September 2	6,600
Pit Stop Auto	September 19	1,100
Reliable Auto Repair	July 15	9,750
Trident Auto	August 24	1,800
Valley Repair & Tow	May 17	4,000

Determine the number of days each account is past due as of October 31.

EX 9-8 Aging of receivables schedule

OBJ. 4

SHOW ME HOW

The accounts receivable clerk for Kirchhoff Industries prepared the following partially completed aging of receivables schedule as of the end of business on August 31:

	A	B	C	D	E	F	G
1			Not	Days Past Due			
2			Past				Over
3	Customer	Balance	Due	1–30	31–60	61–90	90
4	Academy Industries Inc.	3,000	3,000				
5	Ascent Company	4,500		4,500			
21	Zoot Company	5,000			5,000		
22	Subtotals	1,050,000	600,000	220,000	115,000	85,000	30,000
23							

(Continued)

The following accounts were unintentionally omitted from the aging schedule and not included in the preceding subtotals:

Customer	Balance	Due Date
Conover Industries	$30,000	March 22
Keystone Company	18,000	July 1
Moxie Creek Inc.	9,000	July 25
Rainbow Company	26,400	September 10
Swanson Company	46,600	August 3

a. Determine the number of days past due for each of the preceding accounts as of August 31.

b. Complete the aging of receivables schedule by adding the omitted accounts to the bottom of the schedule and updating the totals.

EX 9-9 Estimating allowance for doubtful accounts

OBJ. 4

✔ Allowance for doubtful accounts, $131,712

Kirchhoff Industries has a past history of uncollectible accounts, as follows. Estimate the allowance for doubtful accounts, based on the aging of receivables schedule you completed in Exercise 9-8.

Age Class	Percent Uncollectible
Not past due	2%
1–30 days past due	4
31–60 days past due	18
61–90 days past due	40
Over 90 days past due	75

EX 9-10 Adjustment for uncollectible accounts

OBJ. 4

Using data in Exercise 9-9, assume that the allowance for doubtful accounts for Kirchhoff Industries has a credit balance of $10,112 before adjustment on August 31. Journalize the adjusting entry for uncollectible accounts as of August 31.

EX 9-11 Estimating doubtful accounts

OBJ. 4

SHOW
ME HOW

Performance Bike Co. is a wholesaler of motorcycle supplies. An aging of the company's accounts receivable on December 31 and a historical analysis of the percentage of uncollectible accounts in each age category are as follows:

Age Interval	Balance	Percent Uncollectible
Not past due	$3,250,000	0.8%
1–30 days past due	1,050,000	2.4
31–60 days past due	780,000	7.0
61–90 days past due	320,000	18.0
91–180 days past due	240,000	34.0
Over 180 days past due	150,000	85.0
	$5,790,000	

Estimate the proper balance of the allowance for doubtful accounts as of December 31.

EX 9-12 Entry for uncollectible accounts

OBJ. 4

Using the data in Exercise 9-11, assume that the allowance for doubtful accounts for Performance Bike Co. had a debit balance of $28,400 as of December 31.

Journalize the adjusting entry for uncollectible accounts as of December 31.

EX 9-13 Entries for bad debt expense under the direct write-off and allowance methods

OBJ. 5

✔ c. $8,225 higher

SHOW ME HOW

The following selected transactions were taken from the records of Shipway Company for the first year of its operations ending December 31:

Apr. 13. Wrote off account of Dean Sheppard, $8,450.

May 15. Received $500 as partial payment on the $7,100 account of Dan Pyle. Wrote off the remaining balance as uncollectible.

July 27. Received $8,450 from Dean Sheppard, whose account had been written off on April 13. Reinstated the account and recorded the cash receipt.

Dec. 31. Wrote off the following accounts as uncollectible (record as one journal entry):

Paul Chapman	$2,225
Duane DeRosa	3,550
Teresa Galloway	4,770
Ernie Klatt	1,275
Marty Richey	1,690

31. If necessary, record the year-end adjusting entry for uncollectible accounts.

a. Journalize the transactions under the direct write-off method.

b. Journalize the transactions under the allowance method. Shipway Company uses the percent of credit sales method of estimating uncollectible accounts expense. Based on past history and industry averages, ¾% of credit sales are expected to be uncollectible. Shipway Company recorded $3,778,000 of credit sales during the year.

c. How much higher (lower) would Shipway Company's net income have been under the direct write-off method than under the allowance method?

EX 9-14 Entries for bad debt expense under the direct write-off and allowance methods

OBJ. 5

✔ c. $11,090 higher

SHOW ME HOW

The following selected transactions were taken from the records of Rustic Tables Company for the year ending December 31:

June 8. Wrote off account of Kathy Quantel, $8,440.

Aug. 14. Received $3,000 as partial payment on the $12,500 account of Rosalie Oakes. Wrote off the remaining balance as uncollectible.

Oct. 16. Received the $8,440 from Kathy Quantel, whose account had been written off on June 8. Reinstated the account and recorded the cash receipt.

Dec. 31. Wrote off the following accounts as uncollectible (record as one journal entry):

Wade Dolan	$4,600
Greg Gagne	3,600
Amber Kisko	7,150
Shannon Poole	2,975
Niki Spence	6,630

31. If necessary, record the year-end adjusting entry for uncollectible accounts.

a. Journalize the transactions under the direct write-off method.

b. Journalize the transactions under the allowance method, assuming that the allowance account had a beginning credit balance of $36,000 on January 1 and the company uses the analysis of receivables method. Rustic Tables Company prepared the following aging schedule for its accounts receivable:

Aging Class (Number of Days Past Due)	Receivables Balance on December 31	Estimated Percent of Uncollectible Accounts
0–30 days	$320,000	1%
31–60 days	110,000	3
61–90 days	24,000	10
91–120 days	18,000	33
More than 120 days	43,000	75
Total receivables	$515,000	

(Continued)

c. How much higher (lower) would Rustic Tables' net income have been under the direct write-off method than under the allowance method?

EX 9-15 Effect of doubtful accounts on net income **OBJ. 5**

During its first year of operations, Mack's Plumbing Supply Co. had sales of $3,250,000, wrote off $27,800 of accounts as uncollectible using the direct write-off method, and reported net income of $487,500. Determine what the net income would have been if the allowance method had been used and the company estimated that 1% of sales would be uncollectible.

EX 9-16 Effect of doubtful accounts on net income **OBJ. 5**

✔ b. $11,700 credit balance

Using the data in Exercise 9-15, assume that during the second year of operations, Mack's Plumbing Supply Co. had sales of $4,100,000, wrote off $34,000 of accounts as uncollectible using the direct write-off method, and reported net income of $600,000.

a. Determine what net income would have been in the second year if the allowance method (using 1% of sales) had been used in both the first and second years.

b. Determine what the balance of the allowance for doubtful accounts would have been at the end of the second year if the allowance method had been used in both the first and second years. *Hint:* Use an Allowance for Doubtful Accounts T account.

EX 9-17 Entries for bad debt expense under the direct write-off and allowance methods **OBJ. 5**

✔ c. $9,375 higher

SHOW ME HOW

Casebolt Company wrote off the following accounts receivable as uncollectible for the first year of its operations ending December 31:

Customer	Amount
Shawn Brooke	$ 4,650
Eve Denton	5,180
Art Malloy	11,050
Cassie Yost	9,120
Total	$30,000

a. Journalize the write-offs under the direct write-off method.

b. Journalize the write-offs under the allowance method. Also, journalize the adjusting entry for uncollectible accounts. The company recorded $5,250,000 of credit sales during the year. Based on past history and industry averages, ¾% of credit sales are expected to be uncollectible.

c. How much higher (lower) would Casebolt Company's net income have been under the direct write-off method than under the allowance method?

EX 9-18 Entries for bad debt expense under the direct write-off and allowance methods **OBJ. 5**

Seaforth International wrote off the following accounts receivable as uncollectible for the year ending December 31:

Customer	Amount
Kim Abel	$ 21,550
Lee Drake	33,925
Jenny Green	27,565
Mike Lamb	19,460
Total	$102,500

The company prepared the following aging schedule for its accounts receivable on December 31:

Aging Class (Number of Days Past Due)	Receivables Balance on December 31	Estimated Percent of Uncollectible Accounts
0–30 days	$ 715,000	1%
31–60 days	310,000	2
61–90 days	102,000	15
91–120 days	76,000	30
More than 120 days	97,000	60
Total receivables	$1,300,000	

a. Journalize the write-offs under the direct write-off method.

b. Journalize the write-offs and the year-end adjusting entry under the allowance method, assuming that the allowance account had a beginning credit balance of $95,000 on January 1 and the company uses the analysis of receivables method.

c. How much higher (lower) would Seaforth International's net income have been under the allowance method than under the direct write-off method?

✔ a. Apr. 10, $500

SHOW ME HOW

EXCEL ONLINE

EX 9-19 Determine due date and interest on notes — OBJ. 6

Determine the due date and the amount of interest due at maturity on the following notes:

	Date of Note	Face Amount	Interest Rate	Term of Note
a.	January 10*	$40,000	5%	90 days
b.	March 19	18,000	8	180 days
c.	June 5	90,000	7	30 days
d.	September 8	36,000	3	90 days
e.	November 20	27,000	4	60 days

*Assume that February has 28 days.

✔ b. $94,550

SHOW ME HOW

EX 9-20 Entries for notes receivable — OBJ. 6

Autumn Designs & Decorators issued a 120-day, 5% note for $93,000, dated April 13 to Zebra Furniture Company on account.

a. Determine the due date of the note.

b. Determine the maturity value of the note.

c. Journalize the entries to record the following: (1) receipt of the note by Zebra Furniture and (2) receipt of payment of the note at maturity.

EX 9-21 Entries for notes receivable — OBJ. 6

The series of five transactions recorded in the following T accounts were related to a sale to a customer on account and the receipt of the amount owed. Briefly describe each transaction.

Cash

	Debit		Credit
(e)	76,500		

Accounts Receivable

	Debit		Credit
(a)	75,000	(c)	75,000
(d)	75,400	(e)	75,400

Inventory

	Debit		Credit
		(b)	45,000

Sales

	Debit		Credit
		(a)	75,000

Notes Receivable

	Debit		Credit
(c)	75,000	(d)	75,000

Cost of Goods Sold

	Debit		Credit
(b)	45,000		

Interest Revenue

	Debit		Credit
		(d)	400
		(e)	1,100

EX 9-22 Entries for notes receivable, including year-end entries **OBJ. 6**

The following selected transactions were completed by Fasteners Inc. Co., a supplier of buttons and zippers for clothing:

20Y3

Nov. 21. Received from McKenna Outer Wear Co., on account, a $96,000, 60-day, 3% note dated November 21 in settlement of a past due account.

Dec. 31. Recorded an adjusting entry for accrued interest on the note of November 21.

20Y4

Jan. 20. Received payment of note and interest from McKenna Outer Wear Co.

Journalize the entries to record the transactions.

EX 9-23 Entries for receipt and dishonor of note receivable **OBJ. 6**

Journalize the following transactions of Trapper Jon's Productions:

June 23. Received a $48,000, 90-day, 8% note dated June 23 from Radon Express Co. on account.

Sept. 21. The note is dishonored by Radon Express Co.

Oct. 21. Received the amount due on the dishonored note plus interest for 30 days at 10% on the total amount charged to Radon Express Co. on September 21.

EX 9-24 Entries for receipt and dishonor of notes receivable **OBJ. 6**

Journalize the following transactions in the accounts of Safari Games Co., which operates a riverboat casino:

Apr. 18. Received a $60,000, 30-day, 7% note dated April 18 from Glenn Cross on account.

30. Received a $42,000, 60-day, 8% note dated April 30 from Rhoni Melville on account.

May 18. The note dated April 18 from Glenn Cross is dishonored, and the customer's account is charged for the note, including interest.

June 29. The note dated April 30 from Rhoni Melville is dishonored, and the customer's account is charged for the note, including interest.

Aug. 16. Cash is received for the amount due on the dishonored note dated April 18 plus interest for 90 days at 8% on the total amount debited to Glenn Cross on May 18.

Oct. 22. Wrote off against the allowance account the amount charged to Rhoni Melville on June 29 for the dishonored note dated April 30.

EX 9-25 Receivables on the balance sheet **OBJ. 7**

List any errors you can find in the following partial balance sheet:

Napa Vino Company
Balance Sheet
December 31, 20Y9

Assets		
Current assets:		
Cash		$ 78,500
Notes receivable	$ 300,000	
Less interest receivable	4,500	295,500
Accounts receivable	$1,200,000	
Plus allowance for doubtful accounts	11,500	1,211,500

EX 9-26 Accounts receivable turnover and days' sales in receivables **OBJ. 8**

✓ a. Year 2: 9.45

Ralph Lauren Corporation designs, markets, and distributes a variety of apparel, home decor, accessory, and fragrance products. The company's products include such brands as Polo by Ralph Lauren, Ralph Lauren Purple Label, Ralph Lauren, Polo Jeans Co., and Chaps. Polo Ralph Lauren reported the following (in thousands) for two recent years:

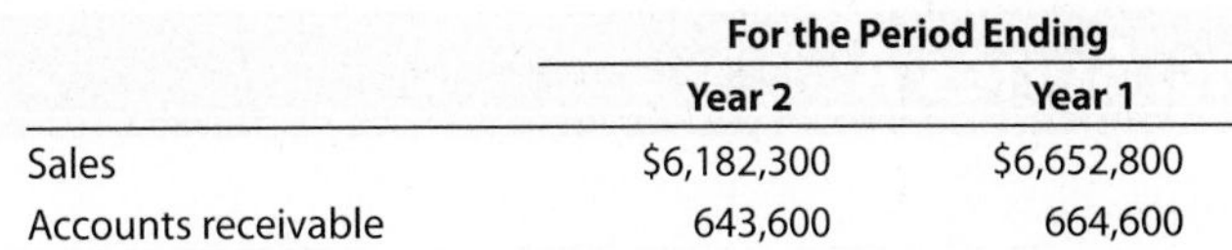

	For the Period Ending	
	Year 2	Year 1
Sales	$6,182,300	$6,652,800
Accounts receivable	643,600	664,600

Assume that accounts receivable (in thousands) were $770,700 at the beginning of Year 1.

a. Compute the accounts receivable turnover for Year 2 and Year 1. Round to two decimal places.

b. Compute the days' sales in receivables for Year 2 and Year 1. Use 365 days and round to one decimal place.

c. What conclusions can be drawn from these analyses regarding Ralph Lauren's efficiency in collecting receivables?

EX 9-27 Accounts receivable turnover and days' sales in receivables — OBJ. 8

✔ a. Year 2: 12.22

The **Campbell Soup Company** manufactures and markets food products throughout the world. The following sales and receivable data (in millions) were reported by Campbell Soup for two recent years:

	Year 2	Year 1
Sales	$8,685	$7,890
Accounts receivable	805	616

Assume that the accounts receivable were $638 million at the beginning of Year 1.

a. Compute the accounts receivable turnover for Year 2 and Year 1. Round average accounts receivable to one decimal place and accounts receivable turnover to two decimal places.

b. Compute the days' sales in receivables for Year 2 and Year 1. Use 365 days and round to one decimal place.

c. What conclusions can be drawn from these analyses regarding Campbell's efficiency in collecting receivables?

EX 9-28 Accounts receivable turnover and days' sales in receivables — OBJ. 8

American Eagle Outfitters, Inc. sells clothing, accessories, and personal care products for men and women through its retail stores. American Eagle reported the following data (in millions) for two recent years:

	Year 2	Year 1
Sales	$4,036	$3,796
Accounts receivable	93	78

Assume that accounts receivable were $87 million at the beginning of Year 1.

a. Compute the accounts receivable turnover for Year 2 and Year 1. Round to two decimal places.

b. Compute the days' sales in receivables for Year 2 and Year 1. Use 365 days and round to one decimal place.

c. What conclusions can be drawn from these analyses regarding American Eagle Outfitters' efficiency in collecting receivables?

EX 9-29 Accounts receivable turnover — OBJ. 8

Use the data in Exercises 9-27 and 9-28 to analyze the accounts receivable turnover ratios of the **Campbell Soup Company** and **American Eagle Outfitters, Inc.**

a. Compute the average accounts receivable turnover ratio for Campbell Soup and American Eagle for the years shown in Exercises 9-27 and 9-28.

b. Does Campbell Soup or American Eagle have the higher average accounts receivable turnover ratio?

c. Explain why the average turnover ratios are different in (b).

Problems: Series A

PR 9-1A Entries related to uncollectible accounts

OBJ. 4

✔ 3. $2,626,670

SHOW ME HOW

The following transactions were completed by Emmanuel Company during the current fiscal year ended December 31:

Jan. 29. Received 40% of the $17,000 balance owed by Jankovich Co., a bankrupt business, and wrote off the remainder as uncollectible.

Apr. 18. Reinstated the account of Vince Karm, which had been written off in the preceding year as uncollectible. Journalized the receipt of $7,560 cash in full payment of Karm's account.

Aug. 9. Wrote off the $22,380 balance owed by Golden Stallion Co., which has no assets.

Nov. 7. Reinstated the account of Wiley Co., which had been written off in the preceding year as uncollectible. Journalized the receipt of $13,220 cash in full payment of the account.

Dec. 31. Wrote off the following accounts as uncollectible (one entry): Claire Moon Inc., $22,860; Jet Set Co., $15,320; Randall Distributors, $41,460; Harmonic Audio, $18,890.

31. Based on an analysis of the $2,740,000 of accounts receivable, it was estimated that $113,330 will be uncollectible. Journalized the adjusting entry.

Instructions

1. Record the January 1 credit balance of $102,380 in a T account for Allowance for Doubtful Accounts.
2. Journalize the transactions. Post each entry that affects the following selected T accounts and determine the new balances:

   Allowance for Doubtful Accounts
   Bad Debt Expense
3. Determine the expected net realizable value of the accounts receivable as of December 31.
4. Assuming that instead of basing the provision for uncollectible accounts on an analysis of receivables the adjusting entry on December 31 had been based on an estimated expense of ½ of 1% of the sales of $24,900,000 for the year, determine the following:
   a. Bad debt expense for the year.
   b. Balance in the allowance account after the adjustment of December 31.
   c. Expected net realizable value of the accounts receivable as of December 31.

PR 9-2A Aging of receivables; estimating allowance for doubtful accounts

OBJ. 4

✔ 3. $121,000

Trophy Fish Company supplies flies and fishing gear to sporting goods stores and outfitters throughout the western United States. The accounts receivable clerk for Trophy Fish prepared the following partially completed aging of receivables schedule as of the end of business on December 31, 20Y6:

	A	B	C	D	E	F	G	H
1			Not	Days Past Due				
2			Past					
3	Customer	Balance	Due	1–30	31–60	61–90	91–120	Over 120
4	AAA Outfitters	20,000	20,000					
5	Brown Trout Fly Shop	7,500			7,500			
30	Zigs Fish Adventures	4,000		4,000				
31	Subtotals	1,300,000	750,000	290,000	120,000	40,000	20,000	80,000
32								

The following accounts were unintentionally omitted from the aging schedule:

Customer	Due Date	Balance
Adams Sports & Flies	May 22, 20Y6	$5,000
Blue Dun Flies	Oct. 10, 20Y6	4,900
Cicada Fish Co.	Sept. 29, 20Y6	8,400
Deschutes Sports	Oct. 20, 20Y6	7,000
Green River Sports	Nov. 7, 20Y6	3,500
Smith River Co.	Nov. 28, 20Y6	2,400
Western Trout Company	Dec. 7, 20Y6	6,800
Wolfe Sports	Jan. 20, 20Y7	4,400

Trophy Fish has a past history of uncollectible accounts by age category, as follows:

Age Class	Percent Uncollectible
Not past due	1%
1–30 days past due	2
31–60 days past due	10
61–90 days past due	30
91–120 days past due	40
Over 120 days past due	80

Instructions

1. Determine the number of days past due for each of the preceding accounts.
2. Complete the aging of receivables schedule by adding the omitted accounts to the bottom of the schedule and updating the totals.
3. Estimate the allowance for doubtful accounts, based on the aging of receivables schedule.
4. Assume that the allowance for doubtful accounts for Trophy Fish Company has a debit balance of $3,600 before adjustment on December 31, 20Y6. Journalize the adjusting entry for uncollectible accounts.
5. Assuming that the adjusting entry in (4) was inadvertently omitted, how would the omission affect the balance sheet and income statement?

PR 9-3A Compare two methods of accounting for uncollectible receivables OBJ. 3, 4, 5

✔ 1. Year 4: Balance of allowance account, end of year, $15,050

Call Systems Company, a telephone service and supply company, has just completed its fourth year of operations. The direct write-off method of recording bad debt expense has been used during the entire period. Because of substantial increases in sales volume and the amount of uncollectible accounts, the company is considering changing to the allowance method. Information is requested as to the effect that an annual provision of 1% of sales would have had on the amount of bad debt expense reported for each of the past four years. It is also considered desirable to know what the balance of Allowance for Doubtful Accounts would have been at the end of each year. The following data have been obtained from the accounts:

			Year of Origin of Accounts Receivable Written Off as Uncollectible			
Year	**Sales**	**Uncollectible Accounts Written Off**	**1st**	**2nd**	**3rd**	**4th**
1st	$ 900,000	$ 4,500	$4,500			
2nd	1,250,000	9,600	3,000	$6,600		
3rd	1,500,000	12,800	1,000	3,700	$8,100	
4th	2,200,000	16,550		1,500	4,300	$10,750

Instructions

1. Assemble the desired data, using the following column headings:

	Bad Debt Expense			
Year	**Expense Actually Reported**	**Expense Based on Estimate**	**Increase (Decrease) in Amount of Expense**	**Balance of Allowance Account, End of Year**

(Continued)

2. Experience during the first four years of operations indicated that the receivables either were collected within two years or had to be written off as uncollectible. Does the estimate of 1% of sales appear to be reasonably close to the actual experience with uncollectible accounts originating during the first two years? Explain.

PR 9-4A Details of notes receivable and related entries — OBJ. 6

✔ 1. Note 2: Due date, June 22; Interest due at maturity, $360

SHOW ME HOW

Flush Mate Co. wholesales bathroom fixtures. During the current fiscal year, Flush Mate Co. received the following notes:

	Date	Face Amount	Interest Rate	Term
1.	Mar. 6	$80,000	5%	45 days
2.	Apr. 23	24,000	9	60 days
3.	July 20	42,000	6	120 days
4.	Sept. 6	54,000	7	90 days
5.	Nov. 29	27,000	6	60 days
6.	Dec. 30	72,000	5	30 days

Instructions

1. Determine for each note (a) the due date and (b) the amount of interest due at maturity, identifying each note by number.
2. Journalize the entry to record the dishonor of Note (3) on its due date.
3. Journalize the adjusting entry to record the accrued interest on Notes (5) and (6) on December 31.
4. Journalize the entries to record the receipt of the amounts due on Notes (5) and (6) in January.

PR 9-5A Notes receivable entries — OBJ. 6

The following data relate to notes receivable and interest for CGH Cable Co., a cable manufacturer and supplier. (All notes are dated as of the day they are received.)

Apr. 10. Received a $144,000, 5%, 60-day note on account.
May 15. Received a $270,000, 7%, 120-day note on account.
June 9. Received $145,200 on note of April 10.
Aug. 22. Received a $150,000, 4%, 45-day note on account.
Sept. 12. Received $276,300 on note of May 15.
30. Received a $210,000, 8%, 60-day note on account.
Oct. 6. Received $150,750 on note of August 22.
18. Received a $120,000, 5%, 60-day note on account.
Nov. 29. Received $212,800 on note of September 30.
Dec. 17. Received $121,000 on note of October 18.

Instructions

Journalize the entries to record the transactions.

PR 9-6A Sales and notes receivable transactions — OBJ. 6

The following were selected from among the transactions completed by Caldemeyer Co. during the current year. Caldemeyer Co. sells and installs home and business security systems.

Jan. 3. Loaned $18,000 cash to Trina Gelhaus, receiving a 90-day, 8% note.
Feb. 10. Sold merchandise on account to Bradford & Co., $24,000. The cost of the merchandise sold was $14,400.
13. Sold merchandise on account to Dry Creek Co., $60,000. The cost of merchandise sold was $54,000.

Mar. 12. Accepted a 60-day, 7% note for $24,000 from Bradford & Co. on account.

14. Accepted a 60-day, 9% note for $60,000 from Dry Creek Co. on account.

Apr. 3. Received the interest due from Trina Gelhaus and a new 120-day, 9% note as a renewal of the loan of January 3. (Record both the debit and the credit to the notes receivable account.)

May 11. Received from Bradford & Co. the amount due on the note of March 12.

13. Dry Creek Co. dishonored its note dated March 14.

July 12. Received from Dry Creek Co. the amount owed on the dishonored note, plus interest for 60 days at 12% computed on the maturity value of the note.

Aug. 1. Received from Trina Gelhaus the amount due on her note of April 3.

Oct. 5. Sold merchandise on account to Halloran Co., $13,500. The cost of the merchandise sold was $8,100.

15. Received from Halloran Co. the amount of the invoice of October 5.

Instructions

Journalize the entries to record the transactions.

Problems: Series B

PR 9-1B Entries related to uncollectible accounts **OBJ. 4**

✔ 3. $2,290,000

SHOW ME HOW

The following transactions were completed by The Wild Trout Gallery during the current fiscal year ended December 31:

Jan. 19. Reinstated the account of Arlene Gurley, which had been written off in the preceding year as uncollectible. Journalized the receipt of $2,660 cash in full payment of Arlene's account.

Apr. 3. Wrote off the $12,750 balance owed by Premier GS Co., which is bankrupt.

July 16. Received 25% of the $22,000 balance owed by Hayden Co., a bankrupt business, and wrote off the remainder as uncollectible.

Nov. 23. Reinstated the account of Harry Carr, which had been written off two years earlier as uncollectible. Recorded the receipt of $4,000 cash in full payment.

Dec. 31. Wrote off the following accounts as uncollectible (one entry): Cavey Co., $3,300; Fogle Co., $8,100; Lake Furniture, $11,400; Melinda Shryer, $1,200.

31. Based on an analysis of the $2,350,000 of accounts receivable, it was estimated that $60,000 will be uncollectible. Journalized the adjusting entry.

Instructions

1. Record the January 1 credit balance of $50,000 in a T account for Allowance for Doubtful Accounts.
2. Journalize the transactions. Post each entry that affects the following T accounts and determine the new balances:

   Allowance for Doubtful Accounts
   Bad Debt Expense
3. Determine the expected net realizable value of the accounts receivable as of December 31.
4. Assuming that instead of basing the provision for uncollectible accounts on an analysis of receivables the adjusting entry on December 31 had been based on an estimated expense of ½ of 1% of the sales of $15,800,000 for the year, determine the following:
   a. Bad debt expense for the year.
   b. Balance in the allowance account after the adjustment of December 31.
   c. Expected net realizable value of the accounts receivable as of December 31.

PR 9-2B Aging of receivables; estimating allowance for doubtful accounts **OBJ. 4**

✔ 3. $123,235

Wig Creations Company supplies wigs and hair care products to beauty salons throughout Texas and the Southwest. The accounts receivable clerk for Wig Creations prepared the following partially completed aging of receivables schedule as of the end of business on December 31, 20Y1:

	A	B	C	D	E	F	G	H
1			Not	Days Past Due				
2			Past					
3	Customer	Balance	Due	1–30	31–60	61–90	91–120	Over 120
4	ABC Beauty	15,000	15,000					
5	Angel Wigs	8,000			8,000			
30	Zodiac Beauty	3,000		3,000				
31	Subtotals	875,000	415,000	210,000	112,000	55,000	18,000	65,000
32								

The following accounts were unintentionally omitted from the aging schedule:

Customer	Due Date	Balance
Arcade Beauty	Aug. 17, 20Y1	$10,000
Creative Images	Oct. 30, 20Y1	8,500
Excel Hair Products	July 3, 20Y1	7,500
First Class Hair Care	Sept. 8, 20Y1	6,600
Golden Images	Nov. 23, 20Y1	3,600
Oh That Hair	Nov. 29, 20Y1	1,400
One Stop Hair Designs	Dec. 7, 20Y1	4,000
Visions Hair & Nail	Jan. 11, 20Y2	9,000

Wig Creations has a past history of uncollectible accounts by age category, as follows:

Age Class	Percent Uncollectible
Not past due	1%
1–30 days past due	4
31–60 days past due	16
61–90 days past due	25
91–120 days past due	40
Over 120 days past due	80

Instructions

1. Determine the number of days past due for each of the preceding accounts.
2. Complete the aging of receivables schedule by adding the omitted accounts to the bottom of the schedule and updating the totals.
3. Estimate the allowance for doubtful accounts, based on the aging of receivables schedule.
4. Assume that the allowance for doubtful accounts for Wig Creations has a credit balance of $7,375 before adjustment on December 31, 20Y1. Journalize the adjustment for uncollectible accounts.
5. Assuming that the adjusting entry in (4) was inadvertently omitted, how would the omission affect the balance sheet and income statement?

PR 9-3B Compare two methods of accounting for uncollectible receivables **OBJ. 3, 4, 5**

✔ 1. Year 4: Balance of allowance account, end of year, $32,550

Digital Depot Company, which operates a chain of 40 electronics supply stores, has just completed its fourth year of operations. The direct write-off method of recording bad debt expense has been used during the entire period. Because of substantial increases in sales volume and the amount of uncollectible accounts, the firm is considering changing to the allowance method. Information is requested as to the effect that an annual provision of ¼% of sales would have had on the amount of bad debt expense reported for each of the past four years. It is also considered desirable to know what the balance of Allowance for Doubtful Accounts would have been at the end of each year. The following data have been obtained from the accounts:

			Year of Origin of Accounts Receivable Written Off as Uncollectible			
Year	**Sales**	**Uncollectible Accounts Written Off**	**1st**	**2nd**	**3rd**	**4th**
1st	$12,500,000	$18,000	$18,000			
2nd	14,800,000	30,200	9,000	$21,200		
3rd	18,000,000	39,900	3,600	9,300	$27,000	
4th	24,000,000	52,600		5,100	12,500	$35,000

Instructions

1. Assemble the desired data, using the following column headings:

	Bad Debt Expense			
Year	**Expense Actually Reported**	**Expense Based on Estimate**	**Increase (Decrease) in Amount of Expense**	**Balance of Allowance Account, End of Year**

2. Experience during the first four years of operations indicated that the receivables either were collected within two years or had to be written off as uncollectible. Does the estimate of ¼% of sales appear to be reasonably close to the actual experience with uncollectible accounts originating during the first two years? Explain.

PR 9-4B Details of notes receivable and related entries — OBJ. 6

✔ 1. Note 1: Due date, Feb. 13; Interest due at maturity, $110

SHOW ME HOW

Gen-X Ads Co. produces advertising videos. During the current fiscal year, Gen-X Ads Co. received the following notes:

	Date	Face Amount	Interest Rate	Term
1.	Jan. 14	$33,000	4%	30 days
2.	Mar. 9	60,000	7	45 days
3.	July 12	48,000	5	90 days
4.	Aug. 23	16,000	6	75 days
5.	Nov. 15	36,000	8	60 days
6.	Dec. 10	24,000	6	60 days

Instructions

1. Determine for each note (a) the due date and (b) the amount of interest due at maturity, identifying each note by number.
2. Journalize the entry to record the dishonor of Note (3) on its due date.
3. Journalize the adjusting entry to record the accrued interest on Notes (5) and (6) on December 31.
4. Journalize the entries to record the receipt of the amounts due on Notes (5) and (6) in January and February.

PR 9-5B Notes receivable entries — OBJ. 6

The following data relate to notes receivable and interest for Owens Co., a financial services company. (All notes are dated as of the day they are received.)

Mar. 8. Received a $33,000, 5%, 60-day note on account.
31. Received an $80,000, 7%, 90-day note on account.
May 7. Received $33,275 on note of March 8.
16. Received a $72,000, 7%, 90-day note on account.

(Continued)

June 11. Received a $36,000, 6%, 45-day note on account.
29. Received $81,400 on note of March 31.
July 26. Received $36,270 on note of June 11.
Aug. 4. Received a $48,000, 9%, 120-day note on account.
14. Received $73,260 on note of May 16.
Dec. 2. Received $49,440 on note of August 4.

Instructions

Journalize the entries to record the transactions.

PR 9-6B Sales and notes receivable transactions **OBJ. 6**

The following were selected from among the transactions completed during the current year by Danix Co., an appliance wholesale company:

Jan. 21. Sold merchandise on account to Black Tie Co., $28,000. The cost of merchandise sold was $16,800.
Mar. 18. Accepted a 60-day, 6% note for $28,000 from Black Tie Co. on account.
May 17. Received from Black Tie Co. the amount due on the note of March 18.
June 15. Sold merchandise on account to Pioneer Co. for $17,700. The cost of merchandise sold was $10,600.
21. Loaned $18,000 cash to JR Stutts, receiving a 30-day, 8% note.
25. Received from Pioneer Co. the amount due on the invoice of June 15.
July 21. Received the interest due from JR Stutts and a new 60-day, 9% note as a renewal of the loan of June 21. (Record both the debit and the credit to the notes receivable account.)
Sept. 19. Received from JR Stutts the amount due on her note of July 21.
22. Sold merchandise on account to Wycoff Co., $20,000. The cost of merchandise sold was $12,000.
Oct. 14. Accepted a 30-day, 6% note for $20,000 from Wycoff Co. on account.
Nov. 13. Wycoff Co. dishonored the note dated October 14.
Dec. 28. Received from Wycoff Co. the amount owed on the dishonored note, plus interest for 45 days at 8% computed on the maturity value of the note.

Instructions

Journalize the entries to record the transactions.

Cases & Projects

ETHICS

CP 9-1 Ethics in Action

Bud Lighting Co. is a retailer of commercial and residential lighting products. Gowen Geter, the company's chief accountant, is in the process of making year-end adjusting entries for uncollectible accounts receivable. In recent years, the company has experienced an increase in accounts that have become uncollectible. As a result, Gowen believes that the company should increase the percentage used for estimating doubtful accounts from 2% to 4% of credit sales. This change will significantly increase bad debt expense, resulting in a drop in earnings for the first time in company history. The company president, Tim Burr, is under considerable pressure to meet earnings goals. He suggests that this is "not the right time" to change the estimate. He instructs Gowen to keep the estimate at 2%. Gowen is confident that 2% is too low, but he follows Tim's instructions.

Evaluate the decision to use the lower percentage to improve earnings. Are Tim and Gowen acting in an ethical manner?

CP 9-2 Ethics in Action

Bev Wynn, vice president of operations for Dillon County Bank, has instructed the bank's computer programmer to use a 365-day year to compute interest on depository accounts (liabilities). Bev also instructed the programmer to use a 360-day year to compute interest on loans (assets).

Discuss whether Bev is behaving in a professional manner.

CP 9-3 Team Activity

In teams, select a public company that interests you and is a business that has accounts receivable. Obtain the company's most recent annual report on Form 10-K. The Form 10-K is a company's annually required filing with the Securities and Exchange Commission (SEC). It includes the company's financial statements and accompanying notes. The Form 10-K can be obtained either (a) by referring to the investor relations section of the company's website or (b) by using the company search feature of the SEC's EDGAR database service found at www.sec.gov/edgar/searchedgar/companysearch.html.

1. Based on the information in the company's most recent annual report, answer the following questions:
   a. What amount of accounts receivable did the company report at the end of the most recent year?
   b. What is the balance in the company's Allowance for Uncollectible Accounts at the end of the most recent year?
   c. What percentage of total current assets is accounts receivable at the end of each of the two years presented? Round to one decimal place. Has this percentage increased, decreased, or remained the same during this period?
   d. How much bad debt expense did the company report for the most recent year?
2. Using the information presented in the company's annual report, compute the company's accounts receivable turnover for the current and previous years. Round to one decimal place. Based on this information, has the company's management of accounts receivable improved? Briefly explain your answer.

CP 9-4 Communication

On January 1, Xtreme Co. began offering credit with terms of n/30. Uncollectible accounts are estimated to be 1% of credit sales, which is the average for the industry. The CEO, Todd Hurley, has no background in accounting and is struggling to understand the allowance method.

Write a brief memo to Todd, explaining the allowance method and how this information is reported in the financial statements.

CP 9-5 Estimate uncollectible accounts

For several years, Xtreme Co.'s sales have been on a "cash only" basis. On January 1, 20Y4, however, Xtreme Co. began offering credit on terms of n/30. The amount of the adjusting entry to record the estimated uncollectible receivables at the end of each year has been ½ of 1% of credit sales, which is the rate reported as the average for the industry. Credit sales and the year-end credit balances in Allowance for Doubtful Accounts for the past four years are as follows:

Year	Credit Sales	Allowance for Doubtful Accounts
20Y4	$4,000,000	$ 5,000
20Y5	4,400,000	8,250
20Y6	4,800,000	10,200
20Y7	5,100,000	14,400

(Continued)

Laurie Jones, president of Xtreme Co., is concerned that the method used to account for and write off uncollectible receivables is unsatisfactory. She has asked for your advice in the analysis of past operations in this area and for recommendations for change.

1. Determine the amount of (a) the addition to Allowance for Doubtful Accounts and (b) the accounts written off for each of the four years.
2. a. Advise Laurie Jones as to whether the estimate of ½ of 1% of credit sales appears reasonable.

   b. Assume that after discussing (a) with Laurie Jones, she asked you what action might be taken to determine what the balance of Allowance for Doubtful Accounts should be at December 31, 20Y7, and what possible changes, if any, you might recommend in accounting for uncollectible receivables. How would you respond?

CP 9-6 Accounts receivable turnover and days' sales in receivables

Best Buy is a specialty retailer of consumer electronics, including personal computers, entertainment software, and appliances. Best Buy operates retail stores in addition to the Best Buy, Media Play, On Cue, and Magnolia Hi-Fi websites. For two recent years, Best Buy reported the following (in millions):

	Year 2	Year 1
Sales	$42,879	$42,151
Accounts receivable at end of year	1,015	1,049

Assume that the accounts receivable (in millions) were $1,347 at the beginning of fiscal Year 1.

1. Compute the accounts receivable turnover for Year 2 and Year 1. Round to two decimal places.
2. Compute the days' sales in receivables at the end of Year 2 and Year 1. Use 365 days and round to one decimal place.
3. What conclusions can be drawn from (1) and (2) regarding Best Buy's efficiency in collecting receivables?
4. What assumption did we make about sales for the Best Buy ratio computations that might distort the ratios and therefore cause the ratios not to be comparable for Year 2 and Year 1?

CP 9-7 Accounts receivable turnover and days' sales in receivables

Apple Inc. designs, manufactures, and markets personal computers and related personal computing and communicating solutions for sale primarily to education, creative, consumer, and business customers. Substantially all of the company's sales over the last five years are from sales of its Macs, iPods, iPads, and related software and peripherals. For two recent fiscal years, Apple reported the following (in millions):

	Year 2	Year 1
Sales	$265,595	$229,234
Accounts receivable at end of year	23,186	17,874

Assume that the accounts receivable (in millions) were $15,754 at the beginning of fiscal Year 1.

1. Compute the accounts receivable turnover for Year 2 and Year 1. Round to two decimal places.
2. Compute the days' sales in receivables at the end of Year 2 and Year 1. Use 365 days and round to one decimal place.
3. What conclusions can be drawn from (1) and (2) regarding Apple's efficiency in collecting receivables?

CP 9-8 Accounts receivable turnover and days' sales in receivables

Costco Wholesale Corporation operates membership warehouses that sell a variety of branded and private label products. Headquartered in Issaquah, Washington, it also sells merchandise online in the United States (Costco.com) and in Canada (Costco.ca). For two recent years, Costco reported the following (in millions):

	Year 2	Year 1
Sales	$138,434	$126,172
Accounts receivable at end of year	1,669	1,432

Assume that the accounts receivable were $1,252 at the beginning of Year 1.

1. Compute the accounts receivable turnover for Year 2 and Year 1. Round to two decimal places.
2. Compute the days' sales in receivables at the end of Year 2 and Year 1. Use 365 days and round to one decimal place.
3. What conclusions can be drawn from (1) and (2) regarding Costco's efficiency in collecting receivables?
4. Given the nature of Costco's operations, do you believe Costco's accounts receivable turnover ratio would be higher or lower than a typical manufacturing company such as the **Campbell Soup Company**? Explain.

CP 9-9 Accounts receivable turnover

The accounts receivable turnover ratio will vary across companies, depending on the nature of the company's operations. For example, an accounts receivable turnover of 6 for a retailer is unacceptable but might be excellent for a manufacturer of specialty milling equipment. A list of well-known companies follows:

Alcoa Corp.	**The Coca-Cola Company**	**Kroger**
AutoZone, Inc.	**Delta Air Lines**	**Procter & Gamble**
Barnes & Noble, Inc.	**The Home Depot**	**Wal-Mart**
Caterpillar	**IBM**	**Whirlpool Corporation**

1. Categorize each of the preceding companies as to whether its turnover ratio is likely to be above or below 15.
2. Based on (1), identify a characteristic of companies with accounts receivable turnover ratios above 15.

CHAPTER

10 Long-Term Assets: Fixed and Intangible

STATEMENT OF OWNER'S EQUITY
For the Year Ended December 31, 20Y6

Owner's capital, Jan. 1, 20Y6		$XXX
Net income	$ XXX	
Withdrawals	(XXX)	
Increase in equity		XXX
Owner's capital, Dec. 31, 20Y6		$XXX

INCOME STATEMENT
For the Year Ended December 31, 20Y6

Sales		$XXX
Cost of merchandise sold		XXX
Gross profit		$XXX
Operating expenses:		
Advertising expense	$XXX	
Depreciation expense	XXX	
Amortization expense	XXX	
Depletion expense	XXX	
...	XXX	
...	XXX	
Total operating expenses		XXX
Income from operations		$XXX
Other revenue and expenses		XXX
Net income		$XXX

STATEMENT OF CASH FLOWS
For the Year Ended December 31, 20Y6

Cash flows from (used for) operating activities	$XXX
Cash flows from (used for) investing activities	XXX
Cash flows from (used for) financing activities	XXX
Net increase (decrease) in cash	$XXX
Cash balance, January 1, 20Y6	XXX

BALANCE SHEET
December 31, 20Y6

Current assets:		
Cash	$XXX	
Accounts receivable	XXX	
Merchandise inventory	XXX	
Total current assets		$XXX
Property, plant, and equipment	$XXX	
Intangible assets	XXX	
Total long-term assets		XXX
Total assets		$XXX
Liabilities:		
Current liabilities	$XXX	
Long-term liabilities	XXX	
Total liabilities		$XXX
Owner's equity		XXX
Total liabilities and owner's equity		$XXX

SON PHOTO/SHUTTERSTOCK.COM

McDonald's

McDonald's began in 1940 in San Bernardino, California, as a Bar-B-Q restaurant operated by two brothers, Dick and Mac McDonald. In 1954, Ray Kroc visited the restaurant and convinced the McDonald brothers to let him franchise its operations nationwide. Ray Kroc opened his first McDonald's in Des Plaines, Illinois, in 1955, with its distinguishing, newly designed Golden Arches. Today, McDonald's operates in more than 100 countries, has more than 37,000 restaurants, employs more than 210,000 people, sells millions of hamburgers each year, and generates yearly revenues in excess of $21 billion.

Would you like to own and operate a McDonald's restaurant? McDonald's grants 20-year franchises to individuals who want to become owner/operators of a restaurant. Individuals may either purchase an existing restaurant or open a new restaurant. When opening a new restaurant, the owner must invest in the store equipment, signs, seating, and décor. McDonald's normally owns the land and the building. McDonald's also provides training for its owner/operators. In return, McDonald's is paid a monthly service charge, which is either a fixed amount or a percent of sales. The total cost of opening a new restaurant may exceed several million dollars.

Obviously, the decision to open a McDonald's restaurant is a major commitment with long-term implications. This chapter discusses the accounting for investments in long-term, fixed assets such as a new restaurant. This accounting addresses such issues as how much of the investment should be recorded as an asset, how much should be written off as an expense each year, and how the disposal of a fixed asset should be recorded. Finally, accounting for natural resources, such as mineral deposits, and for intangible assets, such as patents, copyrights, trademarks, and goodwill, are discussed.

Source: Click on ABOUT at https://corporate.mcdonalds.com.

Link to McDonald's.......... Pages 493, 495, 496, 513

LEARNING OBJECTIVES

After studying this chapter, you should be able to:

Example Exercises (EE) are shown in **red.**

OBJ. 1 **Define, classify, and account for the cost of fixed assets.**

Nature of Fixed Assets
Classifying Costs
The Cost of Fixed Assets
Leasing Fixed Assets

OBJ. 2 **Compute depreciation using the following methods: straight-line, units-of-activity, and double-declining-balance.**

Accounting for Depreciation
Factors in Computing Depreciation Expense
Straight-Line Method EE **10-1**
Units-of-Activity Method EE **10-2**
Double-Declining-Balance Method EE **10-3**
Comparing Depreciation Methods
Partial-Year Depreciation
Revising Depreciation Estimates EE **10-4**
Repair and Improvements EE **10-5**

OBJ. 3 **Journalize the disposal of fixed assets.**

Disposal of Fixed Assets
Discarding Fixed Assets
Selling Fixed Assets EE **10-6**

OBJ. 4 **Describe the accounting for natural resources, including the journal entry for depletion.**

Natural Resources
Compute and Record Depletion EE **10-7**

OBJ. 5 **Describe the accounting for intangible assets, such as patents, copyrights, and goodwill.**

Intangible Assets
Patents EE **10-8**
Copyrights and Trademarks
Goodwill EE **10-8**

OBJ. 6 **Describe how depreciation expense is reported on an income statement and prepare a balance sheet that includes fixed assets and intangible assets.**

Financial Reporting for Long-Term Assets: Fixed and Intangible

OBJ. 7 **Describe and illustrate the fixed asset turnover ratio to assess the efficiency of a company's use of its fixed assets.**

Financial Analysis and Interpretation: Fixed Asset Turnover Ratio
Compute Fixed Asset Turnover Ratio EE **10-9**

APP. OBJ. **Describe and illustrate the accounting for exchanging similar assets.**

At a Glance 10 Page 520

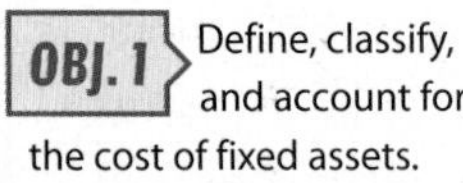

Define, classify, and account for the cost of fixed assets.

Nature of Fixed Assets

Fixed assets are long-term or relatively permanent assets such as equipment, machinery, buildings, and land. Other descriptive titles for fixed assets are *plant assets* or *property, plant, and equipment*. Fixed assets have the following characteristics:

- They exist physically and, thus, are *tangible* assets.
- They are owned and used by the company in its normal operations.
- They are not offered for sale as part of normal operations.

Fixed assets are critical to the success of many businesses. For example, computers and Internet servers are critical fixed assets for a business that provides online retail or technology services.

Classifying Costs

A cost that has been incurred may be classified as a fixed asset, an investment, or an expense. Exhibit 1 shows how to determine the proper classification of a cost and how it should be recorded.

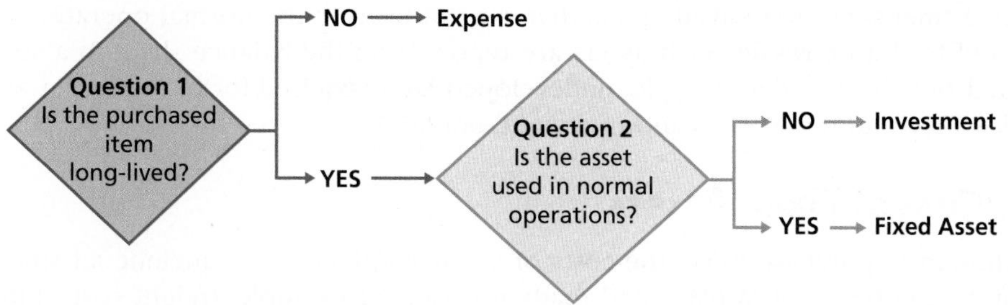

EXHIBIT 1
Classifying Costs

As shown in Exhibit 1, classifying a cost involves the following questions:

Question 1. Is the purchased item long-lived (more than one year)?
If *yes*, the item is recorded as an asset on the balance sheet, either as a fixed asset or an investment. Proceed to Question 2.
If *no*, the item is classified and recorded as an *expense*.

Question 2. Is the asset used in normal operations?
If *yes*, the asset is classified and recorded as a *fixed asset*.
If *no*, the asset is classified and recorded as an *investment*.

Items that are classified and recorded as fixed assets include equipment, buildings, and land. Such assets normally last more than a year and are used in the normal operations of the business. However, standby equipment for use during peak periods or when other equipment breaks down is still classified as a fixed asset, even though it is not used very often. In contrast, fixed assets that have been abandoned or are no longer used in operations are not classified as fixed assets.

Although fixed assets may be sold, they should not be offered for sale as part of normal operations. For example, cars and trucks offered for sale by an automotive dealership are not fixed assets of the dealership. On the other hand, a tow truck used in the normal operations of the dealership is a fixed asset of the dealership.

Link to McDonald's

In a recent financial statement, **McDonald's** reported total property, plant, and equipment of over $37 billion, which consists of land, buildings, and equipment.

Business Connection

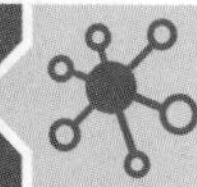

FIXED ASSETS

Fixed assets often represent a significant portion of a company's total assets. The table that follows shows the fixed assets as a percent of total assets for some select companies across a variety of industries. As can be seen, the type of industry will impact the proportion of fixed assets to total assets. Retail has the highest percent of fixed assets to total assets, while social media and software have much lower percentages. High-tech service companies often use fewer fixed assets to deliver their services than companies that use stores, equipment, planes, cell towers, or theme parks.

Company	Industry	Percent of Fixed Assets to Total Assets
McDonald's Corporation	Food Retail	70%
Target Corporation	Merchandise Retail	64%
Delta Air Lines, Inc.	Transportation	47%
Verizon Communications Inc.	Communications	34%
The Walt Disney Company	Entertainment	30%
Facebook, Inc.	Social Media	25%
Alcoa Inc.	Heavy Industry	24%
Microsoft Corporation	Software	11%

Investments are long-lived assets that are not used in the normal operations and are held for future resale. Such assets are reported on the balance sheet in a section entitled *Investments*. For example, undeveloped land acquired for future resale would be classified and reported as an investment, not land.

The Cost of Fixed Assets

In addition to purchase price, the costs of acquiring fixed assets include all amounts spent getting the asset in place and ready for use. For example, freight costs and the costs of installing equipment are part of the asset's total cost.

Exhibit 2 summarizes some of the common costs of acquiring fixed assets. These costs are recorded by debiting the related fixed asset account, such as Land,[1] Building, Land Improvements, or Machinery and Equipment.

EXHIBIT 2 Costs of Acquiring Fixed Assets

Building

- Architects' fees
- Engineers' fees
- Insurance costs incurred during construction
- Interest on money borrowed to finance construction
- Sales taxes
- Repairs (purchase of existing building)
- Reconditioning (purchase of existing building)
- Modifying for use
- Permits from government agencies

Machinery & Equipment

- Sales taxes
- Freight
- Installation
- Repairs (purchase of used equipment)
- Reconditioning (purchase of used equipment)
- Insurance while in transit
- Assembly
- Modifying for use
- Testing for use
- Permits from government agencies

Land

- Purchase price
- Sales taxes
- Permits from government agencies
- Broker's commissions
- Attorney fees
- Title fees
- Surveying fees
- Delinquent real estate taxes
- Removing unwanted building less any salvage
- Grading and leveling

Only costs necessary for preparing the fixed asset for use are included as a cost of the asset. Unnecessary costs that do not increase the asset's usefulness are recorded as an expense. For example, the following costs are recorded as expenses:

- Vandalism
- Mistakes in installation
- Uninsured theft

1 As discussed here, land is assumed to be used only as a location or site and not for its mineral deposits or other natural resources.

- Damage during unpacking and installing
- Fines for not obtaining proper permits from governmental agencies

To illustrate, assume Kimble Inc. purchased equipment for $12,000. Freight costs of $600 were incurred to transport the equipment to the installation site. On site, installation costs of $1,500 were incurred, including $500 due to an error in installation. The journal entry to record the equipment is as follows:

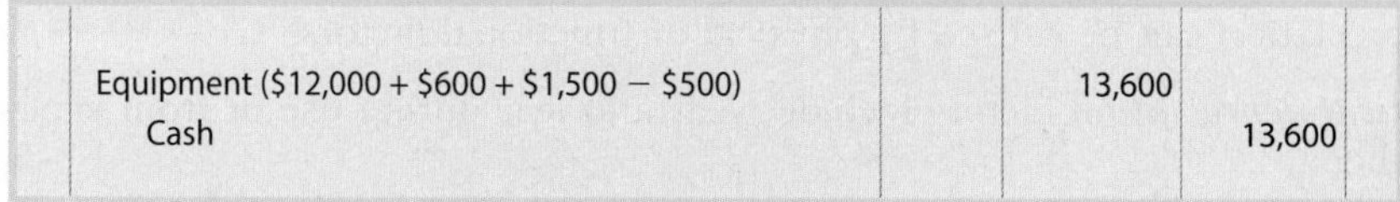

Equipment ($12,000 + $600 + $1,500 − $500)		13,600	
Cash			13,600

The cost of the error in installing the equipment of $500 is not included in the cost of the equipment, but instead is recorded as an expense.

A company may incur costs associated with constructing a fixed asset such as a new building. The direct costs incurred in the construction, such as labor and materials, should be capitalized as a debit to an account entitled *Construction in Progress*. When the construction is complete, the costs are reclassified by crediting Construction in Progress and debiting the proper fixed asset account such as Building.

Leasing Fixed Assets

A *lease* is a contract for the use of an asset for a period of time. Leases are often used in business. For example, automobiles, computers, medical equipment, buildings, and airplanes are often leased.

The two parties to a lease contract are as follows:

- The *lessor* is the party who owns the asset.
- The *lessee* is the party to whom the rights to use the asset are granted by the lessor.

Under a lease contract, the lessee pays rent on a periodic basis for the lease term. An advantage of leasing an asset is that the lessee has access to an asset without having to spend a large amount of funds or borrow to buy the asset. In addition, expenses such as maintenance and repair costs may be the responsibility of the lessor. Finally, the risk of incurring additional cost because the asset becomes obsolete before the end of its useful life can be mitigated by leasing an asset.

> **Link to McDonald's**
>
> **McDonald's** recently reported that it is the lessee in over 12,000 locations. The leases are normally for 20 years with an option to renew.

The Financial Accounting Standards Board (FASB) and the International Accounting Standards Board (IASB) recently completed a project to merge U.S. and international standards on leasing.[2] The new FASB standard distinguishes between finance leases and operating leases. Under a finance lease, the lessee records an asset and a liability similar to having purchased the asset. Under an operating lease, the lessee records prepaid rent (and, if necessary, a liability for future lease payments) and records rent expense as the asset is used.

For purposes of this text, we assume that all leases are operating leases that do not extend beyond one year. Thus, lease payments are recorded by debiting Rent Expense and crediting Cash. In some cases, like those illustrated in earlier chapters, Prepaid Rent is initially recorded with an adjusting entry at the end of the period to record Rent Expense.

Regardless of the type of lease, lease terms should be disclosed in the notes to the financial statements. These disclosures would include such items as the length of the lease, termination rights, and renewal options.

2 Accounting Standards Update, *Leases (Topic 842)*, February 2016, FASB (Norwalk, CT).

OBJ. 2 Compute depreciation using the following methods: straight-line, units-of-activity, and double-declining-balance.

Accounting for Depreciation

Over time, fixed assets, with the exception of land, lose their ability to provide services. Thus, the costs of fixed assets such as equipment, buildings, and land improvements should be recorded as an expense over their useful lives. Recording the cost of fixed assets as an expense is called **depreciation**. Because land has an unlimited life, it is not depreciated.

Depreciation can be caused by physical or functional factors.

- *Physical depreciation* factors include wear and tear during use or from exposure to weather.
- *Functional depreciation* factors include obsolescence and changes in customer needs that cause the asset to no longer provide services for which it was intended. For example, equipment may become obsolete due to changing technology.

Two common misunderstandings about depreciation as used in accounting include:

- Depreciation does not measure a decline in the market value of a fixed asset. Instead, depreciation is an allocation of a fixed asset's cost to expense over the asset's useful life. Thus, the book value of a fixed asset (cost less accumulated depreciation) usually does not agree with the asset's market value. This is justified in accounting because a fixed asset is for use in a company's operations rather than for resale.
- Depreciation does not provide cash to replace fixed assets as they wear out. This misunderstanding may occur because depreciation, unlike many expenses, does not represent an outlay of cash, but instead is an allocation of the asset's initial cost to expense.

Factors in Computing Depreciation Expense

The three factors that determine the depreciation expense for a fixed asset are as follows:

- The asset's initial cost
- The asset's expected useful life
- The asset's estimated residual value

Link to McDonald's

McDonald's uses a useful life of up to 40 years for its buildings and from 3–12 years for its equipment.

The **initial cost** of a fixed asset is the purchase price of the asset plus all costs to obtain and ready it for use. This initial cost is determined using the concepts discussed and illustrated earlier in this chapter.

The **expected useful life** of a fixed asset is the estimated length of time the asset will be used in normal operations. It is estimated at the time the asset is placed into service. Estimates of expected useful lives are available from industry trade associations. The Internal Revenue Service also publishes guidelines for useful lives, which may be helpful for financial reporting purposes. However, it is not uncommon for different companies to use a different useful life for similar assets.

The **residual value** of a fixed asset is the estimated value of the asset at the end of its useful life. It is estimated at the time the asset is placed into service. Residual value is sometimes referred to as *scrap value*, *salvage value*, or *trade-in value*.

The difference between a fixed asset's initial cost and its residual value is called the asset's **depreciable cost**. This is the asset's cost that is allocated over its useful life as depreciation expense. If a fixed asset has no residual value, then its entire cost should be allocated to depreciation.

To illustrate depreciation methods, assume that **Exeter Company** purchased a new forklift on January 1 as follows:

Initial cost	$24,000
Expected useful life	5 years
Estimated residual value	$2,000

Exhibit 3 shows the relationship between depreciation expense and the forklift's initial cost, expected useful life, and estimated residual value.

EXHIBIT 3
Depreciation Expense

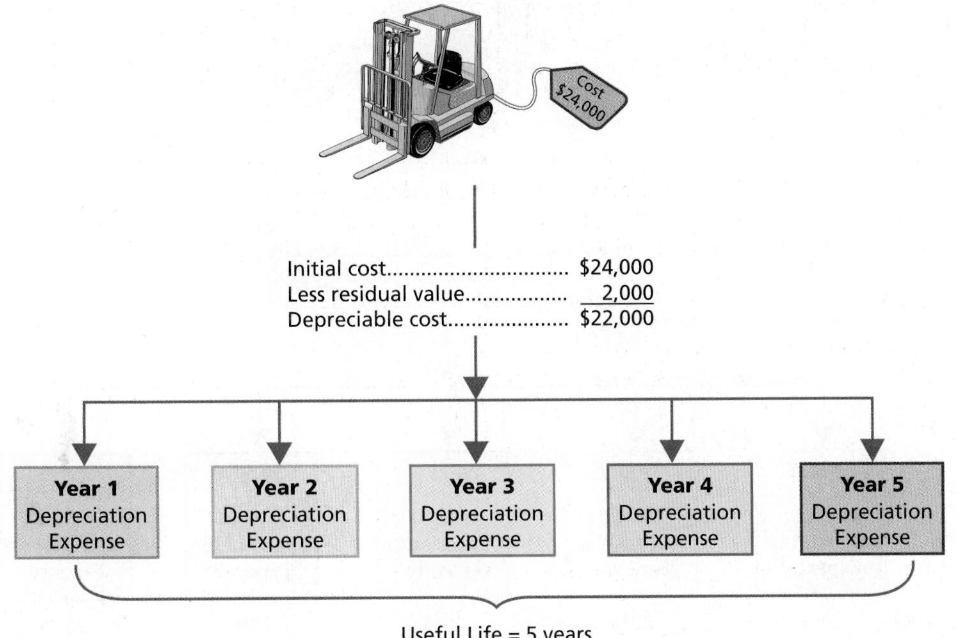

The three depreciation methods used most often are as follows:

- Straight-line depreciation
- Units-of-activity depreciation
- Double-declining-balance depreciation

It is not necessary for a company to use only one method of computing depreciation for all of its fixed assets. For example, a company may use one method for depreciating equipment and another method for depreciating buildings.

Straight-Line Method

The **straight-line method** provides for the same amount of depreciation expense for each year of the asset's useful life. The annual straight-line depreciation for **Exeter**'s forklift is $4,400, computed as follows:

$$\text{Annual Depreciation} = \frac{\text{Cost} - \text{Residual Value}}{\text{Useful Life}} = \frac{\$24{,}000 - \$2{,}000}{\text{5 Years}} = \$4{,}400$$

The straight-line method reports the same amount of depreciation expense each year, as illustrated in Exhibit 4.

Computing straight-line depreciation may be simplified by converting the annual depreciation to a percentage of depreciable cost.[3] The straight-line percentage is

3 The depreciation rate may also be expressed as a fraction. For example, the annual straight-line rate for an asset with a three-year useful life is 1/3.

EXHIBIT 4 **Straight-Line Method**

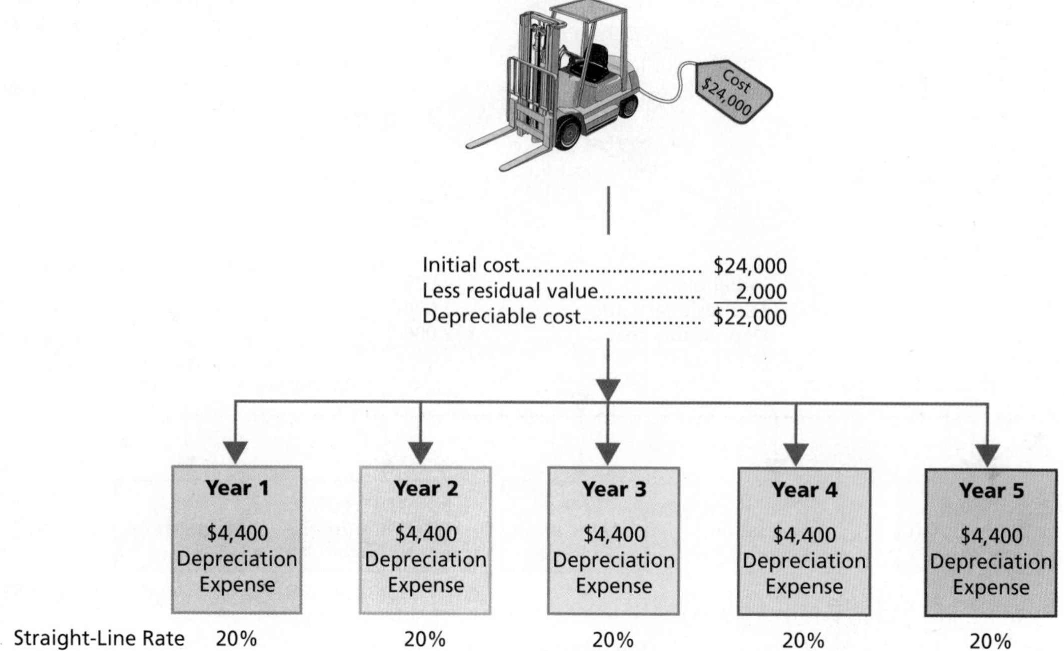

determined by dividing 100% by the number of years of expected useful life, computed as follows:

Expected Years of Useful Life	Straight-Line Percentage
5 years	20% (100% ÷ 5)
8 years	12.5% (100% ÷ 8)
10 years	10% (100% ÷ 10)
20 years	5% (100% ÷ 20)
25 years	4% (100% ÷ 25)

For the preceding equipment, the annual depreciation of $4,400 can be computed by multiplying the depreciable cost of $22,000 by 20% (100% ÷ 5).

Depreciation of the forklift for the first year using the straight-line method is recorded as follows:

Dec.	31	Depreciation Expense—Forklift		4,400	
		Accumulated Depreciation—Forklift			4,400

Accumulated depreciation accounts are called *contra accounts* or *contra asset accounts*. This is because accumulated depreciation accounts are deducted from their related fixed asset accounts on the balance sheet. The difference between the fixed asset account and its related accumulated depreciation account is called the asset's **book value** or *net book value of the asset*.

The book value of the forklift at the end of the first year is $19,600. It would be reported on the balance sheet as follows:

Equipment	$24,000
Less accumulated depreciation	4,400
Book value	$19,600

As shown in Exhibit 5, as depreciation expense is recorded each year, Accumulated Depreciation—Forklift will increase and the book value of the forklift will decrease.

Straight-Line Method: Depreciation Expense and Book Value EXHIBIT 5

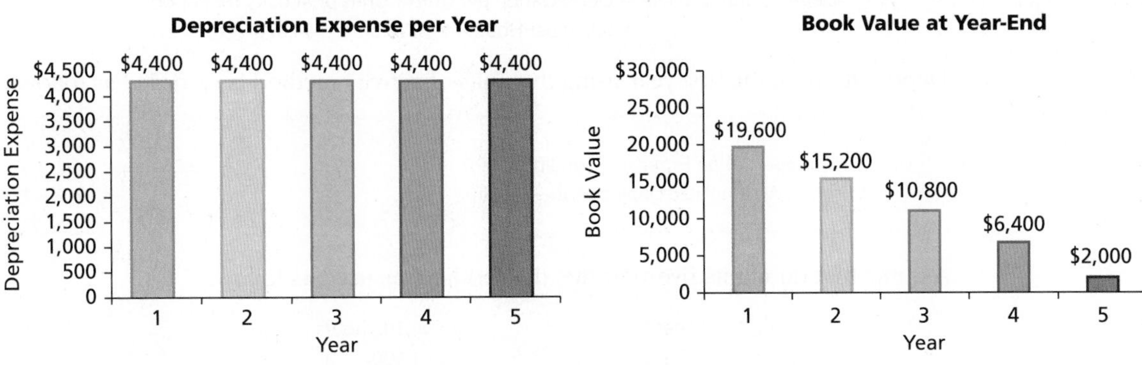

The straight-line method is simple to use. When an asset's revenues are about the same from period to period, straight-line depreciation provides a good matching of depreciation expense with the asset's revenues.

EXAMPLE EXERCISE 10-1 Straight-Line Depreciation **OBJ. 2**

Equipment acquired at the beginning of the year at a cost of $125,000 has an estimated residual value of $5,000 and an estimated useful life of 10 years. Determine (a) the depreciable cost, (b) the straight-line rate, and (c) the annual straight-line depreciation.

Follow My Example 10-1

a. $120,000 ($125,000 − $5,000)

b. 10% = 100% ÷ 10

c. $12,000 ($120,000 × 10%) or ($120,000 ÷ 10 years)

Practice Exercises: PE 10-1A, PE 10-1B

Units-of-Activity Method

The **units-of-activity method** provides the same amount of depreciation expense for each unit of activity of the asset. Depending on the asset, the units of activity can be expressed in terms of hours, miles driven, or quantity produced. For example, the unit of activity for a truck is normally expressed in miles driven. For manufacturing assets, the units of activity are often expressed as units of product. In this case, the units-of-activity method may be called the *units-of-production method* or *units-of-output method*.

The units-of-activity method is applied in the following two steps:

Step 1. Determine the depreciation per unit as follows:

$$\text{Depreciation per Unit} = \frac{\text{Cost} - \text{Residual Value}}{\text{Total Estimated Units of Activity}}$$

Step 2. Compute the depreciation expense as follows:

$$\text{Depreciation Expense} = \text{Depreciation per Unit} \times \text{Units of Activity for Period}$$

To illustrate, assume that **Exeter**'s forklift is estimated to have a useful life of 10,000 operating hours. During the first year, the forklift was operated 2,100 hours. The units-of-activity depreciation for the year is $4,620, computed as follows:

Step 1. Determine the depreciation per hour as follows:

$$\text{Depreciation per Hour} = \frac{\text{Cost} - \text{Residual Value}}{\text{Total Estimated Units of Activity}} = \frac{\$24{,}000 - \$2{,}000}{10{,}000 \text{ Hours}} = \$2.20 \text{ per Hour}$$

Step 2. Compute the depreciation expense as follows:

Depreciation Expense = Depreciation per Unit × Units of Activity for Period
= \$2.20 per Hour × 2,100 Hours = \$4,620

Depreciation for the first year using the units-of-activity method is recorded as follows:

Dec.	31	Depreciation Expense—Forklift	4,620	
		Accumulated Depreciation—Forklift		4,620

Assume that during its five-year life, the forklift was used as follows:

Year 1	2,100 hours
Year 2	1,500
Year 3	2,600
Year 4	1,800
Year 5	2,000
Total	10,000 hours

Exhibit 6 illustrates the depreciation expense and book value of the forklift over its five-year life using the units-of-activity method.

EXHIBIT 6 **Units-of-Activity Method**

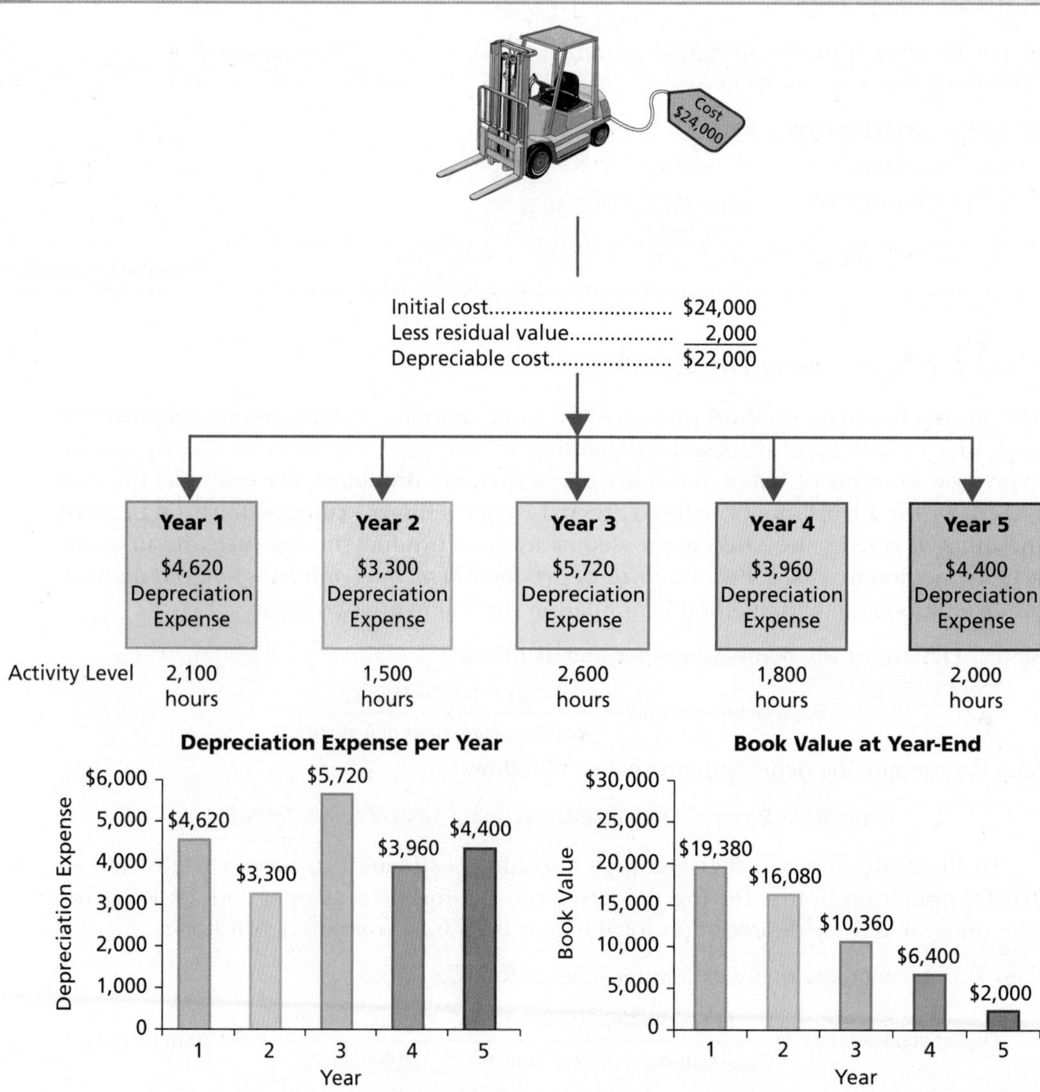

As shown in Exhibit 6, depreciation expense and book value vary each year depending on the hours the forklift is operated.

The units-of-activity method is often used when a fixed asset's use varies from year to year. In such cases, the units-of-activity method matches depreciation expense with the asset's revenues.

EXAMPLE EXERCISE 10-2 Units-of-Activity Depreciation **OBJ. 2**

Equipment acquired at the beginning of the year at a cost of $180,000 has an estimated residual value of $10,000, has an estimated useful life of 40,000 hours, and was operated 3,600 hours during the year. Determine (a) the depreciable cost, (b) the depreciation rate, and (c) the units-of-activity depreciation for the year.

Follow My Example 10-2

a. $170,000 ($180,000 − $10,000)
b. $4.25 per hour ($170,000 ÷ 40,000 hours)
c. $15,300 (3,600 hours × $4.25)

Practice Exercises: PE 10-2A, PE 10-2B

Double-Declining-Balance Method

The **double-declining-balance method** provides for a declining periodic expense over the expected useful life of the asset. The double-declining-balance method is applied in the following three steps:

Step 1. Determine the straight-line percentage, using the expected useful life.

Step 2. Determine the double-declining-balance rate by multiplying the straight-line rate (from Step 1) by 2.

Step 3. Compute the depreciation expense by multiplying the double-declining-balance rate (from Step 2) times the book value of the asset.

To illustrate, the purchase of Exeter's forklift is used to compute double-declining-balance depreciation. For the first year, the depreciation is $9,600, computed as follows:

Step 1. Straight-line percentage = 20% (100% ÷ 5)
Step 2. Double-declining-balance rate = 40% (20% × 2)
Step 3. Depreciation expense = $9,600 ($24,000 × 40%)

Depreciation of the forklift for the first year using the double-declining-balance method is recorded as follows:

Dec.	31	Depreciation Expense—Forklift	9,600	
		Accumulated Depreciation—Forklift		9,600

For the first year, the book value of the equipment is its initial cost of $24,000. After the first year, the book value declines, and thus, the depreciation also declines. The double-declining-balance depreciation for the full five-year life of the forklift is as follows:

Year	Cost	Acc. Dep. at Beginning of Year	Book Value at Beginning of Year		Double-Declining-Balance Rate	Depreciation for Year	Book Value at End of Year
1	$24,000		$24,000.00	×	40%	$9,600.00	$14,400.00
2	24,000	$ 9,600.00	14,400.00	×	40%	5,760.00	8,640.00
3	24,000	15,360.00	8,640.00	×	40%	3,456.00	5,184.00
4	24,000	18,816.00	5,184.00	×	40%	2,073.60	3,110.40
5	24,000	20,889.60	3,110.40		—	1,110.40	2,000.00

When the double-declining-balance method is used, the estimated residual value is *not* considered. However, the asset should not be depreciated below its estimated residual value. In the preceding example, the estimated residual value was $2,000. Therefore, the depreciation for the fifth year is $1,110.40 ($3,110.40 − $2,000.00) instead of $1,244.16 (40% × $3,110.40).

Exhibit 7 illustrates the depreciation expense and book value of the forklift over its five-year life using the double-declining-balance method. As shown in Exhibit 7, the double-declining-balance method has higher depreciation in the first year of the asset's life, followed by declining depreciation amounts. For this reason, the double-declining-balance method is called an **accelerated depreciation method**.

EXHIBIT 7 **Double-Declining-Balance Method**

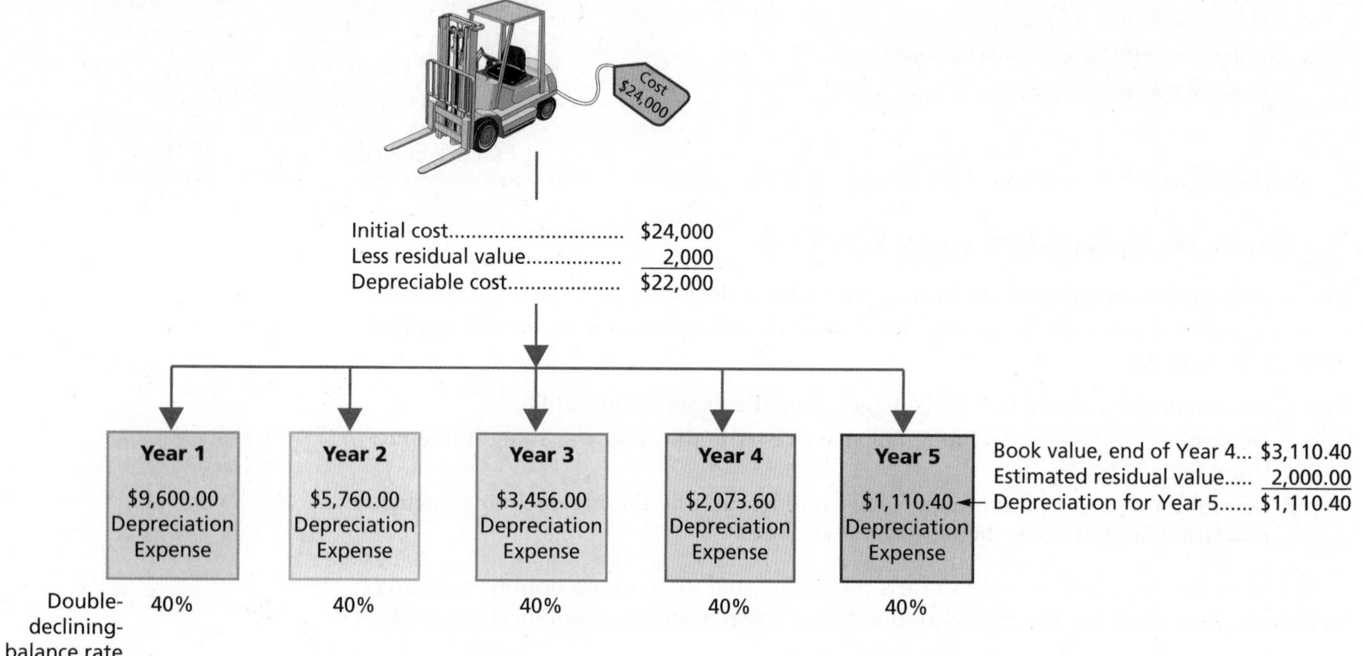

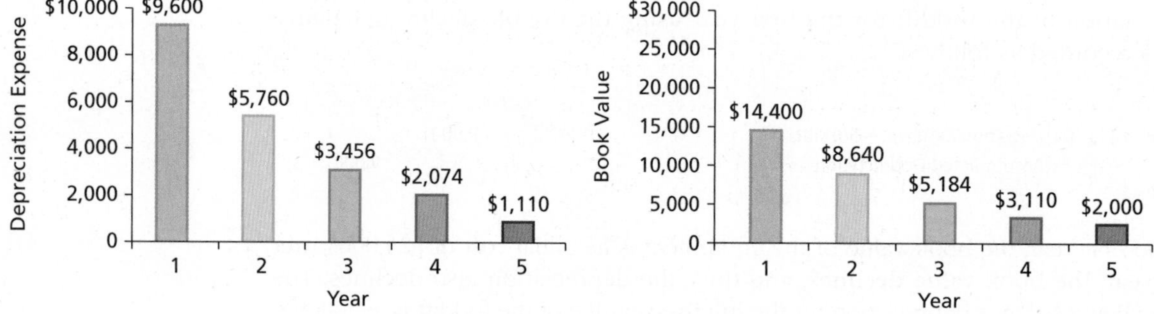

Revenues generated by an asset are often greater in the early years of its use than in later years. In such cases, the double-declining-balance method provides a good matching of depreciation expense with the asset's revenues.

EXAMPLE EXERCISE 10-3 Double-Declining-Balance Depreciation **OBJ. 2**

Equipment acquired at the beginning of the year at a cost of $125,000 has an estimated residual value of $5,000 and an estimated useful life of 10 years. Determine (a) the double-declining-balance rate and (b) the double-declining-balance depreciation for the first year.

Follow My Example 10-3

a. 20% [(100% ÷ 10) × 2]
b. $25,000 ($125,000 × 20%)

Practice Exercises: PE 10-3A, PE 10-3B

Comparing Depreciation Methods

The three depreciation methods are summarized in Exhibit 8. All three methods allocate the total cost of an asset to depreciation expense over the asset's useful life while never depreciating an asset below its residual value.

EXHIBIT 8
Summary of Depreciation Methods

Method	Useful Life	Depreciable Cost	Depreciation Rate	Depreciation Expense
Straight-line	Years	Cost less residual value	Straight-line rate*	Constant
Units-of-activity	Units of activity	Cost less residual value	$\frac{\text{Cost} - \text{Residual value}}{\text{Total units of activity}}$	Variable
Double-declining-balance	Years	Declining book value, but not below residual value	Straight-line rate* × 2	Declining

*Straight-line rate = (100% ÷ Useful life)

The straight-line method provides for the same periodic amounts of depreciation expense over the life of the asset. The units-of-activity method provides for periodic amounts of depreciation expense that vary, depending on the amount the asset is used. The double-declining-balance method provides for a higher depreciation amount in the first year of the asset's use, followed by declining amounts.

Exhibit 9 illustrates depreciation expense for each depreciation method over the five-year life of the forklift.

Partial-Year Depreciation

A fixed asset may be purchased and placed in service other than the first month of an accounting period. In such cases, depreciation is prorated based on the month the asset is placed in service. For example, assume that an asset is placed in service on March 1. For an accounting period ending December 31, depreciation would be computed (prorated) for 10 months (March 1 to December 31).

EXHIBIT 9

Comparing Depreciation Methods

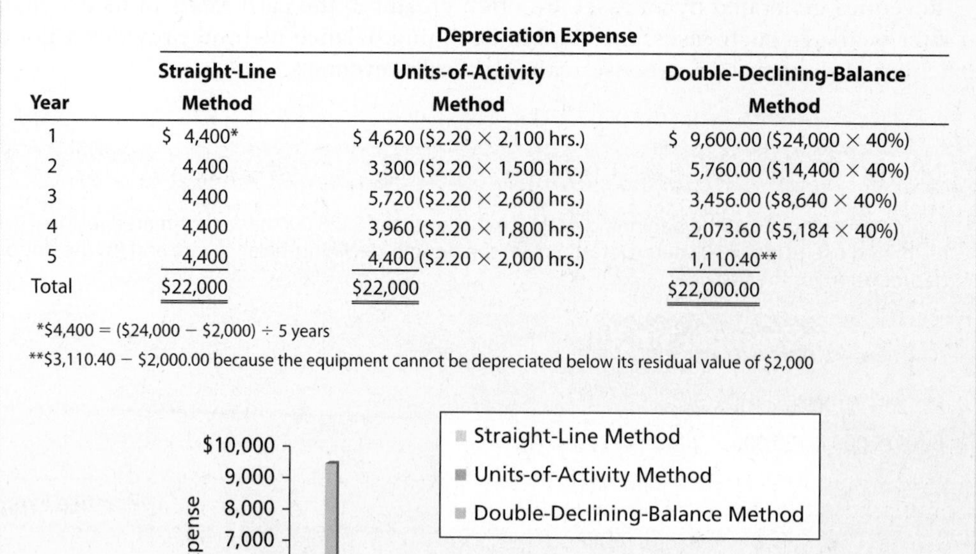

	Depreciation Expense		
Year	**Straight-Line Method**	**Units-of-Activity Method**	**Double-Declining-Balance Method**
1	$ 4,400*	$ 4,620 ($2.20 × 2,100 hrs.)	$ 9,600.00 ($24,000 × 40%)
2	4,400	3,300 ($2.20 × 1,500 hrs.)	5,760.00 ($14,400 × 40%)
3	4,400	5,720 ($2.20 × 2,600 hrs.)	3,456.00 ($8,640 × 40%)
4	4,400	3,960 ($2.20 × 1,800 hrs.)	2,073.60 ($5,184 × 40%)
5	4,400	4,400 ($2.20 × 2,000 hrs.)	1,110.40**
Total	$22,000	$22,000	$22,000.00

*$4,400 = ($24,000 − $2,000) ÷ 5 years

**$3,110.40 − $2,000.00 because the equipment cannot be depreciated below its residual value of $2,000

Assets may also be placed in service other than the first day of a month. In such cases, assets placed in service during the first half of a month are normally treated as having been purchased on the first day of *that* month. Likewise, asset purchases during the second half of a month are treated as having been placed in service on the first day of the *next* month.

Straight-Line Method Under the straight-line method, depreciation is prorated based on the number of months the asset is in service. To illustrate, assume that **Exeter Company** purchased the forklift on October 1 instead of January 1. The first-year

Business Connection

DEPRECIATING ANIMALS

The Internal Revenue Code uses the Modified Accelerated Cost Recovery System (MACRS) to compute depreciation for tax purposes. Under MACRS, various farm animals may be depreciated. The period (years) over which some common classes of farm animals may be depreciated are shown in the table that follows.

Depreciation for farm animals begins when the animal reaches the age of maturity, which is normally when it can be worked, milked, or bred. For racehorses, depreciation begins when a horse is put into training.

Class of Animal	Years
Dairy or breeding cattle	7–10
Goats and sheep	5
Hogs	3
Horses	3–12

depreciation would be based upon three months (October, November, December). First-year depreciation would be $1,100, computed as follows:

Annual Depreciation = ($24,000 − $2,000) ÷ 5 years = $4,400

First-Year Depreciation = $4,400 × (3 ÷ 12) = $1,100

Units-of-Activity Method The units-of-activity method computes depreciation expense using an activity rate and the activity level for the period. To illustrate, assume that Exeter purchased the forklift on October 1 instead of January 1. Assume that during the period from October 1 to December 31, the forklift was used for 400 hours. First-year depreciation would be $880, computed as follows:

Depreciation per Hour = ($24,000 − $2,000) ÷ 10,000 Hours = $2.20 per Hour

First-Year Depreciation = $2.20 per Hour × 400 Hours = $880

Double-Declining-Balance Method Like straight-line depreciation, if an asset is used for only part of a year, the annual double-declining-balance depreciation is prorated based on the number of months the asset is in service. To illustrate, assume that Exeter's forklift was purchased and placed into service on October 1 instead of January 1. First-year depreciation would be based upon three months (October, November, December). First-year depreciation would be $2,400, computed as follows:

Double-Declining-Balance Rate = (100% ÷ 5) × 2 = 40%

First-Year Annual Depreciation = $24,000 × 40% = $9,600

First-Year Partial Depreciation = $9,600 × (3 ÷ 12) = $2,400

The second-year depreciation would be computed by multiplying the book value on January 1 of the second year by the double-declining-balance rate. To illustrate, assume that Exeter purchased the forklift on October 1 and that $2,400 partial depreciation was recorded on December 31. The book value on January 1 of the second year is $21,600 ($24,000 − $2,400). The second-year depreciation would then be $8,640, computed as follows:

Second-Year Annual Depreciation = $21,600 × 40% = $8,640

Revising Depreciation Estimates

Estimates of residual values and useful lives of fixed assets may change due to abnormal wear and tear or obsolescence. When new estimates are made by management, they are used to determine the depreciation expense in future periods. The depreciation expense recorded in earlier years is not affected.[4]

To illustrate, assume the following data for a machine that was purchased on January 1:

Initial machine cost	$140,000
Expected useful life	5 years
Estimated residual value	$10,000
Annual depreciation using the straight-line method [($140,000 – $10,000) ÷ 5 years]	$26,000

At the end of the second year, the machine's book value (undepreciated cost) is $88,000, computed as follows:

Initial machine cost	$140,000
Less accumulated depreciation ($26,000 per year × 2 years)	52,000
Book value (undepreciated cost), end of second year	$ 88,000

4 *FASB Accounting Standards Codification*, Section 250-10-05.

At the beginning of the third year, the company estimates that the machine's remaining useful life is eight years (instead of three) and that its residual value is $8,000 (instead of $10,000). The depreciation expense for each of the remaining eight years is $10,000, computed as follows:

$$\text{Revised Depreciation Expense} = \frac{\text{Book Value} - \text{Revised Residual Value}}{\text{Revised Remaining Useful Life}} = \frac{\$88{,}000 - \$8{,}000}{8 \text{ Years}} = \$10{,}000$$

Exhibit 10 shows the book value of the asset over its original and revised lives. After the depreciation is revised at the end of the second year, book value declines at a slower rate. At the end of the tenth year, the book value reaches the revised residual value of $8,000.

EXHIBIT 10

Book Value of Asset with Change in Estimate

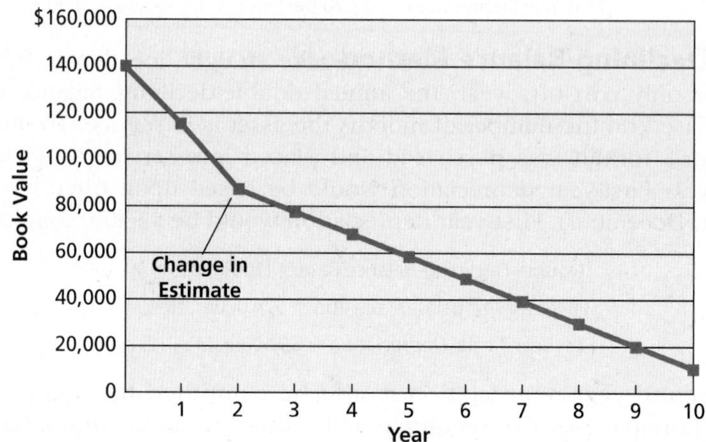

EXAMPLE EXERCISE 10-4 Revision of Depreciation **OBJ. 2**

A warehouse with a cost of $500,000 has an estimated residual value of $120,000, has an estimated useful life of 40 years, and is depreciated by the straight-line method. (a) Determine the amount of the annual depreciation. (b) Determine the book value at the end of the twentieth year of use. (c) Assuming that at the start of the twenty-first year the remaining life is estimated to be 25 years and the residual value is estimated to be $150,000, determine the depreciation expense for each of the remaining 25 years.

Follow My Example 10-4

a. $9,500 [($500,000 − $120,000) ÷ 40]

b. $310,000 [$500,000 − ($9,500 × 20)]

c. $6,400 [($310,000 − $150,000) ÷ 25]

Practice Exercises: PE 10-4A, PE 10-4B

Repair and Improvements

Once a fixed asset has been acquired and placed into service, costs may be incurred for ordinary maintenance and repairs. In addition, costs may be incurred for improving an asset or for extraordinary repairs that extend the asset's useful life. Costs that benefit only the current period are called **revenue expenditures**. Costs that improve the asset or extend its useful life are **capital expenditures**.

Ordinary Maintenance and Repairs Costs related to the ordinary maintenance and repairs of a fixed asset are recorded as an expense of the current period. Such expenditures are *revenue expenditures* and are recorded as debits to Repairs and Maintenance Expense. For example, $300 paid for a tune-up of a delivery truck is recorded as follows:

		Debit	Credit
Repairs and Maintenance Expense		300	
Cash			300

Extraordinary Repairs After a fixed asset has been placed into service, costs may be incurred to extend the asset's useful life. For example, the engine of a forklift that is near the end of its useful life may be overhauled at a cost of $4,500, extending its useful life by eight years. Such costs are *capital expenditures* and are recorded as a decrease in an accumulated depreciation account. In the case of the forklift, the expenditure is recorded as follows:

		Debit	Credit
Accumulated Depreciation—Forklift		4,500	
Cash			4,500

Because the forklift's remaining useful life has changed, depreciation for the forklift will also change based on the new book value of the forklift.

Asset Improvements After a fixed asset has been placed into service, costs may be incurred to improve the asset. For example, the service value of a delivery truck might be improved by adding a $5,500 hydraulic lift to allow for easier and quicker loading of cargo. Such costs are *capital expenditures* and are recorded as increases to the fixed asset account. In the case of the hydraulic lift, the expenditure is recorded as follows:

		Debit	Credit
Delivery Truck		5,500	
Cash			5,500

Because the cost of the delivery truck has increased, depreciation for the truck will also change over its remaining useful life.

Integrity, Objectivity, and Ethics in Business

CAPITAL CRIME

One of the largest accounting frauds in history involved the improper accounting for maintenance expenditures. **WorldCom**, the second largest telecommunications company in the United States at the time, improperly treated maintenance expenditures on its telecommunications network as capital expenditures. As a result, the company had to restate its prior years' earnings downward by nearly $4 billion to correct this error. The company declared bankruptcy within months of disclosing the error, and the CEO was sentenced to 25 years in prison.

The accounting for revenue and capital expenditures is summarized in Exhibit 11.

EXHIBIT 11

Revenue and Capital Expenditures

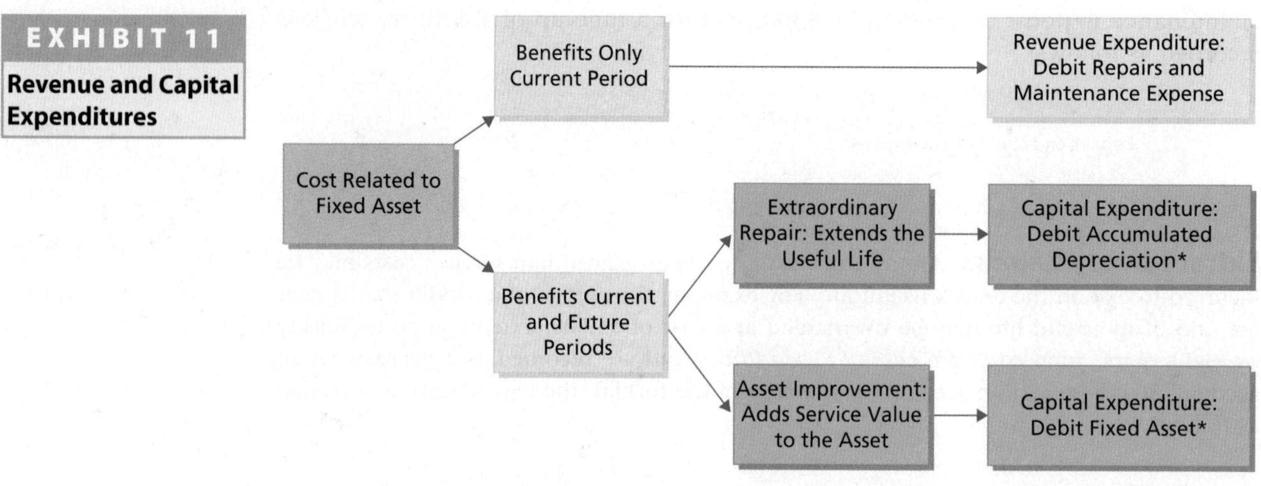

EXAMPLE EXERCISE 10-5 Capital and Revenue Expenditures OBJ. 2

On June 18, GTS Co. paid $1,200 to upgrade a hydraulic lift and $45 for an oil change for one of its delivery trucks. Journalize the entries for the hydraulic lift upgrade and oil change expenditures.

Follow My Example 10-5

June 18	Delivery Truck	1,200	
	Cash		1,200
18	Repairs and Maintenance Expense	45	
	Cash		45

Practice Exercises: PE 10-5A, PE 10-5B

OBJ. 3 Journalize the disposal of fixed assets.

Disposal of Fixed Assets

Fixed assets that are no longer useful may be discarded or sold.[5] In such cases, the fixed asset is removed from the accounts. Just because a fixed asset is fully depreciated, however, does not mean that it should be removed from the accounts.

If a fixed asset is still being used, its cost and accumulated depreciation should remain in the ledger even if the asset is fully depreciated. If the asset was removed from the ledger, the accounts would contain no evidence of their continued existence. In addition, cost and accumulated depreciation data on such assets are often needed for property tax and income tax reports.

Discarding Fixed Assets

If a fixed asset is no longer used and has no residual value, it is discarded. For example, assume that a fixed asset is fully depreciated, has no residual value, and is discarded. The discarded asset and its accumulated depreciation are removed from the accounts and ledger.

5 The accounting for the exchange of fixed assets is described and illustrated in the appendix at the end of this chapter.

To illustrate, assume that equipment acquired at a cost of $25,000 with no residual value is fully depreciated. On February 14, the equipment is discarded. The entry to record the discard is as follows:

Feb.	14	Accumulated Depreciation—Equipment	25,000	
		Equipment		25,000
		To write off equipment discarded.		

If an asset has not been fully depreciated, depreciation should be recorded before removing the asset from the accounting records. To illustrate, assume that equipment costing $6,000 with no estimated residual value is depreciated at a straight-line rate of 10%. The accumulated depreciation balance, after adjusting entries, is $4,650 on December 31. On March 24 of the following year, the asset is removed from service and discarded. The entry to record the depreciation for the three months before the asset is discarded is as follows:

Mar.	24	Depreciation Expense—Equipment	150	
		Accumulated Depreciation—Equipment		150
		To record current depreciation on equipment discarded ($600 × 3/12).		

The discarding of the equipment is then recorded as follows:

Mar.	24	Accumulated Depreciation—Equipment	4,800	
		Loss on Disposal of Equipment	1,200	
		Equipment		6,000
		To write off equipment discarded.		

The loss of $1,200 is recorded because the book value of the asset ($6,000 − $4,800) is greater than the amount received for the asset ($0). Losses on the discarding of fixed assets are reported on the income statement.

Selling Fixed Assets

The entry to record the sale of a fixed asset is similar to the entry for discarding an asset. The only difference is that the receipt of cash is also recorded. If the selling price is more than the book value of the asset, a gain is recorded. If the selling price is less than the book value, a loss is recorded.

To illustrate, assume that equipment is purchased at a cost of $10,000 with no estimated residual value and is depreciated at a straight-line rate of 10%. The equipment is sold for cash on October 12 of the eighth year of its use. The balance of the accumulated depreciation account as of the preceding December 31 is $7,000. The entry to update the depreciation for the nine months of the current year is as follows:

Oct.	12	Depreciation Expense—Equipment	750	
		Accumulated Depreciation—Equipment		750
		To record current depreciation on equipment sold ($10,000 × 9/12 × 10%).		

After the current depreciation is recorded, the book value of the asset is $2,250 ($10,000 − $7,750). The entries to record the sale, assuming three different selling prices, are as follows:

Sold at book value, for $2,250. No gain or loss.

Oct.	12	Cash	2,250	
		Accumulated Depreciation—Equipment	7,750	
		Equipment		10,000

Sold below book value, for $1,000. Loss of $1,250.

Oct.	12	Cash	1,000	
		Accumulated Depreciation—Equipment	7,750	
		Loss on Sale of Equipment	1,250	
		Equipment		10,000

Sold above book value, for $2,800. Gain of $550.

Oct.	12	Cash	2,800	
		Accumulated Depreciation—Equipment	7,750	
		Equipment		10,000
		Gain on Sale of Equipment		550

EXAMPLE EXERCISE 10-6 Sale of Equipment — OBJ. 3

Equipment was acquired at the beginning of the year at a cost of $91,000. The equipment was depreciated using the straight-line method based on an estimated useful life of nine years and an estimated residual value of $10,000.

a. What was the depreciation for the first year?

b. Assuming that the equipment was sold at the end of the second year for $78,000, determine the gain or loss on the sale of the equipment.

c. Journalize the entry to record the sale.

Follow My Example 10-6

a. $9,000 [($91,000 – $10,000) ÷ 9]

b. $5,000 gain {$78,000 – [$91,000 – ($9,000 × 2)]}

c.

Cash	78,000	
Accumulated Depreciation—Equipment	18,000	
Equipment		91,000
Gain on Sale of Equipment		5,000

Practice Exercises: PE 10-6A, PE 10-6B

Business Connection

DOWNSIZING

Management may decide to sell a fixed asset when it is perceived to no longer meet business objectives. This can happen when the strategy of the business changes or the business is downsizing operations. For example, over a recent three-year period, **Ruby Tuesday**, a national restaurant chain, sold stores and equipment at a book value of $30 million for cash proceeds of $34 million, resulting in a $4 million gain. These fixed assets were sold in order to focus on more profitable restaurants.

Natural Resources

OBJ. 4 Describe the accounting for natural resources, including the journal entry for depletion.

Some businesses own natural resources such as timber, minerals, or oil. The characteristics of natural resources are as follows:

- **Naturally Occurring:** An asset that is created through natural growth or naturally through the passage of time. For example, timber is a natural resource that naturally grows over time.
- **Removed for Sale:** The asset is consumed by removing it from its land source. For example, timber is removed for use when it is harvested, and minerals are removed when they are mined.
- **Removed and Sold over More Than One Year:** The natural resource is removed and sold over a period of more than one year.

Natural resources are classified as a type of fixed asset. The cost of a natural resource includes the cost of obtaining and preparing it for use. For example, legal fees incurred in purchasing a natural resource are included as part of its cost.

As natural resources are harvested or mined and then sold, a portion of their cost is debited to an expense account called **depletion expense**.

Depletion is determined as follows:[6]

Step 1. Determine the depletion rate as follows:

$$\text{Depletion Rate} = \frac{\text{Cost of Resource}}{\text{Estimated Total Units of Resource}}$$

Step 2. Multiply the depletion rate by the quantity removed from the resource during the period.

$$\text{Depletion Expense} = \text{Depletion Rate} \times \text{Quantity Removed}$$

To illustrate, assume that Karst Company purchased mining rights as follows:

Cost of mineral deposit	$ 400,000
Estimated total units of resource	1,000,000 tons
Tons mined during year	90,000 tons

The depletion expense of $36,000 for the year is computed as follows:

$$\text{Step 1. Depletion Rate} = \frac{\text{Cost of Resource}}{\text{Estimated Total Units of Resource}} = \frac{\$400{,}000}{1{,}000{,}000\text{ Tons}} = \$0.40\text{ per Ton}$$

$$\text{Step 2. Depletion Expense} = \$0.40\text{ per Ton} \times 90{,}000\text{ Tons} = \$36{,}000$$

The adjusting entry to record the depletion is as follows:

Dec.	31	Depletion Expense		36,000	
		Accumulated Depletion			36,000
		Depletion of mineral deposit.			

Like the accumulated depreciation account, Accumulated Depletion is a contra asset account. It is reported on the balance sheet as a deduction from the cost of the mineral deposit.

6 We assume that there is no significant residual value after all the natural resource is removed.

EXAMPLE EXERCISE 10-7 Depletion OBJ. 4

Earth's Treasures Mining Co. acquired mineral rights for $45,000,000. The mineral deposit is estimated at 50,000,000 tons. During the current year, 12,600,000 tons were mined and sold.

a. Determine the depletion rate.

b. Determine the amount of depletion expense for the current year.

c. Journalize the adjusting entry on December 31 to recognize the depletion expense.

Follow My Example 10-7

a. $0.90 per ton ($45,000,000 ÷ 50,000,000 tons)

b. $11,340,000 (12,600,000 tons × $0.90 per ton)

c.

Dec. 31	Depletion Expense	11,340,000	
	Accumulated Depletion		11,340,000
	Depletion of mineral deposit.		

Practice Exercises: PE 10-7A, PE 10-7B

OBJ. 5 Describe the accounting for intangible assets, such as patents, copyrights, and goodwill.

Intangible Assets

Long-term assets that are used in the operations of the business but do not exist physically are called intangible assets. **Intangible assets** may be acquired through innovative, creative activities or through the purchase of the rights from another company. Examples of intangible assets include patents, copyrights, trademarks, and goodwill.

The accounting for intangible assets is similar to that for fixed assets. The major issues are:

- Determining the initial cost.
- Determining the **amortization**, which is the amount of cost to transfer to expense.

Amortization results from the passage of time or a decline in the usefulness of the intangible asset.

Patents

Manufacturers may acquire exclusive rights to produce and sell goods with one or more unique features. Such rights are granted by **patents**, which the federal government issues to inventors. These rights continue in effect for 20 years. A business may purchase patent rights from others, or it may obtain patents developed by its own research and development.

The initial cost of a purchased patent, including any legal fees, is debited to an asset account. This cost is written off, or amortized, over the years of the patent's expected useful life. The expected useful life of a patent may be less than its legal life. For example, a patent may become worthless due to changing technology or consumer tastes.

Patent amortization is normally computed using the straight-line method. The amortization is recorded by debiting an amortization expense account and crediting the patents account. A separate contra asset account is usually *not* used for intangible assets.

To illustrate, assume that at the beginning of its fiscal year, a company acquires patent rights for $100,000. Although the patent will not expire for 14 years, its remaining useful life is estimated as five years. The adjusting entry to amortize the patent at the end of the year is as follows:

Dec.	31	Amortization Expense—Patents		20,000	
		Patents			20,000
		Patent amortization ($100,000 ÷ 5).			

Some companies develop their own patents through research and development. In such cases, any *research and development costs* are usually recorded as current operating expenses in the period in which they are incurred. This accounting for research and development costs is justified on the basis that any future benefits from current research and development are highly uncertain.

Copyrights and Trademarks

The exclusive right to publish and sell a literary, artistic, or musical composition is granted by a **copyright**. Copyrights are issued by the federal government and extend for 70 years beyond the author's death. The costs of a copyright include all costs of creating the work plus any other costs of obtaining the copyright. A copyright that is purchased is recorded at the price paid for it. Copyrights are amortized over their estimated useful lives.

A **trademark** is a name, term, or symbol used to identify a business and its products. Under federal law, businesses can protect their trademarks by registering them for 10 years and renewing the registration for 10-year periods. Like a copyright, the legal costs of registering a trademark are recorded as an asset. Most businesses identify their registered trademarks with ® in their advertisements and on their products.

If a trademark is purchased from another business, its cost is recorded as an asset. In such cases, the cost of the trademark is considered to have an indefinite useful life. Thus, trademarks are not amortized. Instead, trademarks are reviewed periodically for impaired value. When a trademark is impaired, the trademark should be written down and a loss recognized.

Link to McDonald's

McDonald's Corporation owns trademarks on "McDonald's" and the Golden Arches logo.

Link to McDonald's

On a recent balance sheet, **McDonald's** reported goodwill of $2.3 billion. Most of McDonald's goodwill arises when it purchases existing restaurants from franchisees.

Goodwill

Goodwill refers to an intangible asset of a business that is created from such favorable factors as location, product quality, reputation, and managerial skill. Goodwill allows a business to earn a greater rate of return than normal.

Generally accepted accounting principles (GAAP) allow goodwill to be recorded only if it is objectively determined by a transaction. An example of such a transaction is the purchase of a business at a price in excess of the fair value of its net assets (assets less liabilities). The excess is recorded as goodwill and reported as an intangible asset.

Unlike patents and copyrights, goodwill is not amortized. However, a loss should be recorded if the future prospects of the purchased firm become impaired. This loss would normally be disclosed in the Other Expense section of the income statement.

To illustrate, assume that on December 31, FaceCard Company has determined that $250,000 of the goodwill created from the purchase of Electronic Systems is impaired. The entry to record the impairment is as follows:

Dec.	31	Loss from Impaired Goodwill		250,000	
		Goodwill			250,000
		Impaired goodwill.			

Link to McDonald's

McDonald's compares fair value to book (carrying) value to determine whether goodwill is impaired. In a recent annual report, McDonald's reported $15.6 million of losses from impaired goodwill.

Exhibit 12 shows that intangible assets now represent more value than tangible assets in the S&P 500.

EXHIBIT 12

Frequency of Intangible Asset Disclosures for 500 Firms

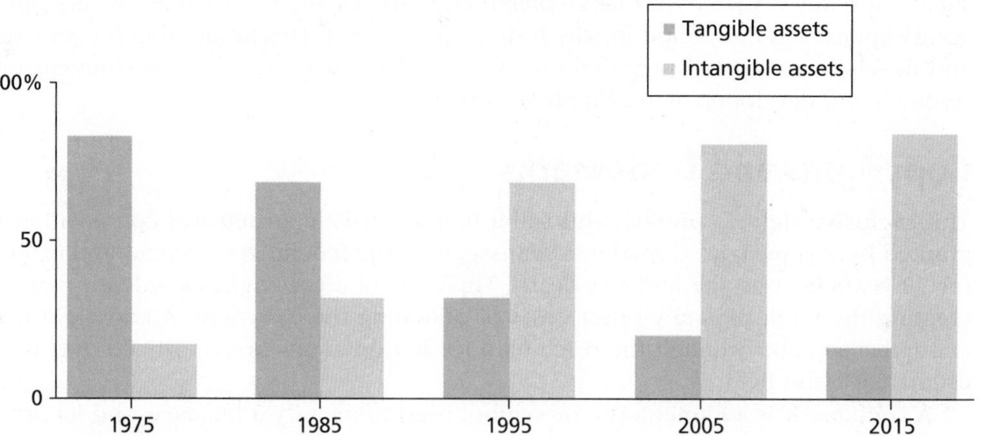

Source: https://www.oceantomo.com/blog/2015/03-05-ocean-tomo-2015-intangible-asset-market-value/.

Exhibit 13 summarizes the characteristics of intangible assets.

EXHIBIT 13

Comparison of Intangible Assets

Intangible Asset	Description	Amortization Period	Periodic Expense
Patent	Exclusive right to benefit from an innovation	Estimated useful life not to exceed legal life	Amortization expense
Copyright	Exclusive right to benefit from a literary, artistic, or musical composition	Estimated useful life not to exceed legal life	Amortization expense
Trademark	Exclusive use of a name, term, or symbol	None	Impairment loss if fair value less than carrying value (impaired)
Goodwill	Excess of purchase price of a business over the fair value of its net assets (assets − liabilities)	None	Impairment loss if fair value less than carrying value (impaired)

EXAMPLE EXERCISE 10-8 Impaired Goodwill and Amortization of Patent — OBJ. 5

On December 31, it was estimated that goodwill of $40,000 was impaired. In addition, a patent with an estimated useful economic life of 12 years was acquired for $84,000 on July 1.

a. Journalize the adjusting entry on December 31 for the impaired goodwill.

b. Journalize the adjusting entry on December 31 for the amortization of the patent rights.

Follow My Example 10-8

a.	Dec. 31	Loss from Impaired Goodwill	40,000	
		Goodwill		40,000
		Impaired goodwill.		
b.	Dec. 31	Amortization Expense—Patents	3,500	
		Patents		3,500
		Amortized patent rights [($84,000 ÷ 12) × (6 ÷ 12)].		

Practice Exercises: PE 10-8A, PE 10-8B

International Connection

IFRS INTERNATIONAL FINANCIAL REPORTING STANDARDS (IFRS)

IFRS allow certain research and development (R&D) costs to be recorded as assets when incurred. Typically, R&D costs are classified as either research costs or development costs. If certain criteria are met, research costs can be recorded as an expense, while development costs can be recorded as an asset. This criterion includes such considerations as the company's intent to use or to sell the intangible asset. For example, **Nokia Corporation** (Finland) reported capitalized development costs of €4.9 billion in a recent statement of financial position (balance sheet), where € represents the euro, the common currency of the European Economic Union.

Financial Reporting for Long-Term Assets: Fixed and Intangible

OBJ. 6 Describe how depreciation expense is reported on an income statement and prepare a balance sheet that includes fixed assets and intangible assets.

On the income statement, depreciation and amortization expense should be reported separately or disclosed in a note. A description of the methods used in computing depreciation should also be reported.

On the balance sheet, each class of fixed assets should be disclosed on the face of the statement along with its related accumulated depreciation. Fixed assets may also be reported at their *book value* (net amount) with accumulated depreciation shown in the notes.

If there are many classes of fixed assets, a single amount may be presented on the balance sheet, supported by a note with a separate listing. Fixed assets may be reported under the more descriptive caption of property, plant, and equipment.

Intangible assets are usually reported on the balance sheet in a separate section following fixed assets. The balance of each class of intangible assets should be disclosed net of any amortization.

The balance sheet presentation for **Mornin' Joe**'s fixed and intangible assets follows:

Mornin' Joe
Balance Sheet
December 31, 20Y6

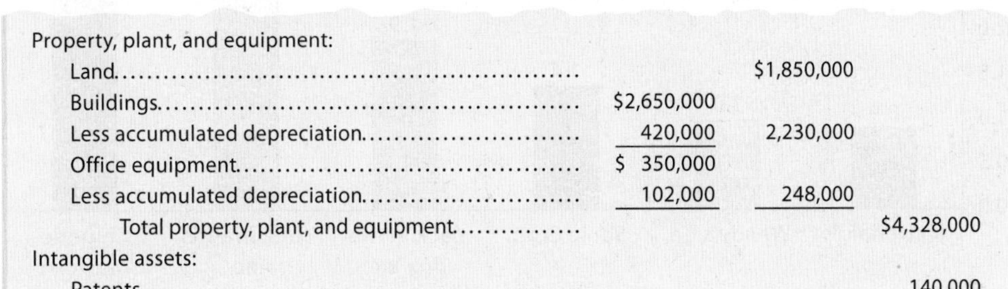

Property, plant, and equipment:			
Land		$1,850,000	
Buildings	$2,650,000		
Less accumulated depreciation	420,000	2,230,000	
Office equipment	$ 350,000		
Less accumulated depreciation	102,000	248,000	
Total property, plant, and equipment			$4,328,000
Intangible assets:			
Patents			140,000

If a company has natural resources, depletion expense is reported on the income statement. In addition, the cost and related accumulated depletion of the natural resources are reported as part of the Property, Plant, and Equipment section of the balance sheet.

OBJ. 7 Describe and illustrate the fixed asset turnover ratio to assess the efficiency of a company's use of its fixed assets.

Financial Analysis and Interpretation: Fixed Asset Turnover Ratio

Fixed Asset Turnover Ratio

The **fixed asset turnover ratio** measures the number of sales dollars earned per dollar of fixed assets. The higher the ratio, the more efficiently a company is using its fixed assets in generating sales. The ratio is computed as follows:

$$\text{Fixed Asset Turnover Ratio} = \frac{\text{Sales}}{\text{Average Book Value of Fixed Assets}}$$

To illustrate, the following data (in millions) were taken from a recent financial statement of **McDonald's Corporation**:

Sales	$21,025
Fixed assets (net):	
Beginning of year	22,448
End of year	22,843

McDonald's fixed asset turnover ratio for the year is computed as follows (rounded to one decimal place):

$$\text{Fixed Asset Turnover Ratio} = \frac{\text{Sales}}{\text{Average Book Value of Fixed Assets}}$$

$$= \frac{\$21{,}025}{(\$22{,}448 + \$22{,}843) \div 2} = \frac{\$21{,}025}{\$22{,}646}$$

$$= 0.9$$

Is McDonald's fixed asset turnover ratio of 0.9 efficient? To answer this question, McDonald's fixed asset turnover ratio can be compared to other quick-service restaurant companies, as shown in Exhibit 14. **Yum! Brands** operates **KFC**, **Pizza Hut**, and **Taco Bell** quick-service restaurants. The other restaurants are likely familiar by name.

EXHIBIT 14

Fixed Asset Turnover: Selected Quick-Service Restaurants

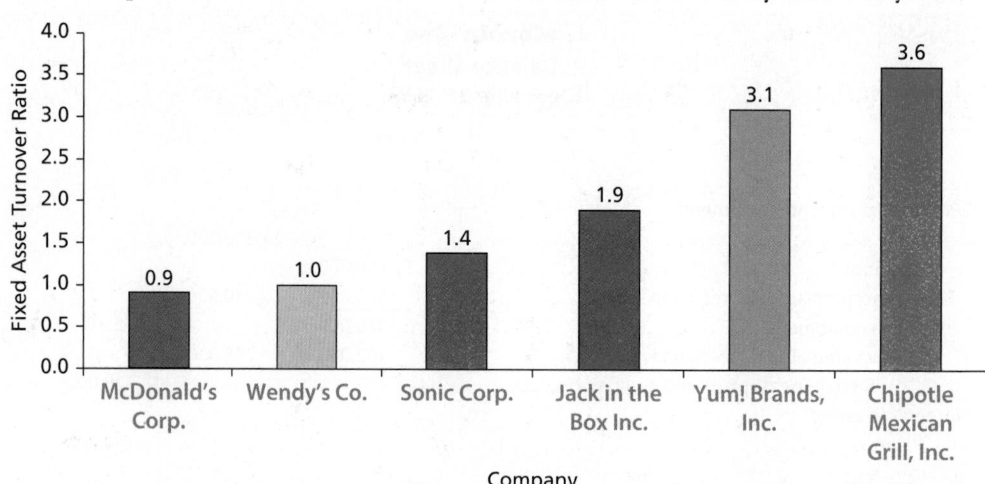

Differences in the fixed asset turnover between these companies can be due to a number of factors, including differences in both the average fixed asset book value and sales per restaurant. Explaining McDonald's low fixed asset turnover ratio relative to the other restaurants would require a deeper analysis into these factors.

The fixed asset turnover ratio will vary across industries because of differences in how industries use fixed assets. For example, the fixed asset turnover ratio for selected companies in different industries is shown in Exhibit 15.

Company (Industry)	Fixed Asset Turnover Ratio
Disney (entertainment)	2.1
ExxonMobil (petrochemical)	1.0
ManpowerGroup (temporary employment)	35.0
McDonald's (quick-service restaurant)	0.9
Union Pacific (railroad)	0.4

EXHIBIT 15

Fixed Asset Turnover Ratio: Various Industries

The smaller fixed asset turnover ratios are associated with industries that require large fixed asset investments to generate revenues. The larger fixed asset turnover ratios are associated with industries that require smaller fixed asset investments to generate revenues. Thus, for example, the difference in the fixed asset turnover ratio between **Union Pacific** and **ManpowerGroup** is due to the difference in the way fixed assets are used in their respective industries. Railroads require extensive investments in track, engines, and railcars, while temporary employment agencies require few investments in fixed assets.

Business Connection

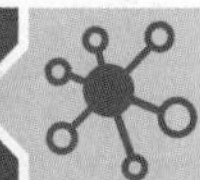

HUB-AND-SPOKE OR POINT-TO-POINT?

Southwest Airlines Co. uses a simple fare structure featuring low, unrestricted, unlimited, everyday coach fares. These fares are made possible by Southwest's use of a point-to-point rather than a hub-and-spoke business approach.

United Airlines, Inc., **Delta Air Lines**, and **American Airlines** employ a hub-and-spoke approach in which an airline establishes major hubs that serve as connecting links to other cities. For example, Delta has major connecting hubs in Atlanta and Salt Lake City.

In contrast, Southwest focuses on nonstop, point-to-point service between selected cities. As a result, Southwest minimizes connections, delays, and total trip time. This operating approach permits Southwest to achieve high utilization of its fixed assets, such as its 750 aircraft.

EXAMPLE EXERCISE 10-9 Fixed Asset Turnover Ratio

OBJ. 7

Financial statement data for years ending December 31 for Broadwater Company follow:

	Year 2	Year 1
Sales	$2,862,000	$2,025,000
Fixed assets:		
Beginning of year	750,000	600,000
End of year	840,000	750,000

a. Determine the fixed asset turnover ratio for Year 1 and Year 2.

b. Does the change in the fixed asset turnover ratio from Year 1 to Year 2 indicate a favorable or an unfavorable change?

(Continued)

Follow My Example 10-9

a. Fixed asset turnover:

	Year 2	Year 1
Sales	$2,862,000	$2,025,000
Fixed assets:		
Beginning of year	$750,000	$600,000
End of year	$840,000	$750,000
Average fixed assets	$795,000	$675,000
	[($750,000 + $840,000) ÷ 2]	[($600,000 + $750,000) ÷ 2]
Fixed asset turnover	3.6	3.0
	($2,862,000 ÷ $795,000)	($2,025,000 ÷ $675,000)

b. The increase in the fixed asset turnover ratio from 3.0 to 3.6 indicates a favorable change in the efficiency of using fixed assets to generate sales.

Practice Exercises: PE 10-9A, PE 10-9B

APPENDIX

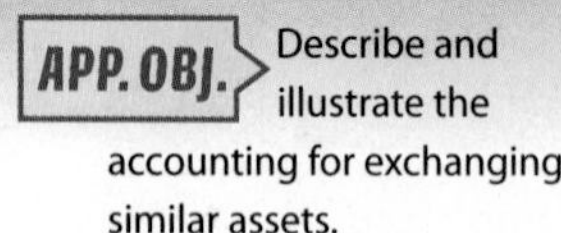
APP. OBJ. Describe and illustrate the accounting for exchanging similar assets.

Exchanging Similar Fixed Assets

Old equipment is often traded in for new equipment having a similar use. In such cases, the seller allows the buyer an amount for the old equipment traded in. This amount, called the **trade-in allowance**, may be either greater or less than the book value of the old equipment. The remaining balance—the amount owed—is either paid in cash or recorded as a liability. It is normally called **boot**, which is its tax name.

Accounting for the exchange of similar assets depends on whether the transaction has *commercial substance*.[7] An exchange has commercial substance if future cash flows change as a result of the exchange. If an exchange of similar assets has commercial substance, a gain or loss is recognized. In such cases, the exchange is accounted for similar to that of a sale of a fixed asset. The gain or loss is determined as the difference between the fair market value (trade-in allowance) of the asset given up (exchanged) and its book value. Alternatively, the gain or loss can be determined as the difference between the fair market value of the new asset received and the assets given up in the exchange (cash and book value of the old asset).

Gain on Exchange

To illustrate a gain on an exchange of similar assets, assume the following:

Similar equipment acquired (new):

Price (fair market value) of new equipment	$5,000
Less trade-in allowance on old equipment	1,100
Cash paid at June 19, date of exchange	$3,900

Equipment traded in (old):

Cost of old equipment	$4,000
Less accumulated depreciation at date of exchange	3,200
Book value at June 19, date of exchange	$ 800

7 *FASB Accounting Standards Codification*, Section 360-10-30.

The entry to record this exchange and payment of cash is as follows:

June	19	Accumulated Depreciation—Equipment		3,200	
		Equipment (new equipment)		5,000	
		Equipment (old equipment)			4,000
		Cash			3,900
		Gain on Exchange of Equipment			300

The gain on the exchange, $300, is the difference between the fair market value (trade-in allowance) of the asset given up (exchanged) of $1,100 and its book value of $800, computed as follows:

Fair market value (trade-in allowance) of old equipment	$1,100
Less book value of old equipment	800
Gain on exchange of assets	$ 300

The gain on the exchange, $300, can also be determined as the difference between the fair market value of the new asset of $5,000 and the book value of the old asset traded in of $800 plus the cash paid of $3,900, computed as follows:

Price (fair market value) of new equipment		$5,000
Assets given up in exchange:		
Book value of old equipment ($4,000 – $3,200)	$ 800	
Cash paid on the exchange	3,900	4,700
Gain on exchange of assets		$ 300

Loss on Exchange

To illustrate a loss on an exchange of similar assets, assume that instead of a trade-in allowance of $1,100, a trade-in allowance of only $675 was allowed in the preceding example. In this case, the cash paid on the exchange is $4,325, computed as follows:

Price (fair market value) of new equipment	$5,000
Less trade-in allowance of old equipment	675
Cash paid at June 19, date of exchange	$4,325

The entry to record this exchange and payment of cash is as follows:

June	19	Accumulated Depreciation—Equipment		3,200	
		Equipment (new equipment)		5,000	
		Loss on Exchange of Equipment		125	
		Equipment (old equipment)			4,000
		Cash			4,325

The loss on the exchange, $125, is the difference between the fair market value (trade-in allowance) of the asset given up (exchanged) of $675 and its book value of $800, computed as follows:

Fair market value (trade-in allowance) of old equipment	$ 675
Less book value of old equipment	800
Loss on exchange of assets	$(125)

The loss on the exchange, $125, can also be determined as the difference between the fair market value of the new asset of $5,000 and the book value of the old asset traded in of $800 plus the cash paid of $4,325, computed as follows:

Price (fair market value) of new equipment		$5,000
Assets given up in exchange:		
Book value of old equipment ($4,000 – $3,200)	$ 800	
Cash paid on the exchange	4,325	5,125
Loss on exchange of assets		$ (125)

In those cases where an asset exchange *lacks commercial substance*, no gain is recognized on the exchange. Instead, the cost of the new asset is reduced by any gain. For example, in the first illustration, the gain of $300 would be subtracted from the purchase price of $5,000 and the new asset would be recorded at $4,700. Accounting for the exchange of assets that lack commercial substance is discussed in more advanced accounting texts.[8]

At a Glance 10

OBJ. 1 Define, classify, and account for the cost of fixed assets.

Key Points Fixed assets are long-term tangible assets used in the normal operations of the business such as equipment, buildings, and land. The initial cost of a fixed asset includes all amounts spent to get the asset in place and ready for use.

Learning Outcomes	Example Exercises	Practice Exercises
• Define *fixed assets*. • List the types of costs that should be included in the cost of a fixed asset.		

8 The exchange of similar assets also involves complex tax issues, which are discussed in advanced accounting courses.

OBJ. 2 Compute depreciation using the following methods: straight-line, units-of-activity, and double-declining-balance.

Key Points All fixed assets except land should be depreciated over time. Three factors are considered in determining depreciation: (1) the fixed asset's initial cost, (2) the useful life of the asset, and (3) the residual value of the asset.

Depreciation may be determined using the straight-line, units-of-activity, and double-declining-balance methods.

Depreciation may be revised into the future for changes in an asset's useful life or residual value.

Learning Outcomes	Example Exercises	Practice Exercises
• Define and describe *depreciation*.		
• List the factors used in determining depreciation.		
• Compute straight-line depreciation.	**EE10-1**	**PE10-1A, 10-1B**
• Compute units-of-activity depreciation.	**EE10-2**	**PE10-2A, 10-2B**
• Compute double-declining-balance depreciation.	**EE10-3**	**PE10-3A, 10-3B**
• Compute revised depreciation for a change in an asset's useful life and residual value.	**EE10-4**	**PE10-4A, 10-4B**
• Provide examples of ordinary repairs, asset improvements, and extraordinary repairs.		
• Prepare journal entries for ordinary repairs, asset improvements, and extraordinary repairs.	**EE10-5**	**PE10-5A, 10-5B**

OBJ. 3 Journalize the disposal of fixed assets.

Key Points When discarding a fixed asset, any depreciation for the current period should be recorded, and the book value of the asset is then removed from the accounts.

When a fixed asset is sold, the book value is removed, and the cash or other asset received is recorded. If the selling price is more than the book value of the asset, the transaction results in a gain. If the selling price is less than the book value, there is a loss.

Learning Outcomes	Example Exercises	Practice Exercises
• Prepare the journal entry for discarding a fixed asset.		
• Prepare journal entries for the sale of a fixed asset.	**EE10-6**	**PE10-6A, 10-6B**

OBJ. 4 Describe the accounting for natural resources, including the journal entry for depletion.

Key Points The amount of periodic depletion is computed by multiplying the quantity of minerals extracted during the period by a depletion rate. The depletion rate is computed by dividing the cost of the mineral deposit by its estimated total units of resource. The entry to record depletion debits a depletion expense account and credits an accumulated depletion account.

Learning Outcomes	Example Exercises	Practice Exercises
• Define and describe *depletion*.		
• Compute a depletion rate.	**EE10-7**	**PE10-7A, 10-7B**
• Prepare the journal entry to record depletion.	**EE10-7**	**PE10-7A, 10-7B**

OBJ. 5 Describe the accounting for intangible assets, such as patents, copyrights, and goodwill.

Key Points Long-term assets such as patents, copyrights, trademarks, and goodwill are intangible assets. The cost of patents and copyrights should be amortized over the years of the asset's expected usefulness by debiting an expense account and crediting the intangible asset account. Trademarks and goodwill are not amortized but are written down only upon impairment.

Learning Outcomes	Example Exercises	Practice Exercises
• Define, describe, and provide examples of *intangible assets*.		
• Prepare a journal entry for the purchase of an intangible asset.		
• Prepare a journal entry to amortize the costs of patents and copyrights.	**EE10-8**	**PE10-8A, 10-8B**
• Prepare the journal entry to record the impairment of goodwill.	**EE10-8**	**PE10-8A, 10-8B**

OBJ. 6 Describe how depreciation expense is reported on an income statement and prepare a balance sheet that includes fixed assets and intangible assets.

Key Points The amount of depreciation expense and the depreciation methods used should be disclosed in the financial statements. Each major class of fixed assets should be disclosed, along with the related accumulated depreciation. Intangible assets are usually presented in a separate section following fixed assets. Each major class of intangible assets should be disclosed net of the amortization recorded to date.

Learning Outcomes	Example Exercises	Practice Exercises
• Describe and illustrate how fixed assets are reported on the income statement and balance sheet.		
• Describe and illustrate how intangible assets are reported on the income statement and balance sheet.		
• Describe and illustrate how natural resources are reported on the income statement and balance sheet.		

OBJ. 7 Describe and illustrate the fixed asset turnover ratio to assess the efficiency of a company's use of its fixed assets.

Key Points A measure of a company's efficiency in using its fixed assets to generate sales is the fixed asset turnover ratio. The fixed asset turnover ratio measures the number of dollars of sales earned per dollar of fixed assets and is computed by dividing sales by the average book value of fixed assets.

Learning Outcomes	Example Exercises	Practice Exercises
• Describe a measure of the efficiency of a company's use of fixed assets to generate revenue.		
• Compute and interpret the fixed asset turnover ratio.	**EE10-9**	**PE10-9A, 10-9B**

Illustrative Problem

McCollum Company, a furniture wholesaler, acquired new equipment at a cost of $150,000 at the beginning of the fiscal year. The equipment has an estimated life of five years and an estimated residual value of $12,000. Ellen McCollum, the president, has requested information regarding alternative depreciation methods.

Instructions

1. Determine the annual depreciation for each of the five years of estimated useful life of the equipment, the accumulated depreciation at the end of each year, and the book value of the equipment at the end of each year by (a) the straight-line method and (b) the double-declining-balance method.
2. Assume that the equipment was depreciated under the double-declining-balance method. In the first week of the fifth year, the equipment was sold for $10,000. Journalize the entry to record the sale.

Solution

1.

	Year	Depreciation Expense	Accumulated Depreciation, End of Year	Book Value, End of Year
a.	1	$27,600*	$ 27,600	$122,400
	2	27,600	55,200	94,800
	3	27,600	82,800	67,200
	4	27,600	110,400	39,600
	5	27,600	138,000	12,000

*$27,600 = ($150,000 − $12,000) ÷ 5

	Year	Depreciation Expense	Accumulated Depreciation, End of Year	Book Value, End of Year
b.	1	$60,000**	$ 60,000	$90,000
	2	36,000	96,000	54,000
	3	21,600	117,600	32,400
	4	12,960	130,560	19,440
	5	7,440***	138,000	12,000

**$60,000 = $150,000 × 40%

***The asset is not depreciated below the estimated residual value of $12,000.
$7,440 = $150,000 − $130,560 − $12,000

2.

Account	Debit	Credit
Cash	10,000	
Accumulated Depreciation—Equipment	130,560	
Loss on Sale of Equipment	9,440	
Equipment		150,000

Key Terms

accelerated depreciation method (502)
amortization (512)
book value (498)
boot (518)
capital expenditures (506)
copyright (513)
depletion expense (511)
depreciable cost (496)
depreciation (496)
double-declining-balance method (501)
expected useful life (496)
fixed asset turnover ratio (516)
fixed assets (492)
goodwill (513)
initial cost (496)
intangible assets (512)
patents (512)
residual value (496)
revenue expenditures (506)
straight-line method (497)
trade-in allowance (518)
trademark (513)
units-of-activity method (499)

Discussion Questions

1. O'Neil Office Supplies has a fleet of automobiles and trucks for use by salespersons and for delivery of office supplies and equipment. Collins Auto Sales Co. has automobiles and trucks for sale. Under what caption would the automobiles and trucks be reported in the balance sheet of (a) O'Neil Office Supplies and (b) Collins Auto Sales Co.?
2. Bullwinkle Co. acquired an adjacent vacant lot with the hope of selling it in the future at a gain. The lot is not intended to be used in Bullwinkle business operations. Where should such real estate be listed on the balance sheet?
3. Alpine Company solicited bids from several contractors to construct an addition to its office building. The lowest bid received was for $1,200,000. Alpine decided to construct the addition itself at a cost of $1,100,000. What amount should be recorded in the building account?
4. Keyser Company purchased a machine that has a manufacturer's suggested life of 20 years. The company plans to use the machine on a special project that will last 12 years. At the completion of the project, the machine will be sold. Over how many years should the machine be depreciated?
5. Is it necessary for a business to use the same method of computing depreciation for all classes of its depreciable assets?
6. a. Under what conditions is the use of the straight-line depreciation method most appropriate?
   b. Under what conditions is the use of the units-of-activity depreciation method most appropriate?
   c. Under what conditions is the use of the double-declining-balance depreciation method most appropriate?
7. Distinguish between the accounting for capital expenditures and revenue expenditures.
8. Immediately after a used truck is acquired, a new motor is installed at a total cost of $3,850. Is this a capital expenditure or a revenue expenditure?
9. For some of the fixed assets of a business, the balance in Accumulated Depreciation is equal to the cost of the asset. (a) Is it permissible to record additional depreciation on the assets if they are still useful to the business? Explain. (b) When should an entry be made to remove the cost and the accumulated depreciation from the accounts?
10. a. Over what period of time should the cost of a patent acquired by purchase be amortized?
    b. In general, what is the required accounting treatment for research and development costs?
    c. How should goodwill be amortized?

Practice Exercises

Example Exercises

EE 10-1 *p. 499*

PE 10-1A Straight-line depreciation **OBJ. 2**

A building acquired at the beginning of the year at a cost of $1,630,000 has an estimated residual value of $340,000 and an estimated useful life of 10 years. Determine (a) the depreciable cost, (b) the straight-line rate, and (c) the annual straight-line depreciation.

EE 10-1 *p. 499*

PE 10-1B Straight-line depreciation **OBJ. 2**

Equipment acquired at the beginning of the year at a cost of $470,000 has an estimated residual value of $62,000 and an estimated useful life of five years. Determine (a) the depreciable cost, (b) the straight-line rate, and (c) the annual straight-line depreciation.

EE 10-2 *p. 501*

PE 10-2A Units-of-activity depreciation **OBJ. 2**

A truck acquired at a cost of $202,800 has an estimated residual value of $18,000, has an estimated useful life of 440,000 miles, and was driven 113,000 miles during the year. Determine (a) the depreciable cost, (b) the depreciation rate, and (c) the units-of-activity depreciation for the year.

SHOW ME HOW

EXCEL ONLINE

EE 10-2 *p. 501*

PE 10-2B Units-of-activity depreciation **OBJ. 2**

A tractor acquired at a cost of $678,000 has an estimated residual value of $48,000, has an estimated useful life of 45,000 hours, and was operated 3,330 hours during the year. Determine (a) the depreciable cost, (b) the depreciation rate, and (c) the units-of-activity depreciation for the year.

SHOW ME HOW

EE 10-3 *p. 503*

PE 10-3A Double-declining-balance depreciation **OBJ. 2**

A building acquired at the beginning of the year at a cost of $1,193,000 has an estimated residual value of $220,000 and an estimated useful life of 40 years. Determine (a) the double-declining-balance rate and (b) the double-declining-balance depreciation for the first year.

SHOW ME HOW

EE 10-3 *p. 503*

PE 10-3B Double-declining-balance depreciation **OBJ. 2**

Equipment acquired at the beginning of the year at a cost of $540,000 has an estimated residual value of $40,000 and an estimated useful life of 10 years. Determine (a) the double-declining-balance rate and (b) the double-declining-balance depreciation for the first year.

SHOW ME HOW

EE 10-4 *p. 506*

PE 10-4A Revision of depreciation **OBJ. 2**

Equipment with a cost of $304,000 has an estimated residual value of $41,600, has an estimated useful life of 16 years, and is depreciated by the straight-line method. (a) Determine the amount of the annual depreciation. (b) Determine the book value at the end of the tenth year of use. (c) Assuming that at the start of the eleventh year the remaining life is estimated to be eight years and the residual value is estimated to be $16,800, determine the depreciation expense for each of the remaining eight years.

SHOW ME HOW

EE 10-4 *p. 506*

PE 10-4B Revision of depreciation **OBJ. 2**

A truck with a cost of $123,000 has an estimated residual value of $24,000, has an estimated useful life of 12 years, and is depreciated by the straight-line method. (a) Determine the amount of the annual depreciation. (b) Determine the book value at the end of the seventh year of use. (c) Assuming that at the start of the eighth year the remaining life is estimated to be five years and the residual value is estimated to be $15,000, determine the depreciation expense for each of the remaining five years.

SHOW ME HOW

EE 10-5 *p. 508*

PE 10-5A Capital and revenue expenditures **OBJ. 2**

On February 14, Foster Associates Co. paid $4,700 to repair the transmission on one of its delivery vans. In addition, Foster paid $920 to install a GPS system in its van. Journalize the entries for the transmission and GPS system expenditures.

SHOW ME HOW

EE 10-5 *p. 508*

PE 10-5B Capital and revenue expenditures **OBJ. 2**

On August 7, Blue Ocean Inflatables Co. paid $2,800 to install a hydraulic lift and $70 for an air filter for one of its delivery trucks. Journalize the entries for the new lift and air filter expenditures.

SHOW ME HOW

EE 10-6 *p. 510*

PE 10-6A Sale of equipment **OBJ. 3**

Equipment was acquired at the beginning of the year at a cost of $280,000. The equipment was depreciated using the double-declining-balance method based on an estimated useful life of 16 years and an estimated residual value of $14,000.

a. What was the depreciation for the first year?

b. Assuming that the equipment was sold at the end of the second year for $230,400, determine the gain or loss on the sale of the equipment.

c. Journalize the entry to record the sale.

SHOW ME HOW

EE 10-6 p. 510

PE 10-6B Sale of equipment OBJ. 3

Equipment was acquired at the beginning of the year at a cost of $287,100. The equipment was depreciated using the straight-line method based on an estimated useful life of nine years and an estimated residual value of $27,000.

a. What was the depreciation for the first year?

b. Assuming the equipment was sold at the end of the fifth year for $138,700, determine the gain or loss on the sale of the equipment.

c. Journalize the entry to record the sale.

SHOW ME HOW

EE 10-7 p. 512

PE 10-7A Depletion OBJ. 4

Snowcap Mining Co. acquired mineral rights for $342,720,000. The mineral deposit is estimated at 306,000,000 tons. During the current year, 55,600,000 tons were mined and sold.

a. Determine the depletion rate.

b. Determine the amount of depletion expense for the current year.

c. Journalize the adjusting entry on December 31 to recognize the depletion expense.

SHOW ME HOW

EE 10-7 p. 512

PE 10-7B Depletion OBJ. 4

Poff Mining Co. acquired mineral rights for $195,650,000. The mineral deposit is estimated at 559,000,000 tons. During the current year, 22,900,000 tons were mined and sold.

a. Determine the depletion rate.

b. Determine the amount of depletion expense for the current year.

c. Journalize the adjusting entry on December 31 to recognize the depletion expense.

SHOW ME HOW

EE 10-8 p. 514

PE 10-8A Impaired goodwill and amortization of patent OBJ. 5

On December 31, it was estimated that goodwill of $4,700,000 was impaired. In addition, a patent with an estimated useful economic life of 12 years was acquired for $1,260,000 on April 1.

a. Journalize the adjusting entry on December 31 for the impaired goodwill.

b. Journalize the adjusting entry on December 31 for the amortization of the patent rights.

SHOW ME HOW

EE 10-8 p. 514

PE 10-8B Impaired goodwill and amortization of patent OBJ. 5

On December 31, it was estimated that goodwill of $1,600,000 was impaired. In addition, a patent with an estimated useful economic life of 15 years was acquired for $594,000 on August 1.

a. Journalize the adjusting entry on December 31 for the impaired goodwill.

b. Journalize the adjusting entry on December 31 for the amortization of the patent rights.

SHOW ME HOW

FAI

EE 10-9 p. 517

PE 10-9A Fixed asset turnover ratio OBJ. 7

Financial statement data for years ending December 31 for Dennis Company follow:

	Year 2	Year 1
Sales	$4,521,000	$3,960,000
Fixed assets:		
Beginning of year	1,140,000	1,060,000
End of year	1,600,000	1,140,000

a. Determine the fixed asset turnover ratio for Year 1 and Year 2.

b. Does the change in the fixed asset turnover ratio from Year 1 to Year 2 indicate a favorable or an unfavorable change?

SHOW ME HOW

FAI

EXCEL ONLINE

EE 10-9 *p. 517*

PE 10-9B Fixed asset turnover ratio **OBJ. 7**

Financial statement data for years ending December 31 for Xiong Company follow:

	Year 2	Year 1
Sales	$1,560,000	$1,026,000
Fixed assets:		
Beginning of year	580,000	500,000
End of year	620,000	580,000

a. Determine the fixed asset turnover ratio for Year 1 and Year 2.

b. Does the change in the fixed asset turnover ratio from Year 1 to Year 2 indicate a favorable or an unfavorable change?

Exercises

EX 10-1 Costs of acquiring fixed assets **OBJ. 1**

Melinda Stoffers owns and operates ABC Print Co. During February, ABC incurred the following costs in acquiring two printing presses. One printing press was new, and the other was purchased from a business that recently filed for bankruptcy.

Costs related to new printing press:

1. Fee paid to factory representative for installation
2. Freight
3. Insurance while in transit
4. New parts to replace those damaged in unloading
5. Sales tax on purchase price
6. Special foundation

Costs related to used printing press:

7. Fees paid to attorney to review purchase agreement
8. Freight
9. Installation
10. Repair of damage incurred in reconditioning the press
11. Replacement of worn-out parts
12. Vandalism repairs during installation

a. Indicate which costs incurred in acquiring the new printing press should be debited to the asset account.

b. Indicate which costs incurred in acquiring the used printing press should be debited to the asset account.

EX 10-2 Determining cost of land **OBJ. 1, 2**

Bridger Ski Co. has developed a tract of land into a ski resort. The company has cut the trees, cleared and graded the land and hills, and constructed ski lifts.

(a) Should the tree cutting, land clearing, and grading costs of constructing the ski slopes be debited to the land account? (b) If such costs are debited to Land, should they be depreciated? Explain.

SHOW ME HOW

EX 10-3 Determining cost of land **OBJ. 1**

On-Time Delivery Company acquired an adjacent lot to construct a new warehouse, paying $90,000 and giving a short-term note for $50,000. Legal fees paid were $1,750, delinquent taxes assumed were $25,000, and fees paid to remove an old building from the land were $9,000. Materials salvaged from the demolition of the building were sold for $1,000. A contractor was paid $415,000 to construct a new warehouse. Determine the cost of the land to be reported on the balance sheet.

EX 10-4 Nature of depreciation OBJ. 2

Tri-City Ironworks Co. reported $44,500,000 for equipment and $29,800,000 for accumulated depreciation—equipment on its balance sheet.

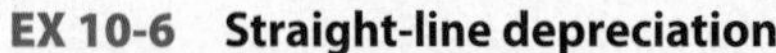 Does this mean (a) that the replacement cost of the equipment is $44,500,000 and (b) that $29,800,000 is set aside in a special fund for the replacement of the equipment? Explain.

EX 10-5 Straight-line depreciation rates OBJ. 2

✓ c. 4%

Convert each of the following estimates of useful life to a straight-line depreciation rate, stated as a percentage: (a) 10 years, (b) 8 years, (c) 25 years, (d) 40 years, (e) 5 years, (f) 4 years, (g) 20 years.

EX 10-6 Straight-line depreciation OBJ. 2

A refrigerator used by a wholesale warehouse has a cost of $66,700, an estimated residual value of $5,100, and an estimated useful life of 14 years. What is the amount of the annual depreciation computed by the straight-line method?

EX 10-7 Depreciation by units-of-activity method OBJ. 2

A diesel-powered tractor with a cost of $136,700 and estimated residual value of $14,500 is expected to have a useful operating life of 18,800 hours. During November, the tractor was operated 160 hours. Determine the depreciation for the month.

EX 10-8 Depreciation by units-of-activity method OBJ. 2

✓ a. Truck #1, credit to Accumulated Depreciation, $5,460

Prior to adjustment at the end of the year, the balance in Trucks is $296,900 and the balance in Accumulated Depreciation—Trucks is $99,740. Details of the subsidiary ledger are as follows:

Truck No.	Cost	Estimated Residual Value	Estimated Useful Life	Accumulated Depreciation at Beginning of Year	Miles Operated During Year
1	$80,000	$15,000	250,000 miles	—	21,000 miles
2	54,000	6,000	300,000	$14,400	33,500
3	72,900	10,900	200,000	60,140	8,000
4	90,000	22,800	240,000	25,200	22,500

a. Determine for each truck the depreciation rate per mile and the amount to be credited to the Accumulated Depreciation section of each subsidiary account for the miles operated during the current year.

b. Journalize the entry on December 31 to record depreciation for the year.

EX 10-9 Depreciation by two methods OBJ. 2

✓ a. $7,000

A computer system acquired on January 1 at a cost of $35,000 has an estimated useful life of five years. Assuming that it will have no residual value, determine the depreciation for each of the first two years (a) by the straight-line method and (b) by the double-declining-balance method.

EX 10-10 Depreciation by two methods OBJ. 2

✓ a. $2,600

A storage tank acquired at the beginning of the fiscal year at a cost of $61,000 has an estimated residual value of $9,000 and an estimated useful life of 20 years. Determine the following: (a) the amount of annual depreciation by the straight-line method and (b) the amount of depreciation for the first and second years computed by the double-declining-balance method.

EX 10-11 Partial-year depreciation — OBJ. 2

✔ a. First year, $6,200

Equipment acquired at a cost of $105,000 has an estimated residual value of $12,000 and an estimated useful life of 10 years. It was placed into service on May 1 of the current fiscal year, which ends on December 31. Determine the depreciation for the current fiscal year and for the following fiscal year by (a) the straight-line method and (b) the double-declining-balance method.

EX 10-12 Revision of depreciation — OBJ. 2

✔ a. $23,750

A building with a cost of $1,200,000 has an estimated residual value of $250,000, has an estimated useful life of 40 years, and is depreciated by the straight-line method. (a) What is the amount of the annual depreciation? (b) What is the book value at the end of the twenty-eighth year of use? (c) If at the start of the twenty-ninth year it is estimated that the remaining life is 10 years and that the residual value is $180,000, what is the depreciation expense for each of the remaining 10 years?

EX 10-13 Capital and revenue expenditures — OBJ. 2

US Freight Lines Co. incurred the following costs related to trucks and vans used in operating its delivery service:

1. Installed GPS systems on the trucks.
2. Replaced the transmission fluid on a truck that had been in service for the past four years.
3. Overhauled the engine on one of the trucks purchased three years ago.
4. Performed annual service of installing new spark plugs, changing the oil, and greasing the joints of all trucks and vans.
5. Rebuilt the engine on one of the vans that had been driven 80,000 miles.
6. Repaired a flat tire on one of the vans.
7. Installed a hydraulic lift to a truck.
8. Tinted the back and side windows of the vans and installed a security system to discourage theft of contents.
9. Replaced a truck's suspension system with a new suspension system, allowing for heavier loads.
10. Installed an optional third-row seat on one of the vans.

Classify each of the costs as a capital expenditure or a revenue expenditure.

EX 10-14 Capital and revenue expenditures — OBJ. 2

Jackie Fox owns and operates Platinum Transport Co. During the past year, Jackie incurred the following costs related to an 18-wheel truck:

1. Changed engine oil.
2. Installed a television in the sleeping compartment of the truck.
3. Installed a wind deflector on top of the cab to increase fuel mileage.
4. Modified the factory-installed turbo charger with a special-order kit designed to add 50 more horsepower to the engine performance.
5. Replaced a headlight that had burned out.
6. Replaced a shock absorber that had worn out.
7. Replaced fog and cab light bulbs.
8. Replaced the hydraulic brake system that had begun to fail during his latest trip through the Rocky Mountains.
9. Removed the old radio and replaced it with a new communications module.
10. Replaced the old radar detector with a newer model that is fastened to the truck with a locking device that prevents its removal.

Classify each of the costs as a capital expenditure or a revenue expenditure.

EX 10-15 Capital and revenue expenditures

OBJ. 1, 2

Quality Move Company made the following expenditures on one of its delivery trucks:

Mar. 20. Replaced the transmission at a cost of $1,890.
June 11. Paid $1,350 for installation of a hydraulic lift.
Nov. 30. Paid $55 to change the oil and air filter.

Prepare journal entries for each expenditure.

EX 10-16 Capital expenditure and depreciation; parital-year depreciation

OBJ. 1, 2

✔ b. Depreciation Expense, $800

Willow Creek Company purchased and installed carpet in its new general offices on April 30 for a total cost of $18,000. The carpet is estimated to have a 15-year useful life and no residual value.

a. Prepare the journal entry necessary for recording the purchase of the new carpet.
b. Record the December 31 adjusting entry for the partial-year depreciation expense for the carpet, assuming that Willow Creek uses the straight-line method.

EX 10-17 Entries for sale of fixed asset

OBJ. 3

✔ a. $134,000

Equipment acquired on January 8 at a cost of $168,000 has an estimated useful life of 18 years, has an estimated residual value of $15,000, and is depreciated by the straight-line method.

a. What was the book value of the equipment at December 31 the end of the fourth year?
b. Assuming that the equipment was sold on April 1 of the fifth year for $125,000, journalize the entries to record (1) depreciation for the three months until the sale date and (2) the sale of the equipment.

EX 10-18 Disposal of fixed asset

OBJ. 3

✔ b. $338,600

Equipment acquired on January 6 at a cost of $401,300 has an estimated useful life of 18 years and an estimated residual value of $25,100.

a. What was the annual amount of depreciation for Years 1–3 using the straight-line method of depreciation?
b. What was the book value of the equipment on January 1 of Year 3?
c. Assuming that the equipment was sold on January 3 of Year 4 for $315,000, journalize the entry to record the sale.
d. Assuming that the equipment had been sold on January 3 of Year 4 for $342,000 instead of $315,000, journalize the entry to record the sale.

EX 10-19 Depletion entries

OBJ. 4

✔ a. $7,000,000

SHOW ME HOW

Backwoods Mining Co. acquired mineral rights for $53,200,000. The mineral deposit is estimated at 19,000,000 tons. During the current year, 2,500,000 tons were mined and sold.

a. Determine the amount of depletion expense for the current year.
b. Journalize the adjusting entry on December 31 to recognize the depletion expense.

EX 10-20 Amortization entries

OBJ. 5

✔ a. $357,600

Kleen Company acquired patent rights on January 10 of Year 1 for $2,800,000. The patent has a useful life equal to its legal life of eight years. On January 7 of Year 4, Kleen successfully defended the patent in a lawsuit at a cost of $38,000.

a. Determine the patent amortization expense for Year 4 ended December 31.
b. Journalize the adjusting entry on December 31 of Year 4 to recognize the amortization.

EX 10-21 Book value of fixed assets OBJ. 6

Apple Inc. designs, manufactures, and markets personal computers and related software. Apple also manufactures and distributes music players (iPod) and mobile phones (iPhone) along with related accessories and services, including online distribution of third-party music, videos, and applications. The following information was taken from a recent annual report of Apple:

Property, Plant, and Equipment (in millions):

	Current Year	Preceding Year
Land and buildings	$ 16,216	$ 13,587
Machinery, equipment, and internal-use software	65,982	54,210
Other fixed assets	8,205	7,279
Accumulated depreciation and amortization	(49,099)	(41,293)

a. Compute the book value of the fixed assets for the current year and the preceding year and explain the differences, if any.

b. Would you normally expect Apple's book value of fixed assets to increase or decrease during the year? Why?

EX 10-22 Balance sheet presentation OBJ. 6

List the errors you find in the following partial balance sheet:

Burnt Red Company
Balance Sheet
December 31, 20Y2

Assets

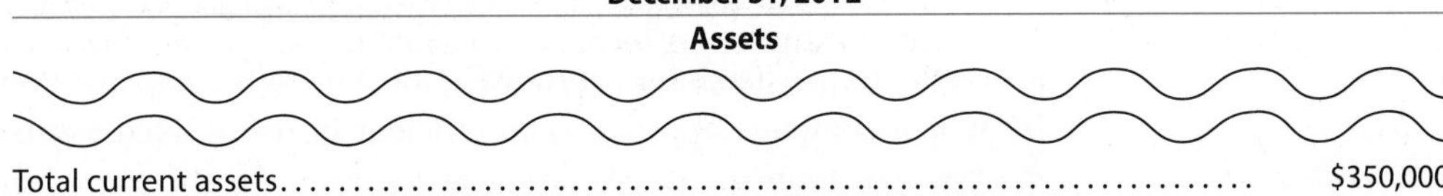

Total current assets.......... $350,000

	Replacement Cost	Accumulated Depreciation	Book Value
Property, plant, and equipment:			
Land	$ 250,000	$ 50,000	$200,000
Buildings	450,000	160,000	290,000
Factory equipment	375,000	140,000	235,000
Office equipment	125,000	60,000	65,000
Patents	90,000	—	90,000
Goodwill	60,000	10,000	50,000
Total property, plant, and equipment	$1,350,000	$420,000	$930,000

EX 10-23 Fixed asset turnover ratio OBJ. 7

Amazon.com, Inc. is the world's leading Internet retailer of merchandise and media. Amazon also designs and sells electronic products, such as e-readers. **Netflix, Inc.** is the world's leading Internet television network. Both companies compete in the digital media and streaming space. However, Netflix is more narrowly focused in the digital streaming business than is Amazon. Sales and average book value of fixed assets information (in millions) are provided for Amazon and Netflix for a recent year as follows:

	Amazon	Netflix
Sales	$232,887	$15,794
Average book value of fixed assets	55,332	369

a. Compute the fixed asset turnover ratio for each company. Round to one decimal place.

b. Which company is more efficient in generating sales from fixed assets?

c. Interpret your results.

EX 10-24 Fixed asset turnover ratio **OBJ. 7**

Verizon Communications Inc. is a major telecommunications company in the United States. Two recent balance sheets for Verizon disclosed the following information regarding fixed assets:

	End of Year (in millions)	Beginning of Year (in millions)
Property, plant, and equipment	$252,835	$246,498
Less accumulated depreciation	163,549	157,930
Property, plant, and equipment (net)	$ 89,286	$ 88,568

Verizon's revenue for the year was $130,863 million. Assume that the fixed asset turnover ratio for the telecommunications industry averages approximately 1.1.

a. Determine Verizon's fixed asset turnover ratio. Round to one decimal place.

b. Interpret this ratio with respect to the industry average.

EX 10-25 Fixed asset turnover ratio **OBJ. 7**

FedEx Corporation and **United Parcel Service, Inc.** compete in the package delivery business. The major fixed assets for each business include aircraft, sorting and handling facilities, delivery vehicles, and information technology. The sales and average book value of fixed assets reported on recent financial statements for each company were as follows:

	FedEx	UPS
Sales (in millions)	$65,450	$71,861
Average book value of fixed assets (in millions)	27,068	24,347

a. Compute the fixed asset turnover ratio for each company. Round to one decimal place.

b. Which company appears more efficient in using fixed assets?

c. Interpret the meaning of the ratio for the more efficient company.

EX 10-26 Fixed asset turnover ratio **OBJ. 7**

The following table shows the sales and average book value of fixed assets for three different companies from three different industries for a recent year:

Company (Industry)	Sales (in millions)	Average Book Value of Fixed Assets (in millions)
Alphabet (Google) Inc. (Internet)	$136,819	$ 51,051
Comcast Corporation (communications)	94,507	41,454
Walmart Inc. (retail)	510,329	113,107

a. For each company, determine the fixed asset turnover ratio. Round to one decimal place.

b. Explain Comcast's fixed asset turnover ratio relative to the other two companies.

Appendix

EX 10-27 Asset traded for similar asset

✔ a. $185,000

A printing press priced at a fair market value of $275,000 is acquired in a transaction that has commercial substance by trading in a similar press and paying cash for the difference between the trade-in allowance and the price of the new press.

a Assuming that the trade-in allowance is $90,000, what is the amount of cash given?

b. Assuming that the book value of the press traded in is $68,000, what is the gain or loss on the exchange?

Appendix

EX 10-28 Asset traded for similar asset

✔ b. $(18,500) loss

Assume the same facts as in Exercise 10-27, except that the book value of the press traded in is $108,500. (a) What is the amount of cash given? (b) What is the gain or loss on the exchange?

Appendix

EX 10-29 Entries for trade of fixed asset

On July 1, Twin Pines Co., a water distiller, acquired new bottling equipment with a list price (fair market value) of $220,000. Twin Pines received a trade-in allowance (fair market value) of $45,000 on the old equipment of a similar type and paid cash of $175,000. The following information about the old equipment is obtained from the account in the equipment ledger: cost, $180,000; accumulated depreciation on December 31, the end of the preceding fiscal year, $120,000; annual depreciation, $12,000. Assuming that the exchange has commercial substance, journalize the entries to record (a) the current depreciation of the old equipment to the date of trade-in and (b) the exchange transaction on July 1.

Appendix

EX 10-30 Entries for trade of fixed asset

On October 1, Bentley Delivery Services acquired a new truck with a list price (fair market value) of $75,000. Bentley Delivery received a trade-in allowance (fair market value) of $24,000 on an old truck of similar type and paid cash of $51,000. The following information about the old truck is obtained from the account in the equipment ledger: cost, $56,000; accumulated depreciation on December 31, the end of the preceding fiscal year, $35,000; annual depreciation, $7,000. Assuming that the exchange has commercial substance, journalize the entries to record (a) the current depreciation of the old truck to the date of trade-in and (b) the transaction on October 1.

Problems: Series A

PR 10-1A Allocating payments and receipts to fixed asset accounts — OBJ. 1

✔ Land, $400,000

The following payments and receipts are related to land, land improvements, and buildings acquired for use in a wholesale ceramic business. The receipts are identified by an asterisk.

a.	Fee paid to attorney for title search	$ 2,500
b.	Cost of real estate acquired as a plant site: Land	285,000
	Building (to be demolished)	55,000
c.	Delinquent real estate taxes on property, assumed by purchaser	15,500
d.	Cost of tearing down and removing building acquired in (b)	5,000
e.	Proceeds from sale of salvage materials from old building	4,000*
f.	Special assessment paid to city for extension of water main to the property	29,000
g.	Architect's and engineer's fees for plans and supervision	60,000
h.	Premium on one-year insurance policy during construction	6,000
i.	Cost of filling and grading land	12,000
j.	Money borrowed to pay building contractor	900,000*
k.	Cost of repairing windstorm damage during construction	5,500
l.	Cost of paving parking lot to be used by customers	32,000
m.	Cost of trees and shrubbery planted	11,000
n.	Cost of floodlights installed on parking lot	2,000
o.	Cost of repairing vandalism damage during construction	2,500
p.	Proceeds from insurance company for windstorm and vandalism damage	7,500*
q.	Payment to building contractor for new building	800,000
r.	Interest incurred on building loan during construction	34,500
s.	Refund of premium on insurance policy (h) canceled after 11 months	500*

(Continued)

Instructions

1. Assign each payment and receipt to Land (unlimited life), Land Improvements (limited life), Building, or Other Accounts. Indicate receipts by an asterisk. Identify each item by letter and list the amounts in columnar form, as follows:

Item	Land	Land Improvements	Building	Other Accounts

2. Determine the amount debited to Land, Land Improvements, and Building.
3. The costs assigned to the land, which is used as a plant site, will not be depreciated, while the costs assigned to land improvements will be depreciated. Explain this seemingly contradictory application of the concept of depreciation.
4. What would be the effect on the current year's income statement and balance sheet if the cost of filling and grading land of $12,000 [payment (i)] was incorrectly classified as Land Improvements rather than Land? Assume that Land Improvements are depreciated over a 20-year life using the double-declining-balance method.

PR 10-2A Comparing three depreciation methods — OBJ. 2

✔ 1. a. Year 1: straight-line depreciation, $22,500

SHOW ME HOW

Dexter Industries purchased packaging equipment on January 8 for $72,000. The equipment was expected to have a useful life of three years, or 18,000 operating hours, and a residual value of $4,500. The equipment was used for 7,600 hours during Year 1, 6,000 hours in Year 2, and 4,400 hours in Year 3.

Instructions

1. Determine the amount of depreciation expense for the three years ending December 31 by (a) the straight-line method, (b) the units-of-activity method, and (c) the double-declining-balance method. Also determine the total depreciation expense for the three years by each method. The following columnar headings are suggested for recording the depreciation expense amounts:

	Depreciation Expense		
Year	Straight-Line Method	Units-of-Activity Method	Double-Declining-Balance Method

2. What method yields the highest depreciation expense for Year 1?
3. What method yields the most depreciation over the three-year life of the equipment?

PR 10-3A Depreciation by three methods; partial years — OBJ. 2

✔ a. Year 1: $65,250

Perdue Company purchased equipment on April 1 for $270,000. The equipment was expected to have a useful life of three years, or 18,000 operating hours, and a residual value of $9,000. The equipment was used for 7,500 hours during Year 1, 5,500 hours in Year 2, 4,000 hours in Year 3, and 1,000 hours in Year 4.

Instructions

Determine the amount of depreciation expense for the years ended December 31, Year 1, Year 2, Year 3, and Year 4, by (a) the straight-line method, (b) the units-of-activity method, and (c) the double-declining-balance method.

PR 10-4A Depreciation by two methods; sale of fixed asset — OBJ. 2, 3

✔ 1. b. Year 1: $320,000 depreciation expense

New lithographic equipment, acquired at a cost of $800,000 on March 1 of Year 1 (beginning of the fiscal year), has an estimated useful life of five years and an estimated residual value of $90,000. The manager requested information regarding the effect of alternative methods on the amount of depreciation expense each year.

On March 4 of Year 5, the equipment was sold for $135,000.

Instructions

1. Determine the annual depreciation expense for each of the estimated five years of use, the accumulated depreciation at the end of each year, and the book value of the equipment at the end of each year by (a) the straight-line method and (b) the double-declining-balance method. The following columnar headings are suggested for each schedule:

Year	Depreciation Expense	Accumulated Depreciation, End of Year	Book Value, End of Year

2. Journalize the entry to record the sale assuming that the manager chose the double-declining-balance method.
3. Journalize the entry to record the sale in (2) assuming that the equipment was sold for $88,750 instead of $135,000.

PR 10-5A Transactions for fixed assets, including sale

OBJ. 1, 2, 3

The following transactions and adjusting entries were completed by Legacy Furniture Co. during a three-year period. All are related to the use of delivery equipment. The double-declining-balance method of depreciation is used.

Year 1

Jan. 4. Purchased a used delivery truck for $28,000, paying cash.

Nov. 2. Paid garage $675 for miscellaneous repairs to the truck.

Dec. 31. Recorded depreciation on the truck for the year. The estimated useful life of the truck is four years, with a residual value of $5,000 for the truck.

Year 2

Jan. 6. Purchased a new truck for $48,000, paying cash.

Apr. 1. Sold the used truck purchased on January 4 of Year 1 for $15,000. (Record depreciation to date in Year 2 for the truck.)

June 11. Paid garage $450 for miscellaneous repairs to the truck.

Dec. 31. Record depreciation for the new truck. It has an estimated residual value of $9,000 and an estimated life of five years.

Year 3

July 1. Purchased a new truck for $54,000, paying cash.

Oct. 2. Sold the truck purchased January 6, Year 2, for $16,750. (Record depreciation to date for Year 3 for the truck.)

Dec. 31. Recorded depreciation on the remaining truck purchased on July 1. It has an estimated residual value of $12,000 and an estimated useful life of eight years.

Instructions

Journalize the transactions and the adjusting entries.

PR 10-6A Amortization and depletion entries

OBJ. 4, 5

✔ 1. a. $352,000

Data related to the acquisition of timber rights and intangible assets during the current year ended December 31 are as follows:

a. Timber rights on a tract of land were purchased for $1,600,000 on February 22. The stand of timber is estimated at 5,000,000 board feet. During the current year, 1,100,000 board feet of timber were cut and sold.
b. On December 31, the company determined that $3,750,000 of goodwill was impaired.
c. Governmental and legal costs of $6,600,000 were incurred on April 3 in obtaining a patent with an estimated economic life of 12 years. Amortization is to be for three-fourths of a year.

Instructions

1. Determine the amount of the amortization, depletion, or impairment for the current year for each of the foregoing items.
2. Journalize the adjusting entries required to record the amortization, depletion, or impairment for each item.

Problems: Series B

PR 10-1B Allocating payments and receipts to fixed asset accounts **OBJ. 1**

✔ Land, $860,000

The following payments and receipts are related to land, land improvements, and buildings acquired for use in a wholesale apparel business. The receipts are identified by an asterisk.

a.	Fee paid to attorney for title search	$ 3,600
b.	Cost of real estate acquired as a plant site: Land	720,000
	Building (to be demolished)	60,000
c.	Finder's fee paid to real estate agency	23,400
d.	Delinquent real estate taxes on property, assumed by purchaser	15,000
e.	Architect's and engineer's fees for plans for new building	75,000
f.	Cost of removing building purchased with land in (b)	10,000
g.	Proceeds from sale of salvage materials from old building	3,400*
h.	Cost of filling and grading land	18,000
i.	Premium on one-year insurance policy during construction	8,400
j.	Money borrowed to pay building contractor	800,000*
k.	Special assessment paid to city for extension of water main to the property	13,400
l.	Cost of repairing windstorm damage during construction	3,000
m.	Cost of repairing vandalism damage during construction	2,000
n.	Cost of trees and shrubbery planted	14,000
o.	Cost of paving parking lot to be used by customers	21,600
p.	Interest incurred on building loan during construction	40,000
q.	Proceeds from insurance company for windstorm and vandalism damage	4,500*
r.	Payment to building contractor for new building	800,000
s.	Refund of premium on insurance policy (i) canceled after 10 months	1,400*

Instructions

1. Assign each payment and receipt to Land (unlimited life), Land Improvements (limited life), Building, or Other Accounts. Indicate receipts by an asterisk. Identify each item by letter and list the amounts in columnar form, as follows:

Item	Land	Land Improvements	Building	Other Accounts

2. Determine the amount debited to Land, Land Improvements, and Building.
3. The costs assigned to the land, which is used as a plant site, will not be depreciated, while the costs assigned to land improvements will be depreciated. Explain this seemingly contradictory application of the concept of depreciation.
4. What would be the effect on the current year's income statement and balance sheet if the cost of paving the parking lot of $21,600 [payment (o)] was incorrectly classified as Land rather than Land Improvements? Assume that Land Improvements are depreciated over a 10-year life using the double-declining-balance method.

PR 10-2B Comparing three depreciation methods **OBJ. 2**

✔ 1. a. Year 1: straight-line depreciation, $71,250

SHOW ME HOW

Waylander Coatings Company purchased waterproofing equipment on January 6 for $320,000. The equipment was expected to have a useful life of four years, or 20,000 operating hours, and a residual value of $35,000. The equipment was used for 7,200 hours during Year 1, 6,400 hours in Year 2, 4,400 hours in Year 3, and 2,000 hours in Year 4.

Instructions

1. Determine the amount of depreciation expense for the years ended December 31, Year 1, Year 2, Year 3, and Year 4, by (a) the straight-line method, (b) the units-of-activity method, and (c) the double-declining-balance method. Also determine the total depreciation expense for the four years by each method. The following columnar headings are suggested for recording the depreciation expense amounts:

	Depreciation Expense		
Year	Straight-Line Method	Units-of-Activity Method	Double-Declining-Balance Method

2. What method yields the highest depreciation expense for Year 1?
3. What method yields the most depreciation over the four-year life of the equipment?

PR 10-3B Depreciation by three methods; partial years — OBJ. 2

✔ a. Year 1, $17,600

McMullen Company purchased tool sharpening equipment on May 1 for $162,000. The equipment was expected to have a useful life of three years, or 12,000 operating hours, and a residual value of $3,600. The equipment was used for 2,400 hours during Year 1, 3,900 hours in Year 2, 4,050 hours in Year 3, and 1,650 hours in Year 4.

Instructions

Determine the amount of depreciation expense for the years ended December 31, Year 1, Year 2, Year 3, and Year 4, by (a) the straight-line method, (b) the units-of-activity method, and (c) the double-declining-balance method.

PR 10-4B Depreciation by two methods; sale of fixed asset — OBJ. 2, 3

✔ 1. b. Year 1, $55,000 depreciation expense

New tire retreading equipment, acquired at a cost of $110,000 on September 1 of Year 1 (beginning of the fiscal year), has an estimated useful life of four years and an estimated residual value of $7,500. The manager requested information regarding the effect of alternative methods on the amount of depreciation expense each year. On the basis of the data presented to the manager, the double-declining-balance method was selected.

On September 6 of Year 4, the equipment was sold for $18,000.

Instructions

1. Determine the annual depreciation expense for each of the estimated four years of use, the accumulated depreciation at the end of each year, and the book value of the equipment at the end of each year by (a) the straight-line method and (b) the double-declining-balance method. The following columnar headings are suggested for each schedule:

Year	Depreciation Expense	Accumulated Depreciation, End of Year	Book Value, End of Year

2. Journalize the entry to record the sale.
3. Journalize the entry to record the sale, assuming that the equipment sold for $10,500 instead of $18,000.

PR 10-5B Transactions for fixed assets, including sale — OBJ. 1, 2, 3

The following transactions and adjusting entries were completed by Robinson Furniture Co. during a three-year period. All are related to the use of delivery equipment. The double-declining-balance method of depreciation is used.

Year 1

Jan. 8. Purchased a used delivery truck for $24,000, paying cash.

Mar. 7. Paid garage $900 for changing the oil, replacing the oil filter, and tuning the engine on the delivery truck.

Dec. 31. Recorded depreciation on the truck for the fiscal year. The estimated useful life of the truck is four years, with a residual value of $4,000 for the truck.

Year 2

Jan. 9. Purchased a new truck for $50,000, paying cash.

Feb. 28. Paid garage $250 to tune the engine and make other minor repairs on the used truck.

Apr. 30. Sold the used truck for $9,500. (Record depreciation to date in Year 2 for the truck.)

Dec. 31. Record depreciation for the new truck. It has an estimated residual value of $12,000 and an estimated life of eight years.

Year 3

Sept. 1. Purchased a new truck for $58,500, paying cash.

4. Sold the truck purchased January 9, Year 2, for $36,000. (Record depreciation to date for Year 3 for the truck.)

Dec. 31. Recorded depreciation on the remaining truck. It has an estimated residual value of $16,000 and an estimated useful life of 10 years.

Instructions

Journalize the transactions and the adjusting entries.

✔ b. $150,000

PR 10-6B Amortization and depletion entries **OBJ. 4, 5**

Data related to the acquisition of timber rights and intangible assets during the current year ended December 31 are as follows:

a. On December 31, the company determined that $3,400,000 of goodwill was impaired.
b. Governmental and legal costs of $4,800,000 were incurred on September 30 in obtaining a patent with an estimated economic life of eight years. Amortization is to be for one-fourth of a year.
c. Timber rights on a tract of land were purchased for $2,975,000 on February 4. The stand of timber is estimated at 12,500,000 board feet. During the current year, 4,150,000 board feet of timber were cut and sold.

Instructions

1. Determine the amount of the amortization, depletion, or impairment for the current year for each of the foregoing items.
2. Journalize the adjusting entries to record the amortization, depletion, or impairment for each item.

Cases & Projects

CP 10-1 Ethics in Action

Hard Bodies Co. is a fitness chain that has just completed its second year of operations. At the beginning of its first fiscal year, the company purchased fitness equipment at a cost of $600,000 and estimated that the equipment would have a useful life of five years and no residual value. The company uses the straight-line depreciation method. The company reported net income for the first two years of operations as follows:

Year	Net Income (Loss)
1	$50,000
2	(2,000)

Mike Gambit, the company's chief financial officer (CFO), has recently run financial models to predict future net income, and he expects net losses to continue at $(2,000) per year for the next three years. James Steed, the president of Hard Bodies, is concerned about these predictions, as he is under pressure from the company's owner to return the company to Year 1 net income levels. If the company does not meet these goals, both he and Mike will likely be fired. Mike suggests that the company change the estimated useful life of the fitness equipment to 10 years and increase the equipment's estimated residual value to $50,000. This will reduce depreciation expense and increase net income.

1. Evaluate the decision to change the equipment's estimated useful life and estimated residual value to improve earnings. How does this change impact the usefulness of the company's net income for external decision makers?
2. If Mike and James make the change, are they acting in an ethical manner? Explain.

CP 10-2 Ethics in Action

Dave Elliott, CPA, is an assistant to the controller of Lyric Consulting Co. In his spare time, Dave also prepares tax returns and performs general accounting services for clients. Frequently, Dave performs these services after his normal working hours, using Lyric Consulting Co.'s computers and laser printers. Occasionally, Dave's clients will call him at the office during regular working hours.

Discuss whether Dave is performing in a professional manner.

CP 10-3 Team Activity

In teams, select a public company that interests you. Obtain the company's most recent annual report on Form 10-K. The Form 10-K is a company's annually required filing with the Securities and Exchange Commission (SEC). It includes the company's financial statements and accompanying notes. The Form 10-K can be obtained either (a) by referring to the investor relations section of the company's website or (b) by using the company search feature of the SEC's EDGAR database service found at www.sec.gov/edgar/searchedgar/companysearch.html.

1. Based on the information in the company's most recent annual report, answer the following questions:
   a. What depreciation methods does the company use to compute depreciation expense?
   b. How much depreciation expense does the company report on its income statement?
   c. What is the initial cost of the company's fixed assets?
   d. What is the book value of the company's fixed assets?
   e. What types of intangible assets, if any, does the company report on its balance sheet?
2. Does the book value of the company's fixed assets reflect its current market value? Explain your answer.

CP 10-4 Team Activity

Go to the Internet and review the procedures for applying for a patent, a copyright, and a trademark. You may find information available on Wikipedia (Wikipedia.org) useful for this purpose. Prepare a brief written summary of these procedures.

CP 10-5 Communication

Godwin Co. owns three delivery trucks. Details for each truck at the end of the most recent year follow:

	Age	Expected Useful Life	Initial Cost	Accumulated Depreciation
Truck 1	3	6	$22,500	$11,250
Truck 2	5	6	26,250	21,875
Truck 3	2	6	28,500	9,500

- At the beginning of the year, a hydraulic lift is added to Truck 1 at a cost of $4,500. The addition of the hydraulic lift will allow the company to deliver much larger objects than could previously be delivered.
- At the beginning of the year, the engine of Truck 2 is overhauled at a cost of $5,000. The engine overhaul will extend the truck's useful life by three years.

Write a short memo to Godwin's chief financial officer explaining the financial statement effects of the expenditures associated with Trucks 1 and 2.

CP 10-6 Financial versus tax depreciation

The following is an excerpt from a conversation between two employees of WXT Technologies, Nolan Sears and Stacy Mays. Nolan is the accounts payable clerk, and Stacy is the cashier.

Nolan: Stacy, could I get your opinion on something?

Stacy: Sure, Nolan.

Nolan: Do you know Rita, the fixed assets clerk?

Stacy: I know who she is, but I don't know her real well. Why?

Nolan: Well, I was talking to her at lunch last Monday about how she liked her job. You know, the usual; and she mentioned something about having to keep two sets of books—one for taxes and one for the financial statements. That can't be good accounting, can it? What do you think?

Stacy: Two sets of books? It doesn't sound right.

Nolan: It doesn't seem right to me either. I was always taught that you had to use generally accepted accounting principles. How can there be two sets of books? What can be the difference between the two?

How would you respond to Nolan and Stacy if you were Rita?

CHAPTER

11 Current Liabilities and Payroll

STATEMENT OF OWNER'S EQUITY
For the Year Ended December 31, 20Y6

Owner's capital, Jan. 1, 20Y6		$XXX
Net income	$ XXX	
Withdrawals	(XXX)	
Increase in capital		XXX
Owner's capital, Dec. 31, 20Y6		$XXX

INCOME STATEMENT
For the Year Ended December 31, 20Y6

Sales		$XXX
Cost of merchandise sold		XXX
Gross profit		$XXX
Operating expenses:		
Wages expense	$XXX	
Advertising expense	XXX	
Depreciation expense	XXX	
Amortization expense	XXX	
Depletion expense	XXX	
...	XXX	
...	XXX	
Total operating expenses		XXX
Income from operations		$XXX
Other revenue and expenses		XXX
Interest expense		XXX
Net income		$XXX

STATEMENT OF CASH FLOWS
For the Year Ended December 31, 20Y6

Cash flows from (used for) operating activities	$XXX
Cash flows from (used for) investing activities	XXX
Cash flows from (used for) financing activities	XXX
Net increase (decrease) in cash	$XXX
Cash balance, January 1, 20Y6	XXX

BALANCE SHEET
December 31, 20Y6

Current assets:		
Cash	$XXX	
Accounts receivable	XXX	
Merchandise inventory	XXX	
Total current assets		$XXX
Property, plant, and equipment	$XXX	
Intangible assets	XXX	
Total long-term assets		XXX
Total assets		$XXX
Liabilities:		
Accounts payable	$XXX	
Payroll liabilities	XXX	
Notes payable	XXX	
Total liabilities		$XXX
Owner's equity		XXX
Total liabilities and owner's equity		$XXX

INCAMERASTOCK/ALAMY STOCK PHOTO

Starbucks

Buying goods on credit is essential for businesses to run efficiently. The use of credit makes transactions more convenient and improves buying power. For *individuals*, the most common form of short-term credit is a credit card. Credit cards allow individuals to purchase items before they are paid for while removing the need for individuals to carry large amounts of cash. They also provide documentation of purchases through a monthly credit card statement.

Short-term credit is used by *businesses* to make purchasing items for manufacture or resale more convenient. It also gives the business control over the payment for goods and services. When **Starbucks** opened its first coffee shop in 1971, it relied on short-term trade credit, or accounts payable, to purchase ingredients for its coffee shop in Seattle's historic Pike Place Market. Today, Starbucks still relies on accounts payable and short-term trade credit, which gives the company control over cash payments by separating the purchase function from the payment function. Thus, the employee responsible for purchasing the ingredients is separated from the employee responsible for paying for the purchase. This separation of duties can help prevent unauthorized purchases or payments.

In addition to accounts payable, a business such as Starbucks can have current liabilities related to payroll, payroll taxes, employee benefits, short-term notes, unearned revenue, and contingencies. This chapter discusses each of these types of current liabilities.

Link to Starbucks .... Pages 542, 545, 556, 558, 559, 560

LEARNING OBJECTIVES

After studying this chapter, you should be able to:

Example Exercises (EE) are shown in **red.**

OBJ. 1 **Describe and illustrate current liabilities related to accounts payable, the current portion of long-term debt, and notes payable.**

Current Liabilities
Accounts Payable
Current Portion of Long-Term Debt
Short-Term Notes Payable — EE **11-1**

OBJ. 2 **Determine employer liabilities for payroll, including liabilities arising from employee earnings and deductions from earnings.**

Payroll and Payroll Taxes
Liability for Employee Earnings
Deductions from Employee Earnings — EE **11-2**
Computing Employee Net Pay — EE **11-3**
Liability for Employer's Payroll Taxes

OBJ. 3 **Describe payroll accounting systems that use a payroll register, employee earnings records, and a general journal.**

Accounting Systems for Payroll and Payroll Taxes
Payroll Register — EE **11-4, 11-5**
Employee's Earnings Record
Payroll Checks
Computerized Payroll System
Internal Controls for Payroll Systems

OBJ. 4 **Journalize entries for employee fringe benefits, including vacation pay and pensions.**

Employees' Fringe Benefits
Vacation Pay
Pensions — EE **11-6**
Postretirement Benefits Other Than Pensions
Current Liabilities on the Balance Sheet

OBJ. 5 **Describe the accounting treatment for contingent liabilities and journalize entries for product warranties.**

Contingent Liabilities
Probable and Estimable — EE **11-7**
Probable and Not Estimable
Reasonably Possible
Remote

OBJ. 6 **Describe and illustrate the use of the quick ratio in analyzing a company's ability to pay its current liabilities.**

Financial Analysis and Interpretation: Quick Ratio
Compute the Quick Ratio — EE **11-8**

At a Glance 11 Page 563

Describe and illustrate current liabilities related to accounts payable, the current portion of long-term debt, and notes payable.

Current Liabilities

When a company or a bank advances *credit,* it is making a loan. The company or bank is called a *creditor* (or *lender*). The individuals or companies receiving the loan are called *debtors* (or *borrowers*).

Debt is recorded as a liability by the debtor. *Long-term liabilities* are debts due beyond one year. Thus, a 30-year mortgage used to purchase property is a long-term liability. *Current liabilities* are debts that will be paid out of current assets and are due within one year.

Three types of current liabilities are discussed in this section—accounts payable, the current portion of long-term debt, and short-term notes payable.

Link to Starbucks

On a recent balance sheet, **Starbucks** reported $1,179.3 million of accounts payable and $2,298.4 million of accrued liabilities, which is almost two-thirds of its current liabilities.

Accounts Payable

Accounts payable transactions have been described and illustrated in earlier chapters. These transactions involve a variety of purchases on account, including the purchase of merchandise and supplies. For most companies, accounts payable is the largest current liability.

Current Portion of Long-Term Debt

Long-term liabilities are often paid back in periodic payments, called *installments.* Such installments that are due *within* the coming year are classified as a current liability. The installments due *after* the coming year are classified as a long-term liability.

To illustrate, **Starbucks Corporation** reported the following debt payments schedule in a recent year (in millions):

Fiscal year ending	
Year 1	$ 349.9
Years 2–3	1,250.0
Years 4–5	1,500.0
Thereafter	6,340.2
Total principal payments	$9,440.1

The debt of $349.9 due in Year 1 would be reported as a current liability on the December 31 balance sheet. The remaining debt of $9,090.2 ($9,440.1 − $349.9) would be reported as a long-term liability on the balance sheet.

Short-Term Notes Payable

Notes may be issued to purchase merchandise or other assets. Notes may also be issued to creditors to satisfy an account payable created earlier.[1]

To illustrate, assume that Nature's Sunshine Company issued a 90-day, 12% note for $1,000, dated August 1, 20Y7, to Murray Co. for a $1,000 overdue account. The entry to record the issuance of the note is as follows:

Aug.	1	Accounts Payable—Murray Co.		1,000	
		Notes Payable			1,000
		Issued a 90-day, 12% note on account.			

When the note matures, the entry to record the payment of $1,000 plus $30 interest ($1,000 × 12% × 90 ÷ 360[2]) is as follows:

Oct.	30	Notes Payable		1,000	
		Interest Expense		30	
		Cash			1,030
		Paid principal and interest due on note.			

The interest expense is reported in the Other Expense section of the income statement for the year ended December 31, 20Y7. The interest expense account is closed at December 31.

Each note transaction affects a debtor (borrower) and creditor (lender). The following illustration shows how the same transactions are recorded by the debtor and creditor. In this illustration, the debtor (borrower) is Bowden Co., and the creditor (lender) is Coker Co.

	Bowden Co. (Borrower)			Coker Co. (Creditor)		
May 1. Bowden Co. purchased merchandise on account from Coker Co., $10,000, 2/10, n/30. The merchandise cost Coker Co. $7,500.	Merchandise Inventory	10,000		Accounts Receivable	10,000	
	Accounts Payable		10,000	Sales		10,000
				Cost of Merchandise Sold	7,500	
				Merchandise Inventory		7,500
May 31. Bowden Co. issued a 60-day, 12% note for $10,000 to Coker Co. on account.	Accounts Payable	10,000		Notes Receivable	10,000	
	Notes Payable		10,000	Accounts Receivable		10,000

(Continued)

1 The accounting for notes received to satisfy an account receivable was described and illustrated in Chapter 9.
2 To simplify computations and rounding, 360 days per year are used. In practice, companies use 365 days.

	Bowden Co. (Borrower)			Coker Co. (Creditor)		
July 30. Bowden Co. paid Coker Co. the amount due on the note of May 31. Interest: \$10,000 × 12% × 60 ÷ 360.	Notes Payable	10,000		Cash	10,200	
	Interest Expense	200		Interest Revenue		200
	Cash		10,200	Notes Receivable		10,000

A company may also borrow from a bank by issuing a note. To illustrate, assume that on September 19, Iceburg Company borrowed cash from First National Bank by issuing a \$4,000, 90-day, 15% note to the bank. The entry to record the issuance of the note and the cash proceeds received by Iceburg is as follows:

Sept.	19	Cash		4,000	
		Notes Payable			4,000
		Issued a 90-day, 15% note to First National Bank.			

On the due date of the note (December 18), Iceburg Company owes First National Bank \$4,000 plus interest of \$150 (\$4,000 × 15% × 90 ÷ 360). The entry to record the payment of the note is as follows:

Dec.	18	Notes Payable		4,000	
		Interest Expense		150	
		Cash			4,150
		Paid principal and interest due on note.			

In some cases, a *discounted note* may be issued rather than an interest-bearing note. A discounted note has the following characteristics:

- The interest rate on the note is called the *discount rate.*
- The amount of interest on the note, called the *discount,* is computed by multiplying the discount rate times the face amount of the note.
- The debtor (borrower) receives the face amount of the note less the discount. The amount of cash received at issuance is called the *proceeds.*
- The debtor must repay the face amount of the note on the due date.

To illustrate, assume that on August 10, Cary Company issues a \$20,000, 90-day discounted note to Western National Bank. The discount rate is 15%, and the amount of the discount is \$750 (\$20,000 × 15% × 90 ÷ 360). Thus, the proceeds received by Cary Company are \$19,250. The entry by Cary Company is as follows:

Aug.	10	Cash		19,250	
		Interest Expense		750	
		Notes Payable			20,000
		Issued a 90-day discounted note to Western National Bank at a 15% discount rate.			

The entry to record the repayment of the discounted note on November 8 is as follows:[3]

Nov.	8	Notes Payable		20,000	
		Cash			20,000
		Paid note due.			

3 If the accounting period ends before a discounted note is paid, an adjusting entry should record the prepaid (deferred) interest that is not yet an expense. This deferred interest would be deducted from Notes Payable in the Current Liabilities section of the balance sheet.

Other current liabilities that have been discussed in earlier chapters include accrued expenses, unearned revenue, and interest payable. The accounting for wages and salaries, termed *payroll accounting*, is discussed next.

EXAMPLE EXERCISE 11-1 Proceeds from Notes Payable **OBJ. 1**

On July 1, Bella Salon Company borrowed cash from Best Bank by issuing a 60-day note with a face amount of $60,000.

a. Determine the proceeds of the note, assuming that the note carries an interest rate of 6%.
b. Determine the proceeds of the note, assuming that the note is discounted at 6%.

Follow My Example 11-1

a. $60,000
b. $59,400 [$60,000 − ($60,000 × 6% × 60 ÷ 360)]

Practice Exercises: PE 11-1A, PE 11-1B

Payroll and Payroll Taxes

OBJ. 2 Determine employer liabilities for payroll, including liabilities arising from employee earnings and deductions from earnings.

In accounting, **payroll** refers to the amount paid to employees for services they provided during the period. A company's payroll is important for the following reasons:

- Payroll and related payroll taxes significantly affect the net income of most companies.
- Payroll is subject to federal and state regulations.
- Good employee morale requires payroll to be paid timely and accurately.

Liability for Employee Earnings

Salary usually refers to payment for managerial and administrative services. Salary is payment to employees for services that is typically expressed in terms of a month or a year. *Wages* usually refers to payment to employees for services that is stated on an hourly or weekly basis. The salary or wage of an employee may be increased by bonuses, commissions, profit sharing, or other adjustments.

Note

Employee salaries and wages are expenses to an employer.

Companies engaged in interstate commerce must follow the Fair Labor Standards Act. This act, sometimes called the Federal Wage and Hour Law, requires employers to pay a minimum rate of 1½ times the regular rate for all hours worked in excess of 40 hours per week. Exemptions are provided for executive, administrative, and some supervisory positions. Increased rates for working overtime, nights, or holidays are common, even when not required by law. These rates may be as much as twice the regular rate.

Link to Starbucks

Starbucks pays employees 1½ times their base hourly rate for any hours worked on holidays such as New Year's Day, Thanksgiving Day, and Christmas Day.

To illustrate computing an employee's earnings, assume that **John T. McGrath** is a salesperson employed by **McDermott Supply Co.** McGrath's regular rate is $34 per hour, and any hours worked in excess of 40 hours per week are paid at 1½ times the regular rate. McGrath worked 42 hours for the week ended December 27. His earnings of $1,462 for the week are computed as follows:

Earnings at regular rate (40 hrs. × $34)	$1,360
Earnings at overtime rate [2 hrs. × ($34 × 1½)]	102
Total earnings	$1,462

Deductions from Employee Earnings

The total earnings of an employee for a payroll period, including any overtime pay, are called **gross pay**. From this amount is subtracted one or more *deductions* to arrive at **net pay**. Deductions include items such as federal, state, and local income taxes; medical insurance; and pension contributions. Net pay is the amount the employee receives after deductions are subtracted from gross pay.

Note

Net Pay = Gross Pay – Deductions

Income Taxes Employers normally withhold a portion of employee earnings for payment of the employees' federal income tax. Each employee authorizes the amount to be withheld by completing an "Employee's Withholding Allowance Certificate," called a W-4. Exhibit 1 is the W-4 form submitted by John T. McGrath.

EXHIBIT 1

Employee's Withholding Allowance Certificate (W-4 Form)

Separate here and give Form W-4 to your employer. Keep the worksheet(s) for your records.

Form **W-4** Department of the Treasury Internal Revenue Service

Employee's Withholding Allowance Certificate

▶ Whether you're entitled to claim a certain number of allowances or exemption from withholding is subject to review by the IRS. Your employer may be required to send a copy of this form to the IRS.

OMB No. 1545-0074 **20Y6**

1 Your first name and middle initial	Last name	2 Your social security number
John T.	McGrath	381 48 9120

Home address (number and street or rural route): 1830 4th Street

3 ☑ Single ☐ Married ☐ Married, but withhold at higher Single rate.
Note. If married filing separately, check "Married, but withhold at higher Single rate."

City or town, state, and ZIP code: Clinton, Iowa 52732-6142

4 If your last name differs from that shown on your social security card, check here. You must call 800-772-1213 for a replacement card. ▶ ☐

5 Total number of allowances you're claiming (from the applicable worksheet on the following pages) . . . . 5 | 1

6 Additional amount, if any, you want withheld from each paycheck . . . . . 6 | $

7 I claim exemption from withholding for 20Y6, and I certify that I meet **both** of the following conditions for exemption.
- Last year I had a right to a refund of **all** federal income tax withheld because I had **no** tax liability, **and**
- This year I expect a refund of **all** federal income tax withheld because I expect to have **no** tax liability.

If you meet both conditions, write "Exempt" here . . . . ▶ 7

Under penalties of perjury, I declare that I have examined this certificate and, to the best of my knowledge and belief, it is true, correct, and complete.

Employee's signature (This form is not valid unless you sign it.) ▶ *John T. McGrath* Date ▶ June 2, 20Y6

8 Employer's name and address (**Employer:** Complete boxes 8 and 10 if sending to IRS and complete boxes 8, 9, and 10 if sending to State Directory of New Hires.)	9 First date of employment	10 Employer identification number (EIN)

For Privacy Act and Paperwork Reduction Act Notice, see page 4. Cat. No. 10220Q Form **W-4** (20Y6)

*The W-4 form is issued yearly by the U.S. Treasury Department.

On the W-4, an employee indicates marital status and the number of withholding allowances. A single employee may claim one withholding allowance. A married employee may claim an additional allowance for a spouse. An employee may also claim an allowance for each dependent other than a spouse. Each allowance reduces the federal income tax withheld from the employee's pay. Exhibit 1 indicates that McGrath is single and, thus, claimed one withholding allowance.

The federal income tax withheld depends on each employee's gross pay and W-4 allowance. Withholding tables issued by the Internal Revenue Service (IRS) are used to determine amounts to withhold. Exhibit 2 is an example of an IRS wage withholding table for a single person who is paid weekly.[4]

In Exhibit 2, each row is the employee's wages after deducting the employee's withholding allowances. Each year, the amount of the standard withholding allowance is determined by the IRS. For ease of computation and because this amount changes

EXHIBIT 2

Wage Bracket Withholding Table

Percentage Method Tables for Income Tax Withholding*
(For Wages Paid in 20Y6)

TABLE 1—WEEKLY Payroll Period

(a) SINGLE person (including head of household)—

If the amount of wages (after subtracting withholding allowances) is: | The amount of income tax to withhold is:

Not over $73 . . . . $0

Over—	But not over—		of excess over—	
$73	—$260 . .	$0.00 plus 10%	—$73	
$260	—$832 . .	$18.70 plus 12%	—$260	
$832	—$1,692 . .	$87.34 plus 22%	—$832	← McGrath wage bracket
$1,692	—$3,164 . .	$276.54 plus 24%	—$1,692	
$3,164	—$3,998 . .	$629.82 plus 32%	—$3,164	
$3,998	—$9,887 . .	$896.70 plus 35%	—$3,998	
$9,887 . . .		$2,957.85 plus 37%	—$9,887	

*Based upon 2019 withholding tables.

4 IRS withholding tables are also available for married employees and for pay periods other than weekly.

each year, we assume that the standard withholding allowance to be deducted in Exhibit 2 for a single person paid weekly is $81.[5] Thus, if two withholding allowances are claimed, $162 ($81 × 2) is deducted.

To illustrate, John T. McGrath made $1,462 for the week ended December 27. McGrath's W-4 claims one withholding allowance of $81. Thus, the wages used in determining McGrath's withholding bracket in Exhibit 2 are $1,381 ($1,462 – $81).

After the person's withholding wage bracket has been computed, the federal income tax to be withheld is determined as follows:

Step 1. Locate the proper withholding wage bracket in Exhibit 2.

McGrath's wages after deducting one standard IRS withholding allowance are $1,381 ($1,462 – $81). Therefore, the wage bracket for McGrath is $832–$1,692.

Step 2. Compute the withholding for the proper wage bracket using the directions in the two right-hand columns in Exhibit 2.

For McGrath's wage bracket, the withholding is computed as "$87.34 plus 22% of the excess over $832." Hence, McGrath's withholding is $208.12, computed as follows:

Initial withholding from wage bracket	*$ 87.34*
Plus [22% × ($1,381 – $832)]	*120.78*
Total withholding	*$208.12*

Employers may also be required to withhold state or city income taxes. The amounts to be withheld are determined on state-by-state and city-by-city bases.

EXAMPLE EXERCISE 11-2 Federal Income Tax Withholding

OBJ. 2

Karen Dunn's weekly gross earnings for the present week were $2,250. Dunn has two exemptions. Using the wage bracket withholding table in Exhibit 2 with an $81 standard withholding allowance for each exemption, what is Dunn's federal income tax withholding?

Follow My Example 11-2

Total wage payment		$ 2,250
One allowance	$81	
Multiplied by allowances claimed on Form W-4	× 2	162
Amount subject to withholding		$ 2,088
Initial withholding from wage bracket in Exhibit 2		$276.54
Plus additional withholding: 24% of excess over $1,692		95.04*
Federal income tax withholding		$371.58

*24% × ($2,088 – $1,692)

Practice Exercises: PE 11-2A, PE 11-2B

FICA Tax Employers are required by the Federal Insurance Contributions Act (FICA) to withhold a portion of the earnings of each employee. The **FICA tax** withheld contributes to the following two federal programs:

- *Social security,* which provides payments for retirees, survivors, and disability insurance.
- *Medicare,* which provides health insurance for senior citizens.

The amount withheld from each employee is based on the employee's earnings *paid* in the *calendar* year. The withholding tax rates and maximum earnings subject

5 The actual IRS standard withholding allowance changes every year and was $80.80 for 2019.

to tax are often revised by Congress.[6] To simplify, this chapter assumes the following rates and earnings subject to tax:

- Social security: 6% on all earnings
- Medicare: 1.5% on all earnings

To illustrate, assume that John T. McGrath's earnings for the week ending December 27 are $1,462 and the total FICA tax to be withheld is $109.65, computed as follows:

Earnings subject to 6% social security tax	$1,462	
Social security tax rate	× 6%	
Social security tax		$ 87.72
Earnings subject to 1.5% Medicare tax	$1,462	
Medicare tax rate	×1.5%	
Medicare tax		21.93
Total FICA tax		$109.65

Other Deductions Employees may choose to have additional amounts deducted from their gross pay. For example, an employee may authorize deductions for retirement savings, charitable contributions, or life insurance. A union contract may also require the deduction of union dues.

Computing Employee Net Pay

Gross earnings less payroll deductions equals *net pay*, sometimes called *take-home pay*. Assuming that John T. McGrath authorized deductions for retirement savings and for a United Fund contribution, McGrath's net pay for the week ended December 27 is $1,119.23, computed as follows:

Gross earnings for the week		$1,462.00
Deductions:		
Federal income tax	$208.12	
Social security tax	87.72	
Medicare tax	21.93	
Retirement savings	20.00	
United Fund	5.00	
Total deductions		342.77
Net pay		$1,119.23

EXAMPLE EXERCISE 11-3 Employee Net Pay — OBJ. 2

Karen Dunn's weekly gross earnings for the week ending December 3 were $2,250, and her federal income tax withholding was $371.58. Assuming that the social security rate is 6% and Medicare is 1.5%, what is Dunn's net pay?

Follow My Example 11-3

Total wage payment		$2,250.00
Less: Federal income tax withholding	$371.58	
Social security tax ($2,250 × 6%)	135.00	
Medicare tax ($2,250 × 1.5%)	33.75	540.33
Net pay		$1,709.67

Practice Exercises: PE 11-3A, PE 11-3B

6 For 2019, the social security tax rate was 6.2% and the Medicare tax rate was 1.45%. Earnings subject to the social security tax are limited to an annual threshold amount, but for text examples and problems, assume that all accumulated annual earnings are below this threshold and subject to the tax.

Liability for Employer's Payroll Taxes

Employers are subject to the following payroll taxes for amounts paid their employees:

- *FICA Tax*: Employers must match the employee's FICA tax contribution.
- *Federal Unemployment Compensation Tax (FUTA)*: This employer tax provides for temporary payments to those who become unemployed. The tax collected by the federal government is allocated among the states for use in state programs rather than paid directly to employees. Congress often revises the FUTA tax rate and maximum earnings subject to tax.
- *State Unemployment Compensation Tax (SUTA)*: This employer tax also provides temporary payments to those who become unemployed. The FUTA and SUTA programs are closely coordinated, with the states distributing the unemployment checks. SUTA tax rates and earnings subject to tax vary by state.[7]

The preceding employer taxes are an operating expense of the company. Exhibit 3 summarizes the responsibility for employee and employer payroll taxes.

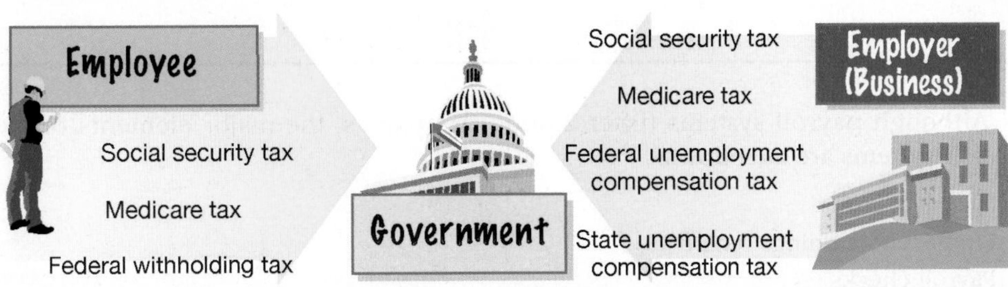

EXHIBIT 3
Responsibility for Tax Payments

Business Connection

THE MOST YOU WILL EVER PAY

In 1936, the Social Security Board described how the tax was expected to affect a worker's pay, as follows:

The taxes called for in this law will be paid both by your employer and by you. For the next 3 years you will pay maybe 15 cents a week, maybe 25 cents a week, maybe 30 cents or more, according to what you earn. That is to say, during the next 3 years, beginning January 1, 1937, you will pay 1 cent for every dollar you earn, and at the same time your employer will pay 1 cent for every dollar you earn, up to $3,000 a year. . . .

. . . Beginning in 1940 you will pay, and your employer will pay, 1½ cents for each dollar you earn, up to $3,000 a year. . . and then beginning in 1943, you will pay 2 cents, and so will your employer, for every dollar you earn for the next three years. After that, you and your employer will each pay half a cent more for 3 years, and finally, beginning in 1949, . . . you and your employer will each pay 3 cents on each dollar you earn, up to $3,000 a year. That is the most you will ever pay.

The rate on January 1, 2015, was 7.65 cents per dollar earned (7.65%). The social security portion was 6.20% on the first $118,500 of earnings. The Medicare portion was 1.45% on all earnings. There is an additional Medicare tax of 0.9% on wages in excess of $200,000 for the calendar year.

Source: Arthur Lodge, "That Is the Most You Will Ever Pay," *Journal of Accountancy*, October 1985, p. 44.

Accounting Systems for Payroll and Payroll Taxes

OBJ. 3 Describe payroll accounting systems that use a payroll register, employee earnings records, and a general journal.

Payroll systems should be designed to:

- Pay employees accurately and timely.
- Meet regulatory requirements of federal, state, and local agencies.
- Provide useful data for management decision-making needs.

7 For 2019, the FUTA tax rate is 6.0% of the first $7,000 of each employee's earnings during a calendar year. Employers may get a credit of up to 5.4% for state unemployment taxes, resulting in a net FUTA rate of 0.6% (6.0% FUTA rate – 5.4% credit).

EXHIBIT 4 **Payroll Register**

		Earnings: Week Ended December 27				
	Employee Name	**Total Hours**	**Regular**	**Overtime**	**Total**	
1	Abrams, Julie S.	40	500.00		500.00	1
2	Elrod, Fred G.	44	392.00	58.80	450.80	2
3	Gomez, Jose C.	40	840.00		840.00	3
4	**McGrath, John T.**	**42**	**1,360.00**	**102.00**	**1,462.00**	4
25	Wilkes, Glenn K.	40	480.00		480.00	25
26	Zumpano, Michael W.	40	600.00		600.00	26
27	Total		13,328.00	574.00	13,902.00	27
28						28

Although payroll systems differ among companies, the major elements of most payroll systems are as follows:

- Payroll register
- Employee's earnings record
- Payroll checks

Payroll Register

The **payroll register** is a multicolumn report used for summarizing the data for each payroll period. Although payroll registers vary by company, a payroll register normally includes the following columns:

- Employee name
- Total hours worked
- Regular earnings
- Overtime earnings
- Total gross earnings
- Social security tax withheld
- Medicare tax withheld
- Federal income tax withheld
- Retirement savings withheld
- Miscellaneous items withheld
- Total withholdings
- Net pay
- Check number of payroll check issued
- Accounts debited for payroll expense

Exhibit 4 illustrates a payroll register for **McDermott Supply Co.** The two right-hand columns of the payroll register indicate the accounts debited for the payroll expense. These columns are often referred to as the *payroll distribution*.

Recording Employees' Earnings The column totals of the payroll register provide the basis for recording the journal entry for payroll. The entry based on the payroll register in Exhibit 4 follows:

				Debit	Credit
Dec.	27	Sales Salaries Expense		11,122.00	
		Office Salaries Expense		2,780.00	
		Social Security Tax Payable			834.12
		Medicare Tax Payable			208.53
		Employees Federal Income Tax Payable			3,332.00
		Retirement Savings Deductions Payable			680.00
		United Fund Deductions Payable			520.00
		Salaries Payable			8,327.35
		Payroll for week ended December 27.			

Payroll Register (*Concluded*) EXHIBIT 4

	Deductions Withheld						Paid		Accounts Debited		
	Social Security Tax	Medicare Tax	Federal Income Tax	Retirement Savings	Misc.	Total	Net Pay	Check No.	Sales Salaries Expense	Office Salaries Expense	
1	30.00	7.50	48.35	20.00	UF 10.00	115.85	384.15	6857	500.00		1
2	27.05	6.76	40.85		UF 50.00	124.66	326.14	6858		450.80	2
3	50.40	12.60	117.90	25.00	UF 10.00	215.90	624.10	6859	840.00		3
4	**87.72**	**21.93**	**208.12**	**20.00**	**UF 5.00**	**342.77**	**1,119.23**	**6860**	**1,462.00**		4
25	28.80	7.20	45.35	10.00		91.35	388.65	6880	480.00		25
26	36.00	9.00	63.35	5.00	UF 2.00	115.35	484.65	6881		600.00	26
27	834.12	208.53	3,332.00	680.00	UF 520.00	5,574.65	8,327.35		11,122.00	2,780.00	27
28											28

Miscellaneous Deductions: UF—United Fund

Recording and Paying Payroll Taxes Payroll taxes are recorded as liabilities when the payroll is *paid* to employees. In addition, employers compute and report payroll taxes on a *calendar-year* basis, which may differ from the company's fiscal year.

Note

Payroll taxes become a liability to the employer when the payroll is paid.

EXAMPLE EXERCISE 11-4 Journalize Period Payroll — OBJ. 3

The payroll register of Chen Engineering Services indicates $900 of social security withheld and $225 of Medicare tax withheld on total salaries of $15,000 for the period. Federal withholding for the period totaled $2,925.

Provide the journal entry for the period's payroll.

Follow My Example 11-4

	Debit	Credit
Salaries Expense	15,000	
Social Security Tax Payable		900
Medicare Tax Payable		225
Employees Federal Income Tax Payable		2,925
Salaries Payable		10,950

Practice Exercises: PE 11-4A, PE 11-4B

On December 27, McDermott Supply has the following payroll data:

Sales salaries	$11,122
Office salaries	2,780
Wages owed employees on December 27	$13,902
Wages subject to payroll taxes:	
Social security tax (6%)	$13,902
Medicare tax (1.5%)	13,902
State (5.4%) and federal (0.6%) unemployment compensation tax	2,710

Employers must match the employees' social security and Medicare tax contributions. In addition, the employer must pay state unemployment compensation tax (SUTA) of 5.4% and federal unemployment compensation tax (FUTA) of 0.6%. When payroll is paid on December 27, these payroll taxes are computed as follows:

Social security tax	$ 834.12 ($13,902 × 6%, and from Social Security Tax column of Exhibit 4)
Medicare tax	208.53 ($13,902 × 1.5%, and from Medicare Tax column of Exhibit 4)
SUTA	146.34 ($2,710 × 5.4%)
FUTA	16.26 ($2,710 × 0.6%)
Total payroll taxes	$1,205.25

The entry to journalize the payroll tax expense for Exhibit 4 follows:

Dec.	27	Payroll Tax Expense		1,205.25	
		Social Security Tax Payable			834.12
		Medicare Tax Payable			208.53
		State Unemployment Tax Payable			146.34
		Federal Unemployment Tax Payable			16.26
		Payroll taxes for week ended December 27.			

The preceding entry records a liability for each payroll tax. When the payroll taxes are paid, an entry is recorded debiting the payroll tax liability accounts and crediting Cash.

EXAMPLE EXERCISE 11-5 Journalize Payroll Tax — OBJ. 3

The payroll register of Chen Engineering Services indicates $900 of social security withheld and $225 of Medicare tax withheld on total salaries of $15,000 for the period. Earnings of $5,250 are subject to state and federal unemployment compensation taxes at the federal rate of 0.6% and the state rate of 5.4%.

Provide the journal entry to record the payroll tax expense for the period.

Follow My Example 11-5

Payroll Tax Expense	1,440.00	
Social Security Tax Payable		900.00
Medicare Tax Payable		225.00
State Unemployment Tax Payable		283.50*
Federal Unemployment Tax Payable		31.50**

*$5,250 × 5.4%
**$5,250 × 0.6%

Practice Exercises: PE 11-5A, PE 11-5B

Employee's Earnings Record

Each employee's earnings to date must be determined at the end of each payroll period. This total is necessary for computing the employee's social security tax withholding and the employer's payroll taxes. Thus, detailed payroll records must be kept for each employee. This record is called an **employee's earnings record**.

Exhibit 5 shows a portion of John T. McGrath's employee's earnings record. An employee's earnings record and the payroll register are interrelated. For example, McGrath's earnings record for December 27 can be traced to the fourth line of the payroll register in Exhibit 4.

EXHIBIT 5

Employee's Earnings Record

John T. McGrath
1830 4th St.
Clinton, IA 52732-6142

PHONE: 555-3148

SINGLE

NUMBER OF WITHHOLDING ALLOWANCES: 1

PAY RATE: $1,360.00 Per Week

OCCUPATION: Salesperson

EQUIVALENT HOURLY RATE: $34

			Earnings				
	Period Ending	Total Hours	Regular Earnings	Overtime Earnings	Total Earnings	Total	
42	SEPT. 27	53	1,360.00	663.00	2,023.00	75,565.00	42
43	THIRD QUARTER		17,680.00	7,605.00	25,285.00		43
44	OCT. 4	51	1,360.00	561.00	1,921.00	77,486.00	44
50	NOV. 15	50	1,360.00	510.00	1,870.00	89,382.00	50
51	NOV. 22	53	1,360.00	663.00	2,023.00	91,405.00	51
52	NOV. 29	47	1,360.00	357.00	1,717.00	93,122.00	52
53	DEC. 6	53	1,360.00	663.00	2,023.00	95,145.00	53
54	DEC.13	52	1,360.00	612.00	1,972.00	97,117.00	54
55	DEC. 20	51	1,360.00	561.00	1,921.00	99,038.00	55
56	DEC. 27	42	1,360.00	102.00	1,462.00	100,500.00	56
57	FOURTH QUARTER		17,680.00	7,255.00	24,935.00		57
58	YEARLY TOTAL		70,720.00	29,780.00	100,500.00		58

SOC. SEC. NO.: 381-48-9120

EMPLOYEE NO.: 814

DATE OF BIRTH: February 15, 1992

DATE EMPLOYMENT TERMINATED:

	Deductions							Paid		
	Social Security Tax	Medicare Tax	Federal Income Tax	Retirement Savings		Other	Total	Net Amount	Check No.	
42	121.38	30.35	336.54	20.00			508.27	1,514.73	6175	42
43	1,517.10	379.28	5,391.71	260.00	UF	40.00	7,588.09	17,696.91		43
44	115.26	28.82	312.06	20.00			476.14	1,444.86	6225	44
50	112.20	28.05	299.82	20.00			460.07	1,409.93	6530	50
51	121.38	30.35	336.54	20.00			508.27	1,514.73	6582	51
52	103.02	25.76	264.22	20.00			413.00	1,304.00	6640	52
53	121.38	30.35	336.54	20.00	UF	5.00	513.27	1,509.73	6688	53
54	118.32	29.58	324.30	20.00			492.20	1,479.80	6743	54
55	115.26	28.82	312.06	20.00			476.14	1,444.86	6801	55
56	87.72	21.93	208.12	20.00	UF	5.00	342.77	1,119.23	6860	56
57	1,506.90	376.73	5,293.71	260.00	UF	15.00	7,452.34	17,482.66		57
58	6,030.00	1,507.50	21,387.65	1,040.00	UF	100.00	30,065.15	70,434.85		58

As shown in Exhibit 5, an employee's earnings record has quarterly and yearly totals. These totals are used for tax, insurance, and other reports. For example, one such report is the Wage and Tax Statement, commonly called a *W-2*. This form is provided annually to each employee as well as to the Social Security Administration. The W-2 shown in Exhibit 6 is based on John T. McGrath's employee's earnings record shown in Exhibit 5.

EXHIBIT 6 **Employee's Wage and Tax Statement (W-2 Form)**

22222	Void ☐	a Employee's social security number 381-48-9120	For Official Use Only ▶ OMB No. 1545-0008
b Employer identification number (EIN) 61-8436524		1 Wages, tips, other compensation 100,500.00	2 Federal income tax withheld 21,387.65
c Employer's name, address, and ZIP code McDermott Supply Co. 415 5th Ave. So. Dubuque, IA 52736-0142		3 Social security wages 100,500.00	4 Social security tax withheld 6,030.00
		5 Medicare wages and tips 100,500.00	6 Medicare tax withheld 1,507.50
		7 Social security tips	8 Allocated tips
d Control number		9	10 Dependent care benefits
e Employee's first name and initial John T.	Last name McGrath / Suff.	11 Nonqualified plans	12a See instructions for box 12
1830 4th St. Clinton, IA 52732-6142		13 Statutory employee ☐ Retirement plan ☐ Third-party sick pay ☐	12b
		14 Other	12c
f Employee's address and ZIP code			12d

15 State	Employer's state ID number	16 State wages, tips, etc.	17 State income tax	18 Local wages, tips, etc.	19 Local income tax	20 Locality name
IA						Dubuque

Form **W-2** **Wage and Tax Statement** **20Y6**

Department of the Treasury—Internal Revenue Service
For Privacy Act and Paperwork Reduction Act Notice, see the separate instructions.
Cat. No. 10134D

Copy A For Social Security Administration — Send this entire page with Form W-3 to the Social Security Administration; photocopies are **not** acceptable.

Do Not Cut, Fold, or Staple Forms on This Page

Payroll Checks

Companies pay employees either by electronic funds transfer or by *payroll checks*. With electronic funds transfers, the employee's net pay is electronically deposited into their bank account each period. Later, the employees receive a payroll statement summarizing how the net pay was computed. A payroll statement for the electronic funds transfer of John T. McGrath's pay is shown in Exhibit 7. Each payroll check includes a detachable statement showing how the net pay was computed, which is typically identical to the payroll statement accompanying electronic funds transfers (EFTs).

Most companies use a special payroll bank account to disburse payroll. In such cases, payroll is processed as follows:

1. The total net pay for the period is determined from the payroll register.
2. The company authorizes an electronic funds transfer (EFT) from its regular bank account to the special payroll bank account for the total net pay.
3. Individual EFTs or payroll checks are disbursed from the payroll account.
4. The numbers of the individual payroll disbursements are inserted in the payroll register.

EXHIBIT 7
Payroll Statement

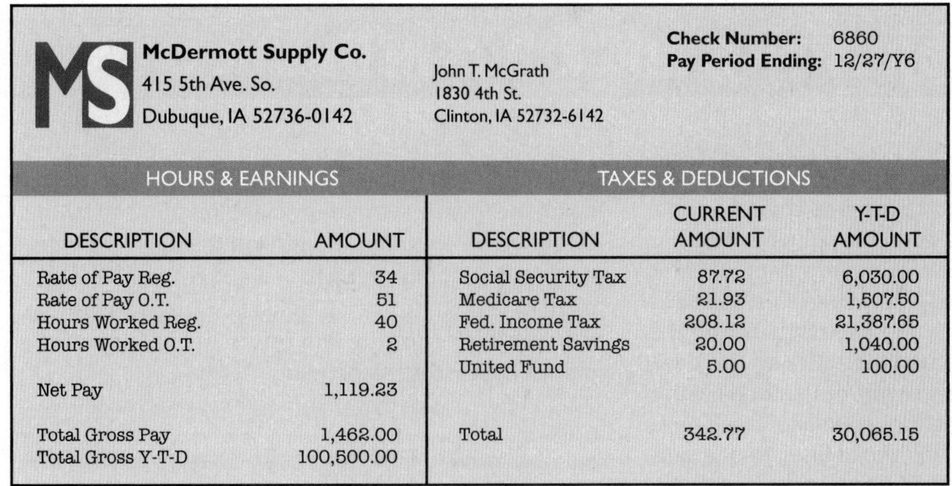

McDermott Supply Co.
415 5th Ave. So.
Dubuque, IA 52736-0142

John T. McGrath
1830 4th St.
Clinton, IA 52732-6142

Check Number: 6860
Pay Period Ending: 12/27/Y6

HOURS & EARNINGS		TAXES & DEDUCTIONS		
DESCRIPTION	AMOUNT	DESCRIPTION	CURRENT AMOUNT	Y-T-D AMOUNT
Rate of Pay Reg.	34	Social Security Tax	87.72	6,030.00
Rate of Pay O.T.	51	Medicare Tax	21.93	1,507.50
Hours Worked Reg.	40	Fed. Income Tax	208.12	21,387.65
Hours Worked O.T.	2	Retirement Savings	20.00	1,040.00
		United Fund	5.00	100.00
Net Pay	1,119.23			
Total Gross Pay	1,462.00	Total	342.77	30,065.15
Total Gross Y-T-D	100,500.00			

An advantage of using a separate payroll bank account is that reconciling the bank statements is simplified. In addition, a payroll bank account establishes control over payroll checks and, thus, prevents their theft or misuse.

Computerized Payroll System

The inputs into a payroll system may be classified as follows:

- *Constants:* Data that remain unchanged from payroll to payroll

  Examples*:* Employee names, social security numbers, marital status, number of income tax withholding allowances, rates of pay, tax rates, and withholding tables
- *Variables:* Data that change from payroll to payroll

  Examples*:* Number of hours or days worked for each employee, accrued days of sick leave, vacation credits, total earnings to date, and total taxes withheld

In a computerized accounting system, constants are stored within a payroll file. The variables are input each pay period by a payroll clerk. In some systems, employees swipe their identification (ID) cards when they report for and leave from work. In such cases, the hours worked by each employee are automatically updated.

A computerized payroll system also maintains electronic versions of the payroll register and employee earnings records. Payroll system outputs, such as payroll checks, electronic funds transfers, and tax records, are automatically produced each pay period.

Internal Controls for Payroll Systems

The cash payment controls described in Chapter 8 also apply to payrolls. Some examples of payroll controls include the following:

- If a check-signing machine is used, blank payroll checks and access to the machine should be restricted to prevent their theft or misuse.
- The hiring and firing of employees should be properly authorized and approved in writing.
- All changes in pay rates should be properly authorized and approved in writing.
- Employees should be observed when arriving for work to verify that employees are "checking in" for work only once and only for themselves. Employees may "check in" for work by using a time card or by swiping their employee ID card.
- Payroll checks should be distributed by someone other than employee supervisors.
- A special payroll bank account should be used.

Integrity, Objectivity, and Ethics in Business

OVERBILLING CLIENTS

The U.S. government makes payments to hospitals for the medical costs of patients covered under Medicaid. In some cases, computer glitches result in hospitals overbilling the U.S. government, causing overpayments to the hospital. When this happens, hospitals must return the overpayments to the U.S. government within 60 days of identifying the overpayment. If a hospital fails to return the funds within this time frame, it is subject to a penalty of three times the original liability plus additional fines. In one case, **Continuum Health Partners, Inc.**, determined that a computer glitch resulted in over $1,000,000 in claims being incorrectly submitted to and reimbursed by the U.S. government. After identifying the overpayments, it took Continuum over two years to return the funds. In 2014, a U.S. attorney filed a claim to recover penalties and fines for the late return of these overpayments. The case is still pending.

Source: Kevin P. Mulry, "Failure to Promptly Return Overpayments Arising from Computer Glitch Leads to False Claims Act Complaint," *New York Health Law*, July 17, 2014.

OBJ. 4 Journalize entries for employee fringe benefits, including vacation pay and pensions.

Employees' Fringe Benefits

Many companies provide their employees with benefits in addition to salary and wages earned. Such **fringe benefits** may include vacation, medical, and retirement benefits.

The cost of employee fringe benefits is recorded as an expense by the employer. To match revenues and expenses, the estimated cost of fringe benefits is recorded as an expense during the period in which employees earn the benefits.

Link to Starbucks

Starbucks offers eligible employees the Starbucks College Achievement Plan, which provides full tuition reimbursement for 80 undergraduate degree programs, delivered online at Arizona State University.

Vacation Pay

Most employers provide employees vacations, sometimes called *compensated absences*. The liability to pay for employee vacations could be accrued as a liability at the end of each pay period. However, many companies wait and record an adjusting entry for accrued vacation at the end of the year.

To illustrate, assume that employees earn one day of vacation for each month worked. The estimated vacation pay for the year ending December 31 is $325,000. The adjusting entry for the accrued vacation is as follows:

Dec.	31	Vacation Pay Expense		325,000	
		Vacation Pay Payable			325,000
		Accrued vacation pay for the year.			

Note

Vacation pay becomes the employer's liability as the employee earns vacation rights.

Employees may be required to take all their vacation time within one year. In such cases, any accrued vacation pay will be paid within one year. Thus, the vacation pay payable is reported as a current liability on the balance sheet. If employees are allowed to accumulate their vacation pay, the estimated vacation pay payable that will *not* be taken within a year is reported as a long-term liability.

When employees take vacations, the liability for vacation pay is decreased by debiting Vacation Pay Payable. Salaries or Wages Payable and the other related payroll accounts for taxes and withholdings are credited.

Pensions

A **pension** is a cash payment to retired employees. Pension benefits are accrued by employees as they work, based on the employer's pension plan. Two basic types of pension plans are defined contribution and defined benefit plans.[8]

Defined Contribution Plans In a **defined contribution plan**, the company invests contributions on behalf of the employee during the employee's working years. Normally, both the employee and employer contribute to the plan. The employee's pension depends on the total contributions and the investment returns earned on those contributions.

One of the more popular defined contribution plans is the 401k plan. Under this plan, employees contribute a portion of their gross pay to investments, such as mutual funds. A 401k plan offers employees two advantages.

- The employee contribution is deducted before taxes.
- The contributions and related earnings are not taxed until withdrawn at retirement.

In most cases, the employer matches some portion of the employee's contribution. The employer's cost is debited to *Pension Expense*. To illustrate, assume that Heaven Scent Perfumes Company contributes 10% of employee monthly salaries to an employee 401k plan. Assuming $500,000 of monthly salaries, the journal entry to record the monthly contribution is as follows:

Dec.	31	Pension Expense		50,000	
		Cash			50,000
		Contributed 10% of monthly salaries to pension plan.			

Defined Benefit Plans In a **defined benefit plan**, the company pays the employee a fixed annual pension based on a formula. The formula is normally based on such factors as the employee's years of service, age, and past salary.

In a defined benefit plan, the employer is obligated to pay for (fund) the employee's future pension benefits. As a result, many companies are replacing their defined benefit plans with defined contribution plans.

The pension cost of a defined benefit plan is debited to *Pension Expense*. Cash is credited for the amount contributed (funded) by the employer. Any unfunded amount is credited to *Unfunded Pension Liability*.

To illustrate, assume that the defined benefit plan of Hinkle Co. requires an annual pension cost of $80,000. This annual contribution is based on estimates of Hinkle's future pension liabilities. On December 31, Hinkle Co. pays $60,000 to the pension fund. The entry to record the payment and the unfunded liability is as follows:

Dec.	31	Pension Expense		80,000	
		Cash			60,000
		Unfunded Pension Liability			20,000
		Annual pension cost and contribution.			

If the unfunded pension liability is to be paid within one year, it is reported as a current liability on the balance sheet. Any portion of the unfunded pension liability that will be paid beyond one year is a long-term liability.

8 The accounting for pensions is complex due to the uncertainties of estimating future pension liabilities. These estimates depend on such factors as employee life expectancies, employee turnover, expected employee compensation levels, and investment income on pension contributions. Additional accounting and disclosures related to pensions are covered in advanced accounting courses.

EXAMPLE EXERCISE 11-6 Vacation Pay and Pension Benefits **OBJ. 4**

Manfield Services Company provides its employees with vacation benefits and a defined contribution pension plan. Employees earned vacation pay of $44,000 for the period. The pension plan requires a contribution to the plan administrator equal to 8% of employee salaries. Salaries were $450,000 during the period.

Provide the journal entry for the (a) vacation pay and (b) pension benefit.

Follow My Example 11-6

		Debit	Credit
a.	Vacation Pay Expense	44,000	
	Vacation Pay Payable		44,000
	Vacation pay accrued for the period.		
b.	Pension Expense	36,000	
	Cash		36,000
	Pension contribution, 8% of $450,000 salary.		

Practice Exercises: PE 11-6A, PE 11-6B

Link to Starbucks

On a recent balance sheet, **Starbucks** reported a $1,642.9 million dollar liability for "Stored Value Cards," which are prepaid purchases loaded onto a gift card or a mobile device, that have not yet been redeemed by customers.

Postretirement Benefits Other Than Pensions

Employees may earn rights to other postretirement benefits from their employer. Such benefits may include dental care, eye care, medical care, life insurance, tuition assistance, tax services, and legal services.

The accounting for other postretirement benefits is similar to that of defined benefit pension plans. The estimate of the annual benefits expense is recorded by debiting *Postretirement Benefits Expense*. If the benefits are fully funded, Cash is credited for the same amount. If the benefits are not fully funded, a postretirement benefits plan liability account is also credited.

The financial statements should disclose the nature of the postretirement benefit liabilities. These disclosures are usually included as notes to the financial statements. Additional accounting and disclosures for postretirement benefits are covered in advanced accounting courses.

Current Liabilities on the Balance Sheet

Accounts payable, the current portion of long-term debt, notes payable, and any other debts that are due within one year are reported as current liabilities on the balance sheet. The balance sheet presentation of current liabilities for **Mornin' Joe** follows:

Mornin' Joe
Balance Sheet
December 31, 20Y6

Liabilities		
Current liabilities:		
Accounts payable	$133,000	
Notes payable (current portion)	200,000	
Salaries and wages payable	42,000	
Payroll taxes payable	16,400	
Interest payable	40,000	
Total current liabilities		$431,400

Contingent Liabilities

OBJ. 5 Describe the accounting treatment for contingent liabilities and journalize entries for product warranties.

Some liabilities may arise from past transactions only if certain events occur in the future. These *potential* liabilities are called **contingent liabilities**.

The accounting for contingent liabilities depends on the following two factors:

- *Likelihood of occurring:* Probable, reasonably possible, or remote
- *Measurement:* Estimable or not estimable

The likelihood that the event creating the liability occurring is classified as *probable*, *reasonably possible*, or *remote*. The ability to estimate the potential liability is classified as *estimable* or *not estimable*.

Probable and Estimable

If a contingent liability is *probable* and the amount of the liability can be *reasonably estimated*, it is recorded and disclosed. The liability is recorded by debiting an expense and crediting a liability.

To illustrate, assume that during June, a company sold a product for $60,000 that includes a 36-month warranty for repairs.[9] The average cost of repairs over the warranty period is estimated at 5% of the sales price. The entry to record the estimated product warranty expense for June is as follows:

June	30	Product Warranty Expense		3,000	
		Product Warranty Payable			3,000
		Warranty expense for June, 5% × $60,000.			

The preceding entry records warranty expense in the same period in which the sale is recorded. In this way, warranty expense is matched with the related revenue (sales).

If the product is repaired under warranty, the repair costs are recorded by debiting *Product Warranty Payable* and crediting *Cash, Supplies, Wages Payable*, or other appropriate accounts. Thus, if a $200 part is replaced under warranty on August 16, the entry is as follows:

Aug.	16	Product Warranty Payable		200	
		Supplies			200
		Replaced defective part under warranty.			

Link to Starbucks

Starbucks terminated a contract with **Kraft Foods** that allowed Kraft to sell bagged Starbucks coffee in grocery stores. The early termination resulted in litigation between Kraft and Starbucks. After an arbitrator found in Kraft's favor, Starbucks recorded a contingent liability for $2.8 billion.

EXAMPLE EXERCISE 11-7 Estimated Warranty Liability **OBJ. 5**

Cook-Rite Co. sold $140,000 of kitchen appliances during August under a six-month warranty. The cost to repair defects under the warranty is estimated at 6% of the sales price. On September 12, a customer required a $200 part replacement plus $90 of labor under the warranty.

Provide the journal entry for (a) the estimated warranty expense on August 31 for August sales and (b) the September 12 warranty work.

Follow My Example 11-7

a.	Product Warranty Expense	8,400	
	Product Warranty Payable		8,400
	To record warranty expense for August, 6% × $140,000.		
b.	Product Warranty Payable	290	
	Supplies		200
	Wages Payable		90
	Replaced defective part under warranty.		

Practice Exercises: PE 11-7A, PE 11-7B

9 This discussion is limited to assurance type warranties. A more detailed discussion of the types of warranties and their accounting is covered in intermediate and advanced accounting texts.

Probable and Not Estimable

A contingent liability may be probable but cannot be estimated. In this case, the contingent liability is disclosed in the notes to the financial statements. For example, a company may have accidentally polluted a local river by dumping waste products. At the end of the period, the cost of the cleanup and any fines may not be able to be estimated.

Reasonably Possible

A contingent liability may be only possible. For example, a company may have lost a lawsuit for infringing on another company's patent rights. However, the verdict is under appeal and the company's lawyers believe that the verdict will be reversed or significantly reduced. In this case, the contingent liability is disclosed in the notes to the financial statements.

Remote

A contingent liability may be remote. For example, a ski resort may be sued for injuries incurred by skiers. In most cases, the courts have found that a skier accepts the risk of injury when participating in the activity. Thus, unless the ski resort is grossly negligent, the resort will not incur a liability for ski injuries. In such cases, no disclosure needs to be made in the notes to the financial statements. The accounting treatment of contingent liabilities is summarized in Exhibit 8.

Common examples of contingent liabilities disclosed in notes to the financial statements are litigation, environmental matters, guarantees, and contingencies from the sale of receivables.

Professional judgment is necessary in distinguishing between classes of contingent liabilities. This is especially the case when distinguishing between probable and reasonably possible contingent liabilities.

Link to Starbucks

In a recent annual report, **Starbucks** reported that in its normal course of business, it is party to a variety of legal actions. However, the management of Starbucks believes none of these actions will have a material effect on its financial statements.

EXHIBIT 8 **Accounting Treatment of Contingent Liabilities**

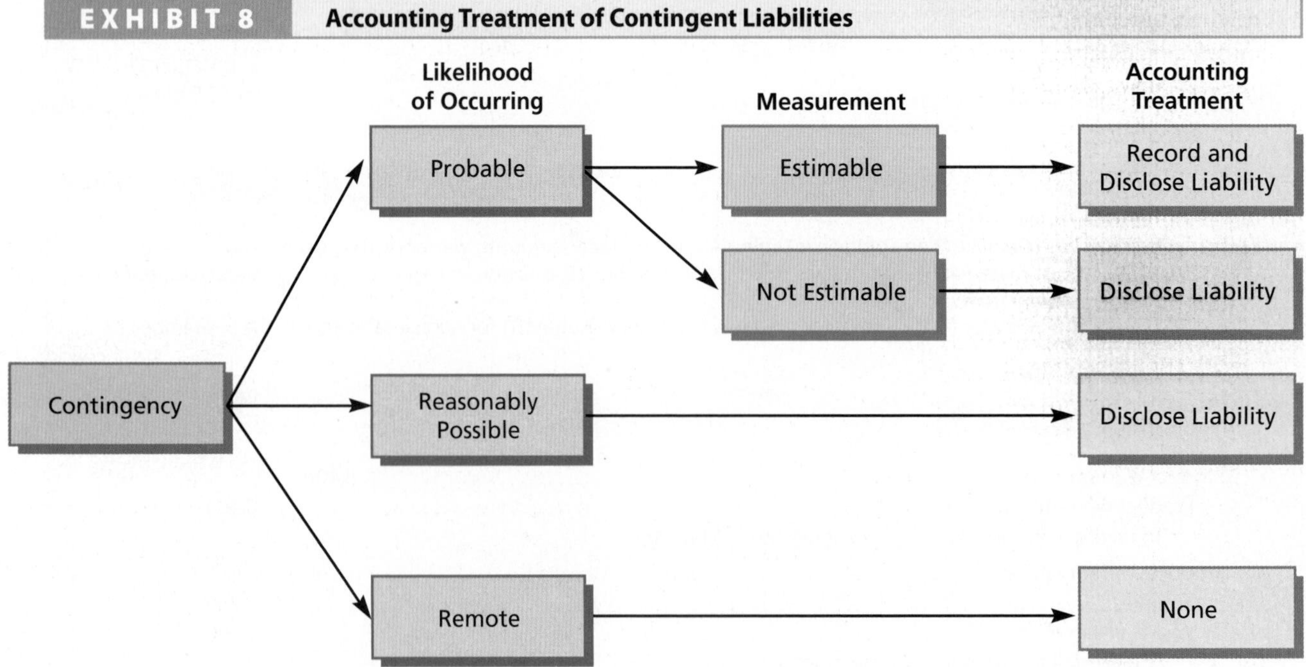

Financial Analysis and Interpretation: Quick Ratio

OBJ. 6 Describe and illustrate the use of the quick ratio in analyzing a company's ability to pay its current liabilities.

FAI

Current position analysis helps creditors evaluate a company's ability to pay its current liabilities. This analysis is based on the following three measures:

- Working capital
- Current ratio
- Quick ratio

Working capital and the current ratio were discussed in Chapter 4 and are computed as follows:

$$\text{Working Capital} = \text{Current Assets} - \text{Current Liabilities}$$

$$\text{Current Ratio} = \frac{\text{Current Assets}}{\text{Current Liabilities}}$$

While these two measures can be used to evaluate a company's ability to pay its current liabilities, they do not provide insight into the company's ability to pay these liabilities within a short period of time. This is because some current assets, such as inventory, cannot be converted into cash as quickly as other current assets, such as cash and accounts receivable.

The **quick ratio** overcomes this limitation by measuring the "instant" debt-paying ability of a company and is computed as follows:

$$\text{Quick Ratio} = \frac{\text{Quick Assets}}{\text{Current Liabilities}}$$

Quick assets are cash and other current assets that can be easily converted to cash. This normally includes cash, temporary investments, and accounts receivable. To illustrate, consider the following data for TechSolutions, Inc., at the end of 20Y7:

Current assets:	
Cash	$2,020
Temporary investments	3,400
Accounts receivable	1,600
Inventory	2,000
Other current assets	160
Total current assets	$9,180
Current liabilities:	
Accounts payable	$3,000
Other current liabilities	2,400
Total current liabilities	$5,400
Working capital (current assets − current liabilities)	$3,780
Current ratio (current assets ÷ current liabilities)	1.7

The quick ratio for TechSolutions, Inc., is computed as follows:

$$\text{Quick Ratio} = \frac{\$2,020 + \$3,400 + \$1,600}{\$5,400} = 1.3$$

The quick ratio of 1.3 indicates that the company has more than enough quick assets to pay its current liabilities in a short period of time. A quick ratio below 1.0 would indicate that the company does not have enough quick assets to cover its current liabilities.

Like the current ratio, the quick ratio is particularly useful in making comparisons across companies. To illustrate, the following selected balance sheet data (excluding ratios) were taken from recent financial statements of **Dunkin' Brands Group, Inc.,** and **Starbucks Corporation** (in thousands):

	Dunkin'	Starbucks
Current assets:		
Cash and cash equivalents	$517,594	$ 8,756,300
Temporary investments	—	181,500
Accounts receivable	75,963	693,100
Inventory	—	1,400,500
Other current assets	219,916	1,462,800
Total current assets	$813,473	$12,494,200
Current liabilities:		
Accounts payable	$ 80,037	$ 1,179,300
Other current liabilities	459,544	4,504,900
Total current liabilities	$ 539,581	$ 5,684,200
Working capital (current assets − current liabilities)	$273,892	$ 6,810,000
Current ratio (current assets ÷ current liabilities)	1.5	2.2
Quick ratio (quick assets ÷ current liabilities)*	1.1	1.7

*The quick ratio for each company is computed as follows:
Dunkin': ($517,594 + $75,963) ÷ $539,581 = 1.1
Starbucks: ($8,756,300 + $181,500 + $693,100) ÷ $5,684,200 = 1.7

Starbucks is larger than Dunkin' and has almost 25 times the amount of working capital. Such size differences make working capital comparisons between companies difficult. In contrast, the current and quick ratios provide better comparisons across companies. In this example, Starbucks has higher current and quick ratios than Dunkin'. Dunkin's quick ratio of 1.1, however, does indicate that the company has more than enough quick assets to meet its current liabilities.

EXAMPLE EXERCISE 11-8 Quick Ratio — OBJ. 6

Sayer Company reported the following current assets and current liabilities for the years ended December 31, 20Y9 and 20Y8:

	20Y9	20Y8
Cash	$1,250	$1,000
Temporary investments	1,925	1,650
Accounts receivable	1,775	1,350
Inventory	1,900	1,700
Accounts payable	2,750	2,500

a. Compute the quick ratio for 20Y9 and 20Y8.

b. Interpret the company's quick ratio across the two time periods.

Follow My Example 11-8

a. December 31, 20Y9:
Quick Ratio = Quick Assets ÷ Current Liabilities
= ($1,250 + $1,925 + $1,775) ÷ $2,750
= 1.8

December 31, 20Y8:
Quick Ratio = Quick Assets ÷ Current Liabilities
= ($1,000 + $1,650 + $1,350) ÷ $2,500
= 1.6

b. The quick ratio of Sayer Company has improved from 1.6 in 20Y8 to 1.8 in 20Y9. This increase is the result of a large increase in the three types of quick assets (cash, temporary investments, and accounts receivable) compared to a relatively smaller increase in the current liability, accounts payable.

Practice Exercises: PE 11-8A, PE 11-8B

At a Glance 11

OBJ. 1 **Describe and illustrate current liabilities related to accounts payable, the current portion of long-term debt, and notes payable.**

Key Points Current liabilities are obligations that are to be paid out of current assets and are due within a short time, usually within one year. The three primary types of current liabilities are accounts payable, notes payable, and the current portion of long-term debt.

Learning Outcomes	Example Exercises	Practice Exercises
• Identify and define the most frequently reported current liabilities on the balance sheet.		
• Determine the interest from interest-bearing and discounted notes payable.	**EE11-1**	**PE11-1A, 11-1B**

OBJ. 2 **Determine employer liabilities for payroll, including liabilities arising from employee earnings and deductions from earnings.**

Key Points An employer's liability for payroll is determined from employee total earnings, including overtime pay. From this amount, employee deductions are subtracted to arrive at the net pay to be paid to each employee. Most employers also incur liabilities for payroll taxes, such as social security tax, Medicare tax, federal unemployment compensation tax, and state unemployment compensation tax.

Learning Outcomes	Example Exercises	Practice Exercises
• Compute the federal withholding tax from a wage bracket withholding table.	**EE11-2**	**PE11-2A, 11-2B**
• Compute employee net pay, including deductions for social security and Medicare tax.	**EE11-3**	**PE11-3A, 11-3B**

OBJ. 3 **Describe payroll accounting systems that use a payroll register, employee earnings records, and a general journal.**

Key Points The payroll register is used in assembling and summarizing the data needed for each payroll period. The payroll register is supported by a detailed payroll record for each employee, called an *employee's earnings record*.

Learning Outcomes	Example Exercises	Practice Exercises
• Journalize the employee's earnings, net pay, and payroll liabilities from the payroll register.	**EE11-4**	**PE11-4A, 11-4B**
• Journalize the payroll tax expense.		
• Describe elements of a payroll system, including the employee's earnings record, payroll checks, and internal controls.	**EE11-5**	**PE11-5A, 11-5B**

OBJ. 4 **Journalize entries for employee fringe benefits, including vacation pay and pensions.**

Key Points Fringe benefits are expenses of the period in which the employees earn the benefits. Fringe benefits are recorded by debiting an expense account and crediting a liability account.

Learning Outcomes	Example Exercises	Practice Exercises
• Journalize vacation pay.	EE11-6	PE11-6A, 11-6B
• Distinguish and journalize defined contribution and defined benefit pension plans.	EE11-6	PE11-6A, 11-6B

OBJ. 5 **Describe the accounting treatment for contingent liabilities and journalize entries for product warranties.**

Key Points A contingent liability is a potential obligation that results from a past transaction but depends on a future event. The accounting for contingent liabilities is summarized in Exhibit 8.

Learning Outcomes	Example Exercises	Practice Exercises
• Describe the accounting for contingent liabilities.		
• Journalize estimated warranty obligations and services granted under warranty.	EE11-7	PE11-7A, 11-7B

OBJ. 6 **Describe and illustrate the use of the quick ratio in analyzing a company's ability to pay its current liabilities.**

Key Points The quick ratio is a measure of a company's ability to pay current liabilities within a short period of time. The quick ratio is computed by dividing quick assets by current liabilities. Quick assets include cash, temporary investments, accounts receivable, and other current assets that can be easily converted into cash. A quick ratio exceeding 1.0 is usually desirable.

Learning Outcomes	Example Exercises	Practice Exercises
• Describe the quick ratio.		
• Compute and evaluate the quick ratio.	EE11-8	PE11-8A, 11-8B

Illustrative Problem

Selected transactions of Taylor Company, completed during the fiscal year ended December 31, 20Y4, are as follows:

Mar. 1. Purchased merchandise on account from Kelvin Co., $20,000.

Apr. 10. Issued a 60-day, 9% note for $20,000 to Kelvin Co. on account.

June 9. Paid Kelvin Co. the amount owed on the note of April 10.

Aug. 1. Issued a $50,000, 90-day note to Harold Co. in exchange for a building. Harold Co. discounted the note at 6%.

Oct. 30. Paid Harold Co. the amount due on the note of August 1.

Dec. 27. Journalized the entry to record the biweekly payroll. A summary of the payroll record follows:

Salary distribution:		
Sales	$63,400	
Officers	36,600	
Office	10,000	$110,000
Deductions:		
Social security tax	$ 6,600	
Medicare tax	1,650	
Federal income tax	17,600	
State income tax	4,950	
Retirement savings	850	
Medical insurance	1,120	32,770
Net amount		$ 77,230

27. Journalized the entry to record payroll taxes for social security and Medicare from the biweekly payroll.

30. Issued a check in payment of liabilities for employees' federal income tax of $17,600, social security tax of $13,200, and Medicare tax of $3,300.

31. Issued a check for $9,500 to the pension fund trustee to fully fund the pension cost for December.

31. Journalized an entry to record the employees' accrued vacation pay, $36,100.

31. Journalized an entry to record the estimated accrued product warranty liability, $37,240.

Instruction

Journalize the preceding transactions.

Solution

20Y4					
Mar.	1	Merchandise Inventory		20,000	
		Accounts Payable—Kelvin Co.			20,000
Apr.	10	Accounts Payable—Kelvin Co.		20,000	
		Notes Payable			20,000
June	9	Notes Payable		20,000	
		Interest Expense		300	
		Cash			20,300
Aug.	1	Building		49,250	
		Interest Expense		750	
		Notes Payable			50,000
Oct.	30	Notes Payable		50,000	
		Cash			50,000

(Continued)

20Y4				
Dec.	27	Sales Salaries Expense	63,400	
		Officers Salaries Expense	36,600	
		Office Salaries Expense	10,000	
		Social Security Tax Payable		6,600
		Medicare Tax Payable		1,650
		Employees Federal Income Tax Payable		17,600
		Employees State Income Tax Payable		4,950
		Retirement Savings Deductions Payable		850
		Medical Insurance Payable		1,120
		Salaries Payable		77,230
	27	Payroll Tax Expense	8,250	
		Social Security Tax Payable		6,600
		Medicare Tax Payable		1,650
	30	Employees Federal Income Tax Payable	17,600	
		Social Security Tax Payable	13,200	
		Medicare Tax Payable	3,300	
		Cash		34,100
	31	Pension Expense	9,500	
		Cash		9,500
	31	Vacation Pay Expense	36,100	
		Vacation Pay Payable		36,100
	31	Product Warranty Expense	37,240	
		Product Warranty Payable		37,240

Key Terms

contingent liabilities (559)
current position analysis (561)
defined benefit plan (557)
defined contribution plan (557)
employee's earnings record (552)
FICA tax (547)
fringe benefits (556)
gross pay (545)
net pay (545)
payroll (545)
payroll register (550)
pension (557)
quick assets (561)
quick ratio (561)

Discussion Questions

1. Does a discounted note payable provide credit without interest? Discuss.
2. Employees are subject to taxes withheld from their paychecks.
   a. List the federal taxes withheld from most employee paychecks.
   b. Give the title of the accounts credited by amounts withheld.
3. Why are deductions from employees' earnings classified as liabilities for the employer?
4. For each of the following payroll-related taxes, indicate whether they generally apply to (a) employees only, (b) employers only, or (c) both employees and employers:
   1. Federal income tax
   2. Medicare tax

3. Social security tax
4. Federal unemployment compensation tax
5. State unemployment compensation tax

5. What are the principal reasons for using a special payroll bank account?
6. In a payroll system, what types of input data are referred to as (a) constants and (b) variables?
7. To match revenues and expenses properly, should the expense for employee vacation pay be recorded in the period during which the vacation privilege is earned or during the period in which the vacation is taken? Discuss.
8. Explain how a defined contribution pension plan works.
9. When should the liability associated with a product warranty be recorded? Discuss.
10. REAL WORLD **General Motors Corporation** reported $2.6 billion of product warranties in the Current Liabilities section of a recent balance sheet. How would costs of repairing a defective product be recorded?

Practice Exercises

Example Exercises

SHOW ME HOW

EE 11-1 p. 545

PE 11-1A Proceeds from notes payable **OBJ. 1**

On May 15, Franklin Co. borrowed cash from Dakota Bank by issuing a 90-day note with a face amount of $180,000.

a. Determine the proceeds of the note, assuming that the note carries an interest rate of 8%.

b. Determine the proceeds of the note, assuming that the note is discounted at 8%.

SHOW ME HOW

EE 11-1 p. 545

PE 11-1B Proceeds from notes payable **OBJ. 1**

On January 26, McMaster Co. borrowed cash from Quantum Bank by issuing a 45-day note with a face amount of $324,000.

a. Determine the proceeds of the note, assuming that the note carries an interest rate of 10%.

b. Determine the proceeds of the note, assuming that the note is discounted at 10%.

SHOW ME HOW

EE 11-2 p. 547

PE 11-2A Federal income tax withholding **OBJ. 2**

Stan Stately's weekly gross earnings for the present week were $2,400. Stately has two exemptions. Using the wage bracket withholding table in Exhibit 2 with an $81 standard withholding allowance for each exemption, what is Stately's federal income tax withholding?

SHOW ME HOW

EE 11-2 p. 547

PE 11-2B Federal income tax withholding **OBJ. 2**

Candy Cane's weekly gross earnings for the present week were $1,370. Cane has one exemption. Using the wage bracket withholding table in Exhibit 2 with an $81 standard withholding allowance for each exemption, what is Cane's federal income tax withholding?

SHOW ME HOW

EE 11-3 p. 548

PE 11-3A Employee net pay **OBJ. 2**

Stan Stately's weekly gross earnings for the week ended April 22 were $2,400, and his federal income tax withholding was $407.58. Assuming that the social security rate is 6% and Medicare is 1.5% of all earnings, what is Stately's net pay?

SHOW ME HOW

EE 11-3 p. 548

PE 11-3B Employee net pay **OBJ. 2**

Candy Cane's weekly gross earnings for the week ended May 23 were $1,370, and her federal income tax withholding was $187.88. Assuming that the social security rate is 6% and Medicare is 1.5% of all earnings, what is Cane's net pay?

SHOW ME HOW EE 11-4 p. 551

PE 11-4A Journalize period payroll OBJ. 3

The payroll register of Clapton Co. indicates $11,340 of social security withheld and $2,835 of Medicare tax withheld on total salaries of $189,000 for the period. Federal withholding for the period totaled $37,420.

Provide the journal entry for the period's payroll.

SHOW ME HOW EE 11-4 p. 551

PE 11-4B Journalize period payroll OBJ. 3

The payroll register of Shortman Co. indicates $3,240 of social security withheld and $810 of Medicare tax withheld on total salaries of $54,000 for the period. Retirement savings withheld from employee paychecks were $3,500 for the period. Federal withholding for the period totaled $10,690.

Provide the journal entry for the period's payroll.

SHOW ME HOW EE 11-5 p. 552

PE 11-5A Journalize payroll tax OBJ. 3

The payroll register of Clapton Co. indicates $11,340 of social security withheld and $2,835 of Medicare tax withheld on total salaries of $189,000 for the period. Earnings of $19,000 are subject to state and federal unemployment compensation taxes at the federal rate of 0.6% and the state rate of 5.4%.

Provide the journal entry to record the payroll tax expense for the period.

SHOW ME HOW EE 11-5 p. 552

PE 11-5B Journalize payroll tax OBJ. 3

The payroll register of Shortman Co. indicates $3,240 of social security withheld and $810 of Medicare tax withheld on total salaries of $54,000 for the period. Earnings of $5,000 are subject to state and federal unemployment compensation taxes at the federal rate of 0.6% and the state rate of 5.4%.

Provide the journal entry to record the payroll tax expense for the period.

SHOW ME HOW EE 11-6 p. 558

PE 11-6A Vacation pay and pension benefits OBJ. 4

Nakajima Company provides its employees with vacation benefits and a defined contribution pension plan. Employees earned vacation pay of $25,500 for the period. The pension plan requires a contribution to the plan administrator equal to 6% of employee salaries. Salaries were $340,000 during the period, and the full amount due was contributed to the pension plan administrator.

Provide the journal entry for the (a) vacation pay and (b) pension benefit.

SHOW ME HOW EE 11-6 p. 558

PE 11-6B Vacation pay and pension benefits OBJ. 4

Vandiver Company provides its employees with vacation benefits and a defined benefit pension plan. Employees earned vacation pay of $62,000 for the period. The pension formula indicated a pension cost of $342,920. Only $298,000 was contributed to the pension plan administrator.

Provide the journal entry for the (a) vacation pay and (b) pension benefit.

SHOW ME HOW EE 11-7 p. 559

PE 11-7A Estimated warranty liability OBJ. 5

Fitzpatrick Co. sold $391,000 of equipment during January under a one-year warranty. The cost to repair defects under the warranty is estimated at 3% of the sales price. On August 15, a customer required a $110 part replacement plus $55 of labor under the warranty.

Provide the journal entry for (a) the estimated warranty expense on January 31 for January sales and (b) the August 15 warranty work.

SHOW ME HOW EE 11-7 p. 559

PE 11-7B Estimated warranty liability OBJ. 5

Gupta Industries sold $436,000 of consumer electronics during July under a nine-month warranty. The cost to repair defects under the warranty is estimated at 4.5% of the sales price. On November 11, a customer was given $480 cash under terms of the warranty.

Provide the journal entry for (a) the estimated warranty expense on July 31 for July sales and (b) the November 11 cash payment.

EE 11-8 *p. 562*

PE 11-8A Quick ratio **OBJ. 6**

Basted Company reported the following current assets and liabilities for December 31 for two recent years:

	Dec. 31, Current Year	Dec. 31, Previous Year
Cash	$2,070	$2,230
Temporary investments	4,780	5,030
Accounts receivable	2,160	2,420
Inventory	3,960	4,550
Accounts payable	5,300	4,400

a. Compute the quick ratio on December 31 of both years.

b. Interpret the company's quick ratio. Is the quick ratio improving or declining?

EE 11-8 *p. 562*

FAI

PE 11-8B Quick ratio **OBJ. 6**

Aloha Company reported the following current assets and liabilities for December 31 for two recent years:

	Dec. 31, Current Year	Dec. 31, Previous Year
Cash	$1,760	$1,680
Temporary investments	2,130	2,090
Accounts receivable	1,430	1,330
Inventory	3,880	3,420
Accounts payable	2,800	3,400

a. Compute the quick ratio on December 31 of both years.

b. Interpret the company's quick ratio. Is the quick ratio improving or declining?

Exercises

EX 11-1 Current liabilities **OBJ. 1**

✔ Total current liabilities, $1,929,750

Bon Nebo Co. sold 25,000 annual subscriptions of *Magazine 20XX* for $85 during December 20Y8. These new subscribers will receive monthly issues, beginning in January 20Y9. In addition, the business had taxable income of $840,000 during the first calendar quarter of 20Y9. The federal tax rate is 40%. A quarterly tax payment will be made on April 12, 20Y9.

Prepare the Current Liabilities section of the balance sheet for Bon Nebo Co. on March 31, 20Y9.

EX 11-2 Entries for notes payable **OBJ. 1**

Laughlin Enterprises issues a $130,000, 45-day, 6% note to Morrison Industries for merchandise inventory.

a. Journalize Laughlin Enterprises' entries to record:
   1. the issuance of the note.
   2. the payment of the note at maturity.

b. Journalize Morrison Industries' entries to record:
   1. the receipt of the note.
   2. the receipt of the payment of the note at maturity.

EX 11-3 Entries for discounting notes payable **OBJ. 1**

Ramsey Company issues an $800,000, 45-day note to Buckner Company for merchandise inventory. Buckner discounts the note at 7%.

a. Journalize Ramsey's entries to record:
   1. the issuance of the note.
   2. the payment of the note at maturity.

b. Journalize Buckner's entries to record:
   1. the receipt of the note.
   2. the receipt of the payment of the note at maturity.

EXCEL ONLINE

EX 11-4 Evaluating alternative notes **OBJ. 1**

A borrower has two alternatives for a loan: (1) issue a $360,000, 60-day, 5% note or (2) issue a $360,000, 60-day note that the creditor discounts at 5%.

a. Compute the amount of the interest expense for each option.

b. Determine the proceeds received by the borrower in each situation.

c. Which alternative is more favorable to the borrower? Explain.

EX 11-5 Entries for notes payable **OBJ. 1**

A business issued a 45-day, 6% note for $210,000 to a creditor on account. Journalize the entries to record (a) the issuance of the note and (b) the payment of the note at maturity, including interest.

EX 11-6 Entries for discounted note payable **OBJ. 1**

A business issued a 45-day note for $80,000 to a creditor on account. The note was discounted at 5%. Journalize the entries to record (a) the issuance of the note and (b) the payment of the note at maturity.

EX 11-7 Entries for notes payable **OBJ. 1**

Bull City Industries is considering issuing a $100,000, 7% note to a creditor on account.

a. If the note is issued with a 45-day term, journalize the entries to record:
   1. the issuance of the note.
   2. the payment of the note at maturity.

b. If the note is issued with a 90-day term, journalize the entries to record:
   1. the issuance of the note.
   2. the payment of the note at maturity.

✔ a. $3,953

REAL WORLD

EX 11-8 Current portion of long-term debt **OBJ. 1**

PepsiCo, Inc., reported the following information about its long-term debt in the notes to a recent financial statement (in millions):

Long-term debt is comprised of the following:

	December 31	
	Current Year	**Previous Year**
Total long term-debt	$32,248	$37,816
Less current portion	(3,953)	(4,020)
Long-term debt	$28,295	$33,796

a. How much of the long-term debt was disclosed as a current liability on the current year's December 31 balance sheet?

b. How much did the total current liabilities change between the preceding year and the current year as a result of the current portion of long-term debt?

c. If PepsiCo did not issue additional long-term debt next year, what would be the total long-term debt on December 31 of the upcoming year?

✔ b. Net pay, $1,043.90

SHOW ME HOW

EX 11-9 Compute payroll **OBJ. 2**

An employee earns $22 per hour and 2 times that rate for all hours in excess of 40 hours per week. Assume that the employee worked 50 hours during the week. Assume further that the social security tax rate was 6.0%, the Medicare tax rate was 1.5%, and federal income tax to be withheld was $177.10.

a. Determine the gross pay for the week.

b. Determine the net pay for the week.

✔ Consultant net pay, $3,434.30

SHOW ME HOW

EX 11-10 Compute payroll **OBJ. 2**

Floatin Away Company has three employees—a consultant, a computer programmer, and an administrator. The following payroll information is available for each employee:

	Consultant	Computer Programmer	Administrator
Regular earnings rate	$5,000 per week	$80 per hour	$50 per hour
Overtime earnings rate*	Not applicable	1.5 times hourly rate	2 times hourly rate
Number of withholding allowances	2	1	2

*For hourly employees, overtime is paid for hours worked in excess of 40 hours per week.

For the current pay period, the computer programmer worked 46 hours and the administrator worked 50 hours. The federal income tax withheld for all three employees, who are single, can be determined from the wage bracket withholding table in Exhibit 2 in the chapter. Assume further that the social security tax rate was 6.0%, the Medicare tax rate was 1.5%, and one withholding allowance is $81.

Determine the gross pay and the net pay for each of the three employees for the current pay period.

✔ a. (3) Total earnings, $540,000

EX 11-11 Summary payroll data **OBJ. 2, 3**

Assume that the social security tax rate is 6% and the Medicare tax rate is 1.5%. In the following summary of data for a payroll period, some amounts have been intentionally omitted:

Earnings:	
1. At regular rate	?
2. At overtime rate	$ 80,000
3. Total earnings	?
Deductions:	
4. Social security tax	32,400
5. Medicare tax	8,100
6. Federal income tax withheld	135,000
7. Medical insurance	18,900
8. Union dues	?
9. Total deductions	201,150
10. Net amount paid	338,850
Accounts debited:	
11. Factory Wages	285,000
12. Sales Salaries	?
13. Office Salaries	120,000

a. Determine the amounts omitted in lines (1), (3), (8), and (12).

b. Journalize the entry to record the payroll accrual.

c. Journalize the entry to record the payment of the payroll.

✔ a. $45,600

SHOW ME HOW

EX 11-12 Payroll tax entries **OBJ. 3**

According to a summary of the payroll of Guthrie Co., $560,000 was subject to the 6.0% social security tax and the 1.5% Medicare tax. Also, $60,000 was subject to state and federal unemployment taxes.

a. Compute the employer's payroll taxes, using the following rates: state unemployment, 5.4%; federal unemployment, 0.6%.

b. Journalize the entry to record the accrual of payroll taxes.

SHOW ME HOW

EX 11-13 Payroll entries **OBJ. 3**

The payroll register for Schmidt Company for the week ended April 29 indicated the following:

Salaries	$1,380,000
Social security tax withheld	82,800
Medicare tax withheld	20,700
Federal income tax withheld	276,000

In addition, state and federal unemployment taxes were computed at the rate of 5.4% and 0.6%, respectively, on $245,000 of salaries.

a. Journalize the entry to record the payroll for the week of April 29.

b. Journalize the entry to record the payroll tax expense incurred for the week of April 29.

SHOW ME HOW

EX 11-14 Payroll entries **OBJ. 3**

Urban Window Company had gross wages of $320,000 during the week ended July 15. The amount of wages subject to social security tax was $320,000, while the amount of wages subject to federal and state unemployment taxes was $40,000. Tax rates are as follows:

Social security	6.0%
Medicare	1.5%
State unemployment	5.4%
Federal unemployment	0.6%

The total amount withheld from employee wages for federal taxes was $75,200.

a. Journalize the entry to record the payroll for the week of July 15.

b. Journalize the entry to record the payroll tax expense incurred for the week of July 15.

EX 11-15 Payroll internal control procedures **OBJ. 3**

Big Howie's Hot Dog Stand is a fast-food restaurant specializing in hot dogs and hamburgers. The store employs 8 full-time and 12 part-time workers. The store's weekly payroll averages $5,600 for all 20 workers.

Big Howie's Hot Dog Stand uses a personal computer to assist in preparing paychecks. Each week, the store's accountant collects employee time cards and enters the hours worked into the payroll program. The payroll program computes each employee's pay and prints a paycheck. The accountant uses a check-signing machine to sign the paychecks. Next, the restaurant's owner authorizes the transfer of funds from the restaurant's regular bank account to the payroll account.

For the week of May 12, the accountant accidentally recorded 100 hours worked instead of 40 hours for one of the full-time employees.

Does Big Howie's Hot Dog Stand have internal controls in place to catch this error? If so, how will this error be detected?

EX 11-16 Internal control procedures **OBJ. 3**

Dave's Scooters is a small manufacturer of specialty scooters. The company employs 14 production workers and four administrative persons. The following procedures are used to process the company's weekly payroll:

a. Whenever an employee receives a pay raise, the supervisor must fill out a wage adjustment form, which is signed by the company president. This form is used to change the employee's wage rate in the payroll system.

b. All employees are required to record their hours worked by clocking in and out on a time clock. Employees must clock out for lunch break. Due to congestion around the time clock area at lunch time, management has not objected to having one employee clock in and out for an entire department.

c. Whenever a salaried employee is terminated, Personnel authorizes Payroll to remove the employee from the payroll system. However, this procedure is not required when an hourly worker is fired. Hourly employees only receive a paycheck if their time cards show hours worked. The computer automatically drops an employee from the payroll system when that employee has six consecutive weeks with no hours worked.

d. Paychecks are signed using a check-signing machine. This machine is located in the main office so that it can be easily accessed by anyone needing a check signed.

e. Dave's Scooters maintains a separate checking account for payroll checks. Each week the total net pay for all employees is transferred from the company's regular bank account to the payroll account.

State whether each of the procedures is appropriate or inappropriate, after considering the principles of internal control. If a procedure is inappropriate, describe the appropriate procedure.

EX 11-17 Accrued vacation pay

OBJ. 4

A business provides its employees with varying amounts of vacation per year, depending on the length of employment. The estimated amount of the current year's vacation pay is $138,000.

a. Journalize the adjusting entry required on January 31, the end of the first month of the current year, to record the accrued vacation pay.

b. How is the vacation pay reported on the company's balance sheet? When is this amount removed from the company's balance sheet?

EX 11-18 Pension plan entries

OBJ. 4

Yuri Co. operates a chain of gift shops. The company maintains a defined contribution pension plan for its employees. The plan requires quarterly installments to be paid to the funding agent, Whims Funds, by the fifteenth of the month following the end of each quarter. Assume that the pension cost is $365,000 for the quarter ended December 31.

a. Journalize the entries to record the accrued pension liability on December 31 and the payment to the funding agent on January 15.

b. How does a defined contribution plan differ from a defined benefit plan?

EX 11-19 Defined benefit pension plan terms

OBJ. 4

In a recent year's financial statements, **Procter & Gamble** showed an unfunded pension liability of $4,391 million and a periodic pension cost of $208 million.

Explain the meaning of the $4,391 million unfunded pension liability and the $208 million periodic pension cost.

EX 11-20 Accrued product warranty

OBJ. 5

Logan Manufacturing Co. warrants its products for one year. The estimated product warranty is 2.5% of sales. Assume that sales were $398,000 for January. In February, a customer received warranty repairs requiring $410 of parts and $250 of labor.

a. Journalize the adjusting entry required at January 31, the end of the first month of the current fiscal year, to record the accrued product warranty.

b. Journalize the entry to record the warranty work provided in February.

EX 11-21 Accrued product warranty

OBJ. 5

General Motors Corporation (GM) disclosed estimated product warranty payable for comparative years as follows:

	(in millions)	
	Year 2	**Year 1**
Current estimated product warranty payable	$2,788	$2,994
Noncurrent estimated product warranty payable	4,802	5,338
Total	$7,590	$8,332

Presume that GM's sales were $147,049 million in Year 2 and that the total paid on warranty claims during Year 2 was $3,000 million.

(Continued)

a. Why are short- and long-term estimated warranty liabilities disclosed separately?

b. Provide the journal entry for the Year 2 product warranty expense.

c. What two conditions must be met in order for a product warranty liability to be reported on the financial statements?

EX 11-22 Contingent liabilities **OBJ. 5**

Several months ago, Ayers Industries Inc. experienced a hazardous materials spill at one of its plants. As a result, the Environmental Protection Agency (EPA) fined the company $240,000. The company is contesting the fine. In addition, an employee is seeking $220,000 in damages related to the spill. Finally, a homeowner has sued the company for $310,000. The homeowner lives 35 miles from the plant but believes that the incident has reduced the home's resale value by $310,000.

Ayers' legal counsel believes that it is probable that the EPA fine will stand. In addition, counsel indicates that an out-of-court settlement of $125,000 has recently been reached with the employee. The final papers will be signed next week. Counsel believes that the homeowner's case is much weaker and will be decided in favor of Ayers. Other litigation related to the spill is possible, but the damage amounts are uncertain.

a. Journalize the contingent liabilities associated with the hazardous materials spill. Use the account "Damage Awards and Fines" to recognize the expense for the period.

b. Prepare a note disclosure relating to this incident.

EX 11-23 Quick ratio **OBJ. 6**

✔ a. Current year: 1.2

FAI

EXCEL ONLINE

Gmeiner Co. had the following current assets and liabilities on December 31 of two recent years:

	Current Year	Previous Year
Current assets:		
Cash	$ 486,000	$ 500,000
Accounts receivable	210,000	200,000
Inventory	375,000	350,000
Total current assets	$1,071,000	$1,050,000
Current liabilities:		
Current portion of long-term debt	$ 145,000	$ 110,000
Accounts payable	175,000	150,000
Accrued and other current liabilities	260,000	240,000
Total current liabilities	$ 580,000	$ 500,000

a. Determine the quick ratio for December 31 of both years.

b. Interpret the change in the quick ratio between the two balance sheet dates.

EX 11-24 Quick ratio **OBJ. 6**

✔ a. Apple, 1.0

REAL WORLD

The current assets and current liabilities for **Apple Inc.** and **HP, Inc.**, are as follows at the end of a recent fiscal period:

	Apple Inc. (in millions)	HP, Inc. (in millions)
Current assets:		
Cash and cash equivalents	$ 25,913	$ 5,166
Short-term investments	40,388	0
Accounts receivable	48,995	5,113
Inventories	3,956	6,062
Other current assets*	12,087	5,046
Total current assets	$131,339	$21,387
Current liabilities:		
Accounts payable	$ 55,888	$14,816
Accrued and other current liabilities	60,978	10,315
Total current liabilities	$116,866	$25,131

* These represent prepaid expense and other nonquick current assets.

a. Determine the quick ratio for both companies. Round to one decimal place.

b. Interpret the quick ratio difference between the two companies.

Problems: Series A

PR 11-1A Liability transactions

OBJ. 1, 5

SHOW ME HOW

The following items were selected from among the transactions completed by Shin Co. during the current year:

Jan. 10. Purchased merchandise on account from Beckham Co., $420,000, terms n/30.

Feb. 9. Issued a 30-day, 6% note for $420,000 to Beckham Co., on account.

Mar. 11. Paid Beckham Co. the amount owed on the note of February 9.

May 1. Borrowed $240,000 from Verity Bank, issuing a 45-day, 5% note.

June 1. Purchased tools by issuing a $312,000, 60-day note to Rassmuessen Co., which discounted the note at the rate of 5%.

15. Paid Verity Bank the interest due on the note of May 1 and renewed the loan by issuing a new 45-day, 7% note for $240,000. (Journalize both the debit and credit to the notes payable account.)

July 30. Paid Verity Bank the amount due on the note of June 15.

30. Paid Rassmuessen Co. the amount due on the note of June 1.

Dec. 1. Purchased office equipment from Lambert Co. for $700,500 paying $160,500 and issuing a series of ten 5% notes for $54,000 each, coming due at 30-day intervals.

15. Settled a product liability lawsuit with a customer for $144,200 payable in January. Shin accrued the loss in a litigation claims payable account.

31. Paid the amount due Lambert Co. on the first note in the series issued on December 1.

Instructions

1. Journalize the transactions.
2. Journalize the adjusting entry for each of the following accrued expenses at the end of the current year:
   a. Product warranty cost, $19,500.
   b. Interest on the nine remaining notes owed to Lambert Co.

PR 11-2A Entries for payroll and payroll taxes

OBJ. 2, 3

✔ **1. (b) Dr. Payroll Tax Expense, $60,675**

The following information about the payroll for the week ended December 30 was obtained from the records of Pharrell Co.:

Salaries:		Deductions:	
Sales salaries	$402,000	Federal income tax withheld	$135,975
Warehouse salaries	210,000	Social security tax withheld	46,620
Office salaries	165,000	Medicare tax withheld	11,655
	$777,000	Retirement savings	17,094
		Group insurance	13,986
			$225,330

Tax rates assumed:

Social security, 6%

Medicare, 1.5%

State unemployment (employer only), 5.4%

Federal unemployment (employer only), 0.6%

(Continued)

Instructions

1. Assuming that the payroll for the last week of the year is to be paid on December 31, journalize the following entries:
   a. December 30, to record the payroll.
   b. December 30, to record the employer's payroll taxes on the payroll to be paid on December 31. Of the total payroll for the last week of the year, $40,000 is subject to unemployment compensation taxes.
2. Assuming that the payroll for the last week of the year is to be paid on January 5 of the following fiscal year, journalize the following entries:
   a. December 30, to record the payroll.
   b. January 5, to record the employer's payroll taxes on the payroll to be paid on January 5. Because it is a new fiscal year, all salaries are subject to unemployment compensation taxes.

PR 11-3A Wage and tax statement data on employer FICA tax

OBJ. 2, 3

✔ 2. (e) $28,450.80

Ehrlich Co. began business on January 2, 20Y8. Salaries were paid to employees on the last day of each month, and social security tax, Medicare tax, and federal income tax were withheld in the required amounts. An employee who is hired in the middle of the month receives half the monthly salary for that month. All required payroll tax reports were filed, and the correct amount of payroll taxes was remitted by the company for the calendar year. Early in 20Y9, before the Wage and Tax Statements (Form W-2) could be prepared for distribution to employees and for filing with the Social Security Administration, the employees' earnings records were inadvertently destroyed.

None of the employees resigned or were discharged during the year, and there were no changes in salary rates. The social security tax was withheld at the rate of 6.0% and Medicare tax at the rate of 1.5%. Data on dates of employment, salary rates, and employees' income taxes withheld, which are summarized as follows, were obtained from personnel records and payroll records:

Employee	Date First Employed	Monthly Salary	Monthly Federal Income Tax Withheld
Arnett	Nov. 16	$ 5,500	$ 944
Cruz	Jan. 2	4,800	833
Edwards	Oct. 1	8,000	1,592
Harvin	Dec. 1	6,000	1,070
Nicks	Feb. 1	10,000	2,350
Shiancoe	Mar. 1	11,600	2,600
Ward	Nov. 16	5,220	876

Instructions

1. Determine the amounts to be reported on each employee's Wage and Tax Statement (Form W-2) for 20Y8, arranging the data in the following form:

Employee	Gross Earnings	Federal Income Tax Withheld	Social Security Tax Withheld	Medicare Tax Withheld

2. Compute the following employer payroll taxes for the year: (a) social security; (b) Medicare; (c) state unemployment compensation at 5.4% on the first $10,000 of each employee's earnings; (d) federal unemployment compensation at 0.6% on the first $10,000 of each employee's earnings; (e) total.

✔ 1. Total net pay $15,424.12

PR 11-4A Payroll register

OBJ. 2, 3

The following data for Throwback Industries Inc. relate to the payroll for the week ended December 9, 20Y8:

Employee	Hours Worked	Hourly Rate	Weekly Salary	Federal Income Tax	Retirement Savings
Aaron	46	$68.00		$750.20	$100
Cobb	41	62.00		537.68	110
Clemente	48	70.00		832.64	120
DiMaggio	35	56.00		366.04	0
Griffey, Jr.	45	62.00		641.84	130
Mantle			$1,800	342.45	120
Robinson	36	54.00		382.56	130
Williams			2,000	398.24	125
Vaughn	42	62.00		584.72	50

Employees Mantle and Williams are office staff, and all of the other employees are sales personnel. All sales personnel are paid 1½ times the regular rate for all hours in excess of 40 hours per week. The social security tax rate is 6.0%, and Medicare tax is 1.5% of each employee's annual earnings. The next payroll check to be used is No. 901.

Instructions

1. Prepare a payroll register for Throwback Industries Inc. for the week ended December 9, 20Y8. Use the following columns for the payroll register: Employee, Total Hours, Regular Earnings, Overtime Earnings, Total Earnings, Social Security Tax, Medicare Tax, Federal Income Tax, Retirement Savings, Total Deductions, Net Pay, Ck. No., Sales Salaries Expense, and Office Salaries Expense.
2. Journalize the entry to record the payroll for the week.

PR 11-5A Payroll accounts and year-end entries

OBJ. 2, 3, 4

The following accounts, with the balances indicated, appear in the ledger of Garcon Co. on December 1 of the current year:

Account	Balance	Account	Balance
211 Salaries Payable	—	218 Retirement Savings Deductions Payable	$ 3,400
212 Social Security Tax Payable	$ 9,273	219 Medical Insurance Payable	27,000
213 Medicare Tax Payable	2,318	411 Operations Salaries Expense	950,000
214 Employees Federal Income Tax Payable	15,455	511 Officers Salaries Expense	600,000
215 Employees State Income Tax Payable	13,909	512 Office Salaries Expense	150,000
216 State Unemployment Tax Payable	1,400	519 Payroll Tax Expense	137,951
217 Federal Unemployment Tax Payable	500		

The following transactions relating to payroll, payroll deductions, and payroll taxes occurred during December:

Dec. 2. Issued Check No. 410 for $3,400 to Jay Bank to invest in a retirement savings account for employees.

2. Issued Check No. 411 to Jay Bank for $27,046, in payment of $9,273 of social security tax, $2,318 of Medicare tax, and $15,455 of employees' federal income tax due.

13. Journalized the entry to record the biweekly payroll. A summary of the payroll record follows:

Salary distribution:		
Operations	$43,200	
Officers	27,200	
Office	6,800	$77,200
Deductions:		
Social security tax	$ 4,632	
Medicare tax	1,158	
Federal income tax withheld	15,440	
State income tax withheld	3,474	
Retirement savings deductions	1,700	
Medical insurance deductions	4,500	30,904
Net amount		$46,296

(Continued)

Dec. 13. Issued Check No. 420 in payment of the net amount of the biweekly payroll to fund the payroll bank account.

13. Journalized the entry to record payroll taxes on employees' earnings of December 13: social security tax, $4,632; Medicare tax, $1,158; state unemployment tax, $350; federal unemployment tax, $125.

16. Issued Check No. 424 to Jay Bank for $27,020, in payment of $9,264 of social security tax, $2,316 of Medicare tax, and $15,440 of employees' federal income tax due.

19. Issued Check No. 429 to Sims-Walker Insurance Company for $31,500, in payment of the semiannual premium on the group medical insurance policy.

27. Journalized the entry to record the biweekly payroll. A summary of the payroll record follows:

Salary distribution:		
Operations	$42,800	
Officers	28,000	
Office	7,000	$77,800
Deductions:		
Social security tax	$ 4,668	
Medicare tax	1,167	
Federal income tax withheld	15,404	
State income tax withheld	3,501	
Retirement savings deductions	1,700	26,440
Net amount		$51,360

27. Issued Check No. 541 in payment of the net amount of the biweekly payroll to fund the payroll bank account.

27. Journalized the entry to record payroll taxes on employees' earnings of December 27: social security tax, $4,668; Medicare tax, $1,167; state unemployment tax, $225; federal unemployment tax, $75.

27. Issued Check No. 543 for $20,884 to State Department of Revenue in payment of employees' state income tax due on December 31.

31. Issued Check No. 545 to Jay Bank for $3,400 to invest in a retirement savings account for employees.

31. Paid $45,000 to the employee pension plan. The annual pension cost is $60,000. (Record both the payment and unfunded pension liability.)

Instructions

1. Journalize the transactions.
2. Journalize the following adjusting entries on December 31:
   a. Salaries accrued: operations salaries, $8,560; officers salaries, $5,600; office salaries, $1,400. The payroll taxes are immaterial and are not accrued.
   b. Vacation pay, $15,000.

Problems: Series B

PR 11-1B Liability transactions **OBJ. 1, 5**

The following items were selected from among the transactions completed by Aston Martin Inc. during the current year:

Apr. 15. Borrowed $225,000 from Audi Company, issuing a 30-day, 6% note for that amount.

May 1. Purchased equipment by issuing a $320,000, 180-day note to Spyder Manufacturing Co., which discounted the note at the rate of 6%.

15. Paid Audi Company the interest due on the note of April 15 and renewed the loan by issuing a new 60-day, 8% note for $225,000. (Record both the debit and credit to the notes payable account.)

July 14. Paid Audi Company the amount due on the note of May 15.

Aug. 16. Purchased merchandise on account from Exige Co., $90,000, terms, n/30.

Sept. 15. Issued a 45-day, 6% note for $90,000 to Exige Co., on account.

Oct. 28. Paid Spyder Manufacturing Co. the amount due on the note of May 1.

30. Paid Exige Co. the amount owed on the note of September 15.

Nov. 16. Purchased store equipment from Gallardo Co. for $450,000, paying $50,000 and issuing a series of twenty 9% notes for $20,000 each, coming due at 30-day intervals.

Dec. 16. Paid the amount due Gallardo Co. on the first note in the series issued on November 16.

28. Settled a personal injury lawsuit with a customer for $87,500, to be paid in January. Aston Martin Inc. accrued the loss in a litigation claims payable account.

Instructions

1. Journalize the transactions.
2. Journalize the adjusting entry for each of the following accrued expenses at the end of the current year:
   a. Product warranty cost, $26,800.
   b. Interest on the 19 remaining notes owed to Gallardo Co.

PR 11-2B Entries for payroll and payroll taxes **OBJ. 2, 3**

✔ 1. (b) Dr. Payroll Tax Expense, $90,675

The following information about the payroll for the week ended December 30 was obtained from the records of Saine Co.:

Salaries:		Deductions:	
Sales salaries	$ 625,000	Federal income tax withheld	$232,260
Warehouse salaries	240,000	Social security tax withheld	71,100
Office salaries	320,000	Medicare tax withheld	17,775
	$1,185,000	Retirement savings	35,500
		Group insurance	53,325
			$409,960

Tax rates assumed:

Social security, 6%

Medicare, 1.5%

State unemployment (employer only), 5.4%

Federal unemployment (employer only), 0.6%

Instructions

1. Assuming that the payroll for the last week of the year is to be paid on December 31, journalize the following entries:
   a. December 30, to record the payroll.
   b. December 30, to record the employer's payroll taxes on the payroll to be paid on December 31. Of the total payroll for the last week of the year, $30,000 is subject to unemployment compensation taxes.
2. Assuming that the payroll for the last week of the year is to be paid on January 4 of the following fiscal year, journalize the following entries:
   a. December 30, to record the payroll.
   b. January 4, to record the employer's payroll taxes on the payroll to be paid on January 4. Because it is a new fiscal year, all $1,185,000 in salaries is subject to unemployment compensation taxes.

PR 11-3B Wage and tax statement data and employer FICA tax **OBJ. 2, 3**

✔ 2. (e) $25,017.38

Jocame Inc. began business on January 2, 20Y7. Salaries were paid to employees on the last day of each month, and social security tax, Medicare tax, and federal income tax were withheld in the required amounts. An employee who is hired in the middle of the month receives half the monthly salary for that month. All required payroll tax reports were filed, and the correct amount of payroll taxes was remitted by the company for the

(Continued)

calendar year. Early in 20Y8, before the Wage and Tax Statements (Form W-2) could be prepared for distribution to employees and for filing with the Social Security Administration, the employees' earnings records were inadvertently destroyed.

None of the employees resigned or were discharged during the year, and there were no changes in salary rates. The social security tax was withheld at the rate of 6.0% and Medicare tax at the rate of 1.5% on salary. Data on dates of employment, salary rates, and employees' income taxes withheld, which are summarized as follows, were obtained from personnel records and payroll records:

Employee	Date First Employed	Monthly Salary	Monthly Federal Income Tax Withheld
Addai	July 16	$ 8,160	$1,704
Kasay	June 1	3,600	533
McGahee	Feb. 16	6,420	1,238
Moss	Jan. 1	4,600	783
Stewart	Dec. 1	4,500	758
Tolbert	Nov. 16	3,250	446
Wells	May 1	10,500	2,359

Instructions

1. Determine the amounts to be reported on each employee's Wage and Tax Statement (Form W-2) for 20Y7, arranging the data in the following form:

Employee	Gross Earnings	Federal Income Tax Withheld	Social Security Tax Withheld	Medicare Tax Withheld

2. Compute the following employer payroll taxes for the year: (a) social security; (b) Medicare; (c) state unemployment compensation at 5.4% on the first $10,000 of each employee's earnings; (d) federal unemployment compensation at 0.6% on the first $10,000 of each employee's earnings; (e) total.

PR 11-4B Payroll register

OBJ. 2, 3

✔ **1. Total net pay, $16,592.58**

The following data for Flexco Inc. relate to the payroll for the week ended December 9, 20Y8:

Employee	Hours Worked	Hourly Rate	Weekly Salary	Federal Income Tax	Retirement Savings
Carlton	52	$50.00		$667.00	$ 60
Grove			$4,000	860.00	100
Johnson	36	52.00		355.68	0
Koufax	45	58.00		578.55	44
Maddux	37	45.00		349.65	62
Seaver			3,200	768.00	120
Spahn	46	52.00		382.20	0
Winn	48	50.00		572.00	75
Young	43	54.00		480.60	80

Employees Grove and Seaver are office staff, and all of the other employees are sales personnel. All sales personnel are paid 1½ times the regular rate for all hours in excess of 40 hours per week. The social security tax rate is 6.0% of each employee's annual earnings, and Medicare tax is 1.5% of each employee's annual earnings. The next payroll check to be used is No. 328.

Instructions

1. Prepare a payroll register for Flexco Inc. for the week ended December 9, 20Y8. Use the following columns for the payroll register: Employee, Total Hours, Regular Earnings, Overtime Earnings, Total Earnings, Social Security Tax, Medicare Tax, Federal Income Tax, Retirement Savings, Total Deductions, Net Pay, Ck. No., Sales Salaries Expense, and Office Salaries Expense.
2. Journalize the entry to record the payroll for the week.

PR 11-5B Payroll accounts and year-end entries **OBJ. 2, 3, 4**

The following accounts, with the balances indicated, appear in the ledger of Codigo Co. on December 1 of the current year:

101 Salaries Payable	—	108 Retirement Savings Deductions Payable	$ 2,300
102 Social Security Tax Payable	$2,913	109 Medical Insurance Payable	2,520
103 Medicare Tax Payable	728	201 Sales Salaries Expense	700,000
104 Employees Federal Income Tax Payable	4,490	301 Officers Salaries Expense	340,000
105 Employees State Income Tax Payable	4,078	401 Office Salaries Expense	125,000
106 State Unemployment Tax Payable	1,260	408 Payroll Tax Expense	59,491
107 Federal Unemployment Tax Payable	360		

The following transactions relating to payroll, payroll deductions, and payroll taxes occurred during December:

Dec. 1. Issued Check No. 815 to Aberderas Insurance Company for $2,520, in payment of the semiannual premium on the group medical insurance policy.

1. Issued Check No. 816 to Alvarez Bank for $8,131, in payment for $2,913 of social security tax, $728 of Medicare tax, and $4,490 of employees' federal income tax due.

2. Issued Check No. 817 for $2,300 to Alvarez Bank to invest in a retirement savings account for employees.

12. Journalized the entry to record the biweekly payroll. A summary of the payroll record follows:

Salary distribution:		
Sales	$14,500	
Officers	7,100	
Office	2,600	$24,200
Deductions:		
Social security tax	$ 1,452	
Medicare tax	363	
Federal income tax withheld	4,308	
State income tax withheld	1,089	
Retirement savings deductions	1,150	
Medical insurance deductions	420	8,782
Net amount		$15,418

12. Issued Check No. 822 in payment of the net amount of the biweekly payroll to fund the payroll bank account.

12. Journalized the entry to record payroll taxes on employees' earnings of December 12: social security tax, $1,452; Medicare tax, $363; state unemployment tax, $315; federal unemployment tax, $90.

15. Issued Check No. 830 to Alvarez Bank for $7,938, in payment of $2,904 of social security tax, $726 of Medicare tax, and $4,308 of employees' federal income tax due.

26. Journalized the entry to record the biweekly payroll. A summary of the payroll record follows:

Salary distribution:		
Sales	$14,250	
Officers	7,250	
Office	2,750	$24,250
Deductions:		
Social security tax	$ 1,455	
Medicare tax	364	
Federal income tax withheld	4,317	
State income tax withheld	1,091	
Retirement savings deductions	1,150	8,377
Net amount		$15,873

26. Issued Check No. 840 for the net amount of the biweekly payroll to fund the payroll bank account.

(Continued)

Dec. 26. Journalized the entry to record payroll taxes on employees' earnings of December 26: social security tax, $1,455; Medicare tax, $364; state unemployment tax, $150; federal unemployment tax, $40.

30. Issued Check No. 851 for $6,258 to State Department of Revenue, in payment of employees' state income tax due on December 31.

30. Issued Check No. 852 to Alvarez Bank for $2,300 to invest in a retirement savings account for employees.

31. Paid $55,400 to the employee pension plan. The annual pension cost is $65,500. (Record both the payment and the unfunded pension liability.)

Instructions

1. Journalize the transactions.
2. Journalize the following adjusting entries on December 31:
   a. Salaries accrued: sales salaries, $4,275; officers salaries, $2,175; office salaries, $825. The payroll taxes are immaterial and are not accrued.
   b. Vacation pay, $13,350.

Comprehensive Problem 3

✔ 5. Total assets, $3,569,290

Selected transactions completed by Kornett Company during its first fiscal year ended December 31, 20Y8, were as follows:

Jan. 3. Issued a check to establish a petty cash fund of $4,500.

Feb. 26. Replenished the petty cash fund, based on the following summary of petty cash receipts: office supplies, $1,680; miscellaneous selling expense, $570; miscellaneous administrative expense, $880.

Apr. 14. Purchased $31,300 of merchandise on account, terms, n/30. The perpetual inventory system is used to account for inventory.

May 13. Paid the invoice of April 14.

17. Received cash from daily cash sales for $21,200. The amount indicated by the cash register was $21,240.

June 2. Received a 60-day, 8% note for $180,000 on the Ryanair account.

Aug. 1. Received amount owed on June 2 note plus interest at the maturity date.

24. Received $7,600 on the Finley account and wrote off the remainder owed on a $9,000 accounts receivable balance. (The allowance method is used in accounting for uncollectible receivables.)

Sept. 15. Reinstated the Finley account written off on August 24 and received $1,400 cash in full payment.

15. Purchased land by issuing a $670,000, 90-day note to Zahorik Co., which discounted it at 9%.

Oct. 17. Sold office equipment in exchange for $135,000 cash plus receipt of a $100,000, 90-day, 9% note. The equipment had a cost of $320,000 and accumulated depreciation of $64,000 as of October 17.

Nov. 30. Journalized the monthly payroll for November, based on the following data:

Salaries		Deductions	
Sales salaries	$135,000	Federal income tax withheld	$39,266
Office salaries	77,250	Social security tax withheld	12,735
	$212,250	Medicare tax withheld	3,184

Unemployment tax rates:	
State unemployment	5.4%
Federal unemployment	0.6%
Amount subject to unemployment taxes:	
State unemployment	$5,000
Federal unemployment	5,000

30. Journalized the employer's payroll taxes on the payroll.

Dec. 14. Journalized the payment of the September 15 note at maturity.

31. The pension cost for the year was $190,400, of which $139,700 was paid to the pension plan trustee.

Instructions

1. Journalize the selected transactions.
2. Based on the following data, prepare a bank reconciliation for December of the current year:
   a. Balance according to the bank statement at December 31, $283,000.
   b. Balance according to the ledger at December 31, $245,410.
   c. Checks outstanding at December 31, $68,540.
   d. Deposit in transit, not recorded by bank, $29,500.
   e. Bank debit memo for service charges, $750.
   f. A check for $12,700 in payment of an invoice was incorrectly recorded in the accounts as $12,000.
3. Based on the bank reconciliation prepared in (2), journalize the entry or entries to be made by Kornett Company.
4. Based on the following selected data, journalize the adjusting entries as of December 31 of the current year:
   a. Estimated uncollectible accounts at December 31, $16,000, based on an aging of accounts receivable. The balance of Allowance for Doubtful Accounts at December 31 was $2,000 (debit).
   b. The physical inventory on December 31 indicated an inventory shrinkage of $3,300.
   c. Prepaid insurance expired during the year, $22,820.
   d. Office supplies used during the year, $3,920.
   e. Depreciation is computed as follows:

Asset	Cost	Residual Value	Acquisition Date	Useful Life in Years	Depreciation Method Used
Buildings	$900,000	$ 0	January 2	50	Double-declining-balance
Office Equip.	246,000	26,000	January 3	5	Straight-line
Store Equip.	112,000	12,000	July 1	10	Straight-line

   f. A patent costing $48,000 when acquired on January 2 has a remaining legal life of 10 years and is expected to have value for eight years.
   g. The cost of mineral rights was $546,000. Of the estimated deposit of 910,000 tons of ore, 50,000 tons were mined and sold during the year.
   h. Vacation pay expense for December, $10,500.
   i. A product warranty was granted beginning December 1 and covering a one-year period. The estimated cost is 4% of sales, which totaled $1,900,000 in December.
   j. Interest was accrued on the note receivable received on October 17.

(Continued)

5. Based on the following information and the post-closing trial balance that follows, prepare a balance sheet in report form at December 31 of the current year:

The merchandise inventory is stated at cost by the LIFO method.
The product warranty payable is a current liability.

Vacation pay payable:

Current liability	$7,140
Long-term liability	3,360

The unfunded pension liability is a long-term liability.

Notes payable:

Current liability	$ 70,000
Long-term liability	630,000

Kornett Company
Post-Closing Trial Balance
December 31, 20Y8

	Debit Balances	Credit Balances
Petty Cash	4,500	
Cash	243,960	
Notes Receivable	100,000	
Accounts Receivable	470,000	
Allowance for Doubtful Accounts		16,000
Merchandise Inventory	320,000	
Interest Receivable	1,875	
Prepaid Insurance	45,640	
Office Supplies	13,390	
Land	654,925	
Buildings	900,000	
Accumulated Depreciation—Buildings		36,000
Office Equipment	246,000	
Accumulated Depreciation—Office Equipment		44,000
Store Equipment	112,000	
Accumulated Depreciation—Store Equipment		5,000
Mineral Rights	546,000	
Accumulated Depletion		30,000
Patents	42,000	
Social Security Tax Payable		25,470
Medicare Tax Payable		4,710
Employees Federal Income Tax Payable		40,000
State Unemployment Tax Payable		270
Federal Unemployment Tax Payable		30
Salaries Payable		157,000
Accounts Payable		131,600
Interest Payable		28,000
Product Warranty Payable		76,000
Vacation Pay Payable		10,500
Unfunded Pension Liability		50,700
Notes Payable		700,000
J. Kornett, Capital		2,345,010
	3,700,290	3,700,290

Cases & Projects

ETHICS

CP 11-1 Ethics in Action

Tonya Latirno is a staff accountant for Cannally and Kennedy, a local CPA firm. For the past 10 years, the firm has given employees a year-end bonus equal to two weeks' salary. On November 15, the firm's management team announced that there would be no annual bonus this year. Because of the firm's long history of giving a year-end bonus, Tonya and her coworkers had come to expect the bonus and believed that Cannally and Kennedy had breached an implicit agreement by discontinuing the bonus. As a result, Tonya decided that she would make up for the lost bonus by working an extra six hours of overtime per week for the rest of the year. Cannally and Kennedy's policy is to pay overtime at 150% of straight time.

Tonya's supervisor was surprised to see overtime being reported, because there is generally very little additional or unusual client service demands at the end of the calendar year. However, the overtime was not questioned, because employees are on the "honor system" in reporting their work hours.

1. Is Cannally and Kennedy acting in an ethical manner by eliminating the bonus? Explain your answer.
2. Is Tonya behaving ethically by making up the bonus with unnecessary overtime? Why or why not?

ETHICS

CP 11-2 Ethics in Action

Marvin Turner was discussing summer employment with Tina Song, president of Motown Construction Service:

Tina: I'm glad you're thinking about joining us for the summer. We certainly can use the help.

Marvin: Sounds good. I enjoy outdoor work, and I could use the money to help with next year's school expenses.

Tina: I've got a plan that can help you out on that. As you know, I'll pay you $14 per hour, but in addition, I'd like to pay you with cash. Since you're only working for the summer, it really doesn't make sense for me to go to the trouble of formally putting you on our payroll system. In fact, I do some jobs for my clients on a strictly cash basis, so it would be easy just to pay you that way.

Marvin: Well, that's a bit unusual, but I guess money is money.

Tina: Yeah, not only that, it's tax-free!

Marvin: What do you mean?

Tina: Didn't you know? Any money that you receive in cash is not reported to the IRS on a W-2 form; therefore, the IRS doesn't know about the income—hence, it's the same as tax-free earnings.

1. Why does Tina Song want to conduct business transactions using cash (not check or credit card)?
2. How should Marvin respond to Tina's suggestion?

TEAM ACTIVITY

CP 11-3 Team Activity

In teams, select a public company that interests you. Obtain the company's most recent annual report on Form 10-K. The Form 10-K is a company's annually required filing with the Securities and Exchange Commission (SEC). It includes the company's financial statements and accompanying notes. The Form 10-K can be obtained either (a) by referring to the investor relations section of the company's website or (b) by using the company search feature of the SEC's EDGAR database service found at www.sec.gov/edgar/searchedgar/companysearch.html.

Based on the information in the company's most recent annual report, answer the following questions:

1. What amount of current liabilities does the company report on its balance sheet at the end of the most recent year? What types of current liabilities does the company report?
2. Have current liabilities increased or decreased from the prior year? If so, by what amount?
3. Does the company disclose any contingent liabilities in the notes to the financial statements? If so, briefly describe the nature of these contingent liabilities.
4. How much of the company's long-term debt will come due in the coming year?

CP 11-4 Payroll forms

Payroll accounting involves the use of government-supplied forms to account for payroll taxes. Three common forms are the W-2, Form 940, and Form 941. Form a team with three of your classmates and retrieve copies of each of these forms. They may be obtained from a local IRS office, a library, or the Internet at www.irs.gov (go to forms and publications).

Briefly describe the purpose of each of the three forms.

CP 11-5 Communication

COMMUNICATION

WBM Motorworks is a manufacturer of high-end touring and off-road motorcycles. On November 30, the company was sued by a customer who was injured when the front shock absorber on the WBM Series 3 motorcycle cracked during use. The company conducted a preliminary investigation into the matter during December and found evidence of a manufacturing defect in the shock absorber. While it is uncertain whether the manufacturing defect is the source of the product failure, the company has voluntarily recalled the front shock absorbers on the Series 3 motorcycles. The company is uncertain how the lawsuit will be resolved. Similar lawsuits against other manufacturers have been settled for approximately $2,000,000.

Write a brief memo to the president of WBM Motorworks, U. D. Mach III, discussing how the lawsuit might be reported on the financial statements.

CP 11-6 Recognizing pension expense

The annual examination of Felton Company's financial statements by its external public accounting firm (auditors) is nearing completion. The following conversation took place between the controller of Felton Company (Francie) and the audit manager from the public accounting firm (Sumana):

Sumana: You know, Francie, we are about to wrap up our audit for this fiscal year. Yet, there is one item still to be resolved.

Francie: What's that?

Sumana: Well, as you know, at the beginning of the year, Felton began a defined benefit pension plan. This plan promises your employees an annual payment when they retire, using a formula based on their salaries at retirement and their years of service. I believe that a pension expense should be recognized this year, equal to the amount of pension earned by your employees.

Francie: Wait a minute. I think you have it all wrong. The company doesn't have a pension expense until it actually pays the pension in cash when the employee retires. After all, some of these employees may not reach retirement, and if they don't, the company doesn't owe them anything.

Sumana: You're not really seeing this the right way. The pension is earned by your employees during their working years. You actually make the payment much later—when they retire. It's like one long accrual—much like incurring wages in one period and paying them in the next. Thus, I think you should recognize the expense in the period the pension is earned by the employees.

Francie: Let me see if I've got this straight. I should recognize an expense this period for something that may or may not be paid to the employees in 20 or 30 years, when they finally retire. How am I supposed to determine what the expense is for the current year? The amount of the final retirement depends on many uncertainties: salary levels, employee longevity, mortality rates, and interest earned on investments to fund the pension. I don't think an amount can be determined even if I accepted your arguments.

Evaluate Sumana's position. Is she right, or is Francie correct?

CP 11-7 Contingent liabilities

Philip Morris International Inc. has numerous pages dedicated to describing contingent liabilities in the notes to recent financial statements. These pages include extensive descriptions of multiple contingent liabilities. Use the Internet to research Philip Morris International Inc. at www.pmi.com.

1. What are the major business units of Philip Morris International Inc.?
2. Based on your understanding of this company, why would Philip Morris International require so many pages of contingency disclosure?

CHAPTER

12 Accounting for Partnerships and Limited Liability Companies

STATEMENT OF PARTNERSHIP EQUITY
For the Year Ended December 31, 20Y6

	J. Stone, Capital	C. Mills, Capital	Total
Balance, Jan. 1, 20Y6	$ XXX	$ XXX	$ XXX
Capital additions	XXX	XXX	XXX
Net income	XXX	XXX	XXX
Partner withdrawals	(XXX)	(XXX)	(XXX)
Balance, Dec. 31, 20Y6	$ XXX	$ XXX	$ XXX

STATEMENT OF CASH FLOWS
For the Year Ended December 31, 20Y6

Cash flows from (used for) operating activities	$XXX
Cash flows from (used for) investing activities	XXX
Cash flows from (used for) financing activities	XXX
Net increase (decrease) in cash	$XXX
Cash balance, January 1, 20Y6	XXX

INCOME STATEMENT
For the Year Ended December 31, 20Y6

Sales		$XXX
Cost of merchandise sold		XXX
Gross profit		$XXX
Operating expenses:		
Advertising expense	$XXX	
Depreciation expense	XXX	
Amortization expense	XXX	
Depletion expense	XXX	
...	XXX	
...	XXX	
Total operating expenses		XXX
Income from operations		$XXX
Other revenue and expenses		XXX
Net income		$XXX

BALANCE SHEET
December 31, 20Y6

Assets:		
Current assets		$XXX
Property, plant, and equipment		XXX
Intangible assets		XXX
Total assets		$XXX
Liabilities:		
Current liabilities	$XXX	
Long-term liabilities	XXX	
Total liabilities		$XXX
Partners' equity:		
Jennifer Stone, capital	$XXX	
Crystal Mills, capital	XXX	
Total partners' equity		XXX
Total liabilities and partners' equity		$XXX

MELISSA MAJCHRZAK/NATIONAL BASKETBALL ASSOCIATION/GETTY IMAGES

Boston Basketball Partners LLC

Boston Basketball Partners (BBP) LLC are the owners of the Boston Celtics NBA basketball franchise. The letters "LLC" stand for *limited liability company*. Unlike sole proprietorships illustrated in prior chapters, an LLC is a business form that normally has multiple owners. BBP LLC is led by Wic Grousbeck, a former venture fund manager from Boston, with the assistance of more than 15 other owners. Grousbeck called investing in the Celtics "a chance of a lifetime." Surprisingly, Grousbeck claims "money would not be the first priority." Even so, Grousbeck and his team have turned their venture capital skills for making money toward the Celtics. Some of their innovations off the court include building a cable partnership, using technology to evaluate seat usage, and adding advertising sponsors.

So why would BBP LLC choose the LLC form of organization?

The entity form chosen by a business has an important impact on the owners' legal liability, taxation, and ability to raise money. The four major forms of business entities discussed in this text are the proprietorship, partnership, limited liability company, and corporation. Proprietorships have been discussed in prior chapters. Partnerships and limited liability companies will be discussed in this chapter, and corporations will be introduced in the next chapter.

Link to Boston Basketball Partners LLC .... Pages 592, 593, 595, 596, 604

LEARNING OBJECTIVES

After studying this chapter, you should be able to:

Example Exercises (EE) are shown in **red.**

OBJ. 1 **Describe the characteristics of proprietorships, partnerships, and limited liability companies.**

Proprietorships, Partnerships, and Limited Liability Companies
Proprietorships
Partnerships
Limited Liability Companies
Comparing Proprietorships, Partnerships, and Limited Liability Companies

OBJ. 2 **Describe and illustrate the accounting for forming a partnership and for dividing the net income or net loss of a partnership.**

Forming a Partnership and Dividing Income
Forming a Partnership EE **12-1**
Dividing Income EE **12-2**

OBJ. 3 **Describe and illustrate the accounting for partner admission and withdrawal.**

Partner Admission and Withdrawal
Admitting a Partner EE **12-3**
Withdrawal of a Partner EE **12-4**
Death of a Partner

OBJ. 4 **Describe and illustrate the accounting for liquidating a partnership.**

Liquidating Partnerships
Gain on Realization
Loss on Realization EE **12-5**
Loss on Realization—Capital Deficiency EE **12-6**

OBJ. 5 **Prepare the statement of partnership equity.**

Statement of Partnership Equity

OBJ. 6 **Analyze and interpret employee efficiency.**

Financial Analysis and Interpretation: Revenue per Employee
Compute and Analyze Revenue per Employee EE **12-7**

At a Glance 12 Page 612

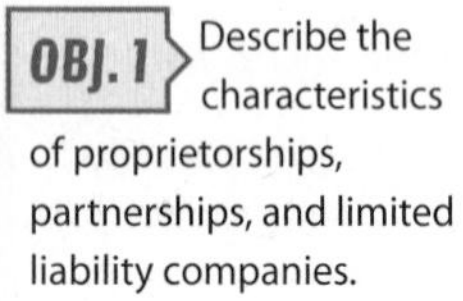
Describe the characteristics of proprietorships, partnerships, and limited liability companies.

Proprietorships, Partnerships, and Limited Liability Companies

The four most common legal forms for organizing and operating a business are as follows:

- Proprietorship
- Corporation
- Partnership
- Limited liability company

In this section, the characteristics of proprietorships, partnerships, and limited liability companies are described. The characteristics of corporations are described in Chapter 13.

Proprietorships

A *proprietorship* is a company owned by a single individual. The most common proprietorships are professional service providers, such as lawyers, architects, realtors, and physicians.

Characteristics of proprietorships include the following:

- *Simple to form.* There are no legal restrictions or forms to file.
- *No limitation on legal liability.* The owner is personally liable for any debts or legal claims against the business. Thus, creditors can take the personal assets of the owner if the business debts exceed the owner's investment in the company.
- *Not taxable.* For federal income tax purposes, a proprietorship is not taxed. Instead, the proprietorship's income or loss is "passed through" to the owner's individual income tax return.[1]

1 The proprietor's statement of income is included on Schedule C of the individual 1040 tax return.

- *Limited life.* When the owner dies or retires, the proprietorship ceases to exist.
- *Limited ability to raise capital (funds).* The ability to raise capital (funds) is limited to what the owner can provide from personal resources or through borrowing.

Partnerships

A **partnership** is an association of two or more persons who own and manage a business for profit.[2] Partnerships are less widely used than proprietorships.

Characteristics of a partnership include the following:

Note

A partnership is a nontaxable entity that has a limited life and unlimited liability.

- *Moderately complex to form.* A partnership is often formed with a partnership agreement. A **partnership agreement** includes matters such as amounts to be invested, limits on withdrawals, distributions of income and losses, and admission and withdrawal of partners. Thus, an attorney is often used in forming a partnership.
- *No limitation on legal liability.* The partners are personally liable for any debts or legal claims against the partnership. Therefore, creditors can take the personal assets of the partners if the business debts exceed the partners' investment in the business.
- *Not taxable.* For federal income tax purposes, a partnership is not taxed. Instead, the partnership's income or loss is "passed through" to the partners' individual income tax returns. However, partnerships must still report revenues, expenses, and income or loss annually to the Internal Revenue Service.
- *Limited life.* When a partner dies or retires, the partnership ceases to exist. Likewise, the admission of a new partner dissolves the old partnership, and a new partnership must be formed if operations are to continue.
- *Limited ability to raise capital (funds).* The ability to raise capital (funds) for the partnership is limited to what the partners can provide from personal resources or through borrowing.

In addition to those characteristics, some unique aspects of partnerships are:

- *Co-ownership of partnership property.* The property invested in a partnership by a partner becomes the joint property of all the partners. When a partnership is dissolved, each partner's share of the partnership assets is the balance in his or her capital account.
- *Mutual agency.* Each partner is an agent of the partnership and may act on behalf of the entire partnership. Thus, any liabilities created by one partner become liabilities of all the partners.
- *Participation in income.* Net income and net loss are distributed among the partners according to their partnership agreement. If the partnership agreement does not provide for distribution of income and losses, then income and losses are divided equally among the partners.

Business Connection

BREAKING UP IS HARD TO DO

Former partners of Adam Carolla filed court papers accusing the star of The Adam Carolla Show (adamcarolla.com) of a breach of their partnership agreement. They claimed the partnership agreement gave 30% ownership to Donny Misraje, 10% to Sandy Ganz, and 60% to Carolla. The suit alleges that Carolla began his popular podcast with the help of his partners at a time when future success of the venture was risky and unknown.

The former partners claim to have given up jobs, invested money and equipment, and provided expertise to launch the show. Once the show achieved success, the former partners claim Carolla unfairly kicked them out of the partnership. The court will, in part, use the partnership agreement to help settle this dispute. A partnership agreement helps protect the interests of all parties to a business venture.

Source: Radar Staff, "Best Friend Sues Adam Carolla Over Hit Podcast Show," January 18, 2013.

2 The definition of a partnership is included in the Uniform Partnership Act, which has been adopted by most states.

Limited Liability Companies

A **limited liability company (LLC)** is a form of legal entity that provides limited liability to its owners but is treated as a partnership for tax purposes. Thus, the LLC organizational form is popular for small businesses.

Characteristics of an LLC include the following:

- *Moderately complex to form.* An LLC requires an agreement among the owners, who are called members. The *operating agreement* includes matters such as amounts to be invested, limits on withdrawals, distributions of income and losses, and admission and withdrawal of members. An attorney is normally used in forming an LLC.
- *Limited legal liability.* The members have *limited liability* even if they are active in the company. Thus, the members' personal assets are legally protected against creditor claims made against the LLC. That is, only the members' investments in the company are subject to claims of creditors.
- *Not taxable.* An LLC may elect to be treated as a partnership for tax purposes. In this way, income passes through the LLC and is taxed on the individual members' tax returns.[3]
- *Unlimited life.* Most LLC operating agreements specify continuity of life for the LLC, even when a member withdraws or new members join the LLC.
- *Moderate ability to raise capital (funds).* Because of their limited liability, LLCs are attractive to many investors, thus allowing for greater access to capital (funds) than is normally the case in a partnership.

Link to Boston Basketball Partners LLC

BBP LLC is formed as an LLC. The LLC members include individuals and **The Abbey Group**, a real estate development company in Boston.

An LLC may elect to operate as a *member-managed* or *manager-managed* company. In a member-managed LLC, individual members may legally bind the LLC, like partners bind a partnership. In a manager-managed LLC, only authorized members may legally bind the LLC. Thus, in a manager-managed LLC, members may share in the income of the LLC without concern for managing the company.

Comparing Proprietorships, Partnerships, and Limited Liability Companies

Exhibit 1 summarizes the characteristics of proprietorships, partnerships, and limited liability companies.

EXHIBIT 1 Characteristics of Proprietorships, Partnerships, and Limited Liability Companies

Organizational Form	Complexity of Formation	Legal Liability	Taxation	Limitation on Life of Entity	Access to Capital
Proprietorship	Simple	No limitation	Nontaxable (pass-through) entity	Limited	Limited
Partnership	Moderate	No limitation	Nontaxable (pass-through) entity	Limited	Limited
Limited Liability Company	Moderate	Limited liability	Nontaxable (pass-through) entity by election	Unlimited	Moderate

Business Connection

ORGANIZATIONAL FORMS IN THE ACCOUNTING INDUSTRY

The four major accounting firms, **KPMG LLP**, **Ernst & Young**, **PricewaterhouseCoopers**, and **Deloitte & Touche**, all began as partnerships. This form was legally required due to the theory of mutual agency. That is, the partnership form was thought to create public trust by requiring all partners to be jointly liable and responsible for each other's judgments. In addition, investment in the partnerships was limited to practicing accountants. This prevented any pressures from outside investors affecting professional decisions.

As these firms grew and the risk increased, all of these firms were allowed to change, by law, to limited liability partnerships (LLPs). Thus, while remaining a partnership, the liability of the partners was limited to their investment in the firm. The LLP form is very similar to an LLC, except that investment is restricted to professionals.

3 An LLC may also be taxed as a separate entity. However, doing so would remove these tax benefits, making this a less common election.

Forming a Partnership and Dividing Income

OBJ. 2 Describe and illustrate the accounting for forming a partnership and for dividing the net income or net loss of a partnership.

Most of the day-to-day accounting for a partnership or an LLC is similar to that illustrated in earlier chapters. However, the formation, division of net income or net loss, dissolution, and liquidation of partnerships and LLCs give rise to unique transactions.

In the remainder of this chapter, the unique transactions for partnerships and LLCs are described and illustrated. The accounting for an LLC is the same as a partnership, except that the terms *member* and *members' equity* are used rather than *partner* or *owners' capital*. For this reason, the journal entries for an LLC are shown alongside the partnership entries.

Link to Boston Basketball Partners LLC

BBP LLC announced the completed purchase of the Boston Celtics basketball team on December 31, 2002, for an estimated $360 million.

Forming a Partnership

In forming a partnership, the investments of each partner are recorded in separate entries. The assets contributed by a partner are debited to the partnership asset accounts. If any liabilities are assumed by the partnership, the partnership liability accounts are credited. The partner's capital account is credited for the net amount.

To illustrate, assume that Joseph Stevens and Earl Foster, owners of competing hardware stores, agree to combine their businesses in a partnership. Stevens agrees to contribute the following:

Cash	$ 7,200	Office equipment	$2,500
Accounts receivable	16,300	Allowance for doubtful accounts	1,500
Merchandise inventory	28,700	Accounts payable	2,600
Store equipment	5,400		

The entry to record the assets and liabilities contributed by Stevens is as follows:

Partnership

Apr.	1	Cash	7,200	
		Accounts Receivable	16,300	
		Merchandise Inventory	28,700	
		Store Equipment	5,400	
		Office Equipment	2,500	
		Allowance for Doubtful Accounts		1,500
		Accounts Payable		2,600
		Joseph Stevens, Capital		56,000

LLC alternative

Apr.	1	Cash	7,200	
		Accounts Receivable	16,300	
		Merchandise Inventory	28,700	
		Store Equipment	5,400	
		Office Equipment	2,500	
		Allowance for Doubtful Accounts		1,500
		Accounts Payable		2,600
		Joseph Stevens, Member Equity		56,000

In the preceding entry, the noncash assets are recorded at values agreed upon by the partners. These values are normally based on current market values. As a result, the previous book value of the assets contributed by the partners normally differs from that recorded by the new partnership.

To illustrate, the store equipment contributed by Stevens may have had a book value of $3,500 in Stevens' ledger (cost of $10,000 less accumulated depreciation of $6,500). However, the store equipment is recorded at its current market value of $5,400 in the preceding entry. The contributions of Foster would be recorded in an entry similar to the entry for Stevens.

EXAMPLE EXERCISE 12-1 Journalizing Partner's Original Investment — OBJ. 2

Reese Howell contributed equipment, inventory, and $34,000 cash to a partnership. The equipment had a book value of $23,000 and a market value of $29,000. The inventory had a book value of $60,000 but only had a market value of $15,000 due to obsolescence. The partnership also assumed a $12,000 note payable owed by Howell that was used originally to purchase the equipment.

Provide the journal entry for Howell's contribution to the partnership.

(Continued)

Follow My Example 12-1

Cash	34,000	
Inventory	15,000	
Equipment	29,000	
Notes Payable		12,000
Reese Howell, Capital		66,000

Practice Exercises: PE 12-1A, PE 12-1B

Dividing Income

Income or losses of the partnership are divided as specified in the partnership agreement. If there is no specification or agreement, income and losses are divided equally.

Common methods of dividing partnership income are based on the following:

- Services of the partners
- Services and investments of the partners

Services of Partners One method of dividing partnership income is based on the services provided by each partner to the partnership. These services are often recognized by partner salary allowances. Such allowances reflect differences in partners' abilities and time devoted to the partnership. Since partners are not employees, such allowances are recorded as divisions of net income and are credited to the partners' capital accounts.

To illustrate, assume that the partnership agreement of Jennifer Stone and Crystal Mills provides for the following:

	Monthly Salary Allowance
Jennifer Stone	$5,000
Crystal Mills	4,000
Remaining net income:	Divided Equally

The division of income may be reported at the bottom of the partnership income statement. Using this format, the division of $150,000 of net income would be reported on the bottom of the partnership income statement as follows:

Revenues	$650,000
Expenses	500,000
Net income	$150,000

Division of net income:

	J. Stone	C. Mills	Total
Annual salary allowance (mo. × 12)	$60,000	$48,000	$108,000
Remaining income	21,000	21,000	42,000
Net income	$81,000	$69,000	$150,000

As with other business forms, a partnership makes two closing entries at the end of the accounting period. The first closing entry closes all revenues and expenses to the partners' equity accounts. Each partner's equity account is credited for the partner's share of net income (or debited for the partner's share of a net loss). The second closing entry closes each partner's drawing account to the partner's equity account.

Based upon the preceding division of income, the first closing entry for the Stone and Mills partnership is as follows:

Partnership				
Dec.	**31**	**Revenues**	**650,000***	
		Expenses		**500,000**
		Jennifer Stone, Capital		**81,000**
		Crystal Mills, Capital		**69,000**

LLC alternative				
Dec.	31	Revenues	650,000*	
		Expenses		500,000
		Jennifer Stone, Member Equity		81,000
		Crystal Mills, Member Equity		69,000

*We illustrate the closing of revenue and expense totals for simplicity, though in practice, the individual revenue and expense accounts would be closed.

The second closing entry, assuming that Stone and Mills only withdrew their monthly salary allowances, is as follows:

Partnership				
Dec.	**31**	**Jennifer Stone, Capital**	**60,000**	
		Crystal Mills, Capital	**48,000**	
		Jennifer Stone, Drawing		**60,000**
		Crystal Mills, Drawing		**48,000**

LLC alternative				
Dec.	31	Jennifer Stone, Member Equity	60,000	
		Crystal Mills, Member Equity	48,000	
		Jennifer Stone, Drawing		60,000
		Crystal Mills, Drawing		48,000

Services of Partners and Investments A partnership agreement may divide income based upon salary allowances, as discussed, and also based upon interest on capital balances of each partner. In this way, partners with more invested in the partnership are rewarded by receiving more of the partnership income. One such method of dividing partnership income would be as follows:

1. Partner salary allowances
2. Interest on capital investments
3. Any remaining income equally

To illustrate, assume that the partnership agreement for Stone and Mills provides for the following:

BBP LLC has a seven-member executive committee responsible for running the business.

1.

	Monthly Salary Allowance
Jennifer Stone	$5,000
Crystal Mills	4,000

2. Interest of 12% on each partner's capital balance as of January 1.

Capital, Jennifer Stone, January 1	$160,000
Capital, Crystal Mills, January 1	120,000

3. Remaining income: Divided equally

The $150,000 net income for the year is divided as follows:

Revenues	$650,000
Expenses	500,000
Net income	$150,000

Division of net income:

	J. Stone	**C. Mills**	**Total**
Annual salary allowance	$60,000	$48,000	$108,000
Interest allowance	19,200[1]	4,400[2]	33,600
Total	$79,200	$62,400	$141,600
Remaining income	4,200	4,200	8,400
Net income	$83,400	$66,600	$150,000

[1]12% × $160,000
[2]12% × $120,000

Link to Boston Basketball Partners LLC

BBP LLC had 14 founding investors.

The entry for closing revenue and expenses and dividing net income is as follows:

Partnership

Dec.	31	Revenues	650,000	
		Expenses		500,000
		Jennifer Stone, Capital		83,400
		Crystal Mills, Capital		66,600

LLC alternative

Dec.	31	Revenues	650,000	
		Expenses		500,000
		Jennifer Stone, Member Equity		83,400
		Crystal Mills, Member Equity		66,600

Integrity, Objectivity, and Ethics in Business

TYRANNY OF THE MAJORITY

Some partnerships involve the contribution of money by one partner and the contribution of effort and expertise by another. This can create a conflict between the two partners, because one works and the other doesn't. Without a properly developed partnership agreement, the working partner could take income in the form of a salary allowance, leaving little for the investor partner. Thus, partnership agreements often require all partners to agree on salary allowances provided to working partners.

Link to Boston Basketball Partners LLC

BBP LLC's estimated operating income for a recent year was $100 million.

Allowances Exceed Net Income In the preceding example, the net income is $150,000. The total of the salary ($108,000) and interest ($33,600) allowances is $141,600. Thus, the net income exceeds the salary and interest allowances. In some cases, however, the net income may be less than the total of the allowances. In this case, the remaining net income to divide is a *negative* amount. This negative amount is divided among the partners as though it were a net loss.

To illustrate, assume the same salary and interest allowances as in the preceding example but the net income is $100,000. In this case, the total of the allowances of $141,600 exceeds the net income by $41,600 ($100,000 − $141,600). This amount is divided equally between Stone and Mills. Thus, $20,800 ($41,600 ÷ 2) is deducted from each partner's share of the allowances. The final division of net income between Stone and Mills is as follows:

Revenues	$600,000
Expenses	500,000
Net income	$100,000

Division of net income:

	J. Stone	C. Mills	Total
Annual salary allowance	$ 60,000	$48,000	$108,000
Interest allowance	19,200	14,400	33,600
Total	$ 79,200	$62,400	$141,600
Deduct excess of allowances over income	20,800	20,800	41,600
Net income[4]	$ 58,400	$41,600	$100,000

The entry for closing revenue and expenses and dividing net income is as follows:

Partnership

Dec.	31	Revenues	600,000	
		Expenses		500,000
		Jennifer Stone, Capital		58,400
		Crystal Mills, Capital		41,600

LLC alternative

Dec.	31	Revenues	600,000	
		Expenses		500,000
		Jennifer Stone, Member Equity		58,400
		Crystal Mills, Member Equity		41,600

4 In the event of a net loss, the amount deducted from the total allowances would be the "excess of allowances over loss" or the sum of the net loss and the allowances, divided according to the sharing ratio.

EXAMPLE EXERCISE 12-2 Dividing Partnership Net Income OBJ. 2

Steve Prince and Chelsy Bernard formed a partnership, dividing income as follows:

1. Annual salary allowance to Prince of $42,000.
2. Interest of 9% on each partner's capital balance on January 1.
3. Any remaining net income divided equally.

Prince and Bernard had $20,000 and $150,000 in their January 1 capital balances, respectively. Net income for the year was $240,000.

How much net income should be distributed to Prince and Bernard?

Follow My Example 12-2

	S. Prince	C. Bernard	Total
Annual salary allowance	$ 42,000	$ 0	$ 42,000
Interest allowance	1,800[1]	13,500[2]	15,300
Total	$ 43,800	$ 13,500	$ 57,300
Remaining income	91,350[3]	91,350	182,700
Net income	$135,150	$104,850	$240,000

[1] $20,000 × 9%
[2] $150,000 × 9%
[3] ($240,000 − $42,000 − $15,300) × 50%

Practice Exercises: PE 12-2A, PE 12-2B

Partner Admission and Withdrawal

OBJ. 3 Describe and illustrate the accounting for partner admission and withdrawal.

Many partnerships provide for admitting new partners and for partner withdrawals by amending the existing partnership agreement. In this way, the company may continue operating without having to form a new partnership and prepare a new partnership agreement.

Admitting a Partner

As shown in Exhibit 2, a person may be admitted to a partnership by either of the following:

- Purchasing an interest from one or more of the existing partners
- Contributing assets to the partnership

Purchasing an Interest from an Existing Partner

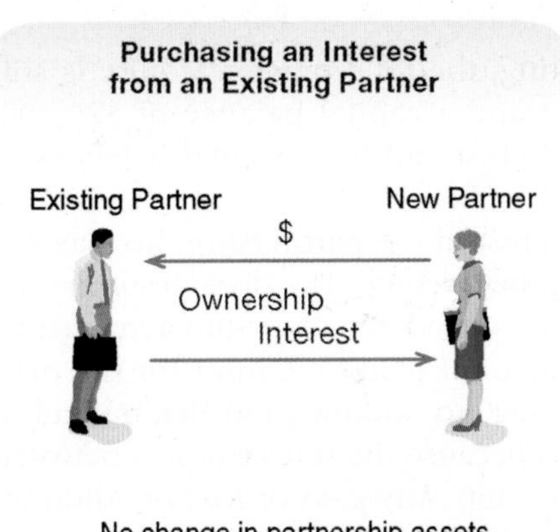

No change in partnership assets

Contributing Assets to a Partnership

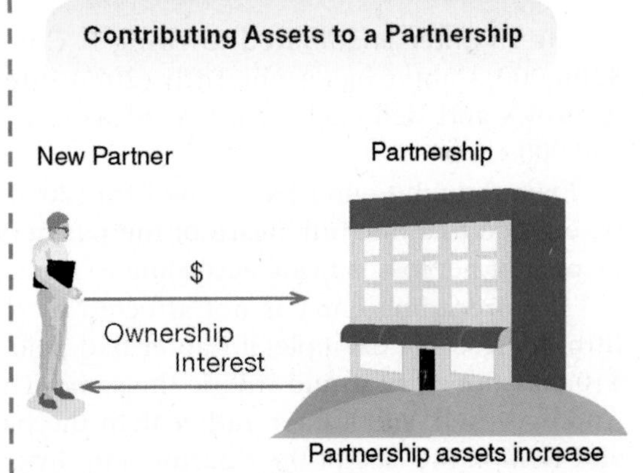

Partnership assets increase

EXHIBIT 2
Two Methods for Admitting a Partner

When a new partner is admitted by *purchasing an interest* from one or more of the existing partners, the total assets and the total owners' equity of the partnership are not affected. The capital (equity) of the new partner is recorded by transferring capital (equity) from the existing partners.

When a new partner is admitted by *contributing assets* to the partnership, the total assets and the total owners' equity of the partnership are increased. The capital (equity) of the new partner is recorded as the amount of assets contributed to the partnership by the new partner.

Purchasing an Interest from Existing Partners When a new partner is admitted by purchasing an interest from one or more of the existing partners, the transaction is between the new and existing partners acting as individuals. The admission of the new partner is recorded by transferring owners' equity amounts from the capital accounts of the selling partners to the capital account of the new partner.

To illustrate, assume that on June 1, Tom Andrews and Nathan Bell each sell one-fifth of their partnership equity of Bring It Consulting to Joe Canter for $10,000 in cash. On June 1, the partnership has total assets of $120,000 and total liabilities of $20,000, or net assets of $100,000 ($120,000 − $20,000). Both existing partners have capital balances of $50,000 each. This transaction is between Andrews, Bell, and Canter. The only entry required by Bring It Consulting is to record the transfer of capital (equity) from Andrews and Bell to Canter, as follows:

Partnership				
June	1	Tom Andrews, Capital	10,000	
		Nathan Bell, Capital	10,000	
		Joe Canter, Capital		20,000

LLC alternative				
June	1	Tom Andrews, Member Equity	10,000	
		Nathan Bell, Member Equity	10,000	
		Joe Canter, Member Equity		20,000

The effect of the transaction on the partnership accounts is as follows:

BRING IT CONSULTING

Partnership Accounts

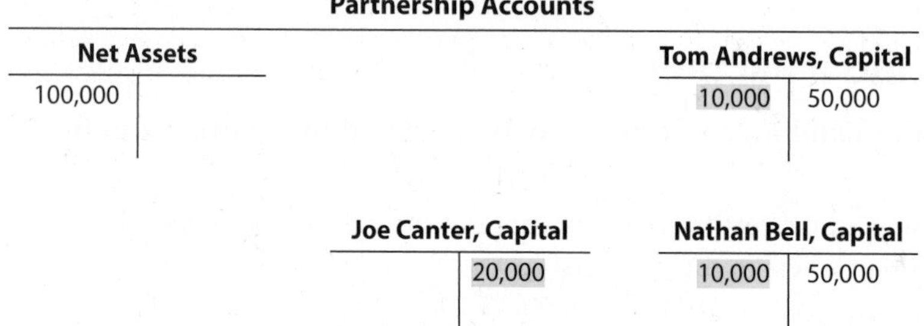

After Canter is admitted to Bring It Consulting, the total owners' equity is still $100,000. Canter has a one-fifth (20%) interest and a capital balance of $20,000. Andrews and Bell each own two-fifths (40%) interest and have capital balances of $40,000 each.

Even though Canter has a one-fifth (20%) interest in the partnership, he may not be entitled to a one-fifth share of the partnership net income. The division of the net income or net loss is made according to the new or amended partnership agreement.

The preceding entry is not affected by the amount paid by Canter for the one-fifth interest. For example, if Canter had paid $15,000 to Andrews and Bell instead of $10,000, the entry would still be the same. This is because the transaction is between Andrews, Bell, and Canter, rather than the partnership. Any gain or loss by Andrews and Bell on the sale of their partnership interest is theirs as individuals and does not affect the partnership.

Contributing Assets to a Partnership When a new partner is admitted by contributing assets to the partnership, the total assets and the total owners' equity of the partnership are increased. This is because the transaction is between the new partner and the partnership.

To illustrate, assume that instead of purchasing a one-fifth ownership in Bring It Consulting directly from Tom Andrews and Nathan Bell, Joe Canter contributes $20,000 cash to Bring It Consulting for ownership equity of $20,000. The entry to record this transaction is as follows:

Partnership				
June	1	Cash	20,000	
		Joe Canter, Capital		20,000

LLC alternative				
June	1	Cash	20,000	
		Joe Canter, Member Equity		20,000

The effect of the transaction on the partnership accounts is as follows:

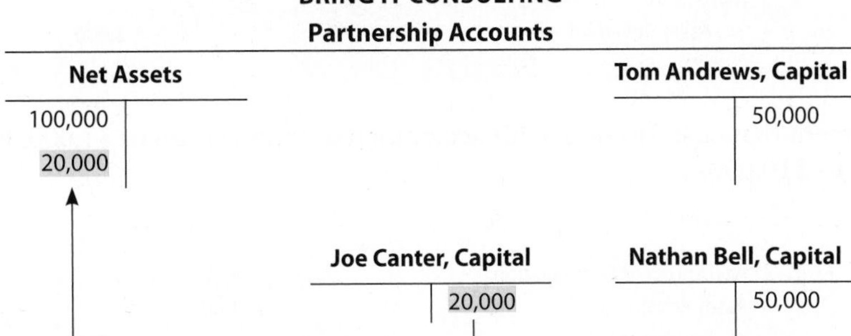

After the admission of Canter, the net assets and total owners' equity of Bring It Consulting increase to $120,000, of which Joe Canter has a $20,000 interest. In contrast, in the prior example, the net assets and total owners' equity of Bring It Consulting did not change from $100,000.

Revaluation of Assets Before a new partner is admitted, the balances of a partnership's asset accounts should be stated at current values. If necessary, the accounts should be adjusted. Any net adjustment (increase or decrease) in asset values is divided among the capital accounts of the existing partners, similar to the division of income.

To illustrate, assume that in the preceding example, the balance of the merchandise inventory account is $14,000 and the current replacement value is $17,000. If Andrews and Bell share net income equally, the revaluation is recorded as follows:

Partnership				
June	1	Merchandise Inventory	3,000	
		Tom Andrews, Capital		1,500
		Nathan Bell, Capital		1,500

LLC alternative				
June	1	Merchandise Inventory	3,000	
		Tom Andrews, Member Equity		1,500
		Nathan Bell, Member Equity		1,500

In the case of fixed assets, the accumulated depreciation is removed and fixed assets are revalued to current value. For example, assume that the partnership of Andrews and Bell in the previous example had equipment of $15,000, with accumulated depreciation of $4,000, that was revalued down to $10,000. The $1,000 ($11,000 – $10,000) revaluation decrease is recorded as follows:

Partnership				
June	1	Accumulated Depreciation	4,000	
		Tom Andrews, Capital	500	
		Nathan Bell, Capital	500	
		Equipment		5,000*

LLC alternative				
June	1	Accumulated Depreciation	4,000	
		Tom Andrews, Member Equity	500	
		Nathan Bell, Member Equity	500	
		Equipment		5,000

* $15,000 – $10,000

An alternative approach to revaluing assets uses a temporary account called Asset Revaluation when a revaluation occurs during the period. For an upward revaluation, the asset account is debited and Asset Revaluation is credited for the amount of the increase. When an asset is decreased, its account is credited and Asset Revaluation is debited for the amount of the decrease.

The capital accounts are only affected at the end of the accounting period when the asset revaluation balance is transferred to the owners' accounts. A credit (debit) balance in Asset Revaluation increases (decreases) the capital accounts.

The following examples are used to illustrate the revaluation transactions using this approach. Andrews and Bell share net income equally.

1. The balance of the merchandise inventory account is $14,000, and the current replacement value is $17,000.

June	1	Merchandise Inventory		3,000	
		Asset Revaluation			3,000

2. Equipment that cost $15,000, with accumulated depreciation of $4,000, is revalued down to $10,000.

June	1	Accumulated Depreciation		4,000	
		Asset Revaluation		1,000	
		Equipment			5,000

3. At the end of the accounting period, the asset revaluation account balance is closed to the partners' capital accounts.

Dec.	31	Asset Revaluation ($3,000 – $1,000)		2,000	
		Tom Andrews, Capital			1,000
		Nathan Bell, Capital			1,000

Failure to adjust the partnership accounts for current values before admitting a new partner may result in the new partner sharing in asset gains or losses that occurred prior to their admission to the partnership.

EXAMPLE EXERCISE 12-3 Revaluing and Contributing Assets to a Partnership — OBJ. 3

Blake Nelson invested $45,000 in the Lawrence & Kerry partnership for ownership equity of $45,000. Prior to the investment, land was revalued to a market value of $260,000 from a book value of $200,000. Lynne Lawrence and Tim Kerry share net income in a 1:2 ratio.

a. Provide the journal entry for the revaluation of land.

b. Provide the journal entry to admit Nelson.

Follow My Example 12-3

a. Land	60,000	
Lynne Lawrence, Capital		20,000
Tim Kerry, Capital		40,000

[1] $60,000 × 1/3

[2] $60,000 × 2/3

b. Cash	45,000	
Blake Nelson, Capital		45,000

Practice Exercises: PE 12-3A, PE 12-3B

Partner Bonuses A new partner may pay existing partners a bonus to join a partnership. In other cases, existing partners may pay a new partner a bonus to join the partnership.

Bonuses are usually paid because of higher than normal profits the new or existing partners are expected to contribute in the future. For example, a new partner may bring special qualities or skills to the partnership. Celebrities such as actors, musicians, or sports figures often provide name recognition that is expected to increase a partnership's profits.

Partner bonuses are illustrated in Exhibit 3. Existing partners receive a bonus when the ownership interest received by the new partner is less than the amount paid. In contrast, the new partner receives a bonus when the ownership interest received by the new partner is greater than the amount paid.

Bonus to Existing Partners To illustrate, assume that on March 1, the partnership of Marsha Jenkins and Helen Kramer is considering a new partner, Alex Diaz. After the assets of the partnership have been adjusted to current market values, the capital balances of Jenkins and Kramer are as follows:

Marsha Jenkins, Capital	$20,000
Helen Kramer, Capital	24,000
Total owners' equity *before* admitting Diaz	$44,000

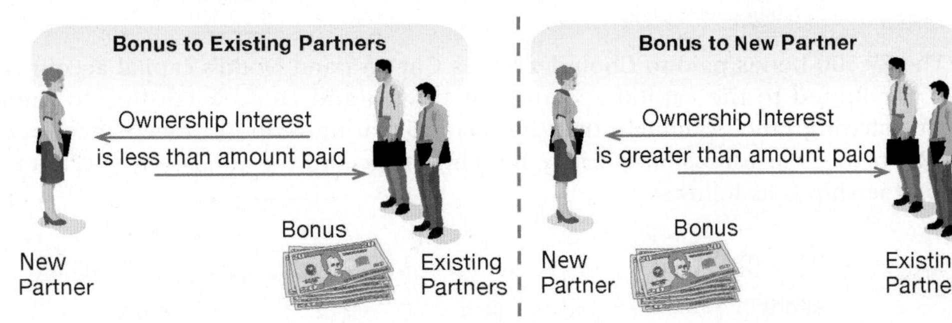

EXHIBIT 3
Partner Bonuses

Jenkins and Kramer agree to admit Diaz to the partnership for $31,000. In return, Diaz will receive a one-third equity in the partnership and will share equally with Jenkins and Kramer in partnership income or losses. In this case, Diaz is paying Jenkins and Kramer a $6,000 bonus to join the partnership, computed as follows:

Marsha Jenkins, Capital	$20,000
Helen Kramer, Capital	24,000
Diaz's contribution	31,000
Total owners' equity *after* admitting Diaz	$75,000
Diaz's equity interest after admission	× 1/3
Alex Diaz, Capital	$25,000
Diaz's contribution	$31,000
Alex Diaz, Capital	25,000
Bonus paid to Jenkins and Kramer	$ 6,000

The $6,000 bonus paid by Diaz increases Jenkins' and Kramer's capital accounts. It is distributed to the capital accounts of Jenkins and Kramer according to their income-sharing ratio.[5] Assuming that Jenkins and Kramer share profits and losses equally, the entry to record the admission of Diaz to the partnership is as follows:

Partnership

Mar.	1	Cash	31,000	
		Alex Diaz, Capital		25,000
		Marsha Jenkins, Capital		3,000
		Helen Kramer, Capital		3,000

LLC alternative

Mar.	1	Cash	31,000	
		Alex Diaz, Member Equity		25,000
		Marsha Jenkins, Member Equity		3,000
		Helen Kramer, Member Equity		3,000

5 Another method used to record the admission of partners attributes goodwill rather than a bonus to the partners. This method is discussed in advanced accounting textbooks.

Bonus to New Partners Existing partners may agree to pay the new partner a bonus to join a partnership. To illustrate, assume that after adjusting assets to market values, the capital balances of Janice Cowen and Steve Dodd are as follows:

Janice Cowen, Capital	$ 80,000
Steve Dodd, Capital	40,000
Total owners' equity *before* admitting Chou	$120,000

Cowen and Dodd agree to admit Ellen Chou to the partnership on June 1 for an investment of $30,000. In return, Chou will receive a one-fourth equity interest in the partnership and will share in one-fourth of the profits and losses. In this case, Cowen and Dodd are paying Chou a $7,500 bonus to join the partnership, computed as follows:

Janice Cowen, Capital	$ 80,000
Steve Dodd, Capital	40,000
Chou's contribution	30,000
Total owners' equity *after* admitting Chou	$150,000
Chou's equity interest after admission	× 1/4
Ellen Chou, Capital	$ 37,500
Ellen Chou, Capital	$ 37,500
Chou's contribution	30,000
Bonus paid to Chou	$ 7,500

The $7,500 bonus paid to Chou decreases Cowen's and Dodd's capital accounts. It is distributed to the capital accounts of Cowen and Dodd according to their income-sharing ratio. Assuming that the income-sharing ratio of Cowen and Dodd was 2:1 before the admission of Chou, the entry to record the admission of Chou to the partnership is as follows:

Partnership

June	1	Cash	30,000	
		Janice Cowen, Capital	5,000[1]	
		Steve Dodd, Capital	2,500[2]	
		Ellen Chou, Capital		37,500

LLC alternative

June	1	Cash	30,000	
		Janice Cowen, Member Equity	5,000[1]	
		Steve Dodd, Member Equity	2,500[2]	
		Ellen Chou, Member Equity		37,500

[1] $7,500 × 2/3

[2] $7,500 × 1/3

EXAMPLE EXERCISE 12-4 Partner Bonus

OBJ. 3

Lowman has a capital balance of $51,000 after adjusting assets to fair market value. Conrad contributes $24,000 to receive a 30% interest in a new partnership with Lowman.

Determine the amount and recipient of the partner bonus.

Follow My Example 12-4

Equity of Lowman	$51,000
Conrad's contribution	24,000
Total equity after admitting Conrad	$75,000
Conrad's equity interest	× 30%
Conrad's equity after admission	$22,500
Conrad's contribution	$24,000
Conrad's equity after admission	22,500
Bonus paid to Lowman	$ 1,500

Practice Exercises: PE 12-4A, PE 12-4B

Withdrawal of a Partner

A partner may retire or withdraw from a partnership. In such cases, the withdrawing partner's interest is normally sold to the:

- Existing partners or
- Partnership

If the *existing partners* purchase the withdrawing partner's interest, the purchase and sale of the partnership interest is between the partners as individuals. The only entry on the partnership's records is to debit the capital account of the partner withdrawing and to credit the capital account of the partner or partners buying the additional interest.

If the *partnership purchases* the withdrawing partner's interest, the assets and the owners' equity of the partnership are reduced by the purchase price. Before the purchase, the asset accounts should be adjusted to current values. The net amount of any adjustment should be divided among the capital accounts of the partners according to their income-sharing ratio.

The entry to record the purchase debits the capital account of the withdrawing partner and credits Cash for the amount of the purchase. If not enough partnership cash is available to pay the withdrawing partner, a liability may be created (credited) for the amount owed the withdrawing partner.

Death of a Partner

When a partner dies, the partnership accounts should be closed as of the date of death. The net income for the current period should then be determined and divided among the partners' capital accounts. The asset accounts should also be adjusted to current values and the amount of any adjustment divided among the capital accounts of the partners.

After the income is divided and any assets are revalued, an entry is recorded to close the deceased partner's capital account. The entry debits the deceased partner's capital account for its balance and credits a liability account, which is payable to the deceased's estate. The remaining partner or partners may then decide to continue the business or liquidate it.

Liquidating Partnerships

Describe and illustrate the accounting for liquidating a partnership.

When a partnership goes out of business, it sells the assets, pays the creditors, and distributes the remaining cash or other assets to the partners. This winding-up process is called the **liquidation** of the partnership. Although *liquidating* refers to the payment of liabilities, it includes the entire winding-up process.

When the partnership goes out of business and the normal operations are discontinued, the accounts should be adjusted and closed. The only accounts remaining open will be the asset, contra asset, liability, and owners' equity accounts.

The liquidation process is illustrated in Exhibit 4. The steps in the liquidation process are as follows:

Step 1. Sell the partnership assets. This step is called **realization**.

Step 2. Distribute any gains or losses from realization to the partners based on their income-sharing ratio.

Step 3. Pay the claims of creditors, using the cash from the step 1 realization.

Step 4. Distribute the remaining cash to the partners based on the balances in their capital accounts.

Note

In liquidation, cash is distributed to partners according to their capital balances.

EXHIBIT 4

Steps in Liquidating a Partnership

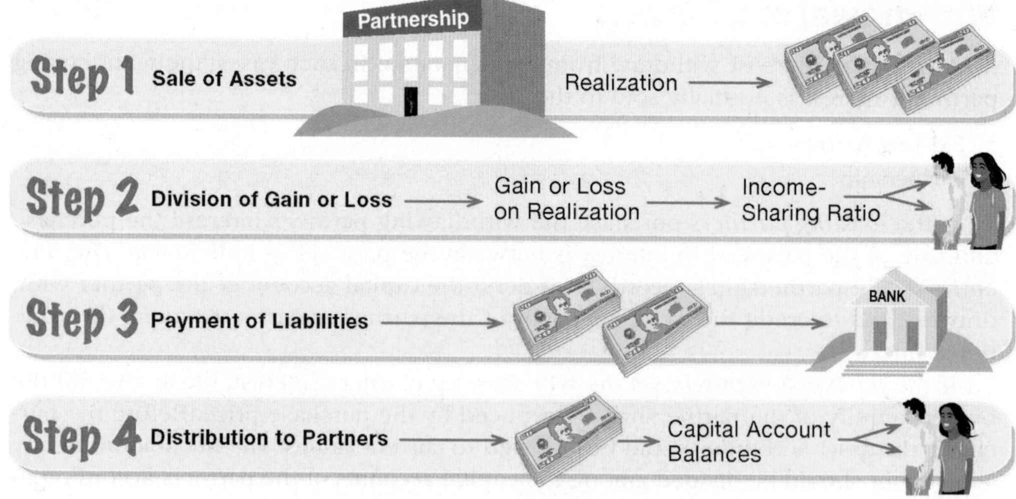

To illustrate, assume that Farley, Green, and Hall decide to liquidate their partnership. On April 9, 20Y5, after discontinuing business operations of the partnership and closing the accounts, the following trial balance is prepared:

Farley, Green, and Hall
Post-Closing Trial Balance
April 9, 20Y5

	Debit Balances	Credit Balances
Cash	11,000	
Noncash Assets	64,000	
Liabilities		9,000
Jean Farley, Capital		22,000
Brad Green, Capital		22,000
Alice Hall, Capital		22,000
	75,000	75,000

Farley, Green, and Hall share income and losses in a ratio of 5:3:2 (50%, 30%, 20%). To simplify, assume that all noncash assets are sold in a single transaction and that all liabilities are paid at one time. In addition, Noncash Assets and Liabilities will be used as account titles in place of the various asset, contra asset, and liability accounts.

Link to Boston Basketball Partners LLC

Forbes Magazine has estimated the Boston Celtics as the fifth most valuable NBA franchise at $2.8 billion.

Source: "The Business of Basketball," *Forbes*, February 2019.

Gain on Realization

Assume that Farley, Green, and Hall sell all noncash assets for $72,000. Thus, a gain of $8,000 ($72,000 – $64,000) is realized. The partnership is liquidated during April as follows:

Step 1. Sale of assets: $72,000 is realized from sale of all the noncash assets.

Step 2. Division of gain: The gain of $8,000 is distributed to Farley, Green, and Hall in the income-sharing ratio of 5:3:2. Thus, the partner capital accounts are credited as follows:

Farley	$4,000 ($8,000 × 50%)
Green	2,400 ($8,000 × 30%)
Hall	1,600 ($8,000 × 20%)

Step 3. Payment of liabilities: Creditors are paid $9,000.

Step 4. Distribution of cash to partners: The remaining cash of $74,000 is distributed to the partners according to their capital balances as follows:

Farley	$26,000
Green	24,400
Hall	23,600

A **statement of partnership liquidation**, which summarizes the liquidation process, is shown in Exhibit 5.

Statement of Partnership Liquidation: Gain on Realization EXHIBIT 5

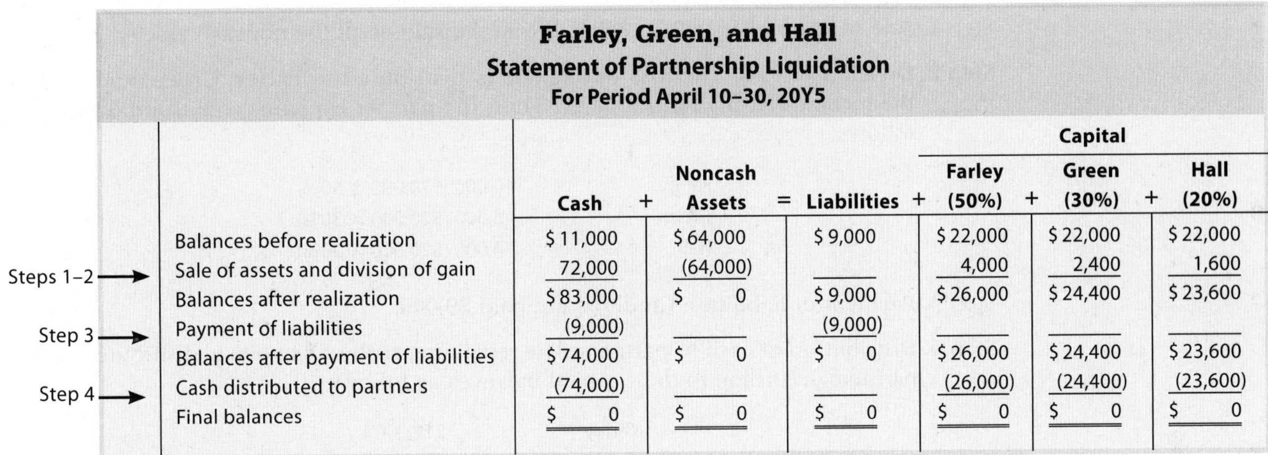

Farley, Green, and Hall
Statement of Partnership Liquidation
For Period April 10–30, 20Y5

		Cash	+ Noncash Assets	= Liabilities	+ Capital Farley (50%)	+ Capital Green (30%)	+ Capital Hall (20%)
	Balances before realization	$ 11,000	$ 64,000	$ 9,000	$ 22,000	$ 22,000	$ 22,000
Steps 1–2 →	Sale of assets and division of gain	72,000	(64,000)		4,000	2,400	1,600
	Balances after realization	$ 83,000	$ 0	$ 9,000	$ 26,000	$ 24,400	$ 23,600
Step 3 →	Payment of liabilities	(9,000)		(9,000)			
	Balances after payment of liabilities	$ 74,000	$ 0	$ 0	$ 26,000	$ 24,400	$ 23,600
Step 4 →	Cash distributed to partners	(74,000)			(26,000)	(24,400)	(23,600)
	Final balances	$ 0	$ 0	$ 0	$ 0	$ 0	$ 0

The entries to record the steps in the liquidating process are as follows:

Sale of assets (Step 1):

Partnership

Account	Debit	Credit
Cash	72,000	
Noncash Assets		64,000
Gain on Realization		8,000

LLC alternative

Account	Debit	Credit
Cash	72,000	
Noncash Assets		64,000
Gain on Realization		8,000

Division of gain (Step 2):

Partnership

Account	Debit	Credit
Gain on Realization	8,000	
Jean Farley, Capital		4,000
Brad Green, Capital		2,400
Alice Hall, Capital		1,600

LLC alternative

Account	Debit	Credit
Gain on Realization	8,000	
Jean Farley, Member Equity		4,000
Brad Green, Member Equity		2,400
Alice Hall, Member Equity		1,600

Payment of liabilities (Step 3):

Partnership

Account	Debit	Credit
Liabilities	9,000	
Cash		9,000

LLC alternative

Account	Debit	Credit
Liabilities	9,000	
Cash		9,000

Distribution of cash to partners (Step 4):

Partnership

Account	Debit	Credit
Jean Farley, Capital	26,000	
Brad Green, Capital	24,400	
Alice Hall, Capital	23,600	
Cash		74,000

LLC alternative

Account	Debit	Credit
Jean Farley, Member Equity	26,000	
Brad Green, Member Equity	24,400	
Alice Hall, Member Equity	23,600	
Cash		74,000

As shown in Exhibit 5, *the cash is distributed to the partners based on the balances of their capital accounts.* These balances are determined after the gain on realization has been divided among the partners and the liabilities are paid. *The income-sharing ratio should not be used as a basis for distributing the cash to partners.*

Loss on Realization

Assume that Farley, Green, and Hall sell all noncash assets for $44,000. Thus, a loss of $20,000 ($64,000 – $44,000) is realized. The liquidation of the partnership is as follows:

Step 1. Sale of assets: $44,000 is realized from the sale of all the noncash assets.

Step 2. Division of loss: The loss of $20,000 is distributed to Farley, Green, and Hall in the income-sharing ratio of 5:3:2. Thus, the partner capital accounts are debited as follows:

Farley	$10,000 ($20,000 × 50%)
Green	6,000 ($20,000 × 30%)
Hall	4,000 ($20,000 × 20%)

Step 3. Payment of liabilities: Creditors are paid $9,000.

Step 4. Distribution of cash to partners: The remaining cash of $46,000 is distributed to the partners according to their capital balances as follows:

Farley	$12,000
Green	16,000
Hall	18,000

The steps in liquidating the partnership are summarized in the statement of partnership liquidation shown in Exhibit 6.

EXHIBIT 6 **Statement of Partnership Liquidation: Loss on Realization**

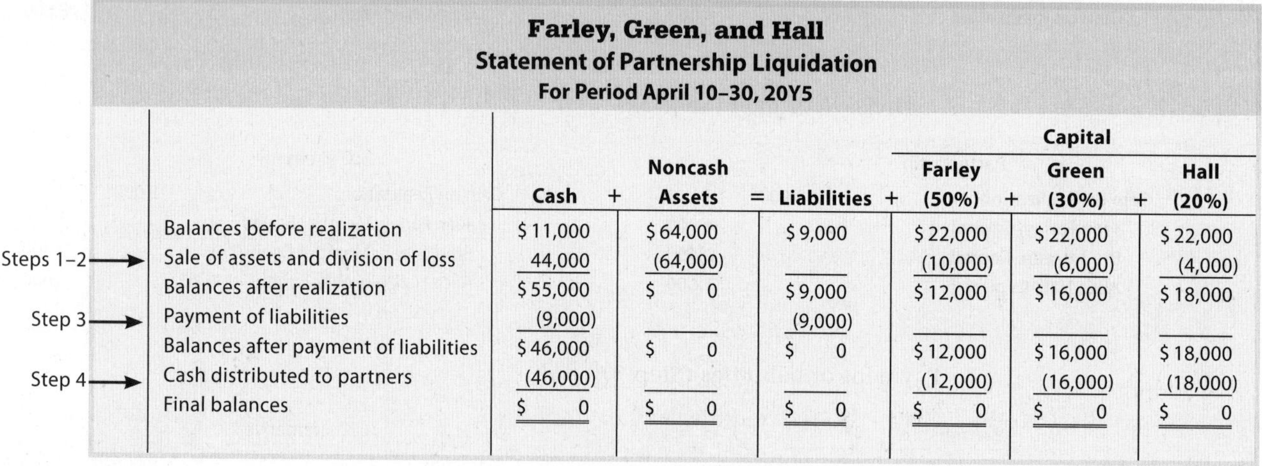

Farley, Green, and Hall
Statement of Partnership Liquidation
For Period April 10–30, 20Y5

		Cash	+	Noncash Assets	=	Liabilities	+	Capital Farley (50%)	+	Capital Green (30%)	+	Capital Hall (20%)
	Balances before realization	$ 11,000		$ 64,000		$ 9,000		$ 22,000		$ 22,000		$ 22,000
Steps 1–2 →	Sale of assets and division of loss	44,000		(64,000)				(10,000)		(6,000)		(4,000)
	Balances after realization	$ 55,000		$ 0		$ 9,000		$ 12,000		$ 16,000		$ 18,000
Step 3 →	Payment of liabilities	(9,000)				(9,000)						
	Balances after payment of liabilities	$ 46,000		$ 0		$ 0		$ 12,000		$ 16,000		$ 18,000
Step 4 →	Cash distributed to partners	(46,000)						(12,000)		(16,000)		(18,000)
	Final balances	$ 0		$ 0		$ 0		$ 0		$ 0		$ 0

The entries to liquidate the partnership are as follows:

Sale of assets (Step 1):

Partnership

Account	Debit	Credit
Cash	44,000	
Loss on Realization	20,000	
Noncash Assets		64,000

LLC alternative

Account	Debit	Credit
Cash	44,000	
Loss on Realization	20,000	
Noncash Assets		64,000

Division of loss (Step 2):

Partnership		
Jean Farley, Capital	10,000	
Brad Green, Capital	6,000	
Alice Hall, Capital	4,000	
Loss on Realization		20,000

LLC alternative		
Jean Farley, Member Equity	10,000	
Brad Green, Member Equity	6,000	
Alice Hall, Member Equity	4,000	
Loss on Realization		20,000

Payment of liabilities (Step 3):

Partnership		
Liabilities	9,000	
Cash		9,000

LLC alternative		
Liabilities	9,000	
Cash		9,000

Distribution of cash to partners (Step 4):

Partnership		
Jean Farley, Capital	12,000	
Brad Green, Capital	16,000	
Alice Hall, Capital	18,000	
Cash		46,000

LLC alternative		
Jean Farley, Member Equity	12,000	
Brad Green, Member Equity	16,000	
Alice Hall, Member Equity	18,000	
Cash		46,000

EXAMPLE EXERCISE 12-5 Liquidating Partnerships **OBJ. 4**

Prior to liquidating their partnership, Todd and Gentry had capital accounts of $50,000 and $100,000, respectively. Prior to liquidation, the partnership had no other cash assets than what was realized from the sale of assets. These assets were sold for $220,000. The partnership had $20,000 of liabilities. Todd and Gentry share income and losses equally. Determine the amount received by Gentry as a final distribution from the liquidation of the partnership.

Follow My Example 12-5

Gentry's equity prior to liquidation		$100,000
Realization of asset sale	$220,000	
Book value of assets ($50,000 + $100,000 + $20,000)	170,000	
Gain on liquidation	$ 50,000	
Gentry's share of gain (50% × $50,000)		25,000
Gentry's cash distribution		$125,000

Practice Exercises: PE 12-5A, PE 12-5B

Loss on Realization—Capital Deficiency

The share of a loss on realization may be greater than the balance in a partner's capital account. The resulting debit balance in the capital account is called a **deficiency**. It represents a claim of the partnership against the partner.

To illustrate, assume that Farley, Green, and Hall sell all noncash assets for $10,000. Thus, a loss of $54,000 ($64,000 – $10,000) is realized. The liquidation of the partnership is as follows:

Step 1. Sale of assets: $10,000 is realized from the sale of all the noncash assets.

Step 2. Division of loss: The loss of $54,000 is distributed to Farley, Green, and Hall in the income-sharing ratio of 5:3:2. The partner capital accounts are debited as follows:

Farley	$27,000 ($54,000 × 50%)
Green	16,200 ($54,000 × 30%)
Hall	10,800 ($54,000 × 20%)

Step 3. Payment of liabilities: Creditors are paid $9,000.

Step 4. Distribution of cash to partners: (a) The share of the loss allocated to Farley, $27,000 (50% × $54,000), exceeds the $22,000 balance in her capital account. This $5,000 deficiency represents an amount that Farley owes the partnership. (b) Assuming that Farley pays the deficiency, the cash of $17,000 is distributed to the partners according to their capital balances as follows:

Farley	$ 0
Green	5,800
Hall	11,200

The steps in liquidating the partnership are summarized in the statement of partnership liquidation shown in Exhibit 7.

EXHIBIT 7 **Statement of Partnership Liquidation: Loss on Realization—Capital Deficiency**

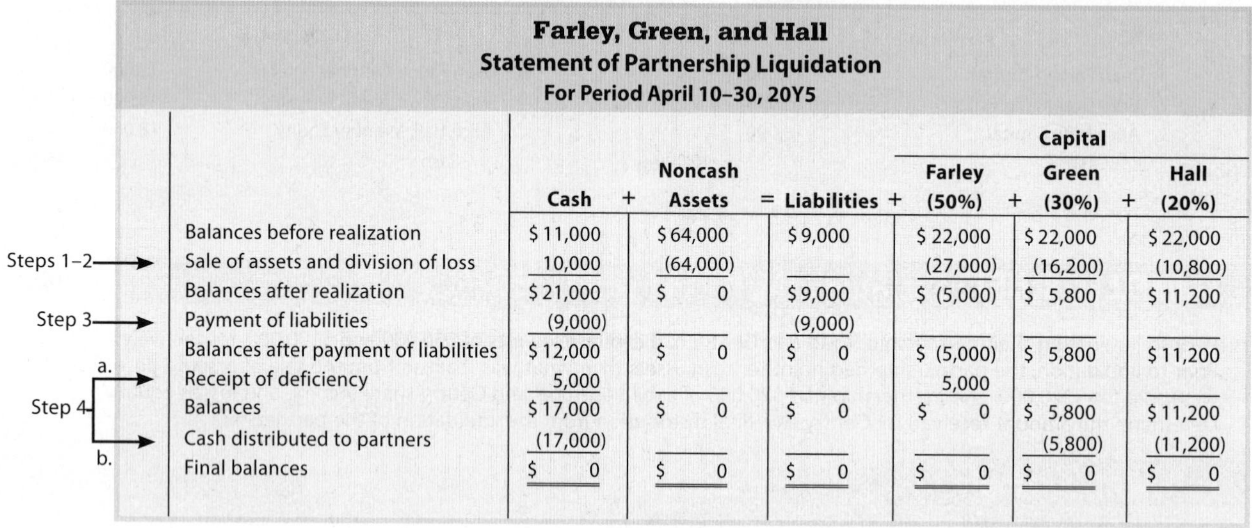

Farley, Green, and Hall
Statement of Partnership Liquidation
For Period April 10–30, 20Y5

		Cash +	Noncash Assets =	Liabilities +	Capital: Farley (50%) +	Green (30%) +	Hall (20%)
	Balances before realization	$ 11,000	$ 64,000	$ 9,000	$ 22,000	$ 22,000	$ 22,000
Steps 1–2 →	Sale of assets and division of loss	10,000	(64,000)		(27,000)	(16,200)	(10,800)
	Balances after realization	$ 21,000	$ 0	$ 9,000	$ (5,000)	$ 5,800	$ 11,200
Step 3 →	Payment of liabilities	(9,000)		(9,000)			
	Balances after payment of liabilities	$ 12,000	$ 0	$ 0	$ (5,000)	$ 5,800	$ 11,200
Step 4 a. →	Receipt of deficiency	5,000			5,000		
	Balances	$ 17,000	$ 0	$ 0	$ 0	$ 5,800	$ 11,200
Step 4 b. →	Cash distributed to partners	(17,000)				(5,800)	(11,200)
	Final balances	$ 0	$ 0	$ 0	$ 0	$ 0	$ 0

The entries to liquidate the partnership are as follows:

Sale of assets (Step 1):

Partnership		
Cash	10,000	
Loss on Realization	54,000	
Noncash Assets		64,000

LLC alternative		
Cash	10,000	
Loss on Realization	54,000	
Noncash Assets		64,000

Division of loss (Step 2):

Partnership		
Jean Farley, Capital	27,000	
Brad Green, Capital	16,200	
Alice Hall, Capital	10,800	
Loss on Realization		54,000

LLC alternative		
Jean Farley, Member Equity	27,000	
Brad Green, Member Equity	16,200	
Alice Hall, Member Equity	10,800	
Loss on Realization		54,000

Payment of liabilities (Step 3):

Partnership		
Liabilities	9,000	
Cash		9,000

LLC alternative		
Liabilities	9,000	
Cash		9,000

Receipt of deficiency (Step 4a):

Partnership				LLC alternative			
	Cash	5,000			Cash	5,000	
	Jean Farley, Capital		5,000		Jean Farley, Member Equity		5,000

Distribution of cash to partners (Step 4b):

Partnership				LLC alternative			
	Brad Green, Capital	5,800			Brad Green, Member Equity	5,800	
	Alice Hall, Capital	11,200			Alice Hall, Member Equity	11,200	
	Cash		17,000		Cash		17,000

If the deficient partner does not pay the partnership the deficiency, there will not be sufficient partnership cash to pay the remaining partners in full. Any uncollected deficiency becomes a loss to the partnership and is divided among the remaining partners' capital balances based on their income-sharing ratio. The cash balance will then equal the sum of the capital account balances. The cash can then be distributed to the remaining partners, based on the balances of their capital accounts.

To illustrate, assume that in the preceding example, Farley could not pay her deficiency. The deficiency would be allocated to Green and Hall based on their income-sharing ratio of 3:2. The remaining cash of $12,000 would then be distributed to Green ($2,800) and Hall ($9,200), computed as follows:

	Capital Balances *Before* Deficiency	Allocated (Deficiency)	Capital Balances *After* Deficiency
Farley	$ (5,000)	$ 5,000	$ 0
Green	5,800	(3,000)*	2,800
Hall	11,200	(2,000)**	9,200
Total	$12,000		$12,000

*$3,000 = ($5,000 × 3/5) or ($5,000 × 60%)

**$2,000 = ($5,000 × 2/5) or ($5,000 × 40%)

The entries to allocate Farley's deficiency and distribute the cash are as follows:

Allocation of deficiency (Step 4a):

Partnership				LLC alternative			
	Brad Green, Capital	3,000			Brad Green, Member Equity	3,000	
	Alice Hall, Capital	2,000			Alice Hall, Member Equity	2,000	
	Jean Farley, Capital		5,000		Jean Farley, Member Equity		5,000

Distribution of cash to partners (Step 4b):

Partnership				LLC alternative			
	Brad Green, Capital	2,800			Brad Green, Member Equity	2,800	
	Alice Hall, Capital	9,200			Alice Hall, Member Equity	9,200	
	Cash		12,000		Cash		12,000

EXAMPLE EXERCISE 12-6 Liquidating Partnerships—Deficiency OBJ. 4

Prior to liquidating their partnership, Short and Bain had capital accounts of $20,000 and $80,000, respectively. The partnership assets were sold for $40,000. The partnership had no liabilities. Short and Bain share income and losses equally.

a. Determine the amount of Short's deficiency.

b. Determine the amount distributed to Bain, assuming that Short is unable to satisfy the deficiency.

(Continued)

Follow My Example 12-6

a. Short's equity prior to liquidation		$ 20,000
Realization of asset sale	$ 40,000	
Book value of assets ($20,000 + $80,000)	100,000	
Loss on liquidation	$ 60,000	
Short's share of loss (50% × $60,000)		30,000
Short's deficiency		$(10,000)

b. $40,000 ($80,000 − $30,000 share of loss − $10,000 Short deficiency)

Practice Exercises: PE 12-6A, PE 12-6B

OBJ. 5 Prepare the statement of partnership equity.

Statement of Partnership Equity

Reporting changes in partnership capital accounts is similar to that for a proprietorship. The primary difference is that there is a capital account for each partner. The changes in partner capital accounts for a period of time are reported in a **statement of partnership equity**.

Exhibit 8 illustrates a statement of partnership equity for Investors Associates, a partnership of Dan Cross and Kelly Baker. Each partner's capital account is shown as a separate column. The partner capital accounts may change due to capital additions, net income, or withdrawals, similar to sole proprietorships.

EXHIBIT 8

Statement of Partnership Equity

Investors Associates
Statement of Partnership Equity
For the Year Ended December 31, 20Y8

	Dan Cross, Capital	Kelly Baker, Capital	Total Partnership Capital
Balance, January 1, 20Y8	$245,000	$365,000	$610,000
Capital additions	50,000		50,000
Net income for the year	40,000	80,000	120,000
Partner withdrawals	(5,000)	(45,000)	(50,000)
Balance, December 31, 20Y8	$330,000	$400,000	$730,000

The equity reporting for an LLC is similar to that of a partnership. Instead of a statement of partnership equity, a statement of members' equity is prepared. The **statement of members' equity** reports the changes in member equity for a period. The statement is similar to Exhibit 8, except that the columns represent member equity rather than partner equity.

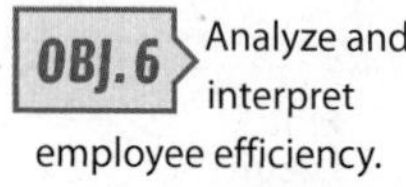

OBJ. 6 Analyze and interpret employee efficiency.

Financial Analysis and Interpretation: Revenue per Employee

Many partnerships and LLCs operate as service-oriented enterprises. This is the case for many professions, such as medical, advertising, and accounting. The performance of such firms can be measured by the amount of net income per partner, as illustrated in this chapter. Another measure used to assess the performance of a service-oriented business is revenue per employee.

Revenue per employee is a measure of the efficiency of the business in generating revenues. It is computed as follows:

$$\text{Revenue per Employee} = \frac{\text{Revenue}}{\text{Number of Employees}}$$

In a partnership, the number of partners may be included with employees, or partners may be evaluated separately. Generally, the higher the revenue per employee, the more efficient the company is in generating revenue from its employees. In evaluating revenue per employee, changes over time as well as comparisons with industry peers or averages are often used.

To illustrate comparisons over time, assume that Washburn & Lovett, CPAs, has the following information for two years:

	20Y5	20Y4
Revenues	$220,000,000	$180,000,000
Number of employees	1,600	1,500

For Washburn & Lovett, the revenue per employee ratio is computed for 20Y5 and 20Y4 as follows:

$$\text{Revenue per employee, 20Y5: } \frac{\$220{,}000{,}000}{1{,}600 \text{ employees}} = \$137{,}500 \text{ per employee}$$

$$\text{Revenue per employee, 20Y4: } \frac{\$180{,}000{,}000}{1{,}500 \text{ employees}} = \$120{,}000 \text{ per employee}$$

Washburn & Lovett increased revenues by $40,000,000 ($220,000,000 − $180,000,000), or 22.2% ($40,000,000 ÷ $180,000,000) from 20Y4 to 20Y5. The number of employees increased by 100, or 6.7% (100 employees ÷ 1,500 employees) between the two years. Thus, the firm increased revenues at a rate faster than the increase in employees. As a result, the revenue per employee improved from $120,000 to $137,500 between the two years, suggesting improved efficiency in generating revenues.

To illustrate comparison within an industry, the revenue per employee for **McDonald's** and **Starbucks** for a recent year is computed as follows:

$$\text{McDonald's: } \frac{\$21{,}025{,}200{,}000}{210{,}000 \text{ employees}} = \$100{,}120 \text{ per employee}$$

$$\text{Starbucks: } \frac{\$24{,}719{,}500{,}000}{291{,}000 \text{ employees}} = \$84{,}947 \text{ per employee}$$

McDonald's is able to generate more revenues per employee than is Starbucks. Many factors may explain this difference, including relative employee efficiency, extent of part-time workforce, and product pricing.

EXAMPLE EXERCISE 12-7 Revenue per Employee — OBJ. 6

AccuTax, CPAs earned $4,200,000 during 20Y7 using 20 employees. During 20Y8, the firm grew revenues to $4,560,000 and expanded the staff to 24 employees.

a. Determine the revenue per employee for each year.

b. Interpret the results.

Follow My Example 12-7

a. 20Y7: $\frac{\$4{,}200{,}000}{20 \text{ employees}} = \$210{,}000 \text{ per employee}$

20Y8: $\frac{\$4{,}560{,}000}{24 \text{ employees}} = \$190{,}000 \text{ per employee}$

b. While AccuTax grew revenues by $360,000 ($4,560,000 – $4,200,000), or 8.6% ($360,000 ÷ $4,200,000), the number of employees expanded by 4, or 20% (4/20). The growth in revenue was less than the growth in the number of employees; thus, the revenue per employee declined between the two years. The firm was less efficient in generating revenues from its employees in 20Y8.

Practice Exercises: PE 12-7A, PE 12-7B

At a Glance 12

OBJ. 1 **Describe the characteristics of proprietorships, partnerships, and limited liability companies.**

Key Points The advantages and disadvantages of proprietorships, partnerships, and limited liability companies are summarized in Exhibit 1.

Learning Outcomes	*Example Exercises*	*Practice Exercises*
• Identify the advantages and disadvantages of proprietorships, partnerships, and limited liability companies.		

OBJ. 2 **Describe and illustrate the accounting for forming a partnership and for dividing the net income or net loss of a partnership.**

Key Points When a partnership is formed, accounts are debited for contributed assets and credited for assumed liabilities, and the partner's capital account is credited for the net amount. The net income of a partnership may be divided among the partners on the basis of services rendered, interest earned on the capital account balance, and the income-sharing ratio.

Learning Outcomes	*Example Exercises*	*Practice Exercises*
• Journalize the initial formation of a partnership and establish partner capital.	**EE12-1**	**PE12-1A, 12-1B**
• Determine and journalize the income distributed to each partner.	**EE12-2**	**PE12-2A, 12-2B**

OBJ. 3 **Describe and illustrate the accounting for partner admission and withdrawal.**

Key Points Partnership assets should be restated to current values prior to the admission or withdrawal of a partner. A new partner may be admitted into a partnership by either purchasing an interest from an existing partner or by purchasing an interest directly from the partnership.

Learning Outcomes	*Example Exercises*	*Practice Exercises*
• Prepare for partner admission by revaluing assets to approximate current values.	**EE12-3**	**PE12-3A, 12-3B**
• Distinguish between partner admission through purchase from an existing partner or purchase from the partnership.	**EE12-3**	**PE12-3A, 12-3B**
• Determine partner bonuses.	**EE12-4**	**PE12-4A, 12-4B**

OBJ. 4 Describe and illustrate the accounting for liquidating a partnership.

Key Points A partnership is liquidated by the (1) sale of partnership assets (realization), (2) distribution of gain or loss on realization to the partners, (3) payments to creditors, and (4) distribution of the remaining cash to partners according to their capital account balances. A partner may be deficient when the amount of loss distribution exceeds the capital balance.

Learning Outcomes	*Example Exercises*	*Practice Exercises*
• Apply the four steps of liquidating a partnership for either gain or loss on realization.	**EE12-5**	**PE12-5A, 12-5B**
• Apply the four steps of partnership liquidation when there is a partner deficiency.	**EE12-6**	**PE12-6A, 12-6B**

OBJ. 5 Prepare the statement of partnership equity.

Key Points A statement of partnership equity reports the changes in partnership equity from capital additions, net income, and withdrawals.

Learning Outcomes	*Example Exercises*	*Practice Exercises*
• Prepare a statement of partnership equity.		

OBJ. 6 Analyze and interpret employee efficiency.

Key Points The revenue per employee ratio is computed as the total annual revenues divided by the total employees. This ratio measures the total revenue earned by each employee and, thus, is a measure of the efficiency of each employee in revenue terms. The ratio is often used to measure efficiency trends over time and across similar firms.

Learning Outcomes	*Example Exercises*	*Practice Exercises*
• Analyze and interpret the revenue per employee ratio.	**EE12-7**	**PE12-7A, 12-7B**

Illustrative Problem

Radcliffe, Sonders, and Towers, who share in income and losses in the ratio of 2:3:5, decided to discontinue operations as of April 30 and liquidate their partnership. After the accounts were closed on April 30, 20Y9, the following trial balance was prepared:

(Continued)

Radcliffe, Sonders, and Towers
Post-Closing Trial Balance
April 30, 20Y9

	Debit Balances	Credit Balances
Cash	5,900	
Noncash Assets	109,900	
Liabilities		26,800
Radcliffe, Capital		14,600
Sonders, Capital		27,900
Towers, Capital		46,500
	115,800	115,800

Between May 1 and May 18, the noncash assets were sold for $27,400, and the liabilities were paid.

Instructions

1. Assuming that the partner with the capital deficiency pays the entire amount owed to the partnership, prepare a statement of partnership liquidation.
2. Journalize the entries to record (a) the sale of the assets, (b) the division of loss on the sale of the assets, (c) the payment of the liabilities, (d) the receipt of the deficiency, and (e) the distribution of cash to the partners.

Solution

1.

Radcliffe, Sonders, and Towers
Statement of Partnership Liquidation
For Period May 1–18, 20Y9

					Capital		
	Cash +	Noncash Assets =	Liabilities +	Radcliffe (20%) +	Sonders (30%) +	Towers (50%)
Balances before realization	$ 5,900	$ 109,900	$ 26,800	$ 14,600	$ 27,900	$ 46,500
Sale of assets and division of loss	27,400	(109,900)		(16,500)	(24,750)	(41,250)
Balances after realization	$ 33,300	$ 0	$ 26,800	$ (1,900)	$ 3,150	$ 5,250
Payment of liabilities	(26,800)		(26,800)			
Balances after payment of liabilities	$ 6,500	$ 0	$ 0	$ (1,900)	$ 3,150	$ 5,250
Receipt of deficiency	1,900			1,900		
Balances	$ 8,400	$ 0	$ 0	$ 0	$ 3,150	$ 5,250
Cash distributed to partners	(8,400)				(3,150)	(5,250)
Final balances	$ 0	$ 0	$ 0	$ 0	$ 0	$ 0

2. a.

			Debit	Credit
Cash			27,400	
Loss on Realization			82,500	
Noncash Assets				109,900

b.

Radcliffe, Capital		16,500	
Sonders, Capital		24,750	
Towers, Capital		41,250	
Loss on Realization			82,500

c.

Liabilities		26,800	
Cash			26,800

d.

Cash		1,900	
Radcliffe, Capital			1,900

e.

Sonders, Capital		3,150	
Towers, Capital		5,250	
Cash			8,400

Key Terms

deficiency (607)
limited liability company (LLC) (592)
liquidation (603)
partnership (591)
partnership agreement (591)
realization (603)
revenue per employee (610)
statement of members' equity (610)
statement of partnership equity (610)
statement of partnership liquidation (605)

Discussion Questions

1. What are the main advantages of (a) proprietorships, (b) partnerships, and (c) limited liability companies?
2. What are the disadvantages of a partnership over a limited liability company form of organization for a profit-making business?
3. Emilio Alvarez and Graciela Zavala joined together to form a partnership. Is it possible for them to lose a greater amount than the amount of their investment in the partnership? Explain.
4. What are the major features of a partnership agreement for a partnership or an operating agreement for a limited liability company?
5. Josiah Barlow, Patty DuMont, and Owen Maholic are contemplating the formation of a partnership. According to the partnership agreement, Barlow is to invest $60,000 and devote one-half time, DuMont is to invest $40,000 and devote three-fourths time, and Maholic is to make no investment and devote full time. Would Maholic be correct in assuming that since he is not contributing any assets to the firm, he is risking nothing? Explain.

6. During the current year, Marsha Engles withdrew $4,000 monthly from the partnership of Engles and Cox Water Management Consultants. Is it possible that her share of partnership net income for the current year might be more or less than $48,000? Explain.
7. a. What accounts are debited and credited to record a partner's cash withdrawal in lieu of salary?
   b. The articles of partnership provide for a salary allowance of $6,000 per month to partner C. If C withdrew only $4,000 per month, would this affect the division of the partnership net income? Explain.
   c. At the end of the fiscal year, what accounts are debited and credited to record the division of net income among partners?
8. Explain the difference between the admission of a new partner to a partnership (a) by purchase of an interest from another partner and (b) by contribution of assets to the partnership.
9. Why is it important to state all partnership assets in terms of current prices at the time of the admission of a new partner?
10. Why might a partnership pay a bonus to a newly admitted partner?

Practice Exercises

Example Exercises

SHOW ME HOW

EE 12-1 p. 593

PE 12-1A Journalizing partner's original investment **OBJ. 2**

Melissa Shallowford contributed a patent, accounts receivable, and $15,000 cash to a partnership. The patent had a book value of $6,000. However, the technology covered by the patent appeared to have significant market potential. Thus, the patent was appraised at $71,000. The accounts receivable control account was $35,000, with an allowance for doubtful accounts of $2,000. The partnership also assumed a $11,000 account payable owed to a Shallowford supplier.

Provide the journal entry for Shallowford's contribution to the partnership.

SHOW ME HOW

EE 12-1 p. 593

PE 12-1B Journalizing partner's original investment **OBJ. 2**

Xi Lin contributed land, inventory, and $38,600 cash to a partnership. The land had a book value of $128,500 and a market value of $187,400. The inventory had a book value of $53,500 and a market value of $45,100. The partnership also assumed a $37,600 note payable owed by Lin that was used originally to purchase the land.

Provide the journal entry for Lin's contribution to the partnership.

SHOW ME HOW

EE 12-2 p. 597

PE 12-2A Dividing partnership net income **OBJ. 2**

Adriana Gonzalez and Sylvester Van Horne formed a partnership, dividing income as follows:

1. Annual salary allowance to Gonzalez of $25,000.
2. Interest of 5% on each partner's capital balance on January 1.
3. Any remaining net income divided to Gonzalez and Van Horne, 2:1.

Gonzalez and Van Horne had $126,000 and $189,000, respectively, in their January 1 capital balances. Net income for the year was $115,000.

How much net income should be distributed to Gonzalez and Van Horne?

SHOW ME HOW

EE 12-2 p. 597

PE 12-2B Dividing partnership net income **OBJ. 2**

Bruce Delew and Nadia Comatof formed a partnership, dividing income as follows:

1. Annual salary allowance to Delew, $18,000, and Comatof, $51,000.
2. Interest of 6% on each partner's capital balance on January 1.
3. Any remaining net income divided equally.

Delew and Comatof had $36,000 and $91,000, respectively, in their January 1 capital balances. Net income for the year was $55,000.

How much net income should be distributed to Delew and Comatof?

SHOW ME HOW

EE 12-3 *p. 600*

PE 12-3A Revaluing and purchasing an interest from existing partner **OBJ. 3**

Greg Thomas purchased one-half of Ian Hamilton's interest in the Freidman and Hamilton partnership for $49,500. Prior to the investment, land was revalued to a market value of $189,200 from a book value of $116,400. Adam Freidman and Ian Hamilton share net income equally. Hamilton had a capital balance of $52,400 prior to these transactions.

a. Provide the journal entry for the revaluation of land.

b. Provide the journal entry to admit Thomas.

SHOW ME HOW

EE 12-3 *p. 600*

PE 12-3B Revaluing and contributing assets to a partnership **OBJ. 3**

Marquis Westbury invested $119,100 in the Trenton and Rainwater partnership for ownership equity of $119,100. Prior to the investment, equipment was revalued to a market value of $77,400 from a book value of $57,300. Daniel Trenton and Ann Marie Rainwater share net income in a 2:1 ratio.

a. Provide the journal entry for the revaluation of equipment.

b. Provide the journal entry to admit Westbury.

SHOW ME HOW

EE 12-4 *p. 602*

PE 12-4A Partner bonus **OBJ. 3**

Patel has a capital balance of $310,000 after adjusting assets to fair market value. Killingsworth contributes $490,000 to receive a 60% interest in a new partnership with Patel.

Determine the amount and recipient of the partner bonus.

SHOW ME HOW

EE 12-4 *p. 602*

PE 12-4B Partner bonus **OBJ. 3**

Todd has a capital balance of $170,600 after adjusting assets to fair market value. Zanetti contributes $45,500 to receive a 40% interest in a new partnership with Todd.

Determine the amount and recipient of the partner bonus.

SHOW ME HOW

EE 12-5 *p. 607*

PE 12-5A Liquidating partnerships **OBJ. 4**

Prior to liquidating their partnership, Cameron and Solivita had capital accounts of $44,000 and $92,000, respectively. Prior to liquidation, the partnership had no cash assets other than what was realized from the sale of assets. These partnership assets were sold for $166,000. The partnership had $9,000 of liabilities. Cameron and Solivita share income and losses equally. Determine the amount received by Cameron as a final distribution from liquidation of the partnership.

SHOW ME HOW

EE 12-5 *p. 607*

PE 12-5B Liquidating partnerships **OBJ. 4**

Prior to liquidating their partnership, Kim and Cheyenne had capital accounts of $304,000 and $190,000, respectively. Prior to liquidation, the partnership had no cash assets other than what was realized from the sale of assets. These partnership assets were sold for $520,000. The partnership had $106,000 of liabilities. Kim and Cheyenne share income and losses equally. Determine the amount received by Kim as a final distribution from liquidation of the partnership.

SHOW ME HOW

EE 12-6 *p. 609*

PE 12-6A Liquidating partnerships—deficiency **OBJ. 4**

Prior to liquidating their partnership, Heller and Warren had capital accounts of $128,000 and $67,000, respectively. The partnership assets were sold for $49,000. The partnership had no liabilities. Heller and Warren share income and losses equally.

a. Determine the amount of Warren's deficiency.

b. Determine the amount distributed to Heller assuming that Warren is unable to satisfy the deficiency.

SHOW ME HOW

EE 12-6 *p. 609*

PE 12-6B Liquidating partnerships—deficiency **OBJ. 4**

Prior to liquidating their partnership, Jacobs and Sanchez had capital accounts of $320,000 and $424,000, respectively. The partnership assets were sold for $52,000. The partnership had no liabilities. Jacobs and Sanchez share income and losses equally.

a. Determine the amount of Jacobs's deficiency.

b. Determine the amount distributed to Sanchez, assuming that Jacobs is unable to satisfy the deficiency.

SHOW ME HOW

FAI

EE 12-7 p. 611

PE 12-7A Revenue per employee **OBJ. 6**

Schwartz and Beer, CPAs earned $9,338,000 during 20Y4 using 46 employees. During 20Y5, the firm grew revenues to $11,825,000 and expanded the staff to 55 employees.

a. Determine the revenue per employee for each year.

b. Interpret the results.

SHOW ME HOW

FAI

EE 12-7 p. 611

PE 12-7B Revenue per employee **OBJ. 6**

Makeman Architects earned $4,400,000 during 20Y1 using 40 employees. During 20Y2, the firm reduced revenues to $3,894,000 and reduced the staff to 33 employees.

a. Determine the revenue per employee for each year.

b. Interpret the results.

Exercises

SHOW ME HOW

EX 12-1 Recording partner's original investment **OBJ. 2**

Vanessa Kaiser and Mariah Newman decide to form a partnership by combining the assets of their separate businesses. Kaiser contributes the following assets to the partnership: cash, $25,800; accounts receivable with a face amount of $187,600 and an allowance for doubtful accounts of $5,400; merchandise inventory with a cost of $118,900; and equipment with a cost of $175,800 and accumulated depreciation of $58,200.

The partners agree that $6,000 of the accounts receivable are completely worthless and are not to be accepted by the partnership, that $5,700 is a reasonable allowance for the uncollectibility of the remaining accounts, that the merchandise inventory is to be recorded at the current market price of $131,400, and that the equipment is to be valued at $104,900.

Journalize the partnership's entry to record Kaiser's investment.

SHOW ME HOW

EX 12-2 Recording partner's original investment **OBJ. 2**

Hannah Freeman and Hugo Hernandez form a partnership by combining assets of their former businesses. The following balance sheet information is provided by Freeman, sole proprietorship:

Hannah Freeman Proprietorship
Balance Sheet
June 1, 20Y3

Cash		$ 65,000
Accounts receivable	$125,000	
Less: Allowance for doubtful accounts	7,200	117,800
Land		215,000
Equipment	$ 78,000	
Less: Accumulated depreciation—equipment	41,000	37,000
Total assets		$434,800
Accounts payable		$ 24,800
Notes payable		76,000
Hannah Freeman, capital		334,000
Total liabilities and owner's equity		$434,800

Freeman obtained appraised values for the land and equipment as follows:

Land	$320,000
Equipment	34,800

An analysis of the accounts receivable indicated that the allowance for doubtful accounts should be increased to $9,500.

Journalize the partnership's entry for Freeman's investment.

EX 12-3 Dividing partnership income **OBJ. 2**

✔ b. Dawson, $285,000

Beau Dawson and Willow McDonald formed a partnership, investing $276,000 and $92,000, respectively. Determine their participation in the year's net income of $380,000 under each of the following independent assumptions: (a) no agreement concerning division of net income; (b) divided in the ratio of original capital investment; (c) interest at the rate of 5% allowed on original investments and the remainder divided in the ratio of 2:3; (d) salary allowances of $47,000 and $59,000, respectively, and the balance divided equally; (e) allowance of interest at the rate of 5% on original investments, salary allowances of $47,000 and $59,000, respectively, and the remainder divided equally.

EX 12-4 Dividing partnership income **OBJ. 2**

✔ c. Dawson, $60,840

Using each of the five assumptions as to income division listed in Exercise 12-3, determine the income participation of Dawson and McDonald if the year's net income is $136,000.

EX 12-5 Dividing partnership net loss **OBJ. 2**

Lynn Carpenter and Matthew Fredrick formed a partnership in which the partnership agreement provided for salary allowances of $58,000 and $41,000, respectively. Determine the division of a $33,000 net loss for the current year, assuming that remaining income or losses are shared equally by the two partners.

EX 12-6 Negotiating income-sharing ratio **OBJ. 2**

Sixty-year-old Wanda Davis retired from her computer consulting business in Boston and moved to Florida. There she met 27-year-old Ava Jain, who had just graduated from Eldon Community College with an associate degree in computer science. Wanda and Ava formed a partnership called D&J Computer Consultants. Wanda contributed $50,000 for startup costs and devoted one-half time to the business. Ava devoted full time to the business. The monthly drawings were $2,500 for Wanda and $5,000 for Ava.

At the end of the first year of operations, the two partners disagreed on the division of net income. Wanda reasoned that the division should be equal. Although she devoted only one-half time to the business, she contributed all of the startup funds. Ava reasoned that the income-sharing ratio should be 2:1 in her favor because she devoted full time to the business and her monthly drawings were twice those of Wanda.

a. What flaws can you identify in the partners' reasoning regarding the income-sharing ratio?

b. How could an income-sharing agreement resolve this dispute?

EX 12-7 Dividing LLC income **OBJ. 2**

✔ a. Farley, $86,800

Martin Farley and Ashley Clark formed a limited liability company with an operating agreement that provided a salary allowance of $40,000 and $30,000 to each member, respectively. In addition, the operating agreement specified an income-sharing ratio of 3:2. The two members withdrew amounts equal to their salary allowances. Revenues were $668,000 and expenses were $520,000, for a net income of $148,000.

a. Determine the division of $148,000 net income for the year.

b. Provide journal entries to close the (1) revenues and expenses and (2) drawing accounts for the two members.

c. If the net income was less than the sum of the salary allowances, how would income be divided between the two members of the LLC?

EX 12-8 LLC net income and statement of members' equity **OBJ. 2, 5**

✔ a. O'Reilly, $190,400

Exploit Media, LLC, has three members: WACS Partners, Elyse O'Reilly, and Encounter Newspaper, LLC. On January 1, 20Y2, the three members had equity of $275,000, $55,000, and $220,000, respectively. WACS Partners contributed an additional $69,000 to Exploit

(Continued)

Media, LLC, on June 1, 20Y2. Elyse O'Reilly received an annual salary allowance of $76,000 during 20Y2. The members' equity accounts are also credited with 10% interest on each member's January 1 capital balance. Any remaining income is to be shared in the ratio of 4:3:3 among the three members. The revenues, expenses, and net income for Exploit Media, LLC, for 20Y2 were $1,730,000, $1,236,000, and $494,000, respectively. Amounts equal to the salary and interest allowances were withdrawn by the members.

a. Determine the division of income among the three members.

b. Prepare the journal entry to close the revenues, expenses, and withdrawals to the individual member equity accounts.

c. Prepare a statement of members' equity for 20Y2.

d. What are the advantages of an income-sharing agreement for the members of this LLC?

SHOW ME HOW

EX 12-9 Admitting new partners **OBJ. 3**

Myles Etter and Crystal Santori are partners who share in the income equally and have capital balances of $210,000 and $62,500, respectively. Etter, with the consent of Santori, sells one-third of his interest to Lonnie Davis. What entry is required by the partnership if the sales price is (a) $60,000? (b) $80,000?

EX 12-10 Admitting new partners who buy an interest and contribute assets **OBJ. 3**

✔ b. Henry, $128,000

SHOW ME HOW

The capital accounts of Trent Henry and Tim Chou have balances of $160,000 and $100,000, respectively. LeAnne Gilbert and Becky Clarke are to be admitted to the partnership. Gilbert buys one-fifth of Henry's interest for $35,000 and one-fourth of Chou's interest for $29,000. Clarke contributes $90,000 cash to the partnership, for which she is to receive an ownership equity of $90,000.

a. Journalize the entries to record the admission of (1) Gilbert and (2) Clarke.

b. What are the capital balances of each partner after the admission of the new partners?

EX 12-11 Admitting new partner who contributes assets **OBJ. 3**

✔ b. Jackson, $61,300

After the tangible assets have been adjusted to current market prices, the capital accounts of Grayson Jackson and Harry Barge have balances of $64,900 and $86,500, respectively. Lewan Gorman is to be admitted to the partnership, contributing $43,300 cash to the partnership, for which he is to receive an ownership equity of $50,500. All partners share equally in income.

a. Journalize the entry to record the admission of Gorman, who is to receive a bonus of $7,200.

b. What are the capital balances of each partner after the admission of the new partner?

c. Why are tangible assets adjusted to current market prices prior to admitting a new partner?

EX 12-12 Admitting new partner with bonus **OBJ. 3**

Cody Jenkins and Lacey Tanner formed a partnership to provide landscaping services. Jenkins and Tanner shared profits and losses equally. After all the tangible assets have been adjusted to current market prices, the capital accounts of Cody Jenkins and Lacey Tanner have balances of $78,000 and $46,000, respectively. Valeria Solano has expertise with using the computer to prepare landscape designs, cost estimates, and renderings. Jenkins and Tanner deem these skills useful; thus, Solano is admitted to the partnership at a 30% interest for a purchase price of $32,000.

a. Determine the recipient and amount of the partner bonus.

b. Provide the journal entry to admit Solano into the partnership.

c. Why would a bonus be paid in this situation?

EX 12-13 Admitting a new LLC member with bonus OBJ. 3

✔ b. (2) Bonus paid to Lin, $7,500

Alert Medical, LLC, consists of two doctors, Abrams and Lipscomb, who share in all income and losses according to a 2:3 income-sharing ratio. Dr. Lin has been asked to join the LLC. Prior to admitting Lin, the assets of Alert Medical were revalued to reflect their current market values. The revaluation resulted in medical equipment being increased by $40,000. Prior to the revaluation, the equity balances for Abrams and Lipscomb were $154,000 and $208,000, respectively.

a. Provide the journal entry for the asset revaluation.

b. Provide the journal entry for the bonus under the following independent situations:
   1. Lin purchased a 30% interest in Alert Medical, LLC, for $228,000.
   2. Lin purchased a 25% interest in Alert Medical, LLC, for $124,000.

EX 12-14 Admitting new partner with bonus OBJ. 3

✔ b. (1) Bonus paid to Ortiz, $9,600

L. Bowers and V. Lipscomb are partners in Elegant Event Consultants. Bowers and Lipscomb share income equally. M. Ortiz will be admitted to the partnership. Prior to the admission, equipment was revalued downward by $8,000. The capital balances of each partner are $96,000 and $40,000, respectively, prior to the revaluation.

a. Provide the journal entry for the asset revaluation.

b. Provide the journal entry for Ortiz's admission under the following independent situations:
   1. Ortiz purchased a 20% interest for $20,000.
   2. Ortiz purchased a 30% interest for $60,000.

EX 12-15 Partner bonuses, statement of partnership equity OBJ. 2, 3, 5

✔ Dennis Overton, Capital, Dec. 31, 20Y5, $226,400

The partnership of Angel Investor Associates began operations on January 1, 20Y5, with contributions from two partners as follows:

Dennis Overton	$180,000
Ben Testerman	120,000

The following additional partner transactions took place during the year:

1. In early January, Randy Campbell is admitted to the partnership by contributing $75,000 cash for a 20% interest.
2. Net income of $150,000 was earned in 20Y5. In addition, Dennis Overton received a salary allowance of $40,000 for the year. The three partners agree to an income-sharing ratio equal to their capital balances after admitting Campbell.
3. The partners' withdrawals are equal to half of the increase in their capital balances from salary allowance and income.

Prepare a statement of partnership equity for the year ended December 31, 20Y5.

EX 12-16 Withdrawal of partner OBJ. 3

Lane Stevens is to retire from the partnership of Stevens and Associates as of March 31, the end of the current fiscal year. After closing the accounts, the capital balances of the partners are as follows: Lane Stevens, $150,000; Cherrie Ford, $70,000; and LaMarcus Rollins, $60,000. They have shared net income and net losses in the ratio of 3:2:2. The partners agree that the merchandise inventory should be increased by $22,300 and the allowance for doubtful accounts should be increased by $1,300. Stevens agrees to accept a note for $100,000 in partial settlement of his ownership equity. The remainder of his claim is to be paid in cash. Ford and Rollins are to share equally in the net income or net loss of the new partnership.

Journalize the entries to record (a) the adjustment of the assets to bring them into agreement with current market prices and (b) the withdrawal of Stevens from the partnership.

EX 12-17 Statement of members' equity, admitting new member

OBJ. 2, 3, 5

✔ a. 3:7

The statement of members' equity for Bonanza, LLC, follows:

Bonanza, LLC
Statement of Members' Equity
For the Years Ended December 31, 20Y3 and 20Y4

	Idaho Properties, LLC, Member Equity	Silver Streams, LLC, Member Equity	Thomas Dunn, Member Equity	Total Members' Equity
Members' equity, January 1, 20Y3	$273,000	$307,000		$ 580,000
Net income	57,000	133,000		190,000
Members' equity, December 31, 20Y3	$330,000	$440,000		$ 770,000
Dunn contribution, January 1, 20Y4	3,000	7,000	$220,000	230,000
Net income	62,500	137,500	50,000	250,000
Member withdrawals	(32,000)	(48,000)	(40,000)	(120,000)
Members' equity, December 31, 20Y4	$363,500	$536,500	$230,000	$1,130,000

a. What was the income-sharing ratio in 20Y3?

b. What was the income-sharing ratio in 20Y4?

c. How much cash did Thomas Dunn contribute to Bonanza, LLC, for his interest?

d. Why do the member equity accounts of Idaho Properties, LLC, and Silver Streams, LLC, have positive entries for Thomas Dunn's contribution?

e. What percentage interest of Bonanza did Thomas Dunn acquire?

f. Why are withdrawals less than net income?

EX 12-18 Distribution of cash upon liquidation

OBJ. 4

✔ a. $11,000 loss

EXCEL ONLINE

Hewitt and Patel are partners, sharing gains and losses equally. They decide to terminate their partnership. Prior to realization, their capital balances are $28,000 and $18,000, respectively. After all noncash assets are sold and all liabilities are paid, there is a cash balance of $35,000.

a. What is the amount of a gain or loss on realization?

b. How should the gain or loss be divided between Hewitt and Patel?

c. How should the cash be divided between Hewitt and Patel?

EX 12-19 Distribution of cash upon liquidation

OBJ. 4

✔ Oliver, $30,000

David Oliver and Umar Ansari, with capital balances of $28,000 and $35,000, respectively, decide to liquidate their partnership. After selling the noncash assets and paying the liabilities, there is $67,000 of cash remaining. If the partners share income and losses equally, how should the cash be distributed?

EX 12-20 Liquidating partnerships—capital deficiency

OBJ. 4

✔ b. $97,500

Lewis, Zapata, and Fowler share equally in net income and net losses. After the partnership sells all assets for cash, divides the losses on realization, and pays the liabilities, the balances in the capital accounts are as follows: Lewis, $73,500 Cr.; Zapata, $41,000 Cr.; Fowler, $17,000 Dr.

a. What term is applied to the debit balance in Fowler's capital account?

b. What is the amount of cash on hand?

c. Journalize the transaction that must take place for Lewis and Zapata to receive cash in the liquidation process equal to their capital account balances.

✔ a. $975

EX 12-21 Distribution of cash upon liquidation **OBJ. 4**

Bray, Lincoln, and Mapes arranged to import and sell orchid corsages for a university dance. They agreed to share equally the net income or net loss of the venture. Bray and Lincoln advanced $225 and $300 of their own respective funds to pay for advertising and other expenses. After collecting for all sales and paying creditors, the partnership has $1,500 in cash.

a. How much net income was earned from the venture?

b. How should the $1,500 be distributed?

c. Assuming that the partnership has only $300 instead of $1,500, do any of the three partners have a capital deficiency? If so, how much?

EX 12-22 Liquidating partnerships—capital deficiency **OBJ. 4**

Nettles, King, and Tanaka are partners sharing income 3:2:1. After the firm's loss from liquidation is distributed, the capital account balances were as follows: Nettles, $15,000 Dr.; King, $46,000 Cr.; and Tanaka, $71,000 Cr. If Nettles is personally bankrupt and unable to pay any of the $15,000, what will be the amount of cash received by King and Tanaka upon liquidation?

SHOW ME HOW

EX 12-23 Statement of partnership liquidation **OBJ. 4, 5**

After closing the accounts on July 1, prior to liquidating the partnership, the capital account balances of Silver, Carillo, and Tingley are $77,700, $51,800, and $25,900, respectively. Cash, noncash assets, and liabilities total $72,500, $124,200, and $41,300, respectively. Between July 1 and July 29, the noncash assets are sold for $116,400, the liabilities are paid, and the remaining cash is distributed to the partners. The partners share net income and loss in the ratio of 3:2:1. Prepare a statement of partnership liquidation for the period July 1–29.

EX 12-24 Statement of LLC liquidation **OBJ. 4, 5**

Lester, Torres, and Hearst are members of Arcadia Sales, LLC, sharing income and losses in the ratio of 2:2:1, respectively. The members decide to liquidate the limited liability company. The members' equity prior to liquidation and asset realization on August 1 are as follows:

Lester	$ 49,000
Torres	61,000
Hearst	27,000
Total	$137,000

In winding up operations during the month of August, noncash assets with a book value of $146,000 are sold for $158,000, and liabilities of $35,000 are satisfied. Prior to realization, Arcadia Sales has a cash balance of $26,000.

a. Prepare a statement of LLC liquidation.

b. Provide the journal entry for the final cash distribution to members.

c. What is the role of the income- and loss-sharing ratio in liquidating an LLC?

✔ b. Grecco, Capital, Dec. 31, $74,000

EX 12-25 Partnership entries and statement of partnership equity **OBJ. 2, 5**

The capital accounts of Lorraine Grecco and Carrie Rosenfeld have balances of $64,000 and $99,000, respectively, on January 1, 20Y4, the beginning of the fiscal year. On March 10, Grecco invested an additional $11,000. During the year, Grecco and Rosenfeld withdrew $43,000 and $53,000, respectively, and net income for the year was $84,000. Revenues were $654,000, and expenses were $570,000. The articles of partnership make no reference to the division of net income.

a. Journalize the entries to close (1) the revenues and expenses and (2) the drawing accounts.

b. Prepare a statement of partnership equity for the current year for the partnership of Grecco and Rosenfeld.

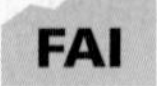

EX 12-26 Revenue per professional staff **OBJ. 6**

The accounting firm of **Deloitte & Touche** is the largest international accounting firm in the world as ranked by total revenues. For two recent years, Deloitte & Touche reported the following for its U.S. operations:

	Current Year	Previous Year
Revenue (in billions)	$19.9	$18.6
Number of professional staff (including partners)	79,347	71,212

a. For the current and previous years, determine the revenue per professional staff. Round to nearest dollar.

b. Interpret the trend between the two years.

FAI

EX 12-27 Revenue per employee **OBJ. 6**

Squeeky Cleaning Services, LLC, provides cleaning services for office buildings. The firm has 10 members in the LLC, which did not change between 20Y8 and 20Y9. During 20Y9, the business terminated two commercial contracts. The following revenue and employee information is provided:

	20Y9	20Y8
Revenues (in thousands)	$27,270	$31,140
Number of employees (excluding members)	135	180

a. For 20Y9 and 20Y8, determine the revenue per employee (excluding members).

b. Interpret the trend between the two years.

Problems: Series A

PR 12-1A Entries and balance sheet for partnership **OBJ. 2**

✔ 3. Keene net income, $33,800

On March 1, 20Y8, Eric Keene and Renee Wallace form a partnership. Keene agrees to invest $23,400 in cash and merchandise inventory valued at $62,600. Wallace invests certain business assets at valuations agreed upon, transfers business liabilities, and contributes sufficient cash to bring her total capital to $60,000. Details regarding the book values of the business assets and liabilities, and the agreed valuations, follow:

	Wallace's Ledger Balance	Agreed-Upon Valuation
Accounts Receivable	$19,900	$19,500
Allowance for Doubtful Accounts	1,200	1,400
Equipment	83,500 }	55,400
Accumulated Depreciation—Equipment	29,800 }	
Accounts Payable	15,000	15,000
Notes Payable (current)	37,500	37,500

The partnership agreement includes the following provisions regarding the division of net income: interest on original investments at 10%, salary allowances of $19,000 (Keene) and $24,000 (Wallace), and the remainder equally.

Instructions

1. Journalize the entries to record the investments of Keene and Wallace in the partnership accounts.
2. Prepare a balance sheet as of March 1, 20Y8, the date of formation of the partnership of Keene and Wallace.
3. After adjustments at February 28, 20Y9, the end of the first full year of operations, the revenues were $300,000 and expenses were $230,000, for a net income of $70,000. The drawing accounts have debit balances of $19,000 (Keene) and $24,000 (Wallace). Journalize the entries to close the revenues and expenses and the drawing accounts at February 28, 20Y9.

PR 12-2A Dividing partnership income **OBJ. 2**

✔ 1. f. Black net income, $108,000

SHOW ME HOW

Black and Shannon have decided to form a partnership. They have agreed that Black is to invest $360,000 and that Shannon is to invest $120,000. Black is to devote one-half time to the business, and Shannon is to devote full time. The following plans for the division of income are being considered:

a. Equal division
b. In the ratio of original investments
c. In the ratio of time devoted to the business
d. Interest of 6% on original investments and the remainder equally
e. Interest of 6% on original investments, salary allowances of $96,000 to Black and $168,000 to Shannon, and the remainder equally
f. Plan (e), except that Shannon is also to be allowed a bonus equal to 20% of the amount by which net income exceeds the total salary allowances

Instructions

For each plan, determine the division of the net income under each of the following assumptions: (1) net income of $276,000 and (2) net income of $480,000. Present the data in tabular form, using the following columnar headings:

	$276,000		$480,000	
Plan	**Black**	**Shannon**	**Black**	**Shannon**

PR 12-3A Financial statements for partnership **OBJ. 2, 5**

✔ 2. Dec. 31 capital—Yost, $125,000

The ledger of Tyler Lambert and Jayla Yost, attorneys-at-law, contains the following accounts and balances after adjustments have been recorded on December 31, 20Y3:

Lambert and Yost
Trial Balance
December 31, 20Y3

	Debit Balances	Credit Balances
Cash	34,000	
Accounts Receivable	47,800	
Supplies	2,000	
Land	120,000	
Building	157,500	
Accumulated Depreciation—Building		67,200
Office Equipment	63,600	
Accumulated Depreciation—Office Equipment		21,700
Accounts Payable		27,900
Salaries Payable		5,100
Tyler Lambert, Capital		135,000
Tyler Lambert, Drawing	50,000	
Jayla Yost, Capital		88,000
Jayla Yost, Drawing	60,000	
Professional Fees		395,300
Salary Expense	154,500	
Depreciation Expense—Building	15,700	
Property Tax Expense	12,000	
Heating and Lighting Expense	8,500	
Supplies Expense	6,000	
Depreciation Expense—Office Equipment	5,000	
Miscellaneous Expense	3,600	
	740,200	740,200

The balance in Yost's capital account includes an additional investment of $10,000 made on April 10, 20Y3.

(Continued)

Instructions

1. Prepare an income statement for 20Y3, indicating the division of net income. The partnership agreement provides for salary allowances of $45,000 to Lambert and $54,700 to Yost, allowances of 10% on each partner's capital balance at the beginning of the fiscal year, and equal division of the remaining net income or net loss.
2. Prepare a statement of partnership equity for 20Y3.
3. Prepare a balance sheet as of the end of 20Y3.

PR 12-4A Admitting new partner

OBJ. 3

✓ 3. Total assets, $326,300

Musa Moshref and Shaniqua Hollins have operated a successful firm for many years, sharing net income and net losses equally. Taylor Anderson is to be admitted to the partnership on July 1 of the current year, in accordance with the following agreement:

a. Assets and liabilities of the old partnership are to be valued at their book values as of June 30, except for the following:
   - Accounts receivable amounting to $2,500 are to be written off, and the allowance for doubtful accounts is to be increased to 5% of the remaining accounts.
   - Merchandise inventory is to be valued at $76,600.
   - Equipment is to be valued at $155,700.

b. Anderson is to purchase $70,000 of the ownership interest of Hollins for $75,000 cash and to contribute another $45,000 cash to the partnership for a total ownership equity of $115,000.

The post-closing trial balance of Moshref and Hollins as of June 30 is as follows:

Moshref and Hollins
Post-Closing Trial Balance
June 30, 20Y7

	Debit Balances	Credit Balances
Cash	8,000	
Accounts Receivable	42,500	
Allowance for Doubtful Accounts		1,600
Merchandise Inventory	72,000	
Prepaid Insurance	3,000	
Equipment	180,500	
Accumulated Depreciation—Equipment		43,100
Accounts Payable		21,300
Notes Payable (current)		35,000
Musa Moshref, Capital		120,000
Shaniqua Hollins, Capital		85,000
	306,000	306,000

Instructions

1. Journalize the entries as of June 30 to record the revaluations, using a temporary account entitled Asset Revaluations. Debits and credits to the asset revaluations account are losses and gains from revaluation, respectively. The balance in the accumulated depreciation account is to be eliminated. After journalizing the revaluations, close the balance of the asset revaluations account to the capital accounts of Musa Moshref and Shaniqua Hollins.
2. Journalize the additional entries to record Anderson's entrance to the partnership on July 1, 20Y7.
3. Present a balance sheet for the new partnership as of July 1, 20Y7.

PR 12-5A Statement of partnership liquidation

OBJ. 4

✓ 1d. Gerloff, $8,500

After the accounts are closed on February 3, prior to liquidating the partnership, the capital accounts of William Gerloff, Joshua Chu, and Courtney Jewett are $19,300, $4,500, and $22,300, respectively. Cash and noncash assets total $5,200 and $55,900, respectively. Amounts owed to creditors total $15,000. The partners share income and losses in the ratio of 2:1:1. Between February 3 and February 28, the noncash assets are sold for $34,300, the partner with the capital deficiency pays the deficiency to the partnership, and the liabilities are paid.

Instructions

1. Prepare a statement of partnership liquidation, indicating (a) the sale of assets and division of loss, (b) the payment of liabilities, (c) the receipt of the deficiency (from the appropriate partner), and (d) the distribution of cash.
2. Assume that the partner with the capital deficiency declares bankruptcy and is unable to pay the deficiency. Journalize the entries to (a) allocate the partner's deficiency and (b) distribute the remaining cash.

PR 12-6A Statement of partnership liquidation

OBJ. 4

On November 1, the firm of Bowes, Simmons, and Ahmed decided to liquidate its partnership. The partners have capital balances of $69,000, $85,000, and $12,000, respectively. The cash balance is $38,000, the book values of noncash assets total $152,000, and liabilities total $24,000. The partners share income and losses in the ratio of 2:2:1.

Instructions

1. Prepare a statement of partnership liquidation, covering the period November 1–30, for each of the following independent assumptions:
   a. All of the noncash assets are sold for $185,000 in cash, the creditors are paid, and the remaining cash is distributed to the partners.
   b. All of the noncash assets are sold for $65,000 in cash, the creditors are paid, the partner with the debit capital balance pays the amount owed to the firm, and the remaining cash is distributed to the partners.
2. Assume that the partner with the capital deficiency in part (b) declares bankruptcy and is unable to pay the deficiency. Journalize the entries to (a) allocate the partner's deficiency and (b) distribute the remaining cash.

Problems: Series B

PR 12-1B Entries and balance sheet for partnership

OBJ. 2

✓ 3. Lang net income, $63,400

SHOW ME HOW

On April 1, 20Y1, Whitney Lang and Eli Capri form a partnership. Lang agrees to invest $18,000 cash and merchandise inventory valued at $50,000. Capri invests certain business assets at valuations agreed upon, transfers business liabilities, and contributes sufficient cash to bring his total capital to $120,000. Details regarding the book values of the business assets and liabilities, and the agreed valuations, follow:

	Capri's Ledger Balance	Agreed-Upon Balance
Accounts Receivable	$45,700	$43,400
Allowance for Doubtful Accounts	3,200	3,500
Merchandise Inventory	31,500	28,900
Equipment	89,500	63,400
Accumulated Depreciation—Equipment	19,000	
Accounts Payable	23,400	23,400
Notes Payable (current)	15,000	15,000

The partnership agreement includes the following provisions regarding the division of net income: interest of 10% on original investments, salary allowances of $36,000 (Lang) and $22,000 (Capri), and the remainder equally.

Instructions

1. Journalize the entries to record the investments of Lang and Capri in the partnership accounts.
2. Prepare a balance sheet as of April 1, 20Y1, the date of formation of the partnership of Lang and Capri.
3. After adjustments at March 31, 20Y2, the end of the first full year of operations, the revenues were $598,000 and expenses were $480,000, for a net income of $118,000.

(Continued)

The drawing accounts have debit balances of $40,000 (Lang) and $30,000 (Capri). Journalize the entries to close the revenues and expenses and the drawing accounts at March 31, 20Y2.

PR 12-2B Dividing partnership income

OBJ. 2

✔ 1. f. Howell net income, $254,550

SHOW ME HOW

Dylan Howell and Demond Nickles have decided to form a partnership. They have agreed that Howell is to invest $50,000 and that Nickles is to invest $75,000. Howell is to devote full time to the business, and Nickles is to devote one-half time. The following plans for the division of income are being considered:

a. Equal division

b. In the ratio of original investments

c. In the ratio of time devoted to the business

d. Interest of 10% on original investments and the remainder in the ratio of 3:2

e. Interest of 10% on original investments, salary allowances of $38,000 to Howell and $19,000 to Nickles, and the remainder equally

f. Plan (e), except that Howell is also to be allowed a bonus equal to 20% of the amount by which net income exceeds the total salary allowances

Instructions

For each plan, determine the division of the net income under each of the following assumptions: (1) net income of $420,000 and (2) net income of $150,000. Present the data in tabular form, using the following columnar headings:

	$420,000		$150,000	
Plan	Howell	Nickles	Howell	Nickles

PR 12-3B Financial statements for partnerships

OBJ. 2, 5

✔ 2. Dec. 31 capital—Xue, $179,100

The ledger of Camila Ramirez and Ping Xue, attorneys-at-law, contains the following accounts and balances after adjustments have been recorded on December 31, 20Y2:

Ramirez and Xue
Trial Balance
December 31, 20Y2

	Debit Balances	Credit Balances
Cash	70,300	
Accounts Receivable	33,600	
Supplies	5,800	
Land	128,000	
Building	175,000	
Accumulated Depreciation—Building		80,000
Office Equipment	42,000	
Accumulated Depreciation—Office Equipment		25,300
Accounts Payable		12,400
Salaries Payable		10,000
Camila Ramirez, Capital		125,000
Camila Ramirez, Drawing	35,000	
Ping Xue, Capital		155,000
Ping Xue, Drawing	50,000	
Professional Fees		555,300
Salary Expense	384,900	
Depreciation Expense—Building	12,900	
Heating and Lighting Expense	10,500	
Depreciation Expense—Office Equipment	6,300	
Property Tax Expense	3,200	
Supplies Expense	3,000	
Miscellaneous Expense	2,500	
	963,000	963,000

The balance in Xue's capital account includes an additional investment of $20,000 made on May 5, 20Y2.

Instructions

1. Prepare an income statement for 20Y2, indicating the division of net income. The partnership agreement provides for salary allowances of $50,000 to Ramirez and $65,000 to Xue, allowances of 12% on each partner's capital balance at the beginning of the fiscal year, and equal division of the remaining net income or net loss.
2. Prepare a statement of partnership equity for 20Y2.
3. Prepare a balance sheet as of the end of 20Y2.

PR 12-4B Admitting new partner

OBJ. 3

✔ 3. Total assets, $173,900

Brian Caldwell and Adriana Estrada have operated a successful firm for many years, sharing net income and net losses equally. Kris Mays is to be admitted to the partnership on September 1 of the current year, in accordance with the following agreement:

a. Assets and liabilities of the old partnership are to be valued at their book values as of August 31, except for the following:
   - Accounts receivable amounting to $1,500 are to be written off, and the allowance for doubtful accounts is to be increased to 5% of the remaining accounts.
   - Merchandise inventory is to be valued at $46,800.
   - Equipment is to be valued at $64,500.

b. Mays is to purchase $26,000 of the ownership interest of Estrada for $30,000 cash and to contribute $32,000 cash to the partnership for a total ownership equity of $58,000.

The post-closing trial balance of Caldwell and Estrada as of August 31 follows:

Caldwell and Estrada
Post-Closing Trial Balance
August 31, 20Y9

	Debit Balances	Credit Balances
Cash	12,300	
Accounts Receivable	19,500	
Allowance for Doubtful Accounts		600
Merchandise Inventory	42,500	
Prepaid Insurance	1,200	
Equipment	67,500	
Accumulated Depreciation—Equipment		15,500
Accounts Payable		8,900
Notes Payable (current)		15,000
Brian Caldwell, Capital		55,000
Adriana Estrada, Capital		48,000
	143,000	143,000

Instructions

1. Journalize the entries as of August 31 to record the revaluations, using a temporary account entitled Asset Revaluations. Debits and credits to the asset revaluations account are losses and gains from revaluation, respectively. The balance in the accumulated depreciation account is to be eliminated. After journalizing the revaluations, close the balance of the asset revaluations account to the capital accounts of Brian Caldwell and Adriana Estrada.
2. Journalize the additional entries to record Mays' entrance to the partnership on September 1, 20Y9.
3. Present a balance sheet for the new partnership as of September 1, 20Y9.

PR 12-5B Statement of partnership liquidation OBJ. 4

✔1d. Fairchild, $33,000

After the accounts are closed on April 10, prior to liquidating the partnership, the capital accounts of Zach Fairchild, Austin Lowes, and Amber Howard are $42,000, $7,500, and $36,500, respectively. Cash and noncash assets total $23,500 and $84,500, respectively. Amounts owed to creditors total $22,000. The partners share income and losses in the ratio of 1:1:2. Between April 10 and April 30, the noncash assets are sold for $48,500, the partner with the capital deficiency pays the deficiency to the partnership, and the liabilities are paid.

Instructions

1. Prepare a statement of partnership liquidation, indicating (a) the sale of assets and division of loss, (b) the payment of liabilities, (c) the receipt of the deficiency (from the appropriate partner), and (d) the distribution of cash.
2. Assume that the partner with the capital deficiency declares bankruptcy and is unable to pay the deficiency. Journalize the entries to (a) allocate the partner's deficiency and (b) distribute the remaining cash.

PR 12-6B Statement of partnership liquidation OBJ. 4

On August 3, the firm of Chapelle, Rock, and Pryor decided to liquidate its partnership. The partners have capital balances of $14,000, $102,000, and $86,000, respectively. The cash balance is $65,000, the book values of noncash assets total $167,000, and liabilities total $30,000. The partners share income and losses in the ratio of 1:2:2.

Instructions

1. Prepare a statement of partnership liquidation, covering the period August 3–29, for each of the following independent assumptions:
   a. All of the noncash assets are sold for $217,000 in cash, the creditors are paid, and the remaining cash is distributed to the partners.
   b. All of the noncash assets are sold for $72,000 in cash, the creditors are paid, the partner with the debit capital balance pays the amount owed to the firm, and the remaining cash is distributed to the partners.
2. Assume that the partner with the capital deficiency in part (b) declares bankruptcy and is unable to pay the deficiency. Journalize the entries to (a) allocate the partner's deficiency and (b) distribute the remaining cash.

Cases & Projects

CP 12-1 Ethics in Action

ETHICS

Taye Barrow, M.D., and James Robbins, M.D., are sole owners of two medical practices that operate in the same medical building. The two doctors agree to combine assets and liabilities of the two businesses to form a partnership. The partnership agreement calls for dividing income equally between the two doctors. After several months, the following conversation takes place between the two doctors:

Barrow: I've noticed that your patient load has dropped over the last couple of months. When we formed our partnership, we were seeing about the same number of patients per week. However, now our patient records show that you have been seeing about half as many patients as I have. Are there any issues that I should be aware of?

Robbins: There's nothing going on. When I was working on my own, I was really putting in the hours. One of the reasons I formed this partnership was to enjoy life a little more and scale back a little bit.

Barrow: I see. Well, I find that I'm working as hard as I did when I was on my own yet making less than I did previously. Essentially, you're sharing in half of my billings and I'm sharing in half of yours. Since you are working much less than I am, I end up on the short end of the bargain.

Robbins: Well, I don't know what to say. An agreement is an agreement. The partnership is based on a 50/50 split. That's what a partnership is all about.

Barrow: If that's so, then it applies equally well on the effort end of the equation as it does on the income end.

 Discuss whether Robbins is acting in an ethical manner. How could Barrow renegotiate the partnership agreement to avoid this dispute?

CP 12-2 Team Activity

In groups of two or three, find the most recent "Accounting Today Top 100 Firms" on the Internet.

a. From this document, create an Excel spreadsheet of the total revenues and total partners for **Deloitte & Touche**, **PwC**, **Ernst & Young**, and **KPMG**.

b. Determine the revenue per partner for each of these four firms. Round to the nearest dollar.

c. Develop a table of the revenue earned per partner of each of these four firms as a percent of the highest revenue per partner firm. Round to the nearest whole percentage.

d. Interpret the differences between the firms in terms of your answer in (c).

CP 12-3 Communication

Lindsey Wilson has agreed to invest $200,000 into an LLC with Lacy Lovett and Justin Lassiter. Lovett and Lassiter will not invest any money but will provide effort and expertise to the LLC. Lovett and Lassiter have agreed that the net income of the LLC should be divided so that Wilson is to receive a 10% preferred return on her capital investment prior to any remaining income being divided equally among the partners. In addition, Lovett and Lassiter have suggested that the operating agreement be written so that all matters are settled by majority vote, with each partner having a one-third voting interest in the LLC.

If you were providing Lindsey Wilson counsel, what might you suggest in forming the final agreement?

CP 12-4 Dividing partnership income

Terry Willard and Jasmine Hill decide to form a partnership. Willard will contribute $300,000 to the partnership, while Hill will contribute only $30,000. However, Hill will be responsible for running the day-to-day operations of the partnership, which are anticipated to require about 45 hours per week. In contrast, Willard will only work five hours per week for the partnership. The two partners are attempting to determine a formula for dividing partnership net income. Willard believes the partners should divide income in the ratio of 7:3, favoring Willard, since Willard provides the majority of the capital. Hill believes the income should be divided 7:3, favoring Hill, since Hill provides the majority of effort in running the partnership business.

How would you advise the partners in developing a method for dividing income?

CHAPTER

13 Corporations: Organization, Stock Transactions, and Dividends

RETAINED EARNINGS STATEMENT
For the Year Ended December 31, 20Y6

Retained earnings, Jan. 1, 20Y6		$XXX
Net income	$ XXX	
Dividends	(XXX)	
Increase in retained earnings		XXX
Retained earnings, Dec. 31, 20Y6		$XXX

STATEMENT OF CASH FLOWS
For the Year Ended December 31, 20Y6

Cash flows from (used for) operating activities	$XXX
Cash flows from (used for) investing activities	XXX
Cash flows from (used for) financing activities	XXX
Net increase (decrease) in cash	$XXX
Cash balance, January 1, 20Y6	XXX
Cash balance, December 31, 20Y6	$XXX

INCOME STATEMENT
For the Year Ended December 31, 20Y6

Sales		$XXX
Cost of merchandise sold		XXX
Gross profit		$XXX
Operating expenses:		
Advertising expense	$XXX	
Depreciation expense	XXX	
Amortization expense	XXX	
Depletion expense	XXX	
...	XXX	
...	XXX	
Total operating expenses		XXX
Income from operations		$XXX
Other revenue and expenses		XXX
Net income		$XXX

BALANCE SHEET
December 31, 20Y6

Assets:		
Current assets		$XXX
Property, plant, and equipment		XXX
Intangible assets		XXX
Total assets		$XXX
Liabilities:		
Current liabilities	$ XXX	
Long-term liabilities	XXX	
Total liabilities		$XXX
Stockholders' equity:		
Common stock	$ XXX	
Preferred stock	XXX	
Paid-in capital in excess of par	XXX	
Paid-in capital from sale of treasury stock	XXX	
Retained earnings	XXX	
Treasury stock	(XXX)	
Total stockholders' equity		XXX
Total liabilities and stockholders' equity		$XXX

CHAPTER 13

BENNY MARTY/SHUTTERSTOCK.COM

Alphabet (Google), Inc.*

If you purchase a share of stock from **Alphabet**, you own a small interest in the company. You may request an Alphabet stock certificate as an indication of your ownership.

Alphabet is one of the most visible companies on the Internet. Many of us cannot visit the Web without using Alphabet to power a search or to retrieve our email using Gmail. In addition, Alphabet has expanded into developing and offering free software platforms for mobile devices such as cell phones. For example, your cell phone may use Google's Android™ operating system. Yet Alphabet's Internet tools are free to online browsers. Alphabet generates most of its revenue through online advertising.

Purchasing a share of stock from Alphabet may be a great gift idea for the "hard-to-shop-for person." However, a stock certificate represents more than just a picture that you can frame. In fact, the stock certificate is a document that reflects legal ownership of the future financial prospects of Alphabet. In addition, as a shareholder, it represents your claim against the assets and earnings of the corporation.

If you are purchasing Alphabet stock as an investment, you should analyze Alphabet's financial statements and management's plans for the future. For example, Google first offered its stock to the public on August 19, 2004, for $100 per share. Alphabet's stock sells for more than $1,000 per share, even though it pays no dividends. In addition, Alphabet is authorized to issue convertible preferred stock, Class A stock, and Class B stock. Shares of Class A and Class B stock have been issued and are currently outstanding.

This chapter describes and illustrates the nature of corporations, including the accounting for stock and dividends. This discussion will aid you in understanding the differences between Alphabet's types of stock.

* In August 2015, Google, Inc., announced that it was reorganizing and changing the name of its company from Google to **Alphabet**. Alphabet will be the parent company for a number of different brands, including Google, Android, and YouTube.

Link to Alphabet........Pages 636, 637, 638, 639, 640, 644, 647, 649, 651

LEARNING OBJECTIVES

After studying this chapter, you should be able to:

Example Exercises (EE) are shown in **red.**

At a Glance 13 Page 656

OBJ. 1 Describe the nature of the corporate form of organization.

Nature of a Corporation

Most large businesses are organized as corporations. As a result, corporations generate more than 90% of the total business dollars in the United States. In contrast, most small businesses are organized as proprietorships, partnerships, or limited liability companies.

Characteristics of a Corporation

A *corporation* is a legal entity, distinct and separate from the individuals who create and operate it. As a legal entity, a corporation may acquire, own, and dispose of property in its own name. It may also incur liabilities and enter into contracts. Most importantly, it can sell shares of ownership, called **stock**. Issuing (selling) stock gives corporations the ability to raise large amounts of capital.

The **stockholders** or *shareholders* who own the stock own the corporation. They can buy and sell stock without affecting the corporation's operations or continued existence. Corporations whose shares of stock are traded in public markets are called *public corporations*. Corporations whose shares of stock are not traded publicly are usually owned by a small group of investors and are called *nonpublic* or *private corporations*.

Note

Corporations have a separate legal existence, transferable units of ownership, and limited stockholder liability.

The stockholders of a corporation have *limited liability*. This means that creditors usually may not go beyond the assets of the corporation to satisfy their claims. Thus, the financial loss that a stockholder may suffer is limited to the amount invested.

Stockholders' Equity

OBJ. 2 Describe the two main sources of stockholders' equity.

The owners' equity in a corporation is called **stockholders' equity**, *shareholders' equity, shareholders' investment,* or *capital.* On the balance sheet, stockholders' equity is reported by its following two main sources, as shown in Exhibit 4:

- Capital contributed to the corporation by the stockholders, called **paid-in capital** or *contributed capital*
- Net income retained in the business, called **retained earnings**

EXHIBIT 4

Sources of Stockholders' Equity

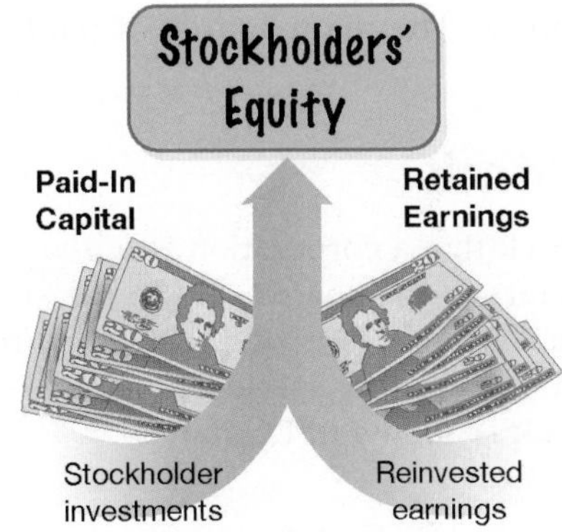

Link to Alphabet

Alphabet recently reported paid-in capital of $45 billion and retained earnings of $135 billion.

A Stockholders' Equity section of a balance sheet follows:[3]

Stockholders' Equity

Paid-in capital:		
Common stock	$330,000	
Retained earnings	80,000	
Total stockholders' equity		$410,000

The paid-in capital contributed by the stockholders is recorded in separate accounts for each class of stock. If there is only one class of stock, the account is entitled *Common Stock* or *Capital Stock.*

Retained earnings is a corporation's cumulative net income that has not been distributed as dividends. **Dividends** are distributions of a corporation's earnings to stockholders. Sometimes retained earnings that are not distributed as dividends are referred to in the financial statements as *earnings retained for use in the business* or *earnings reinvested in the business.*

Net income increases retained earnings, while a net loss and dividends decrease retained earnings. The net increase or decrease in retained earnings for a period is recorded by the following two closing entries:

1. Debit each revenue account for its balance, credit each expense account for its balance, and credit (net income) or debit (net loss) the retained earnings account.
2. Debit the retained earnings account for the balance of each dividend account and credit each dividend account.

Most companies generate net income. In addition, most companies do not pay out all of their net income in dividends. As a result, Retained Earnings normally has a credit balance. However, in some cases, a debit balance in Retained Earnings may occur. A debit balance in Retained Earnings is called a **deficit**. Such a balance results from accumulated net losses. In the Stockholders' Equity section, a deficit is deducted from paid-in capital in determining total stockholders' equity.

3 The reporting of stockholders' equity is further discussed and illustrated later in this chapter.

The balance of Retained Earnings represents earnings that have been reinvested back into the company. As cash is reinvested into the company, Cash decreases and Property, Plant, and Equipment or other assets increase. Because Retained Earnings is unaffected by the investments, its balance does not represent cash or cash available for dividends.

OBJ. 3 Describe and illustrate the characteristics of stock, classes of stock, and entries for issuing stock.

Paid-In Capital from Stock

The two main sources of stockholders' equity are paid-in capital (or contributed capital) and retained earnings. The main source of paid-in capital is from issuing stock.

Characteristics of Stock

The number of shares of stock that a corporation is *authorized* to issue is stated in its charter. The term *issued* refers to the shares sold to the stockholders. A corporation may reacquire some of the stock it has issued. The stock remaining in the hands of stockholders is then called **outstanding stock**. The relationship between authorized, issued, and outstanding stock is shown in Exhibit 5.

EXHIBIT 5

Authorized, Issued, and Outstanding Stock

Number of shares authorized, issued, and outstanding

Upon request, corporations may issue stock certificates to stockholders to document their ownership. Printed on a stock certificate is the name of the company, the name of the stockholder, and the number of shares owned. The stock certificate may also indicate a dollar amount assigned to each share of stock, called **par value**. Stock may be issued without par, in which case it is called *no-par stock*. In some states, the board of directors of a corporation is required to assign a *stated value* to no-par stock.

Corporations have limited liability; thus, creditors have no claim against stockholders' personal assets. To protect creditors, however, some states require corporations to maintain a minimum amount of paid-in capital. This minimum amount, called *legal capital*, usually includes the par or stated value of the shares issued.

Link to Alphabet

The par value of **Alphabet**'s stock is $0.001 per share.

The major rights that accompany ownership of a share of stock are as follows:

- The right to vote in matters concerning the corporation
- The right to share in distributions of earnings
- The right to share in assets upon liquidation

These stock rights normally vary with the class of stock.

Classes of Stock

When only one class of stock is issued, it is called **common stock**. Each share of common stock has equal rights. Recently, many public companies have begun issuing different classes of common stock with different rights.

A corporation may also issue one or more classes of stock with various preference rights, such as a preference to dividends. Such stock is called **preferred stock**. The dividend rights of preferred stock are stated either as dollars per share or as a percent of par. For example, $50 par value preferred stock with a $4-per-share dividend may be described as either:[4]

preferred $4 stock, $50 par
or
preferred 8% stock, $50 par

Alphabet has three classes of common stock outstanding: Class A has one vote per share, Class B has 10 votes per share, and Class C has no voting rights. The current executive chairman and the two original founders control over 60% of the voting power through their ownership of Class B stock.

As shown in Exhibit 6, preferred stockholders have first rights (preference) to any dividends; thus, they have a greater chance of receiving dividends than common stockholders do. However, since dividends are normally based on earnings, a corporation cannot guarantee dividends even to preferred stockholders.

EXHIBIT 6
Dividend Preferences

The payment of dividends is authorized by the corporation's board of directors. When authorized, the directors are said to have *declared* a dividend.

Cumulative preferred stock has a right to receive regular dividends that were not declared (paid) in prior years. Noncumulative preferred stock does not have this right.

Business Connection

YOU HAVE NO VOTE

An emerging trend in technology companies is using multiple classes of stock to concentrate voting control of the company to the founders. For example, Mark Zuckerberg, the founder and CEO of **Facebook**, owns Class B shares of Facebook. The public owns Class A shares. The Class B shares have 10 votes for every one vote in the Class A shares. As a result, Zuckerberg owns 16% of the stock but 60% of the voting rights of Facebook. Other companies using multiple classes of stock in this way include **Groupon**, **Zynga**, and **Yelp!**. While becoming prevalent among new technology companies, using multiple classes of stock is not a new idea. **The Hershey Company** has had two classes of stock since becoming a public company in 1927. **The Hershey Trust Company**, which oversees the Milton Hershey School for orphans, has 80% of the voting control of The Hershey Company by controlling super voting shares. The argument in favor of super voting rights is that the founders can concentrate on the long-term goals of the company without concern for possibly more short-term goals of public shareholders. The argument in opposition is that concentrating control among the founders can eliminate or reduce the public shareholders' ability to hold management accountable.

4 In some cases, preferred stock may receive additional dividends if certain conditions are met. Such stock, called *participating preferred stock*, is not often issued.

Link to Alphabet

Alphabet has 100,000,000 shares of authorized preferred stock with a par of $0.001, which are convertible to common stock. However, there are no shares of preferred stock issued or outstanding.

Cumulative preferred stock dividends that have not been paid in prior years are said to be **in arrears**. Any preferred dividends in arrears must be paid before any common stock dividends are paid. In addition, any dividends in arrears are normally disclosed in notes to the financial statements.

To illustrate, assume that a corporation has issued the following preferred and common stock:

1,000 shares of cumulative preferred $4 stock, $50 par
4,000 shares of common stock, $15 par

The corporation was organized on January 1, 20Y7, and paid no dividends in 20Y7 and 20Y8. In 20Y9, the corporation paid $22,000 in dividends, of which $12,000 was paid to preferred stockholders and $10,000 was paid to common stockholders, computed as follows:

Total dividends paid		$22,000
Preferred stockholders:		
20Y7 dividends in arrears (1,000 shares × $4)	$4,000	
20Y8 dividends in arrears (1,000 shares × $4)	4,000	
20Y9 dividend (1,000 shares × $4)	4,000	
Total preferred dividends paid		12,000
Dividends available to common stockholders		$10,000

Note

The two primary classes of paid-in capital are common stock and preferred stock.

As a result, preferred stockholders received $12.00 per share ($12,000 ÷ 1,000 shares) in dividends, while common stockholders received $2.50 per share ($10,000 ÷ 4,000 shares).

In addition to dividend preference, preferred stock may be given preferences to assets if the corporation goes out of business and is liquidated. However, claims of creditors must be satisfied first. Preferred stockholders are next in line to receive any remaining assets, followed by the common stockholders.

EXAMPLE EXERCISE 13-1 Dividend per Share **OBJ. 3**

Sandpiper Company has 20,000 shares of cumulative preferred 1% stock of $100 par and 100,000 shares of $50 par common stock. The following amounts were distributed as dividends:

Year 1	$10,000
Year 2	45,000
Year 3	80,000

Determine the dividend per share for preferred and common stock for each year.

Follow My Example 13-1

	Year 1	Year 2	Year 3
Amount distributed	$10,000	$45,000	$80,000
Preferred dividend (20,000 shares)	10,000	30,000*	20,000
Common dividend (100,000 shares)	$ 0	$15,000	$60,000
* Year 1 dividends in arrears of $10,000 plus Year 2 dividends of $20,000			
Dividend per share:			
Preferred stock	$0.50	$1.50	$1.00
Common stock	None	$0.15	$0.60

Practice Exercises: PE 13-1A, PE 13-1B

Issuing Stock

A separate account is used for recording the amount of each class of stock issued to investors in a corporation. For example, assume that a corporation is authorized to issue 10,000 shares of $100 par preferred stock and 100,000 shares of $20 par common stock. The corporation issued 5,000 shares of preferred stock and 50,000 shares of common stock at par for cash. The corporation's entry to record the stock issue is as follows:[5]

		Cash	1,500,000	
		Preferred Stock (5,000 shares × $100)		500,000
		Common Stock (50,000 shares × $20)		1,000,000
		Issued preferred stock and common stock at par for cash.		

Stock is often issued by a corporation at a price other than its par. The price at which stock is sold depends on a variety of factors, such as the following:

- The financial condition, earnings record, and dividend record of the corporation
- Investor expectations of the corporation's potential earning power
- General business and economic conditions and expectations

If stock is issued (sold) for a price that is more than its par, the stock has been sold at a **premium**. For example, if common stock with a par of $50 is sold for $60 per share, the stock has sold at a premium of $10.

If stock is issued (sold) for a price that is less than its par, the stock has been sold at a **discount**. For example, if common stock with a par of $50 is sold for $45 per share, the stock has sold at a discount of $5. Many states do not permit stock to be sold at a discount. In other states, stock may be sold at a discount in only unusual cases. For these reasons, the par value of common stock is often set at a low amount ($1 or less). Because stock is rarely sold at a discount, it is not illustrated.

In order to distribute dividends, financial statements, and other reports, a corporation must keep track of its stockholders. Large public corporations normally use a financial institution, such as a bank, for this purpose.[6] In such cases, the financial institution is referred to as a *transfer agent* or *registrar.*

Premium on Stock

When stock is issued at a premium, Cash is debited for the amount received. Common Stock or Preferred Stock is credited for the par amount. The excess of the amount paid over par is part of the paid-in capital. An account entitled *Paid-In Capital in Excess of Par* is credited for this amount.

To illustrate, assume that Caldwell Company issues 2,000 shares of $50 par preferred stock for cash at $55. The entry to record this transaction is as follows:

		Cash (2,000 shares × $55)	110,000	
		Preferred Stock (2,000 shares × $50)		100,000
		Paid-In Capital in Excess of Par—Preferred Stock		10,000
		Issued $50 par preferred stock at $55.		

When stock is issued in exchange for assets other than cash, such as land, buildings, and equipment, the assets acquired are recorded at their fair market value. If this value cannot be determined, the fair market price of the stock issued is used.

5 The accounting for investments in stocks from the point of view of the investor is discussed in Chapter 15.

6 Small corporations may use a subsidiary ledger, called a *stockholders ledger*. In this case, the stock accounts (Preferred Stock and Common Stock) are controlling accounts for the subsidiary ledger.

To illustrate, assume that a corporation acquired land with a fair market value that cannot be determined. In exchange, the corporation issued 10,000 shares of its $10 par common stock. If the stock has a market price of $12 per share, the transaction is recorded as follows:

		Land (10,000 shares × $12)	120,000	
		Common Stock (10,000 shares × $10)		100,000
		Paid-In Capital in Excess of Par—Common Stock		20,000
		Issued $10 par common stock, valued at $12 per share, for land.		

No-Par Stock

In most states, no-par preferred and common stock may be issued. When no-par stock is issued, Cash is debited and Common Stock is credited for the proceeds. As no-par stock is issued over time, this entry is the same even if the issuing price varies.

To illustrate, assume that on January 9, a corporation issues 10,000 shares of no-par common stock at $40 a share. On June 27, the corporation issues an additional 1,000 shares at $36. The entries to record these issuances of the no-par stock are as follows:

Jan.	9	Cash	400,000	
		Common Stock		400,000
		Issued 10,000 shares of no-par common stock at $40.		
Jun.	27	Cash	36,000	
		Common Stock		36,000
		Issued 1,000 shares of no-par common stock at $36.		

In some states, no-par stock may be assigned a *stated value per share*. The stated value is recorded like a par value. Any excess of the proceeds over the stated value is credited to *Paid-In Capital in Excess of Stated Value*.

To illustrate, assume that in the preceding example, the no-par common stock is assigned a stated value of $25. The issuance of the stock on January 9 and June 27 is recorded as follows:

Jan.	9	Cash (10,000 shares × $40)	400,000	
		Common Stock (10,000 shares × $25)		250,000
		Paid-In Capital in Excess of Stated Value		150,000
		Issued 10,000 shares of no-par common stock at $40; stated value, $25.		
Jun.	27	Cash (1,000 shares × $36)	36,000	
		Common Stock (1,000 shares × $25)		25,000
		Paid-In Capital in Excess of Stated Value		11,000
		Issued 1,000 shares of no-par common stock at $36; stated value, $25.		

Integrity, Objectivity, and Ethics in Business

THE PROFESSOR WHO KNEW TOO MUCH

A major Midwestern university released a quarterly "American Customer Satisfaction Index" based on its research of customers of popular U.S. products and services. Before the release of the index to the public, the professor in charge of the research bought and sold stocks of some of the companies in the report. The professor was quoted as saying that he thought it was important to test his theories of customer satisfaction with "real" [his own] money.

Is this proper or ethical? Apparently, the dean of the Business School didn't think so. In a statement to the press, the dean stated: "I have instructed anyone affiliated with the (index) not to make personal use of information gathered in the course of producing the quarterly index, prior to the index's release to the general public, and they [the researchers] have agreed."

Sources: Jon E. Hilsenrath and Dan Morse, "Researcher Uses Index to Buy, Short Stocks," *Wall Street Journal*, February 18, 2003; and Jon E. Hilsenrath, "Satisfaction Theory: Mixed Results," *Wall Street Journal*, February 19, 2003.

EXAMPLE EXERCISE 13-2 Entries for Issuing Stock — OBJ. 3

On March 6, Limerick Corporation issued for cash 15,000 shares of no-par common stock at $30. On April 13, Limerick issued at par 1,000 shares of preferred 4% stock, $40 par for cash. On May 19, Limerick issued for cash 15,000 shares of 4%, $40 par preferred stock at $42.

Journalize the entries to record the March 6, April 13, and May 19 transactions.

Follow My Example 13-2

Date	Account	Debit	Credit
Mar. 6	Cash (15,000 shares × $30)	450,000	
	Common Stock		450,000
Apr. 13	Cash (1,000 shares × $40)	40,000	
	Preferred Stock		40,000
May 19	Cash (15,000 shares × $42)	630,000	
	Preferred Stock (15,000 shares × $40)		600,000
	Paid-In Capital in Excess of Par—Preferred Stock		30,000

Practice Exercises: PE 13-2A, PE 13-2B

Accounting for Dividends

OBJ. 4 Describe and illustrate the accounting for cash dividends and stock dividends.

When a board of directors declares a cash dividend, it authorizes the distribution of cash to stockholders. When a board of directors declares a stock dividend, it authorizes the distribution of its stock. In both cases, declaring a dividend reduces the retained earnings of the corporation.[7]

Cash Dividends

A cash distribution of earnings by a corporation to its shareholders is a **cash dividend**. Although dividends may be paid in other assets, cash dividends are the most common.

Three conditions for a cash dividend are as follows:

- Sufficient retained earnings
- Sufficient cash
- Formal action by the board of directors

7 In rare cases, when a corporation is reducing its operations or going out of business, a dividend may be a distribution of paid-in capital. Such a dividend is called a *liquidating dividend*.

There must be a sufficient (large enough) balance in Retained Earnings to declare a cash dividend. That is, the balance of Retained Earnings must be large enough so that the dividend does not create a debit balance in the retained earnings account. However, a large Retained Earnings balance does not mean that there is cash available to pay dividends. This is because the balances, as discussed earlier, of Cash and Retained Earnings are often unrelated.

Even if there are sufficient retained earnings and cash, a corporation's board of directors is not required to pay dividends. Nevertheless, many corporations pay quarterly cash dividends to make their stock more attractive to investors. *Special* or *extra dividends* may also be paid when a corporation experiences higher than normal profits.

Link to Alphabet

Alphabet has never paid a cash dividend and has no intention of doing so in the foreseeable future.

Three dates included in a dividend announcement are as follows:

1. Date of declaration
2. Date of record
3. Date of payment

The *date of declaration* is the date the board of directors formally authorizes the payment of the dividend. On this date, the corporation incurs the liability to pay the amount of the dividend.

The *date of record* is the date the corporation uses to determine which stockholders will receive the dividend. During the period of time between the date of declaration and the date of record, the stock price is quoted as selling *with-dividends*. This means that any investors purchasing the stock before the date of record will receive the dividend.

The *date of payment* is the date the corporation will pay the dividend to the stockholders who owned the stock on the date of record. During the period of time between the record date and the payment date, the stock price is quoted as selling *ex-dividends*. This means that since the date of record has passed, any new investors will not receive the dividend.

To illustrate, assume that on October 1, Hiber Corporation declares the following cash dividends with a date of record of November 10 and a date of payment of December 2:

	Dividend per Share	Total Dividends
Preferred stock, $100 par, 5,000 shares outstanding....................	$2.50	$12,500
Common stock, $10 par, 100,000 shares outstanding	$0.30	30,000
Total		$42,500

On October 1, the declaration date, Hiber Corporation records the following entry:

Declaration Date

Oct.	1	Cash Dividends		42,500	
		Cash Dividends Payable			42,500
		Declared cash dividends.			

Date of Record

On November 10, the date of record, no entry is necessary. This date merely determines which stockholders will receive the dividends.

On December 2, the date of payment, Hiber Corporation records the payment of the dividends as follows:

Date of Payment

Dec.	2	Cash Dividends Payable		42,500	
		Cash			42,500
		Paid cash dividends.			

At the end of the accounting period, the balance in Cash Dividends will be transferred to Retained Earnings as part of the closing process. This closing entry debits Retained Earnings and credits Cash Dividends for the balance of the cash dividends account. If the cash dividends have not been paid by the end of the period, Cash Dividends Payable will be reported on the balance sheet as a current liability.

EXAMPLE EXERCISE 13-3 Entries for Cash Dividends **OBJ. 4**

The important dates in connection with a cash dividend of $75,000 on a corporation's common stock are February 26, March 30, and April 2. Journalize the entries required on each date.

Follow My Example 13-3

Feb. 26	Cash Dividends	75,000	
	Cash Dividends Payable		75,000
Mar. 30	No entry required.		
Apr. 2	Cash Dividends Payable	75,000	
	Cash		75,000

Practice Exercises: PE 13-3A, PE 13-3B

Stock Dividends

A **stock dividend** is a distribution of shares of stock to stockholders. Stock dividends are normally declared only on common stock and issued to common stockholders.

A stock dividend affects only stockholders' equity. Specifically, the amount of the stock dividend is transferred from Retained Earnings to Paid-In Capital. The amount transferred is normally the fair value (market price) of the shares issued in the stock dividend.[8]

To illustrate, assume that the stockholders' equity accounts of Hendrix Corporation as of December 15 are as follows:

Common Stock, $20 par (2,000,000 shares issued)	$40,000,000
Paid-In Capital in Excess of Par—Common Stock	9,000,000
Retained Earnings	26,600,000

On December 15, Hendrix Corporation declares a stock dividend of 5% or 100,000 shares (2,000,000 shares × 5%) to be issued on January 10 to stockholders of record on December 31. The market price of the stock on December 15 (the date of declaration) is $31 per share.

The entry to record the stock dividend is as follows:

Dec.	15	Stock Dividends (100,000 shares × $31)		3,100,000	
		Stock Dividends Distributable (100,000 shares × $20)			2,000,000
		Paid-In Capital in Excess of Par—Common Stock			1,100,000
		Declared 5% (100,000 shares) stock dividend on $20 par common stock with a market price of $31 per share.			

After the preceding entry is recorded, Stock Dividends will have a debit balance of $3,100,000. Like cash dividends, the stock dividends account is closed to Retained Earnings at the end of the accounting period. This closing entry debits Retained Earnings and credits Stock Dividends.

8 The use of fair market value is justified as long as the number of shares issued for the stock dividend is small (less than 25% of the shares outstanding).

On December 31, the *stock dividends distributable* and *paid-in capital in excess of par—common stock* accounts are reported in the Paid-In Capital section of Hendrix Corporation's balance sheet. The effect of the preceding stock dividend is to transfer $3,100,000 of retained earnings to paid-in capital.

On January 10, the stock dividend is distributed to stockholders by issuing 100,000 shares of common stock. The issuance of the stock is recorded by the following entry:

Jan.	10	Stock Dividends Distributable		2,000,000	
		Common Stock			2,000,000
		Issued stock as stock dividend.			

A stock dividend does not change the assets, liabilities, or total stockholders' equity of a corporation. Likewise, a stock dividend does not change an individual stockholder's proportionate interest (equity) in the corporation.

To illustrate, assume that a stockholder owns 1,000 of a corporation's 10,000 shares outstanding. If the corporation declares a 6% stock dividend, the stockholder's proportionate interest will not change, computed as follows:

	Before **Stock Dividend**	***After*** **Stock Dividend**
Total shares issued	10,000	10,600 [10,000 + (10,000 × 6%)]
Number of shares owned	1,000	1,060 [1,000 + (1,000 × 6%)]
Proportionate ownership	10% (1,000 ÷ 10,000)	10% (1,060 ÷ 10,600)

EXAMPLE EXERCISE 13-4 Entries for Stock Dividends **OBJ. 4**

Vienna Highlights Corporation has 150,000 shares of $100 par common stock outstanding. On June 14, Vienna Highlights declared a 4% stock dividend to be issued August 15 to stockholders of record on July 1. The market price of the stock was $110 per share on June 14.

Journalize the entries required on June 14, July 1, and August 15.

Follow My Example 13-4

June 14	Stock Dividends (150,000 shares × 4% × $110).......................	660,000	
	Stock Dividends Distributable (6,000 shares × $100).............		600,000
	Paid-In Capital in Excess of Par—Common Stock..................		60,000
July 1	No entry required.		
Aug. 15	Stock Dividends Distributable..	600,000	
	Common Stock..		600,000

Practice Exercises: PE 13-4A, PE 13-4B

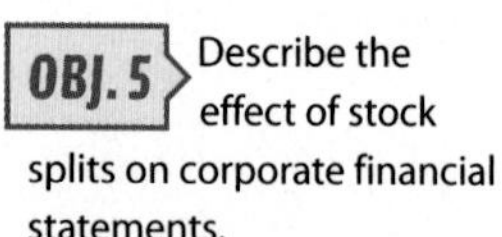
Describe the effect of stock splits on corporate financial statements.

Stock Splits

A **stock split** is a process by which a corporation reduces the par or stated value of its common stock and issues a proportionate number of additional shares. A stock split applies to all common shares including the unissued, issued, and treasury shares.

A major objective of a stock split is to reduce the market price per share of the stock. This attracts more investors and broadens the types and numbers of stockholders.

To illustrate, assume that Rojek Corporation has 10,000 shares of $100 par common stock outstanding with a current market price of $150 per share. The board of directors declares the following stock split:

1. Each common shareholder will receive five shares for each share held. This is called a 5-for-l stock split. As a result, 50,000 shares (10,000 shares × 5) will be outstanding.
2. The par of each share of common stock will be reduced to $20 ($100 ÷ 5).

Link to Alphabet

In 2014, **Alphabet** implemented a 2-for-1 stock split through the issue of Class C common stock.

The par value of the common stock outstanding is $1,000,000 both before and after the stock split, computed as follows:

	Before Split	After Split
Number of shares	10,000	50,000
Par value per share	× $100	× $20
Total	$1,000,000	$1,000,000

In addition, each Rojek Corporation shareholder owns the same total par amount of stock before and after the stock split as shown in Exhibit 7. For example, a stockholder who owned 4 shares of $100 par stock before the split (total par of $400) would own 20 shares of $20 par stock after the split (total par of $400). Only the number of shares and the par value per share have changed.

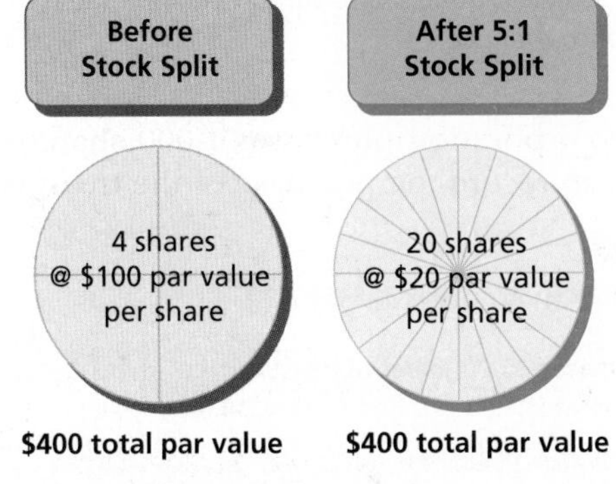

EXHIBIT 7

Stock Split: Before and After

Because there are more shares outstanding after the stock split, the market price of the stock should decrease. For example, in the preceding example, there would be five times as many shares outstanding after the split. Thus, the market price of the stock would be expected to fall from $150 to about $30 ($150 ÷ 5).

Stock splits do not require a journal entry because only the par (or stated) value and number of shares outstanding have changed. However, the details of stock splits are normally disclosed in the notes to the financial statements.

A stock split does not require a journal entry.

Business Connection

BUFFETT ON STOCK SPLITS

Warren E. Buffett, the chairman and chief executive officer of **Berkshire Hathaway Inc.**, opposes stock splits on the basis that they add no value to the company. Since its inception, Berkshire Hathaway has never declared a stock split on its primary (Class A) common stock. As a result, Berkshire Hathaway's Class A common stock sells well above $300,000 per share, which is the most expensive stock on the New York Stock Exchange. Such a high price doesn't bother Buffet because he believes that high stock prices attract more sophisticated and long-term investors and discourage stock speculators and short-term investors.

In contrast, **Microsoft Corporation** has split its stock nine times since it went public in 1986. As a result, one share of Microsoft purchased in 1986 is equivalent to 288 shares today, which would be worth more than $30,000.

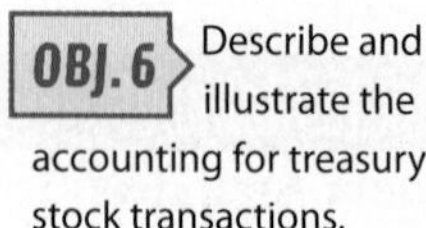

Describe and illustrate the accounting for treasury stock transactions.

Treasury Stock Transactions

Treasury stock is stock that a corporation has issued and then reacquired. A corporation may reacquire (purchase) its own stock for a variety of reasons, including the following:

- To provide shares for resale to employees
- To reissue as bonuses to employees
- To support the market price of the stock

The *cost method* is normally used for recording the purchase and resale of treasury stock.[9] Using the cost method, *Treasury Stock* is debited for the cost (purchase price) of the stock. When the stock is resold, Treasury Stock is credited for its cost. Any difference between the cost and the selling price is debited or credited to *Paid-In Capital from Sale of Treasury Stock.*

To illustrate, assume that a corporation has the following paid-in capital on January 1:

Common stock, $25 par (20,000 shares authorized and issued)	$500,000
Excess of issue price over par	150,000
	$650,000

On February 13, the corporation purchases 1,000 shares of its common stock at $45 per share. The entry to record the purchase of the treasury stock is as follows:

Feb.	13	Treasury Stock (1,000 shares × $45)		45,000	
		Cash			45,000
		Purchased 1,000 shares of treasury stock at $45.			

On April 29, the corporation sells 600 shares of the treasury stock for $60 per share. The entry to record the sale is as follows:

Apr.	29	Cash (600 shares × $60)		36,000	
		Treasury Stock (600 shares × $45)			27,000
		Paid-In Capital from Sale of Treasury Stock			9,000
		Sold 600 shares of treasury stock at $60.			

A sale of treasury stock may result in a decrease in paid-in capital. To the extent that Paid-In Capital from Sale of Treasury Stock has a credit balance, it is debited for any such decrease. Any remaining decrease is then debited to the retained earnings account.

To illustrate, assume that on October 4, the corporation sells the remaining 400 shares of treasury stock for $40 per share. The entry to record the sale is as follows:

Oct.	4	Cash (400 shares × $40)		16,000	
		Paid-In Capital from Sale of Treasury Stock		2,000	
		Treasury Stock (400 shares × $45)			18,000
		Sold 400 shares of treasury stock at $40.			

The preceding October 4 entry decreases paid-in capital by $2,000. Because Paid-In Capital from Sale of Treasury Stock has a credit balance of $9,000, the entire $2,000 was debited to Paid-In Capital from Sale of Treasury Stock.

No dividends (cash or stock) are paid on the shares of treasury stock. To do so would result in the corporation earning dividend revenue from itself.

9 Another method that is used infrequently, called the *par value method*, is discussed in advanced accounting texts.

EXAMPLE EXERCISE 13-5 Entries for Treasury Stock **OBJ. 6**

On May 3, Buzz Off Corporation reacquired 3,200 shares of its common stock at $42 per share. On July 22, Buzz Off sold 2,000 of the reacquired shares at $47 per share. On August 30, Buzz Off sold the remaining shares at $40 per share.

Journalize the transactions of May 3, July 22, and August 30.

Follow My Example 13-5

May 3	Treasury Stock (3,200 × $42)	134,400	
	Cash		134,400
July 22	Cash (2,000 × $47)	94,000	
	Treasury Stock (2,000 × $42)		84,000
	Paid-In Capital from Sale of Treasury Stock [2,000 × ($47 – $42)]		10,000
Aug. 30	Cash (1,200 × $40)	48,000	
	Paid-In Capital from Sale of Treasury Stock [1,200 × ($42 – $40)]	2,400	
	Treasury Stock (1,200 × $42)		50,400

Practice Exercises: PE 13-5A, PE 13-5B

Business Connection

TREASURY STOCK OR DIVIDENDS?

A company has two major ways to return cash to shareholders: paying cash dividends and repurchasing its stock. A shareholder preferring a current cash income may want to receive a steady cash dividend. A shareholder preferring share price appreciation may want stock repurchases. This is because when a company purchases treasury stock, the amount of shares outstanding will decline and the market value per share should increase. Another consideration is that cash dividends are currently taxed at 15% while the gains on share price increases are tax-deferred until sold. A company may prefer returning cash through stock repurchases because it gives management greater flexibility in managing the company's cash flows. It is considered more difficult to decrease a cash dividend than it is to reduce share repurchases over time. So, overall, the answer to the question depends on circumstances. This is likely why many companies pay dividends and repurchase stock.

Reporting Stockholders' Equity

OBJ. 7 Describe and illustrate the reporting of stockholders' equity.

As with other sections of the balance sheet, alternative terms and formats may be used in reporting stockholders' equity. Also, changes in retained earnings and paid-in capital may be reported in separate statements or notes to the financial statements.

Stockholders' Equity on the Balance Sheet

Exhibit 8 shows two methods for reporting stockholders' equity for the December 31, 20Y7, balance sheet for Telex Inc.

Method 1. Each class of stock is reported, followed by its related paid-in capital accounts. Retained earnings is then reported followed by a deduction for treasury stock.

Method 2. The stock accounts are reported, followed by the paid-in capital reported as a single item, additional paid-in capital. Retained earnings is then reported followed by a deduction for treasury stock.

Link to Alphabet

Alphabet has the following shares of common stock outstanding: Class A, 298,470,000; Class B, 46,972,000; and Class C, 349,341,000.

EXHIBIT 8 **Stockholders' Equity Section of a Balance Sheet**

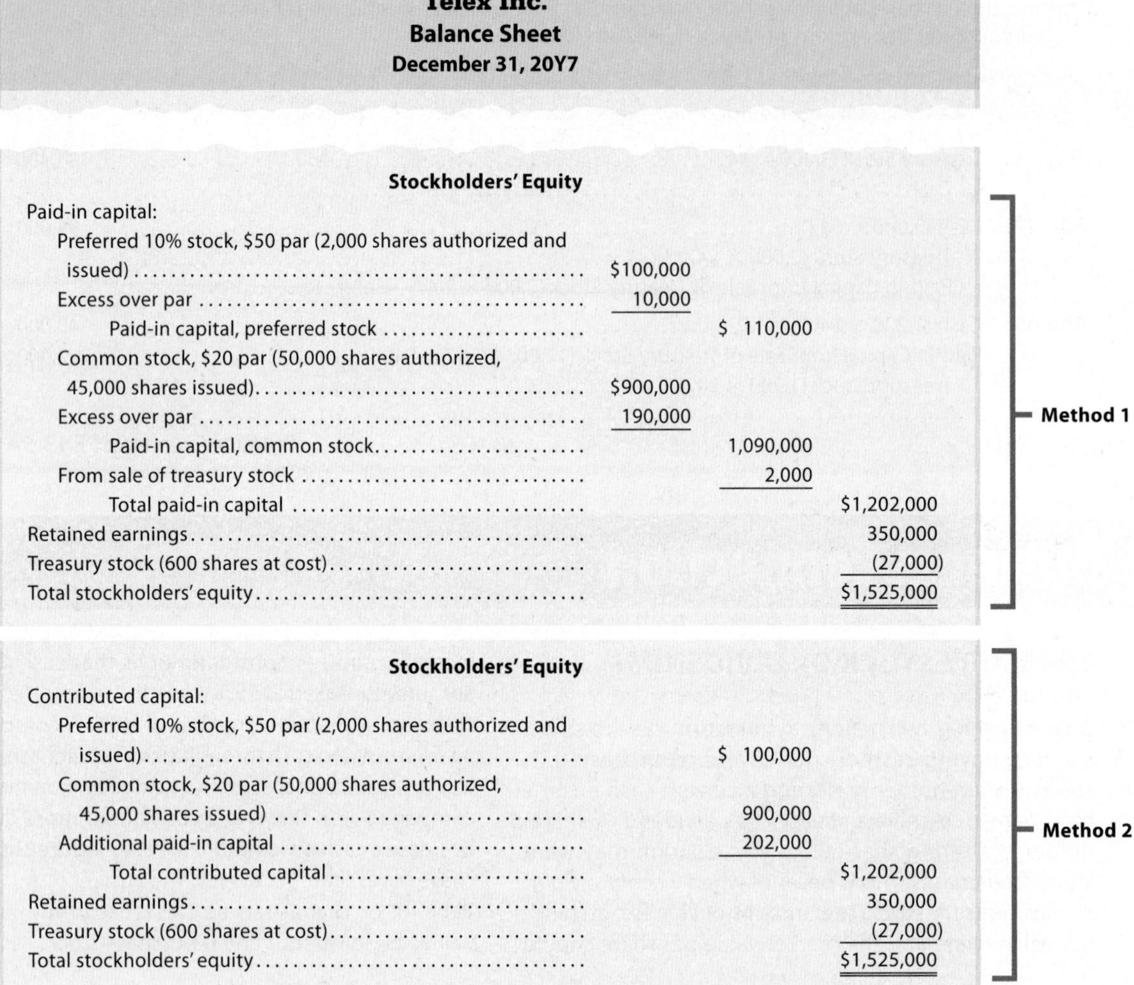

Telex Inc.
Balance Sheet
December 31, 20Y7

Stockholders' Equity (Method 1)

Paid-in capital:			
Preferred 10% stock, $50 par (2,000 shares authorized and issued)	$100,000		
Excess over par	10,000		
Paid-in capital, preferred stock		$ 110,000	
Common stock, $20 par (50,000 shares authorized, 45,000 shares issued)	$900,000		
Excess over par	190,000		
Paid-in capital, common stock		1,090,000	
From sale of treasury stock		2,000	
Total paid-in capital			$1,202,000
Retained earnings			350,000
Treasury stock (600 shares at cost)			(27,000)
Total stockholders' equity			$1,525,000

Stockholders' Equity (Method 2)

Contributed capital:		
Preferred 10% stock, $50 par (2,000 shares authorized and issued)	$ 100,000	
Common stock, $20 par (50,000 shares authorized, 45,000 shares issued)	900,000	
Additional paid-in capital	202,000	
Total contributed capital		$1,202,000
Retained earnings		350,000
Treasury stock (600 shares at cost)		(27,000)
Total stockholders' equity		$1,525,000

Significant changes in stockholders' equity during a period may also be presented in a statement of stockholders' equity or in the notes to the financial statements. The statement of stockholders' equity is illustrated later in this section.

Relevant rights and privileges of the various classes of stock outstanding should also be reported.[10] Examples include dividend and liquidation preferences, conversion rights, and redemption rights. Such information may be disclosed on the face of the balance sheet or in the notes to the financial statements.

EXAMPLE EXERCISE 13-6 Reporting Stockholders' Equity **OBJ. 7**

Using the following accounts and balances, prepare the Stockholders' Equity section of the balance sheet using Method 1 of Exhibit 8. Forty thousand shares of common stock are authorized, and 5,000 shares have been reacquired.

Common Stock, $50 par	$1,500,000
Paid-In Capital from Sale of Treasury Stock	44,000
Paid-In Capital in Excess of Par	160,000
Retained Earnings	4,395,000
Treasury Stock	120,000

10 *FASB Accounting Standards Codification,* Section 505-10-50.

Follow My Example 13-6

Stockholders' Equity

Paid-in capital:			
Common stock, $50 par (40,000 shares authorized, 30,000 shares issued)	$1,500,000		
Excess over par	160,000		
Paid-in capital, common stock		$1,660,000	
From sale of treasury stock		44,000	
Total paid-in capital			$1,704,000
Retained earnings			4,395,000
Treasury stock (5,000 shares at cost)			(120,000)
Total stockholders' equity			$5,979,000

Practice Exercises: PE 13-6A, PE 13-6B

Reporting Retained Earnings

Changes in retained earnings may be reported using one of the following:

- Separate retained earnings statement
- Combined income and retained earnings statement
- Statement of stockholders' equity

Changes in retained earnings may be reported in a separate retained earnings statement. When a separate **retained earnings statement** is prepared, the beginning balance of retained earnings is reported. The net income is then added (or net loss is subtracted) and any dividends are subtracted to arrive at the ending retained earnings for the period.

To illustrate, a retained earnings statement for Telex Inc. is shown in Exhibit 9.

EXHIBIT 9

Retained Earnings Statement

Telex Inc.
Retained Earnings Statement
For the Year Ended December 31, 20Y7

Retained earnings, January 1, 20Y7		$245,000
Net income	$180,000	
Dividends:		
Preferred stock dividends	(10,000)	
Common stock dividends	(65,000)	
Increase in retained earnings		105,000
Retained earnings, December 31, 20Y7		$350,000

Link to Alphabet

Alphabet does not report a separate retained earnings statement but instead reports changes in retained earnings in its statement of stockholders' equity.

Changes in retained earnings may also be reported in combination with the income statement. This format emphasizes net income as the connecting link between the income statement and ending retained earnings. Because this format is not often used, it is not illustrated here.

Changes in retained earnings may also be reported in a statement of stockholders' equity. An example of reporting changes in retained earnings in a statement of stockholders' equity for Telex Inc. is shown in Exhibit 10.

EXAMPLE EXERCISE 13-7 Retained Earnings Statement **OBJ. 7**

Dry Creek Cameras Inc. reported the following results for the year ending March 31, 20Y6:

Retained earnings, April 1, 20Y5	$3,338,500
Net income	461,500
Cash dividends declared	80,000
Stock dividends declared	120,000

Prepare a retained earnings statement for the fiscal year ended March 31, 20Y6.

Follow My Example 13-7

Dry Creek Cameras Inc.
Retained Earnings Statement
For the Year Ended March 31, 20Y6

Retained earnings, April 1, 20Y5		$3,338,500
Net income	$ 461,500	
Dividends declared	(200,000)	
Increase in retained earnings		261,500
Retained earnings, March 31, 20Y6		$3,600,000

Practice Exercises: PE 13-7A, PE 13-7B

Restrictions The use of retained earnings for payment of dividends may be restricted by action of a corporation's board of directors. Such **restrictions**, sometimes called *appropriations*, remain part of the retained earnings.

Restrictions of retained earnings are classified as:

- *Legal.* State laws may require a restriction of retained earnings.

  Example: States may restrict retained earnings by the amount of treasury stock purchased. In this way, legal capital cannot be used for dividends.

- *Contractual.* A corporation may enter into contracts that require restrictions of retained earnings.

  Example: A bank loan may restrict retained earnings so that the amount for repaying the loan cannot be used for dividends.

- *Discretionary.* A corporation's board of directors may restrict retained earnings voluntarily.

  Example: The board may restrict retained earnings and, thus, limit dividend distributions so that earnings are available for expanding the business.

Restrictions of retained earnings must be disclosed in the financial statements. Such disclosures are usually included in the notes to the financial statements.

Prior Period Adjustments An error may arise from a mathematical mistake or from a mistake in applying accounting principles. Such errors may not be discovered within the same period in which they occur. In such cases, the effect of the error should not affect the current period's net income. Instead, the correction of the error, called a **prior period adjustment**, is reported in the retained earnings statement. Such corrections are reported as an adjustment to the beginning balance of retained earnings.[11]

Statement of Stockholders' Equity

When the only change in stockholders' equity is due to net income or net loss and dividends, a retained earnings statement is sufficient. However, when a corporation

11 Prior period adjustments are illustrated in advanced texts.

also has changes in stock and paid-in capital accounts, a **statement of stockholders' equity** is normally prepared.

A statement of stockholders' equity is normally prepared in a columnar format. Each column is a major stockholders' equity classification. Changes in each classification are then described in the left-hand column. Exhibit 10 illustrates a statement of stockholders' equity for Telex Inc.

Statement of Stockholders' Equity **EXHIBIT 10**

Telex Inc.
Statement of Stockholders' Equity
For the Year Ended December 31, 20Y7

	Preferred Stock	Common Stock	Additional Paid-In Capital	Retained Earnings	Treasury Stock	Total
Balance, January 1, 20Y7	$100,000	$850,000	$177,000	$245,000	$(17,000)	$1,355,000
Issuance of additional common stock		50,000	25,000			75,000
Purchase of treasury stock					(10,000)	(10,000)
Net income				180,000		180,000
Dividends on preferred stock				(10,000)		(10,000)
Dividends on common stock				(65,000)		(65,000)
Balance, December 31, 20Y7	$100,000	$900,000	$202,000	$350,000	$(27,000)	$1,525,000

International Connection

IFRS INTERNATIONAL FINANCIAL REPORTING STANDARDS FOR SMEs

In 2010, the International Accounting Standards Board (IASB) issued a set of accounting standards specifically designed for small- and medium-sized enterprises (SMEs) called International Financial Reporting Standards (IFRS) for SMEs. SMEs in the United States are private companies and such small corporations that they do not report to the Securities and Exchange Commission (SEC). IFRS for SMEs consist of only 230 pages, compared to 2,700 pages for full IFRS. These standards are designed to be cost effective for SMEs. Thus, IFRS for SMEs require fewer disclosures and contain no industry-specific standards or exceptions.

The American Institute of CPAs (AICPA) has accepted IFRS for SMEs as part of U.S. generally accepted accounting principles (GAAP) for private companies not reporting to the SEC. If users, such as bankers and investors, accept these financial statements, IFRS for SMEs may become popular in the United States.

Reporting Stockholders' Equity for Mornin' Joe

Mornin' Joe reports stockholders' equity in its balance sheet. Mornin' Joe also includes a retained earnings statement and statement of stockholders' equity in its financial statements.

The Stockholders' Equity section of Mornin' Joe's balance sheet as of December 31, 20Y6, follows:

Mornin' Joe
Balance Sheet
December 31, 20Y6

Stockholders' Equity

Paid-in capital:		
Preferred 10% stock, $50 par (6,000 shares authorized and issued)	$ 300,000	
Excess of issue price over par	50,000	$ 350,000
Common stock, $20 par (50,000 shares authorized, 45,000 shares issued)	$ 900,000	
Excess of issue price over par	1,450,000	2,350,000
Total paid-in capital		$2,700,000
Retained earnings		1,200,300
Treasury stock (1,000 shares at cost)		(46,000)
Total stockholders' equity		$3,854,300
Total liabilities and stockholders' equity		$6,169,700

Mornin' Joe's retained earnings statement for the year ended December 31, 20Y6, is as follows:

Mornin' Joe
Retained Earnings Statment
For the Year Ended December 31, 20Y6

Retained earnings, January 1, 20Y6		$ 852,700
Net income	$421,600	
Dividends:		
Preferred stock	(30,000)	
Common stock	(44,000)	
Increase in retained earnings		347,600
Retained earnings, December 31, 20Y6		$1,200,300

The statement of stockholders' equity for Mornin' Joe follows:

Mornin' Joe
Statement of Stockholders' Equity
For the Year Ended December 31, 20Y6

	Preferred Stock	Common Stock	Additional Paid-In Capital	Retained Earnings	Treasury Stock	Total
Balance, January 1, 20Y6	$300,000	$800,000	$1,325,000	$ 852,700	$(36,000)	$3,241,700
Issuance of additional common stock		100,000	175,000			275,000
Purchase of treasury stock					(10,000)	(10,000)
Net income				421,600		421,600
Dividends on preferred stock				(30,000)		(30,000)
Dividends on common stock				(44,000)		(44,000)
Balance, December 31, 20Y6	$300,000	$900,000	$1,500,000	$1,200,300	$(46,000)	$3,854,300

Financial Analysis and Interpretation: Earnings per Share

Describe and illustrate the use of earnings per share in evaluating a company's profitability.

FAI

Net income is often used by investors and creditors in evaluating a company's profitability. However, net income by itself is difficult to use in comparing companies of different sizes. Also, trends in net income may be difficult to evaluate if there have been significant changes in a company's stockholders' equity. Thus, the profitability of companies is often expressed as earnings per share.

Earnings per share (EPS), sometimes called *earnings per common share* or *basic earnings per share,* is the net income per share of common stock outstanding during a period.[12] Corporations whose stock is traded in a public market must report earnings per common share on their income statements.

Earnings per share is computed as follows:

$$\text{Earnings per Share} = \frac{\text{Net Income} - \text{Preferred Dividends}}{\text{Average Number of Common Shares Outstanding}}$$

If a company has preferred stock outstanding, any preferred dividends are subtracted from net income. This is because the numerator represents only those earnings available to the common shareholders.

To illustrate, the following data (in thousands) were taken from recent financial statements of **Alphabet**:

	Year 2	Year 1
Net income	$30,736,000	$12,662,000
Average number of common shares outstanding	695,170 shares	693,049 shares
Earnings per share	$44.21	$18.27
	($30,736,000 ÷ 695,170 shares)	($12,662,000 ÷ 693,049 shares)

Alphabet had no preferred stock outstanding; thus, no preferred dividends were subtracted in computing earnings per share. As illustrated, Alphabet's earnings per share increased from $18.27 in Year 1 to $44.21 in Year 2. An increase in earnings per share is generally considered a favorable change.

Earnings per share can be used to compare two companies with different net incomes. For example, the following data (in millions) were taken from a recent year's financial statements for **Bank of America Corporation** and **Wells Fargo & Company**:

	Bank of America	Wells Fargo
Net income	$28,147	$22,393
Preferred dividends	$1,451	$1,704
Average number of common shares outstanding	10,097 shares	4,800 shares

Bank of America:

$$\text{Earnings per Share} = \frac{\text{Net Income} - \text{Preferred Dividends}}{\text{Average Number of Common Shares Outstanding}} = \frac{\$28,147 - \$1,451}{10,097 \text{ shares}} = \frac{\$26,696}{10,097 \text{ shares}} = \$2.64$$

Wells Fargo:

$$\text{Earnings per Share} = \frac{\text{Net Income} - \text{Preferred Dividends}}{\text{Average Number of Common Shares Outstanding}} = \frac{\$22,393 - \$1,704}{4,800 \text{ shares}} = \frac{\$20,689}{4,800 \text{ shares}} = \$4.31$$

Based on earnings per share, Wells Fargo is more profitable than Bank of America.

12 For complex capital structures, earnings per share assuming dilution may also be reported as described in Chapter 17.

EXAMPLE EXERCISE 13-8 Earnings per Share

OBJ. 8

Financial statement data for years ending December 31 for Finnegan Company follow:

	20Y2	20Y1
Net income	$350,000	$195,000
Preferred dividends	$20,000	$15,000
Average number of common shares outstanding	75,000 shares	50,000 shares

a. Determine earnings per share for 20Y2 and 20Y1.

b. Does the change in the earnings per share from 20Y1 to 20Y2 indicate a favorable or unfavorable trend?

Follow My Example 13-8

a.

20Y2:

$$\text{Earnings per Share} = \frac{\text{Net Income} - \text{Preferred Dividends}}{\text{Average Number of Common Shares Outstanding}} = \frac{\$350{,}000 - \$20{,}000}{75{,}000 \text{ shares}} = \frac{\$330{,}000}{75{,}000 \text{ shares}} = \$4.40$$

20Y1:

$$\text{Earnings per Share} = \frac{\text{Net Income} - \text{Preferred Dividends}}{\text{Average Number of Common Shares Outstanding}} = \frac{\$195{,}000 - \$15{,}000}{50{,}000 \text{ shares}} = \frac{\$180{,}000}{50{,}000 \text{ shares}} = \$3.60$$

b. The increase in the earnings per share from $3.60 to $4.40 indicates a favorable trend in the company's profitability.

Practice Exercises: PE 13-8A, PE 13-8B

At a Glance 13

OBJ. 1 Describe the nature of the corporate form of organization.

Key Points Corporations have a separate legal existence, transferable units of stock, unlimited life, and limited stockholders' liability. The advantages and disadvantages of the corporate form are summarized in Exhibit 2. Costs incurred in organizing a corporation are debited to Organizational Expenses.

Learning Outcomes	Example Exercises	Practice Exercises
• Describe the characteristics of corporations.		
• List the advantages and disadvantages of the corporate form.		
• Prepare a journal entry for the costs of organizing a corporation.		

OBJ. 2 Describe the two main sources of stockholders' equity.

Key Points The two main sources of stockholders' equity are (1) capital contributed by the stockholders and others, called *paid-in capital*, and (2) net income retained in the business, called *retained earnings*. Stockholders' equity is reported in a corporation balance sheet according to these two sources.

Learning Outcomes	Example Exercises	Practice Exercises
• Describe what is meant by paid-in capital.		
• Describe what is meant by net income retained in the business.		
• Prepare a simple Stockholders' Equity section of the balance sheet.		

OBJ. 3 Describe and illustrate the characteristics of stock, classes of stock, and entries for issuing stock.

Key Points The main source of paid-in capital is from issuing common and preferred stock. Stock issued at par is recorded by debiting Cash and crediting the class of stock issued for its par amount. Stock issued for more than par is recorded by debiting Cash, crediting the class of stock for its par value, and crediting Paid-In Capital in Excess of Par for the difference. When no-par stock is issued, the entire proceeds are credited to the stock account. No-par stock may be assigned a stated value per share, and the excess of the proceeds over the stated value may be credited to Paid-In Capital in Excess of Stated Value.

Learning Outcomes	Example Exercises	Practice Exercises
• Describe the characteristics of common and preferred stock including rights to dividends.	**EE13-1**	**PE13-1A, 13-1B**
• Journalize the entry for common and preferred stock issued at par.	**EE13-2**	**PE13-2A, 13-2B**
• Journalize the entry for common and preferred stock issued at more than par.	**EE13-2**	**PE13-2A, 13-2B**
• Journalize the entry for issuing no-par stock.	**EE13-2**	**PE13-2A, 13-2B**

OBJ. 4 Describe and illustrate the accounting for cash dividends and stock dividends.

Key Points The entry to record a declaration of cash dividends debits Dividends and credits Dividends Payable. When a stock dividend is declared, Stock Dividends is debited for the fair value of the stock to be issued. Stock Dividends Distributable is credited for the par or stated value of the common stock to be issued. The difference between the fair value of the stock and its par or stated value is credited to Paid-In Capital in Excess of Par—Common Stock. When the stock is issued on the date of payment, Stock Dividends Distributable is debited and Common Stock is credited for the par or stated value of the stock issued.

Learning Outcomes	Example Exercises	Practice Exercises
• Journalize the entries for the declaration and payment of cash dividends.	**EE13-3**	**PE13-3A, 13-3B**
• Journalize the entries for the declaration and payment of stock dividends.	**EE13-4**	**PE13-4A, 13-4B**

OBJ. 5 Describe the effect of stock splits on corporate financial statements.

Key Points When a corporation reduces the par or stated value of its common stock and issues a proportionate number of additional shares, a stock split has occurred. There are no changes in the balances of any accounts, and no entry is required for a stock split.

Learning Outcomes	Example Exercises	Practice Exercises
• Define and give an example of a stock split.		
• Describe the accounting for and effects of a stock split on the financial statements.		

OBJ. 6 Describe and illustrate the accounting for treasury stock transactions.

Key Points When a corporation buys its own stock, the cost method of accounting is normally used. Treasury Stock is debited for its cost, and Cash is credited. If the stock is resold, Treasury Stock is credited for its cost and any difference between the cost and the selling price is normally debited or credited to Paid-In Capital from Sale of Treasury Stock.

Learning Outcomes	Example Exercises	Practice Exercises
• Define treasury stock.		
• Describe the accounting for treasury stock.		
• Journalize entries for the purchase and sale of treasury stock.	EE13-5	PE13-5A, 13-5B

OBJ. 7 Describe and illustrate the reporting of stockholders' equity.

Key Points Two alternatives for reporting stockholders' equity are shown in Exhibit 8. Changes in retained earnings are reported in a retained earnings statement, as shown in Exhibit 9. Restrictions to retained earnings should be disclosed. Any prior period adjustments are reported in the retained earnings statement. Changes in stockholders' equity may be reported on a statement of stockholders' equity, as shown in Exhibit 10.

Learning Outcomes	Example Exercises	Practice Exercises
• Prepare the Stockholders' Equity section of the balance sheet.	EE13-6	PE13-6A, 13-6B
• Prepare a retained earnings statement.	EE13-7	PE13-7A, 13-7B
• Describe retained earnings restrictions and prior period adjustments.		
• Prepare a statement of stockholders' equity.		

OBJ. 8 Describe and illustrate the use of earnings per share in evaluating a company's profitability.

Key Points The profitability of companies is often expressed as earnings per share. Earnings per share is computed by subtracting preferred dividends from net income and dividing by the average number of common shares outstanding.

Learning Outcomes	Example Exercises	Practice Exercises
• Describe the use of earnings per share in evaluating a company's profitability.		
• Compute and interpret earnings per share.	EE13-8	PE13-8A, 13-8B

Illustrative Problem

Altenburg Inc. is a lighting fixture wholesaler located in Arizona. During the year ended December 31, 20Y7, Altenburg Inc. completed the following selected transactions:

Feb. 3. Purchased 2,500 shares of its own common stock at $26, recording the stock at cost. (Prior to the purchase, there were 40,000 shares of $20 par common stock outstanding.)

May 1. Declared a semiannual dividend of $1 on the 10,000 shares of preferred stock and a $0.30 dividend on the common stock to stockholders of record on May 31, payable on June 15.

June 15. Paid the cash dividends.

Sept. 23. Sold 1,000 shares of treasury stock at $28, receiving cash.

Nov. 1. Declared semiannual dividends of $1 on the preferred stock and $0.30 on the common stock. In addition, a 5% common stock dividend was declared on the common stock outstanding, to be capitalized at the fair market value of the common stock, which is estimated at $30.

Dec. 1. Paid the cash dividends and issued the certificates for the common stock dividend.

Instructions

Journalize the entries to record the transactions for Altenburg Inc.

Solution

20Y7					
Feb.	3	Treasury Stock		65,000	
		Cash			65,000
May	1	Cash Dividends		21,250	
		Cash Dividends Payable			21,250
		(10,000 × $1) + [(40,000 − 2,500) × $0.30].			
June	15	Cash Dividends Payable		21,250	
		Cash			21,250
Sept.	23	Cash		28,000	
		Treasury Stock			26,000
		Paid-In Capital from Sale of Treasury Stock			2,000
Nov.	1	Cash Dividends		21,550	
		Cash Dividends Payable			21,550
		(10,000 × $1) + [(40,000 − 1,500) × $0.30].			
	1	Stock Dividends		57,750*	
		Stock Dividends Distributable			38,500
		Paid-In Capital in Excess of			
		Par—Common Stock			19,250
		*(40,000 − 1,500) × 5% × $30.			
Dec.	1	Cash Dividends Payable		21,550	
		Stock Dividends Distributable		38,500	
		Cash			21,550
		Common Stock			38,500

Key Terms

cash dividend (643)
common stock (639)
cumulative preferred stock (639)
deficit (637)
discount (641)
dividends (637)
earnings per share (EPS) (655)
in arrears (640)
outstanding stock (638)
paid-in capital (637)
par value (638)
preferred stock (639)
premium (641)
prior period adjustment (652)
restrictions (652)
retained earnings (637)
retained earnings statement (651)
statement of stockholders' equity (653)
stock (634)
stock dividend (645)
stock split (646)
stockholders (634)
stockholders' equity (637)
treasury stock (648)

Discussion Questions

1. Of two corporations organized at approximately the same time and engaged in competing businesses, one issued $80 par common stock and the other issued $1 par common stock. Do the par designations provide any indication as to which stock is preferable as an investment? Explain.

2. A stockbroker advises a client to "buy preferred stock. ... With that type of stock, ... [you] will never have to worry about losing the dividends." Is the broker correct?

3. A corporation with both preferred stock and common stock outstanding has a substantial credit balance in its retained earnings account at the beginning of the current fiscal year. Although net income for the current year is sufficient to pay the preferred dividend of $150,000 each quarter and a common dividend of $90,000 each quarter, the board of directors declares dividends only on the preferred stock. Suggest possible reasons for passing the dividends on the common stock.

4. An owner of 2,500 shares of Simmons Company common stock receives a stock dividend of 50 shares.

   a. What is the effect of the stock dividend on the stockholder's proportionate interest (equity) in the corporation?
   b. How does the total equity of 2,550 shares compare with the total equity of 2,500 shares before the stock dividend?

5. a. Where should a declared but unpaid cash dividend be reported on the balance sheet?
   b. Where should a declared but unissued stock dividend be reported on the balance sheet?

6. What is the primary purpose of a stock split?

7. A corporation reacquires 60,000 shares of its own $10 par common stock for $3,000,000, recording it at cost.

   a. What effect does this transaction have on revenue or expense of the period?
   b. What effect does it have on stockholders' equity?

8. The treasury stock in Discussion Question 7 is resold for $3,750,000.

   a. What is the effect on the corporation's revenue of the period?
   b. What is the effect on stockholders' equity?

9. What are the three classifications of restrictions of retained earnings, and how are such restrictions normally reported on the financial statements?

10. Indicate how prior period adjustments should be reported on the financial statements presented only for the current period.

Practice Exercises

Example Exercises

EE 13-1 *p. 640*

PE 13-1A Dividend per share **OBJ. 3**

Swilley Furniture Company has 50,000 shares of cumulative preferred 2% stock, $75 par, and 100,000 shares of $10 par common stock. The following amounts were distributed as dividends:

Year 1	$ 45,000
Year 2	123,000
Year 3	130,000

Determine the dividend per share for preferred and common stock for each year.

EE 13-1 *p. 640*

PE 13-1B Dividend per share **OBJ. 3**

Castillo Nutrition Company has 14,000 shares of cumulative preferred 1% stock, $130 par, and 70,000 shares of $5 par common stock. The following amounts were distributed as dividends:

Year 1	$35,000
Year 2	6,300
Year 3	80,500

Determine the dividend per share for preferred and common stock for each year.

EE 13-2 *p. 643*

PE 13-2A Entries for issuing stock **OBJ. 3**

On May 23, Washburn Realty Inc. issued for cash 45,000 shares of no-par common stock (with a stated value of $4) at $16. On July 6, Washburn Realty Inc. issued at par value 12,000 shares of preferred 1% stock, $75 par for cash. On September 15, Washburn Realty Inc. issued for cash an additional 20,000 shares of no-par common stock (with a stated value of $4) for $22.

Journalize the entries to record the May 23, July 6, and September 15 transactions.

EE 13-2 *p. 643*

PE 13-2B Entries for issuing stock **OBJ. 3**

On January 22, Micah Corporation issued for cash 125,000 shares of no-par common stock at $6. On February 14, Micah Corporation issued at par value 32,000 shares of preferred 2% stock, $80 par for cash. On August 30, Micah Corporation issued for cash 7,000 shares of preferred 2% stock, $80 par at $94.

Journalize the entries to record the January 22, February 14, and August 30 transactions.

EE 13-3 *p. 645*

PE 13-3A Entries for cash dividends **OBJ. 4**

The declaration, record, and payment dates in connection with a cash dividend of $428,000 on a corporation's common stock are February 28, April 1, and May 15. Journalize the entries required on each date.

EE 13-3 *p. 645*

PE 13-3B Entries for cash dividends **OBJ. 4**

The declaration, record, and payment dates in connection with a cash dividend of $195,000 on a corporation's common stock are February 1, March 18, and May 1. Journalize the entries required on each date.

SHOW ME HOW

EE 13-4 *p. 646*

PE 13-4A Entries for stock dividends **OBJ. 4**

Top-Value Corporation has 900,000 shares of $26 par common stock outstanding. On September 2, Top-Value Corporation declared a 3% stock dividend to be issued November 30 to stockholders of record on October 3. The market price of the stock was $44 per share on September 2.

Journalize the entries required on September 2, October 3, and November 30.

SHOW ME HOW EE 13-4 p. 646

PE 13-4B Entries for stock dividends OBJ. 4

Red Market Corporation has 370,000 shares of $27 par common stock outstanding. On June 8, Red Market Corporation declared a 5% stock dividend to be issued August 12 to stockholders of record on July 13. The market price of the stock was $51 per share on June 8.

Journalize the entries required on June 8, July 13, and August 12.

SHOW ME HOW EE 13-5 p. 649

PE 13-5A Entries for treasury stock OBJ. 6

On January 31, Outback Coast Resorts Inc. reacquired 18,700 shares of its common stock at $45 per share. On April 20, Outback Coast Resorts sold 10,600 of the reacquired shares at $52 per share. On October 4, Outback Coast Resorts sold the remaining shares at $37 per share.

Journalize the transactions of January 31, April 20, and October 4.

SHOW ME HOW EE 13-5 p. 649

PE 13-5B Entries for treasury stock OBJ. 6

On May 27, Idress Clothing Inc. reacquired 64,000 shares of its common stock at $12 per share. On August 3, Idress Clothing sold 41,000 of the reacquired shares at $17 per share. On November 14, Idress Clothing sold the remaining shares at $9 per share.

Journalize the transactions of May 27, August 3, and November 14.

SHOW ME HOW EE 13-6 p. 650

PE 13-6A Reporting stockholders' equity OBJ. 7

Using the following accounts and balances, prepare the Stockholders' Equity section of the balance sheet using Method 1 of Exhibit 8. Two hundred thousand shares of common stock are authorized, and 5,000 shares have been reacquired.

Common Stock, $3 par	$ 270,000
Paid-In Capital from Sale of Treasury Stock	62,000
Paid-In Capital in Excess of Par—Common Stock	1,196,000
Retained Earnings	7,430,000
Treasury Stock	230,000

SHOW ME HOW EE 13-6 p. 650

PE 13-6B Reporting stockholders' equity OBJ. 7

Using the following accounts and balances, prepare the Stockholders' Equity section of the balance sheet using Method 1 of Exhibit 8. Five hundred thousand shares of common stock are authorized, and 35,000 shares have been reacquired.

Common Stock, $120 par	$25,500,000
Paid-In Capital from Sale of Treasury Stock	4,074,000
Paid-In Capital in Excess of Par—Common Stock	7,230,000
Retained Earnings	47,101,000
Treasury Stock	3,920,000

SHOW ME HOW EE 13-7 p. 652

PE 13-7A Retained earnings statement OBJ. 7

Seismic Inc. reported the following results for the year ended June 30, 20Y5:

Retained earnings, July 1, 20Y4	$1,700,000
Net income	311,000
Cash dividends declared	44,000
Stock dividends declared	22,000

Prepare a retained earnings statement for the fiscal year ended June 30, 20Y5.

SHOW ME HOW EE 13-7 p. 652

PE 13-7B Retained earnings statement OBJ. 7

Haggen Cruises Inc. reported the following results for the year ended October 31, 20Y9:

Retained earnings, November 1, 20Y8	$11,775,000
Net income	2,232,000
Cash dividends declared	166,000
Stock dividends declared	285,000

Prepare a retained earnings statement for the fiscal year ended October 31, 20Y9.

SHOW ME HOW

FAI

EE 13-8 p. 656

PE 13-8A Earnings per share **OBJ. 8**

Financial statement data for the years ended December 31 for Cottontop Corporation follow:

	20Y3	20Y2
Net income	$775,000	$966,000
Preferred dividends	$35,000	$35,000
Average number of common shares outstanding	80,000 shares	95,000 shares

a. Determine the earnings per share for 20Y3 and 20Y2.

b. Does the change in the earnings per share from 20Y2 to 20Y3 indicate a favorable or unfavorable trend?

SHOW ME HOW

FAI

EE 13-8 p. 656

PE 13-8B Earnings per share **OBJ. 8**

Financial statement data for the years ended December 31 for Brown Cow Inc. follow:

	20Y6	20Y5
Net income	$4,243,200	$2,855,360
Preferred dividends	$64,000	$64,000
Average number of common shares outstanding	128,000 shares	104,000 shares

a. Determine the earnings per share for 20Y6 and 20Y5.

b. Does the change in the earnings per share from 20Y5 to 20Y6 indicate a favorable or unfavorable trend?

Exercises

✔ Preferred stock, 1st year: $0.70

SHOW ME HOW

EX 13-1 Dividend per share **OBJ. 3**

Internal Insights Inc., a developer of radiology equipment, has stock outstanding as follows: 70,000 shares of cumulative preferred 2% stock, $60 par, and 100,000 shares of $10 par common. During its first four years of operations, the following amounts were distributed as dividends: first year, $49,000; second year, $132,000; third year, $146,000; fourth year, $160,000. Compute the dividend per share on each class of stock for each of the four years.

✔ Preferred stock, 1st year: $0.90

EXCEL ONLINE

EX 13-2 Dividend per share **OBJ. 3**

Lightfoot Inc., a software development firm, has stock outstanding as follows: 40,000 shares of cumulative preferred 1% stock, $125 par, and 100,000 shares of $150 par common. During its first four years of operations, the following amounts were distributed as dividends: first year, $36,000; second year, $58,000; third year, $75,000; fourth year, $124,000. Compute the dividend per share on each class of stock for each of the four years.

SHOW ME HOW

EX 13-3 Entries for issuing par stock **OBJ. 3**

On October 31, Pidgeon Stones Inc., a marble contractor, issued for cash 320,000 shares of $5 par common stock at $12, and on November 19, it issued for cash 45,000 shares of preferred stock, $60 par at $72.

a. Journalize the entries for October 31 and November 19.

b. What is the total amount invested (total paid-in capital) by all stockholders as of November 19?

SHOW ME HOW

EX 13-4 Entries for issuing no-par stock **OBJ. 3**

On February 12, Quality Carpet Inc., a carpet wholesaler, issued for cash 1,000,000 shares of no-par common stock (with a stated value of $0.25) at $1.20, and on August 3, it issued for cash 10,000 shares of preferred stock, $15 par at $21.

a. Journalize the entries for February 12 and August 3, assuming that the common stock is to be credited with the stated value.

b. What is the total amount invested (total paid-in capital) by all stockholders as of August 3?

EX 13-5 Issuing stock for assets other than cash **OBJ. 3**

On April 5, Fenning Corporation, a wholesaler of hydraulic lifts, acquired land in exchange for 30,000 shares of $80 par common stock valued at $112 per share. Journalize the entry to record the transaction.

EX 13-6 Selected stock transactions **OBJ. 3**

Alpha Sounds Corp., an electric guitar retailer, was organized by Michele Kirby, Paul Glenn, and Gretchen Northway. The charter authorized 1,000,000 shares of common stock with a par of $1. The following transactions affecting stockholders' equity were completed during the first year of operations:

a. Issued 100,000 shares of stock at par to Paul Glenn for cash.

b. Issued 3,000 shares of stock at par to Michele Kirby for promotional services provided in connection with the organization of the corporation and issued 45,000 shares of stock at par to Michele Kirby for cash.

c. Purchased land and a building from Gretchen Northway in exchange for stock issued at par. The building is mortgaged for $180,000 for 20 years at 6%, and there is accrued interest of $5,200 on the mortgage note at the time of the purchase. It is agreed that the land is to be priced at $60,000 and the building at $225,000 and that Gretchen Northway's equity will be exchanged for stock at par. The corporation agreed to assume responsibility for paying the mortgage note and the accrued interest.

Journalize the entries to record the transactions.

EX 13-7 Issuing stock **OBJ. 3**

Willow Creek Nursery, with an authorization of 75,000 shares of preferred stock and 200,000 shares of common stock, completed several transactions involving its stock on October 1, the first day of operations. The trial balance at the close of the day follows:

Cash	3,780,000	
Land	840,000	
Buildings	2,380,000	
Preferred 1% Stock, $80 par		2,800,000
Paid-In Capital in Excess of Par—Preferred Stock		420,000
Common Stock, $30 par		3,600,000
Paid-In Capital in Excess of Par—Common Stock		180,000
	7,000,000	7,000,000

All shares within each class of stock were sold at the same price. The preferred stock was issued in exchange for the land and buildings.

Journalize the two entries to record the transactions summarized in the trial balance.

EX 13-8 Issuing stock **OBJ. 3**

Ergonomics Supply Inc., a wholesaler of office products, was organized on July 1 of the current year, with an authorization of 80,000 shares of preferred 2% stock, $70 par, and 900,000 shares of $11 par common stock. The following selected transactions were completed during the first year of operations:

July 1. Issued 260,000 shares of common stock at par for cash.

1. Issued 2,000 shares of common stock at par to an attorney in payment of legal fees for organizing the corporation.

Aug. 7. Issued 60,000 shares of common stock in exchange for land, buildings, and equipment with fair market prices of $320,000, $550,000, and $90,000, respectively.

Sept. 20. Issued 30,000 shares of preferred stock at $74 for cash.

Journalize the transactions.

SHOW ME HOW

EX 13-9 Entries for cash dividends OBJ. 4

The declaration, record, and payment dates in connection with a cash dividend of $135,000 on a corporation's common stock are January 12, March 13, and April 12. Journalize the entries required on each date.

EX 13-10 Entries for stock dividends OBJ. 4

✔ b. (1) $4,000,000
(3) $29,600,000

SHOW ME HOW

Advanced Life Co. is an HMO for businesses in the Albuquerque area. The following account balances appear on the balance sheet of Advanced Life Co.: Common stock (600,000 shares authorized; 400,000 shares issued), $8 par, $3,200,000; Paid-in capital in excess of par—common stock, $800,000; and retained earnings, $25,600,000. The board of directors declared a 2% stock dividend when the market price of the stock was $19 a share. Advanced Life Co. reported no income or loss for the current year.

a. Journalize the entries to record (1) the declaration of the dividend, capitalizing an amount equal to market value, and (2) the issuance of the stock certificates.

b. Determine the following amounts before the stock dividend was declared: (1) total paid-in capital, (2) total retained earnings, and (3) total stockholders' equity.

c. Determine the following amounts after the stock dividend was declared and closing entries were recorded at the end of the year: (1) total paid-in capital, (2) total retained earnings, and (3) total stockholders' equity.

SHOW ME HOW

EXCEL ONLINE

EX 13-11 Effect of stock split OBJ. 5

Yeoman Grill Restaurant Corporation wholesales ovens and ranges to restaurants throughout the Southwest. Yeoman Grill Restaurant Corporation, which had 35,000 shares of common stock outstanding, declared a 3-for-1 stock split.

a. What will be the number of shares outstanding after the split?

b. If the common stock had a market price of $270 per share before the stock split, what would be an approximate market price per share after the split?

EX 13-12 Effect of cash dividend and stock split OBJ. 4, 5

Indicate whether the following actions would (+) increase, (−) decrease, or (0) not affect Indigo Inc.'s total assets, liabilities, and stockholders' equity:

	Assets	Liabilities	Stockholders' Equity
(1) Authorizing and issuing stock certificates in a stock split	______	______	______
(2) Declaring a stock dividend	______	______	______
(3) Issuing stock certificates for the stock dividend declared in (2)	______	______	______
(4) Declaring a cash dividend	______	______	______
(5) Paying the cash dividend declared in (4)	______	______	______

EX 13-13 Selected dividend transactions, stock split OBJ. 4, 5

Selected transactions completed by Canyon Ferry Boating Corporation during the current fiscal year are as follows:

Jan. 8. Split the common stock 2 for 1 and reduced the par from $80 to $40 per share. After the split, there were 150,000 common shares outstanding.

Apr. 30. Declared semiannual dividends of $0.75 on 18,000 shares of preferred stock and $0.28 on the common stock payable on July 1.

July 1. Paid the cash dividends.

Oct. 31. Declared semiannual dividends of $0.75 on the preferred stock and $0.14 on the common stock (before the stock dividend). In addition, a 5% common stock dividend was declared on the common stock outstanding. The fair market value of the common stock is estimated at $52.

Dec. 31. Paid the cash dividends and issued the certificates for the common stock dividend.

Journalize the transactions.

EX 13-14 Treasury stock transactions **OBJ. 6**

✔ b. $210,000 credit

Lava Lake Inc. bottles and distributes spring water. On February 11 of the current year, Lava Lake reacquired 180,000 shares of its common stock at $17 per share. On April 30, Lava Lake Inc. sold 90,000 of the reacquired shares at $20 per share. On August 22, Lava Lake Inc. sold 30,000 shares at $15 per share.

a. Journalize the transactions of February 11, April 30, and August 22.
b. What is the balance in Paid-In Capital from Sale of Treasury Stock on December 31 of the current year?
c. For what reasons might Lava Lake have purchased the treasury stock?

EX 13-15 Treasury stock transactions **OBJ. 6, 7**

✔ b. $181,000 credit

Yard Spray Inc. develops and produces spraying equipment for lawn maintenance and industrial uses. On January 31 of the current year, Yard Spray Inc. reacquired 42,000 shares of its common stock at $36 per share. On June 14, 19,000 of the reacquired shares were sold at $43 per share, and on November 23, 16,000 of the reacquired shares were sold at $39.

a. Journalize the transactions of January 31, June 14, and November 23.
b. What is the balance in Paid-In Capital from Sale of Treasury Stock on December 31 of the current year?
c. What is the balance in Treasury Stock on December 31 of the current year?
d. How will the balance in Treasury Stock be reported on the balance sheet?

EX 13-16 Treasury stock transactions **OBJ. 6, 7**

✔ b. $55,500 credit

Biscayne Bay Water Inc. bottles and distributes spring water. On May 14 of the current year, Biscayne Bay Water Inc. reacquired 23,500 shares of its common stock at $75 per share. On September 6, Biscayne Bay Water Inc. sold 14,000 of the reacquired shares at $81 per share. The remaining 9,500 shares were sold at $72 per share on November 30.

a. Journalize the transactions of May 14, September 6, and November 30.
b. What is the balance in Paid-In Capital from Sale of Treasury Stock on December 31 of the current year?
c. Where will the balance in Paid-In Capital from Sale of Treasury Stock be reported on the balance sheet?
d. For what reasons might Biscayne Bay Water Inc. have purchased the treasury stock?

EX 13-17 Reporting paid-in capital **OBJ. 7**

✔ Total paid-in capital, $12,130,000

The following accounts and their balances were selected from the adjusted trial balance of Block Ayala Group Inc., a freight forwarder, at October 31, the end of the current fiscal year:

Account	Balance
Common Stock, no par, $22 stated value	$ 5,500,000
Paid-In Capital from Sale of Treasury Stock	35,000
Paid-In Capital in Excess of Par—Preferred Stock	165,000
Paid-In Capital in Excess of Stated Value—Common Stock	380,000
Preferred 2% Stock, $110 par	6,050,000
Retained Earnings	31,036,000

Prepare the Paid-In Capital portion of the Stockholders' Equity section of the balance sheet using Method 1 of Exhibit 8. There are 300,000 shares of common stock authorized and 100,000 shares of preferred stock authorized.

✔ Total stockholders' equity, $23,676,000

EX 13-18 Stockholders' Equity section of balance sheet **OBJ. 7**

The following accounts and their balances appear in the ledger of Goodale Properties Inc. on June 30 of the current year:

Common Stock, $45 par	$ 3,060,000
Paid-In Capital from Sale of Treasury Stock	115,000
Paid-In Capital in Excess of Par—Common Stock	272,000
Retained Earnings	20,553,000
Treasury Stock	324,000

Prepare the Stockholders' Equity section of the balance sheet as of June 30 using Method 1 of Exhibit 8. Eighty thousand shares of common stock are authorized, and 9,000 shares have been reacquired.

✔ Total stockholders' equity, $89,100,000

EX 13-19 Stockholders' Equity section of balance sheet **OBJ. 7**

Specialty Auto Racing Inc. retails racing products for BMWs, Porsches, and Ferraris. The following accounts and their balances appear in the ledger of Specialty Auto Racing Inc. on July 31, the end of the current year:

Common Stock, $36 par	$10,080,000
Paid-In Capital from Sale of Treasury Stock—Common	340,000
Paid-In Capital in Excess of Par—Common Stock	420,000
Paid-In Capital in Excess of Par—Preferred Stock	384,000
Preferred 1% Stock, $150 par	7,200,000
Retained Earnings	71,684,000
Treasury Stock—Common	1,008,000

Fifty thousand shares of preferred and 300,000 shares of common stock are authorized. There are 24,000 shares of common stock held as treasury stock.

Prepare the Stockholders' Equity section of the balance sheet as of July 31, the end of the current year using Method 1 of Exhibit 8.

✔ Retained earnings, January 31, $32,123,000

SHOW ME HOW

EX 13-20 Retained earnings statement **OBJ. 7**

Pressure Pumps Corporation, a manufacturer of industrial pumps, reports the following results for the year ended January 31, 20Y2:

Retained earnings, February 1, 20Y1	$29,842,000
Net income	4,082,000
Cash dividends declared	500,000
Stock dividends declared	1,301,000

Prepare a retained earnings statement for the fiscal year ended January 31, 20Y2.

✔ Corrected total stockholders' equity, $84,070,000

EX 13-21 Stockholders' Equity section of balance sheet **OBJ. 7**

The following Stockholders' Equity section of the balance sheet prepared as of the end of the current year:

Stockholders' Equity

Paid-in capital:		
Preferred 2% stock, $60 par (94,000 shares authorized and issued)	$5,640,000	
Excess of issue price over par	375,000	$ 6,015,000
Retained earnings		72,525,000
Treasury stock (56,000 shares at cost)		868,000
Dividends payable		323,000
Total paid-in capital		$ 79,731,000
Common stock, $10 par (750,000 shares authorized, 619,000 shares issued)		6,623,000
Organizing costs		225,000
Total stockholders' equity		$86,579,000

a. List the errors in the preceding statement of stockholders' equity.

b. Prepare a corrected statement of stockholders' equity.

EX 13-22 Statement of stockholders' equity OBJ. 7

✔ Total stockholders' equity, Dec. 31, $21,587,000

The stockholders' equity T accounts of I-Cards Inc. for the fiscal year ended December 31, 20Y9, are as follows. Prepare a statement of stockholders' equity for the year ended December 31, 20Y9.

COMMON STOCK

			Jan. 1	Balance	4,800,000
			Apr. 14	Issued	
				30,000 shares	1,200,000
			Dec. 31	Balance	6,000,000

PAID-IN CAPITAL IN EXCESS OF PAR

			Jan. 1	Balance	960,000
			Apr. 14	Issued	
				30,000 shares	300,000
			Dec. 31	Balance	1,260,000

TREASURY STOCK

Aug. 7	Purchased				
	12,000 shares	552,000			

RETAINED EARNINGS

Mar. 31	Dividend	69,000	Jan. 1	Balance	11,375,000
June 30	Dividend	69,000	Dec. 31	Closing	
Sept. 30	Dividend	69,000		(net income)	3,780,000
Dec. 31	Dividend	69,000			
			Dec. 31	Balance	14,879,000

EX 13-23 EPS OBJ. 8

PickApart Arts, Inc., had earnings of $565,300 for the year. The company had 55,000 shares of common stock outstanding during the year and issued 23,000 shares of $50 par value preferred stock. The preferred stock has a dividend of $2.10 per share. There were no transactions in either common or preferred stock during the year.

Determine the basic earnings per share for PickApart Arts for the year.

EX 13-24 EPS OBJ. 8

✔ a. Year 1, $2.79 per share

REAL WORLD

FAI

Pacific Gas and Electric Company is a large gas and electric utility operating in northern and central California. Three recent years of financial data for Pacific Gas and Electric Company are as follows:

	Fiscal Years Ended (in millions)		
	Year 3	**Year 2**	**Year 1**
Net income (loss)	$(6,837)	$1,660	$1,407
Preferred dividends	$14	$14	$14
Average number of common shares outstanding	517	512	499

a. Determine the earnings per share for fiscal Year 3, Year 2, and Year 1. Round to the nearest cent.

b. Evaluate the growth in earnings per share for the three years in comparison to the growth in net income for the three years.

EX 13-25 EPS OBJ. 8

Caterpillar Inc. and **Deere & Company** are two large companies that manufacture and sell equipment used in the construction, mining, agricultural, and forestry industries. The companies reported the following data (in millions) for two recent years:

	Caterpillar		Deere	
	Year 2	**Year 1**	**Year 2**	**Year 1**
Net income	$6,147	$754	$2,368	$2,159
Average number of common shares outstanding	591	592	323	320

a. Determine the earnings per share in Year 2 and Year 1 for each company. Neither Caterpillar nor Deere have any preferred stock outstanding. Round to the nearest cent.

b. Evaluate the relative profitability of the two companies.

Problems: Series A

PR 13-1A Dividends on preferred and common stock — OBJ. 3

✔ 1. Year 3, Preferred Dividends, $130,000

SHOW ME HOW

Pecan Theatre Inc. owns and operates movie theaters throughout Florida and Georgia. Pecan Theatre has declared the following annual dividends over a six-year period: Year 1, $80,000; Year 2, $90,000; Year 3, $150,000; Year 4, $150,000; Year 5, $160,000; and Year 6, $180,000. During the entire period ended December 31 of each year, the outstanding stock of the company was composed of 250,000 shares of cumulative, preferred 2% stock, $20 par, and 500,000 shares of common stock, $15 par.

Instructions

1. Determine the total dividends and the per-share dividends declared on each class of stock for each of the six years. There were no dividends in arrears at the beginning of Year 1. Summarize the data in tabular form, using the following column headings:

		Preferred Dividends		Common Dividends	
Year	**Total Dividends**	**Total**	**Per Share**	**Total**	**Per Share**
Year 1	$ 80,000				
Year 2	90,000				
Year 3	150,000				
Year 4	150,000				
Year 5	160,000				
Year 6	180,000				

2. Determine the average annual dividend per share for each class of stock for the six-year period.
3. Assuming a market price per share of $25.00 for the preferred stock and $17.50 for the common stock, determine the average annual percentage return on initial shareholders' investment, based on the average annual dividend per share (a) for preferred stock and (b) for common stock.

PR 13-2A Stock transactions for corporate expansion — OBJ. 3

On December 1 of the current year, the following accounts and their balances appear in the ledger of Latte Corp., a coffee processor:

Preferred 2% Stock, $50 par (250,000 shares authorized, 80,000 shares issued)	$ 4,000,000
Paid-In Capital in Excess of Par—Preferred Stock	560,000
Common Stock, $35 par (1,000,000 shares authorized, 400,000 shares issued)	14,000,000
Paid-In Capital in Excess of Par—Common Stock	1,200,000
Retained Earnings	180,000,000

At the annual stockholders' meeting on March 31, the board of directors presented a plan for modernizing and expanding plant operations at a cost of approximately $11,000,000.

(Continued)

The plan provided (a) that a building, valued at $3,375,000, and the land on which it is located, valued at $1,500,000, be acquired in accordance with preliminary negotiations by the issuance of 125,000 shares of common stock valued at $39 per share, (b) that 40,000 shares of the unissued preferred stock be issued through an underwriter, and (c) that the corporation borrow $4,000,000. The plan was approved by the stockholders and accomplished by the following transactions:

May 11. Issued 125,000 shares of common stock in exchange for land and a building, according to the plan.

20. Issued 40,000 shares of preferred stock, receiving $52 per share in cash.

31. Borrowed $4,000,000 from Laurel National, giving a 5% mortgage note.

Instructions

Journalize the entries to record the May transactions.

PR 13-3A Selected stock transactions **OBJ. 3, 4, 6**

✔ f. Cash dividends, $337,600

SHOW ME HOW

The following selected accounts appear in the ledger of Upscale Construction Inc. at the beginning of the current year:

Preferred 2% Stock, $80 par (200,000 shares authorized, 65,000 shares issued)	$ 5,200,000
Paid-In Capital in Excess of Par—Preferred Stock	360,000
Common Stock, $12 par (3,000,000 shares authorized, 1,400,000 shares issued)	16,800,000
Paid-In Capital in Excess of Par—Common Stock	1,290,000
Retained Earnings	110,900,000

During the year, the corporation completed a number of transactions affecting the stockholders' equity. They are summarized as follows:

a. Issued 220,000 shares of common stock at $15, receiving cash.
b. Issued 6,000 shares of preferred 2% stock at $94.
c. Purchased 130,000 shares of treasury common for $19 per share.
d. Sold 70,000 shares of treasury common for $23 per share.
e. Sold 40,000 shares of treasury common for $17 per share.
f. Declared cash dividends of $1.60 per share on preferred stock and $0.14 per share on common stock.
g. Paid the cash dividends.

Instructions

Journalize the entries to record the transactions. Identify each entry by letter.

PR 13-4A Entries for selected corporate transactions **OBJ. 3, 4, 5, 7**

✔ 4. Total stockholders' equity, $44,436,200

Morrow Enterprises Inc. manufactures bathroom fixtures. The stockholders' equity accounts of Morrow Enterprises Inc., with balances on January 1, 20Y5, are as follows:

Common Stock, $20 stated value (500,000 shares authorized, 375,000 shares issued)	$ 7,500,000
Paid-In Capital in Excess of Stated Value—Common Stock	825,000
Retained Earnings	33,600,000
Treasury Stock (25,000 shares, at a cost of $18 per share)	450,000

The following selected transactions occurred during the year:

Jan. 22. Paid cash dividends of $0.08 per share on the common stock. The dividend had been properly recorded when declared on December 1 of the preceding fiscal year for $28,000.

Apr. 10. Issued 75,000 shares of common stock for $24 per share.

June 6. Sold all of the treasury stock for $26 per share.

July 5. Declared a 4% stock dividend on common stock, to be capitalized at the market price of the stock, which is $25 per share.

Aug. 15. Issued the certificates for the dividend declared on July 5.

Nov. 23. Purchased 30,000 shares of treasury stock for $19 per share.

Dec. 28. Declared a $0.10-per-share dividend on common stock.

31. Closed the two dividends accounts to Retained Earnings.

Instructions

1. Enter the January 1 balances in T accounts for the stockholders' equity accounts listed. Also prepare T accounts for the following: Paid-In Capital from Sale of Treasury Stock; Stock Dividends Distributable; Stock Dividends; Cash Dividends.
2. Journalize the entries to record the transactions and post to the eight selected accounts.
3. Prepare a retained earnings statement for the year ended December 31, 20Y5. Assume that Morrow Enterprises had net income for the year ended December 31, 20Y5, of $1,125,000.
4. Prepare the Stockholders' Equity section of the December 31, 20Y5, balance sheet using Method 1 of Exhibit 8.

PR 13-5A Entries for selected corporate transactions — OBJ. 3, 4, 5, 6

✔ Oct. 15, Cash dividends, $324,300

Selected transactions completed by ATV Discount Corporation during the current fiscal year are as follows:

Jan. 5. Split the common stock 4 for 1 and reduced the par from $20 to $5 per share. After the split, there were 4,000,000 common shares outstanding.

Mar. 10. Purchased 100,000 shares of the corporation's own common stock at $30, recording the stock at cost.

Apr. 30. Declared semiannual dividends of $0.25 on 30,000 shares of preferred stock and $0.08 on the common stock to stockholders of record on May 15, payable on June 15.

June 15. Paid the cash dividends.

Aug. 20. Sold 60,000 shares of treasury stock at $40, receiving cash.

Oct. 15. Declared semiannual dividends of $0.25 on the preferred stock and $0.08 on the common stock (before the stock dividend). In addition, a 1% common stock dividend was declared on the common stock outstanding. The fair market value of the common stock is estimated at $35. The dividend date of record is November 15 payable on December 19.

Dec. 19. Paid the cash dividends and issued the certificates for the common stock dividend.

Instructions

Journalize the transactions.

Problems: Series B

PR 13-1B Dividends on preferred and common stock — OBJ. 3

✔ 1. Common dividends in Year 3: $44,000

SHOW ME HOW

Black Bear Bike Corp. manufactures mountain bikes and distributes them through retail outlets in California, Oregon, and Washington. Black Bear Bike Corp. has declared the following annual dividends over a six-year period ended December 31 of each year: Year 1, $42,500; Year 2, $18,000; Year 3, $223,500; Year 4, $178,000; Year 5, $222,000; and Year 6, $222,000. During the entire period, the outstanding stock of the company was composed of 50,000 shares of cumulative preferred 2% stock, $80 par, and 100,000 shares of common stock, $4 par.

Instructions

1. Determine the total dividends and the per-share dividends declared on each class of stock for each of the six years. There were no dividends in arrears on January 1, Year 1. Summarize the data in tabular form, using the following column headings:

(Continued)

Year	Total Dividends	Preferred Dividends Total	Preferred Dividends Per Share	Common Dividends Total	Common Dividends Per Share
Year 1	$ 42,500				
Year 2	18,000				
Year 3	223,500				
Year 4	178,000				
Year 5	222,000				
Year 6	222,000				

2. Determine the average annual dividend per share for each class of stock for the six-year period.
3. Assuming a market price of $100 for the preferred stock and $5 for the common stock, determine the average annual percentage return on initial shareholders' investment, based on the average annual dividend per share (a) for preferred stock and (b) for common stock.

PR 13-2B Stock transaction for corporate expansion

OBJ. 3

Pulsar Optics produces medical lasers for use in hospitals. The accounts and their balances appear in the ledger of Pulsar Optics on April 30 of the current year as follows:

Account	Balance
Preferred 1% Stock, $120 par (300,000 shares authorized, 36,000 shares issued)	$ 4,320,000
Paid-In Capital in Excess of Par—Preferred Stock	180,000
Common Stock, $15 par (2,000,000 shares authorized, 1,400,000 shares issued)	21,000,000
Paid-In Capital in Excess of Par—Common Stock	3,500,000
Retained Earnings	78,000,000

At the annual stockholders' meeting on August 5, the board of directors presented a plan for modernizing and expanding plant operations at a cost of approximately $9,000,000. The plan provided (a) that the corporation borrow $1,500,000, (b) that 20,000 shares of the unissued preferred stock be issued through an underwriter, and (c) that a building, valued at $4,150,000, and the land on which it is located, valued at $800,000, be acquired in accordance with preliminary negotiations by the issuance of 300,000 shares of common stock valued at $16.50 per share. The plan was approved by the stockholders and accomplished by the following transactions:

Oct. 9. Borrowed $1,500,000 from St. Peter City Bank, giving a 4% mortgage note.
17. Issued 20,000 shares of preferred stock, receiving $126 per share in cash.
28. Issued 300,000 shares of common stock in exchange for land and a building, according to the plan.

Instructions

Journalize the entries to record the October transactions.

PR 13-3B Selected stock transactions

OBJ. 3, 4, 6

✔ f. Cash dividends, $234,775

SHOW ME HOW

Diamondback Welding & Fabrication Corporation sells and services pipe welding equipment in Illinois. The following selected accounts appear in the ledger of Diamondback Welding & Fabrication Corporation at the beginning of the current fiscal year:

Account	Balance
Preferred 2% Stock, $80 par (100,000 shares authorized, 60,000 shares issued)	$ 4,800,000
Paid-In Capital in Excess of Par—Preferred Stock	210,000
Common Stock, $9 par (3,000,000 shares authorized, 1,750,000 shares issued)	15,750,000
Paid-In Capital in Excess of Par—Common Stock	1,400,000
Retained Earnings	52,840,000

During the year, the corporation completed a number of transactions affecting the stockholders' equity. They are summarized as follows:

a. Purchased 87,500 shares of treasury common for $8 per share.

b. Sold 55,000 shares of treasury common for $11 per share.

c. Issued 20,000 shares of preferred 2% stock at $84.

d. Issued 400,000 shares of common stock at $13, receiving cash.

e. Sold 18,000 shares of treasury common for $7.50 per share.

f. Declared cash dividends of $1.60 per share on preferred stock and $0.05 per share on common stock.

g. Paid the cash dividends.

Instructions

Journalize the entries to record the transactions. Identify each entry by letter.

PR 13-4B Entries for selected corporate transactions OBJ. 3, 4, 5, 7

✔ 4. Total stockholders' equity, $11,262,432

Nav-Go Enterprises Inc. produces aeronautical navigation equipment. The stockholders' equity accounts of Nav-Go Enterprises Inc., with balances on January 1, 20Y3, are as follows:

Common Stock, $5 stated value (900,000 shares authorized, 620,000 shares issued)	$3,100,000
Paid-In Capital in Excess of Stated Value—Common Stock	1,240,000
Retained Earnings	4,875,000
Treasury Stock (48,000 shares, at a cost of $6 per share)	288,000

The following selected transactions occurred during the year:

Jan. 15. Paid cash dividends of $0.06 per share on the common stock. The dividend had been properly recorded when declared on December 1 of the preceding fiscal year for $34,320.

Mar. 15. Sold all of the treasury stock for $6.75 per share.

Apr. 13. Issued 200,000 shares of common stock for $8 per share.

June 14. Declared a 3% stock dividend on common stock, to be capitalized at the market price of the stock, which is $7.50 per share.

July 16. Issued the certificates for the dividend declared on June 14.

Oct. 30. Purchased 50,000 shares of treasury stock for $6 per share.

Dec. 30. Declared a $0.08-per-share dividend on common stock.

31. Closed the two dividends accounts to Retained Earnings.

Instructions

1. Enter the January 1 balances in T accounts for the stockholders' equity accounts listed. Also prepare T accounts for the following: Paid-In Capital from Sale of Treasury Stock; Stock Dividends Distributable; Stock Dividends; Cash Dividends.
2. Journalize the entries to record the transactions and post to the eight selected accounts.
3. Prepare a retained earnings statement for the year ended December 31, 20Y3. Assume that Nav-Go Enterprises had net income for the year ended December 31, 20Y3, of $775,000.
4. Prepare the Stockholders' Equity section of the December 31, 20Y3, balance sheet using Method 1 of Exhibit 8.

PR 13-5B Entries for selected corporate transactions OBJ. 3, 4, 5, 6

✔ Sept. 1, Cash dividends, $95,200

West Yellowstone Outfitters Corporation manufactures and distributes leisure clothing. Selected transactions completed by West Yellowstone Outfitters during the current fiscal year are as follows:

Jan. 15. Split the common stock 4 for 1 and reduced the par from $120 to $30 per share. After the split, there were 800,000 common shares outstanding.

(Continued)

Mar. 1. Declared semiannual dividends of $0.25 on 100,000 shares of preferred stock and $0.07 on the 800,000 shares of $30 par common stock to stockholders of record on March 31, payable on April 30.

Apr. 30. Paid the cash dividends.

May 31. Purchased 60,000 shares of the corporation's own common stock at $32, recording the stock at cost.

Aug. 17. Sold 40,000 shares of treasury stock at $38, receiving cash.

Sept. 1. Declared semiannual dividends of $0.25 on the preferred stock and $0.09 on the common stock (before the stock dividend). In addition, a 1% common stock dividend was declared on the common stock outstanding, to be capitalized at the fair market value of the common stock, which is estimated at $40. The dividend date of record is September 30, payable on October 31.

Oct. 31. Paid the cash dividends and issued the certificates for the common stock dividend.

Instructions

Journalize the transactions.

Cases & Projects

ETHICS

CP 13-1 Ethics in Action

Tommy Gunn is a division manager for K-Cern Inc., a small pharmaceutical company. Tommy's division has been working on a new drug that has the potential to revolutionize the treatment of skin cancer. Once the drug is proven to be effective in clinical trials, it will be approved for sale by the government and patented by the company. Because of the potential market for this drug, it is highly likely that the company's revenues and net income will increase significantly when it is approved. Tommy recently saw an internal company memo indicating that the drug passed its final clinical trial and that the company has received government approval to sell the drug. The company will issue a press release announcing this news in the next two days, and this announcement is expected to result in a dramatic increase in the company's stock price. Tommy knows that there is "free money" to be made if he invests in the stock before the announcement is made. However, K-Cern has a strict policy against employee purchases of company stock outside of established employee stock purchase plans. To get around this rule, Tommy asks his father to purchase the stock for him. The next morning Tommy's father purchases the stock with the understanding that he will split the profits with Tommy.

Is Tommy behaving ethically? Why or why not?

ETHICS

CP 13-2 Ethics in Action

Lou Hoskins and Shirley Crothers are organizing Red Lodge Metals Unlimited Inc. to undertake a high-risk gold-mining venture in Canada. Lou and Shirley tentatively plan to request authorization for 400,000,000 shares of common stock to be sold to the general public. Lou and Shirley have decided to establish par of $0.03 per share in order to appeal to a wide variety of potential investors. Lou and Shirley believe that investors would be more willing to invest in the company if they received a large quantity of shares for what might appear to be a "bargain" price.

Discuss whether Lou and Shirley are behaving in a professional manner.

CP 13-3 Team Activity

In teams, select a public company that interests you. Obtain the company's most recent annual report on Form 10-K. The Form 10-K is a company's annually required filing with the Securities and Exchange Commission (SEC). It includes the company's financial statements and accompanying notes. The Form 10-K can be obtained either (a) by referring to the investor relations section of the company's website or (b) by using the company search feature of the SEC's EDGAR database service found at www.sec.gov/edgar/searchedgar/companysearch.html.

Based on the information in the company's most recent annual report, determine the following:

1. Name of the corporation
2. State of incorporation
3. Nature of its operations
4. Total assets reported on the most recent balance sheet
5. Total liabilities reported on the most recent balance sheet
6. Total stockholders' equity reported on the most recent balance sheet
7. Total revenues reported on the most recent income statement
8. Net income reported on the most recent income statement
9. The number of shares of common stock authorized, issued, and outstanding
10. The par value per share of each class of stock
11. Basic and diluted earnings per share reported on the income statement
12. Dividend per share reported on the income statement

CP 13-4 Communication

Motion Designs Inc. has paid quarterly cash dividends since 20Y7. These dividends have steadily increased from $0.05 per share to the latest dividend declaration of $0.50 per share. The board of directors would like to continue this trend and is hesitant to suspend or decrease the amount of quarterly dividends. Unfortunately, sales dropped sharply in the fourth quarter of 20Y8 due to worsening economic conditions and increased competition. As a result, the board is uncertain as to whether it should declare a dividend for the last quarter of 20Y8.

On October 1, 20Y8, Motion Designs Inc. borrowed $4,000,000 from Valley National Bank to use in modernizing its retail stores and to expand its product line in response to changes in its industry. The terms of the 10-year, 6% loan require Motion Designs to do the following:

- Pay monthly interest on the last day of the month
- Pay $400,000 of the principal each October 1, beginning in 20Y9
- Maintain a current ratio (current assets ÷ current liabilities) of 2
- Maintain a minimum balance (a compensating balance) of $100,000 in its Valley National Bank account

On December 31, 20Y8, $1,000,000 of the $4,000,000 loan had been disbursed in modernization of the retail stores and in expansion of the product line. Motion Designs Inc.'s balance sheet as of December 31, 20Y8, follows:

(*Continued*)

Motion Designs Inc. Balance Sheet December 31, 20Y8			
Assets			
Current assets:			
Cash		$ 250,000	
Marketable securities		3,000,000	
Accounts reveivable	$ 800,000		
Less allowance for doubtful accounts	50,000		
Accounts receivable, net		750,000	
Inventory		2,980,000	
Prepaid expenses		20,000	
Total current assets			$ 7,000,000
Property, plant, and equipment:			
Land		$1,500,000	
Buildings	$ 5,050,000		
Less accumulated depreciation—buildings	1,140,000		
Buildings, book value		3,910,000	
Equipment	$ 3,320,000		
Less accumulated depreciation equipment	730,000		
Equipment, book value		2,590,000	
Total property, plant, and equipment			8,000,000
Total assets			$15,000,000
Liabilities			
Current liabilities:			
Accounts payable	$ 1,590,000		
Notes payable (Valley National Bank)	400,000		
Salaries payable	10,000		
Total current liabilities		$2,000,000	
Long-term liabilities:			
Notes payable (Valley National Bank)		3,600,000	
Total liabilities			$ 5,600,000
Stockholders' Equity			
Paid-in capital:			
Common stock, $25 par (200,000 shares authorized, 180,000 shares issued)	$ 4,500,000		
Excess of issue price over par	270,000		
Total paid-in capital		$4,770,000	
Retained earnings		4,630,000	
Total stockholders' equity			9,400,000
Total liabilities and stockholders' equity			$15,000,000

The board of directors is scheduled to meet January 10, 20Y9, to discuss the results of operations for 20Y8 and to consider the declaration of dividends for the fourth quarter of 20Y8. The chairman of the board, Matt Cengage, has asked for your advice on the declaration of dividends.

Write a brief memo to the chairman of the board, outlining the factors that the board should consider in deciding whether to declare a cash dividend.

ETHICS

CP 13-5 Ethics in Action

Bernie Ebbers, the CEO of **WorldCom**, a major telecommunications company, was having personal financial troubles. Ebbers pledged a large stake of his WorldCom stock as security for some personal loans. As the price of WorldCom stock sank, Ebbers's bankers threatened to sell his stock in order to protect their loans. To avoid having his stock sold, Ebbers asked the board of directors of WorldCom to loan him nearly $400 million of corporate assets at 2.5% interest to pay off his bankers. The board agreed to lend him the money.

Comment on the decision of the board of directors in this situation.

CP 13-6 Issuing stock

Epstein Engineering Inc. began operations on January 5, 20Y8, with the issuance of 500,000 shares of $80 par common stock. The sole stockholders of Epstein Engineering Inc. are Barb Abrams and Dr. Amber Epstein, who organized Epstein Engineering Inc. with the objective of developing a new flu vaccine. Dr. Epstein claims that the flu vaccine, which is nearing the final development stage, will protect individuals against 90% of the flu types that have been medically identified. To complete the project, Epstein Engineering Inc. needs $25,000,000 of additional funds. The local banks have been unwilling to loan the funds because of the lack of sufficient collateral and the riskiness of the business.

The following is a conversation between Barb Abrams, the chief executive officer of Epstein Engineering Inc., and Amber Epstein, the leading researcher:

Barb: What are we going to do? The banks won't loan us any more money, and we've got to have $25 million to complete the project. We are so close! It would be a disaster to quit now. The only thing I can think of is to issue additional stock. Do you have any suggestions?

Amber: I guess you're right. But if the banks won't loan us any more money, how can we find any investors to buy stock?

Barb: I've been thinking about that. What if we promise the investors that we will pay them 5% of sales until they receive an amount equal to what they paid for the stock?

Amber: What happens when we pay back the $25 million? Do the investors get to keep the stock? If they do, it'll dilute our ownership.

Barb: How about if after we pay back the $25 million, we make them turn in their stock for $120 per share? That's one and one-half times what they paid for it, and they would have already gotten all their money back. That's a $120 profit per share for the investors.

Amber: It could work. We get our money but don't have to pay any interest, dividends, or the $80 per share until we start generating sales. At the same time, the investors could get their money back plus $120 per share profit.

Barb: We'll need current financial statements for the new investors. I'll get our accountant working on them and contact our attorney to draw up a legally binding contract for the new investors. Yes, this could work.

In late 20Y8, the attorney and the various regulatory authorities approved the new stock offering, and 312,500 shares of common stock were privately sold to new investors at the stock's par of $80.

In preparing financial statements for 20Y8, Barb Abrams and Dan Fisher, the controller for Epstein Engineering Inc., have the following conversation:

Dan: Barb, I've got a problem.

Barb: What's that, Dan?

Dan: Issuing common stock to raise that additional $25 million was a great idea. But . . .

Barb: But what?

Dan: I've got to prepare the 20Y8 annual financial statements, and I am not sure how to classify the common stock.

Barb: What do you mean? It's common stock.

Dan: I'm not so sure. I called the auditor and explained how we are contractually obligated to pay the new stockholders 5% of sales until $80 per share is paid. Then we may be obligated to pay them $120 per share.

Barb: So . . .

Dan: So the auditor thinks that we should classify the additional issuance of $25 million as debt, not stock! And if we put the $25 million on the balance sheet as debt, we will violate our other loan agreements with the banks. And if these agreements are violated, the banks may call in all our debt immediately. If they do that, we are in deep trouble. We'll probably have to file for bankruptcy. We just don't have the cash to pay off the banks.

1. Discuss the arguments for and against classifying the issuance of the $25 million of stock as debt.
2. What might be a practical solution to this classification problem?

CHAPTER 14

Long-Term Liabilities: Bonds and Notes

RETAINED EARNINGS STATEMENT
For the Year Ended December 31, 20Y6

Retained earnings, Jan. 1, 20Y6		$XXX
Net income	$ XXX	
Dividends	(XXX)	
Increase in retained earnings		XXX
Retained earnings, Dec. 31, 20Y6		$XXX

INCOME STATEMENT
For the Year Ended December 31, 20Y6

Sales		$XXX
Cost of merchandise sold		XXX
Gross profit		$XXX
Operating expenses:		
Advertising expense	$XXX	
Depreciation expense	XXX	
Amortization expense	XXX	
Depletion expense	XXX	
...	XXX	
...	XXX	
Total operating expenses		XXX
Income from operations		$XXX
Other revenue and expenses		
Interest expense		XXX
Net income		$XXX

STATEMENT OF CASH FLOWS
For the Year Ended December 31, 20Y6

Cash flows from (used for) operating activities	$XXX
Cash flows from (used for) investing activities	XXX
Cash flows from (used for) financing activities	XXX
Net increase (decrease) in cash	$XXX
Cash balance, January 1, 20Y6	XXX

BALANCE SHEET
December 31, 20Y6

Current assets:		
Cash	$XXX	
Accounts receivable	XXX	
Inventory	XXX	
Total current assets		$XXX
Property, plant, and equipment	$XXX	
Intangible assets	XXX	
Total long-term assets		XXX
Total assets		$XXX
Liabilities:		
Current liabilities	$XXX	
Long-term liabilities:	XXX	
Bonds payable	XXX	
Notes payable	XXX	
Total liabilities		$XXX
Stockholders' equity		XXX
Total liabilities and stockholders' equity		$XXX

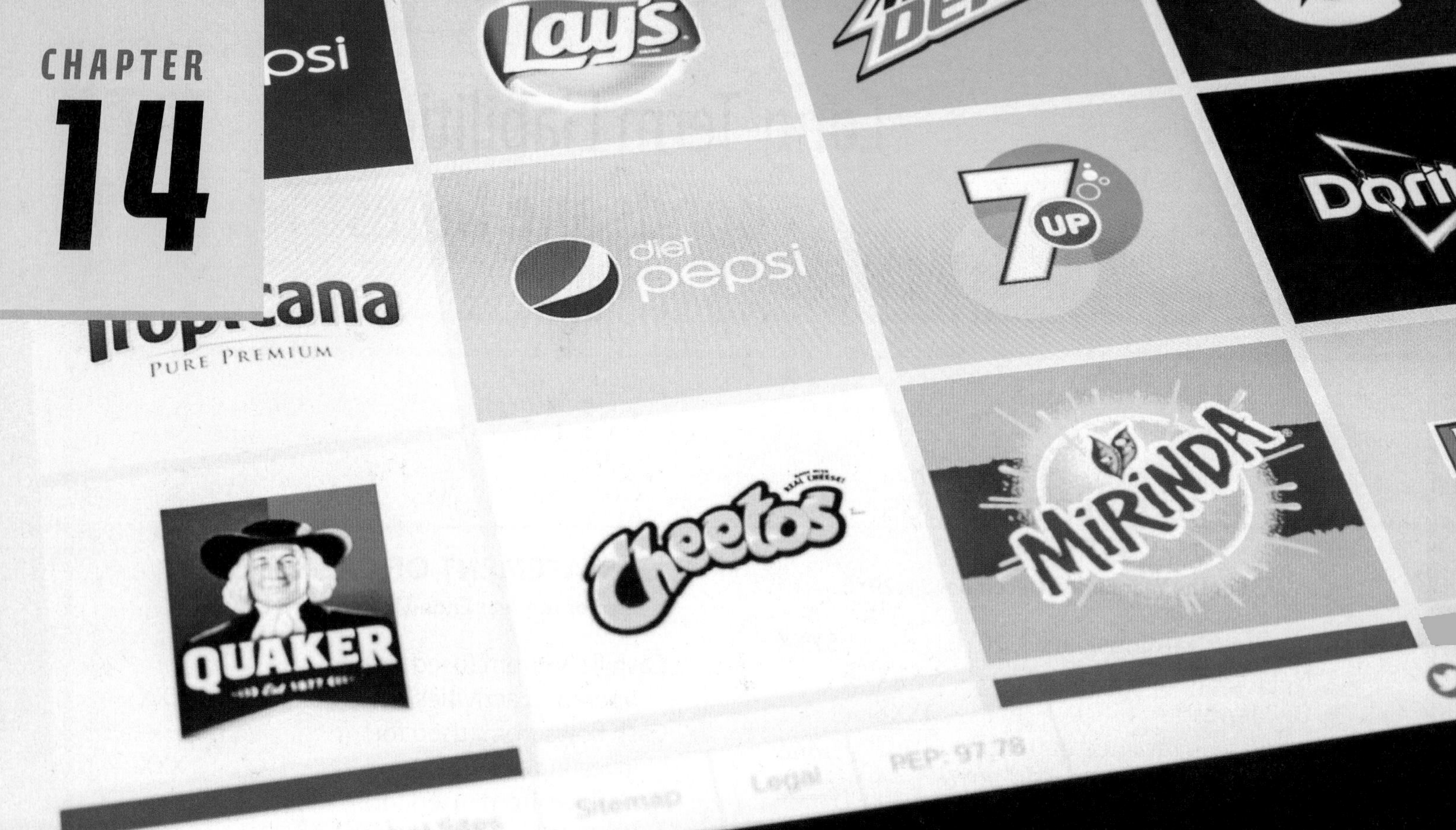

RADU BERCAN/SHUTTERSTOCK.COM

PepsiCo, Inc.

PepsiCo, Inc., is best known for its beverages, which include Pepsi, Diet Pepsi, Gatorade, Mountain Dew, Diet Mountain Dew, Tropicana fruit juices, and Aquafina water.* However, PepsiCo also produces a variety of foods, which include Lay's potato chips, Fritos corn chips, Doritos, Cheetos, Quaker oatmeal, Aunt Jemima mixes and syrups, and Cap'n Crunch cereal. PepsiCo produces, distributes, and sells its products in over 200 countries.

PepsiCo uses a variety of methods to finance its operations, including long-term debt and stock. A recent balance sheet revealed that over 75% of its total assets are financed with liabilities, and 66% of these liabilities are long-term. Included in PepsiCo's long-term liabilities are a variety of notes and bonds. For example, PepsiCo has $16,161 million of bonds maturing throughout 2024–2047 with interest rates of 3.7% and 3.8%. In this chapter, we will discuss the accounting and reporting of bonds payable and installment notes payable.

*The brands listed here are trademarked by PepsiCo.

Link to PepsiCo .... Pages 684, 685, 687

LEARNING OBJECTIVES

After studying this chapter, you should be able to:

Example Exercises (EE) are shown in **red.**

At a Glance 14 Page 704

Financing Corporations

OBJ. 1 Compute the potential impact of long-term borrowing on earnings per share.

Corporations finance their operations using the following sources:

- Short-term debt, such as purchasing goods or services on account
- Long-term debt, such as issuing bonds or notes payable
- Equity, such as issuing common or preferred stock

Short-term debt, including the purchase of goods and services on account and the issuance of short-term notes payable, was discussed in Chapter 11. Issuing equity in the form of common or preferred stock was discussed in Chapter 13. This chapter focuses on the use of long-term debt such as bonds and notes payable to finance a company's operations.

A **bond** is an interest-bearing note that requires periodic interest payments, with the face amount to be repaid at the maturity date. For example, a 12% bond requires the company issuing the bond to pay 12% interest on the face amount of the bonds every year. As creditors of the corporation, bondholder claims on the corporation's assets rank ahead of stockholders.

One of the main factors that influences the decision to issue debt or equity is the effect that various financing alternatives will have on earnings per share. **Earnings per share (EPS)** measures the income earned by each share of common stock. It is computed as follows:[1]

$$\text{Earnings per Share} = \frac{\text{Net Income} - \text{Preferred Dividends}}{\text{Number of Common Shares Outstanding}}$$

1 Earnings per share is also discussed in the *Financial Analysis and Interpretation* section of Chapter 13 and in Chapter 17.

To illustrate the effects that issuing debt can have on earnings per share, consider the following alternative plans for financing Boz Corporation, a $4,000,000 company:

	Plan 1		Plan 2		Plan 3	
	Amount	**Percent**	**Amount**	**Percent**	**Amount**	**Percent**
Issue 12% bonds	—	0%	—	0%	$2,000,000	50%
Issue preferred 9% stock, $50 par value	—	0	$2,000,000	50	1,000,000	25
Issue common stock, $10 par value	$4,000,000	100	2,000,000	50	1,000,000	25
Total amount of financing	$4,000,000	100%	$4,000,000	100%	$4,000,000	100%

The company must choose one of these plans. Each plan finances some of the corporation's operations by issuing common stock. However, the percentage financed by common stock varies from 100% (Plan 1) to 25% (Plan 3).

Assume the following data for Boz Corporation:

- Earnings before interest and income taxes are $800,000.
- The tax rate is 40%.
- All bonds or stocks are issued at their par or face amount.

The effect of the preceding financing plans on Boz's net income and earnings per share is shown in Exhibit 1.

EXHIBIT 1

Effect of Alternative Financing Plans—$800,000 Earnings

	Plan 1	Plan 2	Plan 3
12% bonds	—	—	$2,000,000
Preferred 9% stock, $50 par	—	$2,000,000	1,000,000
Common stock, $10 par	$4,000,000	2,000,000	1,000,000
Total	$4,000,000	$4,000,000	$4,000,000
Earnings before interest and income tax	$ 800,000	$ 800,000	$ 800,000
Interest on bonds	—	—	(240,000)[a]
Income before income tax	$ 800,000	$ 800,000	$ 560,000
Income tax	(320,000)[b]	(320,000)[b]	(224,000)[b]
Net income	$ 480,000	$ 480,000	$ 336,000
Dividends on preferred stock	—	(180,000)[c]	(90,000)[c]
Available for dividends on common stock	$ 480,000	$ 300,000	$ 246,000
Shares of common stock outstanding	÷ 400,000[d]	÷ 200,000[d]	÷ 100,000[d]
Earnings per share on common stock	$ 1.20	$ 1.50	$ 2.46

[a] $2,000,000 bonds × 12%
[b] Income before income tax × 40%
[c] Preferred stock × 9%
[d] Common stock ÷ $10 par value per share

Exhibit 1 indicates that when earnings are strong, Plan 3 has the highest earnings per share, making it most attractive for common shareholders. This is because the company is generating more than enough net income to cover the bond interest. If the estimated earnings are more than $800,000, the difference between the earnings per share to common stockholders under Plans 1 and 3 is even greater.[2]

Lower earnings, however, have the opposite effect. If earnings are reduced to $440,000, as illustrated in Exhibit 2, Plans 1 and 2 become more attractive to common stockholders. This is because more of the company's earnings are being used to pay bond interest, leaving less net income attributable to common stockholders.

2 The higher earnings per share under Plan 3 is due to a finance concept known as *leverage*. This concept is discussed further in Chapter 18.

EXHIBIT 2

Effect of Alternative Financing Plans—$440,000 Earnings

	Plan 1	Plan 2	Plan 3
12% bonds	—	—	$2,000,000
Preferred 9% stock, $50 par	—	$2,000,000	1,000,000
Common stock, $10 par	$4,000,000	2,000,000	1,000,000
Total	$4,000,000	$4,000,000	$4,000,000
Earnings before interest and income tax	$ 440,000	$ 440,000	$ 440,000
Interest on bonds	—	—	(240,000)
Income before income tax	$ 440,000	$ 440,000	$ 200,000
Income tax	(176,000)	(176,000)	(80,000)
Net income	$ 264,000	$ 264,000	$ 120,000
Dividends on preferred stock	—	(180,000)	(90,000)
Available for dividends on common stock	$ 264,000	$ 84,000	$ 30,000
Shares of common stock outstanding	÷ 400,000	÷ 200,000	÷ 100,000
Earnings per share on common stock	$ 0.66	$ 0.42	$ 0.30

In addition to earnings per share, the corporation should consider other factors in deciding among the financing plans. For example, if bonds are issued, the interest and the face value of the bonds at maturity must be paid. If these payments are not made, the bondholders could seek court action and force the company into bankruptcy. In contrast, a corporation is not legally obligated to pay dividends on preferred or common stock.

EXAMPLE EXERCISE 14-1 Alternative Financing Plans

OBJ. 1

Gonzales Co. is considering the following alternative financing plans:

	Plan 1	Plan 2
Issue 10% bonds (at face value)	—	$2,000,000
Issue common stock, $10 par	$3,000,000	1,000,000

Income tax is estimated at 40% of income.

Determine the earnings per share of common stock under the two alternative financing plans, assuming that income before bond interest and income tax is $750,000.

Follow My Example 14-1

	Plan 1	Plan 2
Earnings before bond interest and income tax	$ 750,000	$ 750,000
Interest on bonds	—	200,000[2]
Income before income tax	$ 750,000	$ 550,000
Income tax	(300,000)[1]	(220,000)[3]
Net income	$ 450,000	$ 330,000
Dividends on preferred stock	—	—
Available for dividends on common stock	$ 450,000	$ 330,000
Shares of common stock outstanding	÷300,000	÷100,000
Earnings per share on common stock	$ 1.50	$ 3.30

[1]$750,000 × 40% [2]$2,000,000 × 10% [3]$550,000 × 40%

Practice Exercises: PE 14-1A, PE 14-1B

Nature of Bonds Payable

OBJ. 2 Describe the characteristics and terminology of bonds payable.

Corporate bonds normally differ in face amount, interest rates, interest payment dates, and maturity dates. Bonds also differ in other ways such as whether corporate assets are pledged in support of the bonds.

Bond Characteristics and Terminology

The face amount of each bond is called the *principal*. This is the amount that must be repaid on the dates the bonds mature. The principal is usually $1,000, or a multiple of $1,000. The interest on bonds may be payable annually, semiannually, or quarterly. Most bonds pay interest semiannually.

The underlying contract between the company issuing bonds and the bondholders is called a **bond indenture**. This contract can be written in different ways, depending on the financing needs of the company. The two most common types of bonds are term bonds and serial bonds. When all bonds of an issue mature at the same time, they are called *term bonds*. If the bonds mature over several dates, they are called *serial bonds*. For example, one-tenth of an issue of $1,000,000 bonds, or $100,000, may mature 16 years from the issue date, another $100,000 in the 17th year, and so on.

There are also a variety of more complicated bond structures. For example, *convertible bonds* may be exchanged for shares of common stock, and *callable bonds* may be redeemed by the corporation prior to maturity. These bonds are discussed in intermediate and advanced accounting texts.

Proceeds from Issuing Bonds

When a corporation issues bonds, the proceeds received for the bonds depend on the following:

- The face amount of the bonds, which is the amount due at the maturity date
- The interest rate on the bonds
- The market rate of interest for similar bonds

The face amount and the interest rate on the bonds are identified in the bond indenture. The interest rate to be paid on the face amount of the bond is called the **contract rate** or *coupon rate*.

> **Link to PepsiCo**
>
> **PepsiCo**'s 2.75% bonds maturing in 2023 were recently selling for more than their face value.

The **market rate of interest**, sometimes called the **effective rate of interest**, is the rate determined from sales and purchases of similar bonds. The market rate of interest is affected by a variety of factors, including investors' expectations of current and future economic conditions.

By comparing the market and contract rates of interest, it can be determined whether the bonds will sell for more than, for less than, or at their face amount, as shown in Exhibit 3.

EXHIBIT 3 **Issuing Bonds at a Discount, at Face Amount, and at a Premium**

If: Market Rate > Contract Rate	**If:** Market Rate = Contract Rate	**If:** Market Rate < Contract Rate
< $1,000 Bond	= $1,000 Bond	> $1,000 Bond
Less than $1,000	**$1,000**	**More than $1,000**
Then: Selling Price < Face Amount	**Then:** Selling Price = Face Amount	**Then:** Selling Price > Face Amount
Sold at a DISCOUNT	Sold at FACE AMOUNT	Sold at a PREMIUM

If the market rate equals the contract rate, bonds will sell at the **face amount**.

If the market rate is greater than the contract rate, the bonds will sell for less than their face value. The face amount of the bonds less the selling price is called a **discount**. A bond sells at a discount because buyers are not willing to pay the full face amount for bonds with a contract rate that is lower than the market rate.

If the market rate is less than the contract rate, the bonds will sell for more than their face value. The selling price of the bonds less the face amount is called a **premium**. A bond sells at a premium because buyers are willing to pay more than the face amount for bonds with a contract rate that is higher than the market rate.

The price of a bond is quoted as a percentage of the bond's face value. For example, a $1,000 bond quoted at 98 could be purchased or sold for $980 ($1,000 × 0.98). Likewise, bonds quoted at 109 could be purchased or sold for $1,090 ($1,000 × 1.09).

Link to PepsiCo

PepsiCo's 4.6% bonds maturing in 2045 were recently selling for almost 112% of their face value.

Business Connection

INVESTOR BOND PRICE RISK

Corporate bonds are purchased as investments by both individuals and institutions. Bonds issued by financially strong issuers provide a compelling balance of risk and reward, as they provide the investor with both a steady stream of interest payments and the repayment of the principal at maturity. Thus, high-quality bond investments are considered less risky than equity investments. However, this does not mean that bond investors have no price risk. Bond prices move in the opposite direction as changes in market interest rates, as shown below.

Market Rate of Interest	Market Price of Bonds
Increase	Decrease
Decrease	Increase

The magnitude of a bond's price change depends on its maturity. When market interest rates change, the price of short-term bonds fluctuates less than the price of long-term bonds with a comparable interest rate. This is illustrated in the following table:

Bond Term	Contract Rate	Estimated Price of $1,000 Par Value Bond if Market Interest Rate Doubles	Estimated Price of $1,000 Par Value Bond if Market Interest Rate Halves
1 year	0.5%	$995	$1,002
5 years	1.5%	931	1,037
10 years	2.0%	838	1,095
30 years	3.0%	587	1,360

The greater price variability of long-term bonds makes them a riskier investment than short-term bonds. This is one of the reasons longer-term bonds typically have higher coupon rates than shorter-term bonds. As a result, the bond's term must be considered in evaluating both the risk and return of a bond investment.

Accounting for Bonds Payable

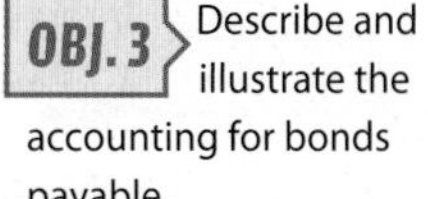

Describe and illustrate the accounting for bonds payable.

Bonds may be issued at their face amount, a discount, or a premium. When bonds are issued at less or more than their face amount, the discount or premium must be amortized over the life of the bonds. At the maturity date, the face amount must be repaid. In some situations, a corporation may redeem bonds before their maturity date by repurchasing them from investors.

Bonds Issued at Face Amount

If the market rate of interest is equal to the contract rate of interest, the bonds will sell for their face amount or at a price of 100. To illustrate, assume that on January 1, 20Y5, Eastern Montana Communications Inc. issued the following bonds:

Face amount	$100,000
Contract rate of interest	12%
Interest paid semiannually on June 30 and December 31.	
Term of bonds	5 years
Market rate of interest	12%

Since the contract rate of interest and the market rate of interest are the same, the bonds will sell at their face amount. The entry to record the issuance of the bonds is as follows:

20Y5				
Jan.	1	Cash	100,000	
		Bonds Payable		100,000
		Issued $100,000 bonds payable at face amount.		

Every six months (on June 30 and December 31) after the bonds are issued, interest of $6,000 ($100,000 × 12% × ½ year) is paid. The first interest payment on June 30, 20Y5, is recorded as follows:

20Y5				
June	30	Interest Expense	6,000	
		Cash		6,000
		Paid six months' interest on bonds.		

At the maturity date, the payment of the principal of $100,000 is recorded as follows:

20Y9				
Dec.	31	Bonds Payable	100,000	
		Cash		100,000
		Paid bond principal at maturity date.		

EXAMPLE EXERCISE 14-2 Issuing Bonds at Face Amount **OBJ. 3**

The first day of the fiscal year, a company issues a $1,000,000, 6%, five-year bond that pays semiannual interest of $30,000 ($1,000,000 × 6% × ½ year), receiving cash of $1,000,000. Journalize the entries to record (a) the issuance of the bonds at their face amount, (b) the first interest payment, and (c) the payment of the principal on the maturity date.

Follow My Example 14-2

a.	Cash	1,000,000	
	Bonds Payable		1,000,000
b.	Interest Expense	30,000	
	Cash		30,000
c.	Bonds Payable	1,000,000	
	Cash		1,000,000

Practice Exercises: PE 14-2A, PE 14-2B

Bonds Issued at a Discount

Note

Bonds will sell at a discount when the market rate of interest is higher than the contract rate.

If the market rate of interest is greater than the contract rate of interest, the bonds will sell for less than their face amount. This is because investors are not willing to pay the full face amount for bonds that pay a lower contract rate of interest than the rate they could earn on similar bonds (market rate). The difference between the face amount and the selling price of the bonds is the bond discount.[3]

3 The price that investors are willing to pay for the bonds depends on present value concepts. Present value concepts, including the computation of bond prices, are described and illustrated in Appendix 1 at the end of this chapter.

To illustrate, assume that on January 1, 20Y5, Western Wyoming Distribution Inc. issued the following bonds:

Face amount	$100,000
Contract rate of interest	12%
Interest paid semiannually on June 30 and December 31.	
Term of bonds	5 years
Market rate of interest	13%

Because the contract rate of interest is less than the market rate of interest, the bonds will sell at less than their face amount. Assuming that the bonds sell for $96,406, the entry to record the issuance of the bonds is as follows:

20Y5					
Jan.	1	Cash		96,406	
		Discount on Bonds Payable		3,594	
		Bonds Payable			100,000
		Issued $100,000 bonds at discount.			

The $96,406 is the amount investors are willing to pay for bonds that have a lower contract rate of interest (12%) than the market rate (13%). The discount is the market's way of adjusting the contract rate of interest to the higher market rate of interest.

The account, Discount on Bonds Payable, is a contra account to Bonds Payable and has a normal debit balance. It is subtracted from Bonds Payable to determine the carrying amount (or book value) of the bonds payable. The **carrying amount** of bonds payable is the face amount of the bonds less any unamortized discount or plus any unamortized premium. Thus, after the preceding entry, the carrying amount of the bonds payable is $96,406 ($100,000 − $3,594).

Link to PepsiCo

PepsiCo's 3.6% bonds maturing in 2042 were selling for less than 97% of their face value, which implies that the market rate of interest for equivalent bonds is more than the 3.6% contract rate.

EXAMPLE EXERCISE 14-3 Issuing Bonds at a Discount **OBJ. 3**

On the first day of the fiscal year, a company issues a $1,000,000, 6%, five-year bond that pays semiannual interest of $30,000 ($1,000,000 × 6% × ½), receiving cash of $936,420. Journalize the entry to record the issuance of the bonds.

Follow My Example 14-3

Cash	936,420	
Discount on Bonds Payable	63,580	
Bonds Payable		1,000,000

Practice Exercises: PE 14-3A, PE 14-3B

Amortizing a Bond Discount

Every period, a portion of the bond discount must be reduced and added to interest expense to reflect the passage of time. This process, called **amortization**, increases the contract rate of interest on a bond to the market rate of interest that existed on the date the bonds were issued. The entry to amortize a bond discount is as follows:

Interest Expense	XXX	
Discount on Bonds Payable		XXX

Business Connection

U.S. GOVERNMENT DEBT

Like many corporations, the U.S. government issues debt to finance its operations. Currently, debt provides approximately 15% of the total annual funding needs of the U.S. government. The remainder comes from taxes. The debt is issued by the U.S. Treasury Department in the form of U.S. Treasury bills, notes, and bonds. An individual investor can purchase these as an investment through the TreasuryDirect® website or through a broker. Treasury securities have the following characteristics:

	Issued at	Interest Paid	Term
U.S. Treasury bills	Discount	None	1 year or less
U.S. Treasury notes	Face value	Semiannual	1 to 10 years
U.S. Treasury bonds	Face value	Semiannual	30 years

Recently, 10-year notes had a contract rate of 2.56%. The contract interest rate for government securities will normally be lowest for Treasury bills and largest for Treasury bonds.

The preceding entry may be made annually as an adjusting entry, or it may be combined with the semiannual interest payment. In the latter case, the entry would be as follows:

		Interest Expense		XXX	
		Discount on Bonds Payable			XXX
		Cash (amount of semiannual interest)			XXX

The straight-line method is used to compute the amortization of a bond discount. This method provides equal amounts of amortization each period.[4] To illustrate, amortization of the Western Wyoming Distribution bond discount of $3,594 is computed as follows:

Discount on bonds payable	$3,594
Term of bonds	5 years
Semiannual amortization	$359.40 ($3,594 ÷ 10 periods)

The combined entry to record the first interest payment and the amortization of the discount is as follows:

20Y5					
June	30	Interest Expense		6,359.40	
		Discount on Bonds Payable			359.40
		Cash			6,000.00
		Paid semiannual interest and amortized 1/10 of bond discount.			

The preceding entry is made on each interest payment date. Thus, the amount of the semiannual interest expense on the bonds ($6,359.40) remains the same over the life of the bonds.

The effect of the discount amortization is to increase the interest expense from $6,000.00 to $6,359.40 on every semiannual interest payment date. In effect, this increases the contract rate of interest from 12% to a rate of interest that approximates the market rate of 13%. In addition, as the discount is amortized, the carrying amount of the bonds increases until it equals the face amount of the bonds on the maturity date.

4 The effective interest rate method is required by generally accepted accounting principles. However, the straight-line method may be used if the results do not differ significantly from the interest method. The straight-line method is used in this chapter. The effective interest rate method is described and illustrated in Appendix 2 at the end of this chapter.

EXAMPLE EXERCISE 14-4 Discount Amortization OBJ. 3

Using the bond from Example Exercise 14-3, journalize the first interest payment and the amortization of the related bond discount.

Follow My Example 14-4

Interest Expense	36,358	
Discount on Bonds Payable		6,358
Cash		30,000
Paid interest and amortized the bond discount ($63,580 ÷ 10).		

Practice Exercises: PE 14-4A, PE 14-4B

Bonds Issued at a Premium

If the market rate of interest is less than the contract rate of interest, the bonds will sell for more than their face amount. This is because investors are willing to pay more for bonds that pay a higher contract rate of interest than the rate they could earn on similar bonds (market rate).

Note

Bonds will sell at a premium when the market rate of interest is less than the contract rate.

To illustrate, assume that on January 1, 20Y5, Northern Idaho Transportation Inc. issued the following bonds:

Face amount	$100,000
Contract rate of interest	12%
Interest paid semiannually on June 30 and December 31.	
Term of bonds	5 years
Market rate of interest	11%

Because the contract rate of interest is more than the market rate of interest, the bonds will sell for more than their face amount. Assuming that the bonds sell for $103,769, the entry to record the issuance of the bonds is as follows:

20Y5					
Jan.	1	Cash		103,769	
		Bonds Payable			100,000
		Premium on Bonds Payable			3,769
		Issued $100,000 bonds at a premium.			

The $3,769 premium is the extra amount investors are willing to pay for bonds that have a higher contract rate of interest (12%) than the market rate (11%). The premium is the market's way of adjusting the contract rate of interest to the lower market rate of interest.

The account Premium on Bonds Payable has a normal credit balance. It is added to Bonds Payable to determine the carrying amount (or book value) of the bonds payable. Thus, after the preceding entry, the carrying amount of the bonds payable is $103,769 ($100,000 + $3,769).

EXAMPLE EXERCISE 14-5 Issuing Bonds at a Premium OBJ. 3

On the first day of the fiscal year, a company issues a $2,000,000, 12%, five-year bond that pays semiannual interest of $120,000 ($2,000,000 × 12% × ½), receiving cash of $2,154,440. Journalize the bond issuance.

(Continued)

Follow My Example 14-5

Cash	2,154,440	
Premium on Bonds Payable		154,440
Bonds Payable		2,000,000

Practice Exercises: PE 14-5A, PE 14-5B

Amortizing a Bond Premium

Like bond discounts, a bond premium must be amortized over the life of the bond. The amortization of a bond premium decreases the contract rate of interest on a bond to the market rate of interest that existed on the date the bonds were issued. The amortization can be computed using either the straight-line or the effective interest rate method. The entry to amortize a bond premium is as follows:

		Premium on Bonds Payable	XXX	
		Interest Expense		XXX

The preceding entry may be made annually as an adjusting entry, or it may be combined with the semiannual interest payment. In the latter case, it would be:

		Interest Expense	XXX	
		Premium on Bonds Payable	XXX	
		Cash (amount of semiannual interest)		XXX

To illustrate, amortization of the preceding premium of $3,769 is computed as follows using the straight-line method:

Premium on bonds payable	$3,769
Term of bonds	5 years
Semiannual amortization	$376.90 ($3,769 ÷ 10 periods)

The combined entry to record the first interest payment and the amortization of the premium is as follows:

20Y5				
June	30	Interest Expense	5,623.10	
		Premium on Bonds Payable	376.90	
		Cash		6,000.00
		Paid semiannual interest and amortized 1/10 of bond premium.		

The preceding entry is made on each interest payment date. Thus, the amount of the semiannual interest expense ($5,623.10) on the bonds remains the same over the life of the bonds.

The effect of the premium amortization is to decrease the interest expense from $6,000.00 to $5,623.10. In effect, this decreases the rate of interest from 12% to a rate of interest that approximates the market rate of 11%. In addition, as the premium is amortized, the carrying amount of the bonds decreases until it equals the face amount of bonds on the maturity date.

EXAMPLE EXERCISE 14-6 Premium Amortization **OBJ. 3**

Using the bond from Example Exercise 14-5, journalize the first interest payment and the amortization of the related bond premium.

Follow My Example 14-6

Interest Expense	104,556	
Premium on Bonds Payable	15,444	
Cash		120,000
Paid interest and amortized the bond premium ($154,440 ÷ 10).		

Practice Exercises: PE 14-6A, PE 14-6B

Business Connection

BOND RATINGS

When purchasing bonds, investors are very interested in understanding how likely it is that the bond issuer will be able to repay the bond principal and associated interest. To help them assess this likelihood, independent rating agencies review and grade the financial condition of companies that issue bonds. For example, the **Standard & Poor's** rating agency rates bonds on a scale from D (lowest) to AAA (highest). Bonds with a rating of BBB- or higher are called *investment grade* because they are issued by companies in sound financial condition and are considered to be reasonably safe investments. Bonds issued by companies in relatively weak financial condition receive ratings below BBB-, reflecting the higher potential for default or nonpayment. These lesser quality bonds are referred to as *non-investment grade* or *junk* bonds. The market rate of interest on junk bonds is much higher than the market rate on investment grade bonds, which compensates bond investors for junk bonds' higher risk of default.

Bond Redemption

A corporation may redeem or call bonds before they mature. This is often done when the market rate of interest declines below the contract rate of interest. In such cases, the corporation may issue new bonds at a lower interest rate and use the proceeds to redeem the original bond issue.

Callable bonds can be redeemed by the issuing corporation within the period of time and at the price stated in the bond indenture. Normally, the call price is above the face value. A corporation may also redeem its bonds by purchasing them on the open market.[5]

A corporation usually redeems its bonds at a price different from the carrying amount (or book value) of the bonds. A gain or loss may be realized on a bond redemption as follows:

- A *gain* is recorded if the price paid for redemption is below the bond carrying amount.
- A *loss* is recorded if the price paid for the redemption is above the carrying amount.

Gains and losses on the redemption of bonds are reported in the *Other Revenue (Loss)* section of the income statement.

To illustrate, assume that on June 30, 20Y5, a corporation has the following bond issue:

Face amount of bonds	$100,000
Premium on bonds payable	4,000*

*After the semiannual interest payment and premium amortization have been recorded.

5 Some bond indentures require the corporation issuing the bonds to transfer cash to a special cash fund, called a *sinking fund*, over the life of the bond. Such funds help assure investors that there will be adequate cash to pay the bonds at their maturity date.

On June 30, 20Y5, the corporation redeemed one-fourth ($25,000) of these bonds in the market for $24,000. The entry to record the redemption is as follows:

20Y5						
June	30	Bonds Payable			25,000	
		Premium on Bonds Payable			1,000	
		Cash				24,000
		Gain on Redemption of Bonds				2,000
		Redeemed $25,000 bonds for $24,000.				

In the preceding entry, only the portion of the premium related to the redeemed bonds ($4,000 × 25% = $1,000) is removed. The difference between the carrying amount of the bonds redeemed, $26,000 ($25,000 + $1,000), and the redemption price, $24,000, is recorded as a gain.

Assume that the corporation calls the remaining $75,000 of outstanding bonds, which are held by a private investor, for $79,500 on July 1, 20Y5. The entry to record the redemption is as follows:

20Y5						
July	1	Bonds Payable			75,000	
		Premium on Bonds Payable			3,000	
		Loss on Redemption of Bonds			1,500	
		Cash				79,500
		Redeemed $75,000 bonds for $79,500.				

EXAMPLE EXERCISE 14-7 Redemption of Bonds Payable OBJ. 3

A $500,000 bond issue on which there is an unamortized discount of $40,000 is redeemed for $475,000. Journalize the redemption of the bonds.

Follow My Example 14-7

Bonds Payable	500,000	
Loss on Redemption of Bonds	15,000	
Discount on Bonds Payable		40,000
Cash		475,000

Practice Exercises: PE 14-7A, PE 14-7B

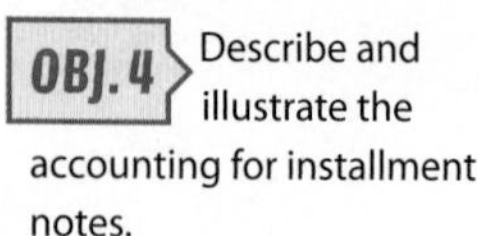

Describe and illustrate the accounting for installment notes.

Installment Notes

Corporations often finance their operations by issuing bonds payable. As an alternative, corporations may issue a different kind of notes payable called installment notes. An **installment note** is a debt that requires the borrower to make equal periodic payments to the lender for the term of the note. Unlike bonds, each note payment includes the following:

- Payment of a portion of the amount initially borrowed, called the *principal*
- Payment of interest on the outstanding balance

At the end of the note's term, the principal will have been repaid in full.

Installment notes are often used to purchase specific assets such as equipment and are often secured by the purchased asset. When a note is secured by an asset, it is called a **mortgage note**. If the borrower fails to pay a mortgage note, the lender has the right to take possession of the pledged asset and sell it to pay off the debt. Mortgage notes are typically issued by an individual bank.

Individuals typically use mortgage notes when buying a house or car.

Issuing an Installment Note

When an installment note is issued, an entry is recorded debiting Cash and crediting Notes Payable. To illustrate, assume that Lewis Company issues the following installment note to City National Bank on January 1, 20Y4:

Principal amount of note	$24,000
Interest rate	6%
Term of note	5 years
Annual payments	$5,698[6]

The entry to record the issuance of the note is as follows:

20Y4				
Jan.	1	Cash	24,000	
		Notes Payable		24,000
		Issued installment note for cash.		

Annual Payments

The preceding note payable requires Lewis Company to repay the principal and interest in equal payments of $5,698 beginning December 31, 20Y4, for each of the next five years. Unlike bonds, however, each installment note payment includes an interest and principal component.

The interest portion of an installment note payment is computed by multiplying the interest rate by the carrying amount (book value) of the note at the beginning of the period. The principal portion of the payment is then computed as the difference between the total installment note payment (cash paid) and the interest component. These computations are illustrated in Exhibit 4 (rounded to the nearest dollar).

Amortization of Installment Notes **EXHIBIT 4**

Year Ending December 31	A January 1 Carrying Amount	B Note Payment (Cash Paid)	C Interest Expense (6% of January 1 Note Carrying Amount)		D Decrease in Notes Payable (B – C)	E December 31 Carrying Amount (A – D)
20Y4	$24,000	$ 5,698	$ 1,440	(6% of $24,000)	$ 4,258	$19,742
20Y5	19,742	5,698	1,185	(6% of $19,742)	4,513	15,229
20Y6	15,229	5,698	914	(6% of $15,229)	4,784	10,445
20Y7	10,445	5,698	627	(6% of $10,445)	5,071	5,374
20Y8	5,374	5,698	324*	(6% of $5,374)	5,374	—
		$28,490	$4,490		$24,000	

*Rounded ($5,698 – $5,374).

1. The January 1, 20Y4, carrying value (Column A) equals the amount borrowed from the bank. The January 1 balance in the following years equals the December 31 balance from the prior year.
2. The note payment (Column B) remains constant at $5,698, the annual cash payment required by the bank.
3. The interest expense (Column C) is computed at 6% times the installment note carrying amount at the beginning of each year. Since the carrying amount decreases each year, the interest expense decreases each year.
4. Notes payable decreases each year by the amount of the principal repayment (Column D). The principal repayment is computed by subtracting the interest expense (Column C) from the total payment (Column B). The principal repayment (Column D) increases each year as the interest expense decreases (Column C).

6 The amount of the annual payment is computed by using the present value concepts discussed in Appendix 1 at the end of this chapter. The annual payment of $5,698 is computed by dividing the $24,000 loan amount by the present value of an annuity of $1 for five periods at 6% (4.21236) from Exhibit 10 (rounded to the nearest dollar).

5. The carrying amount on December 31 (Column E) of the note decreases from $24,000, the initial amount borrowed, to $0 at the end of the five years.

The entry to record the first payment on December 31, 20Y4, is as follows:

20Y4				
Dec.	31	Interest Expense	1,440	
		Notes Payable	4,258	
		Cash		5,698
		Paid principal and interest on installment note.		

The entry to record the second payment on December 31, 20Y5, is as follows:

20Y5				
Dec.	31	Interest Expense	1,185	
		Notes Payable	4,513	
		Cash		5,698
		Paid principal and interest on installment note.		

As the prior entries show, the cash payment is the same in each year. The interest and principal payments, however, change each year. This is because the carrying amount (book value) of the note decreases each year as principal is paid, which decreases the interest component the next period.

The entry to record the final payment on December 31, 20Y8, is as follows:

20Y8				
Dec.	31	Interest Expense	324	
		Notes Payable	5,374	
		Cash		5,698
		Paid principal and interest on installment note.		

After the final payment, the carrying amount on the note is zero, indicating that the note has been paid in full. Any assets that secure the note would then be released by the bank.

EXAMPLE EXERCISE 14-8 Journalizing Installment Notes — OBJ. 4

On the first day of the fiscal year, a company issues a $30,000, 10%, five-year installment note that has annual payments of $7,914. The first note payment consists of $3,000 of interest and $4,914 of principal repayment.

a. Journalize the entry to record the issuance of the installment note.

b. Journalize the first annual note payment.

Follow My Example 14-8

a.	Cash	30,000	
	Notes Payable		30,000
b.	Interest Expense	3,000	
	Notes Payable	4,914	
	Cash		7,914

Practice Exercises: PE 14-8A, PE 14-8B

Integrity, Objectivity, and Ethics in Business

THE RATINGS GAME

In February 2013, the United States Justice Department filed a lawsuit against the three main credit rating agencies (**Moody's**, **Standard & Poor's**, and **Fitch**) for inflating their ratings on high-risk bond issuances between 2004 and 2007. During this time period, the three ratings agencies gave their highest rating (AAA) to debt securities that were, in fact, highly risky. During the financial crisis of 2008, most of these bonds experienced significant drops in value, leaving investors with huge losses. The Justice Department lawsuit alleges that the ratings agencies were aware of the high risks associated with these bonds but inflated their ratings because of the large fee they received for providing a rating on these bonds. In 2015, Standard & Poor's settled this and related lawsuits for $1.5 billion. Moody's agreed to pay nearly $864 million for this and related lawsuits.

Sources: "U.S. vs. S&P: The Rating Game," *Chicago Tribune*, February 6, 2013; "S&P Reaches $1.5 Billion Deal with U.S., States over Crisis-Era Ratings," Reuters, *Business News*, February 3, 2015; "Moody's Pays $864 Million to U.S., States over Pre-crisis Ratings," Reuters, *Business News*, January 13, 2017.

Reporting Long-Term Liabilities

OBJ. 5 Describe and illustrate the reporting of long-term liabilities, including bonds and installment notes payable.

Bonds payable and notes payable are reported as liabilities on the balance sheet. Any portion of the bonds or notes that is due within one year is reported as a current liability. Any remaining bonds or notes are reported as a long-term liability.

Any unamortized premium is reported as an addition to the face amount of the bonds. Any unamortized discount is reported as a deduction from the face amount of the bonds. A description of the bonds and notes should also be reported either on the face of the financial statements or in the accompanying notes.

The reporting of bonds and notes payable for **Mornin' Joe** follows:

Mornin' Joe
Balance Sheet
December 31, 20Y6

Current liabilities:		
Accounts payable	$133,000	
Notes payable (current portion)	200,000	
Salaries and wages payable	42,000	
Payroll taxes payable	16,400	
Interest payable	40,000	
Total current liabilities		$ 431,400
Long-term liabilities:		
Bonds payable, 8%, due in 15 years	$500,000	
Less unamortized discount	16,000	$ 484,000
Notes payable		1,400,000
Total long-term liabilities		$1,884,000
Total liabilities		$2,315,400

Financial Analysis and Interpretation: Times Interest Earned Ratio

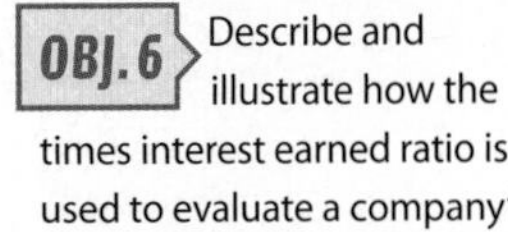

OBJ. 6 Describe and illustrate how the times interest earned ratio is used to evaluate a company's financial condition.

As we have discussed, the assets of a company are subject to (1) the claims of creditors and (2) the rights of owners. As creditors, bondholders are concerned primarily with the company's ability to make its periodic interest payments and repay the face amount of the bonds at maturity.

Analysts assess the risk that bondholders will not receive their interest payments by computing the **times interest earned** ratio during the year as follows:

$$\text{Times Interest Earned} = \frac{\text{Income Before Income Tax Expense} + \text{Interest Expense}}{\text{Interest Expense}}$$

This ratio computes the number of times interest payments could be paid out of current period earnings. Because interest payments reduce income tax expense, the ratio is computed using income before tax. High values of this ratio are considered favorable. In contrast, low values are considered unfavorable. Values of this ratio less than 1.0 suggest that the firm is unable to cover interest payments from current period income before tax. Such a situation could eventually lead to loan defaults.

To illustrate, the following data were taken from recent annual reports of three companies in the soft drink beverage industry—**PepsiCo, Inc.**, **The Coca-Cola Company**, and **Keurig Dr Pepper Inc.** (in thousands):

	PepsiCo	Coca-Cola	Keurig Dr Pepper
Interest expense	$1,525,000	$ 841,000	$401,000
Income before income tax expense	9,189,000	6,742,000	791,000

The times interest earned is computed as follows for all three companies:

	PepsiCo	Coca-Cola	Keurig Dr Pepper
Interest expense	$ 1,525,000	$ 841,000	$ 401,000
Income before income tax expense	9,189,000	6,742,000	791,000
Income before income tax expense + Interest expense	$10,714,000	$7,583,000	$1,192,000
Times interest earned	7.0*	9.0**	3.0***

*$10,714,000 ÷ $1,525,000

**$7,583,000 ÷ $841,000

***$1,192,000 ÷ $401,000

Among the three beverage companies, Coca-Cola has the highest interest coverage. Since all of the ratios are in excess of 1.0, all of the companies generate enough income before tax to pay (cover) their interest payments. As a result, bondholders of these companies have good protection in the event of an earnings decline.

EXAMPLE EXERCISE 14-9 Times Interest Earned

OBJ. 6

Harris Industries reported the following on the company's income statement in 20Y7 and 20Y6:

	20Y7	20Y6
Interest expense	$ 200,000	$180,000
Income before income tax expense	1,000,000	720,000

a. Determine the times interest earned ratio for 20Y7 and 20Y6.

b. Is the times interest earned ratio improving or declining?

Follow My Example 14-9

a. 20Y7:

Times interest earned: $\frac{\$1{,}000{,}000 + \$200{,}000}{\$200{,}000} = 6.0$

20Y6:

Times interest earned: $\frac{\$720{,}000 + \$180{,}000}{\$180{,}000} = 5.0$

b. The times interest earned has increased from 5.0 in 20Y6 to 6.0 in 20Y7. Thus, the debtholders have improved confidence in the company's ability to make its interest payments.

Practice Exercises: PE 14-9A, PE 14-9B

APPENDIX 1

Present Value Concepts and Pricing Bonds Payable

APP. 1 OBJ. Describe and illustrate the use of present value concepts to determine the price of a bond.

When a corporation issues bonds, the price that investors are willing to pay for the bonds depends on the following:

- The face amount of the bonds, which is the amount due at the maturity date
- The periodic interest to be paid on the bonds
- The market rate of interest

An investor determines how much to pay for the bonds by computing the present value of the bond's future cash receipts, using the market rate of interest. A bond's future cash receipts include its face value at maturity and the periodic interest payments.

Present Value Concepts

The concept of present value is based on the time value of money. The *time value of money concept* recognizes that cash received today is worth more than the same amount of cash to be received in the future.

To illustrate, what would you rather have: $1,000 today or $1,000 one year from now? You would rather have the $1,000 today because it could be invested to earn interest. For example, if the $1,000 could be invested to earn 10% interest per year, the $1,000 will accumulate to $1,100 ($1,000 plus $100 interest) in one year. In this sense, you can think of the $1,000 in hand today as the **present value** of $1,100 to be received a year from today. This present value is illustrated in Exhibit 5.

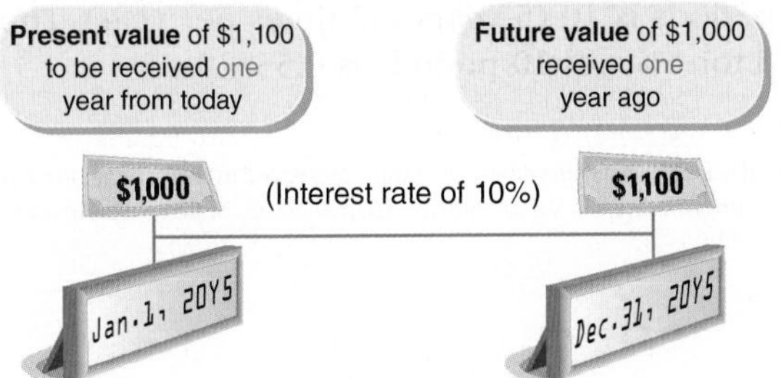

EXHIBIT 5

Present Value and Future Value

A related concept to present value is **future value**. To illustrate, using the preceding example illustrated in Exhibit 5, the $1,100 to be received on December 31, 20Y5, is the *future value* of $1,000 on January 1, 20Y5, assuming an interest rate of 10%.

Present Value of an Amount To illustrate the present value of an amount, assume that $1,000 is to be received in one year. If the market rate of interest is 10%, the present value of the $1,000 is $909.09 ($1,000 ÷ 1.10). This present value is illustrated in Exhibit 6.

EXHIBIT 6

Present Value of an Amount to Be Received in One Year

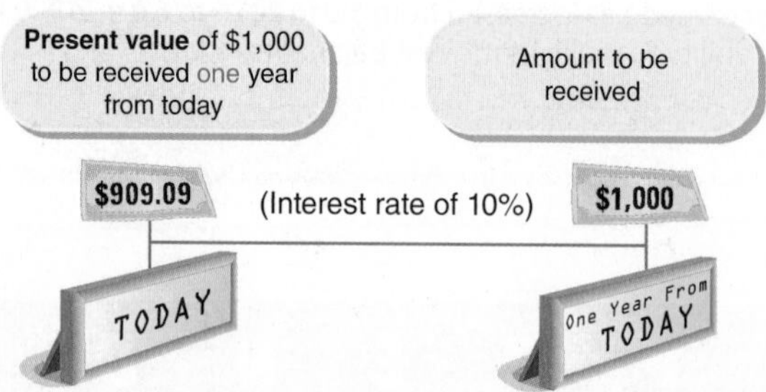

If the $1,000 is to be received in two years, with interest of 10% compounded at the end of the first year, the present value is $826.45 ($909.09 ÷ 1.10). This present value is illustrated in Exhibit 7.

EXHIBIT 7

Present Value of an Amount to Be Received in Two Years

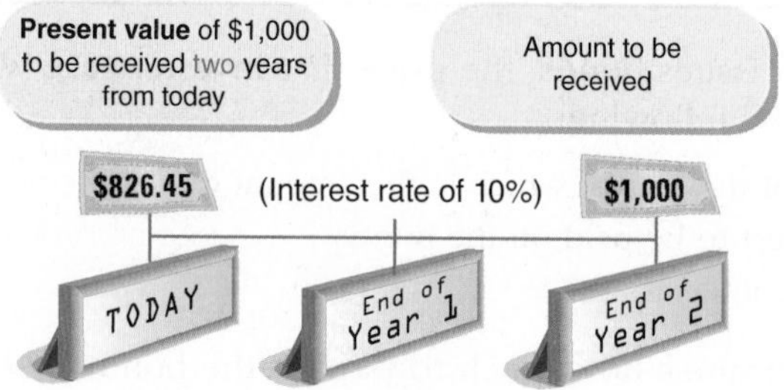

Spreadsheet software and business calculators have built-in present value functions that can also be used to compute present values.

The present value of an amount to be received in the future can be determined by a series of divisions as illustrated in Exhibits 5, 6, and 7. In practice, however, it is easier to use a table of present values.

The *present value of $1* table is used to find the present value factor for $1 to be received after a number of periods in the future. The amount to be received is then multiplied by this factor to determine its present value.

To illustrate, Exhibit 8 is a partial table of the present value of $1.[7] Exhibit 8 indicates that the present value of $1 to be received in two years with a market rate of interest of 10% a year is 0.82645. Multiplying $1,000 to be received in two years by 0.82645 yields $826.45 ($1,000 × 0.82645). This amount is the same as the amount computed earlier. In Exhibit 8, the Periods column represents the number of compounding periods, and the percentage columns represent the compound interest rate per period. Thus, the present value factor from Exhibit 8 for 12% for five years is 0.56743. If the interest is compounded semiannually, the interest rate is 6% (12% ÷ 2), and the number of periods is 10 (5 years × 2 times per year). Thus, the present value factor from Exhibit 8 for 6% and 10 periods is 0.55839.

7 To simplify the illustrations and homework assignments, the tables presented in this chapter are limited to 10 periods for a small number of interest rates and the amounts are carried to only five decimal places. More complete interest tables are presented in Appendix A of the text.

Present Value of $1 at Compound Interest EXHIBIT 8

Periods	4%	4½%	5%	5½%	6%	6½%	7%	10%	11%	12%	13%
1	0.96154	0.95694	0.95238	0.94787	0.94340	0.93897	0.93458	0.90909	0.90090	0.89286	0.88496
2	0.92456	0.91573	0.90703	0.89845	0.89000	0.88166	0.87344	0.82645	0.81162	0.79719	0.78315
3	0.88900	0.87630	0.86384	0.85161	0.83962	0.82785	0.81630	0.75131	0.73119	0.71178	0.69305
4	0.85480	0.83856	0.82270	0.80722	0.79209	0.77732	0.76290	0.68301	0.65873	0.63552	0.61332
5	0.82193	0.80245	0.78353	0.76513	0.74726	0.72988	0.71299	0.62092	0.59345	0.56743	0.54276
6	0.79031	0.76790	0.74622	0.72525	0.70496	0.68533	0.66634	0.56447	0.53464	0.50663	0.48032
7	0.75992	0.73483	0.71068	0.68744	0.66506	0.64351	0.62275	0.51316	0.48166	0.45235	0.42506
8	0.73069	0.70319	0.67684	0.65160	0.62741	0.60423	0.58201	0.46651	0.43393	0.40388	0.37616
9	0.70259	0.67290	0.64461	0.61763	0.59190	0.56735	0.54393	0.42410	0.39092	0.36061	0.33288
10	0.67556	0.64393	0.61391	0.58543	0.55839	0.53273	0.50835	0.38554	0.35218	0.32197	0.29459

Some additional examples using Exhibit 8 follow:

	Number of Periods	Interest Rate	Present Value of $1 Factor from Exhibit 8
10% for *two* years compounded *annually*	2	10%	0.82645
10% for *two* years compounded *semiannually*	4	5%	0.82270
10% for *three* years compounded *semiannually*	6	5%	0.74622
12% for *five* years compounded *semiannually*	10	6%	0.55839

Present Value of the Periodic Receipts A series of equal cash receipts spaced equally in time is called an **annuity**. The **present value of an annuity** is the sum of the present values of each cash receipt. To illustrate, assume that $100 is to be received annually for two years and that the market rate of interest is 10%. Using Exhibit 8, the present value of the receipt of the two amounts of $100 is $173.55, as shown in Exhibit 9.

EXHIBIT 9

Present Value of an Annuity

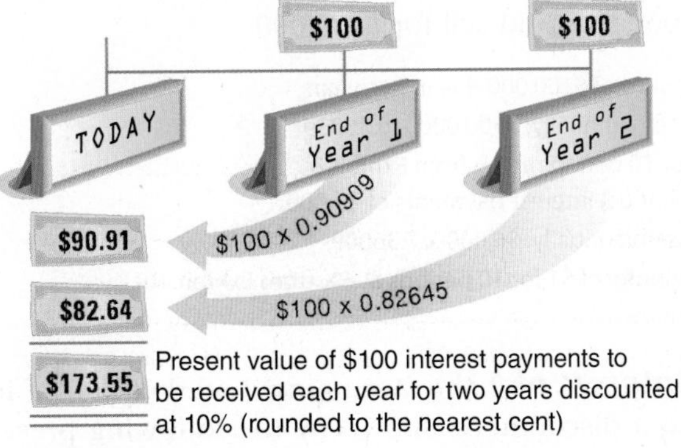

Instead of using present value of $1 tables to determine the present value of each cash flow separately, such as in Exhibit 8, the present value of an annuity can be computed in a single step. Using a value from the *present value of an annuity of $1* table in Exhibit 10, the present value of the entire annuity can be determined by multiplying the equal cash payment times the appropriate present value of an annuity of $1.

To illustrate, the present value of $100 to be received at the end of each of the next two years at 10% compound interest per period is $173.55 ($100 × 1.73554). This amount is the same amount computed previously using the present value of $1.

EXHIBIT 10 **Present Value of an Annuity of $1 at Compound Interest**

Periods	4%	4½%	5%	5½%	6%	6½%	7%	10%	11%	12%	13%
1	0.96154	0.95694	0.95238	0.94787	0.94340	0.93897	0.93458	0.90909	0.90090	0.89286	0.88496
2	1.88609	1.87267	1.85941	1.84632	1.83339	1.82063	1.80802	1.73554	1.71252	1.69005	1.66810
3	2.77509	2.74896	2.72325	2.69793	2.67301	2.64848	2.62432	2.48685	2.44371	2.40183	2.36115
4	3.62990	3.58753	3.54595	3.50515	3.46511	3.42580	3.38721	3.16987	3.10245	3.03735	2.97447
5	4.45182	4.38998	4.32948	4.27028	4.21236	4.15568	4.10020	3.79079	3.69590	3.60478	3.51723
6	5.24214	5.15787	5.07569	4.99553	4.91732	4.84101	4.76654	4.35526	4.23054	4.11141	3.99755
7	6.00205	5.89270	5.78637	5.68297	5.58238	5.48452	5.38929	4.86842	4.71220	4.56376	4.42261
8	6.73274	6.59589	6.46321	6.33457	6.20979	6.08875	5.97130	5.33493	5.14612	4.96764	4.79677
9	7.43533	7.26879	7.10782	6.95220	6.80169	6.65610	6.51523	5.75902	5.53705	5.32825	5.13166
10	8.11090	7.91272	7.72173	7.53763	7.36009	7.18883	7.02358	6.14457	5.88923	5.65022	5.42624

Pricing Bonds

The selling price of a bond is the sum of the present values of:

- The face amount of the bonds due at the maturity date
- The periodic interest to be paid on the bonds

The market rate of interest is used to compute the present value of both the face amount and the periodic interest.[8]

To illustrate the pricing of bonds, assume that Southern Utah Communications Inc. issued the following bond on January 1:

Face amount	$100,000
Contract rate of interest	12%
Interest paid semiannually on June 30 and December 31.	
Term of bonds	5 years

Market Rate of Interest of 12% Assuming a market rate of interest of 12%, the bonds would sell for their face amount. As shown by the following present value computations, the bonds would sell for $100,000:

Present value of face amount of $100,000 due in five years, at 12% compounded semiannually: $100,000 × 0.55839 (present value of $1 for 10 periods at 6% from Exhibit 8)	$ 55,839
Present value of 10 semiannual interest payments of $6,000, at 12% compounded semiannually: $6,000 × 7.36009 (present value of an annuity of $1 for 10 periods at 6% from Exhibit 10)	44,161
Total present value of bonds	$100,000

Market Rate of Interest of 13% Assuming a market rate of interest of 13%, the bonds would sell at a discount. As shown by the following present value computations, the bonds would sell for $96,406:[9]

Present value of face amount of $100,000 due in five years, at 13% compounded semiannually: $100,000 × 0.53273 (present value of $1 for 10 periods at 6½% from Exhibit 8)	$53,273
Present value of 10 semiannual interest payments of $6,000, at 13% compounded semiannually: $6,000 × 7.18883 (present value of an annuity of $1 for 10 periods at 6½% from Exhibit 10)	43,133
Total present value of bonds	$96,406

8 An online appendix, *Computing Present Values*, contains examples of Excel spreadsheets for computing present values and pricing bonds.

9 Some corporations issue bonds called *zero-coupon bonds* that provide for only the payment of the face amount at maturity. Such bonds sell for large discounts. In this example, such a bond would sell for $53,273, which is the present value of the face amount.

Market Rate of Interest of 11% Assuming a market rate of interest of 11%, the bonds would sell at a premium. As shown by the following present value computations, the bonds would sell for $103,769:

Present value of face amount of $100,000 due in five years, at 11% compounded semiannually: $100,000 × 0.58543 (present value of $1 for 10 periods at 5½% from Exhibit 8)	$ 58,543
Present value of 10 semiannual interest payments of $6,000, at 11% compounded semiannually: $6,000 × 7.53763 (present value of an annuity of $1 for 10 periods at 5½% from Exhibit 10)	45,226
Total present value of bonds	$103,769

As shown, the selling price of the bond varies with the present value of the bond's face amount at maturity, interest payments, and the market rate of interest.

APPENDIX 2

Interest Rate Method of Amortization

APP. 2 OBJ. Use the effective interest rate method to amortize bond payable discounts and premiums.

The **effective interest rate method** of amortization is an alternative method for amortizing the discount or premium on a bond, which provides for a constant *rate* of interest over the life of the bonds. As the discount or premium is amortized, the carrying amount of the bonds changes. As a result, interest expense also changes each period. This is in contrast to the straight-line method, which provides for a constant *amount* of interest expense each period.

The interest rate used in the effective interest rate method of amortization, sometimes called the *interest method*, is the market rate on the date the bonds are issued. The carrying amount of the bonds is multiplied by this interest rate to determine the interest expense for the period. The difference between the interest expense and the interest payment is the amount of discount or premium to be amortized for the period.

Amortization of Discount by the Interest Method

To illustrate, the following data taken from the chapter illustration of issuing bonds at a discount are used:

Face value of 12%, five-year bonds, interest compounded semiannually	$100,000
Present value of bonds at effective (market) rate of interest of 13%	96,406
Discount on bonds payable	$ 3,594

Exhibit 11 illustrates the interest method for the preceding bonds. Exhibit 11 begins with six columns. The first column is not lettered. The remaining columns are lettered A through E. The exhibit was then prepared as follows:

Step 1. List the interest payment dates in the first column, which for the preceding bond are 10 interest payment dates (semiannual interest over five years). Also list on the first line (above the first interest payment) the initial amount of discount in Column D and the initial carrying amount (selling price) of the bonds in Column E.

Step 2. List in Column A the semiannual interest payments, which for the preceding bond are $6,000 ($100,000 × 6%).

Step 3. Compute the interest expense in Column B by multiplying the bond carrying amount at the beginning of each period times 6½%, which is the semiannual effective interest (market) rate (13% ÷ 2).

Step 4. In Column C, compute the discount to be amortized each period by subtracting the interest payment in Column A ($6,000) from the interest expense for the period shown in Column B.

EXHIBIT 11 **Amortization of Discount on Bonds Payable**

Interest Payment Date	A Interest Paid (6% of Face Amount)	B Interest Expense (6½% of Bond Carrying Amount)	C Discount Amortization (B – A)	D Unamortized Discount (D – C)	E Bond Carrying Amount ($100,000 – D)
				$3,594	$ 96,406
June 30, 20Y5	$6,000	$6,266 (6½% of $96,406)	$266	3,328	96,672
Dec. 31, 20Y5	6,000	6,284 (6½% of $96,672)	284	3,044	96,956
June 30, 20Y6	6,000	6,302 (6½% of $96,956)	302	2,742	97,258
Dec. 31, 20Y6	6,000	6,322 (6½% of $97,258)	322	2,420	97,580
June 30, 20Y7	6,000	6,343 (6½% of $97,580)	343	2,077	97,923
Dec. 31, 20Y7	6,000	6,365 (6½% of $97,923)	365	1,712	98,288
June 30, 20Y8	6,000	6,389 (6½% of $98,288)	389	1,323	98,677
Dec. 31, 20Y8	6,000	6,414 (6½% of $98,677)	414	909	99,091
June 30, 20Y9	6,000	6,441 (6½% of $99,091)	441	468	99,532
Dec. 31, 20Y9	6,000	6,470 (6½% of $99,532)	468*	—	100,000

*Cannot exceed unamortized discount.

Step 5. Compute the remaining unamortized discount by subtracting the amortized discount in Column C for the period from the unamortized discount at the beginning of the period in Column D.

Step 6. Compute the bond carrying amount at the end of the period by subtracting the unamortized discount at the end of the period in Column D from the face amount of the bonds ($100,000).

Steps 3–6 are repeated for each interest payment.

As shown in Exhibit 11, the interest expense increases each period as the carrying amount of the bond increases. Also, the unamortized discount decreases each period to zero at the maturity date. Finally, the carrying amount of the bonds increases from $96,406 to $100,000 (the face amount) at maturity.

The entry to record the first interest payment on June 30, 20Y5, and the related discount amortization is as follows:

20Y5				
June	30	Interest Expense	6,266	
		Discount on Bonds Payable		266
		Cash		6,000
		Paid semiannual interest and amortized bond discount for ½ year.		

If the amortization is recorded only at the end of the year, the amount of the discount amortized on December 31, Year 1, would be $550. This is the sum of the first two semiannual amortization amounts ($266 and $284) from Exhibit 11.

Amortization of Premium by the Interest Method

To illustrate, the following data taken from the chapter illustration of issuing bonds at a premium are used:

Present value of bonds at effective (market) rate of interest of 11%..............................	$103,769
Face value of 12%, five-year bonds, interest compounded semiannually..........................	100,000
Premium on bonds payable..	$ 3,769

Exhibit 12 illustrates the interest method for the preceding bonds. Exhibit 12 begins with six columns. The first column is not lettered. The remaining columns are lettered A through E.

Amortization of Premium on Bonds Payable EXHIBIT 12

Interest Payment Date	A Interest Paid (6% of Face Amount)	B Interest Expense (5½% of Bond Carrying Amount)	C Premium Amortization (A – B)	D Unamortized Premium (D – C)	E Bond Carrying Amount ($100,000 + D)
				$3,769	$103,769
June 30, 20Y5	$6,000	$5,707 (5½% of $103,769)	$293	3,476	103,476
Dec. 31, 20Y5	6,000	5,691 (5½% of $103,476)	309	3,167	103,167
June 30, 20Y6	6,000	5,674 (5½% of $103,167)	326	2,841	102,841
Dec. 31, 20Y6	6,000	5,656 (5½% of $102,841)	344	2,497	102,497
June 30, 20Y7	6,000	5,637 (5½% of $102,497)	363	2,134	102,134
Dec. 31, 20Y7	6,000	5,617 (5½% of $102,134)	383	1,751	101,751
June 30, 20Y8	6,000	5,596 (5½% of $101,751)	404	1,347	101,347
Dec. 31, 20Y8	6,000	5,574 (5½% of $101,347)	426	921	100,921
June 30, 20Y9	6,000	5,551 (5½% of $100,921)	449	472	100,472
Dec. 31, 20Y9	6,000	5,526 (5½% of $100,472)	472*	—	100,000

*Cannot exceed unamortized premium.

The exhibit was then prepared as follows:

Step 1. List the number of interest payments in the first column, which for the preceding bond are 10 interest payments (semiannual interest over five years). Also list on the first line the initial amount of premium in Column D and the initial carrying amount of the bonds in Column E.

Step 2. List in Column A the semiannual interest payments, which for the preceding bond are $6,000 ($100,000 × 6%).

Step 3. Compute the interest expense in Column B by multiplying the bond carrying amount at the beginning of each period times 5½%, which is the semiannual effective interest (market) rate (11% ÷ 2).

Step 4. In Column C, compute the premium to be amortized each period by subtracting the interest expense for the period shown in Column B from the interest payment in Column A ($6,000).

Step 5. Compute the remaining unamortized premium by subtracting the amortized premium in Column C for the period from the unamortized premium at the beginning of the period in Column D.

Step 6. Compute the bond carrying amount at the end of the period by adding the unamortized premium at the end of the period in Column D to the face amount of the bonds ($100,000).

Steps 3–6 are repeated for each interest payment.

As shown in Exhibit 12, the interest expense decreases each period as the carrying amount of the bond decreases. Also, the unamortized premium decreases each period to zero at the maturity date. Finally, the carrying amount of the bonds decreases from $103,769 to $100,000 (the face amount) at maturity.

The entry to record the first interest payment on June 30, 20Y5, and the related premium amortization is as follows:

20Y5					
June	30	Interest Expense		5,707	
		Premium on Bonds Payable		293	
		Cash			6,000
		Paid semiannual interest and amortized bond premium for ½ year.			

If the amortization is recorded only at the end of the year, the amount of the premium amortized on December 31, Year 1, would be $602. This is the sum of the first two semiannual amortization amounts ($293 and $309) from Exhibit 12.

At a Glance 14

OBJ. 1 Compute the potential impact of long-term borrowing on earnings per share.

Key Points Corporations can finance their operations by issuing short-term debt, long-term debt, or equity. One of the many factors that influence a corporation's decision on whether it should issue long-term debt or equity is the effect each alternative has on earnings per share.

Learning Outcomes	Example Exercises	Practice Exercises
• Define the concept of a bond.		
• Compute and compare the effect of alternative long-term financing plans on earnings per share.	EE14-1	PE14-1A, 14-1B

OBJ. 2 Describe the characteristics and terminology of bonds payable.

Key Points A corporation that issues bonds enters into a contract, or bond indenture.

When a corporation issues bonds, the price that buyers are willing to pay for the bonds depends on (1) the face amount of the bonds, (2) the periodic interest to be paid on the bonds, and (3) the market rate of interest.

Learning Outcomes	Example Exercises	Practice Exercises
• Define the characteristics of a bond.		
• Describe the various types of bonds.		
• Describe the factors that determine the price of a bond.		

OBJ. 3 Describe and illustrate the accounting for bonds payable.

Key Points The journal entry for issuing bonds payable debits Cash and credits Bonds Payable. Any difference between the face amount of the bonds and the selling price is debited to Discount on Bonds Payable or credited to Premium on Bonds Payable when the bonds are issued. The discount or premium on bonds payable is amortized to interest expense over the life of the bonds.

At the maturity date, the entry to record the repayment of the face value of a bond is a debit to Bonds Payable and a credit to Cash.

When a corporation redeems bonds before they mature, Bonds Payable is debited for the face amount of the bonds, the premium (discount) on bonds payable account is debited (credited) for its unamortized balance, Cash is credited, and any gain or loss on the redemption is recorded.

Learning Outcomes	Example Exercises	Practice Exercises
• Journalize the issuance of bonds at face value and the payment of periodic interest.	EE14-2	PE14-2A, 14-2B
• Journalize the issuance of bonds at a discount.	EE14-3	PE14-3A, 14-3B
• Journalize the amortization of a bond discount.	EE14-4	PE14-4A, 14-4B
• Journalize the issuance of bonds at a premium.	EE14-5	PE14-5A, 14-5B
• Journalize the amortization of a bond premium.	EE14-6	PE14-6A, 14-6B
• Describe bond redemptions.		
• Journalize the redemption of bonds payable.	EE14-7	PE14-7A, 14-7B

OBJ.4 Describe and illustrate the accounting for installment notes.

Key Points An installment note requires the borrower to make equal periodic payments to the lender for the term of the note. Unlike bonds, the annual payment in an installment note consists of both principal and interest. The journal entry for the annual payment debits Interest Expense and Notes Payable and credits Cash for the amount of the payment. After the final payment, the carrying amount on the note is zero.

Learning Outcomes	*Example Exercises*	*Practice Exercises*
• Define the characteristics of an installment note.		
• Journalize the issuance of installment notes.	EE14-8	PE14-8A, 14-8B
• Journalize the annual payment for an installment note.		

OBJ.5 Describe and illustrate the reporting of long-term liabilities, including bonds and installment notes payable.

Key Points Bonds payable and notes payable are usually reported as long-term liabilities. If the balance sheet date is within one year, they are reported as current liabilities. A discount on bonds should be reported as a deduction from the related bonds payable. A premium on bonds should be reported as an addition to related bonds payable.

Learning Outcomes	*Example Exercises*	*Practice Exercises*
• Illustrate the balance sheet presentation of bonds payable and notes payable.		

OBJ.6 Describe and illustrate how the times interest earned ratio is used to evaluate a company's financial condition.

Key Points The times interest earned ratio measures the risk to bondholders that a company will not be able to make its interest payments. It is computed by dividing income before income tax plus interest expense by interest expense. This ratio computes the number of times interest payments could be paid out of current period earnings.

Learning Outcomes	*Example Exercises*	*Practice Exercises*
• Describe and compute the times interest earned ratio.	EE14-9	PE14-9A, 14-9B
• Interpret the times interest earned ratio.		

Illustrative Problem

The fiscal year of Russell Inc., a manufacturer of acoustical supplies, ends December 31. Selected transactions for the period 20Y1 through 20Y8, involving bonds payable issued by Russell Inc., are as follows:

20Y1

June 30. Issued $2,000,000 of 25-year, 7% callable bonds dated June 30, 20Y1, for cash of $1,920,000. Interest is payable semiannually on June 30 and December 31.

Dec. 31. Paid the semiannual interest on the bonds. The bond discount is amortized annually in a separate journal entry.

(Continued)

Dec. 31. Recorded straight-line amortization of $1,600 of discount on the bonds.

20Y2

June 30. Paid the semiannual interest on the bonds. The bond discount is amortized annually in a separate journal entry.

Dec. 31. Paid the semiannual interest on the bonds. The bond discount is amortized annually in a separate journal entry.

31. Recorded straight-line amortization of $3,200 of discount on the bonds.

20Y8

June 30. Recorded the redemption of the bonds, which were called at 101.5. The balance in the bond discount account is $57,600 after the payment of interest and amortization of discount have been recorded. Record the redemption only.

Instructions

1. Journalize entries to record the preceding transactions.
2. Determine the amount of interest expense for 20Y1 and 20Y2.
3. Determine the carrying amount of the bonds as of December 31, 20Y2.

Solution

1.

20Y1					
June	30	Cash		1,920,000	
		Discount on Bonds Payable		80,000	
		Bonds Payable			2,000,000
Dec.	31	Interest Expense*		70,000	
		Cash			70,000
	31	Interest Expense		1,600	
		Discount on Bonds Payable			1,600
		Amortization of discount from July 1 to December 31.			
20Y2					
June	30	Interest Expense		70,000	
		Cash			70,000
Dec.	31	Interest Expense		70,000	
		Cash			70,000
	31	Interest Expense		3,200	
		Discount on Bonds Payable			3,200
		Amortization of discount from January 1 to December 31.			
20Y8					
June	30	Bonds Payable		2,000,000	
		Loss on Redemption of Bonds Payable		87,600	
		Discount on Bonds Payable			57,600
		Cash			2,030,000

*$2,000,000 × 7% × ½

2. a. 20Y1: $71,600 = $70,000 + $1,600

   b. 20Y2: $143,200 = $70,000 + $70,000 + $3,200

3.

Initial carrying amount of bonds	$1,920,000
Discount amortized on December 31, 20Y1	1,600
Discount amortized on December 31, 20Y2	3,200
Carrying amount of bonds, December 31, 20Y2	$1,924,800

Key Terms

amortization (687)
annuity (699)
bond (681)
bond indenture (684)
carrying amount (687)
contract rate (684)
discount (684)
earnings per share (EPS) (681)
effective interest rate method (701)
effective rate of interest (684)
face amount (684)
future value (698)
installment note (692)
market rate of interest (684)
mortgage notes (692)
premium (685)
present value (697)
present value of an annuity (699)
times interest earned (696)

Discussion Questions

1. Describe the two distinct obligations incurred by a corporation when issuing bonds.
2. Explain the meaning of each of the following terms as they relate to a bond issue: (a) convertible and (b) callable.
3. If you asked your broker to buy you a 12% bond when the market interest rate for such bonds was 11%, would you expect to pay more or less than the face amount for the bond? Explain.
4. A corporation issues $26,000,000 of 9% bonds to yield interest at the rate of 7%. (a) Was the amount of cash received from the sale of the bonds greater or less than $26,000,000? (b) Identify the following amounts as they relate to the bond issue: (1) face amount, (2) market or effective rate of interest, (3) contract rate of interest, and (4) maturity amount.
5. If bonds issued by a corporation are sold at a discount, is the market rate of interest greater or less than the contract rate?
6. The following data relate to a $2,000,000, 8% bond issued for a selected semiannual interest period:

Bond carrying amount at beginning of period	$2,125,000
Interest paid during period	160,000
Interest expense allocable to the period	148,750

(a) Were the bonds issued at a discount or at a premium? (b) What is the unamortized amount of the discount or premium account at the beginning of the period? (c) What account was debited to amortize the discount or premium?

7. Bonds Payable has a balance of $5,000,000, and Discount on Bonds Payable has a balance of $150,000. If the issuing corporation redeems the bonds at 98, is there a gain or loss on the bond redemption?
8. What is a mortgage note?
9. Fleeson Company needs additional funds to purchase equipment for a new production facility and is considering either issuing bonds payable or borrowing the money from a local bank in the form of an installment note. How does an installment note differ from a bond payable?
10. In what section of the balance sheet would a bond payable be reported if (a) it is payable within one year and (b) it is payable beyond one year?

Practice Exercises

Example Exercises

SHOW ME HOW

EE 14-1 *p. 683* **PE 14-1A Alternative financing plans** **OBJ. 1**

Desmond Co. is considering the following alternative financing plans:

	Plan 1	Plan 2
Issue 5% bonds (at face value)	$3,000,000	$1,000,000
Issue preferred $1 stock, $20 par	—	3,000,000
Issue common stock, $10 par	3,000,000	2,000,000

Income tax is estimated at 40% of income.

Determine the earnings per share of common stock, assuming that income before bond interest and income tax is $400,000.

SHOW ME HOW

EE 14-1 *p. 683* **PE 14-1B Alternative financing plans** **OBJ. 1**

Vatican Co. is considering the following alternative financing plans:

	Plan 1	Plan 2
Issue 10% bonds (at face value)	$6,000,000	$3,750,000
Issue preferred $2.50 stock, $25 par	—	4,500,000
Issue common stock, $20 par	6,000,000	3,750,000

Income tax is estimated at 40% of income.

Determine the earnings per share of common stock, assuming that income before bond interest and income tax is $3,000,000.

SHOW ME HOW

EE 14-2 *p. 686* **PE 14-2A Issuing bonds at face amount** **OBJ. 3**

The first day of the fiscal year, a company issues a $3,500,000, 5%, 10-year bond that pays semiannual interest of $87,500 ($3,500,000 × 5% × ½ year), receiving cash of $3,500,000. Journalize the entries to record (a) the issuance of the bonds, (b) the first interest payment, and (c) the payment of the principal on the maturity date.

SHOW ME HOW

EE 14-2 *p. 686* **PE 14-2B Issuing bonds at face amount** **OBJ. 3**

The first day of the fiscal year, a company issues a $700,000, 6%, 10-year bond that pays semiannual interest of $21,000 ($700,000 × 6% × ½ year), receiving cash of $700,000. Journalize the entries to record (a) the issuance of the bonds, (b) the first interest payment, and (c) the payment of the principal on the maturity date.

SHOW ME HOW

EE 14-3 *p. 687* **PE 14-3A Issuing bonds at a discount** **OBJ. 3**

On the first day of the fiscal year, a company issues a $1,800,000, 6%, five-year bond that pays semiannual interest of $54,000 ($1,800,000 × 6% × ½), receiving cash of $1,725,151. Journalize the entry to record the issuance of the bonds.

SHOW ME HOW

EE 14-3 *p. 687* **PE 14-3B Issuing bonds at a discount** **OBJ. 3**

On the first day of the fiscal year, a company issues a $4,200,000, 10%, five-year bond that pays semiannual interest of $210,000 ($4,200,000 × 10% × ½), receiving cash of $4,041,710. Journalize the entry to record the issuance of the bonds.

SHOW ME HOW

EE 14-4 *p. 689* **PE 14-4A Discount amortization** **OBJ. 3**

Using the bond from Practice Exercise 14-3A, journalize the first interest payment and the amortization of the related bond discount. Round to the nearest dollar.

SHOW ME HOW

EE 14-4 *p. 689* **PE 14-4B Discount amortization** **OBJ. 3**

Using the bond from Practice Exercise 14-3B, journalize the first interest payment and the amortization of the related bond discount. Round to the nearest dollar.

EE 14-5 *p. 689* **PE 14-5A Issuing bonds at a premium** **OBJ. 3**

On the first day of the fiscal year, a company issues an $8,600,000, 11%, five-year bond that pays semiannual interest of $473,000 ($8,600,000 × 11% × ½), receiving cash of $8,932,035. Journalize the bond issuance.

EE 14-5 *p. 689* **PE 14-5B Issuing bonds at a premium** **OBJ. 3**

On the first day of the fiscal year, a company issues a $5,300,000, 8%, five-year bond that pays semiannual interest of $212,000 ($5,300,000 × 8% × ½), receiving cash of $5,520,390. Journalize the bond issuance.

EE 14-6 *p. 691* **PE 14-6A Premium amortization** **OBJ. 3**

Using the bond from Practice Exercise 14-5A, journalize the first interest payment and the amortization of the related bond premium. Round to the nearest dollar.

EE 14-6 *p. 691* **PE 14-6B Premium amortization** **OBJ. 3**

Using the bond from Practice Exercise 14-5B, journalize the first interest payment and the amortization of the related bond premium. Round to the nearest dollar.

SHOW ME HOW

EE 14-7 *p. 692* **PE 14-7A Redemption of bonds payable** **OBJ. 3**

A $2,300,000 bond issue on which there is an unamortized discount of $107,500 is redeemed for $2,231,000. Journalize the redemption of the bonds.

EE 14-7 *p. 692* **PE 14-7B Redemption of bonds payable** **OBJ. 3**

A $1,900,000 bond issue on which there is an unamortized premium of $101,264 is redeemed for $1,979,000. Journalize the redemption of the bonds.

EE 14-8 *p. 694* **PE 14-8A Journalizing installment notes** **OBJ. 4**

On the first day of the fiscal year, a company issues $89,000, 6%, five-year installment notes that have annual payments of $21,128. The first note payment consists of $5,340 of interest and $15,788 of principal repayment.

a. Journalize the entry to record the issuance of the installment notes.

b. Journalize the first annual note payment.

EE 14-8 *p. 694* **PE 14-8B Journalizing installment notes** **OBJ. 4**

On the first day of the fiscal year, a company issues $35,000, 5%, eight-year installment notes that have annual payments of $5,415. The first note payment consists of $1,750 of interest and $3,665 of principal repayment.

a. Journalize the entry to record the issuance of the installment notes.

b. Journalize the first annual note payment.

EE 14-9 *p. 696* **PE 14-9A Times interest earned** **OBJ. 6**

Sprout Company reported the following on the company's income statement in two recent years:

	Current Year	Prior Year
Interest expense	$ 510,000	$ 480,000
Income before income tax expense	5,610,000	6,720,000

(Continued)

a. Determine the times interest earned ratio for the current year and the prior year. Round to one decimal place.

b. Is the times interest earned ratio improving or declining?

EE 14-9 p. 696

PE 14-9B Times interest earned **OBJ. 6**

Mahmood Products Inc. reported the following on the company's income statement in two recent years:

	Current Year	Prior Year
Interest expense	$ 270,000	$ 250,000
Income before income tax expense	4,212,000	3,450,000

a. Determine the times interest earned ratio for the current year and the prior year. Round to one decimal place.

b. Is the times interest earned ratio improving or declining?

Exercises

EX 14-1 Effect of financing on earnings per share **OBJ. 1**

✔ b. $2.10

Henriksen Co., which produces and sells biking equipment, is financed as follows:

Bonds payable, 5% (issued at face amount)	$6,000,000
Preferred $2.00 stock, $100 par	3,000,000
Common stock, $25 par	5,000,000

Income tax is estimated at 40% of income.

Determine the earnings per share of common stock, assuming that the income before bond interest and income tax is (a) $900,000, (b) $1,100,000, and (c) $1,500,000.

EX 14-2 Evaluate alternative financing plans **OBJ. 1**

Based on the data in Exercise 14-1, what factors other than earnings per share should be considered in evaluating these alternative financing plans?

EX 14-3 Corporate financing **OBJ. 1**

The financial statements for **Nike, Inc.**, are presented in Appendix C at the end of the text. What is the major source of financing for Nike?

EX 14-4 Bond price **OBJ. 3**

Stone Energy Corporation's 7.5% bonds due in 2022 were reported as selling for 77.00.

Were the bonds selling at a premium or at a discount? Why is Stone Energy Corporation able to sell its bonds at this price?

EX 14-5 Entries for issuing bonds **OBJ. 3**

Abioye Co. produces and distributes semiconductors for use by computer manufacturers. Abioye Co. issued $700,000 of 10-year, 9% bonds on May 1 of the current year at face value, with interest payable on May 1 and November 1. The fiscal year of the company is the calendar year. Journalize the entries to record the following selected transactions for the current year:

May 1. Issued the bonds for cash at their face amount.

Nov. 1. Paid the interest on the bonds.

Dec. 31. Recorded accrued interest for two months.

EX 14-6 Entries for issuing bonds and amortizing discount by straight-line method OBJ. 2, 3

✔ b. $505,836

SHOW ME HOW

On the first day of its fiscal year, Jacinto Company issued $6,500,000 of six-year, 7% bonds to finance its operations of producing and selling home improvement products. Interest is payable semiannually. The bonds were issued at a market (effective) interest rate of 8%, resulting in Jacinto Company receiving cash of $6,194,985.

a. Journalize the entries to record the following:
   1. Issuance of the bonds.
   2. First semiannual interest payment. The bond discount amortization is combined with the semiannual interest payment. Round to the nearest dollar.
   3. Second semiannual interest payment. The bond discount amortization is combined with the semiannual interest payment. Round to the nearest dollar.

b. Determine the amount of the bond interest expense for the first year.

c. Explain why the company was able to issue the bonds for only $6,194,985 rather than for the face amount of $6,500,000.

EX 14-7 Entries for issuing bonds and amortizing premium by straight-line method OBJ. 2, 3

SHOW ME HOW

Favreau Corporation wholesales repair products to equipment manufacturers. On April 1, Year 1, Favreau Corporation issued $35,000,000 of five-year, 7% bonds at a market (effective) interest rate of 6%, receiving cash of $36,492,785. Interest is payable semiannually on April 1 and October 1. Journalize the entries to record the following:

a. Issuance of bonds on April 1.

b. First interest payment on October 1 and amortization of bond premium for six months, using the straight-line method. The bond premium amortization is combined with the semiannual interest payment. Round to the nearest dollar.

c. Explain why the company was able to issue the bonds for $36,492,785 rather than for the face amount of $35,000,000.

EX 14-8 Entries for issuing and calling bonds; loss OBJ. 3

SHOW ME HOW

Rushton Corp., a wholesaler of music equipment, issued $11,000,000 of 20-year, 9% callable bonds on March 1, 20Y1, at their face amount, with interest payable on March 1 and September 1. The fiscal year of the company is the calendar year. Journalize the entries to record the following selected transactions:

20Y1

Mar. 1. Issued the bonds for cash at their face amount.

Sept. 1. Paid the interest on the bonds.

20Y5

Sept. 1. Called the bond issue at 101, the rate provided in the bond indenture. (Omit entry for payment of interest.)

EX 14-9 Entries for issuing and calling bonds; gain OBJ. 3

SHOW ME HOW

Emil Corp. produces and sells wind-energy-driven engines. To finance its operations, Emil Corp. issued $15,000,000 of 20-year, 9% callable bonds on May 1, 20Y1, at their face amount, with interest payable on May 1 and November 1. The fiscal year of the company is the calendar year. Journalize the entries to record the following selected transactions:

20Y1

May 1. Issued the bonds for cash at their face amount.

Nov. 1. Paid the interest on the bonds.

20Y5

Nov. 1. Called the bond issue at 96, the rate provided in the bond indenture. (Omit entry for payment of interest.)

EX 14-10 Entries for installment note transactions **OBJ. 4, 5**

On the first day of the fiscal year, Shiller Company borrowed $85,000 by giving a seven-year, 7% installment note to Soros Bank. The note requires annual payments of $15,772, with the first payment occurring on the last day of the fiscal year. The first payment consists of interest of $5,950 and principal repayment of $9,822.

a. Journalize the entries to record the following:
   1. Issued the installment note for cash on the first day of the fiscal year.
   2. Paid the first annual payment on the note.

b. Explain how the notes payable would be reported on the balance sheet at the end of the first year.

EX 14-11 Entries for installment note transactions **OBJ. 4**

On January 1, Year 1, Wedekind Company issued a $170,000, five-year, 8% installment note to Shannon Bank. The note requires annual payments of $42,578, beginning on December 31, Year 1. Journalize the entries to record the following:

Year 1

Jan. 1. Issued the note for cash at its face amount.

Dec. 31. Paid the annual payment on the note, which consisted of interest of $13,600 and principal of $28,978.

Year 4

Dec. 31. Paid the annual payment on the note, including $6,074 of interest. The remainder of the payment reduced the principal balance on the note.

EX 14-12 Entries for installment note transactions **OBJ. 4**

On January 1, Year 1, Bryson Company obtained a $147,750, four-year, 7% installment note from Campbell Bank. The note requires annual payments of $43,620, beginning on December 31, Year 1.

a. Prepare an amortization table for this installment note, similar to the one presented in Exhibit 4. Round to nearest dollar.

b. Journalize the entries for the issuance of the note and the four annual note payments.

c. Describe how the annual note payment would be reported in the Year 1 income statement.

EX 14-13 Reporting bonds **OBJ. 5**

At the beginning of the current year, two bond issues (Simmons Industries 7%, 20-year bonds and Hunter Corporation 8%, 10-year bonds) were outstanding. During the year, the Simmons Industries bonds were redeemed and a significant loss on the redemption of bonds was reported as cost of merchandise sold on the income statement. At the end of the year, the Hunter Corporation bonds were reported as a noncurrent liability. The maturity date on the Hunter Corporation bonds was early in the following year.

Identify the flaws in the reporting practices related to the two bond issues.

EX 14-14 Times interest earned **OBJ. 6**

The following data were taken from recent annual reports of **Southwest Airlines**, which operates a low-fare airline service to more than 50 cities in the United States:

	Current Year	Prior Year
Interest expense	$ 131,000,000	$ 114,000,000
Income before income tax expense	3,164,000,000	3,265,000,000

a. Determine the times interest earned ratio for the current and preceding years. Round to one decimal place.

b. What conclusions can you draw?

EX 14-15 Times interest earned

OBJ. 6

Loomis, Inc., reported the following on the company's income statement in two recent years:

	Current Year	Prior Year
Interest expense	$ 13,500,000	$ 16,000,000
Income before income tax expense	310,500,000	432,000,000

a. Determine the times interest earned ratio for the current year and the prior year. Round to one decimal place.

b. Is this ratio improving or declining?

EX 14-16 Times interest earned

OBJ. 6

Iacouva Company reported the following on the company's income statement for two recent years:

	Current Year	Prior Year
Interest expense	$5,000,000	$5,000,000
Income before income tax expense	3,500,000	6,000,000

a. Determine the times interest earned ratio for the current year and the prior year. Round to one decimal place.

b. What conclusions can you draw?

Appendix 1

EXCEL ONLINE

EX 14-17 Present value of amounts due

Tommy John is going to receive $1,000,000 in three years. The current market rate of interest is 10%.

a. Using the present value of $1 table in Exhibit 8, determine the present value of this amount compounded annually.

b. Why is the present value less than the $1,000,000 to be received in the future?

Appendix 1

EX 14-18 Present value of an annuity

Determine the present value of $200,000 to be received at the end of each of four years, using an interest rate of 7%, compounded annually, as follows:

a. By successive computations, using the present value table in Exhibit 8.

b. By using the present value table in Exhibit 10.

c. Why is the present value of the four $200,000 cash receipts less than the $800,000 to be received in the future?

Appendix 1

EX 14-19 Present value of an annuity

✔ $44,160,540

EXCEL ONLINE

On January 1, you win $60,000,000 in the state lottery. The $60,000,000 prize will be paid in equal installments of $6,000,000 over 10 years. The payments will be made on December 31 of each year, beginning on December 31 of the current year. If the current interest rate is 6%, determine the present value of your winnings. Use the present value tables in Appendix A.

Appendix 1

EX 14-20 Present value of an annuity

Assume the same data as in Exercise 14-19, except that the current interest rate is 10%.

Will the present value of your winnings using an interest rate of 10% be more than the present value of your winnings using an interest rate of 6%? Why or why not?

Appendix 1
EX 14-21 Present value of bonds payable; discount

Pinder Co. produces and sells high-quality video equipment. To finance its operations, Pinder Co. issued $25,000,000 of five-year, 7% bonds, with interest payable semiannually, at a market (effective) interest rate of 9%. Determine the present value of the bonds payable, using the present value tables in Exhibits 8 and 10. Round to the nearest dollar.

Appendix 1
EX 14-22 Present value of bonds payable; premium

✔ $45,323,443

Moss Co. issued $42,000,000 of five-year, 11% bonds, with interest payable semiannually, at a market (effective) interest rate of 9%. Determine the present value of the bonds payable using the present value tables in Exhibits 8 and 10. Round to the nearest dollar.

Appendix 2
EX 14-23 Amortize discount by interest method

✔ b. $3,923,959

On the first day of its fiscal year, Ebert Company issued $50,000,000 of 10-year, 7% bonds to finance its operations. Interest is payable semiannually. The bonds were issued at a market (effective) interest rate of 9%, resulting in Ebert Company receiving cash of $43,495,895. The company uses the interest method.

a. Journalize the entries to record the following:
   1. Sale of the bonds.
   2. First semiannual interest payment, including amortization of discount. Round to the nearest dollar.
   3. Second semiannual interest payment, including amortization of discount. Round to the nearest dollar.

b. Compute the amount of the bond interest expense for the first year.

c. Explain why the company was able to issue the bonds for only $43,495,895 rather than for the face amount of $50,000,000.

Appendix 2
EX 14-24 Amortize premium by interest method

✔ b. $1,662,619

Shunda Corporation wholesales parts to appliance manufacturers. On January 1, Year 1, Shunda Corporation issued $22,000,000 of five-year, 9% bonds at a market (effective) interest rate of 7%, receiving cash of $23,829,684. Interest is payable semiannually. Shunda Corporation's fiscal year begins on January 1. The company uses the interest method.

a. Journalize the entries to record the following:
   1. Sale of the bonds.
   2. First semiannual interest payment, including amortization of premium. Round to the nearest dollar.
   3. Second semiannual interest payment, including amortization of premium. Round to the nearest dollar.

b. Determine the bond interest expense for the first year.

c. Explain why the company was able to issue the bonds for $23,829,684 rather than for the face amount of $22,000,000.

Appendix 1 and Appendix 2
EX 14-25 Compute bond proceeds, amortizing premium by interest method, and interest expense

✔ a. $37,702,483
✔ c. $225,620

Ware Co. produces and sells motorcycle parts. On the first day of its fiscal year, Ware Co. issued $35,000,000 of five-year, 12% bonds at a market (effective) interest rate of 10%, with interest payable semiannually. Compute the following, presenting figures used in your computations:

a. The amount of cash proceeds from the sale of the bonds. Use the tables of present values in Exhibits 8 and 10. Round to the nearest dollar.

b. The amount of premium to be amortized for the first semiannual interest payment period, using the interest method. Round to the nearest dollar.

c. The amount of premium to be amortized for the second semiannual interest payment period, using the interest method. Round to the nearest dollar.

d. The amount of the bond interest expense for the first year.

Appendix 1 and Appendix 2

EX 14-26 Compute bond proceeds, amortizing discount by interest method, and interest expense

✔ a. $71,167,524
✔ b. $670,051

EXCEL ONLINE

Boyd Co. produces and sells aviation equipment. On the first day of its fiscal year, Boyd Co. issued $80,000,000 of five-year, 9% bonds at a market (effective) interest rate of 12%, with interest payable semiannually. Compute the following, presenting figures used in your computations:

a. The amount of cash proceeds from the sale of the bonds. Use the tables of present values in Exhibits 8 and 10. Round to the nearest dollar.

b. The amount of discount to be amortized for the first semiannual interest payment period, using the interest method. Round to the nearest dollar.

c. The amount of discount to be amortized for the second semiannual interest payment period, using the interest method. Round to the nearest dollar.

d. The amount of the bond interest expense for the first year.

Problems: Series A

PR 14-1A Effect of financing on earnings per share OBJ. 1

✔ 1. Plan 3: $1.44

Three different plans for financing an $18,000,000 corporation are under consideration by its organizers. Under each of the following plans, the securities will be issued at their par or face amount, and the income tax rate is estimated at 40% of income:

	Plan 1	Plan 2	Plan 3
8% bonds	—	—	$ 9,000,000
Preferred 4% stock, $20 par	—	$ 9,000,000	4,500,000
Common stock, $10 par	$18,000,000	9,000,000	4,500,000
Total	$18,000,000	$18,000,000	$18,000,000

Instructions

1. Determine the earnings per share of common stock for each plan, assuming that the income before bond interest and income tax is $2,100,000.
2. Determine the earnings per share of common stock for each plan, assuming that the income before bond interest and income tax is $1,050,000.
3. Discuss the advantages and disadvantages of each plan.

PR 14-2A Bond discount, entries for bonds payable transactions OBJ. 2, 3

✔ 3. $516,945

SHOW ME HOW

On July 1, Year 1, Khatri Industries Inc. issued $18,000,000 of 10-year, 5% bonds at a market (effective) interest rate of 6%, receiving cash of $16,661,102. Interest on the bonds is payable semiannually on December 31 and June 30. The fiscal year of the company is the calendar year.

Instructions

1. Journalize the entry to record the amount of cash proceeds from the issuance of the bonds on July 1, Year 1.
2. Journalize the entries to record the following:
   a. The first semiannual interest payment on December 31, Year 1, and the amortization of the bond discount, using the straight-line method. Round to the nearest dollar.

(Continued)

b. The interest payment on June 30, Year 2, and the amortization of the bond discount, using the straight-line method. Round to the nearest dollar.

3. Determine the total interest expense for Year 1.
4. Will the bond proceeds always be less than the face amount of the bonds when the contract rate is less than the market rate of interest?
5. (Appendix 1) Compute the price of $16,661,102 received for the bonds by using the present value tables in Appendix A at the end of the text. Round to the nearest dollar.

PR 14-3A Bond premium, entries for bonds payable transactions **OBJ. 2, 3**

✔ 3. $1,151,165

O'Halloran Inc. produces and sells outdoor equipment. On July 1, Year 1, O'Halloran Inc. issued $32,000,000 of six-year, 8% bonds at a market (effective) interest rate of 7%, receiving cash of $33,546,022. Interest on the bonds is payable semiannually on December 31 and June 30. The fiscal year of the company is the calendar year.

Instructions

1. Journalize the entry to record the amount of cash proceeds from the issuance of the bonds on July 1, Year 1.
2. Journalize the entries to record the following:
   a. The first semiannual interest payment on December 31, Year 1, and the amortization of the bond premium, using the straight-line method. Round to the nearest dollar.
   b. The interest payment on June 30, Year 2, and the amortization of the bond premium, using the straight-line method. Round to the nearest dollar.
3. Determine the total interest expense for Year 1.
4. Will the bond proceeds always be greater than the face amount of the bonds when the contract rate is greater than the market rate of interest?
5. (Appendix 1) Compute the price of $33,546,022 received for the bonds by using the present value tables in Appendix A at the end of the text. Round to the nearest dollar.

PR 14-4A Entries for bonds payable and installment note transactions **OBJ. 3, 4**

✔ 3. $64,317,346

SHOW ME HOW

The following transactions were completed by Winklevoss Inc., whose fiscal year is the calendar year:

Year 1

July 1. Issued $74,000,000 of 20-year, 11% callable bonds dated July 1, Year 1, at a market (effective) rate of 13%, receiving cash of $63,532,267. Interest is payable semiannually on December 31 and June 30.

Oct. 1. Borrowed $200,000 by issuing a six-year, 6% installment note to Nicks Bank. The note requires annual payments of $40,673, with the first payment occurring on September 30, Year 2.

Dec. 31. Accrued $3,000 of interest on the installment note. The interest is payable on the date of the next installment note payment.

31. Paid the semiannual interest on the bonds. The bond discount amortization of $261,693 is combined with the semiannual interest payment.

Year 2

June 30. Paid the semiannual interest on the bonds. The bond discount amortization of $261,693 is combined with the semiannual interest payment.

Sept. 30. Paid the annual payment on the note, which consisted of interest of $12,000 and principal of $28,673.

Dec. 31. Accrued $2,570 of interest on the installment note. The interest is payable on the date of the next installment note payment.

31. Paid the semiannual interest on the bonds. The bond discount amortization of $261,693 is combined with the semiannual interest payment.

Year 3

June 30. Recorded the redemption of the bonds, which were called at 98. The balance in the bond discount account is $9,420,961 after payment of interest and amortization of discount have been recorded. Record the redemption only.

Sept. 30. Paid the second annual payment on the note, which consisted of interest of $10,280 and principal of $30,393.

Instructions

1. Journalize the entries to record the foregoing transactions. Round all amounts to the nearest dollar.
2. Indicate the amount of the interest expense in (a) Year 1 and (b) Year 2.
3. Determine the carrying amount of the bonds as of December 31, Year 2.

Appendix 1 and Appendix 2

PR 14-5A Bond discount, entries for bonds payable transactions, interest method of amortizing bond discount

✔ 3. $499,833

On July 1, Year 1, Khatri Industries Inc. issued $18,000,000 of 10-year, 5% bonds at a market (effective) interest rate of 6%, receiving cash of $16,661,102. Interest on the bonds is payable semiannually on December 31 and June 30. The fiscal year of the company is the calendar year.

Instructions

1. Journalize the entry to record the amount of cash proceeds from the issuance of the bonds.
2. Journalize the entries to record the following:
   a. The first semiannual interest payment on December 31, Year 1, and the amortization of the bond discount, using the interest method. Round to the nearest dollar.
   b. The interest payment on June 30, Year 2, and the amortization of the bond discount, using the interest method. Round to the nearest dollar.
3. Determine the total interest expense for Year 1.

Appendix 1 and Appendix 2

PR 14-6A Bond premium, entries for bonds payable transactions, interest method of amortizing bond premium

✔ 3. $1,174,111

O'Halloran, Inc., produces and sells outdoor equipment. On July 1, Year 1, O'Halloran, Inc., issued $32,000,000 of 6-year, 8% bonds at a market (effective) interest rate of 7%, receiving cash of $33,546,022. Interest on the bonds is payable semiannually on December 31 and June 30. The fiscal year of the company is the calendar year.

Instructions

1. Journalize the entry to record the amount of cash proceeds from the issuance of the bonds.
2. Journalize the entries to record the following:
   a. The first semiannual interest payment on December 31, Year 1, and the amortization of the bond premium, using the interest method. Round to the nearest dollar.
   b. The interest payment on June 30, Year 2, and the amortization of the bond premium, using the interest method. Round to the nearest dollar.
3. Determine the total interest expense for Year 1.

Problems: Series B

PR 14-1B Effect of financing on earnings per share **OBJ. 1**

✔ 1. Plan 3: $2.84

Three different plans for financing an $80,000,000 corporation are under consideration by its organizers. Under each of the following plans, the securities will be issued at their par or face amount, and the income tax rate is estimated at 40% of income:

(Continued)

	Plan 1	Plan 2	Plan 3
9% bonds	—	—	$40,000,000
Preferred 5% stock, $25 par	—	$40,000,000	20,000,000
Common stock, $20 par	$80,000,000	40,000,000	20,000,000
Total	$80,000,000	$80,000,000	$80,000,000

Instructions

1. Determine for each plan the earnings per share of common stock, assuming that the income before bond interest and income tax is $10,000,000.
2. Determine for each plan the earnings per share of common stock, assuming that the income before bond interest and income tax is $6,000,000.
3. Discuss the advantages and disadvantages of each plan.

PR 14-2B Bond discount, entries for bonds payable transactions **OBJ. 2, 3**

✔ 3. $2,392,269

SHOW ME HOW

On July 1, Year 1, Livingston Corporation, a wholesaler of manufacturing equipment, issued $46,000,000 of 20-year, 10% bonds at a market (effective) interest rate of 11%, receiving cash of $42,309,236. Interest on the bonds is payable semiannually on December 31 and June 30. The fiscal year of the company is the calendar year.

Instructions

1. Journalize the entry to record the amount of cash proceeds from the issuance of the bonds on July 1, Year 1.
2. Journalize the entries to record the following:
   a. The first semiannual interest payment on December 31, Year 1, and the amortization of the bond discount, using the straight-line method. Round to the nearest dollar.
   b. The interest payment on June 30, Year 2, and the amortization of the bond discount, using the straight-line method. Round to the nearest dollar.
3. Determine the total interest expense for Year 1.
4. Will the bond proceeds always be less than the face amount of the bonds when the contract rate is less than the market rate of interest?
5. (Appendix 1) Compute the price of $42,309,236 received for the bonds by using the present value tables in Appendix A at the end of the text. Round to the nearest dollar.

PR 14-3B Bond premium, entries for bonds payable transactions **OBJ. 2, 3**

✔ 3. $3,494,977

Rodgers Corporation produces and sells football equipment. On July 1, Year 1, Rodgers Corporation issued $65,000,000 of 10-year, 12% bonds at a market (effective) interest rate of 10%, receiving cash of $73,100,469. Interest on the bonds is payable semiannually on December 31 and June 30. The fiscal year of the company is the calendar year.

Instructions

1. Journalize the entry to record the amount of cash proceeds from the issuance of the bonds on July 1, Year 1.
2. Journalize the entries to record the following:
   a. The first semiannual interest payment on December 31, Year 1, and the amortization of the bond premium, using the straight-line method. Round to the nearest dollar.
   b. The interest payment on June 30, Year 2, and the amortization of the bond premium, using the straight-line method. Round to the nearest dollar.
3. Determine the total interest expense for Year 1.
4. Will the bond proceeds always be greater than the face amount of the bonds when the contract rate is greater than the market rate of interest?
5. (Appendix 1) Compute the price of $73,100,469 received for the bonds by using the present value tables in Appendix A at the end of the text. Round to the nearest dollar.

PR 14-4B Entries for bonds payable and installment note transactions **OBJ. 3, 4**

✔ 3. $84,060,660

SHOW ME HOW

The following transactions were completed by Almeda Inc., whose fiscal year is the calendar year:

Year 1

July 1. Issued $75,000,000 of 10-year, 9% callable bonds dated July 1, Year 1, at a market (effective) rate of 7%, receiving cash of $85,659,600. Interest is payable semiannually on December 31 and June 30.

Oct. 1. Borrowed $270,000 by issuing a six-year, 8% installment note to Main Street Bank. The note requires annual payments of $58,405, with the first payment occurring on September 30, Year 2.

Dec. 31. Accrued $5,400 of interest on the installment note. The interest is payable on the date of the next installment note payment.

31. Paid the semiannual interest on the bonds. The bond premium amortization of $532,980 is combined with the semiannual interest payment.

Year 2

June 30. Paid the semiannual interest on the bonds. The bond premium amortization of $532,980 is combined with the semiannual interest payment.

Sept. 30. Paid the annual payment on the note, which consisted of interest of $21,600 and principal of $36,805.

Dec. 31. Accrued $4,664 of interest on the installment note. The interest is payable on the date of the next installment note payment.

31. Paid the semiannual interest on the bonds. The bond premium amortization of $532,980 is combined with the semiannual interest payment.

Year 3

June 30. Recorded the redemption of the bonds, which were called at 103. The balance in the bond premium account is $8,527,680 after payment of interest and amortization of premium have been recorded. Record the redemption only.

Sept. 30. Paid the second annual payment on the note, which consisted of interest of $18,656 and principal of $39,749.

Instructions

1. Journalize the entries to record the foregoing transactions.
2. Indicate the amount of the interest expense in (a) Year 1 and (b) Year 2.
3. Determine the carrying amount of the bonds as of December 31, Year 2.

Appendix 1 and Appendix 2
PR 14-5B Bond discount, entries for bonds payable transactions, interest method of amortizing bond discount

✔ 3. $2,327,008

On July 1, Year 1, Livingston Corporation, a wholesaler of manufacturing equipment, issued $46,000,000 of 20-year, 10% bonds at a market (effective) interest rate of 11%, receiving cash of $42,309,236. Interest on the bonds is payable semiannually on December 31 and June 30. The fiscal year of the company is the calendar year.

Instructions

1. Journalize the entry to record the amount of cash proceeds from the issuance of the bonds.
2. Journalize the entries to record the following:
   a. The first semiannual interest payment on December 31, Year 1, and the amortization of the bond discount, using the interest method. Round to the nearest dollar.
   b. The interest payment on June 30, Year 2, and the amortization of the bond discount, using the interest method. Round to the nearest dollar.
3. Determine the total interest expense for Year 1.

Appendix 1 and Appendix 2
PR 14-6B Bond premium, entries for bonds payable transactions, interest method of amortizing bond premium

✓ 3. $3,655,023

Rodgers Corporation produces and sells football equipment. On July 1, Year 1, Rodgers Corporation issued $65,000,000 of 10-year, 12% bonds at a market (effective) interest rate of 10%, receiving cash of $73,100,469. Interest on the bonds is payable semiannually on December 31 and June 30. The fiscal year of the company is the calendar year.

Instructions

1. Journalize the entry to record the amount of cash proceeds from the issuance of the bonds.
2. Journalize the entries to record the following:
   a. The first semiannual interest payment on December 31, Year 1, and the amortization of the bond premium, using the interest method. Round to the nearest dollar.
   b. The interest payment on June 30, Year 2, and the amortization of the bond premium, using the interest method. Round to the nearest dollar.
3. Determine the total interest expense for Year 1.

Cases & Projects

CP 14-1 Ethics in Action

ETHICS

CEG Capital Inc. is a large holding company that uses long-term debt extensively to fund its operations. At December 31, the company reported total assets of $100 million, total debt of $55 million, and total equity of $45 million. In January, the company issued $11 billion in long-term bonds to investors at par value. This was the largest debt issuance in the company's history, and it significantly increased the company's ratio of total debt to total equity. Five days after the debt issuance, CEG filed legal documents to prepare for an additional $50 billion long-term bond issue. As a result of this filing, the price of the $11 billion in bonds that the company issued earlier in the week dropped to 94 because of the increased risk associated with the company's debt. The investors in the original $11 billion bond issuance were not informed of the company's plans to issue additional debt so quickly after the initial bond issue. Did CEG Capital act unethically by not disclosing to initial bond investors its immediate plans to issue an additional $50 billion debt offering?

CP 14-2 Team Activity

TEAM ACTIVITY

In teams, select a public company that interests you. Obtain the company's most recent annual report on Form 10-K. The Form 10-K is a company's annually required filing with the Securities and Exchange Commission (SEC). It includes the company's financial statements and accompanying notes. The Form 10-K can be obtained either (a) by referring to the investor relations section of the company's website or (b) by using the company search feature of the SEC's EDGAR database service found at www.sec.gov/edgar/searchedgar/companysearch.html.

1. Based on the information in the company's most recent annual report, answer the following questions:
   a. How much long-term debt does the company report at the end of the most recent year presented?
   b. Does the company have any bonds outstanding at the end of the most recent year? If so, read the supporting notes to the financial statements and determine the following:
      (1) The due date of the bond issue(s).
      (2) The contract rate of interest on the bond issue(s).
      (3) The face amount of the bond issue(s).
      (4) The book value of the bond issue(s).
2. Based on your answers to the questions in requirement 1, evaluate the company's debt position.

CP 14-3 Communication

Nordbock Inc. reports the following outstanding bond issue on its December 31, 20Y1, balance sheet:

$1,000,000, 7%, 10-year bonds that pay interest semiannually.

The bonds have been outstanding for five years and were originally issued at face amount. The company is considering redeeming these bonds on January 1, 20Y2, at 103 and issuing new $1,000,000, 5%, five-year bonds at their face amount. These bonds would pay interest semiannually on June 30 and December 31.

Write a brief memo to Liz Nolan, the chief financial officer, discussing the costs of redeeming the existing bonds, the proceeds from issuing the new bonds, and whether this is a good financial decision.

CP 14-4 Present values

Alex Kelton recently won the jackpot in the Colorado lottery while he was visiting his parents. When he arrived at the lottery office to collect his winnings, he was offered the following three payout options:

a. Receive $100,000,000 in cash today.

b. Receive $25,000,000 today and $9,000,000 per year for eight years, with the first payment being received one year from today.

c. Receive $15,000,000 per year for 10 years, with the first payment being received one year from today.

Assuming that the effective rate of interest is 7%, which payout option should Alex select? Use the present value tables in Appendix A. Explain your answer and provide any necessary supporting calculations.

CP 14-5 Preferred stock vs. bonds

Xentec Inc. has decided to expand its operations to owning and operating golf courses. The following is an excerpt from a conversation between the chief executive officer, Peter Kilgallon, and the vice president of finance, Dan Baron:

Peter: Dan, have you given any thought to how we're going to manage the acquisition of Sweeping Bluff Golf Course?

Dan: Well, the two basic options, as I see it, are to issue either preferred stock or bonds. The equity market is a little depressed right now. The rumor is that the Federal Reserve Bank's going to increase the interest rates either this month or next.

Peter: Yes. I've heard the rumor. The problem is that we can't wait around to see what's going to happen. We'll have to move on this next week if we want any chance to complete the acquisition of Sweeping Bluff Golf Course.

Dan: Well, the bond market is strong right now. Maybe we should issue debt this time around.

Peter: That's what I would have guessed as well. Sweeping Bluff Golf Course's financial statements look pretty good, except for the volatility of its income and cash flows. But that's characteristic of the industry.

Discuss the advantages and disadvantages of issuing preferred stock versus bonds.

CP 14-6 Financing business expansion

You hold a 25% common stock interest in YouOwnIt, a family-owned construction equipment company. Your sister, who is the manager, has proposed an expansion of plant facilities at an expected cost of $26,000,000. Two alternative plans have been suggested as methods of financing the expansion. Each plan is briefly described as follows:

Plan 1. Issue $26,000,000 of 20-year, 8% notes at face amount

Plan 2. Issue an additional 550,000 shares of $10 par common stock at $20 per share, and $15,000,000 of 20-year, 8% notes at face amount

(Continued)

The balance sheet as of the end of the previous fiscal year is as follows:

YouOwnIt, Inc.
Balance Sheet
December 31, 20Y7

Assets	
Current assets	$15,000,000
Property, plant, and equipment	22,500,000
Total assets	$37,500,000
Liabilities and Stockholders' Equity	
Liabilities	$11,250,000
Common stock, $10	4,000,000
Paid-in capital in excess of par	500,000
Retained earnings	21,750,000
Total liabilities and stockholders' equity	$37,500,000

Net income has remained relatively constant over the past several years. The expansion program is expected to increase yearly income before bond interest and income tax from $2,667,000 in the previous year to $5,000,000 for this year. Your sister has asked you, as the company treasurer, to prepare an analysis of each financing plan.

1. Prepare a table indicating the expected earnings per share on the common stock under each plan. Assume an income tax rate of 40%. Round to the nearest cent.
2. a. Discuss the factors that should be considered in evaluating the two plans.
   b. Which plan offers greater benefit to the present stockholders? Give reasons for your opinion.

CP 14-7 Times interest earned

The following financial data (in thousands) were taken from recent financial statements of **Office Depot, Inc.**:

	Year 3	Year 2	Year 1
Interest expense	$121,000	$ 62,000	$ 80,000
Earnings before taxes	158,000	299,000	459,000

1. Determine the times interest earned ratio for Office Depot in Year 3, Year 2, and Year 1? Round to one decimal place.
2. Evaluate this ratio for Office Depot.

CHAPTER 15

Investments

RETAINED EARNINGS STATEMENT
For the Year Ended December 31, 20Y6

Retained earnings, Jan. 1, 20Y6		$XXX
Net income	$ XXX	
Dividends	(XXX)	
Increase in retained earnings		XXX
Retained earnings, Dec. 31, 20Y6		$XXX

STATEMENT OF CASH FLOWS
For the Year Ended December 31, 20Y6

Cash flows from (used for) operating activities	$XXX
Cash flows from (used for) investing activities	XXX
Cash flows from (used for) financing activities	XXX

INCOME STATEMENT
For the Year Ended December 31, 20Y6

Sales	$XXX
Cost of merchandise sold	XXX
Gross profit	$XXX
Total operating expenses	XXX
Income from operations	$XXX
Other revenue and expenses:	
Interest revenue	XXX
Gain (loss) on sale of investments	XXX
Unrealized gain (loss) on equity and trading investments	XXX
Equity income in investments	XXX
Net income	$XXX

BALANCE SHEET
December 31, 20Y6

Current assets:		
Cash	$XXX	
Accounts receivable	XXX	
Merchandise inventory	XXX	
Investments	XXX	
Total current assets		$XXX
Long-term assets:		
Property, plant, and equipment	$XXX	
Investments	XXX	
Total long-term assets		XXX
Total assets		$XXX
Liabilities:		
Current liabilities	$XXX	
Long-term liabilities	XXX	
Total liabilities		$XXX
Stockholders' equity:		
Common stock	$XXX	
Retained earnings	XXX	
Unrealized gain (loss) on available-for-sale investments	XXX	
Total stockholders' equity		XXX
Total liabilities and stockholders' equity		$XXX

CHAPTER

15

MARDIS COERS/MOMENT MOBILE/GETTY IMAGES

Deere & Company

You invest cash to earn more cash. For example, you could deposit cash in a bank account to earn interest. You could also invest in preferred or common stocks, or in corporate or U.S. government notes and bonds.

Preferred and common stock can be purchased through a stock exchange such as the New York Stock Exchange (NYSE). Preferred stock is purchased primarily with the expectation of earning dividends. Common stock is purchased with the expectation of earning dividends and realizing gains from an increase in the price of the stock.

Corporate and U.S. government bonds can also be purchased through a bond exchange. Bonds are purchased with the primary expectation of earning interest revenue.

Companies make investments for many of the same reasons you would as an individual. For example, **Deere & Company**, a manufacturer of agricultural and construction machinery, has invested approximately $490 million of available cash in stocks and bonds. These investments are held by Deere & Company for interest, dividends, and expected price increases.

Unlike most individuals, however, companies also purchase significant amounts of the outstanding common stock of other companies for strategic reasons. For example, Deere & Company has more than $207 million invested in companies where it owns between 20% and 50% of the outstanding shares. The vast majority of these investments are international manufacturing partners.

Investments in debt and equity securities give rise to a number of accounting issues. These issues are described and illustrated in this chapter.

Link to Deere & Company .... Pages 730, 731, 733, 738

LEARNING OBJECTIVES

After studying this chapter, you should be able to: Example Exercises (EE) are shown in **red.**

OBJ. 1 **Describe why companies invest in debt and equity securities.**

OBJ. 2 **Describe and illustrate the accounting for equity investments.**

OBJ. 3 **Describe and illustrate the accounting for held-to-maturity investments.**

OBJ. 4 **Describe and illustrate the accounting for and reporting of trading and available-for-sale investments.**

OBJ. 5 **Describe and illustrate the computation of dividend yield.**

APP. OBJ. **Define comprehensive income and describe its reporting on the financial statements.**

At a Glance 15 Page 743

Why Companies Invest

OBJ. 1 Describe why companies invest in debt and equity securities.

Most companies generate cash from their operations. This cash can be used for the following investment purposes:

- Investing in current operations
- Investing in temporary and long-term investments to earn additional revenue and/or realize an appreciation in value
- Investing in long-term investments in stock of other companies for strategic reasons

Investing Cash in Current Operations

Cash is often used to support the current operating activities of a company. For example, cash may be used to replace worn-out equipment or to purchase new, more efficient and productive equipment. In addition, cash may be reinvested in the company to expand its current operations. For example, a retailer based in the northwest United States might decide to expand by opening stores in the Midwest.

The accounting for the use of cash in current operations has been described and illustrated in earlier chapters. For example, Chapter 10 illustrated the use of cash for purchasing property, plant, and equipment. In this chapter, we describe and illustrate the use of cash for investing in the debt and stock of other companies.

Investing Cash in Temporary Investments

A company may temporarily have excess cash that is not needed for use in its current operations. This is often the case when a company has a seasonal operating cycle. For example, a significant portion of the annual merchandise sales of a retailer occurs during the fall holiday season. As a result, retailers often experience a large increase in cash during this period, which is not needed until the spring buying season.

Instead of letting excess cash remain idle in a checking account, most companies invest their excess cash in temporary investments. In doing so, companies invest in securities such as:

- **Equity securities**, which are preferred and common stock that represent ownership in a company and do not have a fixed maturity date.
- **Debt securities**, which are notes and bonds that pay interest and have a fixed maturity date.

Short-term investments in debt and equity securities, termed **investments** or *temporary investments*, are reported in the Current Assets section of the balance sheet.

The primary objective of investing in temporary investments is as follows:

- Receive dividends
- Earn interest revenue
- Realize gains from increases in the market price of the securities

Investing Cash in Long-Term Investments

A company may invest cash in the debt or equity of another company as a long-term investment. Long-term investments may be held for the same investment objectives as temporary investments. Long-term investments may involve the purchase of a significant portion of the stock of another company. Such investments usually have a strategic purpose, such as reduction of costs or expansion into new markets.

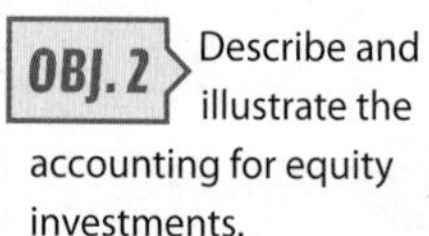

Describe and illustrate the accounting for equity investments.

Equity Investments[1]

A company may invest in the preferred or common stock of another company. The company investing in another company's stock is the **investor**. The company whose stock is purchased is the **investee**.

The percent of the investee's outstanding stock purchased by the investor determines the degree of control that the investor has over the investee. This, in turn, determines the accounting method used to record the stock investment, as shown in Exhibit 1.

EXHIBIT 1

Stock Investments

Percent of Outstanding Stock Owned by Investor	Degree of Control of Investor over Investee	Accounting Method
Less than 20%	No control	Fair value
Between 20% and 50%	Significant influence	Equity
Greater than 50%	Control	Consolidation

Fair Value Method: Less Than 20% Ownership

If the investor purchases less than 20% of the outstanding stock of the investee, the investor is considered to have no control over the investee. In this case, it is assumed that the investor purchased the stock primarily to earn dividends or to realize gains on price increases of the stock.

All equity investments of less than 20% of the investee's outstanding stock are accounted for using the **fair value method**. Under the fair value method, entries are recorded for the following transactions:

- Purchase of stock
- Receipt of dividends
- Sale of stock
- Change in fair value

Purchase of Stock The purchase of stock is recorded at its cost. Any brokerage commissions are included as part of the cost. To illustrate, assume that on May 1, 20Y2, Tindell Company purchases 2,000 shares of Lisa Company common stock

1 This discussion is consistent with *Financial Instruments, Subtopic 825-10, FASB Accounting Standards Update*, Financial Accounting Standards Board, Norwalk, CT, January 2016.

at $49.90 per share plus a brokerage commission of $200. The entry to record the purchase of the stock is as follows:

20Y2				
May	1	Investments—Lisa Company Stock	100,000	
		Cash		100,000
		Purchased 2,000 shares of Lisa Company common stock [($49.90 × 2,000 shares) + $200].		

Receipt of Dividends On July 31, 20Y2, Tindell Company receives a dividend of $0.40 per share from Lisa Company. The entry to record the receipt of the dividend is as follows:

20Y2				
July	31	Cash	800	
		Dividend Revenue		800
		Received dividend on Lisa Company common stock (2,000 shares × $0.40).		

Dividend Revenue is reported as part of Other Revenue on Tindell Company's income statement.

Sale of Stock The sale of a stock investment normally results in a gain or loss. A gain is recorded if the proceeds from the sale exceed the balance of the investment account. A loss is recorded if the proceeds from the sale are less than the balance of the investment account.

To illustrate, on September 1, 20Y2, Tindell Company sells 1,500 shares of Lisa Company stock for $54.50 per share less a $160 commission. The sale results in a gain of $6,590, computed as follows:

Proceeds from sale	$81,590*
Account balance (cost) of the stock	75,000**
Gain on sale	$ 6,590

*($54.50 × 1,500 shares) – $160
**($100,000 ÷ 2,000 shares) × 1,500 shares

The entry to record the sale is as follows:

20Y2				
Sept.	1	Cash	81,590	
		Gain on Sale of Investments		6,590
		Investments—Lisa Company Stock		75,000
		Sold 1,500 shares of Lisa Company common stock.		

The gain on the sale of investments is reported as part of Other Revenue on Tindell Company's income statement.

Change in Fair Value At the end of the accounting period, an adjusting entry is made to record the change in the fair value of the investment. **Fair value** is the market price that the company would receive for a security if it were sold. A change in fair value of an equity investment is recognized in net income as an **unrealized gain or loss** for the period.[2]

To illustrate, assume that Tindell Company's year end is December 31, 20Y2, and that the remaining 500 shares of Lisa Company stock have a fair value of $55 per share. The increase in fair value results in an unrealized gain of $2,500, computed as follows:

Fair value of investment	$27,500*
Less balance of the investment account	25,000**
Change in fair value	$ 2,500

*500 shares × $55
**$100,000 – $75,000

2 *Financial Instruments, Subtopic 825-10, FASB Accounting Standards Update.*

In order to maintain a record of the original cost of the securities, a valuation account, called Valuation Allowance for Equity Investments, is debited for $2,500, and Unrealized Gain on Equity Investments is credited for $2,500. The adjusting entry to record the increase in fair value of the equity investment is as follows:

20Y2				
Dec.	31	Valuation Allowance for Equity Investments	2,500	
		Unrealized Gain on Equity Investments		2,500

The Lisa Company stock would be reported as a current asset on Tindell Company's December 31, 20Y2, balance sheet as follows:

Tindell Company
Balance Sheet
December 31, 20Y2

Current assets:		
Cash		$ 75,000
Accounts receivable		190,000
Equity investment at cost	$25,000	
Valuation allowance	2,500	
Equity investment at fair value		27,500

When a company owns more than one equity security, the securities are valued and reported as a group (portfolio) using the securities' fair values.

EXAMPLE EXERCISE 15-1 Equity Investments: Less Than 20% Ownership — OBJ. 2

On September 1, 1,500 shares of Monroe Company's common stock are acquired at a price of $24 per share plus a $40 brokerage commission. On October 14, a $0.60-per-share dividend was received on the Monroe Company stock. On November 11, 750 shares (half) of Monroe Company stock were sold for $20 per share less a $45 brokerage commission. At the end of the accounting period on December 31, the fair value of Monroe Company's stock is $27 per share. Monroe Company has 175,000 shares of common stock outstanding. Journalize the entries for the original purchase, dividend, sale, and change in fair value under the fair value method.

Follow My Example 15-1

Sept. 1	Investments—Monroe Company Stock	36,040*	
	Cash		36,040
	*(1,500 shares × $24 per share) + $40		
Oct. 14	Cash	900*	
	Dividend Revenue		900
	*$0.60 per share × 1,500 shares		
Nov. 11	Cash	14,955*	
	Loss on Sale of Investments	3,065	
	Investments—Monroe Company Stock		18,020**
	*(750 shares × $20) − $45		
	**$36,040 × ½		
Dec. 31	Valuation Allowance for Equity Investments	2,230*	
	Unrealized Gain on Equity Investments		2,230
	*Fair value of investment (750 shares × $27)	$20,250	
	Balance of the investment account ($36,040 × ½)	18,020	
	Change in fair value	$ 2,230	

Practice Exercises: PE 15-1A, PE 15-1B

Equity Method: Between 20%–50% Ownership

If a company (investor) purchases between 20% and 50% of the outstanding stock of another company (investee), the investor is considered to have a *significant influence* over the investee. Investments of between 20% and 50% of the investee's outstanding stock are accounted for using the **equity method**.

Under the equity method, a stock investment is recorded at its initial cost. However, the investor's share of the investee's operating results and dividends are also recorded in the investment account as follows:

- *Net Income:* The investor records its share (percent) of the net income of the investee as an increase (debit) to the investment account. Its share (percent) of any net loss is recorded as a decrease (credit) to the investment account.
- *Dividends:* The investor's share (percent) of cash dividends received from the investee decreases (credits) the investment account.

Purchase of Stock To illustrate, assume that Simpson Inc. purchased a 40% interest in Flanders Corporation's common stock on January 2, 20Y6, for $350,000. The entry to record the purchase is as follows:

20Y6					
Jan.	2	Investment in Flanders Corporation Stock		350,000	
		Cash			350,000
		Purchased 40% of Flanders Corporation stock.			

Recording Investee Net Income For the year ended December 31, 20Y6, Flanders Corporation reported net income of $105,000. Under the equity method, Simpson Inc. (investor) records its share (percent) of Flanders net income, as follows:

20Y6					
Dec.	31	Investment in Flanders Corporation Stock		42,000	
		Income of Flanders Corporation			42,000
		Recorded 40% share of Flanders Corporation net income ($105,000 × 40%).			

Income of Flanders Corporation is reported on Simpson Inc.'s income statement separately or as part of Other Revenue. If Flanders Corporation had a net loss during the period, the loss would be recorded as a debit to Loss from Flanders Corporation and a credit to Investment in Flanders Corporation Stock.

Recording Investee Dividends During the year ended December 31, 20Y6, Flanders Corporation declared and paid cash dividends of $45,000. Under the equity method, Simpson Inc. (investor) records its share (percent) of Flanders dividends as follows:

20Y6					
Dec.	31	Cash		18,000	
		Investment in Flanders Corporation Stock			18,000
		Recorded 40% share of Flanders Corporation dividends ($45,000 × 40%).			

The effect of recording 40% of Flanders Corporation's net income and dividends is to increase the investment account by $24,000 ($42,000 − $18,000). Thus, Investment in Flanders Corporation Stock increases from $350,000 to $374,000, as shown in Exhibit 2.

EXHIBIT 2

Investment and Dividends

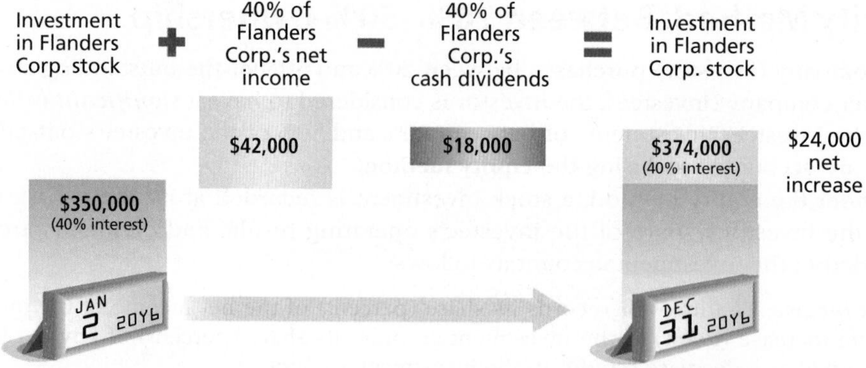

Investments accounted for under the equity method are reported on the balance sheet as noncurrent assets and are not adjusted to fair value.

Sale of Stock Under the equity method, a gain or loss is normally recorded from the sale of an investment. A gain is recorded if the proceeds exceed the balance of the investment account. A loss is recorded if the proceeds are less than the balance of the investment account.

To illustrate, if Simpson Inc. sold Flanders Corporation's stock on January 1, 20Y7, for $400,000, a gain of $26,000 would be reported, computed as follows:

Proceeds from sale	$400,000
Balance in the stock investment account	374,000
Gain on sale	$ 26,000

Link to Deere & Company

In a recent year, **Deere & Company** reported equity method investments of $207.3 million.

The entry to record the sale is as follows:

20Y7					
Jan.	1	Cash		400,000	
		Investment in Flanders Corporation Stock			374,000
		Gain on Sale of Flanders Corporation Stock			26,000
		Sold Flanders Corporation stock.			

EXAMPLE EXERCISE 15-2 Equity Investments: 20%–50% Ownership **OBJ. 2**

On January 2, 20Y1, Olson Company acquired 35% of the outstanding common stock of Bryant Company for $140,000. For the year ended December 31, 20Y1, Bryant Company earned income of $44,000 and paid dividends of $20,000. On January 31, 20Y2, Olson Company sold all of its investment in Bryant Company stock for $152,000. Journalize the entries for Olson Company for the purchase of the stock, the share of Bryant income, the dividends received from Bryant Company, and the sale of the Bryant Company stock.

Follow My Example 15-2

20Y1			
Jan. 2	Investment in Bryant Company Stock	140,000	
	Cash		140,000
Dec. 31	Investment in Bryant Company Stock	15,400*	
	Income of Bryant Company		15,400
	*Recorded 35% of Bryant income, 35% × $44,000		
31	Cash	7,000*	
	Investment in Bryant Company Stock		7,000
	*Recorded 35% of Bryant's $20,000 dividend, 35% × $20,000		
20Y2			
Jan. 31	Cash	152,000	
	Investment in Bryant Company Stock		148,400
	Gain on Sale of Bryant Company Stock		3,600

Practice Exercises: PE 15-2A, PE 15-2B

Consolidation: More Than 50% Ownership

If the investor purchases more than 50% of the outstanding stock of the investee, the investor is considered to have *control* over the investee. The purchase of more than 50% ownership of the investee's stock is termed a **business combination**. The corporation owning all or a majority of the voting stock of another corporation is called a **parent company**. The corporation that is controlled is called the **subsidiary company**.

Parent and subsidiary corporations normally continue to maintain separate accounting records and prepare their own financial statements. In such cases, at the end of the year, the financial statements of the parent and subsidiary are combined and reported as a single company. These combined financial statements are called **consolidated financial statements**. Such statements are normally identified by adding *and Subsidiary(ies)* to the name of the parent corporation or by adding *Consolidated* to the statement title.

Consolidated financial statements are more meaningful than separate statements for each corporation. This is because the parent company, in substance, controls the subsidiaries. The accounting for business combinations, including preparing consolidated financial statements, is described and illustrated in advanced accounting courses and textbooks.

Link to Deere & Company

The financial statements of **Deere & Company** represent the consolidation of all the companies in which Deere & Company owns more than 50%.

Business Connection

MORE CASH MEANS MORE INVESTMENTS FOR DRUG COMPANIES

Patented drugs are the life blood of the pharmaceutical industry. Drug companies with extensive portfolios of patented drugs generate significant cash flows from operating activities. As a result, these companies often have extensive amounts of cash on hand to invest in other companies. Near the end of 2015, the five biggest drug makers had in excess of $45 billion in cash and investments. Many analysts anticipated that these companies would use this excess cash to acquire smaller biotechnology and drug companies for their patented drugs and their ongoing research activities.

Source: "Mergers and Acquisitions on the Rise in 2013 as Big Pharma Companies Hold Record Amounts of Cash on Hand," *Five Star Equities Market Research Report*, February 7, 2013.

Held-to-Maturity Investments

OBJ. 3 Describe and illustrate the accounting for held-to-maturity investments.

Companies often invest in notes and bonds issued by corporations and governmental agencies. Notes and bonds are primarily purchased to earn interest revenue. This section focuses on investments in bonds that are purchased with the intent to earn interest revenue until the bonds mature.

The accounting for bonds involves the following three types of transactions:

- Purchase of bonds
- Receipt of interest revenue
- Sale of bonds

The following transactions are illustrated using the **cost method** of accounting. The cost method is used for bond investments where the investing company's intent and ability is to hold the bonds until they mature. Such bond investments are called **held-to-maturity investments**.

Purchase of Bonds

The purchase of bonds is recorded by debiting an investments account for the cost of acquiring the bonds. This cost includes any fees charged by a broker in acquiring the bonds. If bonds are purchased between interest dates, the buyer must also pay the seller any accrued interest since the last interest payment date. Any accrued interest is debited to an interest receivable account rather than to the investments account.

To illustrate, assume that Homer Company purchases $18,000 of bonds at their face amount on March 17, 20Y3, plus accrued interest. The bonds have an interest rate of 6%, payable on July 31 and January 31.

The entry to record the purchase of the bonds is as follows:

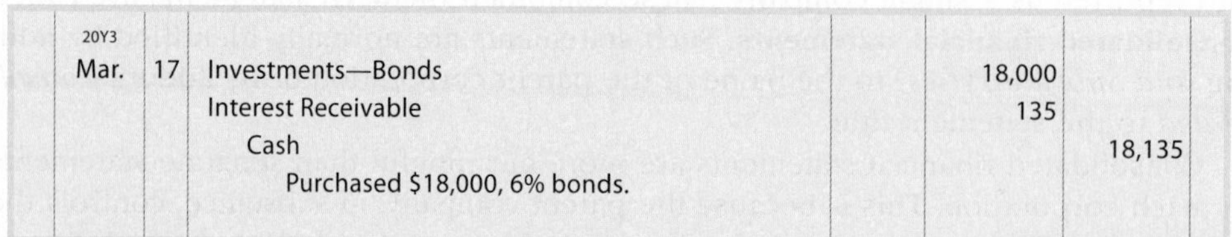

20Y3					
Mar.	17	Investments—Bonds		18,000	
		Interest Receivable		135	
		Cash			18,135
		Purchased $18,000, 6% bonds.			

Because Homer Company purchased the bonds on March 17, it is also purchasing the accrued interest for 45 days (January 31 to March 17), as shown in Exhibit 3.

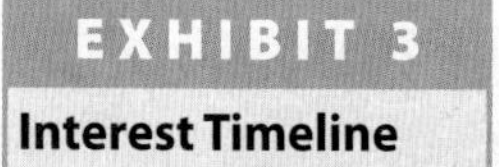

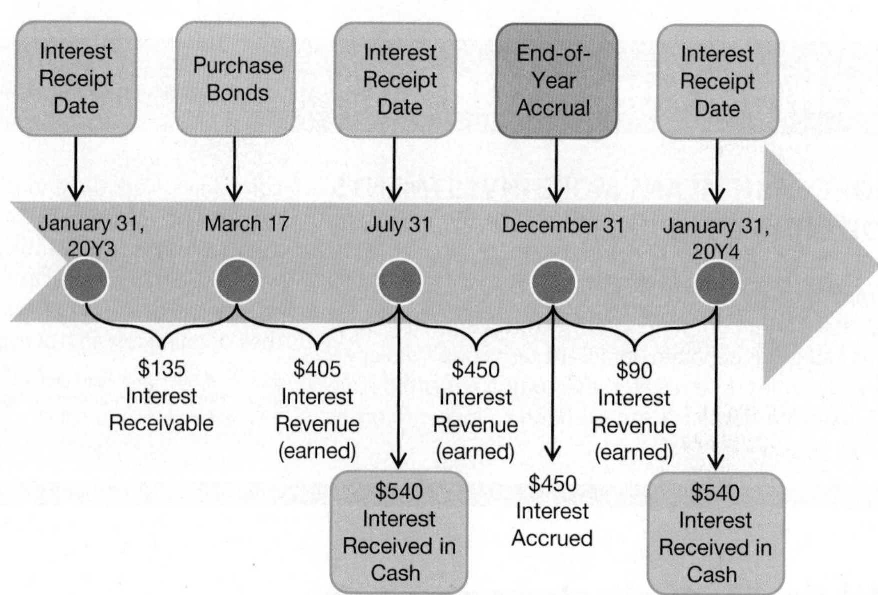

The accrued interest of $135 is computed as follows:[3]

$$\text{Accrued Interest} = \$18,000 \times 6\% \times (45 \div 360) = \$135$$

The accrued interest is recorded by debiting Interest Receivable for $135. Investments—Bonds is debited for the purchase price of the bonds of $18,000.

Receipt of Interest

On July 31, Homer Company receives a semiannual interest payment of $540 ($18,000 × 6% × ½). The $540 interest includes the $135 accrued interest that Homer Company purchased with the bonds on March 17. Thus, Homer has earned $405 ($540 − $135) of interest revenue since purchasing the bonds, as shown in Exhibit 3.

3 To simplify, a 360-day year is used to compute interest.

The receipt of the interest on July 31 is recorded as follows:

20Y3						
July	31	Cash			540	
		Interest Receivable				135
		Interest Revenue				405
		Received semiannual interest.				

Homer Company's accounting period ends on December 31, 20Y3. Thus, an adjusting entry must be made to accrue interest for 5 months (August 1 to December 31) of $450 ($18,000 × 6% × 5/12), as shown in Exhibit 3. The adjusting entry to record the accrued interest is as follows:

20Y3						
Dec.	31	Interest Receivable			450	
		Interest Revenue				450
		Accrued 5 months of interest.				

For the year ended December 31, 20Y3, Homer Company would report Interest Revenue of $855 ($405 + $450) as part of Other Revenue on its income statement.

The receipt of the semiannual interest of $540 on January 31, 20Y4, is recorded as follows:

20Y4						
Jan.	31	Cash			540	
		Interest Revenue				90
		Interest Receivable				450
		Received semiannual interest.				

Sale of Bonds

Although the original intent of a company may have been to hold the bonds until maturity, it may have to sell bonds to raise cash for its operations. In such cases, the sale of bonds normally results in a gain or loss. If the proceeds from the sale exceed the balance of the bond investment account, then a gain is recorded. If the proceeds are less than the balance of the bond investment account, a loss is recorded.

To illustrate, on January 31, 20Y4, Homer Company sells the bonds at 98, which is a price equal to 98% of their face amount. The sale results in a loss of $360, computed as follows:

Proceeds from sale	$17,640*
Less book value (cost) of the bonds	18,000
Loss on sale of bonds	$ (360)

*$18,000 × 98%

The entry to record the sale is as follows:

20Y4						
Jan.	31	Cash			17,640	
		Loss on Sale of Investments			360	
		Investments—Bonds				18,000
		Sold bonds.				

There is no accrued interest upon the sale because the interest payment date is also January 31. If the sale were between interest dates, interest accrued since the last interest payment date would be added to the sale proceeds and credited to Interest Revenue. The loss on the sale of bond investments is reported as part of Other Revenue (Loss) on Homer Company's income statement.

If Homer Company had kept the bonds until their maturity instead of selling them, the entry to record the bonds' maturity would debit Cash and credit Investments—Bonds for $18,000.

Link to Deere & Company

Deere & Company recently reported $297 million of investments in government and corporate bonds.

Reporting on Financial Statements

If a held-to-maturity security will mature within a year, it is reported as a current asset on the balance sheet. Held-to-maturity securities maturing beyond a year are reported as noncurrent assets.

In the preceding illustration, Tyler Company bonds were purchased at their face value. If the interest rate on bonds differs from the market rate of interest, the bonds may be purchased at a premium or discount. In such cases, the premium or discount is amortized over the life of the bonds and the bonds are reported on the balance sheet at their amortized cost. To simplify, we assume that all held-to-maturity securities are purchased at their face value.

EXAMPLE EXERCISE 15-3 Bond (Held-to-Maturity) Investments — OBJ. 3

Journalize the entries to record the following selected bond investment transactions for Fly Company:

a. Purchased for cash $40,000 of Tyler Company 10% bonds at 100 plus accrued interest of $500.

b. Received the first semiannual interest.

c. Sold $30,000 of the bonds at 102 plus accrued interest of $110.

d. Received the face value of the remaining bonds at their maturity.

Follow My Example 15-3

	Account	Debit	Credit
a.	Investments—Tyler Company Bonds	40,000	
	Interest Receivable	500	
	Cash		40,500
b.	Cash	2,000*	
	Interest Receivable		500
	Interest Revenue		1,500
	*$40,000 × 10% × ½		
c.	Cash	30,710*	
	Interest Revenue		110
	Gain on Sale of Investments		600
	Investments—Tyler Company Bonds		30,000

*Sale proceeds ($30,000 × 102%)	$30,600
Accrued interest	110
Total proceeds from sale	$30,710

	Account	Debit	Credit
d.	Cash	10,000	
	Investments—Tyler Company Bonds		10,000

Practice Exercises: PE 15-3A, PE 15-3B

OBJ. 4 Describe and illustrate the accounting for and reporting of trading and available-for-sale investments.

Trading and Available-for-Sale Investments

Generally accepted accounting principles (GAAP) classify debt investments as:

- Held-to-maturity securities
- Trading securities
- Available-for-sale securities

The accounting for and reporting of held-to-maturity investments was discussed in the preceding section. This section discusses the accounting for and reporting of trading and available-for-sale investments.

Trading Securities

Trading securities are debt securities that are purchased to earn profits from short-term changes in their market prices. Trading securities are reported as a current asset on the balance sheet if management expects to sell the securities within a year. Otherwise, the securities are reported as a noncurrent asset. Trading securities are valued as a portfolio (group) of securities using the securities' fair values.[4]

To illustrate, assume that Maggie Company purchased a portfolio of debt securities issued by various companies during 20Y1.[5] On December 31, 20Y1, the cost and fair values of these trading securities were as follows:

Issuing Company	Cost (Face Value)	Fair Value
Armour Company	$ 5,000	$ 7,200
Maven, Inc.	11,000	7,500
Polaris Co.	8,000	10,600
Total	$24,000	$25,300

The portfolio of trading securities is reported with a fair value of $25,300. An adjusting entry is necessary to record the increase in the fair value of $1,300 ($25,300 – $24,000). The adjusting entry on December 31, 20Y1, to record the fair value of the portfolio of trading securities is as follows:

20Y1					
Dec.	31	Valuation Allowance for Trading Investments		1,300	
		Unrealized Gain on Trading Investments			1,300
		To record increase in fair value of trading securities.			

Unrealized Gain on Trading Investments is reported on the income statement. Depending on its significance, it may be reported separately or as Other Revenue on the income statement. The valuation allowance is reported on the December 31, 20Y1, balance sheet as follows:

Maggie Company
Balance Sheet (selected items)
December 31, 20Y1

Current assets:		
Cash		$120,000
Trading investments (at cost)	$24,000	
Valuation allowance for trading investments	1,300	
Trading investments (at fair value)		25,300

If the fair value of the portfolio of trading securities was less than the cost, then the adjustment would debit Unrealized Loss on Trading Investments and credit Valuation Allowance for Trading Investments for the difference. Unrealized Loss on Trading Investments would be reported on the income statement as Other Expenses. Valuation Allowance for Trading Investments would be shown on the balance sheet as a *deduction* from Trading Investments (at cost).

4 The journal entries for the purchase, receipt of interest, and sale of trading and available-for-sale securities are similar to those for held-to-maturity securities, which were illustrated earlier. For this reason, we focus on the end-of-period adjusting entries and reporting of trading and and available-for-sale securities.

5 To simplify, we assume that all trading and available-for-sale securities are purchased at their face value.

Over time, the valuation allowance account is adjusted to reflect the difference between the cost and the fair value of the portfolio. Thus, increases in the valuation allowance account from the beginning of the period will result in an adjustment to record an unrealized gain, similar to the preceding journal entry. Likewise, decreases in the valuation allowance account from the beginning of the period will result in an adjustment to record an unrealized loss.

To illustrate, assume that during 20Y2 no trading securities were purchased or sold and that the fair value of the portfolio of securities is $22,000 on December 31, 20Y2. In this case, the adjusting entry would debit Unrealized Loss on Trading Investments and credit Valuation Allowance for Trading Investments for $3,300 ($25,300 – $22,000). The trading investments would then be reported on the December 31, 20Y2, balance sheet at their fair value of $22,000 (cost of $24,000 less valuation allowance of $2,000).

EXAMPLE EXERCISE 15-4 Trading Securities at Fair Value **OBJ. 4**

On January 1, 20Y6, Valuation Allowance for Trading Investments had a zero balance. On December 31, 20Y6, the cost of the trading securities portfolio was $79,200, and the fair value was $76,800. Journalize the December 31, 20Y6, adjusting entry to record the unrealized gain or loss on trading investments.

Follow My Example 15-4

20Y6			
Dec. 31	Unrealized Loss on Trading Investments	2,400	
	Valuation Allowance for Trading Investments		2,400*
	To record decrease in fair value of trading investments.		

*Trading investments at fair value, December 31, 20Y6	$76,800
Less trading investments at cost, December 31, 20Y6	79,200
Unrealized loss on trading investments	$ (2,400)

Practice Exercises: PE 15-4A, PE 15-4B

Available-for-Sale Securities

Available-for-sale securities are debt securities that a company intends to sell in the future, but not in the near term. Thus, the investment cannot be classified as trading securities or held-to-maturity securities. Available-for-sale securities are recorded at fair value using the fair value method discussed earlier in this chapter. However, changes in the fair values are not reported on the income statement but are reported as part of stockholders' equity.

Integrity, Objectivity, and Ethics in Business

SOCIALLY RESPONSIBLE INVESTING

Socially responsible investing is a growing trend in the United States and Europe that focuses on making investments to improve society. Socially responsible investors attempt to balance investment return with social good by seeking out investments in companies that (1) are environmentally friendly, (2) do not infringe on human rights in the production of a product or provision of a service, and (3) are anti-discriminatory. In some situations, socially responsible investors target emerging markets to both generate a return and help overcome social challenges. In addition, some socially responsible investors refuse to invest in companies that produce alcohol, tobacco, or weapons.

To illustrate, assume that Campbell Company purchased three debt securities during 20Y5 as available-for-sale securities. On December 31, 20Y5, the cost and fair values of the securities were as follows:

Issuing Company	Cost (Face Value)	Fair Value
Bennett Company	$30,000	$32,200
MCT Industries Inc.	10,000	6,500
Randall Co.	50,000	55,000
Total	$90,000	$93,700

The portfolio of available-for-sale securities is reported at its fair value of $93,700. An adjusting entry is made to record the increase in fair value of $3,700 ($93,700 – $90,000). In order to maintain a record of the original cost of the securities, the increase in fair value of $3,700 is debited to Valuation Allowance for Available-for-Sale Investments.

Unlike trading securities, the December 31, 20Y5, adjusting entry credits a stockholders' equity account instead of an income statement account. The $3,700 increase in fair value is credited to Unrealized Gain (Loss) on Available-for-Sale Investments.

The adjusting entry on December 31, 20Y5, to record the fair value of the portfolio of available-for-sale securities is as follows:

20Y5					
Dec.	31	Valuation Allowance for Available-for-Sale Investments		3,700	
		Unrealized Gain on Available-for-Sale Investments			3,700
		To record increase in fair value of available-for-sale securities.			

A credit balance in Unrealized Gain on Available-for-Sale Investments is added to stockholders' equity. In contrast, a debit balance in Unrealized Loss on Available-for-Sale Investments is subtracted from stockholders' equity.

The valuation allowance and the unrealized gain are reported on the December 31, 20Y5, balance sheet as follows:

Campbell Company
Balance Sheet
December 31, 20Y5

Current assets:		
Cash		$120,000
Available-for-sale investments (at cost)	$90,000	
Valuation allowance for available-for-sale investments	3,700	
Available-for-sale investments (at fair value)		93,700
Stockholders' equity:		
Common stock		$ 10,000
Paid-in capital in excess of par		150,000
Retained earnings		250,000
Unrealized gain (loss) on available-for-sale investments		3,700
Total stockholders' equity		$413,700

Equal

Link to Deere & Company

Deere & Company recognizes unrealized fair value changes in equity investments directly in net income.

As shown, Unrealized Gain on Available-for-Sale Investments is reported as an addition to stockholders' equity.[6] In future years, the cumulative effects of unrealized gains and losses are reported in this account.

If the fair value was less than the cost, then the adjustment would debit Unrealized Gain (Loss) on Available-for-Sale Investments and credit Valuation Allowance for Available-for-Sale Investments for the difference. Unrealized Gain (Loss) on Available-for-Sale Investments would be reported in the Stockholders' Equity section as a negative item. Valuation Allowance for Available-for-Sale Investments would be shown on the balance sheet as a deduction from Available-for-Sale Investments (at cost).

Over time, the valuation allowance account is adjusted to reflect the difference between the cost and the fair value of the portfolio. Thus, increases in the valuation allowance from the beginning of the period will result in an adjustment to record an increase in the valuation and unrealized gain (loss) accounts, similar to the journal entry illustrated earlier. Likewise, decreases in the valuation allowance from the beginning of the period will result in an adjustment to record decreases in the valuation and unrealized gain (loss) accounts.

To illustrate, assume that during 20Y6 no available-for-sale securities were purchased or sold and that the fair value of the portfolio of securities is $99,500 on December 31, 20Y6. In this case, the adjusting entry would debit Valuation Allowance for Available-for-Sale Investments and credit Unrealized Gain on Available-for-Sale Investments for $5,800 ($99,500 − $93,700). The trading investments would then be reported on the December 31, 20Y6, balance sheet at their fair value of $99,500 ($90,000 + $9,500).

EXAMPLE EXERCISE 15-5 Available-for-Sale Securities at Fair Value — OBJ. 4

On January 1, 20Y6, Valuation Allowance for Available-for-Sale Investments had a zero balance. On December 31, 20Y6, the cost of the available-for-sale securities was $45,700 and the fair value was $50,000.

Journalize the adjusting entry to record the unrealized gain or loss for available-for-sale investments on December 31, 20Y6.

Follow My Example 15-5

20Y6			
Dec. 31	Valuation Allowance for Available-for-Sale Investments	4,300*	
	Unrealized Gain on Available-for-Sale Investments		4,300
	To record increase in fair value of available-for-sale securities.		

*Available-for-sale investments at fair value, December 31, 20Y6	$50,000
Less available-for-sale investments at cost, December 31, 20Y6	45,700
Unrealized gain on available-for-sale investments	$ 4,300

Practice Exercises: PE 15-5A, PE 15-5B

Summary

Exhibit 4 summarizes the valuation and balance sheet reporting of trading and available-for-sale securities.

EXHIBIT 4

Summary of Valuing and Reporting of Trading and Available-for-Sale Securities

	Trading Securities	Available-for-Sale Securities
Valued at:	Fair value	Fair value
Changes in valuation are reported as:	Unrealized gain or loss on the income statement as Other Revenue (Loss).	Unrealized gain or loss in stockholders' equity on the balance sheet.
Reported on balance sheet as:	Fair value: Cost of investments plus or minus valuation allowance.	Fair value: Cost of investments plus or minus valuation allowance.
Classified on balance sheet as:	Either a current or noncurrent asset, depending on management's intent.	Either a current or noncurrent asset, depending on management's intent.

6 The effects of unrealized gains and losses on available-for-sale investments on stockholders' equity are also reported as part of comprehensive income, which is discussed in the appendix to this chapter.

The balance sheet reporting for the investments of **Mornin' Joe** follows:

Mornin' Joe
Balance Sheet
December 31, 20Y6

Assets			
Current assets:			
Cash and cash equivalents		$235,000	
Trading investments (at cost)	$420,000		
Valuation allowance for trading investments	45,000	465,000	
Accounts receivable	$305,000		
Less allowance for doubtful accounts	12,300	292,700	
Merchandise inventory—at lower of cost (first-in, first-out method) or market		120,000	
Prepaid insurance		24,000	
Total current assets			$1,136,700
Investments:			
Investment in AM Coffee (equity method)			565,000
Property, plant, and equipment:			

Mornin' Joe invests in trading securities and does not have investments in held-to-maturity or available-for-sale securities. Mornin' Joe also owns 40% of AM Coffee Corporation, which is accounted for using the equity method. Mornin' Joe intends to keep its investment in AM Coffee indefinitely for strategic reasons; thus, its investment in AM Coffee is classified as a noncurrent asset. Such investments are normally reported before property, plant, and equipment.

Mornin' Joe reported an Unrealized Gain on Trading Investments of $5,000 and Equity Income in AM Coffee of $57,000 in the Other Revenue and Expense section of its income statement, as follows:

Mornin' Joe
Income Statement
For the Year Ended December 31, 20Y6

Sales		$5,402,100
Cost of merchandise sold		2,160,000
Gross profit		$3,242,100
Total operating expenses		2,608,700
Income from operations		$ 633,400
Other revenue and expense:		
Interest revenue	$ 18,000	
Interest expense	(136,000)	
Loss on disposal of fixed asset	(23,000)	
Unrealized gain (loss) on trading investments	5,000	
Equity income in AM Coffee	57,000	(79,000)
Income before income tax expense		$ 554,400
Income tax expense		132,800
Net income		$ 421,600

Business Connection

WARREN BUFFETT: THE SAGE OF OMAHA

Beginning in 1962, Warren Buffett, one of the world's wealthiest and most successful investors, began buying shares of **Berkshire Hathaway**. He eventually took control of the company and transformed it from a textile manufacturing company into an investment holding company. Today, Berkshire Hathaway holds more than $223 billion in cash and cash equivalents, equity securities, and debt securities. Berkshire's largest holdings include **The Coca-Cola Company, Apple, Wells Fargo**, and **Bank of America**. Berkshire Class A common stock trades near $306,000 per share, the highest priced share on the New York Stock Exchange.

Buffett compares his investment style to hitting a baseball: "Ted Williams, one of the greatest hitters in the game, stated, 'my argument is, to be a good hitter, you've got to get a good ball to hit. It's the first rule of the book. If I have to bite at stuff that is out of my happy zone, I'm not a .344 hitter. I might only be a .250 hitter.'" Buffett states, "Charlie (Buffett's partner) and I agree and will try to wait for (investment) opportunities that are well within our 'happy zone.'" One of Buffet's "happy zone" investments was the acquisition of **Burlington Northern Santa Fe Railroad** for $34 billion.

Warren Buffett as the CEO of Berkshire Hathaway earns a salary of only $100,000 per year, which is the lowest CEO salary for a company of its size in the United States. However, he personally owns approximately 38% of the company, making him worth more than $70 billion. What will Buffett do with this wealth? He has decided to give nearly all of it to philanthropic causes through the **Bill and Melinda Gates Foundation**.

Source: Warren E. Buffett, *The Essays of Warren Buffett: Lessons for Corporate America*, edited by Lawrence A. Cunningham, p. 234.

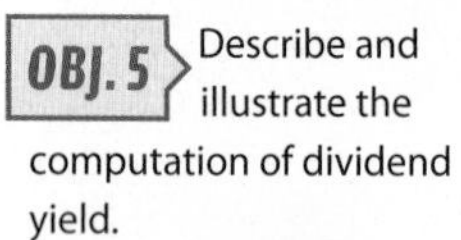
OBJ. 5 Describe and illustrate the computation of dividend yield.

FAI

Financial Analysis and Interpretation: Dividend Yield

The **dividend yield** measures the rate of return to stockholders based on cash dividends. Dividend yield is most often computed for common stock because preferred stock has a stated dividend rate. In contrast, the cash dividends paid on common stock normally vary with the profitability of the corporation.

The dividend yield is computed as follows:

$$\text{Dividend Yield} = \frac{\text{Dividends per Share of Common Stock}}{\text{Market Price per Share of Common Stock}}$$

To illustrate, the market price of **Deere & Company** was $149.17 at the end of a recent fiscal year. During the preceding year, Deere & Company had paid dividends of $2.74 per share. Thus, the dividend yield of Deere & Company's common stock is computed as follows:

$$\text{Dividend Yield} = \frac{\text{Dividends per Share of Common Stock}}{\text{Market Price per Share of Common Stock}} = \frac{\$2.74}{\$149.17} = 1.8\%\ \text{(rounded)}$$

Deere & Company pays a dividend yield of slightly more than 1.8%. The dividend yield depends on a company's profitability, or ability to pay a dividend. Deere & Company has sufficient profitability to pay a dividend. Second, a company's dividend yield depends on management's alternative use of funds. If a company has sufficient growth opportunities, funds may be directed toward internal investment rather than toward paying dividends.

The dividend yield will vary from day to day because the market price of a corporation's stock varies day to day. Current dividend yields are provided with news service quotations of market prices, such as **The Wall Street Journal** or **Yahoo! Finance**.

Recent dividend yields for some selected companies are as follows:

Company	Dividend Yield (%)
Alphabet (Google)	None
Best Buy	2.8
Coca-Cola Company	3.4
Deere & Company	1.8
Duke Energy	4.5
Facebook	None
Microsoft	1.5
Verizon Communications	4.2

As can be seen, the dividend yield varies widely across firms. Growth firms tend to retain their earnings to fund future growth. Thus, **Facebook** and **Alphabet (Google)** pay no dividends. Common stockholders of these companies expect to earn most of their return from stock price appreciation. In contrast, **Duke Energy** and **Verizon Communications** are regulated utilities that provide a return to common stockholders mostly through dividends. **Best Buy**, **Coca-Cola**, **Deere & Company**, and **Microsoft** provide a mix of dividends and expected stock price appreciation to their common stockholders.

EXAMPLE EXERCISE 15-6 Dividend Yield **OBJ. 5**

On March 11, 20Y6, Sheldon Corporation had a market price of $58 per share of common stock. For the previous year, Sheldon paid an annual dividend of $2.90 per share. Compute the dividend yield for Sheldon Corporation.

Follow My Example 15-6

$$\text{Dividend Yield} = \frac{\text{Dividends per Share of Common Stock}}{\text{Market Price per Share of Common Stock}}$$

$$= \frac{\$2.90}{\$58.00} = 0.05\text{, or }5\%$$

Practice Exercises: PE 15-6A, PE 15-6B

APPENDIX

Comprehensive Income

APP. OBJ. Define comprehensive income and describe its reporting on the financial statements.

Comprehensive income is defined as all changes in stockholders' equity during a period, except those resulting from dividends and stockholders' investments. Comprehensive income is computed by adding or subtracting *other comprehensive income* to (from) net income, as follows:

Net income	$XXX
Other comprehensive income	XXX
Comprehensive income	$XXX

Other comprehensive income items include unrealized gains and losses on available-for-sale securities as well as other items such as foreign currency and pension liability adjustments. The *cumulative* effect of other comprehensive income is reported on the balance sheet as **accumulated other comprehensive income**.

Companies are required to report comprehensive income on the financial statements in one of the following two ways:

- On the income statement, or
- In a separate statement of comprehensive income that immediately follows the income statement.

In the earlier illustration, Campbell Company had reported an unrealized gain of $3,700 on available-for-sale investments. This unrealized gain would be reported in the Stockholders' Equity section of Campbell Company's 20Y5 balance sheet, as follows:

Campbell Company
Balance Sheet
December 31, 20Y5

Stockholders' equity:	
Common stock	$ 10,000
Excess of issue price over par	150,000
Retained earnings	250,000
Accumulated other comprehensive income:	
Unrealized gain (loss) on available-for-sale investments	3,700
Total stockholders' equity	$413,700

The accounting for comprehensive income is an advanced accounting topic that will be covered in greater detail in advanced accounting courses.

At a Glance 15

OBJ. 1 Describe why companies invest in debt and equity securities.

Key Points Cash can be used to (1) invest in current operations, (2) invest to earn additional revenue in marketable securities, or (3) invest in marketable securities for strategic reasons.

Learning Outcomes	Example Exercises	Practice Exercises
• Describe the ways excess cash is used by a business.		
• Describe the purpose of temporary investments.		
• Describe the strategic purpose of long-term investments.		

OBJ. 2 Describe and illustrate the accounting for equity investments.

Key Points The accounting for equity investments differs, depending on the degree of control. Accounting for investments of less than 20% of the outstanding stock (no control) of the investee includes recording the purchase of stock, the receipt of dividends, the sale of stock at a gain or loss, and changes in fair value. Investments of 20%–50% of the outstanding stock of an investee are considered to have significant influence and are accounted for under the equity method. An investment for more than 50% of the outstanding stock of an investee is treated as a business combination and is accounted for using consolidated financial statements.

Learning Outcomes	Example Exercises	Practice Exercises
• Describe the accounting for less than 20%, 20%–50%, and greater than 50% investments.		
• Journalize entries to record the purchase of a stock investment.	**EE15-1**	**PE15-1A, 15-1B**
• Journalize entries for the receipt of dividends from a stock investment of less than 20%.	**EE15-1**	**PE15-1A, 15-1B**
• Journalize entries for the sale of a stock investment at a gain or loss.	**EE15-1**	**PE15-1A, 15-1B**
• Journalize entries for changes in fair value.	**EE15-1**	**PE15-1A, 15-1B**
• Journalize entries for the equity earnings of an equity method investee under the equity method.	**EE15-2**	**PE15-2A, 15-2B**
• Journalize entries for the dividends received from an equity method investee under the equity method.	**EE15-2**	**PE15-2A, 15-2B**
• Describe a business combination, parent company, and subsidiary company.		
• Describe consolidated financial statements.		

OBJ. 3 Describe and illustrate the accounting for held-to-maturity investments.

Key Points The accounting for held-to-maturity investments includes recording the purchase, interest revenue, and sale of bonds. Both the purchase and sale may include accrued interest revenue.

Learning Outcomes	*Example Exercises*	*Practice Exercises*
• Journalize entries to record the purchase of a bond, including accrued interest.	EE15-3	PE15-3A, 15-3B
• Journalize entries for interest revenue from bond investments.	EE15-3	PE15-3A, 15-3B
• Journalize entries to record the sale of a bond at a gain or loss.	EE15-3	PE15-3A, 15-3B

OBJ. 4 Describe and illustrate the accounting for and reporting of trading and available-for-sale investments.

Key Points Investments in debt securities can be classified as either (1) trading securities, (2) held-to-maturity securities, or (3) available-for-sale securities. *Trading securities* are valued at *fair value,* with unrealized gains and losses reported on the income statement. *Available-for-sale securities* are reported at fair value with unrealized gains or losses reported in the Stockholders' Equity section of the balance sheet.

Learning Outcomes	*Example Exercises*	*Practice Exercises*
• Describe trading securities.		
• Journalize entries to record the change in the fair value of a trading security portfolio.	EE15-4	PE15-4A, 15-4B
• Describe and illustrate the reporting of trading securities on the balance sheet.		
• Describe available-for-sale securities.		
• Journalize entries to record the change in fair value of an available-for-sale security portfolio.	EE15-5	PE15-5A, 15-5B
• Describe and illustrate the reporting of available-for-sale securities on the balance sheet.		

OBJ. 5 Describe and illustrate the computation of dividend yield.

Key Points The dividend yield measures the cash return from common dividends as a percent of the market price of the common stock. The ratio is computed as dividends per share of common stock divided by the market price per share of common stock.

Learning Outcomes	*Example Exercises*	*Practice Exercises*
• Compute dividend yield.	EE15-6	PE15-6A, 15-6B
• Describe how dividend yield measures the return to stockholders from dividends.		

Illustrative Problem

The following selected investment transactions were completed by Rosewell Company during 20Y3, its first year of operations:

20Y3

Jan. 11. Purchased securities of Bryan Company as available-for-sale securities for $18,400.

Feb. 6. Purchased $40,000 of 8% bonds at their face amount plus accrued interest for 36 days. The bonds pay interest on January 1 and July 1. The bonds were classified as held-to-maturity securities.

Mar. 3. Purchased securities of Cohen Company as trading securities for $90,000.

Apr. 5. Purchased securities of Lyons Inc. as available-for-sale securities for $163,200.

May 12. Purchased 200,000 shares of Myers Company stock at $37 per share plus an $8,000 brokerage commission. Myers Company has 800,000 common shares issued and outstanding. The equity method was used for this investment.

July 1. Received semiannual interest on bonds purchased on February 6.

Aug. 29. Sold Cohen Company securities with a cost of $60,000 for $62,500.

Oct. 1. Received $400 interest on Bryan Company securities.

Nov. 11. Received a $1.10-per-share dividend on Myers Company stock.

16. Purchased securities of Morningside Company as trading securities for $150,000.

Dec. 31. Accrued interest on bonds purchased on February 6.

31. Myers Company earned $1,200,000 during the year. Rosewell recorded its share of Myers Company earnings, using the equity method.

31. Prepared adjusting entries for the portfolios of trading and available-for-sale securities based on the following fair values:

Bryan Company	$ 20,000
Cohen Company	28,300
Lyons Inc.	168,300
Morningside Company	148,700
Myers Company common stock	$40 per share

Instructions

1. Journalize the preceding transactions.
2. Prepare the balance sheet disclosure for Rosewell Company's investments on December 31, 20Y3. Assume that held-to-maturity investments are classified as noncurrent assets.

Solution

1.

20Y3					
Jan.	11	Available-for-Sale Investments—Bryan Company		18,400	
		Cash			18,400

(Continued)

20Y3					
Feb.	6	Investments—Bonds		40,000	
		Interest Receivable		320*	
		Cash			40,320
		*$40,000 × 8% × (36 days ÷ 360 days)			

Mar.	3	Trading Investments—Cohen Company		90,000	
		Cash			90,000

Apr.	5	Available-for-Sale Investments—Lyons Inc.		163,200	
		Cash			163,200

May	12	Investment in Myers Company Stock		7,408,000*	
		Cash			7,408,000
		*(200,000 shares × $37 per share) + $8,000			

July	1	Cash		1,600*	
		Interest Receivable			320
		Interest Revenue			1,280
		*$40,000 × 8% × ½			

Aug.	29	Cash		62,500	
		Trading Investments—Cohen Company			60,000
		Gain on Sale of Trading Investments			2,500

Oct.	1	Cash		400	
		Interest Revenue			400

Nov.	11	Cash		220,000*	
		Investment in Myers Company Stock			220,000
		*200,000 shares × $1.10 per share			

Nov.	16	Trading Investments—Morningside Company		150,000	
		Cash			150,000

20Y3				
Dec.	31	Interest Receivable	1,600	
		Interest Revenue		1,600
		Accrued interest ($40,000 × 8% × ½).		

Dec.	31	Investment in Myers Company Stock	300,000	
		Income of Myers Company		300,000
		Recorded equity income [$1,200,000 × (200,000 shares ÷ 800,000 shares)].		

Dec.	31	Unrealized Loss on Trading Investments	3,000	
		Valuation Allowance for Trading Investments		3,000
		Recorded decrease in fair value of trading investments ($180,000 – $177,000).		

Issuing Company	Cost	Fair Value
Cohen Company	$ 30,000	$ 28,300
Morningside Company	150,000	148,700
Total	$180,000	$177,000

Note: Myers Company is valued using the equity method; thus, the fair value is not used.

Dec.	31	Valuation Allowance for Available-for-Sale Investments	6,700	
		Unrealized Gain on Available-for-Sale Investments		6,700
		Recorded increase in fair value of available-for-sale investments ($188,300 – $181,600).		

Issuing Company	Cost	Fair Value
Bryan Company	$ 18,400	$ 20,000
Lyons Inc.	163,200	168,300
Total	$181,600	$188,300

(Continued)

2.

Rosewell Company **Balance Sheet (Selected)** **December 31, 20Y3**		
Assets		
Current assets:		
Cash		$ XXX,XXX
Trading investments (at cost)	$180,000	
Valuation allowance for trading investments	(3,000)	
Trading investments at fair value		177,000
Available-for-sale investments (at cost)	$181,600	
Valuation allowance for available-for-sale investments	6,700	
Available-for-sale investments at fair value		188,300
Investments:		
Held-to-maturity investments		40,000
Investment in Myers Company (equity method)		7,488,000
Stockholders' equity:		
Common stock		$ XX,XXX
Paid-in capital in excess of par		XXX,XXX
Retained earnings		XXX,XXX
Unrealized gain (loss) on available-for-sale investments		6,700
Total stockholders' equity		$ XXX,XXX

Key Terms

accumulated other comprehensive income (741)
available-for-sale securities (736)
business combination (731)
comprehensive income (741)
consolidated financial statements (731)
cost method (731)
debt securities (726)
dividend yield (740)
equity method (729)
equity securities (726)
fair value (727)
fair value method (726)
held-to-maturity investments (731)
investee (726)
investments (726)
investor (726)
other comprehensive income (741)
parent company (731)
subsidiary company (731)
trading securities (735)
unrealized gain or loss (727)

Discussion Questions

1. Why might a business invest cash in temporary investments?
2. When is the equity method the appropriate accounting for equity investments?
3. How does the accounting for a dividend received differ for equity investments of less than 20% ownership and equity investments of between 20%–50% ownership?
4. If an investor owns more than 50% of an investee, how is the investment treated on the investor's financial statements?
5. What causes a gain or loss on the sale of a bond investment?
6. What is the major difference in the accounting for a portfolio of trading securities and a portfolio of available-for-sale securities?

7. If Valuation Allowance for Trading Investments has a credit balance, how is it reported on the balance sheet?
8. If Valuation Allowance for Available-for-Sale Investments has a debit balance, how is it reported on the balance sheet?
9. How would a debit balance in Unrealized Gain (Loss) on Available-for-Sale Investments be reported on the financial statements?
10. How are the balance sheet and income statement affected by fair value accounting for bond investments?

Practice Exercises

Example Exercises

EE 15-1 *p. 728*

PE 15-1A Equity investments: Less than 20% ownership

OBJ. 2

On January 23, 15,000 shares of Aurora Company's common stock are acquired at a price of $25 per share plus a $150 brokerage commission. On April 12, a $0.50-per-share dividend was received on the Aurora Company stock. On June 10, 6,000 shares of the Aurora Company stock were sold for $31 per share less a $100 brokerage commission. At the end of the accounting period on December 31, the fair value of the remaining 9,000 shares of Aurora Company's stock was $30 per share. Aurora Company has 200,000 shares of common stock outstanding. Journalize the entries for the original purchase, dividend, sale, and change in fair value under the fair value method.

EE 15-1 *p. 728*

PE 15-1B Equity investments: Less than 20% ownership

OBJ. 2

On September 12, 3,000 shares of Denver Company's common stock are acquired at a price of $40 per share plus a $300 brokerage commission. On October 15, an $0.80-per-share dividend was received on the Denver Company stock. On November 10, 1,600 shares of the Denver Company stock were sold for $36 per share less a $150 brokerage commission. At the end of the accounting period on December 31, the fair value of the remaining 1,400 shares of Denver Company's stock was $35 per share. Denver Company has 400,000 shares of common stock outstanding. Journalize the entries for the original purchase, dividend, sale, and change in fair value under the fair value method.

EE 15-2 *p. 730*

PE 15-2A Equity investments: 20%–50% ownership

OBJ. 2

On January 2, 20Y7, Mikedes Company acquired 30% of the outstanding stock of Violet Company for $720,000. For the year ended December 31, 20Y7, Violet Company earned income of $190,000 and paid dividends of $40,000. On January 31, 20Y8, Mikedes Company sold all of its investment in Violet Company stock for $770,000. Journalize the entries for Mikedes Company for the purchase of the stock, the share of Violet income, the dividends received from Violet Company, and the sale of the Violet Company stock.

EE 15-2 *p. 730*

PE 15-2B Equity investments: 20%–50% ownership

OBJ. 2

On January 2, 20Y4, Whitworth Company acquired 40% of the outstanding stock of Aloof Company for $340,000. For the year ended December 31, 20Y4, Aloof Company earned income of $180,000 and paid dividends of $10,000. On January 31 20Y5, Whitworth Company sold all of its investment in Aloof Company stock for $405,000. Journalize the entries for Whitworth Company for the purchase of the stock, the share of Aloof income, the dividends received from Aloof Company, and the sale of the Aloof Company stock.

SHOW ME HOW

EE 15-3 p. 734

PE 15-3A Bond (held-to-maturity) investments **OBJ. 3**

Journalize the entries to record the following selected bond investment transactions for Beacon Trust:

a. Purchased for cash $420,000 of Vasquez City 6% bonds at 100 plus accrued interest of $6,300.
b. Received first semiannual interest payment.
c. Sold $210,000 of the bonds at 99 plus accrued interest of $1,050.
d. Received face value of remaining bonds at their maturity.

SHOW ME HOW

EE 15-3 p. 734

PE 15-3B Bond (held-to-maturity) investments **OBJ. 3**

Journalize the entries to record the following selected bond investment transactions for Marr Products:

a. Purchased for cash $180,000 of Hotline Inc. 5% bonds at 100 plus accrued interest of $1,500.
b. Received first semiannual interest payment.
c. Sold $90,000 of the bonds at 102 plus accrued interest of $750.
d. Received face value of remaining bonds at their maturity.

SHOW ME HOW

EE 15-4 p. 736

PE 15-4A Trading securities at fair value **OBJ. 4**

On January 1, 20Y3, Valuation Allowance for Trading Investments had a zero balance. On December 31, 20Y3, the cost of the trading securities portfolio was $346,000, and the fair value was $309,000. Journalize the December 31, 20Y3, adjusting entry to record the unrealized gain or loss on trading investments.

SHOW ME HOW

EE 15-4 p. 736

PE 15-4B Trading securities at fair value **OBJ. 4**

On January 1, 20Y9, Valuation Allowance for Trading Investments had a zero balance. On December 31, 20Y9, the cost of the trading securities portfolio was $72,600, and the fair value was $79,100. Journalize the December 31, 20Y9, adjusting entry to record the unrealized gain or loss on trading investments.

SHOW ME HOW

EE 15-5 p. 738

PE 15-5A Available-for-sale securities at fair value **OBJ. 4**

On January 1, 20Y5, Valuation Allowance for Available-for-Sale Investments had a zero balance. On December 31, 20Y5, the cost of the available-for-sale securities was $43,290, and the fair value was $39,120. Journalize the adjusting entry to record the unrealized gain or loss on available-for-sale investments on December 31, 20Y5.

SHOW ME HOW

EE 15-5 p. 738

PE 15-5B Available-for-sale securities at fair value **OBJ. 4**

On January 1, 20Y7, Valuation Allowance for Available-for-Sale Investments had a zero balance. On December 31, 20Y7, the cost of the available-for-sale securities was $19,040, and the fair value was $22,870. Journalize the adjusting entry to record the unrealized gain or loss on available-for-sale investments on December 31, 20Y7.

SHOW ME HOW

FAI

EE 15-6 p. 741

PE 15-6A Dividend yield **OBJ. 5**

On June 30, Rae Corporation had a market price of $100 per share of common stock. For the previous year, Rae paid an annual dividend of $8.00 per share. Compute the dividend yield for Rae Corporation.

SHOW ME HOW

FAI

EE 15-6 p. 741

PE 15-6B Dividend yield **OBJ. 5**

On October 23, Brynner Company had a market price of $60 per share of common stock. For the previous year, Brynner paid an annual dividend of $0.90 per share. Compute the dividend yield for Brynner Company.

Exercises

✔ c. Gain on sale of investments, $41,760

SHOW ME HOW

EX 15-1 Entries for equity investments: less than 20% ownership **OBJ. 2**

On February 22, Triangle Corporation acquired 34,000 shares of the 500,000 outstanding common stock of Jupiter Co. at $25 plus commission charges of $680. On June 1, a cash dividend of $1.70 per share was received. On November 12, 7,000 shares were sold at $31 less commission charges of $100. At the end of the accounting period on December 31, the fair value of the remaining 27,000 shares of Jupiter Company's stock was $25.52 per share.

Journalize the entries for (a) the purchase of stock, (b) the receipt of dividends, (c) the sale of 7,000 shares, and (d) the change in fair value.

✔ Sept. 10, Loss on sale of investments, $18,150

SHOW ME HOW

EX 15-2 Entries for equity investments: less than 20% ownership **OBJ. 2**

The following equity investment transactions were completed by Vintage Company during a recent year:

Apr. 10. Purchased 11,000 shares of Delew Company's common stock for a price of $60 per share plus a brokerage commission of $220. Delew Company has 250,000 shares of common stock outstanding.

July 8. Received a quarterly dividend of $0.85 per share on the Delew Company investment.

Sept. 10. Sold 3,000 shares for a price of $54 per share less a brokerage commission of $90.

Dec. 31. At the end of the accounting period, the fair value of the remaining 8,000 shares of Delew Company's stock was $59.90 per share.

Journalize the entries for these transactions.

✔ Sept. 25, Dividend revenue, $310

SHOW ME HOW

EX 15-3 Entries for equity investments: less than 20% ownership **OBJ. 2**

Quan Corp. manufactures construction equipment. Journalize the entries to record the following selected equity investment transactions completed by Quan during a recent year using the fair value method.

Feb. 2. Purchased for cash 3,100 shares of Celeste Inc.'s common stock for $32 per share plus a $124 brokerage commission. Celeste Inc. has 80,000 shares of common stock outstanding.

Mar. 6. Received dividends of $0.45 per share on Celeste Inc. stock.

June 7. Purchased 1,400 shares of Celeste Inc. stock for $38 per share plus a $56 brokerage commission.

July 26. Sold 4,000 shares of Celeste Inc. stock for $41 per share less a $100 brokerage commission. Quan assumes that the first investments purchased are the first investments sold.

Sept. 25. Received dividends of $0.62 per share on Celeste Inc. stock.

Dec. 31. At the end of the accounting period, the fair value of the remaining 500 shares of Celeste Inc. stock was $20,720.

SHOW ME HOW

EX 15-4 Entries for equity investments: less than 20% ownership **OBJ. 2**

Seamus Industries Inc. buys and sells investments as part of its ongoing cash management. The following investment transactions were completed during the year:

Feb. 24. Acquired 1,000 shares of Tett Co.'s common stock for $85 per share plus a $150 brokerage commission.

May 16. Acquired 2,500 shares of Issacson Co.'s common stock for $36 per share plus a $100 commission.

July 14. Sold 400 shares of Tett Co. stock for $100 per share less a $75 brokerage commission.

(Continued)

Aug. 12. Sold 750 shares of Issacson Co. stock for $32.50 per share less an $80 brokerage commission.

Oct. 31. Received dividends of $0.40 per share on Tett Co. stock.

Dec. 31. At the end of the accounting period, the fair value of the remaining 600 shares of Tett Co.'s stock was $85.35 per share. The fair value of the remaining 1,750 shares of Isaacson Co.'s stock was equal to its cost of $36.04 per share.

Journalize the entries for these transactions.

SHOW ME HOW

EX 15-5 Entries for equity investments: 20%–50% ownership **OBJ. 2**

At a total cost of $5,600,000, Herrera Corporation acquired 280,000 shares of Tran Corp. common stock as a long-term investment. Tran Corp. has 800,000 shares of common stock outstanding, including the shares acquired by Herrera Corporation.

a. Journalize the entries by Herrera Corporation to record the following information:
   1. Tran Corp. reports net income of $600,000 for the current period.
   2. A cash dividend of $0.50 per common share is paid by Tran Corp. during the current period.

b. Why is the equity method appropriate for the Tran Corp. investment?

EX 15-6 Entries for equity investments: 20%–50% ownership **OBJ. 2**

✔ b. $14,900,000

SHOW ME HOW

On January 4, 20Y4, Ferguson Company purchased 480,000 shares of Silva Company's common stock directly from one of the founders for a price of $30 per share. Silva has 1,200,000 shares outstanding, including the Daniels shares. On July 2, 20Y4, Silva paid $750,000 in total dividends to its shareholders. On December 31, 20Y4, Silva reported a net income of $2,000,000 for the year.

a. Journalize the Ferguson Company entries for the transactions involving its investment in Silva Company during 20Y4.

b. Determine the December 31, 20Y4, balance of the investment in Silva Company stock account.

EX 15-7 Entries for equity investments: 20%–50% ownership **OBJ. 2**

On January 6, 20Y8, Bulldog Co. purchased 34% of the outstanding common stock of Gator Co. for $212,000. Gator Co. paid total dividends of $24,000 to all shareholders on June 30, 20Y8. Gator had a net loss of $56,000 for 20Y8.

a. Journalize Bulldog's purchase of the stock, receipt of the dividends, and the adjusting entry for the equity loss in Gator Co. stock.

b. Compute the balance of Investment in Gator Co. Stock on December 31, 20Y8.

c. How does valuing an investment under the equity method differ from valuing an investment at fair value?

EX 15-8 Entries for equity investments: 20%–50% ownership **OBJ. 2**

Hawkeye Company's balance sheet reported, under the equity method, its long-term investment in Raven Company for comparative years as follows:

	Dec. 31, 20Y6	Dec. 31, 20Y5
Investment in Raven Company stock (in millions)	$281	$264

In addition, the 20Y6 Hawkeye Company income statement disclosed equity earnings in the Raven Company investment as $25 million. Hawkeye Company neither purchased nor sold Raven Company stock during 20Y6. The fair value of the Raven Company stock investment on December 31, 20Y6, was $310 million.

Explain the change in Investment in Raven Company Stock from December 31, 20Y5, to December 31, 20Y6.

SHOW ME HOW

EX 15-9 Entries for bond (held-to-maturity) investments **OBJ. 3**

Demopoulos Company acquired $150,000 of Marimar Co., 6% bonds on May 1 at their face amount. Interest is paid semiannually on May 1 and November 1. On November 1, Demopoulos Company sold $55,000 of the bonds for 98.

Journalize the entries to record the following:

a. The initial acquisition of the bonds on May 1.

b. The semiannual interest received on November 1.

c. The sale of the bonds on November 1.

d. The accrual of $950 interest on December 31.

SHOW ME HOW

EX 15-10 Entries for bond (held-to-maturity) investments **OBJ. 3**

Bula Investments acquired $240,000 of Effenstein Corp., 8% bonds at their face amount on October 1, 20Y1. The bonds pay interest on October 1 and April 1. On April 1, 20Y2, Bula sold $90,000 of Effenstein Corp. bonds at 102.

Journalize the entries to record the following selected transactions:

a. The initial acquisition of the Effenstein Corp. bonds on October 1, 20Y1.

b. The adjusting entry for 3 months of accrued interest earned on the Effenstein Corp. bonds on December 31, 20Y1.

c. The receipt of semiannual interest on April 1, 20Y2.

d. The sale of $90,000 of Effenstein Corp. bonds on April 1, 20Y2, at 102.

e. The receipt of the face value of the remaining bonds at their maturity on October 1, 20Y8.

✔ c. Oct. 31, Loss on sale of investments, $2,000

SHOW ME HOW

EX 15-11 Entries for bond (held-to-maturity) investments **OBJ. 3**

Gillooly Co. purchased $360,000 of 6%, 20-year Lumpkin County bonds on May 11, Year 1, directly from the county, at their face amount plus accrued interest. The bonds pay semiannual interest on April 1 and October 1. On October 31, Year 1, Gillooly Co. sold $90,000 of the Lumpkin County bonds at 98 plus $450 accrued interest less a $200 brokerage commission.

Journalize the entries to record the following:

a. The purchase of the bonds on May 11 plus 40 days of accrued interest.

b. Semiannual interest on October 1.

c. Sale of the bonds on October 31.

d. Adjusting entry for accrued interest on December 31, Year 1.

e. The receipt of the face value of the remaining bonds at their maturity on April 1, Year 20.

✔ a. Aug. 30, Loss on sale of investments, $700

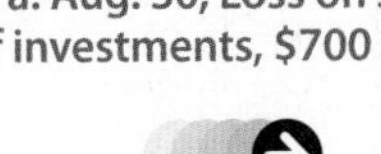

SHOW ME HOW

EX 15-12 Entries for bond (held-to-maturity) investments **OBJ. 3**

The following bond investment transactions were completed by Starks Company:

Jan. 31. Purchased 75, $1,000 government bonds at 100 plus accrued interest of $375 (1 month). The bonds pay 6% annual interest on July 1 and January 1.

July 1. Received semiannual interest on bond investment.

Aug. 30. Sold 35, $1,000 bonds at 98 plus $350 accrued interest (2 months).

a. Journalize the entries for the preceding transactions.

b. Journalize the December 31 adjusting entry for semiannual interest earned on the bonds.

c. Journalize the receipt of $40,000 at the bonds' maturity on July 1.

EX 15-13 Interest for bond (held-to-maturity) investments **OBJ. 3**

On February 1, Hansen Company purchased $120,000 of 5%, 20-year Knight Company bonds at their face amount plus 1 month's accrued interest. The bonds pay interest on January 1 and July 1. On October 1, Hansen Company sold $40,000 of the Knight Company bonds acquired on February 1, plus 3 months' accrued interest. On December 31, 3 months' interest was accrued for the remaining bonds.

Determine the interest earned by Hansen Company on Knight Company bonds for the year.

EX 15-14 Trading invesments: missing financial statement items

OBJ. 4

✔ g. $6,000

JED Capital Inc. makes investments in trading securities. Selected income statement and balance sheet items for the years ended December 31, Year 2 and Year 3, are as follows:

JED Capital Inc.
Selected Income Statement Items
For the Years Ended December 31, Year 2 and Year 3

	Year 2	Year 3
Income from operations	a.	e.
Unrealized loss on trading investments	b.	$(11,000)
Net income	c.	28,000

JED Capital Inc.
Selected Balance Sheet Items
December 31, Year 1, Year 2, and Year 3

	Dec. 31, Year 1	Dec. 31, Year 2	Dec. 31, Year 3
Trading investments, at cost	$144,000	$168,000	$205,000
Valuation allowance for trading investments	(12,000)	17,000	g.
Trading investments, at fair value	d.	f.	h.
Retained earnings	$210,000	$245,000	i.

Determine the missing lettered items assuming JED Capital Inc. paid no dividends.

EX 15-15 Journal entries for trading investments

OBJ. 2, 4

SHOW ME HOW

The investments of Charger Inc. include an investment of trading securities of Raiders Inc. purchased on February 24, 20Y7, for $551,000. The fair value of the securities on December 31, 20Y7, is $609,000.

a. Journalize the entries for the February 24 purchase and the adjustment to fair value on December 31, 20Y7.

b. How is a unrealized gain or loss for trading investments reported on the financial statements?

c. If the Raiders Inc. securities had been classified as available-for-sale securities, how would the investment be reported on the financial statements?

EX 15-16 Journal entries for trading investments

OBJ. 2, 4

✔ a. Unrealized loss on trading investments, $1,950

SHOW ME HOW

Gruden Bancorp Inc. purchased a portfolio of trading securities during 20Y3, its first year of operations. The cost and fair value of this portfolio on December 31, 20Y3, are as follows:

Issuing Company	Cost	Fair Value
Griffin Inc.	$ 40,000	$ 44,800
Luck Company	37,500	33,750
Wilson Company	40,000	37,000
Total	$117,500	$115,550

On May 10, 20Y4, Gruden Bancorp Inc. purchased trading securities of Carroll Inc. for $34,900.

Journalize the entries to record the following:

a. The adjusting entry for the portfolio of trading securities on December 31, 20Y3.

b. The May 10, 20Y4, purchase of Carroll Inc. securities.

c. The adjusting entry for the portfolio of trading securities on December 31, 20Y4. Assume that except for the purchase of Carroll Inc. securities there were no other transactions involving trading securities in 20Y4. In addition, assume that the fair value of the portfolio of trading securities on December 31, 20Y4, is $175,000.

d. What amount should be reported for trading investments on the December 31, 20Y4, balance sheet?

EX 15-17 Journal entries for available-for-sale securities OBJ. 2, 4

✔ a. Dec. 31, 20Y5, Unrealized gain (loss) on available-for-sale investments, $17,500

M. Jones Inc. purchased the following available-for-sale securities during 20Y5, its first year of operations:

Issuing Company	Cost
Arden Enterprises Inc.	$150,000
French Broad Industries Inc.	66,000
Pisgah Construction Inc.	104,000
	$320,000

The fair value of the various available-for-sale securities on December 31, 20Y5, was as follows:

Issuing Company	Fair Value, Dec. 31, 20Y5
Arden Enterprises Inc.	$170,000
French Broad Industries Inc.	71,500
Pisgah Construction Inc.	96,000
	$337,500

a. Journalize the adjusting entry for the fair value of the portfolio of securities on December 31, 20Y5.

b. If the fair value of the portfolio of securities were the same on December 31, 20Y6, what would be the journal entry to adjust the portfolio to fair value?

c. If the fair value of the portfolio of securities was $340,000 on December 31, 20Y6, what would be the journal entry to adjust the portfolio to fair value?

d. If the fair value of the portfolio of securities was $330,000 on December 31, 20Y6, what would be the journal entry to adjust the portfolio to fair value?

EX 15-18 Dividend yield OBJ. 5

At the market close of a recent year, **McDonald's Corporation** had a closing stock price of $198.01. In addition, McDonald's Corporation had a dividend per share of $4.19 during the previous year.

Determine McDonald's Corporation's dividend yield. Round to one decimal place.

EX 15-19 Dividend yield OBJ. 5

✔ a. Dec. 31, current year, 1.65%

The market price for **Microsoft Corporation** closed at $101.57 and $85.95 on December 31, current year, and previous year, respectively. The dividends per share were $1.68 for current year and $1.56 for previous year.

a. Determine the dividend yield for Microsoft on December 31, current year, and previous year. Round percentages to two decimal places.

b. Interpret these measures.

EX 15-20 Dividend yield OBJ. 5

Booking Holdings Inc. is a leading provider of online travel and related services, provided to consumers and local partners through six primary brands: Booking.com, KAYAK, priceline.com, agoda.com, Rentalcars.com, and OpenTable. In a recent annual report, Booking Holdings Inc. published the following dividend policy:

We have not declared or paid any cash dividends on our capital stock since our inception and do not expect to pay any cash dividends for the foreseeable future.

Given Booking Holdings' dividend policy, why would investors be attracted to its stock?

Appendix
EX 15-21 Comprehensive income

On December 31, 20Y7, Valur Co. had the following available-for-sale investment disclosure within the Current Assets section of the balance sheet:

Available-for-sale investments (at cost)	$145,000
Plus valuation allowance for available-for-sale investments	40,000
Available-for-sale investments (at fair value)	$185,000

There were no purchases or sales of available-for-sale investments during 20Y8. On December 31, 20Y8, the fair value of the available-for-sale investment portfolio was $200,000. The net income of Valur Co. was $210,000 for 20Y8.

Compute the comprehensive income for Valur Co. for the year ended December 31, 20Y8.

Problems: Series A

PR 15-1A Transactions for common stock and trading investments OBJ. 2, 4

✔ December 31, 20Y2, Unrealized loss on trading investments, $6,000

Rios Co. is a regional insurance company that began operations on January 1, 20Y2. The following selected transactions relate to investments acquired by Rios Co., which has a fiscal year ending on December 31:

20Y2

Feb. 1. Purchased 7,500 shares of Caldwell Inc. common stock at $50 per share plus a brokerage commission of $75. Caldwell has 100,000 shares of common stock outstanding.

May 1. Purchased securities of Holland Inc. as a trading investment for $126,000.

July 1. Sold 4,500 shares of Caldwell Inc. for $46 per share less a $110 brokerage commission.

31. Received an annual dividend of $0.50 per share on 3,000 shares of Caldwell Inc. stock.

Nov. 15. Sold the remaining shares of Caldwell Inc. for $51 per share less a $90 brokerage commission.

Dec. 31. The trading securities of Holland Inc. have a fair value on December 31 of $120,000.

20Y3

Apr. 1. Purchased securities of Fuller Inc. as a trading investment for $125,000.

Oct. 14. Sold securities of Fuller Inc. that cost $25,000 for $30,000.

Dec. 31. The fair values of the Holland Inc. and Fuller Inc. securities are as follows:

Issuing Company	Cost	Fair Value
Holland Inc.	$126,000	$132,500
Fuller Inc.	100,000	115,600

Instructions

1. Journalize the entries to record the preceding transactions, including any December 31 adjusting entries.
2. Prepare the Trading Investments section of the December 31, 20Y3, balance sheet for Rios Co.
3. How are unrealized gains or losses on trading investments presented on the financial statements of Rios Co.?

PR 15-2A Entries for equity investment of between 20%–50% ownership OBJ. 2

Forte Inc. produces and sells theater set designs and costumes. The company began operations on January 1, 20Y6. The following transactions relate to securities acquired by Forte Inc., which has a fiscal year ending on December 31, 20Y6:

Jan. 10. Purchased an influential interest in Imboden Inc. for $720,000 by purchasing 96,000 shares directly from the estate of the founder of Imboden Inc. There are 300,000 shares of Imboden Inc. stock outstanding.

Dec. 31. Received $57,600 of cash dividends on Imboden Inc. stock. Imboden Inc. reported net income of $450,000 in 20Y6. Forte Inc. uses the equity method of accounting for its investment in Imboden Inc.

Instructions

1. Journalize the entries to record these transactions.
2. Should Forte Inc.'s investment in Imboden Inc. be reported at fair value on its financial statements for the year ending December 31, 20Y6?

PR 15-3A Transactions for bond (held-to-maturity) investments OBJ. 3, 4

Soto Industries Inc. is an athletic footware company that began operations on January 1, 20Y3. The following are bond (held-to-maturity) transactions by Soto Industries Inc., which has a fiscal year ending on December 31:

20Y3

Apr. 1. Purchased $100,000 of Welch Co. 6%, 15-year bonds at their face amount plus accrued interest of $500. The bonds pay interest semiannually on March 1 and September 1.

June 1. Purchased $210,000 of Bailey 4%, 10-year bonds at their face amount plus accrued interest of $700. The bonds pay interest semiannually on May 1 and November 1.

Sept. 1. Received semiannual interest on the Welch Co. bonds.

30. Sold $40,000 of Welch Co. bonds at 97 plus accrued interest of $200.

Nov. 1. Received semiannual interest on the Bailey bonds.

Dec. 31. Accrued interest on the Welch Co. bonds.

31. Accrued interest on the Bailey bonds.

20Y4

Mar. 1. Received semiannual interest on the Welch Co. bonds.

May 1. Received semiannual interest on the Bailey bonds.

Instructions

1. Journalize the entries to record the preceding transactions.
2. If the bond portfolio is classified as an available-for-sale investment, how would it be reported on the financial statements?

PR 15-4A Equity and available-for-sale investments OBJ. 2, 3, 4

✔ h. $(7,800)

O'Brien Industries Inc. is a book publisher. The partial balance sheets for December 31, 20Y4 and 20Y5 are as follows:

O'Brien Industries Inc.
Partial Balance Sheets
December 31

	20Y5	20Y4
Available-for-sale investments (at cost)	$ a.	$103,770
Valuation allowance for available-for-sale investments	b.	(2,500)
Available-for-sale investments (fair value)	$ c.	$101,270
Interest receivable	$ d.	—
Investment in Jolly Roger Co. stock	e.	$ 77,000
Office equipment (net)	115,000	130,000
Total assets	$ f.	$666,270
Accounts payable	$ 69,400	$ 65,000
Common stock	70,000	70,000
Excess of issue price over par	225,000	225,000
Retained earnings	g.	308,770
Unrealized gain (loss) on available-for-sale investments	h.	(2,500)
Total liabilities and stockholders' equity	$ i.	$666,270

(Continued)

The available-for-sale investments at cost and fair value on December 31, 20Y4, are as follows:

Issuing Company	Cost	Fair Value
Bernard Co.	$ 38,250	$ 37,500
Chadwick Co.	65,520	63,770
	$103,770	$101,270

The investment in Jolly Roger Co. stock represents 30% of the outstanding shares of Jolly Roger Co.

The following selected transactions occurred during 20Y5:

Jan. 2. Purchased $94,400 of Gozar Inc. 5%, 10-year bonds at 100. The bonds are classified as an available-for-sale investment. The bonds pay interest on June 30 and December 31.

June 30. Received interest for 6 months on the Gozar Inc. bonds purchased on January 2.

Oct. 1. Purchased $40,000 of Nightline Co. 6%, 10-year bonds at 100. The bonds are classified as an available-for-sale investment. The bonds pay interest on October 1 and April 1.

9. Dividends of $12,500 are received on the Jolly Roger Co. investment.

Dec. 31. Jolly Roger Co. reported a total net income of $112,000 for 20Y5, which O'Brien Industries Inc. recorded using the equity method.

31. Received interest for 6 months on the Gozar Inc. bonds purchased on January 2.

31. Accrued 3 months of interest on the Nightline bonds.

31. Adjusted the available-for-sale investment portfolio to fair value, using the following fair values:

Issuing Company	Fair Value
Bernard Co.	$34,650
Chadwick Co.	57,960
Gozar Inc.	98,560
Nightline Co.	39,200

For the year ending December 31, 20Y5, O'Brien Industries Inc. reported net income of $148,230 and paid no dividends.

Instructions

Determine the missing amounts by letter in the partial balance sheets.

Problems: Series B

PR 15-1B Transactions for common stock and trading investments

OBJ. 2, 4

✔ **Dec. 31, 20Y8, Unrealized gain on trading investments, $6,300**

Zeus Investments Inc. is a regional freight company that began operations on January 1, 20Y8. The following transactions relate to trading securities acquired by Zeus Inc., which has a fiscal year ending on December 31:

20Y8

Feb. 14. Purchased 4,800 shares of Apollo Inc. common stock at $26 per share plus a brokerage commission of $192. Apollo Inc. has 150,000 shares of common stock outstanding.

Apr. 1. Purchased securities of Ares Inc. as a trading investment for $45,000.

June 1. Sold 600 shares of Apollo Inc. for $32 per share less a $100 brokerage commission.

27. Received an annual dividend of $0.20 per share on 4,200 shares of Apollo Inc. stock.

Oct. 15. Sold the remaining shares of Apollo Inc. for $25.50 per share less a $300 brokerage commission.

Dec. 31. The trading securities of Ares Inc. have a fair value on December 31 of $51,300.

20Y9

Mar. 14. Purchased securities of Athena Inc. as a trading investment for $78,000.

July 30. Sold securities of Athena Inc. that cost $28,000 for $25,000.

Dec. 31. The fair values of the Ares Inc. and Athena Inc. securities are as follows:

Issuing Company	Cost	Fair Value
Ares Inc.	$45,000	$54,500
Athena Inc.	50,000	60,000

Instructions

1. Journalize the entries to record the preceding transactions, including any December 31 adjusting entries.
2. Prepare the Trading Investments section of the December 31, 20Y9, balance sheet for Zeus Inc.
3. How are unrealized gains or losses on trading investments presented on the financial statements of Zeus Inc.?

PR 15-2B Entries for equity investment of between 20%–50% ownership

OBJ. 2

Glacier Products Inc. is a wholesaler of rock climbing gear. The company began operations on January 1, 20Y3. The following transactions relate to securities acquired by Glacier Products Inc., which has a fiscal year ending on December 31, 20Y3:

Jan. 25. Purchased 75,000 shares of Helsi Co. common stock for $800,000. There are 250,000 shares of Helsi Co. stock outstanding.

Dec. 31. Received $38,000 of cash dividends on Helsi Co. stock. Helsi Co. reported net income of $170,000 in 20Y3.

Instructions

1. Journalize the entries to record the preceding transactions.
2. Should Glacier Product Inc.'s investment in Helsi Co. be reported at fair value on its financial statements for the year ending December 31, 20Y3?

SHOW ME HOW

PR 15-3B Transactions for bond (held-to-maturity) investments

OBJ. 3, 4

Rekya Mart Inc. is a general merchandise retail company that began operations on January 1, 20Y5. The following are bond (held-to-maturity) transactions by Rekya Mart Inc., which has a fiscal year ending on December 31:

20Y5

Apr. 1. Purchased $90,000 of Smoke Bay 6%, 10-year bonds at their face amount plus accrued interest of $900. The bonds pay interest semiannually on February 1 and August 1.

May 16. Purchased $42,000 of Geotherma Co. 4%, 12-year bonds at their face amount plus accrued interest of $70. The bonds pay interest semiannually on May 1 and November 1.

Aug. 1. Received semiannual interest on the Smoke Bay bonds.

Sept. 1. Sold $12,000 of Smoke Bay bonds at 101 plus accrued interest of $60.

Nov. 1. Received semiannual interest on the Geotherma Co. bonds.

Dec. 31. Accrued interest on the Smoke Bay bonds.

31. Accrued interest on the Geotherma Co. bonds.

20Y6

Feb. 1. Received semiannual interest on the Smoke Bay bonds.

May 1. Received semiannual interest on the Geotherma Co. bonds.

(Continued)

Instructions

1. Journalize the entries to record the preceding transactions.
2. If the bond portfolio is classified as an available-for-sale investment, how would it be reported on the financial statements?

PR 15-4B Equity and available-for-sale investments **OBJ. 2, 3, 4**

✔ b. $4,680

Teasdale Inc. manufactures and sells commercial and residential security equipment. The partial balance sheets for December 31, 20Y7 and 20Y8 are as follows:

Teasdale Inc.
Partial Balance Sheets
December 31

	20Y8	20Y7
Available-for-sale investments (at cost)	$ a.	$ 91,200
Valuation allowance for available-for-sale investments	b.	8,776
Available-for-sale investments (fair value)	$ c.	$ 99,976
Interest receivable	$ d.	—
Investment in Wright Co. stock	e.	$ 69,200
Office equipment (net)	96,000	105,000
Total assets	$ f.	$538,176
Accounts payable	$ 91,000	$ 72,000
Common stock	80,000	80,000
Excess of issue price over par	250,000	250,000
Retained earnings	g.	127,400
Unrealized gain (loss) on available-for-sale investments	h.	8,776
Total liabilities and stockholders' equity	$604,320	$538,176

The available-for-sale investments at cost and fair value on December 31, 20Y7, are as follows:

Issuing Company	Cost	Fair Value
Alvarez Inc.	$36,480	$39,936
Hirsch Inc.	54,720	60,040
	$91,200	$99,976

The Investment in Wright Co. stock represents 30% of the outstanding shares of Wright Co. The following selected investment transactions occurred during 20Y8:

Jan. 2. Purchased $32,000 of Richter Inc. 5%, 10-year bonds at face value as an available-for-sale investment. The bonds pay interest on June 30 and December 31.

June 30. Received interest for 6 months on the Richter Inc. bonds purchased on January 2.

July 12. Dividends of $12,000 are received on the Wright Co. investment.

Oct. 1. Purchased $24,000 of Toon Co. 4%, 10-year bonds at face value as an available-for-sale investment. The bonds pay interest on October 1 and April 1.

Dec. 31. Wright Co. reported a total net income of $80,000 for 20Y8, which Teasdale Inc. recorded using the equity method.

31. Received interest for 6 months on the Richter Inc. bonds purchased on January 2.

31. Accrued interest for 3 months on the Toon Co. bonds purchased on October 1.

31. The fair values of the available-for-sale investments are as follows:

Issuing Company	Fair Value
Alvarez Inc.	$39,840
Hirsch Inc.	49,400
Richter Inc.	38,400
Toon Co.	24,240

For the year ending December 31, 20Y8, Teasdale Inc. reported net income of $51,240 and paid no dividends.

Instructions

Determine the missing amounts by letter in the partial balance sheets.

Comprehensive Problem 4

✔ 2.a. Net income, $326,000

Selected transactions completed by Equinox Products Inc. during the fiscal year ended December 31, 20Y5, were as follows:

a. Issued 15,000 shares of $20 par common stock at $30, receiving cash.

b. Issued 4,000 shares of $80 par preferred $1 stock at $100, receiving cash.

c. Issued $500,000 of 10-year, 5% bonds at 104, with interest payable semiannually.

d. Declared a quarterly dividend of $0.50 per share on common stock and $1.00 per share on preferred stock. On the date of record, 100,000 shares of common stock were outstanding, no treasury shares were held and 20,000 shares of preferred stock were outstanding.

e. Paid the cash dividends declared in (d).

f. Purchased 4% bonds issued by Solstice Corp. as an available-for-sale investment for $300,150.

g. Purchased 8,000 shares of treasury common stock at $33 per share.

h. Purchased 40,000 shares of Pinkberry Co.'s common stock directly from the founders for $24 per share. Pinkberry has 125,000 shares issued and outstanding.

i. Declared a $1.00 quarterly cash dividend per share on preferred stock. On the date of record, 20,000 shares of preferred stock had been issued.

j. Paid the cash dividends to the preferred stockholders.

k. Received $27,500 dividend from Pinkberry Co. investment in (h).

l. Purchased $90,000 of Dream Inc. 10-year, 5% bonds, directly from the issuing company, at their face amount plus accrued interest of $375. The bonds are a held-to-maturity investment.

m. Sold, at $38 per share, 2,600 shares of treasury common stock purchased in (g).

n. Received interest of $6,000 from the Solstice Corp. investment in (f).

o. Sold Solstice Corp. bonds with a face value of $40,020 for $45,000, realizing a gain of $4,980.

p. Recorded the payment of semiannual interest on the bonds issued in (c) and the amortization of the premium for 6 months. The amortization is determined using the straight-line method.

q. Accrued interest for 3 months on the Dream Inc. bonds purchased in (l).

r. Pinkberry Co. reported total earnings of $240,000. Equinox Products recorded its share of Pinkberry Co. net income using the equity method.

s. The Solstice Corp. bonds have a fair value of $253,630 on December 31, 20Y5. Valuation Allowance for Available-for-Sale Investments had a balance of zero on January 1, 20Y5.

Instructions

1. Journalize the selected transactions.
2. The following data were taken from the records of Equinox Products Inc. Assume that these data include all of the transactions and adjusting entries for the year ended December 31, 20Y5, including the transactions and adjusting entries recorded in part (1).
   a. Prepare a multiple-step income statement for the year ended December 31, 20Y5, concluding with earnings per share. In computing earnings per share, assume that the average number of common shares outstanding was 100,000 and preferred dividends were $100,000.
   b. Prepare a retained earnings statement for the year ended December 31, 20Y5.
   c. Prepare a balance sheet in report form as of December 31, 20Y5.

(Continued)

Income statement data:	
Advertising expense	$ 150,000
Cost of merchandise sold	3,700,000
Delivery expense	30,000
Depreciation expense—office buildings and equipment	30,000
Depreciation expense—store buildings and equipment	100,000
Gain on sale of investments	4,980
Income from Pinkberry Co. investment	76,800
Income tax expense	142,000
Interest expense	21,000
Interest revenue	8,720
Miscellaneous administrative expense	7,500
Miscellaneous selling expense	14,000
Office rent expense	50,000
Office salaries expense	170,000
Office supplies expense	10,000
Sales	5,254,000
Sales commissions expense	185,000
Sales salaries expense	385,000
Store supplies expense	21,000
Retained earnings and balance sheet data:	
Accounts payable	$ 194,300
Accounts receivable	545,000
Accumulated depreciation—office buildings and equipment	1,580,000
Accumulated depreciation—store buildings and equipment	4,126,000
Allowance for doubtful accounts	8,450
Available-for-sale investments (at cost)	260,130
Bonds payable, 5%, due in 10 years	500,000
Cash	246,000
Common stock, $20 par (400,000 shares authorized; 100,000 shares issued, 94,600 outstanding)	2,000,000
Dividends:	
Cash dividends for common stock	155,120
Cash dividends for preferred stock	100,000
Goodwill	500,000
Income tax payable	44,000
Interest receivable	1,125
Investment in Pinkberry Co. stock (equity method)	1,009,300
Investment in Dream Inc. bonds (long term)	90,000
Merchandise inventory (December 31, 20Y5), at lower of cost (FIFO) or market	778,000
Office buildings and equipment	4,320,000
Paid-in capital from sale of treasury stock	13,000
Excess of issue price over par—common stock	886,800
Excess of issue price over par—preferred stock	150,000
Preferred $1 stock, $80 par (30,000 shares authorized; 20,000 shares issued)	1,600,000
Premium on bonds payable	19,000
Prepaid expenses	27,400
Retained earnings, January 1, 20Y5	9,319,725
Store buildings and equipment	12,560,000
Treasury stock (5,400 shares of common stock at cost of $33 per share)	178,200
Unrealized gain (loss) on available-for-sale investments	(6,500)
Valuation allowance for available-for-sale investments	(6,500)

Cases & Projects

ETHICS

CP 15-1 Ethics in Action

Financial assets include stocks and bonds. These are fairly simple securities that can often be valued using quoted market prices. However, there are more complex financial instruments that do not have quoted market prices. These complex securities must still be valued on the balance sheet at fair value. Generally accepted accounting principles require that the reporting entity use assumptions in valuing investments when market prices or critical valuation inputs are unobservable.

What are the ethical considerations in making subjective valuations of these complex financial instruments?

TEAM ACTIVITY

CP 15-2 Reporting investments

Team Activity

In groups of three or four, find a recent annual report for **Microsoft Corporation**. The annual report can be found on the company's website at https://www.microsoft.com/en-us/Investor/annual-reports.aspx.

The notes to the financial statements include details of Microsoft's investments. Find the notes that provide details of its investments (Note 4) and the income from its investments (Note 3).

From these disclosures, answer the following questions:

1. What is the total cost of investments?
2. What is the fair value (recorded value) of investments?
3. What is the total unrealized gain from investments?
4. What is the total unrealized loss from investments?
5. What percent of total investments (at fair value) are:
   a. Cash and equivalents?
   b. Short-term investments?
   c. Equity and other investments (long term)?
6. What was the total combined dividend and interest revenue?
7. What was the recognized net gain or loss from sale of investments?

CP 15-3 Warren Buffett and "look-through" earnings

Berkshire Hathaway, the investment holding company of Warren Buffett, reports its "less than 20% ownership" investments according to generally accepted accounting principles. However, it also provides additional disclosures that it terms "look-through" earnings.

Warren Buffett states,

> *Many of these companies (in the less than 20%-owned category) pay out relatively small proportions of their earnings in dividends. This means that only a small proportion of their earning power is recorded in our own current operating earnings. But, while our reported operating earnings reflect only the dividends received from such companies, our economic well-being is determined by their earnings, not their dividends.*
>
> *The value to Berkshire Hathaway of retained earnings (of our investees) is not determined by whether we own 100%, 50%, 20%, or 1% of the businesses in which they reside. . . . Our perspective on such "forgotten-but-not-gone" earnings is simple: the way they are accounted for is of no importance, but their ownership and subsequent utilization is all-important. We care not whether the auditors hear a tree fall in the forest; we do care who owns the tree and what's next done with it.*
>
> *I believe the best way to think about our earnings is in terms of "look-through" results, calculated as follows: Take $250 million, which is roughly our share of the operating earnings retained by our investees (<20% ownership holdings); subtract . . . incremental taxes we would have owed had that $250 million been paid to us in dividends; then add the remainder, $220 million, to our reported earnings of $371 million. Thus, our "look-through" earnings were about $590 million.*

Source: Warren Buffett, *The Essays of Warren Buffett: Lessons for Corporate America*, edited by Lawrence A. Cunningham, pp. 180–183 (excerpted).

Write a brief memo to your instructor, explaining look-through earnings and why Mr. Buffet favors look-through earnings.

CP 15-4 Benefits of fair value

On July 16, 20Y1, Wyatt Corp. purchased 40 acres of land for $350,000. The land has been held for a future plant site until the current date, December 31, 20Y9. On December 18, 20Y9, TexoPete Inc. purchased 40 acres of land for $2,000,000 to be used for a distribution center. The TexoPete land is located next to the Wyatt Corp. land. Thus, both Wyatt Corp. and TexoPete Inc. own nearly identical pieces of land.

1. What are the valuations of land on the balance sheets of Wyatt Corp. and TexoPete Inc. using generally accepted accounting principles?
2. How might fair value accounting aid comparability when evaluating these two companies?

CP 15-5 International fair value accounting

IFRS

International Financial Reporting Standard No. 16 provides companies the option of valuing property, plant, and equipment at either historical cost or fair value. If fair value is selected, then the property, plant, and equipment must be revalued periodically to fair value. Under fair value, if there is an increase in the value of the property, plant, and equipment during the reporting period, then the increase is credited to stockholders' equity. However, if there is a decrease in fair value, then the decrease is reported as an expense for the period.

How is the international accounting treatment for changes in fair value for property, plant, and equipment similar to investments?

CHAPTER 16

Statement of Cash Flows

RETAINED EARNINGS STATEMENT
For the Year Ended December 31, 20Y6

Retained earnings, Jan. 1, 20Y6		$XXX
Net income	$ XXX	
Dividends	(XXX)	
Increase in retained earnings		XXX
Retained earnings, Dec. 31, 20Y6		$XXX

INCOME STATEMENT
For the Year Ended December 31, 20Y6

Sales		$XXX
Cost of merchandise sold		XXX
Gross profit		$XXX
Operating expenses:		
Advertising expense	$XXX	
Depreciation expense	XXX	
Wages expense	XXX	
Utilities expense	XXX	
...	XXX	
...	XXX	
Total operating expenses		XXX
Income from operations		$XXX
Other revenue and expenses		XXX
Net income		$XXX

STATEMENT OF CASH FLOWS
For the Year Ended December 31, 20Y6

Cash flows from (used for) operating activities	$XXX
Cash flows from (used for) investing activities	XXX
Cash flows from (used for) financing activities	XXX
Net increase (decrease) in cash	$XXX
Cash balance, January 1, 20Y6	XXX
Cash balance, December 31, 20Y6	$XXX

BALANCE SHEET
December 31, 20Y6

Current assets:		
Cash	$XXX	
Accounts receivable	XXX	
Inventory	XXX	
Total current assets		$XXX
Property, plant, and equipment	$XXX	
Intangible assets	XXX	
Total long-term assets		XXX
Total assets		$XXX
Liabilities:		
Current liabilities	$XXX	
Long-term liabilities	XXX	
Total liabilities		$XXX
Stockholders' equity:		
Common stock	$XXX	
Retained earnings	XXX	
Total stockholders' equity		XXX
Total liabilities and stockholders' equity		$XXX

CHAPTER 16

VIVIEN KILLILEA/WIREIMAGE/GETTY IMAGES

National Beverage Co.

Suppose you receive $100 from an event. Does it make a difference what the event was? Yes, it does! If you receive $100 for your birthday, then it's a gift. If you receive $100 as a result of working part-time for a week, then it's from earnings. If you receive $100 as a loan, then it's money that you will have to pay back in the future. If you sell your iPod for $100, then it's the result of selling an asset. These examples illustrate that not all cash flows are the same, and the source of the cash has different meanings and implications for your future. You would much rather receive a $100 gift than take out a $100 loan. Likewise, company stakeholders view inflows and outflows of cash differently, depending on their source.

Companies are required to report information about the events causing a change in cash over a period of time. This information is reported on the statement of cash flows. One such company is **National Beverage**, which is known for its innovative soft drinks and alternative beverages. You have probably seen the company's **Shasta** and **Faygo** soft drinks or **LaCroix**, **Everfresh**, and **Crystal Bay** drinks at your local grocery or convenience store. As with any company, cash is important to National Beverage. Without cash, National Beverage would be unable to expand its brands, distribute its product, support extreme sports, or provide a return for its owners. Thus, its managers are concerned about the sources and uses of cash.

In previous chapters, we used the income statement, balance sheet, statement of retained earnings, and other information to analyze the effects of management decisions on a business's financial position and operating performance. In this chapter, we focus on the events causing a change in cash by presenting the preparation and use of the statement of cash flows.

Link to National Beverage.......Pages 769, 770, 775, 779, 782

LEARNING OBJECTIVES

After studying this chapter, you should be able to:

Example Exercises (EE) are shown in **red**.

OBJ. 1 **Describe the cash flow activities reported on the statement of cash flows.**

Reporting Cash Flows

Cash Flows from (used for) Operating Activities	EE **16-1**
Cash Flows from (used for) Investing Activities	EE **16-1**
Cash Flows from (used for) Financing Activities	EE **16-1**
Noncash Investing and Financing Activities	
Format of the Statement of Cash Flows	
Cash Flow per Share	

OBJ. 2 **Prepare the Cash Flows from (used for) Operating Activities section of the statement of cash flows using the indirect method.**

Cash Flows from (used for) Operating Activities

Net Income	
Adjustments to Net Income	EE **16-2**
Changes in Current Operating Assets and Liabilities	EE **16-3**
Determining Cash Flows from (used for) Operating Activities	EE **16-4**

OBJ. 3 **Prepare the Cash Flows from (used for) Investing Activities section of the statement of cash flows.**

Cash Flows from (used for) Investing Activities

Land	EE **16-5**
Building and Accumulated Depreciation—Building	

OBJ. 4 **Prepare the Cash Flows from (used for) Financing Activities section of the statement of cash flows.**

Cash Flows from (used for) Financing Activities

Bonds Payable	EE **16-6**
Common Stock	EE **16-6**
Dividends and Dividends Payable	EE **16-6**

OBJ. 5 **Prepare a statement of cash flows.**

Prepare a Statement of Cash Flows—Indirect Method

OBJ. 6 **Describe and illustrate the use of free cash flow in evaluating a company's cash flow.**

Financial Analysis and Interpretation: Free Cash Flow EE **16-7**

APP. 1 OBJ. **Use a spreadsheet to prepare a statement of cash flows using the indirect method.**

APP. 2 OBJ. **Prepare a statement of cash flows using the direct method.**

At a Glance 16 Page 792

Reporting Cash Flows

OBJ. 1 Describe the cash flow activities reported on the statement of cash flows.

The **statement of cash flows** reports a company's cash inflows and outflows for a period.[1] The statement of cash flows provides useful information about a company's ability to do the following:

- Generate cash from operations
- Maintain and expand its operating capacity
- Meet its financial obligations
- Pay dividends

The statement of cash flows is used by managers in evaluating past operations and in planning future investing and financing activities. It is also used by external users such as investors and creditors to assess a company's profit potential and ability to pay its debt and to pay dividends.

1 As used in this chapter, *cash* refers to cash and cash equivalents. Examples of cash equivalents include short-term, highly liquid investments such as money market accounts, bank certificates of deposit, and U.S. Treasury bills.

The statement of cash flows reports cash flows from operating, investing, and financing activities.

The statement of cash flows reports three types of cash flow activities, as follows:

1. **Cash flows from (used for) operating activities** are the cash flows from transactions that affect the net income of the company.

   Example: Purchase and sale of merchandise by a retailer.
2. **Cash flows from (used for) investing activities** are the cash flows received from or used for transactions that affect investments in the noncurrent assets of the company.

   Example: Purchase and sale of fixed assets, such as equipment and buildings.
3. **Cash flows from (used for) financing activities** are the cash flows received from or used for transactions that affect the debt and equity of the company.

   Example: Issuing or retiring equity and debt securities.

The cash flows are reported on the statement of cash flows as follows:

Cash flows from (used for) operating activities	$XXX
Cash flows from (used for) investing activities	XXX
Cash flows from (used for) financing activities	XXX
Net increase (decrease) in cash	$XXX
Cash at the beginning of the period	XXX
Cash at the end of the period	$XXX

The ending cash on the statement of cash flows equals the cash reported on the company's balance sheet at the end of the year.

Exhibit 1 illustrates the sources (increases) and uses (decreases) of cash by each of the three cash flow activities. A *source* of cash causes the cash flow to increase and is called a *cash inflow*. A *use* of cash causes cash flow to decrease and is called *cash outflow*.

EXHIBIT 1 **Sources and Uses of Cash**

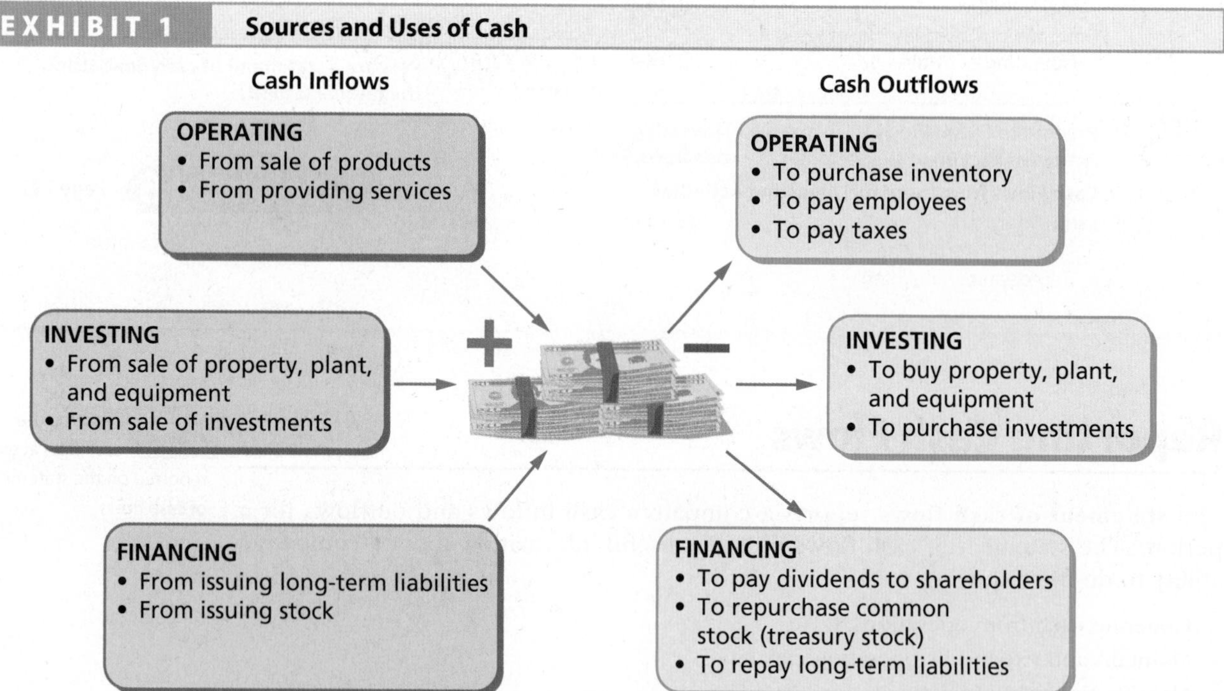

Cash Flows from (used for) Operating Activities

Cash flows from operating activities report the cash inflows and outflows from a company's day-to-day operations. Companies may select one of two alternative methods for reporting cash flows from operating activities on the statement of cash flows:

- The direct method
- The indirect method

Both methods result in the same amount of cash flows from operating activities. They differ in the way they report cash flows from operating activities.

The Direct Method The **direct method** reports operating cash inflows (receipts) and cash outflows (payments) as follows:

Cash flows from (used for) operating activities:		
Cash received from customers	$ XXX	
Cash paid for merchandise	(XXX)	
Cash paid for operating expenses	(XXX)	
Cash paid for interest	(XXX)	
Cash paid for income taxes	(XXX)	
Net cash flows from (used for) operating activities		$XXX

The primary operating cash inflow is cash received from customers. The primary operating cash outflows are cash payments for merchandise, operating expenses, interest, and income tax payments. The cash received from operating activities less the cash paid for operating activities is the net cash flows from operating activities.

The primary advantage of the direct method is that it *directly* reports cash receipts and cash payments on the statement of cash flows. Its primary disadvantage is that these data may not be readily available in the accounting records. Thus, the direct method is normally more costly to prepare and, as a result, is used infrequently in practice. For this reason, the direct method is described and illustrated in Appendix 2 of this chapter.

The Indirect Method The **indirect method** reports cash flows from operating activities by beginning with net income (loss) and adjusting it for revenues and expenses that do not involve the receipt or payment of cash, as follows:

Cash flows from (used for) operating activities:		
Net income (loss)	$XXX	
Adjustments to reconcile net income (loss) to net cash flows from (used for) operating activities	XXX	
Net cash flows from (used for) operating activities		$XXX

The adjustments to reconcile net income to net cash flows from operating activities include such items as depreciation and gains or losses on fixed assets. Changes in current operating assets and liabilities such as accounts receivable or accounts payable are also added or deducted, depending on their effect on cash flows.[2] In effect, these additions and deductions adjust net income, which is reported on an accrual accounting basis, to cash flows from operating activities, which is a cash basis.

A primary advantage of the indirect method is that it reconciles the differences between net income and net cash flows from operations. In doing so, it shows how net income is related to the ending cash balance that is reported on the balance sheet.

Because the data are readily available, the indirect method is less costly to prepare than the direct method. As a result, the indirect method of reporting cash flows from operations is most commonly used in practice.

Link to National Beverage

National Beverage uses the indirect method of reporting the cash flows from operating activities in its statement of cash flows.

Comparing the Direct and Indirect Methods Exhibit 2 illustrates the Cash Flows from (used for) Operating Activities section of the statement of cash flows for NetSolutions. It shows the direct and indirect methods using the NetSolutions data from Chapter 1. As Exhibit 2 illustrates, both methods report the same amount of net cash flows from operating activities, $2,900.

Cash Flows from Operations: Direct and Indirect Methods—NetSolutions **EXHIBIT 2**

Direct Method	
Cash flows from (used for) operating activities:	
Cash received from customers	$ 7,500
Cash paid for expenses and paid to creditors	(4,600)
Net cash flows from operating activities	$ 2,900

Indirect Method	
Cash flows from (used for) operating activities:	
Net income	$3,050
Increase in accounts payable	400
Increase in supplies	(550)
Net cash flows from operating activities	$2,900

the same

2 Current operating assets include all current assets other than cash, and all current liabilities other than dividends payable.

Business Connection

CASH CRUNCH!

The Wet Seal, Inc., a young women's clothing retailer, filed for bankruptcy protection. The cash flows from operating activities for the three years prior to bankruptcy (in thousands) follow:

	Year 3	Year 2	Year 1
Cash provided by (used for) operating activities	$(17,589)	$(26,191)	$61,900

As can be seen, cash flows from operating activities trended into negative territory during the two years prior to the firm's bankruptcy. Thus, when cash flows from operating activities are negative, it can lead to financial distress.

Cash Flows from (used for) Investing Activities

Link to National Beverage

For a recent year, **National Beverage** reported net cash used in investing activities of $31,911,000.

Cash flows from (used for) investing activities show the cash inflows and outflows related to changes in a company's long-term assets. Cash flows from (used for) investing activities are reported on the statement of cash flows as follows:

Cash flows from (used for) investing activities:		
Cash from investing activities	$ XXX	
Cash used for investing activities	(XXX)	
Net cash flows from (used for) investing activities		$XXX

Cash inflows from investing activities normally arise when cash is received from selling fixed assets, investments, and intangible assets. Cash outflows normally include payments to purchase fixed assets, investments, and intangible assets.

Cash Flows from (used for) Financing Activities

Cash flows from (used for) financing activities show the cash inflows and outflows related to changes in a company's long-term liabilities and stockholders' equity. Cash flows from (used for) financing activities are reported on the statement of cash flows as follows:

Link to National Beverage

For a recent year, **National Beverage** reported net cash used in financing activities of $69,318,000.

Cash flows from (used for) financing activities:		
Cash from financing activities	$ XXX	
Cash used for financing activities	(XXX)	
Net cash flows from (used for) financing activities		$XXX

Cash inflows from financing activities normally arise when cash is received from issuing long-term debt or equity securities. For example, issuing bonds, notes payable, preferred stock, and common stock creates cash inflows from financing activities. Cash outflows from financing activities include paying cash dividends, repaying long-term debt, and acquiring treasury stock.

Noncash Investing and Financing Activities

A company may enter into transactions involving investing and financing activities that do not *directly* affect cash. For example, a company may issue common stock to retire long-term debt. Although this transaction does not directly affect cash, it does eliminate future cash payments for interest and for paying the bonds when they mature. Because such transactions *indirectly* affect cash flows, they are reported in a separate section of the statement of cash flows. This section usually appears at the bottom of the statement of cash flows.

Format of the Statement of Cash Flows

The statement of cash flows presents the cash flows generated by, or used for, the three activities previously discussed: operating, investing, and financing. These three activities are always reported in the same order, following the format illustrated in Exhibit 3.

EXHIBIT 3
Format of the Statement of Cash Flows

COMPANY NAME
Statement of Cash Flows
For the Year Ended XXXX

Cash flows from (used for) operating activities:		
(List of individual items, as illustrated in Exhibit 1)	$XXX	
Net cash flows from (used for) operating activities		$XXX
Cash flows from (used for) investing activities:		
(List of individual items, as illustrated in Exhibit 1)	$XXX	
Net cash flows from (used for) investing activities		XXX
Cash flows from (used for) financing activities:		
(List of individual items, as illustrated in Exhibit 1)	$XXX	
Net cash flows from (used for) financing activities		XXX
Net increase (decrease) in cash		$XXX
Cash at the beginning of the period		XXX
Cash at the end of the period		$XXX
Noncash investing and financing activities		$XXX

Cash Flow per Share

Cash flow per share is sometimes reported in the financial press. As reported, cash flow per share is normally computed as net *cash flows from operating activities divided by the number of common shares outstanding.* However, such reporting may be misleading because of the following:

- Users may misinterpret cash flow per share as the per-share amount available for dividends. This would not be the case if the cash generated by operations is required for repaying loans or for reinvesting in the business.
- Users may misinterpret cash flow per share as equivalent to (or better than) earnings per share.

For these reasons, the financial statements, including the statement of cash flows, should not report cash flow per share.

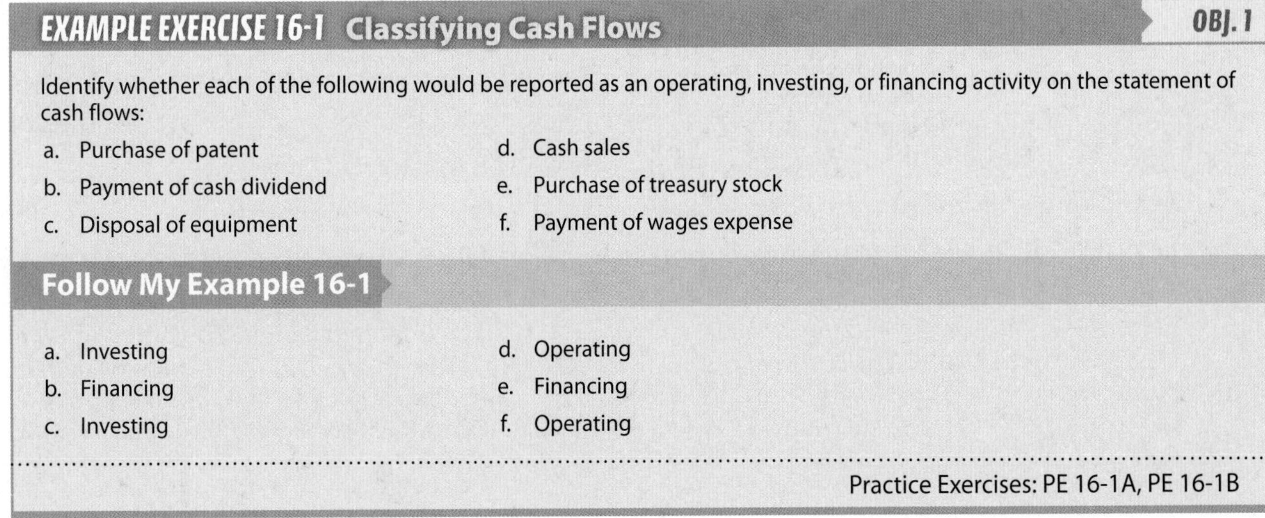

EXAMPLE EXERCISE 16-1 Classifying Cash Flows **OBJ. 1**

Identify whether each of the following would be reported as an operating, investing, or financing activity on the statement of cash flows:

a. Purchase of patent
b. Payment of cash dividend
c. Disposal of equipment
d. Cash sales
e. Purchase of treasury stock
f. Payment of wages expense

Follow My Example 16-1

a. Investing
b. Financing
c. Investing
d. Operating
e. Financing
f. Operating

Practice Exercises: PE 16-1A, PE 16-1B

OBJ. 2 Prepare the Cash Flows from (used for) Operating Activities section of the statement of cash flows using the indirect method.

Cash Flows from (used for) Operating Activities

The indirect method of reporting cash flows from operating activities uses the logic that a change in any balance sheet account (including cash) can be analyzed in terms of changes in the other balance sheet accounts. Thus, by analyzing changes in noncash balance sheet accounts, any change in the cash account can be *indirectly* determined.

To illustrate, the accounting equation can be solved for cash as follows:

Assets = Liabilities + Stockholders' Equity
Cash + Noncash Assets = Liabilities + Stockholders' Equity
Cash = Liabilities + Stockholders' Equity − Noncash Assets

Thus, any change in the cash account can be determined by analyzing changes in the liability, stockholders' equity, and noncash asset accounts as follows:

Change in Cash = *Change* in Liabilities + *Change* in Stockholders' Equity − *Change* in Noncash Assets

Under the indirect method, there is no order in which the balance sheet accounts must be analyzed. However, net income (or net loss) is the first amount reported on the statement of cash flows. Because net income (or net loss) is a component of any change in Retained Earnings, the first account normally analyzed is Retained Earnings.

To illustrate the indirect method, the income statement and comparative balance sheets for Rundell Inc., shown in Exhibit 4, are used. Ledger accounts and other data supporting the income statement and balance sheet are presented as needed.[3]

EXHIBIT 4

Income Statement and Comparative Balance Sheet

Rundell Inc.
Income Statement
For the Year Ended December 31, 20Y8

Sales		$1,180,000
Cost of merchandise sold		790,000
Gross profit		$ 390,000
Operating expenses:		
Depreciation expense	$ 7,000	
Other operating expenses	196,000	
Total operating expenses		203,000
Income from operations		$ 187,000
Other revenue and expense:		
Gain on sale of land	$ 12,000	
Interest expense	(8,000)	4,000
Income before income tax		$ 191,000
Income tax expense		83,000
Net income		$ 108,000

3 Appendix 1 of this chapter discusses using a spreadsheet (work sheet) as an aid in assembling data and preparing the statement of cash flows using the indirect method.

EXHIBIT 4

Income Statement and Comparative Balance Sheet (*Concluded*)

Rundell Inc.
Comparative Balance Sheet
December 31, 20Y8 and 20Y7

	20Y8	20Y7	Increase (Decrease)
Assets			
Cash	$ 97,500	$ 26,000	$ 71,500
Accounts receivable (net)	74,000	65,000	9,000
Inventories	172,000	180,000	(8,000)
Land	80,000	125,000	(45,000)
Building	260,000	200,000	60,000
Accumulated depreciation—building	(65,300)	(58,300)	(7,000)*
Total assets	$618,200	$537,700	$ 80,500
Liabilities			
Accounts payable (merchandise creditors)	$ 43,500	$ 46,700	$ (3,200)
Accrued expenses payable (operating expenses)	26,500	24,300	2,200
Income taxes payable	7,900	8,400	(500)
Dividends payable	14,000	10,000	4,000
Bonds payable	100,000	150,000	(50,000)
Total liabilities	$191,900	$239,400	$ (47,500)
Stockholders' Equity			
Common stock ($2 par)	$ 24,000	$ 16,000	$ 8,000
Paid-in capital in excess of par	120,000	80,000	40,000
Retained earnings	282,300	202,300	80,000
Total stockholders' equity	$426,300	$298,300	$128,000
Total liabilities and stockholders' equity	$618,200	$537,700	$ 80,500

*There is a $7,000 increase to Accumulated Depreciation—Building, which is a contra asset account. As a result, the $7,000 increase in this account must be subtracted in summing to the increase in Total assets of $80,500.

Net Income

Rundell Inc.'s net income for 20Y8 is $108,000, as shown on the income statement in Exhibit 4. Since net income is closed to Retained Earnings, net income also helps explain the change in retained earnings during the year. The retained earnings account for Rundell is as follows:

Account *Retained Earnings* Account No.

Date		Item	Debit	Credit	Balance Debit	Balance Credit
20Y8 Jan.	1	Balance				202,300
June	30	Dividends declared	14,000			188,300
Dec.	31	Net income		108,000		296,300
	31	Dividends declared	14,000			282,300

The retained earnings account indicates that the $80,000 ($108,000 − $28,000) change resulted from net income of $108,000 and cash dividends of $28,000. The net income of $108,000 is the first amount reported in the Cash Flows from (used for) Operating Activities section. The impact of the dividends of $28,000 on cash flows will be included as part of financing activities.

Adjustments to Net Income

The net income of $108,000 reported by Rundell Inc. does not equal the cash flows from operating activities for the period. This is because net income is determined using the accrual method of accounting.

Under the accrual method of accounting, revenues and expenses are recorded at different times from when cash is received or paid. For example, merchandise may be sold on account and the cash received at a later date. Likewise, insurance premiums may be paid in the current period but expensed in a following period.

Thus, under the indirect method, adjustments to net income must be made to determine cash flows from operating activities. The typical adjustments to net income are shown in Exhibit 5.[4]

EXHIBIT 5 **Adjustments to Net Income (Loss) Using the Indirect Method**

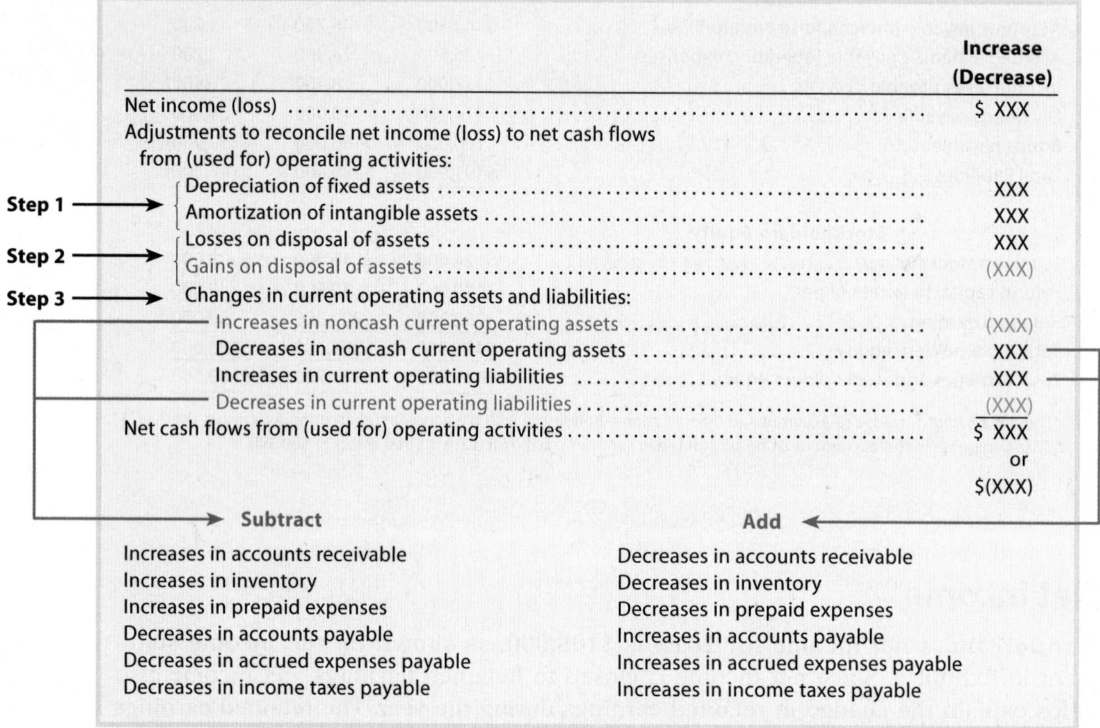

		Increase (Decrease)
	Net income (loss)	$ XXX
	Adjustments to reconcile net income (loss) to net cash flows from (used for) operating activities:	
Step 1	Depreciation of fixed assets	XXX
	Amortization of intangible assets	XXX
Step 2	Losses on disposal of assets	XXX
	Gains on disposal of assets	(XXX)
Step 3	Changes in current operating assets and liabilities:	
	Increases in noncash current operating assets	(XXX)
	Decreases in noncash current operating assets	XXX
	Increases in current operating liabilities	XXX
	Decreases in current operating liabilities	(XXX)
	Net cash flows from (used for) operating activities	$ XXX or $(XXX)

Subtract	Add
Increases in accounts receivable	Decreases in accounts receivable
Increases in inventory	Decreases in inventory
Increases in prepaid expenses	Decreases in prepaid expenses
Decreases in accounts payable	Increases in accounts payable
Decreases in accrued expenses payable	Increases in accrued expenses payable
Decreases in income taxes payable	Increases in income taxes payable

Net income is normally adjusted to cash flows from operating activities, using the following steps:

Step 1. Expenses that do not affect cash are added. Such expenses decrease net income but do not involve cash payments and, thus, are added to net income.

Example: Depreciation of fixed assets and amortization of intangible assets are noncash expenses that are added to net income.

Step 2. Losses on the disposal of assets are added and gains on the disposal of assets are deducted. The disposal (sale) of assets is an investing activity rather than an operating activity. However, the losses and gains are reported as part of net income. As a result, any *losses* on disposal of assets are *added* back to net income. Likewise, any *gains* on disposal of assets are *deducted* from net income.

Example: Land costing $100,000 is sold for $90,000. The loss of $10,000 is added back to net income.

4 Other items that also require adjustments to net income to obtain cash flows from operating activities include amortization of bonds payable discounts (add), losses on debt retirement (add), amortization of bonds payable premiums (deduct), and gains on retirement of debt (deduct). These topics are covered in advanced accounting courses.

Step 3. Changes in current operating assets and liabilities are added or deducted as follows:

- Increases in noncash current operating assets are deducted.
- Decreases in noncash current operating assets are added.
- Increases in current operating liabilities are added.
- Decreases in current operating liabilities are deducted.

Example: A sale of $10,000 on account increases sales, accounts receivable, and net income by $10,000. However, no cash is received or paid. Thus, the $10,000 increase in accounts receivable is deducted from net income. Similar adjustments are required for the changes in the other current asset and liability accounts, such as inventory, prepaid expenses, accounts payable, accrued expenses payable, and income taxes payable, as shown in Exhibit 5.

Link to National Beverage

For a recent year, **National Beverage** reported changes in current asset and liability accounts for accounts receivable, inventory, prepaid assets, accounts payable, and accrued liabilities.

EXAMPLE EXERCISE 16-2 Adjustments to Net Income — OBJ. 2

Omni Corporation's accumulated depreciation increased by $12,000, while $3,400 of patent amortization was recognized between balance sheet dates. There were no purchases or sales of depreciable or intangible assets during the year. In addition, the income statement showed a gain of $4,100 from the sale of land. Reconcile Omni's net income of $50,000 to net cash flows from operating activities.

Follow My Example 16-2

Net income	$50,000
Adjustments to reconcile net income to net cash flows from (used for) operating activities:	
Depreciation	12,000
Amortization of patents	3,400
Gain from sale of land	(4,100)
Net cash flows from operating activities	$61,300

Practice Exercises: PE 16-2A, PE 16-2B

The Cash Flows from (used for) Operating Activities section of **Rundell Inc.**'s statement of cash flows is shown in Exhibit 6.

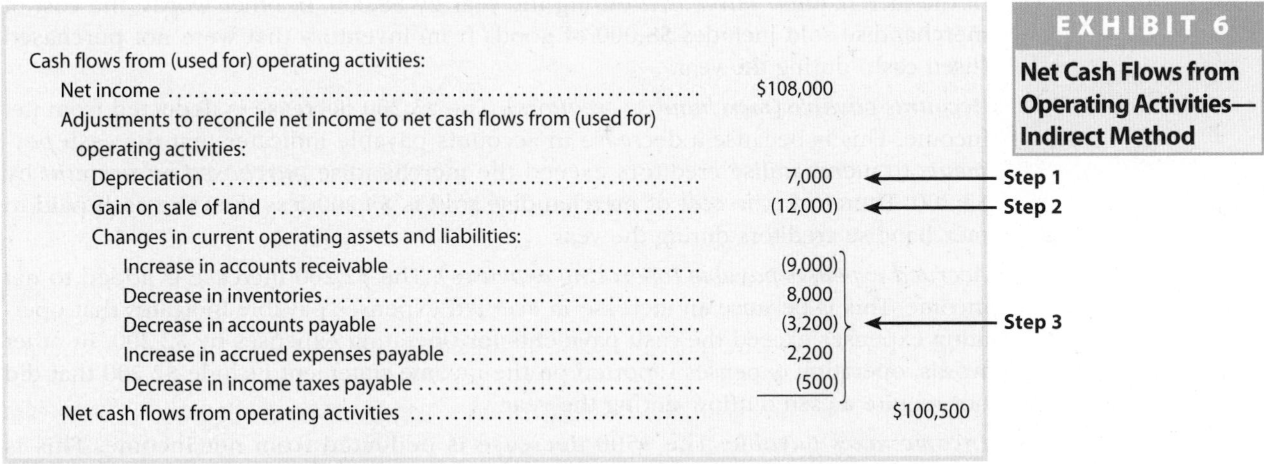

Cash flows from (used for) operating activities:			
Net income		$108,000	
Adjustments to reconcile net income to net cash flows from (used for) operating activities:			
Depreciation	7,000		← Step 1
Gain on sale of land	(12,000)		← Step 2
Changes in current operating assets and liabilities:			
Increase in accounts receivable	(9,000)		Step 3
Decrease in inventories	8,000		Step 3
Decrease in accounts payable	(3,200)		Step 3
Increase in accrued expenses payable	2,200		Step 3
Decrease in income taxes payable	(500)		Step 3
Net cash flows from operating activities		$100,500	

EXHIBIT 6

Net Cash Flows from Operating Activities—Indirect Method

Rundell's net income of $108,000 is converted to cash flows from operating activities of $100,500 as follows:

Step 1. Add depreciation of $7,000.

Analysis: The comparative balance sheet in Exhibit 4 indicates that Accumulated Depreciation—Building increased by $7,000. Given that there was no other activity in this account, as shown on the following page, depreciation expense for the year was $7,000 on the building:

Account *Accumulated Depreciation—Building* Account No.

Date		Item	Debit	Credit	Balance Debit	Balance Credit
20Y8						
Jan.	1	Balance				58,300
Dec.	31	Depreciation for year		7,000		65,300

Step 2. Deduct the gain on the sale of land of $12,000.
Analysis: The income statement in Exhibit 4 reports a gain of $12,000 from the sale of land. The proceeds, which include the gain, are reported in the Investing Activities section of the statement of cash flows.[5] Thus, the gain of $12,000 is deducted from net income in determining cash flows from operating activities.

Step 3. Add and deduct changes in current operating assets and liabilities excluding cash.
Analysis: The increases and decreases in the current operating asset and current liability accounts excluding cash are as follows:

Accounts	December 31 20Y8	December 31 20Y7	Increase (Decrease)
Accounts Receivable (net)	$ 74,000	$ 65,000	$ 9,000
Inventories	172,000	180,000	(8,000)
Accounts Payable (merchandise creditors)	43,500	46,700	(3,200)
Accrued Expenses Payable (operating expenses)	26,500	24,300	2,200
Income Taxes Payable	7,900	8,400	(500)

Accounts receivable (net): The $9,000 increase is deducted from net income. This is because the $9,000 increase in accounts receivable indicates that sales on account were $9,000 more than the cash received from customers. Thus, sales (and net income) includes $9,000 that was not received in cash during the year.

Inventories: The $8,000 decrease is added to net income. This is because the $8,000 decrease in inventories indicates that the cost of merchandise *sold* exceeds the cost of the merchandise *purchased* during the year by $8,000. In other words, the cost of merchandise sold includes $8,000 of goods from inventory that were not purchased (used cash) during the year.

Accounts payable (merchandise creditors): The $3,200 decrease is deducted from net income. This is because a decrease in accounts payable indicates that the cash *payments* to merchandise creditors exceed the merchandise *purchased on account* by $3,200. Therefore, the cost of merchandise sold is $3,200 less than the cash paid to merchandise creditors during the year.

Accrued expenses payable (operating expenses): The $2,200 increase is added to net income. This is because an increase in accrued expenses payable indicates that operating expenses exceed the cash payments for operating expenses by $2,200. In other words, operating expenses reported on the income statement include $2,200 that did not require a cash outflow during the year.

Income taxes payable: The $500 decrease is deducted from net income. This is because a decrease in income taxes payable indicates that taxes paid exceed the amount of taxes incurred during the year by $500. In other words, the amount reported on the income statement for income tax expense is less than the amount paid by $500.

Using the preceding analyses, Rundell's net income of $108,000 is converted to cash flows from operating activities of $100,500 as shown in Exhibit 6.

5 The reporting of the proceeds (cash flows) from the sale of land as part of investing activities is discussed later in this chapter.

EXAMPLE EXERCISE 16-3 Changes in Current Operating Assets and Liabilities

OBJ. 2

Victor Corporation's current operating assets and liabilities from the company's comparative balance sheet were as follows:

	Dec. 31, 20Y8	Dec. 31, 20Y7
Accounts receivable	$ 6,500	$ 4,900
Inventory	12,300	15,000
Accounts payable	4,800	5,200

Adjust Victor's net income of $70,000 for changes in current operating assets and liabilities to arrive at net cash flows from operating activities.

Follow My Example 16-3

Net income	$70,000
Adjustments to reconcile net income to net cash flows from (used for) operating activities:	
Changes in current operating assets and liabilities:	
Increase in accounts receivable	(1,600)
Decrease in inventory	2,700
Decrease in accounts payable	(400)
Net cash flows from operating activities	$70,700

Practice Exercises: PE 16-3A, PE 16-3B

Integrity, Objectivity, and Ethics in Business

CREDIT POLICY AND CASH FLOW

Investors frequently use net cash flows from operating activities to assess a company's financial health. If a company is financially healthy, net cash flows from operating activities should be roughly consistent with accrual basis net income. Questions arise, however, when a company's net cash flows from operating activities significantly lags net income. Two scenarios can cause this to happen:

- Sales on account are never collected in cash.
- Large cash purchases for inventory are never sold or sell at a very slow pace.

Both of these scenarios increase net income, without a corresponding increase in net cash flows from operating activities. Prudent investors are often skeptical when they observe these scenarios and tend to avoid these types of investments until the cash flows become clear.

Source: M. Argersinger, "How Companies Fake It (With Cash Flow)," *Daily Finance Investor Center*, July 17, 2011.

EXAMPLE EXERCISE 16-4 Determining Cash Flows from (used for) Operating Activities

OBJ. 2

Omicron Inc. reported the following data:

Net income	$120,000
Depreciation expense	12,000
Loss on disposal of equipment	15,000
Increase in accounts receivable	5,000
Decrease in accounts payable	2,000

Prepare the Cash Flows from (used for) Operating Activities section of the statement of cash flows, using the indirect method.

(Continued)

Follow My Example 16-4

Cash flows from (used for) operating activities:		
Net income	$120,000	
Adjustments to reconcile net income to net cash flows from (used for) operating activities:		
Depreciation expense	12,000	
Loss on disposal of equipment	15,000	
Changes in current operating assets and liabilities:		
Increase in accounts receivable	(5,000)	
Decrease in accounts payable	(2,000)	
Net cash flows from operating activities		$140,000

Practice Exercises: PE 16-4A, PE 16-4B

OBJ. 3 Prepare the Cash Flows from (used for) Investing Activities section of the statement of cash flows.

Cash Flows from (used for) Investing Activities

The Cash Flows from (used for) Investing Activities section reports the cash inflows and outflows related to changes in a company's long-term assets. Rundell Inc.'s comparative balance sheet in Exhibit 4 lists land, building, and accumulated depreciation—building as long-term assets. Similar to preparing the Cash Flows from (used for) Operating Activities section, the change in each long-term asset account is analyzed for its effect on cash flows from investing activities.

Land

The $45,000 decline in the land account of Rundell Inc. was from two transactions, as follows:

Account *Land* — Account No.

Date		Item	Debit	Credit	Balance Debit	Balance Credit
20Y8						
Jan.	1	Balance			125,000	
June	8	Sold for $72,000 cash		60,000	65,000	
Oct.	12	Purchased for $15,000 cash	15,000		80,000	

The June 8 transaction is the sale of land with a cost of $60,000 for $72,000 in cash. The $72,000 proceeds from the sale are reported in the Cash Flows from (used for) Investing Activities section as follows:

Cash flows from (used for) investing activities:	
Cash received from sale of land	$72,000

The proceeds of $72,000 include the $12,000 gain on the sale of land and the $60,000 cost (book value) of the land. As shown in Exhibit 6, the $12,000 gain is deducted from net income in the Cash Flows from (used for) Operating Activities section. This is so that the $12,000 cash inflow related to the gain is not included twice as a cash inflow.

The October 12 transaction is the purchase of land for cash of $15,000. This transaction is reported as an outflow of cash in the Investing Activities section as follows:

Cash flows from (used for) investing activities:	
Cash paid from purchase of land	$(15,000)

Building and Accumulated Depreciation—Building

The building account of Rundell Inc. increased by $60,000 ($260,000 – $200,000), and the accumulated depreciation—building account increased by $7,000 ($65,300 – $58,300), as follows:

Account *Building* — Account No.

Date		Item	Debit	Credit	Balance Debit	Balance Credit
20Y8						
Jan.	1	Balance			200,000	
Dec.	27	Purchased for cash	60,000		260,000	

Account *Accumulated Depreciation—Building* — Account No.

Date		Item	Debit	Credit	Balance Debit	Balance Credit
20Y8						
Jan.	1	Balance				58,300
Dec.	31	Depreciation for the year		7,000		65,300

Link to National Beverage

In a recent statement of cash flows, **National Beverage Co.** reported cash used for purchases of property, plant, and equipment of $12,140,000 and cash received for selling property, plant, and equipment of $116,000 resulting in net cash flows used for investing activities of $12,024,000.

The purchase of a building for cash of $60,000 is reported as an outflow of cash in the Cash Flows from (used for) Investing Activities section as follows:

Cash flows from (used for) investing activities:	
Cash paid from purchase of building.............................	$(60,000)

The credit in the accumulated depreciation—building account represents depreciation expense for the year. This depreciation expense of $7,000 on the building was added to net income in determining net cash flows from operating activities, as reported in Exhibit 6.

EXAMPLE EXERCISE 16-5 Land Transactions on the Statement of Cash Flows — **OBJ. 3**

Alpha Corporation purchased land for $125,000. Later in the year, the company sold a different piece of land with a book value of $165,000 for $200,000. How are the effects of these transactions reported on the statement of cash flows?

Follow My Example 16-5

The gain on the sale of land is deducted from net income, as follows:

Gain on sale of land..	$ (35,000)

The purchase and sale of land are reported as part of cash flows from (used for) investing activities, as follows:

Cash received from sale of land..	$ 200,000
Cash paid for purchase of land..	(125,000)

Practice Exercises: PE 16-5A, PE 16-5B

Cash Flows from (used for) Financing Activities

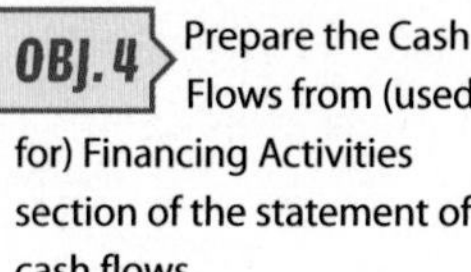

Prepare the Cash Flows from (used for) Financing Activities section of the statement of cash flows.

The Cash Flows from (used for) Financing Activities section reports the cash inflows and outflows related to changes in a company's long-term liabilities and stockholders' equity. Rundell Inc.'s comparative balance sheet in Exhibit 4 reports changes in bonds payable, common stock, and paid-in capital in excess of par. In addition, dividends payable has changed, which impacts retained earnings. Each change must be analyzed to determine its effect on cash flows from financing activities.

Bonds Payable

The bonds payable account of Rundell Inc. decreased by $50,000 ($150,000 − $100,000), as follows:

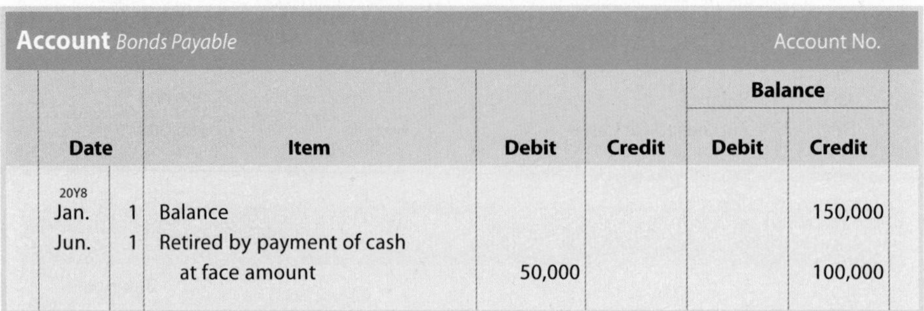

Account *Bonds Payable* — Account No.

Date		Item	Debit	Credit	Balance Debit	Balance Credit
20Y8 Jan.	1	Balance				150,000
Jun.	1	Retired by payment of cash at face amount	50,000			100,000

This decrease is from retiring the bonds by a cash payment for their face amount. This cash outflow is reported in the Financing Activities section as follows:

Cash flows from (used for) financing activities:	
Cash paid to retire bonds payable	$(50,000)

Common Stock

The common stock account of Rundell Inc. increased by $8,000 ($24,000 − $16,000), and the paid-in capital in excess of par—common stock account increased by $40,000 ($120,000 − $80,000), as follows:

Account *Common Stock* — Account No.

Date		Item	Debit	Credit	Balance Debit	Balance Credit
20Y8 Jan.	1	Balance				16,000
Nov.	1	4,000 shares issued for cash		8,000		24,000

Account *Paid-In Capital in Excess of Par—Common Stock* — Account No.

Date		Item	Debit	Credit	Balance Debit	Balance Credit
20Y8 Jan.	1	Balance				80,000
Nov.	1	4,000 shares issued for cash		40,000		120,000

These increases were from issuing 4,000 shares of common stock for $12 per share. This cash inflow is reported in the Financing Activities section as follows:

Cash flows from (used for) financing activities:	
Cash received from issuing common stock	$48,000

Dividends and Dividends Payable

The retained earnings account of Rundell Inc. indicates that cash dividends of $28,000 were declared during the year. However, the following dividends payable account indicates that only $24,000 of dividends were paid during the year:

Account *Dividends Payable* Account No.

Date		Item	Debit	Credit	Balance Debit	Balance Credit
20Y8 Jan.	1	Balance				10,000
	10	Cash paid	10,000		—	—
Jun.	30	Dividends declared		14,000		14,000
Jul.	10	Cash paid	14,000		—	—
Dec.	31	Dividends declared		14,000		14,000

Cash dividends paid during the year can also be computed by adjusting the dividends declared during the year for the change in the dividends payable account as follows:

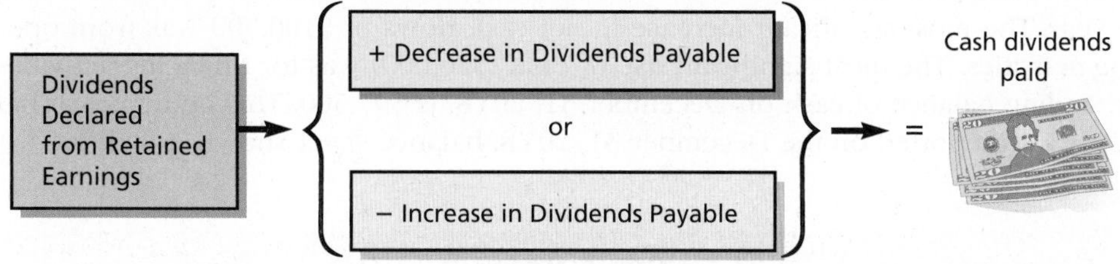

The cash dividends paid by Rundell Inc. during 20Y8 are $24,000, computed as follows:

Dividends declared ($14,000 + $14,000)	$28,000
Increase in dividends payable	(4,000)
Cash dividends paid	$24,000

Because dividend payments are a financing activity, the dividend payment of $24,000 is reported in the Financing Activities section of the statement of cash flows, as follows:

Cash flows from (used for) financing activities:	
Cash dividends	$(24,000)

EXAMPLE EXERCISE 16-6 Financing Activities on the Statement of Cash Flows — OBJ. 4

Mohroman Inc. reported net income of $80,000 for 20Y2. The liability and equity accounts from the company's comparative balance sheet are as follows:

	Dec. 31, 20Y2	Dec. 31, 20Y1	Increase (Decrease)
Accounts payable	$ 42,680	$ 41,500	$ 1,180
Dividends payable	10,000	8,000	2,000
Bonds payable	210,000	300,000	(90,000)
Common stock, $10 par value	120,000	100,000	20,000
Paid-in capital in excess of par—common stock	300,000	200,000	100,000
Retained earnings	240,000	180,000	60,000

During the year, the company retired bonds payable at their face amount, declared dividends of $20,000, and issued 2,000 shares of common stock for $60 per share. Prepare the Cash Flows from (used for) Financing Activities section of the statement of cash flows.

(Continued)

Follow My Example 16-6

Cash flows from (used for) financing activities:		
Cash paid to retire bonds payable	$ (90,000)	
Cash received from issuing common stock	120,000*	
Cash dividends	(18,000)**	
Net cash flows from financing activities		$12,000

* Increase in common stock of $20,000 plus increase in paid-in capital in excess of par—common stock of $100,000.
** Dividends declared of $20,000 less increase in dividends payable of $2,000.

Practice Exercises: PE 16-6A, PE 16-6B

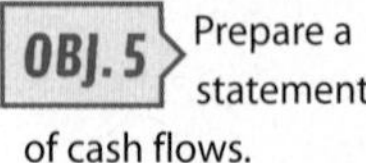
Prepare a statement of cash flows.

Prepare a Statement of Cash Flows—Indirect Method

The statement of cash flows for **Rundell Inc.**, using the indirect method, is shown in Exhibit 7. The statement of cash flows indicates that cash increased by $71,500 during the year. The most significant increase in net cash flows of $100,500 was from operating activities. The most significant use of cash ($26,000) was for financing activities. The ending balance of cash on December 31, 20Y8, is $97,500. This ending cash balance is also reported on the December 31, 20Y8, balance sheet shown in Exhibit 4.

EXHIBIT 7

Statement of Cash Flows—Indirect Method

Rundell Inc.
Statement of Cash Flows
For the Year Ended December 31, 20Y8

Cash flows from (used for) operating activities:		
Net income	$108,000	
Adjustments to reconcile net income to net cash flows from (used for) operating activities:		
Depreciation	7,000	
Gain on sale of land	(12,000)	
Changes in current operating assets and liabilities:		
Increase in accounts receivable	(9,000)	
Decrease in inventories	8,000	
Decrease in accounts payable	(3,200)	
Increase in accrued expenses payable	2,200	
Decrease in income taxes payable	(500)	
Net cash flows from operating activities		$100,500
Cash flows from (used for) investing activities:		
Cash received from sale of land	$ 72,000	
Cash paid for purchase of land	(15,000)	
Cash paid for purchase of building	(60,000)	
Net cash flows used for investing activities		(3,000)
Cash flows from (used for) financing activities:		
Cash received from issuing common stock	$ 48,000	
Cash paid to retire bonds payable	(50,000)	
Cash dividends	(24,000)	
Net cash flows used for financing activities		(26,000)
Net increase in cash		$ 71,500
Cash balance, January 1, 20Y8		26,000
Cash balance, December 31, 20Y8		$ 97,500

Link to National Beverage

In a recent statement of cash flows, **National Beverage** reported net cash provided by operating activities of $154,721,000, net cash used for investing activities of $31,911,000, and net cash used for financing activities of $69,318,000 for a net increase in cash of $53,492,000 for the year.

International Connection

IFRS IFRS FOR STATEMENT OF CASH FLOWS

The statement of cash flows is required under International Financial Reporting Standards (IFRS). The statement of cash flows under IFRS is similar to that reported under U.S. GAAP in that the statement has separate sections for operating, investing, and financing activities. Like U.S. GAAP, IFRS also allow the use of either the indirect or direct method of reporting cash flows from operating activities. IFRS differ from U.S. GAAP in some minor areas, including:

- Interest paid can be reported as either an operating or financing activity, while interest received can be reported as either an operating or investing activity. In contrast, U.S. GAAP reports interest paid or received as an operating activity.
- Dividends paid can be reported as either an operating or financing activity, while dividends received can be reported as either an operating or investing activity. In contrast, U.S. GAAP reports dividends paid as a financing activity and dividends received as an operating activity.
- Cash flows to pay taxes are reported as a separate line in the operating activities, in contrast to U.S. GAAP, which does not require a separate line disclosure.

Financial Analysis and Interpretation: Free Cash Flow

OBJ. 6 Describe and illustrate the use of free cash flow in evaluating a company's cash flow.

A valuable tool for evaluating the profitability of a business is free cash flow. **Free cash flow** measures the operating cash flow available to a company after it purchases the property, plant, and equipment (PP&E) necessary to maintain its current operations. Since the investments in PP&E necessary to maintain current operations cannot often be determined from financial statements, analysts estimate this amount using the cash used to purchase PP&E, as shown on the statement of cash flows. Thus, free cash flow is computed as follows:

Net cash flows from operating activities	$XXX
Less cash used to purchase property, plant, and equipment	XXX
Free cash flow	$XXX

The free cash flow can be expressed as a percentage of sales in order to provide a relative measure that can be compared over time or to other companies. This ratio is computed as follows:

$$\text{Ratio of Free Cash Flow to Sales} = \frac{\text{Free Cash Flow}}{\text{Sales}}$$

Positive free cash flow is considered favorable. A company that has free cash flow is able to fund growth and acquisitions, retire debt, purchase treasury stock, and pay dividends. A company with no free cash flow may have limited financial flexibility, potentially leading to liquidity problems.

To illustrate, information from the annual reports of **National Beverage** for three recent years is as follows (in thousands):

	Year 3	Year 2	Year 1
Net cash flows from operating activities	$154,721	$114,267	$ 80,483
Cash used to purchase property, plant, and equipment	31,974	14,015	12,140
Sales	975,734	826,918	704,785

The free cash flow is computed for the three years as follows:

	Year 3	Year 2	Year 1
Net cash flows from operating activities	$154,721	$114,267	$80,483
Less cash used to purchase property, plant, and equipment	31,974	14,015	12,140
Free cash flow	$122,747	$100,252	$68,343

As can be seen, free cash flow has increased across the three years. In Year 3, it is nearly 80% higher than in Year 1 [($122,747 − $68,343) ÷ $68,343]. The ratio of free cash flow to sales is as follows (rounded to one decimal place):

	Year 3	Year 2	Year 1
Ratio of free cash flow to sales..........	12.6%	12.1%	9.7%
	($122,747 ÷ $975,734)	($100,252 ÷ $826,918)	($68,343 ÷ $704,785)

The ratio of free cash flow to sales has also increased across these three years, from 9.7% in Year 1 to 12.6% in Year 3, which is a 30% increase [(12.6% − 9.7%) ÷ 9.7%].

EXAMPLE EXERCISE 16-7 Free Cash Flow

OBJ. 6

Omnicron Inc. reported the following on the company's cash flow statement in 20Y8 and 20Y7:

	20Y8	20Y7
Net cash flows from operating activities	$ 140,000	$120,000
Net cash flows used for investing activities	(120,000)	(80,000)
Net cash flows used for financing activities	(20,000)	(32,000)

Seventy-five percent of the net cash flows used for investing activities was to replace existing capacity.

a. Determine Omnicron's free cash flow for both years.

b. Has Omnicron's free cash flow improved or declined from 20Y7 to 20Y8?

Follow My Example 16-7

a.

	20Y8	20Y7
Net cash flows from operating activities	$140,000	$120,000
Investments in fixed assets to maintain current production	90,000[1]	60,000[2]
Free cash flow	$ 50,000	$ 60,000

[1] $120,000 × 75%
[2] $80,000 × 75%

b. The change from $60,000 to $50,000 indicates an unfavorable decline.

Practice Exercises: PE 16-7A, PE 16-7B

Business Connection

GROWING PAINS

CONCEPT CLIP

Twitter, Inc., is a global social media platform used for real-time self-expression and conversation within the limits of 140-character tweets. Twitter is a new, fast-growing company. The cash flows from operating, investing, and financing activities are summarized for its first three years as a public company (in thousands):

	Cash Provided from (used in)			
	Operating Activities	Investing Activities	Financing Activities	Net Change for Year
Year 1	$(27,935)	$ 49,443	$ (37,124)	$ (15,616)
Year 2	1,398	(1,306,066)	1,942,176	637,508
Year 3	81,796	(1,097,272)	1,691,722	676,246

One can see the significant improvement in Twitter's cash flows from operations from Year 1 to Year 3. This indicates that Twitter is succeeding as a new company and is able to provide cash from operations after only three years of operating as a public company. However, as a new company, Twitter must make significant investments in order to expand. This is clear in the trend in cash flows used in investing activities. Since the cash flows from operations are insufficient to fund this growth, the company must obtain cash from financing activities. There were significant sources of cash from stockholders in Year 2 and Year 3, which was used to expand and provide future flexibility.

APPENDIX 1

Spreadsheet (Work Sheet) for Statement of Cash Flows—The Indirect Method

APP. 1 OBJ. Use a spreadsheet to prepare a statement of cash flows using the indirect method.

A spreadsheet (work sheet) may be used in preparing the statement of cash flows. However, whether or not a spreadsheet (work sheet) is used, the concepts presented in this chapter are not affected.

The data for Rundell Inc., presented in Exhibit 4, are used as a basis for illustrating the spreadsheet (work sheet) for the indirect method. The steps in preparing this spreadsheet (work sheet), shown in Exhibit 8, are as follows:

Step 1. List the title of each balance sheet account in the Accounts column.

Step 2. For each balance sheet account, enter its balance as of December 31, 20Y7, in the first column and its balance as of December 31, 20Y8, in the last column. Place the credit balances in parentheses.

Step 3. Add the December 31, 20Y7 and 20Y8 column totals, which should total to zero.

Step 4. Analyze the change during the year in each noncash account to determine its net increase (decrease) and classify the change as affecting cash flows from operating activities, investing activities, financing activities, or noncash investing and financing activities.

Step 5. Indicate the effect of the change on cash flows by making entries in the Transactions columns.

Step 6. After all noncash accounts have been analyzed, enter the net increase (decrease) in cash during the period.

Step 7. Add the Debit and Credit Transactions columns. The totals should be equal.

Analyzing Accounts

In analyzing the noncash accounts (Step 4), try to determine the type of cash flow activity (operating, investing, or financing) that led to the change in the account. As each noncash account is analyzed, an entry (Step 5) is made on the spreadsheet (work sheet) for the type of cash flow activity that caused the change. After all noncash accounts have been analyzed, an entry (Step 6) is made for the increase (decrease) in cash during the period.

The entries made on the spreadsheet are not posted to the ledger. They are only used in preparing and summarizing the data on the spreadsheet.

The order in which the accounts are analyzed is not important. However, it is more efficient to begin with Retained Earnings and proceed upward in the account listing.

Retained Earnings

The spreadsheet (work sheet) shows a Retained Earnings balance of $202,300 at December 31, 20Y7, and $282,300 at December 31, 20Y8. Thus, Retained Earnings increased $80,000 during the year. This increase is from the following:

- Net income of $108,000
- Declaring cash dividends of $28,000

To identify the cash flows from these activities, two entries are made on the spreadsheet.

EXHIBIT 8 **End-of-Period Spreadsheet (Work Sheet) for Statement of Cash Flows—Indirect Method**

Step 2

	A	B	C	D	E	F	G
1	Rundell Inc.						
2	End-of-Period Spreadsheet (Work Sheet) for Statement of Cash Flows						
3	For the Year Ended December 31, 20Y8						
4		Balance,		Transactions			Balance,
5	Accounts	Dec. 31, 20Y7		Debit		Credit	Dec. 31, 20Y8
6	Cash	26,000	(o)	71,500			97,500
7	Accounts receivable (net)	65,000	(n)	9,000			74,000
8	Inventories	180,000			(m)	8,000	172,000
9	Land	125,000	(k)	15,000	(l)	60,000	80,000
10	Building	200,000	(j)	60,000			260,000
11	Accumulated depreciation—building	(58,300)			(i)	7,000	(65,300)
12	Accounts payable (merchandise creditors)	(46,700)	(h)	3,200			(43,500)
13	Accrued expenses payable (operating expenses)	(24,300)			(g)	2,200	(26,500)
14	Income taxes payable	(8,400)	(f)	500			(7,900)
15	Dividends payable	(10,000)			(e)	4,000	(14,000)
16	Bonds payable	(150,000)	(d)	50,000			(100,000)
17	Common stock	(16,000)			(c)	8,000	(24,000)
18	Paid-in capital in excess of par	(80,000)			(c)	40,000	(120,000)
19	Retained earnings	(202,300)	(b)	28,000	(a)	108,000	(282,300)
20	Totals Step 3 →	0		237,200		237,200	0 ← Step 3
21	Operating activities:						
22	Net income		(a)	108,000			
23	Depreciation of building		(i)	7,000			
24	Gain on sale of land				(l)	12,000	
25	Increase in accounts receivable				(n)	9,000	
26	Decrease in inventories		(m)	8,000			
27	Decrease in accounts payable				(h)	3,200	
28	Increase in accrued expenses payable		(g)	2,200			
29	Decrease in income taxes payable				(f)	500	
30	Investing activities:						
31	Sale of land		(l)	72,000			
32	Purchase of land				(k)	15,000	
33	Purchase of building				(j)	60,000	
34	Financing activities:						
35	Issuance of common stock		(c)	48,000			
36	Retirement of bonds payable				(d)	50,000	
37	Declaration of cash dividends				(b)	28,000	
38	Increase in dividends payable		(e)	4,000			
39	Increase (decrease) in cash				(o)	71,500	
40	Totals			249,200		249,200	
41							

Step 1 (rows 6–20)

Steps 4–7

The $108,000 is reported on the statement of cash flows as part of cash flows from operating activities. Thus, an entry is made in the Transactions columns on the spreadsheet, as follows:

		Debit	Credit
(a)	Operating Activities—Net Income	108,000	
	Retained Earnings		108,000

The preceding entry accounts for the net income portion of the change to Retained Earnings. It also identifies the cash flow in the bottom portion of the spreadsheet as related to operating activities.

The $28,000 of dividends is reported as a financing activity on the statement of cash flows. Thus, an entry is made in the Transactions columns on the spreadsheet, as follows:

		Debit	Credit
(b)	Retained Earnings	28,000	
	Financing Activities—Declared Cash Dividends		28,000

The preceding entry accounts for the dividends portion of the change to Retained Earnings. It also identifies the cash flow in the bottom portion of the spreadsheet as related to financing activities. The $28,000 of declared dividends will be adjusted later for the actual amount of cash dividends paid during the year.

Other Accounts

The entries for the other noncash accounts are made in the spreadsheet in a manner similar to entries (a) and (b). A summary of these entries follows:

		Debit	Credit
(c)	Financing Activities—Issued Common Stock	48,000	
	Common Stock		8,000
	Paid-In Capital in Excess of Par—Common Stock		40,000
(d)	Bonds Payable	50,000	
	Financing Activities—Retired Bonds Payable		50,000
(e)	Financing Activities—Increase in Dividends Payable	4,000	
	Dividends Payable		4,000
(f)	Income Taxes Payable	500	
	Operating Activities—Decrease in Income Taxes Payable		500
(g)	Operating Activities—Increase in Accrued Expenses Payable	2,200	
	Accrued Expenses Payable		2,200
(h)	Accounts Payable	3,200	
	Operating Activities—Decrease in Accounts Payable		3,200
(i)	Operating Activities—Depreciation of Building	7,000	
	Accumulated Depreciation—Building		7,000
(j)	Building	60,000	
	Investing Activities—Purchase of Building		60,000
(k)	Land	15,000	
	Investing Activities—Purchase of Land		15,000
(l)	Investing Activities—Sale of Land	72,000	
	Operating Activities—Gain on Sale of Land		12,000
	Land		60,000
(m)	Operating Activities—Decrease in Inventories	8,000	
	Inventories		8,000
(n)	Accounts Receivable	9,000	
	Operating Activities—Increase in Accounts Receivable		9,000
(o)	Cash	71,500	
	Net Increase in Cash		71,500

After all the balance sheet accounts are analyzed and the entries made on the spreadsheet (work sheet), all the operating, investing, and financing activities are identified in the bottom portion of the spreadsheet. The accuracy of the entries is verified by totaling the Debit and Credit Transactions columns. The totals of the columns should be equal.

Preparing the Statement of Cash Flows

The statement of cash flows prepared from the spreadsheet is identical to the statement in Exhibit 7. The data for the three sections of the statement are obtained from the bottom portion of the spreadsheet.

APPENDIX 2

Prepare a statement of cash flows using the direct method.

Preparing the Statement of Cash Flows—The Direct Method

The direct method reports cash flows from operating activities as follows:

Cash flows from (used for) operating activities:		
Cash received from customers	$ XXX	
Cash paid for merchandise	(XXX)	
Cash paid for operating expenses	(XXX)	
Cash paid for interest	(XXX)	
Cash paid for income taxes	(XXX)	
Net cash flows from (used for) operating activities		$XXX

The Investing and Financing Activities sections of the statement of cash flows are exactly the same under both the direct and indirect methods. The amount of net cash flows from operating activities is also the same, but the manner in which it is reported is different.

Under the direct method, the income statement is adjusted to cash flows from operating activities as shown in Exhibit 9.

EXHIBIT 9

Converting Income Statement to Cash Flows from (used for) Operating Activities Using the Direct Method

Income Statement	Adjusted to	Cash Flows from (used for) Operating Activities
Sales	→	Cash received from customers
Cost of merchandise sold	→	Cash paid for merchandise
Operating expenses:		
Depreciation expense	N/A	N/A
Other operating expenses	→	Cash paid for operating expenses
Gain on sale of land	N/A	N/A
Interest expense	→	Cash paid for interest
Income tax expense	→	Cash paid for income taxes
Net income	→	Net cash flows from (used for) operating activities

N/A—Not applicable

As shown in Exhibit 9, depreciation expense is not adjusted or reported as part of cash flows from operating activities. This is because deprecation expense does not involve a cash outflow. The gain on the sale of the land is also not adjusted and is not reported as part of cash flows from operating activities. This is because the net cash flows from operating activities is determined directly, rather than by reconciling net income. The cash proceeds from the sale of the land are reported as an investing activity.

To illustrate the direct method, the income statement and comparative balance sheet for Rundell Inc., shown in Exhibit 4, are used.

Cash Received from Customers

The income statement (shown in Exhibit 4) of Rundell Inc. reports sales of $1,180,000. To determine the *cash received from customers*, the $1,180,000 is adjusted for any increase or decrease in accounts receivable. The adjustment is summarized in Exhibit 10.

EXHIBIT 10

Determining the Cash Received from Customers

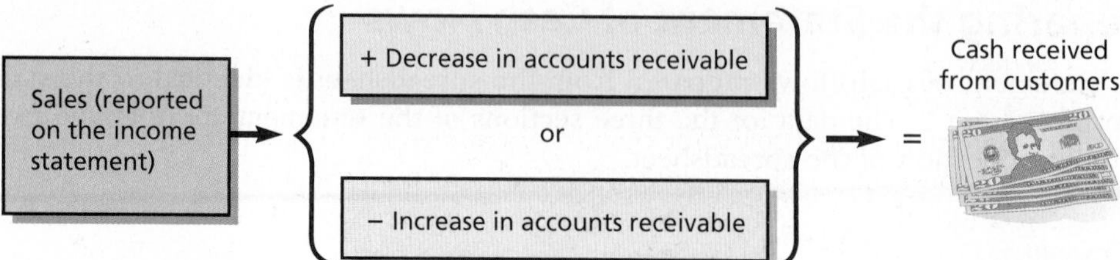

The cash received from customers is $1,171,000, computed as follows:

Sales	$1,180,000
Increase in accounts receivable	(9,000)
Cash received from customers	$1,171,000

The increase of $9,000 in accounts receivable (shown in Exhibit 4) during 20Y8 indicates that sales on account exceeded cash received from customers by $9,000. In other words, sales include $9,000 that did not result in a cash inflow during the year. Thus, $9,000 is deducted from sales to determine the cash received from customers.

Cash Paid for Merchandise

The income statement (shown in Exhibit 4) for Rundell Inc. reports cost of merchandise sold of $790,000. To determine the cash paid for merchandise, the $790,000 is adjusted for any increases or decreases in inventories and accounts payable. Assuming that the accounts payable are owed to merchandise suppliers, the adjustment is summarized in Exhibit 11.

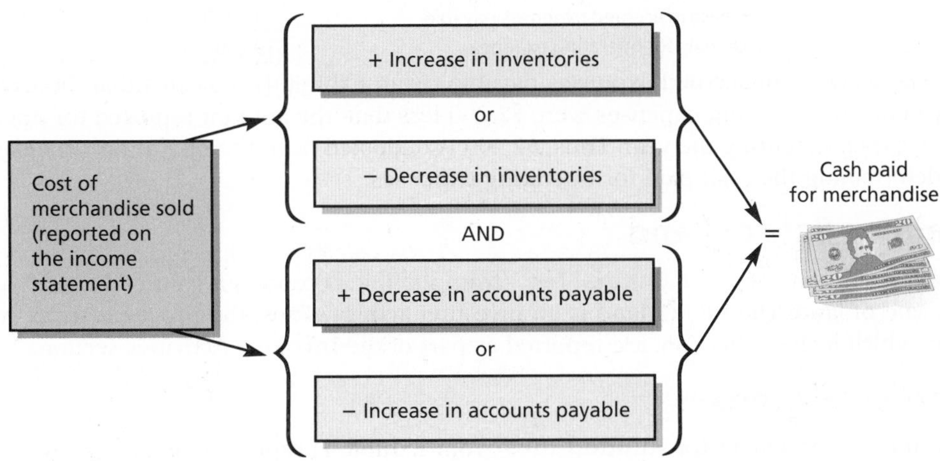

EXHIBIT 11
Determining Cash Paid for Merchandise

The cash paid for merchandise is $785,200, computed as follows:

Cost of merchandise sold	$790,000
Decrease in inventories	(8,000)
Decrease in accounts payable	3,200
Cash paid for merchandise	$785,200

The $8,000 decrease in inventories (from Exhibit 4) indicates that the merchandise sold exceeded the cost of the merchandise purchased by $8,000. In other words, the cost of merchandise sold includes $8,000 of goods sold from inventory that did not require a cash outflow during the year. Thus, $8,000 is deducted from the cost of merchandise sold in determining the cash paid for merchandise.

The $3,200 decrease in accounts payable (from Exhibit 4) indicates that cash payments for merchandise were $3,200 more than the purchases on account during 20Y8. Therefore, $3,200 is added to the cost of merchandise sold in determining the cash paid for merchandise.

Cash Paid for Operating Expenses

The income statement for Rundell Inc. (from Exhibit 4) reports total operating expenses of $203,000, which includes depreciation expense of $7,000. Because depreciation expense does not require a cash outflow, it is omitted from cash paid for operating expenses.

To determine the cash paid for operating expenses, the other operating expenses (excluding depreciation) of $196,000 ($203,000 – $7,000) are adjusted for any increase or decrease in prepaid expenses and accrued expenses. This adjustment is summarized in Exhibit 12.

EXHIBIT 12
Determining the Cash Paid for Operating Expenses

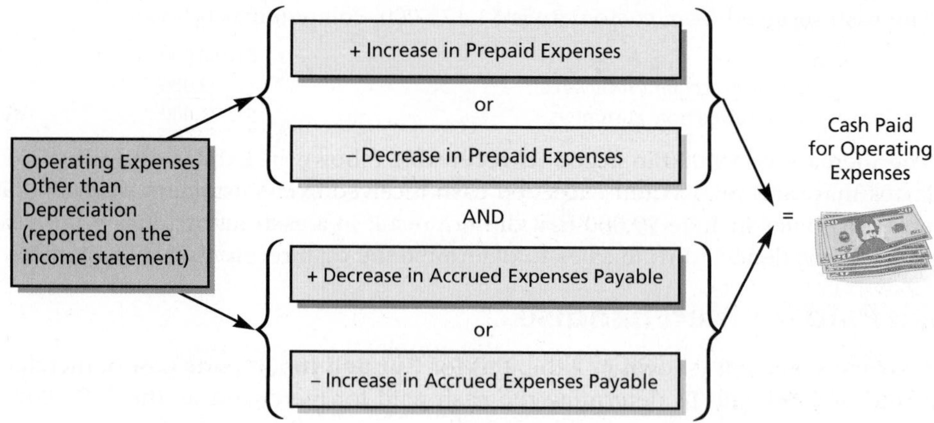

Since Rundell Inc. has no prepaid expenses, the cash paid for operating expenses is $193,800, computed as follows:

Operating expenses other than depreciation	$196,000
Increase in accrued expenses payable	(2,200)
Cash paid for operating expenses	$193,800

The increase in accrued expenses payable (from Exhibit 4) indicates that the cash payments for operating expenses were $2,200 less than the amount reported for operating expenses during the year. Thus, $2,200 is deducted from the operating expenses in determining the cash paid for operating expenses.

Gain on Sale of Land

The income statement for Rundell Inc. (from Exhibit 4) reports a gain of $12,000 on the sale of land. The sale of land is an investing activity. Thus, the proceeds from the sale, which include the gain, are reported as part of the Investing Activities section.

Interest Expense

The income statement for Rundell Inc. (from Exhibit 4) reports interest expense of $8,000. To determine the cash paid for interest, the $8,000 is adjusted for any increases or decreases in interest payable. The adjustment is summarized in Exhibit 13.

EXHIBIT 13
Determining the Cash Paid for Interest

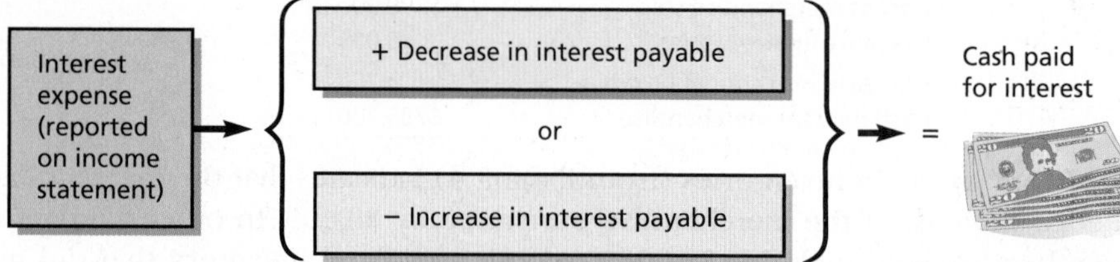

The comparative balance sheet of Rundell in Exhibit 4 indicates no interest payable. This is because the interest expense on the bonds payable is paid on June 1 and December 31. Because there is no interest payable, no adjustment of the interest expense of $8,000 is necessary.

Cash Paid for Income Taxes

The income statement for Rundell Inc. (from Exhibit 4) reports income tax expense of $83,000. To determine the cash paid for income taxes, the $83,000 is adjusted for any increases or decreases in income taxes payable. The adjustment is summarized in Exhibit 14.

EXHIBIT 14
Determining the Cash Paid for Income Taxes

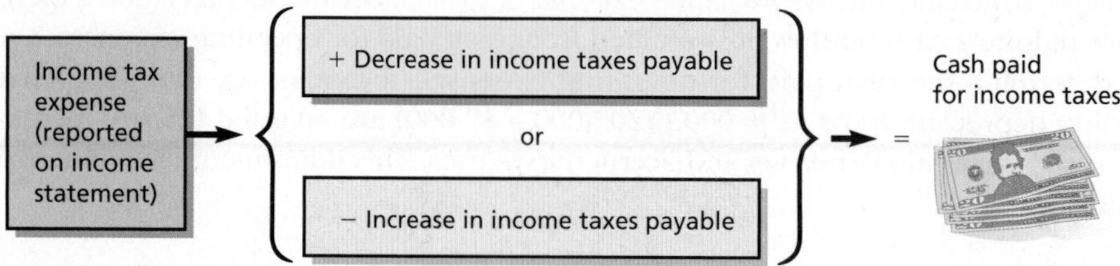

The cash paid for income taxes is $83,500, computed as follows:

Income tax expense	$83,000
Decrease in income taxes payable	500
Cash paid for income taxes	$83,500

The $500 decrease in income taxes payable (from Exhibit 4) indicates that the cash payments for income taxes were $500 more than the amount reported for income tax expense during 20Y8. Thus, $500 is added to the income tax expense in determining the cash paid for income taxes.

Reporting Cash Flows from (used for) Operating Activities—Direct Method

The statement of cash flows for Rundell Inc., using the direct method for reporting cash flows from operating activities, is shown in Exhibit 15. The portions of the statement that differ from those prepared under the indirect method are highlighted.

Exhibit 15 also includes the separate schedule reconciling net income and net cash flows from operating activities. This schedule is included on the statement of cash flows when the direct method is used. This schedule is similar to the Cash Flows from (used for) Operating Activities section prepared under the indirect method.

EXHIBIT 15

Statement of Cash Flows—Direct Method

Rundell Inc.
Statement of Cash Flows
For the Year Ended December 31, 20Y8

Cash flows from (used for) operating activities:		
Cash received from customers	$1,171,000	
Cash paid for merchandise	(785,200)	
Cash paid for operating expenses	(193,800)	
Cash paid for interest	(8,000)	
Cash paid for income taxes	(83,500)	
Net cash flows from operating activities		$100,500
Cash flows from (used for) investing activities:		
Cash received from sale of land	$ 72,000	
Cash paid for purchase of land	(15,000)	
Cash paid for purchase of building	(60,000)	
Net cash flows used for investing activities		(3,000)
Cash flows from (used for) financing activities:		
Cash received from issuing common stock	$ 48,000	
Cash paid to retire bonds payable	(50,000)	
Cash dividends	(24,000)	
Net cash flows used for financing activities		(26,000)
Net increase in cash		$ 71,500
Cash balance, January 1, 20Y8		26,000
Cash balance, December 31, 20Y8		$ 97,500
Schedule Reconciling Net Income with Net Cash Flows from Operating Activities:		
Cash flows from (used for) operating activities:		
Net income		$108,000
Adjustments to reconcile net income to net cash flows from (used for) operating activities:		
Depreciation		7,000
Gain on sale of land		(12,000)
Changes in current operating assets and liabilities:		
Increase in accounts receivable		(9,000)
Decrease in inventory		8,000
Decrease in accounts payable		(3,200)
Increase in accrued expenses payable		2,200
Decrease in income taxes payable		(500)
Net cash flows from operating activities		$100,500

At a Glance 16

OBJ. 1 **Describe the cash flow activities reported on the statement of cash flows.**

Key Points The statement of cash flows reports cash receipts and cash payments by three types of activities: operating activities, investing activities, and financing activities. The Cash Flows from (used for) Operating Activities section reports the cash inflows and outflows from a company's day-to-day operations. The Cash Flows from (used for) Investing Activities section reports the cash inflows and outflows related to changes in a company's long-term assets. The Cash Flows from (used for) Financing Activities section reports the cash inflows and outflows related to changes in a company's long-term liabilities and stockholders' equity. Investing and financing for a business may be affected by transactions that do not involve cash. The effect of such transactions should be reported in a separate schedule accompanying the statement of cash flows.

Learning Outcome	Example Exercises	Practice Exercises
• Classify transactions that either provide or use cash into operating, investing, or financing activities.	**EE16-1**	**PE16-1A, 16-1B**

OBJ. 2 **Prepare the Cash Flows from (used for) Operating Activities section of the statement of cash flows using the indirect method.**

Key Points The indirect method reports cash flows from operating activities by adjusting net income for revenues and expenses that do not involve the receipt or payment of cash. Noncash expenses such as depreciation are added back to net income. Gains and losses on the disposal of assets are added to or deducted from net income. Changes in current operating assets and liabilities are added to or subtracted from net income, depending on their effect on cash.

Learning Outcomes	Example Exercises	Practice Exercises
• Determine net cash flows from (used for) operating activities under the indirect method by adjusting net income for noncash expenses and gains and losses from asset disposals.	**EE16-2**	**PE16-2A, 16-2B**
• Determine net cash flows from (used for) operating activities under the indirect method by adjusting net income for changes in current operating assets and liabilities.	**EE16-3**	**PE16-3A, 16-3B**
• Prepare a Cash Flows from (used for) Operating Activities section of the statement of cash flows, using the indirect method.	**EE16-4**	**PE16-4A, 16-4B**

OBJ. 3 **Prepare the Cash Flows from (used for) Investing Activities section of the statement of cash flows.**

Key Points Cash flows from (used for) investing activities are reported below cash flows from (used for) operating activities on the statement of cash flows. The Cash Flows from (used for) Investing Activities section reports the cash inflows and outflows related to changes in a company's long-term assets.

Learning Outcomes	Example Exercises	Practice Exercises
• Show how purchases and sales of long-term assets are reported in the Investing Activities section of the statement of cash flows.	**EE16-5**	**PE16-5A, 16-5B**
• Describe the effects of depreciation on cash flows from (used for) investing activities.		

OBJ.4 Prepare the Cash Flows from (used for) Financing Activities section of the statement of cash flows.

Key Points Cash flows from (used for) financing activities are reported below cash flows from (used for) investing activities on the statement of cash flows. The Cash Flows from (used for) Financing Activities section reports the cash inflows and outflows related to changes in a company's long-term liabilities and stockholders' equity.

Learning Outcomes	Example Exercises	Practice Exercises
• Show how the retirement of bonds payable is reported in the Financing Activities section of the statement of cash flows.	EE16-6	PE16-6A, 16-6B
• Show how the issuance of common stock is reported in the Financing Activities section of the statement of cash flows.	EE16-6	PE16-6A, 16-6B
• Show how the declaration and payment of dividends are reported in the Financing Activities section of the statement of cash flows.	EE16-6	PE16-6A, 16-6B

OBJ.5 Prepare a statement of cash flows.

Key Points The statement of cash flows reports cash flows from (used for) operating activities followed by cash flows from (used for) investing and financing activities. The result of summing the net cash flows from (used for) operating, investing, and financing activities is the net increase or decrease in cash for the period. Cash at the beginning of the period is added to determine the cash at the end of the period. This ending cash amount must agree with cash reported on the end-of-period balance sheet.

Learning Outcome	Example Exercises	Practice Exercises
Prepare a statement of cash flows using the indirect method.		

OBJ.6 Describe and illustrate the use of free cash flow in evaluating a company's cash flow.

Key Points Free cash flow measures the operating cash flow available for company use after purchasing the fixed assets that are necessary to maintain current productive capacity. It is determined by subtracting these fixed asset purchases from net cash flows from operating activities. A company with strong free cash flow is able to fund internal growth, retire debt, pay dividends, and enjoy financial flexibility. A company with weak free cash flow has much less financial flexibility.

Learning Outcomes	Example Exercises	Practice Exercises
• Describe free cash flow.		
• Compute and evaluate free cash flow.	EE16-7	PE16-7A, 16-7B

Illustrative Problem

The comparative balance sheet of Dowling Company for December 31, 20Y6 and 20Y5, is as follows:

Dowling Company
Comparative Balance Sheet
December 31, 20Y6 and 20Y5

	20Y6	20Y5
Assets		
Cash	$ 140,350	$ 95,900
Accounts receivable (net)	95,300	102,300
Inventories	165,200	157,900
Prepaid expenses	6,240	5,860
Investments (long-term)	35,700	84,700
Land	75,000	90,000
Buildings	375,000	260,000
Accumulated depreciation—buildings	(71,300)	(58,300)
Machinery and equipment	428,300	428,300
Accumulated depreciation—machinery and equipment	(148,500)	(138,000)
Patents	58,000	65,000
Total assets	$1,159,290	$1,093,660
Liabilities and Stockholders' Equity		
Accounts payable (merchandise creditors)	$ 43,500	$ 46,700
Accrued expenses payable (operating expenses)	14,000	12,500
Income taxes payable	7,900	8,400
Dividends payable	14,000	10,000
Mortgage note payable, due in 10 years	40,000	0
Bonds payable	150,000	250,000
Common stock, $30 par	450,000	375,000
Excess of issue price over par—common stock	66,250	41,250
Retained earnings	373,640	349,810
Total liabilities and stockholders' equity	$1,159,290	$1,093,660

The income statement for Dowling Company follows:

Dowling Company
Income Statement
For the Year Ended December 31, 20Y6

Sales		$1,100,000
Cost of merchandise sold		710,000
Gross profit		$ 390,000
Operating expenses:		
Depreciation expense	$ 23,500	
Patent amortization	7,000	
Other operating expenses	196,000	
Total operating expenses		226,500
Income from operations		$ 163,500
Other revenue and expense:		
Gain on sale of investments	$ 11,000	
Interest expense	(26,000)	(15,000)
Income before income tax		$ 148,500
Income tax expense		50,000
Net income		$ 98,500

An examination of the accounting records revealed the following additional information applicable to 20Y6:

a. Land costing $15,000 was sold for $15,000.

b. A mortgage note was issued for $40,000.

c. A building costing $115,000 was constructed.

d. 2,500 shares of common stock were issued at $40 in exchange for the bonds payable.

e. Cash dividends declared were $74,670.

Instruction

Prepare a statement of cash flows, using the indirect method of reporting cash flows from operating activities.

Solution

Dowling Company
Statement of Cash Flows—Indirect Method
For the Year Ended December 31, 20Y6

Cash flows from (used for) operating activities:		
Net income	$ 98,500	
Adjustments to reconcile net income to net cash flows from (used for) operating activities:		
Depreciation	23,500	
Amortization of patents	7,000	
Gain on sale of investments	(11,000)	
Changes in current operating assets and liabilities:		
Decrease in accounts receivable	7,000	
Increase in inventories	(7,300)	
Increase in prepaid expenses	(380)	
Decrease in accounts payable	(3,200)	
Increase in accrued expenses payable	1,500	
Decrease in income taxes payable	(500)	
Net cash flows from operating activities		$115,120
Cash flows from (used for) investing activities:		
Cash received from sale of investments	$ 60,000[1]	
Cash received from sale of land	15,000	
Cash paid for construction of building	(115,000)	
Net cash flows used for investing activities		(40,000)
Cash flows from (used for) financing activities:		
Cash received from issuing mortgage note payable	$ 40,000	
Cash dividends	(70,670)[2]	
Net cash flows used for financing activities		(30,670)
Net increase in cash		$ 44,450
Cash balance, January 1, 20Y6		95,900
Cash balance, December 31, 20Y6		$140,350

Schedule of Noncash Investing and Financing Activities:

Issued common stock to retire bonds payable	$100,000

[1] $60,000 = $11,000 gain + $49,000 (decrease in investments)
[2] $70,670 = $74,670 – $4,000 (increase in dividends)

Key Terms

cash flow per share (771)
cash flows from (used for) financing activities (768)
cash flows from (used for) investing activities (768)
cash flows from (used for) operating activities (768)
direct method (769)
free cash flow (783)
indirect method (769)
statement of cash flows (767)

Discussion Questions

1. What is the principal advantage and the principal disadvantage of the direct method of reporting cash flows from (used for) operating activities?
2. What are the major advantages of the indirect method of reporting cash flows from (used for) operating activities?
3. A corporation issued $2,000,000 of common stock in exchange for $2,000,000 of fixed assets. Where would this transaction be reported on the statement of cash flows?
4. A retail business, using the accrual method of accounting, owed merchandise creditors (accounts payable) $320,000 at the beginning of the year and $350,000 at the end of the year. How would the $30,000 increase be used to adjust net income in determining the amount of cash flows from operating activities by the indirect method?
5. If salaries payable was $100,000 at the beginning of the year and $75,000 at the end of the year, should the $25,000 decrease be added to or deducted from income to determine the amount of cash flows from operating activities by the indirect method? Explain.
6. Fully depreciated equipment costing $50,000 is discarded. What is the effect of the transaction on cash flows if (a) $15,000 cash is received for the equipment, (b) no cash is received for the equipment?
7. A long-term investment in bonds with a cost of $500,000 was sold for $600,000 cash. (a) What was the gain or loss on the sale? (b) What was the effect of the transaction on cash flows? (c) How would the transaction be reported on the statement of cash flows if cash flows from operating activities are reported by the indirect method?
8. A corporation issued $2,000,000 of 20-year bonds for cash at 98. How would the transaction be reported on the statement of cash flows?
9. For the current year, Packers Company decided to switch from the indirect method to the direct method for reporting cash flows from operating activities on the statement of cash flows. Will the change cause the amount of net cash flows from operating activities to be larger, smaller, or the same compared to the indirect method being used? Explain.
10. Name five common major classes of operating cash receipts or operating cash payments presented on the statement of cash flows when the cash flows from operating activities are reported by the direct method.

Practice Exercises

Example Exercises

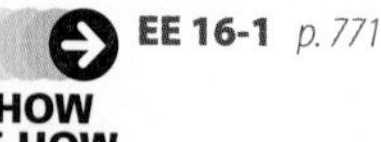
EE 16-1 p. 771

SHOW ME HOW

PE 16-1A Classifying cash flows

OBJ. 1

Identify whether each of the following would be reported as an operating, investing, or financing activity on the statement of cash flows:

a. Retirement of bonds payable
b. Purchase of inventory for cash
c. Cash sales
d. Repurchase of common stock
e. Payment of accounts payable
f. Disposal of equipment

SHOW ME HOW

EE 16-1 p. 771

PE 16-1B Classifying cash flows OBJ. 1

Identify whether each of the following would be reported as an operating, investing, or financing activity on the statement of cash flows:

a. Payment of dividends to common stockholders
b. Purchase of equipment
c. Payment for selling expenses
d. Collection of accounts receivable
e. Cash received from customers
f. Issuance of bonds payable

SHOW ME HOW

EE 16-2 p. 775

PE 16-2A Adjustments to net income OBJ. 2

Nadal Corporation's accumulated depreciation—furniture account increased by $17,720, while $3,800 of patent amortization was recognized between balance sheet dates. There were no purchases or sales of depreciable or intangible assets during the year. In addition, the income statement showed a loss of $5,200 from the sale of land. Reconcile a net income of $343,700 to net cash flows from operating activities.

EXCEL ONLINE

SHOW ME HOW

EE 16-2 p. 775

PE 16-2B Adjustments to net income OBJ. 2

Eastlund Corporation's accumulated depreciation—equipment account increased by $6,320, while $2,450 of patent amortization was recognized between balance sheet dates. There were no purchases or sales of depreciable or intangible assets during the year. In addition, the income statement showed a gain of $13,510 from the sale of investments. Reconcile a net income of $126,300 to net cash flows from operating activities.

SHOW ME HOW

EE 16-3 p. 777

PE 16-3A Changes in current operating assets and liabilities OBJ. 2

Jasneet Corporation's comparative balance sheet for current assets and liabilities was as follows:

	Dec. 31, Year 2	Dec. 31, Year 1
Accounts receivable	$20,200	$22,900
Inventory	13,000	10,700
Accounts payable	10,900	9,400
Dividends payable	25,100	30,700

Adjust net income of $185,000 for changes in operating assets and liabilities to arrive at net cash flows from operating activities.

SHOW ME HOW

EE 16-3 p. 777

PE 16-3B Changes in current operating assets and liabilities OBJ. 2

Paneous Corporation's comparative balance sheet for current assets and liabilities was as follows:

	Dec. 31, Year 2	Dec. 31, Year 1
Accounts receivable	$39,490	$31,590
Inventory	76,340	65,150
Accounts payable	60,750	45,410
Dividends payable	18,000	24,000

Adjust net income of $351,000 for changes in operating assets and liabilities to arrive at net cash flows from operating activities.

SHOW ME HOW

EE 16-4 p. 777

PE 16-4A Determining cash flows from (used for) operating activities OBJ. 2

Featherstone Inc. reported the following data:

Net income	$296,000
Depreciation expense	113,100
Gain on disposal of equipment	58,200
Decrease in accounts receivable	71,300
Decrease in accounts payable	27,100

Prepare the Cash Flows from (used for) Operating Activities section of the statement of cash flows, using the indirect method.

EE 16-4 *p. 777* **PE 16-4B Determining cash flows from (used for) operating activities** **OBJ. 2**

Yeoman Inc. reported the following data:

Net income	$170,000
Depreciation expense	29,000
Loss on disposal of equipment	11,850
Increase in accounts receivable	10,490
Increase in accounts payable	5,430

Prepare the Cash Flows from (used for) Operating Activities section of the statement of cash flows, using the indirect method.

EE 16-5 *p. 779* **PE 16-5A Land transactions on the statement of cash flows** **OBJ. 3**

Lagman Corporation purchased land for $310,000. Later in the year, the company sold a different piece of land with a book value of $114,000 for $81,000. How are the effects of these transactions reported on the statement of cash flows?

EE 16-5 *p. 779* **PE 16-5B Land transactions on the statement of cash flows** **OBJ. 3**

PQR Corporation purchased land for $295,000. Later in the year, the company sold a different piece of land with a book value of $148,000 for $177,000. How are the effects of these transactions reported on the statement of cash flows?

EE 16-6 *p. 781* **PE 16-6A Financing activities on the statement of cash flows** **OBJ. 4**

Takaki Inc. reported net income of $53,000 for 20Y7. The liability and equity accounts from the company's comparative balance sheet are as follows:

	Dec. 31, 20Y7	Dec. 31, 20Y6
Accounts payable	$ 31,900	$28,400
Dividends payable	5,000	3,000
Common stock, $5 par value	80,000	75,000
Paid-in capital in excess of par—common stock	37,000	30,000
Retained earnings	130,600	81,600

During the year, the company declared dividends of $4,000 and issued 1,000 shares of common stock for $12 per share. Prepare the Cash Flows from (used for) Financing Activities section of the statement of cash flows.

EE 16-6 *p. 781* **PE 16-6B Financing activities on the statement of cash flows** **OBJ. 4**

Cosmat Inc. reported net income of $128,000 for 20Y9. The liability and equity accounts from the company's comparative balance sheet are as follows:

	Dec. 31, 20Y9	Dec. 31, 20Y8
Accounts payable	$ 57,920	$ 53,810
Dividends payable	20,000	16,000
Bonds payable	290,000	450,000
Common stock, $10 par value	180,000	120,000
Paid-in capital in excess of par—common stock	328,000	232,000
Retained earnings	488,000	375,000

During the year, the company retired bonds payable at their face amount, declared dividends of $15,000, and issued 6,000 shares of common stock for $26 per share. Prepare the Cash Flows from (used for) Financing Activities section of the statement of cash flows.

EE 16-7 *p. 784* **PE 16-7A Free cash flow** **OBJ. 6**

Burkhalter Inc. reported the following on the company's statement of cash flows in Year 2 and Year 1:

	Year 2	Year 1
Net cash flows from operating activities	$ 385,000	$ 367,000
Net cash flows used for investing activities	(293,000)	(330,000)
Net cash flows used for financing activities	(83,000)	(55,000)

Seventy percent of the net cash flows used for investing activities was used to replace existing capacity.

The changes in the current asset and liability accounts for the year are as follows:

	Increase (Decrease)
Accounts receivable	$ 9,800
Inventory	(5,550)
Prepaid insurance	(1,000)
Accounts payable	(3,700)
Income taxes payable	1,440
Dividends payable	2,200

a. Prepare the Cash Flows from (used for) Operating Activities section of the statement of cash flows, using the indirect method.

b. Briefly explain why net cash flows from operating activities is different from net income.

✔ a. Net income, $341,770

SHOW ME HOW

EX 16-8 Determining net income from net cash flows from operating activities **OBJ. 2**

Curwen Inc. reported net cash flows from operating activities of $357,500 on its statement of cash flows for a recent year ended December 31. The following information was reported in the Cash Flows from (used for) Operating Activities section of the statement of cash flows, using the indirect method:

Decrease in income taxes payable	$ 7,700
Decrease in inventories	19,140
Depreciation	29,480
Gain on sale of investments	13,200
Increase in accounts payable	5,280
Increase in prepaid expenses	2,970
Increase in accounts receivable	14,300

a. Determine the net income reported by Curwen Inc. for the year ended December 31.

b. Briefly explain why Curwen's net income is different from net cash flows from operating activities.

✔ a. Net cash flows from operating activities, $150,296

EXCEL ONLINE

EX 16-9 Cash flows from operating activities **OBJ. 2**

Selected data derived from the income statement and balance sheet of **National Beverage Co.** for a recent year are as follows:

Income statement data (in thousands):	
Net income	$149,774
Loss on disposal of property	(149)
Depreciation expense	13,226
Other items involving noncash expense	837
Balance sheet data (in thousands):	
Increase in accounts receivable	13,041
Increase in inventory	7,565
Increase in prepaid expenses	10,548
Increase in accounts payable and other current liabilities	17,464

a. Prepare the Cash Flows from (used for) Operating Activities section of the statement of cash flows, using the indirect method for National Beverage Co.

b. Interpret your results in part (a).

EX 16-10 Reporting changes in equipment on statement of cash flows **OBJ. 3**

An analysis of the general ledger accounts indicates that office equipment, which cost $202,500 and on which accumulated depreciation totaled $84,375 on the date of sale, was sold for $101,250 during the year. Using this information, indicate the items to be reported on the statement of cash flows.

EX 16-11 Reporting changes in equipment on statement of cash flows **OBJ. 3**

An analysis of the general ledger accounts indicates that delivery equipment, which cost $200,000 and on which accumulated depreciation totaled $60,000 on the date of sale, was sold for $132,500 during the year. Using this information, indicate the items to be reported on the statement of cash flows.

EX 16-12 Reporting land transactions on statement of cash flows **OBJ. 3**

On the basis of the details of the following fixed asset account, indicate the items to be reported on the statement of cash flows:

ACCOUNT ***Land*** **ACCOUNT NO.**

Date		Item	Debit	Credit	Balance Debit	Balance Credit
Jan.	1	Balance			868,000	
Mar.	12	Purchased for cash	104,300		972,300	
Oct.	4	Sold for $95,550		63,840	908,460	

EX 16-13 Reporting land acquisition for cash and mortgage note on statement of cash flows **OBJ. 3**

On the basis of the details of the following fixed asset account, indicate the items to be reported on the statement of cash flows:

ACCOUNT ***Land*** **ACCOUNT NO.**

Date		Item	Debit	Credit	Balance Debit	Balance Credit
Jan.	1	Balance			156,000	
Feb.	10	Purchased for cash	246,000		402,000	
Nov.	20	Purchased with long-term mortgage note	324,000		726,000	

SHOW ME HOW

EX 16-14 Determining cash paid to stockholders **OBJ. 4**

The board of directors declared cash dividends totaling $585,000 during the current year. The comparative balance sheet indicates dividends payable of $167,625 at the beginning of the year and $146,250 at the end of the year. What was the amount of cash paid to stockholders during the year?

EX 16-15 Reporting stockholders' equity items on statement of cash flows **OBJ. 4**

On the basis of the following stockholders' equity accounts, indicate the items, exclusive of net income, to be reported on the statement of cash flows. There were no unpaid dividends at either the beginning or the end of the year.

ACCOUNT ***Common Stock, $40 par*** **ACCOUNT NO.**

Date		Item	Debit	Credit	Balance Debit	Balance Credit
Jan.	1	Balance, 120,000 shares				4,800,000
Apr.	2	30,000 shares issued for cash		1,200,000		6,000,000
June	30	4,400-share stock dividend		176,000		6,176,000

ACCOUNT ***Paid-In Capital in Excess of Par—Common Stock*** **ACCOUNT NO.**

Date		Item	Debit	Credit	Balance Debit	Balance Credit
Jan.	1	Balance				360,000
Apr.	2	30,000 shares issued for cash		720,000		1,080,000
June	30	Stock dividend		114,400		1,194,400

ACCOUNT ***Retained Earnings*** **ACCOUNT NO.**

Date		Item	Debit	Credit	Balance	
					Debit	Credit
Jan.	1	Balance				2,000,000
June	30	Stock dividend	290,440			1,709,560
Dec.	30	Cash dividend	463,200			1,246,360
	31	Net income		1,440,000		2,686,360

EX 16-16 Reporting issuance and retirement of long-term debt **OBJ. 4**

On the basis of the details of the following bonds payable and related discount accounts, indicate the items to be reported in the Financing Activities section of the statement of cash flows, assuming no gain or loss on retiring the bonds:

ACCOUNT ***Bonds Payable*** **ACCOUNT NO.**

Date		Item	Debit	Credit	Balance	
					Debit	Credit
Jan.	1	Balance				750,000
	2	Retire bonds	150,000			600,000
June	30	Issue bonds		450,000		1,050,000

ACCOUNT ***Discount on Bonds Payable*** **ACCOUNT NO.**

Date		Item	Debit	Credit	Balance	
					Debit	Credit
Jan.	1	Balance			33,750	
	2	Retire bonds		12,000	21,750	
June	30	Issue bonds	30,000		51,750	
Dec.	31	Amortize discount		2,625	49,125	

EX 16-17 Statement of cash flows **OBJ. 5**

✔ a. Net cash flows from operating activities, $49

SHOW ME HOW

The comparative balance sheet of Hirayama Industries Inc. for December 31, 20Y2 and 20Y1, is as follows:

	Dec. 31, 20Y2	Dec. 31, 20Y1
Assets		
Cash	$234	$ 18
Accounts receivable (net)	70	63
Inventories	150	127
Land	320	422
Equipment	262	224
Accumulated depreciation—equipment	(87)	(54)
Total assets	$949	$800
Liabilities and Stockholders' Equity		
Accounts payable (merchandise creditors)	$ 65	$ 47
Dividends payable	6	—
Common stock, $1 par	160	102
Paid-in capital in excess of par	109	90
Retained earnings	609	561
Total liabilities and stockholders' equity	$949	$800

(Continued)

The following additional information is taken from the records:

1. Land was sold for $153.
2. Equipment was acquired for cash.
3. There were no disposals of equipment during the year.
4. The common stock was issued for cash.
5. There was a $79 credit to Retained Earnings for net income.
6. There was a $31 debit to Retained Earnings for cash dividends declared.

a. Prepare a statement of cash flows, using the indirect method of presenting cash flows from (used for) operating activities.

b. Was Hirayama Industries Inc.'s net cash flows from operations more or less than net income? What is the source of this difference?

EX 16-18 Statement of cash flows **OBJ. 5**

The following statement of cash flows for Shasta Inc. was not correctly prepared:

Shasta Inc.
Statement of Cash Flows
For the Year Ended December 31, 20Y9

Cash flows from (used for) operating activities:		
Net income	$ 360,000	
Adjustments to reconcile net income to net cash flows from (used for) operating activities:		
Depreciation	100,800	
Gain on sale of investments	17,280	
Changes in current operating assets and liabilities:		
Increase in accounts receivable	27,360	
Increase in inventories	(36,000)	
Increase in accounts payable	(3,600)	
Decrease in accrued expenses payable	(2,400)	
Net cash flows from operating activities		$ 463,440
Cash flows from (used for) investing activities:		
Cash received from sale of investments	$ 240,000	
Cash paid for purchase of land	(259,200)	
Cash paid for purchase of equipment	(432,000)	
Net cash flows used for investing activities		(415,200)
Cash flows from (used for) financing activities:		
Cash received from issuing common stock	$ 312,000	
Cash dividends	(132,000)	
Net cash flows from financing activities		180,000
Net increase in cash		$ 47,760
Cash balance, December 31, 20Y9		192,240
Cash balance, January 1, 20Y9		$ 240,000

a. List the errors you find on the statement of cash flows. The cash balance at the beginning of the year was $240,000. All other amounts are correct, except the cash balance at the end of the year.

b. Prepare a corrected statement of cash flows, using the indirect method.

EX 16-19 Free cash flow **OBJ. 6**

FAI

Sweeter Enterprises Inc. has net cash flows from operating activities of $539,000. Cash flows used for investments in property, plant, and equipment totaled $210,000, of which 75% of this investment was used to replace existing capacity.

a. Determine the free cash flow for Sweeter Enterprises Inc.

b. How might a lender use free cash flow to determine whether or not to give Sweeter Enterprises Inc. a loan?

EX 16-20 Free cash flow **OBJ. 6**

The financial statements for **Nike, Inc.**, are provided in Appendix C at the end of the text.

a. Determine the free cash flow for the most recent fiscal year. Assume that 90% of the additions to property, plant, and equipment were used to maintain productive capacity. Round to the nearest thousand dollars.

b. How might a lender use free cash flow to determine whether or not to give Nike, Inc., a loan?

c. Would you feel comfortable giving Nike a loan, based on the free cash flow determined in (a)?

EX 16-21 Free cash flow **OBJ. 6**

Lovato Motors Inc. has net cash flows from operating activities of $720,000. Cash flows used for investments in property, plant, and equipment totaled $440,000, of which 85% of this investment was used to replace existing capacity.

Determine the free cash flow for Lovato Motors Inc.

Appendix 2

EX 16-22 Cash flows from (used for) operating activities—direct method

✔ a. $801,900

The cash flows from (used for) operating activities are reported by the direct method on the statement of cash flows. Determine the following:

a. If sales for the current year were $753,500 and accounts receivable decreased by $48,400 during the year, what was the amount of cash received from customers?

b. If income tax expense for the current year was $50,600 and income tax payable decreased by $5,500 during the year, what was the amount of cash paid for income taxes?

c. Briefly explain why the cash received from customers in (a) is different from sales.

Appendix 2

EX 16-23 Cash paid for merchandise purchases

The cost of merchandise sold for **Kohl's Corporation** for a recent year was $12,199 million. The balance sheet showed the following current account balances (in millions):

	Balance, End of Year	Balance, Beginning of Year
Merchandise inventories	$3,475	$3,542
Accounts payable	1,187	1,271

Determine the amount of cash paid for merchandise.

Appendix 2

EX 16-24 Determining selected amounts for cash flows from (used for) operating activities—direct method

✔ a. $1,025,800

Selected data taken from the accounting records of Ginis Inc. for the current year ended December 31 are as follows:

	Balance, December 31	Balance, January 1
Accrued expenses payable (operating expenses)	$ 12,650	$ 14,030
Accounts payable (merchandise creditors)	96,140	105,800
Inventories	178,020	193,430

During the current year, the cost of merchandise sold was $1,031,550 and the operating expenses other than depreciation were $179,400. The direct method is used for presenting the cash flows from operating activities on the statement of cash flows.

Determine the amount reported on the statement of cash flows for (a) cash paid for merchandise and (b) cash paid for operating expenses.

Appendix 2

EX 16-25 Cash flows from (used for) operating activities—direct method

✔ a. Net cash flows from operating activities, $96,040

The income statement of Booker T Industries Inc. for the current year ended June 30 is as follows:

Sales		$511,000
Cost of merchandise sold		290,500
Gross profit		$220,500
Operating expenses:		
Depreciation expense	$ 39,200	
Other operating expenses	105,000	
Total operating expenses		144,200
Income before income tax		$ 76,300
Income tax expense		21,700
Net income		$ 54,600

Changes in the balances of selected accounts from the beginning to the end of the current year are as follows:

	Increase (Decrease)
Accounts receivable (net)	$(11,760)
Inventories	3,920
Prepaid expenses	(3,780)
Accounts payable (merchandise creditors)	(7,980)
Accrued expenses payable (operating expenses)	1,260
Income tax payable	(2,660)

a. Prepare the Cash Flows from (used for) Operating Activities section of the statement of cash flows, using the direct method.

b. What does the direct method show about a company's cash flows from operating activities that is not shown using the indirect method?

Appendix 2

EX 16-26 Cash flows from (used for) operating activities—direct method

✔ Net cash flows from operating activities, $104,050

The income statement for Stallion Company for the current year ended June 30 and balances of selected accounts at the beginning and end of the year are as follows:

Sales		$374,500
Cost of merchandise sold		129,500
Gross profit		$245,000
Operating expenses:		
Depreciation expense	$32,400	
Other operating expenses	96,910	
Total operating expenses		129,310
Income before income tax		$115,690
Income tax expense		33,290
Net income		$ 82,400

	End of Year	Beginning of Year
Accounts receivable (net)	$30,510	$26,260
Inventories	77,670	67,500
Prepaid expenses	12,210	13,320
Accounts payable (merchandise creditors)	56,780	52,710
Accrued expenses payable (operating expenses)	16,090	17,600
Income tax payable	3,700	3,700

Prepare the Cash Flows from (used for) Operating Activities section of the statement of cash flows, using the direct method.

Problems: Series A

PR 16-1A Statement of cash flows

OBJ. 2, 3, 4, 5

✓ Net cash flows from operating activities, $588,000

SHOW ME HOW

The comparative balance sheet of Iglesias Inc. for December 31, 20Y3 and 20Y2, is shown as follows:

	Dec. 31, 20Y3	Dec. 31, 20Y2
Assets		
Cash	$ 186,000	$ 180,000
Accounts receivable (net)	540,000	480,000
Inventories	924,000	900,000
Investments	0	120,000
Land	600,000	0
Equipment	1,680,000	1,440,000
Accumulated depreciation—equipment	(720,000)	(600,000)
Total assets	$3,210,000	$2,520,000
Liabilities and Stockholders' Equity		
Accounts payable	$ 408,000	$ 360,000
Accrued expenses payable	54,000	60,000
Dividends payable	36,000	30,000
Common stock, $4 par	840,000	720,000
Paid-in capital in excess of par	240,000	210,000
Retained earnings	1,632,000	1,140,000
Total liabilities and stockholders' equity	$3,210,000	$2,520,000

Additional data obtained from an examination of the accounts in the ledger for 20Y3 are as follows:

a. The investments were sold for $210,000 cash.
b. Equipment and land were acquired for cash.
c. There were no disposals of equipment during the year.
d. The common stock was issued for cash.
e. There was a $600,000 credit to Retained Earnings for net income.
f. There was a $108,000 debit to Retained Earnings for cash dividends declared.

Instructions

Prepare a statement of cash flows, using the indirect method of presenting cash flows from (used for) operating activities.

PR 16-2A Statement of cash flows

OBJ. 2, 3, 4, 5

✓ Net cash flows from operating activities, $425,000

SHOW ME HOW

The comparative balance sheet of Orange Angel Enterprises Inc. at December 31, 20Y8 and 20Y7, is as follows:

	Dec. 31, 20Y8	Dec. 31, 20Y7
Assets		
Cash	$ 151,000	$ 190,000
Accounts receivable (net)	522,000	569,000
Merchandise inventory	968,000	759,000
Prepaid expenses	28,000	19,000
Equipment	2,032,000	1,424,000
Accumulated depreciation—equipment	(380,000)	(304,000)
Total assets	$3,321,000	$2,657,000

(Continued)

	Dec. 31, 20Y8	Dec. 31, 20Y7
Liabilities and Stockholders' Equity		
Accounts payable (merchandise creditors)	$ 190,000	$ 171,000
Mortgage note payable	0	759,000
Common stock, $10 par	1,140,000	380,000
Paid-in capital in excess of par	570,000	190,000
Retained earnings	1,421,000	1,157,000
Total liabilities and stockholders' equity	$3,321,000	$2,657,000

Additional data obtained from the income statement and from an examination of the accounts in the ledger for 20Y8 are as follows:

a. Net income, $359,000.

b. Depreciation reported on the income statement, $218,000.

c. Equipment was purchased at a cost of $750,000, and fully depreciated equipment costing $142,000 was discarded, with no salvage realized.

d. The mortgage note payable was not due for six years, but the terms permitted earlier payment without penalty.

e. 76,000 shares of common stock were issued at $15 for cash.

f. Cash dividends declared and paid, $95,000.

Instructions

Prepare a statement of cash flows, using the indirect method of presenting cash flows from (used for) operating activities.

PR 16-3A Statement of cash flows

OBJ. 2, 3, 4, 5

✔ Net cash flows used for operating activities, $(169,600)

The comparative balance sheet of Whitman Co. at December 31, 20Y2 and 20Y1, is as follows:

	Dec. 31, 20Y2	Dec. 31, 20Y1
Assets		
Cash	$ 918,000	$ 964,800
Accounts receivable (net)	828,900	761,940
Inventories	1,268,460	1,162,980
Prepaid expenses	29,340	35,100
Land	315,900	479,700
Buildings	1,462,500	900,900
Accumulated depreciation—buildings	(408,600)	(382,320)
Equipment	512,280	454,680
Accumulated depreciation—equipment	(141,300)	(158,760)
Total assets	$4,785,480	$4,219,020
Liabilities and Stockholders' Equity		
Accounts payable (merchandise creditors)	$ 922,500	$ 958,320
Bonds payable	270,000	0
Common stock, $25 par	317,000	117,000
Paid-in capital in excess of par	758,000	558,000
Retained earnings	2,517,980	2,585,700
Total liabilities and stockholders' equity	$4,785,480	$4,219,020

The noncurrent asset, noncurrent liability, and stockholders' equity accounts for 20Y2 are as follows:

ACCOUNT *Land* ACCOUNT NO.

Date		Item	Debit	Credit	Balance	
					Debit	Credit
20Y2						
Jan.	1	Balance			479,700	
Apr.	20	Realized $151,200 cash from sale		163,800	315,900	

ACCOUNT ***Buildings*** **ACCOUNT NO.**

Date		Item	Debit	Credit	Balance	
					Debit	Credit
20Y2						
Jan.	1	Balance			900,900	
Apr.	20	Acquired for cash	561,600		1,462,500	

ACCOUNT ***Accumulated Depreciation—Buildings*** **ACCOUNT NO.**

Date		Item	Debit	Credit	Balance	
					Debit	Credit
20Y2						
Jan.	1	Balance				382,320
Dec.	31	Depreciation for year		26,280		408,600

ACCOUNT ***Equipment*** **ACCOUNT NO.**

Date		Item	Debit	Credit	Balance	
					Debit	Credit
20Y2						
Jan.	1	Balance			454,680	
	26	Discarded, no salvage		46,800	407,880	
Aug.	11	Purchased for cash	104,400		512,280	

ACCOUNT ***Accumulated Depreciation—Equipment*** **ACCOUNT NO.**

Date		Item	Debit	Credit	Balance	
					Debit	Credit
20Y2						
Jan.	1	Balance				158,760
	26	Equipment discarded	46,800			111,960
Dec.	31	Depreciation for year		29,340		141,300

ACCOUNT ***Bonds Payable*** **ACCOUNT NO.**

Date		Item	Debit	Credit	Balance	
					Debit	Credit
20Y2						
May	1	Issued 20-year bonds		270,000		270,000

ACCOUNT ***Common Stock, $25 par*** **ACCOUNT NO.**

Date		Item	Debit	Credit	Balance	
					Debit	Credit
20Y2						
Jan.	1	Balance				117,000
Dec.	7	Issued 8,000 shares of common stock for $50 per share		200,000		317,000

(Continued)

ACCOUNT ***Paid-In Capital in Excess of Par—Common Stock*** **ACCOUNT NO.**

Date		Item	Debit	Credit	Balance Debit	Balance Credit
20Y2						
Jan.	1	Balance				558,000
Dec.	7	Issued 8,000 shares of common stock for $50 per share		200,000		758,000

ACCOUNT ***Retained Earnings*** **ACCOUNT NO.**

Date		Item	Debit	Credit	Balance Debit	Balance Credit
20Y2						
Jan.	1	Balance				2,585,700
Dec.	31	Net loss	35,320			2,550,380
	31	Cash dividends	32,400			2,517,980

Instructions

Prepare a statement of cash flows, using the indirect method of presenting cash flows from (used for) operating activities.

Appendix 2

PR 16-4A Statement of cash flows—direct method

✔ Net cash flows from operating activities, $293,600

The comparative balance sheet of Canace Products Inc. for December 31, 20Y6 and 20Y5, is as follows:

	Dec. 31, 20Y6	Dec. 31, 20Y5
Assets		
Cash	$ 643,400	$ 679,400
Accounts receivable (net)	566,800	547,400
Inventories	1,011,000	982,800
Investments	0	240,000
Land	520,000	0
Equipment	880,000	680,000
Accumulated depreciation	(244,400)	(200,400)
Total assets	$3,376,800	$2,929,200
Liabilities and Stockholders' Equity		
Accounts payable	$ 771,800	$ 748,400
Accrued expenses payable	63,400	70,800
Dividends payable	8,800	6,400
Common stock, $2 par	56,000	32,000
Paid-in capital in excess of par	408,000	192,000
Retained earnings	2,068,800	1,879,600
Total liabilities and stockholders' equity	$3,376,800	$2,929,200

The income statement for the year ended December 31, 20Y6, is as follows:

Sales		$5,980,000
Cost of merchandise sold		2,452,000
Gross profit		$3,528,000
Operating expenses:		
Depreciation expense	$ 44,000	
Other operating expenses	3,100,000	
Total operating expenses		3,144,000

Income from operations	$ 384,000
Other expense:	
Loss on sale of investments	(64,000)
Income before income tax	$ 320,000
Income tax expense	102,800
Net income	$ 217,200

Additional data obtained from an examination of the accounts in the ledger for 20Y6 are as follows:

a. Equipment and land were acquired for cash.

b. There were no disposals of equipment during the year.

c. The investments were sold for $176,000 cash.

d. The common stock was issued for cash.

e. There was a $28,000 debit to Retained Earnings for cash dividends declared.

Instructions

Prepare a statement of cash flows, using the direct method of presenting cash flows from (used for) operating activities.

Appendix 2

PR 16-5A Statement of cash flows—direct method applied to PR 16-1A

✔ Net cash flows from operating activities, $588,000

The comparative balance sheet of Iglesias Inc. for December 31, 20Y3 and 20Y2, is as follows:

	Dec. 31, 20Y3	Dec. 31, 20Y2
Assets		
Cash	$ 186,000	$ 180,000
Accounts receivable (net)	540,000	480,000
Inventories	924,000	900,000
Investments	0	120,000
Land	600,000	0
Equipment	1,680,000	1,440,000
Accumulated depreciation—equipment	(720,000)	(600,000)
Total assets	$3,210,000	$2,520,000
Liabilities and Stockholders' Equity		
Accounts payable	$ 408,000	$ 360,000
Accrued expenses payable	54,000	60,000
Dividends payable	36,000	30,000
Common stock, $4 par	840,000	720,000
Paid-in capital in excess of par	240,000	210,000
Retained earnings	1,632,000	1,140,000
Total liabilities and stockholders' equity	$3,210,000	$2,520,000

The income statement for the year ended December 31, 20Y3, is as follows:

Sales		$3,600,000
Cost of merchandise sold		1,680,000
Gross profit		$1,920,000
Operating expenses:		
Depreciation expense	$ 120,000	
Other operating expenses	1,140,000	
Total operating expenses		1,260,000
Income from operations		$ 660,000
Other income:		
Gain on sale of investments		90,000
Income before income tax		$ 750,000
Income tax expense		150,000
Net income		$ 600,000

(Continued)

Additional data obtained from an examination of the accounts in the ledger for 20Y3 are as follows:

a. The investments were sold for $210,000 cash.
b. Equipment and land were acquired for cash.
c. There were no disposals of equipment during the year.
d. The common stock was issued for cash.
e. There was a $108,000 debit to Retained Earnings for cash dividends declared.

Instructions

Prepare a statement of cash flows, using the direct method of presenting cash flows from (used for) operating activities.

Problems: Series B

PR 16-1B Statement of cash flows

OBJ. 2, 3, 4, 5

✔ Net cash flows from operating activities, $154,260

SHOW ME HOW

The comparative balance sheet of Merrick Equipment Co. for December 31, 20Y9 and 20Y8, is as follows:

	Dec. 31, 20Y9	Dec. 31, 20Y8
Assets		
Cash	$ 70,720	$ 47,940
Accounts receivable (net)	207,230	188,190
Inventories	298,520	289,850
Investments	0	102,000
Land	295,800	0
Equipment	438,600	358,020
Accumulated depreciation—equipment	(99,110)	(84,320)
Total assets	$1,211,760	$901,680
Liabilities and Stockholders' Equity		
Accounts payable	$ 205,700	$194,140
Accrued expenses payable	30,600	26,860
Dividends payable	25,500	20,400
Common stock, $1 par	202,000	102,000
Paid-in capital in excess of par	354,000	204,000
Retained earnings	393,960	354,280
Total liabilities and stockholders' equity	$1,211,760	$901,680

Additional data obtained from an examination of the accounts in the ledger for 20Y9 are as follows:

a. Equipment and land were acquired for cash.
b. There were no disposals of equipment during the year.
c. The investments were sold for $91,800 cash.
d. The common stock was issued for cash.
e. There was a $141,680 credit to Retained Earnings for net income.
f. There was a $102,000 debit to Retained Earnings for cash dividends declared.

Instructions

Prepare a statement of cash flows, using the indirect method of presenting cash flows from (used for) operating activities.

PR 16-2B Statement of cash flows

OBJ. 2, 3, 4, 5

✓ Net cash flows from operating activities, $561,400

The comparative balance sheet of Harris Industries Inc. at December 31, 20Y4 and 20Y3, is as follows:

	Dec. 31, 20Y4	Dec. 31, 20Y3
Assets		
Cash	$ 443,240	$ 360,920
Accounts receivable (net)	665,280	592,200
Inventories	887,880	1,022,560
Prepaid expenses	31,640	25,200
Land	302,400	302,400
Buildings	1,713,600	1,134,000
Accumulated depreciation—buildings	(466,200)	(414,540)
Machinery and equipment	781,200	781,200
Accumulated depreciation—machinery and equipment	(214,200)	(191,520)
Patents	106,960	112,000
Total assets	$4,251,800	$3,724,420
Liabilities and Stockholders' Equity		
Accounts payable	$ 837,480	$ 927,080
Dividends payable	32,760	25,200
Salaries payable	78,960	87,080
Mortgage note payable, due in 10 years	224,000	0
Bonds payable	0	390,000
Common stock, $5 par	200,400	50,400
Paid-in capital in excess of par	366,000	126,000
Retained earnings	2,512,200	2,118,660
Total liabilities and stockholders' equity	$4,251,800	$3,724,420

An examination of the income statement and the accounting records revealed the following additional information applicable to 20Y4:

a. Net income, $524,580.

b. Depreciation expense reported on the income statement: buildings, $51,660; machinery and equipment, $22,680.

c. Patent amortization reported on the income statement, $5,040.

d. A building was constructed for $579,600.

e. A mortgage note for $224,000 was issued for cash.

f. 30,000 shares of common stock were issued at $13 in exchange for the bonds payable.

g. Cash dividends declared, $131,040.

Instructions

Prepare a statement of cash flows, using the indirect method of presenting cash flows from (used for) operating activities.

PR 16-3B Statement of cash flows

OBJ. 2, 3, 4, 5

✓ Net cash flows from operating activities, $162,800

The comparative balance sheet of Coulson, Inc., at December 31, 20Y2 and 20Y1, is as follows:

(Continued)

	Dec. 31, 20Y2	Dec. 31, 20Y1
Assets		
Cash	$ 300,600	$ 337,800
Accounts receivable (net)	704,400	609,600
Inventories	918,600	865,800
Prepaid expenses	18,600	26,400
Land	990,000	1,386,000
Buildings	1,980,000	990,000
Accumulated depreciation—buildings	(397,200)	(366,000)
Equipment	660,600	529,800
Accumulated depreciation—equipment	(133,200)	(162,000)
Total assets	$5,042,400	$4,217,400
Liabilities and Stockholders' Equity		
Accounts payable	$ 594,000	$ 631,200
Income taxes payable	26,400	21,600
Bonds payable	330,000	0
Common stock, $20 par	320,000	180,000
Paid-in capital in excess of par	950,000	810,000
Retained earnings	2,822,000	2,574,600
Total liabilities and stockholders' equity	$5,042,400	$4,217,400

The noncurrent asset, noncurrent liability, and stockholders' equity accounts for 20Y2 are as follows:

ACCOUNT *Land* ACCOUNT NO.

Date		Item	Debit	Credit	Balance Debit	Balance Credit
20Y2						
Jan.	1	Balance			1,386,000	
Apr.	20	Realized $456,000 cash from sale		396,000	990,000	

ACCOUNT *Buildings* ACCOUNT NO.

Date		Item	Debit	Credit	Balance Debit	Balance Credit
20Y2						
Jan.	1	Balance			990,000	
Apr.	20	Acquired for cash	990,000		1,980,000	

ACCOUNT *Accumulated Depreciation—Buildings* ACCOUNT NO.

Date		Item	Debit	Credit	Balance Debit	Balance Credit
20Y2						
Jan.	1	Balance				366,000
Dec.	31	Depreciation for year		31,200		397,200

ACCOUNT *Equipment* ACCOUNT NO.

Date		Item	Debit	Credit	Balance Debit	Balance Credit
20Y2						
Jan.	1	Balance			529,800	
	26	Discarded, no salvage		66,000	463,800	
Aug.	11	Purchased for cash	196,800		660,600	

ACCOUNT *Accumulated Depreciation—Equipment* ACCOUNT NO.

Date		Item	Debit	Credit	Balance Debit	Balance Credit
20Y2						
Jan.	1	Balance				162,000
	26	Equipment discarded	66,000			96,000
Dec.	31	Depreciation for year		37,200		133,200

ACCOUNT *Bonds Payable* ACCOUNT NO.

Date		Item	Debit	Credit	Balance Debit	Balance Credit
20Y2						
May	1	Issued 20-year bonds		330,000		330,000

ACCOUNT *Common Stock, $20 par* ACCOUNT NO.

Date		Item	Debit	Credit	Balance Debit	Balance Credit
20Y2						
Jan.	1	Balance				180,000
Dec.	7	Issued 7,000 shares of common stock for $40 per share		140,000		320,000

ACCOUNT *Paid-In Capital in Excess of Par—Common Stock* ACCOUNT NO.

Date		Item	Debit	Credit	Balance Debit	Balance Credit
20Y2						
Jan.	1	Balance				810,000
Dec.	7	Issued 7,000 shares of common stock for $40 per share		140,000		950,000

ACCOUNT *Retained Earnings* ACCOUNT NO.

Date		Item	Debit	Credit	Balance Debit	Balance Credit
20Y2						
Jan.	1	Balance				2,574,600
Dec.	31	Net income		326,600		2,901,200
	31	Cash dividends	79,200			2,822,000

(Continued)

Instructions

Prepare a statement of cash flows, using the indirect method of presenting cash flows from (used for) operating activities.

Appendix 2

PR 16-4B Statement of cash flows—direct method

✔ **Net cash flows from operating activities, $607,790**

SHOW ME HOW

The comparative balance sheet of Suffridge Inc. for December 31, 20Y4 and 20Y3, is as follows:

	Dec. 31, 20Y4	Dec. 31, 20Y3
Assets		
Cash	$ 790,090	$ 815,600
Accounts receivable (net)	1,185,100	1,091,700
Inventories	1,664,800	1,628,200
Investments	0	515,800
Land	1,146,100	0
Equipment	1,461,300	1,174,800
Accumulated depreciation—equipment	(574,800)	(439,800)
Total assets	$5,672,590	$4,786,300
Liabilities and Stockholders' Equity		
Accounts payable	$1,289,400	$ 1,154,000
Accrued expenses payable	80,900	94,600
Dividends payable	120,300	108,900
Common stock, $5 par	155,200	35,800
Paid-in capital in excess of par	1,134,200	537,300
Retained earnings	2,892,590	2,855,700
Total liabilities and stockholders' equity	$5,672,590	$4,786,300

The income statement for the year ended December 31, 20Y4, is as follows:

Sales		$5,386,900
Cost of merchandise sold		2,808,100
Gross profit		$2,578,800
Operating expenses:		
Depreciation expense	$ 135,000	
Other operating expenses	1,605,610	
Total operating expenses		1,740,610
Income from operations		$ 838,190
Other income:		
Gain on sale of investments		186,200
Income before income tax		$1,024,390
Income tax expense		357,100
Net income		$ 667,290

Additional data obtained from an examination of the accounts in the ledger for 20Y4 are as follows:

a. Equipment and land were acquired for cash.
b. There were no disposals of equipment during the year.
c. The investments were sold for $702,000 cash.
d. The common stock was issued for cash.
e. There was a $630,400 debit to Retained Earnings for cash dividends declared.

Instructions

Prepare a statement of cash flows, using the direct method of presenting cash flows from (used for) operating activities.

Appendix 2

PR 16-5B Statement of cash flows—direct method applied to PR 16-1B

✔ **Net cash flows from operating activities, $154,260**

The comparative balance sheet of Merrick Equipment Co. for Dec. 31, 20Y9 and 20Y8, is as follows:

	Dec. 31, 20Y9	Dec. 31, 20Y8
Assets		
Cash	$ 70,720	$ 47,940
Accounts receivable (net)	207,230	188,190
Inventories	298,520	289,850
Investments	0	102,000
Land	295,800	0
Equipment	438,600	358,020
Accumulated depreciation—equipment	(99,110)	(84,320)
Total assets	$1,211,760	$901,680
Liabilities and Stockholders' Equity		
Accounts payable	$ 205,700	$194,140
Accrued expenses payable	30,600	26,860
Dividends payable	25,500	20,400
Common stock, $1 par	202,000	102,000
Paid-in capital in excess of par	354,000	204,000
Retained earnings	393,960	354,280
Total liabilities and stockholders' equity	$1,211,760	$901,680

The income statement for the year ended December 31, 20Y9, is as follows:

Sales		$2,023,898
Cost of merchandise sold		1,245,476
Gross profit		$ 778,422
Operating expenses:		
Depreciation expense	$ 14,790	
Other operating expenses	517,299	
Total operating expenses		532,089
Income from operations		$ 246,333
Other expenses:		
Loss on sale of investments		(10,200)
Income before income tax		$ 236,133
Income tax expense		94,453
Net income		$ 141,680

Additional data obtained from an examination of the accounts in the ledger for 20Y9 are as follows:

a. Equipment and land were acquired for cash.
b. There were no disposals of equipment during the year.
c. The investments were sold for $91,800 cash.
d. The common stock was issued for cash.
e. There was a $102,000 debit to Retained Earnings for cash dividends declared.

Instructions

Prepare a statement of cash flows, using the direct method of presenting cash flows from (used for) operating activities.

Cases & Projects

CP 16-1 Ethics in Action

Lucas Hunter, president of Simmons Industries Inc., believes that reporting operating cash flow per share on the income statement would be a useful addition to the company's just completed financial statements. The following discussion took place between Lucas Hunter and Simmons' controller, John Jameson, in January, after the close of the fiscal year:

Lucas: I've been reviewing our financial statements for the last year. I am disappointed that our net income per share has dropped by 10% from last year. This won't look good to our shareholders. Is there anything we can do about this?

John: What do you mean? The past is the past, and the numbers are in. There isn't much that can be done about it. Our financial statements were prepared according to generally accepted accounting principles, and I don't see much leeway for significant change at this point.

Lucas: No, no. I'm not suggesting that we "cook the books." But look at the cash flow from operating activities on the statement of cash flows. The cash flow from operating activities has increased by 20%. This is very good news—and, I might add, useful information. The higher cash flow from operating activities will give our creditors comfort.

John: Well, the cash flow from operating activities is on the statement of cash flows, so I guess users will be able to see the improved cash flow figures there.

Lucas: This is true, but somehow I think this information should be given a much higher profile. I don't like this information being "buried" in the statement of cash flows. You know as well as I do that many users will focus on the income statement. Therefore, I think we ought to include an operating cash flow per share number on the face of the income statement—someplace under the earnings per share number. In this way, users will get the complete picture of our operating performance. Yes, our earnings per share dropped this year, but our cash flow from operating activities improved! And all the information is in one place where users can see and compare the figures. What do you think?

John: I've never really thought about it like that before. I guess we could put the operating cash flow per share on the income statement, underneath the earnings per share amount. Users would really benefit from this disclosure. Thanks for the idea—I'll start working on it.

Lucas: Glad to be of service.

How would you interpret this situation? Is John behaving in an ethical and professional manner?

CP 16-2 Team Activity

In teams, select a public company that interests you. Obtain the company's most recent annual report on Form 10-K. The Form 10-K is a company's annually required filing with the Securities and Exchange Commission (SEC). It includes the company's financial statements and accompanying notes. The Form 10-K can be obtained either (a) by referring to the investor relations section of the company's website or (b) by using the company search feature of the SEC's EDGAR database service found at www.sec.gov/edgar/searchedgar/companysearch.html.

1. Based on the information in the company's most recent annual report, answer the following questions:
   a. What is the net cash flows from (used for) operating activities reported by the company at the end of the most recent year?
   b. What is the net cash flows from (used for) investing activities reported by the company at the end of the most recent year?
   c. What is the net cash flows from (used for) financing activities reported by the company at the end of the most recent year?
   d. What was the net increase (or decrease) in cash during the year?
2. Evaluate the company's cash inflows and outflows.

CP 16-3 Communication

Tidewater Inc., a retailer, provided the following financial information for its most recent fiscal year:

Net income	$ 945,000
Return on invested capital	8%
Net cash flows used for operating activities	$(1,428,000)
Net cash flows from investing activities	$600,000
Net cash flows from financing activities	$900,000

The company's Cash Flows from (used for) Operating Activities section is as follows:

Net income	$ 945,000
Depreciation	210,000
Increase in accounts receivable	(1,134,000)
Increase in inventory	(1,260,000)
Decrease in accounts payable	(189,000)
Net cash flows used for operating activities	$(1,428,000)

An examination of the financial statements revealed the following additional information:

- Revenues increased during the year as a result of an aggressive marketing campaign aimed at increasing the number of new "Tidewater Card" credit card customers. This is the company's branded credit card, which can only be used at Tidewater stores. The credit card balances are accounts receivable on Tidewater's balance sheet.
- Some suppliers have made their merchandise available at a deep discount. As a result, the company purchased large quantities of these goods in an attempt to improve the company's profitability.
- In recent years, the company has struggled to pay its accounts payable on time. The company has improved on this during the past year and is nearly caught up on overdue payables balances.
- The company reported net losses in each of the two prior years.

Write a brief memo to your instructor evaluating the financial condition of Tidewater Inc.

CP 16-4 Using the statement of cash flows

You are considering an investment in a new start-up company, Giraffe Inc., an Internet service provider. A review of the company's financial statements reveals a negative retained earnings. In addition, it appears as though the company has been running a negative cash flow from operating activities since the company's inception.

How is the company staying in business under these circumstances? Could this be a good investment?

CP 16-5 Analysis of statement of cash flows

Dillip Lachgar is the president and majority shareholder of Argon Inc., a small retail chain store. Recently, Dillip submitted a loan application for Argon Inc. to Compound Bank. It called for a $600,000, 9%, 10-year loan to help finance the construction of a building and the purchase of store equipment, costing a total of $750,000. This will enable Argon Inc. to open a store in the town of Compound. Land for this purpose was acquired last year. The bank's loan officer requested a statement of cash flows in addition to the most recent income statement, balance sheet, and retained earnings statement that Dillip had submitted with the loan application.

As a close family friend, Dillip asked you to prepare a statement of cash flows. From the records provided, you prepared the following statement:

(Continued)

Argon Inc.
Statement of Cash Flows
For the Year Ended December 31, 20Y7

Cash flows from (used for) operating activities:		
Net income	$ 300,000	
Adjustments to reconcile net income to net cash flows from (used for) operating activities:		
Depreciation	84,000	
Gain on sale of investments	(30,000)	
Changes in current operating assets and liabilities:		
Decrease in accounts receivable	21,000	
Increase in inventories	(42,000)	
Increase in accounts payable	30,000	
Decrease in accrued expenses payable	(6,000)	
Net cash flows from operating activities		$ 357,000
Cash flows from (used for) investing activities:		
Cash from investments sold	$ 180,000	
Cash paid for purchase of store equipment	(120,000)	
Net cash flows from investing activities		60,000
Cash flows from (used for) financing activities:		
Cash dividends	$ (126,000)	
Net cash flows used for financing activities		(126,000)
Net increase in cash		$ 291,000
Cash balance, January 1, 20Y7		108,000
Cash balance, December 31, 20Y7		$ 399,000
Schedule of Noncash Financing and Investing Activities:		
Issued common stock for land		$ 240,000

After reviewing the statement, Dillip telephoned you and commented, "Are you sure this statement is right?" Dillip then raised the following questions:

1. How can depreciation be a cash flow?
2. Issuing common stock for the land is listed in a separate schedule. This transaction has nothing to do with cash! Shouldn't this transaction be eliminated from the statement?
3. How can the gain on the sale of investments be a deduction from net income in determining the cash flow from operating activities?
4. Why does the bank need this statement anyway? It can compute the increase in cash from the balance sheets for the last two years.

After jotting down Dillip's questions, you assured him that this statement was "right." But to alleviate Dillip's concern, you arranged a meeting for the following day.

a. How would you respond to each of Dillip's questions?

b. Do you think that the statement of cash flows enhances the chances of Argon Inc. receiving the loan? Discuss.

CP 16-6 Team Activity

This activity will require two teams to retrieve cash flow statement information from the Internet. One team is to obtain the most recent year's statement of cash flows for **Johnson & Johnson**; the other team, the most recent year's statement of cash flows for **JetBlue Airways Corp.**

The statement of cash flows is included as part of the annual report information that is a required disclosure to the Securities and Exchange Commission (SEC). SEC documents can be retrieved using the EdgarScan™ service at www.sec.gov/edgar/searchedgar/companysearch.html.

To obtain annual report information, key a company name in the appropriate space. EdgarScan will list the reports available to you for the company you've selected. Select the most recent annual report filing, identified as a 10-K or 10-K405. EdgarScan provides an outline of the report, including the separate financial statements.

As a group, compare the two statements of cash flows.

a. How are Johnson & Johnson and JetBlue Airways Corp. similar or different regarding cash flows?

b. Compute and compare the free cash flow for each company, assuming that additions to property, plant, and equipment replace current capacity.

CHAPTER 17

Financial Statement Analysis

RETAINED EARNINGS STATEMENT
For the Year Ended December 31, 20Y6

Retained earnings, Jan. 1, 20Y6		$XXX
Net income	$ XXX	
Dividends	(XXX)	
Increase in retained earnings		XXX
Retained earnings, Dec. 31, 20Y6		$XXX

STATEMENT OF CASH FLOWS
For the Year Ended December 31, 20Y6

Cash flows from (used for) operating activities	$XXX
Cash flows from (used for) investing activities	XXX
Cash flows from (used for) financing activities	XXX
Net increase (decrease) in cash	$XXX
Cash balance, January 1, 20Y6	XXX

INCOME STATEMENT
For the Year Ended December 31, 20Y6

Sales		$XXX
Cost of merchandise sold		XXX
Gross profit		$XXX
Operating expenses:		
Advertising expense	$XXX	
Depreciation expense	XXX	
Amortization expense	XXX	
Depletion expense	XXX	
…	XXX	
…	XXX	
Total operating expenses		XXX
Income from operations		$XXX
Other revenue and expenses		XXX
Net income		$XXX

BALANCE SHEET
December 31, 20Y6

Current assets:		
Cash	$XXX	
Accounts receivable	XXX	
Inventory	XXX	
Total current assets		$XXX
Long-term assets:		
Fixed assets	$XXX	
Intangible assets	XXX	
Total long-term assets		XXX
Total assets		$XXX
Liabilities:		
Current liabilities	$XXX	
Long-term liabilities	XXX	
Total liabilities		$XXX
Stockholders' equity		XXX
Total liabilities and stockholders' equity		$XXX

CHAPTER

17

JOSHUA RAINEY PHOTOGRAPHY/SHUTTERSTOCK.COM

Nike, Inc.

"Just do it." These three words identify one of the most recognizable brands in the world, **Nike**. While this phrase inspires athletes to "compete and achieve their potential," it also defines the company.

Nike began in 1964 as a partnership between University of Oregon track coach Bill Bowerman and one of his former student-athletes, Phil Knight. The two began by selling shoes imported from Japan out of the back of Knight's car to athletes at track-and-field events. As sales grew, the company opened retail outlets, calling itself **Blue Ribbon Sports**. The company also began to develop its own shoes. In 1971, the company commissioned a graphic design student at Portland State University to develop the swoosh logo for a fee of $35. In 1978, the company changed its name to Nike, and in 1980, it sold its first shares of stock to the public.

Nike would have been a great company to invest in at the time. If you had invested in Nike's common stock back in 1990, you would have paid $5 per share. As of June 2019, Nike's stock was worth over $83 per share. Unfortunately, you can't invest using hindsight.

How can you select companies in which to invest? Like any significant purchase, you should do some research to guide your investment decision. If you were buying a car, for example, you might go to **Edmunds.com** to obtain reviews, ratings, prices, specifications, options, and fuel economies to evaluate different vehicles. In selecting companies in which to invest, you can use financial analysis to gain insight into a company's past performance and future prospects. This chapter describes and illustrates common financial data that can be analyzed to assist you in making investment decisions such as whether or not to invest in Nike's stock.

Source: http://news.nike.com

Link to Nike..........Pages 826, 827, 829, 830, 834, 836, 837, 840, 843, 845

LEARNING OBJECTIVES

After studying this chapter, you should be able to:

Example Exercises (EE) are shown in **red.**

OBJ. 1 **Describe the techniques and tools used to analyze financial statement information.**

Analyzing and Interpreting Financial Statements
The Value of Financial Statement Information
Techniques for Analyzing Financial Statements

OBJ. 2 **Describe and illustrate basic financial statement analytical methods.**

Basic Analytical Methods
Horizontal Analysis EE **17-1**
Vertical Analysis EE **17-2**
Common-Sized Statements

OBJ. 3 **Describe and illustrate how to use financial statement analysis to assess liquidity.**

Analyzing Liquidity
Current Position Analysis EE **17-3**
Accounts Receivable Analysis EE **17-4**
Inventory Analysis EE **17-5**

OBJ. 4 **Describe and illustrate how to use financial statement analysis to assess solvency.**

Analyzing Solvency
Ratio of Fixed Assets to Long-Term Liabilities
Ratio of Liabilities to Stockholders' Equity EE **17-6**
Times Interest Earned EE **17-7**

OBJ. 5 **Describe and illustrate how to use financial statement analysis to assess profitability.**

Analyzing Profitability
Asset Turnover EE **17-8**
Return on Total Assets EE **17-9**
Return on Stockholders' Equity
Return on Common Stockholders' Equity EE **17-10**
Earnings per Share on Common Stock
Price-Earnings Ratio EE **17-11**
Dividends per Share
Dividend Yield
Summary of Analytical Measures

OBJ. 6 **Describe the contents of corporate annual reports.**

Corporate Annual Reports
Management Discussion and Analysis
Report on Internal Control
Report on Fairness of the Financial Statements

APP. OBJ. **Define and describe the reporting of unusual items on the income statement.**

At a Glance 17 Page 850

Analyzing and Interpreting Financial Statements

OBJ. 1 Describe the techniques and tools used to analyze financial statement information.

The objective of accounting is to provide relevant and timely information to support the decision-making needs of financial statement users. Bankers, creditors, and investors all rely on financial statements to provide insight into a company's financial condition and performance. This chapter discusses the value of financial statement information, techniques used to evaluate financial statements, and how this information can be used in decision making.

The Value of Financial Statement Information

General-purpose financial statements are distributed to a wide range of potential users, providing each group with valuable information about a company's economic performance and financial condition. Users typically evaluate this information along three dimensions: liquidity, solvency, and profitability.

Liquidity Short-term creditors such as banks and financial institutions are concerned primarily with whether a company will be able to repay short-term borrowings such as loans and notes. As such, they are most interested in evaluating a company's ability to convert assets into cash, which is called **liquidity**.

Solvency Long-term creditors such as bondholders loan money for long periods of time. Thus, they are interested in evaluating a company's ability to make its periodic interest payments and repay the face amount of debt at maturity, which is called **solvency**.

Profitability Investors such as stockholders are the owners of the company. They benefit from increases in the price of a company's shares and are interested in evaluating the potential for the price of the company's stock to increase. The price of a company's stock depends on a variety of factors, including the company's current and potential future earnings. As such, investors focus on evaluating a company's ability to generate earnings, which is called **profitability**.

Techniques for Analyzing Financial Statements

Financial statement users rely on the following techniques to analyze and interpret a company's financial performance and condition:

- **Analytical methods** examine changes in the amount and percentage of financial statement items within and across periods.
- **Ratios** express a financial statement item or set of financial statement items as a percentage of another financial statement item in order to measure an important economic relationship as a single number.

Both analytical methods and ratios can be used to compare a company's financial performance over time or to another company.

- *Comparisons over Time:* The comparison of a financial statement item or ratio with the same item or ratio from a prior period often helps the user identify trends in a company's economic performance, financial condition, liquidity, solvency, and profitability.
- *Comparisons Between Companies:* The comparison of a financial statement item or ratio to another company in the same industry can provide insight into a company's economic performance and financial condition relative to its competitors.

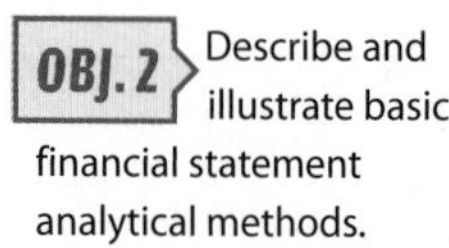

Describe and illustrate basic financial statement analytical methods.

Basic Analytical Methods

Users analyze a company's financial statements using a variety of analytical methods. Three such methods are:

- Horizontal analysis
- Vertical analysis
- Common-sized statements

Horizontal Analysis

The analysis of increases and decreases in the amount and percentage of comparative financial statement items is called **horizontal analysis**. Each item on the most recent statement is compared with the same item on one or more earlier statements in terms of the following:

- *Amount* of increase or decrease
- *Percent* of increase or decrease

When comparing statements, the earlier statement is normally used as the base year for computing increases and decreases.

Exhibit 1 illustrates horizontal analysis for the December 31, 20Y6 and 20Y5 balance sheets of **Lincoln Company**. In Exhibit 1, the December 31, 20Y5, balance sheet (the earliest year presented) is used as the base year.

EXHIBIT 1

Comparative Balance Sheet—Horizontal Analysis

Lincoln Company
Comparative Balance Sheet
December 31, 20Y6 and 20Y5

	Dec. 31, 20Y6	Dec. 31, 20Y5	Increase (Decrease) Amount	Increase (Decrease) Percent
Assets				
Current assets	$ 550,000	$ 533,000	$ 17,000	3.2%
Long-term investments	95,000	177,500	(82,500)	(46.5%)
Property, plant, and equipment (net)	444,500	470,000	(25,500)	(5.4%)
Intangible assets	50,000	50,000	—	—
Total assets	$1,139,500	$1,230,500	$ (91,000)	(7.4%)
Liabilities				
Current liabilities	$ 210,000	$ 243,000	$ (33,000)	(13.6%)
Long-term liabilities	100,000	200,000	(100,000)	(50.0%)
Total liabilities	$ 310,000	$ 443,000	$(133,000)	(30.0%)
Stockholders' Equity				
Preferred 6% stock, $100 par	$ 150,000	$ 150,000	$ —	—
Common stock, $10 par	500,000	500,000	—	—
Retained earnings	179,500	137,500	42,000	30.5%
Total stockholders' equity	$ 829,500	$ 787,500	$ 42,000	5.3%
Total liabilities and stockholders' equity	$1,139,500	$1,230,500	$ (91,000)	(7.4%)

Exhibit 1 indicates that total assets decreased by $91,000 (7.4%), liabilities decreased by $133,000 (30.0%), and stockholders' equity increased by $42,000 (5.3%). Since the long-term investments account decreased by $82,500, it appears that most of the decrease in long-term liabilities of $100,000 was achieved through the sale of long-term investments.

The balance sheets in Exhibit 1 may be expanded or supported by a separate schedule that includes the individual asset and liability accounts. For example, Exhibit 2 is a supporting schedule of Lincoln Company's current asset accounts.

EXHIBIT 2

Comparative Schedule of Current Assets—Horizontal Analysis

Lincoln Company
Comparative Schedule of Current Assets
December 31, 20Y6 and 20Y5

	Dec. 31, 20Y6	Dec. 31, 20Y5	Increase (Decrease) Amount	Increase (Decrease) Percent
Cash	$ 90,500	$ 64,700	$ 25,800	39.9%
Temporary investments	75,000	60,000	15,000	25.0%
Accounts receivable, net	115,000	120,000	(5,000)	(4.2%)
Inventories	264,000	283,000	(19,000)	(6.7%)
Prepaid expenses	5,500	5,300	200	3.8%
Total current assets	$550,000	$533,000	$ 17,000	3.2%

Exhibit 2 indicates that while cash and temporary investments increased, accounts receivable and inventories decreased. The decrease in accounts receivable could be caused by improved collection policies, which would increase cash. The decrease in inventories could be caused by increased sales.

Exhibit 3 illustrates horizontal analysis for the 20Y6 and 20Y5 income statements of Lincoln Company. Exhibit 3 indicates an increase in sales of $298,000, or 24.8%.

EXHIBIT 3

Comparative Income Statement—Horizontal Analysis

Lincoln Company
Comparative Income Statement
For the Years Ended December 31, 20Y6 and 20Y5

			Increase (Decrease)	
	20Y6	**20Y5**	**Amount**	**Percent**
Sales	$1,498,000	$1,200,000	$298,000	24.8%
Cost of merchandise sold	1,043,000	820,000	223,000	27.2%
Gross profit	$ 455,000	$ 380,000	$ 75,000	19.7%
Selling expenses	$ 191,000	$ 147,000	$ 44,000	29.9%
Administrative expenses	104,000	97,400	6,600	6.8%
Total operating expenses	$ 295,000	$ 244,400	$ 50,600	20.7%
Income from operations	$ 160,000	$ 135,600	$ 24,400	18.0%
Other revenue and expense:				
Other revenue	8,500	11,000	(2,500)	(22.7%)
Other expense (interest)	(6,000)	(12,000)	(6,000)	(50.0%)
Income before income tax expense	$ 162,500	$ 134,600	$ 27,900	20.7%
Income tax expense	71,500	58,100	13,400	23.1%
Net income	$ 91,000	$ 76,500	$ 14,500	19.0%

However, the percentage increase in sales of 24.8% was accompanied by an even greater percentage increase in the cost of merchandise sold of 27.2%. Thus, gross profit increased by only 19.7% compared to the 24.8% increase in sales.

Exhibit 3 also indicates that selling expenses increased by 29.9%. Thus, the 24.8% increase in sales could have been caused by an advertising campaign, which increased selling expenses. Administrative expenses increased by only 6.8%, total operating expenses increased by 20.7%, and income from operations increased by 18.0%. Interest expense decreased by 50.0%. This decrease was probably caused by the 50.0% decrease in long-term liabilities (Exhibit 1). Overall, net income increased by 19.0%, a favorable result.

Exhibit 4 illustrates horizontal analysis for the 20Y6 and 20Y5 retained earnings statements of **Lincoln Company**. Exhibit 4 indicates that retained earnings increased by 30.5% for the year. The increase is due to net income of $91,000 for the year, less dividends of $49,000.

Link to Nike

For a recent year, **Nike**'s net income decreased by 54.4%.

EXHIBIT 4

Comparative Retained Earnings Statement—Horizontal Analysis

Lincoln Company
Comparative Retained Earnings Statement
For the Years Ended December 31, 20Y6 and 20Y5

			Increase (Decrease)	
	20Y6	**20Y5**	**Amount**	**Percent**
Retained earnings, January 1	$137,500	$100,000	$37,500	37.5%
Net income	91,000	76,500	14,500	19.0%
Dividends:				
Preferred stock dividends	(9,000)	(9,000)	—	—
Common stock dividends	(40,000)	(30,000)	10,000	33.3%
Retained earnings, December 31	$179,500	$137,500	$42,000	30.5%

EXAMPLE EXERCISE 17-1 Horizontal Analysis

OBJ. 2

The comparative cash and accounts receivable balances for a company follow:

	Dec. 31, Current Year	Dec. 31, Prior Year
Cash	$62,500	$50,000
Accounts receivable (net)	74,400	80,000

Based on this information, what is the amount and percentage of increase or decrease that would be shown on a balance sheet with horizontal analysis?

Follow My Example 17-1

Cash	$12,500 increase ($62,500 – $50,000), or 25%
Accounts receivable	$5,600 decrease ($74,400 – $80,000), or (7%)

Practice Exercises: PE 17-1A, PE 17-1B

Vertical Analysis

The percentage analysis of the relationship of each component in a financial statement to a total within the statement is called **vertical analysis**. Although vertical analysis is applied to a single statement, it may be applied on the same statement over time. This enhances the analysis by showing how the percentages of each item have changed over time.

In vertical analysis of the balance sheet, the percentages are computed as follows:

- Each asset item is stated as a percent of the total assets.
- Each liability and stockholders' equity item is stated as a percent of the total liabilities and stockholders' equity.

Exhibit 5 illustrates the vertical analysis of the December 31, 20Y6 and 20Y5 balance sheets of **Lincoln Company**. Exhibit 5 indicates that current assets have increased from 43.3% to 48.3% of total assets. Long-term investments decreased from 14.4% to 8.3% of total assets. Stockholders' equity increased from 64.0% to 72.8%, with a comparable decrease in liabilities.

Link to Nike

For a recent year, **Nike**'s current assets were 67.2% of total assets.

EXHIBIT 5

Comparative Balance Sheet—Vertical Analysis

Lincoln Company
Comparative Balance Sheet
December 31, 20Y6 and 20Y5

	Dec. 31, 20Y6		Dec. 31, 20Y5	
	Amount	**Percent**	**Amount**	**Percent**
Assets				
Current assets	$ 550,000	48.3%	$ 533,000	43.3%
Long-term investments	95,000	8.3	177,500	14.4
Property, plant, and equipment (net)	444,500	39.0	470,000	38.2
Intangible assets	50,000	4.4	50,000	4.1
Total assets	$1,139,500	100.0%	$1,230,500	100.0%
Liabilities				
Current liabilities	$ 210,000	18.4%	$ 243,000	19.7%
Long-term liabilities	100,000	8.8	200,000	16.3
Total liabilities	$ 310,000	27.2%	$ 443,000	36.0%
Stockholders' Equity				
Preferred 6% stock, $100 par	$ 150,000	13.2%	$ 150,000	12.2%
Common stock, $10 par	500,000	43.9	500,000	40.6
Retained earnings	179,500	15.7	137,500	11.2
Total stockholders' equity	$ 829,500	72.8%	$ 787,500	64.0%
Total liabilities and stockholders' equity	$1,139,500	100.0%	$1,230,500	100.0%

In a vertical analysis of the income statement, each item is stated as a percent of sales. Exhibit 6 illustrates the vertical analysis of the 20Y6 and 20Y5 income statements of Lincoln Company.

EXHIBIT 6

Comparative Income Statement—Vertical Analysis

Lincoln Company
Comparative Income Statement
For the Years Ended December 31, 20Y6 and 20Y5

	20Y6		20Y5	
	Amount	Percent	Amount	Percent
Sales	$1,498,000	100.0%	$1,200,000	100.0%
Cost of merchandise sold	1,043,000	69.6	820,000	68.3
Gross profit	$ 455,000	30.4%	$ 380,000	31.7%
Selling expenses	$ 191,000	12.8%	$ 147,000	12.3%
Administrative expenses	104,000	6.9	97,400	8.1
Total operating expenses	$ 295,000	19.7%	$ 244,400	20.4%
Income from operations	$ 160,000	10.7%	$ 135,600	11.3%
Other revenue and expense:				
Other revenue	8,500	0.6	11,000	0.9
Other expense (interest)	(6,000)	(0.4)	(12,000)	(1.0)
Income before income tax expense	$ 162,500	10.9%	$ 134,600	11.2%
Income tax expense	71,500	4.8	58,100	4.8
Net income	$ 91,000	6.1%	$ 76,500	6.4%

Exhibit 6 indicates a decrease in the gross profit rate from 31.7% in 20Y5 to 30.4% in 20Y6. Although this is only a 1.3 percentage point (31.7% – 30.4%) decrease, in dollars of potential gross profit, it represents a decrease of $19,474 (1.3% × $1,498,000) based on 20Y6 sales. Thus, a small percentage decrease can have a large dollar effect.

EXAMPLE EXERCISE 17-2 Vertical Analysis **OBJ. 2**

Income statement information for Lee Corporation follows:

Sales	$100,000
Cost of merchandise sold	65,000
Gross profit	$ 35,000

Prepare a vertical analysis of the income statement for Lee Corporation.

Follow My Example 17-2

	Amount	Percentage	
Sales	$100,000	100%	($100,000 ÷ $100,000)
Cost of merchandise sold	65,000	65	($65,000 ÷ $100,000)
Gross profit	$ 35,000	35%	($35,000 ÷ $100,000)

Practice Exercises: PE 17-2A, PE 17-2B

Common-Sized Statements

In a **common-sized statement**, all items are expressed as percentages, with no dollar amounts shown. Common-sized statements are often useful for comparing one company with another or for comparing a company with industry averages.

Exhibit 7 illustrates common-sized income statements for **Lincoln Company** and Madison Corporation. Exhibit 7 indicates that Lincoln has a slightly higher gross profit percentage (30.4%) than Madison (30.0%). However, Lincoln has a higher percentage of selling expenses (12.8%) and administrative expenses (6.9%) than does Madison (11.5% and 4.1%, respectively). As a result, the income from operations as a percentage of sales of Lincoln (10.7%) is less than that of Madison (14.4%).

EXHIBIT 7

Common-Sized Income Statements

	Lincoln Company	Madison Corporation
Sales	100.0%	100.0%
Cost of merchandise sold	69.6	70.0
Gross profit	30.4%	30.0%
Selling expenses	12.8%	11.5%
Administrative expenses	6.9	4.1
Total operating expenses	19.7%	15.6%
Income from operations	10.7%	14.4%
Other revenue and expense:		
Other revenue	0.6	0.6
Other expense (interest)	(0.4)	(0.5)
Income before income tax expense	10.9%	14.5%
Income tax expense	4.8	5.5
Net income	6.1%	9.0%

The unfavorable difference of 3.7 (14.4% – 10.7%) percentage points in income from operations would concern the managers and other stakeholders of Lincoln. The underlying causes of the difference should be investigated and possibly corrected. For example, Lincoln may decide to outsource some of its administrative duties so that its administrative expenses are more comparative to that of Madison.

Link to Nike

For a recent year, **Nike**'s net income was 5.3% of sales.

Analyzing Liquidity

OBJ. 3 Describe and illustrate how to use financial statement analysis to assess liquidity.

Liquidity analysis evaluates the ability of a company to convert current assets into cash. Banks and other short-term creditors rely heavily on liquidity analysis, because they are interested in evaluating a company's ability to repay loans and short-term notes. Exhibit 8 shows three categories of measures used to evaluate a company's liquidity. These ratios and measures focus upon a company's current position (current assets and liabilities), accounts receivable, and inventory.

EXHIBIT 8

Liquidity Ratios and Measures

Current Position Analysis	Accounts Receivable Analysis	Inventory Analysis
Working Capital	Accounts Receivable Turnover	Inventory Turnover
Current Ratio	Number of Days' Sales in Receivables	Number of Days' Sales in Inventory
Quick Ratio		

Current Position Analysis

Current position analysis evaluates a company's ability to pay its current liabilities. This information helps short-term creditors determine how quickly they will be repaid. This analysis includes:

- Working capital
- Current ratio
- Quick ratio

Working Capital A company's **working capital** is computed as follows:

Working Capital = Current Assets − Current Liabilities

To illustrate, the working capital for **Lincoln Company** for 20Y6 and 20Y5 is computed as follows:

	20Y6	20Y5
Current assets	$550,000	$533,000
Less current liabilities	210,000	243,000
Working capital	$340,000	$290,000

The working capital is used to evaluate a company's ability to pay current liabilities. A company's working capital is often monitored monthly, quarterly, or yearly by creditors and other debtors. However, it is difficult to use working capital to compare companies of different sizes. For example, working capital of $250,000 may be adequate for a local sporting goods store, but it would be inadequate for **Nike**.

Current Ratio The **current ratio**, sometimes called the *working capital ratio*, is computed as follows:

$$\text{Current Ratio} = \frac{\text{Current Assets}}{\text{Current Liabilities}}$$

To illustrate, the current ratio for **Lincoln Company** is computed as follows:

	20Y6	20Y5
Current assets	$550,000	$533,000
Current liabilities	$210,000	$243,000
Current ratio	2.6 ($550,000 ÷ $210,000)	2.2 ($533,000 ÷ $243,000)

> **Link to Nike**
>
> For a recent five-year period, **Nike**'s average current ratio was 2.7.

The current ratio is a more reliable indicator of a company's ability to pay its current liabilities than is working capital, and it is much easier to compare across companies. To illustrate, assume that as of December 31, 20Y6, the working capital of a competitor is much greater than Lincoln's $340,000, but its current ratio is only 1.3. Considering these facts alone, Lincoln is in a more favorable position to obtain short-term credit than the competitor because it has a higher current ratio.

Quick Ratio One limitation of working capital and the current ratio is that they do not consider the types of current assets a company has and how easily they can be turned into cash. Because of this, two companies may have the same working capital and current ratios but differ significantly in their ability to pay their current liabilities.

To illustrate, the current assets and liabilities for Lincoln Company and Jefferson Company as of December 31, 20Y6, are as follows:

	Lincoln Company	Jefferson Company
Current assets:		
Cash	$ 90,500	$ 45,500
Temporary investments	75,000	25,000
Accounts receivable (net)	115,000	90,000
Inventories	264,000	380,000
Prepaid expenses	5,500	9,500
Total current assets	$550,000	$550,000
Current assets	$550,000	$550,000
Current liabilities	210,000	210,000
Working capital	$340,000	$340,000
Current ratio (Current assets ÷ Current liabilities)	2.6	2.6

Lincoln and Jefferson both have a working capital of $340,000 and current ratios of 2.6. Jefferson, however, has more of its current assets in inventories. These inventories must be sold and the receivables collected before all the current liabilities can be paid. This takes time. In addition, if the market for its product declines, Jefferson may have difficulty selling its inventory. This, in turn, could impair its ability to pay its current liabilities.

In contrast, Lincoln's current assets contain more cash, temporary investments, and accounts receivable, which can easily be converted to cash. Thus, Lincoln is in a stronger current position than Jefferson to pay its current liabilities.

A ratio that captures this difference and measures the "instant" debt-paying ability of a company is the **quick ratio**, sometimes called the *acid-test ratio*. The quick ratio is computed as follows:

$$\text{Quick Ratio} = \frac{\text{Quick Assets}}{\text{Current Liabilities}}$$

Quick assets are cash and other current assets that can be easily converted to cash. Quick assets normally include cash, temporary investments, and receivables but exclude inventories and prepaid assets.

To illustrate, the quick ratios for Lincoln Company and Jefferson Company are computed as follows:

	Lincoln Company	Jefferson Company
Quick assets:		
Cash	$ 90,500	$ 45,500
Temporary investments	75,000	25,000
Accounts receivable (net)	115,000	90,000
Total quick assets	$280,500	$160,500
Current liabilities	$210,000	$210,000
Quick ratio	1.3 ($280,500 ÷ $210,000)	0.8 ($160,500 ÷ $210,000)

EXAMPLE EXERCISE 17-3 Current Position Analysis

OBJ. 3

The following items are reported on a company's balance sheet:

Cash	$300,000
Temporary investments	100,000
Accounts receivable (net)	200,000
Inventory	200,000
Accounts payable	400,000

Determine (a) the current ratio and (b) the quick ratio. Round to one decimal place.

(Continued)

Follow My Example 17-3

a. Current Ratio = Current Assets ÷ Current Liabilities
= ($300,000 + $100,000 + $200,000 + $200,000) ÷ $400,000
= 2.0

b. Quick Ratio = Quick Assets ÷ Current Liabilities
= ($300,000 + $100,000 + $200,000) ÷ $400,000
= 1.5

Practice Exercises: PE 17-3A, PE 17-3B

Accounts Receivable Analysis

A company's ability to collect its accounts receivable is called **accounts receivable analysis**. It includes the computation and analysis of the following:

- Accounts receivable turnover
- Number of days' sales in receivables

Collecting accounts receivable as quickly as possible improves a company's liquidity. In addition, the cash collected from receivables may be used to improve or expand operations. Quick collection of receivables also reduces the risk of uncollectible accounts.

Accounts Receivable Turnover The **accounts receivable turnover** is computed as follows:

$$\text{Accounts Receivable Turnover} = \frac{\text{Sales}^1}{\text{Average Accounts Receivable}}$$

To illustrate, the accounts receivable turnover for Lincoln Company for 20Y6 and 20Y5 is computed as follows. Lincoln's accounts receivable balance at the beginning of 20Y5 is $140,000.

	20Y6	20Y5
Sales	$1,498,000	$1,200,000
Accounts receivable (net):		
Beginning of year	$ 120,000	$ 140,000
End of year	115,000	120,000
Total	$ 235,000	$ 260,000
Average accounts receivable	$117,500 ($235,000 ÷ 2)	$130,000 ($260,000 ÷ 2)
Accounts receivable turnover	12.7 ($1,498,000 ÷ $117,500)	9.2 ($1,200,000 ÷ $130,000)

The increase in Lincoln's accounts receivable turnover from 9.2 to 12.7 indicates that the collection of receivables has improved during 20Y6. This may be due to a change in how credit is granted, collection practices, or both.

For Lincoln, the average accounts receivable was computed using the accounts receivable balance at the beginning and end of the year. When sales are seasonal and, thus, vary throughout the year, monthly balances of receivables are often used. Also, if sales on account include notes receivable as well as accounts receivable, notes and accounts receivable are normally combined for analysis.

1 If known, *credit* sales should be used in the numerator. Because credit sales are not normally known by external users, we use sales in the numerator.

Number of Days' Sales in Receivables The **number of days' sales in receivables** is computed as follows:

$$\text{Number of Days' Sales in Receivables} = \frac{\text{Average Accounts Receivable}}{\text{Average Daily Sales}}$$

where

$$\text{Average Daily Sales} = \frac{\text{Sales}}{\text{365 days}}$$

To illustrate, the number of days' sales in receivables for **Lincoln Company** is computed as follows:

	20Y6	20Y5
Average accounts receivable	\$117,500 (\$235,000 ÷ 2)	\$130,000 (\$260,000 ÷ 2)
Average daily sales	\$4,104 (\$1,498,000 ÷ 365)	\$3,288 (\$1,200,000 ÷ 365)
Number of days' sales in receivables	28.6 (\$117,500 ÷ \$4,104)	39.5 (\$130,000 ÷ \$3,288)

The number of days' sales in receivables is an estimate of the time (in days) that the accounts receivable have been outstanding. The number of days' sales in receivables is often compared with a company's credit terms to evaluate the efficiency of the collection of receivables.

To illustrate, if Lincoln's credit terms are 2/10, n/30, then Lincoln was very *inefficient* in collecting receivables in 20Y5. In other words, receivables should have been collected in 30 days or less but were being collected in 39.5 days. Although collections improved during 20Y6 to 28.6 days, there is probably still room for improvement. On the other hand, if Lincoln's credit terms are n/45, then there is probably little room for improving collections.

EXAMPLE EXERCISE 17-4 Accounts Receivable Analysis **OBJ. 3**

A company reports the following:

Sales	\$960,000
Average accounts receivable (net)	48,000

Determine (a) the accounts receivable turnover and (b) the number of days' sales in receivables. Round to one decimal place.

Follow My Example 17-4

a. Accounts Receivable Turnover = Sales ÷ Average Accounts Receivable
= \$960,000 ÷ \$48,000
= 20.0

b. Number of Days' Sales in Receivables = Average Accounts Receivable ÷ Average Daily Sales
= \$48,000 ÷ (\$960,000 ÷ 365) = \$48,000 ÷ \$2,630
= 18.3 days

Practice Exercises: PE 17-4A, PE 17-4B

Inventory Analysis

A company's ability to manage its merchandise inventory effectively is evaluated using **inventory analysis**. It includes the computation and analysis of the following:

- Inventory turnover
- Number of days' sales in inventory

Excess inventory decreases liquidity by tying up funds (cash) in inventory. In addition, excess inventory increases insurance expense, property taxes, storage costs, and other related expenses. These expenses further reduce funds that could be used elsewhere to improve or expand operations.

Excess inventory also increases the risk of losses because of price declines or obsolescence of the inventory. On the other hand, a company should keep enough inventory in stock so that it doesn't lose sales because of lack of inventory.

Inventory Turnover The **inventory turnover** is computed as follows:

$$\text{Inventory Turnover} = \frac{\text{Cost of Merchandise Sold}}{\text{Average Merchandise Inventory}}$$

To illustrate, the inventory turnover for Lincoln Company for 20Y6 and 20Y5 is computed as follows. Lincoln's inventory balance at the beginning of 20Y5 is $311,000.

	20Y6	20Y5
Cost of merchandise sold	$1,043,000	$820,000
Merchandise inventories:		
Beginning of year	$ 283,000	$311,000
End of year	264,000	283,000
Total	$ 547,000	$594,000
Average merchandise inventory	$273,500 ($547,000 ÷ 2)	$297,000 ($594,000 ÷ 2)
Inventory turnover	3.8 ($1,043,000 ÷ $273,500)	2.8 ($820,000 ÷ $297,000)

The increase in Lincoln's inventory turnover from 2.8 to 3.8 indicates that the management of inventory has improved in 20Y6. The inventory turnover improved because of an increase in the cost of merchandise sold, which indicates more sales and a decrease in the average inventories.

What is considered a good inventory turnover varies by type of inventory, company, and industry. For example, grocery stores have a higher inventory turnover than jewelers or furniture stores. Likewise, within a grocery store, perishable foods have a higher turnover than the soaps and cleansers.

Link to Nike

For a recent five-year period, **Nike**'s average inventory turnover was 3.9.

Number of Days' Sales in Inventory The **number of days' sales in inventory** is computed as follows:

$$\text{Number of Days' Sales in Inventory} = \frac{\text{Average Merchandise Inventory}}{\text{Average Daily Cost of Merchandise Sold}}$$

where

$$\text{Average Daily Cost of Merchandise Sold} = \frac{\text{Cost of Merchandise Sold}}{\text{365 days}}$$

To illustrate, the number of days' sales in inventory for Lincoln Company is computed as follows:

	20Y6	20Y5
Average merchandise inventory	$273,500 ($547,000 ÷ 2)	$297,000 ($594,000 ÷ 2)
Average daily cost of merchandise sold	$2,858 ($1,043,000 ÷ 365)	$2,247 ($820,000 ÷ 365)
Number of days' sales in inventory	95.7 ($273,500 ÷ $2,858)	132.2 ($297,000 ÷ $2,247)

The number of days' sales in inventory is a rough measure of the length of time it takes to purchase, sell, and replace the inventory. Lincoln's number of days' sales in inventory improved from 132.2 days to 95.7 days during 20Y6. This is a major improvement in managing inventory.

EXAMPLE EXERCISE 17-5 Inventory Analysis OBJ. 3

A company reports the following:

Cost of merchandise sold	$560,000
Average merchandise inventory	112,000

Determine (a) the inventory turnover and (b) the number of days' sales in inventory. Round to one decimal place.

Follow My Example 17-5

a. Inventory Turnover = Cost of Merchandise Sold ÷ Average Merchandise Inventory
= $560,000 ÷ $112,000
= 5.0

b. Number of Days' Sales in Inventory = Average Merchandise Inventory ÷ Average Daily Cost of Merchandise Sold
= $112,000 ÷ ($560,000 ÷ 365) = $112,000 ÷ $1,534
= 73.0 days

Practice Exercises: PE 17-5A, PE 17-5B

Business Connection

FLYING OFF THE SHELVES

Two companies with a fast inventory turnover relative to their industries are **Apple Inc.** and **Costco Wholesale Corporation**:

	Inventory Turnover	Industry	Industry Average
Apple	37.2	Technology	6.5
Costco	11.8	Retail	10.4

Apple turns over its merchandise inventory approximately every week and a half. There are two primary reasons for this performance. First, Apple does not manufacture its products, but contracts their manufacture by others. Thus, Apple has no inventory related to manufacturing. Second, the Apple Store inventory moves very quickly due to the popularity of its products. Costco is ranked number one in the retail industry for inventory turns. This is because Costco employs a club warehouse model that stocks a minimum variety of highly popular products. Products that don't sell quickly are removed from its offerings.

Analyzing Solvency

OBJ. 4 Describe and illustrate how to use financial statement analysis to assess solvency.

Solvency analysis evaluates a company's ability to pay its long-term debts. Bondholders and other long-term creditors use solvency analysis to evaluate a company's ability to (1) repay the face amount of debt at maturity and (2) make periodic interest payments. Three common solvency ratios are shown in Exhibit 9.

EXHIBIT 9
Solvency Ratios

Solvency Ratios		
Ratio of Fixed Assets to Long-Term Liabilities	Ratio of Liabilities to Stockholders' Equity	Times Interest Earned

Ratio of Fixed Assets to Long-Term Liabilities

Fixed assets are often pledged as security for long-term notes and bonds. The **ratio of fixed assets to long-term liabilities** provides a measure of how much fixed assets a company has to support its long-term debt. This measures a company's ability to repay the face amount of debt at maturity and is computed as follows:

$$\text{Ratio of Fixed Assets to Long-Term Liabilities} = \frac{\text{Fixed Assets (net)}}{\text{Long-Term Liabilities}}$$

To illustrate, the ratio of fixed assets to long-term liabilities for **Lincoln Company** is computed as follows:

	20Y6	20Y5
Fixed assets (net)	$444,500	$470,000
Long-term liabilities	$100,000	$200,000
Ratio of fixed assets to long-term liabilities	4.4 ($444,500 ÷ $100,000)	2.4 ($470,000 ÷ $200,000)

Link to Nike

For a recent year, **Nike**'s ratio of fixed assets to long-term liabilities was 1.2.

During 20Y6, Lincoln's ratio of fixed assets to long-term liabilities increased from 2.4 to 4.4. This increase was due primarily to Lincoln paying off one-half of its long-term liabilities in 20Y6.

Ratio of Liabilities to Stockholders' Equity

The **ratio of liabilities to stockholders' equity** measures how much of the company is financed by debt and equity. It is computed as follows:

$$\text{Ratio of Liabilities to Stockholders' Equity} = \frac{\text{Total Liabilities}}{\text{Total Stockholders' Equity}}$$

To illustrate, the ratio of liabilities to stockholders' equity for **Lincoln Company** is computed as follows:

	20Y6	20Y5
Total liabilities	$310,000	$443,000
Total stockholders' equity	$829,500	$787,500
Ratio of liabilities to stockholders' equity	0.4 ($310,000 ÷ $829,500)	0.6 ($443,000 ÷ $787,500)

Link to Nike

For a recent five-year period, **Nike**'s average ratio of liabilities to stockholders' equity was 0.2.

Lincoln's ratio of liabilities to stockholders' equity decreased from 0.6 to 0.4 during 20Y6. The lower ratio indicates that Lincoln's liabilities as a proportion of equity is decreasing. This is an improvement and indicates that the margin of safety for Lincoln's creditors is improving.

EXAMPLE EXERCISE 17-6 Solvency Analysis — OBJ. 4

The following information was taken from Acme Company's balance sheet:

Fixed assets (net)	$1,400,000
Long-term liabilities	400,000
Total liabilities	560,000
Total stockholders' equity	1,400,000

Determine the company's (a) ratio of fixed assets to long-term liabilities and (b) ratio of liabilities to total stockholders' equity. Round to one decimal place.

Follow My Example 17-6

a. Ratio of Fixed Assets to Long-Term Liabilities = Fixed Assets ÷ Long-Term Liabilities
= $1,400,000 ÷ $400,000
= 3.5

b. Ratio of Liabilities to Total Stockholders' Equity = Total Liabilities ÷ Total Stockholders' Equity
= $560,000 ÷ $1,400,000
= 0.4

Practice Exercises: PE 17-6A, PE 17-6B

Times Interest Earned

The **times interest earned**, sometimes called the *coverage ratio*, measures the risk that interest payments will not be made if earnings decrease. It is computed as follows:

$$\text{Times Interest Earned} = \frac{\text{Income Before Income Tax} + \text{Interest Expense}}{\text{Interest Expense}}$$

Interest expense is paid before income taxes. In other words, interest expense is deducted in determining taxable income and, thus, income tax. For this reason, income *before taxes* is used in computing the times interest earned.

The *higher* the ratio, the more likely interest payments will be paid if earnings decrease. To illustrate, the times interest earned for **Lincoln Company** is computed as follows:

	20Y6	20Y5
Income before income tax expense	$162,500	$134,600
Interest expense	6,000	12,000
Amount available to pay interest	$168,500	$146,600
Times interest earned	28.1 ($168,500 ÷ $6,000)	12.2 ($146,600 ÷ $12,000)

The times interest earned improved from 12.2 to 28.1 during 20Y6. The higher ratio indicates that the relationship between the amount of income available to pay interest and the amount of interest expense has improved. Lincoln has more than enough earnings (28 times) to make its interest payments.

Link to Nike

For a recent year, **Nike**'s times interest earned ratio was approximately three times higher than the industry average.

EXAMPLE EXERCISE 17-7 Times Interest Earned

OBJ. 4

Acme Company reports the following:

Income before income tax expense	$250,000
Interest expense	100,000

Determine the times interest earned ratio. Round to one decimal place.

Follow My Example 17-7

Times Interest Earned = (Income Before Income Tax + Interest Expense) ÷ Interest Expense
= ($250,000 + $100,000) ÷ $100,000
= 3.5

Practice Exercises: PE 17-7A, PE 17-7B

Business Connection

LIQUIDITY CRUNCH

RadioShack Corporation, an electronics retailer, filed for bankruptcy protection. Information on the company's liquidity and solvency for the three years prior to bankruptcy follow:

	20Y3	20Y2	20Y1
Liquidity measures:			
Working capital (in thousands)	$748,400	$1,003,700	$1,176,700
Current ratio	2.3	2.0	2.9
Quick ratio	0.7	1.0	1.5
Solvency measures:			
Ratio of liabilities to stockholders' equity	6.7	2.8	1.9
Ratio of fixed assets to long-term liabilities	0.2	0.3	0.3

The data show that the company's liquidity and solvency measures deteriorated in the years prior to the firm's bankruptcy. All three of the company's liquidity measures declined significantly during the three-year period, indicating a growing risk that the company would not be able to repay its current liabilities. The ratio of liabilities to stockholders' equity also increased significantly during this period, indicating that the company might not be able to repay its long-term debts. Finally, the ratio of fixed assets to long-term liabilities began to deteriorate in 20Y3, indicating that fewer assets would be available to secure the company's long-term liabilities.

OBJ. 5 Describe and illustrate how to use financial statement analysis to assess profitability.

Analyzing Profitability

Profitability analysis evaluates the ability of a company to generate future earnings. This ability depends on the relationship between the company's operating results and the assets the company has available for use in its operations. Thus, the relationships between income statement and balance sheet items are used to evaluate profitability.

Common profitability ratios are shown in Exhibit 10.

EXHIBIT 10
Profitability Ratios

Profitability Ratios		
Asset Turnover	Return on Stockholders' Equity	Price-Earnings Ratio
Return on Total Assets	Return on Common Stockholders' Equity	Dividends per Share
	Earnings per Share on Common Stock	Dividend Yield

Asset Turnover

The **asset turnover** ratio measures how effectively a company uses its assets. It is computed as follows:

$$\text{Asset Turnover} = \frac{\text{Sales}}{\text{Average Total Assets}}$$

To illustrate, the asset turnover for **Lincoln Company** is computed as follows. Total assets are $1,187,500 at the beginning of 20Y5.

	20Y6	20Y5
Sales	$1,498,000	$1,200,000
Total assets:		
Beginning of year	$1,230,500	$1,187,500
End of year	1,139,500	1,230,500
Total	$2,370,000	$2,418,000
Average total assets	$1,185,000 ($2,370,000 ÷ 2)	$1,209,000 ($2,418,000 ÷ 2)
Asset turnover	1.3 ($1,498,000 ÷ $1,185,000)	1.0 ($1,200,000 ÷ $1,209,000)

For Lincoln, the average total assets was computed using total assets at the beginning and end of the year. The average total assets could also be based on monthly or quarterly averages.

The asset turnover ratio indicates that Lincoln's use of its assets has improved in 20Y6. This was due primarily to the increase in sales in 20Y6.

EXAMPLE EXERCISE 17-8 Asset Turnover **OBJ. 5**

A company reports the following:

Sales	$2,250,000
Average total assets	1,500,000

Determine the asset turnover ratio. Round to one decimal place.

Follow My Example 17-8

Asset Turnover Ratio = Sales ÷ Average Total Assets
= $2,250,000 ÷ $1,500,000
= 1.5

Practice Exercises: PE 17-8A, PE 17-8B

Return on Total Assets

The **return on total assets** measures the profitability of total assets, without considering how the assets are financed. In other words, this rate is not affected by the portion of assets financed by creditors or stockholders. It is computed as follows:

$$\text{Return on Total Assets} = \frac{\text{Net Income} + \text{Interest Expense}}{\text{Average Total Assets}}$$

The return on total assets is computed by adding interest expense to net income. By adding interest expense to net income, the effect of whether the assets are financed by creditors (debt) or stockholders (equity) is eliminated. Because net income includes any income earned from long-term investments, the average total assets includes long-term investments as well as the net operating assets.

To illustrate, the return on total assets by **Lincoln Company** is computed as follows. Total assets are $1,187,500 at the beginning of 20Y5.

	20Y6	20Y5
Net income	$ 91,000	$ 76,500
Interest expense	6,000	12,000
	$ 97,000	$ 88,500
Total assets:		
Beginning of year	$1,230,500	$1,187,500
End of year	1,139,500	1,230,500
Total	$2,370,000	$2,418,000
Average total assets	$1,185,000 ($2,370,000 ÷ 2)	$1,209,000 ($2,418,000 ÷ 2)
Return on total assets	8.2% ($97,000 ÷ $1,185,000)	7.3% ($88,500 ÷ $1,209,000)

The return on total assets improved from 7.3% to 8.2% during 20Y6.

The *return on operating assets* is sometimes computed when there are large amounts of nonoperating income and expense. It is computed as follows:

$$\text{Return on Operating Assets} = \frac{\text{Income from Operations}}{\text{Average Operating Assets}}$$

Because Lincoln does not have a significant amount of nonoperating income and expense, the return on operating assets is not illustrated.

EXAMPLE EXERCISE 17-9 Return on Total Assets **OBJ. 5**

A company reports the following income statement and balance sheet information for the current year:

Net income	$ 125,000
Interest expense	25,000
Average total assets	2,000,000

Determine the return on total assets. Round percentage to one decimal place.

Follow My Example 17-9

Return on Total Assets = (Net Income + Interest Expense) ÷ Average Total Assets
= ($125,000 + $25,000) ÷ $2,000,000
= $150,000 ÷ $2,000,000
= 7.5%

Practice Exercises: PE 17-9A, PE 17-9B

Return on Stockholders' Equity

The **return on stockholders' equity** measures the rate of income earned on the amount invested by the stockholders. It is computed as follows:

$$\text{Return on Stockholders' Equity} = \frac{\text{Net Income}}{\text{Average Total Stockholders' Equity}}$$

To illustrate, the return on stockholders' equity for **Lincoln Company** is computed as follows. Total stockholders' equity is $750,000 at the beginning of 20Y5.

	20Y6	20Y5
Net income	$ 91,000	$ 76,500
Total stockholders' equity:		
Beginning of year	$ 787,500	$ 750,000
End of year	829,500	787,500
Total	$1,617,000	$1,537,500
Average total stockholders' equity	$808,500 ($1,617,000 ÷ 2)	$768,750 ($1,537,500 ÷ 2)
Return on stockholders' equity	11.3% ($91,000 ÷ $808,500)	10.0% ($76,500 ÷ $768,750)

Link to Nike

For a recent five-year period, **Nike**'s average return on stockholders' equity was 23.4%.

The return on stockholders' equity improved from 10.0% to 11.3% during 20Y6.

Leverage involves using debt to increase the return on an investment. The return on stockholders' equity is normally higher than the return on total assets. This is because of the effect of leverage.

For **Lincoln Company**, the effect of leverage for 20Y6 is 3.1% and for 20Y5 is 2.7%, computed as follows:

	20Y6	20Y5
Return on stockholders' equity	11.3%	10.0%
Less return on total assets	8.2	7.3
Effect of leverage	3.1%	2.7%

Exhibit 11 shows the 20Y6 and 20Y5 effects of leverage for Lincoln.

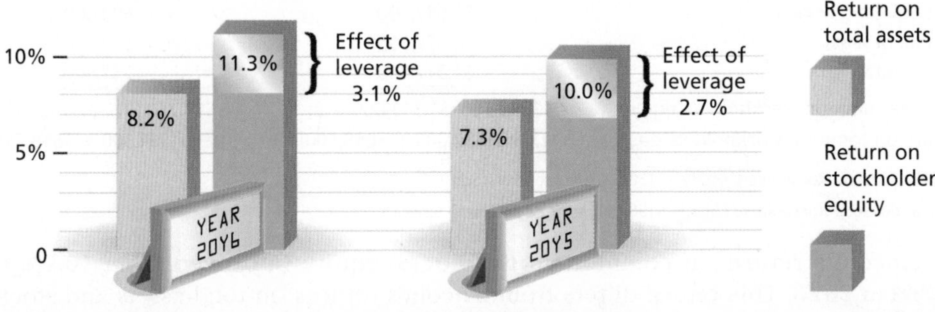

EXHIBIT 11
Effect of Leverage

Business Connection

GEARING FOR PROFIT

Another term for leverage is "financial gearing." **Exxon Mobil Corporation**, a worldwide-integrated energy company, is an example of a company that uses leverage for financial advantage. Exxon had a return on total assets of 6.02% for a recent year, while its return on stockholders' equity was 10.87%. Thus, Exxon is "geared" almost 2:1 by using debt on its balance sheet. Exxon is very profitable; thus, leverage is beneficial. In contrast, **Chesapeake Energy**, an oil and gas exploration company, had return on assets of 7.3% for a recent 12-month period and return on stockholders' equity of 187.8%. In this case, the over 25:1 leverage (187.8% ÷ 7.3%) is not a financial advantage, because its large amount of long-term debt was used to cover previous years' losses.

Return on Common Stockholders' Equity

The **return on common stockholders' equity** measures the rate of profits earned on the amount invested by the common stockholders. It is computed as follows:

$$\text{Return on Common Stockholders' Equity} = \frac{\text{Net Income} - \text{Preferred Dividends}}{\text{Average Common Stockholders' Equity}}$$

Because preferred stockholders rank ahead of the common stockholders in their claim on earnings, any preferred dividends are subtracted from net income in computing the return on common stockholders' equity.

Lincoln Company had $150,000 par value of 6% preferred stock outstanding on December 31, 20Y6 and 20Y5. Thus, preferred dividends of $9,000 ($150,000 × 6%) are deducted from net income. Lincoln's common stockholders' equity is determined as follows:

	December 31		
	20Y6	20Y5	20Y4
Common stock, $10 par	$500,000	$500,000	$500,000
Retained earnings	179,500	137,500	100,000
Common stockholders' equity	$679,500	$637,500	$600,000

The retained earnings on December 31, 20Y4, of $100,000 is the same as the retained earnings on January 1, 20Y5, as shown in Lincoln's retained earnings statement in Exhibit 4.

Using this information, the return on common stockholders' equity for Lincoln is computed as follows:

	20Y6	20Y5
Net income	$ 91,000	$ 76,500
Less preferred dividends	9,000	9,000
Total	$ 82,000	$ 67,500
Common stockholders' equity:		
Beginning of year	$ 637,500	$ 600,000
End of year	679,500*	637,500**
Total	$1,317,000	$1,237,500
Average common stockholders' equity	$658,500 ($1,317,000 ÷ 2)	$618,750 ($1,237,500 ÷ 2)
Return on common stockholders' equity	12.5% ($82,000 ÷ $658,500)	10.9% ($67,500 ÷ $618,750)

*($829,500 total stockholders' equity – $150,000 preferred 6% stock)

**($787,500 total stockholders' equity – $150,000 preferred 6% stock)

Lincoln's return on common stockholders' equity improved from 10.9% to 12.5% in 20Y6. This return differs from Lincoln's returns on total assets and stockholders' equity, which follow:

	20Y6	20Y5
Return on total assets	8.2%	7.3%
Return on stockholders' equity	11.3%	10.0%
Return on common stockholders' equity	12.5%	10.9%

These returns differ because of leverage, as discussed in the preceding section.

EXAMPLE EXERCISE 17-10 Return on Stockholders' Equity OBJ. 5

A company reports the following:

Net income	$ 125,000
Preferred dividends	5,000
Average stockholders' equity	1,000,000
Average common stockholders' equity	800,000

Determine (a) the return on stockholders' equity and (b) the return on common stockholders' equity. Round percentages to one decimal place.

Follow My Example 17-10

a. Return on Stockholders' Equity = Net Income ÷ Average Stockholders' Equity
= $125,000 ÷ $1,000,000
= 12.5%

b. Return on Common Stockholders' Equity = (Net Income – Preferred Dividends) ÷ Average Common Stockholders' Equity
= ($125,000 – $5,000) ÷ $800,000
= 15.0%

Practice Exercises: PE 17-10A, PE 17-10B

Earnings per Share on Common Stock

Earnings per share (EPS) on common stock measures the share of profits that are earned by a share of common stock. Earnings per share must be reported on the income statement. As a result, earnings per share (EPS) is often reported in the financial press. It is computed as follows:

$$\text{Earnings per Share (EPS) on Common Stock} = \frac{\text{Net Income} - \text{Preferred Dividends}}{\text{Shares of Common Stock Outstanding}}$$

When preferred and common stock are outstanding, preferred dividends are subtracted from net income to determine the income related to the common shares.

To illustrate, the earnings per share (EPS) of common stock for Lincoln Company is computed as follows:

	20Y6	20Y5
Net income	$91,000	$76,500
Less preferred dividends	9,000	9,000
Total	$82,000	$67,500
Shares of common stock outstanding	50,000	50,000
Earnings per share on common stock	$1.64 ($82,000 ÷ 50,000)	$1.35 ($67,500 ÷ 50,000)

Lincoln had $500,000 par value of $10 common stock, and $150,000 par value of 6% preferred stock outstanding on December 31, 20Y6 and 20Y5. The preferred dividends of $9,000 ($150,000 × 6%) are deducted from net income in computing earnings per share on common stock. This amount is divided by the 50,000 common shares outstanding, which is computed by dividing the $500,000 par value of the common stock by the $10 par value per share.

Lincoln did not issue any additional shares of common stock in 20Y6. If Lincoln had issued additional shares in 20Y6, a weighted average of common shares outstanding during the year would have been used.

Lincoln's earnings per share (EPS) on common stock improved from $1.35 to $1.64 during 20Y6.

Lincoln has a simple capital structure with only common stock and preferred stock outstanding. Many corporations, however, have complex capital structures with various types of equity securities outstanding, such as convertible preferred stock, stock options, and stock warrants. In such cases, the possible effects of such securities on the shares of common stock outstanding are considered in reporting earnings per share. These possible effects are reported separately as *earnings per common share assuming dilution* or *diluted earnings per share*. This topic is described and illustrated in advanced accounting courses and textbooks.

Link to Nike

On a recent income statement, **Nike** reported net income of $1,933 million.

Price-Earnings Ratio

The **price-earnings (P/E) ratio** on common stock measures a company's future earnings prospects. It is often quoted in the financial press and is computed as follows:

$$\text{Price-Earnings (P/E) Ratio} = \frac{\text{Market Price per Share of Common Stock}}{\text{Earnings per Share on Common Stock}}$$

To illustrate, the price-earnings (P/E) ratio for Lincoln Company is computed as follows:

	20Y6	20Y5
Market price per share of common stock	$41.00	$27.00
Earnings per share on common stock	$1.64	$1.35
Price-earnings ratio on common stock	25 ($41 ÷ $1.64)	20 ($27 ÷ $1.35)

The price-earnings ratio improved from 20 to 25 during 20Y6. In other words, a share of common stock of Lincoln was selling for 20 times earnings per share at the end of 20Y5. At the end of 20Y6, the common stock was selling for 25 times earnings per share. This indicates that the market expects Lincoln to experience favorable earnings in the future.

EXAMPLE EXERCISE 17-11 Earnings per Share and Price-Earnings Ratio — OBJ. 5

A company reports the following:

Net income	$250,000
Preferred dividends	$15,000
Shares of common stock outstanding	20,000
Market price per share of common stock	$35.25

a. Determine the company's earnings per share on common stock.

b. Determine the company's price-earnings ratio. Round to one decimal place.

Follow My Example 17-11

a. Earnings per Share on Common Stock = (Net Income – Preferred Dividends) ÷ Shares of Common Stock Outstanding
= ($250,000 – $15,000) ÷ 20,000
= $11.75

b. Price-Earnings Ratio = Market Price per Share of Common Stock ÷ Earnings per Share on Common Stock
= $35.25 ÷ $11.75
= 3.0

Practice Exercises: PE 17-11A, PE 17-11B

Dividends per Share

Dividends per share measures the extent to which earnings are being distributed to common shareholders. It is computed as follows:

$$\text{Dividends per Share} = \frac{\text{Dividends on Common Stock}}{\text{Shares of Common Stock Outstanding}}$$

To illustrate, the dividends per share for **Lincoln Company** are computed as follows:

	20Y6	20Y5
Dividends on common stock	$40,000	$30,000
Shares of common stock outstanding	50,000	50,000
Dividends per share of common stock	$0.80 ($40,000 ÷ 50,000)	$0.60 ($30,000 ÷ 50,000)

The dividends per share of common stock increased from $0.60 to $0.80 during 20Y6.

Dividends per share are often reported with earnings per share. Comparing the two per-share amounts indicates the extent to which earnings are being retained for use in operations. To illustrate, the dividends and earnings per share for **Lincoln Company** are shown in Exhibit 12.

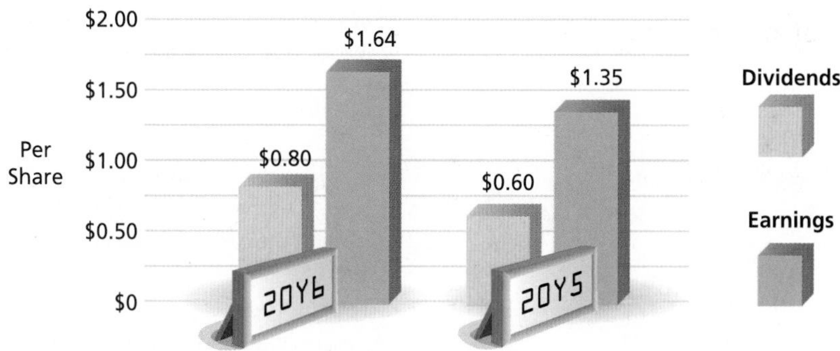

EXHIBIT 12

Dividends and Earnings per Share of Common Stock

Dividend Yield

The **dividend yield** on common stock measures the rate of return to common stockholders from cash dividends. It is of special interest to investors whose objective is to earn revenue (dividends) from their investment. It is computed as follows:

$$\text{Dividend Yield} = \frac{\text{Dividends per Share of Common Stock}}{\text{Market Price per Share of Common Stock}}$$

To illustrate, the dividend yield for **Lincoln Company** is computed as follows:

	20Y6	20Y5
Dividends per share of common stock	$0.80	$0.60
Market price per share of common stock	$41.00	$27.00
Dividend yield on common stock	2.0% ($0.80 ÷ $41)	2.2% ($0.60 ÷ $27)

The dividend yield declined slightly from 2.2% to 2.0% in 20Y6. This decline was due primarily to the increase in the market price of Lincoln's common stock.

Link to Nike

For a recent five-year period, **Nike**'s average dividend yield was 1.16%.

Business Connection

INVESTING FOR YIELD

Companies that provide attractive dividend yields are often mature companies found in stable industries. Examples of such industries are public utilities and food. **Coca-Cola**, **Procter & Gamble**, **Kellogg's**, **Consolidated Edison**, **Southern Company**, and **General Mills** all have attractive dividend yields in excess of 3%. Procter & Gamble has had 58 consecutive years of dividend payouts, and Kellogg's has not reduced its dividend for 56 years. The stability of the food industry has allowed these companies to maintain dividends for many years. Growth companies such as **Google** and **Facebook** do not pay dividends, because they use their cash to grow the business. Investors in such growth companies expect to make their return from stock price appreciation rather than dividends. Mark Cuban, billionaire, Shark Tank® investor, and owner of the **Dallas Mavericks**, stated, "I believe non-dividend stocks aren't much more than baseball cards. They are worth what you can convince someone to pay for it."

Quote source: Tim Parker, "The Top Ten Dividend Quotes," *Dividend.com*, August 29, 2012.

Summary of Analytical Measures

Exhibit 13 shows a summary of the liquidity, solvency and profitability measures discussed in this chapter. The type of industry and the company's operations usually affect which measures are used. In many cases, additional measures are used for a specific industry. For example, airlines use *revenue per passenger mile* and *cost per available seat* as profitability measures. Likewise, hotels use *occupancy rates* as a profitability measure.

EXHIBIT 13 Summary of Analytical Measures

Liquidity Measures

	Method of Computation	Use
Working Capital	Current Assets – Current Liabilities	Measures the company's ability to pay current liabilities.
Current Ratio	$\frac{\text{Current Assets}}{\text{Current Liabilities}}$	
Quick Ratio	$\frac{\text{Quick Assets}}{\text{Current Liabilities}}$	Measures the company's instant debt-paying ability.
Accounts Receivable Turnover	$\frac{\text{Sales}}{\text{Average Accounts Receivable}}$	Measures the company's efficiency in collecting receivables and in the management of credit.
Numbers of Days' Sales in Receivables	$\frac{\text{Average Accounts Receivable}}{\text{Average Daily Sales}}$	
Inventory Turnover	$\frac{\text{Cost of Merchandise Sold}}{\text{Average Merchandise Inventory}}$	Measures the company's efficiency in managing merchandise inventory.
Number of Days' Sales in Inventory	$\frac{\text{Average Merchandise Inventory}}{\text{Average Daily Cost of Merchandise Sold}}$	

Solvency Measures

	Method of Computation	Use
Ratio of Fixed Assets to Long-Term Liabilities	$\frac{\text{Fixed Assets (net)}}{\text{Long-Term Liabilities}}$	Measures the margin of safety available to long-term creditors.
Ratio of Liabilities to Stockholders' Equity	$\frac{\text{Total Liabilities}}{\text{Total Stockholders' Equity}}$	Measures how much of the company is financed by debt and equity.
Times Interest Earned	$\frac{\text{Income Before Income Tax + Interest Expense}}{\text{Interest Expense}}$	Measures the risk that interest payments will not be made if earnings decrease.

Profitability Measures

	Method of Computation	Use
Asset Turnover	$\frac{\text{Sales}}{\text{Average Total Assets}}$	Measures how effectively a company uses its assets.
Return on Total Assets	$\frac{\text{Net Income + Interest Expense}}{\text{Average Total Assets}}$	Measures the profitability of a company's assets.
Return on Stockholders' Equity	$\frac{\text{Net Income}}{\text{Average Total Stockholders' Equity}}$	Measures the profitability of the investment by stockholders.
Return on Common Stockholders' Equity	$\frac{\text{Net Income – Preferred Dividends}}{\text{Average Common Stockholders' Equity}}$	Measures the profitability of the investment by common stockholders.
Earnings per Share (EPS) on Common Stock	$\frac{\text{Net Income – Preferred Dividends}}{\text{Shares of Common Stock Outstanding}}$	
Price-Earnings (P/E) Ratio	$\frac{\text{Market Price per Share of Common Stock}}{\text{Earnings per Share on Common Stock}}$	Measures future earnings prospects, based on the relationship between market value of common stock and earnings.
Dividends per Share	$\frac{\text{Dividends on Common Stock}}{\text{Shares of Common Stock Outstanding}}$	Measures the extent to which earnings are being distributed to common stockholders.
Dividend Yield	$\frac{\text{Dividends per Share of Common Stock}}{\text{Market Price per Share of Common Stock}}$	Measures the rate of return to common stockholders in terms of dividends.

The analytical measures shown in Exhibit 13 are a useful starting point for analyzing a company's liquidity, solvency, and profitability. However, they are not a substitute for sound judgment. The general economic and business environment should always be considered in analyzing a company's future prospects. In addition, any trends and interrelationships among the measures should be studied carefully.

Corporate Annual Reports

OBJ. 6 Describe the contents of corporate annual reports.

Public corporations issue annual reports summarizing their operating activities for the past year and plans for the future. Such annual reports include the financial statements and the accompanying notes. In addition, annual reports normally include the following sections:

- Management discussion and analysis
- Report on internal control
- Report on fairness of the financial statements

Management Discussion and Analysis

Management's Discussion and Analysis (MD&A) is required in annual reports filed with the Securities and Exchange Commission. It includes management's analysis of current operations and its plans for the future. Typical items included in the MD&A are as follows:

- Management's analysis and explanations of any significant changes between the current and prior years' financial statements.
- Important accounting principles or policies that could affect interpretation of the financial statements, including the effect of changes in accounting principles or the adoption of new accounting principles.
- Management's assessment of the company's liquidity and the availability of capital to the company.
- Significant risk exposures that might affect the company.
- Any "off-balance-sheet" arrangements such as leases not included in the financial statements. Such arrangements are discussed in advanced accounting courses and textbooks.

Report on Internal Control

The Sarbanes-Oxley Act of 2002 requires a report on internal control by management. The report states management's responsibility for establishing and maintaining internal control. In addition, management's assessment of the effectiveness of internal controls over financial reporting is included in the report.

Integrity, Objectivity, and Ethics in Business

CHARACTERISTICS OF FINANCIAL STATEMENT FRAUD

Each year, the Association of Certified Fraud Examiners conducts a worldwide survey examining the characteristics of corporate fraud. The most recent study found the following:

- 50% of frauds were detected by a tip from an employee or someone close to the company.
- Frauds committed by owners and executives tended to be much larger than those caused by employees.
- Most people who are caught committing fraud are first-time offenders with clean employment histories.
- In 85% of the cases, the person committing the fraud displayed one or more behavioral red flags, such as living beyond his or her means, having financial difficulties, and having excessive control issues.

Fraud examiners can use these trends to help them narrow their focus when searching for fraud.

Source: *2018 Report to the Nations*, Association of Certified Fraud Examiners, 2018.

Sarbanes-Oxley also requires a public accounting firm to verify management's conclusions on internal control. Thus, two reports on internal control, one by management and one by a public accounting firm, are included in the annual report. In some situations, these may be combined into a single report on internal control.

Report on Fairness of the Financial Statements

All publicly held corporations are required to have an independent audit (examination) of their financial statements. The Certified Public Accounting (CPA) firm that conducts the audit renders an opinion, called the *Report of Independent Registered Public Accounting Firm*, on the fairness of the statements.

An opinion stating that the financial statements present fairly the financial position, results of operations, and cash flows of the company is said to be an *unmodified opinion*, sometimes called a *clean opinion*. Any report other than an unmodified opinion raises a red flag for financial statement users and requires further investigation as to its cause. The types and nature of audit opinions are covered in more detail in advanced courses on auditing.

The annual report of **Nike Inc.** is shown in Appendix C. The Nike report includes the financial statements as well as Management's Discussion and Analysis, Report on Internal Control, and the Report on Fairness of the Financial Statements.

APPENDIX

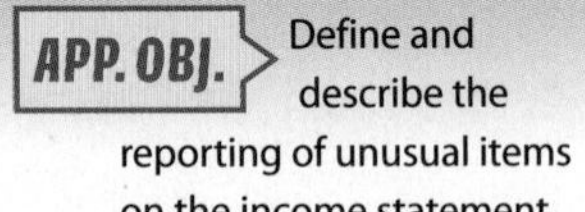

Define and describe the reporting of unusual items on the income statement.

Unusual Items on the Income Statement

Generally accepted accounting principles require that unusual items be reported separately on the income statement. These **unusual income statement items** do not occur frequently and are typically unrelated to current operations. Without separate reporting of these items, users of the financial statements might be misled about current and future operations.

Unusual items on the income statement are classified as one of the following:

- Affecting the *current period* income statement
- Affecting a *prior-period* income statement

Unusual Items Affecting the Current Period's Income Statement

Discontinued operations are an unusual item that affects the current period's:

- Income statement presentation
- Earnings per share presentation

Discontinued operations are reported separately on the income statement for any period in which they occur.

Income Statement Presentation A company may discontinue a component of its operations by selling or abandoning the component's operations. For example, a retailer might decide to sell its product only online and, thus, discontinue selling its merchandise at its retail outlets (stores).

If the discontinued component is (1) the result of a strategic shift and (2) has a major effect on the entity's operations and financial results, any gain or loss on discontinued operations is reported on the income statement as a *Gain (or loss) from discontinued operations*. It is reported immediately following *Income from continuing operations*.

To illustrate, assume that Jones Corporation produces and sells electrical products, hardware supplies, and lawn equipment. Because of a lack of profits, Jones discontinues its electrical products operation and sells the remaining inventory and other assets at a loss of $100,000. Exhibit 14 illustrates the reporting of the loss on discontinued operations.[2]

EXHIBIT 14

Unusual Items on the Income Statement

Jones Corporation **Income Statement** **For the Year Ended December 31, 20Y2**	
Sales	$12,350,000
Cost of merchandise sold	5,800,000
Gross profit	$ 6,550,000
Selling and administrative expenses	5,240,000
Income from continuing operations before income tax expense	$ 1,310,000
Income tax expense	620,000
Income from continuing operations	$ 690,000
Loss on discontinued operations	(100,000)
Net income	$ 590,000

In addition, a note to the financial statements should describe the operating component sold, including the date operations were discontinued and details about the assets, liabilities, income, and expenses of the discontinued component.

Earnings per Share Presentation Earnings per share on common stock should be reported separately for discontinued operations. To illustrate, a partial income statement for Jones Corporation is shown in Exhibit 15. The company has 200,000 shares of common stock outstanding.

EXHIBIT 15

Income Statement with Earnings per Share

Jones Corporation **Income Statement** **For the Year Ended December 31, 20Y2**	
Earnings per share:	
Income from continuing operations	$ 3.45
Loss on discontinued operations	(0.50)
Net income	$ 2.95

Exhibit 15 reports earnings per share for income from continuing operations and discontinued operations. However, only earnings per share for income from continuing operations and net income are required by generally accepted accounting principles. The other per-share amounts may be presented in the notes to the financial statements.

2 The gain or loss on discontinued operations is reported net of any tax effects. To simplify, the tax effects are not specifically identified in Exhibit 14.

Unusual Items Affecting the Prior Period's Income Statement

An unusual item may occur that affects a prior period's income statement. Two such items are as follows:

- Errors in applying generally accepted accounting principles
- Changes from one generally accepted accounting principle to another

If an error is discovered in a prior period's financial statement, the prior-period statement and all following statements are restated and thus corrected.

A company may change from one generally accepted accounting principle to another. In this case, the prior-period financial statements are restated as if the new accounting principle had always been used as discussed in Chapter 11.

For both of the preceding items, the current period earnings are not affected. That is, only the earnings reported in prior periods are restated. However, because the prior earnings are restated, the beginning balance of Retained Earnings may also have to be restated. This, in turn, may cause the restatement of other balance sheet accounts. Illustrations of these types of adjustments and restatements are provided in advanced accounting courses.

At a Glance 17

OBJ. 1 Describe the techniques and tools used to analyze financial statement information.

Key Points Financial statements provide important information that users rely on to make economic decisions. This information is evaluated along three dimensions: liquidity, solvency, and profitability. Two common techniques are used to analyze a company's financial performance and condition: analytical methods and ratios. Both analytical methods and ratios can be used to compare a company's financial performance over time or to another company.

Learning Outcome	*Example Exercises*	*Practice Exercises*
• Describe the techniques used to analyze a company's financial performance.		

OBJ. 2 Describe and illustrate basic financial statement analytical methods.

Key Points Financial statements provide much of the information users need to make economic decisions. Analytical procedures are used to compare items on a current financial statement with related items on earlier financial statements or to examine relationships within a financial statement.

Learning Outcomes	*Example Exercises*	*Practice Exercises*
• Prepare a horizontal analysis from a company's financial statements.	**EE17-1**	**PE17-1A, 17-1B**
• Prepare a vertical analysis from a company's financial statements.	**EE17-2**	**PE17-2A, 17-2B**
• Prepare a common-sized financial statement.		

OBJ. 3 Describe and illustrate how to use financial statement analysis to assess liquidity.

Key Points Liquidity analysis evaluates a company's ability to convert current assets into cash. Short-term creditors use liquidity analysis to evaluate a company's ability to repay short-term debts by focusing on a company's current position, accounts receivable, and inventory. The measures and ratios used to evaluate a company's liquidity include (1) working capital, (2) current ratio, (3) quick ratio, (4) accounts receivable turnover, (5) number of days' sales in receivables, (6) inventory turnover, and (7) number of days' sales in inventory.

Learning Outcomes	*Example Exercises*	*Practice Exercises*
• Determine working capital.		
• Compute and interpret the current ratio.		
• Compute and interpret the quick ratio.	**EE17-3**	**PE17-3A, 17-3B**
• Compute and interpret accounts receivable turnover.	**EE17-4**	**PE17-4A, 17-4B**
• Compute and interpret the number of days' sales in receivables.		
• Compute and interpret inventory turnover.		
• Compute and interpret the number of days' sales in inventory.	**EE17-5**	**PE17-5A, 17-5B**

OBJ. 4 Describe and illustrate how to use financial statement analysis to assess solvency.

Key Points Solvency analysis evaluates the ability of a company to pay its long-term debts. Long-term creditors use solvency analysis to evaluate a company's ability to make its periodic interest payments and repay the face amount of bonds at maturity. Solvency is normally assessed by examining (1) the ratio of fixed assets to long-term liabilities, (2) the ratio of liabilities to stockholders' equity, and (3) the times interest earned ratio.

Learning Outcomes	*Example Exercises*	*Practice Exercises*
• Compute and interpret the ratio of fixed assets to long-term liabilities.		
• Compute and interpret the ratio of liabilities to stockholders' equity.	**EE17-6**	**PE17-6A, 17-6B**
• Compute and interpret the times interest earned ratio.	**EE17-7**	**PE17-7A, 17-7B**

OBJ. 5 Describe and illustrate how to use financial statement analysis to assess profitability.

Key Points Profitability analysis focuses on the relationship between operating results (income statement) and assets (balance sheet). Profitability analyses include (1) the asset turnover ratio, (2) the return on total assets, (3) the return on stockholders' equity, (4) the return on common stockholders' equity, (5) earnings per share on common stock, (6) the price-earnings ratio, (7) dividends per share, and (8) dividend yield.

Learning Outcomes	*Example Exercises*	*Practice Exercises*
• Compute and interpret the asset turnover ratio.	**EE17-8**	**PE17-8A, 17-8B**
• Compute and interpret the return on total assets.	**EE17-9**	**PE17-9A, 17-9B**
• Compute and interpret the return on stockholders' equity.		
• Compute and interpret the return on common stockholders' equity.	**EE17-10**	**PE17-10A, 17-10B**
• Compute and interpret the price-earnings ratio.	**EE17-11**	**PE17-11A, 17-11B**
• Compute and interpret dividends per share and dividend yield.		
• Describe the uses and limitations of analytical measures.		

OBJ. 6 Describe the contents of corporate annual reports.

Key Points Public corporations issue annual reports summarizing their operating activities for the past year and plans for the future. In addition to the financial statements and accompanying notes, annual reports include Management's Discussion and Analysis (MD&A), a report on internal control, and a report on fairness of the financial statements.

Learning Outcome	*Example Exercises*	*Practice Exercises*
• Describe the elements of a corporate annual report.		

Illustrative Problem

Rainbow Paint Co.'s comparative financial statements for the years ending December 31, 20Y9 and 20Y8, are as follows. The market price of Rainbow Paint's common stock was $25 on December 31, 20Y9, and $30 on December 31, 20Y8.

Rainbow Paint Co.
Comparative Income Statement
For the Years Ended December 31, 20Y9 and 20Y8

	20Y9	20Y8
Sales	$5,000,000	$3,200,000
Cost of merchandise sold	3,400,000	2,080,000
Gross profit	$1,600,000	$1,120,000
Selling expenses	$ 650,000	$ 464,000
Administrative expenses	325,000	224,000
Total operating expenses	$ 975,000	$ 688,000
Income from operations	$ 625,000	$ 432,000
Other revenue and expense:		
Other revenue	25,000	19,200
Other expense (interest)	(105,000)	(64,000)
Income before income tax expense	$ 545,000	$ 387,200
Income tax expense	300,000	176,000
Net income	$ 245,000	$ 211,200

Rainbow Paint Co.
Comparative Retained Earnings Statement
For the Years Ended December 31, 20Y9 and 20Y8

	20Y9	20Y8
Retained earnings, January 1	$723,000	$581,800
Net income	245,000	211,200
Dividends:		
Preferred stock dividends	(40,000)	(40,000)
Common stock dividends	(45,000)	(30,000)
Retained earnings, December 31	$883,000	$723,000

(Continued)

Rainbow Paint Co.
Comparative Balance Sheet
December 31, 20Y9 and 20Y8

	20Y9	20Y8
Assets		
Current assets:		
Cash	$ 175,000	$ 125,000
Temporary investments	150,000	50,000
Accounts receivable (net)	425,000	325,000
Inventories	720,000	480,000
Prepaid expenses	30,000	20,000
Total current assets	$1,500,000	$1,000,000
Long-term investments	250,000	225,000
Property, plant, and equipment (net)	2,093,000	1,948,000
Total assets	$3,843,000	$3,173,000
Liabilities		
Current liabilities	$ 750,000	$ 650,000
Long-term liabilities:		
Mortgage note payable, 10%, due in five years	$ 410,000	$ —
Bonds payable, 8%, due in 15 years	800,000	800,000
Total long-term liabilities	$1,210,000	$ 800,000
Total liabilities	$1,960,000	$1,450,000
Stockholders' Equity		
Preferred 8% stock, $100 par	$ 500,000	$ 500,000
Common stock, $10 par	500,000	500,000
Retained earnings	883,000	723,000
Total stockholders' equity	$1,883,000	$1,723,000
Total liabilities and stockholders' equity	$3,843,000	$3,173,000

Instructions

Determine the following measures for 20Y9, rounding percentages and ratios other than per-share amounts to one decimal place:

1. Working capital
2. Current ratio
3. Quick ratio
4. Accounts receivable turnover
5. Number of days' sales in receivables
6. Inventory turnover
7. Number of days' sales in inventory
8. Ratio of fixed assets to long-term liabilities
9. Ratio of liabilities to stockholders' equity
10. Times interest earned
11. Asset turnover
12. Return on total assets
13. Return on stockholders' equity
14. Return on common stockholders' equity
15. Earnings per share on common stock
16. Price-earnings ratio
17. Dividends per share
18. Dividend yield

Solution

(Ratios are rounded to one decimal place.)

1. Working capital: $750,000

   $1,500,000 – $750,000

2. Current ratio: 2.0

   $1,500,000 ÷ $750,000

3. Quick ratio: 1.0

   $750,000 ÷ $750,000

4. Accounts receivable turnover: 13.3

   $5,000,000 ÷ [($425,000 + $325,000) ÷ 2]

5. Number of days' sales in receivables: 27.4 days

   $5,000,000 ÷ 365 days = $13,699 average daily sales

   $375,000 ÷ $13,699

6. Inventory turnover: 5.7

   $3,400,000 ÷ [($720,000 + $480,000) ÷ 2]

7. Number of days' sales in inventory: 64.4 days

   $3,400,000 ÷ 365 days = $9,315 average daily cost of merchandise sold

   $600,000 ÷ $9,315

8. Ratio of fixed assets to long-term liabilities: 1.7

   $2,093,000 ÷ $1,210,000

9. Ratio of liabilities to stockholders' equity: 1.0

   $1,960,000 ÷ $1,883,000

10. Times interest earned: 6.2

    ($545,000 + $105,000) ÷ $105,000

11. Asset turnover: 1.4

    $5,000,000 ÷ [($3,843,000 + $3,173,000) ÷ 2]

12. Return on total assets: 10.0%

    ($245,000 + $105,000) ÷ [($3,843,000 + $3,173,000) ÷ 2]

13. Return on stockholders' equity: 13.6%

    $245,000 ÷ [($1,883,000 + $1,723,000) ÷ 2]

14. Return on common stockholders' equity: 15.7%

    ($245,000 – $40,000) ÷ [($1,383,000 + $1,223,000) ÷ 2]

15. Earnings per share on common stock: $4.10

    ($245,000 – $40,000) ÷ 50,000 shares

16. Price-earnings ratio: 6.1

    $25 ÷ $4.10

17. Dividends per share: $0.90

    $45,000 ÷ 50,000 shares

18. Dividend yield: 3.6%

    $0.90 ÷ $25

Key Terms

accounts receivable analysis (832)
accounts receivable turnover (832)
analytical methods (824)
asset turnover (838)
common-sized statement (828)
current position analysis (830)
current ratio (830)
dividend yield (845)
dividends per share (844)
earnings per share (EPS) on common stock (842)
horizontal analysis (824)
inventory analysis (833)
inventory turnover (834)
leverage (840)
liquidity (823)
Management's Discussion and Analysis (MD&A) (847)
number of days' sales in inventory (834)
number of days' sales in receivables (833)
price-earnings (P/E) ratio (843)
profitability (824)
quick assets (831)
quick ratio (831)
ratio of fixed assets to long-term liabilities (836)
ratio of liabilities to stockholders' equity (836)
ratios (824)
return on common stockholders' equity (841)
return on stockholders' equity (840)
return on total assets (839)
solvency (824)
times interest earned (837)
unusual income statement items (848)
vertical analysis (827)
working capital (830)

Discussion Questions

1. Briefly explain the difference between liquidity, solvency, and profitability analysis.
2. What is the advantage of using comparative statements for financial analysis rather than statements for a single date or period?
3. A company's current year net income (after income tax) is 25% larger than that of the preceding year. Does this indicate improved operating performance? Why or why not?
4. How would the current and quick ratios of a service business compare?
5. a. Why is a high inventory turnover considered to be a positive indicator?

   b. Is it possible to have a high inventory turnover and a high number of days' sales in inventory? Why?
6. What do the following data, taken from a comparative balance sheet, indicate about the company's ability to borrow additional long-term debt in the current year as compared to the preceding year?

	Current Year	Preceding Year
Fixed assets (net)	$1,260,000	$1,360,000
Total long-term liabilities	300,000	400,000

7. a. How does the return on total assets differ from the return on stockholders' equity?

   b. Which ratio is normally higher? Why?
8. REAL WORLD **Kroger**, a grocery store chain, recently had a price-earnings ratio of 7.6, while the average price-earnings ratio in the grocery store industry was 18.6. What might explain this difference?
9. REAL WORLD The dividend yield of **Suburban Propane** was 10.2% in a recent year, and the dividend yield of **Alphabet** was 0% in the same year. What might explain the difference between these ratios?
10. Describe two reports provided by independent auditors in the annual report to shareholders.

Practice Exercises

Example Exercises

SHOW ME HOW

EE 17-1 *p. 827*

PE 17-1A Horizontal analysis **OBJ. 2**

The comparative temporary investments and inventory balances of a company follow:

	Current Year	Prior Year
Temporary investments	$36,000	$30,000
Inventory	72,000	75,000

Based on this information, what is the amount and percentage of increase or decrease that would be shown on a balance sheet with horizontal analysis?

SHOW ME HOW

EE 17-1 *p. 827*

PE 17-1B Horizontal analysis **OBJ. 2**

The comparative accounts payable and long-term debt balances for a company follow:

	Current Year	Prior Year
Accounts payable	$176,000	$200,000
Long-term debt	168,950	155,000

Based on this information, what is the amount and percentage of increase or decrease that would be shown on a balance sheet with horizontal analysis?

SHOW ME HOW

EE 17-2 *p. 828*

PE 17-2A Vertical analysis **OBJ. 2**

Income statement information for Turay Corporation follows:

Sales	$200,000
Cost of merchandise sold	140,000
Gross profit	60,000

Prepare a vertical analysis of the income statement for Turay Corporation.

SHOW ME HOW

EE 17-2 *p. 828*

PE 17-2B Vertical analysis **OBJ. 2**

Income statement information for Ivanoff Corporation follows:

Sales	$1,400,000
Cost of merchandise sold	812,000
Gross profit	588,000

Prepare a vertical analysis of the income statement for Ivanoff Corporation.

SHOW ME HOW

EE 17-3 *p. 831*

PE 17-3A Current position analysis **OBJ. 3**

The following items are reported on a company's balance sheet:

Cash	$120,000
Marketable securities	40,000
Accounts receivable (net)	50,000
Inventory	90,000
Accounts payable	150,000

Determine (a) the current ratio and (b) the quick ratio. Round to one decimal place.

SHOW ME HOW

EE 17-3 p. 831

PE 17-3B Current position analysis **OBJ. 3**

The following items are reported on a company's balance sheet:

Cash	$320,000
Marketable securities	170,000
Accounts receivable (net)	140,000
Inventory	450,000
Accounts payable	300,000

Determine (a) the current ratio and (b) the quick ratio. Round to one decimal place.

SHOW ME HOW

EE 17-4 p. 833

PE 17-4A Accounts receivable analysis **OBJ. 3**

A company reports the following:

Sales	$1,460,000
Average accounts receivable (net)	100,000

Determine (a) the accounts receivable turnover and (b) the number of days' sales in receivables. Round to one decimal place.

SHOW ME HOW

EE 17-4 p. 833

PE 17-4B Accounts receivable analysis **OBJ. 3**

A company reports the following:

Sales	$6,862,000
Average accounts receivable (net)	365,000

Determine (a) the accounts receivable turnover and (b) the number of days' sales in receivables. Round to one decimal place.

SHOW ME HOW

EE 17-5 p. 835

PE 17-5A Inventory analysis **OBJ. 3**

A company reports the following:

Cost of merchandise sold	$558,000
Average merchandise inventory	45,000

Determine (a) the inventory turnover and (b) the number of days' sales in inventory. Round to one decimal place.

SHOW ME HOW

EE 17-5 p. 835

PE 17-5B Inventory analysis **OBJ. 3**

A company reports the following:

Cost of merchandise sold	$680,400
Average merchandise inventory	94,500

Determine (a) the inventory turnover and (b) the number of days' sales in inventory. Round to one decimal place.

SHOW ME HOW

EE 17-6 p. 836

PE 17-6A Solvency analysis **OBJ. 4**

The following information was taken from Tyson Company's balance sheet:

Fixed assets (net)	$ 774,000
Long-term liabilities	430,000
Total liabilities	1,218,000
Total stockholders' equity	580,000

Determine the company's (a) ratio of fixed assets to long-term liabilities and (b) ratio of liabilities to stockholders' equity. Round to one decimal place.

SHOW ME HOW

EE 17-6 p. 836

PE 17-6B Solvency analysis

OBJ. 4

The following information was taken from Jacobus Company's balance sheet:

Fixed assets (net)	$630,000
Long-term liabilities	140,000
Total liabilities	957,000
Total stockholders' equity	290,000

Determine the company's (a) ratio of fixed assets to long-term liabilities and (b) ratio of liabilities to stockholders' equity. Round to one decimal place.

SHOW ME HOW

EE 17-7 p. 837

PE 17-7A Times interest earned

OBJ. 4

A company reports the following:

Income before income tax expense	$6,000,000
Interest expense	300,000

Determine the times interest earned ratio. Round to one decimal place.

SHOW ME HOW

EE 17-7 p. 837

PE 17-7B Times interest earned

OBJ. 4

A company reports the following:

Income before income tax expense	$4,300,000
Interest expense	600,000

Determine the times interest earned ratio. Round to one decimal place.

SHOW ME HOW

EE 17-8 p. 839

PE 17-8A Asset turnover

OBJ. 5

A company reports the following:

Sales	$6,480,000
Average total assets	2,400,000

Determine the asset turnover ratio. Round to one decimal place.

SHOW ME HOW

EE 17-8 p. 839

PE 17-8B Asset turnover

OBJ. 5

A company reports the following:

Sales	$5,580,000
Average total assets	3,100,000

Determine the asset turnover ratio. Round to one decimal place.

SHOW ME HOW

EE 17-9 p. 840

PE 17-9A Return on total assets

OBJ. 5

A company reports the following income statement and balance sheet information for the current year:

Net income	$ 110,000
Interest expense	77,000
Average total assets	1,700,000

Determine the return on total assets. Round percentage to one decimal place.

SHOW ME HOW

EE 17-9 p. 840

PE 17-9B Return on total assets **OBJ. 5**

A company reports the following income statement and balance sheet information for the current year:

Net income	$ 502,100
Interest expense	113,500
Average total assets	3,800,000

Determine the return on total assets. Round percentage to one decimal place.

SHOW ME HOW

EE 17-10 p. 842

PE 17-10A Return on stockholders' equity **OBJ. 5**

A company reports the following:

Net income	$ 750,000
Preferred dividends	150,000
Average stockholders' equity	5,000,000
Average common stockholders' equity	3,750,000

Determine (a) the return on stockholders' equity and (b) the return on common stockholders' equity. Round percentages to one decimal place.

SHOW ME HOW

EE 17-10 p. 842

PE 17-10B Return on stockholders' equity **OBJ. 5**

A company reports the following:

Net income	$ 500,000
Preferred dividends	25,000
Average stockholders' equity	3,125,000
Average common stockholders' equity	1,900,000

Determine (a) the return on stockholders' equity and (b) the return on common stockholders' equity. Round percentages to one decimal place.

SHOW ME HOW

EE 17-11 p. 844

PE 17-11A Earnings per share and price-earnings ratio **OBJ. 5**

A company reports the following:

Net income	$460,000
Preferred dividends	$40,000
Shares of common stock outstanding	150,000
Market price per share of common stock	$40.60

a. Determine the company's earnings per share on common stock.

b. Determine the company's price-earnings ratio. Round to one decimal place.

SHOW ME HOW

EE 17-11 p. 844

PE 17-11B Earnings per share and price-earnings ratio **OBJ. 5**

A company reports the following:

Net income	$640,000
Preferred dividends	$82,000
Shares of common stock outstanding	60,000
Market price per share of common stock	$120.90

a. Determine the company's earnings per share on common stock.

b. Determine the company's price-earnings ratio. Round to one decimal place.

Exercises

EX 17-1 Vertical analysis of income statement

OBJ. 2

✔ a. Current year net income: $360,000; 9% of sales

Revenue and expense data for Innovation Quarter Inc. for two recent years are as follows:

	Current Year	Prior Year
Sales	$4,000,000	$3,600,000
Cost of merchandise sold	2,280,000	1,872,000
Selling expenses	600,000	648,000
Administrative expenses	520,000	360,000
Income tax expense	240,000	216,000

a. Prepare an income statement in comparative form, stating each item for both years as a percent of sales. Round to the nearest whole percentage.

b. Comment on the significant changes disclosed by the comparative income statement.

EX 17-2 Vertical analysis of income statement

OBJ. 2

✔ a. Current fiscal year income from continuing operations, 11.6% of revenues

The following comparative income statement (in thousands of dollars) for two recent fiscal years was adapted from the annual report of **Speedway Motorsports, Inc.**, owner and operator of several major motor speedways, such as the Atlanta, Texas, and Las Vegas Motor Speedways.

	Current Year	Prior Year
Revenues:		
Admissions	$ 78,332	$ 86,949
Event-related revenue	140,210	133,632
NASCAR broadcasting revenue	216,592	209,155
Other operating revenue	26,780	28,622
Total revenues	$461,914	$458,358
Expenses and other:		
Direct expense of events	$101,876	$ 98,973
NASCAR event management fees	123,212	119,101
Other direct operating expenses	18,502	18,782
General and administrative	164,949	177,132
Total expenses and other	$408,539	$413,988
Income from continuing operations	$ 53,375	$ 44,370

a. Prepare a comparative income statement for these two years in vertical form, stating each item as a percent of revenues. Round percentages to one decimal place.

b. Comment on the significant changes.

EX 17-3 Common-sized income statement

OBJ. 2

✔ a. Tannenhill net income: $120,000; 3% of sales

Revenue and expense data for the current calendar year for Tannenhill Company and for the electronics industry are as follows. Tannenhill's data are expressed in dollars. The electronics industry averages are expressed in percentages.

(Continued)

	Tannenhill Company	Electronics Industry Average
Sales	$4,000,000	100%
Cost of merchandise sold	2,120,000	60
Gross profit	$1,880,000	40%
Selling expenses	$1,080,000	24%
Administrative expenses	640,000	14
Total operating expenses	$1,720,000	38%
Income from operations	$ 160,000	2%
Other revenue and expense:		
Other revenue	120,000	3
Other expense	(80,000)	2
Income before income tax expense	$ 200,000	3%
Income tax expense	80,000	2
Net income	$ 120,000	1%

a. Prepare a common-sized income statement comparing the results of operations for Tannenhill Company with the industry average. Round to the nearest whole percentage.

b. As far as the data permit, comment on significant relationships revealed by the comparisons.

EX 17-4 Vertical analysis of balance sheet **OBJ. 2**

✔ **Retained earnings, Current year, 33.0%**

SHOW ME HOW

Balance sheet data for Kwan Company on December 31, the end of two recent fiscal years, follow:

	Current Year	Prior Year
Current assets	$2,352,000	$1,900,000
Property, plant, and equipment	4,536,000	4,712,000
Intangible assets	1,512,000	988,000
Current liabilities	1,848,000	1,444,000
Long-term liabilities	2,520,000	2,888,000
Common stock	1,260,000	836,000
Retained earnings	2,772,000	2,432,000

Prepare a comparative balance sheet for both years, stating each asset as a percent of total assets and each liability and stockholders' equity item as a percent of the total liabilities and stockholders' equity. Round percentages to one decimal place.

EX 17-5 Horizontal analysis of the income statement **OBJ. 2**

✔ **a. Net income increase, 66.0%**

SHOW ME HOW

Income statement data for Winthrop Company for two recent years ended December 31 are as follows:

	Current Year	Prior Year
Sales	$2,280,000	$2,000,000
Cost of merchandise sold	1,960,000	1,750,000
Gross profit	$ 320,000	$ 250,000
Selling expenses	$ 156,500	$ 125,000
Administrative expenses	122,000	100,000
Total operating expenses	$ 278,500	$ 225,000
Income before income tax expense	$ 41,500	$ 25,000
Income tax expense	16,600	10,000
Net income	$ 24,900	$ 15,000

a. Prepare a comparative income statement with horizontal analysis, indicating the increase (decrease) for the current year when compared with the prior year. Round percentages to one decimal place.

b. What conclusions can be drawn from the horizontal analysis?

EX 17-6 Current position analysis OBJ. 3

✔ a. Current year working capital, $1,120,000

SHOW ME HOW

EXCEL ONLINE

The following data were taken from the balance sheet of Albertini Company at the end of two recent fiscal years:

	Current Year	Prior Year
Current assets:		
Cash	$ 372,400	$ 285,500
Marketable securities	425,900	326,400
Accounts and notes receivable (net)	531,700	408,100
Inventories	343,200	210,600
Prepaid expenses	146,800	89,400
Total current assets	$1,820,000	$1,320,000
Current liabilities:		
Accounts and notes payable (short-term)	$ 404,000	$ 352,000
Accrued liabilities	296,000	248,000
Total current liabilities	$ 700,000	$ 600,000

a. Determine for each year (1) the working capital, (2) the current ratio, and (3) the quick ratio. Round ratios to one decimal place.

b. What conclusions can be drawn from these data as to the company's ability to meet its currently maturing debts?

EX 17-7 Current position analysis OBJ. 3

✔ a. (1) Current year's current ratio, 1.0

REAL WORLD

EXCEL ONLINE

PepsiCo, Inc., the parent company of Frito-Lay snack foods and Pepsi beverages, had the following current assets and current liabilities at the end of two recent years:

	Current Year (in millions)	Prior Year (in millions)
Cash and cash equivalents	$ 8,721	$10,610
Short-term investments, at cost	272	8,900
Accounts and notes receivable, net	7,142	7,024
Inventories	3,128	2,947
Prepaid expenses and other current assets	2,630	1,546
Accounts payable	18,112	15,017
Other short-term liabilities	4,026	5,485

a. Determine the (1) current ratio and (2) quick ratio for both years. Round to one decimal place.

b. What conclusions can you draw from these data about PepsiCo's liquidity?

EX 17-8 Current position analysis OBJ. 3

The bond indenture for the 10-year, 9% debenture bonds issued January 2, 20Y5, required working capital of $100,000, a current ratio of 1.5, and a quick ratio of 1.0 at the end of each calendar year until the bonds mature. At December 31, 20Y6, the three measures were computed as follows:

1. Current assets:

Cash	$102,000	
Temporary investments	48,000	
Accounts and notes receivable (net)	120,000	
Merchandise inventory	36,000	
Prepaid expenses	24,000	
Intangible assets	124,800	
Property, plant, and equipment	55,200	
Total current assets (net)		$510,000
Current liabilities:		
Accounts and short-term notes payable	$ 96,000	
Accrued liabilities	204,000	
Total current liabilities		300,000
Working capital		$210,000

(Continued)

2. Current ratio..	1.7	\$510,000 ÷ \$300,000
3. Quick ratio..	1.2	\$115,200 ÷ \$ 96,000

a. List the errors in the determination of the three measures of current position analysis.

b. Is the company satisfying the terms of the bond indenture? Explain.

✔ a. (1) Accounts receivable turnover, 20Y3, 9.2

SHOW ME HOW

EXCEL ONLINE

EX 17-9 Accounts receivable analysis **OBJ. 3**

The following data are taken from the financial statements of Basinger Inc. Terms of all sales are 2/10, n/45.

	20Y3	20Y2	20Y1
Accounts receivable, end of year	\$ 476,800	\$ 420,000	\$377,000
Sales on account	4,125,280	3,347,400	

a. For 20Y2 and 20Y3, determine (1) the accounts receivable turnover and (2) the number of days' sales in receivables. Round to the nearest dollar and one decimal place.

b. What conclusions can be drawn from these data concerning accounts receivable and credit policies?

✔ a. (1) Lestrade, 7.0

EX 17-10 Accounts receivable analysis **OBJ. 3**

Xavier Stores Company and Lestrade Stores Inc. are large retail department stores. Both companies offer credit to their customers through their own credit card operations. Information from the financial statements for both companies for two recent years is as follows (in millions):

	Xavier	Lestrade
Sales	\$8,500,000	\$4,585,000
Credit card receivables—beginning	820,000	600,000
Credit card receviables—ending	880,000	710,000

a. Determine the (1) accounts receivable turnover and (2) the number of days' sales in receivables for both companies. Round to one decimal place.

b. Compare the two companies with regard to their credit card policies.

✔ a. (1) Inventory turnover, current year, 10.8

SHOW ME HOW

EX 17-11 Inventory analysis **OBJ. 3**

The following data were extracted from the income statement of Shriver Inc.:

	Current Year	Prior Year
Sales	\$17,900,000	\$18,100,000
Beginning inventories	760,000	700,000
Cost of merchandise sold	8,964,000	9,782,000
Ending inventories	900,000	760,000

a. Determine for each year (1) the inventory turnover and (2) the number of days' sales in inventory. Round to the nearest dollar and one decimal place.

b. What conclusions can be drawn from these data concerning the inventories?

✔ a. (1) QT inventory turnover, 32.1

EX 17-12 Inventory analysis **OBJ. 3**

QT, Inc., and Elppa Computers, Inc., compete with each other in the personal computer market. QT assembles computers to customer orders, building and delivering a computer within four days of a customer entering an order online. Elppa, on the other hand, builds computers for inventory prior to receiving an order. These computers are sold from inventory once an order is received. Selected financial information for both companies from recent financial statements follows (in millions):

	QT	Elppa
Sales	$56,940	$120,357
Cost of merchandise sold	44,754	92,385
Inventory, beginning of period	1,382	6,317
Inventory, end of period	1,404	7,490

a. Determine for both companies (1) the inventory turnover and (2) the number of days' sales in inventory. Round to one decimal place.

b. Interpret the inventory ratios in the context of both companies' operating strategies.

EX 17-13 Ratio of liabilities to stockholders' equity and times interest earned **OBJ. 4**

✔ **a. Ratio of liabilities to stockholders' equity, current year, 0.9**

The following data were taken from the financial statements of Hunter Inc. for December 31 of two recent years:

	Current Year	Prior Year
Accounts payable	$ 924,000	$ 800,000
Current maturities of serial bonds payable	200,000	200,000
Serial bonds payable, 10%	1,000,000	1,200,000
Common stock, $10 par value	250,000	250,000
Paid-in capital in excess of par	1,250,000	1,250,000
Retained earnings	860,000	500,000

The income before income tax expense was $480,000 and $420,000 for the current and prior years, respectively.

a. Determine the ratio of liabilities to stockholders' equity at the end of each year. Round to one decimal place.

b. Determine the times interest earned ratio for both years. Round to one decimal place.

c. What conclusions can be drawn from these data as to the company's ability to meet its currently maturing debts?

EX 17-14 Ratio of liabilities to stockholders' equity and times interest earned **OBJ. 4**

✔ **a. Hasbro, 2.0**

Hasbro, Inc., and **Mattel, Inc.**, are the two largest toy companies in North America. Condensed liabilities and stockholders' equity from a recent balance sheet are shown for each company as follows (in thousands):

	Hasbro	Mattel
Liabilities:		
Current liabilities	$ 1,274,324	$ 1,252,608
Long-term debt	1,695,092	2,851,723
Other liabilities	539,086	469,669
Total liabilities	$ 3,508,502	$ 4,574,000
Stockholders' equity:		
Common stock	$ 104,847	$ 441,369
Additional paid-in capital	1,275,059	1,812,682
Retained earnings	4,184,374	1,629,257
Accumulated other comprehensive loss and other equity items	(294,514)	(859,226)
Treasury stock, at cost	(3,515,280)	(2,354,617)
Total stockholders' equity	$ 1,754,486	$ 669,465
Total liabilities and stockholders' equity	$ 5,262,988	$ 5,243,465

The income from operations and interest expense from the income statement for each company were as follows (in thousands):

(Continued)

	Hasbro	Mattel
Income (loss) from operations (before income tax expense)	$270,402	$(419,261)
Interest expense	90,826	181,886

a. Determine the ratio of liabilities to stockholders' equity for both companies. Round to one decimal place.

b. Determine the times interest earned ratio for both companies. Round to one decimal place.

c. Interpret the ratio differences between the two companies.

EX 17-15 Ratio of liabilities to stockholders' equity and ratio of fixed assets to long-term liabilities **OBJ. 4**

✔ a. Mondelez International, Inc., 1.4

Recent balance sheet information for two companies in the food industry, **Mondelez International, Inc.**, and **The Hershey Company**, is as follows (in thousands):

	Mondelez	Hershey
Net property, plant, and equipment	$ 8,482,000	$2,130,294
Current liabilities	16,737,000	2,418,566
Long-term debt	12,532,000	3,254,280
Other long-term liabilities	7,747,000	622,908
Stockholders' equity	25,713,000	1,407,266

a. Determine the ratio of liabilities to stockholders' equity for both companies. Round to one decimal place.

b. Determine the ratio of fixed assets to long-term liabilities for both companies. Round to one decimal place.

c. Interpret the ratio differences between the two companies.

EX 17-16 Asset turnover **OBJ. 5**

✔ a. YRC, 3.2

Three major segments of the transportation industry are motor carriers such as **YRC Worldwide**, railroads such as **Union Pacific**, and transportation logistics services such as **C.H. Robinson Worldwide, Inc.** Recent financial statement information for these three companies follows (in thousands):

	YRC	Union Pacific	C.H. Robinson
Sales	$5,092,000	$22,832,000	$16,631,172
Average total assets	1,601,300	58,476,500	4,331,623

a. Determine the asset turnover for all three companies. Round to one decimal place.

b. Assume that the asset turnover for each company represents its respective industry segment. Interpret the differences in the asset turnover in terms of the operating characteristics of each of the respective segments.

EX 17-17 Profitability ratios **OBJ. 5**

✔ a. Return on total assets, 20Y7, 11.0%

The following selected data were taken from the financial statements of Vidahill Inc. for December 31, 20Y7, 20Y6, and 20Y5:

	20Y7	20Y6	20Y5
Total assets	$5,200,000	$5,000,000	$4,800,000
Notes payable (6% interest)	2,500,000	2,500,000	2,500,000
Common stock	250,000	250,000	250,000
Preferred 2.5% stock, $100 par (no change during year)	500,000	500,000	500,000
Retained earnings	1,574,000	1,222,000	750,000

The 20Y7 net income was $411,000, and the 20Y6 net income was $462,500. No dividends on common stock were declared between 20Y5 and 20Y7. Preferred dividends were declared and paid in full in 20Y6 and 20Y7.

a. Determine the return on total assets, the return on stockholders' equity, and the return on common stockholders' equity for the years 20Y6 and 20Y7. Round percentages to one decimal place.

b. What conclusions can be drawn from these data as to the company's profitability?

EX 17-18 Profitability ratios **OBJ. 5**

✔a. Year 3 return on total assets, 3.1%

Ralph Lauren Corporation sells apparel through company-owned retail stores. Recent financial information for Ralph Lauren follows (in thousands):

	Fiscal Year 3	Fiscal Year 2
Net income (loss)	$162,800	$(99,300)
Interest expense	18,200	12,400

	Fiscal Year 3	Fiscal Year 2	Fiscal Year 1
Total assets (at end of fiscal year)	$6,143,300	$5,652,000	$6,213,100
Total stockholders' equity (at end of fiscal year)	3,457,400	3,299,600	3,743,500

Assume that the apparel industry average return on total assets is 11.4% and the average return on stockholders' equity is 26.4% for the year ended April 2, Year 3.

a. Determine the return on total assets for Ralph Lauren for fiscal Years 2 and 3. Round percentages to one decimal place.

b. Determine the return on stockholders' equity for Ralph Lauren for fiscal Years 2 and 3. Round percentages to one decimal place.

c. Evaluate the two-year trend for the profitability ratios determined in (a) and (b).

EX 17-19 Six measures of solvency or profitability **OBJ. 4, 5**

✔ c. Asset turnover, 2.8

The following data were taken from the financial statements of Loveseth Inc. for the current fiscal year.

Property, plant, and equipment (net)			$ 3,040,000
Liabilities:			
Current liabilities		$1,200,000	
Note payable, 6%, due in 15 years		1,600,000	
Total liabilities			$ 2,800,000
Stockholders' equity:			
Preferred $10 stock, $100 par (no change during year)			$ 800,000
Common stock, $10 par (no change during year)			1,600,000
Retained earnings:			
Balance, beginning of year	$1,072,000		
Net income	928,000	$2,000,000	
Preferred dividends	$ 80,000		
Common dividends	320,000	400,000	
Balance, end of year			1,600,000
Total stockholders' equity			$ 4,000,000
Sales			$17,920,000
Interest expense			$ 96,000

Assuming that total assets were $6,000,000 at the beginning of the current fiscal year, determine the following: (a) ratio of fixed assets to long-term liabilities, (b) ratio of liabilities to stockholders' equity, (c) asset turnover, (d) return on total assets, (e) return on stockholders' equity, and (f) return on common stockholders' equity. Round ratios and percentages to one decimal place as appropriate.

EX 17-20 Five measures of solvency or profitability — OBJ. 4, 5

✔ c. Price-earnings ratio, 11.0

The balance sheet for Quigg Inc. at the end of the current fiscal year indicated the following:

Bonds payable, 8%	$7,500,000
Preferred $4 stock, $50 par	3,750,000
Common stock, $10 par	7,500,000

Income before income tax expense was $5,280,000 and income taxes were $1,305,000 for the current year. Cash dividends paid on common stock during the current year totaled $1,950,000. The common stock was selling for $53.90 per share at the end of the year. Determine each of the following: (a) times interest earned ratio, (b) earnings per share on common stock, (c) price-earnings ratio, (d) dividends per share of common stock, and (e) dividend yield. Round ratios and percentages to one decimal place, except for per-share amounts.

EX 17-21 Earnings per share, price-earnings ratio, dividend yield — OBJ. 5

✔ b. Price-earnings ratio, 15.0

The following information was taken from the financial statements of Zeil Inc. for December 31 of the current fiscal year:

Common stock, $20 par (no change during the year)	$8,000,000
Preferred $3 stock, $50 par (no change during the year)	1,500,000

The net income was $2,010,000, and the declared dividends on the common stock were $1,728,000 for the current year. The market price of the common stock is $72 per share.

For the common stock, determine (a) the earnings per share, (b) the price-earnings ratio, (c) the dividends per share, and (d) the dividend yield. Round ratios and percentages to one decimal place, except for per-share amounts.

EX 17-22 Price-earnings ratio; dividend yield — OBJ. 5

✔ a. Alphabet, 23.4

The table that follows shows the stock price, earnings per share, and dividends per share for three companies for a recent year:

	Price	Earnings per Share	Dividends per Share
Deere & Company	$ 135.44	$ 7.34	$2.58
Alphabet	1,035.61	44.22	0.00
The Coca-Cola Company	47.35	1.58	1.56

a. Determine the price-earnings ratio and dividend yield for the three companies. Round ratios and percentages to one decimal place as appropriate.

b. Explain the differences in these ratios across the three companies.

Appendix

EX 17-23 Earnings per share, discontinued operations

✔ b. Earnings per share on common stock, $7.60

The net income reported on the income statement of Cutler Co. was $4,000,000. There were 500,000 shares of $10 par common stock and 100,000 shares of $2 preferred stock outstanding throughout the current year. The income statement included a gain on discontinued operations of $400,000 after applicable income tax. Determine the per-share figures for common stock for (a) income before discontinued operations and (b) net income.

Appendix

EX 17-24 Income statement and earnings per share for discontinued operations

Apex Inc. reports the following for a recent year:

Income from continuing operations before income tax expense	$1,000,000
Loss from discontinued operations	$240,000*
Weighted average number of shares outstanding	20,000
Applicable tax rate	40%

*Net of any tax effect.

a. Prepare a partial income statement for Apex Inc., beginning with income from continuing operations before income tax expense.

b. Determine the earnings per common share for Apex Inc., including per-share amounts for unusual items.

Appendix

EX 17-25 Unusual items

Explain whether Colston Company correctly reported the following items in the financial statements:

a. In a recent year, the company discovered a clerical error in the prior year's accounting records. As a result, the reported net income for the previous year was overstated by $45,000. The company corrected this error by restating the prior-year financial statements.

b. In a recent year, the company voluntarily changed its method of accounting for long-term construction contracts from the percentage of completion method to the completed contract method. Both methods are acceptable under generally acceptable accounting principles. The cumulative effect of this change was reported as a separate component of income on the current period income statement.

Problems: Series A

PR 17-1A Horizontal analysis of income statement — OBJ. 2

✔ 1. Sales, 12.0% increase

SHOW ME HOW

For 20Y2, McDade Company reported a decline in net income. At the end of the year, T. Burrows, the president, is presented with the following condensed comparative income statement:

McDade Company
Comparative Income Statement
For the Years Ended December 31, 20Y2 and 20Y1

	20Y2	20Y1
Sales	$16,800,000	$15,000,000
Cost of merchandise sold	11,500,000	10,000,000
Gross profit	$ 5,300,000	$ 5,000,000
Selling expenses	$ 1,770,000	$ 1,500,000
Administrative expenses	1,220,000	1,000,000
Total operating expenses	$ 2,990,000	$ 2,500,000
Income from operations	$ 2,310,000	$ 2,500,000
Other revenue	256,950	225,000
Income before income tax expense	$ 2,566,950	$ 2,725,000
Income tax expense	1,413,000	1,500,000
Net income	$ 1,153,950	$ 1,225,000

Instructions

1. Prepare a comparative income statement with horizontal analysis for the two-year period, using 20Y1 as the base year. Round percentages to one decimal place.
2. To the extent the data permit, comment on the significant relationships revealed by the horizontal analysis prepared in (1).

PR 17-2A Vertical analysis of income statement — OBJ. 2

✔ 1. Net income, 20Y2, 10.0%

For 20Y2, Tri-Comic Company initiated a sales promotion campaign that included the expenditure of an additional $50,000 for advertising. At the end of the year, Lumi Neer, the president, is presented with the following condensed comparative income statement:

(Continued)

Tri-Comic Company
Comparative Income Statement
For the Years Ended December 31, 20Y2 and 20Y1

	20Y2	20Y1
Sales	$1,500,000	$1,250,000
Cost of merchandise sold	510,000	475,000
Gross profit	$ 990,000	$ 775,000
Selling expenses	$ 270,000	$ 200,000
Administrative expenses	180,000	156,250
Total operating expenses	$ 450,000	$ 356,250
Income from operations	$ 540,000	$ 418,750
Other revenue	60,000	50,000
Income before income tax expense	$ 600,000	$ 468,750
Income tax expense	450,000	375,000
Net income	$ 150,000	$ 93,750

Instructions

1. Prepare a comparative income statement for the two-year period, presenting an analysis of each item in relationship to sales for each of the years. Round percentages to one decimal place.
2. To the extent the data permit, comment on the significant relationships revealed by the vertical analysis prepared in (1).

PR 17-3A Effect of transactions on current position analysis **OBJ. 3**

✔ 2. c. Current ratio, 2.2

Data pertaining to the current position of Forte Company follow:

Cash	$412,500
Marketable securities	187,500
Accounts and notes receivable (net)	300,000
Inventories	700,000
Prepaid expenses	50,000
Accounts payable	200,000
Notes payable (short-term)	250,000
Accrued expenses	300,000

Instructions

1. Compute (a) the working capital, (b) the current ratio, and (c) the quick ratio. Round ratios in parts b through j to one decimal place.
2. List the following captions on a sheet of paper:

Transaction	Working Capital	Current Ratio	Quick Ratio

Compute the working capital, the current ratio, and the quick ratio after each of the following transactions and record the results in the appropriate columns. *Consider each transaction separately* and assume that only that transaction affects the data given. Round to one decimal place.

a. Sold marketable securities at no gain or loss, $70,000.
b. Paid accounts payable, $125,000.
c. Purchased goods on account, $110,000.
d. Paid notes payable, $100,000.
e. Declared a cash dividend, $150,000.
f. Declared a common stock dividend on common stock, $50,000.
g. Borrowed cash from bank on a long-term note, $225,000.
h. Received cash on account, $125,000.
i. Issued additional shares of stock for cash, $600,000.
j. Paid cash for prepaid expenses, $10,000.

PR 17-4A Measures of liquidity, solvency, and profitability **OBJ. 3, 4, 5**

✔ 5. Number of days' sales in receivables, 18.3

The comparative financial statements of Marshall Inc. are as follows. The market price of Marshall common stock was $82.60 on December 31, 20Y2.

Marshall Inc.
Comparative Retained Earnings Statement
For the Years Ended December 31, 20Y2 and 20Y1

	20Y2	20Y1
Retained earnings, January 1	$3,704,000	$3,264,000
Net income	600,000	550,000
Dividends:		
On preferred stock	(10,000)	(10,000)
On common stock	(100,000)	(100,000)
Retained earnings, December 31	$4,194,000	$3,704,000

Marshall Inc.
Comparative Income Statement
For the Years Ended December 31, 20Y2 and 20Y1

	20Y2	20Y1
Sales	$10,850,000	$10,000,000
Cost of merchandise sold	6,000,000	5,450,000
Gross profit	$ 4,850,000	$ 4,550,000
Selling expenses	$ 2,170,000	$ 2,000,000
Administrative expenses	1,627,500	1,500,000
Total operating expenses	$ 3,797,500	$ 3,500,000
Income from operations	$ 1,052,500	$ 1,050,000
Other revenue and expense:		
Other revenue	99,500	20,000
Other expense (interest)	(132,000)	(120,000)
Income before income tax expense	$ 1,020,000	$ 950,000
Income tax expense	420,000	400,000
Net income	$ 600,000	$ 550,000

Marshall Inc.
Comparative Balance Sheet
December 31, 20Y2 and 20Y1

	20Y2	20Y1
Assets		
Current assets:		
Cash	$1,050,000	$ 950,000
Marketable securities	301,000	420,000
Accounts receivable (net)	585,000	500,000
Inventories	420,000	380,000
Prepaid expenses	108,000	20,000
Total current assets	$ 2,464,000	$2,270,000
Long-term investments	800,000	800,000
Property, plant, and equipment (net)	5,760,000	5,184,000
Total assets	$ 9,024,000	$8,254,000
Liabilities		
Current liabilities	$ 880,000	$ 800,000
Long-term liabilities:		
Mortgage note payable, 6%	$ 200,000	$ 0
Bonds payable, 4%	3,000,000	3,000,000
Total long-term liabilities	$ 3,200,000	$3,000,000
Total liabilities	$ 4,080,000	$3,800,000
Stockholders' Equity		
Preferred 4% stock, $5 par	$ 250,000	$ 250,000
Common stock, $5 par	500,000	500,000
Retained earnings	4,194,000	3,704,000
Total stockholders' equity	$ 4,944,000	$4,454,000
Total liabilities and stockholders' equity	$ 9,024,000	$8,254,000

(Continued)

Instructions

Determine the following measures for 20Y2, rounding to one decimal place, including percentages, except for per-share amounts:

1. Working capital
2. Current ratio
3. Quick ratio
4. Accounts receivable turnover
5. Number of days' sales in receivables
6. Inventory turnover
7. Number of days' sales in inventory
8. Ratio of fixed assets to long-term liabilities
9. Ratio of liabilities to stockholders' equity
10. Times interest earned
11. Asset turnover
12. Return on total assets
13. Return on stockholders' equity
14. Return on common stockholders' equity
15. Earnings per share on common stock
16. Price-earnings ratio
17. Dividends per share of common stock
18. Dividend yield

PR 17-5A Solvency and profitability trend analysis — OBJ. 4, 5

✔ 1. c. 20Y8, 1.5

Addai Company has provided the following comparative information:

	20Y8	20Y7	20Y6	20Y5	20Y4
Net income	$ 273,406	$ 367,976	$ 631,176	$ 884,000	$ 800,000
Interest expense	616,047	572,003	528,165	495,000	440,000
Income tax expense	31,749	53,560	106,720	160,000	200,000
Total assets (ending balance)	4,417,178	4,124,350	3,732,443	3,338,500	2,750,000
Total stockholders' equity (ending balance)	3,706,557	3,433,152	3,065,176	2,434,000	1,550,000
Average total assets	4,270,764	3,928,396	3,535,472	3,044,250	2,475,000
Average total stockholders' equity	3,569,855	3,249,164	2,749,588	1,992,000	1,150,000

You have been asked to evaluate the historical performance of the company over the last five years.

Selected industry ratios have remained relatively steady at the following levels for the last five years:

	20Y4–20Y8
Return on total assets	28%
Return on stockholders' equity	18%
Times interest earned	2.7
Ratio of liabilities to stockholders' equity	0.4

Instructions

1. Prepare four line graphs with the ratio on the vertical axis and the years on the horizontal axis for the following four ratios, rounding to one decimal place:
   a. Return on total assets
   b. Return on stockholders' equity
   c. Times interest earned
   d. Ratio of liabilities to stockholders' equity

   Display both the company ratio and the industry benchmark on each graph. That is, each graph should have two lines.
2. Prepare an analysis of the graphs in (1).

Problems: Series B

PR 17-1B Horizontal analysis of income statement OBJ. 2

✔ 1. Sales, 32.0% increase

SHOW ME HOW

For 20Y2, Gerhardt Inc. reported a significant increase in net income. At the end of the year, John Mayer, the president, is presented with the following condensed comparative income statement:

Gerhardt Inc.
Comparative Income Statement
For the Years Ended December 31, 20Y2 and 20Y1

	20Y2	20Y1
Sales	$805,200	$610,000
Cost of merchandise sold	365,400	280,000
Gross profit	$439,800	$330,000
Selling expenses	$117,200	$ 92,000
Administrative expenses	87,400	68,000
Total operating expenses	$204,600	$160,000
Income from operations	$235,200	$170,000
Other revenue	43,700	40,000
Income before income tax expense	$278,900	$210,000
Income tax expense	69,700	51,500
Net income	$209,200	$158,500

Instructions

1. Prepare a comparative income statement with horizontal analysis for the two-year period, using 20Y1 as the base year. Round percentages to one decimal place.
2. To the extent the data permit, comment on the significant relationships revealed by the horizontal analysis prepared in (1).

PR 17-2B Vertical analysis of income statement OBJ. 2

✔ 1. Net income, 20Y1, 14.0%

For 20Y2, Fielder Industries Inc. initiated a sales promotion campaign that included the expenditure of an additional $40,000 for advertising. At the end of the year, Leif Grando, the president, is presented with the following condensed comparative income statement:

Fielder Industries Inc.
Comparative Income Statement
For the Years Ended December 31, 20Y2 and 20Y1

	20Y2	20Y1
Sales	$1,300,000	$1,180,000
Cost of merchandise sold	682,500	613,600
Gross profit	$ 617,500	$ 566,400
Selling expenses	$ 260,000	$ 188,800
Adminstrative expenses	169,000	177,000
Total operating expenses	$ 429,000	$ 365,800
Income from operations	$ 188,500	$ 200,600
Other revenue	78,000	70,800
Income before income tax expense	$ 266,500	$ 271,400
Income tax expense	117,000	106,200
Net income	$ 149,500	$ 165,200

Instructions

1. Prepare a comparative income statement for the two-year period, presenting an analysis of each item in relationship to sales for each of the years. Round percentages to one decimal place.
2. To the extent the data permit, comment on the significant relationships revealed by the vertical analysis prepared in (1).

PR 17-3B Effect of transactions on current position analysis

OBJ. 3

✔ 2. g. Quick ratio, 1.6

Data pertaining to the current position of Lucroy Industries Inc. follow:

Cash	$ 800,000
Marketable securities	550,000
Accounts and notes receivable (net)	850,000
Inventories	700,000
Prepaid expenses	300,000
Accounts payable	1,200,000
Notes payable (short-term)	700,000
Accrued expenses	100,000

Instructions

1. Compute (a) the working capital, (b) the current ratio, and (c) the quick ratio. Round ratios in parts b through j to one decimal place.
2. List the following captions on a sheet of paper:

Transaction	Working Capital	Current Ratio	Quick Ratio

Compute the working capital, the current ratio, and the quick ratio after each of the following transactions and record the results in the appropriate columns. *Consider each transaction separately* and assume that only that transaction affects the data given. Round to one decimal place.

a. Sold marketable securities at no gain or loss, $500,000.
b. Paid accounts payable, $287,500.
c. Purchased goods on account, $400,000.
d. Paid notes payable, $125,000.
e. Declared a cash dividend, $325,000.
f. Declared a common stock dividend on common stock, $150,000.
g. Borrowed cash from bank on a long-term note, $1,000,000.
h. Received cash on account, $75,000.
i. Issued additional shares of stock for cash, $2,000,000.
j. Paid cash for prepaid expenses, $200,000.

PR 17-4B Measures of liquidity, solvency, and profitability

OBJ. 3, 4, 5

✔ 9. Ratio of liabilities to stockholders' equity, 0.4

The comparative financial statements of Stargel Inc. are as follows. The market price of Stargel common stock was $119.70 on December 31, 20Y2.

Stargel Inc.
Comparative Retained Earnings Statement
For the Years Ended December 31, 20Y2 and 20Y1

	20Y2	20Y1
Retained earnings, January 1	$5,375,000	$4,545,000
Net income	900,000	925,000
Dividends:		
Preferred stock dividends	(45,000)	(45,000)
Common stock dividends	(50,000)	(50,000)
Retained earnings, December 31	$6,180,000	$5,375,000

Stargel Inc.
Comparative Income Statement
For the Years Ended December 31, 20Y2 and 20Y1

	20Y2	20Y1
Sales	$10,000,000	$9,400,000
Cost of merchandise sold	5,350,000	4,950,000
Gross profit	$ 4,650,000	$4,450,000
Selling expenses	$ 2,000,000	$1,880,000
Administrative expenses	1,500,000	1,410,000
Total operating expenses	$ 3,500,000	$3,290,000
Income from operations	$ 1,150,000	$1,160,000
Other revenue and expense:		
Other revenue	150,000	140,000
Other expense (interest)	(170,000)	(150,000)
Income before income tax expense	$ 1,130,000	$1,150,000
Income tax expense	230,000	225,000
Net income	$ 900,000	$ 925,000

Stargel Inc.
Comparative Balance Sheet
December 31, 20Y2 and 20Y1

	20Y2	20Y1
Assets		
Current assets:		
Cash	$ 500,000	$ 400,000
Marketable securities	1,010,000	1,000,000
Accounts receivable (net)	740,000	510,000
Inventories	1,190,000	950,000
Prepaid expenses	250,000	229,000
Total current assets	$3,690,000	$3,089,000
Long-term investments	2,350,000	2,300,000
Property, plant, and equipment (net)	3,740,000	3,366,000
Total assets	$9,780,000	$8,755,000
Liabilities		
Current liabilities	$ 900,000	$ 880,000
Long-term liabilities:		
Mortgage note payable, 10%	$ 200,000	$ 0
Bonds payable, 10%	1,500,000	1,500,000
Total long-term liabilities	$1,700,000	$1,500,000
Total liabilities	$2,600,000	$2,380,000
Stockholders' Equity		
Preferred $0.90 stock, $10 par	$ 500,000	$ 500,000
Common stock, $5 par	500,000	500,000
Retained earnings	6,180,000	5,375,000
Total stockholders' equity	$7,180,000	$6,375,000
Total liabilities and stockholders' equity	$9,780,000	$8,755,000

Instructions

Determine the following measures for 20Y2, rounding to one decimal place including percentages, except for per-share amounts:

1. Working capital
2. Current ratio
3. Quick ratio
4. Accounts receivable turnover
5. Number of days' sales in receivables

(Continued)

6. Inventory turnover
7. Number of days' sales in inventory
8. Ratio of fixed assets to long-term liabilities
9. Ratio of liabilities to stockholders' equity
10. Times interest earned
11. Asset turnover
12. Return on total assets
13. Return on stockholders' equity
14. Return on common stockholders' equity
15. Earnings per share on common stock
16. Price-earnings ratio
17. Dividends per share of common stock
18. Dividend yield

PR 17-5B Solvency and profitability trend analysis

OBJ. 4, 5

✔ 1. b. 20Y7, 32.9%

Crosby Company has provided the following comparative information:

	20Y8	20Y7	20Y6	20Y5	20Y4
Net income	$ 5,571,720	$ 3,714,480	$ 2,772,000	$ 1,848,000	$ 1,400,000
Interest expense	1,052,060	891,576	768,600	610,000	500,000
Income tax expense	1,225,572	845,222	640,320	441,600	320,000
Total assets (ending balance)	29,378,491	22,598,839	17,120,333	12,588,480	10,152,000
Total stockholders' equity (ending balance)	18,706,200	13,134,480	9,420,000	6,648,000	4,800,000
Average total assets	25,988,665	19,859,586	14,854,406	11,370,240	8,676,000
Average total stockholders' equity	15,920,340	11,277,240	8,034,000	5,724,000	4,100,000

You have been asked to evaluate the historical performance of the company over the last five years.

Selected industry ratios have remained relatively steady at the following levels for the last five years:

	20Y4–20Y8
Return on total assets	19%
Return on stockholders' equity	26%
Times interest earned	3.4
Ratio of liabilities to stockholders' equity	1.4

Instructions

1. Prepare four line graphs with the ratio on the vertical axis and the years on the horizontal axis for the following four ratios, rounding ratios and percentages to one decimal place:
   a. Return on total assets
   b. Return on stockholders' equity
   c. Times interest earned
   d. Ratio of liabilities to stockholders' equity

   Display both the company ratio and the industry benchmark on each graph. That is, each graph should have two lines.
2. Prepare an analysis of the graphs in (1).

Nike, Inc., Problem

Financial statement analysis

The financial statements for **Nike, Inc.**, are presented in Appendix C at the end of the text. Use the following additional information (in millions):

Accounts receivable at May 31, 2018	$ 3,498
Inventories at May 31, 2018	5,261
Total assets at May 31, 2018	22,536
Stockholders' equity at May 31, 2018	9,812

Instructions

1. Determine the following measures for the fiscal years ended May 31, 2018, and May 31, 2017. Round ratios and percentages to one decimal place.
   a. Working capital
   b. Current ratio
   c. Quick ratio
   d. Accounts receivable turnover
   e. Number of days' sales in receivables
   f. Inventory turnover
   g. Number of days' sales in inventory
   h. Ratio of liabilities to stockholders' equity
   i. Asset turnover
   j. Return on total assets.
   k. Return on common stockholders' equity
   l. Price-earnings ratio, assuming that the market price was $72.12 per share on May 29, 2018, and $53.06 per share on May 30, 2017
2. What conclusions can be drawn from these analyses?

Cases & Projects

ETHICS

CP 17-1 Ethics in Action

Rodgers Industries Inc. completed its fiscal year on December 31. Near the end of the fiscal year, the company's Internal Audit Department determined that an important internal control procedure had not been functioning properly. The head of Internal Audit, Dash Riprock, reported the internal control failure to the company's chief accountant, Todd Barleywine. Todd reported the failure to the company's chief financial officer, Josh McCoy. After discussing the issue, Josh instructed Todd not to inform the external auditors of the internal control failure and to fix the problem quietly after the end of the fiscal year. The external auditors did not discover the internal control failure during their audit. In March, after the audit was complete, the company released its annual report, including associated reports by management. As chief financial officer, Josh authorized the release of Management's Report on Internal Control, which stated that the management team believed that the company's internal controls were effective during the period covered by the annual report.

Did Josh behave ethically in this situation? Explain your answer.

CP 17-2 Team Activity

In teams, select a public company that interests you. Obtain the company's most recent annual report on Form 10-K. The Form 10-K is a company's annually required filing with the Securities and Exchange Commission (SEC). It includes the company's financial statements and accompanying notes. The Form 10-K can be obtained either (a) by referring to the investor relations section of the company's website or (b) by using the company search feature of the SEC's EDGAR database service found at www.sec.gov/edgar/searchedgar/companysearch.html.

1. Based on the information in the company's most recent annual report, compute the following, rounding ratios and percentages to one decimal place, except for per-share amounts:
   a. Liquidity analysis:
      (1) Working capital
      (2) Current ratio
      (3) Quick ratio
      (4) Accounts receivable turnover
      (5) Number of days' sales in receivables
      (6) Inventory turnover
      (7) Number of days' sales in inventory
   b. Solvency analysis:
      (1) Ratio of liabilities to stockholders' equity
      (2) Times interest earned
   c. Profitability analysis:
      (1) Asset turnover
      (2) Return on total assets
      (3) Return on common stockholders' equity
      (4) Earnings per share
      (5) Price-earnings ratio

CP 17-3 Communication

The president of Freeman Industries Inc. made the following statement in the annual report to shareholders: "The founding family and majority shareholders of the company do not believe in using debt to finance future growth. The founding family learned from hard experience during the Great Depression that debt can cause loss of flexibility and eventual loss of corporate control. The company will not place itself at such risk again. As such, all future growth will be financed either by stock sales to the public or by internally generated resources."

Write a brief memo to the company's president, Boss Freeman, outlining the errors in his logic.

CP 17-4 Common-sized income statements

The condensed income statements through income from operations for **Amazon.com, Inc.**, **Best Buy, Inc.**, and **Walmart Inc.**, for a recent fiscal year follow (in millions):

	Amazon	Best Buy	Walmart
Sales	$232,887	$42,879	$514,405
Cost of sales	139,156	32,918	385,301
Gross profit	$ 93,731	$ 9,961	$129,104
Selling, general, and administrative expenses	81,310	8,015	107,147
Other operating expenses	0	46	0
Income from operations	$ 12,421	$ 1,900	$ 21,957

1. Prepare comparative common-sized income statements for each company. Round percentages to one decimal place.
2. Use the common-sized analysis to compare the financial performance of the three companies.

CP 17-5 Profitability analysis

Deere & Company manufactures and distributes farm and construction machinery that it sells around the world. In addition to its manufacturing operations, Deere's credit division loans money to customers to finance the purchase of their farm and construction equipment.

The following information is available for three recent years (in millions except per-share amounts):

	Year 3	Year 2	Year 1
Net income	$2,368.4	$2,159.1	$1,523.9
Preferred dividends	$0.00	$0.00	$0.00
Interest expense	$1,203.6	$899.5	$763.7
Shares outstanding for computing earnings per share	323	320	315
Cash dividend per share	$2.58	$2.40	$2.40
Average total assets	$67,947	$61,852	$57,933
Average stockholders' equity	$10,426	$8,046	$6,644
Average stock price per share	$134.16	$110.59	$83.94

1. Compute the following ratios for each year, rounding ratios and percentages to one decimal place, except for per-share amounts:
   a. Return on total assets
   b. Return on stockholders' equity
   c. Earnings per share
   d. Dividend yield
   e. Price-earnings ratio
2. Based on these data, evaluate Deere's profitability.

CP 17-6 Comprehensive profitability and solvency analysis

Marriott International, Inc., and **Hyatt Hotels Corporation** are two major owners and managers of lodging and resort properties in the United States. Abstracted income statement information for the two companies is as follows for a recent year (in millions):

	Marriott	Hyatt
Operating profit before other expenses and interest	$ 2,366	$332
Other revenue	319	695
Interest expense	(340)	(76)
Income before income tax expense	$ 2,345	$951
Income tax expense	438	182
Net income	$ 1,907	$769

Balance sheet information is as follows:

	Marriott	Hyatt
Total liabilities	$ 21,471	$3,966
Total stockholders' equity	2,225	3,677
Total liabilities and stockholders' equity	$23,696	$7,643

(Continued)

The average liabilities, average stockholders' equity, and average total assets are as follows:

	Marriott	Hyatt
Average total liabilities	$20,868	$3,848
Average total stockholders' equity	2,903	3,760
Average total assets	23,771	7,608

1. Determine the following ratios for both companies, rounding ratios and percentages to one decimal place:
   a. Return on total assets
   b. Return on stockholders' equity
   c. Times interest earned
   d. Ratio of total liabilities to stockholders' equity
2. Based on the information in (1), analyze and compare the two companies' solvency and profitability.

Financial Statements for Mornin' Joe

The financial statements for **Mornin' Joe** follow. Mornin' Joe is a fictitious coffeehouse chain featuring drip and espresso coffee in cafés. The financial statements for Mornin' Joe are provided to illustrate the complete financial statements of a corporation, using the terms, formats, and reporting illustrated throughout this text. In addition, excerpts of the Mornin' Joe financial statements are used to illustrate the financial reporting for the topics discussed in Chapters 7–15.

The complete financial statements for Mornin' Joe follow.

Mornin' Joe
Income Statement
For the Year Ended December 31, 20Y6

Sales			$5,402,100
Cost of merchandise sold			2,160,000
Gross profit			$3,242,100
Operating expenses			
Selling expenses:			
Wages expense	$825,000		
Advertising expense	678,900		
Depreciation expense—buildings	124,300		
Miscellaneous selling expense	26,500		
Total selling expenses		$1,654,700	
Administrative expenses:			
Office salaries expense	$325,000		
Rent expense	425,600		
Payroll tax expense	110,000		
Depreciation expense—office equipment	68,900		
Bad debt expense	14,000		
Amortization expense	10,500		
Total administrative expenses		954,000	
Total operating expenses			2,608,700
Income from operations			$ 633,400
Other income and expense:			
Interest revenue		$ 18,000	
Interest expense		(136,000)	
Loss on disposal of fixed asset		(23,000)	
Unrealized gain on trading investments		5,000	
Equity income in AM Coffee		57,000	(79,000)
Income before income tax expense			$ 554,400
Income tax expense			132,800
Net income			$ 421,600
Earnings per share [($421,600 – $30,000) ÷ 44,000 shares issued and outstanding]			$ 8.90

Mornin' Joe
Balance Sheet
December 31, 20Y6

Assets			
Current assets:			
Cash and cash equivalents		$ 235,000	
Trading investments (at cost)	$ 420,000		
Plus valuation allowance for trading investments	45,000	465,000	
Accounts receivable	$ 305,000		
Less allowance for doubtful accounts	12,300	292,700	
Merchandise inventory—at lower of cost (first-in, first-out method) or market		120,000	
Prepaid insurance		24,000	
Total current assets			$1,136,700
Investments:			
Investment in AM Coffee (equity method)			565,000
Property, plant, and equipment:			
Land		$1,850,000	
Buildings	$2,650,000		
Less accumulated depreciation	420,000	2,230,000	
Office equipment	$ 350,000		
Less accumulated depreciation	102,000	248,000	
Total property, plant, and equipment			4,328,000
Intangible assets:			
Patents			140,000
Total assets			$6,169,700
Liabilities			
Current liabilities:			
Accounts payable		$ 133,000	
Notes payable (current portion)		200,000	
Salaries and wages payable		42,000	
Payroll taxes payable		16,400	
Interest payable		40,000	
Total current liabilities			$ 431,400
Long-term liabilities:			
Bonds payable, 8%, due in 15 years	$ 500,000		
Less unamortized discount	16,000	$ 484,000	
Notes payable		1,400,000	
Total long-term liabilities			1,884,000
Total liabilities			$2,315,400
Stockholders' Equity			
Paid-in capital:			
Preferred 10% stock, $50 par (6,000 shares authorized and issued)	$ 300,000		
Excess of issue price over par	50,000	$ 350,000	
Common stock, $20 par (50,000 shares authorized, 45,000 shares issued)	$ 900,000		
Excess of issue price over par	1,450,000	2,350,000	
Total paid-in capital			$2,700,000
Retained earnings			1,200,300
Treasury stock (1,000 shares at cost)			(46,000)
Total stockholders' equity			$3,854,300
Total liabilities and stockholders' equity			$6,169,700

Mornin' Joe
Retained Earnings Statement
For the Year Ended December 31, 20Y6

Retained earnings, January 1, 20Y6		$ 852,700
Net income	$421,600	
Dividends:		
Preferred stock	(30,000)	
Common stock	(44,000)	
Increase in retained earnings		347,600
Retained earnings, December 31, 20Y6		$1,200,300

Mornin' Joe
Statement of Stockholders' Equity
For the Year Ended December 31, 20Y6

	Preferred Stock	Common Stock	Additional Paid-In Capital	Retained Earnings	Treasury Stock	Total
Balance, January 1, 20Y6	$300,000	$800,000	$1,325,000	$ 852,700	$(36,000)	$3,241,700
Issuance of additional common stock		100,000	175,000			275,000
Purchase of treasury stock					(10,000)	(10,000)
Net income				421,600		421,600
Dividends on preferred stock				(30,000)		(30,000)
Dividends on common stock				(44,000)		(44,000)
Balance, December 31, 20Y6	$300,000	$900,000	$1,500,000	$1,200,300	$(46,000)	$3,854,300

Appendix A

Interest Tables

Present Value of $1 at Compound Interest Due in *n* Periods

Periods	3%	3.5%	4%	4.5%	5%	5.5%	6%	6.5%	7%
1	0.97087	0.96618	0.96154	0.95694	0.95238	0.94787	0.94340	0.93897	0.93458
2	0.94260	0.93351	0.92456	0.91573	0.90703	0.89845	0.89000	0.88166	0.87344
3	0.91514	0.90194	0.88900	0.87630	0.86384	0.85161	0.83962	0.82785	0.81630
4	0.88849	0.87144	0.85480	0.83856	0.82270	0.80722	0.79209	0.77732	0.76290
5	0.86261	0.84197	0.82193	0.80245	0.78353	0.76513	0.74726	0.72988	0.71299
6	0.83748	0.81350	0.79031	0.76790	0.74622	0.72525	0.70496	0.68533	0.66634
7	0.81309	0.78599	0.75992	0.73483	0.71068	0.68744	0.66506	0.64351	0.62275
8	0.78941	0.75941	0.73069	0.70319	0.67684	0.65160	0.62741	0.60423	0.58201
9	0.76642	0.73373	0.70259	0.67290	0.64461	0.61763	0.59190	0.56735	0.54393
10	0.74409	0.70892	0.67556	0.64393	0.61391	0.58543	0.55839	0.53273	0.50835
11	0.72242	0.68495	0.64958	0.61620	0.58468	0.55491	0.52679	0.50021	0.47509
12	0.70138	0.66178	0.62460	0.58966	0.55684	0.52598	0.49697	0.46968	0.44401
13	0.68095	0.63940	0.60057	0.56427	0.53032	0.49856	0.46884	0.44102	0.41496
14	0.66112	0.61778	0.57748	0.53997	0.50507	0.47257	0.44230	0.41410	0.38782
15	0.64186	0.59689	0.55526	0.51672	0.48102	0.44793	0.41727	0.38883	0.36245
16	0.62317	0.57671	0.53391	0.49447	0.45811	0.42458	0.39365	0.36510	0.33873
17	0.60502	0.55720	0.51337	0.47318	0.43630	0.40245	0.37136	0.34281	0.31657
18	0.58739	0.53836	0.49363	0.45280	0.41552	0.38147	0.35034	0.32189	0.29586
19	0.57029	0.52016	0.47464	0.43330	0.39573	0.36158	0.33051	0.30224	0.27651
20	0.55368	0.50257	0.45639	0.41464	0.37689	0.34273	0.31180	0.28380	0.25842
21	0.53755	0.48557	0.43883	0.39679	0.35894	0.32486	0.29416	0.26648	0.24151
22	0.52189	0.46915	0.42196	0.37970	0.34185	0.30793	0.27751	0.25021	0.22571
23	0.50669	0.45329	0.40573	0.36335	0.32557	0.29187	0.26180	0.23494	0.21095
24	0.49193	0.43796	0.39012	0.34770	0.31007	0.27666	0.24698	0.22060	0.19715
25	0.47761	0.42315	0.37512	0.33273	0.29530	0.26223	0.23300	0.20714	0.18425
26	0.46369	0.40884	0.36069	0.31840	0.28124	0.24856	0.21981	0.19450	0.17220
27	0.45019	0.39501	0.34682	0.30469	0.26785	0.23560	0.20737	0.18263	0.16093
28	0.43708	0.38165	0.33348	0.29157	0.25509	0.22332	0.19563	0.17148	0.15040
29	0.42435	0.36875	0.32065	0.27902	0.24295	0.21168	0.18456	0.16101	0.14056
30	0.41199	0.35628	0.30832	0.26700	0.23138	0.20064	0.17411	0.15119	0.13137
31	0.39999	0.34423	0.29646	0.25550	0.22036	0.19018	0.16425	0.14196	0.12277
32	0.38834	0.33259	0.28506	0.24450	0.20987	0.18027	0.15496	0.13329	0.11474
33	0.37703	0.32134	0.27409	0.23397	0.19987	0.17087	0.14619	0.12516	0.10723
34	0.36604	0.31048	0.26355	0.22390	0.19035	0.16196	0.13791	0.11752	0.10022
35	0.35538	0.29998	0.25342	0.21425	0.18129	0.15352	0.13011	0.11035	0.09366
40	0.30656	0.25257	0.20829	0.17193	0.14205	0.11746	0.09722	0.08054	0.06678
45	0.26444	0.21266	0.17120	0.13796	0.11130	0.08988	0.07265	0.05879	0.04761
50	0.22811	0.17905	0.14071	0.11071	0.08720	0.06877	0.05429	0.04291	0.03395

Present Value of $1 at Compound Interest Due in *n* Periods

Periods	8%	9%	10%	11%	12%	13%	14%
1	0.92593	0.91743	0.90909	0.90090	0.89286	0.88496	0.87719
2	0.85734	0.84168	0.82645	0.81162	0.79719	0.78315	0.76947
3	0.79383	0.77218	0.75131	0.73119	0.71178	0.69305	0.67497
4	0.73503	0.70843	0.68301	0.65873	0.63552	0.61332	0.59208
5	0.68058	0.64993	0.62092	0.59345	0.56743	0.54276	0.51937
6	0.63017	0.59627	0.56447	0.53464	0.50663	0.48032	0.45559
7	0.58349	0.54703	0.51316	0.48166	0.45235	0.42506	0.39964
8	0.54027	0.50187	0.46651	0.43393	0.40388	0.37616	0.35056
9	0.50025	0.46043	0.42410	0.39092	0.36061	0.33288	0.30751
10	0.46319	0.42241	0.38554	0.35218	0.32197	0.29459	0.26974
11	0.42888	0.38753	0.35049	0.31728	0.28748	0.26070	0.23662
12	0.39711	0.35553	0.31863	0.28584	0.25668	0.23071	0.20756
13	0.36770	0.32618	0.28966	0.25751	0.22917	0.20416	0.18207
14	0.34046	0.29925	0.26333	0.23199	0.20462	0.18068	0.15971
15	0.31524	0.27454	0.23939	0.20900	0.18270	0.15989	0.14010
16	0.29189	0.25187	0.21763	0.18829	0.16312	0.14150	0.12289
17	0.27027	0.23107	0.19784	0.16963	0.14564	0.12522	0.10780
18	0.25025	0.21199	0.17986	0.15282	0.13004	0.11081	0.09456
19	0.23171	0.19449	0.16351	0.13768	0.11611	0.09806	0.08295
20	0.21455	0.17843	0.14864	0.12403	0.10367	0.08678	0.07276
21	0.19866	0.16370	0.13513	0.11174	0.09256	0.07680	0.06383
22	0.18394	0.15018	0.12285	0.10067	0.08264	0.06796	0.05599
23	0.17032	0.13778	0.11168	0.09069	0.07379	0.06014	0.04911
24	0.15770	0.12640	0.10153	0.08170	0.06588	0.05323	0.04308
25	0.14602	0.11597	0.09230	0.07361	0.05882	0.04710	0.03779
26	0.13520	0.10639	0.08391	0.06631	0.05252	0.04168	0.03315
27	0.12519	0.09761	0.07628	0.05974	0.04689	0.03689	0.02908
28	0.11591	0.08955	0.06934	0.05382	0.04187	0.03264	0.02551
29	0.10733	0.08215	0.06304	0.04849	0.03738	0.02889	0.02237
30	0.09938	0.07537	0.05731	0.04368	0.03338	0.02557	0.01963
31	0.09202	0.06915	0.05210	0.03935	0.02980	0.02262	0.01722
32	0.08520	0.06344	0.04736	0.03545	0.02661	0.02002	0.01510
33	0.07889	0.05820	0.04306	0.03194	0.02376	0.01772	0.01325
34	0.07305	0.05339	0.03914	0.02878	0.02121	0.01568	0.01162
35	0.06763	0.04899	0.03558	0.02592	0.01894	0.01388	0.01019
40	0.04603	0.03184	0.02209	0.01538	0.01075	0.00753	0.00529
45	0.03133	0.02069	0.01372	0.00913	0.00610	0.00409	0.00275
50	0.02132	0.01345	0.00852	0.00542	0.00346	0.00222	0.00143

Present Value of Ordinary Annuity of $1 per Period

Periods	3%	3.5%	4%	4.5%	5%	5.5%	6%	6.5%	7%
1	0.97087	0.96618	0.96154	0.95694	0.95238	0.94787	0.94340	0.93897	0.93458
2	1.91347	1.89969	1.88609	1.87267	1.85941	1.84632	1.83339	1.82063	1.80802
3	2.82861	2.80164	2.77509	2.74896	2.72325	2.69793	2.67301	2.64848	2.62432
4	3.71710	3.67308	3.62990	3.58753	3.54595	3.50515	3.46511	3.42580	3.38721
5	4.57971	4.51505	4.45182	4.38998	4.32948	4.27028	4.21236	4.15568	4.10020
6	5.41719	5.32855	5.24214	5.15787	5.07569	4.99553	4.91732	4.84101	4.76654
7	6.23028	6.11454	6.00205	5.89270	5.78637	5.68297	5.58238	5.48452	5.38929
8	7.01969	6.87396	6.73274	6.59589	6.46321	6.33457	6.20979	6.08875	5.97130
9	7.78611	7.60769	7.43533	7.26879	7.10782	6.95220	6.80169	6.65610	6.51523
10	8.53020	8.31661	8.11090	7.91272	7.72173	7.53763	7.36009	7.18883	7.02358
11	9.25262	9.00155	8.76048	8.52892	8.30641	8.09254	7.88687	7.68904	7.49867
12	9.95400	9.66333	9.38507	9.11858	8.86325	8.61852	8.38384	8.15873	7.94269
13	10.63496	10.30274	9.98565	9.68285	9.39357	9.11708	8.85268	8.59974	8.35765
14	11.29607	10.92052	10.56312	10.22283	9.89864	9.58965	9.29498	9.01384	8.74547
15	11.93794	11.51741	11.11839	10.73955	10.37966	10.03758	9.71225	9.40267	9.10791
16	12.56110	12.09412	11.65230	11.23402	10.83777	10.46216	10.10590	9.76776	9.44665
17	13.16612	12.65132	12.16567	11.70719	11.27407	10.86461	10.47726	10.11058	9.76322
18	13.75351	13.18968	12.65930	12.15999	11.68959	11.24607	10.82760	10.43247	10.05909
19	14.32380	13.70984	13.13394	12.59329	12.08532	11.60765	11.15812	10.73471	10.33560
20	14.87747	14.21240	13.59033	13.00794	12.46221	11.95038	11.46992	11.01851	10.59401
21	15.41502	14.69797	14.02916	13.40472	12.82115	12.27524	11.76408	11.28498	10.83553
22	15.93692	15.16712	14.45112	13.78442	13.16300	12.58317	12.04158	11.53520	11.06124
23	16.44361	15.62041	14.85684	14.14777	13.48857	12.87504	12.30338	11.77014	11.27219
24	16.93554	16.05837	15.24696	14.49548	13.79864	13.15170	12.55036	11.99074	11.46933
25	17.41315	16.48151	15.62208	14.82821	14.09394	13.41393	12.78336	12.19788	11.65358
26	17.87684	16.89035	15.98277	15.14661	14.37519	13.66250	13.00317	12.39237	11.82578
27	18.32703	17.28536	16.32959	15.45130	14.64303	13.89810	13.21053	12.57500	11.98671
28	18.76411	17.66702	16.66306	15.74287	14.89813	14.12142	13.40616	12.74648	12.13711
29	19.18845	18.03577	16.98371	16.02189	15.14107	14.33310	13.59072	12.90749	12.27767
30	19.60044	18.39205	17.29203	16.28889	15.37245	14.53375	13.76483	13.05868	12.40904
31	20.00043	18.73628	17.58849	16.54439	15.59281	14.72393	13.92909	13.20063	12.53181
32	20.38877	19.06887	17.87355	16.78889	15.80268	14.90420	14.08404	13.33393	12.64656
33	20.76579	19.39021	18.14765	17.02286	16.00255	15.07507	14.23023	13.45909	12.75379
34	21.13184	19.70068	18.41120	17.24676	16.19290	15.23703	14.36814	13.57661	12.85401
35	21.48722	20.00066	18.66461	17.46101	16.37419	15.39055	14.49825	13.68696	12.94767
40	23.11477	21.35507	19.79277	18.40158	17.15909	16.04612	15.04630	14.14553	13.33171
45	24.51871	22.49545	20.72004	19.15635	17.77407	16.54773	15.45583	14.48023	13.60552
50	25.72976	23.45562	21.48218	19.76201	18.25593	16.93152	15.76186	14.72452	13.80075

Present Value of Ordinary Annuity of $1 per Period

Periods	8%	9%	10%	11%	12%	13%	14%
1	0.92593	0.91743	0.90909	0.90090	0.89286	0.88496	0.87719
2	1.78326	1.75911	1.73554	1.71252	1.69005	1.66810	1.64666
3	2.57710	2.53129	2.48685	2.44371	2.40183	2.36115	2.32163
4	3.31213	3.23972	3.16987	3.10245	3.03735	2.97447	2.91371
5	3.99271	3.88965	3.79079	3.69590	3.60478	3.51723	3.43308
6	4.62288	4.48592	4.35526	4.23054	4.11141	3.99755	3.88867
7	5.20637	5.03295	4.86842	4.71220	4.56376	4.42261	4.28830
8	5.74664	5.53482	5.33493	5.14612	4.96764	4.79677	4.63886
9	6.24689	5.99525	5.75902	5.53705	5.32825	5.13166	4.94637
10	6.71008	6.41766	6.14457	5.88923	5.65022	5.42624	5.21612
11	7.13896	6.80519	6.49506	6.20652	5.93770	5.68694	5.45273
12	7.53608	7.16073	6.81369	6.49236	6.19437	5.91765	5.66029
13	7.90378	7.48690	7.10336	6.74987	6.42355	6.12181	5.84236
14	8.22424	7.78615	7.36669	6.96187	6.62817	6.30249	6.00207
15	8.55948	8.06069	7.60608	7.19087	6.81086	6.46238	6.14217
16	8.85137	8.31256	7.82371	7.37916	6.97399	6.60388	6.26506
17	9.12164	8.54363	8.02155	7.54879	7.11963	6.72909	6.37286
18	9.37189	8.75563	8.20141	7.70162	7.24967	6.83991	6.46742
19	9.60360	8.95011	8.36492	7.83929	7.36578	6.93797	6.55037
20	9.81815	9.12855	8.51356	7.96333	7.46944	7.02475	6.62313
21	10.01680	9.29224	8.64869	8.07507	7.56200	7.10155	6.68696
22	10.20074	9.44243	8.77154	8.17574	7.64465	7.16951	6.74294
23	10.37106	9.58021	8.88322	8.26643	7.71843	7.22966	6.79206
24	10.52876	9.70661	8.98474	8.34814	7.78432	7.28288	6.83514
25	10.67478	9.82258	9.07704	8.42174	7.84314	7.32998	6.87293
26	10.80998	9.92897	9.16095	8.48806	7.89566	7.37167	6.90608
27	10.93516	10.02658	9.23722	8.54780	7.94255	7.40856	6.93515
28	11.05108	10.11613	9.30657	8.60162	7.98442	7.44120	6.96066
29	11.15841	10.19828	9.36961	8.65011	8.02181	7.47009	6.98304
30	11.25778	10.27365	9.42691	8.69379	8.05518	7.49565	7.00266
31	11.34980	10.34280	9.47901	8.73315	8.08499	7.51828	7.01988
32	11.43500	10.40624	9.52638	8.76860	8.11159	7.53830	7.03498
33	11.51389	10.46444	9.56943	8.80054	8.13535	7.55602	7.04823
34	11.58693	10.51784	9.60857	8.82932	8.15656	7.57170	7.05985
35	11.65457	10.56682	9.64416	8.85524	8.17550	7.58557	7.07005
40	11.92461	10.75736	9.77905	8.95105	8.24378	7.63438	7.10504
45	12.10840	10.88120	9.86281	9.00791	8.28252	7.66086	7.12322
50	12.23348	10.96168	9.91481	9.04165	8.30450	7.67524	7.13266

Appendix B

Revenue Recognition

Companies recognize revenue when services have been performed or products have been delivered to customers. For example, when **McDonald's** sells a hamburger, the revenue is earned when the hamburger is delivered to the customer. In this example, revenue recognition is simple because the hamburger is delivered and cash is received at a single point in time.

Revenue recognition is more complex, however, when a transaction includes several items that are sold together, items that are delivered over time, or items whose prices depend upon future events. To address these more complex transactions, the Financial Accounting Standards Board (FASB) issued a new accounting standard in May 2014.[1] The new Standard uses a five-step method for determining when revenue should be recognized. The five steps are as follows:

Step 1. *Identify the contract with the customer.* The new Standard treats every revenue transaction as a contract. A contract is an agreement by the seller to provide a good or service in exchange for payment from the buyer. A contract may be verbal and implicit, such as the purchase of a **McDonald's** hamburger, or written and explicit, such as a cell phone contract.

Step 2. *Identify the separate performance obligations in the contract.* Every contract requires the seller and buyer to perform. For example, when you purchase a **McDonald's** hamburger, you (the buyer) perform by paying and McDonald's (the seller) performs by delivering a hamburger. When you purchase a cell phone from **Verizon**, the transaction is more complex. You perform by paying cash or charging your credit card and signing a written contract. Verizon performs by delivering you the phone and promising to provide you cellular service in the future. In this case, Verizon has two performance obligations: (1) to provide the phone and (2) to provide cellular service in the future.

Step 3. *Determine the transaction price.* The transaction price is the amount the seller is entitled to receive in exchange for the goods and services they have provided. In the case of the **McDonald's** hamburger, the transaction price is the amount paid for the hamburger. In the case of **Verizon**, the transaction price must be estimated for the phone (the first performance obligation) and cellular service (the second performance obligation).

Step 4. *Allocate the transaction price to the separate performance obligations.* Since the sale of a **McDonald's** hamburger involves the sale of a single item that is immediately delivered, the entire transaction price is allocated to the hamburger. In more complex transactions, such as a **Verizon** cellular service contract, the revenue received from the customer must be allocated among the performance obligations. This allocation is often based on the stand-alone (separate) price of each good or service. For example, Verizon should allocate the revenue from the

1 Accounting Standards Update, *Revenue from Contracts with Customers (Topic 606)*, Financial Accounting Standards Board, May 2014, Norwalk, CT.

customer between the phone (first performance obligation) and the commitment to provide cellular service (second performance obligation).

Step 5. *Recognize revenue when each separate performance obligation is satisfied.* The seller should recognize (record) revenue as each performance obligation is satisfied. In the case of **McDonald's**, the performance obligation is satisfied when the clerk delivers the hamburger to the customer. At this point, the control of the hamburger has passed to the customer. In the case of **Verizon**, it satisfies its first performance obligation when it delivers you the phone. Verizon satisfies its second performance obligation over time by providing you cellular service. Thus, Verizon should record a portion of the total revenue at the time you sign the contract and receive your phone and the remaining revenue over the period cellular service is provided.

To illustrate, assume that on March 1, Chandler Evans upgrades (replaces) his cell phone with Star Cellular at no cost by signing a two-year agreement. The new agreement cannot be cancelled and requires a payment of $90 per month. The cell phone selected by Evans cost Star Cellular $250.

The five-step method for recognizing revenue from this transaction would be applied as follows:

Step 1. *Identify the contract with the customer.* The contract with Chandler Evans is the two-year cellular service agreement that includes delivery of a new cell phone.

Step 2. *Identify the separate performance obligations in the contract.* Star Cellular has two separate performance obligations under this contract. First, Star Cellular must deliver a new cell phone at the time that Evans signs the service agreement. Second, Star Cellular must provide Evans with cell service for two years.

Step 3. *Determine the transaction price.* The transaction price is the total amount Star Cellular will receive over the contract period. In this case, Star Cellular will receive $2,160 ($90 × 24 months) over the contract period.[2]

Step 4. *Allocate the transaction price to the separate performance obligations.* If Star Cellular sold the cell phone and cell service separately, the individual prices would be as follows:

Cell phone (sold separately)	$ 600
Cell service for two years	3,000
Total price if sold separately	$3,600

The transaction price is allocated to each performance obligation based upon what each obligation would sell for separately as a stand-alone product. To illustrate, the cell phone is allocated $360 of the transaction price of $2,160, computed as follows:

$$\text{Cell Phone} = \text{Transaction Price} \times \frac{\text{Price of Cell Service Sold Separately}}{\text{Total Price of Cell Phone and Cell Service Sold Separately}}$$

$$= \$2{,}160 \times \frac{\$600}{\$3{,}600} = \$360$$

The cell service is allocated $1,800 of the transaction price of $2,160, computed as follows:

$$\text{Cell Service} = \text{Transaction Price} \times \frac{\text{Price of Cell Service Sold Separately}}{\text{Total Price of Cell Phone and Cell Service Sold Separately}}$$

$$= \$2{,}160 \times \frac{\$3{,}000}{\$3{,}600} = \$1{,}800$$

Step 5. *Recognize revenue when each separate performance obligation is satisfied.* The $360 of revenue assigned to the cell phone is recognized when the customer signs the service agreement and receives the phone. At this point, the first performance obligation has been satisfied by Star Cellular and the control of the phone has passed to the customer. The journal entry for revenue on March 1 is as follows:

2 An interest component may need to be considered in long-term contracts. To simplify, we ignore interest.

Mar.	1	Accounts Receivable—Chandler Evans	360	
		Sales		360
	1	Cost of Merchandise Sold	250	
		Merchandise Inventory		250

The $1,800 of cell service revenue recognized as the performance obligation is satisfied over the two-year term of the contract. For example, $75 ($1,800 ÷ 24 months) of service revenue would be recorded each month. The journal entry for the service revenue for March is as follows:

Mar.	31	Cash	90	
		Accounts Receivable ($360 ÷ 24 months)		15
		Cell Service Revenue ($1,800 ÷ 24 months)		75

The preceding journal entries illustrate how over the life of the two-year contract the total revenue from the contract of $2,160 is divided between the sale of the cell phone ($360 of revenue) and providing of cell service ($1,800 of revenue). In addition, the journal entries illustrate when revenue from the phone and service is recorded.

Exhibit 1 summarizes the division of revenue and its recording over the two-year contract.

EXHIBIT 1 **Recording Revenue over Two-Year Contract**

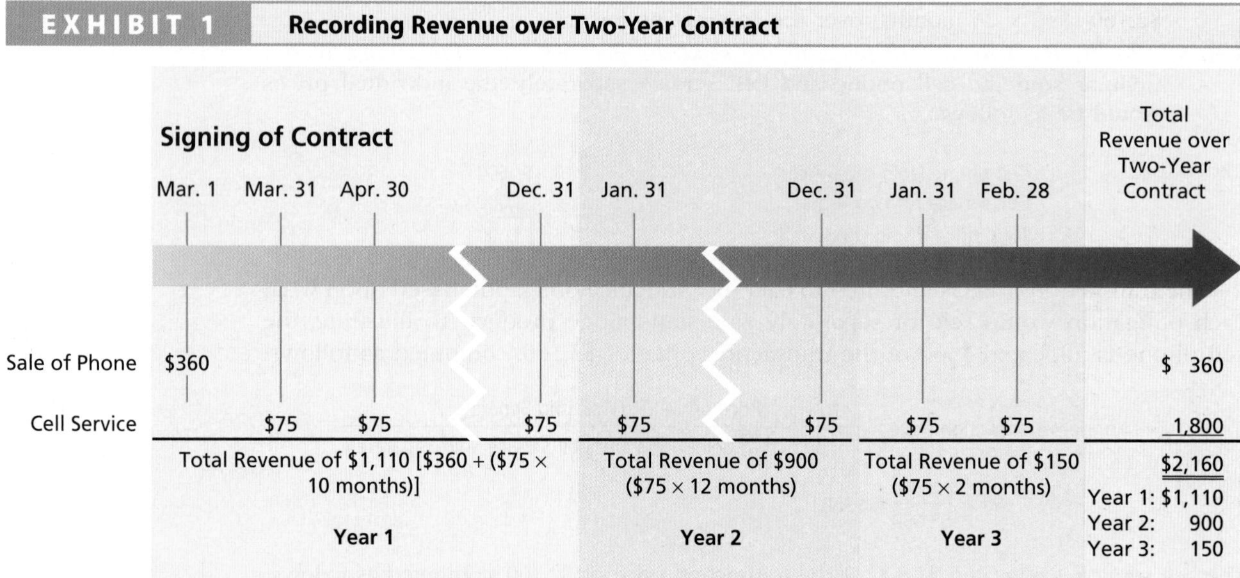

Appendix C

Selected Excerpts from Nike Inc., Form 10-K for the Fiscal Year Ended May 31, 2018

NIKE, Inc.

Management's Annual Report on Internal Control Over Financial Reporting

Management is responsible for establishing and maintaining adequate internal control over financial reporting, as such term is defined in Rule 13(a) - 15(f) and Rule 15(d) - 15(f) of the Securities Exchange Act of 1934, as amended. Internal control over financial reporting is a process designed to provide reasonable assurance regarding the reliability of financial reporting and the preparation of the financial statements for external purposes in accordance with generally accepted accounting principles in the United States of America. Internal control over financial reporting includes those policies and procedures that: (i) pertain to the maintenance of records that, in reasonable detail, accurately and fairly reflect the transactions and dispositions of assets of the Company; (ii) provide reasonable assurance that transactions are recorded as necessary to permit preparation of financial statements in accordance with generally accepted accounting principles, and that receipts and expenditures of the Company are being made only in accordance with authorizations of our management and directors; and (iii) provide reasonable assurance regarding prevention or timely detection of unauthorized acquisition, use or disposition of assets of the Company that could have a material effect on the financial statements.

While "reasonable assurance" is a high level of assurance, it does not mean absolute assurance. Because of its inherent limitations, internal control over financial reporting may not prevent or detect every misstatement and instance of fraud. Controls are susceptible to manipulation, especially in instances of fraud caused by the collusion of two or more people, including our senior management. Also, projections of any evaluation of effectiveness to future periods are subject to the risk that controls may become inadequate because of changes in conditions, or that the degree of compliance with the policies or procedures may deteriorate.

Under the supervision and with the participation of our Chief Executive Officer and Chief Financial Officer, our management conducted an evaluation of the effectiveness of our internal control over financial reporting based upon the framework in *Internal Control — Integrated Framework (2013)* issued by the Committee of Sponsoring Organizations of the Treadway Commission (COSO). Based on the results of our evaluation, our management concluded that our internal control over financial reporting was effective as of May 31, 2018 .

PricewaterhouseCoopers LLP, an independent registered public accounting firm, has audited (1) the Consolidated Financial Statements and (2) the effectiveness of our internal control over financial reporting as of May 31, 2018 , as stated in their report herein.

Mark G. Parker
Chairman, President and Chief Executive Officer

Andrew Campion
Chief Financial Officer

Report of Independent Registered Public Accounting Firm

To the Board of Directors and Shareholders of NIKE, Inc.

Opinions on the Financial Statements and Internal Control over Financial Reporting

We have audited the accompanying consolidated balance sheets of NIKE, Inc. and its subsidiaries as of May 31, 2018 and 2017, and the related consolidated statements of income, comprehensive income, shareholders' equity and cash flows for each of the three years in the period ended May 31, 2018, including the related notes and financial statement schedule listed in the index appearing under Item 15(a)(2) (collectively referred to as the "consolidated financial statements"). We also have audited the Company ' s internal control over financial reporting as of May 31, 2018, based on criteria established in *Internal Control - Integrated Framework* (2013) issued by the Committee of Sponsoring Organizations of the Treadway Commission (COSO).

In our opinion, the consolidated financial statements referred to above present fairly, in all material respects, the financial position of the Company as of May 31, 2018 and 2017 , and the results of their operations and their cash flows for each of the three years in the period ended May 31, 2018 in conformity with accounting principles generally accepted in the United States of America. Also in our opinion, the Company maintained, in all material respects, effective internal control over financial reporting as of May 31, 2018, based on criteria established in *Internal Control - Integrated Framework* (2013) issued by the COSO.

Change in Accounting Principle

As discussed in Note 1 to the consolidated financial statements, the Company changed the manner in which it accounts for share-based payment awards to employees as of June 1, 2017.

Basis for Opinions

The Company's management is responsible for these consolidated financial statements, for maintaining effective internal control over financial reporting, and for its assessment of the effectiveness of internal control over financial reporting, included in Management's Annual Report on Internal Control over Financial Reporting appearing under Item 8. Our responsibility is to express opinions on the Company's consolidated financial statements and on the Company's internal control over financial reporting based on our audits. We are a public accounting firm registered with the Public Company Accounting Oversight Board (United States) ("PCAOB") and are required to be independent with respect to the Company in accordance with the U.S. federal securities laws and the applicable rules and regulations of the Securities and Exchange Commission and the PCAOB.

We conducted our audits in accordance with the standards of the PCAOB. Those standards require that we plan and perform the audits to obtain reasonable assurance about whether the consolidated financial statements are free of material misstatement, whether due to error or fraud, and whether effective internal control over financial reporting was maintained in all material respects.

Our audits of the consolidated financial statements included performing procedures to assess the risks of material misstatement of the consolidated financial statements, whether due to error or fraud, and performing procedures that respond to those risks. Such procedures included examining, on a test basis, evidence regarding the amounts and disclosures in the consolidated financial statements. Our audits also included evaluating the accounting principles used and significant estimates made by management, as well as evaluating the overall presentation of the consolidated financial statements. Our audit of internal control over financial reporting included obtaining an understanding of internal control over financial reporting, assessing the risk that a material weakness exists, and testing and evaluating the design and operating effectiveness of internal control based on the assessed risk. Our audits also included performing such other procedures as we considered necessary in the circumstances. We believe that our audits provide a reasonable basis for our opinions.

Definition and Limitations of Internal Control over Financial Reporting

A company's internal control over financial reporting is a process designed to provide reasonable assurance regarding the reliability of financial reporting and the preparation of financial statements for external purposes in accordance with generally accepted accounting principles. A company's internal control over financial reporting includes those policies and procedures that (i) pertain to the maintenance of records that, in reasonable detail, accurately and fairly reflect the transactions and dispositions of the assets of the company; (ii) provide reasonable assurance that transactions are recorded as necessary to permit preparation of financial statements in accordance with generally accepted accounting principles, and that receipts and expenditures of the company are being made only in accordance with authorizations of management and directors of the company; and (iii) provide reasonable assurance regarding prevention or timely detection of unauthorized acquisition, use, or disposition of the company's assets that could have a material effect on the financial statements.

Because of its inherent limitations, internal control over financial reporting may not prevent or detect misstatements. Also, projections of any evaluation of effectiveness to future periods are subject to the risk that controls may become inadequate because of changes in conditions, or that the degree of compliance with the policies or procedures may deteriorate.

/S/ PricewaterhouseCoopers LLP

Portland, Oregon

July 24, 2018

NIKE, Inc. Consolidated Statements of Income

	Year Ended May 31,		
(In millions, except per share data)	2018	2017	2016
Revenues	$ 36,397	$ 34,350	$ 32,376
Cost of sales	20,441	19,038	17,405
Gross profit	15,956	15,312	14,971
Demand creation expense	3,577	3,341	3,278
Operating overhead expense	7,934	7,222	7,191
Total selling and administrative expense	11,511	10,563	10,469
Interest expense (income), net	54	59	19
Other expense (income), net	66	(196)	(140)
Income before income taxes	4,325	4,886	4,623
Income tax expense	2,392	646	863
NET INCOME	**$ 1,933**	**$ 4,240**	**$ 3,760**
Earnings per common share:			
Basic	$ 1.19	$ 2.56	$ 2.21
Diluted	$ 1.17	$ 2.51	$ 2.16
Dividends declared per common share	$ 0.78	$ 0.70	$ 0.62

The accompanying Notes to the Consolidated Financial Statements are an integral part of this statement.

NIKE, Inc. Consolidated Statements of Comprehensive Income

	Year Ended May 31,		
(In millions)	2018	2017	2016
Net income	$ 1,933	$ 4,240	$ 3,760
Other comprehensive income (loss), net of tax:			
Change in net foreign currency translation adjustment	(6)	16	(176)
Change in net gains (losses) on cash flow hedges	76	(515)	(757)
Change in net gains (losses) on other	34	(32)	5
Total other comprehensive income (loss), net of tax	104	(531)	(928)
TOTAL COMPREHENSIVE INCOME	**$ 2,037**	**$ 3,709**	**$ 2,832**

The accompanying Notes to the Consolidated Financial Statements are an integral part of this statement.

NIKE, Inc. Consolidated Balance Sheets

	May 31,	
(In millions)	**2018**	**2017**
ASSETS		
Current assets:		
Cash and equivalents	$ 4,249	$ 3,808
Short-term investments	996	2,371
Accounts receivable, net	3,498	3,677
Inventories	5,261	5,055
Prepaid expenses and other current assets	1,130	1,150
Total current assets	15,134	16,061
Property, plant and equipment, net	4,454	3,989
Identifiable intangible assets, net	285	283
Goodwill	154	139
Deferred income taxes and other assets	2,509	2,787
TOTAL ASSETS	**$ 22,536**	**$ 23,259**
LIABILITIES AND SHAREHOLDERS' EQUITY		
Current liabilities:		
Current portion of long-term debt	$ 6	$ 6
Notes payable	336	325
Accounts payable	2,279	2,048
Accrued liabilities	3,269	3,011
Income taxes payable	150	84
Total current liabilities	6,040	5,474
Long-term debt	3,468	3,471
Deferred income taxes and other liabilities	3,216	1,907
Commitments and contingencies (Note 15)		
Redeemable preferred stock	—	—
Shareholders' equity:		
Common stock at stated value:		
Class A convertible — 329 and 329 shares outstanding	—	—
Class B — 1,272 and 1,314 shares outstanding	3	3
Capital in excess of stated value	6,384	5,710
Accumulated other comprehensive loss	(92)	(213)
Retained earnings	3,517	6,907
Total shareholders' equity	9,812	12,407
TOTAL LIABILITIES AND SHAREHOLDERS' EQUITY	**$ 22,536**	**$ 23,259**

The accompanying Notes to the Consolidated Financial Statements are an integral part of this statement.

NIKE, Inc. Consolidated Statements of Cash Flows

	Year Ended May 31,		
(In millions)	2018	2017	2016
Cash provided by operations:			
Net income	$ 1,933	$ 4,240	$ 3,760
Adjustments to reconcile net income to net cash provided by operations:			
Depreciation	747	706	649
Deferred income taxes	647	(273)	(80)
Stock-based compensation	218	215	236
Amortization and other	27	10	13
Net foreign currency adjustments	(99)	(117)	98
Changes in certain working capital components and other assets and liabilities:			
Decrease (increase) in accounts receivable	187	(426)	60
(Increase) in inventories	(255)	(231)	(590)
Decrease (increase) in prepaid expenses and other current and non-current assets	35	(120)	(161)
Increase (decrease) in accounts payable, accrued liabilities and other current and non-current liabilities	1,515	(158)	(586)
Cash provided by operations	4,955	3,846	3,399
Cash provided (used) by investing activities:			
Purchases of short-term investments	(4,783)	(5,928)	(5,367)
Maturities of short-term investments	3,613	3,623	2,924
Sales of short-term investments	2,496	2,423	2,386
Investments in reverse repurchase agreements	—	—	150
Additions to property, plant and equipment	(1,028)	(1,105)	(1,143)
Disposals of property, plant and equipment	3	13	10
Other investing activities	(25)	(34)	6
Cash provided (used) by investing activities	276	(1,008)	(1,034)
Cash used by financing activities:			
Net proceeds from long-term debt issuance	—	1,482	981
Long-term debt payments, including current portion	(6)	(44)	(106)
Increase (decrease) in notes payable	13	327	(67)
Payments on capital lease and other financing obligations	(23)	(17)	(7)
Proceeds from exercise of stock options and other stock issuances	733	489	507
Repurchase of common stock	(4,254)	(3,223)	(3,238)
Dividends — common and preferred	(1,243)	(1,133)	(1,022)
Tax payments for net share settlement of equity awards	(55)	(29)	(22)
Cash used by financing activities	(4,835)	(2,148)	(2,974)
Effect of exchange rate changes on cash and equivalents	45	(20)	(105)
Net increase (decrease) in cash and equivalents	441	670	(714)
Cash and equivalents, beginning of year	3,808	3,138	3,852
CASH AND EQUIVALENTS, END OF YEAR	**$ 4,249**	**$ 3,808**	**$ 3,138**
Supplemental disclosure of cash flow information:			
Cash paid during the year for:			
Interest, net of capitalized interest	$ 125	$ 98	$ 70
Income taxes	529	703	748
Non-cash additions to property, plant and equipment	294	266	252
Dividends declared and not paid	320	300	271

The accompanying Notes to the Consolidated Financial Statements are an integral part of this statement.

NIKE, Inc. Consolidated Statements of Shareholders' Equity

	Common Stock				Capital in Excess of Stated Value	Accumulated Other Comprehensive Income	Retained Earnings	Total
	Class A		Class B					
(In millions, except per share data)	**Shares**	**Amount**	**Shares**	**Amount**				
Balance at May 31, 2015	**355**	**$ —**	**1,357**	**$ 3**	**$ 4,165**	**$ 1,246**	**$ 7,293**	**$ 12,707**
Stock options exercised			22		680			680
Conversion to Class B Common Stock	(2)	—	2	—				—
Repurchase of Class B Common Stock			(55)		(148)		(3,090)	(3,238)
Dividends on common stock ($0.62 per share) and preferred stock ($0.10 per share)							(1,053)	(1,053)
Issuance of shares to employees, net of shares withheld for employee taxes			3		105		(11)	94
Stock-based compensation					236			236
Net income							3,760	3,760
Other comprehensive income (loss)						(928)		(928)
Balance at May 31, 2016	**353**	**$ —**	**1,329**	**$ 3**	**$ 5,038**	**$ 318**	**$ 6,899**	**$ 12,258**
Stock options exercised			17		525			525
Conversion to Class B Common Stock	(24)	—	24	—				—
Repurchase of Class B Common Stock			(60)		(189)		(3,060)	(3,249)
Dividends on common stock ($0.70 per share) and preferred stock ($0.10 per share)							(1,159)	(1,159)
Issuance of shares to employees, net of shares withheld for employee taxes			4		121		(13)	108
Stock-based compensation					215			215
Net income							4,240	4,240
Other comprehensive income (loss)						(531)		(531)
Balance at May 31, 2017	**329**	**$ —**	**1,314**	**$ 3**	**$ 5,710**	**$ (213)**	**$ 6,907**	**$ 12,407**
Stock options exercised			24		600			600
Conversion to Class B Common Stock	—	—	—	—				—
Repurchase of Class B Common Stock			(70)		(254)		(4,013)	(4,267)
Dividends on common stock ($0.78 per share) and preferred stock ($0.10 per share)							(1,265)	(1,265)
Issuance of shares to employees, net of shares withheld for employee taxes			4		110		(28)	82
Stock-based compensation					218			218
Net income							1,933	1,933
Other comprehensive income (loss)						104		104
Reclassifications to retained earnings in accordance with ASU 2018-02						17	(17)	—
Balance at May 31, 2018	**329**	**$ —**	**1,272**	**$ 3**	**$ 6,384**	**$ (92)**	**$ 3,517**	**$ 9,812**

The accompanying Notes to the Consolidated Financial Statements are an integral part of this statement.

Glossary

A

accelerated depreciation method A depreciation method that provides for a higher depreciation amount in the first year of the asset's use, followed by a gradually declining amount of depreciation. (Ch. 10)

account An accounting form that is used to record the increases and decreases in each financial statement item. (Ch. 2)

account form The form of balance sheet that resembles the basic format of the accounting equation, with assets on the left side and Liabilities and Owner's Equity sections on the right side. (Ch. 1)

account payable The liability created by a purchase on account. (Ch. 1)

account(s) receivable The claim against customers created by selling merchandise or services on account, normally collected within a short period and classified as a current asset. (Chs. 1, 2, 9)

accounting An information system that provides reports to stakeholders about the economic activities and condition of a business. (Ch. 1)

accounting cycle The process that begins with analyzing and journalizing transactions and ends with the post-closing trial balance. (Ch. 4)

accounting equation Assets = Liabilities + Owner's Equity. (Ch. 1)

Accounting Standards Codification An electronic database maintained by the Financial Accounting Standards Board (FASB) that contains all of the accounting standards that make up the generally accepted accounting principles (GAAP). (Ch. 1)

Accounting Standards Updates Published changes to accounting standards that are the source of updates to the Accounting Standards Codification. (Ch. 1)

accounting system The methods and procedures used by a business to collect, classify, summarize, and report financial data for use by management and external users. (Ch. 5)

accounts payable subsidiary ledger The subsidiary ledger containing the individual accounts with creditors (suppliers). (Ch. 5)

accounts receivable analysis An evaluation of a company's ability to collect its accounts receivable. (Ch. 17)

accounts receivable subsidiary ledger The subsidiary ledger containing the individual accounts with customers. (Ch. 5)

accounts receivable turnover The relationship between sales and accounts receivable, computed by dividing sales by the average accounts receivable; measures how frequently during the year the accounts receivable are being converted to cash. (Chs. 9, 17)

accrual An accrual occurs when revenue has been earned or an expense has been incurred but has not been recorded. (Ch. 3)

accrual basis of accounting A basis of accounting in which revenues and their related expenses are reported on the income statement in the period in which a service has been performed or a product has been delivered, regardless of when cash has been received. (Ch. 3)

Accumulated Depreciation The contra asset account credited when recording the depreciation of a fixed asset. (Ch. 3)

accumulated other comprehensive income The cumulative effects of other comprehensive income items reported separately in the Stockholders' Equity section of the balance sheet. (Ch. 15)

adjusted trial balance The trial balance prepared after all the adjusting entries have been posted. (Ch. 3)

adjusting entries The journal entries that bring the accounts up to date at the end of the accounting period. (Ch. 3)

adjusting process An analysis and updating of the accounts when financial statements are prepared. (Ch. 3)

administrative expenses Expenses incurred in the administration or general operations of the business. (Ch. 6)

aging the receivables The process of analyzing the accounts receivable and classifying them according to various age groupings, with the due date being the base point for determining age. (Ch. 9)

Allowance for Doubtful Accounts The contra asset account for accounts receivable credited for estimated bad debts. (Ch. 9)

allowance method The method of accounting for uncollectible accounts that provides an expense for uncollectible receivables in advance of their write-off. (Ch. 9)

amortization The periodic transfer of the cost of an intangible asset to expense. (Ch. 10) A portion of a bond discount or bond premium transferred to interest expense over time. (Ch. 14)

analytical methods Methods of financial statement analysis that examine changes in the amount and percentage of financial statement items within and across periods. (Ch. 17)

annuity A series of equal cash flows at fixed intervals. (Ch. 14)

asset turnover A measure of how effectively a business is using its assets to generate sales, computed as sales divided by average total assets. (Chs. 6, 17)

assets The resources owned by a business. (Chs. 1, 2)

available-for-sale securities Securities that management expects to sell in the future but not in the near term. (Ch. 15)

B

bad debt expense The operating expense incurred because of the failure to collect receivables. (Ch. 9)

balance of the account The amount of the difference between the debits and the credits that have been entered into an account. (Ch. 2)

balance sheet A list of the assets, liabilities, and owner's equity as of a specific date, usually at the close of the last day of a month or a year. (Ch. 1)

bank reconciliation The analysis that details the items responsible for the difference between the cash balance reported in the bank statement and the balance of the cash account in the ledger. (Ch. 8)

bank statement A summary of all transactions mailed to the depositor or made available online by the bank each month. (Ch. 8)

bond An interest-bearing note that requires periodic interest payments, with the face amount to be repaid at the maturity date. (Ch. 14)

bond indenture The contract between a corporation issuing bonds and the bondholders. (Ch. 14)

book value The cost of a fixed asset minus accumulated depreciation on the asset. (Ch. 10)

book value of the asset The difference between the cost of a fixed asset and its accumulated depreciation. (Ch. 3)

boot The amount a buyer owes a seller when a fixed asset is traded in on a similar asset. (Ch. 10)

business An organization in which basic resources (inputs), such as materials and labor, are assembled and processed to provide goods or services (outputs) to customers. (Ch. 1)

business combination A business making an investment in another business by acquiring a controlling share, often greater than 50%, of the outstanding voting stock of another corporation by paying cash or exchanging stock. (Ch. 15)

business entity concept A concept of accounting that limits the economic data in the accounting system to data related directly to the activities of the business. (Ch. 1)

business transaction An economic event or condition that directly changes an entity's financial condition or directly affects its results of operations. (Ch. 1)

C

capital account An account used for a proprietorship that represents the owner's equity. (Ch. 2)

capital expenditures The costs of acquiring fixed assets, adding to a fixed asset, improving a fixed asset, or extending a fixed asset's useful life. (Ch. 10)

carrying amount The book value of bonds payable, computed as the face amount less any unamortized discount or plus any unamortized premium. (Ch. 14)

cash Coins, currency (paper money), checks, money orders, and money on deposit that is available for unrestricted withdrawal from banks and other financial institutions. (Ch. 8)

cash basis of accounting A basis of accounting in which revenues and expenses are reported on the income statement in the period in which cash is received or paid. (Ch. 3)

cash dividend A cash distribution of earnings by a corporation to its shareholders. (Ch. 13)

cash equivalents Highly liquid investments that are usually reported with cash on the balance sheet. (Ch. 8)

cash flow per share The net cash flows from operating activities divided by the number of common shares outstanding. (Ch. 16)

cash flows from (used for) financing activities The section of the statement of cash flows that reports cash flows from transactions affecting the equity and debt of the business. (Ch. 16)

cash flows from (used for) investing activities The section of the statement of cash flows that reports cash flows from transactions affecting investments in noncurrent assets. (Ch. 16)

cash flows from (used for) operating activities The section of the statement of cash flows that reports the cash transactions affecting the determination of net income. (Ch. 16)

cash payments journal The special journal in which all cash payments are recorded. (Ch. 5)

cash receipts journal The special journal in which all cash receipts are recorded. (Ch. 5)

cash refund An amount paid by the seller to the buyer for merchandise that is defective, is damaged during shipment, or does not meet the buyer's expectations. (Ch. 6)

cash short and over account An account which has recorded errors in cash sales or errors in making change causing the amount of actual cash on hand to differ from the beginning amount of cash plus the cash sales for the day. (Ch. 8)

Certified Public Accountants (CPA) Public accountants who have met a state's education, experience, and examination requirements. (Ch. 1)

chart of accounts A list of the accounts in the ledger. (Ch. 2)

closing entries The entries that transfer the balances of the revenue, expense, and drawing accounts to the owner's capital account. (Ch. 4)

closing process The transfer process of converting temporary account balances to zero by transferring the revenue and expense account balances to the owner's capital account, and transferring the owner's drawing account balance to the owner's capital account. (Ch. 4)

closing the books The process of transferring temporary accounts balances to permanent accounts at the end of the accounting period. (Ch. 4)

common stock The stock outstanding when a corporation has issued only one class of stock. (Ch. 13)

common-sized statement A financial statement in which all items are expressed as percentages, with no dollar amounts shown. (Ch. 17)

compensating balance A requirement by some banks requiring depositors to maintain minimum cash balances in their bank accounts. (Ch. 8)

comprehensive income All changes in stockholders' equity during a period, except those resulting from dividends and stockholders' investments. (Ch. 15)

consigned inventory Merchandise that is shipped by manufacturers to retailers who act as the manufacturer's selling agent. (Ch. 7)

consignee The name for the retailer in a consigned inventory arrangement. (Ch. 7)

consignor The name for the manufacturer in a consigned inventory arrangement. (Ch. 7)

consolidated financial statements Financial statements resulting from combining parent and subsidiary statements. (Ch. 15)

contingent liabilities Liabilities that may arise from past transactions if certain events occur in the future. (Ch. 11)

contra accounts (or contra asset accounts) An account offset against another account. (Ch. 3)

contract rate The periodic interest to be paid on the bonds that is identified in the bond indenture; expressed as a percentage of the face amount of the bond. (Ch. 14)

control environment The overall attitude of management and employees about the importance of controls. (Ch. 8)

controlling account The account in the general ledger that summarizes the balances of the accounts in a subsidiary ledger. (Ch. 5)

copyright An exclusive right to publish and sell a literary, artistic, or musical composition. (Ch. 10)

corporation A business organized under state or federal statutes as a separate business entity. (Ch. 1)

correcting journal entry An entry that is prepared to correct an error that has already been journalized and posted. (Ch. 2)

cost concept A concept of accounting that determines the amount initially entered into the accounting records for purchases. (Ch. 1)

cost method A method of accounting for bond investments in which the purchase is recorded at original cost, including any fees charged by a broker in acquiring the bonds, and any accrued interest is recorded separately. (Ch. 15)

cost of merchandise sold The cost of merchandise inventory that is reported as an expense when merchandise is sold; on the income statement of a merchandising business, determined by subtracting ending merchandise inventory from the cost of merchandise available for sale. (Ch. 6)

credit Amount entered on the right side of an account. (Ch. 2)

credit memorandum (credit memo) A form used by a seller to inform the buyer of the amount the seller proposes to credit to the account receivable due from the buyer. (Ch. 6)

credit period The amount of time the buyer is allowed in which to pay the seller. (Ch. 6)

credit terms Terms for payment on account by the buyer to the seller. (Ch. 6)

cumulative preferred stock Stock that has a right to receive regular dividends that were not declared (paid) in prior years. (Ch. 13)

current assets Cash and other assets that are expected to be converted to cash or sold or used up, usually within one year or less, through the normal operations of the business. (Ch. 4)

current liabilities Liabilities that will be due within a short time (usually one year or less) and that are to be paid out of current assets. (Ch. 4)

current position analysis An evaluation of a company's ability to pay its current liabilities. (Chs. 11, 17)

current ratio A financial ratio that measures a company's ability to pay its current liabilities, computed by dividing current assets by current liabilities. (Chs. 4, 17)

customer allowance Returns to the seller by the customer or reductions from the initial selling price due to defective or damaged merchandise or goods that did not meet the customer's expectations. (Ch. 6)

customer discounts A variety of discounts offered by the seller as incentive for the customer to act in a way benefiting the seller. (Ch. 6)

Customer Refunds Payable A liability account for estimated refunds and allowances that will be paid or granted to customers in the future. (Ch. 6)

D

days' sales in inventory The relationship between the volume of sales and inventory, computed by dividing the inventory at the end of the year by the average daily cost of merchandise sold. (Ch. 7)

days' sales in receivables An estimate of the length of time the accounts receivable have been outstanding, computed by dividing the average accounts receivable by the average daily sales. (Ch. 9)

debit Amount entered on the left side of an account. (Ch. 2)

debit memorandum (debit memo) A form used by a buyer to inform the seller of the amount the buyer proposes to debit to the account payable due the seller. (Ch. 6)

debt securities Notes and bond investments that provide interest revenue over a fixed maturity. (Ch. 15)

deferral A deferral occurs when cash related to a future revenue or expense has been initially recorded as a liability or an asset. (Ch. 3)

deficiency A debit balance in a partner's capital account, representing a claim of the partnership against the partner. (Ch. 12)

deficit A debit balance in the retained earnings account. (Ch. 13)

defined benefit plan A pension plan that promises employees a fixed annual pension benefit at retirement, based on years of service and compensation levels. (Ch. 11)

defined contribution plan A pension plan that requires a fixed amount of money to be invested on the employee's behalf during the employee's working years. (Ch. 11)

depletion expense A portion of the cost of a natural resource debited to expense as it is harvested or mined and then sold. (Ch. 10)

depreciable cost The difference between a fixed asset's initial cost and its residual value. (Ch. 10)

depreciate To lose usefulness as all fixed assets except land do. (Ch. 3)

depreciation The systematic periodic transfer of the cost of a fixed asset to an expense account during its expected useful life. (Chs. 3, 10)

depreciation expense The portion of the cost of a fixed asset that is recorded as an expense each year of its useful life. (Ch. 3)

direct method A method of reporting the cash flows from operating activities as the difference between the operating cash receipts and the operating cash payments. (Ch. 16)

direct write-off method The method of accounting for uncollectible accounts that recognizes the expense only when accounts are judged to be worthless. (Ch. 9)

discount The excess of the par value of stock over its issue price, the interest deducted from the maturity value of a note, or the excess of the face amount of bonds over their issue price. (Chs. 13, 14)

dishonored note receivable A note that the maker fails to pay on the due date. (Ch. 9)

dividend yield A profitability ratio that indicates the rate of return to common stockholders from cash dividends, computed as dividends per share of common stock divided by the market price per share of common stock. (Chs. 15, 17)

dividends Distribution of a corporation's earnings to stockholders. (Ch. 13)

dividends per share A profitability ratio that measures the extent to which earnings are being distributed to common shareholders, computed as dividends on common stock divided by shares of common stock outstanding. (Ch. 17)

double-declining-balance method A method of depreciation that provides a declining periodic expense over an asset's expected useful life, applied at twice the straight-line rate to the book value of the asset. (Ch. 10)

double-entry accounting system A system of accounting for recording transactions, based on recording increases and decreases in accounts so that debits equal credits. (Ch. 2)

drawing The account used to record amounts withdrawn by an owner of a proprietorship. (Ch. 2)

E

e-commerce The use of the Internet for performing business transactions. (Ch. 5)

earnings The amount by which revenues exceed expenses. (Ch. 1)

earnings per share (EPS) The profitability ratio that measures the share of profits that are earned by a share of common stock, computed by dividing net income, reduced by preferred dividend requirements, by the shares of common stock outstanding. (Chs. 13, 14)

earnings per share (EPS) on common stock The profitability ratio that measures the share of profits that are earned by a share of common stock, computed by dividing net income, reduced by preferred dividend requirements, by the shares of common stock outstanding. (Ch. 17)

effective interest rate method A method of amortizing a bond discount or premium that provides for a constant rate of interest over the life of the bonds. (Ch. 14)

effective rate of interest The market rate of interest at the time bonds are issued. (Ch. 14)

electronic funds transfer (EFT) A system in which computers rather than paper (money, checks, etc.) are used to effect cash transactions. (Ch. 8)

elements of internal control The control environment, risk assessment, control activities, information and communication, and monitoring. (Ch. 8)

employee fraud The intentional act of deceiving an employer for personal gain. (Ch. 8)

employee's earnings record A detailed record of each employee's earnings. (Ch. 11)

equity method A method of accounting for an investment in common stock representing between 20% and 50% ownership of the investee. The purchase is recorded at original cost, and the investment account is adjusted for the investor's share of periodic net income and cash dividends of the investee. (Ch. 15)

equity securities The common and preferred stock of a firm. (Ch. 15)

estimated returns inventory A current asset that is reported on the balance sheet after inventory. (Ch. 6)

ethics Moral principles that guide the conduct of individuals. (Ch. 1)

expected useful life The estimated length of time a fixed asset will be used in normal operations. (Ch. 10)

expense recognition principle A principle, sometimes called the *matching principle*, that requires expenses to be recorded in the same period as the related revenue. (Ch. 3)

expenses Assets used up or services consumed in the process of generating revenues. (Chs. 1, 2)

F

face amount The amount specified on a bond to be repaid at maturity. (Ch. 14)

fair value The price that would be received for selling an asset or paying off a liability, often the market price for an equity or debt security. (Ch. 15)

fair value method A method of accounting for equity investments representing less than 20% of the outstanding shares of the investee. The purchase is recorded at original cost, and any gains or losses upon sale are recognized by the difference between the sale proceeds and the original cost. (Ch. 15)

fees earned Revenue from providing services. (Ch. 1)

FICA tax Federal Insurance Contributions Act tax used to finance federal programs for old-age and disability benefits (social security) and health insurance for the aged (Medicare). (Ch. 11)

financial accounting The branch of accounting that is concerned with recording transactions using generally accepted accounting principles (GAAP) for a business or other economic unit and with a periodic preparation of various statements from such records. (Ch. 1)

Financial Accounting Standards Board (FASB) The authoritative body that has the primary responsibility for developing accounting principles. (Ch. 1)

financial statements Financial reports that summarize the effects of events on a business. (Ch. 1)

first closing entry The first journal entry in the closing process that transfers revenue and the expense account balances to the owner's capital account as either a net income or a net loss. (Ch. 4)

first-in, first-out (FIFO) inventory cost flow method The method of inventory costing based on the assumption that the costs of merchandise sold should be charged against revenue in the order in which the costs were incurred. (Ch. 7)

fiscal year The annual accounting period adopted by a business. (Ch. 1)

fixed asset turnover ratio The number of sales dollars earned per dollar of fixed assets, computed by dividing sales by the average book value of fixed assets. (Ch. 10)

fixed assets Long-term or relatively permanent tangible assets such as equipment, machinery, and buildings that are used in the normal business operations and that depreciate over time. (Chs. 3, 4, 10)

FOB (free on board) destination Freight terms in which the seller pays the transportation costs from the shipping point to the final destination. (Ch. 6)

FOB (free on board) shipping point Freight terms in which the seller pays the transportation costs from the shipping point to the final destination. (Ch. 6)

four-column account An account format used for posting journal entries with columns for debits, credits, and a debit or credit balance. (Ch. 2)

free cash flow A measure of the operating cash flow available to a company after it purchases the property, plant, and equipment (PP&E) necessary to maintain its current operations. (Ch. 16)

fringe benefits Benefits provided to employees in addition to wages and salaries. (Ch. 11)

future value The value of an asset or cash at a specified date in the future that is equivalent in value to a specified sum today. (Ch. 14)

G

general expenses Expenses incurred in the administration or general operations of the business. (Ch. 6)

general journal The two-column form used for entries that do not "fit" in any of the special journals. (Ch. 5)

general ledger The primary ledger, when used in conjunction with subsidiary ledgers, that contains all of the balance sheet and income statement accounts. (Ch. 5)

general-purpose financial statements A type of financial accounting report that is distributed to external users. The term *general purpose* refers to the wide range of decision-making needs that the reports are designed to serve. (Ch. 1)

generally accepted accounting principles (GAAP) Generally accepted guidelines for the preparation of financial statements. (Ch. 1)

goodwill An intangible asset that is created from such favorable factors as location, product quality, reputation, and managerial skill. (Ch. 10)

gross method (of recording sales discounts) A method of recording sales discounts in which a sale is initially recorded at the gross amount of the invoice and the discount is recognized when payment is received within the discount period. (Ch. 6)

gross pay The total earnings of an employee for a payroll period. (Ch. 11)

gross profit Sales minus the cost of merchandise sold. (Ch. 6)

gross profit method A method of estimating inventory cost that is based on the relationship of gross profit to sales. (Ch. 7)

H

held-to-maturity investments Investments in bonds or other debt securities that management intends to hold to their maturity. (Ch. 15)

horizontal analysis The analysis of increases and decreases in the amount and percentage of comparative financial statement items. (Chs. 2, 17)

I

in arrears A condition of being behind in regards to a financial obligation; said of preferred stock dividends that have not been paid in prior years. (Ch. 13)

income from operations Gross profit less operating expenses. (Ch. 6)

income statement A summary of the revenue and expenses for a specific period of time, such as a month or a year. (Ch. 1)

indirect method A method of reporting the cash flows from operating activities as the net income from operations adjusted for all deferrals of past cash receipts and payments and all accruals of expected future cash receipts and payments. (Ch. 16)

initial cost The purchase price of a fixed asset plus all costs to obtain and ready it for use. (Ch. 10)

installment note A debt that requires the borrower to make equal periodic payments to the lender for the term of the note. (Ch. 14)

intangible assets Long-term assets that are used in the operations of a business but do not exist physically. (Ch. 10)

interest revenue Money received for interest. (Ch. 1)

internal control The policies and procedures used to safeguard assets, ensure accurate business information, and ensure compliance with laws and regulations. (Chs. 5, 8)

International Accounting Standards Board (IASB) An organization that issues International Financial Reporting Standards for many countries outside the United States. (Ch. 1)

inventory analysis An evaluation of a company's ability to manage its inventory effectively. (Ch. 17)

inventory shrinkage (inventory shortage) The amount by which the merchandise for sale, as indicated by the balance of the merchandise inventory account, is larger than the total amount of merchandise counted during the physical inventory. (Ch. 6)

inventory turnover The relationship between the cost of merchandise sold and inventory, computed by dividing the cost of merchandise sold by the average merchandise inventory. (Chs. 7, 17)

investee The company whose stock is purchased by the investor. (Ch. 15)

investments Debt and equity securities obtained for the purpose of earning interest, receiving dividends, or realizing gains from increases in the market price. (Ch. 15)

investor The company (or person) investing in another company's stock. (Ch. 15)

invoice The bill that the seller sends to the buyer. (Chs. 5, 6)

J

journal The initial record in which the effects of a transaction are recorded. (Ch. 2)

journal entry The form of recording a transaction in a journal. (Ch. 2)

journalizing The process of recording a transaction in the journal. (Ch. 2)

L

last-in, first-out (LIFO) inventory cost flow method A method of inventory costing based on the assumption that the most recent merchandise inventory costs should be charged against revenue. (Ch. 7)

ledger A group of accounts for a business. (Ch. 2)

leverage Using debt to increase the return on an investment. (Ch. 17)

liabilities The rights of creditors that represent debts of the business. (Chs. 1, 2)

limited liability company (LLC) A business form consisting of one or more persons or entities filing an operating agreement with a state to conduct business with limited liability to the owners, yet treated as a partnership for tax purposes. (Chs. 1, 12)

liquidation The winding-up process when a partnership goes out of business. (Ch. 12)

liquidity The ability to convert assets into cash. (Chs. 4, 17)

long-term liabilities Liabilities that usually will not be due for more than one year. (Ch. 4)

lower-of-cost-or-market (LCM) method A method of valuing inventory that reports the inventory at the lower of its cost or current market value (replacement cost). (Ch. 7)

M

management (or managerial) accounting The branch of accounting that uses both historical and estimated data in providing information that management uses in conducting daily operations, in planning future operations, and in developing overall business strategies. (Ch. 1)

Management's Discussion and Analysis (MD&A) An annual report disclosure that provides management's analysis of current operations and its plans for the future. (Ch. 17)

manufacturing business A type of business that changes basic inputs into products that are sold to individual customers. (Ch. 1)

market rate of interest The rate determined from sales and purchases of similar bonds. (Ch. 14)

matching concept A concept of accounting in which expenses are matched with the revenue generated during a period by those expenses. (Ch. 1)

matching principle A concept of accounting in which expenses are matched with the revenue generated during a period by those expenses. (Ch. 3)

maturity value The amount that is due at the maturity or due date of a note. (Ch. 9)

merchandise inventory Merchandise on hand (not sold) at the end of an accounting period. (Ch. 6)

merchandising business A type of business that purchases products from other businesses and sells them to customers. (Ch. 1)

mortgage note An installment note that is secured by a pledge of the borrower's assets. (Ch. 14)

multiple-step income statement A form of income statement that contains several sections, subsections, and subtotals. (Ch. 6)

N

natural business year A fiscal year that ends when business activities have reached the lowest point in an annual operating cycle. (Ch. 1)

net income (or net profit) The amount by which revenues exceed expenses. (Ch. 1)

net loss The amount by which expenses exceed revenues. (Ch. 1)

net pay The amount an employee receives after deductions are subtracted from gross pay. (Ch. 11)

net realizable value The estimated selling price of an item of inventory less any direct costs of disposal, such as sales commissions. (Ch. 7) The amount of receivables expected to be collected or realized, determined by subtracting the allowance for doubtful accounts from the accounts receivable balance. (Ch. 9)

normal balance of an account The normal balance of an account can be either a debit or a credit depending on whether increases in the account are recorded as debits or credits. (Ch. 2)

notes receivable A customer's written promise to pay an amount and possibly interest at an agreed-upon rate. (Chs. 4, 9)

number of days' sales in inventory The relationship between sales and inventory, computed by dividing the average merchandise inventory by the average daily cost of merchandise sold. (Ch. 17)

number of days' sales in receivables An estimate of the length of time the accounts receivable have been outstanding, computed by dividing the average accounts receivable by the average daily sales. (Ch. 17)

O

objectivity concept A concept of accounting that requires accounting records and the data reported in financial statements to be based on objective evidence. (Ch. 1)

operating cycle The process by which a company spends cash, generates revenues, and receives cash either at the time the revenues are generated or later by collecting accounts receivable. (Ch. 6)

operating income Gross profit less operating expenses. (Ch. 6)

other comprehensive income Specified items that are reported separately from net income, including unrealized gains and losses on available-for-sale securities and foreign currency and pension liability adjustments. (Ch. 15)

other expense An expense that cannot be traced directly to the normal operations of the business. (Ch. 6)

other revenue Revenue from sources other than the primary operating activity of a business. (Ch. 6)

outstanding stock The stock in the hands of stockholders. (Ch. 13)

owner's equity The owner's right to the assets of the business. (Chs. 1, 2)

P

paid-in capital Capital contributed to a corporation by the stockholders and others. (Ch. 13)

par value A dollar amount assigned to each share of stock. (Ch. 13)

parent company The corporation owning all or a majority of the voting stock of the other corporation. (Ch. 15)

partnership An unincorporated business form consisting of two or more persons conducting business as co-owners for profit. (Chs. 1, 12)

partnership agreement The formal written contract creating a partnership, which includes matters such as amounts to be invested, limits on withdrawals, distributions of income and losses, and admission and withdrawal of partners. (Ch. 12)

patents Exclusive rights to produce and sell goods with one or more unique features. (Ch. 10)

payroll The total amount paid to employees for a certain period. (Ch. 11)

payroll register A multicolumn report used to assemble and summarize payroll data at the end of each payroll period. (Ch. 11)

pension A cash payment to retired employees. (Ch. 11)

periodic inventory system The inventory system in which the inventory records do not show the amount available for sale or sold during the period. (Ch. 6)

permanent accounts Term for balance sheet accounts because they are relatively permanent and carried forward from year to year. (Ch. 4)

perpetual inventory system The inventory system in which each purchase and sale of merchandise is recorded in an inventory account. (Ch. 6)

petty cash fund A special cash fund to pay relatively small amounts. (Ch. 8)

physical inventory A detailed listing of merchandise on hand. (Chs. 6, 7)

plant assets Long-term or relatively permanent tangible assets such as equipment, machinery, and buildings that are used in the normal business operations and that depreciate over time. (Chs. 3, 4)

posting The process of transferring the debits and credits from the journal entries to the accounts. (Ch. 2)

preferred stock A class of stock with preferential rights over common stock. (Ch. 13)

premium The excess of the issue price of a stock over its par value or the excess of the issue price of bonds over their face amount. (Chs. 13, 14)

prepaid expenses Items such as supplies that will be used in the business in the future. (Chs. 1, 3)

present value The value of an asset or cash at present that is equivalent in value to a specified sum in the future. (Ch. 14)

present value of an annuity The sum of the present values of a series of equal cash flows to be received at fixed intervals. (Ch. 14)

price-earnings (P/E) ratio A profitability ratio that measures a company's future earnings prospects, computed as the market price per share of common stock divided by earnings per share on common stock. (Ch. 17)

prior period adjustment Corrections of material errors related to a prior period or periods, reported as an adjustment to beginning retained earnings and excluded from the determination of the current period's net income. (Ch. 13)

private accounting The field of accounting whereby accountants are employed by a business firm or a not-for-profit organization. (Ch. 1)

profit The difference between the amounts received from customers for goods or services provided and the amounts paid for the inputs used to provide the goods or services. (Ch. 1)

profitability The ability of a firm to earn income. (Ch. 17)

proprietorship A business owned by one individual. (Ch. 1)

public accounting The field of accounting where accountants and their staff provide services on a fee basis. (Ch. 1)

Public Company Accounting Oversight Board (PCAOB) A new oversight body for the accounting profession that was established by the Sarbanes-Oxley Act. (Ch. 1)

purchase order The purchase order authorizes the purchase of the inventory from an approved vendor. (Ch. 7)

purchases discounts Discounts taken by the buyer for early payment of an invoice. (Ch. 6)

purchases journal The journal in which all items purchased on account are recorded. (Ch. 5)

purchases returns and allowances From the buyer's perspective, returned merchandise or an adjustment for defective merchandise. (Ch. 6)

Q

quick assets Cash and other current assets that can be quickly converted to cash, such as marketable securities and receivables. (Chs. 11, 17)

quick ratio A financial ratio that measures the ability to pay current liabilities with quick assets. (Chs. 11, 17)

R

ratio of cash to monthly cash expenses Ratio that helps assess how long a company can continue to operate without additional financing or generating positive cash flows from operations. (Ch. 8)

ratio of fixed assets to long-term liabilities A leverage ratio that measures the margin of safety of long-term creditors, computed as the net fixed assets divided by the long-term liabilities. (Ch. 17)

ratio of liabilities to owner's (stockholders') equity A comprehensive leverage ratio that measures the relationship of the claims of creditors to owner's (stockholders') equity. (Chs. 1, 17)

ratios A number that expresses a financial statement item or set of financial statement items as a percentage of another financial statement item in order to measure an important economic relationship as a single number. (Ch. 17)

real accounts Term for balance sheet accounts because they are relatively permanent and carried forward from year to year. (Ch. 4)

realization The sale of assets when a partnership is being liquidated. (Ch. 12)

receivables All money claims against other entities, including people, business firms, and other organizations. (Ch. 9)

receiving report The form or electronic transmission used by the receiving personnel to indicate that materials have been received and inspected. (Ch. 7)

rent revenue Money received for rent. (Ch. 1)

report form The form of balance sheet with the Liabilities and Owner's Equity sections presented below the Assets section. (Ch. 1)

residual value The estimated value of a fixed asset at the end of its useful life. (Ch. 10)

restrictions Amounts of retained earnings that have been limited for use as dividends. (Ch. 13)

retail inventory method A method of estimating inventory cost that is based on the relationship of gross profit to sales. (Ch. 7)

retained earnings Net income retained in a corporation. (Ch. 13)

retained earnings statement A summary of the changes in the retained earnings in a corporation for a specific period of time, such as a month or a year. (Ch. 13)

return on common stockholders' equity A measure of the rate of income earned on the amount invested by the common stockholders; computed by dividing net income, reduced by preferred dividend requirements, by average common stockholders' equity. (Ch. 17)

return on stockholders' equity A measure of the rate of income earned on the amount invested by the stockholders, computed by dividing net income by average total stockholders' equity. (Ch. 17)

return on total assets A measure of the profitability of total assets, without considering how the assets are financed; computed as income plus interest expense divided by average total assets. (Ch. 17)

revenue expenditures Costs that benefit only the current period or costs incurred for normal maintenance and repairs of fixed assets. (Ch. 10)

revenue journal The journal in which all sales and services on account are recorded. (Ch. 5)

revenue per employee A measure of the efficiency of a business in generating revenues, which is computed as revenue divided by number of employees. (Ch. 12)

revenue recognition The process of recognizing revenue. (Ch. 3)

revenue recognition principle The concept that supports recording revenues when they are earned, which is when services have been performed or products delivered to customers. (Ch. 3)

revenue(s) Increases in assets from performing services or delivering products to customers. (Chs. 1, 2)

rules of debit and credit In the double-entry accounting system, specific rules for recording debits and credits based on the type of account. (Ch. 2)

S

sales The revenue reported for merchandise sold. (Chs. 1, 6)

sales discount From the seller's perspective, discounts that a seller may offer the buyer for early payment. (Ch. 6)

Sarbanes-Oxley Act (SOX) An act passed by Congress to restore public confidence and trust in the financial statements of companies. (Chs. 1, 8)

second closing entry The second journal entry of the closing process that transfers the owner's drawing account balance to the owner's capital account. (Ch. 4)

Securities and Exchange Commission (SEC) An agency of the U.S. government that has authority over the accounting and financial disclosures for companies whose shares of ownership (stock) are traded and sold to the public. (Ch. 1)

selling expenses Expenses that are incurred directly in the selling of merchandise. (Ch. 6)

service business A business providing services rather than products to customers. (Ch. 1)

single-step income statement A form of income statement in which the total of all expenses is deducted from the total of all revenues. (Ch. 6)

slide An error in which the entire number is moved one or more spaces to the right or the left, such as writing $542.00 as $54.20 or $5,420.00. (Ch. 2)

solvency The ability of a firm to pay its debts as they come due. (Chs. 4, 17)

special journals Journals designed to be used for recording a single type of transaction. (Ch. 5)

special-purpose funds Cash funds used for a special business need. (Ch. 8)

specific identification inventory cost flow method Inventory method in which the unit sold is identified with a specific purchase. (Ch. 7)

statement of cash flows A summary of the cash receipts and cash payments for a specific period of time, such as a month or a year. (Chs. 1, 16)

statement of members' equity A summary of the changes in members' equity in a limited liability corporation during a specific period of time. (Ch. 12)

statement of owner's equity A summary of the changes in owner's equity that have occurred during a specific period of time, such as a month or a year. (Ch. 1)

statement of partnership equity A summary of the changes in the partners' capital accounts during a specific period of time. (Ch. 12)

statement of partnership liquidation A summary of the liquidation process whereby cash is distributed to the partners based on the balances in their capital accounts. (Ch. 12)

statement of stockholders' equity A summary of the changes in the stockholders' equity in a corporation that have occurred during a specific period of time. (Ch. 13)

stock Shares of ownership of a corporation. (Ch. 13)

stock dividend A distribution of additional shares of stock to existing stockholders. (Ch. 13)

stock split A process by which a corporation reduces the par or stated value of its common stock and issues a proportionate number of additional shares. (Ch. 13)

stockholders The owners of a corporation. (Ch. 13)

stockholders' equity The owners' equity in a corporation. (Chs. 1, 13)

straight-line method A method of depreciation that provides for equal periodic depreciation expense over the estimated useful life of a fixed asset. (Ch. 10)

subsidiary company The corporation that is controlled by a parent company. (Ch. 15)

subsidiary inventory ledger The subsidiary ledger containing individual accounts for items of inventory. (Ch. 7)

subsidiary ledger A ledger containing individual accounts with a common characteristic. (Ch. 5)

T

T account The simplest form of an account. (Ch. 2)

temporary accounts Accounts that report amounts for only one period. (Ch. 4)

time period concept A concept of accounting that requires a company to report its economic activities on a regular basis for a specific period of time. (Ch. 1)

times interest earned A ratio that measures creditor margin of safety for interest payments, computed as income before interest and taxes divided by interest expense. (Chs. 14, 17)

trade discounts Discounts from the list prices in published catalogs or special discounts offered to certain classes of buyers. (Ch. 6)

trade-in allowance The amount a seller allows a buyer for a fixed asset that is traded in for a similar asset. (Ch. 10)

trademark A name, term, or symbol used to identify a business and its products. (Ch. 10)

trading securities Equity and debt securities that are purchased to earn profits from changes in their market prices. (Ch. 15)

transposition An error in which the order of the digits is changed, such as writing $542 as $452 or $524. (Ch. 2)

treasury stock Stock that a corporation has issued and then reacquired. (Ch. 13)

trial balance A summary listing of the titles and balances of accounts in the ledger. (Ch. 2)

two-column journal A journal format with a debit column and a credit column. (Ch. 2)

U

unadjusted trial balance A summary listing of the titles and balances of accounts in the ledger prior to the posting of adjusting entries. (Ch. 2)

unearned revenue The liability created by receiving revenue in advance. (Chs. 2, 3)

unit of measure concept A concept of accounting requiring that economic data be recorded in dollars. (Ch. 1)

units-of-activity method A method of depreciation that provides for depreciation expense based on each unit of activity of a fixed asset. (Ch. 10)

unrealized gain or loss Changes in the fair value of held equity or debt securities for a period. (Ch. 15)

unusual income statement items Items affecting income that do not occur frequently and are typically unrelated to current operations. (Ch. 17)

V

vertical analysis The percentage analysis of the relationship of each component in a financial statement to a total within the statement. (Chs. 3, 17)

voucher A special form for recording relevant data about a liability and the details of its payment. (Ch. 8)

voucher system A set of procedures for authorizing and recording liabilities and cash payments. (Ch. 8)

W

weighted average inventory cost flow method A method of inventory costing in which the cost of the units sold and in ending inventory is a weighted average of the purchase costs. (Ch. 7)

wholesalers Companies that sell merchandise to other businesses rather than to the public. (Ch. 6)

working capital The excess of the current assets of a business over its current liabilities. (Chs. 4, 17)

Index

A

C

D

J

K

L

Q

R

S

T

The Basics

Accounting Equation:

Assets = Liabilities + Owner's Equity

T Account:

Account Title	
Left side	Right side
debit	credit

Rules of Debit and Credit:

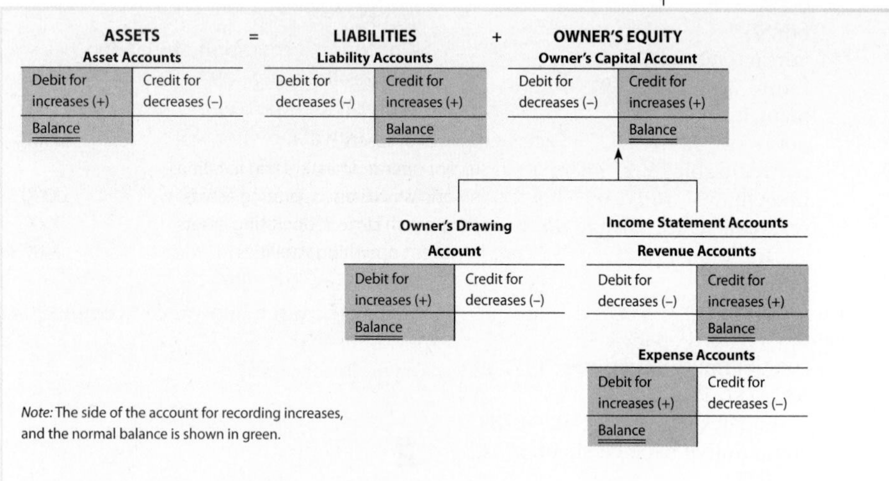

Analyzing and Journalizing Transactions

1. Carefully read the description of the transaction to determine whether an asset, a liability, an owner's equity, a revenue, an expense, or a drawing account is affected.
2. For each account affected by the transaction, determine whether the account increases or decreases.
3. Determine whether each increase or decrease should be recorded as a debit or a credit, following the rules of debit and credit.
4. Record the transaction using a journal entry.
5. Periodically post journal entries to the accounts in the ledger.
6. Prepare an unadjusted trial balance at the end of the period.

Financial Statements:

- **Income statement:** A summary of the revenue and expenses of a business entity for a specific period of time, such as a month or a year.
- **Statement of owner's equity:** A summary of the changes in the owner's equity of a business entity that have occurred during a specific period of time, such as a month or a year.
- **Balance sheet:** A list of the assets, liabilities, and owner's equity of a business entity as of a specific date, usually at the close of the last day of a month or a year.
- **Statement of Cash Flows:** A summary of the cash receipts and cash payments of a business entity for a specific period of time, such as a month or a year.

Accounting Cycle:

1. Transactions are analyzed and recorded in the journal.
2. Transactions are posted to the ledger.
3. An unadjusted trial balance is prepared.
4. Adjustment data are assembled and analyzed.
5. An optional end-of-period spreadsheet is prepared.
6. Adjusting entries are journalized and posted to the ledger.
7. An adjusted trial balance is prepared.
8. Financial statements are prepared.
9. Closing entries are journalized and posted to the ledger.
10. A post-closing trial balance is prepared.

Types of Adjusting Entries:

- Accrued revenue (accrued asset)
- Accrued expense (accrued liability)
- Unearned revenue (deferred revenue)
- Prepaid expense (deferred expense)
- Depreciation expense

Each entry will always affect both a balance sheet account and an income statement account.

Closing Entries:

1. Debit each revenue account for its balance, credit each expense account for its balance, and credit (net income) or debit (net loss) the owner's capital account.
2. Debit the owner's capital account for the balance of the drawing account and credit the drawing account.

Special Journals:

Providing services on account	⟶ recorded in	⟶ Revenue journal
Receipt of cash from any source	⟶ recorded in	⟶ Cash receipts journal
Purchase of items on account	⟶ recorded in	⟶ Purchases journal
Payments of cash for any purpose	⟶ recorded in	⟶ Cash payments journal

Shipping Terms:

	FOB Shipping Point	FOB Destination
Ownership (title) passes to buyer when merchandise is..................	delivered to freight carrier	delivered to buyer
Freight costs are paid by..........................	buyer	seller

Format for Bank Reconciliation:

Cash balance according to bank statement		$XXX
Add: Additions by company not on bank statement	$XXX	
Bank errors	XXX	XXX
		$XXX
Deduct: Deductions by company not on bank statement	$XXX	
Bank errors	XXX	XXX
Adjusted balance		$XXX
Cash balance according to company's records		$XXX
Add: Additions by bank not recorded by company	$XXX	
Company errors	XXX	XXX
		$XXX
Deduct: Deductions by bank not recorded by company	$XXX	
Company errors	XXX	XXX
Adjusted balance		$XXX

Note: Additions and deductions to company records require journal entries by the company.

Inventory Costing Methods:

- First-in, First-out (FIFO)
- Last-in, First-out (LIFO)
- Weighted-Average

Interest Computations:

Interest = Face Amount (or Principal) × Rate × Time

Methods of Determining Annual Depreciation:

Straight-Line: $\frac{\text{Cost} - \text{Estimated Residual Value}}{\text{Estimated Life}}$

Double-Declining-Balance: Rate* × Book Value at Beginning of Period

*Rate is commonly twice the straight-line rate (1 ÷ Estimated Life).

Units-of-Activity: $\frac{\text{Cost} - \text{Residual Value}}{\text{Total Estimated Units of Activity}}$ × Units of Activity for Period

Adjustments to Net Income (Loss) Using the Indirect Method:

	Increase (Decrease)
Net income (loss)	$ XXX
Adjustments to reconcile net income to net cash flow from operating activities:	
Depreciation of fixed assets	XXX
Amortization of intangible assets	XXX
Losses on disposal of assets	XXX
Gains on disposal of assets	(XXX)
Changes in current operating assets and liabilities:	
Increases in noncash current operating assets	(XXX)
Decreases in noncash current operating assets	XXX
Increases in current operating liabilities	XXX
Decreases in current operating liabilities	(XXX)
Net cash flow from operating activities	$ XXX or $(XXX)

Abbreviations and Acronyms Commonly Used in Business and Accounting

AAA	American Accounting Association
AICPA	American Institute of Certified Public Accountants
B2B	Business-to-business
B2C	Business-to-consumer
CFO	Chief Financial Officer
CMA	Certified Management Accountant
COGS	Cost of goods sold
CPA	Certified Public Accountant
Cr.	Credit
Dr.	Debit
EFT	Electronic funds transfer
EPS	Earnings per share
ERP	Enterprise resource planning
FASB	Financial Accounting Standards Board
FICA tax	Federal Insurance Contributions Act tax
FIFO	First-in, first-out
FOB	Free on board
FUTA	Federal unemployment compensation tax
GAAP	Generally accepted accounting principles
IASB	International Accounting Standards Board
IFRS	International Financial Reporting Standards
IMA	Institute of Management Accountants
IRC	Internal Revenue Code
IRS	Internal Revenue Service
LIFO	Last-in, first-out
LCM	Lower of cost or market
MACRS	Modified Accelerated Cost Recovery System
MD&A	Management's Discussion and Analysis
n/30	Net 30
n/eom	Net, end-of-month
NSF	Not sufficient funds
P/E Ratio	Price-earnings ratio
POS	Point of sale
R&D	Research and development
SCM	Supply chain management
SEC	Securities and Exchange Commission
SOX	Sarbanes-Oxley Act
W-4	Employee's Withholding Allowance Certificate

Classification of Accounts

Account Title	*Account Classification*	*Normal Balance*	*Financial Statement*
Accounts Payable	Current liability	Credit	Balance sheet
Accounts Receivable	Current asset	Debit	Balance sheet
Accumulated Depletion	Contra fixed asset	Credit	Balance sheet
Accumulated Depreciation	Contra fixed asset	Credit	Balance sheet
Advertising Expense	Operating expense	Debit	Income statement
Allowance for Doubtful Accounts	Contra current asset	Credit	Balance sheet
Amortization Expense	Operating expense	Debit	Income statement
Bonds Payable	Long-term liability	Credit	Balance sheet
Building	Fixed asset	Debit	Balance sheet
____________ Capital	Owner's equity	Credit	Statement of owner's equity/ Balance sheet
Cash	Current asset	Debit	Balance sheet
Cash Dividends	Stockholders' equity	Debit	Retained earnings statement
Cash Dividends Payable	Current liability	Credit	Balance sheet
Common Stock	Stockholders' equity	Credit	Balance sheet
Cost of Merchandise (Goods) Sold	Cost of merchandise (goods) sold	Debit	Income statement
Customer Refunds Payable	Current liability	Credit	Balance sheet
Delivery Expense	Operating expense	Debit	Income statement
Depletion Expense	Operating expense	Debit	Income statement
Discount on Bonds Payable	Long-term liability	Debit	Balance sheet
Dividend Revenue	Other income	Credit	Income statement
Dividends	Stockholders' equity	Debit	Retained earnings statement
____________ Drawing	Owner's equity	Debit	Statement of owner's equity
Employees Federal Income Tax Payable	Current liability	Credit	Balance sheet
Equipment	Fixed asset	Debit	Balance sheet
Estimated Returns Inventory	Current asset	Debit	Balance sheet
Federal Income Tax Payable	Current liability	Credit	Balance sheet
Federal Unemployment Tax Payable	Current liability	Credit	Balance sheet
Freight In	Cost of merchandise sold	Debit	Income statement
Freight Out	Operating expense	Debit	Income statement
Gain (Loss) on Disposal of Fixed Assets	Other income or expense	Debit or Credit	Income statement
Gain (Loss) on Redemption of Bonds	Other income or expense	Debit or Credit	Income statement
Gain (Loss) on Sale of Investments	Other income or expense	Debit or Credit	Income statement
Goodwill	Intangible asset	Debit	Balance sheet
Income Tax Expense	Income tax	Debit	Income statement
Income Tax Payable	Current liability	Credit	Balance sheet
Insurance Expense	Operating expense	Debit	Income statement
Interest Expense	Other expense	Debit	Income statement
Interest Receivable	Current asset	Debit	Balance sheet
Interest Revenue	Other income	Credit	Income statement
Investment in Bonds	Investment	Debit	Balance sheet
Investment in Stocks	Investment	Debit	Balance sheet
Investment in Subsidiary	Investment	Debit	Balance sheet
Land	Fixed asset	Debit	Balance sheet

Account Title	*Account Classification*	*Normal Balance*	*Financial Statement*
Marketable Securities	Current asset	Debit	Balance sheet
Medicare Tax Payable	Current liability	Credit	Balance sheet
Merchandise Inventory	Current asset/Cost of merchandise sold	Debit	Balance sheet/Income statement
Net Sales	Revenue from sales	Credit	Income statement
Notes Payable	Current liability/ Long-term liability	Credit	Balance sheet
Notes Receivable	Current asset/Investment	Debit	Balance sheet
Patents	Intangible asset	Debit	Balance sheet
Paid-In Capital from Sale of Treasury Stock	Stockholders' equity	Credit	Balance sheet
Paid-In Capital in Excess of Par (Stated Value)	Stockholders' equity	Credit	Balance sheet
Payroll Tax Expense	Operating expense	Debit	Income statement
Pension Expense	Operating expense	Debit	Income statement
Petty Cash	Current asset	Debit	Balance sheet
Preferred Stock	Stockholders' equity	Credit	Balance sheet
Premium on Bonds Payable	Long-term liability	Credit	Balance sheet
Prepaid Insurance	Current asset	Debit	Balance sheet
Prepaid Rent	Current asset	Debit	Balance sheet
Purchases	Cost of merchandise sold	Debit	Income statement
Purchases Discounts	Cost of merchandise sold	Credit	Income statement
Purchases Returns and Allowances	Cost of merchandise sold	Credit	Income statement
Rent Expense	Operating expense	Debit	Income statement
Rent Revenue	Other income	Credit	Income statement
Retained Earnings	Stockholders' equity	Credit	Balance sheet/Retained earnings statement
Salaries Expense	Operating expense	Debit	Income statement
Salaries Payable	Current liability	Credit	Balance sheet
Sales Tax Payable	Current liability	Credit	Balance sheet
Social Security Tax Payable	Current liability	Credit	Balance sheet
State Unemployment Tax Payable	Current liability	Credit	Balance sheet
Stock Dividends	Stockholders' equity	Debit	Retained earnings statement
Stock Dividends Distributable	Stockholders' equity	Credit	Balance sheet
Supplies	Current asset	Debit	Balance sheet
Supplies Expense	Operating expense	Debit	Income statement
Treasury Stock	Stockholders' equity	Debit	Balance sheet
Uncollectible Accounts Expense	Operating expense	Debit	Income statement
Unearned Rent	Current liability	Credit	Balance sheet
Unrealized Gain (Loss) on Available-for-Sale Investments	Addition or deduction to stockholders' equity	Debit or Credit	Statement of stockholders' equity
Unrealized Gain (Loss) on Trading Investments	Other income or expense	Debit or Credit	Income statement
Utilities Expense	Operating expense	Debit	Income statement
Vacation Pay Expense	Operating expense	Debit	Income statement
Vacation Pay Payable	Current liability/ Long-term liability	Credit	Balance sheet
Valuation Allowance for Available-for-Sale Investments	Asset or contra asset	Debit or Credit	Balance sheet
Valuation Allowance for Trading Investments	Asset or contra asset	Debit or Credit	Balance sheet

Abbreviations and Acronyms Commonly Used in Business and Accounting

AAA	American Accounting Association
ABC	Activity-based costing
AICPA	American Institute of Certified Public Accountants
B2B	Business-to-business
B2C	Business-to-consumer
CFO	Chief Financial Officer
CMA	Certified Management Accountant
COGM	Cost of goods manufactured
COGS	Cost of goods sold
CPA	Certified Public Accountant
Cr.	Credit
CVP	Cost-volume-profit
Dr.	Debit
EFT	Electronic funds transfer
EPS	Earnings per share
ERP	Enterprise resource planning
FASB	Financial Accounting Standards Board
FICA tax	Federal Insurance Contributions Act tax
FIFO	First-in, first-out
FOB	Free on board
FUTA	Federal unemployment compensation tax
GAAP	Generally accepted accounting principles
IASB	International Accounting Standards Board
IFRS	International Financial Reporting Standards
IMA	Institute of Management Accountants
IRC	Internal Revenue Code
IRR	Internal rate of return
IRS	Internal Revenue Service
JIT	Just-in-time
LIFO	Last-in, first-out
LCM	Lower of cost or market
MACRS	Modified Accelerated Cost Recovery System
MD&A	Management's Discussion and Analysis
n/30	Net 30
n/eom	Net, end-of-month
NPV	Net present value
NSF	Not sufficient funds
P/E Ratio	Price-earnings ratio
POS	Point of sale
ROI	Return on investment
R&D	Research and development
SCM	Supply chain management
SEC	Securities and Exchange Commission
SOX	Sarbanes-Oxley Act
TQC	Total quality control
W-4	Employee's Withholding Allowance Certificate
WIP	Work in process

Classification of Accounts

Account Title	*Account Classification*	*Normal Balance*	*Financial Statement*
Accounts Payable	Current liability	Credit	Balance sheet
Accounts Receivable	Current asset	Debit	Balance sheet
Accumulated Depletion	Contra fixed asset	Credit	Balance sheet
Accumulated Depreciation	Contra fixed asset	Credit	Balance sheet
Advertising Expense	Operating expense	Debit	Income statement
Allowance for Doubtful Accounts	Contra current asset	Credit	Balance sheet
Amortization Expense	Operating expense	Debit	Income statement
Bonds Payable	Long-term liability	Credit	Balance sheet
Building	Fixed asset	Debit	Balance sheet
___________ Capital	Owner's equity	Credit	Statement of owner's equity/ Balance sheet
Cash	Current asset	Debit	Balance sheet
Cash Dividends	Stockholders' equity	Debit	Retained earnings statement
Cash Dividends Payable	Current liability	Credit	Balance sheet
Common Stock	Stockholders' equity	Credit	Balance sheet
Cost of Merchandise (Goods) Sold	Cost of merchandise (goods) sold	Debit	Income statement
Customer Refunds Payable	Current liability	Credit	Balance sheet
Delivery Expense	Operating expense	Debit	Income statement
Depletion Expense	Operating expense	Debit	Income statement
Discount on Bonds Payable	Long-term liability	Debit	Balance sheet
Dividend Revenue	Other income	Credit	Income statement
Dividends	Stockholders' equity	Debit	Retained earnings statement
___________ Drawing	Owner's equity	Debit	Statement of owner's equity
Employees Federal Income Tax Payable	Current liability	Credit	Balance sheet
Equipment	Fixed asset	Debit	Balance sheet
Estimated Returns Inventory	Current asset	Debit	Balance sheet
Factory Overhead (Overapplied)	Deferred credit	Credit	Balance sheet (interim)
Factory Overhead (Underapplied)	Deferred debit	Debit	Balance sheet (interim)
Federal Income Tax Payable	Current liability	Credit	Balance sheet
Federal Unemployment Tax Payable	Current liability	Credit	Balance sheet
Finished Goods	Current asset	Debit	Balance sheet
Freight In	Cost of merchandise sold	Debit	Income statement
Freight Out	Operating expense	Debit	Income statement
Gain (Loss) on Disposal of Fixed Assets	Other income or expense	Debit or Credit	Income statement
Gain (Loss) on Redemption of Bonds	Other income or expense	Debit or Credit	Income statement
Gain (Loss) on Sale of Investments	Other income or expense	Debit or Credit	Income statement
Goodwill	Intangible asset	Debit	Balance sheet
Income Tax Expense	Income tax	Debit	Income statement
Income Tax Payable	Current liability	Credit	Balance sheet
Insurance Expense	Operating expense	Debit	Income statement
Interest Expense	Other expense	Debit	Income statement
Interest Receivable	Current asset	Debit	Balance sheet
Interest Revenue	Other income	Credit	Income statement
Investment in Bonds	Investment	Debit	Balance sheet
Investment in Stocks	Investment	Debit	Balance sheet
Investment in Subsidiary	Investment	Debit	Balance sheet
Land	Fixed asset	Debit	Balance sheet